ADVANCE PRAISE FOR
THE AMERICAN STORY

"The writing style in the text is very good. It's brisk, written at a level that will be accessible to my students, and nicely detailed without getting bogged down."

Jamie Bronstein, New Mexico State University

"The American Story is something between a full edition and a concise edition, giving it just the right breadth and depth—not to mention portability and price. The writing is crisp and clear and pulls the reader along."

Stephen William Berry II, University of North Carolina, Pembroke

"The American Story is a fine book and an up-to-date one in covering the new social and cultural history. The authors maintained symmetry by keeping chapters to about thirty pages without losing substance or broad coverage. That is a real skill and advantage."

Bruce Tyler, University of Louisville

"The American Story stands out because it is lavishly produced and priced within the reach of almost all students. Now that I have used the textbook, I appreciate not only the affordable cost but also the exceptional writing and appearance. I have had great success with The American Story."

Thomas H. Appleton, Jr., Eastern Kentucky University

"Strengths are the accessible writing style, the tendency to cut to the chase and not overwhelm with details, and its integration of social, political, and economic history."

Robyn Rosen, Marist College

"The writing is clear and concise. The maps and illustrations are well chosen, and the captions are fitting. Three main strengths of the book are its price, readability, and organization. I used it before and students responded well."

Leslie Heaphy, Kent State University, Stark Campus

ABOUT
THE AUTHORS

ROBERT A. DIVINE

Robert A. Divine, George W. Littlefield Professor Emeritus in American History at the University of Texas at Austin, received his Ph.D. from Yale University in 1954. A specialist in American diplomatic history, he taught from 1954 to 1996 at the University of Texas, where he was honored by both the student association and the graduate school for teaching excellence. His extensive published work includes *The Illusion of Neutrality* (1962); *Second Chance: The Triumph of Internationalism in America During World War II* (1967); and *Blowing on the Wind* (1978). His most recent work is *Perpetual War for Perpetual Peace* (2000), a comparative  analysis of twentieth-century American wars. He is also the author of *Eisenhower and the Cold War* (1981) and editor of three volumes of essays on the presidency of Lyndon Johnson. His book, *The Sputnik Challenge* (1993), won the Eugene E. Emme Astronautical Literature Award for 1993. He has been a fellow at the Center for Advanced Study in the Behavioral Sciences and has given the Albert Shaw Lectures in Diplomatic History at Johns Hopkins University.

T. H. BREEN

T. H. Breen, William Smith Mason Professor of American History at Northwestern University, received his Ph.D. from Yale University in 1968. He has taught at Northwestern since 1970. Breen's major books include *The Character of the Good Ruler: A Study of Puritan Political Ideas in New England* (1974); *Puritans and Adventurers: Change and Persistence in Early America* (1980); *Tobacco Culture: The Mentality of the Great Tidewater Planters on the Eve of Revolution* (1985); and, with Stephen Innes of the University of Virginia, *"Myne Owne Ground": Race and Freedom on Virginia's Eastern Shore* (1980). His *Imagining the Past* (1989) won the 1990  Historic Preservation Book Award. His most recent books are *Colonial America in an Atlantic World* (2003) and *Marketplace of Revolution: How Consumer Politics Shaped American Independence* (2004). In addition to receiving several awards for outstanding undergraduate teaching at Northwestern, Breen has been the recipient of research grants from the American Council of Learned Societies, the Guggenheim Foundation, the Institute for Advanced Study (Princeton), the National Humanities Center, the Huntington Library, and the Alexander von Humboldt Foundation (Germany). He has served as the Fowler

Hamilton Fellow at Christ Church, Oxford University (1987–1988), the Pitt Professor of American History and Institutions, Cambridge University (1990–1991), and the Harmsworth Professor of American History at Oxford University (2000–2001). He is currently completing a book tentatively entitled *America's Insurgency: The People's Revolution, 1774–1776*.

GEORGE M. FREDRICKSON

George M. Fredrickson is Edgar E. Robinson Professor Emeritus of United States History at Stanford University. He is the author or editor of several books, including *The Inner Civil War* (1965), *The Black Image in the White Mind* (1971), and *White Supremacy: A Comparative Study in American and South African History* (1981), which won both the Ralph Waldo Emerson Award from Phi Beta Kappa and the Merle Curti Award from the Organization of American Historians. His most recent books are *Black Liberation: A Comparative History of Black Ideologies in the United States and South Africa* (1995); *The Comparative*

Imagination: Racism, Nationalism, and Social Movements (1997); and *Racism: A Short History* (2002). He received his A.B. and Ph.D. degrees from Harvard and has been the recipient of a Guggenheim Fellowship, two National Endowment for the Humanities Senior Fellowships, and a Fellowship from the Center for Advanced Studies in the Behavioral Sciences. Before coming to Stanford in 1984, he taught at Northwestern. He has also served as Fulbright lecturer in American History at Moscow University and as the Harmsworth Professor of American History at Oxford. He served as president of the Organization of American Historians in 1997–1998.

R. HAL WILLIAMS

R. Hal Williams is Professor of History at Southern Methodist University. He received his A.B. degree from Princeton University (1963) and his Ph.D. degree from Yale University (1968). His books include *The Democratic Party and California Politics, 1880–1896* (1973); *Years of Decision: American Politics in the 1890s* (1978); and *The Manhattan Project: A Documentary Introduction to the Atomic Age* (1990). A specialist in American political history, he taught at Yale University from 1968 to 1975 and came to SMU in 1975 as chair of the Department of History. From 1980 to 1988, he served as dean of Dedman College, the

school of humanities and sciences, at SMU, where he is currently dean of Research and Graduate Studies. In 1980, he was a visiting professor at University College, Oxford University. Williams has received grants from the American Philosophical Society and the National Endowment for the Humanities, and he has served on the Texas Committee for the Humanities. He is currently working on a study of the presidential election of 1896 and a biography of James G. Blaine, the late-nineteenth-century speaker of the House, secretary of state, and Republican presidential candidate.

ARIELA J. GROSS

Ariela Gross is professor of law and history at the University of Southern California. She received her B.A. from Harvard University, her J.D. from Stanford Law School, and her Ph.D. from Stanford University. She is the author of *Double Character: Slavery and Mastery in the Antebellum Southern Courtroom* (2000) and numerous law review articles and book chapters, including "'The Caucasian Cloak': Mexican Americans and the Politics of Whiteness in the Twentieth Century Southwest" in the *Georgetown Law Journal* (2006). Her current work in progress, *What Blood Won't Tell: Racial Identity on Trial in America*, Farrar, Straus & Giroux, is supported by fellowships from the Guggenheim Foundation, the National Endowment for the Humanities, and the American Council for Learned Societies.

H. W. BRANDS

H. W. Brands is the Dickson Allen Anderson Centennial Professor of History at the University of Texas at Austin. He is the author of numerous works of history and international affairs, including *The Devil We Knew: Americans and the Cold War* (1993), *Into the Labyrinth: The United States and the Middle East* (1994), *The Reckless Decade: America in the 1890s* (1995), *TR: The Last Romantic* (a biography of Theodore Roosevelt) (1997), *What America Owes the World: The Struggle for the Soul of Foreign Policy* (1998), *The First American: The Life and Times of Benjamin Franklin* (2000), *The Strange Death of American Liberalism* (2001), *The Age of Gold: The California Gold Rush and the New American Dream* (2002), *Woodrow Wilson* (2003), and *Andrew Jackson* (2005). His writing has received critical and popular acclaim; *The First American* was a finalist for the Pulitzer Prize and a national best-seller. He lectures frequently across North America and in Europe. His essays and reviews have appeared in the *New York Times*, the *Wall Street Journal*, the *Washington Post*, the *Los Angeles Times*, and *Atlantic Monthly*. He is a regular guest on radio and television, and has participated in several historical documentary films.

Penguin Academics

THE AMERICAN STORY
Third Edition

ROBERT A. DIVINE
University of Texas

T. H. BREEN
Northwestern University

GEORGE M. FREDRICKSON
Stanford University

R. HAL WILLIAMS
Southern Methodist University

ARIELA J. GROSS
University of Southern California

H. W. BRANDS
University of Texas

PEARSON
Longman

New York San Francisco Boston
London Toronto Sydney Tokyo Singapore Madrid
Mexico City Munich Paris Cape Town Hong Kong Montreal

Executive Editor:	Michael Boezi
Development Editor:	Karen Helfrich
Executive Marketing Manager:	Sue Westmoreland
Production Manager:	Ellen MacElree
Project Coordination and Electronic Page Makeup:	Elm Street Publishing Services, Inc.
Senior Cover Designer/Manager:	Nancy Danahy
Cover Image:	The Branch Libraries, The New York Public Library, Astor, Lenox, and Tilden Foundations
Art Studios:	Elm Street Publishing Services, Inc. and Maps.com
Photo Researcher:	Photosearch, Inc.
Senior Manufacturing Buyer:	Dennis J. Para
Printer and Binder:	R. R. Donnelley at Crawfordsville
Cover Printer:	Phoenix Color Corporation

For permission to use copyrighted material, grateful acknowledgment is made to the copyright holders on pp. C-1–C-3, which are hereby made part of this copyright page.

Library of Congress Cataloging-in-Publication Data

The American story / Robert A. Divine . . . [et al.].
    p. cm.
    Includes bibliographical reference and index.
    ISBN 0-321-44502-3 (single v. ed.)—ISBN 0-321-42184-1 (v. 1)—ISBN 0-321-42185-X (v. 2)
    1. United States—History. I. Divine, Robert A.

Please visit our website at http://www.ablongman.com/divine.

For more information about the Penguin Academics series, please contact us by mail at Longman Publishers, attn. Marketing Department, 1185 Avenue of the Americas, 25th Floor, New York, NY 10036, or by e-mail at www.ablongman.com/feedback.

ISBN 0-321-44502-3 (Complete Edition)
ISBN 0-321-42184-1 (Volume I)
ISBN 0-321-42185-X (Volume II)

1 2 3 4 5 6 7 8 9 10—DOC—09 08 07 06

BRIEF CONTENTS

DETAILED CONTENTS

MAPS

FIGURES

TABLES

PREFACE

For many decades, the traditional narratives that framed the story of the United States assumed a unified society in which men and women of various races and backgrounds shared a common culture. In recent years, however, many historians have come to believe that traditional narratives stressing the rise of democracy or the advance of free enterprise undervalue the complexity and diversity of the American story. This research makes it hard to sustain a perspective that presumes the inevitability of progress for all men and women and that allows one dominant group to speak for so many others who have struggled over the centuries to make themselves heard. Nevertheless, an awareness that the past is as much about controversy as agreement, as much concerned with diversity as with unity, does not preclude the possibility of a coherent narrative. To create such a narrative while still paying attention to the differences of race and class, ethnicity, and gender is the goal.

The authors of this volume accept the challenge, believing strongly that it is possible to craft a coherent story without silencing difference. We start with the conviction that to tell this story it is essential to listen closely to what people in the past have had to say about their own aspirations, frustrations, and passions. After all, they were the ones who had to figure out how to live with other Americans, many of them totally unsympathetic, even hostile to the demands of others who happened to march to different drummers. Readers of this book will encounter many of these individuals and discover how, in their own terms, they tried to make sense of everyday events connected to family and work, church, and community.

We have done our best to avoid the tendency to lump individuals arbitrarily together in groups. It is true, for example, that many early colonists in America were called Puritans, and presumably in their private lives they reflected religious values and beliefs known as Puritanism. But we must not conclude that an abstraction—in this case Puritanism—made history. To do so misses the complexity and diversity masked by the abstraction, for at the end of the day, what for the sake of convenience we term Puritanism was in fact a rich, spirited, often truculent conversation among men and women who disagreed to the point of violence on many details of the theology they allegedly shared. The same observation could be made about other movements in American history, for example, unions or civil rights, political parties or antebellum reform. A narrative that sacrifices the rough edges of dissent in the interest of getting on with the story may propel the reader smoothly through the centuries, but a subtler, more complex tale is more honest about how people in the past actually made events.

Even as we stress the significance of human agency, we resist transforming the long history of the peoples of the United States into a form of highbrow antiquarianism. The men and women who appear in this book lived for the most part in small communities. Even in the large cities that drew so many migrants after the Industrial Revolution, individuals defined their daily routines around family, friends, and neighborhoods. But it would be misleading to conclude that these people were effectively cut off from a larger world. However strong and vibrant their local cultures may have been, their social identities were also the product of the experience of accommodation and resistance to external forces, many of them beyond their own control. Industrialization changed the nature of life in the small communities. So, too, did nationalism, imperialism, global capitalism, and world war. In our accounts of such diverse events as the American Revolution, the Civil War, the New Deal, and the Cold War, we seek the drama of history in the efforts of ordinary people to make sense of the demands imposed upon them by economic and social change.

It was during these confrontations—moments of unexpected opportunity and frightening vulnerability—that ordinary Americans came to understand better those processes of justice and oppression, national security, and distribution of natural resources that we call politics. The outcome of international wars, the policies legislated by Congress, and the decisions handed down by the Supreme Court must be included in a proper narrative history of the peoples of the United States since these occurrences sparked fresh controversies. They were the stuff of expectations as well as disappointments. What one group interpreted as progress, another almost always viewed as a curtailment of rights. For some, the conquest of the West, a process that went on for several centuries, opened the door to prosperity; for others, it brought degradation and removal. The point is not to turn the history of the United States into a chronicle of broken dreams. Rather, we seek to reconstruct the tensions behind events, demonstrating as best we can why good history can never be written entirely from the perspective of the winners.

From the start of the project, we recognized the risk of treating minorities and women as a kind of afterthought, as if their contributions to the defining events of American history were postscripts, to be taken up only after the reader had learned of important battles and transforming elections. Our treatment of the American Revolution is one example of our balanced and integrated approach to telling the story of the past. Women were not spectators during the war for independence. They understood the language of rights and equality, and while they could not vote for representatives in the colonial assemblies, they made known in other ways their protests against British taxation. They formed the backbone of consumer boycotts that helped mobilize popular opinion during the prelude to armed confrontation. And they made it clear that they expected liberation from the legal and economic constraints that consigned them to second-class citizenship in the new republic. Their aspirations were woven into every aspect of the American Revolution, and although they were surely disappointed with the male response to their appeals, they deserve—and here receive—attention not as marginal participants in shaping events but as central figures in an ongoing conversation about gender and power in a liberal society.

The story of how African Americans organized after World War II to demand that the nation live up to the promise of the Declaration of Independence offers yet another example of this book's integrated approach. Our account of the civil rights struggle ranges from the eloquent leadership of Martin Luther King, Jr., to the key roles played by unheralded blacks in the ranks at Selma and Birmingham. These brave men, women, and children suffered the blows of local sheriffs and the indignity of being swept off the streets by fire hoses, yet their travails ultimately persuaded white America to enact the landmark civil rights laws of the 1960s. The United States has yet to accord African Americans full equality, but the strides taken after World War II constitute a major step toward racial justice. Similarly, the stories of other grand events integrate the hopes and fears of other groups—Native Americans, new immigrants from Third World nations—into what philosopher Horace Kallen once described as "a multiplicity in a unity, an orchestration of mankind."

An overriding goal in our crafting of this narrative has been to produce a volume that would be enjoyable to read. Striving for this goal, we have sought to avoid the clumsy jargon that can be so irksome to the reader who—like us—believes that good history involves well-told stories. The structure and features of the book are intended to stimulate student interest and reinforce learning. Chapters begin with vignettes or incidents that introduce the specific chapter themes that drive the narrative and preview the topics to be discussed. Our interpretation of the central events of American history is based on the best scholarship of the past as well as the most recent historiography.

NEW TO THIS EDITION

In this edition, we have reviewed each chapter carefully to take account of recent scholarly work and to streamline the presentation in the most contemporary chapters for a more straightforward and manageable overview of recent American history. To provide students with a convenient and informative review of events, we have included a chronology at the end of each chapter. We have also included new and expanded material in several chapters. Chapter 3 includes an expanded discussion of mercantilism and free markets in the seventeenth century. Chapter 5 begins with a new opening vignette about the personal sacrifices of one family in the Revolutionary fight for liberty. Chapter 7 includes a new discussion of George Washington's mastery of symbolic political power and bringing the new federal government to the people. Chapter 9 includes a new section on Native American societies before the Indian Removal, noting the cultural transformation of Southeastern Indians under pressure of contact from white settlers. Chapter 12 includes an expanded discussion of marriage for love in the American middle class and additional information on the experience of childhood across class and ethnic lines in the mid-nineteenth century. Chapter 29 includes an expanded discussion of Truman's Fair Deal reforms. Chapters 31 through 33 have been revised, restructured, and condensed into two chapters.

Chapter 31, "To a New Conservatism," covers the period 1969–1988 and Chapter 32, "To the Twenty-first Century," covers 1989–2006. Although some material in the previous edition's final three chapters has been carefully trimmed to make these chapters more manageable, we have also updated content and added new sections. These enhancements include discussions of the new environmentalism of the oil shock 1970s and challenges of the new century, including the continued war in Iraq, renewed culture wars, immigration issues, and concerns about American quality of life, particularly employment and health care. Chapter 32 begins with a new opening vignette about George H. W. Bush, the first Persian Gulf War, and the initiation of a new foreign policy in the post–Cold War Era.

The authors are grateful to the reviewers whose thoughtful and constructive work contributed greatly to this edition:

Samantha Barbas, Chapman University
James Baumgardner, Carson-Newman College
Joseph E. Bisson, San Joaquin Delta College
Cynthia Carter, Florida Community College at Jacksonville
Katherine Chavigny, Sweet Briar College
Cole Dawson, Warner Pacific College
James Denham, Florida Southern College
Kathleen Feely, University of Redlands
Jennifer Fry, King's College
Paul B. Hatley, Rogers State University
Sarah Heath, Texas A&M University-Corpus Christi
Ben Johnson, Southern Arkansas University
Carol Keller, San Antonio College
Elizabeth Kuebler-Wolf, Indiana University-Purdue University Fort Wayne
Rick Murray, College of the Canyons
Carrie Pritchett, Northeast Texas Community College
Thomas S. Reid, Valencia Community College
Mark Schmellor, Binghamton University
C. Edward Skeen, University of Memphis
Ronald Spiller, Edinboro University of Pennsylvania
Pat Thompson, University of Texas, San Antonio
Stephen Tootle, University of North Colorado
Stephen Warren, Augustana College
Stephen Webre, Louisiana Tech University

Although this book is a joint effort, each author took primary responsibility for a set of chapters. T. H. Breen contributed the first eight chapters, going from the earliest Native American period to the second decade of the nineteenth century. George M. Fredrickson wrote Chapters 9 through 16, carrying the narrative through the Civil War and Reconstruction. Ariela J. Gross revised Chapters 9, 11, 12, and 16. R. Hal Williams was responsible for Chapters 17 through 24, focusing on the industrial transformation, urbanization, and the events culminating in World War I. The final eight chapters, bringing the story through the Great Depression, World War II, the Cold War and its aftermath, and the early twenty-first century, were the work of H. W. Brands, especially Chapters 25 through 27 and Chapters 31 and 32, and Robert A. Divine, primarily Chapters 28 through 30. Each author reviewed and revised the work of his or her colleagues and helped shape the story into its final form.

The Authors

1

NEW WORLD ENCOUNTERS

New world conquest sparked unexpected, even embarrassing contests over the alleged superiority of European culture. Not surprisingly, the colonizers insisted they brought the benefits of civilization to the savage peoples of North America. Native Americans never shared this perspective, voicing a strong preference for their own values and institutions. In early seventeenth-century Maryland the struggle over cultural superiority turned dramatically on how best to punish the crime of murder, an issue about which both Native Americans and Europeans had strong opinions.

The actual events that occurred at Captain William Claiborne's trading post in 1635 may never be known. Surviving records indicate that several young Native American males identified as Wicomess Indians apparently traveled to Claiborne's on business, but to their great annoyance, they found the proprietor entertaining Susquehannock Indians, their most hated enemies. The situation deteriorated rapidly after the Susquehannock men ridiculed the Wicomess youths, "whereat some of Claiborne's people that saw it, did laugh." Unwilling to endure public disrespect, the Wicomess later ambushed the Susquehannock, killing five, and then returned to the trading post, where they murdered three Englishmen.

Wicomess leaders realized immediately that something had to be done. They dispatched a trusted messenger to inform the governor of Maryland that they intended "to offer satisfaction for the harm . . . done to the English." The murder of the Susquehannock Indians was another matter, best addressed by the Native Americans themselves. The governor praised the Wicomess for coming forward, announcing that "I expect that those men, who have done this outrage, should be delivered unto me, to do with them as I shall think fit." The Wicomess spokesman was dumbfounded. The governor surely did not understand Native American legal procedure. "It is the manner amongst us Indians, that if any such like accident happens," he explained, "we do redeem the life of a man that is so slain with a 100 Arms length of *Roanoke* (which is a sort of Beads that they make, and use for money)." The governor's demand for prisoners seemed doubly

1

impertinent, "since you [English settlers] are here strangers, and coming into our Country, you should rather conform your selves to the Customs of our Country, than impose yours upon us." At this point the governor ended the conversation, perhaps uncomfortably aware that if the legal tables had been turned and the murders committed in England, he would be the one loudly appealing to "the Customs of our Country."

Europeans sailing in the wake of Admiral Christopher Columbus constructed a narrative of dominance that survived long after the Wicomess had been dispersed—a fate that befell them in the late seventeenth century. The story recounted first in Europe and then in the United States depicted heroic adventures, missionaries, and soldiers sharing Western civilization with the peoples of the New World and opening a vast virgin land to economic development. The familiar tale celebrated material progress, the inevitable spread of European values, and the taming of frontiers. It was a history crafted by the victors—usually by white leaders such as Maryland's governor—and by the children of the victors to explain how they had come to inherit the land.

This narrative of events no longer provides an adequate explanation for European conquest and settlement. It is not so much wrong as partisan, incomplete, even offensive. History recounted from the perspective of the victors inevitably silences the voices of the victims, the peoples who, in the victors' view, foolishly resisted economic and technological progress. Heroic tales of the advance of Western values only serve to deflect modern attention away from the rich cultural and racial diversity that characterized North American societies for a very long time. More disturbing, traditional tales of European conquest also obscure the sufferings of the millions of Native Americans who perished, as well as the huge numbers of Africans sold in the New World as slaves.

By placing these complex, often unsettling, experiences within an interpretive framework of *creative adaptations*—rather than of *exploration* or *settlement*—we go a long way toward recapturing the full human dimensions of conquest and resistance. While the New World witnessed tragic violence and systematic betrayal, it allowed ordinary people of three different races and many different ethnic identities opportunities to shape their own lives as best they could. Neither the Native Americans nor the Africans were passive victims of European exploitation. Within their own families and communities they made choices, sometimes rebelling, sometimes accommodating, but always trying to make sense in terms of their own cultures of what was happening to them. Of course, that was precisely what the Wicomess messenger told the governor of Maryland.

NATIVE AMERICAN HISTORIES BEFORE CONQUEST

As almost any Native American could have informed the first European adventurers, the peopling of America did not begin in 1492. In fact, although Spanish invaders such as Columbus proclaimed the discovery of a "New World," they really brought into contact three worlds—Europe, Africa, and America—that in the fifteenth century were already old. The first migrants reached the North

American continent some fifteen to twenty thousand years ago. The precise dating of this great human trek remains a contested topic. Although some archaeologists maintain that settlement began as early as thirty thousand years ago, the scientific evidence in support of this thesis is not persuasive.

Environmental conditions played a major part in the story. Twenty thousand years ago the earth's climate was considerably colder than it is today. Huge glaciers, often a mile thick, extended as far south as the present states of Illinois and Ohio and covered broad sections of western Canada. Much of the world's moisture was transformed into ice, and the oceans dropped hundreds of feet below their current levels. The receding waters created a land bridge connecting Asia and North America, a region now submerged beneath the Bering Sea that modern archaeologists named Beringia.

Even at the height of the last Ice Age, much of the far North remained free of glaciers. Small bands of spear-throwing Paleo-Indians pursued giant mammals (megafauna)—woolly mammoths and mastodons, for example—across the vast tundra of Beringia. These hunters were the first human beings to set foot on a vast, uninhabited continent. Because these migrations took place over a long period of time and involved small, independent bands of highly nomadic people, the Paleo-Indians never developed a sense of common identity. Each group focused on its own immediate survival, adjusting to the opportunities presented by various microenvironments.

The material culture of the Paleo-Indians differed little from that of other Stone Age peoples found in Asia, Africa, and Europe. In terms of human health, however, something occurred on the Beringian tundra that forever altered the history of Native Americans. For complex reasons, the members of these small migrating groups stopped hosting a number of communicable diseases—smallpox and measles being the deadliest—and although Native Americans experienced illnesses such as tuberculosis, they no longer suffered major epidemics. The physical isolation of the various bands may have protected them from the spread of contagious disease. Another theory notes that epidemics have frequently been associated with prolonged contact with domestic animals such as cattle and pigs. Since the Paleo-Indians did not domesticate animals, not even horses, they may have avoided the microbes that caused virulent European and African diseases.

Whatever the explanation for this epidemiological record, Native Americans did not possess immunities that later might have protected them from many contagious germs. Thus when they first came into contact with Europeans and Africans, Native Americans had no defense against the great killers of the Early Modern world. And, as medical researchers have discovered, dislocations resulting from violence and malnutrition made the Indians even more vulnerable to infectious disease.

ENVIRONMENTAL CHALLENGE: FOOD, CLIMATE, AND CULTURE

Some twelve thousand years ago global warming substantially reduced the glaciers, allowing nomadic hunters to pour into the heart of the North American continent. Within just a few thousand years, Native Americans had journeyed from Colorado to the southern tip of South America. Blessed with a seemingly inexhaustible supply of meat, the early migrants experienced rapid population growth. As archaeologists have discovered, however, the sudden expansion of human population coincided with the loss of scores of large mammals, many of them the spear-throwers' favorite sources of food. The animals exterminated during this period included mammoths and mastodons; camels and, amazingly, horses were eradicated from the land. The peoples of the Great Plains did not obtain horses until the Spanish reintroduced them in the New World in 1547. Climatic warming, which transformed well-watered regions into arid territories, probably put the large mammals under severe stress, and the early humans simply contributed to an ecological process over which they ultimately had little control.

The Indian peoples adjusted to the changing environmental conditions. As they dispersed across the North American continent, they developed new food sources, at first smaller mammals and fish, nuts and berries, and then about five thousand years ago, they discovered how to cultivate certain plants. Knowledge of maize (corn), squash, and beans spread north from central Mexico. The peoples living in the Southwest acquired cultivation skills long before the bands living along the Atlantic Coast. The shift to basic crops—a transformation that is sometimes termed the *Agricultural Revolution*—profoundly altered Native American societies. The availability of a more reliable store of food helped liberate nomadic groups from the insecurities of hunting and gathering. It was during this period that Native Americans began to produce ceramics, a valuable technology for the storage of grain. The vegetable harvest made possible the establishment of permanent villages, that often were governed by clearly defined hierarchies of elders and kings, and as the food supply increased, the Native American population greatly expanded. Scholars currently estimate that approximately four million Native Americans lived north of Mexico at the time of initial encounter with Europeans.

MYSTERIOUS DISAPPEARANCES

Several magnificent sites in North America provide powerful testimony to the cultural and social achievements of native peoples during the final two thousand years before European conquest. One of the more impressive is Chaco Canyon on the San Juan River in present-day New Mexico. The massive pueblo was the center of Anasazi culture, serving both political and religious functions, and it is estimated that its complex structures may have housed as many as fifteen thousand people. The Anasazis sustained their agriculture through a huge, technologically sophisticated network of irrigation canals that carried water long distances. They also constructed a transportation system connecting Chaco Canyon by road to more than seventy outlying villages.

During this period equally impressive urban centers developed throughout the Ohio and Mississippi Valleys. In present-day southern Ohio, the Adena and Hopewell peoples—names assigned by archaeologists to distinguish differences in material culture—built large ceremonial mounds, where they buried the families of local elites. Approximately a thousand years after the birth of Christ, the groups gave way to the Mississippian culture, a loose collection of communities dispersed along the Mississippi River from Louisiana to Illinois that shared similar technologies and beliefs. Cahokia, a huge fortification and ceremonial site in Illinois that originally rose high above the river, represented the greatest achievement of the Mississippian peoples. Covering almost twenty acres, Cahokia once supported a population of almost twenty thousand, a city rivaling in size many encountered in late medieval Europe.

Recent research reveals that the various Native American peoples did not live in isolated communities. To be sure, over the millennia they developed many different cultural and social practices, reflecting the specific constraints of local ecologies. More than three hundred separate languages had evolved in North America before European conquest. But members of the groups traded goods over extremely long distances. Burial mounds found in the Ohio Valley, for example, have yielded obsidian from western Wyoming, shells from Florida, mica quarried in North Carolina and Tennessee, and copper found near Lake Superior.

However advanced the Native American cultures of the Southwest and Mississippi Valley may have been, both cultures disappeared rather mysteriously just before the arrival of the Europeans. No one knows what events brought down the great city of Cahokia or persuaded the Anasazis to abandon Chaco Canyon. Some scholars have suggested that climatic changes coupled

The urban center of Mississippian culture was Cahokia, a city of nearly 20,000 inhabitants at its peak. This artist's reconstruction of downtown Cahokia circa 1100 A.D. shows the central plaza dominated by Monks Mound, an earthen platform temple 100 feet high. Several smaller platforms, temples, and burial mounds circled the plaza, which was enclosed by a wooden palisade.

with continuing population growth put too much pressure on food supplies; others insist that chronic warfare destabilized the social order. It has even been argued that diseases carried to the New World by the first European adventurers ravaged the cultures. About one point modern commentators are in full agreement: The breakdown of Mississippian culture caused smaller bands to disperse, construct new identities, and establish different political structures. They were the peoples who first encountered the Europeans along the Atlantic coast and who seemed to the newcomers to have lived in the same places and followed the same patterns of behavior since the dawn of time.

AZTEC DOMINANCE

The stability resulting from the Agricultural Revolution allowed the Indians of Mexico and Central America to structure their societies in more complex ways. Like the Incas who lived in what is now known as Peru, the Mayan and Toltec peoples of Central Mexico built vast cities, formed government bureaucracies that dominated large tributary populations, and developed hieroglyphic writing as well as an accurate solar calendar.

Not long before Columbus began his first voyage across the Atlantic, the Aztecs, an aggressive, warlike people, swept through the Valley of Mexico, conquering the great cities that their enemies had constructed. Aztec warriors ruled by force, reducing defeated rivals to tributary status. In 1519, the Aztecs' main ceremonial center, Tenochtitlán, contained as many as 250,000 people as compared with only 50,000 in Seville, the port from which the early Spaniards had sailed. Elaborate human sacrifice associated with Huitzilopochtli, the Aztec sun god, horrified Europeans, who apparently did not find the savagery of their own civilization so objectionable. The Aztec ritual killings were connected to the agricultural cycle, and the Indians believed the blood of their victims possessed extraordinary fertility powers.

EASTERN WOODLAND CULTURES

In the northeast region along the Atlantic coast, the Indians did not practice intensive agriculture. These peoples, numbering less than a million at the time of conquest, generally supplemented farming with seasonal hunting and gathering. Most belonged to what ethnographers term the Eastern Woodland Cultures. Small bands formed villages during the warm summer months. The women cultivated maize and other crops while the men hunted and fished. During the winter, difficulties associated with feeding so many people forced the communities to disperse. Each family lived off the land as best it could.

Seventeenth-century English settlers most frequently encountered the Algonquian-speaking peoples who occupied much of the territory along the Atlantic coast from North Carolina to Maine. Included in this large linguistic family were the Powhatan of Tidewater Virginia, the Narragansett of Rhode Island, and the Abenaki of northern New England.

Despite common linguistic roots, however, the scattered Algonquian communities would have found communication difficult. They had developed very different dialects. A sixteenth-century Narragansett, for example, would have found

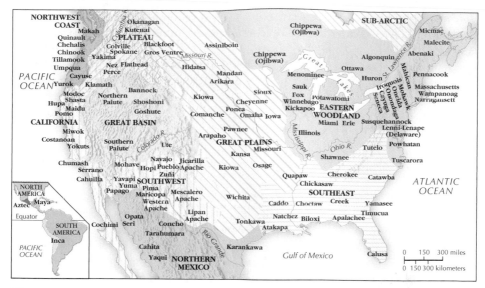

The First Americans: Location of Major Indian Groups and Culture Areas in the 1600s
Native Americans had complex social structures and religious systems and well-developed agricultural techniques before they came into contact with Europeans.

it hard to comprehend a Powhatan. The major groups of the Southeast, such as the Creek, belonged to a separate language group (Muskogean); the Indians of the eastern Great Lakes region and upper St. Lawrence Valley generally spoke Iroquoian dialects.

Linguistic ties had little effect on Indian politics. Algonquian groups who lived in different regions, exploited different resources, and spoke different dialects did not develop strong ties of mutual identity, and when their own interests were involved, they were more than willing to ally themselves with Europeans or "foreign" Indians against other Algonquian speakers. Divisions among Indian groups would in time facilitate European conquest. Local Native American peoples outnumbered the first settlers, and had the Europeans not forged alliances with the Indians, they could not so easily have gained a foothold on the continent.

However divided the Indians of eastern North America may have been, they shared many cultural values and assumptions. Most Native Americans, for example, defined their place in society through kinship. Such personal bonds determined the character of economic and political relations. The farming bands living in areas eventually claimed by England were often matrilineal, which meant in effect that the women owned the planting fields and houses, maintained tribal customs, and had a role in tribal government. Among the native communities of Canada and the northern Great Lakes, patrilineal forms were much more common. In these groups, the men owned the hunting grounds that the family needed to survive.

Eastern Woodland communities organized diplomacy, trade, and war around reciprocal relationships that impressed Europeans as being extraordinarily egalitarian, even democratic. Chains of native authority were loosely structured. Native leaders were such renowned public speakers because persuasive rhetoric was often their only effective source of power. It required considerable oratorical skills for an Indian leader to persuade independent-minded warriors to support a certain policy.

Before the arrival of the white settlers, Indian wars were seldom very lethal. Young warriors attacked neighboring bands largely to exact revenge for a previous insult or the death of a relative, or to secure captives. Fatalities, when they did occur, sparked cycles of revenge. Some captives were tortured to death; others were adopted into the community as replacements for fallen relatives.

A WORLD TRANSFORMED

The arrival of large numbers of white men and women on the North American continent profoundly altered Native American cultures. Indian villages located on the Atlantic coast came under severe pressure almost immediately; inland groups had more time to adjust. Wherever they lived, however, Indians discovered that conquest strained traditional ways of life, and as daily patterns of experience changed almost beyond recognition, native peoples had to devise new answers, new responses, and new ways to survive in physical and social environments that eroded tradition.

Cultural change was not the only effect of Native Americans' contact with Europeans. The ecological transformation, known as the Columbian Exchange, profoundly affected both groups of people. Some aspects of the exchange were beneficial. Europeans introduced into the Americas new plants—bananas, oranges, and sugar, for example—and animals—pigs, sheep, cattle, and especially horses—that altered the diet, economy, and way of life for the native peoples. Native American plants and foods, such as maize, squash, tomatoes, and potatoes, radically transformed the European diet.

Other aspects of the Columbian Exchange were far more destructive, especially for Native Americans. The most immediate biological consequence of contact between Europeans and Indians was the transfer of disease. Native Americans lacked immunity to many common European diseases and when exposed to influenza, typhus, measles, and especially smallpox, they died by the millions.

CULTURAL NEGOTIATIONS

Native Americans were not passive victims of geopolitical forces beyond their control. So long as they remained healthy, they held their own in the early exchanges, and although they eagerly accepted certain trade goods, they generally resisted other aspects of European cultures. The earliest recorded contacts between Indians and explorers suggest curiosity and surprise rather than hostility. A Southeastern Indian who encountered Hernando de Soto in 1540 expressed awe (at least that is what a Spanish witness claimed): "The things that seldom happen bring astonishment. Think, then, what must be the effect on me and mine, the sight of you and your people, whom we have at no time seen . . . things so altogether new, as to strike awe and terror to our hearts."

What Indians desired most was peaceful trade. The earliest French explorers reported that natives waved from shore, urging the Europeans to exchange metal items for beaver skins. In fact, the Indians did not perceive themselves at a disadvantage in these dealings. They could readily see the technological advantage of guns over bows and arrows. Metal knives made daily tasks much easier. And to acquire such goods they gave up pelts, which to them seemed in abundant supply. "The English have no sense," one Indian informed a French priest. "They give us twenty knives like this for one Beaver skin."

Trading sessions along the eastern frontier were really cultural seminars. The Europeans tried to make sense out of Indian customs, and although they may have called the natives "savages," they quickly discovered that the Indians drove hard bargains. They demanded gifts; they set the time and place of trade.

The Indians used the occasions to study the newcomers. They formed opinions about the Europeans, some flattering, some less so, but they never concluded from their observations that Indian culture was inferior to that of the colonizers. They regarded the beards worn by European men as particularly revolting. As an eighteenth-century Englishman said of the Iroquois, "They seem always to have Looked upon themselves as far Superior to the rest of Mankind and accordingly Call themselves *Ongwehoenwe*, i.e., Men Surpassing all other men."

For Europeans, communicating with the Indians was an ordeal. The invaders reported having gained deep insight into Native American cultures through sign languages. How much accurate information explorers and traders took from these crude improvised exchanges is a matter of conjecture. In a letter written in 1493, Columbus expressed frustration: "I did not understand those people nor they me, except for what common sense dictated, although they were saddened and I much more so, because I wanted to have good information concerning everything."

In the absence of meaningful conversation, Europeans often concluded that the Indians held them in high regard, perhaps seeing the newcomers as gods. Such one-sided encounters involved a good deal of projection, a mental process of translating alien sounds and gestures into messages that Europeans wanted to hear. Sometimes the adventurers did not even try to communicate, assuming from superficial observation—as did the sixteenth-century explorer Giovanni da Verrazzano—"that they have no religion, and that they live in absolute freedom, and that everything they do proceeds from Ignorance."

Ethnocentric Europeans tried repeatedly to "civilize" the Indians. In practice that meant persuading natives to dress like the colonists, attend white schools, live in permanent structures, and, most important, accept Christianity. The Indians listened more or less patiently, but in the end, they usually rejected European values. One South Carolina trader explained that when Indians were asked to become more English, they said no, "for they thought it hard, that we should desire them to change their manners and customs, since they did not desire us to turn Indians."

To be sure, some Indians were strongly attracted to Christianity, but most paid it lip service or found it irrelevant to their needs. As one Huron announced, he did not fear punishment after death since "we cannot tell whether everything that appears faulty to Men, is so in the Eyes of God."

Among some Indian groups, gender figured significantly in a person's willingness to convert to Christianity. Native men who traded animal skins for European goods had frequent contact with the whites, and they proved more receptive to the arguments of missionaries. But native women jealously guarded traditional culture, a system that often sanctioned polygamy—a husband having several wives—and gave women substantial authority over the distribution of food within the village. Missionaries insisted on monogamous marriages, an institution based on Christian values but that made little sense in Indian societies where constant warfare against the Europeans killed off large numbers of young males and increasingly left native women without sufficient marriage partners.

The white settlers' educational system proved no more successful than their religion had in winning cultural converts. Young Indian scholars deserted stuffy classrooms at the first chance. In 1744, Virginia offered several Iroquois boys a free education at the College of William and Mary. The Iroquois leaders rejected the invitation because they found that boys who had gone to college "were absolutely good for nothing being neither acquainted with the true methods of killing deer, catching Beaver, or surprising an enemy."

Even matrimony seldom eroded the Indians' attachment to their own customs. When Native Americans and whites married—unions the English found less desirable than did the French or Spanish—the European partner usually elected to live among the Indians. Impatient settlers who regarded the Indians simply as an obstruction to progress sometimes developed more coercive methods, such as enslavement, to achieve cultural conversion. Again, from the white perspective, the results were disappointing. Indian slaves ran away or died. In either case, they did not become Europeans.

THREATS TO SURVIVAL: TRADE AND DISEASE

Over time, cooperative encounters between the Native Americans and Europeans became less frequent. The Europeans found it almost impossible to understand the Indians' relation to the land and other natural resources. English planters cleared the forests and fenced the fields and, in the process, radically altered the ecological systems on which the Indians depended. The European system of land use inevitably reduced the supply of deer and other animals essential to traditional native cultures.

Dependency also came in more subtle forms. The Indians welcomed European commerce, but like so many consumers throughout recorded history, they discovered that the objects they most coveted inevitably brought them into debt. To pay for the trade goods, the Indians hunted more aggressively and even further reduced the population of fur-bearing mammals. Commerce eroded Indian independence in other ways. After several disastrous wars—the Yamasee War in South Carolina (1715), for example—the natives learned that demonstrations of force usually resulted in the suspension of normal trade, on which the Indians had grown quite dependent for guns and ammunition, among other things.

It was disease, however, that ultimately destroyed the cultural integrity of many North American tribes. European adventurers exposed the Indians to bacteria and viruses against which they possessed no natural immunity. Smallpox, measles, and influenza decimated the Native American population. Other diseases such as alcoholism took a terrible toll.

Within a generation of initial contact with Europeans, the Caribs, who gave the Caribbean its name, were virtually extinct. The Algonquian communities of New England experienced appalling rates of death. One Massachusetts colonist reported in 1630 that the Indian peoples of his region "above twelve years since were swept away by a great &

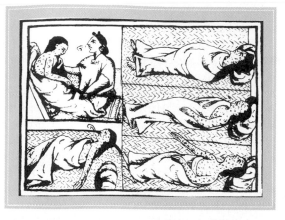

These drawings made soon after the Conquest testify to the lethal impact of common Old World diseases, particularly smallpox, on Native Americans.

grievous Plague . . . so that there are verie few left to inhabit the Country." Settlers speculated that a Christian God had providentially cleared the wilderness of heathens.

Historical demographers now estimate that some tribes suffered a 90 to 95 percent population loss within the first century of European contact. The death of so many Indians decreased the supply of indigenous laborers, who were needed by the Europeans to work the mines and to grow staple crops such as sugar and tobacco. The decimation of native populations may have persuaded colonists throughout the New World to seek a substitute labor force in Africa. Indeed, the enslavement of blacks has been described as an effort by Europeans to "repopulate" the New World.

Indians who survived the epidemics often found that the fabric of traditional culture had come unraveled. The enormity of the death toll and the agony that accompanied it called traditional religious beliefs and practices into question. The survivors lost not only members of their families, but also elders who might have told them how properly to bury the dead and give spiritual comfort to the living.

Some native peoples, such as the Iroquois, who lived some distance from the coast and thus had more time to adjust to the challenge, withstood the crisis better than did those who immediately confronted the Europeans and Africans. Refugee Indians from the hardest hit eastern communities were absorbed into healthier western groups.

WEST AFRICA: ANCIENT AND COMPLEX SOCIETIES

During the era of the European slave trade, roughly from the late fifteenth through the mid-nineteenth centuries, a number of enduring myths about sub-Saharan West Africa were propagated. Even today, commentators claim that the people who inhabited this region four hundred years ago were isolated from the rest of the world and had a simple, self-sufficient economy. Indeed, some scholars still depict the vast region stretching from the Senegal River south to modern Angola as a single cultural unit, as if at one time all the men and women living there must have shared a common set of African political, religious, and social values.

Sub-Saharan West Africa defies such easy generalizations. The first Portuguese who explored the African coast during the fifteenth century encountered a great variety of political and religious cultures. Many hundreds of years earlier, Africans living in this region had come into contact with Islam, the religion founded by the Prophet Muhammad during the seventh century. Islam spread slowly from Arabia into West Africa. Not until A.D. 1030 did a kingdom located in the Senegal Valley accept the Muslim religion. Many other West Africans, such as those in ancient Ghana, resisted Islam and continued to observe traditional religions.

Muslim traders expanded sophisticated trade networks that linked the villagers of Senegambia with urban centers in northwest Africa, Morocco, Tunisia, and Cyrenaica. Great camel caravans regularly crossed the Sahara carrying trade goods that were exchanged for gold and slaves. Sub-Saharan Africa's well-

Artists in West Africa depicted the European traders who arrived in search of gold and slaves. This sixteenth-century Benin bronze relief sculpture shows two Portuguese men.

developed links with Islam surprised a French priest who in 1686 observed African pilgrims going "to visit Mecca to visit Mahomet's tomb, although they are eleven or twelve hundred leagues distance from it."

West Africans spoke many languages and organized themselves into diverse political systems. Several populous states, sometimes termed "empires," exercised loose control over large areas. Ancient African empires such as Ghana were vulnerable to external attack as well as internal rebellion, and the oral and written histories of this region record the rise and fall of several large kingdoms. When European traders first arrived, the list of major states would have included Mali, Benin, and Kongo. Many other Africans lived in what are known as stateless societies, really largely autonomous communities organized around lineage structures.

Whatever the form of government, men and women constructed their primary social identity within well-defined lineage groups, which consisted of persons claiming descent from a common ancestor. Disputes among members of lineage groups were generally settled by clan elders. The senior leaders allocated economic and human resources. They determined who received land and who might take a wife—critical decisions because within the villages of West Africa, women and children cultivated the fields. The communities were economically self-sufficient. Not only were they able to grow enough food to feed themselves, but they also produced trade goods, such as iron, kola, and gum.

The first Europeans to reach the West African coast by sail were the Portuguese. Strong winds and currents along the Atlantic coast moved southward, which meant a ship could sail with the wind from Portugal to West Africa without difficulty. The problem was returning. Advances in maritime technology allowed the Portuguese to overcome these difficulties. By constructing a new type of ship, one uniting European hull design with lateen (triangular) sails from the Middle East, Portuguese caravels were able to navigate successfully against African winds and currents.

The Portuguese journeyed to Africa in search of gold and slaves. Mali and Joloff officials were willing partners in this commerce but insisted that Europeans respect trade regulations established by Africans. They required the Europeans to pay tolls and other fees and restricted the foreign traders to conducting their business in small forts or castles located at the mouths of the major rivers. Local merchants acquired some slaves and gold in the interior and transported them to the coast, where they were exchanged for European manufactures. Transactions were calculated in terms of local African currencies: a slave would be offered to a European trader for so many bars of iron or ounces of gold.

European slave traders accepted these terms largely because they had no other choice. The African states fielded formidable armies, and outsiders soon discovered they could not impose their will on the region simply by demonstrations of force. Moreover, local diseases proved so lethal for Europeans—six out of ten of whom would die within a single year's stay in Africa—that they were happy to avoid dangerous trips to the interior. The slaves were usually men and women taken captive during wars; others were victims of judicial practices designed specifically to supply the growing American market.

Even before Europeans colonized the New World, the Portuguese were purchasing almost a thousand slaves a year on the West African coast. The slaves were frequently forced to work on the sugar plantations of Madeira (Portuguese)

Local African rulers allowed European traders to build compounds along the West African coast. Constructed to expedite the slave trade, each of these "slave factories" served a different European interest. Cape Coast Castle, which changed hands several times as rival nations fought for its control, became one of the largest slave trading posts in the world after the British captured and reinforced it in 1665.

and the Canaries (Spanish), Atlantic islands on which Europeans experimented with forms of unfree labor that would later be more fully and more ruthlessly established in the American colonies. It is currently estimated that approximately 10.7 million Africans were taken to the New World as slaves. The figure for the eighteenth century alone is about 5.5 million, of which more than one-third came from West Central Africa. The Bight of Benin, the Bight of Biafra, and the Gold Coast supplied most of the others. The peopling of the New World is usually seen as a story of European migrations. But in fact, during every year between 1650 and 1831, more Africans than Europeans came to the Americas.

EUROPE ON THE EVE OF CONQUEST

In ancient times, the West possessed a mythical appeal to people living along the shores of the Mediterranean Sea. Classical writers speculated about the fate of Atlantis, a fabled Western civilization said to have sunk beneath the ocean. Fallen Greek heroes allegedly spent eternity in an uncharted western paradise. But because the ships of Greece and Rome were ill designed to sail the open ocean, the lands to the west remained the stuff of legend and fantasy.

In the tenth century, Scandinavian seafarers known as Norsemen or Vikings actually established settlements in the New World, but almost a thousand years passed before they received credit for their accomplishment. In the year 984, a band of Vikings led by Eric the Red sailed west from Iceland to a large island in the North Atlantic. Eric, who possessed a fine sense of public relations, named the island Greenland, reasoning that others would more willingly colonize the icebound region "if the country had a good name." A few years later, Eric's son Leif founded a small settlement he named Vinland at a location in northern Newfoundland now called L'Anse aux Meadows. At the time, the Norse voyages went unnoticed by other Europeans. The hostility of Native Americans, poor lines of communication, climatic cooling, and political upheavals in Scandinavia made maintenance of these distant outposts impossible.

POWERFUL NEW NATION-STATES

At the time of the Viking settlement, other Europeans were unprepared to sponsor transatlantic exploration. Nor would they be in a position to do so for several more centuries. Medieval kingdoms were loosely organized, and until the early fifteenth century, fierce provincial loyalties, widespread ignorance of classical learning, and dreadful plagues such as the Black Death discouraged people from thinking expansively about the world beyond their own immediate communities.

In the fifteenth century, however, these conditions began to change. Europe became more prosperous, political authority was more centralized, and a newly revived humanistic culture fostered a more expansive outlook among literate

Materials excavated at L'Anse aux Meadows, on the northernmost tip of Newfoundland, provide evidence of a Viking settlement in North America. Using the evidence discovered at the site, archaeologists have reconstructed the typically Norse dwellings, which had turf walls and roofs and wooden doors and doorframes.

people. A major element in the shift was the slow but steady growth of population after 1450. Historians are uncertain about the cause of the increase—after all, neither the quality of medicine nor sanitation improved much—but the result was a substantial rise in the price of land, since there were more mouths to feed. Landlords profited from these trends, and as their income expanded, they demanded more of the luxury items, such as spices, silks, and jewels, that came from distant Asian ports. Economic prosperity created powerful new incentives for exploration and trade.

This period also witnessed the centralization of political authority under a group of rulers known collectively as the New Monarchs. Before the mid-fifteenth century, feudal nobles dominated small districts throughout Europe. Conceding only nominal allegiance to larger territorial leaders, the local barons taxed the peasants and waged war pretty much as they pleased. They also dispensed what passed for justice. The New Monarchs challenged the nobles' autonomy. The changes that accompanied the challenges came slowly, and in many areas violently, but the results altered traditional political relationships between the nobility and the crown, and between the citizen and the state. The New Monarchs of Europe recruited armies and supported these expensive organizations with revenues from national taxes. They created effective national courts. While these monarchs were often despotic, they personified the emergent nation-states of Europe and brought a measure of peace to local communities weary of chronic feudal war.

The story was the same throughout most of western Europe. The Tudors of England, represented by Henry VII (r. 1485–1509), ended a long civil war known as the Wars of the Roses. Louis XI, the French monarch (r. 1461–1483), strengthened royal authority by reorganizing state finances. The political unification of Spain began in 1469 with the marriage of Ferdinand of Aragon and Isabella of Castile, setting off a nation-building process that involved driving both the Jews and Muslims out of Spain. These strong-willed monarchs forged nations out of groups of independent kingdoms. If political centralization had not occurred, the major European countries could not possibly have generated the financial and military resources necessary for worldwide exploration.

A final prerequisite to exploration was reliable technical knowledge. Ptolemy (second century A.D.) and other ancient geographers had mapped the known world and had even demonstrated that the world was round. During the Middle Ages, however, Europeans lost effective contact with classical tradition. Within Arab societies, the old learning had survived, indeed flourished, and when Europeans eventually rediscovered the classical texts they drew heavily on the work of Arab scholars. This "new" learning generated great intellectual curiosity about the globe and about the world that existed beyond the Mediterranean.

The invention of printing from movable type by Johann Gutenberg in the 1440s greatly facilitated the spread of technical knowledge. Indeed, printing sparked a communications revolution whose impact on the lives of ordinary people was as far-reaching as that caused by telephones, television, and computers in modern times. Sea captains published their findings as quickly as they could engage a printer, and by the beginning of the sixteenth century, a small, though growing, number of educated readers throughout Europe was well informed about the exploration of the New World.

IMAGINING A NEW WORLD

By 1500, centralization of political authority and advances in geographic knowledge brought Spain to the first rank as a world power. In the early fifteenth century, though, Spain consisted of several autonomous kingdoms. It lacked rich natural resources and possessed few good seaports. In fact, there was little about this land to suggest its people would take the lead in conquering and colonizing the New World.

By the end of the century, however, Spain suddenly came alive with creative energy. The union of Ferdinand and Isabella sparked a drive for political consolidation that, because of the monarchs' fervid Catholicism, took on the characteristics of a religious crusade. Spurred by the militant faith of their monarchs, the armies of Castile and Aragon waged holy war—known as the *Reconquista*—against the independent states in southern Spain that earlier had been captured by Muslims. In 1492, the Moorish (Islamic) kingdom of Granada fell, and, for the first time in centuries, the entire Iberian peninsula was united under Christian rulers.

During the Reconquista, thousands of Jews and Moors were driven from the country. Indeed, Columbus undoubtedly encountered such refugees as he was preparing for his famous voyage. From this volatile social and political environment came the *conquistadores,* men eager for personal glory and material gain, uncompromising in matters of religion, and unswerving in their loyalty to the crown. They were prepared to employ fire and sword in any cause sanctioned by God and king, and these adventurers carried European culture to the most populous regions of the New World.

MYTHS AND REALITY

If it had not been for Christopher Columbus (Cristoforo Colombo), Spain might never have gained an American empire. Born in Genoa in 1451 of humble parentage, Columbus devoured the classical learning that had so recently been rediscovered and made available in printed form. He mastered geography, and—perhaps while sailing the coast of West Africa—he became obsessed with the idea of voyaging west across the Atlantic Ocean to reach Cathay, as China was then known.

In 1484, Columbus presented his plan to the king of Portugal. However, while the Portuguese were just as interested as Columbus in reaching Cathay, they elected to voyage around the continent of Africa instead of following the route suggested by Columbus. They suspected that Columbus had substantially underestimated the circumference of the earth and that for all his enthusiasm, he would almost certainly starve before reaching Asia. The Portuguese decision eventually paid off quite handsomely. In 1498, one of their captains, Vasco da Gama, returned from the coast of India carrying a fortune in spices and other luxury goods.

Undaunted by rejection, Columbus petitioned Isabella and Ferdinand for financial backing. Columbus's stubborn lobbying on behalf of the "Enterprise of the Indies" gradually wore down opposition in the Spanish court, and the two sovereigns provided him with a small fleet that contained two of the most famous caravels ever constructed, the *Niña* and the *Pinta,* as well as the square-rigged *nao Santa Maria.* The indomitable admiral set sail for Cathay in August 1492, the year of Spain's unification.

Educated Europeans of the fifteenth century knew the world was round. No one seriously believed that Columbus and his crew would tumble off the edge of the earth. The concern was with size, not shape. Columbus estimated the distance to the mainland of Asia to be about 3000 nautical miles, a voyage his small ships would have no difficulty completing. The actual distance is 10,600 nautical miles, however, and had the New World not been in his way, he and his crew would have run out of food and water long before they reached China, as the Portuguese had predicted.

When the tiny Spanish fleet sighted an island in the Bahamas after only thirty-three days at sea, the admiral concluded he had reached Asia. Since his mathematical calculations had obviously been correct, he assumed he would soon encounter the Chinese. It never occurred to Columbus that he had stumbled upon a new world. He assured his men, his patrons, and perhaps himself that the islands were part of the fabled "Indies." Or if not the Indies themselves, then they were surely an extension of the great Asian landmass. He searched for splendid cities, but instead of meeting wealthy Chinese, Columbus encountered Native Americans, whom he appropriately, if mistakenly, called "Indians."

After his first voyage of discovery, Columbus returned to the New World three more times. But despite his considerable courage and ingenuity, he could never find the treasure his financial supporters in Spain angrily demanded. Columbus died in 1506 a frustrated but wealthy entrepreneur, unaware that he had reached a previously unknown continent separating Asia from Europe. The final disgrace came in December 1500 when an ambitious falsifier, Amerigo Vespucci, published a sensational account of his travels across the Atlantic that convinced German mapmakers he had proved America was distinct from Asia. Before the misconception could be corrected, the name *America* gained general acceptance throughout Europe.

Only two years after Columbus's first voyage, Spain and Portugal almost went to war over the anticipated treasure of Asia. Pope Alexander VI negotiated a settlement that pleased both kingdoms. Portugal wanted to exclude the Spanish from the west coast of Africa and, what was more important, from Columbus's new route to "India." Spain insisted on maintaining complete control over lands discovered by Columbus, which then still were regarded as extensions of China. The Treaty of Tordesillas (1494) divided the entire world along a line located 270 leagues west of the Azores. Any new lands discovered west of the line belonged to Spain. At the time, no European had ever seen Brazil, which turned out to be on Portugal's side of the line. (To this day, Brazilians speak Portuguese.) The treaty failed to discourage future English, Dutch, and French adventurers from trying their luck in the New World.

CONQUISTADORES: FAITH AND GREED

Spain's new discoveries unleashed a horde of conquistadores on the Caribbean. These independent adventurers carved out small settlements on Cuba, Hispaniola, Jamaica, and Puerto Rico in the 1490s and early 1500s. They were not interested in creating a permanent society in the New World. Rather, they

Ships like this seventeenth-century freighter made the trip from Europe to America in six to ten weeks, depending upon the weather and winds. One of the most difficult tasks was keeping water fresh and food dry, and ships' passengers sometimes found themselves desperate for rations midway across the Atlantic. The transoceanic voyage was so full of such hardships that it acquired almost mythic meaning as a rite of passage for European settlers.

came for instant wealth, preferably in gold, and were not squeamish about the means they used to obtain it. In less than two decades, the Indians who had inhabited the Caribbean islands had been exterminated, victims of exploitation and disease.

For a quarter century, the conquistadores concentrated their energies on the major islands that Columbus had discovered. Rumors of fabulous wealth in Mexico, however, aroused the interest of many Spaniards, including Hernán Cortés, a minor government functionary in Cuba. Like so many members of his class, he dreamed of glory, military adventure, and riches that would transform him from an ambitious court clerk into an honored *hidalgo*. On November 18, 1518, Cortés and a small army left Cuba to verify the stories of Mexico's treasure.

His adversary was the legendary Aztec emperor, Montezuma. The confrontation between the two powerful personalities is one of the more dramatic of early American history. A fear of competition from rival conquistadores coupled with a burning desire to conquer a vast new empire drove Cortés forward. Determined to push his men through any obstacle, he destroyed the ships that had carried them to Mexico in order to prevent them from retreating. Cortés led his band of six hundred followers across rugged mountains and on the way gathered allies from among the Tlaxcalans, a tributary people eager to free themselves from Aztec domination.

At first contact with Cortés's army, the Aztecs, led by Montezuma, thought the Spaniards were demigods. The psychological advantage of their perceived omnipotence helped the Spanish score a decisive victory in Mexico. This Aztec drawing is believed to depict Cortés's conquest of the Aztecs.

In matters of war, Cortés possessed obvious technological superiority over the Aztecs. The sound of gunfire initially frightened the Indians. Moreover, Aztec troops had never seen horses, much less armored horses carrying sword-wielding Spaniards. But these elements would have counted for little had Cortés not also gained a psychological advantage over his opponents. At first, Montezuma thought that the Spaniards were gods, representatives of the fearful plumed serpent, Quetzalcoatl. Instead of resisting immediately, the emperor hesitated. When Montezuma's resolve hardened, it was too late. Cortés's victory in Mexico, coupled with other conquests in South America, transformed Spain, at least temporarily, into the wealthiest state in Europe.

FROM PLUNDER TO SETTLEMENT

Following the conquest of Mexico, renamed New Spain, the Spanish crown confronted a difficult problem. Ambitious conquistadores, interested chiefly in their own wealth and glory, had to be brought under royal authority, a task easier imagined than accomplished. Adventurers like Cortés were stubbornly independent, quick to take offense, and thousands of miles away from the seat of imperial government.

The crown found a partial solution in the *encomienda* system. The monarch rewarded the leaders of the conquest with Indian villages. The people who lived in the settlements provided the *encomenderos* with labor tribute in exchange for legal protection and religious guidance. The system, of course, cruelly exploited Indian laborers.

Spain's rulers attempted to maintain tight personal control over their American possessions. The volume of correspondence between the two continents, much of it concerning mundane matters, was staggering. All documents were duplicated several times by hand. Because the trip to Madrid took many months, a year often passed before receipt of an answer to a simple request. But somehow the cumbersome system worked.

The Spanish also brought Catholicism to the New World. The Dominicans and Franciscans, the two largest religious orders, established Indian missions throughout New Spain. Some friars tried to protect the Native Americans from the worst forms of exploitation. One outspoken Dominican, Fra Bartolomé de las Casas, published an eloquent defense of Indian rights, *Historia de las Indias,* which among other things questioned the legitimacy of European conquest of the New World. Las Casas's work provoked heated debate in Spain, and while the crown had no intention of repudiating the vast American empire, it did initiate reforms designed to bring greater "love and moderation" to Spanish-Indian relations. It is impossible to ascertain how many converts the friars made. In 1531, however, a newly converted Christian reported a vision of the Virgin, a dark-skinned woman of obvious Indian ancestry, who became known throughout the region as the Virgin of Guadalupe. This figure—the result of a creative blending of Indian and European cultures—served as a powerful symbol of Mexican nationalism during the wars for independence fought against Spain almost three centuries later.

About 250,000 Spaniards migrated to the New World during the sixteenth century. Another 200,000 made the journey between 1600 and 1650. Most colonists were single males in their late twenties seeking economic opportunities. They generally came from the poorest agricultural regions of southern Spain— almost 40 percent migrating from Andalusia. Since so few Spanish women migrated, especially in the sixteenth century, the men often married Indians and

Indian Slaves Working at a Spanish Sugar Plantation on the Island of Hispaniola *(1595) by Theodore de Bry. Contemporaries recognized that Spanish treatment of the Native Americans was brutal.*

blacks, unions which produced *mestizos* and *mulattoes*. The frequency of inter-racial marriage indicated that, among other things, the people of New Spain were more tolerant of racial differences than were the English who settled in North America. For the people of New Spain, social standing was affected as much, or more, by economic worth as it was by color.

Spain claimed far more of the New World than it could possibly manage. Spain's rulers regarded the American colonies primarily as a source of precious metal, and between 1500 and 1650, an estimated 200 tons of gold and 16,000 tons of silver were shipped back to the Spanish treasury in Madrid. This great wealth, however, proved a mixed blessing. The sudden acquisition of so much money stimulated a horrendous inflation that hurt ordinary Spaniards. They were hurt further by long, debilitating European wars funded by American gold and silver. Moreover, instead of developing its own industry, Spain became dependent on the annual shipment of bullion from America, and in 1603, one insightful Spaniard declared, "The New World conquered by you, has conquered you in its turn."

THE FRENCH CLAIM CANADA

French interest in the New World developed slowly. More than three decades after Columbus's discovery, King Francis I sponsored the unsuccessful efforts of Giovanni da Verrazzano to find a short water route to China, via a northwest passage around or through North America. In 1534, the king sent Jacques Cartier on a similar quest. The rocky, barren coast of Labrador depressed the explorer. He grumbled, "I am rather inclined to believe that this is the land God gave to Cain."

Discovery of a large, promising waterway the following year raised Cartier's spirits. He reconnoitered the Gulf of Saint Lawrence, traveling up the magnificent river as far as modern Montreal. Despite his high expectations, however, Cartier got no closer to China, and discouraged by the harsh winters, he headed home in 1542. Not until sixty-five years later did Samuel de Champlain resettle this region for France. He founded Quebec in 1608.

As was the case with other colonial powers, the French declared they had migrated to the New World in search of wealth as well as in hopes of converting the Indians to Christianity. As it turned out, these economic and spiritual goals required full cooperation between the French and the Native Americans. In contrast to the English settlers, who established independent farms and who regarded the Indians at best as obstacles in the path of civilization, the French viewed the natives as necessary economic partners. Furs were Canada's most valuable export, and to obtain the pelts of beaver and other animals, the French were absolutely dependent on Indian hunters and trappers. French traders lived among the Indians, often taking native wives and studying local cultures.

Frenchmen known as *coureurs de bois* (forest runners), following Canada's great river networks, paddled deep into the heart of the continent in search of fresh sources of furs. Some intrepid traders penetrated beyond the Great Lakes into the Mississippi Valley. In 1673, Père Jacques Marquette journeyed down the Mississippi River, and nine years later, Sieur de La Salle traveled all the way to the Gulf of Mexico. In the early eighteenth century, the French established small settlements in Louisiana, the most important being New Orleans.

Catholic missionaries also depended on Indian cooperation. Canadian priests were drawn from two orders, the Jesuits and the Recollects, and although measuring their success in the New World is difficult, it seems they converted more Indians to Christianity than did their English Protestant counterparts to the south. Like the fur traders, the missionaries lived among the Indians and learned to speak their languages.

The French dream of a vast American empire suffered from serious flaws. The crown remained largely indifferent to Canadian affairs. Royal officials stationed in New France received limited and sporadic support from Paris. An even greater problem was the decision to settle what seemed to many rural peasants and urban artisans a cold, inhospitable land. Throughout the colonial period, Canada's European population remained small. A census of 1663 recorded a mere 3035 French residents. By 1700, the figure had reached only 15,000. Moreover, because of the colony's geography, all exports and imports had to go through Quebec. It was relatively easy, therefore, for crown officials to control that traffic, usually by awarding fur-trading monopolies to court favorites. Such practices created political tensions and hindered economic growth.

ENGLISH DREAMS OF EMPIRE

The first English visit to North America remains shrouded in mystery. Fishermen working out of Bristol and other western English ports may have landed in Nova Scotia and Newfoundland as early as the 1480s. John Cabot (Giovanni Caboto), a Venetian sea captain, completed the first recorded transatlantic voyage by an English vessel in 1497, while attempting to find a northwest passage to Asia.

Cabot died during a second attempt to find a direct route to Cathay in 1498. Although Sebastian Cabot continued his father's explorations in the Hudson Bay region in 1508–1509, England's interest in the New World waned. For the next three-quarters of a century, the English people were preoccupied with more pressing domestic and religious concerns. When curiosity about the New World revived, however, Cabot's voyages established England's belated claim to American territory.

PROTESTANTISM AND NATIONALISM

At the time of Cabot's death, England was not prepared to compete with Spain and Portugal for the riches of the Orient. Although Henry VII, the first Tudor monarch, brought peace to England after a bitter civil war, the country still contained too many "over-mighty subjects," powerful local magnates who maintained armed retainers and who often paid little attention to royal authority. Henry possessed no standing army; his small navy intimidated no one. The Tudors gave nominal allegiance to the pope in Rome, but unlike the rulers of Spain, they were not crusaders for Catholicism.

By the end of the sixteenth century, however, conditions within England had changed dramatically, in part as a result of the Protestant Reformation. As they did, the English began to consider their former ally, Spain, to be the greatest threat to English aspirations. Tudor monarchs, especially Henry VIII (r. 1509–1547) and his daughter Elizabeth I (r. 1558–1603), developed a strong central administration, while England became more and more a Protestant society. The merger of English Protestantism and English nationalism affected all aspects of public life. It helped propel England into a central role in European affairs and was crucial in creating a powerful sense of an English identity among all classes of people.

The catalyst for Protestant Reformation in England was the king's desire to rid himself of his wife, Catherine of Aragon, who happened to be the daughter of the former king of Spain. Their marriage had produced a daughter, Mary, but, as the years passed, no son. The need for a male heir obsessed Henry. The answer seemed to be remarriage. Henry petitioned Pope Clement VII for a divorce (technically, an annulment), but the Spanish had other ideas. Unwilling to tolerate the public humiliation of Catherine, they forced the pope to procrastinate. In 1527, time ran out. The passionate Henry fell in love with Anne Boleyn, who later bore him a daughter, Elizabeth. The king decided to divorce Catherine with or without papal consent.

The final break with Rome came swiftly. Between 1529 and 1536, the king, acting through Parliament, severed all ties with the pope, seized church lands, and dissolved many of the monasteries. In March 1534, the Act of Supremacy boldly announced, "The King's Majesty justly and rightfully is supreme head of the Church of England." Land formerly owned by the Catholic Church passed quickly into private hands, and within a short period, property holders throughout England had acquired a vested interest in Protestantism. Beyond breaking with the papacy, Henry showed little enthusiasm for theological change. Many Catholic ceremonies survived.

The split with Rome, however, opened the door to increasingly radical religious ideas. The year 1539 saw the publication of the first Bible in English. Before then the Scripture had been available only in Latin, the language of an educated elite. For the first time in English history, ordinary people could read the word of God in the vernacular. It was a liberating experience that persuaded some men and women that Henry had not sufficiently reformed the English church.

With Henry's death in 1547, England entered a period of acute political and religious instability. Edward VI, Henry's young son by his third wife, Jane Seymour, came to the throne, but he was still a child and sickly besides. Militant Protestants took advantage of the political uncertainty, insisting the Church of England remove every trace of its Catholic origins. With the death of young Edward in 1553, these ambitious efforts came to a sudden halt. Henry's eldest daughter, Mary, next ascended the throne. Fiercely loyal to the Catholic faith of her mother, Catherine of Aragon, Mary I vowed to return England to the pope.

However misguided were the queen's plans, she possessed her father's iron will. Hundreds of Protestants were executed; others scurried off to the safety of Geneva and Frankfurt, where they absorbed the most radical Calvinist doctrines of the day. When Mary died in 1558 and was succeeded by Elizabeth, the "Marian exiles" flocked back to England, more eager than ever to rid the Tudor church of Catholicism.

MILITANT PROTESTANTISM

By the time Mary Tudor came to the throne, the vast popular movement known as the Reformation had swept across northern and central Europe, and as much as any of the later great political revolutions, it had begun to transform the character of the modern world. The Reformation started in Germany when, in 1517, a relatively obscure German monk, Martin Luther, publicly challenged the central tenets of Roman Catholicism. Within a few years, the religious unity of Europe was permanently shattered. The Reformation divided kingdoms, sparked bloody wars, and unleashed an extraordinary flood of religious publication.

Luther's message was straightforward, one that ordinary people could easily comprehend. God spoke through the Bible, Luther maintained, not through the pope or priests. Scripture taught that women and men were saved by faith alone. Pilgrimages, fasts, alms, indulgences—none of the traditional ritual observances could assure salvation. The institutional structure of Catholicism was challenged as Luther's radical ideas spread rapidly across northern Germany and Scandinavia.

After Luther, other Protestant theologians—religious thinkers who would determine the course of religious reform in England, Scotland, and the early American colonies—mounted an even more strident attack on Catholicism. The most influential of these was John Calvin, a lawyer turned theologian, who lived most of his adult life in the Swiss city of Geneva. Calvin stressed God's omnipotence over human affairs. The Lord, he maintained, chose some persons for "election," the gift of salvation, while condemning others to eternal damnation. A man or woman could do nothing to alter this decision.

Common sense suggests that such a bleak doctrine—known as predestination—might lead to fatalism or hedonism. After all, why not enjoy the world's pleasures to the fullest if such actions have no effect on God's judgment? But many sixteenth-century Europeans did not share modern notions of what constitutes common sense. Indeed, Calvinists were constantly "up and doing," searching for signs that they had received God's gift of grace. The uncertainty of their eternal state proved a powerful psychological spur, for as long as people did not know whether they were scheduled for heaven or hell, they worked diligently to demonstrate that they possessed at least the seeds of grace. In Scotland, people of Calvinist persuasion founded the Presbyterian Church. And in seventeenth-century England and America, most of those who put Calvin's teachings into practice were called Puritans.

ENGLAND'S PROTESTANT QUEEN

Queen Elizabeth demonstrated that Henry and his advisers had been mistaken about the capabilities of female rulers. She was a woman of such talent that modern biographers find little to criticize in her decisions. She governed the English people from 1558 to 1603, an intellectually exciting period during which some of her subjects took the first halting steps toward colonizing the New World.

Elizabeth recognized her most urgent duty as queen was to end the religious turmoil that had divided the country for a generation. She had no desire to restore Catholicism. After all, the pope openly referred to her as a woman of illegitimate birth. Nor did she want to re-create the church exactly as it had been in the final years of her father's reign. Rather, Elizabeth established a unique institution, Catholic in much of its ceremony and government but clearly Protestant in doctrine. Under her so-called Elizabethan settlement, the queen assumed the title "Supreme Head of the Church."

The state of England's religion was not simply a domestic concern. One scholar aptly termed this period of European history "the Age of Religious Wars." Indeed, it is helpful to view Protestantism and Catholicism as warring ideologies, bundles of deeply held beliefs that divided countries and families much as communism and capitalism did during the late twentieth century. The confrontations between the two faiths affected Elizabeth's entire reign. Soon after she became queen, Pope Pius V excommunicated her, and in his papal bull *Regnans in Exelsis* (1570), he stripped Elizabeth of her "pretended title to the kingdom." Spain, the most fervently Catholic state in Europe, vowed to restore England to the "true" faith, and Catholic militants constantly plotted to overthrow the Tudor monarchy.

Slowly, but steadily, English Protestantism and English national identity merged. A loyal English subject in the late sixteenth century loved the queen, supported the Church of England, and hated Catholics, especially those who happened to live in Spain. Elizabeth herself came to symbolize this militant new chauvinism. Her subjects adored the Virgin Queen, and they applauded when her famed "Sea Dogs"—dashing figures such as Sir Francis Drake and Sir John Hawkins—seized Spanish treasure ships in American waters. The English sailors' raids were little more than piracy, but in this undeclared state of war, such instances of harassment passed for national victories.

In the mid-1580s, Philip II, who had united the empires of Spain and Portugal in 1580, decided that England's arrogantly Protestant queen could be tolerated no longer. He ordered the construction of a mighty fleet, hundreds of transport vessels designed to carry Spain's finest infantry across the English Channel. When one of Philip's lieutenants viewed the Armada at Lisbon in May 1588, he described it as *la felicissima armada,* the invincible fleet. The king believed that with the support of England's oppressed Catholics, Spanish troops would sweep Elizabeth from power.

It was a grand scheme; it was an even grander failure. In 1588, a smaller, more maneuverable English navy dispersed Philip's Armada, and severe storms finished it off. Spanish hopes for Catholic England lay wrecked along the rocky coasts of Scotland and Ireland. English Protestants interpreted victory in providential terms: "God breathed and they were scattered."

THE MYSTERY OF THE LOST COLONY

By the 1570s, English interest in the New World revived. An increasing number of wealthy gentlemen were in an expansive mood, ready to challenge Spain and reap the profits of Asia and America. Yet the adventurers who directed Elizabethan expeditions were only dimly aware of Cabot's voyages, and their sole experience in settling distant outposts was in Ireland. Over the last three decades of the sixteenth century, English adventurers made almost every mistake one could possibly imagine.

One such adventurer was the dashing courtier Sir Walter Ralegh. In 1584, he dispatched two captains to the coast of present-day North Carolina to claim land granted to him by Elizabeth. Ralegh diplomatically renamed this region Virginia, in honor of his patron, the Virgin Queen. But his enterprise known as Roanoke seemed ill-fated from the start. The settlement was poorly situated. To make matters worse, a series of accidents led the adventurers to abandon Ralegh's settlement. In the spring of 1586, Sir Francis Drake visited Roanoke. Since an anticipated shipment of supplies was long overdue, the colonists climbed aboard Drake's ships and went home.

In 1587, Ralegh launched a second colony. Once again, Ralegh's luck turned sour. The Spanish Armada severed communication between England and America. Every available English vessel was pressed into military service, and between 1587 and 1590, no ship visited the Roanoke colonists. When rescuers eventually reached the island, they found the village deserted. The fate of the "lost" colonists remains a mystery. The best guess is that they were absorbed by neighboring groups of natives.

John White, a late sixteenth-century artist, depicted several fishing techniques practiced by the Algonquian Indians of the present-day Carolinas. In the canoe, dip nets and multipronged spears are used. In the background, Indians stab at fish with long spears. At left, a weir traps fish by taking advantage of the river current's natural force.

SELLING ENGLISH AMERICA

Had it not been for Richard Hakluyt, English historian and geographer, the dream of American colonization might have died in England. Hakluyt, a supremely industrious man, never saw America. Nevertheless, his vision of the New World powerfully shaped English public opinion. He interviewed captains and sailors upon their return from distant voyages and carefully collected their stories in a massive book titled *The Principall Navigations, Voyages, and Discoveries of the English Nation* (1589).

The work appeared to be a straightforward description of what these sailors had seen across the sea. That was its strength. In reality, Hakluyt edited each piece so it would drive home the book's central point: England needed American colonies. Indeed, they were essential to the nation's prosperity and independence. In Hakluyt's America, there were no losers. "The earth bringeth fourth all things in aboundance, as in the first creations without toil or labour," he wrote of Virginia. His blend of piety, patriotism, and self-interest proved immensely popular.

Hakluyt's enthusiasm for the spread of English trade throughout the world may have blinded him to the aspirations of other peoples who actually inhabited those distant lands. He continued to collect testimony from adventurers and sailors who claimed to have visited Asia and America. In an immensely popular new edition of his work published between 1598 and 1600 and entitled *Voyages,* he catalogued in extraordinary detail the commercial opportunities awaiting courageous and ambitious English colonizers. Hakluyt's entrepreneurial perspective served to obscure other aspects of the European Conquest, which within only a short amount of time would transform the face of the New World. He paid little attention, for example, to the rich cultural diversity of the Native Americans; he said not a word about the pain of the Africans who traveled to North and South America as slaves. Instead, he and many other polemicists for English colonization led the ordinary men and women who crossed the Atlantic to expect nothing less than a paradise on earth. By fanning such unrealistic expectations, Hakluyt persuaded European settlers that the New World was theirs for the taking, a self-serving view that invited ecological disaster and continuous human suffering.

CHRONOLOGY

24,000–17,000 B.C.	Indians cross the Bering Strait into North America
2000–1500 B.C.	Agricultural Revolution transforms Native American life
A.D. 1001	Norsemen establish a small settlement in Vinland (Newfoundland)
1030	Death of War Jaabi (king of Takrur), first Muslim ruler in West Africa
1450	Gutenberg perfects movable type
1469	Marriage of Isabella and Ferdinand leads to the unification of Spain
1481	Portuguese build castle at Elmina on the Gold Coast of Africa
1492	Columbus lands at San Salvador
1497	Cabot leads first English exploration of North America
1498	Vasco da Gama of Portugal reaches India by sailing around Africa
1502	Montezuma becomes emperor of the Aztecs
1506	Columbus dies in Spain after four voyages to America
1517	Martin Luther's protest sparks Reformation in Germany
1521	Cortés defeats the Aztecs at Tenochtitlán
1529–1536	Henry VIII provokes English Reformation
1534	Cartier claims Canada for France
1536	Calvin's *Institutes* published
1540	Coronado explores the Southwest for Spain
1558	Elizabeth I becomes queen of England
1585	First Roanoke settlement established on coast of North Carolina
1588	Spanish Armada defeated by the English
1598–1600	Hakluyt publishes the *Voyages*
1608	Champlain founds Quebec

2

ENGLAND'S COLONIAL EXPERIMENTS
The Seventeenth Century

In the spring of 1644, John Winthrop, governor of Massachusetts Bay, learned that Native Americans had overrun the scattered tobacco plantations of Virginia, killing as many as five hundred colonists. Winthrop never thought much of the Chesapeake settlements. He regarded the people who had migrated to that part of America as grossly materialistic, and because Virginia had recently expelled several Puritan ministers, Winthrop decided the hostilities were God's way of punishing the tobacco planters for their worldliness. "It was observable," he related, "that this massacre came upon them soon after they had driven out the godly ministers we had sent to them." When Virginians appealed to Massachusetts for military supplies, they received a cool reception. "We were weakly provided ourselves," Winthrop explained, "and so could not afford them any help of that kind."

In 1675, the tables turned. Native Americans declared all-out war against the New Englanders, and soon reports of the destruction of Puritan communities circulated in Virginia. "The Indians in New England have burned Considerable Villages," wrote one leading tobacco planter, "and have made them [the New Englanders] desert more than one hundred and fifty miles of those places they had formerly seated."

Sir William Berkeley, Virginia's royal governor, was not displeased by news of New England's adversity. He and his friends held the Puritans in contempt. Indeed, the New Englanders reminded them of the religious fanatics who had provoked civil war in England. The governor, sounding like a Puritan himself, described the warring Indians as the "Instruments" with which God intended "to destroy the King's Enemies." For good measure, Virginia outlawed the export of foodstuffs to their embattled northern neighbors.

Such disunity in the colonies—not to mention lack of compassion—comes as a surprise to anyone searching for the roots of modern nationalism in this early period. English colonization in the seventeenth century did not spring from a desire to build a centralized empire in the New World similar to that of Spain or France. Instead, the English crown awarded colonial charters to a wide variety of entrepreneurs, religious idealists, and aristocratic adventurers who established separate and profoundly different colonies.

Migration itself helps to explain this striking competition and diversity. At different times, different colonies appealed to different sorts of people. Men and women moved to the New World for various reasons, and as economic, political, and religious conditions changed on both sides of the Atlantic during the course of the seventeenth century, so too did patterns of English migration.

PROFIT AND PIETY

English people in the early decades of the seventeenth century experienced what seemed to them an accelerating pace of social change. What was most striking was the rapid growth of population. Between 1580 and 1650, a period during which many men and women elected to journey to the New World, the population of England expanded from about 3.5 million to more than 5 million. Among other things, the expansion strained the nation's agrarian economy. Competition for food and land drove up prices, and people desperate for work took to the roads. Those migrants, many of them drawn into the orbit of London by tales of opportunity, frightened the propertied leaders of English society.

Even by modern standards, the English population of this period was quite mobile. To be sure, most men and women lived out their days rooted in the tiny country villages of their birth. A growing number of English people, however, were migrant laborers who took seasonal work. Many others relocated from the countryside to London, already a city of several hundred thousand inhabitants by the early seventeenth century.

Other, more distant destinations also beckoned. A large number of English settlers migrated to Ireland, while lucrative employment and religious freedom attracted people to Holland. The Pilgrims, people who separated themselves from the established Church of England, initially hoped to make a new life in Leyden. The migrations within Europe serve as reminders that ordinary people had choices. A person who was upset about the state of the Church of England or who had lost a livelihood did not have to move to America. That some men and women consciously selected this much more dangerous and expensive journey set them apart from contemporaries.

English colonists crossed the Atlantic for many reasons. Some wanted to institute a purer form of worship, more closely based on their interpretation of Scripture. Others dreamed of owning land and improving their social position. A few came to the New World to escape bad marriages, jail terms, or the dreary prospect of lifelong poverty. Since most seventeenth-century migrants left almost no records of their previous lives in England, it is futile to try to isolate a single explanation for their decision to leave home.

In the absence of detailed personal information, historians usually have assumed that poverty, or the fear of soon falling into poverty, drove people across the Atlantic. No doubt economic considerations figured heavily in the final decision. But so too did religion, and it was not uncommon for the poor of early modern England to be among those demanding the most radical ecclesiastical reform.

Whatever their reasons for crossing the ocean, English migrants to America in this period left a nation wracked by recurrent, often violent political and religious controversy. During the 1620s, autocratic Stuart monarchs—James I (r. 1603–1625) and his son Charles I (r. 1625–1649)—who succeeded Queen Elizabeth on the English throne fought constantly with the elected members of Parliament. At stake were rival notions of constitutional and representative government.

Many royal policies—the granting of lucrative commercial monopolies to court favorites, for example—fueled popular discontent, but the Crown's hostility to far-reaching religious reform sparked the most vocal protest. Throughout the kingdom, Puritans became adamant in their demand for radical purification of ritual.

Tensions grew so severe that in 1629, Charles attempted to rule the country without Parliament's assistance. The autocratic strategy backfired. When Charles finally was forced to recall Parliament in 1640 because he was running out of money, Parliament demanded major constitutional reforms. Militant Puritans, supported by many members of Parliament, insisted on restructuring the church—abolishing the office of bishop was high on their list. In this angry political atmosphere, Charles took up arms against the supporters of Parliament. The confrontation between Royalists and Parliamentarians set off a long and bloody civil war. In 1649, the victorious Parliamentarians executed Charles, and for almost a decade, Oliver Cromwell, a skilled general and committed Puritan, governed England, as Lord Protector.

In 1660, following Cromwell's death from natural causes, the Stuarts returned to the English throne. During a period known as the Restoration, neither Charles II (r. 1660–1685) nor James II (r. 1685–1688)—both sons of Charles I—was able to establish genuine political stability. When the authoritarian James lifted some of the restrictions governing Catholics, a Protestant nation rose up in what the English people called the Glorious Revolution (1688) and sent James into permanent exile.

The Glorious Revolution altered the course of English political history and, therefore, that of the American colonies as well. The monarchs who followed James II surrendered some of the prerogative powers that had destabilized English politics for almost a century. The Crown was still a potent force in the political life of the nation, but never again would an English king or queen attempt to govern without Parliament.

Such political events, coupled with periodic economic recession and religious repression, determined, in large measure, the direction and flow of migration to America. During times of political turmoil, religious persecution, and economic insecurity, men and women thought more seriously about transferring to the

New World than they did during periods of peace and prosperity. Obviously, people who moved to America at different times came from different social and political environments. A person who emigrated to Pennsylvania in the 1680s, for example, left an England unlike the one that a Virginian in 1607 or a Bay Colony in 1630 might have known. Moreover, the young men and women who migrated to London in search of work and who then, in their frustration and poverty, decided to move to the Chesapeake carried a very different set of assumptions than did those people who moved directly to New England from the small rural villages of their homeland.

THE CHESAPEAKE: THE LURE OF WEALTH

After the Roanoke debacle in 1590, only a few visionaries such as Richard Hakluyt kept alive the dream of colonies in the New World. These advocates argued that the North American mainland contained resources of incalculable value. Innovative entrepreneurs, they insisted, might reap great profits and at the same time supply England with raw materials that it would otherwise be forced to purchase from European rivals.

Moreover, any enterprise that annoyed Catholic Spain or revealed its weakness in America seemed a desirable end in itself to patriotic English Protestants. Anti-Catholicism and hatred of Spain became an integral part of English national identity during this period, and unless one appreciates just how deeply those sentiments ran in the popular mind, one cannot fully understand why ordinary people who had no direct financial stake in the New World so generously supported English efforts to colonize America. Soon after James I ascended to the throne, adventurers were given an opportunity to put their theories into practice in the colonies of Virginia and Maryland, an area known as the Chesapeake.

ENTREPRENEURS IN VIRGINIA

During Elizabeth's reign, the major obstacle to successful colonization of the New World had been raising money. No single person, no matter how rich or well connected, could underwrite the vast expenses a New World settlement required. The solution to this financial problem was the joint-stock company, a business organization in which scores of people could invest without fear of bankruptcy. A merchant or landowner could purchase a share of stock at a stated price, and at the end of several years the investor could anticipate recovering the initial amount plus a portion of whatever profits the company had made. Some projects were able to amass large amounts of capital, enough certainly to launch a new colony in Virginia.

On April 10, 1606, James issued the first Virginia charter. The document authorized the London Company to establish plantations in Virginia. The London Company was an ambitious business venture. Its leader, Sir Thomas Smith, was reputedly London's wealthiest merchant. Smith and his partners gained possession of the territory lying between present-day North Carolina and the Hudson

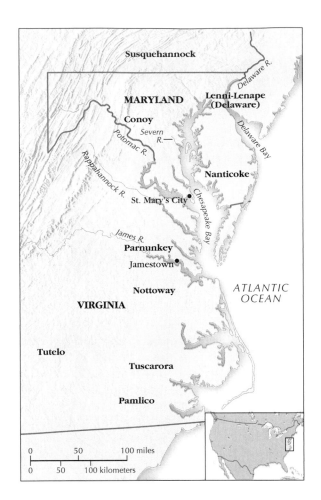

Chesapeake Colonies, 1640
The many deep rivers flowing into the Chesapeake Bay provided scattered Virginia and Maryland planters with a convenient transportation system, linking them directly to European markets.

River. These were generous but vague boundaries, to be sure, but the Virginia Company—as the London Company soon called itself—set out immediately to find the treasures Hakluyt had promised.

In December 1606, the *Susan Constant,* the *Godspeed,* and the *Discovery* sailed for America. The ships carried 104 men and boys who had been instructed to establish a fortified outpost some hundred miles up a large navigable river. The leaders of the colony selected—without consulting resident Native Americans—what the Europeans considered a promising location more than thirty miles from the mouth of the James River. A marshy peninsula jutting out into the river became the site for one of America's most unsuccessful villages, Jamestown. The low-lying ground proved to be a disease-ridden death trap; even the drinking water was contaminated with salt. But the first Virginians were neither stupid nor suicidal. Jamestown seemed the ideal place to build a fort, since surprise attack by Spaniards or Native Americans rather than sickness appeared the more serious threat in the early months of settlement.

Almost immediately, dispirited colonists began quarreling. The adventurers were not prepared for the challenges that confronted them in America. Avarice exacerbated the problems. The adventurers had traveled to the New World in search of the sort of instant wealth they imagined the Spaniards to have found in Mexico and Peru. Published tales of rubies and diamonds lying on the beach probably inflamed their expectations. Even when it must have been apparent that such expectations were unfounded, the first settlers often behaved in Virginia as if they fully expected to become rich. Instead of cooperating for the common good— guarding or farming, for example—individuals pursued personal interests.

BRINK OF FAILURE

Virginia might have gone the way of Roanoke had it not been for Captain John Smith. Before coming to Jamestown, he had traveled throughout Europe and fought with the Hungarian army against the Turks—and, if Smith is to be believed, he was saved from certain death by various beautiful women. Because of his reputation for boasting, historians have discounted Smith's account of life in early Virginia. Recent scholarship, however, has affirmed the truthfulness of his curious story. In Virginia, Smith brought order out of anarchy. While members of the council in Jamestown debated petty politics, he traded with the local Indians for food, mapped the Chesapeake Bay, and may even have been rescued from execution by a young Indian girl, Pocahontas. In the fall of 1608, he seized control of the ruling council and instituted a tough military discipline. Under Smith, no one enjoyed special privilege. Individuals whom he forced to work came to hate him. But he managed to keep them alive, no small achievement in such a deadly environment.

Leaders of the Virginia Company in London recognized the need to reform the entire enterprise. After all, they had spent considerable sums and had received nothing in return. In 1609, the company directors obtained a new charter from the king, which completely reorganized the Virginia government. Moreover, in an effort to raise scarce capital, the original partners opened the joint-stock company to the general public. For a little more than £12—approximately one year's wages for an unskilled English laborer—a person or group of persons could purchase a stake in Virginia.

The burst of energy came to nothing. Bad luck and poor planning plagued the Virginia Company. A vessel carrying additional settlers and supplies went aground in Bermuda. Even the indomitable Captain Smith suffered a gunpowder accident and was forced to return to England.

Between 1609 and 1611, the remaining Virginia settlers lacked capable leadership, and perhaps as a result, they lacked food. The terrible winter of 1609–1610 was termed the "starving time." A few desperate colonists were driven to cannibalism, an ironic situation since early explorers had assumed that only Native Americans would eat human flesh. In England, Smith heard that one colonist had killed his wife, powdered [salted] her, and "had eaten part of her before it was known; for which he was executed." The captain, who possessed a droll sense of

Ætatis suæ 21. Aᵒ 1616.

Matoaks als Rebecka daughter to the mighty Prince Powhatan Emperour of Attanoughkomouck als Virginia converted and baptized in the Christian faith, and Wife to the wor.ᵗ Mʳ Tho: Rolff.

Pocahontas bore no relation to the woman caricatured in modern film. She married John Rolfe, a settler who pioneered the cultivation of tobacco as a cash crop. She converted to Christianity, taking the name Rebecka. This portrait, painted during a visit to London, shows her in court dress.

humor, observed, "Now, whether she was better roasted, broiled, or carbonadoed [sliced], I know not, but such a dish as powdered wife I never heard of."

The presence of so many Native Americans heightened the danger. The first colonists found themselves living—or attempting to live—in territory controlled by what was probably the most powerful Indian confederation east of the Mississippi River. Under the leadership of their *werowance*, Powhatan, these Indians had by 1608 created a loose association of some thirty tribes, and when Captain John Smith arrived to lead several hundred adventurers, the Powhatan Indians (named for their king) numbered some 14,000 people, of whom 3200 were warriors. The Powhatan hoped initially to enlist the Europeans as allies against native enemies. When it became clear that the two groups, holding such different notions about labor and property and about the exploitation of the natural environment, could not coexist in peace, the Powhatan tried to drive the English out of Virginia, once in 1622 and again in 1644. The failure of the second campaign ended in the complete destruction of the Powhatan empire.

In June 1610, the settlers who had survived despite starvation and conflicts with the Indians actually abandoned Virginia. Through a stroke of luck, however, they encountered their new governor Lord De La Warr just as they commenced their voyage down the James River. The governor and the deputy governors who succeeded him, Sir Thomas Gates and Sir Thomas Dale, ruled by martial law. Such methods saved the colony but could not make it flourish. In 1616, company shareholders received no profits. Their only reward was the right to a piece of unsurveyed land located three thousand miles from London.

CASH CROP

The economic solution to Virginia's problems grew in the vacant lots of Jamestown. Only Indians bothered to cultivate tobacco until John Rolfe, a settler who achieved notoriety by marrying Pocahontas, realized this local weed might be a valuable export. Rolfe experimented with the crop, eventually growing in Virginia a milder variety that had been developed in the West Indies and was more appealing to European smokers.

Virginians suddenly possessed a means to make money. Tobacco proved relatively easy to grow, and settlers who had avoided work now threw themselves into its production with single-minded diligence. In 1617, one observer found that Jamestown's "streets and all other spare places [are] planted with tobacco . . . the Colony dispersed all about planting tobacco."

The company sponsored another ambitious effort to transform Virginia into a profitable enterprise. In 1618, Sir Edwin Sandys (pronounced Sands) led a faction of stockholders that began to pump life into the dying organization by instituting a series of sweeping reforms and eventually ousting Sir Thomas Smith and his friends. Sandys wanted private investors to develop their own estates in Virginia. Before 1618, there had been little incentive to do so, but by relaxing Dale's martial law and promising an elective representative assembly called the House of Burgesses, Sandys thought he could make the colony more attractive to wealthy speculators. Even more important was Sandys's method for distributing land. Colonists who paid their own transportation cost to America were guaranteed a "headright," a 50-acre lot for which they paid only a small annual rent. Adventurers were granted additional headrights for each dependent worker they brought to the colony. This procedure allowed prosperous planters to build up huge estates while they also acquired dependent laborers. This land system persisted long after the company's collapse. So too did the notion that the wealth of a few justified the exploitation of many others.

Despite warnings about the danger of smoking to good health, the habit spread quickly. Since tobacco imports generated customs revenue, its sudden popularity produced a lot of money for the government.

BITTER HARVEST

Between 1619 and 1622, the company sent 3570 individuals to the colony. People seldom moved to Virginia in families. Although the first women arrived in Jamestown in 1608, most emigrants were single males in their teens or early twenties who came to the New World as indentured servants. In exchange for transportation across the Atlantic, they agreed to serve a master for a stated number of years. The length of service depended in part on the age of the servant. The younger the servant, the longer he or she served. In return, the master promised to give the laborers proper care and, at the conclusion of their contracts, to provide them with tools and clothes according to "the custom of the country."

Whenever possible, planters in Virginia purchased able-bodied workers, in other words, persons (preferably male) capable of performing hard agricultural labor. This preference dramatically skewed the colony's sex ratio. In the early decades, men outnumbered women by as much as six to one. Such gender imbalance meant that even if a male servant lived to the end of his indenture—an unlikely prospect—he could not realistically expect to start a family of his own. Moreover, despite apparent legal safeguards, masters could treat dependent workers as they pleased; after all, these people were legally considered property. Servants were sold, traded, even gambled away in games of chance. It does not require much imagination to see that a society that tolerated such an exploitative labor system might later embrace slavery.

Most Virginians did not live long enough to worry about marriage. Death was omnipresent. Indeed, extraordinarily high mortality was a major reason the Chesapeake colonies developed so differently from those of New England. On the eve of the 1618 reforms, Virginia's population stood at approximately 700. The company sent at least 3000 more people, but by 1622 only 1240 were still alive. "It Consequentilie followes," declared one angry shareholder, "that we had then lost 3000 persons within those 3 yeares." The major killers were contagious diseases. And on Good Friday, March 22, 1622, the Powhatans slew 347 Europeans in a well-coordinated surprise attack.

No one knows for certain what effect such a horrendous mortality rate had on the men and women who survived. At the very least, it must have created a sense of impermanence, a desire to escape Virginia with a little money before sickness or violence ended the adventure.

CORRUPTION AND REFORM

On both sides of the Atlantic, people asked why so many colonists died in a land so rich in potential. The burden of responsibility lay in large measure with the Virginia Company. Sandys and his supporters were in too great a hurry to make a profit. Settlers were shipped to America, but neither housing nor food awaited them in Jamestown. Weakened by the long sea voyage, they quickly succumbed to contagious disease.

Company officials in Virginia also bore a share of guilt. They were so eager to line their own pockets that they consistently failed to provide for the common good. Various governors and their councilors grabbed up the indentured servants and sent them to their own private plantations to cultivate tobacco, and, as the 1622 surprise attack demonstrated, officials ignored the colony's crumbling defenses. Jamestown took on all the most unattractive characteristics of a boomtown. There was no shared sense of purpose, no common ideology, except perhaps unrestrained self-advancement, to keep the society from splintering into highly individualistic, competitive fragments.

The company's scandalous mismanagement embarrassed the king, and in 1624, he dissolved the bankrupt enterprise and transformed Virginia into a royal colony. The crown appointed a governor and a council. No provision was made, however, for continuing the local representative assembly. The House of Burgesses had first convened in 1619. While elections to the Burgesses were hardly democratic, the assembly did provide wealthy planters with a voice in government. Even without the king's authorization, the representatives gathered annually after 1629, and in 1639, the king recognized the body's existence.

He had no choice. The colonists who served on the council or in the assembly were strong-willed, ambitious men. They had no intention of surrendering control over local affairs. In 1634, the assembly divided the colony into eight counties. In each one, a group of appointed justices of the peace—the wealthy planters of the area—convened as a court of law as well as a governing body. The "county court" was the most important institution of local government in Virginia, serving as a center for social, political, and commercial activities.

A reconstruction of an independent planter's house from the late seventeenth-century Chesapeake. Even well-to-do colonists lived in structures that seemed by contemporary English standards quite primitive.

Changes in government had little impact on the character of daily life in Virginia. The planters continued to grow tobacco, ignoring advice to diversify, and as the Indians were killed, reduced to dependency, or pushed north and south, Virginians took up large tracts of land along the colony's many navigable rivers. The focus of their lives was the isolated plantation, a small cluster of buildings housing the planter's family and dependent workers. These were modest wooden structures. Not until the eighteenth century did the Chesapeake gentry build the great Georgian mansions that still attract tourists. The dispersed pattern of settlement retarded the development of institutions such as schools and churches. Besides Jamestown there were no population centers, and as late as 1705, Robert Beverley, a leading planter, reported that Virginia did not have a single place "that may reasonably bear the Name of a Town."

MARYLAND: A TROUBLED CATHOLIC EXPERIMENT

By the end of the seventeenth century, Maryland society looked remarkably like that of its Chesapeake neighbor, Virginia. At the time of first settlement in 1634, however, no one would have predicted that Maryland, a colony wholly owned by a Catholic nobleman, would have survived, much less flourished.

The driving force behind the founding of Maryland was Sir George Calvert, later Lord Baltimore. Calvert, a talented and well-educated man, enjoyed the patronage of James I. He was awarded lucrative positions in the government, the most important being the king's secretary of state. In 1625, Calvert shocked almost everyone by publicly declaring his Catholicism; in this fiercely anti-Catholic society, persons who openly supported the Church of Rome were immediately stripped of civil office. Although forced to resign as secretary of state, Calvert retained the Crown's favor.

On June 30, 1632, Charles I granted George Calvert's son, Cecilius, a charter for a colony to be located north of Virginia. The boundaries of the settlement, named Maryland in honor of Charles's queen, were so vaguely defined that they generated legal controversies not fully resolved until the mid-eighteenth century when Charles Mason and Jeremiah Dixon surveyed their famous line between Pennsylvania and Maryland.

Cecilius, the second Lord Baltimore, wanted to create a sanctuary for England's persecuted Catholics. He also intended to make money. Without Protestant settlers, it seemed unlikely Maryland would prosper, and Cecilius instructed his brother Leonard, the colony's governor, to do nothing that might frighten off hypersensitive Protestants. On March 25, 1634, the *Ark* and *Dove*, carrying about 150 settlers, landed safely, and within days, the governor purchased from the Yaocomico Indians a village that became St. Mary's City, the capital of Maryland.

The colony's charter was a throwback to an earlier feudal age. It transformed Baltimore into a "palatine lord," a proprietor with almost royal powers. Settlers swore an oath of allegiance not to the king of England but to Lord Baltimore. In England, such practices had long ago passed into obsolescence. As the proprietor, Lord Baltimore owned outright almost 6 million acres; he possessed absolute authority over anyone living in his domain.

On paper, at least, everyone in Maryland was assigned a place in an elaborate social hierarchy. Members of a colonial ruling class, persons who purchased 6000 acres from Baltimore, were called lords of the manor. These landed aristocrats were permitted to establish local courts of law. People holding less acreage enjoyed fewer privileges, particularly in government. Baltimore anticipated that land sales and rents would finance the entire venture.

Baltimore's feudal system never took root in Chesapeake soil. People simply refused to play the social roles the lord proprietor had assigned. These tensions affected the operation of Maryland's government. Baltimore assumed that his brother, acting as his deputy in America, and a small appointed council of local aristocrats would pass necessary laws and carry out routine administration. When an elected assembly first convened in 1635, Baltimore allowed the delegates to discuss only those acts he had prepared. The members of the assembly bridled at such restrictions, insisting on exercising traditional parliamentary privileges. Neither side gained a clear victory in the assembly, and for almost twenty-five years, legislative squabbling contributed to the political instability that almost destroyed Maryland.

The colony drew both Protestants and Catholics, and the two groups might have lived in harmony had civil war not broken out in England. When Cromwell and the Puritan faction executed Charles, transforming England briefly into a republic, it seemed Baltimore might lose his colony. To head off such an event and to placate Maryland's restless Protestants, in 1649, the proprietor drafted the famous "Act concerning Religion," which extended toleration to all individuals who accepted the divinity of Christ. At a time when European rulers regularly persecuted people for their religious beliefs, Baltimore championed liberty of conscience.

However laudable the act may have been, it did not heal religious divisions in Maryland, and when local Puritans seized the colony's government, they promptly repealed the act. For almost two decades, vigilantes roamed the countryside, and during the "Plundering Time" (1644–1646), one armed group temporarily drove Leonard Calvert out of Maryland. In 1655, civil war flared again.

In this troubled sanctuary, ordinary planters and their workers cultivated tobacco on plantations dispersed along riverfronts. Europeans sacrificed much by coming to the Chesapeake. For most of the century, their standard of living was primitive when compared with that of people of the same social class who had remained in England. Two-thirds of the planters, for example, lived in houses of only two rooms and of a type associated with the poorest classes in contemporary English society.

REFORMING ENGLAND IN AMERICA

The Pilgrims enjoy mythic status in American history. These brave refugees crossed the cold Atlantic in search of religious liberty, signed a democratic compact aboard the *Mayflower*, landed at Plymouth Rock, and invented Thanksgiving Day. As with most legends, this one contains only a core of truth.

The Pilgrims were not crusaders who set out to change the world. Rather, they were humble English farmers. Their story began in the early 1600s in Scrooby Manor, a small community located approximately 150 miles north of London. Many people living in this area believed the Church of England retained too many traces of its Catholic origin. To support such a corrupt institution was like winking at the devil, and so, in the early years of the reign of James I, the Scrooby congregation formally left the established state church. Like others who followed this logic, they were called Separatists. Since English statute required citizens to attend Anglican services, the Scrooby Separatists moved to Holland in 1608–1609 rather than compromise.

The Netherlands provided the Separatists with a good home—too good. The members of the little church feared they were losing their distinct identity; their children were becoming Dutch. In 1617, therefore, a portion of the original Scrooby congregation vowed to sail to America. Included in this group was William Bradford, who wrote *Of Plymouth Plantation,* one of the first and certainly most lyrical accounts of an early American settlement.

Poverty presented the major obstacle to the Pilgrims' plans. They petitioned for a land patent from the Virginia Company of London. At the same time, they looked for someone willing to underwrite the staggering costs of colonization. The negotiations went well, or so it seemed. After stopping in England to take on supplies and laborers, the Pilgrims set off for America in 1620 aboard the *Mayflower,* armed with a patent to settle in Virginia and indebted to a group of English investors who were only marginally interested in religious reform.

Because of an error in navigation, the Pilgrims landed not in Virginia but in New England. The patent for which they had worked so diligently had no validity in the region. In fact, the Crown had granted New England to another company. Without a patent, the colonists possessed no authorization to form a civil government. To preserve the struggling community from anarchy, 41 men agreed on November 11 to "covenant and combine our selves together into a civil body politick," a document known as the Mayflower Compact.

During the first months in Plymouth, death claimed approximately half of the 102 people who had initially set out from England. Moreover, debts contracted in England severely burdened the new colony. To their credit, the Pilgrims honored their financial obligations, but it took almost twenty years to satisfy the English investors.

Almost anyone who has heard of the Plymouth Colony knows of Squanto, a Patuxt Indian who welcomed the first Pilgrims in excellent English. In 1614 unscrupulous adventurers kidnapped Squanto and sold him in Spain as a slave. Somehow this resourceful man escaped bondage, making his way to London, where a group of merchants who owned land in Newfoundland taught him to speak English. They apparently hoped that he would deliver moving public testimonials about the desirability of moving to the New World. In any case, Squanto returned to the Plymouth area just before the Pilgrims arrived. Squanto joined Massasoit, a local Native American leader, in teaching the Pilgrims much about hunting and agriculture, a debt that Bradford freely acknowledged. Although evidence for the so-called First Thanksgiving is extremely sketchy, it is certain that without Native American support the Europeans would have starved.

"THE GREAT MIGRATION"

In the early decades of the seventeenth century, an extraordinary spirit of religious reform burst forth in England, and before it had burned itself out, Puritanism had transformed the face of England and America. Modern historians have difficulty comprehending this powerful spiritual movement. Some consider the Puritans rather neurotic individuals who condemned liquor and sex, dressed in drab clothes, and minded their neighbors' business.

The crude caricature is based on a profound misunderstanding of the actual nature of this broad popular movement. The seventeenth-century Puritans were more like today's radical political reformers, men and women committed to far-reaching institutional change, than like naive do-gooders or narrow fundamentalists. To their enemies, of course, the Puritans were irritants, always pointing out civil and ecclesiastical imperfections and urging everyone to try to fulfill the commands of Scripture.

The Puritans accepted a Calvinist notion that an omnipotent God predestined some people to salvation and damned others throughout eternity (see Chapter 1). But instead of waiting passively for Judgment Day, the Puritans examined themselves for signs of grace, for hints that God had in fact placed them among his "elect." A member of this select group, they argued, would try to live according to Scripture, to battle sin and eradicate corruption.

For the Puritans, the logic of everyday life was clear. If the Church of England contained unscriptural elements—clerical vestments, for example—then they must be eliminated. If the pope in Rome was in league with the Antichrist, then Protestant kings had better not form alliances with Catholic states. If God condemned licentiousness and intoxication, then local officials should punish whores and drunks. There was nothing improper about an occasional beer or passionate physical love within marriage, but when sex and drink became ends in themselves, the Puritans thought England's ministers and magistrates should speak out.

From the Puritan perspective, the early Stuarts, James I and Charles I, seemed unconcerned about the spiritual state of the nation. James tolerated corruption within his own court; he condoned gross public extravagance. His foreign policy appeased European Catholic powers. At one time, he even tried to marry his son to a Catholic princess. Neither king showed interest in purifying the Anglican Church. As long as Parliament met, Puritan voters in the various boroughs and countries throughout England elected men sympathetic to their point of view. These outspoken representatives criticized royal policies. Because of their defiance, Charles decided in 1629 to rule England without Parliament; the last door to reform slammed shut. The corruption remained.

John Winthrop, the future governor of Massachusetts Bay, was caught up in these events. Little about his background suggested an auspicious future. He owned a small manor in Suffolk. He dabbled in law. But the core of Winthrop's life was his faith in God, a faith so intense his contemporaries immediately identified him as a Puritan. The Lord, he concluded, was displeased with England. In May 1629, he declared, "I am verily perswaded God will bringe some heavye Affliction upon this lande, and that speedylye." He was, however, confident that the Lord would "provide a shelter and a hidinge place for us."

Other Puritans, some wealthier and politically better connected than Winthrop, reached similar conclusions about England's future. They turned their attention to the possibility of establishing a colony in America, and on March 4, 1629, their Massachusetts Bay Company obtained a charter directly from the king. Charles and his advisers apparently thought the Massachusetts Bay Company was a commercial venture no different from the dozens of other joint-stock companies that had recently sprung into existence.

Winthrop and his associates knew better. On August 26, 1629, twelve of them met secretly and signed the Cambridge Agreement. They pledged to be "ready in our persons and with such of our severall familyes as are to go with us . . . to embark for the said plantation by the first of March next." There was one loophole. The charters of most joint-stock companies designated a specific place where business meetings were to be held. For reasons not entirely clear—a timely bribe is a good guess—the charter of the Massachusetts Bay Company did not contain this standard clause. It could hold meetings anywhere the stockholders, called "freemen," desired, even America, and if they were in America, the king and his archbishop could not easily interfere in their affairs.

Voters in Massachusetts reelected John Winthrop governor many times, an indication of his success in translating Puritan values into practical policy.

"A CITY ON A HILL"

The Winthrop fleet departed England in March 1630. By the end of the first year, almost 2000 people had arrived in Massachusetts Bay, and before the "Great Migration" concluded in the early 1640s, more than 16,000 men and women had arrived in the new Puritan colony.

A great deal is known about the background of these particular settlers. A large percentage of them originated in an area northeast of London called East Anglia, a region in which Puritan ideas had taken deep root. London, Kent, and the West Country also contributed to the stream of emigrants. In some instances, entire villages were reestablished across the Atlantic. Many Bay Colonists had worked as farmers in England, but a surprisingly large number came from industrial centers, such as Norwich, where cloth was manufactured for the export trade.

Whatever their backgrounds, they moved to Massachusetts as nuclear families, fathers, mothers, and their dependent children, a form of migration strikingly different from the one that peopled Virginia and Maryland. Moreover, because the settlers had already formed families in England, the colony's sex ratio was more balanced than that found in the Chesapeake colonies. Finally, and perhaps more significantly, once they had arrived in Massachusetts, these men and women survived. Indeed, their life expectancy compares favorably to that of modern Americans.

The first settlers possessed another source of strength and stability. They were bound together by a common sense of purpose. God, they insisted, had formed a special covenant with the people of Massachusetts Bay. On his part, the Lord expected them to live according to Scripture, to reform the church, in other words, to create an Old Testament "city on a hill" that would stand as a beacon of righteousness for the rest of the Christian world. If they fulfilled their side of the bargain, the settlers could anticipate peace and prosperity. No one, not even the lowliest servant, was excused from this divine covenant, for as Winthrop stated, "Wee must be knitt together in this worke as one man."

The Bay Colonists came to accept a highly innovative form of church government known as Congregationalism. Under the system, each village church was independent of outside interference. The American Puritans, of course, wanted nothing of bishops. The people (the "saints") were the church, and as a body, they pledged to uphold God's law. In the Salem Church, for example, the members covenanted "with the Lord and with one another and do bind ourselves in the presence of God to walk together in all his ways."

Simply because a person happened to live in a certain community did not mean he or she automatically belonged to the local church. The churches of Massachusetts were voluntary institutions, and in order to join one a man or woman had to provide testimony—a confession of faith—before neighbors who had already been admitted as full members. It was a demanding process. Whatever the personal strains, however, most men and women in early Massachusetts aspired to full membership, which entitled them to the sacraments, and gave some of them responsibility for choosing ministers, disciplining backsliders, and determining difficult questions of theology. Although women and blacks could not vote for ministers, they did become members of the Congregational churches. Over the course of the seventeenth century, women made up an increasingly large share of the membership.

In creating a civil government, the Bay Colonists faced a particularly difficult challenge. Their charter allowed the investors in a joint-stock company to set up a business organization. When the settlers arrived in America, however, company leaders—men like Winthrop—moved quickly to transform the commercial structure into a colonial government. An early step in this direction took place on May 18, 1631, when the category of "freeman" was extended to all adult males who had become members of a Congregational church. This decision greatly expanded the franchise of Massachusetts Bay, and during the 1630s, at least 40 percent of the colony's adult males could vote in elections. This percentage was higher than anything the emigrants would have known in England. The freemen voted annually for a governor, a group of magistrates called the Court of Assistants, and after 1634, deputies who represented the interests of the individual towns. Even military officers were elected every year in Massachusetts Bay.

In New England, the town became the center of public life. In other regions of British America where the county was the focus of local government, people

An early Congregational meetinghouse is the Old Ship Meetinghouse in Hingham, Massachusetts. Its name derives from its interior design, which resembles the hull of a ship. The oldest wooden church in the United States, it could accommodate some seven hundred people, about the entire population of seventeenth-century Hingham, who would have sat on backless wooden benches in the unheated building, listening to the preacher address the congregation not from an altar but from an undecorated square speaking box.

did not experience the same density of social and institutional interaction. In Massachusetts, groups of men and women voluntarily covenanted together to observe common goals. The community constructed a meetinghouse where religious services and town meetings were held. Acquisitiveness never got out of control, and entrepreneurial practices rarely disturbed the peace of the Puritan communities. Inhabitants generally received land sufficient to build a house to support a family. Although villagers escaped the kind of feudal dues collected in other parts of America, they were expected to contribute to the minister's salary, pay local and colony taxes, and serve in the militia.

THE CHALLENGE OF RELIGIOUS DISSENT

The European settlers of Massachusetts Bay managed to live in peace—at least with each other. This was a remarkable achievement considering the chronic instability that plagued other colonies at this time. They believed in a rule of law, and in 1648 the colonial legislature, called the General Court, drew up the *Lawes and Liberties,* the first alphabetized code of law printed in English. This is a document of fundamental importance in American constitutional history. In clear prose, it explained to ordinary colonists their rights and responsibilities as citizens of the commonwealth. The code engendered public trust in government and discouraged magistrates from the arbitrary exercise of authority.

The Puritans never supported the concept of religious toleration. They transferred to the New World to preserve *their own* freedom of worship; about religious freedom of those deemed heretics, they expressed little concern. The most serious challenges to Puritan orthodoxy in Massachusetts Bay came from two brilliantly charismatic individuals.

The first, Roger Williams, arrived in 1631 and immediately attracted a body of followers. Williams preached extreme separatism. The Bay Colonists, he exclaimed, were impure in the sight of the Lord so long as they remained even nominal members of the Church of England. Moreover, he questioned the validity of the colony's charter, since the king had not first purchased the land from the Indians, a view that threatened the integrity of the entire colonial experiment. Williams also insisted that the civil rulers of Massachusetts had no business punishing settlers for their religious beliefs. It was God's responsibility, not men's, to monitor people's consciences. The Bay magistrates were prepared neither to tolerate heresy nor to accede to Williams's other demands, and in 1636, after attempts to reach a compromise had failed, they banished him from the colony. Williams worked out the logic of his ideas in Providence, a village he founded in what would become Rhode Island.

The magistrates of Massachusetts Bay concluded that the second individual, Anne Hutchinson, posed an even graver threat to the peace. This intelligent woman followed John Cotton to the New World in 1634. Even contemporaries found her religious ideas, usually termed Antinomianism, somewhat confusing.

Hutchinson shared her ideas with other Bostonians, many of them women. Her outspoken views scandalized orthodox leaders of church and state. She suggested that all but two ministers in the colony were preaching a doctrine in the Congregational churches that was little better than that of the Church of England.

When authorities demanded she explain her unusual opinions, she insisted that she experienced divine inspiration independently of either the Bible or the clergy. In other words, Hutchinson's teachings could not be tested by Scripture, a position that seemed dangerously subjective. Indeed, Hutchinson's theology called the very foundation of Massachusetts Bay into question. Without clear, external standards, one person's truth was as valid as anyone else's, and from Winthrop's perspective, Hutchinson's teachings invited civil and religious anarchy. But her challenge to authority was not simply theological. As a woman, her aggressive speech sparked a deeply misogynist response from the colony's male leaders.

For two very tense days in 1637, the ministers and magistrates of Massachusetts Bay cross-examined Hutchinson; in this intense theological debate, she more than held her own. Hutchinson defied the ministers and magistrates to demonstrate exactly where she had gone wrong. Just when it appeared Hutchinson had outmaneuvered—indeed, thoroughly embarrassed—her male opponents, she let down her guard, declaring forcefully that what she knew of God came "by an immediate revelation. . . . By the voice of his own spirit to my soul." Here was what her accusers had suspected all along but could not prove. She had confessed in open court that one can experience the Spirit directly without the help of ministers or Scripture. This Antinomian statement fulfilled the worst fears of the Bay rulers, and they exiled Hutchinson and her followers to Rhode Island.

MOBILITY AND DIVISION

Massachusetts Bay spawned four new colonies, three of which survived to the American Revolution. New Hampshire became a separate colony in 1677. Its population grew very slowly, and for much of the colonial period, New Hampshire remained economically dependent on Massachusetts, its commercial neighbor to the south.

Far more people were drawn to the fertile lands of the Connecticut River Valley. In 1636, settlers founded the villages of Hartford, Windsor, and Wethersfield. No one forced these men and women to leave Massachusetts, and in their new surroundings, they created a society that looked much like the one they had known in the Bay Colony. Through his writings, Thomas Hooker, Connecticut's most prominent minister, helped all New Englanders define Congregational church polity. Puritans on both sides of the Atlantic read Hooker's beautifully crafted works. In 1639, representatives from the Connecticut towns passed the Fundamental Orders, a blueprint for civil government, and in 1662, Charles II awarded the colony a charter of its own.

In 1638, another group, led by Theophilus Eaton and the Reverend John Davenport, settled New Haven and several adjoining towns along Long Island Sound. These emigrants, many of whom had come from London, lived briefly in Massachusetts Bay but then insisted on forming a Puritan commonwealth of their own, one that established a closer relationship between church and state than the Bay Colonists had allowed. The New Haven colony never prospered, and in 1662, it was absorbed into Connecticut.

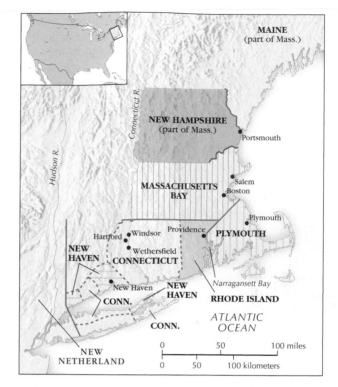

New England Colonies, 1650

The early settlers quickly carved up New England. New Haven briefly flourished as a separate colony before being absorbed by Connecticut in 1662. Long Island later became part of New York; Plymouth was incorporated into Massachusetts; and New Hampshire became a separate colony.

Rhode Island experienced a wholly different history. From the beginning, it drew people of a highly independent turn of mind, and according to one Dutch visitor, Rhode Island was "the receptacle of all sorts of riff-raff people.... All the cranks of New-England retire thither." This description, of course, was an exaggeration. Roger Williams founded Providence in 1636; two years later, Anne Hutchinson took her followers to Portsmouth. Other groups settled around Narragansett Bay. In 1644, Parliament issued a patent for the "Providence Plantations," and in 1663, the Rhode Islanders obtained a royal charter. For most of the seventeenth century, colonywide government existed in name only. Despite their constant bickering, the settlers of Rhode Island built up a profitable commerce in agricultural goods.

CULTURAL DIVERSITY: THE MIDDLE COLONIES

New York, New Jersey, Pennsylvania, and Delaware were settled for quite different reasons. William Penn, for example, envisioned a Quaker sanctuary; the Duke of York worried chiefly about his own income. Despite the founders' intentions, however, some common characteristics emerged. Each colony developed a strikingly heterogeneous population, men and women of different ethnic and religious backgrounds. This cultural diversity became a major influence on the economic, political, and ecclesiastical institutions of the Middle Colonies.

ANGLO-DUTCH RIVALRY ON THE HUDSON

By the early decades of the seventeenth century, the Dutch had established themselves as Europe's most aggressive traders. Holland—a small, loosely federated nation—possessed the world's largest merchant fleet. Dutch rivalry with Spain, a fading though still formidable power, was in large measure responsible for the settlement of New Netherland. While searching for the elusive Northwest Passage in 1609, Henry Hudson, an English explorer employed by a Dutch company, sailed up the river that now bears his name. Further voyages led to the establishment of trading posts in New Netherland, although permanent settlement did not occur until 1624.

The directors of the Dutch West India Company sponsored two small outposts, Fort Orange (Albany) located well up the Hudson River and New Amsterdam (New York City) on Manhattan Island. The first Dutch settlers were salaried employees, and their superiors in Holland expected them to spend most of their time gathering animal furs. They did not receive land for their troubles. Needless to say, this arrangement attracted relatively few Dutch immigrants.

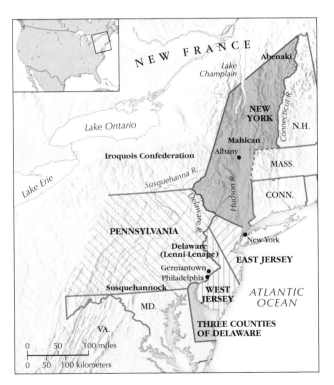

Middle Colonies, 1685
Until the Revolution, the Iroquois resisted European expansion into Western New York. The Jerseys and Pennsylvania initially attracted English and Irish Quakers, who were soon joined by thousands of Scots-Irish and Germans.

The colony's population may have been small, only 270 in 1628, but it contained an extraordinary ethnic mix. One visitor to New Amsterdam in 1644 maintained he had heard "eighteen different languages" spoken in the city. Even if this report was exaggerated, there is no doubt the Dutch colony drew English, Finns, Germans, and Swedes. By the 1640s, a sizable community of free blacks (probably former slaves who had gained their freedom through self-purchase) had developed in New Amsterdam, adding African tongues to the cacophony of languages.

New Netherland lacked capable leadership. The company sent a number of director-generals to oversee judicial and political affairs. Without exception, these men were temperamentally unsuited to govern an American colony. They adopted autocratic procedures, lined their own pockets, and, in one case, blundered into a war that needlessly killed scores of Indians and settlers. The company made no provision for an elected assembly. As much as they were able, the scattered inhabitants living along the Hudson River ignored company directives. They felt no loyalty to the trading company that had treated them so shabbily.

In August 1664, the Dutch lost their tenuous hold on New Netherland. The English Crown, eager to score an easy victory over a commercial rival, dispatched warships to New Amsterdam. The commander of this force, Colonel Richard Nicolls, ordered the colonists to surrender. The last director-general, a colorful character named Peter Stuyvesant (1647–1664), rushed wildly about the city urging the settlers to resist the English. No one obeyed. Even the Dutch remained deaf to Stuyvesant's appeals. They accepted the Articles of Capitulation, a generous agreement that allowed Dutch nationals to remain in the province and to retain their property.

Charles II had already granted his brother, James, the Duke of York, a charter for the newly captured territory and much else besides. The duke became absolute proprietor over Maine, Martha's Vineyard, Nantucket, Long Island, and the rest of New York all the way to Delaware Bay. The king perhaps wanted to encircle New England's potentially disloyal Puritan population, but whatever his aims may have been, he created a bureaucratic nightmare.

During the English Civil War, the duke had acquired a thorough aversion to representative government. The new proprietor had no intention of letting such a participatory system take root in New York. "I cannot *but* suspect," the duke announced, that an assembly "would be of dangerous consequence." In part to appease these outspoken critics, Governor Nicolls—one of the few competent administrators to serve in the Middle Colonies—drew up in March 1665 a legal code known as the Duke's Laws. It guaranteed religious toleration and created local governments.

There was no provision, however, for an elected assembly or, for that matter, for democratic town meetings. The legal code disappointed the Puritan migrants on Long Island, and when the duke's officers attempted to collect taxes, these people protested that they were "inslav'd under an Arbitrary Power."

The Dutch kept silent. For several decades they remained a large unassimilated ethnic group. They continued to speak their own language, worship in their own churches (Dutch Reformed Calvinist), and eye their English neighbors with suspicion. In fact, the colony seemed little different from what it had been under the Dutch West India Company: a loose collection of independent communities ruled by an ineffectual central government.

CONFUSION IN NEW JERSEY

Only three months after receiving a charter for New York, the Duke of York made a terrible mistake. As a gift to two courtiers who had served Charles during the English Civil War, the duke awarded the land lying between the Hudson and Delaware Rivers to John, Lord Berkeley, and Sir George Carteret. This colony was named New Jersey in honor of Carteret's birthplace, the Isle of Jersey in the English Channel. When Nicolls heard what the duke had done, he exploded. In his estimation, this fertile region contained the "most improveable" land in all New York, and to give it away so casually seemed the height of folly.

The duke's impulsive act bred confusion. Soon it was not clear who owned what in New Jersey. Before Nicolls had learned of James's decision, the governor had allowed migrants from New England to take up farms west of the Hudson River. He promised the settlers an opportunity to establish an elected assembly, a headright system, and liberty of conscience. In exchange for these privileges, Nicolls asked only that they pay a small annual rent to the duke. The new proprietors, Berkeley and Carteret, recruited colonists on similar terms. They assumed, of course, that they would receive the rent money.

The result was chaos. Some colonists insisted that Nicolls had authorized their assembly. Others, equally insistent, claimed that Berkeley and Carteret had done so. Both sides were wrong. Neither the proprietors nor Nicolls possessed any legal right whatsoever to set up a colonial government. James could transfer land to favorite courtiers, but no matter how many times the land changed hands, the government remained his personal responsibility. Knowledge of the law failed to quiet the controversy. Through it all, the duke showed not the slightest interest in the peace and welfare of the people of New Jersey.

Berkeley grew tired of the venture. It generated headaches rather than income, and in 1674, he sold his proprietary rights to a group of surprisingly quarrelsome Quakers. The sale necessitated the division of the colony into two separate governments known as East and West Jersey. Neither half prospered. Carteret and his heirs tried unsuccessfully to turn a profit in East Jersey. In 1677, the Quaker proprietors of West Jersey issued a remarkable democratic plan of government, the Laws, Concessions, and Agreements. But they fought among themselves with such intensity that not even William Penn could bring tranquility to their affairs. Penn wisely turned his attention to the unclaimed territory across the Delaware River. The West Jersey proprietors went bankrupt, and in 1702, the Crown reunited the two Jerseys into a single royal colony.

QUAKERS IN AMERICA

The founding of Pennsylvania cannot be separated from the history of the Quaker movement. Believers in a highly personal form of religious experience, the Quakers saw no need for a learned ministry, since one person's interpretation of Scripture was as valid as anyone else's. This radical religious sect, a product of the social upheaval in England during the Civil War, gained its name from the derogatory term that English authorities sometimes used to describe those who "tremble at the word of the Lord." The name persisted even though the Quakers preferred being called Professors of the Light or, more commonly, Friends.

QUAKER BELIEFS AND PRACTICE

By the time the Stuarts regained the throne in 1660, the Quakers had developed strong support throughout England. One person responsible for their remarkable success was George Fox (1624–1691), a shoemaker whose spiritual anxieties sparked a powerful new religious message that pushed beyond traditional reformed Protestantism. According to Fox, he experienced despair "so that I had nothing outwardly to help me . . . [but] then, I heard a voice which said, 'There is one, even Christ Jesus, that can speak to thy condition.'" Throughout his life, Fox and his growing number of followers gave testimony to the working of the Holy Spirit. Indeed, they informed ordinary men and women that if only they would look, they too would discover they possessed an "Inner Light." This was a wonderfully liberating invitation, especially for persons of lower-class origin.

Quakers practiced humility in their daily lives. They wore simple clothes and employed old-fashioned forms of address that set them apart from their neighbors. Friends refused to honor worldly position and accomplishment or to swear oaths in courts of law. They were also pacifists. According to Fox, all persons were equal in the sight of the Lord, a belief that generally annoyed people of rank and achievement.

PENN'S "HOLY EXPERIMENT"

William Penn lived according to the Inner Light, a commitment that led eventually to the founding of Pennsylvania. Penn possessed a curiously complex personality. He was an athletic person who threw himself into intellectual pursuits. He was a bold visionary capable of making pragmatic decisions. He came from an aristocratic family and yet spent his entire adult life involved with a religious movement associated with the lower class.

Precisely when Penn's thoughts turned to America is not known. He was briefly involved with the West Jersey proprietorship. This venture may have suggested the possibility of an even larger enterprise. In any case, Penn negotiated in 1681 one of the more impressive land deals in the history of American real estate. Charles II awarded Penn a charter making him the sole proprietor of a vast area called Pennsylvania (literally, "Penn's woods").

Why the king bestowed such generosity on a leading Quaker who had recently been released from prison remains a mystery. The monarch may have regarded the colony as a means of ridding England of its troublesome Quaker population, or, quite simply, he may have liked Penn. In 1682, the new proprietor purchased from the Duke of York the so-called Three Lower Counties that eventually became Delaware. This astute move guaranteed that Pennsylvania would have access to the Atlantic and determined even before Philadelphia had been established that it would become a commercial center.

Penn lost no time in launching his "Holy Experiment." In 1682, he set forth his ideas in an unusual document known as the Frame of Government. The charter gave Penn the right to create any form of government he desired, and his imagination ran wild. His plan blended traditional notions about the privileges of a landed aristocracy with quite daring concepts of personal liberty. Penn guaranteed that settlers would enjoy among other things liberty of conscience, freedom from persecution, no taxation without representation, and due process of law.

In designing his government, Penn decided that both the rich and poor had to have a voice in political affairs; neither should be able to overrule the legitimate interests of the other class. The Frame of Government envisioned a governor appointed by the proprietor, a 72-member Provincial Council responsible for initiating legislation, and a 200-person assembly that could accept or reject the bills presented to it. Penn apparently thought the council would be filled by the colony's richest landholders, or in the words of the Frame, "persons of most note for their wisdom, virtue and ability." The governor and council were charged with the routine administration of justice. Smaller landowners spoke through the assembly. It was a clumsy structure, and in America the entire edifice crumbled under its own weight.

PROMOTING PENNSYLVANIA

Penn promoted his colony aggressively throughout England, Ireland, and Germany. He had no choice. His only source of revenue was the sale of land and the collection of rents. Penn commissioned pamphlets in several languages extolling the quality of Pennsylvania's rich farmland. The response was overwhelming. People poured into Philadelphia and the surrounding area. In 1685 alone, eight thousand immigrants arrived. Most of the settlers were Irish, Welsh, and English Quakers. But Penn opened the door to men and women of all nations.

Penn himself emigrated to America in 1682. His stay, however, was unexpectedly short and unhappy. The council and assembly—reduced now to more manageable size—fought over the right to initiate legislation. Wealthy Quaker merchants, most of them residents of Philadelphia, dominated the council. By contrast, the assembly included men from rural settlements and the Three Lower Counties who showed no concern for the Holy Experiment.

Penn did not see his colony again until 1699. During his absence, much had changed. The settlement had prospered. Its agricultural products, especially its excellent wheat, were in demand throughout the Atlantic world. Despite this economic success, however, the population remained divided. Even the Quakers had briefly split into hostile factions. Penn's handpicked governors had failed to win general support for the proprietor's policies, and one of them exclaimed in anger that each Quaker "prays for his neighbor on First Days and then preys on him the other six."

In 1701, legal challenges in England again forced Penn to depart for the mother country. Just before he sailed, Penn signed the Charter of Liberties, a new frame of government that established a unicameral or one-house legislature (the only one in colonial America) and gave the representatives the right to initiate bills. Penn also allowed the assembly to conduct its business without proprietary

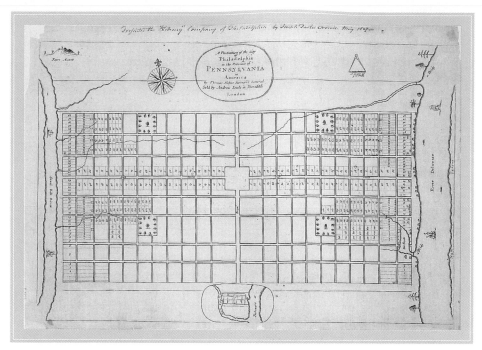

William Penn's plan for Philadelphia shows the city laid out where the Scool Kill (Schuylkill) and Delaware rivers parallel each other. Four of the five public squares were intended to be parks while the fifth (at the center) was designated for public buildings. Today, it is the site of Philadelphia's city hall.

interference. The charter provided for the political separation of the Three Lower Counties (Delaware) from Pennsylvania, something people living in the area had demanded for years. This hastily drafted document served as Pennsylvania's constitution until the American Revolution.

PLANTING THE CAROLINAS

In some ways, Carolina society looked much like the one that had developed in Virginia and Maryland. In both areas, white planters forced African slaves to produce staple crops for a world market. But such superficial similarities masked substantial regional differences. In fact, "the South"—certainly the fabled solid South of the early nineteenth century—did not exist during the colonial period. As a historian of colonial Carolina explained, "the southern colonies were never a cohesive section in the same way that New England was. The great diversity of population groups . . . discouraged southern sectionalism."

PROPRIETORS OF THE CAROLINAS

Carolina was a product of the restoration of the Stuarts to the English throne. Court favorites who had followed the Stuarts into exile during the Civil War demanded tangible rewards for their loyalty. New York and New Jersey were obvious plums. So too was Carolina. Sir John Colleton, a successful English planter returned from Barbados, organized a group of eight powerful courtiers who styled themselves the True and Absolute Lords Proprietors of Carolina. On March 24, 1663, the king granted these proprietors a charter to the vast territory between Virginia and Florida and running west as far as the "South Seas."

The Carolina proprietors divided their grant into three distinct jurisdictions, anticipating no doubt that these areas would become the centers of settlement. The first region, called Albemarle, abutted Virginia. As the earlier ill-fated Roanoke colonists had discovered, the region lacked a good deepwater port. Nevertheless, it attracted a number of dissatisfied Virginians who drifted south in search of fresh land. Farther south, the mouth of the Cape Fear River seemed a second likely site for development. And third, within the present state of South Carolina, the Port Royal region contained a maze of fertile islands and meandering tidal streams.

Colleton and his associates waited for the money to roll in, but to their dismay, no one seemed particularly interested in moving to the Carolina frontier. A tiny settlement at Port Royal failed. One group of New Englanders briefly considered taking up land in the Cape Fear area, but these people were so disappointed by what they saw that they departed, leaving behind only a sign that "tended not only to the disparagement of the Land . . . but also to the great discouragement of all those that should hereafter come into these parts to settle." By this time, a majority of surviving proprietors had given up on Carolina.

THE INFLUENCE OF BARBADOS ON SOUTH CAROLINA

Anthony Ashley Cooper, later Earl of Shaftesbury, was not so easily discouraged. In 1669, he persuaded the remaining Carolinian proprietors to invest their own capital in the colony. Without such financial support, Cooper recognized, the project would surely fail. Once he received sufficient funds, this energetic organizer dispatched three hundred English colonists to Port Royal under the command of Joseph West. The fleet put in briefly at Barbados to pick up additional recruits, and in March 1670, after being punished by Atlantic gales that destroyed one ship, the expedition arrived at its destination. Only one hundred people were still alive. The unhappy settlers did not remain long at Port Royal, an unappealing, low-lying place badly exposed to Spanish attack. They moved northward, locating eventually along the more secure Ashley River. Later the colony's administrative center, Charles Town (it did not become Charleston until 1783) was established at the junction of the Ashley and Cooper rivers.

Cooper also wanted to bring order to the new society. With assistance from John Locke, the famous English philosopher (1632–1704), Cooper devised the Fundamental Constitutions of Carolina. The constitutions created a local aristocracy consisting of proprietors and lesser nobles called *landgraves* and *cassiques,* terms as inappropriate to the realities of the New World as was the idea of creating a hereditary landed elite. Persons who purchased vast tracts of land automatically received a title and the right to sit in the Council of Nobles, a body designed to administer justice, oversee civil affairs, and initiate legislation. A parliament in which smaller landowners had a voice could accept or reject bills drafted by the council. The very poor were excluded from political life altogether. Not surprisingly, the constitutions had little impact on the actual structure of government.

Before 1680, almost half the men and women who settled in the Port Royal area came from Barbados. This small Caribbean island, which produced an annual fortune in sugar, depended on slave labor. By the third quarter of the seventeenth century, Barbados had become overpopulated. Wealthy families could not provide their sons and daughters with sufficient land to maintain social status, and as the crisis intensified, Barbadians looked to Carolina for relief.

These migrants, many of whom were quite rich, traveled to Carolina as both individuals and family groups. Some even brought gangs of slaves with them to the American mainland. The Barbadians carved out plantations on the tributaries of the Cooper River and established themselves immediately as the colony's most powerful political faction.

Much of the planters' time was taken up with the search for a profitable crop. The most successful items turned out to be beef, skins, and naval stores (especially tar used to maintain ocean vessels). By the 1680s, some Carolinians had built up great herds of cattle—seven or eight hundred head in some cases. Traders who dealt with Indians brought back thousands of deerskins from the interior, and they often returned with Indian slaves as well. These commercial resources, together with tar and turpentine, enjoyed a good market. It was not until the 1690s that the planters came to appreciate fully the value of rice, but once they had done so, it quickly became the colony's main staple.

Proprietary Carolina was in a constant political uproar. Factions vied for special privilege. The Barbadian settlers, known locally as the Goose Creek Men, resisted the proprietors' policies at every turn. A large community of French Huguenots located in Craven County distrusted the Barbadians. The proprietors—an ineffectual group following the death of Cooper—appointed a series of utterly incompetent governors who only made things worse. By the end of the century, the Commons House of Assembly had assumed the right to initiate legislation. In 1719, the colonists overthrew the last proprietary governor, and in 1729, the king created separate royal governments for North and South Carolina.

THE FOUNDING OF GEORGIA

The early history of Georgia was strikingly different from that of Britain's other mainland colonies. Its settlement was really an act of aggression against Spain, a country that had as good a claim to this area as did the English. During the eighteenth century, the two nations were often at war (see Chapter 4), and South Carolinians worried that the Spaniards moving up from bases in Florida would occupy the disputed territory between Florida and the Carolina grant.

The colony owed its existence primarily to James Oglethorpe, a British general and member of Parliament who believed that he could thwart Spanish designs on the area south of Charles Town while at the same time providing a fresh

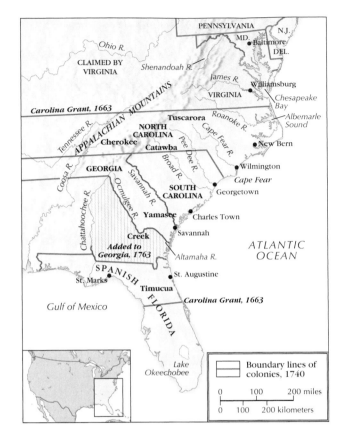

The Carolinas and Georgia
Caribbean sugar planters migrated to the Goose Creek area near Charles Town where, with knowledge supplied by African slaves, they eventually mastered rice cultivation. Poor harbors in North Carolina retarded the spread of European settlement in that region.

start for London's worthy poor, saving them from debtors' prison. In 1732, the king granted Oglethorpe and a board of trustees a charter for a new colony to be located between the Savannah and Altamaha rivers and from "sea to sea." The trustees living in the mother country were given complete control over Georgia politics, a condition the settlers soon found intolerable.

During the first years of colonization, Georgia fared no better than had earlier utopian experiments. The poor people of England showed little desire to move to an inclement frontier, and the trustees, in their turn, provided little incentive for emigration. Slavery was prohibited. So too was rum.

Almost as soon as they arrived in Georgia, the settlers complained. The colonists demanded slaves, pointing out to the trustees that unless the new planters possessed an unfree labor force, they could not compete economically with their South Carolina neighbors. The settlers also wanted a voice in local government. In 1738, 121 people living in Savannah petitioned for fundamental reforms in the colony's constitution.

While the colonists grumbled about various restrictions, Oglethorpe tried and failed to capture the Spanish fortress at Saint Augustine (1740). This personal disappointment coupled with the growing popular unrest destroyed his interest in Georgia. The trustees were forced to compromise their principles. In 1750, they

ENGLAND'S PRINCIPAL MAINLAND COLONIES

NAME	ORIGINAL PURPOSE	PRINCIPAL FOUNDER, DATE OF FOUNDING
Virginia	Commercial venture	Captain John Smith, 1607
New Amsterdam (New York)	Commercial venture	Peter Stuyvesant, Duke of York, 1613 (made English colony, 1664)
Plymouth	Refuge for English Separatists	William Bradford, 1620 (absorbed by Massachusetts, 1691)
New Hampshire	Commercial venture	John Mason, 1623
Massachusetts	Refuge for English Puritans	John Winthrop, 1628
Maryland	Refuge for English Catholics	Lord Baltimore (George Calvert), 1634
Connecticut	Expansion of Massachusetts	Thomas Hooker, 1635
Rhode Island	Refuge for dissenters from Massachusetts	Roger Williams, 1636
New Sweden (Delaware)	Commercial venture	Peter Minuit, William Penn, 1638 (included in Penn grant, 1681; given separate assembly, 1703)
North Carolina	Commercial venture	Anthony Ashley Cooper, 1663
South Carolina	Commercial venture	Anthony Ashley Cooper, 1663
New Jersey	Consolidation of new English territory, Quaker settlement	Sir George Carteret, 1664
Pennsylvania	Refuge for English Quakers	William Penn, 1681
Georgia	Discourage Spanish expansion; charity	James Oglethorpe, 1733

Sources: U.S. Bureau of the Census, *Historical Statistics of the United States: Colonial Times to 1970,* Washington, D.C., 1975; John J. McCusker and Russell R. Menard, *The Economy of British America, 1607–1789,* Chapel Hill, 1985.

permitted the settlers to import slaves. Soon Georgians could drink rum. In 1751, the trustees returned Georgia to the king, undoubtedly relieved to be free of what had become a hard-drinking, slave-owning plantation society much like that in South Carolina. The king authorized an assembly in 1751, but even with these so-cial and political changes, Georgia attracted very few new settlers.

LANDSCAPE OF FRAGMENTS

Over the course of the seventeenth century, women and men had followed lead-ers such as Baltimore, Smith, Winthrop, Bradford, Penn, and Berkeley to the New World in anticipation of creating a successful new society. Some people were religious visionaries; others were hardheaded entrepreneurs. The results of their efforts, their struggles to survive in an often hostile environment, and their interactions with various Native American groups yielded a spectrum of settlements along the Atlantic coast.

The diversity of early English colonization must be emphasized precisely because it is so easy to overlook. Even though the colonists eventually banded together and fought for independence, persistent differences separated New Englanders from Virginians, Pennsylvanians from Carolinians. The interpretive challenge, of course, is to explain how European colonists managed over the course of the eighteenth century to develop the capacity to imagine themselves a single nation.

CHRONOLOGY

1607	First English settlers arrive at Jamestown
1608–1609	Scrooby congregation (Pilgrims) leaves England for Holland
1609–1610	"Starving time" in Virginia threatens survival of the colonists
1616–1618	Plague destroys Native American populations of coastal New England
1619	Virginia assembly, called House of Burgesses, meets for the first time
	First slaves sold at Jamestown
1620	Pilgrims sign the Mayflower Compact
1622	Surprise Indian attack devastates Virginia
1624	Dutch investors create permanent settlements along Hudson River
	James I, king of England, dissolves Virginia Company
1625	Charles I ascends English throne
1630	John Winthrop transfers Massachusetts Bay charter to New England
1634	Colony of Maryland is founded
1636	Harvard College is established
	Puritan settlers found Hartford and other Connecticut Valley towns
1638	Anne Hutchinson exiled to Rhode Island
	Theophilus Eaton and John Davenport lead settlers to New Haven Colony
1639	Connecticut towns accept Fundamental Orders
1644	Second major Indian attack in Virginia
1649	Charles I executed during English Civil War
1660	Stuarts restored to the English throne
1663	Rhode Island obtains royal charter
	Proprietors receive charter for Carolina
1664	English soldiers conquer New Netherland
1677	New Hampshire becomes a royal colony
1681	William Penn granted patent for his "Holy Experiment"
1702	East and West Jersey unite to form single colony
1732	James Oglethorpe receives charter for Georgia

3

PUTTING DOWN ROOTS
Families in an Atlantic Empire

The Witherspoon family moved from Great Britain to the South Carolina backcountry early in the eighteenth century. Although otherwise indistinguishable from the thousands of other ordinary families who put down roots in British America, the Witherspoons entered history through a candid account of pioneer life produced by their son, Robert, who was only a small child at the time of their arrival.

The Witherspoons' initial reaction to the New World—at least, that of the mother and children—was despondence. "My mother and us children were still in expectation that we were coming to an agreeable place," Robert confessed, "but when we arrived and saw nothing but a wilderness and instead of a fine timbered house, nothing but a very mean dirt house, our spirits quite sunk." For many years, the Witherspoons feared they would be killed by Indians, become lost in the woods, or be attacked by snakes.

The Witherspoons managed to survive the early difficult years on the Black River. To be sure, the Carolina backcountry did not look very much like the world they had left behind. The discrepancy, however, apparently did not greatly discourage Robert's father. He had a vision of what the Black River settlement might become. "My father," Robert recounted, "gave us all the comfort he [could] by telling us we would get all these trees cut down and in a short time [there] would be plenty of inhabitants, [and] that we could see from house to house."

Robert Witherspoon's account reminds us just how much the early history of colonial America was a history created by families, and not, as some commentators would have us believe, by individuals. Neither the peopling of the Atlantic frontier, the cutting down of the forests, nor the creation of new communities where one could see from "house to house" was a process that involved what we would today recognize as state policy. Men and women made significant decisions about the character of their lives within families. It was within this primary social unit that most colonists earned their livelihoods, educated their children, defined gender, sustained religious tradition, and nursed each other in sickness. In short, the family was the source of their societal and cultural identities.

Early colonial families did not exist in isolation but were part of larger societies. As we have already discovered, the character of the first English settlements in the New World varied substantially. During much of the seventeenth century, these initial differences grew stronger as each region acquired its own history and developed its own traditions. The various local societies in which families like the Witherspoons put down roots reflected several critical elements: supply of labor, abundance of land, unusual demographic patterns, and commercial ties with European markets. In the Chesapeake, for example, an economy based almost entirely on a single staple—tobacco—created an insatiable demand for indentured servants and black slaves. In Massachusetts Bay, the extraordinary longevity of the founders generated a level of social and political stability that Virginians and Marylanders did not attain until the very end of the seventeenth century.

By 1660, it seemed regional differences had undermined the idea of a unified English empire in America. During the reign of Charles II, however, a trend toward cultural convergence began. Although subcultures had evolved in strikingly different directions, countervailing forces such as common language and religion gradually pulled English American settlers together. Parliament took advantage of this trend and began to establish a uniform set of rules for the expanding American empire. The process was slow and uneven, often sparking violent colonial resistance. By the end of the seventeenth century, however, England had made significant progress toward transforming its New World provinces into an empire that produced needed raw materials and purchased manufactured goods.

SOURCES OF STABILITY: FAMILY VALUES IN SEVENTEENTH-CENTURY NEW ENGLAND

Seventeenth-century New Englanders successfully replicated in America a traditional social order they had known in England. The transfer of a familiar way of life to the New World seemed less difficult for these Puritan migrants than it did for the many English men and women who settled in the Chesapeake colonies. Their contrasting experiences, fundamental to an understanding of the development of both cultures, can be explained, at least in part, by the development of Puritan families.

TRADITION AND A NEW SOCIAL ORDER

Early New Englanders believed God ordained the family for human benefit. It was essential to the maintenance of social order, since outside the family, men and women succumbed to carnal temptation. Such people had no one to sustain them or remind them of Scripture.

The godly family, at least in theory, was ruled by a patriarch, father to his children, husband to his wife, the source of authority and object of unquestioned obedience. The wife shared responsibility for the raising of children, but in decisions of importance, especially those related to property, she was expected to defer to her spouse.

The New Englanders' concern about the character of the godly family is not surprising. This institution played a central role in shaping their society. In contrast to those who migrated to Virginia and Maryland, New Englanders crossed the Atlantic within nuclear families. That is, they moved within established units consisting of a father, mother, and their dependent children rather than as single youths and adults. People who migrated to America within families preserved local English customs more fully than did the youths who traveled to other parts of the continent as single men and women. The comforting presence of immediate family members reduced the shock of adjusting to a strange environment three thousand miles from home. Even in the 1630s, the ratio of men to women in New England was fairly well balanced, about three males for every two females. Persons who had not already married in England before coming to the New World could expect to form nuclear families of their own.

The great migration of the 1630s and 1640s brought approximately 20,000 persons to New England. After 1642, the English Civil War reduced the flood of people moving to Massachusetts Bay to a trickle. Nevertheless, by the end of the century, the population of New England had reached almost 120,000, an amazing increase considering the small number of original immigrants. Historians have been hard pressed to explain this striking rate of growth. Some have suggested that New Englanders married very young, thus giving couples extra years in which to produce large families. Other scholars have maintained that New England women must have been more fertile than their Old World counterparts.

Neither demographic theory adequately explains how so few migrants produced such a large population. Early New England marriage patterns, for example, did not differ substantially from those recorded in seventeenth-century England. The average age for men at first marriage was the mid-twenties. Wives were slightly younger than their husbands, the average age being about twenty-two. There is no evidence that New Englanders favored child brides. Nor, for that matter, were Puritan families unusually large by European standards of the period.

The explanation for the region's extraordinary growth turned out to be survival rather than fertility. Put simply, people who, under normal conditions, would have died in contemporary Europe lived in New England. Indeed, the life expectancy of seventeenth-century settlers was not very different from our own. Males who survived infancy might have expected to see their seventieth birthday. Twenty percent of the men of the first generation reached the age of eighty. The figures for women were only slightly lower. Longer life altered family relations. New England males lived not only to see their own children reach adulthood but also to witness the birth of grandchildren. In other words, this society produced real patriarchs.

COMMONWEALTH OF FAMILIES

The life cycle of the seventeenth-century New England family began with marriage. Young men and women generally initiated courtships. If parents exercised a voice in such matters, it was to discourage union with a person of unsound moral character. Puritan ministers advised single people to choose godly partners, warning:

The Wretch that is alone to Mammon Wed,
May chance to find a Satan in the bed.

In this highly religious society, there was not much chance that young people would stray far from shared community values. The overwhelming majority of the region's population married, for in New England, the single life was not only morally suspect but also economically difficult.

A couple without land could not support an independent and growing family in these agrarian communities. While men generally brought farmland to the marriage, prospective brides were expected to provide a dowry worth approximately one-half what the bridegroom offered. Women often contributed money or household goods. During the seventeenth century, men and women generally lived in the communities of their parents and grandparents. New Englanders usually managed to fall in love with a neighbor, and most marriages took place between men and women living less than 13 miles apart.

The household was primarily a place of work—very demanding work. The primary goal, of course, was to clear enough land to feed the family. Additional cultivation allowed the farmer to produce a surplus that could then be sold or bartered, and since agrarian families required items that could not be manufactured at home—metal tools, for example—they usually grew more than they consumed. Early American farmers were not economically self-sufficient.

Towns were collections of families, not individuals. Over time, these families intermarried, so the community became an elaborate kinship network. Social

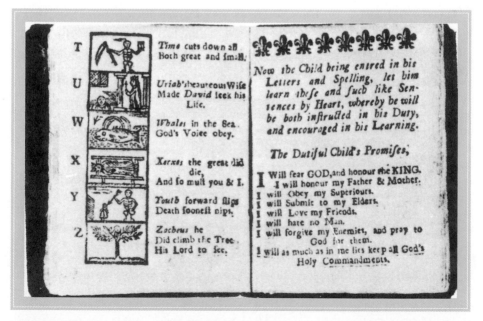

New England parents took seriously their responsibility for the spiritual welfare of their children. To seek the word of God, young people had to learn to read. The New-England Primer, *shown here,* was their primary vehicle.

historians have discovered that in many New England towns, the original founders dominated local politics and economic affairs for several generations. Not surprisingly, newcomers who were not absorbed into the family system tended to move away from the village with greater frequency than did the sons and daughters of the established lineage groups. Congregational churches were also built on a family foundation. During the earliest years of settlement, the churches accepted persons who could demonstrate they were among God's "elect."

Colonists regarded education as primarily a family responsibility. Parents were supposed to instruct children in the principles of Christianity, and so it was necessary to teach boys and girls how to read. In 1642, the Massachusetts General Court reminded the Bay Colonists of their obligation to catechize their families. Five years later, the legislature ordered towns containing at least fifteen families to open an elementary school supported by local taxes. Villages of a hundred or more families had to maintain more advanced grammar schools, which taught a basic knowledge of Latin. At least eleven schools were operating in 1647, and despite their expense, new schools were established throughout the century.

After 1638, young men could attend Harvard College, the first institution of higher learning founded in England's mainland colonies. This family-based education system worked. A large majority of the region's adult males could read and write, an accomplishment not achieved in the Chesapeake colonies for another century. The literacy rate for women was somewhat lower, but by the standards of the period, it was still impressive. A printing press operated in Cambridge as early as 1639.

WOMEN'S LIVES IN PURITAN NEW ENGLAND

Women worked on family farms. They did not, however, necessarily do the same jobs that men performed. Women usually handled separate tasks, including cooking, washing, clothes making, dairying, and gardening. Their production of food was absolutely essential to the survival of most households. Sometimes wives—and the overwhelming majority of adult seventeenth-century women were married—raised poultry, and by selling surplus birds they achieved some economic independence. In fact, during this period women were often described as "deputy husbands," a label that drew attention to their dependence on family patriarchs as well as to their roles as decision makers.

Women also joined churches in greater number than men. Within a few years of founding, many New England congregations contained two female members for every male, a process historians describe as the "feminization of colonial religion." Contemporaries offered different explanations for the gender shift. Cotton Mather, the leading Congregational minister of Massachusetts Bay, argued that God had created "far more *godly Women*" than men. Others thought that the life-threatening experience of childbirth gave women a deeper appreciation of religion. The Quakers gave women an even larger role in religious affairs, which may help to explain the popularity of this sect among ordinary women.

In political and legal matters, society sharply curtailed the rights of colonial women. According to English common law, a wife exercised no control over property. She could not, for example, sell land, although if her husband decided to dispose of their holdings, he was free to do so without her permission. Divorce was extremely difficult to obtain in any colony before the American Revolution. Indeed, a person married to a cruel or irresponsible spouse had little recourse but to run away or accept the unhappy situation.

Most women were neither prosperous entrepreneurs nor abject slaves. Surviving letters indicate that men and women generally accommodated themselves to the gender roles they thought God had ordained. One of early America's most creative poets, Anne Bradstreet, wrote movingly of the fulfillment she had found with her husband. In a piece titled "To my Dear and loving Husband," Bradstreet declared:

> *If ever two were one, then surely we.*
> *If ever man were lov'd by wife, then thee;*
> *If ever wife was happy in a man,*
> *Compare with me ye women if you can.*

Although Puritan couples worried that the affection they felt for a husband or a wife might turn their thoughts away from God's perfect love, they were willing to accept the risk.

RANK AND STATUS IN NEW ENGLAND SOCIETY

During the seventeenth century, the New England colonies attracted neither noblemen nor paupers. The absence of these social groups meant that the American social structure seemed incomplete by contemporary European standards. The settlers were not displeased that the poor remained in the Old World. The lack of very rich persons—and in this period great wealth frequently accompanied noble title—was quite another matter. According to the prevailing hierarchical view of the structure of society, well-placed individuals were natural rulers, people intended by God to exercise political authority over the rank and file. Migration forced the colonists, however, to choose their rulers from men of more modest status. Persons who would never have been "natural rulers" in England became provincial gentry in the various northern colonies.

The problem was that while most New Englanders accepted a hierarchical view of society, they disagreed over their assigned places. Both Massachusetts Bay and Connecticut passed sumptuary laws—statutes that limited the wearing of fine apparel to the wealthy and prominent—to curb the pretensions of those of lower status. Yet such restraints could not prevent some people from rising and others from falling within the social order.

Most northern colonists were yeomen (independent farmers) who worked their own land. While few became rich in America, even fewer fell hopelessly into debt. Their daily lives, especially for those who settled New England, centered on scattered little communities where they participated in village meetings, church-related matters, and militia training. Possession of land gave agrarian families a sense of independence from external authority. As one man bragged to those who had stayed behind in England, "Here are no hard landlords to rack us with high rents or extorting fines. . . . Here every man may be master of his own labour and land . . . and if he have nothing but his hands he may set up his trade, and by industry grow rich."

It was not unusual for northern colonists to work as servants at some point in their lives. This system of labor differed greatly from the pattern of servitude that developed in seventeenth-century Virginia and Maryland. New Englanders seldom recruited servants from the Old World. The forms of agriculture practiced in this region, mixed cereal and dairy farming, made employment of large gangs of dependent workers uneconomic. Rather, New England families placed their adolescent children in nearby homes. These young persons contracted for four or five years and seemed more like apprentices than servants. Servitude was not simply a means by which one group exploited another. It was a form of vocational training.

By the end of the seventeenth century, the New England Puritans had developed a compelling story about their own history in the New World. The founders had been extraordinarily godly men and women, and in a heroic effort to establish a purer form of religion, pious families had passed "over the vast ocean into this vast and howling wilderness." Although the children and grandchildren of the first generation sometimes questioned their own ability to please the Lord, they recognized the mission to the New World had been a success: They were "as Prosperous as ever, there is Peace & Plenty, & the Country flourisheth."

THE PLANTERS' WORLD

Unlike New England's settlers, the men and women who emigrated to the Chesapeake region did not move in family units. They traveled to the New World as young unmarried servants, young people cut off from the security of traditional kin relations. Although these immigrants came from a cross section of English society, most had been middling farmers. It is now estimated that 70 to 85 percent of the white colonists who went to Virginia and Maryland during the seventeenth century were not free; that is, they owed four or five years' labor in exchange for the cost of passage to America. If the servant was under age 15, he or she had to serve a full seven years. The overwhelming majority of these laborers were males between the ages of 18 and 22. In fact, before 1640, the ratio of males to females stood at 6 to 1. This figure dropped to about $2\frac{1}{2}$ to 1 by the end of the century, but the sex ratio in the Chesapeake was never as favorable as it had been in early Massachusetts.

FAMILY LIFE IN A PERILOUS ENVIRONMENT

Most immigrants to the Chesapeake region died soon after arriving. It is difficult to ascertain the exact cause of death in most cases, but malaria and other diseases took a frightful toll. Recent studies also indicate that drinking water conta-

Seventeenth-century Puritan carvers transformed the production of gravestones into a distinctive folk art form.

minated with salt killed many colonists living in low-lying areas. Throughout the entire seventeenth century, high mortality rates had a profound effect on this society. Life expectancy for Chesapeake males was about forty-three, some ten to twenty years less than for men born in New England. For women, life was even shorter. A full 25 percent of all children died in infancy; another 25 percent did not see their twentieth birthdays. The survivors were often weak or ill, unable to perform hard physical labor.

These demographic conditions retarded normal population increase. Young women who might have become wives and mothers could not do so until they had completed their terms of servitude. They thus lost several reproductive years, and in a society in which so many children died in infancy, late marriage greatly restricted family size. Moreover, because of the unbalanced sex ratio, many adult males simply could not find wives. Migration not only cut them off from their English families but also deprived them of an opportunity to form new ones. Without a constant flow of immigrants, the population of Virginia and Maryland would have actually declined.

High mortality compressed the family life cycle into a few short years. One partner in a marriage usually died within seven years. Only one in three Chesapeake marriages survived as long as a decade. Not only did children not meet grandparents—they often did not even know their own parents. Widows and widowers quickly remarried, bringing children by former unions into their new homes, and it was not uncommon for a child to grow up with persons to whom he or she bore no blood relation. The psychological effects of such experiences on Chesapeake settlers cannot be measured. People probably learned to cope with a high degree of personal insecurity. However they adjusted, it is clear family life in this region was vastly more impermanent than it was in the New England colonies during the same period.

Women were obviously in great demand in the early southern colonies. Some historians have argued that scarcity heightened the woman's bargaining power in the marriage market. If she was an immigrant, she did not have to worry about obtaining parental consent. She was on her own in the New World and free to select whomever she pleased.

Nevertheless, liberation from traditional restraints on seventeenth-century women must not be exaggerated. As servants, women were vulnerable to sexual exploitation by their masters. Moreover, in this unhealthy environment, childbearing was extremely dangerous, and women in the Chesapeake usually died twenty years earlier than their New England counterparts.

RANK AND STATUS IN PLANTATION SOCIETY

Colonists who managed to survive grew tobacco—as much tobacco as they possibly could. This crop became the Chesapeake staple, and since it was relatively easy to cultivate, anyone with a few acres of cleared land could harvest leaves for export. Cultivation of tobacco did not, however, produce a society roughly equal in wealth and status. To the contrary, tobacco generated inequality. Some planters amassed large fortunes; others barely subsisted. Labor made the difference, for to succeed in this staple economy, one had to control the labor of other men and women. More workers in the fields meant larger harvests, and, of course, larger profits. Since free persons showed no interest in growing another man's tobacco, not even for wages, wealthy planters relied on white laborers who were not free, as well as on slaves. The social structure that developed in the seventeenth-century Chesapeake reflected a wild, often unscrupulous scramble to bring men and women of three races—black, white, and Indian—into various degrees of dependence.

Great planters dominated Chesapeake society. The group was small, only a trifling portion of the population of Virginia and Maryland. During the early decades of the seventeenth century, the composition of Chesapeake gentry was continually in flux. Some gentlemen died before they could establish a secure claim to high social status; others returned to England, thankful to have survived. Not until the 1650s did the family names of those who would become famous eighteenth-century gentry appear in the records.

These ambitious men arrived in America with capital. They invested immediately in laborers, and one way or another, they obtained huge tracts of the best tobacco-growing land. The members of this gentry were not technically aristocrats, for they did not possess titles that could be passed from generation to generation. They gave themselves military titles, served as justices of the peace on the county courts, and directed local (Anglican) church affairs as members of the vestry. Over time, these gentry families intermarried so frequently that they created a vast network of cousins. During the eighteenth century, it was not uncommon to find a half dozen men with the same surname sitting simultaneously in the Virginia legislature.

Freemen formed the largest class in Chesapeake society. Their origins were strikingly different from those of the gentry, or for that matter, from those of New England's yeomen farmers. Chesapeake freemen traveled to the New World as indentured servants and, by sheer good fortune, managed to remain alive to the end of their contracts. If they had dreamed of becoming great planters, they were gravely disappointed. Most seventeenth-century freemen lived on the edge of poverty. Some freemen, of course, did better in America than they would have in contemporary England, but in both Virginia and Maryland, historians have found a sharp economic division separating the gentry from the rest of white society.

Below the freemen came indentured servants. Membership in this group was not demeaning; after all, servitude was a temporary status. But servitude in the Chesapeake colonies was not the benign institution it was in New England. Great planters purchased servants to grow tobacco. No one seemed overly concerned whether these laborers received decent food and clothes, much less whether they acquired trade skills. Young people, thousands of them, cut off from family ties, sick often to the point of death, unable to obtain normal sexual release, regarded their servitude as a form of slavery. Not surprisingly, the gentry worried that unhappy servants and impoverished freemen, what the planters called the "giddy multitude," would rebel at the slightest provocation, a fear that turned out to be fully justified.

The character of social mobility—and this observation applies only to whites—changed considerably during the seventeenth century. Until the 1680s, it was relatively easy for a newcomer who possessed capital to become a member of the planter elite. No one paid much attention to the reputation or social standing of one's English family.

Sometime after the 1680s, however—the precise date is impossible to establish—a dramatic demographic shift occurred. Although infant mortality remained high, life expectancy rates for those who survived childhood in the Chesapeake improved significantly, and for the first time in the history of Virginia and Maryland, important leadership positions went to men who had actually been born in America. This transition has been described by one political historian as the "emergence of a creole majority," in other words, as the creation of an indigenous ruling elite. The rise of this class helped give the tobacco colonies the kind of political and cultural stability that had eluded earlier generations of planter adventurers.

The key to success in this creole society was ownership of slaves. Those planters who held more blacks could grow more tobacco and thus could acquire fresh capital needed to purchase additional laborers. Over time, the rich not only became richer; they also formed a distinct ruling elite that newcomers found increasingly difficult to enter.

Opportunities for advancement also decreased for freemen in the region. Studies of mid-seventeenth-century Maryland reveal that some servants managed to become moderately prosperous farmers and small officeholders. But as the gentry consolidated its hold on political and economic institutions, ordinary people discovered it was much harder to rise in Chesapeake society. Those men and women with more ambitious dreams headed for Pennsylvania, North Carolina, or western Virginia.

Social institutions that figured importantly in the daily experience of New Englanders were either weak or nonexistent in the Chesapeake colonies. In part, the sluggish development resulted from the continuation of high infant mortality rates. There was little incentive to build elementary schools, for example, if half the children would die before reaching adulthood.

Tobacco influenced the spread of other institutions in the region. Planters were scattered along the rivers, often separated from their nearest neighbors by miles of poor roads. Since the major tobacco growers traded directly with English merchants, they had no need for towns. Whatever items they required were either made on the plantation or imported from Europe. Other than the centers of colonial government, Jamestown (and later Williamsburg) and St. Mary's City (and later Annapolis), there were no villages capable of sustaining a rich community life before the late eighteenth century. Seventeenth-century Virginia did not even possess a printing press.

RACE AND FREEDOM IN BRITISH AMERICA

Many people who landed in the colonies were Africans taken as slaves to cultivate rice, sugar, and tobacco. As the Native Americans were exterminated and the supply of white indentured servants dried up, European planters demanded even more African laborers.

ROOTS OF SLAVERY

Between the sixteenth and nineteenth centuries, slave traders carried almost eleven million blacks to the Americas. Most of these men and women were sold in Brazil or in the Caribbean. A relatively small number of Africans reached British North America, and of this group, the majority arrived after 1700. Because slaves performed hard physical labor, planters preferred purchasing young males. In many early slave communities, men outnumbered women by a ratio of two to one.

English colonists did not hesitate to enslave black people or, for that matter, Native Americans. While the institution of slavery had long before died out in the mother country, New World settlers quickly discovered how well this particular labor system operated in the Spanish and Portuguese colonies. The decision to bring African slaves to the colonies, therefore, was based primarily on economic considerations.

English masters, however, seldom justified the practice purely in terms of planter profits. Indeed, they adopted a quite different pattern of rhetoric. English writers associated blacks in Africa with heathen religion, barbarous behavior, sexual promiscuity—in fact, with evil itself. From such a racist perspective, the enslavement of Africans seemed unobjectionable. The planters maintained that if black slaves converted to Christianity, shedding their supposedly savage ways, they would actually benefit from their loss of freedom.

Africans first landed in Virginia in 1619. For the next fifty years, the status of the colony's black people remained unclear. English settlers classified some black laborers as slaves for life, as chattel to be bought and sold at the master's will. But other Africans became servants, presumably for stated periods of time, and it was even possible for a few blacks to purchase their freedom. Several seventeenth-century Africans became successful Virginia planters.

One reason Virginia lawmakers tolerated such confusion was that the black population remained very small. By 1660, fewer than fifteen hundred people of African origin lived in the entire colony (compared to a white population of approximately twenty-six thousand), and it hardly seemed necessary for the legislature to draw up an elaborate slave code to control so few men and women. If the planters could have obtained more black laborers, they certainly would have done so. The problem was supply. During this period, slave traders sold their cargoes on Barbados or the other sugar islands of the West Indies, where they fetched higher prices than Virginians could afford. In fact, before 1680, most blacks who reached England's colonies on the North American mainland came from Barbados or through New Netherland rather than directly from Africa.

By the end of the seventeenth century, the legal status of Virginia's black people was no longer in doubt. They were slaves for life, and so were their children after them. This transformation reflected changes in the supply of Africans to British North America. After 1672, the Royal African Company was chartered to meet the colonial planters' demands for black laborers. Between 1695 and 1709, more than eleven thousand Africans were sold in Virginia alone; many others went to Maryland and the Carolinas. Although American merchants—most of them based in Rhode Island—entered the trade during the eighteenth century, the

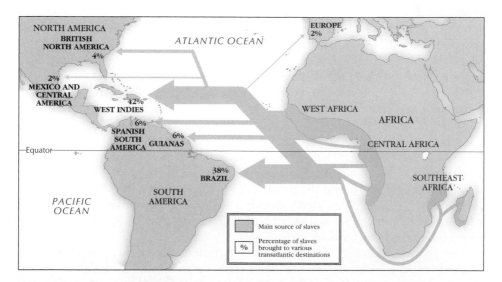

The African Slave Trade
Between 1619 and 1760, about a half million African captives were brought to the thirteen main-land English colonies, far fewer than were taken to other parts of the Americas.

British continued to supply the bulk of the slaves to the mainland market for the entire colonial period.

The expanding black population apparently frightened white colonists, for as the number of Africans increased, lawmakers drew up ever stricter slave codes. It was during this period that racism, always a latent element in New World societies, was fully revealed. By 1700, slavery was unequivocally based on the color of a person's skin. Blacks fell into this status simply because they were black. A vicious pattern of discrimination had been set in motion. Even conversion to Christianity did not free the African from bondage. The white planter could deal with his black property as he alone saw fit, and one revolting Virginia statute excused masters who killed slaves, on the grounds that no rational person would purposely "destroy his own estate." Black women constantly had to fear sexual violation by a master or his sons. Children born to a slave woman became slaves regardless of the father's race. Unlike the Spanish colonies, where persons of lighter color enjoyed greater privileges in society, the English colonies tolerated no mixing of the races. Mulattoes and pure Africans received the same treatment.

CONSTRUCTING AFRICAN AMERICAN IDENTITIES

The slave experience varied substantially from colony to colony. The daily life of a black person in South Carolina, for example, was quite different from that of an African American who happened to live in Pennsylvania or Massachusetts Bay. The size and density of the slave population determined in large measure how successfully blacks could maintain a separate cultural identity. In the lowlands of South Carolina during the eighteenth century, 60 percent of the population was black. The men and women were placed on large, isolated rice plantations, and their contact with whites was limited. In these areas blacks developed creole languages, which mixed the basic vocabulary of English with words borrowed from various African tongues. Slaves on the large rice plantations also were able to establish elaborate and enduring kinship networks that may have helped reduce the more dehumanizing aspects of bondage.

In the New England and Middle Colonies, and even in Virginia, African Americans made up a smaller percentage of the population: 40 percent in Virginia, 8 percent in Pennsylvania, and 3 percent in Massachusetts. In such environments, contact between blacks and whites was more frequent than in South Carolina and Georgia. These population patterns had a profound effect on northern and Chesapeake blacks, for while they escaped the physical drudgery of rice cultivation, they found the preservation of an independent African identity difficult. In northern cities, slaves working as domestics and living in the houses of their masters saw other blacks but had little opportunity to develop creole languages or reaffirm a common African past.

In eighteenth-century Virginia, native-born or creole blacks, people who had learned to cope with whites on a daily basis, looked with contempt on slaves who had just arrived from Africa. These "outlandish" Negroes, as they were called, were forced by blacks as well as whites to accept elements of English culture. It was especially important for newcomers to speak English.

Old Plantation, *a watercolor by an unknown artist (about 1800), shows that African customs survived plantation slavery. The man and women in the center dance (possibly to celebrate a wedding) to the music of drum and banjo. Instruments, turbans, and scarves reflect a distinctive African American culture in the New World.*

Newly arrived men and women from Africa were far more likely to run away, assault their masters, and organize rebellion than were the creole slaves. The people described in colonial newspaper advertisements as "New Negroes" desperately tried to regain control over their lives. In 1770—just to cite one example—two young Africans, both recently sold in Virginia, "went off with several others, being persuaded that they could find their way back to their own Country."

Despite such wrenching experiences, black slaves creatively preserved elements of an African heritage. The process of establishing African American traditions involved an imaginative reshaping of African and European customs into something that was neither African nor European. It was African American. The slaves accepted Christianity, but they did so on their own terms—terms their masters seldom fully understood. Blacks transformed Christianity into an expression of religious feeling in which an African element remained vibrant. In music and folk art, they gave voice to a cultural identity that even the most degrading conditions could not eradicate.

A major turning point in the history of African American people occurred during the early decades of the eighteenth century. At this time, blacks living in England's mainland colonies began to reproduce successfully. The number of live births exceeded deaths, and from that date, the expansion of the African American population owed more to natural increase than to the importation of new slaves. Even though thousands of new Africans arrived each year, the creole population was always much larger than that of the immigrant blacks.

Although mainland blacks lived longer than the blacks of Jamaica or Barbados, they were, after all, still slaves. They protested their debasement in many ways, some in individual acts of violence, others in organized revolt. The most serious slave rebellion of the colonial period was the Stono Uprising, which took place in September 1739. One hundred fifty South Carolina blacks rose up and, seizing guns and ammunition, murdered several white planters. "With Colours displayed, and two Drums beating," they marched toward Spanish Florida, where they had been promised freedom. The local militia soon overtook the rebellious slaves and killed most of them. Although the uprising was short-lived, such incidents helped persuade whites everywhere that their own blacks might secretly be planning bloody revolt. Fear bred paranoia. When a white servant woman in New York City announced in 1741 that blacks intended to burn the town, frightened authorities executed 34 suspected arsonists and dispatched 72 others, either to the West Indies or to Madeira, off the coast of Morocco. While the level of interracial violence in colonial society was quite low, everyone recognized that the blacks—in the words of one Virginia governor—longed "to Shake off the fetters of Slavery."

COMMERCIAL BLUEPRINT FOR EMPIRE

Unlike the Spanish Empire which ruled its New World possessions from Madrid, the English Crown was slow to exercise direct authority over the American mainland colonies. The early Stuarts had other, more pressing matters with which to deal, and it was only after the Restoration of Charles II in 1660 that administrators in London began to develop a clear plan for empire. No one doubted that the colonists should be brought more tightly under the control of the mother country. The question before those who shaped imperial policies—a group of courtiers, merchants, and parliamentarians—was how to intervene most effectively in the affairs of men and women who lived so far away and who had learned to make decisions about local governance for themselves. The regulatory system that evolved during this period formed a framework for commercial empire that survived with only minor adjustment until 1776.

ECONOMIC COMPETITION

By the 1660s the dominant commercial powers of Europe adopted economic principles that later critics would term *mercantilism*. Proponents of this position argued that since trading nations were engaged in a fierce competition for the world's resources—mostly for raw materials transported from dependent colonies—one nation's commercial success translated directly into a loss for its rivals. It seemed logical, therefore, that England would want to protect its own markets from France or Holland. Later advocates of free trade, such as the famous eighteenth-century Scottish economist Adam Smith, claimed that mercantilism actually worked against the nation's true economic interests. Smith insisted that an open competition among merchants would stimulate trade and raise everyone's standard of living. But for seventeenth-century planners free markets made no sense. They argued that trade tightly regulated by the central government represented the only way to increase the nation's wealth at the expense of competitors.

Smith's discussion of mercantilism suggested that English policymakers during the reign of Charles II had developed a well-integrated set of ideas about the nature of international commerce and a carefully planned set of mercantilist government policies to implement them. They did nothing of the sort. Administrators responded to particular problems, usually on an individual basis. National interest alone did not shape public policy. Instead, the needs of several powerful interest groups led to the rise of English commercial regulation.

Each group looked to colonial commerce to solve a different problem. For his part, the king wanted money. For their part, English merchants were eager to exclude Dutch rivals from lucrative American markets and needed government assistance to compete successfully with the Dutch, even in Virginia or Massachusetts Bay. From the perspective of the landed gentry who sat in Parliament, England needed a stronger navy, and that in turn meant expansion of the domestic shipbuilding industry. And almost everyone agreed England should establish a more favorable balance of trade, that is, increase exports, decrease imports, and grow richer at the expense of other European states. None of these ideas was particularly innovative, but taken together they provided a blueprint for England's first empire.

CONTROLLING THE MARKETPLACE

Parliament passed a Navigation Act in 1660. The statute was the most significant piece of imperial legislation drafted before the American Revolution. Colonists from New Hampshire to Georgia paid close attention to the details of this statute, which stated (1) that no ship could trade in the colonies unless it had been constructed in either England or America and carried a crew that was at least 75 percent English (for these purposes, colonists counted as Englishmen), and (2) that certain enumerated goods of great value that were not produced in England—tobacco, sugar, cotton, indigo, dyewoods, ginger—could be transported from the colonies *only* to an English or another colonial port. In 1704, Parliament added rice and molasses to the enumerated list; in 1705, rosins, tars, and turpentines needed for shipbuilding were included.

The act of 1660 was masterfully conceived. It encouraged the development of domestic shipbuilding and prohibited European rivals from obtaining enumerated goods anywhere except in England. Since the Americans had to pay import duties in England (for this purpose colonists did not count as Englishmen) on such items as sugar and tobacco, the legislation also provided the crown with another source of income.

Over the next several decades Parliament strengthened the laws governing imperial commerce. In 1663, for example, it declared in the Staple Act that the colonists could only transport crops such as tobacco directly to England, thus cutting the Americans off from a larger, and potentially more lucrative world market for their products. English rulers wanted to keep Dutch rivals from dealing directly with colonial planters, but however much sense the new trade policy made in London, Americans protested that the Navigation Acts under-mined their own prosperity. When some colonial merchants began to circum-vent the commercial restrictions, sailing directly to Holland and France with goods such as sugar and tobacco, Parliament responded with further restric-tions that made it impossible for the colonists to avoid paying regular English customs duties.

Parliament passed the last major piece of imperial legislation in 1696. Among other things, the statute tightened enforcement procedures, putting pres-sure specifically on the colonial governors to keep England's competitors out of American ports. The act of 1696 also expanded the American customs service and for the first time set up vice-admiralty courts in the colonies. The year 1696 witnessed one other significant change in the imperial system. William III created a body of policy advisers known as the Board of Trade. This group monitored colonial affairs closely and provided government officials with the best available advice on commercial and other problems. For several decades, at least, it ener-getically carried out its responsibilities.

The members of Parliament believed these reforms would belatedly compel the colonists to accept the Navigation Acts, and in large measure they were cor-rect. By 1700, American goods transshipped through the mother country ac-counted for a quarter of all English exports, an indication the colonists found it profitable to obey the commercial regulations. In fact, during the eighteenth cen-tury, smuggling from Europe to America dried up almost completely.

PROVINCES IN REVOLT, 1676–1691

The Navigation Acts created an illusion of unity. English administrators superim-posed a system of commercial regulation on a number of different, often unstable American colonies and called it an empire. But these statutes did not remove long-standing differences. Within each society, men and women struggled to bring order out of disorder, to establish stable ruling elites, to diffuse ethnic and racial tensions, and to cope with population pressures that imperial planners only dimly understood. During the final decades of the seventeenth century, these efforts sometimes sparked revolt.

First, the Virginians rebelled, and then a few years later, political violence swept through Maryland, New York, and Massachusetts Bay, England's most populous mainland colonies. The uprisings certainly did not involve confronta-tions between ordinary people and their rulers. Indeed, the events were not in any modern sense of the word ideological. In each colony, the local gentry split into factions, usually the "outs" versus the "ins," and each side proclaimed its political legitimacy.

CIVIL WAR IN VIRGINIA: BACON'S REBELLION

After 1660, the Virginia economy steadily declined. Returns from tobacco had not been good for some time, and the Navigation Acts reduced profits even fur-ther. Into this unhappy environment came thousands of indentured servants, people drawn to Virginia, as the governor explained, "in hope of bettering their condition in a Growing Country."

The reality bore little relation to their dreams. A hurricane destroyed one entire tobacco crop, and in 1667, Dutch warships captured the tobacco fleet just as it was about to sail for England. Indentured servants complained about lack of food and clothing. No wonder that Virginia's governor, Sir William Berkeley, despaired of ever ruling "a People where six parts of seven at least are Poor, Endebted, Discontented and Armed."

Enter Nathaniel Bacon. This ambitious young man arrived in Virginia in 1674. He came from a respectable English family and set himself up immediately as a substantial planter. But he wanted more. Bacon envied the government patronage monopolized by Berkeley's cronies, a group known locally as the Green Spring faction. When Bacon attempted to obtain a license to engage in the fur trade, he was rebuffed. If Bacon had been willing to wait, he probably would have been accepted into the ruling clique, but as subsequent events would demonstrate, Bacon was not a man of patience.

Elements beyond Bacon's control thrust him suddenly into the center of Virginia politics. In 1675, Indians reacting to white encroachment attacked several outlying plantations, killing a few colonists, and Virginians expected the governor to send an army to retaliate. Instead, early in 1676, Berkeley called for the construction of a line of defensive forts, a plan that seemed to the settlers both expensive and ineffective. Indeed, the strategy raised embarrassing questions. Was Berkeley protecting his own fur monopoly? Was he planning to reward his friends with contracts to build useless forts?

While people speculated about such matters, Bacon stepped forward. He boldly offered to lead a volunteer army against the Indians at no cost to the hard-pressed Virginia taxpayers. All he demanded was an official commission from Berkeley giving him military command and the right to attack other Indians, not just the hostile Susquehannock group. The governor steadfastly refused. With some justification, Berkeley regarded his upstart rival as a fanatic on the subject of Indians. The governor saw no reason to exterminate peaceful tribes simply to avenge the death of a few white settlers.

What followed would have been comic had not so many people died. Bacon thundered against the governor's treachery; Berkeley labeled Bacon a traitor. Both men appealed to the populace for support. On several occasions, Bacon marched his followers to the frontier, but they either failed to find the enemy or, worse, massacred friendly Indians. At one point, Bacon burned Jamestown to the ground, forcing the governor to flee to the colony's Eastern Shore.

As the civil war dragged on, it became increasingly apparent that Bacon and his supporters had only the vaguest notion of what they were trying to achieve. The members of the planter elite never seemed fully to appreciate that the rank-and-file soldiers, often black slaves and poor white servants, had serious, legitimate grievances against Berkeley's corrupt government and were demanding substantial reforms, not just a share in the governor's fur monopoly.

When Charles II learned of the fighting in Virginia, he dispatched a thousand regular soldiers to Jamestown. By the time they arrived, Berkeley had regained full control over the colony's government. In October 1676, Bacon died after a brief illness, and within a few months, his band of rebel followers had dispersed.

THE GLORIOUS REVOLUTION IN THE BAY COLONY

During John Winthrop's lifetime, Massachusetts settlers developed an inflated sense of their independence from the mother country. After 1660, however, it became difficult even to pretend that the Puritan colony was a separate state. Royal officials such as Edward Randolph demanded full compliance with the Navigation Acts. A few Puritan ministers and magistrates regarded compromise with England as treason, a breaking of the Lord's covenant. Other spokesmen, recognizing the changing political realities within the empire, urged a more moderate course.

In 1675, in the midst of this ongoing political crisis, the Indians dealt the New Englanders a terrible setback. Metacomet, a Wampanoag chief the whites called King Philip, declared war against the colonists. The powerful Narragansett, whose lands the settlers had long coveted, joined Metacomet, and in little more than a year of fighting, the Indians destroyed scores of frontier vil-

Metacomet, the Wampanoag chief known to English colonists as King Philip, led Native Americans in a major war designed to remove the Europeans from New England.

lages, killed hundreds of colonists, and disrupted the entire regional economy. More than one thousand Indians and New Englanders died in the conflict.

In 1684, the debate over the Bay Colony's relation to the mother country ended abruptly. The Court of Chancery, sitting in London and acting on a petition from the king, annulled the charter of the Massachusetts Bay Company. In one stroke of a pen, the patent that Winthrop had so lovingly carried to America in 1630, the foundation for a "city on a hill," was gone. The decision forced the most stubborn Puritans to recognize they were part of an empire run by people who did not share their particular religious vision.

James II decided to restructure the government of the entire region as the Dominion of New England. In various stages from 1686 to 1689, the Dominion incorporated Massachusetts, Connecticut, Rhode Island, Plymouth, New York, New Jersey, and New Hampshire under a single appointed royal governor. For this demanding position, James selected Sir Edmund Andros (pronounced Andrews), a military veteran of tyrannical temperament. Andros arrived in Boston in 1686, and within a matter of months he had alienated everyone: Puritans, moderates, and even Anglican merchants. Not only did Andros abolish elective assemblies, but he also enforced the Navigation Acts with such rigor that he brought about commercial depression.

Early in 1689, news of the Glorious Revolution reached Boston. The previous fall, the ruling class of England had deposed James II, an admitted Catholic, and placed his daughter Mary and her husband, William of Orange, on the throne as joint monarchs. As part of the settlement, William and Mary accepted a Bill of Rights, a document stipulating the constitutional rights of all Englishmen. Almost immediately, the Bay Colonists overthrew the hated Andros regime. The New England version of the Glorious Revolution (April 18, 1689) was so popular that no one came to the governor's defense.

However united as they may have been, the Bay Colonists could not take the Crown's support for granted. William III could have declared the New Englanders rebels and summarily reinstated Andros. But thanks largely to the tireless efforts of Increase Mather, Cotton's father, who pleaded the colonists' case in London, William abandoned the Dominion of New England, and in 1691, Massachusetts received a new royal charter. The freemen no longer selected their governor. The choice now belonged to the king. Moreover, the franchise was determined on the basis of personal property rather than church membership, a change that brought Massachusetts into conformity with general English practice. On the local level, town government remained much as it had been in Winthrop's time.

TERROR OF WITCHCRAFT

The instability of the Massachusetts government following Andros's arrest allowed what under normal political conditions would have been an isolated, though ugly, local incident to expand into a major colonial crisis. Excessively fearful men and women living in Salem Village, a small, unprosperous farming community, nearly overwhelmed the new rulers of Massachusetts Bay.

Accusations of witchcraft were not uncommon in seventeenth-century New England. Puritans believed that an individual might make a compact with the devil, but during the first decades of settlement, authorities executed only about fifteen alleged witches. Sometimes villagers simply left suspected witches alone. Never before had fears of witchcraft plunged an entire community into panic.

The terror in Salem Village began in late 1691, when several adolescent girls began to behave in strange ways. They cried out for no apparent reason; they twitched on the ground. When concerned neighbors asked what caused their suffering, the girls announced they were victims of witches, seemingly innocent persons who lived in the community. The arrest of several alleged witches did not relieve the girls' "fits," nor did prayer solve the problem. Additional accusations were made, and at least one person confessed, providing a frightening description of the devil as "a thing all over hairy, all the face hairy, and a long nose." In June 1692, a special court convened and began to send men and women to the gallows. By the end of the summer, the court had hanged nineteen people; another was pressed to death. Several more suspects died in jail awaiting trial.

Then suddenly, the storm was over. Led by Increase Mather, a group of prominent Congregational ministers belatedly urged leniency and restraint. Especially troubling to the clergymen was the court's decision to accept "spectral evidence," that is, reports of dreams and visions in which the accused appeared as the devil's agent. Worried about convicting people on such dubious testimony, Mather declared, "It were better that ten suspected witches should escape, than

The publication of Cotton Mather's Memorable Providences, Relating to Witchcrafts and Possessions *(1689) contributed to the hysteria that resulted in the Salem witchcraft trials of the 1690s, but he did not take part in the trials. He is shown here surrounded by some of the forms a demon assumed in the "documented" case of an English family besieged by witches.*

that one innocent person should be condemned." The colonial government accepted the ministers' advice and convened a new court, which promptly acquitted, pardoned, or released the remaining suspects. After the Salem nightmare, witchcraft ceased to be a capital offense.

No one knows exactly what sparked the terror in Salem Village. The community had a history of religious discord, and during the 1680s, the people split into angry factions over the choice of a minister. Economic tensions played a part as well. Poorer, more traditional farmers accused members of prosperous, commercially oriented families of being witches. The underlying misogyny of the entire culture meant the victims were more often women than men. Terror of attack by Native Americans may also have played a part in this ugly affair. Indians in league with the French in Canada had recently raided nearby communities, killing people related to the families of the bewitched Salem girls, and significantly, during the trials some victims described the Devil as a "tawny man."

Whatever the ultimate social and psychological sources of this event may have been, jealousy and bitterness apparently festered to the point that adolescent girls who normally would have been disciplined were allowed to incite judicial murder.

ETHNIC VIOLENCE IN NEW YORK

The Glorious Revolution in New York was more violent than it had been in Massachusetts Bay. Divisions within New York's ruling class ran deep and involved ethnic as well as religious differences. English newcomers and powerful Anglo-Dutch families who had recently risen to commercial prominence in New York City opposed the older Dutch elite.

Much like Nathaniel Bacon, Jacob Leisler was a man entangled in events beyond his control. Leisler, the son of a German minister, emigrated to New York in 1660 and through marriage aligned himself with the Dutch elite. While he achieved moderate prosperity as a merchant, Leisler resented the success of the Anglo-Dutch.

When news of the Glorious Revolution reached New York City in May 1689, Leisler raised a group of militiamen and seized the local fort in the name of William and Mary. He apparently expected an outpouring of popular support, but it was not forthcoming. His rivals waited, watching while Leisler desperately attempted to legitimize his actions. Through bluff and badgering, Leisler managed to hold the colony together, especially after French forces burned Schenectady (February 1690), but he never established a secure political base.

In March 1691, a new royal governor, Henry Sloughter, reached New York. He ordered Leisler to surrender his authority, but Leisler hesitated. The pause cost Leisler his life. Sloughter declared Leisler a rebel, and in a hasty trial, a court sentenced him and his chief lieutenant, Jacob Milbourne, to be hanged "by the Neck and being Alive their bodyes be Cutt downe to Earth and Their Bowells to be taken out and they being Alive, burnt before their faces. . . ." In 1695, Parliament officially pardoned Leisler, but he not being "Alive," the decision arrived a bit late.

COMMON EXPERIENCES, SEPARATE CULTURES

"It is no little Blessing of God," Cotton Mather announced proudly in 1700, "that we are part of the *English* nation." A half century earlier, John Winthrop would not have spoken these words, at least not with such enthusiasm. The two men were, of course, products of different political cultures. It was not so much that the character of Massachusetts society had changed. In fact, the Puritan families of 1700 were much like those of the founding generation. Rather, the difference was in England's attitude toward the colonies. Rulers living more than three thousand miles away now made political and economic demands that Mather's contemporaries could not ignore.

The creation of a new imperial system did not, however, erase profound sectional differences. By 1700, for example, the Chesapeake colonies were more, not less, committed to the cultivation of tobacco and slave labor. Although the separate regions were being pulled slowly into England's commercial orbit, they did not have much to do with each other. The elements that sparked a powerful sense of nationalism among colonists dispersed over a huge territory would not be evident for a very long time. It would be a mistake, therefore, to anticipate the coming of the American Revolution.

CHRONOLOGY

1619	First blacks arrive in Virginia
1660	Charles II is restored to the English throne
	First Navigation Act passed by Parliament
1663	Second Navigation (Staple) Act passed
1673	Plantation duty imposed to close loopholes in commercial regulations
1675	King Philip's (Metacomet's) War devastates New England
1676	Bacon's Rebellion threatens Governor Berkeley's government in Virginia
1681	William Penn receives charter for Pennsylvania
1684	Charter of the Massachusetts Bay Company revoked
1685	Duke of York becomes James II
1686	Dominion of New England established
1688	James II driven into exile during Glorious Revolution
1689	Rebellions break out in Massachusetts, New York, and Maryland
1691	Jacob Leisler executed
1692	Salem Village wracked by witch trials
1696	Parliament establishes Board of Trade
1739	Stono Uprising of South Carolina slaves terrifies white planters

4

COLONIES IN AN EMPIRE
Eighteenth-Century America

William Byrd II (1674–1744) represented a type of British American one would not have encountered during the earliest years of settlement. This successful Tidewater planter was a product of a new, more cosmopolitan environment, and as an adult, Byrd seemed as much at home in London as in his native Virginia. In 1728, at the height of his political influence in Williamsburg, the capital of colonial Virginia, Byrd accepted a commission to help survey a disputed boundary between North Carolina and Virginia. During his long journey into the distant backcountry, Byrd kept a detailed journal, a satiric, often bawdy chronicle of daily events now regarded as a classic of early American literature.

On his trip into the wilderness, Byrd encountered many different people. No sooner had he departed a comfortable world of tobacco plantations than he came across a self-styled "Hermit," an Englishman who apparently preferred the freedom of the woods to the constraints of society. "He has no other Habitation but a green Bower or Harbour," Byrd reported, "with a Female Domestick as wild & as dirty as himself."

As the commissioners pushed west into the backcountry, they encountered highly independent men and women of European descent, small frontier families that Byrd regarded as living no better than savages. He attributed their uncivilized behavior to a pork diet. "The Truth of it is, these People live so much upon Swine's flesh . . . [that it] makes them . . . extremely hoggish in their Temper, & many of them seem to Grunt rather than Speak in their ordinary conversation." The wilderness journey also brought Byrd's party of surveyors into contact with Native Americans, whom he properly distinguished as Catawba, Tuscarora, Usheree, and Sapponi Indians.

Byrd's journal invites us to view the rapidly developing eighteenth-century backcountry from a fresh perspective. It was not a vast empty territory awaiting the arrival of European settlers. Maps often sustain this erroneous impression, depicting cities and towns, farms and plantations clustered along the Atlantic coast; they suggest a "line of settlement" steadily pushing outward into a huge blank area with no mark of civilization. The people Byrd met on his journey into the backcountry would not have understood such maps. After all, the empty space on the maps was their home. They experienced the frontier as a populous multicultural zone stretching from the English and French settlements in the north all the way to the Spanish borderlands in the far southwest.

The point is not to discount the significance of the older Atlantic settlements. During the eighteenth century, Britain's thirteen mainland colonies underwent a profound transformation. The population in the colonies grew at unprecedented rates. German and Scots-Irish immigrants arrived in huge numbers. So too did African slaves.

Wherever they lived, colonial Americans of this period were less isolated from one another than colonists had been during most of the seventeenth century. Indeed, after 1690, men and women expanded their cultural horizons, becoming part of the British empire. The change was striking. Colonists whose parents or grandparents had come to the New World to confront a "howling wilderness" now purchased imported European manufactures, read English journals, participated in imperial wars, and sought favors from a growing number of resident royal officials. No one—not even the inhabitants of the distant frontiers—could escape the influence of Britain. The cultural, economic, and political links connecting the colonists to the imperial center in London grew stronger with time.

This surprising development raises a difficult question. If the eighteenth-century colonists were so powerfully attracted to Great Britain, then why did they ever declare independence? The answer may well be that as the colonists became *more* British, they inevitably became *more* American as well. This was a development of major significance, for it helps to explain the appearance after midcentury of genuine nationalist sentiment. Political, commercial, and military links that brought the colonists into more frequent contact with Great Britain also made them more aware of other colonists. It was within an expanding, prosperous empire that they first began seriously to consider what it meant to be American.

THE CHALLENGE OF GROWTH

The phenomenal growth of British America during the eighteenth century amazed Benjamin Franklin, one of the first persons to bring scientific rigor to the study of demography. The population of the English colonies doubled approximately every twenty-five years, and, according to calculations Franklin made in 1751, if the expansion continued at such an extraordinary rate for another century or so, "the greatest Number of Englishmen will be on this Side [of] the water." Not only was the total population increasing at a very rapid rate; it also was becoming more dispersed and heterogeneous. Each year witnessed the arrival of thousands of non-English Europeans, most of whom soon moved to the backcountry of Pennsylvania and the Southern Colonies.

As white settlement spread westward from the coastal zones, the forests and swamps of the interior presented major challenges. In this engraving from the mid-eighteenth century, note the vast clearing of trees whose stumps would either be pulled up or left to decay. The water traffic represented the colonists' and Indians' best means of travel and communication.

Accurate population data from the colonial period are extremely difficult to find. The first national census did not occur until 1790. Still, various sources surviving from prerevolutionary times indicate that the total white population of Britain's thirteen mainland colonies rose from about 250,000 in 1700 to 2,150,000 in 1770, an annual growth rate of 3 percent.

Few societies in recorded history have expanded so rapidly. Natural reproduction was responsible for most of the growth. More families bore children who in turn lived long enough to have children of their own. Because of this sudden expansion, the population of the late colonial period was strikingly young; approximately one-half of the populace at any given time was under age sixteen.

CONVICTS SENT TO AMERICA

Since the story of European migration tends to be upbeat—men and women engaged in a largely successful quest for a better material life—it often is forgotten that British courts compelled many people to come to America. Indeed, the African slaves were not the only large group of people coerced into moving to the New World. In 1718, Parliament passed the Transportation Act, allowing judges in England, Scotland, and Ireland to send convicted felons to the American colonies.

Between 1718 and 1775, the courts shipped approximately fifty thousand convicts across the Atlantic. Some of these men and women may actually have been dangerous criminals, but the majority seem to have committed minor crimes against property. Although transported convicts—almost 75 percent of whom were young males—escaped the hangman, they found life difficult in the colonies. Eighty percent of them were sold in the Chesapeake colonies as indentured servants.

ETHNIC CULTURES OF THE BACKCOUNTRY

The eighteenth century also witnessed fresh waves of voluntary European migration. Unlike those seventeenth-century English settlers who had moved to the New World in search of religious sanctuary or to obtain instant wealth (see Chapter 2), the newcomers generally transferred in the hope of obtaining their own land and setting up as independent farmers. These people often traveled to the backcountry, a region stretching approximately eight hundred miles from western Pennsylvania to Georgia.

SCOTS-IRISH FLEE ENGLISH OPPRESSION

Non-English colonists poured into American ports throughout the eighteenth century, creating rich ethnic diversity in areas originally settled by the English. The largest group of newcomers consisted of Scots-Irish. The experiences of these people in Great Britain influenced not only their decision to move to the New World but also their behavior once they arrived.

During the seventeenth century, English rulers thought they could thoroughly dominate Catholic Ireland by transporting thousands of lowland Scottish Presbyterians to the northern region of that war-torn country. The plan failed. English officials who were members of the Anglican Church discriminated against the Presbyterians. They passed laws that placed the Scots-Irish at a severe disadvantage when they traded in England; they taxed them at exorbitant rates.

After several poor harvests, many Scots-Irish elected to emigrate to America, hoping to find the freedom and prosperity that had been denied them in Ireland. Often entire Presbyterian congregations followed charismatic ministers to the New World, intent on replicating a distinctive, fiercely independent culture on the frontier. It is estimated that 150,000 Scots-Irish migrated to the colonies before the Revolution.

Most Scots-Irish immigrants landed initially in Philadelphia, but instead of remaining in that city, they carved out farms on Pennsylvania's western frontier. The colony's proprietors welcomed the influx of new settlers, for it seemed they would form an ideal barrier between the Indians and the older, coastal communities. The Penn family soon had second thoughts, however. The Scots-Irish squatted on whatever land looked best, and when colony officials pointed out that large tracts had already been reserved, the immigrants retorted that "it was against the laws of God and nature that so much land should be idle when so many Christians wanted it to labour on and to raise their bread."

GERMANS SEARCH FOR A BETTER LIFE

A second large body of non-English settlers, more than 100,000 people, came from the upper Rhine Valley, the German Palatinate. Some of the migrants, especially those who relocated to America around the turn of the century, belonged to small pietistic Protestant sects whose religious views were somewhat similar to those of the Quakers. These Germans moved to the New World primarily in the hope of finding religious toleration. Under the guidance of Francis Daniel Pastorius (1651–1720), a group of Mennonites established in Pennsylvania a prosperous community known as Germantown.

By midcentury, however, the characteristics of the German migration had begun to change. Large numbers of Lutherans transferred to the middle colonies. Unlike members of the pietistic sects, these men and women were not in search of religious freedom. Rather, they traveled to the New World looking to better their material lives. The Lutheran Church in Germany initially tried to maintain control over the distant congregations, but even though the migrants themselves fiercely preserved many aspects of traditional German culture, they were eventually forced to accommodate to new social conditions. Henry Melchior Mühlenberg (1711–1787), a tireless leader, helped German Lutherans through a difficult cultural adjustment, and in 1748, Mühlenberg organized a meeting of local pastors and lay delegates that ordained ministers of their own choosing, an act of spiritual independence that has been called "the most important single event in American Lutheran history."

The German migrants—mistakenly called Pennsylvania Dutch because the English confused *deutsch* (meaning "German") with *Dutch* ("a person from Holland")—began reaching Philadelphia in large numbers after 1717, and by 1766, persons of German origin accounted for more than one-third of Pennsylvania's total population. Even their most vocal detractors admitted the Germans were the best farmers in the colony.

Ethnic differences in Pennsylvania bred disputes. The Scots-Irish as well as the Germans preferred to live with people of their own background, and they sometimes fought to keep members of the other nationality out of their neighborhoods. The English were suspicious of both groups. They could not comprehend why the Germans insisted on speaking German in America.

Such prejudice may have persuaded members of both groups to search for new homes. After 1730, Germans and Scots-Irish pushed south from western Pennsylvania into the Shenandoah Valley, thousands of them settling in the backcountry of Virginia and the Carolinas. The Germans usually remained wherever they found unclaimed fertile land. By contrast, the Scots-Irish often moved two or three times, acquiring a reputation as a rootless people.

Wherever the newcomers settled, they often found themselves living beyond the effective authority of the various colonial governments. To be sure, backcountry residents petitioned for assistance during wars against the Indians, but most of the time they preferred to be left alone. These conditions heightened the importance of religious institutions within the small ethnic communities. Although the original stimulus for coming to America may have been a desire for

This folk art painting from the cover of a clothes box depicts a well-dressed German-American farmer. The farmer's hat, his coat, and walking stick indicate that he enjoyed a middling to high status.

economic independence and prosperity, backcountry families—especially the Scots-Irish—flocked to evangelical Protestant preachers, to Presbyterian and later Baptist and Methodist ministers who not only fulfilled the settlers' spiritual needs but also gave the scattered backcountry communities a pronounced moral character that survived long after the colonial period.

NATIVE AMERICANS: STRATEGIES FOR SURVIVAL

During much of the seventeenth century, various Indian groups who contested the English settlers for control of coastal lands suffered terribly, sometimes from war, but more often from the spread of contagious diseases such as smallpox. The two races found it very difficult to live in close proximity. As one Indian informed the members of the Maryland assembly in 1666, "Your hogs & Cattle injure Us, You come too near Us to live & drive Us from place to place. We can fly no farther; let us know where to live & how to be secured for the future from the Hogs & Cattle."

Against such odds the Indians managed to survive. By the eighteenth century, the site of the most intense and creative contact between the races had shifted to the cis-Mississippian west, that is, to the huge territory between the Appalachian Mountains and the Mississippi River, where several hundred thousand Native Americans made their homes.

William Johnson, British superintendent of Indian affairs, issued a certificate with this illustration to announce an alliance between the English colonists and the Native Americans who occupied the "middle ground." Both Johnson and Indian leaders understood that if the British disappointed the Native Americans in these negotiations, the Indians could turn to the French for support.

Many Indians had only recently migrated to the area. The Delaware, for example, retreated to far western Pennsylvania and the Ohio Valley to escape almost continuous confrontation with advancing European invaders. Other Indians drifted west in less happy circumstances. They were refugees, the remnants of Native American groups who had lost so many people that they could no longer sustain an independent cultural identity. These survivors joined with other Indians to establish new multiethnic communities.

Stronger groups of Indians such as the Creek, Choctaw, Chickasaw, Cherokee, and Shawnee generally welcomed the refugees. Strangers were formally adopted to take the places of family members killed in battle or overcome by sickness, and it should be appreciated that many seemingly traditional Indian villages of the eighteenth century actually represented innovative responses to rapidly shifting external conditions.

The concept of a *middle ground* helps us more fully to comprehend how eighteenth-century Indians held their own in the backcountry beyond the Appalachian Mountains. The Native Americans never intended to isolate themselves completely from European contact. They relied on white traders, French as well as English, to provide essential metal goods and weapons. The goal of the Indian confederacies was rather to maintain a strong independent voice in these commercial exchanges, whenever possible playing the French off against the British, and so long as they had sufficient military strength—that is, large numbers of healthy armed warriors—they compelled everyone who came to negotiate in the "middle ground" to give them proper respect. It would be incorrect, therefore, to characterize their relations with the Europeans as a stark choice between resistance or accommodation, between total war or abject surrender. Native Americans took advantage of rivals when possible; they compromised when necessary. It is best to imagine the Indians' middle ground as an open, dynamic process of creative interaction.

The survival of the middle ground depended ultimately on factors over which the Native Americans had little control. Imperial competition between France and Great Britain enhanced the Indians' bargaining position, but after the British defeated the French in 1763, the Indians no longer received the same solicitous attention as they had in earlier times. Keeping old allies happy seemed to the British a needless expense. Moreover, contagious disease continued to take a fearful toll. In the southern backcountry between 1685 and 1790, the Indian population dropped an astounding 72 percent. By the time the United States took control of this region, the middle ground itself had become a casualty of history.

SPANISH BORDERLANDS

The Spanish empire continued to shape the character of borderlands societies well into the eighteenth century. As anyone who visits the modern American Southwest discovers, Spanish administrators and priests—not to mention ordinary settlers—left a lasting imprint on the cultural landscape of this country.

Until 1821, when Mexico declared independence from Madrid, Spanish authorities struggled to control a vast northern frontier. During the eighteenth century, the Spanish empire in North America included widely dispersed settlements such as San Francisco, San Diego, Santa Fe, San Antonio, and St. Augustine. In these borderland communities, European colonists mixed with peoples of other races and backgrounds, forming multicultural societies.

TURBULENCE ON THE NORTHERN FRONTIER

Not until late in the sixteenth century did Spanish settlers, led by Juan de Oñate, establish European communities north of the Rio Grande. The Pueblos resisted the invasion of colonists, soldiers, and missionaries, and in a major rebellion in 1680 led by El Popé, the native peoples drove the whites completely out of New Mexico. "The heathen have conceived a mortal hatred for our holy faith and enmity for the Spanish nation," concluded one imperial bureaucrat. Not until 1692 were the Spanish able to reconquer this fiercely contested area. By then, Native American hostility coupled with the settlers' failure to find precious metal had cooled Spain's enthusiasm for the northern frontier.

Concern over French encroachment in the Southeast led Spain to colonize St. Augustine (Florida) in 1565. Pedro Menéndez de Avilés brought some fifteen hundred soldiers and settlers to St. Augustine, where they constructed an impressive fort, but the colony failed to attract additional Spanish migrants.

California never figured prominently in Spain's plans for the New World. Early explorers reported finding only impoverished Indians living along the Pacific coast. Adventurers saw no natural resources worth mentioning, and since the area proved extremely difficult to reach from Mexico City—the overland trip could take months—California received little attention. Fear that the Russians might seize the entire region belatedly sparked Spanish activity, however, and after 1769, two indomitable servants of empire, Fra Junípero Serra and Don Gaspar de Portolá, organized permanent missions and *presidios* (forts) at San Diego, Monterey, San Francisco, and Santa Barbara.

PEOPLES OF THE SPANISH BORDERLANDS

In sharp contrast to the English frontier settlements of the eighteenth century, the Spanish outposts in North America grew very slowly. A few Catholic priests and imperial administrators traveled to the northern provinces, but the danger of

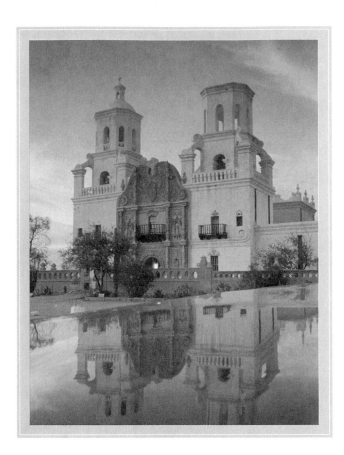

Baroque-style eighteenth-century Spanish mission at San Xavier del Bac in present-day Arizona. Catholic missions dotted the frontier of northern New Spain from Florida to California.

Indian attack as well as a harsh physical environment discouraged ordinary colonists. The European migrants were overwhelmingly male, most of them soldiers in the pay of the empire. Although some colonists came directly from Spain, most had been born in other Spanish colonies such as Minorca, the Canaries, or New Spain, and because European women rarely appeared on the frontier, Spanish males formed relationships with Indian women, fathering large numbers of mestizos, children of mixed race.

The Spanish exploited Native American labor, reducing entire Indian villages to servitude. Many Indians moved to the Spanish towns, and although they lived in close proximity to the Europeans—something rare in British America—they were consigned to the lowest social class, objects of European contempt. However much their material conditions changed, the Indians of the Southwest resisted strenuous efforts to convert them to Catholicism. The Pueblos maintained their own religious forms—often at great personal risk—and they sometimes murdered priests who became too intrusive.

The Spanish empire never had the resources necessary to secure the northern frontier fully. The small military posts were intended primarily to discourage other European powers such as France, Great Britain, and Russia from taking possession of territory claimed by Spain. It would be misleading, however, to stress the fragility of Spanish colonization. The urban design and public architecture of many southwestern cities still reflect the vision of the early Spanish settlers, and to a large extent, the old borderlands remain Spanish speaking to this day.

BRITISH COLONIES IN AN ATLANTIC WORLD

The character of the older, more established British colonies changed almost as rapidly as that of the backcountry. The swift growth of an urban cosmopolitan culture impressed eighteenth-century commentators, and even though most Americans still lived on scattered farms, they had begun to participate aggressively in an exciting consumer marketplace that expanded their imaginative horizons.

PROVINCIAL CITIES

Considering the rate of population growth, it is surprising to discover how few eighteenth-century Americans lived in cities. Boston, Newport, New York, Philadelphia, and Charles Town—the five largest cities—contained only about 5 percent of the colonial population. In 1775, none had more than forty thousand persons. The explanation for the relatively slow development of colonial American cities lies in their highly specialized commercial character. Colonial port towns served as entrepôts, intermediary trade and shipping centers where bulk cargoes were broken up for inland distribution and where agricultural products were gathered for export.

Yet despite the limited urban population, cities profoundly influenced colonial culture. It was in the cities that Americans learned about the latest English ideas. Wealthy colonists—merchants and lawyers—tried to emulate the culture of the mother country. They sponsored concerts and plays; they learned to dance. Women as well as men picked up the new fashions quickly, and even though most of them had never been outside the colony of their birth, they sometimes appeared to be the products of London's best families.

It was in the cities, also, that wealthy merchants transformed commercial profits into architectural splendor, for, in their desire to outdo one another, they built grand homes of enduring beauty. Most of these buildings are described as Georgian because they were constructed during the reign of Britain's early Hanoverian kings, who all happened to be named George. These homes were provincial copies of grand country houses of Great Britain. They drew their inspiration from the great Italian Renaissance architect Andrea Palladio (1508–1580), who had incorporated classical themes into a rigidly symmetrical form. Their owners filled the houses with fine furniture. Each city patronized certain skilled craftsmen, but the artisans of Philadelphia were known for producing magnificent copies of the works of Thomas Chippendale, Great Britain's most famous furniture designer.

ENLIGHTENMENT: AMERICAN STYLE

European historians often refer to the eighteenth century as an Age of Reason. During this period, a body of new, often radical, ideas swept through learned society, altering how educated Europeans thought about God, nature, and society. This intellectual revolution, called the Enlightenment, involved the work of Europe's greatest minds, men such as Newton and Locke, Voltaire and Hume. The writings of these thinkers eventually reached the colonies, where they received a mixed reception. On the whole, the American Enlightenment was a rather tame affair compared to its French counterpart, for while the colonists welcomed experimental science, they seldom questioned the tenets of traditional Christianity.

Philosophers of the Enlightenment replaced the concept of original sin with a much more optimistic view of human nature. A benevolent God, having set the universe in motion, gave human beings the power of reason to enable them to comprehend the orderly workings of his creation. Everything, even human society, operated according to these mechanical rules. The responsibility of right-thinking men and women, therefore, was to make certain that institutions such as church and state conformed to self-evident natural laws. It was possible—or so some of the *philosophes* claimed—to achieve perfection in this world. In fact, human suffering had come about only because people had lost touch with the fundamental insights of reason.

For many Americans, the appeal of the Enlightenment was its search for useful knowledge, ideas, and inventions that would improve the quality of human life. What mattered was practical experimentation. The Enlightenment spawned scores of earnest scientific tinkerers, people who dutifully recorded changes in temperature, the appearance of strange plants and animals, and the details of astronomic phenomena.

Benjamin Franklin exemplified the scientific curiosity and search for practical knowledge characteristic of Enlightenment thinkers of the eighteenth century. Franklin's experiments on electricity became world famous and inspired others to study the effects of the strange force.

BENJAMIN FRANKLIN: THE PRACTICAL SCIENTIST

Benjamin Franklin (1706–1790) absorbed the new cosmopolitan culture. European thinkers regarded him as a genuine *philosophe*, a person of reason and science, a role that he self-consciously cultivated when he visited England and France in later life. Franklin had little formal education, but as a young man working in his brother's print shop, he managed to keep up with the latest intellectual currents.

Franklin's first publication appeared in August 1721 when he and his brother founded the *New England Courant,* a weekly newspaper that satirized Boston's leaders in the manner of the contemporary British press. Writing under the name Silence Dogood, young Franklin asked "Whether a Commonwealth suffers more by hypocritical Pretenders to Religion, or by the openly Profane?" Proper Bostonians were not prepared for a journal that one minister described as "full freighted with Nonesense." Franklin got the point; he left Massachusetts in 1723 in search of a more welcoming intellectual environment.

After he had moved to Philadelphia, leaving behind an irritable brother as well as New England Puritanism, Franklin devoted himself to the pursuit of useful knowledge, ideas that would increase the happiness of his fellow Americans. Franklin never denied the existence of God. Rather, he pushed the Lord aside, making room for the free exercise of human reason. Franklin tinkered, experimented, and reformed. Almost everything he encountered in his daily life aroused his curiosity. His investigation of electricity brought him world fame, but Franklin was never satisfied with his work in this field until it yielded practical application. In 1756, he invented the lightning rod. He also designed a marvelously efficient stove that is still used today.

ECONOMIC TRANSFORMATION

The colonial economy kept pace with the stunning growth in population. Even with so many additional people to feed and clothe, the per capita income did not decline. Indeed, with the exception of poor urban dwellers, such as sailors whose employment varied with the season, white Americans did quite well. An abundance of land and the extensive growth of agriculture accounted for their economic success. New farmers were able not only to provide for their families' well-being but also to sell their crops in European and West Indian markets. Each year, more Americans produced more tobacco, wheat, or rice—to cite just the major export staples—and by this means, they maintained a high level of individual prosperity without developing an industrial base.

At midcentury, colonial exports flowed along well-established routes. More than half of American goods produced for export went to Great Britain. The Navigation Acts (see Chapter 3) were still in effect, and "enumerated" items such as tobacco had to be landed first at a British port. The Molasses Act of 1733—also called the Sugar Act—placed a heavy duty on molasses imported from foreign ports; the Hat and Felt Act of 1732 and the Iron Act of 1750 attempted to limit the production of colonial goods that competed with British exports.

These statutes might have created tensions between the colonists and the mother country had they been rigorously enforced. Crown officials, however, generally ignored the new laws. New England merchants imported molasses from French Caribbean islands without paying the full customs; ironmasters in the middle colonies continued to produce iron. Even without the Navigation Acts, however, a majority of colonial exports would have been sold on the English market. The emerging consumer society in Great Britain was beginning to create a new generation of buyers who possessed enough income to purchase American goods, especially sugar and tobacco. This rising demand was the major market force shaping the colonial economy.

Colonial merchants operating out of Boston, Newport, and Philadelphia also carried substantial tonnage to the West Indies. In 1768, this market accounted for 27 percent of all American exports. Colonial ships carrying wheat and wood products sailed for the Caribbean and returned immediately to the middle colonies or New England with cargoes of molasses, sugar, and rum. The West Indies helped preserve American credit in Europe. Without this source of income, colonists would not have been able to pay for the manufactured items they purchased in the mother country.

BIRTH OF A CONSUMER SOCIETY

The balance of trade was always a problem. After midcentury, it turned dramatically against the colonists. The reasons for this change were complex, but, in simplest terms, Americans began buying more English goods than their parents or grandparents had done. Between 1740 and 1770, English exports to the American colonies increased by an astounding 360 percent.

In part, this shift reflected a fundamental transformation in the British economy. Although the Industrial Revolution was still far in the future, the pace of the British economy picked up dramatically after 1690. Small factories produced certain goods more efficiently and more cheaply than the colonists could. The availability of these products altered the lives of most Americans, even those with modest incomes. Staffordshire china replaced crude earthenware; imported cloth replaced homespun. In this manner, British industrialization undercut American handicraft and folk art.

To help Americans purchase manufactured goods, British merchants offered generous credit. Colonists deferred settlement by agreeing to pay interest on their debts. The temptation to acquire English finery blinded many people to hard economic realities. They gambled on the future, hoping bumper farm crops would reduce their dependence on the large merchant houses of London and Glasgow. Some persons lived within their means, but the aggregate American debt continued to grow. Colonial leaders tried various expedients to remain solvent—issuing paper money, for example—and while these efforts delayed a crisis, the balance-of-payments problem remained a major structural weakness.

The eighteenth century also saw a substantial increase in intercoastal trade. Southern planters sent tobacco and rice to New England and the middle colonies, where these staples were exchanged for meat and wheat as well as goods imported from Great Britain. By 1760, approximately 30 percent of the colonists' total tonnage capacity was involved in this extensive "coastwise" commerce. In addition, backcountry farmers in western Pennsylvania and the Shenandoah Valley carried their grain to market along an old Iroquois trail that became known as the Great Wagon Road, a rough, hilly highway that by the time of the Revolution stretched 735 miles along the Blue Ridge Mountains to Camden, South Carolina.

The shifting patterns of trade had immense effects on the development of an American culture. First, the flood of British imports eroded local and regional identities. Commerce helped to "Anglicize" American culture by exposing colonial consumers to a common range of British manufactured goods. Deep sectional differences remained, of course, but Americans from New Hampshire to Georgia were increasingly drawn into a sophisticated economic network centered in London. Second, the expanding coastal and overland trade brought colonists of different backgrounds into more frequent contact. Ships that sailed between New England and South Carolina, and between Virginia and Pennsylvania, provided Americans with a means to exchange ideas and experiences on a more regular basis. Mid-eighteenth-century printers, for example, established several dozen new journals; these were weekly newspapers that carried information not only about the mother country and world commerce but also about events in other colonies.

REVIVAL: THE APPEAL OF EVANGELICAL RELIGION

A sudden, spontaneous series of Protestant revivals known as the Great Awakening had a profound impact on the lives of ordinary people. This unprecedented evangelical outpouring altered the course of American history. The new, highly personal appeal to a "new birth" in Christ caused men and women of all backgrounds to rethink basic assumptions about church and state, institutions and society.

THE GREAT AWAKENING

Only with hindsight does the Great Awakening seem a unified religious movement. Revivals occurred in different places at different times; the intensity of the events varied from region to region. The first signs of a spiritual awakening appeared in New England during the 1730s, but within a decade the revivals in this area had burned themselves out. It was not until the 1750s and 1760s that the Awakening made more than a superficial impact on the people of Virginia. The revivals were most important in Massachusetts, Connecticut, Rhode Island, Pennsylvania, New Jersey, and Virginia. Their effect on religion in New York, Delaware, and the Carolinas was marginal. No single religious denomination or sect monopolized the Awakening. In New England, revivals shattered Congregational churches, and in the South, especially in Virginia, they had an impact on Presbyterians, Methodists, and Baptists.

Whatever their origins, the seeds of revival were sown on fertile ground. In the early decades of the century, many Americans—but especially New Englanders—complained that organized religion had lost vitality. They looked back at Winthrop's generation with nostalgia, assuming that ordinary people at that time must have possessed greater piety than did later, more worldly colonists. Congregational ministers seemed obsessed with dull, scholastic matters; they no longer touched the heart. And in the Southern Colonies, there were simply not enough ordained ministers to tend to the religious needs of the population.

The Great Awakening arrived unexpectedly in Northampton, a small farm community in western Massachusetts, sparked by Jonathan Edwards, the local Congregational minister. Edwards accepted the traditional teachings of Calvinism (see Chapter 1), reminding his parishioners that since their eternal fate had been determined by an omnipotent God, there was nothing they could do to save themselves. They were totally dependent on the Lord's will. Edwards thought his fellow ministers had grown soft. They left men and women with the mistaken impression that sinners might somehow avoid eternal damnation simply by performing good works.

Why this uncompromising message set off several religious revivals during the mid-1730s is not known. Whatever the explanation for the popular response to Edwards's preaching, young people began flocking to the church. They experienced a searing conversion, a sense of "new birth" and utter dependence on God. "Surely," Edwards pronounced, "this is the Lord's doing, and it is marvelous in our eyes." The excitement spread, and evangelical ministers concluded that God must be preparing Americans, his chosen people, for the millennium, when Christ would rule on earth. "What is now seen in America and especially in New England," Edwards explained, "may prove the dawn of that glorious day."

VOICE OF POPULAR RELIGION

Edwards did not possess the dynamic personality required to sustain the revival. That responsibility fell to George Whitefield, a young, charismatic preacher from England who toured the colonies from New Hampshire to Georgia. While Whitefield was not an original thinker, he was an extraordinarily effective public speaker. And like his friend Benjamin Franklin, he came to symbolize the powerful cultural forces that were transforming the Atlantic world.

Whitefield's audiences came from all groups of American society: rich and poor, young and old, rural and urban. While Whitefield described himself as a Calvinist, he welcomed all Protestants. He spoke from any pulpit that was available. "Don't tell me you are a Baptist, an Independent, a Presbyterian, a dissenter," he thundered, "tell me you are a Christian, that is all I want."

Whitefield was a brilliant entrepreneur. Like Franklin, with whom he published many popular volumes, the itinerant minister possessed an almost intuitive sense of how this burgeoning consumer society could be turned to his own advantage, and he embraced the latest merchandising techniques. He appreciated, for example, the power of the press in selling the revival, and he regularly promoted his own work in advertisements placed in British and American newspapers. The crowds flocked to hear Whitefield, while his critics grumbled about the commercialization of religion. One anonymous writer in Massachusetts noted that there was "a very wholesome law of the province to discourage Pedlars in Trade" and it seemed high time "to enact something for the discouragement of Pedlars in Divinity also."

Other, American-born itinerant preachers followed Whitefield's example. The most famous was Gilbert Tennent, a Presbyterian of Scots-Irish background

The fervor of the Great Awakening was intensified by the eloquence of itinerant preachers such as the Reverend George Whitefield, the most popular evangelical of the mid-eighteenth century.

who had been educated in the middle colonies. His sermon, "On the Danger of an Unconverted Ministry," printed in 1741, set off a storm of protest from established ministers who were understandably insulted. Lesser known revivalists traveled from town to town, colony to colony, challenging local clergymen who seemed hostile to evangelical religion. Men and women who thronged to hear the itinerants were called "New Lights," and during the 1740s and 1750s, many congregations split between defenders of the new emotional preaching and those who regarded the entire movement as dangerous nonsense.

While Tennent did not condone the excesses of the Great Awakening, his attacks on formal learning invited the crude anti-intellectualism of such fanatics as James Davenport. This deranged revivalist traveled along the Connecticut coast in 1742 playing upon popular emotion. At night, under the light of smoky torches, he danced and stripped, shrieked and laughed. He also urged people to burn books written by authors who had not experienced the New Light as defined by Davenport. Like so many fanatics throughout history who have claimed a special knowledge of the "truth," Davenport later recanted and begged pardon for his disruptive behavior.

To concentrate on the bizarre activities of Davenport obscures the positive ways in which this vast revival changed American society. First, despite occasional anti-intellectual outbursts, the New Lights founded several important centers of higher learning. They wanted to train young men who would carry on the good works of Edwards, Whitefield, and Tennent. In 1746, New Light Presbyterians established the College of New Jersey, which later became Princeton University. Just before his death, Edwards was appointed its president.

The evangelical minister Eleazar Wheelock launched Dartmouth (1769); other revivalists founded Brown (1764) and Rutgers (1766).

The Great Awakening also encouraged men and women who had been taught to remain silent before traditional figures of authority to speak up, to take an active role in their salvation. They could no longer rely on ministers or institutions. The individual alone stood before God. Knowing this, New Lights made religious choices that shattered the old harmony among Protestant sects, and in its place, they introduced a noisy, often bitterly fought competition. As one New Jersey Presbyterian explained, "There are so many particular *sects* and *Parties* among professed Christians . . . that we know not . . . in which of these different *paths*, to steer our course for *Heaven*."

Expressive evangelicalism struck a particularly responsive chord among African Americans. Itinerant ministers frequently preached to large sympathetic audiences of slaves. Richard Allen (1760–1831), founder of the African Methodist Episcopal Church, reported he owed his freedom in part to a traveling Methodist minister who persuaded Allen's master of the sinfulness of slavery. Allen himself was converted, as were thousands of other black colonists.

With religious contention came an awareness of a larger community, a union of fellow believers that extended beyond the boundaries of town and colony. In fact, evangelical religion was one of several forces at work during the mid-eighteenth century that brought scattered colonists into contact with one another for the first time. In this sense, the Great Awakening was a "national" event long before a nation actually existed.

People who had been touched by the Great Awakening shared an optimism about the future of America. With God's help, social and political progress was possible, and from this perspective, of course, the New Lights did not sound much different than the mildly rationalist American spokesmen of the Enlightenment. Both groups prepared the way for the development of a revolutionary mentality in colonial America.

CLASH OF POLITICAL CULTURES

The political history of this period illuminates a growing tension within the empire. Americans of all regions repeatedly stated their desire to replicate British political institutions. Parliament, they claimed, provided a model for the American assemblies. They revered the English constitution. However, the more the colonists studied British political theory and practice—in other words, the more they attempted to become British—the more aware they became of major differences. By trying to copy Great Britain, they unwittingly discovered something about being American.

THE ENGLISH CONSTITUTION

During the eighteenth century, the British constitution was the object of universal admiration. Unlike the U.S. Constitution of 1788, the British constitution was not a formal written document. It was something much more elusive. The

English constitution found expression in a growing body of law, court decisions, and statutes, a sense of traditional political arrangements that people of all classes believed had evolved from the past, preserving life, liberty, and property. Almost everyone regarded change as dangerous and destabilizing, a threat to the political tradition that seemed to explain Britain's greatness.

In theory, the English constitution contained three distinct parts. The monarch was at the top, advised by handpicked court favorites. Next came the House of Lords, a body of 180 aristocrats who served with 26 Anglican bishops as the upper house of Parliament. And third was the House of Commons, composed of 558 members elected by various constituencies scattered throughout the realm.

Political theorists waxed eloquent on workings of the British constitution. Each of the three parts of government, it seemed, represented a separate socioeconomic interest: king, nobility, and common people. Acting alone, each body would run to excess, even tyranny, but operating within a mixed system, they automatically checked each other's ambitions for the common good.

THE REALITY OF BRITISH POLITICS

The reality of daily political life in Great Britain, however, bore little relation to theory. The three elements of the constitution did not, in fact, represent distinct socioeconomic groups. Men elected to the House of Commons often came from the same social background as those who served in the House of Lords. All represented the interests of Britain's landed elite. Moreover, there was no attempt to maintain strict constitutional separation. The king, for example, organized parliamentary associations, loose groups of political followers who sat in the House of Commons and who openly supported the monarch's policies in exchange for patronage.

The claim that the members of the House of Commons represented all the people of England also seemed far-fetched. As of 1715, no more than 20 percent of Britain's adult males had the right to vote. Property qualifications or other restrictions often greatly reduced the number of eligible voters. In addition, the size of the electoral districts varied throughout the kingdom. In some boroughs, representatives to Parliament were chosen by several thousand voters. In many districts, however, a handful of electors controlled the result. These tiny, or "rotten," boroughs were an embarrassment. Since these districts were so small, a wealthy lord or ambitious politician could easily bribe or otherwise "influence" the entire constituency, something done regularly throughout the century.

Before 1760, few people spoke out against these constitutional abuses. The main exception was a group of radical publicists whom historians have labeled the Commonwealthmen. These writers decried the corruption of political life, noting that a nation that compromised civic virtue, that failed to stand vigilant against fawning courtiers and would-be despots, deserved to lose its liberty and property. The most famous Commonwealthmen were John Trenchard and Thomas Gordon, who penned a series of essays titled *Cato's Letters* between 1720 and 1723. If England's rulers were corrupt, they warned, then the people could not expect the balanced constitution to save them from tyranny.

However loudly these writers protested, they won little support for political reforms. Most eighteenth-century Englishmen admitted there was more than a grain of truth in the commonwealth critique, but they were not willing to tamper with a system of government that had so recently survived a civil war and a Glorious Revolution. Americans, however, took Trenchard and Gordon to heart.

THE AWKWARD REALITIES OF COLONIAL GOVERNMENT

The colonists assumed—perhaps naively—that their own governments were modeled on the balanced constitution of Great Britain. They argued that within their political systems, the governor corresponded to the king and the governor's council to the House of Lords. The colonial assemblies were perceived as American reproductions of the House of Commons and were expected to preserve the interests of the people against those of the monarch and aristocracy. As the colonists discovered, however, general theories about a mixed constitution were even less relevant in America than they were in Britain.

By midcentury a majority of the mainland colonies had royal governors appointed by the Crown. Many were career army officers who through luck, charm, or family connection had gained the ear of someone close to the king. These patronage posts did not generate income sufficient to interest the most powerful or talented personalities of the period, but they did draw middle-level bureaucrats who were ambitious, desperate, or both.

Whatever their demerits, royal governors in America possessed enormous powers. In fact, royal governors could do certain things in America that a king could not do in eighteenth-century Britain. Among these were the right to veto legislation and dismiss judges. The governors also served as military commanders in each province.

Political practice in America differed from the British model in another crucial respect. Royal governors were advised by a council, usually a body of about twelve wealthy colonists selected by the Board of Trade in London upon the recommendation of the governor. During the seventeenth century, the council had played an important role in colonial government, but its ability to exercise independent authority declined steadily over the course of the eighteenth century. Its members certainly did not represent a distinct aristocracy within American society.

If royal governors did not look like kings, nor American councils like the House of Lords, colonial assemblies bore little resemblance to the eighteenth-century House of Commons. The major difference was the size of the American franchise. In most colonies, adult white males who owned a small amount of land could vote in colonywide elections. One historian estimates that 95 percent of this group in Massachusetts was eligible to participate in elections. The number in Virginia was about 85 percent. These figures—much higher than those in contemporary England—have led some scholars to view the colonies as "middle-class democracies," societies run by moderately prosperous yeomen farmers who—in politics at least—exercised independent judgment.

Colonial governments were not democracies in the modern sense of that term. Possessing the right to vote was one thing, exercising it quite another. Americans participated in elections when major issues were at stake—the formation of banks in mid-eighteenth-century Massachusetts, for example—but most of the time they were content to let members of the rural and urban elite represent them in the assemblies. To be sure, unlike modern democracies, these colonial politics excluded women and nonwhites from voting. The point to remember, however, is that the power to expel legislative rascals was always present in America, and it was this political reality that kept autocratic gentlemen from straying too far from the will of the people.

REPRESENTATIVES OF THE PEOPLE

Elected members of the colonial assemblies believed that they had a special obligation to preserve colonial liberties. They perceived any attack on the legislature as an assault on the rights of Americans. The elected representatives brooked no criticism, and several colonial printers landed in jail because they questioned actions taken by a lower house.

So aggressive were these bodies in seizing privileges, determining procedures, and controlling money bills that some historians have described the political development of eighteenth-century America as "the rise of the assemblies." The long series of imperial wars against the French, demanding large public expenditures, transformed the small, amateurish assemblies of the seventeenth century into the more professional, vigilant legislatures of the eighteenth.

This political system seemed designed to generate controversy. There was simply no reason for the colonial legislators to cooperate with appointed royal governors. Alexander Spotswood, Virginia's governor from 1710 to 1722, for example, attempted to institute a bold new land program backed by the Crown. He tried persuasion and gifts and, when these failed, chicanery. But the members of the House of Burgesses refused to support a plan that did not suit their own interests. Before leaving office, Spotswood gave up trying to carry out royal policy in America. Instead, he allied himself with the local Virginia elite who controlled the House as well as the Council, and because they awarded their new friend with large tracts of land, he became a wealthy man.

A major source of shared political information was the weekly journal, a new and vigorous institution in American life. In New York and Massachusetts especially, weekly newspapers urged readers to preserve civic virtue, to exercise extreme vigilance against the spread of privileged power. In the first issue of the *Independent Reflector*, published in New York (November 30, 1752), the editor announced defiantly that no discouragement shall "deter me from vindicating the *civil and religious RIGHTS* of my Fellow-Creatures." Through such journals, a pattern of political rhetoric that in Britain had gained only marginal respectability became after 1765 America's normal form of political discourse.

The rise of the assemblies shaped American culture in other, subtler ways. Over the course of the century, the language of the law became increasingly Anglicized. The Board of Trade, the Privy Council, and Parliament scrutinized court decisions and legislative actions from all thirteen mainland colonies. As a result, varying local legal practices that had been widespread during the seventeenth century became standardized. Indeed, according to one historian, the colonial legal system by 1750 "was substantially that of the mother country." Not surprisingly, many men who served in colonial assemblies were either lawyers or persons who had received legal training. When Americans from different regions met—as they frequently did in the years before the Revolution—they discovered that they shared a commitment to the preservation of the English common law.

As eighteenth-century political developments drew the colonists closer to the mother country, they also brought Americans a greater awareness of each other. As their horizons widened, they learned they operated within the same general imperial system, and the problems confronting the Massachusetts House of Representatives were not too different from those facing Virginia's House of Burgesses or South Carolina's Commons House. Like the revivalists and merchants—people who crossed old boundaries—colonial legislators laid the foundation for a larger cultural identity.

FIGHTING BRITAIN'S WARS IN AMERICA

The scope and character of warfare in the colonies changed radically during the eighteenth century. The founders of England's mainland colonies had engaged in intense local conflicts with the Indians, such as King Philip's War (1675–1676) in New England. But after 1690, the colonists were increasingly involved in hostilities that originated on the other side of the Atlantic, in imperial rivalries between Great Britain and France over political and commercial ambitions. The external threat to security forced people in different colonies to devise unprecedented measures of military and political cooperation.

On paper, at least, the British colonies enjoyed military superiority over the settlements of New France. Louis XIV (r. 1643–1715) possessed an impressive army of 100,000 well-armed troops, but he dispatched few of them to the New World. He left the defense of Canada and the Mississippi Valley to the companies engaged in the fur trade. Meeting this challenge seemed almost impossible for the French outposts strung out along the St. Lawrence River and the Great Lakes. In 1754, New France contained only 75,000 inhabitants as compared to 1.2 million people living in Britain's mainland colonies.

For most of the century, the theoretical advantages enjoyed by the English colonists did them little good. While the British settlements possessed a larger and more prosperous population, they were divided into separate governments that sometimes seemed more suspicious of each other than of the French. When war came, French officers and Indian allies exploited these jealousies with considerable skill.

EUROPEAN AMBITIONS IN AMERICA

Colonial involvement in imperial war began in 1689, when England's new king, William III, declared war on Louis XIV. Europeans called this struggle the War of the League of Augsburg, but to the Americans, it was simply King William's War.

North America, 1750
By 1750, the French had established a chain of settlements southward through the heart of the continent from Quebec to New Orleans. The English saw this development as a threat to their own seaboard colonies, which were expanding westward.

Canadians commanded by the Comte de Frontenac raided the northern frontiers of New York and New England, and while they made no territorial gains, they caused considerable suffering among the civilian populations of Massachusetts and New York.

The war ended with the Treaty of Ryswick (1697), but the colonists were drawn almost immediately into a new conflict. Queen Anne's War, known in Europe as the War of the Spanish Succession (1702–1713), was fought across a large geographic area. The bloody combat along the American frontier ended in 1713 when Great Britain and France signed the Treaty of Utrecht. European negotiators showed little interest in the military situation in the New World. Their major concern was preserving a balance of power among the European states. More than two decades of intense fighting had taken a heavy toll in North America, but neither French nor English colonists had much to show for their sacrifice.

Both sides viewed this great contest over control of the West in conspiratorial terms. From South Carolina to Massachusetts Bay, colonists believed the French planned to "encircle" the English settlements, to confine the English to a narrow strip of land along the Atlantic coast. The English noted that in 1682, La Salle had claimed for the king of France a territory—Louisiana—that included all the people and resources located on "streams and Rivers" flowing into the Mississippi River. To make good on their claim, the French constructed forts on the Chicago and Illinois rivers. In 1717, they established a military post two hundred miles up the Alabama River, well within striking distance of the Carolina frontier, and in 1718, they settled New Orleans.

Native Americans often depended on trade goods supplied by the British and sometimes adopted British dress. Here the Mohawk chief Theyanoguin, called King Hendrick by the British, wears a cloak he received from Queen Anne of England during a visit to London in 1710. During the Seven Years' War, Theyanoguin mobilized Mohawk support for the British.

On their part, the French suspected their rivals intended to seize all of North America. Land speculators and frontier traders pushed aggressively into territory claimed by the French and owned by the Native Americans. In 1716, one Frenchman urged his government to hasten the development of Louisiana, since "it is not difficult to guess that their [the British] purpose is to drive us entirely out . . . of North America."

To their great sorrow and eventual destruction, the original inhabitants of the frontier, the Native Americans, were swept up in this undeclared war. The Indians maneuvered to hold their own in the "middle ground." The Iroquois favored the British; the Algonquian peoples generally supported the French. But regardless of the groups to which they belonged, Indian warriors—acting independently and for their own strategic reasons—found themselves enmeshed in the imperial policies of distant European kings.

EXPANDING CONFLICT

In 1743, the Americans were dragged once again into the imperial conflict. During King George's War (1743–1748), known in Europe as the War of the Austrian Succession, New

England colonists scored a magnificent victory over the French. Louisbourg, a gigantic fortress on Cape Breton Island, the easternmost promontory of Canada, guarded the approaches to the Gulf of St. Lawrence and Quebec.

The Americans, however, were in for a shock. When the war ended with the signing of the Treaty of Aix-la-Chapelle in 1748, the British government handed Louisbourg back to the French in exchange for concessions elsewhere. Such decisions exposed the deep and continuing ambivalence the colonists felt about participation in imperial wars. They were proud to support Great Britain, of course, but the Americans seldom fully understood why the wars were being fought, why certain tactics had been adopted, and why the British accepted treaty terms that so blatantly ignored colonial interests.

The French were not prepared to surrender an inch. But as they recognized, time was running against them. Not only were the English colonies growing more populous, but they also possessed a seemingly inexhaustible supply of manufactured goods to trade with the Indians. The French decided in the early 1750s, therefore, to seize the Ohio Valley before the Virginians could do so. They established forts throughout the region, the most formidable being Fort Duquesne, located at the strategic fork in the Ohio River and later renamed Pittsburgh.

Although France and England had not officially declared war, British officials advised the governor of Virginia to "repell force by force." The Virginians needed little encouragement. They were eager to make good their claim to the Ohio Valley, and in 1754, militia companies under the command of a promising young officer, George Washington, constructed Fort Necessity not far from Fort Duquesne. The plan failed. French and Indian troops overran the badly exposed outpost (July 3, 1754). Among other things, the humiliating setback revealed that a single colony could not defeat the French.

APPEALS FOR INTERCOLONIAL COOPERATION

Benjamin Franklin, for one, appreciated the need for intercolonial cooperation. When British officials invited representatives from Virginia and Maryland as well as the northern colonies to Albany (June 1754) to discuss relations with the Iroquois, Franklin used the occasion to present a bold blueprint for colonial union. His so-called Albany Plan envisioned the formation of a Grand Council, made up of elected delegates from the various colonies, to oversee matters of common defense, western expansion, and Indian affairs. A President General appointed by the king would preside. Franklin's most daring suggestion involved taxation. He insisted the council be authorized to collect taxes to cover military expenditures.

Initial reaction to the Albany Plan was enthusiastic. To take effect, however, it required the support of the separate colonial assemblies as well as Parliament. It received neither. The assemblies were jealous of their fiscal authority, and the English thought the scheme undermined the Crown's power over American affairs.

In 1755, the Ohio Valley again became the scene of fierce fighting. Even though there was still no formal declaration of war, the British resolved to destroy Fort Duquesne, and to that end, they dispatched units of the regular army

The first political cartoon to appear in an American newspaper was created by Benjamin Franklin in 1754 to emphasize the importance of the Albany Plan.

to America. In command was Major General Edward Braddock, a humorless veteran who inspired neither fear nor respect.

On July 9, Braddock led a joint force of twenty-five hundred British redcoats and colonists to humiliating defeat. The French and Indians opened fire as Braddock's army waded across the Monongahela River, about eight miles from Fort Duquesne. Nearly 70 percent of Braddock's troops were killed or wounded in western Pennsylvania. The general himself died in battle. The French, who suffered only light casualties, remained in firm control of the Ohio Valley.

The entire affair profoundly angered Washington, who fumed, "We have been most scandalously beaten by a trifling body of men." The British thought their allies the Iroquois might desert them after the embarrassing defeat. The Indians, however, took the news in stride, observing that "they were not at all surprised to hear it, as they [Braddock's redcoats] were men who had crossed the Great Water and were unacquainted with the arts of war among the Americans."

SEVEN YEARS' WAR

Britain's imperial war effort flirted with failure. No one in England or America seemed to possess the leadership necessary to drive the French from the Mississippi Valley. The cabinet of George II (r. 1727–1760) lacked the will to organize and finance a sustained military campaign in the New World, and colonial assemblies balked every time Britain asked them to raise men and money. On May 18, 1756, the British officially declared war on the French, a conflict called the French and Indian War in America and the Seven Years' War in Europe.

Had it not been for William Pitt, the most powerful minister in George's cabinet, the military stalemate might have continued. This supremely self-confident Englishman believed he was the only person capable of saving the British empire, an opinion he publicly expressed. When he became effective head of the ministry in December 1756, Pitt had an opportunity to demonstrate his talents.

In the past, warfare on the European continent had worked mainly to France's advantage. Pitt saw no point in continuing to concentrate on Europe, and in 1757 he advanced a bold new imperial policy, one based on commercial assumptions. In Pitt's judgment, the critical confrontation would take place in North America, where Britain and France were struggling to control colonial markets and raw materials. Indeed, according to Pitt, America was "where England and Europe are to be fought for." He was determined, therefore, to expel the French from the continent, however great the cost.

To effect this ambitious scheme, Pitt took personal command of the army and navy. He mapped strategy. He even promoted young promising officers over the heads of their superiors. He also recognized that the success of the war effort could not depend on the generosity of the colonial assemblies. Great Britain would have to foot most of the bill. Pitt's military expenditures, of course, created an enormous national debt that would soon haunt both Britain and its colonies, but at the time, no one foresaw the fiscal consequences of victory in America.

To direct the grand campaign, Pitt selected two relatively obscure officers, Jeffrey Amherst and James Wolfe. It was a masterful choice, one that a less self-assured man than Pitt would never have risked. Both officers were young, talented, and ambitious, and on July 26, 1758, forces under their direction captured Louisbourg, the same fortress the colonists had taken a decade earlier.

The climax to a century of war came dramatically in September 1759. Wolfe, now a major general, assaulted Quebec with nine thousand men. But it was not simply force of arms that brought victory. Wolfe proceeded as if he were preparing to attack the city directly, but under cover of darkness, his troops scaled a cliff to dominate a less well defended position. At dawn on September 13, 1759, they took the French from the rear by surprise. The decisive action occurred on the Plains of Abraham, a bluff high above the St. Lawrence River.

The Peace of Paris signed on February 10, 1763, almost fulfilled Pitt's grandiose dreams. Great Britain took possession of an empire that stretched around the globe. Only Guadeloupe and Martinique, Caribbean sugar islands, were given back to the French. After a centurylong struggle, the French had been driven from the mainland of North America. Even Louisiana passed out of France's control into Spanish hands. The treaty gave Britain title to Canada, Florida, and all the land east of the Mississippi River. Moreover, with the stroke of a diplomat's pen, eighty thousand French-speaking Canadians, most of them Catholics, became the subjects of George III. The Americans were overjoyed. It was a time of good feelings and national pride. Together, the English and their colonial allies had thwarted the "Gallic peril."

IMPERIAL PATRIOTISM

The Seven Years' War made a deep impression on American society. Even though Franklin's Albany Plan had failed, the military struggle had forced the colonists to cooperate on an unprecedented scale. It also drew them into closer contact with Britain. They became aware of being part of a great empire, military and commercial, but in the very process of waging war, they acquired a more intimate

A CENTURY OF CONFLICT: MAJOR WARS, 1689–1763

DATES	EUROPEAN NAME	AMERICAN NAME	ALLIES
1689–1697	War of the League of Augsburg	King William's War	Britain, Holland, Spain, their colonies, and Native American allies against France, its colonies, and Native American allies
1702–1713	War of the Spanish Succession	Queen Anne's War	Britain, Holland, their colonies, and Native American allies against France, Spain, their colonies, and Native American allies
1743–1748	War of the Austrian Succession (War of Jenkin's Ear)	King George's War	Britain, its colonies and Native American allies, and Austria against France, Spain, their Native American allies, and Prussia
1756–1763	Seven Years' War	French and Indian War	Britain, its colonies, and Native American allies against France, its colonies, and Native American allies

sense of an America that lay beyond the plantation and the village. Conflict had carried thousands of young men across colonial boundaries, exposing them to a vast territory full of opportunities for a booming population.

British officials later accused the Americans of ingratitude. England, they claimed, had sent troops and provided funds to liberate the colonists from the threat of French attack. The Americans, appreciative of the aid from England, cheered on the British but dragged their feet at every stage, refusing to pay the bills. These charges were later incorporated into a general argument justifying parliamentary taxation in America.

The British had a point. The colonists were, in fact, slow in providing the men and materials needed to fight the French. Nevertheless, they did make a significant contribution to the war effort, and it was perfectly reasonable for Americans to regard themselves at the very least as junior partners in the empire. After all, they had supplied almost twenty thousand soldiers and spent well over £2 million. In a single year, in fact, Massachusetts enlisted five thousand men out of an adult male population of about fifty thousand. After making such a sacrifice—indeed, after demonstrating their loyalty to the mother country—the colonists would surely have been disturbed to learn that General James Wolfe, the hero of Quebec, had stated, "The Americans are in general the dirtiest, the most contemptible, cowardly dogs that you can conceive. There is no depending upon them in action. They fall down in their own dirt and desert in battalions, officers and all."

ISSUES	MAJOR AMERICAN BATTLE	TREATY
Opposition to French bid for control of Europe	New England troops assault Quebec under Sir William Phips (1690)	Treaty of Ryswick (1697)
Austria and France hold rival claims to Spanish throne	Attack on Deerfield (1704)	Treaty of Utrecht (1713)
Struggle among Britain, Spain, and France for control of New World territory; among France, Prussia, and Austria for control of central Europe	New England forces capture Louisbourg under William Pepperrell (1745)	Treaty of Aix-la-Chapelle (1748)
Struggle among Britain, Spain, and France for worldwide control of colonial markets and raw materials	British and Continental forces capture Quebec under Major General James Wolfe (1759)	Peace of Paris (1763)

IMPERIAL PATRIOTISM

Whatever people such as Wolfe may have said in private, the general mood at midcentury was positive. James Thomson, an Englishman, understood the hold of empire on the popular imagination. In 1740, he composed words that British patriots have proudly sung for more than two centuries:

> *Rule Britannia, rule the waves,*
> *Britons never will be slaves.*

Colonial Americans—at least, those of British background—joined the chorus. By midcentury they took their political and cultural cues from Great Britain. They fought its wars, purchased its consumer goods, flocked to hear its evangelical preachers, and read its many publications. Without question, the empire provided the colonists with a compelling source of identity.

Americans hailed Britannia. In 1763, they were the victors, the conquerors of the backcountry. In their moment of glory, the colonists assumed that Britain's rulers saw the Americans as "Brothers," as equal partners in the business of empire. Only slowly would they learn the British had a different perception. For them, "American" was a way of saying "not quite English."

CHRONOLOGY

1680	El Popé leads Pueblo revolt against the Spanish in New Mexico
1689	William and Mary accede to the English throne
1706	Birth of Benjamin Franklin
1714	George I of Hanover becomes monarch of Great Britain
1732	Colony of Georgia is established
	Birth of George Washington
1734–1736	First expression of the Great Awakening at Northampton, Massachusetts
1740	George Whitefield electrifies listeners at Boston
1745	Colonial troops capture Louisbourg
1748	American Lutheran ministers ordained in Philadelphia
1754	Albany Congress meets
1755	Braddock is defeated by the French and Indians in western Pennsylvania
1756	Seven Years' War is formally declared
1759	British are victorious at Quebec; Wolfe and Montcalm are killed in battle
1760	George III becomes king of Great Britain
1763	Peace of Paris ending French and Indian War is signed
1769	Junípero Serra begins to build missions in California
1821	Mexico declares independence from Spain

5

THE AMERICAN REVOLUTION
From Elite Protest to Popular Revolt, 1763–1783

Even as the British army poured into Boston in 1774 and demanded complete obedience to king and Parliament, few Americans welcomed the possibility of revolutionary violence. For many colonial families, it would have been easier, certainly safer, to accede to imperial demands for taxes enacted without their representation. But they did not do so.

For the Patten family, the moment of reckoning arrived in spring of 1775. Matthew Patten had been born in Ulster, a Protestant Irishman, and with Scots-Irish friends and relatives, he migrated to New Hampshire, where they founded a settlement of fifty-six families known as Bedford. Matthew farmed the unpromising, rocky soil that he, his wife Elizabeth, and their children called home. In time, distant decisions about taxes and representation shattered the peace of Bedford, and the Pattens found themselves drawn into a war not of their own making but which, nevertheless, compelled them to sacrifice the security of everyday life for liberty.

On April 20, 1775, accounts of Lexington and Concord reached Bedford. Matthew noted in his diary, "I Received the Melancholy news in the morning that General Gage's troops had fired on our Countrymen at Concord yesterday." His son John marched with neighbors in support of the Massachusetts soldiers. The departure was tense. The entire family helped John prepare. "Our Girls sit up all night baking bread and fitting things for him," Matthew wrote.

The demands of war had only just begun. In late 1776 John volunteered for an American march on British Canada. On the long trek over impossible terrain, the boy died. The father recorded his emotions in the diary. John "was shot through his left arm at Bunker Hill fight and now was lead after suffering much fategue to the place where he now lyes in defending the just Rights of America to whose end he came in the prime of life by means of that wicked Tyrannical Brute (Nea worse than Brute) of Great Britain [George III]. He was 24 years and 31 days old."

The initial stimulus for rebellion came from the gentry, from the rich and wellborn, who resented Parliament's efforts to curtail their rights within the British empire. But as these influential planters, wealthy merchants, and prominent clergymen discovered, the revolutionary movement generated a momentum that they could not control. As relations with Britain deteriorated, particularly after 1765, the traditional leaders of colonial society encouraged the ordinary folk to join the protest—as rioters, as petitioners, and finally, as soldiers. Newspapers, sermons, and pamphlets helped transform what had begun as a squabble among the gentry into a mass movement, and as so many gentry leaders learned, once the people had become involved in shaping the nation's destiny, they could never again be excluded.

Had it not been for ordinary militiamen like John Patten in the various colonies, the British would have easily crushed American resistance. Although some accounts of the Revolution downplay the military side of the story, leaving the impression that a few famous "Founding Fathers" effortlessly carried the nation to independence, a more persuasive explanation must recognize the centrality of armed violence in achieving nationhood. The American Revolution involved a massive military commitment. If common American soldiers had not been willing to stand up to seasoned British troops, to face the terror of the bayonet charge, independence would have remained a dream of intellectuals.

CHARACTER OF COLONIAL SOCIETY

Colonists who were alive during the 1760s did not anticipate the coming of national independence. It is only from a modern perspective that we see how the events of this period would lead to the formation of the United States. The colonists, of course, did not know what the future would bring. They would probably have characterized these years as "postwar," as a time of heightened economic and political expectation following the successful conclusion of the Seven Years' War (see Chapter 4).

For many Americans, the period generated optimism. The population continued to grow. Indeed, in 1776, approximately 2.5 million people, black and white, were living in Great Britain's thirteen mainland colonies. The striking ethnic and racial diversity of these men and women amazed European visitors who apparently rated homogeneity more highly than did the Americans. In 1775, for example, a traveler corrected the impression in London that the "colonists are the offspring of Englishmen." To be sure, many families traced their roots to Great Britain, but one also encountered "French, Dutch, Germans, innumerable Indians, Africans, and a multitude of felons."

The American population on the eve of independence was also extraordinarily young, a fact of great importance in understanding the development of effective political resistance. Nearly 60 percent of the American people were under age twenty-one. At any given time, most people in this society were small children, and many of the young men who fought the British during the Revolution either had not been born or had been infants during the Stamp Act crisis. Any explanation for the coming of independence, therefore, must take into account the continuing political mobilization of so many young people.

Postwar Americans also experienced a high level of prosperity. To be sure, some major port cities went through a difficult period as colonists who had been employed during the fighting were thrown out of work. Sailors and ship workers, for example, were especially vulnerable to layoffs of this sort. In general, however, white Americans did very well. The quality of their material lives was not substantially lower than that of the English.

Wealth, however, was not evenly distributed in this society. Regional variations were striking. The Southern Colonies enjoyed the highest levels of personal wealth in America, which can be explained in part by the ownership of slaves. More than 90 percent of America's unfree workers lived in the South, and they represented a huge capital investment. Even without including the slaves in these wealth estimates, the South did quite well. In terms of aggregate wealth, the middle colonies also scored impressively. In fact, only New England lagged noticeably behind, a reflection of its relative inability to produce large amounts of exports for a growing world market.

BREAKDOWN OF POLITICAL TRUST

Ultimate responsibility for preserving the empire fell to George III. When he became king of Great Britain in 1760, he was only twenty-two years of age. In public, contemporaries praised the new monarch. In private, however, they expressed grave reservations. The youth had led a sheltered, loveless life; his father, an irresponsible playboy, had died in 1751 before ascending the throne. Young George had not received a good education.

The new monarch was determined to play an aggressive role in government. This decision caused considerable dismay among England's political leaders. For decades, a powerful, though loosely associated, group of men who called themselves Whigs had set policy and controlled patronage. George II, his grandfather, had accepted this situation, and so long as the Whigs in Parliament did not meddle with his beloved army, the king had let them rule the nation.

George III destroyed this cozy relationship. He selected as his chief minister the Earl of Bute, a Scot whose chief qualification for office appeared to be his friendship with the young king. The Whigs who dominated Parliament were outraged. Bute had no ties with the members of the House of Commons; he owed them no favors. It seemed to the Whigs that with the appointment of Bute, George was trying to establish a personal monarchy free from traditional constitutional restraints.

By 1763 Bute had left office. His departure, however, neither restored the Whigs to preeminence nor dampened the king's enthusiasm for domestic politics. Everyone agreed George had the right to select whomever he desired for cabinet posts, but until 1770, no one seemed able to please the monarch. Ministers came and went, often for no other reason than George's personal distaste. Because of this chronic instability, subministers (minor bureaucrats who directed routine colonial affairs) did not know what was expected of them. In the absence of clear long-range policy, some ministers made narrowly based decisions; others did nothing. Most devoted their energies to finding a political patron capable of satisfying the fickle king. With such turbulence surrounding him, the king showed little interest in the American colonies.

The king, however, does not bear the sole responsibility for England's loss of empire. The members of Parliament who actually drafted the statutes that gradually drove a wedge between the colonies and Britain must share the blame, for they failed to provide innovative answers to the explosive constitutional issues of the day.

In part, the impasse resulted from sheer ignorance. Few Englishmen active in government had ever visited America. For those who attempted to follow colonial affairs, accurate information proved extremely difficult to obtain. Packet boats carrying passengers and mail sailed regularly between London and the various colonial ports, but the voyage across the Atlantic required at least four weeks. Furthermore, all correspondence was laboriously copied in longhand by overworked clerks serving in understaffed offices. One could not expect to receive from America an answer to a specific question in less than three months. As a result of the lag in communication between England and America, rumors sometimes passed for true accounts, and misunderstanding influenced the formulation of colonial policy.

But failure of communication alone was not to blame for the widening gap between the colonies and England. Even when complete information was avail-

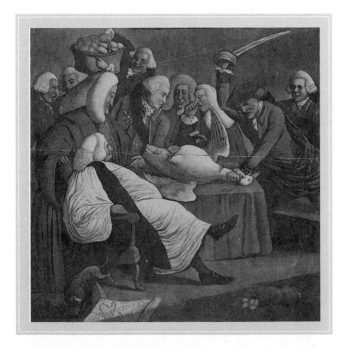

Cartoons became a popular means of criticizing the government during this period. Here, King George III watches as the kilted Lord Bute slaughters the goose America. A cabinet member holds a basket of golden eggs at the rear. At front left, a dog relieves itself on a map of North America.

able, the two sides were often unable to understand each other's positions. The central element in this Anglo-American debate was a concept known as parliamentary sovereignty. The English ruling classes viewed the role of Parliament from a historical perspective that most colonists never shared. They insisted that Parliament was the dominant element within the constitution. Indeed, this elective body protected rights and property from an arbitrary monarch. Almost no one, including George III, would have dissented from a speech made in 1766 before the House of Commons, in which a representative declared, "The parliament hath, and must have, from the nature and essence of the constitution . . . a sovereign supreme power and jurisdiction over every part of the dominions of the state, *to make laws in all cases whatsoever.*"

Such a constitutional position did not leave much room for compromise. Most members of Parliament took a hard line on this issue. The notion of dividing or sharing sovereignty simply made no sense to the English ruling class. In fact, parliamentary leaders could never quite understand why the colonists were so difficult to persuade. In frustration, Lord Hillsborough, the British secretary of state, admonished the colonial agent for Connecticut, "It is essential to the constitution to preserve the supremacy of Parliament inviolate; and tell your friends in America . . . that it is as much their interest to support the constitution and preserve the supremacy of Parliament as it is ours."

No Taxation Without Representation: The American Perspective

Americans most emphatically did not see it in their "interest" to maintain the "supremacy of Parliament." The crisis in imperial relations forced the colonists first to define and then to defend principles deeply rooted in their own political culture.

By 1763, certain fundamental American beliefs had become clear. From Massachusetts to Georgia, colonists aggressively defended the powers of the provincial assemblies. They drew on a rich legislative history of their own. Over the course of the century, the American assemblies had steadily expanded their authority over taxation and expenditure. Since no one in Britain bothered to clip their legislative wings, these provincial bodies assumed a major role in policymaking and routine administration. In other words, by midcentury the assemblies looked like American copies of Parliament. It seemed unreasonable, therefore, for the British suddenly to insist on the supremacy of Parliament.

The constitutional debate turned ultimately on the meaning of representation itself. In 1764, a British official informed the colonists that even though they had not elected members to Parliament—indeed, even though they had had no direct contact with the current members—they were nevertheless "virtually" represented by that august body. The members of Parliament, he declared, represented the political interests of everyone who lived in the British empire. It did not really matter whether everyone had cast a vote.

The colonists ridiculed this argument. The only representatives the Americans recognized as legitimate were those actually chosen by the people for whom they spoke. On this crucial point they would not compromise. As John Adams insisted, a representative assembly should actually mirror its constituents: "It should think, feel, reason, and act like them." Since the members of Parliament could not possibly "think" like Americans, it followed logically they could not represent them. And if they were not genuine representatives, the members of Parliament had no business taxing the American people.

APPEAL TO POLITICAL VIRTUE

The political ideology that had the greatest popular appeal among the colonists contained a strong moral component, one that British rulers and American Loyalists (people who sided with the king and Parliament during the Revolution) never fully understood. The origins of this highly religious perspective on civil government are difficult to locate with precision, but certainly, the Great Awakening created a general awareness of an obligation to conduct public as well as private affairs according to Scripture (see Chapter 4).

Americans expressed their political beliefs in a language they had borrowed from English writers. The person most frequently cited was John Locke, the influential seventeenth-century philosopher whose *Two Treatises of Government* (first published in 1690) seemed, to colonial readers at least, a brilliant description of what was in fact American political practice. Locke claimed that all people possessed natural and inalienable rights. In order to preserve these God-given rights—the rights of life, liberty, and property, for example—free men (the status of women in Locke's work was less clear) formed contracts. These agreements were the foundation of human society as well as civil government, and they required the consent of the people who were actually governed. There could be no coercion. Locke justified rebellion against arbitrary forms of government that were by their very nature unreasonable. Americans delighted in Locke's ability to unite traditional religious values with a spirited defense of popular government.

Colonial Americans also enthusiastically subscribed to the so-called Commonwealthman tradition, a body of political assumptions generally identified with two eighteenth-century English publicists, John Trenchard and Thomas Gordon (see Chapter 4). The writings of such figures helped persuade the colonists that *power* was extremely dangerous, a force that would surely destroy liberty unless it was countered by *virtue*. Persons who shared this highly charged moral outlook regarded bad policy as not simply the result of human error. Rather, it was an indication of sin and corruption.

Insistence on public virtue—sacrifice of self-interest to the public good—became the dominant theme of revolutionary political writing. American pamphleteers seldom took a dispassionate, legalistic approach to their analysis of power and liberty. More commonly, they exposed plots hatched by corrupt courtiers, such as the Earl of Bute. None of them—or their readers—had any doubt that Americans were more virtuous than were the people of England.

During the 1760s, however, popular writers were not certain how long the colonists could hold out against arbitrary taxation, standing armies, Anglican bishops—in other words, against a host of external threats designed to crush American liberty. In 1774, for example, the people of Farmington, Connecticut, declared that "the present ministry, being instigated by the devil and led by their wicked and corrupt hearts, have a design to take away our liberties and properties, and to enslave us forever."

Colonial newspapers spread these ideas through a large dispersed population. A majority of adult white males—especially those in the Northern Colonies—were literate, and it is not surprising that the number of journals published in this country increased dramatically during the revolutionary period. For the first time in American history, persons living in various parts of the continent could closely follow events that occurred in distant American cities.

THE ARMY AS PROVOCATION: ERODING THE BONDS OF EMPIRE

The Seven Years' War saddled Great Britain with a national debt so huge that more than half the annual national budget went to pay the interest on it. Almost everyone in government assumed that with the cessation of hostilities, the troops would be disbanded, thus saving a lot of money; George III had other plans. He insisted on keeping the largest peacetime army in British history on active duty, supposedly to protect Indians from predatory frontiersmen and to preserve order in the newly conquered territories of Florida and Quebec.

The growing financial burden weighed heavily on English taxpayers and sent government leaders scurrying in search of new sources of revenue. For their part, colonists doubted the value of this very expensive army. First, Britain did not leave enough troops in America to maintain peace on the frontier effectively. The weakness of the army was dramatically demonstrated during the spring of 1763. The native peoples of the backcountry—the Seneca, Ottawa, Miami, Creek, and Cherokee—had begun discussing how they might turn back the tide of white settlement. The powerful spiritual leader Neolin, known as the Delaware Prophet, and claiming vision from the "Master of Life," helped these Indians articulate their fear and anger. He urged them to restore their cultures to the "original state that they were in before the white people found out their country." If moral regeneration required violence, so be it. Neolin converted Pontiac, an Ottawa warrior, to the cause, and he, in turn, coordinated an uprising among the western Indians who had been French allies and who hated all British people—even those sent to protect them from land-grabbing colonists. In May, Pontiac attacked Detroit; other Indians harassed the Pennsylvania and Virginia frontiers. At the end of the year, after his followers began deserting, Pontiac sued for peace. During even this brief outbreak, the British army proved unable to defend exposed colonial settlements, and several thousand people lost their lives.

From the perspective of the Native Americans who inhabited the Ohio Valley this was a period of almost unmitigated disaster. In fact, more than any other group, the Indians suffered as a direct result of imperial reorganization. The defeat of the French made it impossible for native peoples to play off one imperial power against European rivals (see Chapter 4), and the victorious British demonstrated that they regarded their former Indian allies as little more than a nuisance. Diplomatic gifts stopped; humiliating restrictions were placed on trade. But even worse, Pontiac's rising unloosed vicious racism along the colonial frontier, and American colonists often used any excuse to attack local Indians, peaceful or not. Late in 1763, a group of vigilantes known as the Paxton Boys murdered a score of Christian Indians, women and children, living near Lancaster, Pennsylvania. White neighbors treated the killers as heroes, and the atrocity ended only after the Paxton Boys threatened to march on Philadelphia in search of administrators who dared to criticize such cold-blooded crimes. One of the administrators, Benjamin Franklin, observed sadly, "It grieves me to hear that our Frontier People are yet greater Barbarians than the Indians, and continue to murder them in time of Peace."

Whatever happened to the Indians, the colonists fully intended to settle the fertile region west of the Appalachian Mountains. After the British government issued the Proclamation of 1763, which prohibited governors from granting land beyond the headwaters of rivers flowing into the Atlantic, disappointed Americans viewed the army as an obstruction to legitimate economic development, a domestic police force that cost too much money.

PAYING OFF THE NATIONAL DEBT

The task of reducing England's debt fell to George Grenville, the rigid, somewhat unimaginative chancellor of the exchequer who replaced Bute in 1763 as the king's first minister. After reviewing the state of Britain's finances, Grenville concluded that the colonists would have to contribute to the maintenance of the army. The first bill he steered through Parliament was the Revenue Act of 1764, known as the Sugar Act.

This legislation placed a new burden on the Navigation Acts that had regulated the flow of colonial commerce for almost a century (see Chapter 3). Those acts had forced Americans to trade almost exclusively with Britain. The statutes were not, however, primarily intended as a means to raise money for the British government. The Sugar Act—and the acts that soon followed—redefined the relationship between America and Great Britain. Parliament now expected the colonies to generate revenue. The preamble of the Sugar Act proclaimed explicitly: "It is just and necessary that a revenue be raised . . . in America for defraying the expenses of defending, protecting, and securing the same." The purpose of the Sugar Act was to discourage smuggling, bribery, and other illegalities that prevented the Navigation Acts from being profitable. Parliament reduced the duty on molasses (set originally by the Molasses Act of 1733) from 6 to 3 pence per gallon. At so low a rate, Grenville reasoned, colonial merchants would have little incentive to bribe customs collectors. Much needed revenue would be diverted from the pockets of corrupt officials into the treasury so that it might be used to maintain the army.

Grenville had been too clever by half. The Americans immediately saw through his unconstitutional scheme. According to the members of the Rhode Island Assembly, the Sugar Act taxed the colonists in a manner "inconsistent with their rights and privileges as British subjects." James Otis, a fiery orator from Massachusetts, exclaimed the legislation deprived Americans of "the right of assessing their own taxes."

MOBILIZING THE PEOPLE

Passage of the Stamp Act in 1765 transformed debate among gentlemen into a mass political movement. The imperial crisis might have been avoided. Colonial agents had presented Grenville with alternative schemes for raising money in America. But Grenville was a stubborn man, and he had little fear of parliamentary opposition. The majority of the House of Commons assumed that Parliament possessed the right to tax the colonists, and when the chancellor of the exchequer announced a plan to squeeze £60,000 annually out of the Americans by requiring them to purchase special seals or stamps to validate legal documents, the members responded with enthusiasm. The Stamp Act was scheduled to go into effect on November 1, 1765, and in anticipation of brisk sales, Grenville appointed stamp distributors for every colony.

Word of the Stamp Act reached America in May, sparking widespread protest. The most dramatic incident occurred in Virginia's House of Burgesses. Patrick Henry, young and eloquent, who contemporaries compared in fervor to evangelical preachers, introduced five resolutions protesting the Stamp Act on the floor of the assembly. He timed his move carefully. It was late in the session; many of the more conservative burgesses had already departed for their plantations. Even then, Henry's resolves declaring that Virginians had the right to tax themselves as they alone saw fit passed by narrow margins. The fifth resolution, stricken almost immediately from the legislative records, announced that any attempt to collect stamp revenues in America was "illegal, unconstitutional, and unjust, and has a manifest tendency to destroy British as well as American liberty."

The Virginia Resolves might have remained a local matter had it not been for the colonial press. Newspapers throughout America printed Henry's resolutions,

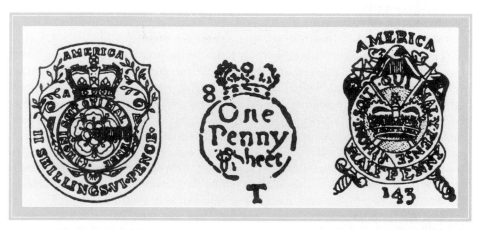

The Stamp Act placed a tax on documents and printed matter—newspapers, marriage licenses, wills, deeds, even playing cards and dice. The stamps (like those shown here) varied in denomination. A tax stamp affixed to a legal document or bill of sale signified that the required tax had been paid.

but, perhaps because editors did not really know what had happened in Williamsburg, they reported that all five resolutions had received the burgesses' full support. Several journals even carried two resolves that Henry had not dared to introduce. A result of this misunderstanding, of course, was that the Virginians appeared to have taken an extremely radical position on the issue of the supremacy of Parliament, one that other Americans now trumpeted before their own assemblies.

Not to be outdone by Virginia, Massachusetts called a general meeting to protest Grenville's policy. Nine colonies sent representatives to the Stamp Act Congress that convened in New York City in October 1765. It was the first intercolonial gathering held since the abortive Albany Congress of 1754; if nothing else, the new congress provided leaders from different regions with an opportunity to discuss common problems. The delegates drafted petitions to the king and Parliament that restated the colonists' belief "that no taxes should be imposed on them, but with their own consent, given personally, or by their representatives."

Resistance to the Stamp Act soon spread to the streets. By taxing deeds, marriage licenses, and playing cards, the Stamp Act touched the lives of ordinary women and men. Anonymous artisans and seamen, angered by Parliament's apparent insensitivity and fearful that the statute would increase unemployment and poverty, organized mass protests in the major colonial ports.

In Boston, the "Sons of Liberty" burned in effigy the local stamp distributor, Andrew Oliver, and when that action failed to bring about his resignation, they tore down one of his office buildings. Even after he resigned, the mob nearly demolished the elegant home of Oliver's close associate, Lieutenant Governor Thomas Hutchinson. After 1765, it was impossible for either royal governors or patriot leaders to take the ordinary folk for granted.

By November 1, 1765, stamp distributors in almost every American port had resigned, and without distributors, the hated revenue stamps could not be sold. The courts soon reopened; most newspapers were published. Daily life in the colonies was undisturbed with one exception: the Sons of Liberty persuaded— some said coerced—colonial merchants to boycott British goods until Parliament repealed the Stamp Act. The merchants showed little enthusiasm for such tactics, but the threat of tar and feathers stimulated cooperation.

The boycott movement was in itself a masterful political innovation. Never before had a resistance movement organized itself so centrally around the market decisions of ordinary consumers. The colonists depended on British imports— cloth, metal goods, and ceramics—and each year they imported more consumer goods than they could possibly afford. In this highly charged moral atmosphere, one in which ordinary people talked constantly of conspiracy and corruption, it is not surprising that Americans of different classes and backgrounds advocated a radical change in buying habits. Personal excess threatened to contaminate the entire political community. This logic explains the power of an appeal made in a Boston newspaper: "Save your money and you can save your country."

The boycotts mobilized colonial women. They were excluded from voting and civil office, but such legal discrimination did not mean that women were not part of the broader political culture. Since wives and mothers spent their days involved with household chores, they assumed special responsibility to reform consumption, to root out luxury, and to promote frugality. Indeed, in this realm they possessed

The boycott movement drew many colonial women into popular politics. In this 1774 woodcut, a Daughter of Liberty stands ready to resist British oppression.

real power; they monitored the ideological commitment of the entire family. Throughout the colonies, women altered styles of dress, made homespun cloth, and shunned imported items on which Parliament had placed a tax.

CONCILIATION AND COERCION

What most Americans did not yet know—after all, communication with Britain required months—was that in July, Grenville had fallen from power. This unexpected shift came about not because the king thought Grenville's policies inept, but rather because George did not like the man. His replacement as first lord of the treasury, Lord Rockingham, was young, inexperienced, and terrified of public speaking, a serious handicap to launching a parliamentary career. Rockingham wanted to repeal the Stamp Act, but because of the shakiness of his own political coalition, he could not announce such a decision until it enjoyed broad parliamentary support.

Grenville, now simply a member of Parliament, would tolerate no retreat on the issue of supremacy. He urged his colleagues in the House of Commons to be tough, to condemn "the outrageous tumults and insurrections which have been excited and carried on in North America." But William Pitt, the architect of victory in the Seven Years' War and a hero throughout America, eloquently defended the colonists' position, and after the Rockingham ministry gathered additional support from prominent figures such as Benjamin Franklin, who happened to be visiting England, Parliament felt strong enough to recommend repeal. On March 18, 1766, the House of Commons voted 275 to 167 to rescind the Stamp Act.

Lest its retreat on the Stamp Act be interpreted as weakness, the House of Commons passed the Declaratory Act (March 1766), a shrill defense of parliamentary supremacy over the Americans "in all cases whatsoever." The colonists' insistence on no taxation without representation failed to impress British rulers.

The Stamp Act crisis eroded the colonists' respect for imperial officeholders in America. Suddenly, these men—royal governors, customs collectors, military personnel—appeared alien, as if their interests were not those of the people over whom they exercised authority. One person who had been forced to resign the post of stamp distributor for South Carolina noted several years later, "The Stamp Act had introduc'd so much Party Rage, Faction, and Debate that the ancient Harmony, Generosity, and Urbanity for which these People were celebrated is destroyed, and at an End."

A FOOLISH BOAST: TEA AND SOVEREIGNTY

Rockingham's ministry soon gave way to a government headed once again by William Pitt, who was now the Earl of Chatham. The aging Pitt suffered horribly from gout, and during his long absences from London, Charles Townshend, his chancellor of the exchequer, made important policy decisions. Townshend was an impetuous man whose mouth often outran his mind. During a parliamentary debate in January 1767, he surprised everyone by blithely announcing that he knew a way to obtain revenue from the Americans.

His scheme turned out to be a grab bag of duties on American imports of paper, glass, paint, lead, and tea, which collectively were known as the Townshend Revenue Acts (June–July 1767). He hoped to generate sufficient funds to pay the salaries of royal governors and other imperial officers, thus freeing them from dependence on the colonial assemblies.

The chancellor recognized that without tough instruments of enforcement, his duties would not produce the promised revenues. Therefore, he created an American Board of Customs Commissioners, a body based in Boston and supported by reorganized vice-admiralty courts located in Boston, Philadelphia, and Charles Town. And for good measure, Townshend induced Parliament to order the governor of New York to veto all bills passed by that colony's assembly until it supplied resident British troops in accordance with the Quartering Act (May 1765). Many Americans regarded this as more taxation without representation, and in New York, at least, colonists refused to pay.

Colonists showed no more willingness to pay Townshend's duties than they had to buy Grenville's stamps. No congress was called; none was necessary. Recent events had taught people how to coordinate protest, and they moved to resist the unconstitutional revenue acts. In major ports, the Sons of Liberty organized boycotts of British goods. Men and women took oaths before neighbors promising not to purchase certain goods until Parliament repealed unconstitutional taxation.

On February 11, 1768, the Massachusetts House of Representatives drafted a circular letter, a provocative appeal that it sent directly to the other colonial assemblies. The letter requested suggestions on how best to thwart the Townshend Acts; not surprisingly, legislators in other parts of America, busy with local matters, simply ignored this general appeal. But not Lord Hillsborough, England's secretary for American affairs. This rather mild attempt to create a united colonial front struck him as gross treason, and he ordered the Massachusetts representatives to rescind their "seditious paper." After considering Hillsborough's demand, the legislators voted 92 to 17 to defy him.

Suddenly, the circular letter became a cause célèbre. The royal governor of Massachusetts hastily dissolved the House of Representatives. That decision compelled the other colonies to demonstrate their support for Massachusetts. Assembly after assembly now felt obligated to take up the circular letter, an action Hillsborough had specifically forbidden. Assemblies in other colonies were dissolved, creating a much broader crisis of representative government. Throughout America, the number 92 (the number of legislators who voted against Hillsborough) immediately became a symbol of patriotism. In fact, Parliament's challenge had brought about the very results it most wanted to avoid: a foundation for intercolonial communication and a strengthening of conviction among the colonists of the righteousness of their position.

CREATING PATRIOTIC MARTYRS

In October 1768, British rulers made another mistake. At the heart of the trouble was the army. In part to save money and in part to intimidate colonial troublemakers, the ministry transferred four thousand regular troops from Nova Scotia and Ireland to Boston. Most of the army had already been withdrawn from the frontier to the seacoast to save revenue, thereby raising more acutely than ever the issue of why troops were in America at all. The armed strangers camped on the Boston Common, and when citizens passed the site, redcoats shouted obscenities.

When colonists questioned why the army had been sent to a peaceful city, pamphleteers responded that it was there to further a conspiracy originally conceived by Bute to oppress Americans, to take away their liberties, to collect illegal revenues. Colonists had no difficulty interpreting the violence that erupted in Boston on March 5, 1770. In the gathering dusk of that afternoon, young boys and street toughs threw rocks and snowballs at soldiers in a small, isolated patrol outside the offices of the hated customs commissioners in King Street. The details of this incident are obscure, but it appears that as the mob grew and became more threatening, the soldiers panicked. In the confusion, the troops fired, leaving five Americans dead.

Pamphleteers promptly labeled the incident a massacre. The victims were seen as martyrs. Paul Revere's engraving of the massacre, appropriately splattered with blood, became an instant best-seller. Confronted with such intense reaction and with the possibility of massive armed resistance, Crown officials wisely moved the army to an island in Boston Harbor.

At this critical moment, the king's new first minister restored a measure of tranquility. Lord North, congenial, well-meaning, but not very talented, became chancellor of the exchequer following Townshend's death in 1767. North was appointed the first minister in 1770, and for the next twelve years—indeed, throughout most of the American crisis—he managed to retain his office. His formula seems to have been an ability to get along with George III and to build an effective majority in Parliament.

Outrage over the Boston Massacre was fanned by propaganda, such as this engraving by Paul Revere, which showed British redcoats firing on ordinary citizens. In subsequent editions, the blood spurting from the dying Americans became more conspicuous.

North recommended to Parliament the repeal of the Townshend duties. Not only had these ill-conceived duties angered the colonists, but they also hurt English manufacturers. By taxing British exports such as glass and paint, Parliament had only encouraged the Americans to develop their own industries; thus, without much prodding, the House of Commons dropped all the Townshend duties—with the notable exception of tea. The tax on tea was retained not for revenue purposes, North insisted, but as a reminder that England's rulers still subscribed to the principles of the Declaratory Act. They would not compromise the supremacy of Parliament.

COLLAPSE OF THE OLD IMPERIAL ORDER, 1770–1773

For a short while, American colonists and British officials put aside their recent animosities. Like England's rulers, some colonial gentry were beginning to pull back from protest, especially violent confrontation with established authority, in fear that the lower orders were becoming too assertive. It was probably in this period that Loyalist Americans emerged as an identifiable group. Colonial merchants returned to familiar patterns of trade, pleased no doubt to end the local boycotts that had depressed the American economy. British goods flooded into colonial ports; the level of American indebtedness soared to new highs.

Appearances were deceiving. The bonds of imperial loyalty remained fragile, and even as Lord North attempted to win the colonists' trust, Crown officials in America created new strains. Customs commissioners whom Townshend had appointed to collect his duties remained in the colonies long after his Revenue Acts had been repealed. If they had been honest, unobtrusive administrators, perhaps no one would have taken notice of their behavior. But the customs commissioners regularly abused their powers of search and seizure and in the process lined their own pockets. In Massachusetts, Rhode Island, and South Carolina—to cite the most notorious cases—these officials drove local citizens to distraction by enforcing the

Navigation Acts with such rigor that a small boat could not cross Narragansett Bay with a load of firewood without first obtaining a sheaf of legal documents. One slip, no matter how minor, could bring confiscation of ship and cargo.

The commissioners were not only corrupt; they were also shortsighted. If they had restricted their extortion to ordinary folk, they might have avoided becoming a major American grievance. But they could not control their greed. Some customs officers harassed the wealthiest, most powerful men such as John Hancock of Boston and Henry Laurens of Charles Town. The commissioners' actions drove some members of the colonial ruling class into opposition to the king's government. When in the summer of 1772 a group of disguised Rhode Islanders burned a customs vessel, the *Gaspee,* Americans cheered. A special royal commission sent to arrest the culprits discovered that not a single Rhode Islander had the slightest idea how the ship could have come to such an end.

During the early 1770s, while colonial leaders turned to other matters, Samuel Adams (1722–1803) kept the cause alive with a drumfire of publicity. He reminded the people of Boston that the tax on tea remained in force. He organized public anniversaries commemorating the repeal of the Stamp Act and the Boston Massacre.

With each new attempt by Parliament to assert its supremacy over the colonists, more and more Bostonians listened to what Adams had to say. He observed ominously that the British intended to use the tea revenue to pay judicial salaries, thus freeing the judges from dependence on the assembly. When in November 1772 Adams suggested the formation of a committee of correspondence to communicate grievances to villagers throughout Massachusetts, he received broad support. Americans living in other colonies soon copied his idea. It was a brilliant stroke. Adams developed a structure of political cooperation completely independent of royal government.

THE FINAL PROVOCATION: THE BOSTON TEA PARTY

In May 1773, Parliament passed the Tea Act, legislation the Americans might have welcomed. After all, it lowered the price for their favorite beverage. Parliament wanted to save one of Britain's largest businesses, the East India Company, from possible bankruptcy. This commercial giant imported Asian tea into England, where it was resold to wholesalers. The tea was also subject to heavy duties. The company tried to pass these charges on to the consumers, but American tea drinkers preferred the cheaper leaves that were smuggled in from Holland.

The Tea Act changed the rules. Parliament not only allowed the company to sell directly to American retailers, thus cutting out intermediaries, but also eliminated the duties paid in England. If all had gone according to plan, the agents of the East India Company in America would have undersold their competitors, including the Dutch smugglers, and with the new profits would have saved the business.

Parliament's logic was flawed. First, since the tax on tea, collected in American ports, remained in effect, this new act seemed a devious scheme to win popular support for Parliament's right to tax the colonists without representation. Second, the act threatened to undercut powerful colonial merchants who did a

This bottle of tea leaves preserved from the Boston Tea Party of December 16, 1773, suggests that one participant or onlooker was mindful of the historical importance of the colonial protest.

good business trading in smuggled Dutch tea. Considering the American reaction, the British government might have been well advised to devise another plan to rescue the ailing company. In Philadelphia, and then at New York City, colonists turned back the tea ships before they could unload.

In Boston, however, the issue was not so easily resolved. Governor Hutchinson, a strong-willed man, would not permit the vessels to return to England. Local Patriots would not let them unload. And so, crammed with the East India Company's tea, the ships sat in Boston Harbor waiting for the colonists to make up their minds. On the night of December 16, 1773, they did so in dramatic style. A group of men disguised as Mohawk Indians boarded the ships and pitched 340 chests of tea worth £10,000 over the side.

When news of the Tea Party reached London in January 1774, the North ministry was stunned. The people of Boston had treated parliamentary supremacy with utter contempt, and British rulers saw no humor whatsoever in the destruction of private property by subjects of the Crown dressed as Indians. To quell such rebelliousness, Parliament passed a series of laws called the Coercive Acts. (In America, they were referred to as the Intolerable Acts.) The legislation (1) closed the port of Boston until the city fully compensated the East India Company for the lost tea; (2) restructured the Massachusetts government by transforming the upper house from an elective to an appointed body and restricting the number of legal town meetings to one a year; (3) allowed the royal governor to transfer British officials arrested for offenses committed in the line of duty to England, where there was little likelihood they would be convicted; and (4) authorized the army to quarter troops wherever they were needed, even if this required the compulsory requisition of uninhabited private buildings. George III enthusiastically supported this tough policy; he appointed General Thomas Gage to serve as the colony's new royal governor. Gage apparently won the king's favor by announcing that in America, "Nothing can be done but by forcible means."

In the midst of the constitutional crisis, Parliament announced plans to establish a new civil government for the Canadian province of Quebec (Quebec Act, June 22, 1774). This territory had been ruled by military authority following the Seven Years' War. The Quebec Act not only failed to create an elective assembly—an institution the Americans regarded as essential for the protection of liberty—but also awarded French Roman Catholics a large voice in political affairs. Moreover, since Quebec extended all the way south to the Ohio River and west to the Mississippi River, Americans concluded that Parliament wanted to deny the American settlers and traders in this fast-developing region their constitutional rights, a threat that affected all colonists, not just those of Massachusetts Bay.

MAJOR PARLIAMENTARY ACTS:
OPPRESSION OR REGULATION?

LEGISLATION	DATE	PROVISIONS	COLONIAL REACTION
Sugar Act	April 5, 1764	Revised duties on sugar, coffee, tea, wine, other imports; expanded jurisdiction of vice-admiralty courts	Several assemblies protest taxation for revenue
Stamp Act	March 22, 1765; repealed March 18, 1766	Printed documents (deeds, newspapers, marriage licenses, etc.) issued only on special stamped paper purchased from stamp distributors	Riots in cities; collectors forced to resign; Stamp Act Congress (October 1765)
Quartering Act	May 1765	Colonists must supply British troops with housing, other items (candles, firewood, etc.)	Protest in assemblies; New York Assembly punished for failure to comply, 1767
Declaratory Act	March 18, 1766	Parliament declares its sovereignty over the colonies "in all cases whatsoever"	Ignored in celebration over repeal of the Stamp Act
Townshend Revenue Acts	June 26, 29, July 2, 1767; all repealed— except duty on tea, March 1770	New duties on glass, lead, paper, paints, tea; customs collections tightened in America	Nonimportation of British goods; assemblies protest; newspapers attack British policy
Tea Act	May 10, 1773	Parliament gives East India Company right to sell tea directly to Americans; some duties on tea reduced	Protests against favoritism shown to monopolistic company; tea destroyed in Boston (December 16, 1773)
Coercive Acts (Intolerable Acts)	March–June 1774	Closes port of Boston; restructures Massachusetts government; restricts town meetings; troops quartered in Boston; British officials accused of crimes sent to England or Canada for trial	Boycott of British goods; First Continental Congress convenes (September 1774)
Prohibitory Act	December 22, 1775	Declares British intention to coerce Americans into submission; embargo on American goods; American ships seized	Drives Continental Congress closer to decision for independence

The sticking point remained—as it had in 1765—the sovereignty of Parliament. No one in Britain could think of a way around this constitutional impasse. In 1773, Benjamin Franklin had offered a suggestion. "The Parliament," he observed, "has no right to make any law whatever, binding on the colonies . . . the king, and not the king, lords, and commons collectively, is their sovereign." But so long as it still seemed possible to coerce the Americans into obedience, to punish these errant children, Britain's rulers had little incentive to accept.

DECISION FOR INDEPENDENCE

During the summer of 1774, committees of correspondence analyzed the perilous situation in which the colonists found themselves. Something, of course, had to be done. But what? Would the Southern Colonies support resistance in New England? Would Pennsylvanians stand up to Parliament? Not surprisingly, the committees endorsed a call for a Continental Congress, a gathering of fifty-five elected delegates from twelve colonies (Georgia sent none but agreed to support the action taken). This momentous gathering convened in Philadelphia on September 5. It included some of America's most articulate, respected leaders, including John Adams, Samuel Adams, Patrick Henry, Richard Henry Lee, Christopher Gadsden, and George Washington.

Differences of opinion soon surfaced. Delegates from the middle colonies—Joseph Galloway of Pennsylvania, for example—wanted to proceed with caution, but Samuel Adams and other more radical members pushed the moderates toward confrontation. Boston's master politician engineered congressional commendation of the Suffolk Resolves, a bold statement drawn up in Suffolk County, Massachusetts, that encouraged forcible resistance of the Coercive Acts.

After this decision, the tone of the meeting was established. Moderate spokesmen introduced conciliatory measures, which received polite discussion but failed to win a majority vote. Just before returning to their homes (September 1774), the delegates created the "Association," an intercolonial agreement to halt all commerce with Britain until Parliament repealed the Intolerable Acts. This was a totally revolutionary decision. The Association authorized a vast network of local committees to enforce nonimportation. Violators were exposed, shamed, forced either to apologize publicly for their actions or to be shunned by all their Patriot neighbors. In many of the communities, the committees *were* the government, distinguishing, in the words of James Madison, "Friends from Foes."

SHOTS HEARD AROUND THE WORLD

Before Congress reconvened, shots were fired at Lexington and Concord, two small farm villages in eastern Massachusetts. On the evening of April 18, 1775, General Gage dispatched troops from Boston to seize rebel supplies. Paul Revere, a renowned silversmith and active Patriot, warned the colonists that the redcoats were coming. The militia of Lexington, a collection of ill-trained farmers, boys as well as old men, decided to stand on the village green on the following morning, April 19, as the British soldiers passed on the road to Concord. No one planned to fight, but in a moment of confusion, someone (probably a colonist) fired; the redcoats discharged a volley, and eight Americans lay dead.

Word of the incident spread rapidly, and by the time the British force reached its destination, the countryside swarmed with "minutemen," special companies of Massachusetts militia prepared to respond instantly to military emergencies.

This 1775 engraving by Amos Doolittle shows the American attack on the British regulars as they marched from Concord back to Boston. The minutemen fired from cover, killing and wounding many redcoats who expected little armed resistance.

The long march back to Boston turned into a rout. Lord Percy, a British officer who brought up reinforcements, remarked that "whoever looks upon them [the American soldiers] as an irregular mob, will find himself much mistaken." On June 17, colonial militiamen again held their own against seasoned troops at the battle of Bunker Hill.

Beginning "the World over Again"

Members of the Second Continental Congress gathered in Philadelphia in May 1775. They faced an awesome responsibility. British government in the mainland colonies had almost ceased to function, and with Americans fighting redcoats, the country desperately needed strong central leadership. Slowly, often reluctantly, Congress took control of the war. The delegates formed a Continental Army and appointed George Washington its commander, in part because he seemed to have greater military experience than anyone else available and in part because he looked like he should be commander in chief. The delegates were also eager to select someone who did not come from Massachusetts, a colony that seemed already to possess too much power in national councils. The members of Congress purchased military supplies and, to pay for them, issued paper money. But while they were assuming the powers of a sovereign government, the congressmen refused to declare independence. They debated and fretted, listened to the appeals of moderates who played on the colonists' remaining loyalty to Britain, and then did nothing.

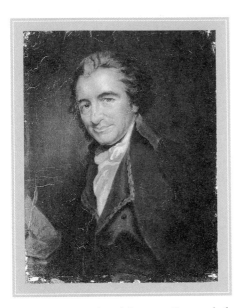

Thomas Paine authored Common Sense, *a brilliantly original pamphlet that persuaded many Americans that since monarchy was an illegitimate form of government, they should create a new independent republic.*

Indecision drove men like John Adams nearly mad. Haste, however, would have been a terrible mistake. While Adams and Richard Henry Lee of Virginia were willing to sever ties with Britain, many Americans were not convinced that such a step was either desirable or necessary. If Congress had moved too quickly, it might have become vulnerable to charges of extremism, in which case the rebellion would have seemed—and indeed, might have been—more like an overthrow by a faction or clique than an expression of popular will.

In December 1775, Parliament passed the Prohibitory Act, declaring war on American commerce. Until the colonists begged for pardon, they could not trade with the rest of the world. The British navy blockaded their ports and seized American ships on the high seas. Lord North also hired German mercenaries (the Russians drove too hard a bargain) to put down the rebellion. And in America, Virginia's royal governor Lord Dunmore further undermined the possibility of reconciliation by urging the colony's slaves to take up arms against their masters.

Thomas Paine (1737–1809) pushed the colonists even closer to independence. Nothing in this man's background suggested he would write the most important pamphlet in American history. In England, Paine had failed in a number of jobs, and exactly why he elected to move to America in 1774 is not clear. While still in England, Paine had the good fortune to meet Benjamin Franklin, who presented him with letters of introduction to the leading patriots of Pennsylvania. At the urging of his new American friends, Paine produced an essay that became an instant best-seller. In only three months, it sold more than 120,000 copies.

Common Sense systematically stripped kingship of historical and theological justification. For centuries, the English had maintained the fiction that the monarch could do no wrong. When the government oppressed the people, the royal counselors received the blame. The Crown was above suspicion. To this, Paine cried nonsense. Monarchs ruled by force. George III was simply a "royal brute," who by his arbitrary behavior had surrendered his claim to the colonists' obedience.

Paine's greatest contribution to the revolutionary cause was persuading ordinary people to sever their ties with Great Britain. It was not reasonable, he argued, to regard England as the mother country. "Europe, and not England," he explained, "is the parent country of America. This new world hath been the asylum

for the persecuted lovers of civil and religious liberty from *every part* of Europe."
No doubt that message made a deep impression on Pennsylvania's German population. The time had come for the colonists to form an independent republic.
"We have it in our power," Paine wrote in one of his most moving statements,
"to begin the world over again . . . the birthday of a new world is at hand."

On July 2, 1776, after a long and tedious debate, Congress finally voted for
independence. The motion passed: twelve states for, none against (with New
York abstaining). Thomas Jefferson, a young Virginia lawyer and planter who
enjoyed a reputation as a graceful writer, drafted a formal declaration that was
accepted with alterations two days later. Much of the Declaration of
Independence consisted of a list of specific grievances against George III and his
government. The document did not become famous for those passages. Long after the establishment of the new republic, the Declaration challenged Americans
to make good on the principle that "all men are created equal." John Adams
nicely expressed the Patriots' fervor when he wrote on July 3, "Yesterday the
greatest question was decided, which ever was debated in America, and a greater
perhaps, never was or will be decided among men."

Many revolutionary leaders throughout the modern world—in Europe as in
Asia—have echoed Adams's assessment. Of all the documents written during this
period, including the Constitution, the Declaration remains the most powerful
and radical invitation to Americans of all backgrounds to demand their equality
and full rights as human beings.

FIGHTING FOR INDEPENDENCE

Only fools and visionaries expressed optimism about America's prospects of winning independence in 1776. The Americans had taken on a formidable military
power. The population of Britain was perhaps four times that of its former
colonies. England also possessed a strong manufacturing base, a well-trained regular army supplemented by thousands of hired German troops (Hessians), and a
navy that dominated the world's oceans. Many British officers had battlefield experience. They already knew what the Americans would slowly learn: waging
war requires discipline, money, and sacrifice.

The British government entered the conflict fully confident that it could beat
the Americans. In 1776, Lord North and his colleagues regarded the war as a police action. They anticipated that a mere show of armed force would intimidate the
upstart colonists. As soon as the rebels in Boston had been humbled, the British argued, people living in other colonies would desert the cause for independence.

As later events demonstrated, of course, Britain had become involved in an
impossible military situation, in some ways analogous to that in which the
United States would find itself more than two hundred years later in Vietnam.
Three separate elements neutralized advantages held by the larger power over its
adversary. First, the British had to transport men and supplies across the
Atlantic, a logistic challenge of unprecedented complexity. Unreliable lines of
communication broke down under the strain of war.

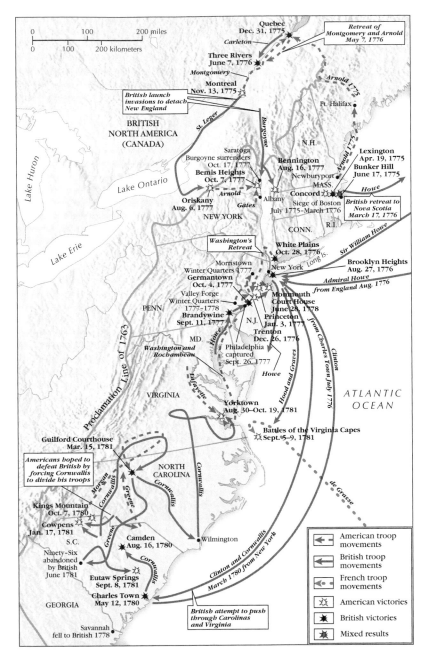

The American Revolution, 1775–1781

The War for Independence ranged over a huge area. The major battles of the first years of the war, from the spontaneous rising at Concord in 1775 to Washington's well-coordinated attack on Trenton in December 1776, were fought in the northern colonies. In the middle theater of war, Burgoyne's attempt in 1777 to cut off New England from the rest of the colonies failed when his army was defeated at Saratoga. Action in the final years of the war, from the battles at Camden, King's Mountain, Cowpens, and Guilford Courthouse to the final victory at Yorktown, occurred in the southern theater of war.

Second, America was too vast to be conquered by conventional military methods. Redcoats might gain control over the major port cities, but as long as the Continental Army remained intact, the rebellion continued. As Washington explained, "the possession of our Towns, while we have an Army in the field, will avail them little . . . It is our Arms, not defenceless Towns, they have to subdue." Even if England had recruited enough soldiers to occupy the entire country, it would still have lost the war. As one Loyalist instructed the king, "if all America becomes a garrison, she is not worth your attention." Britain could only win by crushing the American will to resist.

And third, British strategists never appreciated the depth of the Americans' commitment to a political ideology. In the wars of eighteenth-century Europe, such beliefs had seldom mattered. European troops before the French Revolution served because they were paid or because the military was a vocation, but most certainly not because they hoped to advance a set of constitutional principles. Americans were different. To be sure, some young men were drawn to the military by bounty money or by the desire to escape unhappy families. A few were drafted. But taking such people into account, one still encounters among the American troops a remarkable commitment to republican ideals.

BUILDING A PROFESSIONAL ARMY

During the earliest months of rebellion, American soldiers—especially those of New England—suffered no lack of confidence. Indeed, they interpreted their courageous stands at Concord and Bunker Hill as evidence that brave yeomen farmers could lick British regulars on any battlefield. George Washington spent the first years of the war disabusing the colonists of this foolishness, for as he had learned during the French and Indian War, military success depended on endless drill, careful planning, and tough discipline—rigorous preparation that did not characterize the minutemen's methods.

Washington insisted on organizing a regular well-trained field army. Some advisers urged the commander in chief to wage a guerrilla war, one in which small partisan bands would sap Britain's will to rule Americans. But Washington rejected that course. He recognized that the Continental Army served not only as a fighting force but also as a symbol of the republican cause. Its very existence would sustain American hopes, and so long as the army survived, American agents could plausibly solicit foreign aid. This thinking shaped Washington's wartime strategy; he studiously avoided "general actions" in which the Continental Army might be destroyed. Critics complained about Washington's caution, but as they soon discovered, he understood better than they what independence required.

For the half million African American colonists, most of them slaves, the fight for independence took on special poignancy. After all, they wanted to achieve personal as well as political freedom, and many African Americans supported those who seemed most likely to deliver them from bondage. It is estimated that some five thousand African Americans took up arms to fight against the British. The Continental Army included two all-black units, one from Massachusetts and the other from Rhode Island. In 1778, the legislature of Rhode Island voted to free any slave who volunteered to serve, since, according to the lawmakers, history taught that "the wisest, the freest, and bravest nations . . . liberated their slaves, and enlisted them as soldiers to fight in defence of their country." In the South, especially in Georgia and South Carolina, more than ten thousand African Americans supported the British, and after the Patriots had won the war, these men and women left the United States, relocating to Nova Scotia, Florida, and Jamaica, with some eventually resettling in Africa.

TESTING THE POPULAR WILL

After the embarrassing defeats in Massachusetts, the king appointed General Sir William Howe to replace the ill-fated Gage. British rulers now understood that a simple police action would not be sufficient to crush the American rebellion. Parliament authorized sending more than fifty thousand troops to the mainland colonies, and after evacuating Boston—an untenable strategic position—the British forces stormed ashore at Staten Island in New York Harbor on July 3, 1776. From this more central location, Howe believed he could cut the New Englanders off from the rest of America. He enjoyed the powerful support of the British navy under the command of his brother, Admiral Lord Richard Howe.

When Washington learned the British were planning to occupy New York City, he transferred many of his inexperienced soldiers to Long Island, where they suffered a major defeat (August 27, 1776). In a series of engagements disastrous for the Americans, Howe drove the Continental Army across the Hudson River into New Jersey. Because of his failure to take full advantage of the situation, however, General Howe lost what seemed in retrospect an excellent opportunity to annihilate Washington's entire army. Nevertheless, the Americans were on the run, and in the fall of 1776, contemporaries predicted the rebels would soon capitulate.

"TIMES THAT TRY MEN'S SOULS"

Swift victories in New York and New Jersey persuaded General Howe that few Americans enthusiastically supported independence. He issued a general pardon, therefore, to anyone who would swear allegiance to George III. The results were encouraging. More than three thousand men and women who lived in areas occupied by the British army took the oath. Howe perceived that a lasting peace in America would require his troops to treat "our enemies as if they might one day become our friends." A member of Lord North's cabinet grumbled that this was "a sentimental manner of making war," a shortsighted view considering England's failure to pacify the Irish through fire and sword. In America, the pardon plan eventually failed because as soon as the redcoats left a pardoned region, the rebel militia retaliated against those who had deserted the Patriot cause.

In December 1776, Washington's bedraggled army retreated across the Delaware River into Pennsylvania. American prospects appeared bleaker than at any other time during the war. The Continental Army lacked basic supplies, and many men who had signed up for short-term enlistments prepared to go home. "These are the times that try men's souls," Paine wrote in a pamphlet titled *American Crisis.* "The summer soldier and the sunshine patriot will, in this crisis, shrink from the service of their country, but he that stands it *now* deserves . . . love and thanks . . ." Before winter, Washington determined to attempt one last desperate stroke.

Howe played into Washington's hands. The British forces were dispersed in small garrisons across the state of New Jersey, and while the Americans could not possibly have defeated the combined British army, they did possess the capacity—with luck—to capture an exposed post. On the night of December 25, Continental soldiers slipped over the ice-filled Delaware River and at Trenton took nine hundred sleeping Hessian mercenaries by complete surprise.

Cheered by success, Washington returned a second time to Trenton, but on this occasion the Continental Army was not so fortunate. A large British force under Lord Cornwallis trapped the Americans. Instead of standing and fighting—really an impossible challenge—Washington secretly, by night, marched his little army around Cornwallis's left flank. On January 3, 1777, the Americans surprised a British garrison at Princeton.

VICTORY IN A YEAR OF DEFEAT

In 1777, Britain's chief military strategist, Lord George Germain, still perceived the war in conventional European terms. A large field army would somehow maneuver Washington's Continental troops into a decisive battle in which the British would enjoy a clear advantage. Complete victory over the Americans certainly seemed within England's grasp. Unfortunately for the men who advocated this plan, the Continental forces proved extremely elusive, and while one British army vainly tried to corner Washington in Pennsylvania, another was forced to surrender in the forests of upstate New York.

In the summer of 1777, General John Burgoyne, a dashing though overbearing officer, descended from Canada with a force of more than seven thousand troops. They intended to clear the Hudson Valley of rebel resistance; join Howe's army, which was to come up to Albany; and thereby cut New England off from the other states. The campaign was a disaster. Military units, mostly from New England, cut the enemy force apart in the deep woods north of Albany. At the battle of Bennington (August 16), the New Hampshire militia under Brigadier General John Stark overwhelmed a thousand German mercenaries. After this setback, Burgoyne's forces struggled forward, desperately hoping that Howe would rush to their rescue, but when it became clear that their situation at Saratoga was hopeless, Burgoyne was forced to surrender fifty-eight hundred men to the American General Horatio Gates (October 17).

Soon after Burgoyne left Canada, General Howe unexpectedly decided to move his main army from New York City to Philadelphia. Exactly what he hoped to achieve was not clear, even to Britain's rulers, and of course, when Burgoyne called for assistance, Howe was sitting in the new nation's capital still trying to devise a way to destroy the Continental Army. Howe's campaign began in late July. The British forces sailed to the head of the Chesapeake Bay and then marched north to Philadelphia. Washington's troops obstructed the enemy's progress, first at Brandywine Creek (September 11) and then at Paoli (September 20), but the outnumbered Americans could not stop the British from entering Philadelphia.

Anxious lest these defeats discourage Congress and the American people, Washington attempted one last battle before the onset of winter. In an engagement at Germantown (October 4), the Americans launched a major counterattack on a fog-covered battlefield, but just at the moment when success seemed assured, they broke off the fight. A discouraged Continental Army dug in at Valley Forge, twenty miles outside of Philadelphia, where camp diseases took twenty-five hundred American lives.

THE FRENCH ALLIANCE

Even before the Americans declared independence, agents of the government of Louis XVI began to explore ways to aid the colonists, not so much because the French monarchy favored the republican cause but because it hoped to embarrass the English. The French deeply resented the defeat they had sustained during the Seven Years' War. During the early months of the Revolution, the French covertly sent tons of essential military supplies to the Americans. The negotiations for these arms involved secret agents and fictitious trading companies, the type of clandestine operation more typical of modern times than of the eighteenth century. But when American representatives, Benjamin Franklin for one, pleaded for official recognition of American independence or for outright military alliance, the French advised patience. The international stakes were too great for the king openly to back a cause that had little chance of success.

The American victory at Saratoga convinced the French that the rebels had formidable forces and were serious in their resolve. Indeed, Lord North drew the same conclusion. In April 1778, he tried to avert a greatly expanded war by sending a peace commission to America. He instructed this group, headed by the Earl of Carlisle, to bargain with the Continental Congress "as if it were a legal body." If the colonists would agree to drop their demand for independence, they could turn the imperial calendar back to 1763. Parliament belatedly conceded the right of Americans to tax themselves, even to elect their own governors. It also promised to remove all British troops in times of peace. The proposal might have gained substantial support in 1776. The war, however, had hardened American resolve; the Congress refused to deal with Carlisle.

In Paris, Franklin performed brilliantly. In meetings with French officials, he hinted that the Americans might accept a British peace initiative. If the French wanted the war to continue, if they really wanted to embarrass their old rival, then they had to do what the English refused: formally recognize the independence of the United States.

The stratagem paid off. On February 6, 1778, the French presented American representatives with two separate treaties. The first, called the Treaty of Amity and Commerce, established commercial relations between France and the United States. It tacitly accepted the existence of a new, independent republic. The Treaty of Alliance was even more generous, considering America's obvious military and economic weaknesses. In the event that France and England went to war (they did so on June 14, as everyone expected), the French agreed to reject "either Truce or Peace with Great Britain . . . until the independence of the United States shall have been formally or tacitly assured by the Treaty or Treaties that shall terminate the War." Even more amazing, France surrendered its claim to all territories formerly owned by Great Britain east of the Mississippi River. The Americans pledged they would not sign a separate peace with Britain without first informing their new ally. And in return, France made no claim to Canada, asking only for the right to take possession of certain British islands in the Caribbean. Never had Franklin worked his magic to greater effect.

French intervention instantly transformed British military strategy. What had been a colonial rebellion suddenly became a world conflict, a continuation of the great wars for empire of the late seventeenth century (see Chapter 4). Scarce military resources, especially newer fighting ships, had to be diverted from the American theater to guard the English Channel. In fact, there was talk in London of a possible French invasion.

THE FINAL CAMPAIGN

Military strategists calculated that Britain's last chance of winning the war lay in the Southern Colonies, a region largely untouched in the early years of fighting. Intelligence reports reaching London indicated that Georgia and South Carolina contained a sizable body of Loyalists, men who would take up arms for the Crown if only they received support and encouragement from the regular army. The southern strategy devised by Germain and General Henry Clinton in 1779 turned the war into a bitter guerrilla conflict.

The southern campaign opened in the spring of 1780. Savannah had already fallen, and Clinton reckoned that if the British could take Charles Town, they would be able to control the entire South. A large fleet carrying nearly eight thousand redcoats reached South Carolina in February. Complacent Americans had allowed the city's fortifications to decay, and in a desperate, last-minute effort to preserve Charles Town, General Benjamin Lincoln's forces dug trenches and reinforced walls, but to no avail. On May 12, Lincoln surrendered an American army of almost six thousand men.

The defeat took Congress by surprise, and without making proper preparations, it dispatched a second army to South Carolina under Horatio Gates, the hero of Saratoga. He too failed. At Camden, General Cornwallis, Clinton's second in command, outmaneuvered the raw American recruits, capturing or killing 750 during the course of battle (August 16).

Even at this early stage of the southern campaign, the dangers of partisan warfare had become evident. Tory raiders showed little interest in serving as regular soldiers in Cornwallis's army. They preferred night riding, indiscriminate plundering, or murdering of neighbors against whom they harbored ancient grudges. The British had unleashed a horde of banditti across South Carolina. Men who genuinely supported independence or who had merely fallen victim to Loyalist guerrillas bided their time. They retreated westward, waiting for their enemies to make a mistake. Their chance came on October 7 at King's Mountain, South Carolina. In the most vicious fighting of the Revolution, the backwoodsmen decimated a force of British regulars and Tory raiders who had strayed too far from base.

Cornwallis, badly confused and poorly supplied, squandered his strength chasing American forces across the Carolinas. In early 1781, Congress sent General Nathanael Greene to the South with a new army. In a series of tactically brilliant engagements, it sapped the strength of Cornwallis's army, first at Cowpens, South

French assistance on land and sea helped the Americans defeat the British in the American Revolution. In this French print of the battle at Yorktown, French ships block the entrance of Chesapeake Bay, preventing British vessels from resupplying their troops on land. Yorktown, which was unknown to the French artist who made this print, is depicted as a European walled city.

Carolina (January 17, 1781), and later at Guilford Courthouse, North Carolina (March 15).

Cornwallis pushed north into Virginia, planning apparently to establish a base of operations on the coast. He selected Yorktown, a sleepy tobacco market located on a peninsula bounded by the York and James rivers. Washington watched these maneuvers closely. The canny Virginia planter knew this territory intimately, and he sensed that Cornwallis had made a serious blunder. When Washington learned the French fleet could gain temporary dominance in the Chesapeake Bay, he rushed south from New Jersey. With him marched thousands of well-trained French troops under the Comte de Rochambeau. All the pieces fell into place. The French admiral, the Comte de Grasse, cut Cornwallis off from the sea, while Washington and his lieutenants encircled the British on land. On October 19, 1781, Cornwallis surrendered his entire army of six thousand men. When Lord North heard of the defeat at Yorktown, he moaned, "Oh God! It is all over." The British still controlled New York City and Charles Town, but except for a few skirmishes, the fighting ended.

THE LOYALIST DILEMMA

No one knows for certain how many Americans actually supported the Crown during the Revolution. Some Loyalists undoubtedly kept silent and avoided making a public commitment that might have led to banishment or loss of property.

But for many persons, neutrality proved impossible. Almost 100,000 men and women permanently left America. While a number of these exiles had served as imperial officeholders—Thomas Hutchinson, for example—in the main, they came from all ranks and backgrounds. A large number of humble farmers, more than 30,000, resettled in Canada. Others relocated to England, the West Indies, or Africa.

The political ideology of the Loyalists was not substantially different from that of their opponents. Like other Americans, they believed that men and women were entitled to life, liberty, and the pursuit of happiness. The Loyalists were also convinced that independence would destroy those values by promoting disorder. By turning their backs on Britain, a source of tradition and stability, the rebels seemed to have encouraged licentiousness, even anarchy in the streets. The Loyalists suspected that Patriot demands for freedom were self-serving, even hypocritical, for as Perserved Smith, a Loyalist from Ashfield, Massachusetts, observed, "Sons of liberty . . . did not deserve the name, for it was evident all they wanted was liberty from oppression that they might have liberty to oppress!"

The Loyalists were caught in a difficult squeeze. The British never quite trusted them. After all, they were Americans. During the early stages of the war, Loyalists organized militia companies and hoped to pacify large areas of the countryside with the support of the regular army. The British generals were unreliable partners, however, for no sooner had they called on loyal Americans to come forward than the redcoats marched away, leaving the Tories exposed to rebel retaliation. And in England, the exiles found themselves treated as second-class citizens.

Americans who actively supported independence saw these people as traitors who deserved their fate of constant, often violent, harassment. In many states— but especially in New York—revolutionary governments confiscated Loyalist property. Other friends of the king received beatings, or as the rebels called them, "grand Toory [sic] rides." A few were even executed. According to one Patriot, "A Tory is a thing whose head is in England, and its body in America, and its neck ought to be stretched."

Long after the victorious Americans turned their attentions to the business of building a new republic, Loyalists remembered a receding colonial past, a comfortable, ordered world that had been lost forever at Yorktown. Although many Loyalists eventually returned to their homes, a sizable number could not do so. For them, the sense of loss remained a heavy emotional burden. Perhaps the most poignant testimony came from a young mother living in exile in Nova Scotia. "I climbed to the top of Chipman's Hill and watched the sails disappear in the distance," she recounted, "and such a feeling of loneliness came over me that though I had not shed a tear through all the war I sat down on the damp moss with my baby on my lap and cried bitterly."

Winning the Peace

Congress appointed a skilled delegation to negotiate a peace treaty: Benjamin Franklin, John Adams, and John Jay. According to their official instructions, they were to insist only on the recognition of the independence of the United States.

On other issues, Congress ordered its delegates to defer to the counsel of the French government.

But the political environment in Paris was much different from what the diplomats had been led to expect. The French had formed a military alliance with Spain, and French officials announced that they could not consider the details of an American settlement until after the Spanish had recaptured Gibraltar from the British. The prospects for a Spanish victory were not good, and in any case, it was well known that Spain coveted the lands lying between the Appalachian Mountains and the Mississippi River. Indeed, there were even rumors afloat in Paris that the great European powers might intrigue to deny the United States its independence.

While the three American delegates publicly paid their respects to French officials, they secretly entered into negotiations with an English agent. The peacemakers drove a remarkable bargain, a much better one than Congress could have expected. The preliminary agreement signed on September 3, 1783, not only guaranteed the independence of the United States; it also transferred all the territory east of the Mississippi River, except Spanish Florida, to the new republic. The treaty established generous boundaries on the north and south and gave the Americans important fishing rights in the North Atlantic. In exchange, Congress promised to help British merchants collect debts contracted before the Revolution and compensate Loyalists whose lands had been confiscated by the various state governments. Even though the Americans negotiated separately with the British, they did not sign a separate peace. The preliminary treaty did not become effective until France reached its own agreement with Great Britain. Thus did the Americans honor the French alliance. It is difficult to imagine how Franklin, Adams, and Jay could have negotiated a more favorable conclusion to the war. In the fall of 1783, the last redcoats sailed from New York City, ending 176 years of colonial rule.

UNCERTAIN PROSPECTS: LIBERTY OR ANARCHY

The American people had waged war against the most powerful nation in Europe and emerged victorious. The treaty marked the conclusion of a colonial rebellion, but it remained for the men and women who had resisted taxation without representation to work out the full implications of republicanism. What would be the shape of the new government? What powers would be delegated to the people, the states, the federal authorities? How far would the wealthy, well-born leaders of the rebellion be willing to extend political, social, and economic rights? No wonder Philadelphia physician Dr. Benjamin Rush explained, "There is nothing more common than to confound the terms of American Revolution with those of the late American war. The American war is over, but this is far from being the case with the American Revolution. On the contrary, nothing but the first act of the great drama is closed."

CHRONOLOGY

1763   Peace of Paris ends the Seven Years' War

1764   Parliament passes Sugar Act to collect American revenue

1765   Stamp Act receives support of House of Commons (March)

        Stamp Act Congress meets in New York City (October)

1766   Stamp Act repealed the same day that Declaratory Act becomes law (March 18)

1767   Townshend Revenue Acts stir American anger (June–July)

1768   Massachusetts assembly refuses to rescind circular letter (February)

1770   Parliament repeals all Townshend duties except one on tea (March)

        British troops "massacre" Boston civilians (March)

1772   Samuel Adams forms committee of correspondence

1773   Lord North's government passes Tea Act (May)

        Bostonians hold Tea Party (December)

1774   Parliament punishes Boston with Coercive Acts (March–June)

        First Continental Congress convenes (September)

1775   Patriots take stand at Lexington and Concord (April)

        Second Continental Congress gathers (May)

        Americans hold their own at Bunker Hill (June)

1776   Congress votes for independence; Declaration of Independence is signed

        British defeat Washington at Long Island (August)

        Americans score victory at Trenton (December)

1777   General Burgoyne surrenders at Saratoga (October)

1778   French treaties recognize independence of the United States (February)

1780   British take Charles Town (May)

1781   Washington forces Cornwallis to surrender at Yorktown (October)

1783   Peace treaty signed (September)

        British evacuate New York City (November)

6

❧ ——————— ❧

THE REPUBLICAN EXPERIMENT

In 1788, Lewis Hallam and John Henry petitioned the General Assembly of Pennsylvania to open a theater. Although a 1786 state law banned the performance of stage plays and other "disorderly sports," many Philadelphia leaders favored the request to hold "dramatic representation" in their city. A committee appointed to study the issue concluded that a theater would contribute to "the general refinement of manners and the polish of society." Some supporters even argued that the sooner the United States had a professional theater the sooner the young republic would escape the "foreign yoke" of British culture.

The Quakers of Philadelphia dismissed such claims out of hand. They warned such "seminaries of lewdness and irreligion" would undermine "the virtue of the people." They pointed out that "no sooner is a playhouse opened than it becomes surrounded with . . . brothels." Since Philadelphia was already suffering from a "stagnation of commerce [and] a scarcity of money"—unmistakable signs of God's displeasure—it seemed to them unwise to risk divine punishment by encouraging new "hot-beds of vice."

Such rhetoric did not sit well with other citizens who interpreted the revolutionary experience from an entirely different perspective. At issue, they insisted, was not popular morality, but state censorship. If the government silenced the stage, then "the same authority . . . may, with equal justice, dictate the shape and texture of our dress, or the modes and ceremonies of our worship." Depriving those who wanted to see plays of an opportunity to do so, they argued, "will abridge the natural right of every freeman, to dispose of his time and money, according to his own tastes and dispositions."

Throughout post–Revolutionary America, apparently trivial matters such as the opening of a new playhouse provoked passionate public debate. These divisions were symptomatic of a new, uncertain political culture struggling to find the proper balance between public morality and private freedom. During the long fight against Great Britain, Americans had defended individual rights. The problem was that the same people also believed that a republic that compromised its virtue could not long preserve liberty and independence. During the 1780s, Americans understood their responsibility not only to each other, but also to history. They worried, however, that they might not successfully meet the challenge.

A NEW POLITICAL CULTURE

Today, the term *republican* no longer possesses the evocative power it did for eighteenth-century Americans. For them, it defined an entire political culture. After all, they had done something that no other people had achieved for a very long time. They founded a national government without a monarch or aristocracy, in other words, a genuine republic. Making the new system work was a daunting task. Those Americans who read deeply in ancient and renaissance history knew that most republics had failed, often within a few years, only to be replaced by tyrants who cared not at all what ordinary people thought about the public good. To preserve their republic from such a fate, victorious revolutionaries such as Samuel Adams recast fundamental political values. For them, republicanism represented more than a particular form of government. It was a way of life, a core ideology, an uncompromising commitment to liberty, and a total rejection of aristocracy.

Adams and his contemporaries certainly believed that creating a new nation-state involved more than simply winning independence from Great Britain. If American citizens substituted "luxury, prodigality, and profligacy" for "prudence, virtue, and economy," then their revolution surely would have been in vain. Maintaining popular virtue was crucial to success. An innocent stage play, therefore, set off alarm bells. Such "foolish gratifications" in Philadelphia seemed to compromise republican goals. It is not surprising that confronted by such temptations Adams thundered, "Rome, Athens, and all the cities of renown, whence came your fall?"

White Americans were optimistic about their country's chances. This expansive outlook, encountered among so many ordinary men and women, owed much to the spread of Protestant evangelicalism. However skeptical Jefferson and Franklin may have been about revealed religion, the great mass of American people subscribed to an almost utopian belief that God had promised the new republic progress and prosperity.

Such optimism did not translate easily into the creation of a strong central government. Modern Americans tend to take for granted the acceptance of the Constitution. Its merits seem self-evident largely because it has survived for two centuries. But in the early 1780s, no one could have predicted that the Constitution as we know it would have been written, much less ratified. It was equally possible that the Americans would have supported a weak confederation or perhaps allowed the various states and regions to go their separate ways.

In this political atmosphere, Americans divided sharply over the relative importance of *liberty* and *order*. The revolutionary experience had called into question the legitimacy of older forms of aristocratic privilege that had held monarchical society together. As one republican informed an elitist colleague in the

South Carolina assembly, "the day is Arrived when *goodness,* and not *Wealth,* are the only *Criterions of greatness."* Liberty was contagious, and Americans of all backgrounds began to insist on having a voice in shaping the new society.

Other Americans, however, worried that the citizens of the new nation were caught up in a wild, destructive scramble for material wealth. Democratic liberty seemed to threaten order, to endanger the rights of property. Surely a republic could not long survive unless its citizens showed greater self-control. For people concerned about the loss of order, the state assemblies appeared to be the greatest source of instability. Popularly elected representatives lacked what men of property defined as real civic virtue, an ability to work for the common good rather than their private interests.

Working out the tensions between order and liberty, between property and equality, generated an outpouring of political genius. At other times in American history, persons of extraordinary talent have been drawn to theology, commerce, or science, but during the 1780s, the country's intellectual leaders—Thomas Jefferson, James Madison, Alexander Hamilton, and John Adams, among others—focused their creative energies on the problem of how republicans ought to govern themselves.

LIVING IN THE SHADOW OF REVOLUTION

Revolution transformed American society, often in ways no one had planned. National independence compelled people to reevaluate hierarchical social relations that they had taken for granted during the colonial period. The faltering first steps of independence raised fundamental questions about the meaning of equality in American society, some of which remain as pressing today as during the 1780s.

SOCIAL AND POLITICAL REFORM

Following the war, Americans aggressively denounced any traces of aristocratic pretense. As colonists, they had long resented the claims that certain Englishmen made to special privilege simply because of noble birth. Even so committed a republican as George Washington had to be reminded that artificial status was contrary to republican principles. In 1783, he and the officers who had served during the Revolution formed the Society of the Cincinnati, a hereditary organization in which membership passed from father to eldest son. The soldiers meant no harm; they simply wanted to maintain old friendships. But anxious republicans throughout America let out a howl of protest, and one South Carolina legislator, Aedanus Burke, warned that the Society intended to create "an hereditary peerage . . . [which would] undermine the Constitution and destroy civil liberty." After an embarrassed Washington called for appropriate reforms of the Society's bylaws, the Cincinnati crisis receded.

The appearance of equality was as important as its actual achievement. In fact, the distribution of wealth in postwar America was more uneven than it had been in the mid-eighteenth century. The sudden accumulation of large fortunes by new families made other Americans particularly sensitive to aristocratic display, for it seemed intolerable that a revolution waged against a monarchy should produce a class of persons legally, or even visibly, distinguished from their fellow citizens.

In an effort to root out the notion of a privileged class, states abolished laws of primogeniture and entail. In colonial times, these laws allowed a landholder either to pass his entire estate to his eldest son or to declare that his property could never be divided, sold, or given away. Jefferson claimed that the repeal of these practices would eradicate "antient [sic] and future aristocracy; a foundation [has been] laid for a government truly republican." Republican legislators who wanted to cleanse traces of the former feudal order from the statute books agreed with Jefferson and outlawed primogeniture and entail.

Republican ferment also encouraged many states to lower property requirements for voting. As one group of farmers declared, no man can be "free & independent" unless he possesses "a voice . . . in the choice of the most important Officers in the Legislature."

Demand for equality in the new republic extended to the rights of women. In this illustration, which appeared as the frontispiece in the 1792 issue of The Lady's Magazine and Repository of Entertaining Knowledge, *the "Genius of the* Ladies Magazine" *and the "Genius of Emulation" (holding in her hand a laurel crown) present to Liberty a petition for the rights of women.*

Pennsylvania and Georgia allowed all white male taxpayers to participate in elections. Other states were less democratic, but with the exception of Massachusetts, they reduced property qualifications. But many people were still excluded. During the 1780s, republican lawmakers were not prepared to experiment with universal manhood suffrage. As John Adams observed, if the states pushed the reforms too far, "New claims will arise, women will demand a vote . . . and every man who has not a farthing, will demand an equal vote with any other."

The most important changes in voting patterns resulted from western migration. As Americans moved to the frontier, they received full political representation in their state legislatures, and because new districts tended to be poorer than established coastal settlements, their representatives seemed less cultured, less well trained than those sent by eastern voters. Moreover, western delegates who resented traveling so far to attend legislative meetings lobbied successfully to transfer state capitals to more convenient locations.

After gaining independence, Americans also reexamined the relation between church and state. Republican spokespersons such as Thomas Jefferson insisted that rulers had no right to interfere with the free expression of an individual's religious beliefs. As governor of Virginia, he strenuously advocated the disestablishment of the Anglican Church, an institution that had received tax monies and other benefits during the colonial period. Jefferson and his allies regarded such special privilege not only as a denial of religious freedom—after all, rival denominations did not receive tax money—but also as a vestige of aristocratic society.

In 1786, Virginia cut the last ties between church and state. Other southern states disestablished the Anglican Church, but in Massachusetts and New Hampshire, Congregational churches continued to enjoy special status.

AFRICAN AMERICANS IN THE NEW REPUBLIC

Revolutionary fervor forced Americans to confront the most appalling contradiction to republican principles—slavery. The Quaker leader John Woolman (1720–1772) probably did more than any other white person of the era to remind people of the evils of this institution. A trip he took through the Southern Colonies as a young man forever impressed upon Woolman "the dark gloominess" of slavery. In a sermon, the outspoken humanitarian declared "that though we made slaves of the Negroes, and the Turks made Slaves of the Christians, I believed that Liberty was the natural Right of all Men equally."

During the revolutionary period, abolitionist sentiment spread. Both in private and in public, people began to criticize slavery in other than religious language. No doubt, the double standard of their own political rhetoric embarrassed many white Americans. They hotly demanded liberation from British enslavement at the same time that they held several hundred thousand blacks in bondage.

By keeping the issue of slavery before the public through writing and petitioning, African Americans powerfully undermined arguments advanced in favor of human bondage. They demanded freedom, reminding white lawmakers that African American men and women had the same natural right to liberty as did other Americans.

The scientific accomplishments of Benjamin Banneker (1731–1806), Maryland's African American astronomer and mathematician, and the international fame of Phillis Wheatley (1753–1784), Boston's celebrated "African muse," made it increasingly difficult for white Americans to maintain credibly that African Americans could not hold their own in a free society. Wheatley's poems went through many editions, and after reading her work, the French philosopher Voltaire rebuked a friend who had claimed "there never would be Negro poets." As Voltaire discovered, Wheatley "writes excellent verse in English." Banneker, like Wheatley, enjoyed a well-deserved reputation, in his case for contributions as a scientist. After receiving a copy of an almanac that Banneker had published in Philadelphia, Thomas Jefferson concluded "that nature has given to our black brethren, talents equal to those of the other colors of men."

In the northern states, where there was no economic justification for slavery, white laborers resented having to compete in the workplace against slaves. This economic situation, combined with the acknowledgment of the double standard represented by slavery, contributed to the establishment of antislavery societies. In 1775, Franklin helped organize a group in Philadelphia called the Society for the Relief of Free Negroes, Unlawfully Held. John Jay, Alexander Hamilton, and other prominent New Yorkers founded a Manumission Society in 1785. By 1792, antislavery societies were meeting from Virginia to Massachusetts, and in the northern states at least, these groups, working for the same ends as various Christian evangelicals, put slaveholders on the intellectual defensive for the first time in American history.

In several states north of Virginia, the abolition of slavery took a number of different forms. Even before achieving statehood, Vermont drafted a constitution (1777) that specifically prohibited slavery. In 1780, the Pennsylvania legislature passed a law effecting the gradual emancipation of slaves. Although the Massachusetts assembly refused to address the issue directly, the state courts took up the challenge and liberated the African Americans. By 1800, slavery was well on the road to extinction in the North.

These developments did not mean that white people accepted blacks as equals. In fact, in the very states that outlawed slavery, African Americans faced systematic discrimination. Free blacks were generally excluded from voting, juries, and militia duty—they were denied rights and responsibilities usually associated with full citizenship. They rarely enjoyed access to education, and in cities such as Philadelphia and New York, where African Americans went to look for work, they ended up living in segregated wards or neighborhoods. Even in the churches—institutions that had often spoken out against slavery—free African Americans were denied equal standing with white worshipers. Humiliations of this sort persuaded African Americans to form their own churches. In Philadelphia, Richard Allen, a former slave, founded the Bethel Church for Negro Methodists (1793) and later organized the African Methodist Episcopal Church (1814), an institution of great cultural as well as religious significance for nineteenth-century American blacks.

Born to slaves, Richard Allen became a zealous evangelical minister. Allen organized the African Methodist Episcopal Church in 1814.

Even in the South, where African Americans made up a large percentage of the population, slavery disturbed thoughtful white republicans. Some planters simply freed their slaves, and by 1790, the number of free blacks living in Virginia was 12,766. By 1800, the figure had reached 30,750. Richard Randolph, one of Virginia's wealthier planters, explained that he freed his slaves "to make restitution, as far as I am able, to an unfortunate race of bond-men, over whom my ancestors have usurped and exercised the most lawless and monstrous tyranny." George Washington also manumitted his slaves.

But these were exceptional acts. The southern states did not abolish slavery. The economic incentives to maintain a servile labor force, especially after the invention of the cotton gin in 1793 and the opening up of the Alabama and Mississippi frontier, overwhelmed the initial abolitionist impulse. An opportunity to translate the principles of the American Revolution into social practice had been lost, at least temporarily.

THE CHALLENGE OF WOMEN'S RIGHTS

The revolutionary experience accelerated changes in how ordinary people viewed the family. At the beginning of the eighteenth century, fathers claimed authority over other members of their families simply on the grounds that they were fathers. As patriarchs, they demanded obedience. If they behaved like brutal despots, so be it; fathers could treat wives and children however they pleased. The English philosopher John Locke (1632–1704) powerfully undermined arguments of this sort. In his popular treatise *Some Thoughts Concerning Education* (1693), Locke insisted that the mind was not formed at birth. The child learned from experience, and if the infant witnessed violent, arbitrary behavior, then the baby would become an unattractive adult. Locke warned that harsh physical punishment—even if allegedly delivered with the best of intentions—usually persuaded children that their parents were morally deficient. Enlightened mothers and fathers condemned tyranny in the home.

At the time of the American Revolution few seriously accepted the notion that fathers—be they tyrannical kings or heads of ordinary families—enjoyed unlimited powers over women and children. Indeed, people in England as well as America increasingly described the family in terms of love and companionship. Instead of duties, they spoke of affection. This transformation in the way men and women viewed relations of power within the family was most evident in the popular novels of the period. Americans devoured *Pamela* and *Clarissa,* stories by the English writer Samuel Richardson about women who were the innocent victims of unreformed males, usually deceitful lovers and unforgiving fathers.

In this changing intellectual environment American women began making new demands not only on their husbands but also on republican institutions. Abigail Adams, one of the generation's most articulate women, instructed her husband, John, as he set off for the opening of the Continental Congress: "I desire you would Remember the Ladies, and be more generous and favourable to them than your ancestors. Do not put such unlimited power into the hands of the

Westtown Boarding School in Pennsylvania was established by the Society of Friends to expand educational opportunities for women in the Middle Atlantic states. Instituted in 1794, the school opened in 1799.

Husbands." John responded in a condescending manner. The "Ladies" would have to wait until the country achieved independence. In 1777, Lucy Knox took an even stronger line with her husband, General Henry Knox. When he was about to return home from the army, she warned him, "I hope you will not consider yourself as commander in chief in your own house—but be convinced . . . that there is such a thing as equal command."

If Knox accepted Lucy's argument, he did so because she was a good republican wife and mother. In fact, women justified their assertiveness largely on the basis of political ideology. If survival of republics really depended on the virtue of their citizens, they argued, then it was the special responsibility of women as mothers to nurture the right values in their children and as wives to instruct their husbands in proper behavior.

Ill-educated women could not possibly fulfill these high expectations. They required education that was at least comparable to what men received. Scores of female academies were established during this period to meet what many Americans, men as well as women, now regarded as a pressing social need. The schools may have received widespread encouragement precisely because they did not radically alter traditional gender roles. After all, the educated republican woman of the late eighteenth century did not pursue a career; she returned to the home, where she followed a familiar routine as wife and mother.

During this period, women petitioned for divorce on new grounds. One case is particularly instructive concerning changing attitudes toward women and the family. In 1784, John Backus, an undistinguished Massachusetts silversmith, was hauled before a local court and asked why he beat his wife. He responded that "it was Partly owing to his Education for his father treated his mother in the same manner." The difference between Backus's case and his father's was that Backus's wife refused to tolerate such abuse, and she sued successfully for divorce. Studies of divorce patterns in Connecticut and Pennsylvania show that after 1773, women divorced on about the same terms as men.

The war itself presented some women with fresh opportunities. Women ran family farms and businesses while their husbands fought the British. And in 1790, the New Jersey legislature explicitly allowed women who owned property to vote. Despite these scattered gains, republican society still defined women's roles exclusively in terms of mother, wife, and homemaker. Other pursuits seemed unnatural, even threatening, and it is perhaps not surprising, therefore, that in 1807, New Jersey lawmakers—angry over a close election in which women voters may have determined the result—repealed female suffrage in the interests of "safety, quiet, and good order and dignity of the state."

POSTPONING FULL LIBERTY

The Revolution did not bring about a massive restructuring of American society, at least not in the short term. Nevertheless, republicans such as Samuel Adams and Thomas Jefferson raised issues of immense significance for the later history of the United States. They insisted that equality, however narrowly defined, was an essential element of republican government. Even though they failed to abolish slavery, institute universal manhood suffrage, or apply equality to women, they vigorously articulated a set of assumptions about people's rights and liberties that challenged future generations of Americans to make good on the promise of the Revolution.

THE STATES:
PUTTING REPUBLICANISM INTO PRACTICE

In May 1776, the Second Continental Congress invited the states to adopt constitutions. The old colonial charters filled with references to king and Parliament were no longer adequate, and within a few years, most states had taken action. Rhode Island and Connecticut already enjoyed republican government by virtue of their unique seventeenth-century charters that allowed the voters to select both governors and legislators. Eleven other states plus Vermont created new political structures, and their deliberations reveal how Americans reacting to different social pressures defined fundamental republican principles.

Several constitutions were boldly experimental, and some states later rewrote documents that had been drafted in the first flush of independence. Although these early constitutions were provisional, they provided the framers of the federal Constitution of 1787 with invaluable insights into the strengths and weaknesses of government based on the will of the people.

BLUEPRINTS FOR STATE GOVERNMENT

Despite disagreements over details, Americans who wrote the various state constitutions shared certain political assumptions. They insisted on preparing *written* documents. For many of them, of course, this seemed a natural step. As colonists, they had lived under royal charters, documents that described the workings of local government in detail.

However logical the decision to produce written documents may have seemed to the Americans, it represented a major break with English practice. Political philosophers in the mother country had long boasted of Britain's unwritten constitution, a collection of judicial reports and parliamentary statutes. But this highly vaunted system had not protected the colonists from oppression; hence, after declaring independence, Americans demanded that their state constitutions explicitly define the rights of the people as well as the power of their rulers.

NATURAL RIGHTS AND THE STATE CONSTITUTIONS

The authors of the state constitutions believed men and women possessed certain natural rights over which government exercised no control whatsoever. So that future rulers—potential tyrants—would know the exact limits of authority, these fundamental rights were carefully spelled out. Indeed, the people of Massachusetts rejected the proposed state constitution of 1778 largely because it lacked a full statement of their basic rights.

Eight state constitutions contained specific declarations of rights. The length and character of these lists varied, but, in general, they affirmed three fundamental freedoms: religion, speech, and press. They protected citizens from unlawful searches and seizures; they upheld trial by jury.

In almost every state, delegates to constitutional conventions drastically reduced the power of the governor. The constitutions of Pennsylvania and Georgia abolished the governor's office. In four other states, terms such as *president* were substituted for *governor.* Even when those who designed the new state governments provided for a governor, they severely circumscribed his authority. He was allowed to make almost no political appointments, and while the state legislators closely monitored his activities, he possessed no veto over their decisions (Massachusetts being the lone exception).

Most early constitutions lodged nearly all effective power in the legislature. This decision made good sense to men who had served under powerful royal governors during the late colonial period. These ambitious crown appointees had used executive patronage to influence members of the colonial assemblies, and as the Americans drafted their new republican constitutions, they were determined to bring their governors under tight control.

The legislature dominated early state government. The constitutions of Pennsylvania and Georgia provided for a unicameral, or one-house, system, and since any male taxpayer could cast a ballot in these states, their legislatures became the nation's most democratic. Other states authorized the creation of two houses, but even as they did so, some of the more demanding republicans wondered why America needed a senate or upper house at all. What social and economic interests, they asked, did that body represent that could not be more fully and directly voiced in the lower house? After all, America had just freed itself of an aristocracy. The two-house form survived the Revolution largely because it was familiar and because some persons had already begun to suspect that certain checks on the popular will, however arbitrary they might have appeared, were necessary to preserve minority rights.

POWER TO THE PEOPLE

Massachusetts did not adopt a constitution until 1780, several years after the other states had done so. The experience of the people of Massachusetts is particularly significant because in their efforts to establish a workable system of republican government, they hit on a remarkable political innovation. After the rejection of two constitutions drafted by the state legislature, the responsibility fell to a specially elected convention of delegates whose sole purpose was the "formation of a new Constitution."

John Adams took a position of leadership at this convention and served as the chief architect of the governmental framework of Massachusetts. This framework included a house and senate, a popularly elected governor—who, unlike the chief executives of other states, possessed a veto over legislative bills—and property qualifications for officeholders as well as voters. The most striking aspect of the 1780 constitution, however, was the wording of its opening sentence: "We . . . the people of Massachusetts . . . agree upon, ordain, and establish." This powerful statement would be echoed in the federal Constitution. The Massachusetts experiment reminded Americans that ordinary officeholders could not be trusted to define fundamental rights. That important task required a convention of delegates who could legitimately claim to speak for the people.

In 1780, no one knew whether the state experiments would succeed. There was no question that a different type of person had begun to appear in public office, one who seemed, to the local gentry at least, a little poorer and less polished than they would have liked. When one Virginian surveyed the newly elected House of Burgesses in 1776, he discovered it was "composed of men not quite so well dressed, nor so politely educated, nor so highly born as some Assemblies I have formerly seen." This particular Virginian approved of such change, for he believed that "the People's men," however plain they might appear, possessed honesty and sincerity. They were, in fact, representative republicans, people who insisted they were anyone's equal in this burgeoning society.

STUMBLING TOWARD A NEW NATIONAL GOVERNMENT

When the Second Continental Congress convened in 1775, the delegates found themselves waging war in the name of a country that did not yet exist. As the military crisis deepened, Congress gradually—often reluctantly—assumed greater authority over national affairs, but everyone agreed such narrowly conceived measures were a poor substitute for a legally constituted government. The separate states could not possibly deal with the range of issues that now confronted the American people. Indeed, if independence meant anything in a world of sovereign nations, it implied the creation of a central authority capable of conducting war, borrowing money, regulating trade, and negotiating treaties.

ARTICLES OF CONFEDERATION

The challenge of creating a viable central government proved more difficult than anyone anticipated. Congress appointed a committee to draw up a plan for confederation. John Dickinson headed the committee. He envisioned the creation of a strong central government, and the report his committee presented on July 12, 1776, shocked delegates who assumed that the constitution would authorize a loose confederation of states. Dickinson's plan placed the western territories, land claimed by the separate states, under congressional control. In addition, Dickinson's committee called for equal state representation in Congress.

Since some states, such as Virginia and Massachusetts, were more populous than others, the plan fueled tensions between large and small states. Also unsettling was Dickinson's recommendation that taxes be paid to Congress on the basis of a state's total population, black as well as white, a formula that angered Southerners who did not think slaves should be counted. Indeed, even before the British evacuated Boston, Dickinson's committee raised many difficult political questions that would divide Americans for several decades.

Not surprisingly, the draft of the plan—the Articles of Confederation—that Congress finally approved in November 1777 bore little resemblance to Dickinson's original plan. The Articles jealously guarded the sovereignty of the states. The delegates who drafted the framework shared a general republican conviction that power—especially power so far removed from the people—was inherently dangerous and that the only way to preserve liberty was to place as many constraints as possible on federal authority.

The result was a government that many people regarded as powerless. The Articles provided for a single legislative body consisting of representatives selected annually by the state legislatures. Each state possessed a single vote in Congress. It could send as many as seven delegates, as few as two, but if they divided evenly on a certain issue, the state lost its vote. There was no independent executive and no veto over legislative decisions. The Articles also denied Congress the power of taxation, a serious oversight in time of war. The national government could obtain funds only by asking the states for contributions, called requisitions, but if a state failed to cooperate—and many did—Congress limped along without financial support. Amendments to this constitution required assent by all thirteen states. The authors of the new system expected the weak national government to handle foreign relations, military matters, Indian affairs, and interstate disputes. They most emphatically did not award Congress ownership of the lands west of the Appalachian Mountains.

The new constitution sent to the states for ratification encountered apathy and hostility. Most Americans were far more interested in local affairs than in the actions of Congress. When a British army marched through a state, creating a need for immediate military aid, people spoke positively about central government, but as soon as the threat had passed, they sang a different tune. During this period, even the slightest encroachment on state sovereignty rankled republicans who feared centralization would inevitably promote corruption.

WESTERN LAND: KEY TO THE FIRST CONSTITUTION

The major bone of contention with the Articles was the disposition of the vast, unsurveyed territory west of the Appalachians that everyone hoped the British would soon surrender. Although the region was claimed by the various states, most of it actually belonged to the Native Americans. In a series of land grabs that federal negotiators called treaties, the United States government took the land comprising much of modern Ohio, Indiana, Illinois, and Kentucky. Since the Indians had put their faith in the British during the war, they could do little to resist the humiliating treaty agreements at Fort McIntosh (1785), Fort Stanwix (1784), and Fort Finney (1786).

Some states, such as Virginia and Georgia, claimed land all the way from the Atlantic Ocean to the elusive "South Seas," in effect extending their boundaries to the Pacific coast by virtue of royal charters. State legislators—their appetites whetted by aggressive land speculators—anticipated generating large revenues through land sales. Connecticut, New York, Pennsylvania, and North Carolina also announced intentions to seize blocks of western land.

Other states were not blessed with vague or ambiguous royal charters. The boundaries of Maryland, Delaware, and New Jersey had been established many years earlier, and it seemed as if people living in these states would be permanently cut off from the anticipated bounty. In protest, these "landless" states stubbornly refused to ratify the Articles of Confederation. Marylanders were particularly vociferous. All the states had made sacrifices for the common good during the Revolution, they complained, and it appeared only fair that all states should profit from the fruits of victory, in this case, from the sale of western lands. Maryland's spokesmen feared that if Congress did not void Virginia's excessive claims to all of the Northwest Territory (the land west of Pennsylvania and north of the Ohio River) as well as to a large area south of the Ohio, beyond the Cumberland Gap, known as Kentucky, then Marylanders would desert their home state in search of cheap Virginia farms, leaving Maryland an underpopulated wasteland.

Virginians scoffed at the pleas for equity. They suspected that behind the Marylanders' statements of high purpose lay the greed of speculators. Private land companies had sprung up before the Revolution and purchased large tracts from the Indians in areas claimed by Virginia. Their agents petitioned Parliament to legitimize these questionable transactions. Their efforts failed. After the Declaration of Independence, however, the companies shifted the focus of their lobbying to Congress, particularly to the representatives of landless states like Maryland. By liberally distributing shares of stock, officials of the Indiana, Illinois, and Wabash companies gained powerful supporters such as Benjamin

Franklin, Robert Morris, and Thomas Johnson, governor of Maryland. These activities encouraged Delaware and New Jersey to modify their demands and join the Confederation, while Maryland held out for five years. The leaders of Virginia, though, remained firm. Why, they asked, should Virginia surrender its historic claims to western lands to enrich a handful of selfish speculators?

The states resolved the bitter controversy in 1781 as much by accident as by design. Virginia agreed to cede its holdings north of the Ohio River to the Confederation on condition that Congress nullify the land companies' earlier purchases from the Indians. A practical consideration had softened Virginia's resolve. Republicans such as Jefferson worried about expanding their state beyond the mountains; with poor transportation links, it seemed impossible to govern such a large territory effectively from Richmond. The western settlers might even come to regard Virginia as a colonial power. Marylanders prudently accepted the Articles (March 1, 1781). Other landed states followed Virginia's example. These transfers established an important principle, for after 1781, it was agreed that the West belonged not to the separate states but to the United States.

No one greeted ratification of the Articles with enthusiasm. When they thought about national politics at all, Americans concerned themselves primarily with winning independence. The new government gradually developed an administrative bureaucracy, and in 1781, it formally created the Departments of War, Foreign Affairs, and Finance.

Northwest Territory
The U.S. government auctioned off the land in the Northwest Territory, the region defined by the Ohio River, the Great Lakes, and the Mississippi River. Proceeds from the sale of one section in each township were set aside for the creation and support of public schools.

NORTHWEST ORDINANCE:
THE CONFEDERATION'S MAJOR ACHIEVEMENT

Whatever the weaknesses of Congress may have been, it did score one impressive triumph. Congressional action brought order to western settlement, especially in the Northwest Territory, and incorporated frontier Americans into an expanding federal system. With thousands of men and women, most of them squatters, pouring across the Appalachian Mountains, Congress had to act quickly to avoid the past errors of royal and colonial authorities.

The initial attempt to deal with this explosive problem came in 1784. Jefferson, then serving as a member of Congress, drafted an ordinance that became the basis for later, more enduring legislation. Jefferson recommended carving ten new states out of the western lands located north of the Ohio River and recently ceded to the United States by Virginia. He specified that each new state establish a republican form of government. When the population of a territory equaled that of the smallest state already in the Confederation, the region could apply for full statehood. In the meantime, free white males could participate in local government.

The impoverished Congress was eager to sell off the western territory as quickly as possible. After all, the frontier represented a source of income that did not depend on the unreliable generosity of the states. A second ordinance, passed in 1785 and called the Land Ordinance, established an orderly process for laying out new townships and marketing public lands. Surveyors marked off townships, each running directly from east to west. These units, 6 miles square, were subdivided into 36 separate sections of 640 acres (1 square mile) each. The government planned to auction off its holdings at prices of not less than $1 an acre. Congress set the minimum purchase at 640 acres, and near-worthless paper money was not accepted as payment. Section 16 was set aside for public education; the federal government reserved four other sections for its own use.

Public response disappointed Congress. Surveying the lands took far longer than anticipated, and few persons possessed enough hard currency to make even the minimum purchase. Finally, a solution to the problem came from Manasseh Cutler, a New England minister turned land speculator and congressional lobbyist.

He and his associates offered to purchase more than 6 million unsurveyed acres of land located in present-day southeastern Ohio by persuading Congress to accept, at full face value, government loan certificates that had been issued to soldiers during the Revolution. On the open market, the speculators could pick up the certificates for as little as 10 percent of their face value and, thus, stood to make a fortune.

Like so many other get-rich-quick schemes this one failed to produce the anticipated millions. Small homesteaders settled wherever they pleased, refusing to pay either government or speculators for the land. Congress worried about the excess liberty on the frontier. In the 1780s, the West seemed to be filling up with people who by eastern standards were uncultured. Timothy Pickering, a New Englander, declared that "the emigrants to the frontier lands are the least worthy subjects in the United States."

These various currents shaped the Ordinance of 1787. The bill, also called the Northwest Ordinance, provided a new structure for government of the Northwest Territory. The plan authorized the creation of between three and five territories, each to be ruled by a governor, a secretary, and three judges appointed by Congress. When the population reached five thousand, voters who owned property could elect an assembly, but its decisions were subject to the governor's absolute veto. Once sixty thousand persons resided in a territory, they could write a constitution and petition for full statehood. While these procedures represented a retreat from Jefferson's original proposal, the Ordinance of 1787 contained several significant features. A bill of rights guaranteed the settlers the right to trial by jury, freedom of religion, and due process of law. In addition, the act outlawed slavery, a prohibition that freed the future states of Ohio, Indiana, Illinois, Michigan, and Wisconsin from the curse of human bondage.

By contrast, settlement south of the Ohio River received far less attention from Congress. Long before the end of the war, thousands of Americans streamed through the Cumberland Gap into a part of Virginia known as Kentucky. The most famous of these settlers was Daniel Boone. In 1775, the population of Kentucky was approximately one hundred; by 1784, it had jumped to thirty thousand. Speculators purchased large tracts from the Indians, planning to resell this acreage to settlers at handsome profits. By 1790, the entire region south of the Ohio River had been transformed into a crazy quilt of claims and counterclaims that generated lawsuits for many years to come.

STRENGTHENING FEDERAL AUTHORITY

Despite its success in bringing order to the Northwest Territory, the Confederation increasingly came under heavy fire from critics who wanted a stronger central government. Complaints varied from region to region, from person to person, but most criticism focused on the alleged weakness of the national economy.

THE NATIONALIST CRITIQUE

Even before England signed a treaty with America, its merchants flooded American ports with consumer items and offered easy credit. Families that had postponed purchases of imported goods—either because of British blockade or personal hardship—now rushed to buy European manufactures.

This renewal of trade with Great Britain on such a large scale strained the American economy. Gold and silver flowed back across the Atlantic, leaving the United States desperately short of hard currency. When large merchant houses called in their debts, ordinary American consumers often faced bankruptcy.

Critics of the Confederation pointed to the government's inability to regulate trade. Whenever a northern congressman suggested restricting British access to American markets, southern representatives, who feared any controls on the export of tobacco or rice, bellowed in protest. Southerners anticipated that such regulation of commerce would put planters under the yoke of northern shipping interests.

*"Not worth a Continental"
became a common oath
when inflation eroded the
value of the Continental
currency. Most currency issued by the states was
equally worthless.*

The country's chronic fiscal instability increased public anxiety. While the war was still in progress, Congress printed well over $200 million in paper money, but because of extraordinarily high inflation, the rate of exchange for Continental bills soon declined to a fraction of their face value. In 1781, Congress, facing insolvency, turned to the states for help. They were asked to retire the depreciated currency. The situation was spinning out of control. Several states—pressed to pay their own war-related debts—not only recirculated the Continental bills but also issued nearly worthless money of their own.

A heavy burden of state and national debt compounded the general sense of economic crisis. Revolutionary soldiers had yet to be paid. Creditors clamored for reimbursement. Foreign lenders demanded interest on funds advanced during the Revolution. These pressures grew, but Congress was unable to respond. The Articles specifically prohibited Congress from taxing the American people. It seemed that the Confederation would soon default on its legal obligations unless something was done quickly.

In response, an aggressive group of men known as the "nationalists"—persons such as Alexander Hamilton, James Madison, and Robert Morris—called for major constitutional reforms. They demanded an amendment allowing Congress to collect a 5 percent tax on imported goods sold in the states. Revenues generated by the proposed Impost of 1781 would be used by the Confederation to reduce the national debt. On this point the nationalists were adamant. They recognized that whoever paid the public debt would gain the public trust. If the states assumed the responsibility, then the country could easily fragment into separate republics. Twelve states accepted the Impost amendment, but Rhode Island—where local interests argued that the tax would make Congress "independent of their constituents"—refused to cooperate. One negative vote killed the taxing scheme.

The nationalists insisted that a country with the potential of the United States required a complex, centralized fiscal system. But for all their pretensions to realism, the nationalists of the early 1780s were politically inept. They underestimated the depth of republican and localist fears, and in their rush to strengthen the Articles, they overplayed their hand.

A group of extreme nationalists appealed to the army for support. To this day, no one knows the full story of the Newburgh Conspiracy of 1783. Officers of the Continental Army stationed at Newburgh, New York, worried that Congress would disband them without funding their pensions, lobbied intensively for relief. In March, they scheduled general meetings to protest the weakness and duplicity of Congress. The officers' initial efforts were harmless enough, but frustrated nationalists such as Morris and Hamilton hoped that if the army exerted sufficient pressure on the government, perhaps even threatened a military takeover, then the states might be compelled to amend the Articles.

The conspirators failed to take George Washington's integrity into account. No matter how much he wanted a strong central government, he would not tolerate insubordination by the military. Washington confronted the officers directly at Newburgh, intending to read a prepared statement. Fumbling with his glasses before his men, he commented, "Gentlemen, you must pardon me. I have grown gray in your service and now find myself growing blind." The unexpected vulnerability of this great soldier reduced the mutinous troops to tears, and in an instant, the conspiracy ended. Washington deserves credit for preserving civilian rule in this country.

In April 1783, a second impost failed to win unanimous ratification. Even a personal appeal by Washington could not save the amendment. With this defeat, nationalists gave up on the Confederation.

DIPLOMATIC HUMILIATION

In foreign affairs, Congress endured further embarrassment. It could not even enforce the provisions of its own peace treaty. American negotiators had promised Great Britain that its citizens could collect debts contracted before the Revolution. The states, however, dragged their heels, and several even passed laws obstructing the settlement of legitimate prewar claims. Congress was powerless to force compliance. The British responded to this apparent provocation by refusing to evacuate troops from posts located in the Northwest Territory.

Congress's postrevolutionary dealings with Spain were equally humiliating. That nation refused to accept the southern boundary of the United States established by the Treaty of Paris. Spain claimed sovereignty over much of the land located between Georgia and the Mississippi River. On July 21, 1784, it fueled the controversy by closing the lower Mississippi River to citizens of the United States.

This unexpected decision devastated western farmers. Free use of the Mississippi was essential to the economic development of the entire Ohio Valley. Because of the prohibitively high cost of transporting freight for long distances over land, western settlers—and southern planters eyeing future opportunities in this area—demanded a secure water link with the world's markets. Their spokesmen in Congress denounced anyone who claimed that navigation of the Mississippi was a negotiable issue.

In 1786, a Spanish official, Don Diego de Gardoqui, opened talks with John Jay, a New Yorker appointed by Congress to obtain rights to navigation of the Mississippi. Jay soon discovered that Gardoqui would not compromise. After making little progress, Jay seized the initiative. If Gardoqui would allow American merchants to trade directly with Spain, thus opening up an important new market to ships from New England and the middle states, then the United States might forgo navigation of the Mississippi for twenty-five years. When southern delegates heard of Jay's concessions, they were outraged. It appeared to them as if representatives of northern commerce were attempting to divide the United States into separate confederations. Congress wisely terminated the negotiations with Spain.

By the mid-1780s, the Confederation could claim several notable achievements. Still, as anyone could see, the government was struggling. Congress met irregularly. Some states did not even bother to send delegates, and pressing issues often had to be postponed for lack of a quorum. The nation even lacked a permanent capital, and Congress drifted from Philadelphia to Princeton to Annapolis to New York City.

"HAVE WE FOUGHT FOR THIS?"

By 1785, the country seemed to have lost direction. The buoyant optimism that sustained revolutionary Patriots had dissolved. Many Americans, especially those who had provided leadership during the Revolution, agreed something had to be done. In 1786, Washington bitterly observed, "What astonishing changes a few years are capable of producing. Have we fought for this? Was it with these expectations that we launched into a sea of trouble, and have bravely struggled through the most threatening dangers?"

THE GENIUS OF JAMES MADISON

The conviction of people such as Washington that the nation was indeed in a state of crisis reflected tensions within republican thought. To be sure, they supported open elections and the right of individuals to advance their own economic well-being, but when these elements seemed to undermine social and political order, they expressed the fear that perhaps liberty might bring anarchy. The situation had changed quite rapidly. As recently as the 1770s, men of republican persuasion had insisted that the greatest threat to the American people was concentration of power in the hands of unscrupulous rulers. With this principle in mind, they transformed state governors into mere figureheads and weakened the Confederation in the name of popular liberties.

By the mid-1780s, persons of property and standing saw the problem in a different light. Recent experience suggested to them that ordinary citizens did not in fact possess sufficient virtue to sustain a republic. The states had not in fact been plagued by executive tyranny but by an excess of democracy, by a failure of the majority to preserve the property rights of the minority, by an unrestrained individualism that promoted anarchy rather than good order.

As Americans tried to interpret these experiences within a republican framework, they were checked by the most widely accepted political wisdom of the age. Baron de Montesquieu (1689–1755), a French political philosopher of immense international reputation and author of *The Spirit of the Laws* (1748), declared flatly that a republican government could not flourish in a large territory. The reasons were clear. If the people lost direct control over their representatives, they would fall prey to tyrants. Large distances allowed rulers to hide their corruption.

In the United States, Montesquieu's theories were received as self-evident truths. His writings seemed to demonstrate the importance of preserving the sovereignty of the states, for however much these small republics abused the rights of property and ignored minority interests, it was plainly unscientific to maintain that a republic consisting of thirteen states, several million people, and thousands of acres of territory could long survive.

James Madison challenged Montesquieu's argument, and in so doing, he helped Americans to think of republican government in radical new ways. This soft-spoken, rather unprepossessing Virginian was the most brilliant American political thinker of his generation.

Madison delved into the writings of a group of Scottish philosophers, the most prominent being David Hume (1711–1776), and discovered that Americans need not fear a greatly expanded republic. Madison perceived that it was in small states such as Rhode Island that legislative majorities tyrannized the propertied minority. In a large territory, Madison explained, "the Society becomes broken into a greater variety of interest, of pursuits, of passions, which check each other, whilst those who may feel a common sentiment have less opportunity of communication and contact."

Madison did not, however, advocate a modern "interest-group" model of political behavior. The contending parties were incapable of working for the common good. They were too mired in their own local, selfish concerns. Rather, Madison thought competing factions would neutralize each other, leaving the business of running the central government to the ablest, most virtuous persons the nation could produce. In other words, Madison's federal system was not a small state writ large; it was something entirely different, a government based on the will of the people and yet detached from their narrowly based demands. This thinking formed the foundation of Madison's most famous political essay, *The Federalist* No. 10.

CONSTITUTIONAL REFORM

A concerted movement to overhaul the Articles of Confederation began in 1786, when Madison and his friends persuaded the Virginia assembly to recommend a convention to explore the creation of a unified system of "commercial regulations." Congress supported the idea. In September, delegates from five states arrived in Annapolis, Maryland. The occasion provided strong nationalists with an opportunity to hatch an even bolder plan. The Annapolis delegates advised Congress to hold a second meeting in Philadelphia "to take into consideration the situation of the United States, to devise such further provisions as shall appear to them necessary to render the constitution of the Federal Government

This 1787 woodcut portrays Daniel Shays with one of his chief officers, Jacob Shattucks. Shays led farmers from western Massachusetts in revolt against a state government that seemed insensitive to rural needs. Their rebellion strengthened the demand for a strong new federal government.

adequate to the exigencies of the Union." Whether states' rights advocates in Congress knew what was afoot is not clear. In any case, Congress authorized a grand convention to gather in May 1787.

Events played into Madison's hands. Soon after the Annapolis meeting, an uprising known as Shays's Rebellion, involving several thousand impoverished farmers, shattered the peace of western Massachusetts. They complained of high taxes, of high interest rates, and, most of all, of a state government insensitive to their problems. In 1786, Daniel Shays, a veteran of the battle of Bunker Hill, and his armed neighbors closed a county courthouse where creditors were suing to foreclose farm mortgages. At one point, the rural insurgents threatened to seize the federal arsenal located at Springfield. Congress did not have funds sufficient to support an army, and the arsenal might have fallen had not a group of wealthy Bostonians raised an army of four thousand troops to put down the insurrection.

For the Nationalists throughout the United States, Shays's Rebellion symbolized the breakdown of law and order. "Great commotions are prevailing in Massachusetts," Madison wrote. "An appeal to the sword is exceedingly dreaded." The time had come for sensible people to speak up for a strong national government. The unrest in Massachusetts persuaded persons who might otherwise have ignored the Philadelphia meeting to participate in drafting a new constitution.

THE PHILADELPHIA CONVENTION

In the spring of 1787, fifty-five men representing twelve states traveled to Philadelphia. Rhode Island refused to take part in the proceedings. The delegates were practical people—lawyers, merchants, and planters—many of whom had fought in the Revolution and served in the Congress of the Confederation. The majority were in their thirties or forties. The gathering included George Washington, James Madison, George Mason, Robert Morris, James Wilson,

John Dickinson, Benjamin Franklin, and Alexander Hamilton, just to name the more prominent participants.

As soon as the Constitutional Convention opened on May 25, the delegates made several procedural decisions of great importance. First, they voted "that nothing spoken in the House be printed, or communicated without leave." The rule was stringently enforced. As Madison explained, the secrecy rule saved "both the convention and the community from a thousand erroneous and perhaps mischievous reports." It also has made it extremely difficult for modern lawyers and judges to determine exactly what the delegates actually intended when they wrote the Constitution.

In a second procedural move, the delegates decided to vote by state, but, in order to avoid the kinds of problems that had plagued the Confederation, they ruled that key proposals needed the support of only a majority instead of the nine states required under the Articles.

INVENTING A FEDERAL REPUBLIC

Even before all the delegates had arrived, Madison drew up a framework for a new federal system known as the Virginia Plan. He persuaded Edmund Randolph, Virginia's popular governor, to present this scheme to the convention on May 29. Randolph claimed that the Virginia Plan merely revised sections of the Articles, but everyone, including Madison, knew better. "My ideas," Madison confessed, "strike . . . deeply at the old Confederation." He was determined to restrain the state assemblies, and in the original Virginia Plan, Madison gave the federal government power to veto state laws.

The Virginia Plan envisioned a national legislature consisting of two houses, one elected *directly* by the people, the other chosen by the first house from nominations made by the state assemblies. Representation in both houses was proportional to the state's population. The Virginia Plan also provided for an executive elected by Congress. Since most delegates at the Philadelphia convention sympathized with the nationalist position, Madison's blueprint for a strong federal government initially received broad support.

The Virginia Plan had been pushed through the convention so fast that opponents hardly had an opportunity to present their objections. On June 15, they spoke up. William Paterson, a New Jersey lawyer, advanced the so-called New Jersey Plan, a scheme that retained the unicameral legislature in which each state possessed one vote and that at the same time gave Congress extensive new powers to tax and regulate trade. Paterson argued that these revisions, while more modest than Madison's plan, would have greater appeal for the American people. The delegates listened politely and then soundly rejected the New Jersey Plan on June 19. Indeed, only New Jersey, New York, and Delaware voted in favor of Paterson's scheme.

Rejection of this framework did not resolve the most controversial issue before the convention. Paterson and others feared that under the Virginia Plan small states would lose their separate identities. These delegates maintained that unless each state possessed an equal vote in Congress, the small states would find themselves at the mercy of their larger neighbors.

This argument outraged the delegates who favored a strong federal government. Paterson awarded too much power to the states. "For whom [are we] forming a Government?" Wilson cried. "Is it for men, or for the imaginary beings called States?" It seemed absurd to claim that the 68,000 people of Rhode Island should have the same voice in Congress as Virginia's 747,000 inhabitants.

COMPROMISE SAVES THE CONVENTION

Despite growing pessimism, the gathering did not break up. The delegates desperately wanted to produce a constitution, and they refused to give up until they had explored every avenue of reconciliation. Perhaps cooler heads agreed with Washington: "To please all is impossible, and to attempt it would be vain."

Mediation offered the only way to overcome potential deadlock. On July 2, a "grand committee" of one person from each state was elected by the convention to resolve persistent differences between the large and small states. It recommended that the states be equally represented in the upper house of Congress, while representation was to be proportionate in the lower house. Only the lower house could initiate money bills. The committee also decided that one member of the lower house should be selected for every thirty thousand inhabitants of a state.

Southern delegates insisted that this number include slaves. In the so-called three-fifths rule, the committee agreed that for the purpose of determining representation in the lower house, slaves would be counted, but not as much as free persons. For every five slaves, a congressional district received credit for three free voters, a deal that gave the South much greater power in the new government than it would have otherwise received. As with most compromise solutions, this one fully satisfied no one. It did, however, overcome a major impasse, and after the small states gained an assured voice in the upper house, the Senate, they cooperated enthusiastically in creating a strong central government.

SLAVERY: A NATIONAL EMBARRASSMENT

During the final days of August, a deeply disturbing issue came before the convention. It was a harbinger of the great sectional crisis of the nineteenth century. Northern representatives detested the slave trade and wanted it to end immediately. They despised the three-fifths ruling that awarded slaveholders extra power in government simply because they owned slaves. "It seemed now to be pretty well understood," Madison jotted in his private notes, "that the real difference of interest lay, not between the large and small but between the N. and Southn. States. The institution of slavery and its consequences formed a line of discrimination."

Whenever northern delegates—and on this point they were by no means united—pushed too aggressively, Southerners threatened to bolt the convention, thereby destroying any hope of establishing a strong national government. Curiously, even recalcitrant Southerners avoided using the word *slavery*. They seemed embarrassed to call the institution by its true name, and in the

REVOLUTION OR REFORM? THE ARTICLES OF CONFEDERATION AND THE CONSTITUTION COMPARED

POLITICAL CHALLENGE	ARTICLES OF CONFEDERATION	CONSTITUTION
Mode of ratification or amendment	Require confirmation by every state legislature	Requires confirmation by three-fourths of state conventions or legislatures
Number of houses in legislature	One	Two
Mode of representation	Two to seven delegates represent each state; each state holds only one vote in Congress	Two senators represent each state in upper house; each senator holds one vote. One representative to lower house represents every 30,000 people (in 1788) in a state; each representative holds one vote
Mode of election and term of office	Delegates appointed annually by state legislatures	Senators chosen by state legislatures for six-year term (direct election after 1913); representatives chosen by vote of citizens for two-year term
Executive	No separate executive: delegates annually elect one of their number as president, who possesses no veto, no power to appoint officers or to conduct policy. Administrative functions of government theoretically carried out by Committee of States, practically by various single-headed departments	Separate executive branch: president elected by electoral college to four-year term; granted veto, power to conduct policy and to appoint ambassadors, judges, and officers of executive departments established by legislation
Judiciary	Most adjudication left to state and local courts; Congress is final court of appeal in disputes between states	Separate branch consisting of Supreme Court and inferior courts established by Congress to enforce federal law
Taxation	States alone can levy taxes; Congress funds the Common Treasury by making requisitions for state contributions	Federal government granted powers of taxation
Regulation of commerce	Congress regulates foreign commerce by treaty but holds no check on conflicting state regulations	Congress regulates foreign commerce by treaty; all state regulations must obtain congressional consent

Constitution itself, slaves were described as "other persons," "such persons," "persons held to Service or Labour," in other words, as everything but slaves.

Largely ignoring northern attacks, the delegates reached an uneasy compromise on the continuation of the slave trade. Southerners feared that the new Congress would pass commercial regulations adversely affecting the planters—taxes on the export of rice and tobacco, for example. They demanded, therefore, that no trade laws be passed without a two-thirds majority of the federal legislature. They backed down on this point, however, in exchange for guarantees that

Congress would not interfere with the slave trade until 1808 (see Chapter 8). The South even came away with a clause assuring the return of fugitive slaves.

Although these deals disappointed many Northerners, they conceded that establishing a strong national government was of greater immediate importance than ending the slave trade. "Great as the evil is," Madison wrote, "a dismemberment of the union would be worse."

THE LAST DETAILS

On July 26, the convention formed a Committee of Detail to prepare a rough draft of the Constitution. After the committee completed its work—writing a document that still, after so many hours of debate, preserved the fundamental points of the Virginia Plan—the delegates reconsidered each article. The task required the better part of a month.

During these sessions, the members of the convention concluded that the president, as they now called the executive, should be selected by an electoral college, a body of prominent men in each state chosen by local voters. The number of "electoral" votes held by each state equaled its number of representatives and senators. This elitist device guaranteed that the president would not be indebted to the Congress for his office. Whoever received the second largest number of votes in the electoral college automatically became vice president. In the event that no person received a majority of the votes, the election would be decided by the lower house—the House of Representatives—with each state casting a single vote. Delegates also armed the chief executive with veto power over legislation as well as the right to nominate judges. Both privileges, of course, would have been unthinkable a decade earlier, but the state experiments revealed the importance of having an independent executive to maintain a balanced system of republican government.

As the meeting was concluding, some delegates expressed concern about a bill of rights. Such declarations had been included in most state constitutions, and Virginians such as George Mason insisted that the states and their citizens needed explicit protection from possible excesses by the federal government. While many delegates sympathized with Mason's appeal, they noted that the hour was late and, in any case, that the proposed Constitution provided sufficient security for individual rights. During the hard battles over ratification, the delegates to the convention may have regretted passing over the issue so lightly.

WE, THE PEOPLE

The delegates adopted an ingenious procedure for ratification. Instead of submitting the Constitution to the various state legislatures, all of which had a vested interest in maintaining the status quo and most of which had two houses, either of which could block approval, they called for the election of thirteen state conventions especially chosen to review the new federal government. The delegates may have picked up this idea from the Massachusetts experiment of 1780. Moreover, the Constitution would take effect after the assent of only nine states.

There was no danger, therefore, that the proposed system would fail simply because a single state like Rhode Island withheld approval. On September 17, thirty-nine men signed the Constitution.

WHOSE CONSTITUTION?
STRUGGLE FOR RATIFICATION

The convention had been authorized only to revise the Articles. Instead, it produced a new plan that fundamentally altered relations between the states and the central government. The delegates dutifully dispatched copies of the Constitution to the Congress of Confederation, then meeting in New York City, and that powerless body referred the document to the separate states without any specific recommendation. The fight for ratification had begun.

FEDERALISTS AND ANTIFEDERALISTS

Proponents of the Constitution enjoyed great advantages over the opposition. In the contest for ratification, they took no chances. Their most astute move was the adoption of the label *Federalist.* The term cleverly suggested that they stood for a confederation of states rather than for the creation of a supreme national authority. In fact, they envisioned the creation of a strong centralized national government capable of fielding a formidable army. Critics of the Constitution, who tended to be somewhat poorer, less urban, and less well educated than their opponents, cried foul, but there was little they could do. They were stuck with the name *Antifederalist,* a misleading term that made their cause seem a rejection of the very notion of a federation of the states.

The Federalists recruited the most prominent public figures of the day. In every state convention, speakers favoring the Constitution were more polished and more fully prepared than were their opponents. In New York, the campaign to win ratification sparked publication of *The Federalist,* a brilliant series of essays written by Madison, Hamilton, and Jay during the fall and winter of 1787 and 1788. The nation's newspapers threw themselves overwhelmingly behind the new government. In some states, the Federalists adopted tactics of questionable propriety in order to gain ratification. In Pennsylvania, for example, they achieved a legal quorum for a crucial vote by dragging several opposition delegates into the meeting from the streets. In New York, Hamilton intimidated upstate Antifederalists with threats that New York City would secede from the state unless the state ratified the Constitution.

In these battles, the Antifederalists articulated a political philosophy that had broad popular appeal. Like the extreme republicans who drafted the first state constitutions, the Antifederalists were deeply suspicious of centralized political power. During the debates over ratification, they warned that public officials, however selected, would be constantly scheming to expand their authority. The preservation of individual liberty required constant vigilance. It seemed obvious that the larger the republic, the greater the opportunity for political corruption.

Local voters could not possibly know what their representatives in a distant national capital were doing.

Antifederalists demanded direct, personal contact with their representatives. They argued that elected officials should reflect the character of their constituents as closely as possible. It seemed unlikely that in large congressional districts, the people would be able to preserve such close ties with their representatives. According to the Antifederalists, the Constitution favored persons wealthy enough to have forged a reputation that extended beyond a single community. Samuel Chase told the members of the Maryland ratifying convention that under the new system, "the distance between the people and their representatives will be so great that there is no probability of a farmer or planter being chosen . . . only the *gentry*, the *rich*, and the well-born will be elected."

Federalist speakers mocked their opponents' localist perspective. The Constitution deserved general support precisely because it ensured that future Americans would be represented by "natural aristocrats," individuals possessing greater insights, skills, and training than did the ordinary citizen. These talented leaders, the Federalists insisted, could discern the interests of the entire population.

It would be a mistake, however, to see the Antifederalists as "losers" or as persons who could not comprehend social and economic change. Although their rhetoric echoed an older moral view of political culture, they accepted more easily than did many Federalists a liberal marketplace in which ordinary citizens competed as equals with the rich and well-born. They believed the public good was best served by allowing individuals like themselves to pursue their own private interests.

The Constitution drew support from many different types of people. In general, Federalists lived in more commercialized areas than did their opponents. In the cities, artisans as well as merchants called for ratification, while those farmers who were only marginally involved in commercial agriculture frequently voted Antifederalist.

Despite passionate pleas from Patrick Henry and other Antifederalists, most state conventions quickly adopted the Constitution. Delaware acted first (December 7, 1787), and within eight months of the Philadelphia meeting, eight of the nine states required to launch the government had ratified the document. The contests in Virginia (June 1788) and New York (July 1788) generated bitter debate, but they too joined the union, leaving only North Carolina and Rhode Island outside the United States. Eventually (November 21, 1789, and May 29, 1790), these states ratified the Constitution. The vote had been very close. The Constitution was ratified in New York by a tally of 30 to 27, in Massachusetts by 187 to 168, and in Virginia by 89 to 79. A swing of a few votes in several key states could have defeated the new government.

ADDING THE BILL OF RIGHTS

The first ten amendments to the Constitution are the major legacy of the Antifederalist argument. In almost every state convention, opponents of the Constitution pointed to the need for greater protection of individual liberties,

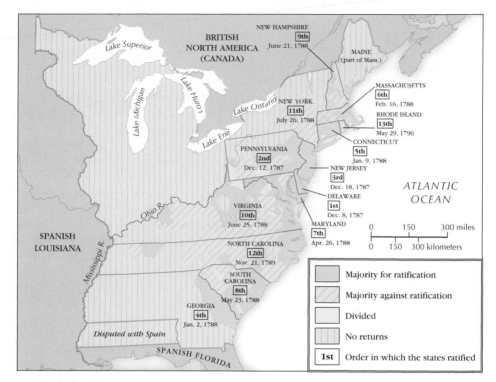

NEW HAMPSHIRE 9th June 21, 1788

BRITISH NORTH AMERICA (CANADA)

Lake Superior

Lake Michigan

Lake Huron

Lake Ontario

Lake Erie

NEW YORK 11th July 26, 1788

MAINE (part of Mass.)

MASSACHUSETTS 6th Feb. 16, 1788

RHODE ISLAND 13th May 29, 1790

CONNECTICUT 5th Jan. 9, 1788

PENNSYLVANIA 2nd Dec. 12, 1787

NEW JERSEY 3rd Dec. 18, 1787

DELAWARE 1st Dec. 8, 1787

ATLANTIC OCEAN

Ohio R.

VIRGINIA 10th June 25, 1788

MARYLAND 7th Apr. 26, 1788

0   150   300 miles

0   150   300 kilometers

SPANISH LOUISIANA

Mississippi R.

NORTH CAROLINA 12th Nov. 21, 1789

SOUTH CAROLINA 8th May 23, 1788

GEORGIA 4th Jan. 2, 1788

Disputed with Spain

SPANISH FLORIDA

	Majority for ratification
	Majority against ratification
	Divided
	No returns
1st	Order in which the states ratified

Ratification of the Constitution

Advocates of the new Constitution called themselves Federalists, and those who opposed its ratification were known as Antifederalists.

rights that people presumably had possessed in a state of nature. The list of fundamental rights varied from state to state, but most Antifederalists demanded specific guarantees for jury trial and freedom of religion. They wanted prohibitions against cruel and unusual punishments. There was also considerable, though not universal, support for freedom of speech and freedom of the press.

Madison and others regarded the proposals with little enthusiasm. In *The Federalist* No. 84, Hamilton bluntly reminded the American people that "the constitution is itself . . . a BILL OF RIGHTS." But after the adoption of the Constitution had been assured, Madison moderated his stand. If nothing else, passage of a bill of rights would appease able Antifederalists who might otherwise remain alienated from the new federal system.

The crucial consideration was caution. A number of people throughout the nation advocated calling a second constitutional convention, one that would take Antifederalist criticism into account. Madison wanted to avoid such a meeting, and he feared that some members of the first Congress might use a bill of rights as an excuse to revise the entire Constitution.

Madison carefully reviewed these recommendations as well as the various declarations of rights that had appeared in the early state constitutions, and on June 8, 1789, he placed before the House of Representatives a set of amendments designed to protect individual rights from government interference. Madison told the members of Congress that the greatest dangers to popular liberties came from "the majority [operating] against the minority." A committee compressed and revised his original ideas into ten amendments that were ratified and became known collectively as the Bill of Rights.

The Bill of Rights protected the freedoms of assembly, speech, religion, and the press; guaranteed speedy trial by an impartial jury; preserved the people's right to bear arms; and prohibited unreasonable searches. Other amendments dealt with legal procedure. Some opponents of the Constitution urged Congress to provide greater safeguards for states' rights, but Madison had no intention of backing away from a strong central government. Only the Tenth Amendment addressed the states' relation to the federal system. This crucial article, designed to calm Antifederalist fears, specified that those "powers not delegated to the United States by the Constitution, nor prohibited by it to the States, are reserved to the States respectively, or to the people." On September 25, 1789, the Bill of Rights passed both houses of Congress, and by December 15, 1791, the amendments had been ratified by three-fourths of the states.

CAN THE PEOPLE BE TRUSTED?

By 1789, one phase of American political experimentation had come to an end. During these years, the people gradually, often haltingly, learned that in a republican society, they themselves were sovereign. They could no longer blame the failure of government on inept monarchs or greedy aristocrats. They bore a great responsibility. Americans had demanded a government of the people only to discover during the 1780s that in some situations, the people could not be trusted with power, majorities could tyrannize minorities, and the best of governments could abuse individual rights.

Although contemporaries had difficulty deciding just what had been accomplished, most Americans probably would have accepted Franklin's optimistic assessment. As he watched the delegates to the Philadelphia convention come forward to sign the Constitution, he noted that there was a sun carved on the back of George Washington's chair. "I have," the aged philosopher noted, ". . . often in the course of the session . . . looked at [the sun] behind the President without being able to tell whether it was rising or setting; but now at length I have the happiness to know that it is a rising and not a setting sun."

CHRONOLOGY

1776 Second Continental Congress authorizes colonies to create republican government (May)

Eight states draft new constitutions; two others already enjoy republican government by virtue of former colonial charters

1777 Congress accepts Articles of Confederation after long debate (November)

1780 Massachusetts finally ratifies state constitution

1781 States ratify Articles of Confederation following settlement of Virginia's western land claims

British army surrenders at Yorktown (October)

1782 States fail to ratify proposed Impost tax

1783 Newburgh Conspiracy thwarted (March)

Society of the Cincinnati raises a storm of criticism

Treaty of peace signed with Great Britain (September)

1785 Land Ordinance for Northwest Territory passed by Congress

1786 Jay-Gardoqui negotiations over Mississippi navigation anger southern states

Annapolis Convention suggests second meeting to revise the Articles of Confederation (September)

Shays's Rebellion frightens American leaders

1787–1788 The federal Constitution is ratified by all states except North Carolina and Rhode Island

1791 Bill of Rights (first ten amendments to the Constitution) ratified by states

7

❖———————————❖

DEMOCRACY AND DISSENT

The Violence of Party Politics, 1788–1800

W hile presiding over the first meeting of the U.S. Senate in 1789, Vice President John Adams called the senators' attention to a procedural question: How would they address George Washington, the newly elected president? Adams insisted that Washington deserved an impressive title, lending dignity and weight to his office. The vice president warned the senators that if they called Washington simply "president of the United States," the "common people of foreign countries [as well as] the sailors and soldiers [would] despise him to all eternity." Adams recommended "His Highness, the President of the United States, and Protector of their Liberties," but some senators favored "His Elective Majesty" or "His Excellency."

Adams's initiative caught many persons, including Washington, completely by surprise. They regarded the entire debate as ridiculous. James Madison, a member of the House of Representatives, announced that pretentious European titles were ill suited to the "genius of the people" and "the nature of our Government." Thomas Jefferson, then residing in Paris, could not comprehend what motivated the vice president, and in private correspondence, he repeated Benjamin Franklin's judgment that Adams "means well for his Country, is always an honest Man, often a wise one, but sometimes, and in some things, absolutely out of his senses." When the senators learned that their efforts embarrassed Washington, they dropped the topic. The leader of the new republic would be called president of the United States. One humorist, however, dubbed the portly Adams "His Rotundity."

POWER OF PUBLIC OPINION

The comic-opera quality of the debate about how to address Washington should not obscure the participants' serious concern about the future of republican government. All of them, of course, wanted to secure the Revolution. The recently ratified Constitution transferred sovereignty from the states to the people, a bold and unprecedented decision that many Americans feared would generate chronic instability. Translating constitutional abstractions into practical legislation would have been difficult, even under the most favorable conditions. But these were especially trying times. Great Britain and France, rivals in a world war, put nearly unbearable pressures on the leaders of the new republic and, in the process, made foreign policy a bitterly divisive issue.

Although no one welcomed them, political parties gradually took shape during this period. Neither the Jeffersonians nor the Federalists—as the two major groups were called—doubted that the United States would one day become a great commercial power. They differed, however, on how best to manage the transition from an agrarian household economy to an international system of trade and industry. The Federalists encouraged rapid integration of the United States into a world economy, but however enthusiastic they were about capitalism, they did not trust the people or local government to do the job effectively. A modern economy, they insisted, required strong national institutions that would be directed by a social elite who understood the financial challenge and who would work in the best interests of the people.

Such claims frightened persons who came to identify themselves as Jeffersonians. Strong financial institutions, they thought, had corrupted the government of Great Britain from which they had just separated themselves. They searched for alternative ways to accommodate the needs of commerce and industry. Unlike the Federalists, the Jeffersonians put their faith in the people, defined for the most part politically as white yeoman farmers. The Jeffersonians insisted that ordinary entrepreneurs, if they could be freed from intrusive government regulations, could be trusted to resist greed and crass materialism and to sustain the virtue of the republic.

Leaders of every persuasion had to learn to live with "public opinion." Revolutionary leaders had invited the people to participate in government, but the gentlemen assumed that ordinary voters would automatically defer to their social betters. Instead, the Founders discovered they had created a rough-and-tumble political culture, a robust public sphere of cheap newspapers and street demonstrations. The newly empowered "public" followed the great debates of the period through articles they read in hundreds of highly partisan journals and magazines.

Just as the Internet has done in our own times, print journalism opened politics to a large audience that previously might have been indifferent to the activities of elected officials. By the time John Adams left the presidency in 1800, he had learned this lesson well. The ordinary workers and farmers of the United

The front pages of Benjamin Franklin Bache's Aurora General Advertiser, *February 22, 1798, and William Cobbett's* Porcupine's Gazette, *February 27, 1798. The two partisan editors traded insults in print, referring to rivals as "reptiles," "impudent dogs," "prostitute hireling wretches," and worse.*

States, feisty individuals who thought they were as good as anyone else and who were not afraid to let their political opinions be known, were not likely to let their president become an "Elective Majesty."

ESTABLISHING A NEW GOVERNMENT

In 1788, George Washington enjoyed great popularity throughout the nation. The people remembered him as the selfless leader of the Continental Army, and even before the states had ratified the Constitution, everyone assumed he would be chosen president of the United States. He received the unanimous support of the electoral college, an achievement that no subsequent president has duplicated. Adams, a respected Massachusetts lawyer who championed national independence in 1776, was selected vice president. As Washington left his beloved Virginia plantation, Mount Vernon, for New York City, he recognized that the people—now so vocal in his support—could be fickle. "I fear," he mused, "if the issue of public measures should not correspond with their sanguine expectations, they will turn the extravagant . . . praise . . . into equally extravagant . . . censures."

Washington owed much of his success as the nation's first president to an instinctive feeling for the symbolic possibilities of political power. Although he possessed only modest speaking abilities and never matched the intellectual brilliance of some contemporaries, Washington sensed that he had come to embody the hopes and fears of the new republic, and thus, without ever quite articulating the attributes necessary to achieve charisma—an ability that some leaders have to merge their own personality with the abstract goals of the government—he carefully monitored his official behavior. Washington knew that if he did not convincingly demonstrate the existence of a strong republic, people who championed the sovereignty of the individual states would attempt to weaken federal authority before it was ever properly established.

No example better illustrates Washington's mastery of symbolic power than his grand trips in 1789 and 1791. Accompanied by only a secretary and a few servants, he journeyed from the present state of Maine to Georgia. Along the way ordinary men and women flocked to see the president and to celebrate the new political order. His sacrifice—the roads were terrible and the food worse— visibly brought the new federal government to the people. In Boston, organizers honored Washington with a huge arch on which they inscribed on one side "To the Man who united all hearts" and on the other "To Columbia's favorite Son." Civic leaders in Charleston, South Carolina, outdid themselves. They arranged to have Washington taken over the water to the city "in a 12 oared barge rowed by

This unfinished portrait of George Washington was done by the portrait painter Gilbert Stuart in 1796. Because of the large demand for images of the first president, Stuart developed a brisk business copying his original painting. The image of Washington that appears on the U.S. dollar bill is based on this "Athenaeum" portrait.

12 American Captains of Ships, most elegantly dressed. There were a great number of other Boats with Gentlemen and ladies in them; and two Boats with Music; all of whom attended me across." It all worked as Washington planned. By celebrating a visit from the president of the United States, the people also recognized the power and unity of the new nation.

The first Congress quickly established executive departments. Some congressmen wanted to prohibit presidents from dismissing cabinet-level appointees without Senate approval, but James Madison—still a voice for an independent executive—led a successful fight against this restriction on presidential authority. Madison recognized that the chief executive could not function unless he had personal confidence in the people with whom he worked. In 1789, Congress created the Departments of War, State, and the Treasury, and as secretaries, Washington nominated Henry Knox, Thomas Jefferson, and Alexander Hamilton, respectively. Edmund Randolph served as part-time attorney general, a position that ranked slightly lower in prestige than the head of a department. Since the secretary of the treasury oversaw the collection of customs and other future federal taxes, Hamilton could anticipate having several thousand jobs to dispense, an obvious source of political patronage.

To modern Americans accustomed to a huge federal bureaucracy, the size of Washington's government seems amazingly small. When Jefferson arrived in New York to take over the State Department, for example, he found two chief clerks, two assistants, and a part-time translator. With this tiny staff, he not only maintained contacts with the representatives of foreign governments, collected information about world affairs, and communicated with U.S. officials living overseas, but also organized the entire federal census! The situation in other de-

This Liverpool Ware jug records the results of the nation's first census in 1790. Symbols of prosperity surround the census figures, even though the results disappointed many people who hoped the final count would show a population of more than four million people. Perhaps the "Not Known" number of persons living northwest of Ohio would have brought the total to the expected figure.

partments was similar. Overworked clerks scribbled madly just to keep up with the burden of correspondence.

Congress also provided for a federal court system. The Judiciary Act of 1789, the work primarily of Connecticut Congressman Oliver Ellsworth, created a Supreme Court staffed by a chief justice and five associate justices. In addition, the statute set up thirteen district courts authorized to review the decisions of the state courts. John Jay, a leading figure in New York politics, agreed to serve as chief justice, but since federal judges in the 1790s were expected to travel hundreds of miles over terrible roads to attend sessions of the inferior courts, few persons of outstanding talent and training joined Jay on the federal bench.

Remembering the financial insecurity of the old Confederation government, the newly elected congressmen passed the tariff of 1789, a tax of approximately 5 percent on imports. The new levy generated considerable revenue. Even before it went into effect, however, the act sparked controversy. Southern planters, who relied heavily on European imports, claimed that the tariff discriminated against southern interests.

Conflicting Visions: Jefferson and Hamilton

Washington's first cabinet included two extraordinary personalities, Alexander Hamilton and Thomas Jefferson. Both had served the country with distinction during the Revolution, were recognized by contemporaries as men of special genius as well as high ambition, and brought to public office a powerful vision of how the American people could achieve greatness. The story of their opposing views during the decade of the 1790s reveals how a common political ideology, republicanism (see Chapter 6), could be interpreted in such vastly different ways that decisions about government policy turned friends into adversaries. Indeed, the falling out of Hamilton and Jefferson reflected deep, potentially explosive political divisions within American society.

Hamilton was a brilliant, dynamic lawyer who had distinguished himself as Washington's aide-de-camp during the Revolution. Born in the West Indies, the child of an adulterous relationship, Hamilton employed charm, courage, and intellect to serve his inexhaustible ambition. He strove not for wealth but for reputation. Men and women who fell under his spell found him almost irresistible, but to enemies, Hamilton appeared a dark, calculating, even evil, genius. He advocated a strong central government and refused to be bound by the strict wording of the Constitution, a document Hamilton once called "a shilly shally thing." While he had fought for American independence, he admired British culture, and during the 1790s, he advocated closer commercial and diplomatic ties with England, with whom, he said, "we have a similarity of tastes, language, and general manners."

Jefferson possessed a profoundly different temperament. This tall Virginian was more reflective and shone less brightly in society than Hamilton.

During the first years of Washington's administration, neither Hamilton (left) nor Jefferson (right) recognized the full extent of their differences. But as events forced the federal government to make decisions on economic and foreign affairs, the two secretaries increasingly came into open conflict.

Contemporaries sometimes interpreted his retiring manner as lack of ambition. They misread Jefferson. He thirsted not for power or wealth but for an opportunity to advance the democratic principles that he had stated so eloquently in the Declaration of Independence. When Jefferson became secretary of state in January 1790, he had just returned from Paris where he witnessed the first exhilarating moments of the French Revolution. These earthshaking events, he believed, marked the beginning of a worldwide republican assault on absolute monarchy and aristocratic privilege. His European experiences persuaded Jefferson to favor France over Great Britain when the two nations clashed.

The differences dividing these two men could not long be contained. Washington's secretaries disagreed on precisely how the United States should fulfill its destiny. As head of the Treasury Department, Hamilton urged fellow citizens to think in terms of bold commercial development, of farms and factories embedded within a complex financial network that would reduce the nation's reliance on foreign trade. Because Great Britain had already established an elaborate system of banking and credit, the secretary looked to that country for economic models that might be reproduced on this side of the Atlantic.

Hamilton also voiced concerns about the role of the people in shaping public policy. He assumed that in a republican society, the gravest threat to political stability was anarchy rather than monarchy. "The truth," he claimed, "unquestionably is, that the only path to a subversion of the republican system of the Country is, by flattering the prejudices of the people, and exciting their jealousies and apprehensions." The best hope for the survival of the republic, Hamilton believed, lay with the country's monied classes. If the wealthiest people could be persuaded their economic self-interest could be advanced—or at least made less insecure—by the central government, then they would work to strengthen it, and by so doing, bring a greater measure of prosperity to the common people. From Hamilton's perspective, there was no conflict between private greed and public good; one was the source of the other.

On almost every detail, Jefferson rejected Hamilton's analysis. The secretary of state assumed that the strength of the American economy lay not in its industrial potential but in its agricultural productivity. The "immensity of land" represented the country's major economic resource. Contrary to the claims of some critics, Jefferson did not advocate agrarian self-sufficiency or look back nostalgically to a golden age dominated by simple yeomen. He recognized the necessity of change, and while he thought that persons who worked the soil were more responsible citizens than were those who labored in factories for wages, he encouraged the nation's farmers to participate in an expanding international market.

Unlike Hamilton, Jefferson expressed faith in the ability of the American people to shape policy. Throughout this troubled decade, even when the very survival of constitutional government seemed in doubt, Jefferson maintained a boundless optimism in the judgment of the common folk. He instinctively trusted the people, feared that uncontrolled government power might destroy their liberties, and insisted public officials follow the letter of the Constitution, a frame of government he described as "the wisest ever presented to men." The greatest threat to the young republic, he argued, came from the corrupt activities of pseudoaristocrats, persons who placed the protection of "property" and "civil order" above the preservation of "liberty." To tie the nation's future to the selfish interests of a privileged class—bankers, manufacturers, and speculators—seemed cynical as well as dangerous. He despised speculators who encouraged "the rage of getting rich in a day," since such "gaming" activities inevitably promoted the kinds of public vice that threatened republican government. To mortgage the future of the common people by creating a large national debt struck Jefferson as particularly insane.

HAMILTON'S PLAN FOR ECONOMIC DEVELOPMENT

The unsettled state of the nation's finances presented the new government with a staggering challenge. In August 1789, the House of Representatives announced that "adequate provision for the support of public credit [is] a matter of high importance to the national honor and prosperity." However pressing the problem appeared, no one was prepared to advance a solution, and the House asked the secretary of the treasury for suggestions.

Congress may have received more than it bargained for. Hamilton threw himself into the task. He read deeply in abstruse economic literature. He even developed a questionnaire designed to find out how the U.S. economy really worked and sent it to scores of commercial and political leaders throughout the country. But when Hamilton's three major reports—on public credit, on banking, and on manufacturers—were complete, they bore the unmistakable stamp of his own creative genius.

The secretary presented his *Report on the Public Credit* to Congress on January 14, 1790. His research revealed that the nation's outstanding debt stood at approximately $54 million. This sum represented various obligations that the U.S. government had incurred during the Revolutionary War. In addition to foreign loans, the figure included loan certificates the government had issued to its own citizens and soldiers. But that was not all. The states still owed creditors approximately $25 million. During the 1780s, Americans desperate for cash had been forced to sell government certificates to speculators at greatly discounted prices, and it was estimated that approximately $40 million of the nation's debt was owed to twenty thousand people, only 20 percent of whom were the original creditors.

FUNDING AND ASSUMPTION

Hamilton's *Report on the Public Credit* contained two major recommendations covering the areas of funding and assumption. First, under his plan, the United States promised to fund its foreign and domestic obligations at full face value. Current holders of loan certificates, whoever they were and no matter how they obtained them, could exchange the old certificates for new government bonds bearing a moderate rate of interest. Second, the secretary urged the federal government to assume responsibility for paying the remaining state debts.

Hamilton reasoned that his credit system would accomplish several desirable goals. It would significantly reduce the power of the individual states in shaping national economic policy, something Hamilton regarded as essential in maintaining a strong federal government. Moreover, the creation of a fully funded national debt signaled to investors throughout the world that the United States was now solvent, that its bonds represented a good risk. Hamilton argued that investment capital, which might otherwise flow to Europe, would remain in this country, providing a source of money for commercial and industrial investment. In short, Hamilton invited the country's wealthiest citizens to invest in the future of the United States.

To Hamilton's surprise, Madison—his friend and collaborator in writing *The Federalist*—attacked the funding scheme in the House of Representatives. The Virginia congressman agreed that the United States should honor its debts. He worried, however, about the citizens and soldiers who, because of personal financial hardship, had been compelled to sell their certificates at prices far below face value. Why should wealthy speculators now profit from their hardship? If the government treated the current holders of certificates less generously, Madison declared, then there might be sufficient funds to provide equitable treatment for the distressed Patriots. Whatever the moral justification for Madison's plan may have been, it proved unworkable on the national level. Far too many records had been lost since the Revolution for the Treasury Department to be able to identify all the original holders. In February 1790, Congress soundly defeated Madison's proposal.

The assumption portion of Hamilton's plan unleashed even greater criticism. Some states had already paid their revolutionary debts, and Hamilton's program seemed designed to reward certain states—Massachusetts and South Carolina, for example—simply because they had failed to put their finances in order. In addition, the secretary's opponents in Congress became suspicious that assumption was merely a ploy to increase the power and wealth of Hamilton's immediate friends.

Some of those who protested, however, were simply looking after their own speculative schemes. These men had contracted to purchase huge tracts of vacant western lands from the state and federal governments. They anticipated that when settlers finally arrived in these areas, the price of land would skyrocket. In the meantime, the speculators had paid for the land with revolutionary certificates, often purchased on the open market at fifteen cents on the dollar. This meant that one could obtain 1,000 acres for only $150. Hamilton's assumption proposal threatened to destroy these lucrative transactions by cutting off the supply of cut-rate securities. On April 12, a rebellious House led by Madison defeated assumption.

The victory was short-lived. Hamilton and congressional supporters resorted to legislative horse trading to revive his foundering program. In exchange for locating the new federal capital on the Potomac River, a move that would stimulate the depressed economy of northern Virginia, several key congressmen who shared Madison's political philosophy changed their votes on assumption. In August, Washington signed assumption and funding into law.

Interpreting the Constitution:
The Bank Controversy

The persistent Hamilton submitted his second report to Congress in January 1791. He proposed that the U.S. government charter a national bank. This privately owned institution would be funded in part by the federal government. Indeed, since the Bank of the United States would own millions of dollars of new U.S. bonds, its financial stability would be tied directly to the strength of the federal government and, of course, to the success of Hamilton's program. The secretary of the treasury argued that a growing financial community required a central bank to facilitate increasingly complex commercial transactions. The institution not only would serve as the main depository of the U.S. government but also would issue currency acceptable in payment of federal taxes. Because of that guarantee, the money would maintain its value while in circulation.

Madison and others in Congress immediately protested. While they were not oblivious to the many important services a national bank might provide for a growing country, they suspected that banks—especially those modeled on British institutions—might "perpetuate a large monied interest" in the United States. Moreover, the Constitution said nothing about chartering financial corporations, and they warned that if Hamilton and his supporters were allowed to stretch fundamental law on this occasion, popular liberties would be at the mercy of whoever happened to be in office.

This intense controversy involving his closest advisers worried the president. Even though the bank bill passed Congress (February 8), Washington considered vetoing the legislation on constitutional grounds. Before doing so, however, he requested written opinions from the members of his cabinet. Jefferson's rambling, wholly predictable attack on the bank was not one of his more persuasive performances. By contrast, in only a few days, Hamilton prepared a masterful essay titled "Defense of the Constitutionality of the Bank." He assured the president that Article I, Section 8 of the Constitution—"The Congress shall have Power . . . To make all Laws which shall be necessary and proper for carrying into Execution the foregoing Powers"—justified issuing charters to national banks. The "foregoing Powers" on which Hamilton placed so much weight were taxation, regulation of commerce, and making war. He boldly articulated a doctrine of *implied powers,* an interpretation of the Constitution that neither Madison nor Jefferson had anticipated. Hamilton's "loose construction" carried the day, and on February 25, 1791, Washington signed the bank act into law.

The general public looked on Hamilton's actions with growing hostility. Many persons associated huge national debts and privileged banks with the decay of public virtue. Men of Jefferson's temperament believed that Great Britain—a country Hamilton held in high regard—had compromised the purity of its own constitution by allowing speculators to worm their way into positions of political power.

Hamilton seemed intent on reproducing this corrupt system in the United States. When news of his proposal to fund the national debt at full face value leaked out, for example, urban speculators rushed to rural areas, where they purchased loan certificates from unsuspecting citizens at bargain prices. When the greed of a former Treasury Department official led to several serious bankruptcies in 1792, ordinary citizens began to listen more closely to what Madison, Jefferson, and their associates were saying about growing corruption in high places.

SETBACK FOR HAMILTON

In his third major report, *Report on Manufactures,* submitted to Congress in December 1791, Hamilton revealed the final details of his grand design for the economic future of the United States. This lengthy document suggested ways by which the federal government might stimulate manufacturing. If the country wanted to free itself from dependence on European imports, Hamilton observed, then it had to develop its own industry, textile mills for example. Without direct government intervention, however, the process would take decades. Americans would continue to invest in agriculture. But, according to the secretary of the treasury, protective tariffs and special industrial bounties would greatly accelerate the growth of a balanced economy, and with proper planning, the United States would soon hold its own with England and France.

In Congress, the battle lines were drawn. Hamilton's opponents—a loose coalition of men who shared Madison's and Jefferson's misgivings about the secretary's program—ignored his economic arguments. Instead, they engaged him on moral and political grounds. Madison railed against the dangers of "consolidation," a process that threatened to concentrate all power in the federal government, leaving the states defenseless. Under the Confederation, of course, Madison had stood with the nationalists against the advocates of extreme states' rights. His disagreements with Hamilton over economic policy, coupled with the necessity of pleasing the voters of his Virginia congressional district every two years, transformed Madison into a spokesman for the states.

Jefferson attacked the *Report on Manufactures* from a different angle. He assumed—largely because he had been horrified by Europe's urban poverty—that cities bred vice. The government, Jefferson argued, should do nothing to promote their development. He believed that Hamilton's proposal guaranteed that American workers would leave the countryside and crowd into urban centers. "I think our government will remain virtuous for many centuries," Jefferson explained, "as long as they [the people] are chiefly agricultural. . . . When they get piled upon one another in large cities, as in Europe, they will become corrupt as in Europe." And southern congressmen saw tariffs and bounties as vehicles for enriching Hamilton's northern friends at the planters' expense. The recommendations in the *Report on Manufactures* were soundly defeated in the House of Representatives.

Washington detested political squabbling. The president, of course, could see that the members of his cabinet disagreed on many issues, but in 1792, he still believed that Hamilton and Jefferson—and the people who looked to them for advice—could be reconciled. In August, he personally begged them to rise above the "internal dissensions [that are] . . . harrowing and tearing at our vitals." The appeal came too late. By the conclusion of Washington's first term, neither secretary trusted the other's judgment. Their sparring had produced congressional factions, but as yet no real political parties with permanent organizations that engaged in campaigning had come into existence.

CHARGES OF TREASON: THE BATTLE OVER FOREIGN AFFAIRS

During Washington's second term (1793–1797), war in Europe dramatically thrust foreign affairs into the forefront of American life. The impact of this development on the conduct of domestic politics was devastating. Officials who had formerly disagreed on economic policy now began to identify their interests with either Britain or France, Europe's most powerful nations. Differences of political opinion, however trivial, were suddenly cited as evidence that one group or the other had entered into treasonous correspondence with external enemies eager to compromise the independence and prosperity of the United States.

Formal political organizations—the Federalists and Republicans—were born in this poisonous atmosphere. The clash between the groups developed over how best to preserve the new republic. The Republicans (Jeffersonians) advocated states' rights, strict interpretation of the Constitution, friendship with France, and vigilance against "the avaricious, monopolizing Spirit of Commerce and Commercial Men." The Federalists urged a strong national government, central economic planning, closer ties with Great Britain, and maintenance of public order, even if that meant calling out federal troops.

THE PERIL OF NEUTRALITY

Great Britain treated the United States with arrogance. Weakness justified such a policy. The young republic could not even compel its old adversary to comply with the Treaty of 1783, in which the British had agreed to vacate military posts in the Northwest Territory. In 1794, approximately a thousand British soldiers still occupied American land. Moreover, even though 75 percent of American imports came from Great Britain, that country refused to grant the United States full commercial reciprocity. Among other provocations, it barred American shipping from the lucrative West Indian trade.

France presented a very different challenge. In May 1789, Louis XVI, desperate for revenue, authorized a meeting of a representative assembly known as the Estates General. By so doing, the king unleashed explosive revolutionary forces that toppled the monarchy and cost him his life (January 1793). The men who seized power—and they came and went rapidly—were militant republicans, ideologues eager to liberate all Europe from feudal institutions. In the early years of the Revolution, France drew on the American experience, and Thomas Paine and the Marquis de Lafayette enjoyed great popularity. But the French found they could not contain the violence of revolution. Constitutional reform turned into bloody purges, and one radical group, the Jacobins, guillotined thousands of people who were suspected of monarchist sympathies during the so-called Reign of Terror (October 1793–July 1794). These horrific events left Americans confused. While those who shared Jefferson's views cheered the spread of republicanism, others who sided with Hamilton condemned French expansionism and political excess.

In the face of growing international tension, neutrality seemed the most prudent course for the United States. But that policy was easier for a weak country to proclaim than to defend. In February 1793, France declared war on Great Britain—what the leaders of revolutionary France called the "war of all peoples against all kings"—and these powerful European rivals immediately challenged the official American position on shipping: "free ships make free goods," meaning that belligerents should not interfere with the shipping of neutral carriers. To make matters worse, no one was certain whether the Franco-American treaties of 1778 (see Chapter 5) legally bound the United States to support its old ally against Great Britain.

Both Hamilton and Jefferson wanted to avoid war. The secretary of state, however, believed that nations desiring American goods should be forced to

The execution of Louis XVI by French revolutionaries served to deepen the growing political division in America. Although Jeffersonian Republicans deplored the excesses of the Reign of Terror, they continued to support the French people. Federalists feared that the violence and lawlessness would spread to the United States.

honor American neutrality and, therefore, that if Britain treated the United States as a colonial possession, if the Royal Navy stopped American ships on the high seas and forced seamen to serve the king—in other words, if it impressed American sailors—then the United States should award France special commercial advantages. Hamilton thought Jefferson's scheme insane. He pointed out that Britain possessed the largest navy in the world and was not likely to be coerced by American threats. The United States, he counseled, should appease the former mother country even if that meant swallowing national pride.

A newly appointed French minister to the United States, Edmond Genêt, precipitated the first major diplomatic crisis. This incompetent young man arrived in Charleston, South Carolina, in April 1793. He found considerable popular enthusiasm for the French Revolution, and, buoyed by this reception, he authorized privately owned American vessels to seize British ships in the name of France. Such actions violated U.S. neutrality and invited British retaliation. When U.S. government officials warned Genêt to desist, he threatened to take his appeal directly to the American people, who presumably loved France more than did members of Washington's administration.

This confrontation particularly embarrassed Jefferson, the most outspoken pro-French member of the cabinet. He described Genêt as "hot headed." Washington did not wait to discover whether the treaties of 1778 were still in force. Before he had formally received the impudent French minister, the president issued a Proclamation of Neutrality (April 22).

JAY'S TREATY SPARKS DOMESTIC UNREST

Great Britain failed to take advantage of Genêt's insolence. Instead, it pushed the United States to the brink of war. British forts in the Northwest Territory remained a constant source of tension. In June 1793, a new element was added. The London government blockaded French ports to neutral shipping, and in November, its navy captured several hundred American vessels trading in the French West Indies. The British had not even bothered to give the United States advance warning of a change in policy. Outraged members of Congress, especially those who identified with Jefferson and Madison, demanded retaliation, an embargo, a stoppage of debt payment, even war.

Before this rhetoric produced armed struggle, Washington made one final effort to preserve peace. In May 1794, he sent Chief Justice John Jay to London to negotiate a formidable list of grievances. Jay's main objectives were removal of the British forts on U.S. territory, payment for ships taken in the West Indies, improved commercial relations, and acceptance of the American definition of neutral rights.

Jefferson's supporters—by now openly called the Republican interest—anticipated a treaty favorable to the United States. After all, they explained, the war with France had not gone well for Great Britain, and the British people were surely desperate for American foodstuffs. Even before Jay departed, however, his mission stood little chance of success. Hamilton, anxious to placate the British, had already secretly informed British officials that the United States was prepared to compromise on most issues.

Not surprisingly, when Jay reached London, he encountered polite but firm resistance. The chief justice did persuade the British to abandon their frontier posts and to allow small American ships to trade in the British West Indies, but they rejected out of hand the U.S. position on neutral rights. The Royal Navy would continue to search American vessels on the high seas for contraband and to impress sailors suspected of being British citizens. Moreover, there would be no compensation for the ships seized in 1793 until the Americans paid British merchants for debts contracted before the Revolution. And to the particular annoyance of Southerners, not a word was said about the slaves the British army had carried off at the conclusion of the war. While Jay salvaged the peace, he appeared to have betrayed the national interest.

News of Jay's Treaty—perhaps more correctly called Hamilton's Treaty—produced an angry outcry in the nation's capital. Even Washington was apprehensive. He submitted the document to the Senate without recommending ratification, a sign that the president was not entirely happy with the results of Jay's mission. After an extremely bitter debate, the upper house, controlled by Federalists, accepted a revised version of the treaty (June 1795). The vote was 20 to 10, a bare two-thirds majority.

The details of the Jay agreement soon leaked to the press. This was an important moment in American political history. The popular journals sparked a firestorm of protest. Throughout the country, people who had generally been apathetic about national politics were swept up in a wave of protest. Urban mobs condemned Jay's alleged sellout; rural settlers burned him in effigy.

A storm broke in the House of Representatives. Republican congressmen, led by Madison, thought they could stop Jay's Treaty by refusing to appropriate funds for its implementation. As part of their plan, they demanded that Washington show the House state papers relating to Jay's mission. The challenge raised complex issues of constitutional law. The House, for example, was claiming a voice in treaty ratification, a power explicitly reserved to the Senate. Second, there was the question of executive secrecy in the interest of national security. Could the president withhold information from the public? According to Washington—as well as all subsequent presidents—the answer was yes.

The president had a trump card to play. He raised the possibility that the House was really contemplating his impeachment. Such an action was, of course, unthinkable. Even criticizing Washington in public was politically dangerous, and as soon as he redefined the issue before Congress, petitions supporting the president flooded into the nation's capital. The Federalists won a stunning tactical victory over the opposition. A less popular man than Washington would not have fared so well. The division between the two parties was beyond repair. The Republicans labeled the Federalists "the British party"; the Federalists believed that the Republicans were in league with the French.

By the time Jay's Treaty became law (June 14, 1795), the two giants of Washington's first cabinet had retired. Late in 1793, Jefferson returned to his Virginia plantation, Monticello, where, despite his separation from day-to-day political affairs, he remained the chief spokesman for the Republican party. His rival, Hamilton, left the Treasury in January 1795 to practice law in New York City. He maintained close ties with important Federalist officials.

PUSHING THE NATIVE AMERICANS ASIDE

Before Great Britain finally withdrew its troops from the Great Lakes and Northwest Territory, its military officers encouraged local Indian groups—the Shawnee, Chippewa, and Miami—to attack settlers and traders from the United States. The Indians, who even without British encouragement fully appreciated that the newcomers intended to seize their land, won several impressive victories over federal troops in the area that would become western Ohio and Indiana. In 1790, General Josiah Harmar led his soldiers into an ambush. The following year, an army under General Arthur St. Clair suffered more than nine hundred casualties near the Wabash River. But the Indians were militarily

At the Treaty of Greenville in 1795, negotiators shared this calumet, or peace pipe, a spiritually symbolic act for Native Americans. This superficial recognition of the legitimacy of Native American cultures barely disguised the Indians' crushing loss of sovereignty.

more vulnerable than they realized, for when confronted with a major U.S. army under the command of General Anthony Wayne, they received no support from their former British allies. At the battle of Fallen Timbers (August 20, 1794), Wayne's forces crushed Indian resistance in the Northwest Territory, and the native peoples were compelled to sign the Treaty of Greenville, formally ceding to the U.S. government the land that became Ohio. In 1796, the last British soldiers departed for Canada.

Shrewd negotiations mixed with pure luck helped secure the nation's southwestern frontier. For complex reasons having to do with the state of European diplomacy, Spanish officials in 1795 encouraged the U.S. representative in Madrid to discuss the navigation of the Mississippi River. Before this initiative, the Spanish government not only had closed the river to American commerce but also had incited the Indians of the region to harass settlers from the United States (see Chapter 6). Relations between the two countries probably would have deteriorated further had the United States not signed Jay's Treaty. The Spanish assumed—quite erroneously—that Great Britain and the United States had formed an alliance to strip Spain of its North American possessions.

To avoid this imagined disaster, officials in Madrid offered the American envoy, Thomas Pinckney, extraordinary concessions: the opening of the Mississippi, the right to deposit goods in New Orleans without paying duties, a secure southern boundary on the 31st parallel (a line roughly parallel to the northern boundary of Florida and running west to the Mississippi), and a promise to stay out of Indian affairs. An amazed Pinckney signed the Treaty of San Lorenzo (also called Pinckney's Treaty) on October 27, 1795, and in March the Senate ratified the document without a single dissenting vote.

POPULAR POLITICAL CULTURE

More than any other event during Washington's administration, ratification of Jay's Treaty generated intense political strife. Even as members of Congress voted as Republicans or Federalists, they condemned the rising partisan spirit as a grave threat to the stability of the United States. Popular writers equated "party" with "faction" and "faction" with "conspiracy to overthrow legitimate authority." Contemporaries did not appreciate the beneficial role that parties could play by presenting alternative solutions to foreign and domestic problems. Organized opposition smacked of disloyalty and therefore had to be eliminated by any means—fair or foul.

AN INFORMED PUBLIC: NEWS AND POLITICS

Newspapers transformed the political culture of the United States. John Fenno established the *Gazette of the United States* (1789), a journal that supported Hamilton's political philosophy. The Republicans responded in October 1790 with Philip Freneau's influential *National Gazette*. While the format of the publications was similar to that of the colonial papers, their tone was quite different. These fiercely partisan journals presented rumor and opinion as fact. Jefferson, for example, was accused of cowardice; Hamilton, vilified as an adulterer. As

Conquest of the West

Withdrawal of the British, defeat of Native Americans, and negotiations with Spain secured the nation's frontiers.

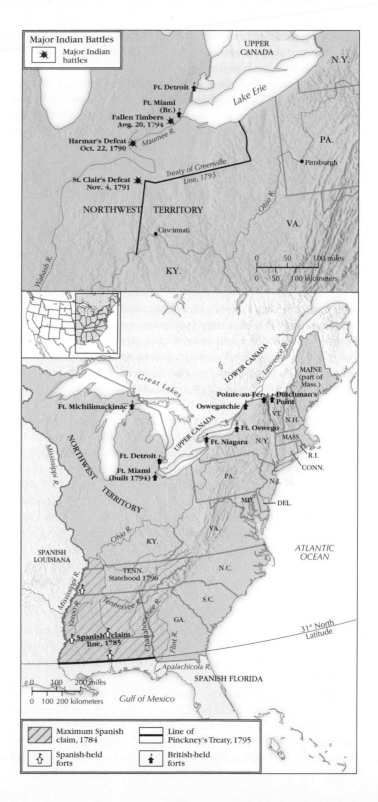

Major Indian Battles

✳ Major Indian battles

UPPER CANADA

N.Y.

Ft. Detroit

Ft. Miami (Br.)

Fallen Timbers Aug. 20, 1794

Lake Erie

Harmar's Defeat Oct. 22, 1790

Maumee R.

PA.

Pittsburgh

Treaty of Greenville Line, 1795

St. Clair's Defeat Nov. 4, 1791

Ohio R.

NORTHWEST TERRITORY

VA.

Cincinnati

0   50   100 miles
0 50   100 kilometers

KY.

UPPER CANADA

LOWER CANADA

St. Lawrence R.

MAINE (part of Mass.)

Pointe-au-Fer

Dutchman's Point

Oswegatchie

Great Lakes

Ft. Michilimackinac

VT.   N.H.

Ft. Oswego

UPPER CANADA

Ft. Niagara   N.Y.

MASS.

R.I.

Mississippi R.

NORTHWEST TERRITORY

Ft. Detroit

Ft. Miami (built 1794)

PA.

CONN.

N.J.

Ohio R.

MD.   DEL.

SPANISH LOUISIANA

KY.

VA.

ATLANTIC OCEAN

TENN. Statehood 1796

N.C.

Mississippi R.

Yazoo R.

Tennessee R.

Chattahoochee R.

S.C.

31° North Latitude

Spanish claim line, 1785

GA.

Flint R.

Apalachicola R.

SPANISH FLORIDA

0   100   200 miles
0 100 200 kilometers

Gulf of Mexico

▨ Maximum Spanish claim, 1784

⬆ Spanish-held forts

▬ Line of Pinckney's Treaty, 1795

⬆ British-held forts

party competition became more bitter, editors showed less restraint. One Republican paper suggested that George Washington had been a British agent during the Revolution.

This decade also witnessed the birth of political clubs. These "Democratic" or "Republican" associations, as they were called, first appeared in 1793 and were modeled on the political debating societies that sprang up in Paris during the early years of the French Revolution. Perhaps because of the French connection, Federalists assumed that the American clubs represented the interests of the Republican party. Their purpose seemed to be political indoctrination. A Democratic club in New York City asked each member to declare himself a "firm and steadfast friend of the EQUAL RIGHTS OF MAN." By 1794, at least twenty-four clubs were holding regular meetings.

WHISKEY REBELLION:
CHARGES OF REPUBLICAN CONSPIRACY

Political tensions became explosive in 1794. The Federalists convinced themselves that the Republicans were actually prepared to employ violence against the U.S. government. Although the charge was without foundation, it took on plausibility in the context of growing party strife.

The crisis developed when a group of farmers living in western Pennsylvania protested a federal excise tax on distilled whiskey that Congress had originally passed in 1791. This tax struck them as particularly unfair, since the excise threatened to put them out of business.

Largely because the Republican governor of Pennsylvania refused to suppress the angry farmers, Washington and other leading Federalists assumed that the insurrection represented a direct political challenge. The president called out fifteen thousand militiamen, and, accompanied by Hamilton, who came out of retirement, he marched against the rebels. The expedition was an embarrassing fiasco. The distillers disappeared, and predictably enough, no one living in the Pittsburgh region seemed to know where the troublemakers had gone. As peace returned to the frontier, Republicans gained much electoral support from voters the Federalists had alienated.

In the national political forum, however, the Whiskey Rebellion had just begun. Spokesmen for both parties offered sinister explanations for a seemingly innocuous affair. Washington blamed the Republican clubs for promoting civil unrest. He apparently believed that the opposition party had dispatched French agents to western Pennsylvania to undermine the authority of the federal government. In November 1794, Washington informed Congress that these "self-created societies"—in other words, the Republican political clubs—had inspired "a spirit inimical to all order."

The president's interpretation of this rural tax revolt was no less charitable than the conspiratorial explanation offered by the Republicans. Jefferson labeled the entire episode a Hamiltonian device to create an army for the purpose of intimidating Republicans. The response of both parties reveals a pervasive fear of some secret evil design to destroy the republic. The clubs and newspapers—as yet unfamiliar tools for mobilizing public opinion—fanned these anxieties, convincing many government officials that the First Amendment should not be interpreted as protecting political dissent.

WASHINGTON'S FAREWELL

In September 1796, Washington published his famed Farewell Address, formally declaring his intention to retire from the presidency. In the address, which was printed in newspapers throughout the country, Washington warned against all political factions. Written in large part by Hamilton, who drew on a draft prepared several years earlier by Madison, the address served narrowly partisan ends. The product of growing political strife, it sought to advance the Federalist cause in the forthcoming election. By waiting until September to announce his retirement, Washington denied the Republicans valuable time to organize an effective campaign.

Washington also spoke to foreign policy matters in the address. He counseled the United States to avoid making permanent alliances with distant nations that had no interest in promoting American security. This statement guided foreign relations for many years and became the credo of later American isolationists, who argued that the United States should steer clear of foreign entanglements.

THE ADAMS PRESIDENCY

The election of 1796 took place in an atmosphere of mutual distrust. Jefferson, soon to be the vice president, informed a friend that "an Anglican and aristocratic" party has sprung up. On their part, the Federalists were convinced their Republican opponents wanted to hand the government over to French radicals. By modern standards, the structures of both political parties were primitive. Leaders of national stature, such as Madison and Hamilton, wrote letters encouraging local gentlemen around the country to support a certain candidate, but no one attempted to canvass the voters in advance of the election.

During the campaign, the Federalists sowed the seeds of their eventual destruction. Party stalwarts agreed that John Adams should stand against the Republican candidate, Thomas Jefferson. Hamilton, however, could not leave well enough alone. From New York City, he schemed to deprive Adams of the presidency, fearing that an independent-minded Adams would be difficult to manipulate. He was correct.

Hamilton exploited an awkward feature of the electoral college. In accordance with the Constitution, each elector cast two ballots, and the person who gained the most votes became president. The runner-up, regardless of party affiliation, served as vice president. Ordinarily the Federalist electors would have cast one vote for Adams and one for Thomas Pinckney, the hero of the negotiations with Spain and the party's choice for vice president. Everyone hoped, of course, there would be no tie. Hamilton secretly urged southern Federalists to support only Pinckney, even if that meant throwing away an elector's second vote. If

THE ELECTION OF 1796

CANDIDATE	PARTY	ELECTORAL VOTE
J. Adams	Federalist	71
Jefferson	Republican	68
T. Pinckney	Federalist	59
Burr	Republican	30

everything had gone according to plan, Pinckney would have received more votes than Adams, but when New Englanders loyal to Adams heard of Hamilton's maneuvering, they dropped Pinckney. When the votes were counted, Adams had 71, Jefferson 68, and Pinckney 59. Hamilton's treachery heightened tensions within the Federalist party.

Adams assumed the presidency under intolerable conditions. He found himself saddled with the members of Washington's old cabinet, a group of second-raters who regularly consulted with Hamilton behind Adams's back. The two most offensive were Timothy Pickering, secretary of state, and James McHenry, secretary of war. But to have dismissed them summarily would have called Washington's judgment into question, and Adams was not prepared to take that risk publicly.

Adams also had to work with a Republican vice president. Adams hoped that he and Jefferson could cooperate as they had during the Revolution—they had served together on the committee that drafted the Declaration of Independence—but partisan pressures soon overwhelmed the president's good intentions.

THE XYZ AFFAIR AND DOMESTIC POLITICS

Foreign affairs immediately occupied Adams's full attention. The French government regarded Jay's Treaty as an affront. By allowing Great Britain to define the conditions for neutrality, the United States had in effect sided with that nation against the interests of France.

Relations between the two countries steadily deteriorated. The French refused to receive Charles Cotesworth Pinckney, the U.S. representative in Paris. Pierre Adet, the French minister in Philadelphia, openly tried to influence the 1796 election in favor of the Republicans. His meddling in domestic politics not only embarrassed Jefferson, but also offended the American people. In 1797, French privateers began seizing American ships. Since neither the United States nor France officially declared war, the hostilities came to be known as the Quasi-War.

The High Federalists—as members of Hamilton's wing of the party were called—counseled the president to prepare for all-out war, hoping that war would purge the United States of French influence. Adams was not persuaded to escalate the conflict. He dispatched a special commission in a final attempt to remove the sources of antagonism. This famous negotiating team consisted of Charles Pinckney, John Marshall, and Elbridge Gerry. They were instructed to obtain compensation for the ships seized by French privateers as well as release from the treaties of 1778. Federalists still worried that this old agreement might oblige the United States to defend French colonies in the Caribbean against

British attack, something they were extremely reluctant to do. In exchange, the commission offered France the same commercial privileges granted to Great Britain in Jay's Treaty. While the diplomats negotiated for peace, Adams talked of strengthening American defenses, rhetoric that pleased the militant members of his own party.

The commission was shocked by the outrageous treatment it received in France. The commission reported that the French representative would not open negotiations without a bribe of $250,000. In addition, the French government expected a "loan" of millions of dollars. The Americans refused to play this insulting game. When they arrived home, Marshall offered a much-quoted toast: "Millions for defense, but not one cent for tribute."

Diplomatic humiliation set off a domestic political explosion. When Adams presented the commission's official correspondence before Congress—the names of the French agents were labeled X, Y, and Z—the Federalists burst out with a war cry. At last, they would be able to even old scores with the Republicans. In April 1798, a Federalist newspaper in New York City announced ominously that any American who refused to censure France "must have a soul black enough to be *fit for treasons, strategems,* and *spoils.*" Rumors of conspiracy—termed the XYZ Affair—spread throughout the country. Personal friendships between Republicans and Federalists were shattered.

CRUSHING DISSENT IN THE NAME OF NATIONAL SECURITY

In the spring of 1798, High Federalists assumed that it was just a matter of time until Adams asked Congress for a formal declaration of war. In the meantime, they pushed for a general rearmament, new fighting ships, additional harbor fortifications, and most important, a greatly expanded U.S. Army. About the need for land forces, Adams remained understandably skeptical. He saw no likelihood of French invasion.

The army the High Federalists wanted was intended not to thwart French aggression but to stifle internal opposition. Indeed, militant Federalists used the XYZ Affair as the occasion to institute what Jefferson termed the "reign of witches." The threat to the Republicans was not simply a figment of Jefferson's overwrought imagination. When Theodore Sedgwick, a Federalist senator from Massachusetts, first learned of the commission's failure, he observed in words that captured the High Federalists' vindictiveness, "It will afford a glorious opportunity to destroy faction."

During the summer of 1798, a provisional army gradually came into existence. George Washington agreed to lead the troops, but he would do so only on condition that Adams appoint Hamilton as second in command. This demand placed the president in a terrible dilemma. Several revolutionary veterans— Henry Knox, for example—outranked Hamilton. Moreover, the former secretary of the treasury had consistently undermined Adams's authority, and to give Hamilton a position of real power in the government seemed awkward at best. When Washington insisted, however, Adams was forced to support his political enemy. Hamilton threw himself into the task of recruiting and supplying the troops. He and Secretary of War McHenry made certain that in this political army, only loyal Federalists received commissions.

Hamilton should not have treated Adams with such open contempt. After all, the Massachusetts statesman was still the president, and without presidential cooperation, Hamilton could not fulfill his grand military ambitions. Whenever pressing questions concerning the army arose, Adams was nowhere to be found. He let commissions lie on his desk unsigned; he took overlong vacations to New England. Adams further infuriated the High Federalists by refusing to ask Congress for a formal declaration of war. When they pressed him, Adams threatened to resign, making Jefferson president. As the weeks passed, the American people increasingly regarded the idle army as an expensive extravagance.

SACRIFICING RIGHTS FOR POLITICAL GOALS: THE ALIEN AND SEDITION ACTS

The Federalists did not rely solely on the army to crush political dissent. During the summer of 1798, the party's majority in Congress passed a group of bills known collectively as the Alien and Sedition Acts. This legislation authorized the use of federal courts and the powers of the presidency to silence the Republicans. The acts were born of fear and vindictiveness, and in their efforts to punish the followers of Jefferson, the Federalists created the nation's first major crisis over civil liberties.

Congress drew up three separate Alien Acts. The first, the Alien Enemies Law, vested the president with extraordinary wartime powers. On his own authority, he could detain or deport citizens of nations with which the United States was at war and who behaved in a suspicious manner. Since Adams refused to ask for a declaration of war, this legislation never went into effect. A second act, the Alien Law, empowered the president to expel any foreigner from the United States simply by executive decree. Congress limited the acts to two years, and Adams did not attempt to enforce them. The third act, the Naturalization Law, was the most flagrantly political of the group. The act established a fourteen-year probationary period before foreigners could apply for U.S. citizenship. Federalists recognized that recent immigrants, especially the Irish, tended to vote Republican. The Naturalization Law, therefore, was designed to keep "hordes of wild Irishmen" away from the polls for as long as possible.

The Sedition Law struck at the heart of free political exchange. It defined criticism of the U.S. government as criminal libel; citizens found guilty by a jury were subject to fines and imprisonment. Congress entrusted enforcement of the act to the federal courts. Republicans were justly worried that the Sedition Law undermined rights guaranteed by the First Amendment. When they protested, however, the High Federalists dismissed their complaints. The Constitution, they declared, did not condone "the most groundless and malignant lies, striking at the safety and existence of the nation."

Americans living in widely scattered regions of the country soon witnessed political repression firsthand. District courts staffed by Federalist appointees indicted seventeen people for criticizing the government. The most celebrated trial occurred in Vermont. A Republican congressman, Matthew Lyon, who was running for reelection, publicly accused the Adams administration of mishandling the Quasi-War. This was not the first time this Irish immigrant had angered the Federalists. On the floor of the House of Representatives, Lyon once spit in the eye of a Federalist congressman from Connecticut. Lyon was immediately labeled the "Spitting Lyon." A Federalist court convicted him of libel. Lyon had the last laugh. While he sat in jail, his constituents reelected him to Congress.

The federal courts had become political tools. While the fumbling efforts at enforcement of the Sedition Law did not silence opposition—indeed, they sparked even greater criticism—the actions of the administration persuaded Republicans that the survival of free government was at stake. "There is no event," Jefferson warned, ". . . however atrocious, which may not be expected."

KENTUCKY AND VIRGINIA RESOLUTIONS

By the fall of 1798, Jefferson and Madison were convinced that the Federalists wanted to create a police state. The Sedition Law threatened the free communication of ideas that Madison "deemed the only effectual guardian of every other right." Some extreme Republicans recommended secession from the Union; others advocated armed resistance. But Jefferson counseled against such extreme strategies. "This is not the kind of opposition the American people will permit," he reminded his desperate supporters. The last best hope for American freedom lay in the state legislatures.

As the crisis deepened, Jefferson and Madison drafted separate protests known as the Virginia and Kentucky Resolutions. In the Kentucky Resolutions (November 1798), Jefferson described the federal union as a compact. The states transferred certain explicit powers to the national government, but, in his opinion, they retained full authority over all matters not specifically mentioned in the Constitution. Jefferson rejected Hamilton's broad interpretation of the "general welfare" clause. "Every state," Jefferson argued, "has a natural right in cases not within the compact . . . to nullify of their own authority all assumptions of power by others within their limits." Carried to an extreme, this logic could have led to the breakup of the federal government, and in 1798, Kentucky legislators were not prepared to take such a radical stance. While they diluted Jefferson's prose, they fully accepted his belief that the Alien and Sedition Acts were unconstitutional and ought to be repealed.

When Madison drafted the Virginia Resolutions in December, he took a stand more temperate than Jefferson's. Madison urged the states to defend the rights of the American people, but he resisted the notion that a single state legislature could or should overthrow federal law.

The Virginia and Kentucky Resolutions were not intended as statements of abstract principles and most certainly not as a justification for southern secession. They were pure political party propaganda. Jefferson and Madison dramatically reminded American voters during a period of severe domestic tension that the Republicans offered a clear alternative to Federalist rule. No other state legislatures passed the Resolutions.

PRESIDENTIAL COURAGE

In February 1799, President Adams belatedly declared his independence from the Hamiltonian wing of the Federalist party. Throughout the confrontation with France, Adams had shown little enthusiasm for war. A French foreign minister now told American agents that the bribery episode had been an unfortunate misunderstanding. The High Federalists ridiculed this report. But Adams, still brooding over Hamilton's appointment to the army, decided to throw his own waning prestige behind peace. In February, he suddenly asked the Senate to confirm William Vans Murray as U.S. representative to France.

The move caught the High Federalists totally by surprise. They sputtered with outrage. "It is solely the President's act," Pickering cried, "and we were all thunderstruck when we heard of it." Adams was just warming to the task. In May, he fired Pickering and McHenry.

When the new negotiators—Oliver Ellsworth and William Davie joined Murray—finally arrived in France in November 1799, they discovered that yet another group had come to power there. This government, headed by Napoleon Bonaparte, cooperated in drawing up an agreement known as the Convention of Mortefontaine. The French refused to compensate the Americans for vessels taken during the Quasi-War, but they did declare the treaties of 1778 null and void. Moreover, the convention removed annoying French restrictions on U.S. commerce. Not only had Adams avoided war, but he had also created an atmosphere of mutual trust that paved the way for the purchase of the Louisiana Territory. In the short run, however, political courage cost Adams reelection.

THE PEACEFUL REVOLUTION: THE ELECTION OF 1800

On the eve of the election of 1800, the Federalists were fatally divided. Adams enjoyed wide popularity among the Federalist rank and file, especially in New England, but party leaders such as Hamilton vowed to punish the president for his betrayal of their militant policies. Hamilton even composed a scathing pamphlet titled *Letter Concerning the Public Conduct and Character of John Adams*, an essay that questioned Adams's ability to hold high office.

Once again the former secretary of the treasury attempted to rig the voting in the electoral college so that the party's vice presidential candidate, Charles Cotesworth Pinckney, would receive more ballots than Adams and America would be saved from "the fangs of Jefferson." As in 1796, the conspiracy backfired. The Republicans gained 73 votes while the Federalists trailed with 65.

To everyone's surprise, however, the election was not resolved in the electoral college. When the ballots were counted, Jefferson and his running mate, Aaron Burr, had tied. This accident—a Republican elector should have thrown away his second vote—sent the selection of the next president to the House of Representatives, a lame-duck body still controlled by members of the Federalist party.

As the House began its work on February 27, 1801, excitement ran high. Each state delegation cast a single vote, with nine votes needed for election. On the first ballot, Jefferson received the support of eight states, Burr six, and two states divided evenly. People predicted a quick victory for Jefferson, but after dozens of ballots, the House had still not selected a president.

THE ELECTION OF 1800

CANDIDATE	PARTY	ELECTORAL VOTE
Jefferson	Republican	73
Burr	Republican	73
J. Adams	Federalist	65
C. Pinckney	Federalist	64

The logjam finally broke when leading Federalists decided that Jefferson, whatever his faults, would make a more responsible president than would the shifty Burr. On the thirty-sixth ballot, Representative James A. Bayard of Delaware announced he no longer supported Burr, giving Jefferson the presidency, ten states to four.

The Twelfth Amendment, ratified in 1804, saved the American people from repeating this potentially dangerous turn of events. Henceforth, the electoral college cast separate ballots for president and vice president.

During the final days of his presidency, Adams appointed as many Federalists as possible to the federal bench. Jefferson protested the hasty manner in which these "midnight judges" were selected. One of them, John Marshall, became chief justice of the United States, a post he held with distinction for thirty-four years.

Jefferson attempted to quiet partisan fears. "We are all republicans; we are all federalists," the new president declared. By this statement, he did not mean to suggest that party differences no longer mattered. Rather, whatever the politicians might say, the people shared a deep commitment to a federal union based on republican ideals set forth during the American Revolution. Indeed, the president interpreted the election of 1800 as a revolutionary episode, as the fulfillment of the principles of 1776.

The Federalists were thoroughly dispirited by the entire experience. In the end, it had not been Hamilton's foolish electoral schemes that destroyed the party's chances in 1800. Rather, the Federalists had lost touch with a majority of the American people. In office, Adams and Hamilton—whatever their own differences may have been—betrayed their doubts about popular sovereignty too often, and when it came time to marshal broad support, to mobilize public opinion in favor of the party of wealth and privilege, few responded.

DANGER OF POLITICAL EXTREMISM

From a broader historical perspective, the election of 1800 seems noteworthy for what did not occur. There were no riots in the streets, no attempted coup by military officers, no secession from the Union, nothing except the peaceful transfer of government from the leaders of one political party to those of the opposition. Americans had weathered the Alien and Sedition Acts, the meddling by predatory foreign powers in domestic affairs, the shrilly partisan rhetoric of hack journalists, and now, at the start of a new century, they were impressed with their own achievement. But as they well understood—indeed, as modern Americans must constantly relearn—extremism in the name of partisan political truth can easily unravel the delicate fabric of representative democracy and leave the republic at the mercy of those who would employ fear to advance a narrow party agenda.

CHRONOLOGY

1787   Constitution of the United States signed (September)

1789   George Washington inaugurated (April)

          Louis XVI of France calls meeting of the Estates General (May)

1790   Congress approves Hamilton's plan for funding and assumption (July)

1791   Bank of the United States is chartered (February)

          Hamilton's *Report on Manufactures* rejected by Congress (December)

1793   France's revolutionary government announces a "war of all people against all kings" (February)

          Genêt affair strains relations with France (April)

          Washington issues Proclamation of Neutrality (April)

          Spread of "Democratic" clubs alarms Federalists

          Jefferson resigns as secretary of state (December)

1794   Whiskey Rebellion put down by U.S. Army (July–November)

          General Anthony Wayne defeats Indians at battle of Fallen Timbers (August)

1795   Hamilton resigns as secretary of the treasury (January)

          Jay's Treaty divides the nation (June)

          Pinckney's Treaty with Spain is a welcome surprise (October)

1796   Washington publishes Farewell Address (September)

          John Adams elected president (December)

1797   XYZ Affair poisons U.S. relations with France (October)

1798–1800   Quasi-War with France

1798   Congress passes the Alien and Sedition Acts (June and July)

          Provisional army is formed

          Virginia and Kentucky Resolutions protest the Alien and Sedition Acts (November and December)

1799   George Washington dies (December)

1800   Convention of Mortefontaine is signed with France, ending Quasi-War (September)

1801   House of Representatives elects Thomas Jefferson president (February)

8

REPUBLICAN ASCENDANCY
The Jeffersonian Vision

British visitors often expressed contempt for Jeffersonian society. Wherever they traveled in the young republic, they met ill-mannered people who championed liberty and equality. Charles William Janson, an Englishman who lived in the United States for thirteen years, recounted an exchange that had occurred at the home of an American acquaintance. "On knocking at the door," he reported, "it was opened by a servant maid, whom I had never before seen." The woman's behavior astonished Janson. "The following is the dialogue, word for word, which took place on this occasion:—'Is your master at home?'—'I have no master.'—'Don't you live here?'—'I *stay* here.'—'And who are you then?'—'Why, I am Mr.———'s *help*. I'd have you know, *man*, that I am no *sarvant* [sic]; none but *negers* [sic] are *sarvants*.'"

Standing on his friend's doorstep, Janson encountered the authentic voice of Jeffersonian republicanism—self-confident, assertive, blatantly racist, and having no intention of being relegated to low social status. The maid who answered the door believed she was her employer's equal, perhaps not in wealth but surely in character.

American society fostered such ambition. In the early nineteenth century, thousands of settlers poured across the Appalachian Mountains or moved to cities in search of opportunity. Thomas Jefferson and individuals who stood for public office under the banner of the Republican party claimed to speak for these people.

The limits of the Jeffersonian vision were obvious even to contemporaries. The people who argued most eloquently for equal opportunity often owned slaves. As early as the 1770s, the famed English essayist Samuel Johnson had chided Americans for their hypocrisy. "How is it," he asked the indignant rebels, "that we hear the loudest yelps for liberty from the drivers of Negroes?" Little had changed since the Revolution. African Americans, who represented one-fifth of the population of the United States, were excluded from the new opportunities opening up in the cities and the West.

It is not surprising that in this highly charged racial climate leaders of the Federalist party accused the Republicans, especially those who lived in the South, of disingenuousness, and in 1804, one Massachusetts Federalist sarcastically defined "Jeffersonian" as "an Indian word, signifying '*a great tobacco planter, who had herds of black slaves.*'" The race issue was always just beneath the surface of political maneuvering.

In other areas, the Jeffersonians did not fulfill even their own high expectations. As members of an opposition party during the presidency of John Adams, they insisted on a strict interpretation of the Constitution, peaceful foreign relations, and a reduction of the role of the federal government in the lives of the average citizens. But following the election of 1800, Jefferson and his supporters discovered that unanticipated pressures, foreign and domestic, forced them to moderate these goals. Before he retired from public office, Jefferson interpreted the Constitution in a way that permitted the government to purchase the Louisiana Territory when the opportunity arose; he regulated the national economy with a rigor that would have surprised Alexander Hamilton; and he led the country to the brink of war. Some Americans praised the president's pragmatism; others felt betrayed. For a man who played a leading role in the revolt against George III, it must have been shocking in 1807 to find himself labeled a "despot" in a popular New England newspaper.

REGIONAL IDENTITIES IN A NEW REPUBLIC

During the early decades of the nineteenth century, the population of the United States experienced substantial growth. The 1810 census counted 7,240,000 Americans, a jump of almost 2 million in just ten years. Of this total, approximately 20 percent were black slaves, the majority of whom lived in the South. The large population increase in the nation was the result primarily of natural reproduction, since during Jefferson's presidency few immigrants moved to the New World. The largest single group in this society was children under the age of sixteen, boys and girls who were born after Washington's election and who defined their own futures at a time when the nation's boundaries were rapidly expanding.

Americans were also forming strong regional identifications. In commerce and politics, they perceived themselves as representatives of distinct subcultures—as Southerners, New Englanders, or Westerners. No doubt, the broadening geographic horizons reflected improved transportation links that enabled people to travel more easily within the various sections. But the growing regional mentality was also the product of defensiveness. While local writers celebrated New England's cultural distinctiveness, for example, they were clearly uneasy about the region's rejection of the democratic values that were sweeping the rest of the nation. Moreover, during this period people living south of the Potomac River began describing themselves as Southerners, not as citizens of the Chesapeake or the Carolinas as they had done in colonial times.

This shifting focus of attention resulted not only from an awareness of shared economic interests but also from a sensitivity to outside attacks on slavery. Several

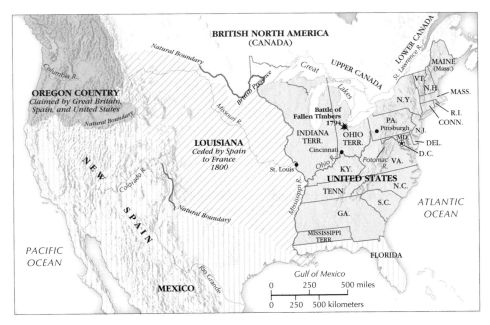

North America in 1800
In the 1790s, diplomatic agreements with Britain and Spain and defeat of the Native Americans at the battle of Fallen Timbers opened the way to U.S. settlement of the land beyond the Appalachian Mountains.

times during the first fifteen years of the nineteenth century, conspirators actually advocated secession, and though the schemes failed, they revealed the powerful sectional loyalties that threatened national unity.

WESTWARD THE COURSE OF EMPIRE

The West dominated popular imagination. Before the end of the American Revolution, only Indian traders and a few hardy settlers had ventured across the Appalachians. After 1790, however, a flood of people rushed west to stake out farms. Many settlers followed the so-called northern route across Pennsylvania or New York into the old Northwest Territory. Pittsburgh and Cincinnati, both strategically located on the Ohio River, became important commercial ports. In 1803, Ohio joined the Union, and territorial governments were formed in Indiana (1800), Louisiana (1805), Michigan (1805), Illinois (1809), and Missouri (1812). Southerners poured into the new states of Kentucky (1792) and Tennessee (1796). Wherever they located, Westerners depended on water transportation. Because of the extraordinarily high cost of hauling goods overland, riverboats provided the only economical means of carrying agricultural products to distant markets. The Mississippi River was the crucial commercial link for the entire region, and Westerners did not feel secure so long as New Orleans, the southern gate to the Mississippi, remained under Spanish control.

Families that moved west attempted to transplant familiar eastern customs to the frontier. In some areas such as the Western Reserve, a narrow strip of land along Lake Erie in northern Ohio, the influence of New England remained strong. In general, however, a creative mixing of peoples of different backgrounds in a strange environment generated distinctive folkways. Westerners developed their own heroes, such as Mike Fink, the legendary keelboatman of the Mississippi River; Daniel Boone, the famed trapper and Indian fighter; and the eye-gouging "alligatormen" of Kentucky and Tennessee.

NATIVE AMERICAN RESISTANCE

At the beginning of the nineteenth century, a substantial number of Native Americans lived in the greater Ohio Valley; the land belonged to them. These Indians, many dependent on trade with the white people and ravaged by disease, lacked unity. Small groups of Native Americans, allegedly representing the interests of an entire tribe, sold off huge pieces of land, often for whiskey and trinkets.

Such fraudulent transactions disgusted the Shawnee leaders Tenskwatawa (known as the Prophet) and his brother Tecumseh. Tecumseh rejected classification as a Shawnee and may have been the first native leader to identify himself as "Indian." These men attempted to revitalize native cultures, and against overwhelming odds, they briefly persuaded Native Americans living in the Indiana Territory to avoid contact with whites, to resist alcohol, and, most important, to hold on to their land. White intruders saw Tecumseh as a threat to

Tenskwatawa, known as the Prophet, provided spiritual leadership for the union of the native peoples he and his brother Tecumseh organized to resist white encroachment on Native American lands.

progress, and during the War of 1812, they shattered the Indians' dream of cultural renaissance. The populous Creek nation, located in the modern states of Alabama and Mississippi, also resisted the settlers' advance, but its warriors were crushed by Andrew Jackson's Tennessee militia at the battle of Horseshoe Bend (March 1814).

Jeffersonians disclaimed any intention to destroy the Indians. The president talked of creating a vast reservation beyond the Mississippi River, just as the British had talked before the Revolution of a sanctuary beyond the Appalachian Mountains. He sent federal agents to "civilize" the Indians, to transform them into yeoman farmers. But even the most enlightened white thinkers of the day did not believe the Indians possessed cultures worth preserving.

COMMERCIAL LIFE IN THE CITIES

Before 1820, the prosperity of the United States depended on its agriculture and trade. Jeffersonian America was by no stretch of the imagination an industrial economy. The overwhelming majority of the population—84 percent in 1810—was directly involved in agriculture. Southerners concentrated on the staple crops of tobacco, rice, and cotton, which they sold on the European market. In the North, people generally produced livestock and cereal crops. Regardless of location, however, the nation's farmers followed a backbreaking work routine that did not differ substantially from that of their parents and grandparents. Except for the cotton gin, important chemical and mechanical inventions did not appear in the fields for another generation.

The merchant marine represented an equally important element in America's economy. At the turn of the century, ships flying the Stars and Stripes transported a large share of the world's trade. Merchants in Boston, New York, and Philadelphia received handsome profits from such commerce. Their vessels provided essential links between European countries and their Caribbean colonies. France, for example, relied heavily on American transport for its sugar. These lucrative transactions, coupled with the export of domestic staples, especially cotton, generated impressive fortunes. Between 1793 and 1807, the year Jefferson imposed the embargo against Britain and France, American commerce enjoyed a more than 300 percent increase in the value of exports and in net earnings. The boom did not last. The success of the "carrying trade" depended in large measure on friendly relations between the United States and the major European powers. When England and France began seizing American ships—as they both did after 1805—national prosperity suffered.

The cities of Jeffersonian America functioned chiefly as depots for international trade. Only about 7 percent of the nation's population lived in urban centers, and most of these people owed their livelihoods either directly or indirectly to the carrying trade. Recent studies revealed that several major port cities of the early republic—New York, Philadelphia, and Baltimore, for example—had some of the highest population densities ever recorded in this country's history. In 1800, more than 40,000 New Yorkers crowded into an area of only 1.5 square miles; in Philadelphia, some 46,000 people were packed into less than one square mile. As is common today, many city dwellers rented living space, and since the demand for housing exceeded the supply, the rents were high.

American cities exercised only a marginal influence on the nation's vast hinterland. Because of the high cost of land transportation, urban merchants seldom purchased goods for export—flour, for example—from a distance of more than 150 miles. The separation between rural and urban Americans was far more pronounced during Jefferson's presidency than it was after the development of canals and railroads a few decades later.

The booming carrying trade may actually have retarded the industrialization of the United States. The lure of large profits drew investment capital—a scarce resource in a developing society—into commerce. By contrast, manufacturing seemed too risky. To be sure, Samuel Slater, an English-born designer of textile machinery, established several cotton-spinning mills in New England, but until the 1820s these plants employed only a small number of workers. Another farsighted inventor, Robert Fulton, sailed the first American steamship up the Hudson River in 1807. In time, this marvelous innovation opened new markets for domestic manufacturers, especially in the West. At the end of the War of 1812, however, few people anticipated how greatly power generated by fossil fuel would transform the character of the American economy.

JEFFERSON AS PRESIDENT

The District of Columbia seemed an appropriate capital for a Republican president. At the time of Jefferson's first inauguration, Washington was still an isolated rural village, a far cry from the crowded centers of Philadelphia and New York. Jefferson fit comfortably into Washington society. He despised formal ceremony and sometimes shocked foreign dignitaries by meeting them in his slippers or a threadbare jacket.

The president was a poor public speaker. He wisely refused to deliver annual addresses before Congress. In personal conversation, however, Jefferson exuded considerable charm. His dinner parties were major intellectual as well as social events, and in this forum, the president regaled politicians with his knowledge of literature, philosophy, and science.

Notwithstanding his commitment to the life of the mind, Jefferson was a politician to the core. He ran for the presidency to achieve specific goals: the reduction of the size and cost of federal government, the repeal of obnoxious Federalist legislation such as the Alien Acts, and the maintenance of international peace. To accomplish his program, Jefferson realized he needed the full cooperation of congressional Republicans, some of whom were stubbornly independent men. Over such figures Jefferson exercised political mastery. He established close ties with the leaders of both houses of Congress, and while he seldom announced his plans in public, he made certain his legislative lieutenants knew exactly what he desired. Contemporaries who described Jefferson as a weak president—and some Federalists did just that—did not read the scores of memoranda he sent to political friends or witness the informal meetings he held at the executive mansion with important Republicans. In two terms as president, Jefferson never had to veto a single act of Congress.

Jefferson carefully selected the members of his cabinet. During Washington's administration, he had witnessed—even provoked—severe infighting; as president, he nominated only those who enthusiastically supported his programs. James Madison, the leading figure at the Constitutional Convention, became secretary of state. For the Treasury, Jefferson chose Albert Gallatin, a Swiss-born financier who understood the complexities of the federal budget.

JEFFERSONIAN REFORMS

A top priority of the new government was reducing the national debt. Jefferson and Gallatin regarded a large federal deficit as dangerous to the health of republican institutions. In fact, both men associated debt with Alexander Hamilton's Federalist financial programs, measures they considered harmful to republicanism.

Jefferson also wanted to diminish the activities of the federal government. He urged Congress to repeal all direct taxes, including the tax that had sparked the Whiskey Rebellion in 1794. Secretary Gallatin linked federal income to the carrying trade. He calculated that the entire cost of national government could be borne by customs receipts. As long as commerce flourished, revenues provided sufficient sums. When international war closed foreign markets, however, the flow of funds dried up.

To help pay the debt inherited from the Adams administration, Jefferson ordered substantial cuts in the national budget. The president closed several American embassies in Europe. He also slashed military spending. In his first term, Jefferson reduced the size of the U.S. Army by 50 percent. This decision left only three thousand soldiers to guard the entire frontier. In addition, he retired a majority of the navy's warships.

More than budgetary considerations prompted Jefferson's military reductions. He was deeply suspicious of standing armies. In the event of foreign attack, he reasoned, local militias would rise in defense of the republic. No doubt, his experiences during the Revolution influenced his thinking on military affairs, for in 1776, an aroused populace had taken up arms against the British. To ensure that the citizen soldiers would receive professional leadership in battle, Jefferson created the Army Corps of Engineers and the military academy at West Point in 1802.

Political patronage burdened the new president. Loyal Republicans throughout the United States had worked hard for Jefferson's victory, and as soon as he took office, they stormed the executive mansion seeking federal employment. While the president controlled several hundred jobs, he refused to dismiss all the Federalists. To be sure, he acted quickly to remove the so-called midnight appointees, highly partisan selections that Adams had made after learning of Jefferson's election. But to transform federal hiring into an undisciplined spoils system, especially at the highest levels of the federal bureaucracy, seemed to Jefferson shortsighted. Moderate Federalists might be converted to the Republican party, and, in any case, there was a good chance they possessed the expertise needed to run the government. At the end of his first term, half of the people holding office were appointees of Washington and Adams.

Jefferson's political moderation helped hasten the demise of the Federalist party. This loose organization had nearly destroyed itself during the election of 1800, and following Adams's defeat, prominent Federalist spokesmen such as Fisher Ames and John Jay withdrew from national affairs. The mere prospect of flattering the common people was odious enough to drive these Federalists into political retirement.

After 1804, a group of younger Federalists belatedly attempted to pump life into the dying party. They experimented with popular election techniques. In some states, they tightened party organization, held nominating conventions, and campaigned energetically for office. These were essential reforms, but with the exception of a brief Federalist revival in the Northeast between 1807 and 1814, the results of these activities were disappointing. Even the younger Federalists thought it demeaning to appeal for votes. Diehards such as Timothy Pickering promoted wild secessionist schemes in New England, while the most promising moderates—John Quincy Adams, for example—joined the Republicans.

THE LOUISIANA PURCHASE

When Jefferson first took office, he was confident that Louisiana as well as Florida would eventually become part of the United States. After all, Spain owned the territory, and Jefferson assumed he could persuade the rulers of that nation to sell their colonies. If that peaceful strategy failed, the president was prepared to threaten forcible occupation.

In May 1801, however, prospects for the easy acquisition of Louisiana suddenly darkened. Jefferson learned that Spain had secretly transferred title to the entire region to France. To make matters worse, the French leader Napoleon seemed intent on reestablishing an empire in North America. Even as Jefferson sought additional information concerning the details of the transfer, Napoleon was dispatching a large army to put down a rebellion in France's sugar-rich Caribbean colony, Haiti. From that island stronghold in the West Indies, French troops could occupy New Orleans and close the Mississippi River to American trade.

A sense of crisis enveloped Washington. Some congressmen urged Jefferson to prepare for war against France. Tensions increased when the Spanish officials who still governed New Orleans announced the closing of that port to American commerce (October 1802). Jefferson and his advisers assumed that the Spanish had acted on orders from France, but despite this serious provocation, the president preferred negotiations to war. In January 1803, he asked James Monroe, a loyal Republican from Virginia, to join the American minister, Robert Livingston, in Paris. The president instructed the two men to explore the possibility of purchasing the city of New Orleans. Lest they underestimate the importance of their diplomatic mission, Jefferson reminded them, "There is on the globe one single spot, the possessor of which is our natural and habitual enemy. It is New Orleans." If Livingston and Monroe failed, Jefferson realized he would

President Jefferson recognized the strategic location of New Orleans and determined to buy it from the French. By 1803, when this view was painted, New Orleans was already a thriving port and an important outlet for exports produced by new communities in the Ohio and Mississippi valleys.

be forced to turn to Great Britain for military assistance. Dependence on that country seemed repellent, but he recognized that as soon as French troops moved into Louisiana, "we must marry ourselves to the British fleet and nation."

By the time Monroe joined Livingston in France, Napoleon had lost interest in establishing an American empire. The army he sent to Haiti succumbed to tropical diseases. The diplomats from the United States knew nothing of these developments. They were taken by complete surprise, therefore, when they learned that Talleyrand, the French minister for foreign relations, had offered to sell the entire Louisiana Territory in April 1803. For only $15 million, the Americans doubled the size of the United States. In fact, Livingston and Monroe were not certain how much land they had actually purchased. When they asked Talleyrand whether the deal included Florida, he responded ambiguously, "You have made a noble bargain for yourselves, and I suppose you will make the most of it." Even at that moment, Livingston realized that the transaction would alter the course of American history. "From this day," he wrote, "the United States take their place among the powers of first rank."

Jefferson, of course, was immensely relieved. The nation had avoided war with France. Nevertheless, he worried that the purchase might be unconstitutional. The president pointed out that the Constitution did not specifically authorize the acquisition of vast new territories and the incorporation of thousands of foreign citizens. To escape this apparent legal dilemma, Jefferson proposed an amendment to the Constitution. Few persons, even his closest advisers, shared

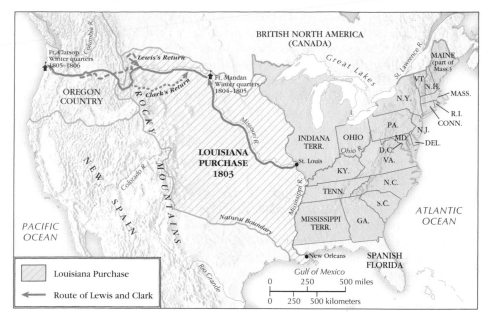

The Louisiana Purchase and the Route of Lewis and Clark
Not until Lewis and Clark had explored the Far West did citizens of the United States realize just how much territory Jefferson had acquired through the Louisiana Purchase.

the president's scruples. Events in France soon forced Jefferson to adopt a more pragmatic course. When he heard that Napoleon had become impatient for his money, Jefferson rushed the papers to a Senate eager to ratify the agreement, and nothing more was said about the Constitution.

The purchase raised other difficult problems. The area that eventually became the state of Louisiana (1812) contained many people of French and Spanish background who possessed no familiarity with representative institutions. Their laws had been autocratic, their local government corrupt. To allow such persons to elect a representative assembly struck the president as dangerous. He did not even know whether the population of Louisiana would remain loyal to the United States. Jefferson, therefore, recommended to Congress a transitional government consisting entirely of appointed officials. In March 1804, the Louisiana Government Bill narrowly passed the House of Representatives. Members of the president's own party attacked the plan since it imposed taxes on the citizens of Louisiana without their consent. Most troubling perhaps was the fact that the legislation ran counter to Jefferson's well-known republican principles.

THE LEWIS AND CLARK EXPEDITION

In the midst of the Louisiana controversy, Jefferson dispatched a secret message to Congress requesting funds for the exploration of the Far West (January 1803). How closely this decision was connected to the Paris negotiations is not clear. Whatever the case may have been, the president asked his private secretary,

Meriwether Lewis, to discover whether the Missouri River "may offer the most direct & practicable water communication across this continent for the purposes of commerce." The president also regarded the expedition as an opportunity to collect data about flora and fauna. He personally instructed Lewis in the latest techniques of scientific observation. While preparing for this adventure, Lewis's second in command, William Clark, assumed such a prominent role that the effort became known as the Lewis and Clark Expedition. The effort owed much of its success to a young Shoshoni woman known as Sacagawea. She served as a translator and helped persuade suspicious Native Americans that the explorers meant no harm. As Clark explained, "A woman with a party of men is a token of peace."

The exploring party set out from St. Louis in May 1804, and after crossing the snow-covered Rocky Mountains, with their food supply running dangerously low, the Americans reached the Pacific Ocean in November 1805. The group returned safely the following September. The results of the expedition not only fulfilled Jefferson's scientific expectations but also reaffirmed his faith in the future economic prosperity of the United States.

CONFLICT WITH THE BARBARY STATES

During this period, Jefferson dealt with another problem. For several decades, the North African states of Tangier, Algiers, Tripoli, and Tunis—the Barbary States—had preyed on commercial shipping. Most European nations paid the pirates tribute, hoping thereby to protect merchants trading in the Mediterranean. In 1801, Jefferson decided the extortion had become intolerable and dispatched a small fleet to the Barbary Coast, where, according to one commander, the Americans intended to negotiate "through the mouth of a cannon." Tripoli put up stiff resistance, however, and in one mismanaged engagement it captured the U.S. frigate *Philadelphia*. Ransoming the crew cost Jefferson's government another $60,000. An American land assault across the Libyan desert provided inspiration for the words of the "Marines' Hymn"—"to the shores of Tripoli"—but no smashing victory.

Despite a generally unimpressive American military record, a vigorous naval blockade brought hostilities to a conclusion. In 1805, the president signed a treaty formally ending the Barbary War. One diplomat crowed, "It must be mortifying to some of the neighboring European powers to see that the Barbary States have been taught their first lessons of humiliation from the Western World."

Jefferson concluded his first term on a wave of popularity. He had maintained the peace, reduced taxes, and expanded the boundaries of the United States.

THE ELECTION OF 1804

CANDIDATE	PARTY	ELECTORAL VOTE
Jefferson	Republican	162
C. Pinckney	Federalist	14

Not surprisingly, he overwhelmed Charles Cotesworth Pinckney, his Federalist opponent in the presidential election of 1804.

JEFFERSON'S CRITICS

At the moment of Jefferson's greatest electoral victory, a perceptive person might have seen signs of serious division within the Republican party and within the country. The president's heavy-handed attempts to reform the federal courts stirred deep animosities. Republicans had begun sniping at other Republicans, and one leading member of the party, Aaron Burr, became involved in a bizarre plot to separate the West from the rest of the nation. Congressional debates over the future of the slave trade revealed the existence of powerful sectional loyalties.

ATTACK ON THE JUDGES

Jefferson's controversy with the federal bench commenced the moment he became president. The Federalists, realizing they would soon lose control over the executive branch, had passed the Judiciary Act of 1801. This bill created several circuit courts and sixteen new judgeships. Through his "midnight" appointments, Adams had quickly filled these positions with stalwarts of the Federalist party. Such blatantly partisan behavior angered Jefferson. Even more infuriating was Adams's appointment of John Marshall as the new chief justice. This shrewd, largely self-educated Virginian of Federalist background, whose training in the law consisted of a series of lectures he attended at the College of William and Mary in 1780, held his own against the new president.

In January 1802, Jefferson's congressional allies called for repeal of the Judiciary Act. In public debate, they studiously avoided the obvious political issue. The new circuit courts, they claimed, were needlessly expensive. The judges did not hear enough cases to warrant continuance. The Federalists mounted an able defense. The Constitution, they observed, provided for the removal of federal judges only when they were found guilty of high crimes and misdemeanors. By repealing the Judiciary Act, the legislative branch would in effect be dismissing judges without a trial, a clear violation of their constitutional rights. This argument made little impression on the Republican party. In March, the House, following the Senate, voted for repeal.

While Congress debated the Judiciary Act, another battle erupted. One of Adams's "midnight" appointees, William Marbury, complained that the new administration would not give him his commission for the office of justice of the peace for the District of Columbia. He sought redress before the Supreme Court, demanding that the federal justices compel James Madison, the secretary of state, to deliver the necessary papers. When they learned that Marshall had agreed to hear this case, the Republicans were furious. Apparently the chief justice wanted to provoke a confrontation with the executive branch.

Marshall was too clever to jeopardize the independence of the Supreme Court over such a relatively minor issue. In his celebrated *Marbury* v. *Madison* decision (February 1803), Marshall berated the secretary of state for withholding

Marbury's commission. Nevertheless, he concluded that the Supreme Court did not possess jurisdiction over such matters. Poor Marbury was out of luck. The Republicans proclaimed victory. In fact, they were so pleased with the outcome that they failed to examine the logic of Marshall's decision. He had ruled that part of the earlier act of Congress, the one on which Marbury based his appeal, was unconstitutional. This was the first time the Supreme Court asserted its right to judge the constitutionality of congressional acts, and while contemporaries did not fully appreciate the significance of Marshall's doctrine, *Marbury v. Madison* later served as an important precedent for judicial review of federal statutes.

Neither Marbury's defeat nor repeal of the Judiciary Act placated extreme Republicans. They insisted that federal judges should be made more responsive to the will of the people. One solution, short of electing federal judges, was impeachment. This clumsy device provided the legislature with a way of removing particularly offensive individuals. By the spring of 1803, Jefferson found an appealing target. In a Baltimore newspaper, the president stumbled on the transcript of a speech allegedly delivered before a federal grand jury. The words seemed almost treasonous. The person responsible was Samuel Chase, a justice of the Supreme Court, who had frequently attacked Republican policies. Jefferson leapt at the chance to remove Chase from office. In a matter of weeks, the Republican-controlled House of Representatives indicted Chase.

Even at this early stage of the impeachment, some members of Congress expressed uneasiness. The charges drawn up against the judge were purely political. There was no doubt that the judge's speech had been indiscreet. He had told the Baltimore jurors that "our late reformers"—in other words, the Republicans—threatened "peace and order, freedom and property." But while Chase lacked good judgment, his attack on the Jefferson administration hardly seemed criminal. It was clear that if the Senate convicted Chase, every member of the Supreme Court, including Marshall, might also be dismissed.

Chase's trial before the U.S. Senate was one of the most dramatic events in American legal history. Aaron Burr, the vice president, organized the proceedings. For reasons known only to himself, Burr redecorated the Senate chamber so that it looked more like the British House of Lords than the meeting place of a republican legislature. In this luxurious setting, Chase and his lawyers conducted a masterful defense. By contrast, John Randolph, the congressman who served as chief prosecutor, behaved in an erratic manner, betraying repeatedly his ignorance of relevant points of law. While most Republican senators personally disliked the arrogant Chase, they refused to expand the constitutional definition of impeachable offenses to suit Randolph's argument, and on March 1, 1805, the Senate acquitted Chase of all charges.

POLITICS OF DESPERATION

The collapse of the Federalists on the national level encouraged dissension within the Republican party. Extremists in Congress insisted on monopolizing the president's ear, and when he listened to political moderates, they rebelled.

The members of the most vociferous faction called themselves "the *good old republicans*"; the newspapers labeled them the "Tertium Quids," loosely translated as "nothings" or "no accounts." During Jefferson's second term, the Quids argued that the president's policies, foreign and domestic, sacrificed virtue for pragmatism. Their chief spokesmen were two members from Virginia, John Randolph and John Taylor of Caroline (the name of his plantation), both of whom were convinced that Jefferson had betrayed the republican purity of the Founders. They both despised commercial capitalism. Taylor urged Americans to return to a simple agrarian way of life.

The Yazoo controversy raised the Quids from political obscurity. This complex legal battle began in 1795 when a thoroughly corrupt Georgia assembly sold 35 million acres of western land, known as the Yazoo claims, to private companies at bargain prices. It soon became apparent that every member of the legislature had been bribed, and in 1796, state lawmakers rescinded the entire agreement. Unfortunately, some land had already changed hands. When Jefferson became president, a specially appointed federal commission attempted to clean up the mess. It recommended that Congress set aside 5 million acres for buyers who had unwittingly purchased land from the discredited companies.

Randolph immediately cried foul. Such a compromise, however well-meaning, condoned fraud. Republican virtue hung in the balance. For months, the Quids harangued Congress about the Yazoo business, but in the end, their impassioned oratory accomplished nothing. The Marshall Supreme Court upheld the rights of the original purchasers in *Fletcher* v. *Peck* (1810). The justices unanimously declared that legislative fraud did not impair private contracts and that the Georgia assembly of 1796 did not have authority to take away lands already sold to innocent buyers. This important case upheld the Supreme Court's authority to rule on the constitutionality of state laws.

MURDER AND CONSPIRACY: THE CURIOUS CAREER OF AARON BURR

Vice President Aaron Burr created far more serious difficulties for the president. Burr's strange behavior during the election of 1800 raised suspicions that he had conspired to deprive Jefferson of the presidency. Whatever the truth may have been, the vice president entered the new administration under a cloud.

In the spring of 1804, Burr decided to run for governor of New York. Although he was a Republican, he entered into political negotiations with High Federalists who were plotting the secession of New England and New York from the Union. In a particularly scurrilous contest—and New York politics were always abusive—Alexander Hamilton described Burr as ". . . a dangerous man . . . who ought not to be trusted with the reins of government" and urged Federalists in the state to vote for another candidate.

Burr blamed Hamilton for his subsequent defeat and challenged him to a duel. Even though Hamilton condemned this form of violence—his own son had recently been killed in a duel—he accepted Burr's "invitation," describing the foolishness as

Flintlock pistols used in the duel between Aaron Burr and Alexander Hamilton on July 11, 1804. Burr was not hit, but Hamilton was mortally wounded and died the next day.

a matter of personal honor. On July 11, 1804, at Weehawken, New Jersey, the vice president shot and killed the former secretary of the treasury. Both New York and New Jersey indicted Burr for murder. His political career lay in shambles.

In his final weeks as vice president, Burr hatched a scheme so audacious that the people with whom he dealt could not decide whether he was a genius or a madman. On a trip down the Ohio River in April 1805, after his term as vice president was over, he hinted broadly that he was planning a private military adventure against a Spanish colony, perhaps Mexico. Burr also suggested that he envisioned separating the western states and territories from the Union. The region certainly seemed ripe for secession. The citizens of New Orleans acted as if they wanted no part of the United States. Burr covered his tracks well. No two contacts ever heard the same story. Wherever Burr traveled, he recruited adventurers; he mingled with the leading politicians of Kentucky, Ohio, and Tennessee. James Wilkinson, commander of the U.S. Army in the Mississippi Valley, accepted an important role in this vaguely defined conspiracy.

In the late summer of 1806, Burr put his ill-defined plan into action. A group of volunteers constructed riverboats on a small island in the Ohio River owned by Harman Blennerhassett, an Irish immigrant who, like so many contemporaries, found Burr's charm irresistible. By the time this armed band set out to join Wilkinson's forces, however, the general had experienced a change of heart. He frantically dispatched letters to Jefferson denouncing Burr. Wilkinson's betrayal destroyed any chance of success, and conspirators throughout the West rushed pell-mell to save their own skins. Facing certain defeat, Burr tried to escape to Spanish Florida. It was already too late. Federal authorities arrested Burr in February 1807 and took him to Richmond to stand trial for treason.

The trial judge was John Marshall, a strong Federalist not likely to do the Republican administration any favors. During the entire proceedings, Marshall insisted on a narrow constitutional definition of treason. He refused to hear testimony regarding Burr's supposed intentions. "Troops must be embodied," Marshall thundered, "men must be actually assembled." He demanded two witnesses to each overt act of treason.

Burr, of course, had been too clever to leave this sort of evidence. While Jefferson complained bitterly about the miscarriage of justice, the jurors declared on September 1, 1807, that the defendant was "not proved guilty by any evidence submitted to us." The public was outraged, and Burr prudently went into exile in Europe. The president threatened to introduce an amendment to the Constitution calling for the election of federal judges. Nothing came of his proposal. And Marshall, who behaved in an undeniably partisan manner, inadvertently helped protect the civil rights of all Americans. If the chief justice had allowed circumstantial evidence into the Richmond courtroom, if he had listened to rumor and hearsay, he would have made it much easier for later presidents to use trumped-up conspiracy charges to silence political opposition.

THE SLAVE TRADE

Slavery sparked angry debate at the Constitutional Convention of 1787 (see Chapter 6). If delegates from the northern states had refused to compromise on this issue, Southerners would not have supported the new government. The slave states demanded a great deal in return for cooperation. According to an agreement that determined the size of a state's congressional delegation, a slave counted as three-fifths of a free white male. This political formula meant that while blacks did not vote, they helped increase the number of southern representatives. The South in turn gave up very little, agreeing only that after 1808 Congress *might consider* banning the importation of slaves into the United States. Slaves even influenced the outcome of national elections. Had the three-fifths rule not been in effect in 1800, for example, Adams would have had the votes to defeat Jefferson in the electoral college.

In an annual message sent to Congress in December 1806, Jefferson urged the representatives to prepare legislation outlawing the slave trade. During the early months of 1807, congressmen debated various ways of ending the embarrassing commerce. It was clear that the issue cut across party lines. Northern representatives generally favored a strong bill; some even wanted to make smuggling slaves into the country a capital offense. But there was a serious problem. The northern congressmen could not figure out what to do with black people captured by the customs agents who would enforce the legislation. To sell these

Although the external slave trade was officially outlawed in 1808, the commerce in humans persisted. An estimated 250,000 African slaves were brought illicitly to the United States between 1808 and 1860. The internal slave trade continued as well. Folk artist Lewis Miller sketched this slave coffle marching from Virginia to new owners in Tennessee under the watchful eyes of mounted white overseers.

Africans would involve the federal government in slavery, which many Northerners found morally repugnant. Nor was there much sympathy for freeing them. Ignorant of the English language and subject to intense racism, these blacks seemed unlikely long to survive free in the American South.

Southern congressmen responded with threats and ridicule. They explained to their northern colleagues that no one in the South regarded slavery as evil. It appeared naive, therefore, to expect local planters to enforce a ban on the slave trade or to inform federal agents when they spotted a smuggler. The notion that these culprits deserved capital punishment seemed viciously inappropriate.

The bill that Jefferson finally signed in March 1807 pleased no one. The law prohibited the importation of slaves into the United States after the new year. Whenever customs officials captured a smuggler, the slaves were to be turned over to state authorities and disposed of according to local custom. Southerners did not cooperate, and for many years African slaves continued to pour into southern ports. Even more blacks would have been imported had Great Britain not outlawed the slave trade in 1807. As part of their ban of the slave trade, ships of the Royal Navy captured American slave smugglers off the coast of Africa, and when anyone complained, the British explained that they were merely enforcing the laws of the United States.

EMBARRASSMENTS OVERSEAS

During Jefferson's second term (1805–1809), the United States found itself in the midst of a world at war. A brief peace in Europe ended abruptly in 1803, and the two military giants of the age, France and Great Britain, fought for supremacy on land and sea. This was a kind of total war unknown in the eighteenth century. Napoleon's armies carried the ideology of the French Revolution across the Continent. The emperor—as Napoleon Bonaparte called himself after December 1804—transformed conquered nations into French satellites. Only Britain offered effective resistance. On October 21, 1805, Admiral Horatio Nelson destroyed the main French fleet at the battle of Trafalgar, demonstrating decisively the supremacy of the Royal Navy. But only a few weeks later (December 2, 1805), Napoleon crushed Britain's allies, Austria and Russia, at the battle of Austerlitz and confirmed his superiority on land.

During the early stages of the war, the United States profited from European adversity. As "neutral carriers," American ships transported goods to any port in the world where they could find buyers, and American merchants grew wealthy serving Britain and France. Since the Royal Navy did not allow direct trade between France and its colonies, American captains conducted "broken voyages." American vessels sailing out of French ports in the Caribbean would put in briefly in the United States, pay nominal customs, and then leave for France. For several years, the British did little to halt this obvious subterfuge.

Napoleon's successes on the battlefield, however, strained Britain's economic resources. In July 1805, a British admiralty court announced in the *Essex* decision that henceforth "broken voyages" were illegal. The Royal Navy began seizing American ships in record number. Moreover, as the war continued, the British stepped up the impressment of sailors on ships flying the U.S. flag. Estimates of the number of men impressed ranged as high as nine thousand.

Beginning in 1806, the British government issued a series of trade regulations known as the Orders in Council. These proclamations forbade neutral commerce with the Continent and threatened seizure of any ship that violated these orders. The declarations created what were in effect "paper blockades," for even the powerful British navy could not monitor the activities of every Continental port.

Napoleon responded to Britain's commercial regulations with his own paper blockade called the Continental System. In the Berlin Decree of November 1806 and the Milan Decree of December 1807, he announced the closing of all continental ports to British trade. Since French armies occupied most of the territory between Spain and Germany, the decrees obviously cut the British out of a large market. The French emperor also declared that neutral vessels carrying British goods were liable to seizure. The Americans were caught between two conflicting systems. The British ordered American ships to stop off to pay duties and secure clearances in England on the way to the Continent; Napoleon was determined to seize any vessel that obeyed the British.

This unhappy turn of international events baffled Jefferson. He had assumed that civilized countries would respect neutral rights; justice obliged them to do so. Appeals to reason, however, made little impression on states at war. In an attempt to avoid hostilities for which the United States was ill prepared, Jefferson ordered James Monroe and William Pinckney to negotiate a commercial treaty with Great Britain. The document they signed on December 31, 1806, said nothing about impressment, and an angry president refused to submit the treaty to the Senate for ratification.

The United States soon suffered an even greater humiliation. A ship of the Royal Navy, the *Leopard,* sailing off the coast of Virginia, commanded an American warship to submit to a search for deserters (June 22, 1807). When the captain of the *Chesapeake* refused to cooperate, the *Leopard* opened fire, killing three men and wounding eighteen. The attack violated the sovereignty of the United States and the American people demanded revenge.

Jefferson played for time. He recognized that the United States was unprepared for war against a powerful nation such as Great Britain. The president worried that an expensive conflict with Great Britain would quickly undo the fiscal reforms of his first term. As Gallatin explained, in the event of war, the United States "will be poorer, both as a nation and as a government, our debt and taxes will increase, and our progress in every respect be interrupted."

EMBARGO DIVIDES THE NATION

Jefferson responded to European powers with a policy called "peaceable coercion." If Britain and France refused to respect the rights of neutral carriers, then the United States would keep its ships at home. Not only would this action protect them from seizure, but it would also deprive the European powers of much needed American goods, especially food. The president predicted that a total embargo of American commerce would soon force Britain and France to negotiate with the United States in good faith.

"Peaceable coercion" turned into a Jeffersonian nightmare. The president apparently believed the American people would enthusiastically support the embargo. He was wrong. Compliance required a series of enforcement acts that over fourteen months became increasingly harsh.

By the middle of 1808, Jefferson and Gallatin were involved in the regulation of the smallest details of American economic life. The federal government super-

The Ograbme (embargo spelled backward) snapping turtle, created by cartoonist Alexander Anderson, is shown here biting an American tobacco smuggler who is breaking the embargo.

vised the coastal trade, lest a ship sailing between two states slip away to Europe or the West Indies. Overland trade with Canada was proscribed. When violations still occurred, Congress gave customs collectors the right to seize a vessel merely on suspicion of wrongdoing. A final desperate act, passed in January 1809, prohibited the loading of any U.S. vessel, regardless of size, without authorization from a customs officer who was supported by the army, navy, and local militia. Jefferson's eagerness to pursue a reasonable foreign policy blinded him to the fact that he and a Republican Congress would have had to establish a police state to make it work.

New Englanders regarded the embargo as lunacy. Merchants of the region were willing to take their chances on the high seas, but for reasons that few people understood, the president insisted that it was better to preserve ships from possible seizure than to make profits. Sailors and artisans were thrown out of work. The popular press maintained a constant howl of protest. One writer observed that embargo in reverse spelled "O grab me!"

The embargo never damaged the British economy. In fact, British merchants rushed to take over the lucrative markets that the Americans had been forced to abandon. Napoleon liked the embargo, since it seemed to harm Great Britain more than it did France. Faced with growing popular opposition, the Republicans in Congress panicked. One newly elected representative declared that "peaceful coercion" was a "miserable and mischievous failure" and joined his colleagues in repealing the embargo a few days before James Madison's inauguration.

A New Administration Goes to War

As president, James Madison suffered from several political handicaps. Although his intellectual abilities were great, he lacked the personal qualities necessary for effective leadership. In public gatherings, he impressed people as being "exceedingly modest."

During the election of 1808, Randolph and the Quids tried unsuccessfully to persuade James Monroe to challenge Madison's candidacy. Jefferson favored his old friend Madison. In the end, a caucus of Republican congressmen gave the official nod to Madison, the first time in American history that such a congressional group controlled a presidential nomination. The former secretary of state defeated his Federalist rival, Charles Cotesworth Pinckney, in the electoral college by a vote of 122 to 47, with New Yorker George Clinton receiving 6 ballots. The margin of victory was substantially lower than Jefferson's had been in 1804, a warning of political troubles ahead. The Federalists also made impressive gains in the House of Representatives, raising their delegation from 24 to 48.

The new president confronted the same foreign policy

THE ELECTION OF 1808		
CANDIDATE	PARTY	ELECTORAL VOTE
Madison	Republican	122
C. Pinckney	Federalist	47

problems that had occupied his predecessor. Neither Britain nor France showed the slightest interest in respecting American neutral rights. Threats against either nation rang hollow so long as the United States lacked military strength. Out of weakness, therefore, Madison was compelled to put the Non-Intercourse Act into effect. Congress passed this clumsy piece of legislation at the same time as it repealed the embargo (March 1, 1809). The new bill authorized the resumption of trade between the United States and all nations of the world *except* Britain and France. Either of these countries could restore full commercial relations simply by promising to observe the rights of neutral carriers.

The British immediately took advantage of this offer. Their minister to the United States, David M. Erskine, informed Madison that the British government had modified its position on a number of sensitive commercial issues. The president was so encouraged by these talks that he publicly announced that trade with Great Britain could resume in June 1809. Unfortunately, Erskine had not conferred with his superiors on the details of these negotiations. George Canning, the British foreign secretary, rejected the agreement out of hand, and while an embarrassed Madison fumed in Washington, the Royal Navy seized the American ships that had already put to sea.

Canning's apparent betrayal led the artless Madison straight into a French trap. In May 1810, Congress passed Macon's Bill Number Two, an act sponsored by Nathaniel Macon of North Carolina. In a complete reversal of strategy, this poorly drafted legislation reestablished trade with *both* England and France. It also contained a curious carrot-and-stick provision. As soon as either of these European states repealed restrictions upon neutral shipping, the U.S. government promised to halt all commerce with the other.

Napoleon spotted a rare opportunity. He informed the U.S. minister in Paris that France would no longer enforce the hated Berlin and Milan Decrees. Again, Madison acted impulsively. Without waiting for further information from Paris, he announced that unless Britain repealed the Orders in Council by November, the United States would cut off commercial relations. Only later did the president learn that Napoleon had no intention of living up to his side of the bargain; his agents continued to seize American ships. Madison, who had been humiliated by the Erskine experience, decided to ignore the French provocations, to pretend the emperor was behaving in an honest manner. The British could not explain why the United States tolerated such obvious deception. No one in London suspected that the president really had no other options.

Events unrelated to international commerce fueled anti-British sentiment in the newly conquered parts of the United States. Westerners believed—incorrectly, as it turned out—that British agents operating out of Canada had persuaded Tecumseh's warriors to resist the spread of American settlement. According to the rumors that ran through the region, the British dreamed of monopolizing the fur trade. In any case, General William Henry Harrison, governor of the Indiana Territory, marched an army to the edge of a large Shawnee village at the mouth of Tippecanoe Creek near the banks of the Wabash River. On the morning of November 7, 1811, the American troops routed the Indians at the battle of Tippecanoe. Harrison immediately became a national hero, and several decades later the American people rewarded "Tippecanoe" by electing him president. This incident forced Tecumseh—a brilliant leader who was trying to restore the confidence and revitalize tribal cultures of the Indians of the Indiana Territory—to seek British military assistance in battling the Americans, something he probably would not have done had Harrison left him alone.

FUMBLING TOWARD CONFLICT

In 1811, the anti-British mood of Congress intensified. A group of militant representatives, some of them elected to Congress for the first time in the election of 1810, announced they would no longer tolerate national humiliation. They called for action, for resistance to Great Britain, for any course that promised to win respect for the United States. These aggressive nationalists, many of them elected in the South and West, have sometimes been labeled the War Hawks. The group included Henry Clay, an earthy Kentucky congressman who served as speaker of the House, and John C. Calhoun, a brilliant South Carolinian.

On June 1, 1812, Madison sent Congress a declaration of war against Great Britain. The timing of his action was peculiar. Over the preceding months, tensions between the two nations had relaxed. No new attacks had occurred. Indeed, at the very moment Madison called for war, the British government was suspending the Orders in Council, a conciliatory gesture that in all likelihood would have preserved the peace.

Patriotic symbols abound in this print by John Archibald Woodside, Jr. Miss Liberty, carrying a liberty cap on a pole, crowns an American sailor with a laurel wreath, signifying that American liberty is victorious. The sentiment expressed visually and emphatically, "We Owe Allegiance to No Crown," seems appropriate for the revolutionary era, but in fact this print dates much later, to the early nineteenth century, when the War of 1812 sparked nationalism.

THE ELECTION OF 1812

CANDIDATE	PARTY	ELECTORAL VOTE
Madison	Republican	128
Clinton	Republican* (antiwar faction)	89

*Clinton was nominated by a convention of antiwar Republicans and endorsed by the Federalists.

However confused Madison may have seemed, he did have a plan. The president's problem was to figure out how a militarily weak nation like the United States could bring effective pressure on Great Britain. Madison's answer was Canada. This colony supplied Britain's Caribbean possessions with much needed foodstuffs. The president reasoned, therefore, that by threatening to seize Canada, the Americans might compel the British to make concessions on maritime issues.

Congressional War Hawks, of course, may have had other goals in mind. Some expansionists were probably more concerned about conquering Canada than they were about the impressment of American seamen. For others, the whole affair may have truly been a matter of national pride. The vote in Congress was close, 79 to 49 in the House, 19 to 13 in the Senate. With this doubtful mandate, the country marched to war against the most powerful maritime nation in Europe. Division over the war question was reflected in the election of 1812. A faction of antiwar Republicans nominated De Witt Clinton of New York, who was endorsed by the Federalists. Nevertheless Madison, the Republican, won narrowly, gaining 128 electoral votes to Clinton's 89.

THE STRANGE WAR OF 1812

The War Hawks insisted that even though the United States possessed only a small army and navy, it could easily sweep the British out of Canada. Such predictions flew in the face of political and military realities. Not only did the Republicans fail to appreciate how unprepared the country was for war, but they also refused to mobilize needed resources. The House rejected proposals for direct taxes and authorized naval appropriations only with the greatest reluctance. Indeed, even as they planned for battle, the Republican members of Congress did not seem to understand that a weak, highly decentralized government—the one that Jeffersonians championed—was incapable of waging an expensive war against the world's greatest sea power.

American military operations focused initially on the western forts. The results were discouraging. On August 16, 1812, Major General William Hull surrendered an entire army to a smaller British force at Detroit. Michilimackinac was lost. Poorly coordinated marches against the enemy at Niagara and Montreal achieved nothing. On the sea, the United States did better. In August, Captain Isaac Hull's *Constitution* defeated the HMS *Guerrière* in a fierce battle.

The campaigns of 1813 revealed that conquering Canada would be more difficult than the War Hawks ever imagined. On September 10, 1813, Oliver

Hazard Perry destroyed a British fleet at Put-in-Bay, and in a much quoted letter written immediately after the battle, Perry exclaimed, "We have met the enemy; and they are ours." On the other fronts, however, the war went badly for the Americans. General Wilkinson suffered an embarrassing defeat near Montreal (battle of Chrysler's Farm, November 11), and the British navy held its own on Lake Ontario.

In 1814, the British took the offensive. Warships harassed the Chesapeake coast. The British found the region almost totally undefended, and on August 24, 1814, in retaliation for the Americans' destruction of the capital of Upper Canada (York, Ontario), a small force of British marines burned the American capital. Encouraged by their easy success, the British launched a full-scale attack on Baltimore (September 13–14). To everyone's surprise, the fort guarding the harbor held out against a heavy naval bombardment, and the British gave up the operation. The survival of Fort McHenry inspired Francis Scott Key to write "The Star-Spangled Banner."

The battle of New Orleans should never have occurred. The British landed a large assault force under General Edward Pakenham at precisely the same time as diplomats in Europe were preparing the final drafts of a peace treaty. The combatants, of course, knew nothing of these distant developments, and on January 8, 1815, Pakenham ordered a frontal attack against General Andrew Jackson's well-defended positions. In a short time, the entire British force had been destroyed. The victory not only transformed Jackson into a national folk hero, but it also provided the people of the United States with a much needed source of pride.

HARTFORD CONVENTION: THE DEMISE OF THE FEDERALISTS

In the fall of 1814, leading New England politicians, most of them moderate Federalists, gathered in Hartford to discuss relations between the people of their region and the federal government. The delegates protested the Madison administration's seeming insensitivity to the economic interests of the New England states.

The men who met at Hartford on December 15 did not advocate secession from the Union. Although people living in other sections of the country cried treason, the convention delegates only recommended changes in the Constitution. They drafted a number of amendments that reflected the New Englanders' growing frustration. One proposal suggested that congressional representation be calculated on the basis of the number of white males living in a state. New England congressmen were tired of the three-fifths rule that gave southern slaveholders a disproportionately large voice in the House. The convention also wanted to limit each president to a single term in office, a reform that New Englanders hoped might end Virginia's monopoly of the executive mansion. And finally, the delegates insisted that a two-thirds majority was necessary before Congress could declare war, pass commercial regulations, or admit new states to the Union.

The Hartford Convention dispatched its resolutions to Washington, but soon after an official delegation reached the federal capital, the situation

This engraving by Joseph Yeager (ca. 1815) depicts the battle of New Orleans and the death of British Major General Pakenham. The Americans suffered only light casualties in the battle, but more than two thousand British soldiers were killed or wounded.

became extremely awkward. Everyone was celebrating the victory of New Orleans and the announcement of peace. Republican leaders in Congress accused the hapless New Englanders of disloyalty, and people throughout the country were persuaded that a group of wild secessionists had attempted to destroy the Union.

TREATY OF GHENT ENDS THE WAR

In August 1814, the United States dispatched a distinguished negotiating team to Ghent, a Belgian city where the Americans opened talks with British counterparts. During the early weeks of discussion, the British made impossible demands. Fatigue finally broke the diplomatic deadlock. The British government realized that no amount of military force could significantly alter the outcome of hostilities in the United States. Weary negotiators signed the Treaty of Ghent on Christmas Eve 1814. The document dealt with virtually none of the topics contained in Madison's original war message. Neither side surrendered territory; Great Britain refused even to discuss the topic of impressment. In fact, after more than two years of hostilities, the adversaries merely agreed to end the fighting, postponing the vexing issues of neutral rights. The Senate apparently concluded that stalemate was preferable to continued conflict and ratified the treaty 35 to 0.

Most Americans—except perhaps the diehard Federalists of New England—viewed the War of 1812 as an important success. Even though the country's military accomplishments had been unimpressive, the people of the United States had been swept up in a contagion of nationalism. "The war," reflected Gallatin, had made Americans "feel and act more as a nation; and I hope that the permanency of the Union is thereby better secured."

REPUBLICAN LEGACY

During the 1820s, it became fashionable to visit retired presidents. These were not, of course, ordinary leaders. Jefferson, Adams, and Madison linked a generation of younger men and women to the heroic moments of the early republic. When they spoke about the Declaration of Independence or the Constitution of the United States, their opinions carried symbolic weight for a burgeoning society anxious about its political future.

A remarkable coincidence occurred on July 4, 1826, the fiftieth anniversary of the Declaration of Independence. On that day, Thomas Jefferson died at Monticello. His last words were, "Is it the Fourth?" On the same day, several hundred miles to the north, John Adams also passed his last day on earth. His mind was on his old friend and sometimes adversary, and during his final moments, Adams found comfort in the assurance that "Thomas Jefferson still survives."

James Madison lived on at his Virginia plantation, the last of the Founders. Throughout a long and productive career, he had fought for republican values. He championed a Jeffersonian vision of a prosperous nation in which virtuous, independent citizens pursued their own economic interests. He tolerated no aristocratic pretensions.

But many visitors who journeyed to Madison's home at Montpelier before he died in 1836 were worried about another legacy of the founding generation. Why, they asked the aging president, had the early leaders of this nation allowed slavery to endure? How did African Americans fit into the republican scheme? Try as they would, neither Madison nor the politicians who claimed the Jeffersonian mantle could provide satisfactory answers. In an open, egalitarian society, there seemed no place for slaves, and a few months before Madison died, a visitor reported sadly, "With regard to slavery, he owned himself almost to be in despair."

CHRONOLOGY

1800	Thomas Jefferson elected president
1801	Adams makes "midnight" appointments of federal judges
1802	Judiciary Act is repealed (March)
1803	Chief Justice John Marshall rules on *Marbury* v. *Madison* (February); sets precedent for judicial review
	Louisiana Purchase concluded with France (May)
1803–1806	Lewis and Clark explore the Northwest
1804	Aaron Burr kills Alexander Hamilton in a duel (July)
	Jefferson elected to second term
1805	Justice Samuel Chase acquitted by Senate (March)
1807	Burr is tried for conspiracy (August–September)
	Embargo Act passed (December)
1808	Slave trade is ended (January)
	Madison elected president
1809	Embargo is repealed; Non-Intercourse Act passed (March)
1811	Harrison defeats Indians at Tippecanoe (November)
1812	Declaration of war against Great Britain (June)
	Madison elected to second term, defeating De Witt Clinton of New York
1813	Perry destroys British fleet at battle of Put-in-Bay (September)
1814	Jackson crushes Creek Indians at Horseshoe Bend (March)
	British marines burn Washington, D.C. (August)
	Hartford Convention meets to recommend constitutional changes (December)
	Treaty of Ghent ends War of 1812 (December)
1815	Jackson routs British at battle of New Orleans (January)

9

NATION BUILDING
AND NATIONALISM

The return of the Marquis de Lafayette to the United States in 1824 created a public sensation and an occasion for national stock-taking. For more than a year, the great French hero of the American Revolution toured the country that he had helped to bring into being, and he marveled at how much had changed since he had fought beside George Washington more than forty years before. Lafayette hailed "the immense improvements" and "admirable communications" that he had witnessed and declared himself deeply moved by "all the grandeur and prosperity of these happy United States, which . . . reflect on every part of the world the light of a far superior political civilization."

Americans had good reasons to make Lafayette's return the occasion for patriotic celebration and reaffirmation. Since the War of 1812, the nation had been free from serious foreign threats to its independence and way of life. It was growing rapidly in population, size, and wealth. Its republican form of government, which many had considered a risky experiment at the time of its origin, was apparently working well. James Monroe, the current president, had proclaimed in his first inaugural address that "the United States have flourished beyond example. Their citizens individually have been happy and the nation prosperous." Expansion "to the Great Lakes and beyond the sources of the great rivers which communicate through our whole interior" meant that "no country was ever happier with respect to its domain." As for the government, it was so near to perfection that "in respect to it we have no essential improvement to make."

Beneath the optimism and self-confidence, however, lay undercurrents of doubt and anxiety about the future. The visit of the aged Lafayette signified the passing of the Founders. Less than a year after his departure, Jefferson and Adams, except for Madison the last of the great Founders, died within hours of each other on the fiftieth anniversary of the Declaration of Independence. Most Americans saw the coincidence as a good omen for the nation. But, some asked, could their example of republican virtue and self-sacrifice be maintained in an increasingly prosperous and materialistic society? And what about the place of black slavery in a "perfect" democratic republic? Lafayette himself noted with disappointment that the United States had not yet extended freedom to southern slaves.

But the peace following the War of 1812 did open the way for a great surge of nation building. As new lands were acquired or opened up for settlement, hordes of pioneers often rushed in. Improvements in transportation soon gave many of them access to distant markets, and advances in the processing of raw materials led to the first stirrings of industrialization. Politicians looked for ways to encourage the process of growth and expansion, and an active judiciary handed down decisions that served to promote economic development and assert the priority of national over state and local interests. To guarantee the peace and security essential for internal progress, statesmen proclaimed a foreign policy designed to insulate America from external involvements. A new nation of great potential wealth and power was emerging.

EXPANSION AND MIGRATION

The peace concluded with Great Britain in 1815 allowed Americans to shift their attention from Europe and the Atlantic to the vast lands of North America. Two treaties negotiated with Great Britain dealt with northern borders. The Rush-Bagot Agreement (1817) limited U.S. and British naval forces on the Great Lakes and Lake Champlain and guaranteed that the British would never try to invade the United States from Canada and that the United States would never try to take Canada from the British. The Anglo-American Convention of 1818 set the border between the lands of the Louisiana Purchase and Canada at the 49th parallel and provided for joint U.S. and British occupation of Oregon.

Between the Appalachians and the Mississippi, settlement had already begun, especially in the new states of Ohio, Kentucky, and Tennessee. In the lower Mississippi Valley, the former French colony of Louisiana had been admitted as a state in 1812, and a thriving settlement existed around Natchez in the Mississippi Territory. Elsewhere in the trans-Appalachian West, white settlement was sparse and much land remained in Indian hands. U.S. citizens, eager to expand into lands held by Indian nations as well as by Spain, used diplomacy, military action, force, and fraud to "open" lands for U.S. settlement and westward migration.

EXTENDING THE BOUNDARIES

The Americans' first goal was to obtain Florida from Spain. The Spanish claimed possession of land extending along the Gulf Coast to the Mississippi. Between 1810 and 1812, however, the United States had annexed the area between the Mississippi and the Perdido River in what became Alabama, claiming that it was part of the Louisiana Purchase. The remainder, known as East Florida, became a prime object of territorial ambition for President James Monroe and his energetic secretary of state, John Quincy Adams. Spanish claims east and west of the Mississippi stood in the way of Adams's grand design for continental expansion.

General Andrew Jackson provided Adams with an opportunity to acquire the Spanish claims. In 1816, U.S. troops crossed into East Florida in pursuit of hostile Seminole Indians. After taking command in late 1817, Jackson went beyond his official orders and occupied East Florida in April and May of 1818. This operation became known as the First Seminole War. Despite widespread condemnation by government officials of this aggressive action no disciplinary action was taken, mainly because public opinion rallied behind the hero of New Orleans.

In November 1818, Adams informed the Spanish government that the United States had acted in self-defense and that further conflict would be avoided only if East Florida was ceded to the United States. The weakened Spanish government was in no position to resist American bullying. As part of the Adams-Onís Treaty, signed on February 22, 1819, Spain relinquished Florida to the United States. In return, the United States assumed $5 million of the financial claims of American citizens against Spain.

Adams used the confrontation over Florida to force Spain to cede its claim to the Pacific Coast north of California, thus opening a path for future American expansion. He induced the Spanish minister Luis de Onís to agree to the creation of a new boundary between American and Spanish territory that ran north of Texas but extended all the way to the Pacific. Great Britain and Russia still had competing claims to the Pacific Northwest, but the United States was now in a better position to acquire frontage on a second ocean.

Interest in exploitation of the Far West continued to grow between 1810 and 1830. In 1811, New York merchant John Jacob Astor founded the fur-trading post of Astoria at the mouth of the Columbia River in the Oregon Country. Astor's American Fur Company operated out of St. Louis in the 1820s and 1830s, with fur traders working their way up the Missouri to the northern Rockies and beyond. First they limited themselves to trading for furs with the Indians, but later businesses, such as the Rocky Mountain Fur Company founded in 1822, relied on trappers or "mountain men" who went after game on their own and sold the furs to agents of the company at an annual "rendezvous."

These colorful characters, who included such legendary figures as Jedediah Smith, Jim Bridger, Kit Carson, and Jim Beckwourth (one of the many African Americans who contributed to the opening of the West as fur traders, scouts, or settlers), accomplished prodigious feats of survival under harsh natural conditions. Following Indian trails, they explored many parts of the Rockies and the Great Basin.

Reports of military expeditions provided better documented information about the Far West than did the tales of illiterate mountain men. The most notable of the postwar expeditions was mounted by Major Stephen S. Long in 1819–1820. Long surveyed parts of the Great Plains and Rocky Mountains, but his reports encouraged the misleading view that the Plains were a "great American desert" unfit for cultivation or settlement. The focus of attention

Mountain men such as Jim Beckwourth and Native Americans met at a rendezvous to trade their furs to company agents in exchange for food, ammunition, and other goods. Feasting, drinking, gambling, and sharing exploits were also part of the annual event. Moccasins trimmed with trade beads, worn by both Native Americans and trappers, show how trade influenced both cultures. The painting Rendezvous (ca. 1837) is by Alfred Jacob Miller.

between 1815 and the 1840s was the rich agricultural lands between the Appalachians and the Mississippi that were inhabited by numerous Indian tribes.

NATIVE AMERICAN SOCIETIES UNDER PRESSURE

Five Indian nations, with a combined population of nearly 60,000, occupied much of what later became Mississippi, Alabama, Georgia, and Florida. These nations—the Cherokee, Chickasaw, Choctaw, Creek, and Seminole—became known as the "Five Civilized Tribes" because by 1815 they had adopted many of the features of the surrounding white Southern society: an agricultural economy; a republican form of government; and the institution of slavery. Indeed, the cultural transformation of the Southeastern Indians was part of a conscious strategy to respond to Jeffersonian exhortations toward "civilization," and the promise of citizenship that came with it. But between 1815 and 1833, it became increasingly clear that however "civilized" Indians had become, most white Americans were not interested in incorporating them into U.S. society, whether as nations or as individuals.

The five nations varied in their responses to white encroachment on their lands. So-called mixed-blood leaders like John Ross convinced the Cherokee to adopt a strategy of accommodation to increase their chances of survival; the Creek and Seminole, by contrast, took up arms in resistance.

The Cherokee were the largest of the five nations. Traditional Cherokee society had combined hunting by men and subsistence farming by women. In the early nineteenth century, the shift to a more agrarian, market-based economy led to an erosion of the traditional matrilineal kinship system, in which a person belonged to his mother's clan, and also helped introduce American-style slavery to Cherokee society.

Discrimination against Africans in all five nations grew under pressure of contact with whites. Beginning in the 1820s, the Cherokee Council passed laws limiting the rights of slaves and free blacks. By the time of Indian Removal, a few Cherokees owned plantations with hundreds of slaves, and there were more than 1500 slaves in the Cherokee Nation.

In an effort to head off encroachments by southern states, the Cherokee in the 1820s tried to centralize power in a republican government, including all three branches of government modeled on the United States. This process culminated in the 1827 adoption of a formal written constitution based on the U.S. Constitution.

At the same time, a renaissance of Cherokee culture was spurred by Sequoyah's invention of a written Cherokee language in 1821–1822. While the system was not perfect, "Sequoyan" provided Cherokees a new means of self-expression and a reinvigorated sense of Cherokee identity.

The Seminole Nation, the smallest of the five nations, presents perhaps the starkest cultural contrast to the Cherokee, both because the Seminole reacted to pressure from white settlers with armed resistance rather than accommodation, and because their multicultural history gave them a very different relationship to slavery.

Sequoyah's invention of the Cherokee alphabet enabled thousands of Cherokee to read and write primers and newspapers published in their own language.

The Seminole Nation in Florida formed after the European conquest of America, an amalgam of many different peoples with roots in Africa as well as other parts of the New World. Disparate groups of Creek Indians migrating from Georgia and Alabama in the wake of war and disease mingled with the remnants of native Floridians to form the new tribe known as the Seminoles. At the same time, Spain had granted asylum to runaway African American slaves from the Carolinas, who created "maroon communities" in Florida, striking up alliances with the Seminoles to ward off slave catchers. African Americans and Native Americans intermingled, and by the late eighteenth century, some African Americans were already known as "Seminole Negroes" or "estelusti."

Although the Seminoles adopted African slavery at some point in the first decades of the nineteenth century, it was very different from slavery as it existed among whites, or even among the Cherokee and Creek. Seminole "slaves" lived in separate towns, planted and cultivated fields in common, owned large herds of livestock, and paid their "owners" only an annual tribute, similar to that paid by Seminole towns to the *micco* or chief.

During the 1820s and 1830s, the estelusti and the Seminoles were allies in a series of wars against the Americans although their alliance came under increasing strain. During the 1830s, the estelusti played a major role in the Second Seminole War, fought in resistance to Indian removal from 1835 to 1842. General Thomas W. Jesup, the leader of the U.S. Army, claimed, "This, you may be assured is a negro and not an Indian war."

The federal government used a combination of deception, bribery, and threats to induce the five nations to give up their land; sometimes they convinced a few individuals to sign treaties, purporting to represent the entire tribe. When federal action did not yield results fast enough to suit southern whites who coveted Indian land for mining, speculation, and cotton production, state governments began to act on their own, proclaiming state jurisdiction over lands still allotted by federal treaty to Indians within the state's borders. The stage was thus set for the forced removal of the five civilized tribes to the trans-Mississippi West during the administration of Andrew Jackson.

Farther north, in the Ohio Valley and the Northwest Territory, Native Americans had already suffered military defeat in the conflict between Britain and the United States, leaving them only a minor obstacle to the ambitions of white settlers and land speculators. British withdrawal from the Old Northwest in 1815 left their former Indian allies virtually defenseless before the white advance. Most of the tribes were eventually forced west of the Mississippi. The last stand of the Indians in this region occurred in 1831–1832, when a faction of the confederated Sac and Fox Indians under Chief Black Hawk refused to abandon their lands east of the Mississippi. Federal troops and Illinois state militia pursued Black Hawk's band and drove the Indians back to the river, where they were almost exterminated while attempting to cross to the western bank.

Uprooting once populous Indian communities of the Old Northwest was part of a national program for removing Indians of the eastern part of the country to an area beyond the Mississippi. Not everyone agreed with Thomas Jefferson's belief that Indians, unlike blacks, had the natural ability to adopt white ways and become useful citizens of the republic. People living on the frontier who coveted Indian land and risked violent retaliation for trying to take it were more likely to think of Native Americans as irredeemable savages, or even as vermin to be exterminated if necessary. Furthermore, Indians based property rights to land on use rather than absolute ownership; white settlers regarded this practice as an insuperable obstacle to economic development. As originally conceived by Thomas Jefferson, removal would have allowed those Indians who became "civilized" to remain behind on individually owned farms and qualify for American citizenship. This policy would reduce Indian holdings without appearing to violate American standards of justice. During the Monroe era, however, it became clear that white settlers wanted nothing less than the removal of all Indians, "civilized" or not. Andrew Jackson, who made his name as an Indian fighter in the 1810s, presided over a shift to a far more aggressive Indian removal policy.

SETTLEMENT TO THE MISSISSIPPI

While Indians were being driven beyond the Mississippi, settlers poured into the agricultural heartland of the United States. In 1810, only about one-seventh of the American population lived beyond the Appalachians; by 1840, more than one-third did. Eight new western states were added to the Union during this period. The government took care of Indian removal, but the settlers faced the difficult task of taking possession of the land and deriving a livelihood from it.

Much of the vast acreage opened up by the westward movement passed through the hands of land speculators before it reached farmers and planters. After a financial panic in 1819 brought ruin to many who had purchased tracts on credit, the minimum price was lowered from $2.00 to $1.25 an acre, but full payment was required in cash. Since few settlers could afford the necessary outlays, wealthy speculators continued to acquire most good land.

Eventually, most of the land did find its way into the hands of actual cultivators. In some areas, squatters arrived before the official survey and formed claims associations that policed land auctions to prevent "outsiders" from bidding up the price and buying their farms out from under them. Squatters also insisted that they had the right to purchase at the minimum price land they had already improved, a practice called "preemption." In 1841, Congress formally acknowledged the right to farm on public lands with the assurance of a *future* preemption right.

Settlers who arrived after speculators had secured title had to deal with land barons. Fortunately for the settlers, most speculators operated on credit and needed a quick return on their investment. They did this by selling land at a profit to settlers who had some capital and by arranging finance plans for tenants who did not. Thus the family farm or owner-operated plantation became the typical unit of western agriculture.

Since the pioneer family was likely to be saddled with debt of one kind or another, farmers were often forced from the beginning to do more than simply raise enough food to subsist; they also had to produce something for market. Much of the earliest settlement occurred along rivers that provided a natural means of transportation for flatboats loaded with corn, wheat, cotton, or cured meat. Farmers from more remote areas drove livestock over primitive trails and roads to eastern markets. To turn bulky grain, especially corn, into a more easily transportable commodity, farmers in remote regions often distilled grain into whiskey. To meet the needs of farmers, local marketing centers quickly sprang up, usually at river junctions. In the Midwest especially, the rapid rise of towns and cities serving surrounding farming areas greatly accelerated regional development.

THE PEOPLE AND CULTURE OF THE FRONTIER

Most of the settlers who populated the West were farmers from the seaboard states. Rising land prices and declining fertility of the soil in the older regions often motivated their migration. Most moved in family units and tried to re-create their former ways of life as soon as possible. Women were often reluctant to migrate in the first place, and when they arrived in new areas, they strove valiantly to recapture the comfort and stability they had left behind.

In general, pioneers sought out the kind of terrain and soil with which they were already familiar. People from eastern uplands favored western hill country. Piedmont and Tidewater farmers or planters usually made for the lower and flatter areas. Early settlers avoided the fertile prairies of the Midwest preferring instead river bottoms or wooded sections because they were more like home and could be farmed by tried-and-true methods. Rather than being the bold and deliberate innovators pictured in American mythology, typical agricultural pioneers were deeply averse to changing their habits.

The log cabin and split-rail fence of this frontier farmstead were cut from trees on the land. Settlers often burned trees to clear the land for farming.

Yet adjustments were necessary simply to survive under frontier conditions. Initially, at least, isolated homesteads required a high degree of self-sufficiency. Crops had to be planted, harvested, and readied for home consumption with simple tools brought in wagons from the East—often little more than an axe, a plow, and a spinning wheel. Men usually cut down trees, built cabins, broke the soil, and put in crops. Women made clothes, manufactured soap and other household necessities, churned butter, preserved food for the winter, and worked in the fields at busy times in addition to cooking, keeping house, and caring for children.

But this picture of frontier self-reliance is not the whole story. Most settlers in fact found it extremely difficult to accomplish all the tasks using only family labor. A more common practice was the sharing of work by a number of pioneer families. Except in parts of the South, where frontier planters had taken slaves with them, the normal way to get heavy labor done in newly settled regions was through mutual aid. Assembling the neighbors to raise a house, burn the woods, roll logs, harvest wheat, husk corn, pull flax, or make quilts helped turn collective work into a festive social occasion. These communal events represented a creative response to the shortage of labor and at the same time provided a source for community solidarity. They probably tell us more about the "spirit of the frontier" than the conventional image of the pioneer as a lonely individualist.

Americans who remained in the East often imagined the West as an untamed American wilderness inhabited by Indians and solitary white "pathfinders" who turned their backs on civilization and learned to live in harmony with nature. James Fenimore Cooper, the first great American novelist, fostered this mythic view of the West in his series of novels featuring Natty Bumppo, or "Leatherstocking"—a character who became the prototype for the western hero of popular fiction. Natty Bumppo was a hunter and scout who preferred the freedom of living in the forest to the constraints of civilization. Through Natty

Bumppo, Cooper engendered a main theme of American romanticism—the superiority of a solitary life in the wilderness to the kind of settled existence among the families, schools, and churches to which most real pioneers aspired.

TRANSPORTATION AND THE MARKET ECONOMY

It took more than the spread of settlements to bring prosperity to new areas and ensure that they would identify with older regions or with the country as a whole. Along the eastern seaboard, land transportation was so primitive that in 1813 it took seventy-five days for a horse-drawn wagon of goods to travel the thousand miles from Worcester, Massachusetts, to Charleston, South Carolina. Coastal shipping eased the problem somewhat and stimulated the growth of port cities. Traveling west over the mountains, however, meant months on the trail.

After the War of 1812, political leaders realized that national security, economic progress, and political unity would require a greatly improved transportation network. Accordingly, President Madison called for a federally supported program of "internal improvements" in 1815. In the ensuing decades, the nationalists' vision of a transportation revolution was realized to a considerable extent, although the direct role of the federal government proved to be less important than anticipated.

A REVOLUTION IN TRANSPORTATION: ROADS AND STEAMBOATS

The first great federal transportation project was the building between 1811 and 1818 of the National Road between Cumberland, Maryland, on the Potomac and Wheeling, Virginia, on the Ohio. This impressive gravel-surfaced toll road was subsequently extended to Vandalia, Illinois, in 1838. By about 1825, thousands of miles of turnpikes—privately owned toll roads chartered by the states—crisscrossed southern New England, upstate New York, much of Pennsylvania, and northern New Jersey.

Toll roads, however, failed to meet the demand for low-cost transportation over long distances. Transporters of bulky freight usually found that total expenses—toll plus the cost and maintenance of heavy wagons and great teams of horses—were too high to guarantee a satisfactory profit from haulage. Hence traffic was less than anticipated, and the tolls collected failed to provide an adequate return to investors.

Even the National Road could not offer the low freight costs required for the long-distance hauling of wheat, flour, and the other bulky agricultural products of the Ohio Valley. For these commodities, water transportation of some sort was required.

The United States' natural system of river transportation was one of the most significant reasons for its rapid economic development. The Ohio-Mississippi system in particular provided ready access to the rich agricultural areas of the interior and a natural outlet for their products. By 1815, flatboats loaded with wheat, flour, salt pork, and cotton were floating toward New Orleans. Even after the coming of the steamboat, flatboats continued to carry a major share of the downriver trade.

The flatboat trade, however, was necessarily one-way. A farmer from Ohio or Illinois, or someone hired to do the job, could float down to New Orleans easily enough, but there was generally no way to get back except by walking overland through rough country. Until the problem of upriver navigation was solved, the Ohio-Mississippi could not carry the manufactured goods that farmers desired in exchange for their crops.

Fortunately, a solution was readily at hand: the use of steam power. In 1807, inventor Robert Fulton, backed by Robert R. Livingston—a New Yorker of great wealth and political prominence—demonstrated the full potential of the steamboat by successfully propelling the *Clermont* 150 miles up the Hudson River. The first steamboat launched in the West was the *New Orleans*, which made the long trip from Pittsburgh to New Orleans in 1811–1812. The river steamboat revolutionized western commerce. By 1820, sixty-nine steamboats with a total capacity of 13,890 tons were plying western waters.

Steam transport was a great boon for farmers and merchants. It reduced costs, increased the speed of moving goods and people, and allowed a two-way commerce on the Mississippi and Ohio. Eastern manufacturers and merchants now had a better way to reach interior markets.

The steamboat quickly captured the American imagination. Great paddle wheelers became luxurious floating hotels, the natural habitats of gamblers and

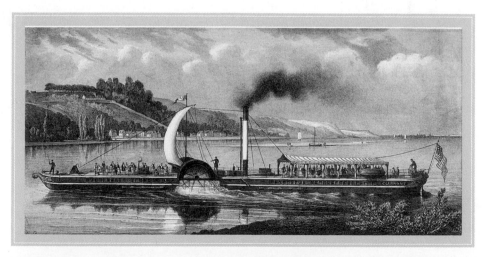

The Clermont on the Hudson *(ca. 1830–1835) by Charles Pensee. Although some called his* Clermont *"Fulton's Folly," Robert Fulton immediately turned a profit from his fleet of steamboats, which reduced the cost and increased the speed of river transport.*

confidence men. But the boats also had a lamentable safety record, frequently running aground, colliding, or blowing up. As a result of such accidents, the federal government began in 1838 to regulate steamboats and monitor their construction and operation. This legislation stands as virtually the only federal effort in the pre–Civil War period to regulate domestic transportation.

THE CANAL BOOM

A transportation system based solely on rivers and roads had one enormous gap—it did not provide an economical way to ship western farm produce directly east to the growing urban market of the seaboard states. The solution offered by the politicians and merchants of the Middle Atlantic and midwestern states was to build a system of canals to link seaboard cities directly to the Great Lakes, the Ohio, and ultimately the Mississippi.

The best natural location for a canal connecting a river flowing into the Atlantic with one of the Great Lakes was between Albany and Buffalo, a relatively flat stretch of 364 miles. When the New York legislature approved the bold project in 1817, no more than about 100 miles of canal existed in the entire United States. Credit for the project belongs mainly to New York's governor De Witt Clinton, who persuaded the state legislature to underwrite the project by issuing bonds. Begun in 1818, the completed canal opened in 1825, to great public acclaim.

At 364 miles long, 40 feet wide, and 4 feet deep, and containing 84 locks, the Erie Canal was the most spectacular engineering achievement of the young repub-

Illustration of a lock on the Erie Canal at Lockport, New York, 1838. The canal facilitated trade by linking the Great Lakes region to the eastern seaports.

lic. Furthermore, it was a great economic success. It reduced the cost of moving goods from Buffalo to Albany to one-twelfth the previous rate, thus allowing both Easterners and Westerners to buy each other's products at sharply lower costs. It also helped make New York City the commercial capital of the nation.

The great success of the Erie Canal inspired other states to extend public credit for canal building. During the 1830s and 1840s, Pennsylvania, Ohio, Illinois, and Michigan embarked on ambitious canal construction projects, from Philadelphia to Pittsburgh, from the Ohio River to Cleveland, and from Chicago to the Illinois River and the Mississippi.

The canal boom ended when it became apparent in the 1830s and 1840s that most of the waterways were unprofitable. State credit had been overextended, and the panic and depression of the late 1830s and early 1840s forced retrenchment. Moreover, by this time railroads were beginning to compete successfully for the same traffic, and a new phase in the transportation revolution was beginning.

But canals should not be written off as economic failures that contributed little to the improvement of transportation. Some of them continued to be important arteries up to the time of the Civil War and well beyond. Furthermore, the "failure" of many of the canals was due solely to their inability to yield an adequate return to investors. Had the canals been thought of as providing a service rather than yielding a profit their vital contribution to the nation's economic development would have been better appreciated.

EMERGENCE OF A MARKET ECONOMY

The desire to reduce the costs and increase the speed of shipping heavy freight over great distances laid the groundwork for a new economic system. With the advent of steamboats and canals, western farmers could inexpensively ship their crops to the east, while eastern manufacturers gained ready access to an interior market. Hence improved transport both increased farm income and stimulated commercial agriculture.

At the beginning of the nineteenth century, the typical farming household consumed most of what it produced and sold only a small surplus in nearby markets. Most manufactured articles were produced at home. Easier and cheaper access to distant markets caused a decisive change in this pattern. Between 1800 and 1840, agricultural output increased at an annual rate of approximately 3 percent, and a rapidly growing portion of this production consisted of commodities grown for sale rather than consumed at home. The rise in productivity was partly due to technological advances. Iron or steel plows proved better than wooden ones, the grain cradle displaced the scythe for harvesting, and better varieties or strains of crops, grasses, and livestock were introduced. But the availability of good land and the revolution in marketing were the most important spurs to profitable commercial farming. Transportation facilities made distant markets available and plugged farmers into a commercial network that provided credit and relieved them of the need to do their own selling.

The emerging exchange network encouraged movement away from diversified farming and toward regional concentration on staple crops. Wheat was the main cash crop of the North, and the center of its cultivation moved westward as soil depletion, pests, and plant diseases lowered yields in older regions. On the rocky hillsides of New England, sheep raising was displacing the mixed farming of an earlier era. But the prime examples of successful staple production in this era were in the South. Tobacco continued to be a major cash crop of the upper South, rice was important in coastal South Carolina, and sugar was a staple of southern Louisiana. Cotton, however, was the "king" crop in the lower South as a whole. In the course of becoming the nation's principal export commodity, it brought wealth and prosperity to a belt of states running from South Carolina to Louisiana.

A number of factors made the Deep South the world's greatest producer of cotton. First was the great demand generated by the rise of textile manufacturing in England and, to a lesser extent, in New England. Second was the effect of the cotton gin on processing. Invented by Eli Whitney in 1793, this simple device cut the labor costs involved in cleaning short-staple cotton, thus making it an easily marketable commodity. Third was the availability of good land in the Southeast. The center of cotton growing moved steadily westward from South Carolina and Georgia, primarily, toward the fertile plantation areas of Alabama, Mississippi, and Louisiana.

A fourth factor was the existence of slavery, which permitted operations on a scale impossible for the family labor system of the agricultural North. Finally, the cotton economy benefited from the South's natural transportation system—its great network of navigable rivers extending deep into the interior. The South had less need than other agricultural regions for artificial internal improvements such as canals and good roads. Planters could simply establish themselves on or near a river and ship their crops to market via natural waterways.

COMMERCE AND BANKING

As regions specialized in growing commercial crops, a new system of marketing emerged. During the early years of expansion, farmers did their marketing personally. With the growth of country towns, local merchants took charge of the crops near their sources, bartering clothing and other manufactured goods for produce. These intermediaries shipped the farmers' crops to larger local markets such as Pittsburgh, Cincinnati, and St. Louis. From there the commodities could be sent on to Philadelphia, New York, or New Orleans.

Credit was a crucial element in the whole system. Farmers borrowed from local merchants, who received an advance of their own when they consigned crops to a commission house or factor. The commission agents relied on credit from merchants or manufacturers at the ultimate destination, which might be Liverpool or New York City. Even though the intermediaries all charged fees and interest, the net cost to the farmers was less than it had been when they had handled their own marketing.

Before the revolutions in transportation and marketing, small-scale local economies could survive to a considerable extent on barter. But long-distance transactions involving credit and deferred payment required money and lots of it. Under the Constitution, only the U.S. government is authorized to coin money and regulate its value. But in the early to mid-nineteenth century, the government printed no paper money and produced gold and silver coins in such small quantities that it failed to meet the expanding economy's need for a circulating currency.

Private or state banking institutions filled the void by issuing banknotes, promises to redeem their paper in *specie*—gold or silver—on the bearer's demand. The demand for money and credit during the economic boom after 1815 led to a vast increase in the number of state banks—from 88 to 208 within two years. The resulting flood of state banknotes caused this form of currency to depreciate well below its face value and threatened a runaway inflation. In an effort to stabilize the currency, Congress established a second Bank of the United States in 1816.

The Bank was expected to serve as a check on the state banks by forcing them to resume specie payments. But it did not perform this task well in its early years. In fact, its own free lending policies contributed to the overextension of credit that led to financial panic and depression in 1819. When the economy collapsed, many Americans questioned whether the new system of banking and credit was as desirable as it had seemed to be in times of prosperity. As a result, hostility to banks became a prominent feature of American politics.

EARLY INDUSTRIALISM

The growth of a market economy also created new opportunities for industrialists. In 1815, most manufacturing in the United States was carried on in households, in the workshops of skilled artisans, or in small mills. The factory form of production, in which supervised workers tended or operated machines under one roof, was rare. Even in the American textile industry, most spinning of thread, as well as the weaving, cutting, and sewing of cloth, was still done in the home.

As late as 1820, most clothing worn by Americans was made entirely by female family members. But a growing proportion was produced for market, rather than direct home consumption. Under the "putting-out" system of manufacturing, merchant capitalists provided raw material to people in their own homes, picked up finished or semifinished products, paid the workers, and took charge of distribution. Simple shoes and hats, as well as clothing, were made under the putting-out system, which was centered in the Northeast.

Artisans working in small shops in towns produced articles that required greater skill—such as high-quality shoes and boots, carriages or wagons, mill wheels, and barrels or kegs. But in the decades after 1815, shops expanded in size, masters tended to become entrepreneurs rather than working artisans, and journeymen often became wage earners rather than aspiring masters. At the same time, the growing market for low-priced goods led to a stress on speed, quantity, and standardization in the methods of production.

A fully developed factory system emerged first in textile manufacturing. The establishment of the first cotton mills utilizing the power loom as well as spinning machinery—thus making it possible to turn fiber into cloth in a single factory—resulted from the efforts of a trio of Boston merchants: Francis Cabot Lowell, Nathan Appleton, and Patrick Tracy Jackson.

As the Boston Manufacturing Company, the associates began their operation in Waltham, Massachusetts, in 1813. Their phenomenal success led to the erection of a larger and even more profitable mill at Lowell, Massachusetts, in 1822 and another at Chicopee in 1823. Lowell became the great showplace for early American industrialization. Its large and seemingly contented workforce of unmarried young women residing in supervised dormitories, its unprecedented scale of operation, its successful mechanization of almost every stage of the production process—all captured the American middle-class imagination in the 1820s and 1830s. Other mills using similar methods sprang up throughout New England, and the region became the first important manufacturing area in the United States.

The shift away from the putting-out system to factory production changed the course of capitalist activity in New England. Before the 1820s, New England merchants concentrated mainly on international trade. A major source of capital was the lucrative China trade carried on by fast, well-built New England vessels. When the success of Waltham and Lowell became clear, many merchants shifted their capital away from oceanic trade and into manufacturing. Politically, this change meant that representatives from New England no longer advocated a low tariff that favored importers over exporters. Instead, they championed a high duty designed to protect manufacturers from foreign competition.

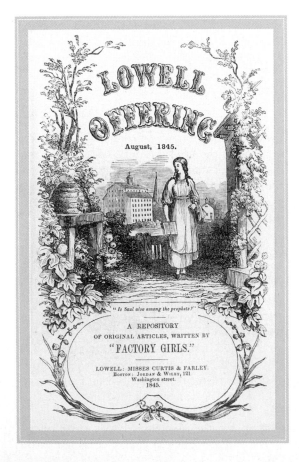

The young women who worked in the Lowell mills wrote and edited their own monthly magazine, the Lowell Offering, from 1840 to 1845. The magazine's editors, Harriot F. Curtis and Harriet Farley, said that the cover represented "The New England school-girl, of which our factories are made up, standing near a beehive, emblem of industry and intelligence, and in the background the Yankee schoolhouse, church, and factory."

The development of other "infant industries" after the War of 1812 was less dramatic and would not come to fruition until the 1840s and 1850s. Technology imported from England to improve the rolling and refining of iron gradually encouraged a domestic iron industry centered in Pennsylvania. The use of interchangeable parts in the manufacture of small arms helped modernize the weapons industry while also contributing to the growth of new forms of mass production.

One should not assume, however, that America had already experienced an industrial revolution by 1840. Most of the nation's labor force was still employed in agriculture. Fewer than 10 percent of workers were directly involved in factory production. The revolution that did occur during these years was essentially one of distribution rather than production. The growth of a market economy of national scope was the major economic development of this period. And it was one that had vast repercussions for all aspects of American life.

For those who benefited from it most directly, the market economy provided firm evidence of progress and improvement. But many of those who suffered from its periodic panics and depressions were receptive to politicians and reformers who attacked corporations and "the money power."

THE POLITICS OF NATION BUILDING AFTER THE WAR OF 1812

Geographic expansion, economic growth, and the changes in American life that accompanied them were bound to generate political controversy. Farmers, merchants, manufacturers, and laborers were affected by the changes in different ways, as were Northerners, Southerners, and Westerners. Federal and state policies that were meant to encourage or control growth and expansion did not benefit all these groups or sections equally, and conflicts of interest inevitably arose.

But the temporary lack of a party system during the period following the War of 1812 meant that politicians did not have to offer voters a choice of programs and ideologies. A myth of national harmony prevailed, culminating in the Era of Good Feeling during James Monroe's two terms as president. Behind this façade, individuals and groups fought for advantage, as always, but without the public accountability and need for broad popular approval that a party system would have required.

The absence of a party system did not completely immobilize the federal government. The president took important initiatives in foreign policy, Congress legislated on matters of national concern, and the Supreme Court made far-reaching decisions. The common theme of the public policies that emerged between the War of 1812 and the age of Andrew Jackson was an awakening nationalism—a sense of American pride and purpose that reflected the events of the period.

THE REPUBLICANS IN POWER

By the end of the War of 1812, the Federalist party was no longer a significant force in national politics, although Jefferson's party, now known simply as the Republicans, had adopted some of their rivals' programs and policies. Retreating from their original philosophy of states' rights and limited government, Republican party leaders now supported reestablishment of a national bank, a mildly protective tariff for industry, and a program of federally financed internal improvements.

Congressman Henry Clay of Kentucky advocated that the government take action to promote economic development. The keystone of what Clay called the "American System" was a high protective tariff to stimulate industrial growth and provide a "home market" for the farmers of the West, making the nation economically self-sufficient and free from dependence on Europe.

In 1816, Congress took the first step toward Clay's goal by enacting a tariff that raised import duties an average of 25 percent. Passed to protect American industry from British competition, the tariff had substantial support in all parts of the country. Americans viewed the act as a move toward economic independence, a necessity to protect political independence.

Later the same year, Congress voted to establish the second Bank of the United States. Organized much like the first Bank, it was a mixed public-private institution, with the federal government owning one-fifth of its stock and appointing five of its twenty-five directors. The Bank provided a depository for government funds, an outlet for marketing its securities, and a source of redeemable banknotes that could be used to pay taxes or purchase public lands. State banking interests and strict constructionists opposed the bank bill, but the majority of Congress found it a necessary and proper means for promoting financial stability and meeting the federal government's constitutional responsibility to raise money from taxation and loans.

Legislation dealing with internal improvements aroused stronger constitutional objections and sparked disagreements among sectional groups over who would benefit from specific projects. Except for the National Road, the federal government undertook no major transportation projects during the Madison and Monroe administrations. Public aid for the building of roads and canals continued to come mainly from state and local governments.

MONROE AS PRESIDENT

As did Jefferson before him, President Madison chose his own successor in 1816. James Monroe thus became the third successive Virginian to occupy the White House. He served two full terms and was virtually uncontested in his election to each. Experienced, reliable, dignified, and high principled, Monroe was also stolid and unimaginative, lacking the intellectual depth and agility of his predecessors.

Monroe avoided controversy in his effort to maintain the national harmony that was the keynote of his presidency. His first inaugural address expressed the complacency and optimism

THE ELECTION OF 1816

CANDIDATE	PARTY	ELECTORAL VOTE
Monroe	Republican	183
King	Federalist	34

of the time, and he followed it up with a goodwill tour of the country, the first made by a president since Washington. A local newspaper was so impressed with Monroe's warm reception in Federalist Boston that it announced that party strife was a thing of the past and that an "era of good feeling" had begun. A principal aim of Monroe's administrations was to see that the good feelings persisted. He hoped to conciliate all the sectional or economic interests of the country and devote his main attention to the task of asserting American power and influence on the world stage. For example, during the Panic of 1819, an economic depression that followed the postwar boom, Congress acted by passing debt relief legislation, but Monroe himself had no program to relieve the economic crisis because he did not feel called on to exert that kind of leadership.

Monroe prized national harmony above economic prosperity. But during his first administration, a bitter controversy developed between the North and the South over the admission of Missouri to the Union. Once again Monroe remained outside the battle and suffered little damage to his own prestige. It was left entirely to Congress to deal with the nation's most serious domestic political crisis between the War of 1812 and the late 1840s.

THE MISSOURI COMPROMISE

In 1817, the Missouri territorial assembly applied for statehood. Because the petition made no provision for emancipation of the two to three thousand slaves already in the territory or for curbing further introduction of slaves, it was clear that Missouri expected to enter the Union as a slave state.

When the question came before Congress in early 1819, sectional fears and anxieties bubbled to the surface. Many Northerners resented southern control of the presidency and the fact that the three-fifths clause of the Constitution, by which every five slaves were counted as three persons in figuring the state's population, gave the South's free population added weight in the House of Representatives and the electoral college. Southerners feared for the future of what they saw as a necessary balance of power between the sections. Up until 1819, strict equality had been maintained by alternately admitting slave and free states. But northern population was growing more rapidly than southern, and the North had built up a decisive majority in the House of Representatives. Hence the South saw its equal vote in the Senate as essential for preservation of the balance.

In February 1819, Congressman James Tallmadge of New York introduced an amendment to the statehood bill, banning further introduction of slaves into Missouri and requiring steps toward the gradual elimination of slavery within the state. The House approved the Tallmadge amendment by a narrow margin,

THE ELECTION OF 1820

CANDIDATE	PARTY	ELECTORAL VOTE
Monroe	Republican	231
J. Q. Adams	No party designation	1

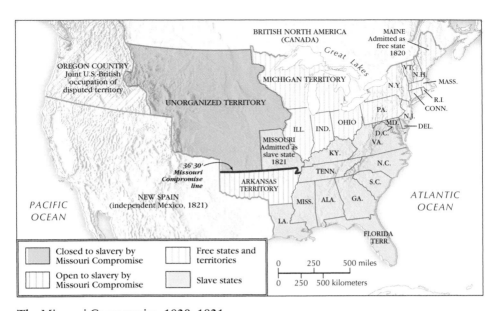

The Missouri Compromise, 1820–1821

The Missouri Compromise kept the balance of power in the Senate by admitting Missouri as a slave state and Maine as a free state. The agreement temporarily settled the argument over slavery in the territories.

but the Senate voted it down. The issue remained unresolved until a new Congress convened in December 1819. In the great debate that ensued in the Senate, Federalist leader Rufus King of New York argued that Congress was within its rights to require restriction of slavery before Missouri could become a state. Southern senators protested that denying Missouri's freedom in this matter was an attack on the principle of equality among the states and showed that Northerners were conspiring to upset the balance of power between the sections.

A statehood petition from the people of Maine, who were seeking to be separated from Massachusetts, suggested a way out of the impasse. In February 1820, the Senate voted to couple the admission of Missouri as a slave state with the admission of Maine as a free state. A further amendment was also passed prohibiting slavery in the rest of the Louisiana Purchase north of the southern border of Missouri, or above the latitude of 36°30', and allowing it below that line. The Senate's compromise then went to the House. Through the adroit maneuvering of Henry Clay—who broke the proposal into three separate bills—it eventually won House approval. The measure authorizing Missouri to frame a constitution and apply for admission as a slave state passed by a razor-thin margin of 90 to 87, with most northern representatives remaining opposed.

A major sectional crisis had been resolved. But the Missouri affair had ominous overtones for the future of North-South relations. Thomas Jefferson described the controversy as "a fire bell in the night," threatening the peace of the Union. The congressional furor had shown that when the issue of slavery or its extension came directly before the people's representatives, regional loyalties took precedence over party or other considerations. An emotional rhetoric of morality and fundamental rights issued from both sides, and votes followed sectional lines much more closely than on any other issue. If the United States were to acquire any new territories in which the status of slavery had to be determined by Congress, renewed sectional strife would be inevitable.

POSTWAR NATIONALISM AND THE SUPREME COURT

While the Monroe administration was proclaiming national harmony and congressional leaders were struggling to reconcile sectional differences, the Supreme Court was making a more substantial and enduring contribution to the growth of nationalism and a strong federal government. Much of this achievement was due to the firm leadership and fine legal mind of the chief justice of the United States, John Marshall. A Virginian, a Federalist, and the devoted disciple and biographer of George Washington, Marshall served as chief justice from 1801 to 1835, and during that entire period he dominated the Court as no other chief justice has ever done.

As the author of most of the major opinions issued by the Supreme Court during its formative period, Marshall gave shape to the Constitution and clarified the crucial role of the Court in the American system of government. The role of the Court, in Marshall's view, was to interpret and enforce the Constitution in a way that encouraged economic development, especially against efforts of state legislatures to interfere with the constitutionally protected rights of individuals or combinations of individuals to acquire property through productive activity. Under Marshall's lead, the Supreme Court approved broad powers for the federal government so that the latter could fulfill its constitutional responsibility to promote the general welfare by encouraging economic growth and prosperity.

In a series of major decisions between 1819 and 1824, the Marshall Court enhanced judicial power and used the contract clause of the Constitution to limit the power of state legislatures. It also strengthened the federal government by sanctioning a broad or loose construction of its constitutional powers and by clearly affirming its supremacy over the states.

In *Dartmouth College* v. *Woodward* (1819), the Court was asked to rule whether New Hampshire had the right to convert Dartmouth from a private college into a state university. Daniel Webster, arguing for the college, contended that Dartmouth's original charter of 1769 was a valid and irrevocable contract. The Court accepted his argument. Speaking for all the justices, Marshall made the far-reaching determination that any charter granted by a state to a private corporation was fully protected by the contract clause.

The decision increased the power and independence of business corporations by weakening the ability of the states to regulate them or withdraw their privileges. The ruling helped foster the growth of the modern corporation as a profit-making enterprise with limited public responsibilities.

In March 1819, the Marshall Court handed down its most important decision. The case of *McCulloch* v. *Maryland* arose because the state of Maryland had levied a tax on the Baltimore branch of the Bank of the United States. The unanimous opinion of the Court, delivered by Marshall, was that the Maryland tax was unconstitutional. The two main issues were whether Congress had the

Chief Justice John Marshall affirmed the Supreme Court's authority to overrule state laws and congressional legislation that it held to be in conflict with the Constitution. The portrait is by Chester Harding, ca. 1829.

right to establish a national bank and whether a state had the power to tax or regulate an agency or institution created by Congress.

In response to the first question, Marshall set forth his doctrine of "implied powers." Conceding that no specific authorization to charter a bank could be found in the Constitution, the chief justice argued that such a right could be deduced from more general powers and from an understanding of the "great objects" for which the federal government had been founded. Marshall thus struck a blow for loose construction of the Constitution.

In answer to the second question—the right of a state to tax or regulate a federal agency—Marshall held that the Bank was indeed such an agency and that giving a state the power to tax it would also give the state the power to destroy it. In an important assertion of the supremacy of the national government, Marshall argued that the American people "did not design to make their government dependent on the states." This opinion ran counter to the view of many Americans, particularly in the South, that the Constitution did not take away sovereignty from the states.

The *Gibbons* v. *Ogden* decision of 1824 bolstered the power of Congress to regulate interstate commerce. A steamboat monopoly granted by the state of New York was challenged by a competing ferry service operating between New York and New Jersey. The Court declared the New York grant unconstitutional because it amounted to state interference with Congress's exclusive right to regulate interstate commerce. The Court's ruling went a long way toward freeing private interests engaged in furthering the transportation revolution from state interference.

The actions of the Marshall Court provide the clearest and most consistent example of the main nationalistic trends of the postwar period—the acknowledgment of the federal government's major role in promoting the growth of a powerful and prosperous America and the rise of a nationwide capitalist economy.

NATIONALISM IN FOREIGN POLICY: THE MONROE DOCTRINE

The new spirit of nationalism was also reflected in foreign affairs. The main diplomatic challenge facing Monroe after his reelection in 1820 was how to respond to the successful revolt of most of Spain's Latin American colonies after the Napoleonic wars. Henry Clay and many other Americans called for immediate recognition of the new republics, arguing that these neighbors to the south were simply following the example of the United States in its own struggle for independence.

Before 1822, the administration stuck to a policy of neutrality. Monroe and Secretary of State Adams feared that recognizing the revolutionary governments would antagonize Spain and impede negotiations to acquire Florida. But pressure for recognition continued to mount in Congress. After ratification of the Adams-Onís treaty in 1821, Monroe agreed to recognition and the establishment of diplomatic ties with the Latin American republics. Mexico and Colombia were recognized in 1822, Chile and Argentina in 1823, Brazil and the Federation of Central American States in 1824, and Peru in 1826.

Recognizing the republics put the United States on a possible collision course with the major European powers. Austria, Russia, and Prussia were committed to rolling back the tides of liberalism, self-government, and national self-determination that had arisen during the French Revolution and its Napoleonic aftermath. After Napoleon's first defeat in 1814, the monarchs of Europe had joined in a "Grand Alliance" to protect "legitimate" authoritarian governments from democratic challenges. Great Britain was originally a member of this concert of nations but withdrew when it found that its own interests conflicted with those of the other members. In 1822, the remaining alliance members, joined now by the restored French monarchy, gave France the green light to invade Spain and restore a Bourbon regime that might be disposed to reconquer the empire. Both Great Britain and the United States were alarmed by this prospect.

The threat from the Grand Alliance compelled the United States to closer cooperation with Great Britain, for whom independent nations offered better and more open markets for British manufactured goods than the colonies of other nations. In 1823, British foreign secretary George Canning sought to involve the United States in a joint policy to prevent the Grand Alliance from intervening in Latin America.

In August, Canning broached the possibility of joint Anglo-American action against the Alliance to Richard Rush, U.S. minister to Great Britain, and Rush referred the suggestion to the president. Monroe welcomed the British initiative because he believed the United States should take an active role in transatlantic affairs by playing one European power against another. Secretary of State Adams, however, favored a different approach. Adams believed the national interest would best be served by avoiding all entanglements in European politics while at the same time discouraging European intervention in the Americas.

In the end, Adams managed to swing Monroe around to his viewpoint. In his annual message to Congress on December 2, 1823, Monroe included a far-reaching statement on foreign policy that was actually written mainly by Adams, who did become president in 1824. What came to be known as the Monroe Doctrine solemnly declared that the United States opposed any further colonization in the Americas or any effort by European nations to extend their political systems outside their own hemisphere. In return, the United States pledged not to involve itself in the internal affairs of Europe or to take part in European wars. The statement envisioned a North and South America composed entirely of independent republics—with the United States preeminent among them.

Although the Monroe Doctrine made little impression on the great powers of Europe at the time it was proclaimed, it signified the rise of a new sense of independence and self-confidence in American attitudes toward the Old World. The United States would now go its own way free of involvement in European conflicts and would energetically protect its own sphere of influence from European interference.

THE END OF THE ERA OF GOOD FEELING

The consensus on national goals and leadership that Monroe had represented could not sustain itself. The Era of Good Feeling turned out to be a passing phase and something of an illusion. Although the pursuit of national greatness would continue, there would be sharp divisions over how it should be achieved. A general commitment to settlement of the West and the development of agriculture, commerce, and industry would endure despite serious differences over what role government should play in the process; but the idea that an elite of nonpartisan statesmen could define common purposes and harmonize competing elements—the concept of leadership that Monroe and Adams had advanced—would no longer be viable in the more contentious and democratic America of the Jacksonian era.

CHRONOLOGY

1813	Boston Manufacturing Company founds cotton mill at Waltham, Massachusetts
1815	War of 1812 ends
1816	James Monroe elected president
1818	Andrew Jackson invades Florida
1819	Supreme Court hands down far-reaching decision in Dartmouth College case and in *McCulloch* v. *Maryland*
	Adams-Onís treaty cedes Spanish territory to the United States
	Financial panic is followed by a depression lasting until 1823
1820	Missouri Compromise resolves nation's first sectional crisis
	Monroe reelected president almost unanimously
1823	Monroe Doctrine proclaimed
1824	Lafayette revisits the United States
	Supreme Court decides *Gibbons* v. *Ogden*
	John Quincy Adams elected president
1825	Erie Canal completed; canal era begins

10

THE TRIUMPH OF WHITE MEN'S DEMOCRACY

So many Americans were moving about in the 1820s and 1830s that new industries sprang up just to meet their needs. To service the rising tide of travelers, transients, and new arrivals, entrepreneurs erected large hotels in the center of major cities. By the 1830s, imposing hotels were springing up in commercial centers all over the country. The grandest of these was New York's Astor House, completed in 1836.

According to historian Doris Elizabeth King, "the new hotels were so obviously 'public' and 'democratic' in their character that foreigners were often to describe them as a true reflection of American society." Their very existence showed that many people, white males in particular, were on the move geographically and socially. Among the hotels' patrons were traveling salesmen, ambitious young men seeking to establish themselves in a new city, and restless pursuers of economic opportunities who were not yet ready to put down roots.

Hotel managers shocked European visitors by failing to enforce traditional social distinctions among their clientele. Under the "American plan," guests were required to pay for their meals and to eat at a common "table d'hôte" with anyone who happened to be there, including servants traveling with their employers. Ability to pay was the only requirement for admission (unless one happened to be an unescorted woman or dark-skinned), and every white male patron, regardless of social background and occupation, enjoyed the kind of personal service previously available only to a privileged class.

The hotel culture also revealed some of the limitations of the new era of democratic ideals and aspirations. African Americans, Native Americans, and women were excluded or discriminated against, just as they were denied suffrage at a time when it was being extended to all white males. The genuinely poor—of whom there were more than met the eye of most European visitors—simply could not afford to patronize the hotels and were consigned to squalid rooming houses. If the social equality *within* the hotel reflected a decline in traditional status distinctions, the broad gulf between potential patrons and those who could not pay the rates signaled the growth of inequality based squarely on wealth rather than inherited status.

The hotel life also reflected the emergence of democratic politics. Professional politicians of a new breed, pursuing the votes of a mass electorate, spent much of their time in hotels as they traveled about. Those elected to Congress or a state legislature often stayed in hotels during the session, there conducting political deals and bargains.

When Andrew Jackson arrived in Washington to prepare for his administration in 1829, he took residence at the new National Hotel. The hotel was more than a public and "democratic" gathering place; it could also serve as a haven where the rising men of politics and business could find rest and privacy. In its lobbies, salons, and private rooms, the spirit of an age was expressing itself.

DEMOCRACY IN THEORY AND PRACTICE

During the 1820s and 1830s, the term *democracy* first became a generally accepted term to describe how American institutions were supposed to work. The Founders had defined democracy as direct rule by the people; most of them rejected this concept of a democratic approach to government because it was at odds with their conception of a well-balanced republic led by a "natural aristocracy." For champions of popular government in the Jacksonian period, however, the people were truly sovereign and could do no wrong. Conservatives were less certain of the wisdom of the common folk. But even they were coming to recognize that public opinion had to be won over before major policy decisions could be made.

Besides evoking a heightened sense of "popular sovereignty," the democratic impulse seemed to stimulate a process of social leveling. By the 1830s, the disappearance of inherited social ranks and clearly defined aristocracies or privileged groups struck European visitors such as Alexis de Tocqueville as the most radical feature of democracy in America. Historians have described this development as a decline of the spirit of "deference."

The decline of deference meant that "self-made men" of lowly origins could now rise more readily to positions of power and influence and that exclusiveness and aristocratic pretensions were likely to provoke popular hostility or scorn. But economic equality, in the sense of an equitable sharing of wealth, was not part of the mainstream agenda of the Jacksonian period. This was, after all, a competitive capitalist society. The watchword was equality of *opportunity*, not equality of *reward*. Historians now generally agree that economic inequality was actually increasing during this period of political and social democratization.

DEMOCRACY AND SOCIETY

Although some types of inequality persisted or even grew during the age of democracy, they did so in the face of a growing belief that equality was the governing principle of American society. What this meant in practice was that no one could expect special privileges because of family connections. The plain folk, who in an earlier period would have deferred to their betters, were now likely to greet claims for special treatment with indifference or scorn. High-status Europeans who traveled in America were constantly affronted by democratic attitudes and manners.

With the exception of slaveholders, wealthy Americans could not depend on a distinctive social class for domestic service. Instead of keeping "servants," they hired "help"—household workers who refused to wear livery, agreed to work for only short periods of time, and sometimes insisted on eating at the same table as their employers. No true American was willing to be considered a member of a servant class, and those who engaged in domestic work regarded it as a temporary stopgap.

The decline of distinctive modes of dress for upper and lower classes conveyed the principle of equality in yet another way. The elaborate periwigs and knee breeches worn by eighteenth-century gentlemen gave way to short hair and pantaloons, a style that was adopted by men of all social classes. Serving girls on their day off wore the same kind of finery as the wives and daughters of the wealthy. Those with a good eye for detail might detect subtle differences in taste or in quality of materials, but the casual observer of crowds in a large city could easily conclude that all Americans belonged to a single social class.

Of course, Americans were not all of one social class. In fact, inequality based on control of productive resources was increasing during the Jacksonian period. The rise of industrialization was creating a permanent class of landless, low-paid, unorganized wage earners in urban areas. In rural areas, there was a significant division between successful commercial farmers and smallholders, or tenants who subsisted on marginal land, as well as enormous inequality of status between southern planters and their slaves. But the attention of most foreign observers was riveted on the fact that all white males appeared to be equal before the law and at the polls, a situation that was genuinely radical by European standards.

Traditional forms of privilege and elitism were also under strong attack, as evidenced by changes in the organization and status of the learned professions. State legislatures abolished the licensing requirements for physicians, previously administered by local medical societies. As a result, practitioners of unorthodox modes of healing were permitted to compete freely with established medical doctors. The legal profession was similarly opened up to far more people. The result was not always beneficial.

For the clergy, "popular sovereignty" meant being increasingly under the thumb of the laity. Ministers had ceased to command respect merely because of their office, and to succeed in their calling, they were forced to develop a more popular and emotional style of preaching. Preachers, as much as politicians, prospered by pleasing the public.

In this atmosphere of democratic leveling, the popular press came to play an increasingly important role as a source of information and opinion. Written and read by common folk, hundreds of newspapers and magazines ushered the mass of white Americans into the political arena. New political views—which in a previous generation might have been silenced by those in power—could now find an audience. Reformers of all kinds could easily publicize their causes, and

Interior of an American Inn *(1813) by John Lewis Krimmel. In the early republic, people gathered in taverns to catch up on news—both the local news exchanged with their neighbors and the national news printed in newspapers and often read aloud to the patrons.*

the press became the venue for the great national debates on issues such as the government's role in banking and the status of slavery in new states and territories. As a profession, journalism was open to those who were literate and thought they had something to say. The editors of newspapers with a large circulation were the most influential opinion makers of the age.

DEMOCRATIC CULTURE

The democratic spirit also found expression in the rise of new forms of literature and art directed at a mass audience. The intentions of individual artists and writers varied considerably. Some sought success by pandering to popular taste. Others tried to capture the spirit of the age by portraying the everyday life of ordinary Americans. A notable few hoped to use literature and art as a way of improving popular taste and instilling deeper moral and spiritual values. But all of them were aware that their audience was the broad citizenry of a democratic nation rather than a refined elite.

The romantic movement in literature, which came to the fore in the early nineteenth century in both Europe and America, valued strong feeling and mystical intuition over the calm rationality and appeal to common experience that had prevailed in much of the writing of the eighteenth century. Romanticism was not necessarily connected with democracy; in Europe, it sometimes went along with a reaffirmation of the right of a superior few to rule over the masses. In America, however, romanticism often appealed to the feelings and intuitions of ordinary people: the innate love of goodness, truth, and beauty that all people were thought to possess. Writers in search of popularity and economic success, however, often deserted the high plane of romantic art for crass sentimentalism—a willingness to pull out all emotional stops to thrill readers or bring tears to their eyes.

A rise in literacy and a revolution in the technology of printing created a mass market for popular literature. An increase in the number of potential readers and a decrease in publishing costs led to a flood of lurid and sentimental novels, some of which became the first American best-sellers. Many of the new sentimental novels were written by and for women. Some women writers implicitly protested against their situation by portraying men as tyrannical, unreliable, or vicious and the women they abandoned or failed to support as resourceful individualists capable of making their own way in a man's world. But the standard happy endings sustained the convention that a woman's place was in the home, for a virtuous and protective man usually turned up and saved the heroine from independence.

In the theater, melodrama became the dominant genre. The standard fare involved the inevitable trio of beleaguered heroine, mustachioed villain, and a hero who asserted himself in the nick of time. Patriotic comedies extolling the common sense of the rustic Yankee who foiled the foppish European aristocrat were also popular and served to arouse the democratic sympathies of the audience. Men and women of all classes went to the theater, and those in the cheap seats often openly voiced their displeasure with an actor or a play.

The spirit of "popular sovereignty" expressed itself less dramatically in the visual arts, but its influence was felt nonetheless. Beginning in the 1830s, painters turned from portraying great events and famous people to depicting scenes from everyday life. Democratic genre painters such as William Sidney Mount and George Caleb Bingham captured the lives of plain folk with great skill and understanding. Mount, who painted lively rural scenes, expressed the credo of the democratic artist: "Paint pictures that will take with the public—never paint for the few but the many."

Sculpture was intended for public admiration or inspiration, and its principal subjects were the heroes of the republic. The sculptors who accepted public commissions had to make sure their work met the expectations of politicians and taxpayers, who favored stately, idealized images. Horatio Greenough, the greatest sculptor of the pre–Civil War era, got into trouble when he unveiled a seated George Washington, dressed in classical garb and nude from the waist up. Much more acceptable was the equestrian figure of Andrew Jackson executed for the federal government by Clark Mills and unveiled in 1853. What most impressed the public was that Mills had succeeded in balancing the horse on two legs.

Serious exponents of a higher culture and a more refined sensibility sought to reach the new public in the hope of enlightening or uplifting it. The "Brahmin poets" of New England—Henry Wadsworth Longfellow, James Russell Lowell, and Oliver Wendell Holmes—offered lofty sentiments and moral messages to a receptive middle class; Ralph Waldo Emerson carried his philosophy of spiritual self-reliance to lyceums and lecture halls across the country; and great novelists

William Sidney Mount, Rustic Dance After a Sleigh Ride, *1830. Mount's portrayals of country people folk dancing, gambling, playing music, or horse trading were pieces that appealed strongly to contemporaries. Art historians have found much to praise in his use of architecture, particularly that of the common barn, to achieve striking compositional effects.*

such as Nathaniel Hawthorne and Herman Melville experimented with the popular romantic genres. But the ironic and pessimistic view of life that pervaded the work of these two authors clashed with the optimism of the age and they failed to gain a large readership. Later generations of American critics, however, regarded the works of Melville and Hawthorne as the centerpieces of the American literary "renaissance" of the mid-nineteenth century. The most original of the antebellum poets, Walt Whitman, sought to be a direct mouthpiece for the rising democratic spirit, but his abandonment of traditional verse forms and his freedom in dealing with the sexual side of human nature left him relatively isolated and unappreciated during his most creative years.

THE DEMOCRATIC FERMENT

The supremacy of democracy was most obvious in the new politics of universal white manhood suffrage and mass political parties. By the 1820s, most states had removed the last remaining barriers to voting participation by all white males.

Accompanying this broadening of the electorate was a rise in the proportion of public officials who were elected rather than appointed. More and more judges, as well as legislative and executive officeholders, were chosen by the people. As a result, a new style of politicking developed, emphasizing dramatic speeches that appealed to voters' fears and concerns. Electoral politics began to assume a more festive quality.

Skillful and farsighted politicians—such as Martin Van Buren in New York—began in the 1820s to build stable statewide political organizations out of what had been loosely organized factions. Earlier politicians had regarded political parties as a threat to republican virtue and had embraced them only as a temporary expedient. But in Van Buren's opinion, regular parties were an effective check on the temptation to abuse power. The major breakthrough in American political thought during the 1820s and 1830s was the idea of a "loyal opposition," ready to capitalize politically on the mistakes or excesses of the "ins" without denying the right of the "ins" to act the same way when they became the "outs."

Changes in the method of nominating and electing a president fostered the growth of a two-party system on the national level. By 1828, presidential electors were chosen by popular vote rather than by state legislatures in all but two of the twenty-four states. The need to mobilize grassroots support behind particular candidates required national organization. Coalitions of state parties that could agree on a single standard-bearer gradually evolved into the great national parties of the Jacksonian era—the Democrats and the Whigs. When national nominating conventions made their appearance in 1831, candidate selection became a task for representative party assemblies, not congressional caucuses or ad hoc political alliances.

New political institutions and practices encouraged a great upsurge of popular interest and participation. Between 1824 and 1840, the percentage of eligible voters who cast their ballot in presidential elections tripled.

Economic questions dominated the political controversies of the 1820s and 1830s. The Panic of 1819 and the subsequent depression heightened popular interest in government economic policy. Americans proposed a number of ways to keep the economy healthy. Many small farmers favored a return to a simpler and more "honest" economy without banks, paper money, and the easy credit that encouraged speculation. Emerging entrepreneurs tended to see salvation in government aid and protection for venture capital, and they appealed to state governments for charters that granted special privileges to banks, transportation enterprises, and manufacturing corporations. Out of the economic distress of the early 1820s came a rapid growth of state-level political activity and organization that foreshadowed the rise of national parties, which would be organized around economic programs.

Party disputes involved more than the direct economic concerns of particular interest groups. They also reflected the republican ideology that feared conspiracy against American liberty and equality. Whenever any group appeared to be exerting decisive influence over public policy, people who did not identify with that group's aspirations were quick to charge its members with corruption and the unscrupulous pursuit of power.

The notion that the American experiment was a fragile one, constantly threatened by power-hungry conspirators, eventually took two principal forms. Jacksonians believed that "the money power" endangered the survival of republicanism; their opponents feared that populist politicians like Jackson himself—alleged "rabble-rousers"—would gull the electorate into ratifying high-handed and tyrannical actions contrary to the true interests of the nation.

An object of increasing concern for both sides was the role of the federal government. Almost everyone favored equality of opportunity, but there was serious disagreement over whether this goal could best be achieved by active government support of commerce and industry or by divorcing the government from the economy in the name of laissez-faire and free competition. National Republicans, and later the Whigs, favored an active role for the government; Jacksonians simply wanted to end "special privileges."

For one group of dissenters, democracy took on a more radical meaning. Leaders of workingmen's parties and trade unions condemned the growing gap between the rich and the poor resulting from early industrialization and the growth of a market economy. They argued that employers' dominance over workers was endangering the American tradition of "equal rights." To them, society was divided between "producers"—laborers, artisans, farmers, and small-business owners who ran their own enterprises—and nonproducing "parasites"—bankers, speculators, and merchant capitalists. Workingmen's parties aimed to give the producers greater control over the fruits of their labor.

These radicals advocated a number of reforms to achieve their goal of equal rights, including abolition of inheritance and a redistribution of property, extended and improved systems of public education, cooperative production, a ten-hour workday, abolition of imprisonment for debt, and a currency system based exclusively on hard money so workers could no longer be paid in depreciated banknotes.

In the 1830s and 1840s, northern abolitionists and early proponents of women's rights also attempted to extend the meaning and scope of democracy. But Jacksonian America was too permeated with racism and male chauvinism to give much heed to claims that the equal rights prescribed by the Declaration of Independence should be extended to blacks and women. Most of those who advocated democratization explicitly limited its application to white males, and in some ways, the civil and political status of blacks and women actually deteriorated during "the age of the common *man*."

JACKSON AND THE POLITICS OF DEMOCRACY

The public figure who came to symbolize the triumph of democracy was Andrew Jackson, although he lost the presidential election of 1824. His victory four years later, his actions as president, and the great political party that formed around him refashioned national politics in a more democratic mold.

THE ELECTION OF 1824
AND J. Q. ADAMS'S ADMINISTRATION

As Monroe's second term ended, the ruling Republican party was in disarray and could not agree on who should succeed to the presidency. The party's congressional caucus chose William Crawford of Georgia, an old-line Jeffersonian. But a majority of congressmen disapproved of this outmoded method of nominating candidates and refused to attend the caucus. Monroe himself favored John Quincy Adams of Massachusetts. Supporters of Henry Clay and John C. Calhoun mounted campaigns for their favorites, and a group of local leaders in his home state of Tennessee tossed Jackson's hat into the ring.

Initially, Jackson was not given much of a chance. Although he was a famous military hero, not even his original supporters believed this would be sufficient to catapult him into the White House. But then Calhoun withdrew and chose instead to run for vice president. Crawford suffered a debilitating stroke that weakened his chances. These developments made Jackson the favorite in the South. He also found support among Northerners and Westerners who were disenchanted with the economic nationalism of Clay and Adams.

Jackson won a plurality of the electoral votes, but he lacked the required majority. The contest was thrown into the House of Representatives, where the legislators were to choose from among the three top candidates. Adams emerged victorious over Jackson and Crawford when Clay, who had just missed making the final three, persuaded his supporters to vote for Adams. When Adams then appointed Clay as his secretary of state, Jacksonians charged that a "corrupt bargain" had deprived their favorite of the presidency. Even though the charge was unproven, Adams assumed office under a cloud of suspicion.

Adams had a difficult and frustrating presidency. The political winds were blowing against nationalistic programs, partly because the country was just recovering from a depression that many thought had been caused or exacerbated by federal banking and tariff policies. Adams refused to bow to public opinion and called for an expansion of federal activity, including government funding of scientific research and the establishment of a national university. Congress, however, firmly rejected the administration's ambitious domestic program.

The new Congress elected in 1826 was clearly under the control of men hostile to the administration and favorable to the presidential aspirations of Andrew Jackson. The tariff issue was the main business on their agenda.

THE ELECTION OF 1824

CANDIDATE	PARTY	POPULAR VOTE	ELECTORAL VOTE*
J. Q. Adams	No party designation	108,740	84
Jackson		153,544	99
Clay		47,136	37
Crawford		46,618	41

*No candidate received a majority of the electoral votes. Adams was elected by the House of Representatives.

Pressure for greater protection came not only from manufacturers but also from many farmers. The cotton-growing South—the only section where tariffs of all kinds were unpopular—was assumed to be safely in Jackson's camp. Therefore, promoters of Jackson's candidacy felt safe in supporting a high tariff to swing critical votes in Jackson's direction. Jackson himself had never categorically opposed protective tariffs so long as they were "judicious."

As it turned out, the resulting 1828 tariff law was anything but judicious. Congress had operated on a give-and-take principle, trying to provide something for everybody. The substantial across-the-board increase in duties that resulted, however, angered southern free traders and became known as the "tariff of abominations."

JACKSON COMES TO POWER

The campaign of 1828 actually began with Adams's election in 1824. Rallying around the charge of a corrupt bargain between Adams and Clay, Jackson's supporters began to organize to get their candidate elected in 1828. So successful were their efforts that influential state or regional leaders who had supported other candidates in 1824 now rallied behind the Tennessean to create a formidable coalition.

The most significant of these were Vice President Calhoun, who now spoke for the militant states' rights sentiment of the South; Senator Martin Van Buren, who dominated New York politics through the political machine known as the Albany Regency; and two Kentucky editors, Francis P. Blair and Amos Kendall, who worked in the West to mobilize opposition to Henry Clay and his "American System," which advocated government encouragement of economic development through such measures as protective tariffs and federally funded internal improvements. These leaders and their many local followers laid the foundations for the first modern American political party—the Democrats. The fact that the Democratic party was founded to promote the cause of a particular presidential candidate revealed a central characteristic of the emerging two-party system. From this time on, according to historian Richard P. McCormick, national parties existed primarily "to engage in a contest for the presidency."

The election of 1828 saw the birth of a new era of mass democracy. Jackson's supporters made widespread use of such electioneering techniques as huge public rallies, torchlight parades, and lavish barbecues or picnics paid for by the candidate's supporters. Personalities and mudslinging dominated the

THE ELECTION OF 1828

CANDIDATE	PARTY	POPULAR VOTE	ELECTORAL VOTE
Jackson	Democratic	647,286	178
Adams	National Republican	508,064	83

An 1835 painting of Andrew Jackson in the heroic style by Thomas Sully. The painting shows Jackson as the common people saw him.

campaign of 1828, which reached its low point when Adams's supporters accused Jackson's wife, Rachel, of bigamy and adultery because she had unwittingly married Jackson before being officially divorced from her first husband. The Democrats then countered with the utterly false charge that Adams's wife had been born out of wedlock!

What gave Jacksonians the edge was their success in portraying their candidate as an authentic man of the people, despite his substantial fortune in land and slaves. His backwoods upbringing, his record as a popular military hero and Indian fighter, and even his lack of education were touted as evidence that he was a true representative of the common people, especially the common folk of the South and the West. Adams, according to Democratic propagandists, was the exact opposite—an overeducated aristocrat, more at home in the salon and the study than among common people. Nature's nobleman was pitted against the aloof New England intellectual, and Adams never really had a chance.

Jackson won by a popular vote margin of almost 150,000 and by more than 2 to 1 in the electoral college. He had piled up massive majorities in the Deep South, but the voters elsewhere divided fairly evenly. Adams, in fact, won a majority of the electoral vote in the northern states. Furthermore, it was not clear what kind of mandate Jackson had won. Most of the politicians in his camp favored states' rights and limited government, but "Old Hickory," as Jackson was called, had never taken a clear public stand on such issues as banks, tariffs, and internal improvements. He did, however, stand for the removal of Indians from the Gulf states, and this was a key to his immense popularity in that region.

Jackson turned out to be one of the most forceful and domineering of American presidents. His most striking character traits were an indomitable will, an intolerance of opposition, and a prickly pride that would not permit him to forgive or forget an insult or supposed act of betrayal. His violent temper had led him to fight a number of duels, and as a soldier his critics charged him with using excessive force. His experiences had made him tough and resourceful but had also deprived him of the flexibility normally associated with successful politicians. Yet he generally got what he wanted.

Jackson's presidency commenced with his open endorsement of rotation of officeholders or what his critics called "the spoils system." Although he did not actually depart radically from his predecessors in the extent to which he removed federal officeholders and replaced them with his supporters, he was the first president to defend this practice as a legitimate application of democratic doctrine.

Midway through his first administration, Jackson completely reorganized his cabinet, replacing almost all of his original appointees. At the root of this upheaval was a growing feud between Jackson and Vice President Calhoun, but the incident that brought it to a head was the Peggy Eaton affair. Peggy O'Neale Eaton, the daughter of a Washington tavern owner, married Secretary of War John Eaton in 1829. Because of gossip about her moral character, the wives of other cabinet members refused to receive her socially. Jackson became her fervent champion, partly because he found the charges against her reminiscent of the slanders against his late wife, who had died in 1828. When he raised the issue of Mrs. Eaton's social status at a cabinet meeting, only Secretary of State Van Buren, a widower, supported his stand. This seemingly trivial incident led to the resignation of all but one of the cabinet members, and the president was able to begin again with a fresh slate. Although Van Buren resigned with the rest, his loyalty was rewarded by his appointment as minister to England and strong prospects of future favor.

INDIAN REMOVAL

The first major policy question facing the Jackson administration concerned the fate of Native Americans. Jackson had long favored removing eastern Indians to lands beyond the Mississippi. Jackson's support of removal was no different from the policy of previous administrations. The only real issues to be determined were how rapidly and thoroughly the process should be carried out and by what means. At the time of Jackson's election, the states of Georgia, Alabama, and Mississippi were clamoring for quick action.

The greatest obstacle to voluntary relocation was the Cherokee Nation, which held lands in Georgia, Alabama, North Carolina, and Tennessee. The Cherokee, who had instituted a republican form of government among themselves, refused to move. In response, Georgia and Alabama extended their state

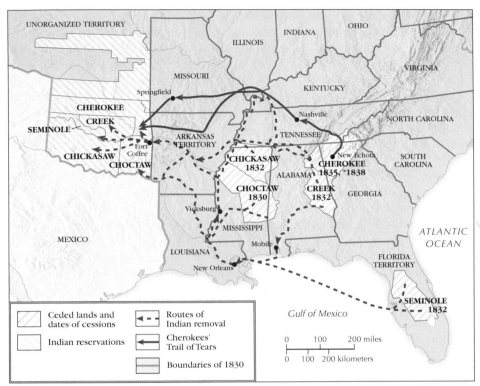

Treaty signed in 1835 by a minority faction was met with defiance from the majority, but removal was forced in 1838.

Indian Removal
Because so many Native Americans, uprooted from their lands in the East, died on the forced march to Oklahoma, the route they followed became known as the Trail of Tears.

laws over the Cherokee, actions which defied provisions of the Constitution that gave the federal government exclusive jurisdiction over Indian affairs and also violated specific treaties. As anticipated, Jackson quickly gave his endorsement to the state actions. His own attitude toward Indians was that they were children when they did the white man's bidding and savage beasts when they resisted. In his December 1829 message to Congress, he advocated a new and more coercive removal policy. He denied Cherokee autonomy, asserted the primacy of states' rights over Indian rights, and called for the speedy and thorough removal of all eastern Indians to designated areas beyond the Mississippi.

Early in 1830, the president's congressional supporters introduced a bill to implement this policy. The ensuing debate was vigorous and heated, but with strong support from the South and the western border states, the removal bill passed both the Senate and the House.

Jackson then moved quickly to conclude the necessary treaties, using the threat of unilateral state action to bludgeon the tribes into submission. In 1832, he condoned Georgia's defiance of a Supreme Court decision (*Worcester* v. *Georgia*) that denied the right of a state to extend its jurisdiction over tribal lands. By 1833, all the southeastern tribes except the Cherokee had agreed to evacuate their ancestral homes. A stubbornly resisting majority faction of the Cherokee held out until 1838 when military pressure forced them to march to Oklahoma. This trek—known as the Trail of Tears—was made under such harsh conditions that almost four thousand of approximately sixteen thousand marchers died on the way.

THE NULLIFICATION CRISIS

During the 1820s, Southerners became increasingly fearful of federal encroachment on states' rights. Behind this concern, in South Carolina at least, was a strengthened commitment to the preservation of slavery and a resulting anxiety about possible uses of federal power to strike at the peculiar institution. Hoping to keep the explosive slavery issue out of the political limelight, South Carolinians seized on another genuine grievance, the protective tariff, as the issue on which to take their stand in favor of a state veto power over federal actions they viewed as contrary to their interests. Tariffs that increased the prices that southern agriculturists paid for manufactured goods and threatened to undermine their foreign markets by inciting counterprotection hurt the economy of the staple-producing and exporting South.

Vice President John C. Calhoun emerged as the leader of the states' rights insurgency in South Carolina. After the passage of the tariff of abominations in 1828, the state legislature declared the new duties unconstitutional and endorsed a lengthy statement—written anonymously by Calhoun—that affirmed the right of an individual state to nullify federal law. Calhoun supported Jackson in 1828 and expected Jackson to support his native region on questions involving the tariff and states' rights. He also entertained hopes of succeeding Jackson as president.

In the meantime, however, a bitter personal feud developed between Jackson and Calhoun. Jackson considered the vice president and his wife prime movers in the ostracism of Peggy Eaton. Furthermore, evidence came to light that Calhoun, as secretary of war in Monroe's cabinet in 1818, had privately advocated punishing Jackson for his incursion into Florida. As Calhoun lost favor with Jackson, it became clear that Van Buren rather than the vice president would be Jackson's designated successor. The personal breach between Jackson and Calhoun colored and intensified their confrontation over nullification and the tariff.

The two men differed on matters of principle as well. Although generally a defender of states' rights and strict construction of the Constitution, Jackson opposed the theory of nullification as a threat to the survival of the Union. In his view, federal power should be held in check, but this did not mean the states were truly sovereign. The differences between Jackson and Calhoun came into the open at the Jefferson Day dinner in 1830, when Jackson offered the toast "Our Union: It must be preserved," to which Calhoun responded, "The Union. Next to Liberty, the most dear. May we always remember that it can only be preserved by distributing equally the benefits and the burdens of the Union."

In 1830 and 1831, the movement against the tariff gained strength in South Carolina. In 1832, Congress passed a new tariff that lowered the rates slightly but retained the principle of protection. Supporters of nullification persuaded the South Carolina state legislature to call a special convention. When the convention met in November 1832, the members voted overwhelmingly to nullify the tariffs of 1828 and 1832 and to forbid the collection of customs duties within the state.

Jackson reacted with characteristic decisiveness. He alerted the secretary of war to prepare for possible military action, issued a proclamation denouncing nullification as a treasonous attack on the Union, and asked Congress to vote him the authority to use the army to enforce the tariff. At the same time, he sought to pacify the nullifiers somewhat by recommending a lower tariff. Congress responded by enacting the Force Bill, which gave the president the military powers he sought, and the compromise tariff of 1833. Faced with this combination of force and appeasement, South Carolina rescinded the nullification ordinance in March 1833. But to demonstrate that they had not conceded their constitutional position, the convention delegates concluded their deliberations by nullifying the Force Bill.

The nullification crisis revealed that South Carolinians would not tolerate any federal action that seemed contrary to their interests or raised doubts about the institution of slavery. The nullifiers' philosophy implied the right of secession as well as the right to declare laws of Congress null and void. As subsequent events would show, a fear of northern meddling with slavery was the main spur to the growth of a militant doctrine of state sovereignty in the South. At the time of the nullification crisis, the other slave states had not yet developed such strong anxieties about the future of the peculiar institution. Jackson was himself a Southerner and a slaveholder, and in general, he was a proslavery president.

Some farsighted southern loyalists, however, were alarmed by the Unionist doctrines that Jackson propounded in his proclamation against nullification. More strongly than any previous president, he had asserted that the federal government was supreme over the states and that the Union was indivisible. What was more, he had justified the use of force against states that denied federal authority.

THE BANK WAR AND THE SECOND PARTY SYSTEM

Jackson's most important and controversial use of executive power was his successful attack on the Bank of the United States. The "Bank war" revealed some of the deepest concerns of Jackson and his supporters and dramatically expressed their concept of democracy. It also aroused intense opposition to the president and his policies, an opposition that crystallized in a new national party—the Whigs. The destruction of the Bank and the economic disruption that followed brought to the forefront the issue of the government's relationship to the nation's financial system. Differences on this question helped to sustain and strengthen the new two-party system.

BIDDLE, THE BANK VETO, AND THE ELECTION OF 1832

The Bank of the United States had long been embroiled in public controversy. Many, especially in the South and the West, blamed the Bank and its policies for the Panic of 1819 and the subsequent depression. But after Nicholas Biddle took over the Bank's presidency in 1823, the institution regained public confidence. Cultured, well-educated, and politically experienced, Biddle probably understood the mysteries of banking and currency better than any other American of his generation.

Old-line Jeffersonians had always opposed the Bank on the grounds that its establishment was unconstitutional and that it placed too much power in the hands of a small, privileged group. A chartered monopoly, the Bank was an essentially private corporation performing public services in return for exclusive economic rights. Because of its great influence, the Bank tended to be blamed for anything that went wrong with the economy. For those who had misgivings about the rise of the national market, the Bank epitomized the forces threatening the independence and prosperity of small producers. In an era of rising white men's democracy, an obvious and telling objection to the Bank was simply that it possessed great power and privilege without being under popular control.

Jackson came into office with strong reservations about banking and paper money in general—in part as a result of his own brushes with bankruptcy. He also harbored suspicions that branches of the Bank of the United States had illicitly used their influence on behalf of his opponent in the presidential election. In his annual messages in 1829 and 1830, Jackson called on Congress to begin discussing ways to curb the Bank's power.

Biddle began to worry about the fate of the Bank's charter when it came up for renewal in 1836. At the same time, Jackson was listening to the advice of his "Kitchen Cabinet," especially Amos Kendall and Francis P. Blair, who thought an attack on the Bank would provide a good party issue for the election of 1832. Biddle then made a fateful blunder. He determined to seek recharter by Congress in 1832, four years ahead of schedule. Senator Henry Clay, leader of the anti-administration forces on Capitol Hill, encouraged this move because he was convinced that Jackson had chosen the unpopular side of the issue and would be embarrassed or even discredited by a congressional endorsement of the Bank. The bill to recharter, therefore, was introduced in the House and Senate in early 1832. Despite the opposition of Jackson and his administration, it passed Congress with ease.

THE ELECTION OF 1832

CANDIDATE	PARTY	POPULAR VOTE	ELECTORAL VOTE
Jackson	Democratic	688,242	219
Clay	National Republican	473,462	49
Wirt	Anti-Masonic	101,051	7
Floyd	Independent Democratic	*	11

*Delegates chosen by South Carolina legislature.

The next move was Jackson's, and he made the most of the opportunity. He vetoed the bill and defended his action with ringing statements of principle. The Bank was unconstitutional, he claimed (notwithstanding the Supreme Court's ruling on the issue). He argued further that it violated the fundamental rights of the people in a democratic society: "In the full enjoyment of the gifts of Heaven and the fruits of superior industry, economy, and virtue, every man is equally entitled to protection by law; but when the laws undertake . . . to grant . . . exclusive privileges, the humble members of society—the farmers, mechanics, and laborers—who have neither the time nor the means of securing like favors to themselves, have a right to complain of the injustice of their government." Government, he added, should "confine itself to equal protection."

Jackson thus called on the common people to join him in fighting the "monster" corporation. His veto message was the first ever to use more than strictly constitutional arguments and to deal directly with social and economic issues. Congressional attempts to override the veto failed, and Jackson resolved to take the entire issue to the people in the upcoming presidential election.

The 1832 election, the first in which candidates were chosen by national nominating conventions, pitted Jackson against Henry Clay, standard-bearer of the National Republicans. The Bank recharter was the major issue. In the end, Jackson won a great personal triumph, garnering 219 electoral votes to 49 for Clay. As far as Jackson was concerned, he had his mandate for continuing the war against the Bank.

KILLING THE BANK

Not content with preventing the Bank from getting a new charter, Jackson now resolved to attack it directly by removing federal deposits from Biddle's vaults. Jackson told Van Buren, "The bank . . . is trying to kill me, but I will kill it." The Bank, in an act of self-defense, had indeed used all the political influence it could muster in an attempt to prevent Jackson's reelection. Old Hickory regarded Biddle's actions during the presidential race as a personal attack.

In order to remove the deposits from the Bank, Jackson had to overcome strong resistance in his own cabinet. When one secretary of the treasury refused to support the policy, he was shifted to another cabinet post. When a second balked at carrying out removal, he was replaced by Roger B. Taney, a Jackson loyalist and dedicated opponent of the Bank. Beginning in late September 1833, Taney ceased depositing government money in the Bank of the United States and began to withdraw the funds already there. The problem of how to dispose of the funds was resolved by an ill-advised decision to place them in selected state banks. By the end of 1833, twenty-three state banks had been chosen as depositories. Opponents charged that the banks had been selected for political rather than fiscal reasons and dubbed them Jackson's "pet banks." Since Congress refused to approve administration proposals to regulate the credit policies of these banks, Jackson's effort to shift to a hard-money economy was quickly nullified by the use the state banks made of the new deposits. They extended credit more recklessly than before and increased the amount of paper money in circulation.

The Bank of the United States counterattacked by calling in outstanding loans and instituting a policy of credit contraction that helped bring on an economic recession. Biddle hoped to win support for recharter by demonstrating that weakening the Bank's position would be disastrous for the economy. But all he showed, at least to the president's supporters, was that they had been right all along about the Bank's excessive power. They blamed the economic distress on Biddle, and the Bank never did regain its charter.

Strong opposition to Jackson's fiscal policies developed in Congress. Led by Henry Clay, the Senate approved a motion of censure against Jackson, charging him with exceeding his constitutional authority when he removed the deposits from the Bank. Jacksonians in the House were able to block such action, but the president was further humiliated when the Senate refused to confirm Taney as secretary of the treasury. Some congressmen who originally defended Jackson's veto now became disenchanted with the president because they thought he had gone too far in asserting the powers of his office.

THE EMERGENCE OF THE WHIGS

The coalition that passed the censure resolution in the Senate provided the nucleus for a new national party, the Whigs. The leadership of the new party and a majority of its support came from National Republicans and ex-Federalists. The Whigs also picked up critical support from southern proponents of states' rights who had been upset by Jackson's stand on nullification and then saw an unconstitutional abuse of power in his withdrawal of federal deposits from the Bank of the United States. The Whig label was chosen because of its associations with both English and American revolutionary opposition to royal power and prerogatives. The initial rallying cry for this diverse anti-Jackson coalition was "executive usurpation" by the tyrannical designs of "King Andrew" and his court.

The Whigs also gradually absorbed the Anti-Masonic party, a surprisingly strong political movement that had arisen in the northeastern states in the late 1820s and early 1830s. The Anti-Masons exploited traditional American fears of secret societies and conspiracies. They also appealed successfully to the moral concerns of the northern middle class under the sway of an emerging evangelical Protestantism. Anti-Masons detested Jacksonianism mainly because it stood for a toleration of diverse lifestyles. They believed that the government should restrict such "sinful" behavior as drinking, gambling, and breaking the Sabbath.

As the election of 1836 approached, the government's fiscal policies also provoked a localized rebellion among the urban working-class elements of the Democratic coalition. In New York City, a dissident faction broke with the regular Democratic organization. These radicals—called Loco-Focos after the matches they used for illumination when their opponents turned off the gaslights at a party meeting—favored a strict hard-money policy and condemned Jackson's transfer of federal deposits to the state banks as inflationary. The Loco-Focos went beyond opposition to the Bank of the United States and attacked state banks as well. Seeing no basis for cooperation with the Whigs, they established the independent Equal Rights party and nominated a separate state ticket for 1836.

Jackson himself had hard-money sentiments and regarded the "pet bank" solution as a stopgap measure rather than a final solution to the money problem. Nonetheless, in early 1836, he surrendered to congressional pressure and signed legislation allocating surplus federal revenues to the deposit banks, increasing their numbers and weakening federal controls over them. The result was runaway inflation as state banks in the South and West responded to demands from land-speculating interests by issuing a new flood of paper money. Reacting somewhat belatedly to the speculative mania he had helped to create, on July 11, 1836, Jackson issued his "specie circular," requiring that after August 15 only gold and silver would be accepted in payment for public lands. The action did curb inflation and land speculation but in such a sudden and drastic way that it helped precipitate the financial panic of 1837.

THE RISE AND FALL OF VAN BUREN

As his successor, Jackson chose Martin Van Buren, a master of practical politics. In accepting the nomination of the Democratic National Convention in 1835, Van Buren promised to "tread generally in the footsteps of General Jackson."

The newly created Whig party, reflecting the diversity of its constituency, did not try to decide on a single standard-bearer and instead supported three regional candidates—Daniel Webster in the East, William Henry Harrison of Ohio (also the Anti-Masonic nominee) in the Old Northwest, and Hugh Lawson White of Tennessee (a former Jackson supporter) in the South. Whigs hoped to deprive Van Buren of enough electoral votes to throw the election into the House of Representatives where one of the Whigs might stand a chance.

The strategy proved unsuccessful. Van Buren won a clear victory. But the election foreshadowed future trouble for the Democrats, particularly in the South. There the Whigs ran virtually even. The emergence of a two-party system in the previously solid Deep South resulted from opposition to some of Jackson's policies and the image of Van Buren as an unreliable Yankee politician. The division did not reflect basic disagreement on the slavery issue. Both Southern Whigs and Democrats shared a commitment to protecting slavery, and each tried to persuade the electorate they could do the job better than the opposition.

As he took office, Van Buren was immediately faced with a catastrophic depression. The price of cotton fell by almost 50 percent, banks all over the nation suspended specie payments, and many businesses went bankrupt. The sale of public lands fell off so drastically that the federal surplus became a deficit.

The Panic of 1837, however, was not exclusively, or even primarily, the result of government policies. It was in fact international in scope and reflected some complex changes in the world economy that were beyond the control of American policymakers. But the Whigs were quick to blame the state of the economy on Jacksonian finance. Committed to a policy of laissez-faire on the federal level, Van Buren and his party could do little or nothing to relieve economic distress through subsidies or relief measures. But Van Buren could at least try to salvage the federal funds deposited in shaky state banks and devise a new system of public finance that would not contribute to future panics by fueling speculation and credit expansion.

An adroit politician and a loyal vice president to Jackson, Martin Van Buren was Jackson's choice and the Democratic party's nominee for president in 1836.

Van Buren's solution was to establish a public depository for government funds with no connections whatsoever to commercial banking. His proposal for such an "independent subtreasury" aroused intense opposition from the congressional Whigs, who strongly favored the reestablishment of a national bank as the only way to restore economic stability. Whig resistance stalled the Independent Subtreasury Bill for three years, and it was not enacted into law until 1840.

The state of the economy undoubtedly hurt Van Buren's chances for reelection in 1840. The Whigs had the chance to offer alternative policies that

THE ELECTION OF 1836

CANDIDATE	PARTY	POPULAR VOTE	ELECTORAL VOTE
Van Buren	Democratic	764,198	170
Harrison	Whig	549,508	73
White	Whig	145,342	26
Webster	Whig	41,287	14
Mangum	Independent Democratic	*	11

*Delegates chosen by South Carolina legislature.

THE ELECTION OF 1840

CANDIDATE	PARTY	POPULAR VOTE	ELECTORAL VOTE
Harrison	Whig	1,274,624	234
Van Buren	Democratic	1,127,781	60

promised to restore prosperity. The Whigs passed over the true leader of their party, Henry Clay, and nominated William Henry Harrison, a military hero of advanced age who was associated in the public mind with the battle of Tippecanoe and the winning of the West. To balance the ticket and increase its appeal in the South, they chose John Tyler of Virginia, a converted states' rights Democrat, to be Harrison's running mate.

Using the slogan "Tippecanoe and Tyler, too," the Whigs pulled out all stops in their bid for the White House. Matching the Democrats in grassroots organization and popular electioneering, the Whigs staged rallies and parades in every locality, complete with posters, placards, campaign hats and emblems, special songs, and even movable log cabins filled with coonskin caps and barrels of cider for the faithful. Imitating the Jacksonian propaganda against Adams in 1828, they portrayed Van Buren as a luxury-loving aristocrat and compared him with their own homespun candidate. Election day saw an enormous turnout—78 percent of those eligible to vote. Harrison carried 19 of the 26 states and won 234 electoral votes to 60 for Van Buren. Buoyed by the electorate's belief that their policies might revive the economy, the Whigs also won control of both houses of Congress.

HEYDAY OF THE SECOND PARTY SYSTEM

America's "second party system" came of age in the election of 1840. The rivalry of Democrats and Whigs made the two-party pattern a normal feature of electoral politics in the United States. During the 1840s, the two national parties competed on fairly equal terms for the support of the electorate. Allegiance to one party or the other became an important source of personal identity for many Americans and increased their interest and participation in politics.

In addition to drama and entertainment, the parties offered the voters a real choice of programs and ideologies. Whigs stood for a "positive liberal state," in which government had the right and duty to subsidize or protect enterprises that could contribute to general prosperity and economic growth. Democrats normally advocated a "negative liberal state" in which government should keep its hands off the economy.

Political candidates of the Jacksonian era traveled from town to town giving stump speeches. The political gatherings at which they spoke provided entertainment as well as an excellent source of political news. This painting, Stump Speaking, *is by George Caleb Bingham, one of the most prolific of the democratic genre painters.*

Conflict over economic issues helped determine each party's base of support. In the Whig camp were industrialists who wanted tariff protection, merchants who favored internal improvements as a stimulus to commerce, and farmers and planters who had adapted successfully to a market economy. Democrats appealed mainly to smaller farmers, workers, declining gentry, and emerging entrepreneurs who were excluded from the established commercial groups that stood to benefit most from Whig programs. To some extent, this division pitted richer, more privileged Americans against those who were poorer and less economically or socially secure. But it did not follow class lines in any simple or direct way. Many businessmen were Democrats, and large numbers of wage earners voted Whig. Merchants engaged in the import trade had no use for Whiggish high tariffs, whereas workers in industries clamoring for protection often concluded that their jobs depended on such duties.

Lifestyles and ethnic or religious identities also strongly affected party loyalties during this period. In the northern states, one way to tell the typical Whig from the typical Democrat was to see what each did on Sunday. A person who went to one of the evangelical Protestant churches was very likely to be a Whig. On the other hand, the person who attended a ritualized service—Catholic, Lutheran, or Episcopalian—or did not go to church at all was most probably a Democrat.

The Democrats were the favored party of immigrants, Catholics, freethinkers, backwoods farmers, and those of all classes who enjoyed traditional amusements condemned by the new breed of moral reformers. One thing all these groups had in common was a desire to be left alone, free of restrictions on their freedom to think and behave as they liked. The Whigs enjoyed particularly strong support among Protestants of old stock living in smaller cities, towns, and prosperous rural areas devoted to market farming. In general, the Whigs welcomed a market economy but wanted to restrain the individualism and disorder it created by enforcing cultural and moral values derived from the Puritan tradition.

Nevertheless, party conflict in Congress continued to center on national economic policy. Whigs stood firm for a loose construction of the Constitution and federal support for business and economic development. The Democrats persisted in their defense of strict construction, states' rights, and laissez-faire. Debates over tariffs, banking, and internal improvements remained vital and vigorous during the 1840s.

True believers in both parties saw a deep ideological or moral meaning in the clash over economic issues. Whigs and Democrats had conflicting views of the good society, and their policy positions reflected these differences. The Democrats were the party of white male equality and personal liberty. They perceived the American people as a collection of independent and self-sufficient white men. The role of government was to see to it that the individual was not interfered with—in his economic activity, in his personal habits, and in his religion (or lack of it). Democrats were ambivalent about the rise of the market economy because of the ways it threatened individual independence. The Whigs, by contrast, were the party of orderly progress under the guidance of an enlightened elite. They believed that the propertied, the well-educated, and the pious were responsible for guiding the masses toward the common good. Believing sincerely that a market economy would benefit everyone in the long run, they had no qualms about the rise of a commercial and industrial capitalism.

TOCQUEVILLE'S WISDOM

The French traveler Alexis de Tocqueville, author of the most influential account ever written of the emergence of American democracy, visited the United States in 1831 and 1832. He had relatively little to say about national politics and the formation of political parties. For him, the essence of American democracy was local self-government, such as he observed in the town meetings of New England. The participation of ordinary citizens in the affairs of their communities impressed him greatly, and he praised Americans for not conceding their liberties to a centralized state.

Despite his generally favorable view of the American experiment, Tocqueville was acutely aware of the limitations of American democracy and of the dangers facing the republic. He believed the nullification crisis foreshadowed destruction of the Union and predicted the problem of slavery would lead eventually to civil war and racial conflict. He also noted the power of white supremacy, providing an unforgettable firsthand description of the sufferings of an Indian community in the course of forced migration to the West, as well as a graphic account of the way free blacks were segregated and driven from the polls in northern cities like Philadelphia. White Americans, he believed, were deeply prejudiced against people of color, and he doubted it was possible "for a whole people to rise . . . above itself." Tocqueville was equally sure that the kind of democracy men were practicing was not meant for women. Observing how women were strictly assigned to a separate domestic sphere, he concluded that Americans had never supposed "that democratic principles should undermine the husband's authority and make it doubtful who is in charge of the family." His observations have value because of their clear-sighted insistence that the democracy and equality of the Jacksonian era were meant for only some of the people. The democratic idea could not be so limited; it would soon begin to burst the boundaries of white male supremacy.

CHRONOLOGY

1824	House of Representatives elects John Quincy Adams president
1828	Congress passes "tariff of abominations"
	Jackson elected president over J. Q. Adams
1830	Jackson vetoes the Maysville Road Bill
	Congress passes Indian Removal Act
1831	Jackson reorganizes his cabinet
	First national nominating conventions meet
1832	Jackson vetoes the bill rechartering the Bank of the United States
	Jackson reelected, defeating Henry Clay (National Republican candidate)
1832–1833	Crisis erupts over South Carolina's attempt to nullify the tariff of 1832
1833	Jackson removes federal deposits from the Bank of the United States
1834	Whig party comes into existence
1836	Jackson issues "specie circular"
	Martin Van Buren elected president
1837	Financial panic occurs, followed by depression lasting until 1843
1840	Congress passes the Independent Subtreasury Bill
	Harrison (Whig) defeats Van Buren (Democrat) for the presidency

11

SLAVES AND MASTERS

On August 22, 1831, the worst nightmare of southern slaveholders became reality. A group of slaves in Southampton County, Virginia, rose in open and bloody rebellion. Their leader was Nat Turner, a preacher and prophet who believed God had given him a sign that the time was ripe to strike for freedom.

Beginning with a few followers and rallying others as he went along, Turner led his band from plantation to plantation and oversaw the killing of nearly sixty whites. The rebellion was short-lived; after only forty-eight hours, white forces dispersed the rampaging slaves. The rebels were then rounded up and executed, along with dozens of other slaves who were vaguely suspected of complicity. Nat Turner was the last to be captured, and he went to the gallows unrepentant, convinced he had acted in accordance with God's will.

White Southerners were determined to prevent another such uprising. Their anxiety and resolve were strengthened by the fact that a more militant northern abolitionism began to emerge in 1831. Although no evidence came to light that Turner was directly influenced by abolitionist propaganda, many whites believed that he must have been or that future rebels might be. Consequently, they launched a massive campaign to quarantine the slaves from possible exposure to antislavery ideas and attitudes.

A series of new laws severely restricted the rights of slaves to move about, assemble without white supervision, or learn to read and write. Other laws and the threat of mob action prevented white dissenters from publicly criticizing or even questioning the institution of slavery. Proslavery agitators sought to create a mood of crisis requiring absolute single-mindedness among whites. This embattled attitude lay behind the rise of Southern nationalism and inspired threats to secede from the Union if necessary to protect the South's peculiar institution.

The campaign for repression apparently achieved its original aim. Between 1831 and the Civil War, there were no further uprisings resulting in the mass killing of whites. But resistance to slavery simply took less dangerous forms than open revolt. The response to Turner's rebellion provided slaves with a more realistic sense of the odds against direct confrontation with white power. As a result, they perfected other methods of asserting their humanity and maintaining their self-esteem. The heroic effort to endure slavery without surrendering to it gave rise to a resilient African American culture.

This culture combined unique family arrangements, religious ideas of liberation, and creative responses to the oppression of servitude. Among white Southerners, the need to police and control this huge population of enslaved people influenced every aspect of daily life and produced an increasingly isolated, divided, and insecure society. While long-standing racial prejudice contributed to the divided society, the determination of whites to preserve the institution of slavery derived in large part from the important role slavery played in the southern economy.

THE DIVIDED SOCIETY OF THE OLD SOUTH

Slavery would not have lasted as long as it did—and Southerners would not have reacted so strongly to real or imagined threats to its survival—if an influential class of whites had not had a vital and growing economic interest in this form of human exploitation. Since the early colonial period, forced labor had been considered essential to the South's plantation economy. In the period between the 1790s and the Civil War, plantation agriculture expanded enormously, and so did dependence on slave labor.

The fact that all whites were free and most blacks were slaves created a sharp cleavage between the races in Southern society. Yet the overwhelming importance of race gives an impression of a basic equality within the "master race" that some would say is an illusion. The truth may lie somewhere in between. In the language of sociologists, inequality in the Old South was determined in two ways: by class (differences in status resulting from unequal access to wealth and productive resources) and by caste (inherited advantages or disadvantages associated with racial ancestry). Awareness of both systems of social ranking is necessary for an understanding of southern society.

White society was divided by class and by region; both were important for determining a white Southerner's relationship to the institution of slavery. More than any other factor, the ownership of slaves determined gradations of social prestige and influence among whites. In 1860, only one-quarter of all white Southerners belonged to families owning slaves. The dominant class of planters (defined as those who owned twenty or more slaves) were just 4 percent of the total white population of the South in 1860, and tended to live in the plantation areas of the "Cotton Belt" stretching from Georgia across Alabama, Mississippi, Louisiana, and Texas, as well as low-country South Carolina. The majority of whites were nonslaveholding yeoman farmers who were concentrated in up-country and frontier areas. Thus, Southern society was dominated by a geographically isolated minority; inequalities of class became divisions of region as well.

There were also divisions within black society. Most African Americans in the South were slaves, but a small number, about 6 percent, were free. Even free blacks faced increasing restrictions on their rights during the antebellum era. Among slaves, the great majority lived on plantations and worked in agriculture, but a small number worked in industrial or urban jobs. Even on plantations, there were some differences in status and experience between field hands and servants who worked in the house or in skilled jobs such as carpentry or blacksmithing. Yet because all blacks, even those who were free, suffered under the yoke of racial prejudice and legal inequality, these diverse experiences did not translate into the kind of class divisions that caused rifts within white Southern society. Rather, most blacks shared the goal of ending slavery.

THE WORLD OF SOUTHERN BLACKS

Most African Americans of the early to mid-nineteenth century experienced slavery on plantations; the majority of slaves lived on units owned by planters who had twenty or more slaves. The masters of these agrarian communities sought to ensure their personal safety and the profitability of their enterprises by using all the means—physical and psychological—at their command to make slaves docile and obedient. Despite these pressures, most African Americans managed to retain an inner sense of their own worth and dignity. When conditions were right, they openly asserted their desire for freedom and equality and showed their disdain for white claims that slavery was a positive good. Although slave culture did not normally provoke violent resistance to the slaveholders' regime, the inner world that slaves made for themselves gave them the spiritual strength to thwart the masters' efforts to take over their hearts and minds.

SLAVES' DAILY LIFE AND LABOR

Slaves' daily life varied enormously depending on the region in which they lived and the type of plantation or farm on which they worked. On large plantations in the Cotton Belt, most slaves worked in "gangs" under an overseer. White overseers, sometimes helped by black "drivers," enforced a workday from sunup to sundown, six days a week. Cotton cultivation required year-round labor, so there was never a slack season under "King Cotton." Enslaved women and children were expected to work in the fields as well, often bringing babies and young children to the fields where they could be cared for by older children, and nursed by their mothers during brief breaks. Some older children worked in "trash gangs," doing lighter tasks such as weeding and yard cleaning.

Not all slaves in agriculture worked in gangs. In the low country of South Carolina and Georgia, slaves who cultivated rice worked under a "task system" that gave them more control over the pace of labor. With less supervision, many were able to complete their tasks within an eight-hour day. Likewise, slaves who lived on small farms often worked side by side with their masters rather than in large groups of slaves. While about three-quarters of slaves were field workers, slaves performed many other kinds of labor. They dug ditches, built houses,

Although cotton cultivation required constant attention, many of the tasks involved were relatively simple. Thus on a plantation the majority of slaves, including women and children, were field hands who performed the same tasks. Here, a slave family stands behind baskets of picked cotton in a Georgia cotton field.

worked on boats and in mills (often hired out by their masters for a year at a time), and labored as house servants, cooking, cleaning and gardening. Some slaves, especially women, also worked within the slave community as preachers, caretakers of children, and healers.

A small number of slaves, about 5 percent, worked in industry in the South, including mills, iron works, and railroad building. Slaves in cities took on a wider range of jobs than plantation slaves—as porters, waiters, cooks, and skilled laborers in tradesmen's shops—and in general enjoyed more autonomy. Some urban slaves even lived apart from their masters and hired out their own time, returning a portion of their wages to their owners.

In addition to the work they did for their masters in the fields or in other jobs, most slaves kept gardens or small farm plots for themselves, and some fished, hunted, or trapped animals. Many also worked "overtime" for their own masters on Sundays or holidays in exchange for money or goods, or hired out their overtime hours to others. This underground economy suggests slaves' overpowering desire to provide for their families, sometimes even raising enough funds to purchase their freedom.

SLAVE FAMILIES, KINSHIP, AND COMMUNITY

More than any other, the African American family was the institution that prevented slavery from becoming utterly demoralizing. Slaves had a strong and abiding sense of family and kinship. But the nature of the families or households that predominated on particular plantations or farms varied according to local circumstances. On large plantations with relatively stable slave populations, a substantial majority of slave children lived in two-parent households, and many marriages lasted for as long as twenty to thirty years. They were more often broken up by the death or sale of one of the partners than by voluntary dissolution of the union. Close bonds united mothers, fathers, and children, and parents shared child-rearing responsibilities (within the limits allowed by the masters).

But in areas where most slaves lived on farms or small plantations, and especially in areas of the upper South where the trading and hiring out of slaves was frequent, a different pattern seems to have prevailed. Under these circumstances, slaves frequently had spouses who resided on other plantations or farms, often some distance away, and ties between husbands and wives were looser and more fragile. The result was that female-headed families were the norm, and responsibility for child rearing was vested in mothers, assisted in most cases by female relatives and friends. But whether the basic family form was nuclear or matrifocal (female-headed), the ties that it created were infinitely precious to its members. Masters acquired great leverage over the behavior of slaves by invoking the threat of family breakup through sale to enforce discipline.

The terrible anguish that usually accompanied the breakup of families through sale showed the depth of kinship feelings. Masters knew that the first place to look for a fugitive was in the neighborhood of a family member who had been sold away. Indeed, many slaves tried to shape their own sales in order to be sold with family members. After emancipation, thousands of freed slaves wandered about looking for spouses, children, or parents from whom they had been forcibly separated years before.

Feelings of kinship and mutual obligation extended beyond the primary family. Grandparents, uncles, aunts, and even cousins were often known to slaves through direct contact or family lore. Nor were kinship ties limited to blood relations. Slaves sold to plantations far from home were likely to be "adopted" into new kinship networks. Orphans or children without responsible parents were quickly absorbed without prejudice into new families.

Kinship provided a model for personal relationships and the basis for a sense of community. Elderly slaves were addressed by everyone else as "uncle" and "aunty," and younger unrelated slaves commonly called each other "brother" or "sister." Slave culture was a family culture, and this was one of its greatest sources of strength and cohesion. The kinship network also provided a vehicle for the transmission of African American folk traditions from one generation to the next. Together with slave religion, kinship gave African Americans some

Some slave families managed to stay together, as shown by the footnote to this 1835 bill of sale: "I did intend to leave Nancy['s] child but she made such a damned fuss I had to let her take it. . . ."

sense that they were members of a community, not just a collection of individuals victimized by oppression.

AFRICAN AMERICAN RELIGION

From the realm of culture and fundamental beliefs, African Americans drew the strength to hold their heads high and look beyond their immediate condition. Religion was the cornerstone of this emerging African American culture. Black Christianity may have owed its original existence to the efforts of white missionaries, but it was far from a mere imitation of white religious forms and beliefs. This distinctive variant of evangelical Protestantism incorporated elements of African religion and stressed those portions of the Bible that spoke to the aspirations of an enslaved people thirsting for freedom.

Most slaves did not encounter Christianity in a church setting. There were a few independent black churches in the antebellum South, which mainly served free blacks and some urban slaves with indulgent masters. These included a variety of autonomous Baptist groups as well as Southern branches of the highly successful African Methodist Episcopal (AME) Church, a national denomination founded by Reverend Richard Allen of Philadelphia in 1816. But the mass of blacks did not have access to the independent churches.

John Antrobus, Plantation Burial, *ca. 1860. The painting depicts slaves gathering in a forest to bury a fellow slave. Many spirituals sung by the slaves on such occasions portrayed death as a welcome release from bondage and created an image of an afterlife in which the trials and cares of this life were unknown.*

Plantation slaves who were exposed to Christianity either attended the neighboring white churches or worshiped at home. On large estates, masters or white missionaries often conducted Sunday services. But white-sanctioned religious activity was only a superficial part of the slaves' spiritual life. The true slave religion was practiced at night, often secretly, and was led by black preachers.

This covert slave religion was a highly emotional affair that featured singing, shouting, and dancing. In some ways, the atmosphere resembled a backwoods revival meeting. But much of what went on was actually an adaptation of African religious beliefs and customs. The chanting mode of preaching—with the congregation responding at regular intervals—and the expression of religious feelings through rhythmic movements, especially the counterclockwise movement known as the ring shout, were clearly African in origin. The black conversion experience was normally a state of ecstasy more akin to possession by spirits—a major form of African religious expression—than to the agony of those "struck down" at white revivals. The emphasis on sinfulness and fear of damnation that were core themes of white Evangelicalism played a lesser role among blacks. For them, religion was more an affirmation of the joy of life than a rejection of worldly pleasures and temptations.

Slave sermons and religious songs spoke directly to the plight of a people in bondage and implicitly asserted their right to be free. The most popular of all biblical subjects was the deliverance of the children of Israel from slavery in Egypt. The book of Exodus provided more than its share of texts for sermons and images for songs. In one moving spiritual, God commands Moses to "tell Old Pharaoh" to "let my people Go." Many sermons and songs refer to the crossing of Jordan and the arrival in the Promised Land. Other songs invoked the liberation theme by recalling that Jesus had "set poor sinners free," or prophesying, "We'll soon be free, when the Lord will call us home."

Most of the songs of freedom and deliverance can be interpreted as referring exclusively to religious salvation and the afterlife—and this was undoubtedly how slaves hoped their masters would understand them. But the slaves did not forget that God had once freed a people from slavery in this life and punished their masters. The Bible thus gave African Americans the hope that they, as a people, would repeat the experience of the Israelites and be delivered from bondage.

Religion also helped the slaves endure bondage without losing their sense of inner worth. Unless their masters were unusually pious, religious slaves could regard themselves as superior to their owners. Some slaves even believed that all whites were damned because of their unjust treatment of blacks, while all slaves would be saved because any sins they committed were the involuntary result of their condition.

As important, slave religion gave African Americans a chance to create and control a world of their own. Preachers, elders, and other leaders of slave congregations acquired status within their own community that had not been conferred by whites. Although religion seldom inspired slaves to open rebellion, it helped create community, solidarity, and self-esteem among slaves by giving them something infinitely precious of their own.

RESISTANCE AND REBELLION

Open rebellion, the bearing of arms against the oppressors by organized groups of slaves, was the most dramatic and clear-cut form of slave resistance. Between 1800 and 1831, a number of slaves participated in revolts that showed their willingness to risk their lives in a desperate bid for liberation. In 1800, a Virginia slave named Gabriel Prosser mobilized a large band of his fellows to march on Richmond, but whites suppressed the uprising without any loss of white life. In 1811, several hundred Louisiana slaves marched on New Orleans brandishing guns, waving flags, and beating drums. It took three hundred soldiers of the U.S. Army, aided by armed planters and militiamen, to stop the advance and to end the rebellion. In 1822, whites in Charleston, South Carolina, uncovered an extensive and well-planned conspiracy, organized by a free black man named Denmark Vesey, to seize local armories, arm the slave population, and take possession of the city.

As we have seen, the most bloody and terrifying of all slave revolts was the Nat Turner insurrection of 1831. Although it was the last slave rebellion of this kind during the pre–Civil War period, armed resistance had not ended. In Florida, hundreds of black fugitives fought in the Second Seminole War (1835–1842) alongside the Indians who had given them a haven. The Seminole were resisting removal to Oklahoma, but for the blacks who took part, the war was a struggle for their own freedom. When it ended, most blacks accompanied their Indian allies to the trans-Mississippi West.

Slaveowners doggedly pursued their runaway slaves, publishing descriptions of the fugitives in newspapers and offering rewards for their capture and return.

Only a tiny fraction of all slaves ever took part in organized acts of violent resistance against white power. Most realized that the odds against a successful revolt were very high, and bitter experience had shown them that the usual outcome was death to the rebels. As a consequence, they characteristically devised safer or more ingenious ways to resist white dominance.

Thousands of slaves showed their discontent and desire for freedom by running away. Most fugitives never got beyond the neighborhood of the plantation; after "lying out" for a time, they would return, often after negotiating immunity from punishment. But many escapees remained free for years by hiding in swamps or other remote areas, and a fraction escaped to the North or Mexico, stowing away aboard ships or traveling overland for hundreds of miles. Light-skinned blacks sometimes made it to freedom by passing for white. The Underground Railroad, an informal network of sympathetic free blacks (and a few whites), helped many fugitives make their way North. For the majority of slaves, however, flight was not a real option. Either they lived too deep in the South to have any chance of reaching free soil, or they were reluctant to leave family and friends behind.

Slaves who did not revolt or run away often expressed discontent by engaging in passive or indirect resistance. Many slaves worked slowly and inefficiently, not because they were naturally lazy (as whites supposed) but as a gesture of protest. Others withheld labor by feigning illness or injury. Stealing provisions—a very common activity on most plantations—was another way to show contempt for authority. According to the code of ethics prevailing in the slave quarters, theft from the master was no sin; it was simply a way for slaves to get a larger share of the fruits of their own labors.

Substantial numbers of slaves committed acts of sabotage. Tools and agricultural implements were deliberately broken, animals were willfully neglected or mistreated, and barns or other outbuildings were set afire. Often masters could not identify the culprits because slaves did not readily inform on one another. The ultimate act of clandestine resistance was poisoning the master's food. Some slaves, especially the "conjure" men and women who practiced a combination of folk medicine and witchcraft, knew how to mix rare, virtually untraceable poisons; and a suspiciously large number of plantation whites became suddenly and mysteriously ill.

The basic attitude behind such actions was revealed in the folktales that slaves passed down from generation to generation. The famous Brer Rabbit stories showed how a small, apparently defenseless animal could overcome a bigger and stronger one through cunning and deceit. Although these tales often had an African origin, they also served as an allegory for the black view of the master-slave relationship. Other stories—which were not told in front of whites—openly portrayed the slave as a clever trickster outwitting the master.

FREE BLACKS IN THE OLD SOUTH

Free blacks occupied an increasingly precarious position in the antebellum South. White Southerners' fears of free blacks inciting slave revolts, and their reaction to attacks by abolitionists, led slaveholders after 1830 increasingly to defend slavery as a positive good rather than a necessary evil. Southerners articulated this defense of slavery in terms of race, emphasizing a dual image of the black person: under the "domesticating" influence of a white master, the slave was a child, a happy Sambo; outside of this influence, he was a savage beast. As whites strove to convince themselves and Northerners that blacks were happy in slavery, they more frequently portrayed free blacks as savages who needed to be reined in.

Beginning in the 1830s, all of the Southern states passed a series of laws cracking down on free blacks. These laws forced free people of color to register or have white guardians who were responsible for their behavior. Invariably, free blacks were required to carry papers proving their free status, and in some states, they had to obtain official permission to move from one county to another. Licensing laws were invoked to exclude blacks from several occupations, and attempts by blacks to hold meetings or form organizations were frequently blocked by the authorities. Sometimes vagrancy and apprenticeship laws were used to force free blacks into a state of economic dependency barely distinguishable from outright slavery.

Although beset by special problems of their own, most free blacks identified with the suffering of the slaves; when circumstances allowed, they protested against the peculiar institution and worked for its abolition. Many of them had once been slaves themselves or were the children of slaves; often they had close relatives who were still in bondage. Furthermore, they knew that as long as slavery existed, their own rights were likely to be denied, and even their freedom was at risk. Kidnapping or fraudulent seizure by slave-catchers was always a possibility.

Because of the elaborate system of control and surveillance, free blacks in the South were in a relatively weak position to work against slavery. Most free blacks found that survival depended on creating the impression of loyalty to the planter regime. In some parts of the lower South, groups of relatively privileged free Negroes, mostly of racially mixed origin, were sometimes persuaded that it was to their advantage to preserve the status quo. As skilled artisans and small-business owners dependent on white favors and patronage, they had little incentive to risk everything by taking the side of the slaves. In southern Louisiana, there was even a small group of mulatto planters who lived in luxury, supported by the labor of other African Americans.

However, although some free blacks were able to create niches of relative freedom, their position in southern society became increasingly precarious in the late antebellum period. Beginning in the 1830s, Southern whites sought to draw the line between free and unfree more firmly as a line between black and white. Free blacks were an anomaly in this system; increasingly, the Southern answer was to exclude, degrade, and even enslave those free people of color who remained within their borders. Just before the outbreak of the Civil War, a campaign developed in some southern states to carry the pattern of repression and discrimination to its logical conclusion: Several state legislatures proposed laws giving free people of color the choice of emigrating from the state or being enslaved.

WHITE SOCIETY IN THE ANTEBELLUM SOUTH

Those who know the Old South only from modern novels, films, and television programs are likely to envision a land filled with majestic plantations, where courtly gentlemen and elegant ladies are attended by hordes of uniformed black servants. It is easy to conclude from such images that the typical white Southerner was an aristocrat who belonged to a family that owned large numbers of slaves. Certainly, the great houses existed, and some wealthy slaveholders did maintain as aristocratic a lifestyle as was ever seen in the United States. But this was the world of only a small percentage of slaveowners and a minuscule portion of the total white population.

Most Southern whites were nonslaveholding yeoman farmers. Yet even those who owned no slaves grew to depend on slavery in other ways, whether economically, because they hired slaves, or psychologically, because having a degraded class of blacks below them made them feel better about their own place in society. However, the class divisions between slaveholders and nonslaveholders did contribute to the political rifts that became increasingly apparent on the eve of the Civil War.

THE PLANTERS' WORLD

Although few in number, the great planters set the tone and values for much of the rest of society. While many of them were too busy tending to their plantations to become openly involved in politics, wealthy planters held more than their share of high offices and often exerted a decisive influence on public policy. In regions where plantation agriculture predominated, they were a ruling class in every sense of the term.

Contrary to legend, a majority of the great planters of the pre–Civil War period were self-made rather than descendants of the old colonial gentry. Some were ambitious young men who married planters' daughters. Others started as lawyers and used their fees and connections to acquire plantations.

As the Cotton Kingdom spread westward, the men who became the largest slaveholders were less and less likely to have come from old and well-established planter families. A large proportion of them began as hard-driving businessmen who built up capital from commerce, land speculation, banking, and even slave trading. They then used their profits to buy plantations. The highly competitive, boom-or-bust economy of the western Gulf states put a greater premium on sharp dealing and business skills than on genealogy. To be successful, a planter had to be not only a good plantation manager, but a shrewd entrepreneur who kept a careful eye on the market, the prices of slaves and land, and the extent of his indebtedness. Hence few planters could be men of leisure.

Likewise, the responsibility of running an extended household that produced much of its own food and clothing kept most plantation mistresses from being the idle ladies of legend—few southern women fit the stereotype of the southern belle sipping tea on the veranda. Not only were plantation mistresses a tiny minority of the women who lived and worked in the slave states before the Civil War, but even those who were part of the planter elite rarely led lives of leisure.

A small number of the richest and most secure plantation families did aspire to live in the manner of a traditional landed aristocracy, with big houses, elegant carriages, fancy-dress balls, and excessive numbers of house servants. Dueling, despite efforts to repress it, remained the standard way to settle "affairs of honor" among gentlemen. Another sign of gentility was the tendency of planters' sons to avoid "trade" as a primary or secondary career in favor of law or the military. Planters' daughters were trained from girlhood to play the piano, speak French, dress in the latest fashions, and sparkle in the drawing room or on the dance floor. The aristocratic style originated among the older gentry of the seaboard slave states, but by the 1840s and 1850s it had spread southwest as a second generation of wealthy planters began to displace the rough-hewn pioneers of the Cotton Kingdom.

PLANTERS, RACISM, AND PATERNALISM

No assessment of the planters' outlook or worldview can be made without considering their relations with their slaves. Planters owned more than half of all the slaves in the South and set standards for treatment and management. Most planters liked to think of themselves as benevolent masters and often referred to their slaves as if they were members of an extended patriarchal family—a favorite phrase was "our people." According to this ideology of paternalism, blacks were a race of perpetual children requiring constant care and supervision by superior whites. Paternalistic rhetoric increased greatly after abolitionists began to charge that most slaveholders were sadistic monsters.

Paternalism went hand in hand with racism. In a typical proslavery apology, Georgia lawyer Thomas Reade Cobb wrote that "a state of bondage, so far from doing violence to the law of [the African's] nature, develops and perfects it; and that, in that state, he enjoys the greatest amount of happiness, and arrives at the greatest degree of perfection of which his nature is capable." Slaveholders justified slavery by the supposed mental and moral inferiority of Africans. While one can find scattered evidence that Europeans had drawn negative associations with blackness for centuries, it was only in the 1830s and 1840s that full-blown modern racism developed on both sides of the Atlantic. Racial "scientists" developed theories relating skull size to mental ability, and some proslavery apologists even developed religious theories of "polygenesis," arguing that blacks were not descended from Adam and Eve. This racial ideology helped slaveholders believe that a benevolent Christian could enslave another human being.

While some historians have argued that paternalism was part of a social system that was organized like a family hierarchy rather than a brutal, profit-making arrangement, there was no inconsistency between planters' paternalism and capitalism. Slaves were themselves a form of capital; that is, they were both the main tools of production for a booming economy as well as an asset in themselves valuable for their rising prices, like shares in the stock market today. It was in the interest of masters to see that their slave property remained in good enough condition to work hard and produce large numbers of children. Furthermore, a good return on their investment enabled southern planters to spend more on slave maintenance than could masters in less prosperous plantation economies.

Much of the slaveholders' paternalist writing discussed "the coincidence of humanity and interest," by which they meant that treating slaves well (including firm discipline) was in their best economic interest. Thus, there was a grain of truth in the planters' claim that their slaves were relatively well provided for. Slaves' food, clothing, and shelter usually were sufficient to sustain life and labor at slightly above a bare subsistence level, and the rapid increase of the slave population in the Old South stands in sharp contrast to the usual failure of slave populations to reproduce themselves. But some planters failed to control their tempers or tried to work more slaves than they could afford to maintain. Consequently, there were more cases of physical abuse and undernourishment than a purely economic calculation would lead us to expect.

The testimony of slaves themselves and of some independent white observers suggests that masters of large plantations generally did not have close and intimate relationships with the mass of field slaves. The kind of affection and concern associated with a father figure appears to have been limited mainly to relationships with a few favored house servants or other elite slaves, such as drivers and highly skilled artisans. The field hands on large estates dealt mostly with overseers who were hired or fired based on their ability to meet production quotas.

The limits of paternalism were revealed in the slave market. Planters who looked down on slave traders as less than respectable gentlemen nevertheless broke apart families by selling slaves "down river" when they found themselves in need of money. Even slaveholders who claimed not to participate in the slave market themselves often mortgaged slaves to secure debts; as many as one third of all slave sales in the South were court-ordered sheriff's auctions when such masters defaulted on their debts.

While paternalism may have moderated planters' behavior to some extent, especially when economic self-interest reinforced "humanity," it is important to remember that most departures from unremitting labor and harsh conditions were concessions wrested from owners through slaves' defiance and resistance, at great personal risk.

Furthermore, when they were being most realistic, planters conceded that the ultimate basis of their authority was the slaves' fear of force and intimidation. Scattered among their statements are admissions that they relied on the "principle of fear," "more and more on the power of fear," or—most graphically—that it was necessary "to make them stand in fear." Devices for inspiring fear included whipping—a common practice on most plantations—and the threat of sale away from family and friends. Planters' manuals and instructions to overseers reveal that certain and swift punishment for any infraction of the rules or even for a surly attitude was the preferred method for maintaining order and productivity.

Slaves had little recourse against masters' abuse. Slaves lacked legal protection because their testimony was not accepted in court. Abolitionists were correct in condemning slavery on principle because it gave one human being nearly absolute power over another. This system was bound to result in atrocities and

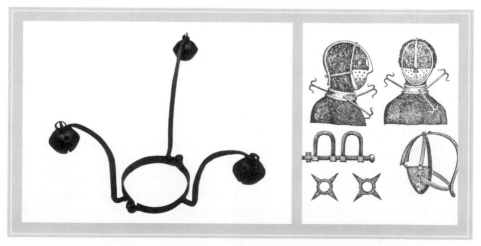

Not all slaves and masters had the benevolent relationship cited in defense of slavery. In fact, masters devised various instruments of torture and punishment to control their slaves. For example, a slave fitted with a belled slave collar could not make a move without alerting the master. Iron masks, leg shackles, and spurs were other devices slaveowners used to punish and torture their slaves.

violence. Even Harriet Beecher Stowe acknowledged in *Uncle Tom's Cabin,* her celebrated antislavery novel of 1852, that most slaveholders were not as sadistic and brutish as Simon Legree. But—and this was her real point—there was something terribly wrong with an institution that made a Simon Legree possible.

SMALL SLAVEHOLDERS

As we have seen, 88 percent of all slaveholders in 1860 owned fewer than twenty slaves and thus were not planters in the usual sense of the term. Of these, the great majority had fewer than ten. Some of the small slaveholders were urban merchants or professional men who needed slaves only for domestic service, but more typical were farmers who used one or two slave families to ease the burden of their own labor. Life on these small slaveholding farms was relatively spartan. Masters lived in log cabins or small frame cottages, and slaves lived in lofts or sheds that were not usually up to plantation housing standards.

For better or worse, relations between owners and their slaves were more intimate than on larger estates. Unlike planters, these farmers often worked in the fields alongside their slaves and sometimes ate at the same table or slept under the same roof. But such closeness did not necessarily result in better treatment. Given a choice, most slaves preferred to live on plantations because they offered the sociability, culture, and kinship of the slave quarters, as well as better prospects for adequate food, clothing, and shelter.

YEOMAN FARMERS

Just below the small slaveholders on the social scale was a substantial class of yeoman farmers who owned land they worked themselves. Contrary to another myth about the Old South, most of these people did not fit the image of the degraded, shiftless poor white. The majority of the nonslaveholding rural population were proud, self-reliant farmers whose way of life did not differ markedly from that of family farmers in the Midwest during the early stages of settlement. If they were disadvantaged in comparison with farmers elsewhere in the United States, it was because the lack of economic development and urban growth perpetuated frontier conditions and denied them the opportunity to produce a substantial surplus for market.

The yeomen were mostly concentrated in the backcountry where slaves and plantations were rarely seen. The foothills or interior valleys of the Appalachians and the Ozarks were unsuitable for plantation agriculture but offered reasonably good soils for mixed farming, and long stretches of piney barrens along the Gulf Coast were suitable for raising livestock. Slaveless farmers concentrated in such regions, giving rise to the "white counties" that complicated southern politics. A somewhat distinct group were the genuine mountaineers, who lived too high up to succeed at farming and relied heavily on hunting, lumbering, and distilling whiskey.

Yeoman women, much more than their wealthy plantation counterparts, participated in every dimension of household labor. They worked in the garden, made handicrafts and clothing, and even labored in the fields when it was necessary. Women in the most dire economic circumstances even worked for wages in small businesses or on nearby farms. They raised much larger families than their wealthier neighbors because having many children supplied a valuable labor pool for the family farm.

There were also a greater number of lower-class women who lived outside of male-headed households. Despite the pressures of respectability, there was a greater acceptance and sympathy in less affluent communities for women who bore illegitimate children or were abandoned by their husbands. Working women created a broader definition of "proper households" and navigated the challenges of holding families together in precarious economic conditions.

The lack of transportation facilities, more than some failure of energy or character, limited the prosperity of the yeomen. A large part of their effort was devoted to growing subsistence crops, mainly corn. They raised a small percentage of the South's cotton and tobacco, but the difficulty of marketing severely limited production. Their main source of cash was livestock, especially hogs, which could be walked to market over long distances. But southern livestock was of poor quality and did not bring high prices or big profits to raisers.

Although they did not benefit directly from the peculiar institution, most yeomen and other nonslaveholders tolerated slavery and were fiercely opposed to abolitionism in any form. A few antislavery Southerners, most notably Hinton R. Helper of North Carolina, tried to convince the yeomen that slavery and the plantation system created a privileged class and circumscribed the economic opportunities of the nonslaveholding white majority.

Most yeomen were staunch Jacksonians who resented aristocratic pretensions and feared concentrations of power and wealth in the hands of the few. In state and local politics, they sometimes expressed such feelings by voting against planter interests on issues involving representation, banking, and internal improvements. Why, then, did they fail to respond to antislavery appeals that called on them to strike at the real source of planter power and privilege?

One reason was that some nonslaveholders hoped to get ahead in the world, and in the South this meant acquiring slaves of their own. Just enough of the more prosperous yeomen broke into the slaveholding classes to make this dream seem believable. Planters, anxious to ensure the loyalty of nonslaveholders, strenuously encouraged the notion that every white man was a potential master.

Even if they did not aspire to own slaves, white farmers often viewed black servitude as providing a guarantee of their own liberty and independence. Although they had no natural love of planters and slavery, they believed—or could be induced to believe—that abolition would threaten their liberty and independence. In part, their anxieties were economic; freed slaves would compete with them for land or jobs. But an intense racism deepened their fears and made their opposition to black freedom implacable. Emancipation was unthinkable because it would remove the pride and status that automatically went along with a white skin in this acutely race-conscious society. Slavery, despite its drawbacks, served to keep blacks "in their place" and to make all whites, however poor and uneducated they might be, feel they were free and equal members of a master race.

A CLOSED MIND AND A CLOSED SOCIETY

Despite the tacit assent of most nonslaveholders, the dominant planters never lost their fear that lower-class whites would turn against slavery. They felt threatened from two sides: from the slave quarters where a new Nat Turner might be gathering his forces, and from the backcountry where yeomen and poor whites might heed the call of abolitionists and rise up against planter domination. Beginning in the 1830s, the ruling element tightened their grip on southern society and culture.

Before the 1830s, open discussion of the rights or wrongs of slavery had been possible in many parts of the South. Apologists commonly described the institution as "a necessary evil." In the upper South, as late as the 1820s, there had been significant support for the American Colonization Society's program of gradual voluntary emancipation accompanied by deportation of the freedmen. In 1831 and 1832, the Virginia state legislature debated a gradual emancipation plan. But the proposal met defeat as the argument that slavery was "a positive good"—rather than an evil slated for gradual elimination—won the day.

The "positive good" defense of slavery was an answer to the abolitionist charge that the institution was inherently sinful. The message was carried in a host of books, pamphlets, and newspaper editorials published between the 1830s and the Civil War. Who was it meant to persuade? Partly, the argument was aimed at

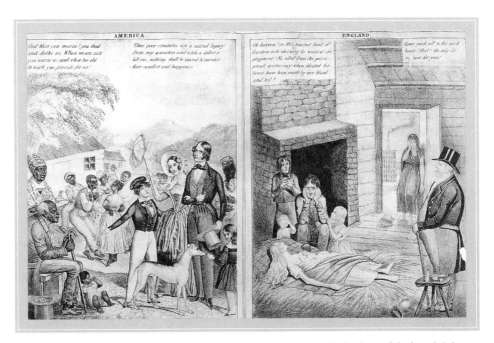

This proslavery cartoon of 1841 contends that the slave in America had a better life than did the working-class white in England. Supposedly, the grateful slaves were clothed, fed, and cared for in their old age by kindly and sympathetic masters, while starving English workers were mercilessly exploited by factory owners.

the North, as a way of bolstering the strong current of anti-abolitionist sentiment. But Southerners themselves were a prime target; the message was clearly calculated to resolve doubts and misgivings about slavery and to arouse racial anxieties that tended to neutralize antislavery sentiment among the lower classes.

The proslavery argument was based on three main propositions. The first and foremost was that enslavement was the natural and proper status for people of African descent. Blacks, it was alleged, were innately inferior to whites and suited only for slavery. Biased scientific and historical evidence was presented to support this claim. Second, slavery was held to be sanctioned by the Bible and Christianity—a position made necessary by the abolitionist appeal to Christian ethics. Ancient Hebrew slavery was held up as a divinely sanctioned model, and Saint Paul was quoted endlessly on the duty of servants to obey their masters. Third, efforts were made to show that slavery was consistent with the humanitarian spirit of the nineteenth century. The premise that blacks were naturally dependent led to the notion that they needed some kind of special protective environment. The plantation was portrayed as a sort of asylum, where benevolent masters guided and ruled this race of "perpetual children."

By the 1850s, the proslavery argument had gone beyond mere apology for the South and its peculiar institution and featured an ingenious attack on the free-labor system of the North. According to Virginian George Fitzhugh, the master-slave relationship was more humane than the one prevailing between employers and wage laborers in the North. Slaves had security against unemployment and a guarantee of care in old age, whereas free workers might face destitution and even starvation at any time.

In addition to arguing against the abolitionists, proslavery Southerners attempted to seal off their region from antislavery ideas and influences. Whites who criticized slavery publicly were mobbed or persecuted. Clergymen who questioned the morality of slavery were driven from their pulpits, and northern travelers suspected of being abolitionist agents were tarred and feathered. When abolitionists tried to send their literature through the mails during the 1830s, it was seized in southern post offices and publicly burned.

Such flagrant denials of free speech and civil liberties were inspired in part by fears that nonslaveholding whites and slaves would get subversive ideas about slavery. Hinton R. Helper's 1857 book, *The Impending Crisis of the South,* an appeal to nonslaveholders to resist the planter regime, was suppressed with particular vigor. But the deepest fear was that slaves would hear the abolitionist talk or read antislavery literature and be inspired to rebel. Consequently, new laws were passed making it a crime to teach slaves to read and write. Other repressive legislation aimed at slaves banned meetings unless a white man was present, severely restricted the activities of black preachers, and suppressed independent black churches. Free blacks, thought to be possible instigators of slave revolt, were denied basic civil liberties and were the object of growing surveillance and harassment.

All these efforts at thought control and internal security did not allay planters' fears of abolitionist subversion, lower-class white dissent, and, above all, slave revolt. The persistent barrage of proslavery propaganda and the course of national events in the 1850s created a mood of panic and desperation. By this time, an increasing number of Southerners had become convinced that safety from abolitionism and its associated terrors required a formal withdrawal from the Union—secession.

SLAVERY AND THE SOUTHERN ECONOMY

Despite the internal divisions of southern society, white Southerners from all regions and classes came to perceive their interests tied up with slavery. Southern society transformed itself according to the needs of the slave system because slavery was the cornerstone of the Southern economy. For the most part, the expansion of slavery—the number of slaves in the South more than tripled between 1810 and 1860 to nearly 4 million—can be attributed to the rise of King Cotton. The cotton-growing areas of the South were becoming more and more dependent on slavery, at the same time that agriculture in the upper South was actually moving away from the institution. Yet slavery continued to remain important to the economy of the upper South in a different way, through the slave trade. To understand Southern thought and behavior, it is necessary to bear in mind this major regional difference between a slave plantation society and a farming and slave trading region.

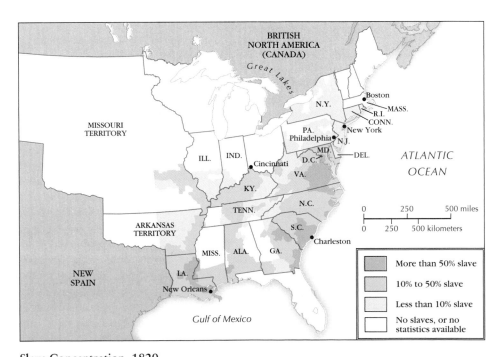

Slave Concentration, 1820
In 1820, most slaves lived in the eastern seaboard states of Virginia and South Carolina and in Louisiana on the Gulf of Mexico.

THE INTERNAL SLAVE TRADE

Tobacco, the original plantation crop of the colonial period, continued to be the principal slave-cultivated commodity of the upper tier of southern states during the pre–Civil War era. But markets were often depressed, and profitable tobacco cultivation was hard to sustain for very long in one place because the crop rapidly depleted the soil. As slave prices rose (because of high demand in the lower South) and demand for slaves in the upper South fell, the "internal" slave trade took off. Some economic historians have concluded that the most important crop produced in the tobacco kingdom was not the "stinking weed" but human beings cultivated for the auction block. Increasingly, the most profitable business for slaveholders in the upper South was selling "surplus" slaves to regions of the lower South, where staple crop production was more profitable. This interstate slave trade sent an estimated six to seven hundred thousand slaves in a southwesterly direction between 1815 and 1860. A slave child in the Upper South in the 1820s had a 30 percent chance of being "sold downriver" by 1860. Such sales were wrenching, not only splitting families, but also making it especially unlikely that the slaves sold would ever see friends or family again.

The slave trade provided a crucial source of capital in a period of transition and innovation in the Upper South. Nevertheless, the fact that slave labor was

Slave Concentration, 1860
In 1860, slavery had extended throughout the southern states, with the greatest concentrations of slaves in the states of the Deep South. There were also sizable slave populations in the new states of Missouri, Arkansas, Texas, and Florida.

declining in importance in that region meant the peculiar institution had a weaker hold on public loyalty there than in the cotton states. Diversification of agriculture was accompanied by a more rapid rate of urban and industrial development than was occurring elsewhere in the South. As a result, Virginians, Marylanders, and Kentuckians were seriously divided on whether their ultimate future lay with the Deep South's plantation economy or with the industrializing free-labor system that was flourishing just north of their borders.

THE RISE OF THE COTTON KINGDOM

The warmer climate and good soils of the lower tier of southern states made it possible to raise crops more naturally suited than tobacco or cereals to the plantation form of agriculture and the heavy use of slave labor, including rice and long-staple cotton along the coast of South Carolina and Georgia, and sugar in lower Louisiana. But cultivation of rice, long-staple cotton, and sugar was limited by natural conditions to peripheral, semitropical areas. It was the rise of short-staple cotton as the South's major crop that strengthened the hold of slavery and the plantation on the southern economy.

Short-staple cotton differed from the long-staple variety in two important ways: its bolls contained seeds that were much more difficult to extract by hand, and it could be grown almost anywhere south of Virginia and Kentucky—the main requirement was a guarantee of two hundred frost-free days. The invention of the cotton gin in 1793 resolved the seed extraction problem and opened vast areas for cotton cultivation. Unlike rice and sugar, cotton could be grown on small farms as well as on plantations. But large planters enjoyed certain advantages that made them the main producers. Only relatively large operators could afford their own gins or possessed the capital to acquire the fertile bottomlands that brought the highest yields. They also had lower transportation costs because they were able to monopolize land along rivers and streams that were the South's natural arteries of transportation.

The first major cotton-producing regions were inland areas of Georgia and South Carolina but the center of production shifted rapidly westward during the nineteenth century, first to Alabama and Mississippi and then to Arkansas, northwest Louisiana, and east Texas. The rise in total production that accompanied this geographic expansion was phenomenal. Between 1792 and 1817, the South's output of cotton rose from about 13,000 bales to 461,000; by 1840, it was 1.35 million; and in 1860, production peaked at the colossal figure of 4.8 million bales. Most of the cotton went to supply the booming textile industry of Great Britain.

Despite its overall success, however, the rise of the Cotton Kingdom did not bring a uniform or steady prosperity to the lower South. Many planters worked the land until it was exhausted and then took their slaves westward to richer soils, leaving depressed and ravaged areas in their wake. Fluctuations in markets and prices also ruined many planters. Widespread depressions, including a wave of bankruptcies, followed the boom periods of 1815–1819, 1832–1837, and 1849–1860. But during the eleven years of rising output and high prices preceding the Civil War, the planters gradually forgot their earlier troubles and began to imagine they were immune to future economic disasters.

Despite the insecurities associated with its cultivation, cotton production represented the Old South's best chance for profitable investment. Prudent planters who had not borrowed too heavily during flush times could survive periods of depression by cutting costs, making their plantations self-sufficient by shifting acreage away from cotton and planting subsistence crops. Those with worn-out land could sell their land and move west, or they could sell their slaves to raise capital for fertilization, crop rotation, and other improvements that could help them survive where they were. Hence planters had little incentive to seek alternatives to slavery, the plantation, and dependence on a single cash crop. From a purely economic point of view, they had every reason to defend slavery and to insist on their right to expand it.

SLAVERY AND INDUSTRIALIZATION

As the sectional quarrel with the North intensified, Southerners became increasingly alarmed by their region's lack of economic self-sufficiency. Dependence on the North for capital, marketing facilities, and manufactured goods was seen as evidence of a dangerous subservience to "external" economic interests. During the 1850s, southern nationalists such as J. D. B. DeBow, editor of the influential *DeBow's Review,* called for the South to develop its own industries, commerce, and shipping. As a fervent defender of slavery, DeBow saw no reason why slaves could not be used as the main workforce in an industrial revolution. But his call for a diversified economy went unanswered. Men with capital were doing too well in plantation agriculture to risk their money in other ventures.

In the 1840s and 1850s, a debate raged among white capitalists over whether the South should use free whites or enslaved blacks as the labor supply for industry. William Gregg of South Carolina, the foremost promoter of cotton mills in the Old South, defended a white labor policy, arguing that factory work would provide new economic opportunities for a degraded class of poor whites. But other advocates of industrialization feared that the growth of a free working class would lead to social conflict among whites and preferred using slaves for all supervised manual labor. In fact, a minority of slaves—about 5 percent during the 1850s—were successfully employed in industrial tasks such as mining, construction, and mill work. Some factories employed slaves, others white workers, and a few even experimented with integrated workforces. It is clear, however, that the union of slavery and cotton that was central to the South's prosperity impeded industrialization and left the region dependent on a one-crop agriculture and on the North for capital and marketing.

THE "PROFITABILITY" ISSUE

Some Southerners were making money, and a great deal of it, using slave labor to raise cotton. But did slavery yield a good return for the great majority of slaveholders who were not large planters? Did it provide the basis for general prosperity and a relatively high standard of living for the southern population in general, or at least for the two-thirds of it who were white and free? In short, was slavery profitable?

For many years historians believed that slave-based agriculture was, on the average, not very lucrative. Planters' account books seemed to show at best a modest return on investment. In the 1850s, the price of slaves rose at a faster rate than the price of cotton, allegedly squeezing many operators. Some historians even concluded that slavery was a dying institution by the time of the Civil War. Profitability, they argued, depended on access to new and fertile land suitable for plantation agriculture, and virtually all such land within the limits of the United States had already been taken up by 1860. Hence slavery had allegedly reached its natural limits of expansion and was on the verge of becoming so unprofitable that it would fall of its own weight in the near future.

A more recent interpretation holds that slavery was in fact still an economically sound institution in 1860 and showed no signs of imminent decline. A reexamination of planters' records using modern accounting methods shows that during the 1850s, planters usually could expect an annual return of 8 to 10 percent on capital invested. This yield was roughly equivalent to the best that could then be obtained from the most lucrative sectors of northern industry and commerce.

Furthermore, it is no longer clear that plantation agriculture had reached its natural limits of expansion by 1860. Production in Texas had not yet peaked, and construction of railroads and levees was opening up new areas for cotton growing elsewhere in the South. With the advantage of hindsight, economic historians have pointed out that improvements in transportation and flood control would enable the post–Civil War South to double its cotton acreage. Those who now argue that slavery was profitable and had an expansive future have made a strong and convincing case.

But the larger question remains: What sort of economic development did a slave plantation system foster? The system may have made slaveholders wealthy, but did the benefits trickle down to the rest of the population—to the majority of whites who owned no slaves and to the slaves themselves? Did it promote efficiency and progressive change? Economists Robert Fogel and Stanley Engerman have argued that the plantation's success was due to an internally efficient enterprise with good managers and industrious, well-motivated workers. Other economic historians have attributed the profitability almost exclusively to favorable market conditions.

In any case, only large plantation owners profited substantially. Because of various factors—lack of credit, high transportation costs, and a greater vulnerability to market fluctuations—small slaveholders and nonslaveholders had to devote a larger share of their acreage to subsistence crops, especially corn and hogs, than did the planters. This kept their standard of living lower than that of most northern farmers. Slaves received sufficient food, clothing, and shelter for their subsistence and to make them capable of working well enough to keep the plantation afloat economically, but their living standard was below that of the poorest free people in the United States. It was proslavery propaganda, rather than documented fact, to maintain that slaves were better off than northern wage laborers.

The South's economic development was skewed in favor of a single route to wealth, open only to the minority possessing both white skin and access to capital. The concentration of capital and business energies on cotton production foreclosed the kind of diversified industrial and commercial growth that would have provided wider opportunities. Thus, in comparison to the industrializing North, the South was an underdeveloped region in which much of the population had little incentive to work hard. A lack of public education for whites and the denial of even minimal literacy to slaves represented a critical failure to develop human resources. The South's economy was probably condemned so long as it was based on slavery.

WORLDS IN CONFLICT

If slaves lived to some extent in a separate and distinctive world of their own, so did planters, less affluent whites, and even free blacks. The Old South was thus a deeply divided society. The northern traveler Frederick Law Olmsted, who made three journeys through the slave states in the 1850s, provided a vivid sense of how diverse in outlook and circumstances southern people could be. Visiting a great plantation, he watched the slaves stop working as soon as the overseer turned away; on a small farm, he saw a slave and his owner working in the fields together. Treatment of slaves, he found, ranged from humane paternalism to flagrant cruelty. Olmsted heard nonslaveholding whites damn the planters as "cotton snobs" but also talk about blacks as "niggers" and express fear of interracial marriages if slaves were freed. He received hospitality from poor whites living in crowded one-room cabins as well as from fabulously wealthy planters in pillared mansions, and he found life in the backcountry radically different from that in the plantation belts.

In short, he showed that the South was a kaleidoscope of groups divided by class, race, culture, and geography. What held it together and provided some measure of unity was a booming plantation economy and a web of customary relationships and loyalties that could obscure the underlying cleavages and antagonisms. The fractured and fragile nature of this society would soon become apparent when it was subjected to the pressures of civil war.

CHRONOLOGY

1793	Eli Whitney invents the cotton gin
1800	Gabriel Prosser leads abortive slave rebellion in Virginia
1811	Slaves revolt in Point Coupée section of Louisiana
1822	Denmark Vesey conspiracy uncovered in Charleston, South Carolina
1829	David Walker publishes *Appeal* calling for slave insurrection
1830	First National Negro Convention meets
1831	Slaves under Nat Turner rebel in Virginia, killing almost sixty whites
1832	Virginia legislature votes against gradual emancipation
1835–1842	Blacks fight alongside Indians in the Second Seminole War
1837	Panic of 1837 is followed by major depression of the cotton market
1847	Frederick Douglass publishes the *North Star*, a black antislavery newspaper
1849	Cotton prices rise, and a sustained boom commences
1851	Group of free blacks rescues escaped slave Shadrack from federal authorities in Boston
1852	Harriet Beecher Stowe's antislavery novel *Uncle Tom's Cabin* is published and becomes a best-seller
1857	Hinton R. Helper attacks slavery on economic grounds in *The Impending Crisis of the South*; the book is suppressed in the southern states
1860	Cotton prices and production reach all-time peak

12

THE PURSUIT OF PERFECTION

In the winter of 1830 to 1831, a wave of religious revivals swept the northern states. The most dramatic and successful took place in Rochester, New York. For six months, Presbyterian evangelist Charles G. Finney preached almost daily, emphasizing that every man or woman had the power to choose Christ and a godly life.

Finney broke with his church's traditional belief that it was God's inscrutable will that decided who would be saved when he preached that "sinners ought to be made to feel that they have something to do, and that something is to repent. That is something that no other being can do for them, neither God nor man, and something they can do and do now." He converted hundreds, and church membership doubled during his stay. The newly awakened Christians of Rochester were urged to convert relatives, neighbors, and employees. If enough people enlisted in the evangelical crusade, Finney proclaimed, the millennium would be achieved within months.

Finney's call for religious and moral renewal fell on fertile ground in Rochester. The bustling boomtown on the Erie Canal was suffering from severe growing pains and tensions arising from rapid economic development. Leading families were divided into quarreling factions, and workers were threatening to break free from the control their employers had previously exerted over their daily lives. Most of the early converts were from the middle class. Businessmen who had been heavy drinkers and irregular churchgoers now abstained from alcohol and went to church at least twice a week. They also pressured the employees in their workshops, mills, and stores to do likewise. More rigorous standards of proper behavior and religious conformity unified Rochester's elite and increased its ability to control the rest of the community. Evangelical Protantism provided the middle class with a stronger sense of identity and purpose.

But the war on sin was not always so unifying. Finney concentrated on religious conversion and moral uplift of the individual, trusting that the purification of American society and politics would automatically follow. Other religious and moral reformers crusaded against social and political institutions that failed to measure up to the standards of Christian perfection. They attacked such collective "sins" as the liquor traffic, war, slavery, and even government. Religiously inspired reformism cut two ways. On the one hand, it imposed a new order and cultural unity to previously divided and troubled communities. But it also inspired a variety of more radical movements that threatened to undermine established institutions. One of these movements—abolitionism—challenged the central social and economic institution of the southern states and helped trigger political upheaval and civil war.

THE RISE OF EVANGELICALISM

American Protestantism was in a state of constant ferment during the early nineteenth century. The separation of church and state, a process that began during the Revolution, was now complete. Government sponsorship and funding had ended, or would soon end, for the established churches of the colonial era. Dissenting groups, such as Baptists and Methodists, welcomed full religious freedom because it offered a better chance to win new converts. All pious Protestants, however, were concerned about the spread of "infidelity"—a term they applied to Catholics, freethinkers, Unitarians, Mormons, and anyone else who was not an evangelical Christian. But they faced opposition to their effort to make the nation officially Protestant. As deism—the belief in a God who expressed himself through natural laws accessible to human reason—declined in popularity in the early to mid-nineteenth century, Catholic immigration increased, and the spread of popery became the main focus of evangelical concern.

Revivalism proved to be a very effective means to extend religious values and build up church membership. The Great Awakening of the mid-eighteenth century had shown the wonders that evangelists could accomplish, and new revivalists repeated this success by greatly increasing the proportion of the population that belonged to Protestant churches. Spiritual renewals were often followed by mobilization of the faithful into associations to spread the gospel and reform American morals.

Although both evangelical reformers and Jacksonian politicians sought popular favor and assumed that individuals were free agents capable of self-direction and self-improvement, leaders of the two types of movements made different kinds of demands on ordinary people. Jacksonians idealized common folk pretty much as they found them and saw no danger to the community if individuals pursued their worldly interests. Evangelical reformers, by contrast, believed that the common people needed to be redeemed and uplifted. They did not trust a democracy of unbelievers and sinners. The republic would be safe, they insisted, only if a right-minded minority preached, taught, and agitated until the mass of ordinary citizens was reborn into a higher life.

THE SECOND GREAT AWAKENING: THE FRONTIER PHASE

The Second Great Awakening began in earnest on the southern frontier around the turn of the century. In 1801, a crowd estimated at nearly fifty thousand gathered at Cane Ridge, Kentucky. According to a contemporary observer:

> *The noise was like the roar of Niagara. . . . I counted seven ministers all preaching at once. . . . At one time I saw at least five hundred swept down in a moment, as if a battery of a thousand guns had been opened upon them, and then followed immediately shrieks and shouts that rent the heavens.*

Highly emotional camp meetings, organized usually by Methodists or Baptists but sometimes by Presbyterians, became a regular feature of religious life in the South and the lower Midwest. On the frontier, the camp meeting met social as well as religious needs. In the sparsely settled southern backcountry, for many people the only way to get baptized or married or to have a communal religious experience was to attend a camp meeting.

Rowdies and scoffers also attended, drinking whiskey, carousing, and fornicating on the fringes of the small city of tents and wagons. Sometimes they were "struck down" by a mighty blast from the pulpit. Evangelists loved to tell stories of such conversions or near conversions. According to Methodist preacher Peter Cartwright, one scoffer was seized by the "jerks"—a set of involuntary bodily

Lithograph depicting a camp meeting. Religious revival meetings on the frontier attracted hundreds of people who camped for days to listen to the preacher and to share with their neighbors in a communal religious experience. Notice that the men and women are seated in separate sections.

movements often observed at camp meetings. Normally such an experience would lead to conversion, but this particular sinner refused to surrender to God. The result was that he kept jerking until his neck was broken.

In the southern states, Baptists and Presbyterians eventually deemphasized camp meetings in favor of "protracted meetings" in local churches, which featured guest preachers holding forth day after day for up to two weeks. Southern evangelical churches, especially Baptist and Methodist, grew rapidly in membership and influence during the first half of the nineteenth century and became the focus of community life in rural areas. Although they encouraged temperance and discouraged dueling, they generally shied away from social reform. The conservatism of a slaveholding society discouraged radical efforts to change the world.

THE SECOND GREAT AWAKENING IN THE NORTH

Reformist tendencies were more evident in the revivalism that originated in New England and western New York. Northern evangelists were mostly Congregationalists and Presbyterians, strongly influenced by New England Puritan traditions. Their revivals, although less extravagantly emotional than the camp meetings of the South, found fertile soil in the small and medium-sized cities and towns of the North. Northern evangelism gave rise to societies devoted to the redemption of the human race in general and American society in particular.

The reform movement in New England began as an effort to defend Calvinism against the liberal views of religion fostered by the Enlightenment. The Reverend Timothy Dwight, who became president of Yale College in 1795, was alarmed by the younger generation's growing acceptance of the belief that the Deity was the benevolent master architect of a rational universe rather than an all-powerful, mysterious God. Dwight was particularly disturbed by those religious liberals who denied the doctrine of the Trinity and proclaimed themselves to be "Unitarians." Horrified when Unitarians won control of the Harvard Divinity School, Dwight fought back by preaching to Yale undergraduates that they were "dead in sin" and succeeded in provoking a series of campus revivals. But the harshness and pessimism of orthodox Calvinist doctrine, with its stress on original sin and predestination, had limited appeal in a republic committed to human freedom and progress.

A younger generation of Congregational ministers reshaped New England Puritanism to increase its appeal to people who shared the prevailing optimism about human capabilities. The main theologian of early nineteenth-century neo-Calvinism was Nathaniel Taylor, a disciple of Dwight. Taylor softened the doctrine of predestination by contending that every individual was a free agent who had the ability to overcome a natural inclination to sin.

The first great practitioner of the new evangelical Calvinism was Lyman Beecher, another of Dwight's pupils. In the period just before and after the War of 1812, Beecher helped promote a series of revivals in the Congregational churches of New England. Using his own homespun version of Taylor's doctrine of free agency, Beecher induced thousands to acknowledge their sinfulness and surrender to God.

During the late 1820s, Beecher was forced to confront the new and more radical form of revivalism being practiced in western New York by Charles G. Finney. Upstate New York was a seedbed for religious enthusiasms of various kinds. A majority of its population were transplanted New Englanders who had left behind their close-knit village communities and ancestral churches but not their Puritan consciences. Troubled by rapid economic changes and the social dislocations that went with them, they were ripe for a new faith and a fresh moral direction.

Beginning in 1823, Finney conducted a series of highly successful revivals in towns and cities of western New York. Even more controversial than his free-wheeling approach to theology were the means he used to win converts. Seeking instantaneous conversions, Finney held protracted meetings that lasted all night or several days in a row, placed an "anxious bench" in front of the congregation where those in the process of repentance could receive special attention, and encouraged women to pray publicly for the souls of male relatives.

The results could be dramatic. Sometimes listeners fell to the floor in fits of excitement. Although he appealed to emotion, Finney had a practical, almost manipulative, attitude toward the conversion process: it "is not a miracle or dependent on a miracle in any sense. . . . It is purely a philosophical result of the right use of constituted means."

Finney's new methods and the emotionalism that accompanied them disturbed Lyman Beecher and other eastern evangelicals. They were also upset because Finney violated long-standing Christian tradition by allowing women to pray aloud in church. Beecher and Finney met in an evangelical summit at New Lebanon, New York, in 1827, but failed to reach agreement on this and other issues. But it soon became clear that Finney was not merely stirring people to temporary peaks of excitement; he also was leaving strong and active churches behind him, and eastern opposition gradually weakened.

FROM REVIVALISM TO REFORM

Northern revivalists inspired a great movement for social reform. Converts were organized into voluntary associations that sought to stamp out sin and social evil and win the world for Christ. Most of the converts were middle-class citizens already active in the lives of their communities. They were seeking to adjust to the bustling world of the market revolution in ways that would not violate their traditional moral and social values. Their generally optimistic and forward-looking attitudes led to hopes that a wave of conversions would save the nation and the world.

In New England, Beecher and his evangelical associates were behind the establishment of a great network of missionary and benevolent societies. In 1810, Presbyterians and Congregationalists founded a Board of Commissioners for Foreign Missions and soon dispatched two missionaries to India. In 1816, the Reverend Samuel John Mills took the leading role in organizing the American Bible Society. By 1821, the society had distributed 140,000 Bibles, mostly in parts of the West where churches and clergymen were scarce.

Evangelicals founded moral reform societies as well as missions. Some of these aimed at curbing irreligious activity on the Sabbath; others sought to stamp out

Temperance propaganda warned that the drinker who began with "a glass with a friend" would inevitably follow the direct path to poverty, despair, and death.

dueling, gambling, and prostitution. In New York in 1831, a zealous young clergyman published a sensational report claiming there were ten thousand prostitutes in the city laying their snares for innocent young men. As a result of this exposé, an asylum was established for the redemption of "abandoned women." When middle-class women became involved in this crusade, they shifted its focus to the men who patronized prostitutes, and they proposed that teams of observers record and publish the names of men seen entering brothels. The plan was abandoned because it offended those who thought the cause of virtue would be better served by suppressing public discussion and investigation of sexual vices.

Beecher was especially influential in the temperance crusade, the most successful of the reform movements. The temperance movement was directed at a real social evil. Since the Revolution, whiskey had become the most popular American beverage. Made from corn by individual farmers or, by the 1820s, in commercial distilleries, it was cheaper than milk or beer and safer than water (which was often contaminated). Hard liquor was frequently consumed with food as a table beverage, even at breakfast, and children sometimes imbibed along with adults. Per capita annual consumption of distilled beverages in the 1820s was almost triple what it is today, and alcoholism had reached epidemic proportions.

The temperance reformers viewed indulgence in alcohol as a threat to public morality. Drunkenness was seen as a loss of self-control and moral responsibility that spawned crime, vice, and disorder. Above all, it threatened the family. The main target of temperance propaganda was the husband and father who abused, neglected, or abandoned his wife and children because he was a slave to the bottle. Women played a vital role in the movement and were instrumental in making it a crusade for the protection of the home. The drinking habits of the poor or laboring classes also aroused great concern. Particularly in urban areas, the "respectable" and propertied elements lived in fear that lower-class mobs, crazed with drink, would attack private property.

Many evangelical reformers regarded intemperance as the greatest single obstacle to a republic of God-fearing, self-disciplined citizens. In 1826, a group of clergymen organized the American Temperance Society to encourage abstinence from "ardent spirits" or hard liquor (there was no agreement on the evils of beer and wine) and to educate people about the evils of "demon rum." Agents of the society organized revival meetings and called on those in attendance to sign a pledge promising abstinence from spirits.

The campaign was enormously effective. Although it may be doubted whether huge numbers of confirmed drunkards were cured, the movement did succeed in altering the drinking habits of middle-class American males. Per capita consumption of hard liquor declined more than 50 percent during the 1830s.

Cooperating missionary and reform societies—collectively known as "the benevolent empire"—were a major force in American culture by the early 1830s. A new ethic of self-control and self-discipline was being instilled in the middle class, equipping individuals to confront a new world of economic growth and social mobility without losing their cultural and moral bearings.

DOMESTICITY AND CHANGES IN THE AMERICAN FAMILY

The evangelical culture of the 1820s and 1830s influenced the family as an institution and inspired new conceptions of its role in American society. Many parents viewed children's rearing as essential preparation for self-disciplined Christian life and performed their nurturing duties with great seriousness and self-consciousness. Women—regarded as particularly susceptible to religious and moral influences—were increasingly confined to the domestic circle, but they assumed a greater importance within it.

MARRIAGE AND GENDER ROLES

The white middle-class American family underwent major changes in the decades between the Revolution and the mid-nineteenth century. A new ideal of marriage for love arose among the American middle class. Many nineteenth-century Americans placed new value on ties of affection among family members, especially a married couple joined by romantic love. Parents now exercised even less control over their children's selection of mates than they had in the colonial period. The desire to protect family property and maintain social status remained strong, but mutual affection was now considered absolutely essential to a proper union.

Wives began to behave more like the companions of their husbands and less like their servants or children. In the main, eighteenth-century correspondence between spouses had been formal and distant in tone. The husband often assumed a patriarchal role, even using such salutations as "my dear child" and rarely confessing that he missed his wife or craved her company.

By the early nineteenth century, first names, pet names, and terms of endearment such as "honey" or "darling" were increasingly used by both sexes, and absent husbands frequently confessed they felt lost without their mates. In their replies, wives assumed a more egalitarian tone and offered counsel on a wide range of subjects.

The change in middle- and upper-class marriage should not be exaggerated or romanticized. In law, and in cases of conflict between spouses, the husband remained the unchallenged head of the household. True independence or equality for women was impossible at a time when men held exclusive legal authority over a couple's property and children. Divorce was difficult for everyone, but the double standard made it easier for husbands than wives to dissolve a marriage on grounds of adultery. Letters also reveal the strains spouses felt between their

The sentiment on this sampler, stitched in 1820 by Ruth Titus, typifies beliefs about woman's proper role, according to the Cult of True Womanhood.

ideals of mutual love and the reality of very different gender roles and life paths—husbands away from home for long periods pursuing financial gain as "self-made men," while women stayed at home in the domestic sphere.

The notion that women belonged in the home while the public sphere belonged to men has been called the ideology of "separate spheres." In particular, the view that women had a special role to play in the domestic sphere as guardians of virtue and spiritual heads of the home has been described as the "Cult of Domesticity" or the "Cult of True Womanhood." In the view of most men, a woman's place was in the home and on a pedestal. The ideal wife and mother was "an angel in the house," a model of piety and virtue who exerted a wholesome moral and religious influence over members of the coarser sex.

The sociological reality behind the Cult of True Womanhood was a growing division between the working lives of middle-class men and women. In the eighteenth century and earlier, most economic activity had been centered in and near the home, and husbands and wives often worked together in a common enterprise. By the early to mid-nineteenth century this way of life was declining, especially in the Northeast. In towns and cities, the rise of factories and counting-houses severed the home from the workplace. Men went forth every morning to their places of labor, leaving their wives at home to tend the house and the children. The Cult of Domesticity made a virtue of the fact that men were solely responsible for running the affairs of the world and building up the economy.

A new conception of gender roles justified and glorified this pattern. The doctrine of separate spheres—as set forth in novels, advice literature, and the new women's magazines—sentimentalized the woman who kept a spotless house, nurtured her children, and offered her husband a refuge from the heartless world of commerce and industry. From a modern point of view, it is easy to condemn the Cult of Domesticity as a rationalization for male dominance. Yet, by the standards of evangelical culture, women in the domestic sphere could be viewed as superior to men, since women were in a good position to cultivate the "feminine" virtues of love and self-sacrifice and thus act as official guardians of religious and moral values. Furthermore, many women used domestic ideology to fashion a role for themselves in the public sphere. Membership in evangelical church–based associations inspired and prepared women for new roles as civilizers of men and guardians of domestic culture and morality. Female reform societies taught women the strict ethical code they were to instill in other family members; organized mothers' groups gave instruction in how to build character and encourage piety in children.

While many working-class women read about and aspired to the ideal of true womanhood, domestic ideology only affected the daily lives of relatively affluent women. Working-class wives were not usually employed outside the home during this period, but they labored long and hard within the household, often taking in washing or piecework to supplement a meager family income. Their endless domestic drudgery made a sham of the notion that women had the time and energy for the "higher things of life." Life was especially hard for African American women. Most of those who were free blacks rather than slaves did not have husbands who made enough to support them, and they were obliged to serve in white households or work long hours at home doing other people's washing and sewing.

In urban areas, unmarried working-class women often lived on their own and toiled as household servants, in the sweatshops of the garment industry, and in factories. Barely able to support themselves and at the mercy of male sexual predators, they were in no position to identify with the middle-class ideal of elevated, protected womanhood.

For middle-class women whose husbands or fathers earned a good income, freedom from industrial or farm labor offered some tangible benefits. They now had the leisure to read extensively the new literature directed primarily at housewives, to participate in female-dominated charitable activities, and to cultivate deep and lasting friendships with other women. The result was a distinctively feminine subculture emphasizing "sisterhood" or "sorority." This growing sense of solidarity with other women could transcend the barriers of social class. Beginning in the 1820s, middle- and upper-class urban women organized societies for the relief and rehabilitation of poor or "fallen" women. The aim of the organizations was not economic and political equality with men but the elevation of all women to true womanhood.

For some women, the domestic ideal even sanctioned efforts to extend their sphere until it conquered the masculine world outside the home. This domestic feminism was reflected in women's involvement in crusades to stamp out such masculine sins as intemperance, gambling, and sexual vice.

The desire to extend the feminine sphere was the motivating force behind Catharine Beecher's campaign to make schoolteaching a woman's occupation. A prolific and influential writer on the theory and practice of domesticity, this unmarried daughter of Lyman Beecher saw the spinster-teacher as equivalent to a mother. By instilling in young males the virtues that only women could teach, the schoolmarm could help liberate America from corruption and materialism.

But Beecher and other domestic feminists continued to emphasize the role of married women who stayed home and did their part simply by being wives and mothers. Because husbands were away from home much of the time and tended to be preoccupied with business, women bore primary responsibility for the rearing of children. Since women were considered particularly well qualified to transmit piety and morality to future citizens of the republic, the Cult of Domesticity exalted motherhood and encouraged a new concern with childhood as the time of life when "character" was formed.

THE DISCOVERY OF CHILDHOOD

The nineteenth century has been called "the century of the child." More than before, childhood was seen as a distinct stage of life requiring the special and sustained attention of adults, at least until the age of thirteen or fourteen. The middle-class family now became "child-centered," viewing its main function as the care, nurture, and rearing of children.

New customs and fashions heralded the "discovery" of childhood. Books aimed specifically at juveniles began to roll off the presses. Parents became more self-conscious about their responsibilities and sought help from a new literature providing expert advice on child rearing. One early nineteenth-century mother wrote, "There is scarcely any subject concerning which I feel more anxiety than the proper education of my children. It is a difficult and delicate subject, the more I feel how much is to be learnt by myself."

The new concern for children resulted in more intimate relations between parents and children. The ideal family described in the advice manuals and sentimental literature was bound together by affection rather than authority. Firm discipline remained at the core of "family government," but there was a change in the preferred method of enforcing good behavior. Corporal punishment declined, partially displaced by shaming or withholding of affection. Disobedient middle-class children were now more likely to be confined to their rooms to reflect on their sins than to receive a good thrashing. The purpose of discipline was to induce repentance and change basic attitudes. The intended result was often described as "self-government"; to achieve it, parents used guilt, rather than fear, as their main source of leverage. A mother's sorrow or a father's stern and prolonged silence was deemed more effective in forming character than were blows or angry words.

Some shared realities of childhood cut across class and ethnic lines. For example, there was a high rate of mortality for infants and young children throughout the nineteenth century. Even wealthy families could expect to lose one child out of five or six before the age of five. But class and region made a big difference to children's lives. Farm children tended livestock, milked cows, churned butter, scrubbed laundry, harvested crops, and hauled water; working-class urban children did "outwork" in textiles, worked in street markets, and scavenged.

One important explanation for the growing focus on childhood is the smaller size of families. If nineteenth-century families had remained as large as those of earlier times, it would have been impossible to lavish so much care and attention on individual offspring. The average number of children born to each woman during her fertile years dropped from 7.04 in 1800 to 5.42 in 1850. As a result, the average number of children per family declined about 25 percent.

The practice of various forms of birth control undoubtedly contributed to this demographic revolution. Ancestors of the modern condom and diaphragm were openly advertised and sold during the pre–Civil War period, but it is likely that most couples controlled family size by practicing the withdrawal method or limiting the frequency of intercourse. Abortion was also surprisingly common and was on the rise.

Parents seemed to understand that having fewer children meant they could provide their offspring with a better start in life. Such attitudes were appropriate in a society that was beginning to shift from agriculture to commerce and industry.

INSTITUTIONAL REFORM

The family could not carry the whole burden of socializing and reforming individuals. Children needed schooling as well as parental nurturing. Some adults, too, seemed to require special kinds of attention and treatment. Seeking to extend the advantages of "family government" beyond the domestic circle, reformers worked to establish or improve public institutions that were designed to shape individual character and instill a capacity for self-discipline.

THE EXTENSION OF EDUCATION

Before the 1820s, schooling in the United States was a haphazard affair. The wealthy sent their children to private schools, and some of the poor sent their children to charity or "pauper" schools that were usually financed in part by local governments. Public education was most highly developed in the New England states, where towns were required by law to support elementary schools. It was weakest in the South, where almost all education was private.

Agitation for expanded public education began in the 1820s and early 1830s as a central demand of the workingmen's movements in eastern cities. These hard-pressed artisans viewed free schools open to all as a way of countering the growing gap between rich and poor. Initially, strong opposition came from more affluent taxpayers who did not see why they should pay for the education of other people's children. But middle-class reformers soon seized the initiative, shaped educational reform to the goal of social discipline, and provided the momentum needed for legislative success.

The most influential supporter of the common school movement was Horace Mann of Massachusetts. As a lawyer and member of the state legislature, Mann worked tirelessly to establish a state board of education and adequate tax support for local schools. In 1837, he persuaded the legislature to enact his proposals, and he subsequently resigned his seat to become the first secretary of the new board, an office he held with great distinction until 1848. He believed children were clay in the hands of teachers and school officials and could be molded to a state of perfection. Like advocates of child rearing through moral influence rather than physical force, he discouraged corporal punishment except as a last resort.

Against those who argued that school taxes violated property rights, Mann contended that private property was actually held in trust for the good of the community. Mann's conception of public education as a means of social discipline converted the middle and upper classes to the cause. By teaching middle-class morality and respect for order, the schools could turn potential rowdies and revolutionaries into law-abiding citizens. They could also encourage social mobility by opening doors for lower-class children who were determined to do better than their parents.

In practice, new or improved public schools often alienated working-class pupils and their families rather than reforming them. Compulsory attendance laws in Massachusetts and other states deprived poor families of needed wage earners without guaranteeing new occupational opportunities for those with an elementary education. As the laboring class became increasingly immigrant and Catholic in the 1840s and 1850s, dissatisfaction arose over the evangelical Protestant tone of "moral instruction" in the schools. Quite consciously, Mann and his disciples were trying to impose a uniform culture on people who valued differing traditions.

In addition to the "three Rs" ("reading, 'riting, and 'rithmetic"), the public schools of the mid-nineteenth century taught the "Protestant ethic"—industry, punctuality, sobriety, and frugality. These were the virtues stressed in the famous *McGuffey's Eclectic Readers,* which first appeared in 1836. Millions of children learned to read by digesting McGuffey's parables about the terrible fate of those who gave in to sloth, drunkenness, or wastefulness. Such moral indoctrination helped produce generations of Americans with personalities and beliefs adapted to the needs of an industrializing society—people who could be depended on to adjust to the precise and regular routines of the factory or the office. But as an education for self-government—in the sense of learning to think for oneself—it left much to be desired.

THE ECLECTIC SERIES. 77

LESSON XXI.

1. In'do-lent; *adj.* lazy; idle.
2. Com-mer'cial; *adj.* trading.
3. Com'ic-al; *adj.* amusing.
3. Drone; *n.* an idler.
4. Nav'i-ga-ble; *adj.* in which boats can sail.

THE IDLE SCHOOL-BOY.

Pronounce correctly. Do not say *indorlunt* for *in-do-lent; creepin* for *creep-ing; zylubble* for *syl-la-*ble*; colud* for *col-ored; scarlit* for *scar-let; ignerunt* for *ig-no-rant.*

1. I will tell you about the †laziest boy you ever heard of. He was indolent about every thing. When he played, the boys said he played as if the teacher told him to. When he went to school, he went creep-·ing along like a snail. The boy had sense enough; but he was too lazy to learn any thing.

2. When he spelled a word, he †drawled out one syllable after another, as if he were afraid the †syllables would quarrel, if he did not keep them a great way apart.

3. Once when he was †reciting, the teacher asked him, "What is said of †Hartford?" He answered, "Hartford is a †flourishing *comical* town." He meant that it was a "flourishing *commercial* town;" but he was such a drone, that he never knew what he was about.

4. When asked how far the River †Kennebec was navigable, he said, "it was navigable for *boots* as far as †Waterville." The boys all laughed, and the teacher could not help laughing, too. The idle boy †colored like scarlet.

5. "I say it is so in my book," said he. When one of the boys showed him the book, and pointed to the

The lessons and examples in McGuffey's Eclectic Readers *upheld the virtues of thrift, honesty, and charity and taught that evil deeds never went unpunished.*

DISCOVERING THE ASYLUM

Some segments of the population were obviously beyond the reach of family government and character training provided in homes and schools. In the 1820s and 1830s, reformers became acutely aware of the danger to society posed by an apparently increasing number of criminals, lunatics, and paupers. Their answer was to establish special institutions to house those deemed incapable of self-discipline. Their goals were humanitarian; they believed reform and rehabilitation were possible in a carefully controlled environment.

In earlier times, the existence of paupers, lawbreakers, and insane persons had been taken for granted. Their presence was viewed as the consequence of divine judgment or original sin. For the most part, these people were dealt with in ways that did not isolate them from local communities. The insane were allowed to wander about if harmless and were confined at home if they were dangerous; the poor were supported by private charity or the dole provided by towns or counties; convicted criminals were whipped, held for limited periods in local jails, or—in the case of very serious offenses—executed.

By the early nineteenth century, these traditional methods had come to seem both inadequate and inhumane. Dealing with deviants in a neighborly way broke down as economic development and urbanization made communities less cohesive. At the same time, reformers were concluding that all defects of mind and character were correctable—the insane could be cured, criminals reformed, and paupers taught to pull themselves out of destitution. The result was the invention and establishment of special institutions for the confinement and reformation of deviants.

The 1820s and 1830s saw the emergence of state-supported prisons, insane asylums, and poorhouses. New York and Pennsylvania led the way in prison reform. Institutions at Auburn, New York, and Philadelphia attracted international attention as model penitentiaries, mainly because of their experiments in isolating inmates from one another. Solitary confinement was viewed as a humanitarian and therapeutic policy because it gave inmates a chance to reflect on their sins, free from the corrupting influence of other convicts. In theory, prisons and asylums substituted for the family. Custodians were meant to act as parents, providing moral advice and training.

Prisons, asylums, and poorhouses did not achieve the aims of their founders. Public support was inadequate to meet the needs of a growing inmate population, and the personnel of the institutions often lacked the training needed to help the incarcerated. The results were overcrowding and the use of brutality to keep order. For the most part, prisons failed to reform hardened criminals, and the primitive psychotherapy known as "moral treatment" failed to cure most asylum patients. Poorhouses rapidly degenerated into sinkholes of despair. A combination of naive theories and poor performance doomed the institutions to a custodial rather than a reformatory role.

Dorothea Dix (1802–1887). Her efforts on behalf of the mentally ill led to the building of more than thirty institutions in the United States and the reform and restaffing—with well-trained personnel— of existing hospitals. She died in Trenton, New Jersey, in 1887, in a hospital that she had founded.

Conditions would have been even worse had it not been for Dorothea Dix. Between 1838 and the Civil War, this remarkable woman devoted her energies and skills to publicizing the inhumane treatment prevailing in prisons, almshouses, and insane asylums and to lobbying for corrective action. As a direct result of her activities, fifteen states opened new hospitals for the insane and others improved their supervision of penitentiaries, asylums, and poorhouses. Dix ranks as one of the most practical and effective of all the reformers of the pre–Civil War era.

REFORM TURNS RADICAL

During the 1830s, internal dissension split the great reform movement spawned by the Second Great Awakening. Efforts to promote evangelical piety, improve personal and public morality, and shape character through familial or institutional discipline continued and even flourished. But bolder spirits went beyond such goals and set their sights on the total liberation and perfection of the individual.

DIVISIONS IN THE BENEVOLENT EMPIRE

Early nineteenth-century reformers were, for the most part, committed to changing existing attitudes and practices gradually and in ways that would not invite conflict or disrupt society. But by the mid-1830s, a new mood of impatience and perfectionism surfaced within the benevolent societies. In 1836, for example, the Temperance Society split over two issues: whether the abstinence pledge should be extended to include beer and wine and whether pressure should be applied to producers and sellers of alcoholic beverages as well as to consumers.

A similar rift occurred in the American Peace Society, an antiwar organization founded in 1828 by clergymen seeking to promote Christian concern for world peace. Most of the founders admitted the propriety of "defensive wars," but some members of the society denounced all use of force as a violation of the Sermon on the Mount.

The new perfectionism realized its most dramatic and important success within the antislavery movement. Before the 1830s, most people who expressed religious and moral concern over slavery were affiliated with the American Colonization Society, a benevolent organization founded in 1817. Most colonizationists admitted that slavery was an evil, but they also viewed it as a deeply rooted social and economic institution that could be eliminated only very gradually and with the cooperation of slaveholders. Reflecting the power of racial prejudice, they proposed to provide transportation to Africa for free blacks who chose to go, or were emancipated for the purpose, as a way of relieving southern fears that a race war would erupt if slaves were simply released from bondage and allowed to remain in America. In 1821, the society established the colony of Liberia in West Africa, and during the next decade a few thousand African Americans were settled there.

In the inaugural issue of his antislavery weekly, the Liberator, *William Lloyd Garrison announced that he was launching a militant battle against the evil and sin of slavery. The stirring words that appeared in that first issue are repeated on the* Liberator's *banner.*

Colonization proved to be grossly inadequate as a step toward the elimination of slavery. Many of the blacks transported to Africa were already free, and those liberated by masters influenced by the movement represented only a tiny percentage of the southern slave population. Northern blacks denounced the enterprise because it denied the prospect of racial equality in America. Black opposition to colonizationism helped persuade William Lloyd Garrison and other white abolitionists to repudiate the Colonization Society and support immediate emancipation without emigration.

Garrison launched a new and more radical antislavery movement in 1831 in Boston, when he began to publish a journal called the *Liberator*. Besides calling for immediate and unconditional emancipation, Garrison denounced colonization as a slaveholder's plot to remove troublesome free blacks and as an ignoble surrender to un-Christian prejudices. His rhetoric was as severe as his proposals were radical. As he wrote in the first issue of the *Liberator*, "I will be as harsh as truth and as uncompromising as justice. . . . I am in earnest—I will not equivocate—I will not excuse—I will not retreat a single inch—And I WILL BE HEARD!" Heard he was. In 1833, Garrison and other abolitionists founded the American Anti-Slavery Society. The colonization movement was placed on the defensive, and during the 1830s, many of its most active northern supporters became abolitionists.

THE ABOLITIONIST ENTERPRISE

The abolitionist movement, like the temperance crusade, was a direct outgrowth of the Second Great Awakening. Many leading abolitionists were already committed to a life of Christian activism before they dedicated themselves to freeing the slaves. Several were ministers or divinity students seeking a mission in life that would fulfill spiritual and professional ambitions.

Antislavery orators and organizers tended to have their greatest successes in the small- to medium-sized towns of the upper North. The typical convert came from an upwardly mobile family engaged in small business, the skilled trades, or market farming. In larger towns and cities, or when they ventured close to the Mason-Dixon line, abolitionists were more likely to encounter fierce and effective opposition. In 1835, Garrison was mobbed in the streets of Boston and almost lynched.

Abolitionists who thought of taking their message to the fringes of the South had reason to pause, given the fate of the antislavery editor Elijah Lovejoy. In 1837, while attempting to defend himself and his printing press from a mob in Alton, Illinois, just across the Mississippi River from slaveholding Missouri, Lovejoy was shot and killed.

Racism was a major cause of anti-abolitionist violence in the North. Rumors that abolitionists advocated or practiced interracial marriage could easily incite an urban crowd. If it could not find white abolitionists, the mob was likely to turn on local blacks. Working-class whites tended to fear that economic and social competition with blacks would increase if abolitionists succeeded in freeing slaves and making them citizens. But a striking feature of many of the mobs was that they were dominated by "gentlemen of property and standing." Solid citizens resorted to violence, it would appear, because abolitionism threatened their conservative notions of social order and hierarchy.

By the end of the 1830s, the abolitionist movement was under great stress. Besides the burden of external repression, there was dissension within the movement. Becoming an abolitionist required an exacting conscience and an unwillingness to compromise on matters of principle. These character traits also made it difficult for abolitionists to work together and maintain a united front.

During the late 1830s, Garrison, the most visible proponent of the cause, began to adopt positions that some other abolitionists found extreme and divisive. Embracing the "no-government" philosophy, he urged abolitionists to abstain from voting or otherwise participating in a corrupt political system. He also attacked the clergy and the churches for refusing to take a strong antislavery stand and encouraged his followers to "come out" of the established denominations rather than continuing to work within them.

These positions alienated those members of the Anti-Slavery Society who continued to hope that organized religion and the existing political system could be influenced or even taken over by abolitionists. But it was Garrison's stand on women's rights that led to an open break at the national convention of the American Anti-Slavery Society in 1840. Following their leader's principle that women should be equal partners in the crusade, a Garrison-led majority elected a woman abolitionist to the society's executive committee. A minority then withdrew to form a competing organization—the American and Foreign Anti-Slavery Society.

The schism weakened Garrison's influence within the abolitionist movement. When he later repudiated the U.S. Constitution as a proslavery document and called for northern secession from the Union, few antislavery people in the

Middle Atlantic or midwestern states went along. Outside New England, most abolitionists worked within the churches and the political system and avoided controversial side issues such as women's rights and nonresistant pacifism. The Liberty party, organized in 1840, was their first attempt to enter the electoral arena under their own banner; it signaled a new effort to turn antislavery sentiment into political power.

BLACK ABOLITIONISTS

From the beginning, the abolitionist movement depended heavily on the support of the northern free black community. Most of the early subscribers to Garrison's *Liberator* were African Americans. Black orators, especially escaped slaves such as Frederick Douglass, made northern audiences aware of the realities of bondage. But relations between white and black abolitionists were often tense and uneasy. Blacks protested that they did not have their fair share of leadership positions or influence over policy. Eventually a black antislavery movement emerged that was largely independent of the white-led crusade. In addition to Douglass, prominent black male abolitionists included Charles Redmond, William Wells Brown, Robert Purvis, and Henry Highland Garnet. Outspoken women such as Sojourner Truth, Maria Stewart, and Frances Harper also played a significant role in black antislavery activity. The Negro Convention movement, which sponsored national meetings of black leaders beginning in 1830, provided an important forum for independent black expression.

Black newspapers, such as *Freedom's Journal*, first published in 1827, and the *North Star,* founded by Douglass in 1847, gave black writers a chance to

A leader in the abolitionist movement was Frederick Douglass, who escaped from slavery in 1838 and became one of the most effective voices in the crusade against slavery.

preach their gospel of liberation to black readers. African American authors also produced a stream of books and pamphlets attacking slavery, refuting racism, and advocating various forms of resistance. One of the most influential publications was David Walker's *Appeal to the Colored Citizens of the World,* which appeared in 1829. Walker denounced slavery in the most vigorous language possible and called for a black revolt against white tyranny.

Free blacks in the North did more than make verbal protests against racial injustice. They were also the main conductors of the fabled Underground Railroad that opened a path for fugitives from slavery. Courageous ex-slaves such as Harriet Tubman and Josiah Henson made regular forays into the slave states to lead other blacks to freedom, and many of the "stations" along the way were run by free blacks. In northern towns and cities, free blacks organized "vigilance committees" to protect fugitives and thwart the slave-catchers. Groups of blacks even used force to rescue recaptured fugitives from the authorities.

Although it failed to convert a majority of Americans, the abolitionist movement brought the slavery issue to the forefront of public consciousness and convinced a substantial and growing segment of the northern population that the South's peculiar institution was morally wrong and potentially dangerous to the American way of life. The South helped the antislavery cause in the North by responding hysterically and repressively to abolitionist agitation. In 1836, Southerners in Congress forced adoption of a "gag rule" requiring that abolitionist petitions be tabled without being read; at about the same time, the post office refused to carry antislavery literature into the slave states. Prominent Northerners who had not been moved to action by abolitionist depictions of slave suffering became more responsive to the movement when it appeared their own civil liberties might be threatened. The politicians who later mobilized the North against the expansion of slavery into the territories drew strength from the antislavery and antisouthern sentiments that abolitionists had already called forth.

FROM ABOLITIONISM TO WOMEN'S RIGHTS

Abolitionism also served as a catalyst for the women's rights movement. From the beginning, women were active participants in the abolitionist crusade. More than half of the thousands of antislavery petitions sent to Washington had women's signatures on them.

Some antislavery women defied conventional ideas of their proper sphere by becoming public speakers and demanding an equal role in the leadership of antislavery societies. The most famous of these were the Grimké sisters, Sarah and Angelina, who attracted enormous attention because they were the rebellious daughters of a South Carolina slaveholder. When some male abolitionists objected to their speaking in public to mixed audiences of men and women, Garrison came to their defense and helped forge a link between blacks' and women's struggles for equality.

The battle to participate equally in the antislavery crusade made a number of women abolitionists acutely aware of male dominance and oppression. For them,

Elizabeth Cady Stanton, a leader of the women's rights movement, reared seven children. In addition to her pioneering work, especially for woman suffrage, she also lectured frequently on family life and child care.

the same principles that justified the liberation of the slaves also applied to the emancipation of women from all restrictions on their rights as citizens. In 1840, Garrison's American followers withdrew from the first World's Anti-Slavery Convention in London because the sponsors refused to seat the women in their delegation. Among the women thus excluded were Lucretia Mott and Elizabeth Cady Stanton.

Wounded by men's reluctance to extend the cause of emancipation to include women, Stanton and Mott organized a new and independent movement for women's rights. The high point of their campaign was the famous convention at Seneca Falls, New York, in 1848. The Declaration of Sentiments issued by this first national gathering of feminists charged that "the history of mankind is a history of repeated injuries and usurpations on the part of man toward woman, having in direct object the establishment of an absolute tyranny over her." It went on to demand that all women be given the right to vote and that married women be freed from unjust laws giving husbands control of their property, persons, and children. Rejecting the Cult of Domesticity with its doctrine of separate spheres, these women and their male supporters launched the modern movement for gender equality.

RADICAL IDEAS AND EXPERIMENTS

Hopes for individual or social perfection were not limited to reformers inspired by evangelicalism. Between the 1820s and 1850s, a great variety of schemes for human redemption came from those who had rejected orthodox Protestantism. Some were secular humanists carrying on the freethinking tradition of the Enlightenment, but most were seekers of new paths to spiritual or religious fulfillment. These philosophical and religious radicals attacked established institutions, prescribed new modes of living, and founded utopian communities to put their ideas into practice.

A radical movement of foreign origin that gained a toehold in Jacksonian America was utopian socialism. In 1825–1826, the British manufacturer and reformer Robert Owen visited the United States and founded a community based on common and equal ownership of property at New Harmony, Indiana. The rapid demise of this model community suggested that utopian socialism did not easily take root in American soil.

But the impulse survived. In the 1840s, a number of Americans became interested in the ideas of the French utopian theorist Charles Fourier, who called for cooperative communities in which everyone did a fair share of the work and tasks were allotted to make use of the natural abilities and instincts of the members. Between 1842 and 1852, about thirty Fourierist "phalanxes" were established in the northeastern and midwestern states. Like the Owenite communities, the Fourierist phalanxes were short-lived, surviving for an average of only two years. The common complaint of the founders was that Americans were too individualistic to cooperate in the ways that Fourier's theories required.

Two of the most successful and long-lived manifestations of pre–Civil War utopianism were the Shakers and the Oneida community. The Shakers—officially known as the Millennial Church or the United Society of Believers—began as a religious movement in England. In 1774, a Shaker leader, Mother Ann Lee, brought their radical beliefs to the United States. Lee believed herself to be the feminine incarnation of Christ and advocated a new theology based squarely on the principle of gender equality. The Shakers, named for their expressions of religious fervor through vigorous dancelike movements, believed in communal ownership and strict celibacy. They lived simply and minimized their contact with the outside world because they expected Christ's Second Coming to occur momentarily. The Oneida community was established in 1848 at Oneida, New York, and was inspired by an unorthodox brand of Christian perfectionism. Its founder, John Humphrey Noyes, believed the Second Coming of Christ had already occurred; hence human beings were no longer obliged to follow the moral rules that their previously fallen state had required. At Oneida, traditional marriage was outlawed, and a carefully regulated form of "free love" was put into practice.

It was a literary and philosophical movement known as transcendentalism that inspired the era's most memorable experiments in thinking and living on a higher plane. The main idea was that the individual could transcend material reality and ordinary understanding, attaining through a higher form of reason—or intuition—a oneness with the universe as a whole and with the spiritual forces that lay behind it. Transcendentalism was the major American version of the romantic and idealist thought that emerged in the early nineteenth century. Throughout the Western world, romanticism was challenging the rationalism and materialism of the Enlightenment. Most American transcendentalists were Unitarians or ex-Unitarians who were dissatisfied with the sober rationalism of their denomination and sought a more intense kind of spiritual experience.

Their prophet was Ralph Waldo Emerson, a brilliant essayist and lecturer who preached that each individual could commune directly with a benign spiritual force that animated nature and the universe, which he called the "oversoul." A radical individualist committed to "self-culture" and "the sufficiency of the private man," Emerson avoided all involvement in organized movements or associations because he believed they limited the freedom of the individual to develop inner resources and find a personal path to spiritual illumination. In the vicinity of Emerson's home in Concord, Massachusetts, a group of like-minded seekers of truth and spiritual fulfillment gathered during the 1830s and 1840s. Among them for a time was Margaret Fuller, the leading woman intellectual of the age. In *Woman in the Nineteenth Century* (1845), she made a strong claim for the spiritual and artistic equality of women.

One group of transcendentalists, led by the Reverend George Ripley, rejected Emerson's radical individualism and founded a cooperative community at Brook Farm, near Roxbury, Massachusetts, in 1841. For the next eight years, group members worked the land in common, conducted an excellent school on the principle that spontaneity rather than discipline was the key to education, and allowed ample time for conversation, meditation, communion with nature, and artistic activity of all kinds.

Another experiment in transcendental living adhered more closely to the individualistic spirit of the movement. Between 1845 and 1847, Henry David Thoreau, a young disciple of Emerson, lived by himself in the woods along the shore of Walden Pond and carefully recorded his thoughts and impressions. In a sense, he pushed the ideal of self-culture to its logical outcome—a utopia of one. The result was *Walden* (published in 1854), one of the greatest achievements in American literature.

FADS AND FASHIONS

Not only venturesome intellectuals experimented with new beliefs and lifestyles. Between the 1830s and 1850s, a number of fads, fashions, and medical cure-alls appeared on the scene, indicating that a large segment of the middle class was obsessed with the pursuit of personal health, happiness, and moral perfection. Dietary reformers such as Sylvester Graham convinced many people to give up meat, coffee, tea, and pastries in favor of fruit, vegetables, and whole wheat bread. Some women, especially feminists, began to wear loose-fitting pantalettes, or "bloomers," popularized by Amelia Bloomer. The clothes were more convenient and less restricting than the elaborate structure of corsets, petticoats, and hoopskirts then in fashion. A concern with understanding and improving personal character and abilities was reflected in the craze for phrenology, a popular

Henry David Thoreau explained that he went to live in solitude in the woods because he wanted to "front only the essential facts of life." The sketch at right appeared on the title page of the first edition of Walden *(1854), the remarkable record of his experiment in living.*

pseudoscience that studied the shape of the skull to determine natural aptitudes and inclinations. In the 1850s, another craze swept through the United States—spiritualism. Spiritualists convinced an extraordinary number of people that it was possible to communicate with spirits and ghosts. Séances were held in parlors around the country as Americans sought advice and guidance from the world beyond. Spiritualism was one more manifestation of the American quest for the perfection of human beings.

COUNTERPOINT ON REFORM

One great American writer observed at close quarters the perfectionist ferment of the age but held himself aloof, suggesting in his novels and tales that pursuit of the ideal led to a distorted view of human nature and possibilities. Nathaniel Hawthorne's sense of human frailty made him skeptical about the claims of transcendentalism and utopianism. He satirized transcendentalism as unworldly and overoptimistic in his allegorical tale "The Celestial Railroad" and gently lampooned the denizens of Brook Farm in his novel *The Blithedale Romance* (1852). His view of the dangers of pursuing perfection too avidly came out in his tale of a father who kills his beautiful daughter by trying to remove her one blemish, a birthmark. His greatest novels, *The Scarlet Letter* (1850) and *The House of the Seven Gables* (1851), imaginatively probed New England's Puritan past and the shadows it cast on the present. By dwelling on original sin as a psychological reality, Hawthorne told his contemporaries that their efforts to escape from guilt and evil were futile. One simply had to accept the world as an imperfect place.

One does not have to agree with Hawthorne's view of the human condition to acknowledge that the dreams of perfectionist reformers promised more than they could possibly deliver. Revivals could not make all men like Christ; temperance could not solve all social problems; abolitionist agitation could not bring a peaceful end to slavery; and transcendentalism could not fully emancipate people from the limitations and frustrations of daily life. The consequences of perfectionist efforts were often far different from what their proponents expected. Yet, if the reform impulse was long on inspirational rhetoric but somewhat short on durable, practical achievements, it did at least disturb the complacent and opportunistic surface of American life and open the way to necessary changes. Nothing could possibly change for the better unless people were willing to dream of improvement.

CHRONOLOGY

1801	Massive revival held at Cane Ridge, Kentucky
1826	American Temperance Society organized
1830–1831	Charles G. Finney evangelizes Rochester, New York
1831	William Lloyd Garrison publishes first issue of the *Liberator*
1833	Abolitionists found American Anti-Slavery Society
1835–1836	Theodore Weld advocates abolition in Ohio and upstate New York
1836	American Temperance Society splits into factions
1837	Massachusetts establishes a state board of education
	Abolitionist editor Elijah Lovejoy killed by a proslavery mob
1840	American Anti-Slavery Society splits over women's rights and other issues
1841	Transcendentalists organize a model community at Brook Farm
1848	Feminists gather at Seneca Falls, New York, and adopt the Declaration of Sentiments
1854	Henry David Thoreau's *Walden* published

13

AN AGE OF EXPANSIONISM

In the 1840s and early 1850s, politicians, journalists, writers, and entrepreneurs frequently proclaimed themselves champions of "Young America." One of the first to use the phrase was Ralph Waldo Emerson, who told an audience of merchants and manufacturers in 1844 that the nation was entering a new era of commercial development, technological progress, and territorial expansion. Emerson suggested that a progressive new generation—the Young Americans—would lead this surge of physical development. More than a slogan and less than an organized movement, Young America stood for a positive attitude toward the market economy and industrial growth, a more aggressive and belligerent foreign policy, and a celebration of America's unique strengths and virtues.

Young Americans favored enlarging the national market by acquiring new territory. They called for annexation of Texas, assertion of an American claim to much of the Pacific Northwest, and the appropriation of vast new territories from Mexico. They also celebrated the technological advances that would knit this new empire together, especially the telegraph and the railroad.

Young America was a cultural and intellectual as well as an economic and political movement. In 1845, a Washington journal hailed the election of forty-nine-year-old James K. Polk, the youngest man yet to become president. During the Polk administration, Young American writers and critics—mostly based in New York City—called for a new and distinctive national literature, free of subservience to European themes or models and expressive of the democratic spirit. Their organ was the *Literary World,* founded in 1847, and its ideals influenced two of the greatest writers the nation has produced: Walt Whitman and Herman Melville.

In his free verse poetry, Whitman captured much of the exuberance, optimism, and expansionism of Young America.

From this hour I ordain myself loos'd of limits and imaginary lines,
Going where I list, my own master total and absolute,
. . . .
I inhale great draughts of space,
The east and the west are mine, and the north and the south are mine.
I am larger, better than I thought.

In *Moby-Dick,* Herman Melville produced a novel sufficiently original in form and conception to more than fulfill the demand of Young Americans for "a New Literature to fit the New Man in the New Age." But Melville was too deep a thinker not to see the perils that underlay the soaring ambition and aggressiveness of the new age. The whaling captain Ahab, who brings destruction on himself and his ship by his relentless pursuit of the white whale, symbolized—among other things—the dangers facing a nation that was overreaching itself by indulging its pride and exalted sense of destiny with too little concern for moral and practical consequences.

The Young American ideal—the idea of a young country led by young men into new paths of prosperity and greatness—appealed to many people and found support across political party lines. But the attitude came to be identified primarily with young Democrats who wanted to move their party away from its traditional fear of the expansion of commerce and industry. Unlike old-line Jeffersonians and Jacksonians, Young Americans had no qualms about the market economy and the speculative, materialistic spirit it called forth.

Before 1848, the Young American impulse focused mainly on the great expanse of western lands that lay just beyond the nation's borders. After the Mexican-American War, when territorial gains extended the nation's boundaries from the Atlantic to the Pacific, attention shifted to internal development. New discoveries of gold in the nation's western territories fostered economic growth, technological advances spurred industrialization, and increased immigration brought more people to populate the lands newly acquired—by agreement or by force.

MOVEMENT TO THE FAR WEST

In the 1830s and 1840s, the westward movement of population penetrated the Far West all the way to the Pacific. Pioneers pursued fertile land and economic opportunity beyond the existing boundaries of the United States and thus helped set the stage for the annexations and international crises of the 1840s. Some went for material gain, others went for adventure, and a significant minority sought freedom from religious persecution. Whatever their reasons, they brought American attitudes into regions that were already occupied or claimed by Mexico or Great Britain.

BORDERLANDS OF THE 1830s

U.S. expansionists directed their ambitions to the north, west, and southwest. For a time, it seemed that both Canada and Mexico might be frontiers for expansionism. Conflicts over the border between the United States and British North America led periodically to calls for diplomatic or military action to wrest the northern half of the continent from the British; similar conflicts in Mexican territory led ultimately to the United States's capture and acquisition of much of northern Mexico.

A long-standing dispute over the boundary between Maine and the Canadian province of New Brunswick was finally resolved in 1842, when Secretary of State Daniel Webster concluded an agreement with the British government, represented by Lord Ashburton. The Webster-Ashburton Treaty gave more than half of the disputed territory to the United States and established a definite northeastern boundary with Canada.

On the other side of the continent, the United States and Britain both laid claim to Oregon, a vast area that lay between the Rockies and the Pacific from the 42nd parallel (the northern boundary of California) to the latitude of 54°40' (the southern boundary of Alaska). Although in 1818 the two nations agreed to joint occupation, each side managed to strengthen its claim. The United States acquired Spain's rights to the Pacific Northwest in the Adams-Onís Treaty, and Britain gained effective control of the northern portion of the Oregon Country through the activities of the Hudson's Bay Company. Neither side, however, wanted to surrender access to the Columbia River basin and the adjacent territory extending north to the 49th parallel (which later became the northern border of the state of Washington).

The Oregon Country was scarcely populated before 1840. The same could not be said of the Mexican borderlands that lay directly west of Jacksonian America. Spanish settlements in present-day New Mexico date from the late sixteenth century. By 1820, about forty thousand people of Spanish descent populated this province, engaging mainly in sheep raising and mining. In 1821, Spain granted independence to Mexico, which then embraced areas that currently make up the states of Texas, New Mexico, Arizona, California, Nevada, Utah, and much of Colorado. The Republic of Mexico instituted a free-trade policy that stimulated commercial prosperity but also whetted expansionist appetites on the Anglo side of the border.

California was the other major northward extension of Mexico. In the 1820s and 1830s, this land of huge estates and enormous cattle herds was far less populous than New Mexico—only about four thousand Mexicans of Spanish origin lived in California in 1827. The region's other inhabitants were the thirty thousand Indians, many of whom were forced to work on vast land tracts owned by Spanish missions. At the beginning of the 1830s, a chain of twenty-one mission stations, stretching from San Diego to Sonoma, well north of San Francisco, controlled most of the province's land and wealth. The Indian population had experienced a catastrophic decline during the sixty years of Spanish rule. The stresses and strains of forced labor and exposure to European diseases had taken an enormous toll.

In 1833, the Mexican Congress's "secularization act" emancipated the Indians from church control and opened the mission lands to settlement. The government awarded immense tracts of the mission land to Mexican citizens and left the Indians landless. A new class of large landowners, or *rancheros*, replaced the *padres* as masters of the province's indigenous population. The rancheros subjected the Indians to a new and even harsher form of servitude. During the

Territorial Expansion by the Mid-Nineteenth Century
Fervent nationalists identified the growth of America through territorial expansion as the divinely ordained "Manifest Destiny" of a chosen people.

fifteen years they held sway, the rancheros created an American legend through their lavish hospitality, extravagant dress, superb horsemanship, and taste for violent and dangerous sports.

The Americans who saw California in the 1830s were mostly merchants and sailors involved in the oceanic trade between Boston and California ports. By the mid-1830s, several Yankee merchants had taken up permanent residence in towns such as Monterey and San Diego in order to conduct the California end of the business. The reports they sent back about the Golden West sparked interest in eastern business circles.

THE TEXAS REVOLUTION

At the same time as some Americans were trading with California, others were taking possession of Texas. In the early 1820s, Mexican officials encouraged settlers from the United States to settle in Texas. Newly independent Mexico granted Stephen F. Austin, son of a onetime Spanish citizen, a huge piece of land in hopes he would help attract and settle new colonists from the United States. Some fifteen other Anglo-American *empresarios* received land grants in the 1820s. In 1823, three hundred families from the United States were settled on the Austin grant, and within a year, the colony's population had swelled to 2021. The offer of fertile and inexpensive land attracted many American immigrants.

Friction soon developed between the Mexican government and the Anglo-American colonists over the status of slavery and the authority of the Catholic Church. Under the terms of settlement, all people living in Texas had to become Mexican citizens and adopt the Roman Catholic faith. Settlers either converted to Catholicism only superficially or ignored the requirement entirely. Slavery presented another problem, for in 1829 Mexico freed all slaves under its jurisdiction. Slaveholders in Texas were given a special exemption that allowed them to emancipate their slaves and then sign them to lifelong contracts as indentured servants, but many refused to limit their ownership rights in any way.

A Mexican government commission reported in 1829 that Americans were the great majority of the Texas population and were flagrantly violating Mexican law—refusing to emancipate their slaves, evading import duties on goods from the United States, and failing to convert to Catholicism. The following year, the Mexican Congress prohibited further American immigration and importation of slaves to Texas.

Enforcement of the new law was feeble, and the flow of settlers, slaves, and smuggled goods continued virtually unabated. A long-standing complaint of the Texans was the failure of the Mexican constitution to grant them local self-government. Under the Mexican federal system, Texas was joined to the state of Coahuila, and Texan representatives were outnumbered three to one in the state legislature. In 1832, the colonists rioted in protest against the arrest of several Anglo-Americans by a Mexican commander.

A threat to the Texans' status as "tolerated guests" occurred in 1834 when General Antonio López de Santa Anna made himself dictator of Mexico and abolished the federal system of government. News of these developments reached Texas late in the year, accompanied by rumors of the impending disfranchisement and even expulsion of American immigrants. The rebels, already aroused by earlier restrictive policies, were influenced by the rumors and prepared to resist Santa Anna's effort to enforce tariff regulations by military force.

When he learned that Texans were resisting customs collections, Santa Anna sent reinforcements. The settlers first engaged Mexican troops at Gonzales in October and forced the retreat of a cavalry detachment. Shortly thereafter, Austin laid siege to San Antonio with a force of five hundred men and after six weeks forced its surrender, thereby capturing most of the Mexican troops then in Texas.

THE REPUBLIC OF TEXAS

While this early fighting was going on, delegates from the American communities in Texas convened and after some hesitation voted overwhelmingly to declare their independence on March 2, 1836. A constitution, based closely on that of the United States, was adopted for the new Republic of Texas, and a temporary government was installed to carry on the military struggle. Although the ensuing conflict was largely one of Americans against Mexicans, some Texas Mexicans, or *Tejanos,* joined the fray on the side of the Anglo rebels. They too wanted to be free of Santa Anna's heavy-handed rule.

Within days after Texas declared itself a republic, rebels and Mexican troops in San Antonio fought the famous battle of the Alamo. Myths about that battle have magnified the Anglo rebels' valor at the Mexicans' expense. The folklore is based on fact—only 187 rebels fought off a far larger number of Mexican soldiers for more than a week before eventually capitulating—but it is not true that all rebels, including the folk hero Davy Crockett, fought to the death. Crockett and seven other survivors were captured and then executed. Nevertheless, a tale that combined actual and mythical bravery inspired the rallying cry "Remember the Alamo."

The revolt ended with an exchange of slaughters. A few days after the Alamo battle, another Texas detachment was surrounded and captured in an open plain near the San Antonio River and was marched to the town of Goliad, where most of its 350 members were executed. The next month, on April 21, 1836, the main Texas army, under General Sam Houston, assaulted Santa Anna's troops at an encampment near the San Jacinto River. The final count showed that 630 Mexicans and only a handful of Texans had been killed. Santa Anna was captured and marched to Velasco, the meeting place of the Texas government, where he was forced to sign treaties recognizing the independence of Texas and its claim to territory all the way to the Rio Grande.

Sam Houston, the hero of San Jacinto, became the first president of Texas. His platform sought annexation to the United States, but Andrew Jackson and others believed that domestic politics and fear of a war with Mexico made immediate annexation impossible. Congress and the Jackson administration did, however, formally recognize Texas sovereignty.

In its ten-year existence as the Lone Star Republic, Texas drew settlers from the United States at an accelerating rate. The Panic of 1837 impelled many debt-ridden and land-hungry farmers to take advantage of the free grants of 1280 acres that Texas offered to immigrating heads of white families. In the decade after independence, the population of Texas soared from 30,000 to 142,000. Most of the newcomers assumed, as did the old settlers, that they would soon be annexed and restored to American citizenship.

TRAILS OF TRADE AND SETTLEMENT

After New Mexico opened its trade to American merchants, a thriving commerce developed along the trail that ran from Missouri to Santa Fe. To protect themselves from the hostile Indians whose territory they had to cross, the traders traveled in large caravans, one or two of which would arrive in Santa Fe every summer.

Deteriorating relations between the United States and Mexico following the Texas revolution had a devastating effect on the Santa Fe trade. In April 1842, the Mexican government passed a new tariff banning the importation of many of the goods sold by American merchants and prohibiting the export of gold and silver. Further restrictions in 1843 denied American traders full access to the Santa Fe market.

The famous Oregon Trail was the great overland route that brought the wagon trains of American migrants to the West Coast during the 1840s. The journey took about six months; most parties departed in May, hoping to arrive in November before the great snows hit the last mountain barriers. After small groups had made their way to both Oregon and California in 1841 and 1842, a mass migration—mostly to Oregon—began in 1843. These migrants were quick to demand the extension of full American sovereignty over the Oregon Country.

THE MORMON TREK

An important and distinctive group of pioneers followed the Oregon Trail as far as South Pass and then veered southwestward to establish a thriving colony in the region of the Great Salt Lake. These were Mormons, members of the largest religious denomination founded on American soil—the Church of Jesus Christ of Latter-day Saints.

The background of the Mormon trek was a history of persecution in the eastern states. Joseph Smith of Palmyra, New York, the founder of Mormonism, revealed in 1830 that he had received a series of revelations that called upon him to establish Christ's pure church on earth. As the prophet of this faith, he published the *Book of Mormon,* a new scripture that he claimed to have discovered and translated with the aid of an angel. Smith and those he converted to his new faith were committed to restoring the pure religion that they believed had once thrived on American soil by founding a western Zion where they could practice their faith unmolested and carry out their special mission to convert the Native Americans.

In the 1830s, the Mormons established communities in Ohio and Missouri, but the former went bankrupt in the Panic of 1837 and the latter was the target of angry mobs and vigilante violence. In 1839, Smith led his followers back across the Mississippi to Illinois, where they found a temporary haven in the

Carl Christian Anton Christensen, Handcart, *ca. 1840. Instead of buying wagons and oxen, some groups of Mormon colonists made their trek to Deseret on foot, hauling their possessions in handcarts and working together as families to move their heavy loads.*

town of Nauvoo. But Smith soon reported new revelations that engendered dissension among his followers and hostility from neighboring "gentiles." Most controversial was his authorization of polygamy, or plural marriage. In 1844, Smith was killed by a mob while being held in jail in Carthage, Illinois, on a charge stemming from his quarrels with dissident Mormons who objected to his new policies.

Smith's death convinced Mormon leaders that they needed to move beyond the borders of the United States to establish their Zion in the wilderness. In late 1845, Smith's successor, Brigham Young, sent a party of fifteen hundred men to assess the chances of a colony in the vicinity of the Great Salt Lake (then part of Mexico). Twelve thousand Mormons took to the trail in 1846. Young himself arrived in Utah in 1847 and sent back word to the thousands encamped along the trail that he had found the promised land.

The Mormon community that Young established in Utah is one of the great success stories of western settlement. In contrast to the rugged individualism and disorder that often characterized mining camps and other new communities, "the state of Deseret" (the name the Mormons originally applied to Utah) was a model of discipline and cooperation. Because of its communitarian form of social organization, its centralized government, and the religious dedication of its inhabitants, this frontier society was able to expand settlement in a planned and efficient way and develop a system of irrigation that "made the desert bloom."

After Utah came under American sovereignty in 1848, the state of Deseret fought to maintain its autonomy and its custom of polygamy against the efforts of the federal government to extend American law and set up the usual type of territorial administration. In 1857, President Buchanan dispatched a military force to Utah, and the Mormons prepared to repel this "invasion." But after a heavy snow prevented the army from crossing the Rockies, Buchanan proposed a general pardon for Mormons who had violated federal law but agreed to cooperate with U.S. authorities in the future. The Mormons accepted, and in return, Brigham Young called off his plan to resist the army by force and accepted the nominal authority of an appointed territorial governor.

MANIFEST DESTINY AND THE MEXICAN-AMERICAN WAR

The rush of settlers beyond the nation's borders in the 1830s and 1840s inspired politicians and propagandists to call for annexation of those areas occupied by migrants. Some went further and proclaimed it was the "manifest destiny" of the United States to expand until it had absorbed all of North America, including Canada and Mexico. Such ambitions—and the policies they inspired—led to a major diplomatic confrontation with Great Britain and a war with Mexico.

TYLER AND TEXAS

President John Tyler initiated the politics of Manifest Destiny. He was vice president when William Henry Harrison died in office in 1841 after serving scarcely a month. Tyler was a states' rights, proslavery Virginian who had been picked as

Harrison's running mate to broaden the appeal of the Whig ticket. Profoundly out of sympathy with the mainstream of his own party, he soon broke with the Whigs in Congress, who had united behind the latest version of Henry Clay's "American System." Although he lacked a base in either of the major parties, Tyler hoped to be elected president in his own right in 1844. To accomplish this difficult feat, he needed a new issue around which he could build a following that would cut across established party lines.

In 1843, Tyler decided upon the annexation of Texas as his issue. He anticipated that incorporation of the Lone Star Republic would be a popular move, especially in the slaveholding South. With Southern support, Tyler expected to have a good chance in the election of 1844.

To prepare the public for annexation, the Tyler administration launched a propaganda campaign in the summer of 1843. Rumors were circulated that the British were preparing to guarantee Texas independence and make a loan to the financially troubled republic in return for the abolition of slavery. Although the reports were groundless, they were believed and used to give urgency to the annexation cause.

Secretary of State John C. Calhoun successfully negotiated an annexation treaty that was brought before the Senate in 1844. Denouncing the British for attempting to subvert the South's essential system of labor and racial control, Calhoun argued that the South's security and well-being—and by extension that of the nation—required the immediate incorporation of Texas into the Union.

The strategy of linking annexation explicitly to the interests of the South and slavery backfired. Northern antislavery Whigs charged that the whole scheme was a proslavery plot meant to advance the interest of one section of the nation against the other. Consequently, the Senate rejected the treaty by a decisive vote of 35 to 16 in June 1844. Tyler then attempted to bring Texas into the Union through a joint resolution of both houses of Congress admitting it as a state, but Congress adjourned before the issue came to a vote. The whole question hung fire in anticipation of the election of 1844.

THE TRIUMPH OF POLK AND ANNEXATION

Tyler's initiative made the future of Texas the central issue in the 1844 campaign. But the president was unable to capitalize on the issue because his stand was not in line with the views of either party. He tried to run as an independent, but his failure to gain significant support eventually forced him to withdraw from the race.

If the Democratic party convention had been held in 1843, as it was originally scheduled, former President Martin Van Buren would have won the nomination. But postponement of the Democratic conclave until May 1844 weakened his chances. Forced to take a stand on the annexation question, Van Buren persisted in the view he had held as president—that incorporation of Texas would risk war with Mexico, arouse sectional strife, and destroy the unity of the Democratic party. In an effort to keep the issue out of the campaign, Van Buren struck a gentleman's agreement with Henry Clay, the overwhelming favorite for the Whig nomination, that both of them would publicly oppose immediate annexation.

THE LIBERTY PARTY SWINGS AN ELECTION

CANDIDATE	PARTY	ACTUAL VOTE IN NEW YORK	NATIONAL ELECTORAL VOTE	IF LIBERTY VOTERS HAD VOTED WHIG	PROJECTED ELECTORAL VOTE
Polk	Democratic	237,588	170	237,588	134
Clay	Whig	232,482	105	248,294	141
Birney	Liberty	15,812	0	—	—

Van Buren's letter opposing annexation appeared shortly before the Democratic convention, and it cost him the nomination. Angry southern delegates, who secured a rule requiring approval by a two-thirds vote, blocked Van Buren's nomination. After several ballots, a dark horse candidate—James K. Polk of Tennessee—emerged triumphant. Polk, a protégé of Andrew Jackson, had been speaker of the House of Representatives and governor of Tennessee.

An avowed expansionist, Polk ran on a platform calling for the simultaneous annexation of Texas and assertion of American claims to all of Oregon. He identified himself and his party with the popular cause of turning the United States into a continental nation, an aspiration that attracted support from all parts of the country.

Polk won the fall election by a relatively narrow popular margin. His triumph in the electoral college was secured by victories in New York and Michigan, where the Liberty party candidate, James G. Birney, had taken away enough votes from Clay to affect the outcome. Although the close election was hardly a clear mandate for expansionism, the Democrats claimed that the people had backed an aggressive campaign to extend the borders of the United States.

After the election, Congress reconvened to consider the annexation of Texas. The mood had changed as a result of Polk's victory, and some leading senators from both parties who had initially opposed Tyler's scheme for annexation by joint resolution of Congress now changed their position. As a result, annexation was approved a few days before Polk took office.

THE ELECTION OF 1844

CANDIDATE	PARTY	POPULAR VOTE	ELECTORAL VOTE
Polk	Democratic	1,338,464	170
Clay	Whig	1,300,097	105
Birney	Liberty	62,300	—

THE DOCTRINE OF MANIFEST DESTINY

The expansionist mood that accompanied Polk's election and the annexation of Texas was given a name and a rationale in the summer of 1845. John L. O'Sullivan, a proponent of the Young America movement and editor of the influential *United States Magazine and Democratic Review,* charged that foreign governments were conspiring to block the annexation of Texas in an effort to thwart "the fulfillment of our manifest destiny to overspread the continent allotted by providence for the free development of our yearly multiplying millions."

Besides coining the phrase Manifest Destiny, O'Sullivan pointed to the three main ideas that lay behind it. One was that God was on the side of American expansionism. This notion arose from the long tradition that identified the growth of America with the divinely ordained success of a chosen people. A second idea, implied in the phrase *free development,* was that the spread of American rule meant the extension of democratic institutions and local self-government if areas claimed by autocratic foreign governments were annexed to the United States. O'Sullivan's third premise was that population growth required the outlet that territorial acquisitions would provide.

In its most extreme form, the doctrine of Manifest Destiny meant that the United States would someday occupy the entire North American continent; nothing less would appease its land-hungry population. "Make way, I say, for the young American Buffalo," bellowed a Democratic orator in 1844, "—he has not yet got land enough. . . . I tell you we will give him Oregon for his summer shade, and the region of Texas as his winter pasture. (Applause) Like all of his race, he wants salt, too. Well, he shall have the use of two oceans—the mighty Pacific and the turbulent Atlantic. . . . He shall not stop his career until he slakes his thirst in the frozen ocean. (Cheers)"

POLK AND THE OREGON QUESTION

In 1845 and 1846, the United States came closer to armed conflict with Great Britain than at any time since the War of 1812. The willingness of some Americans to go to war over Oregon was expressed in the rallying cry "Fifty-four forty or fight." This slogan was actually coined by Whigs seeking to ridicule Democratic expansionists, but Democrats later took it over as a vivid expression of their demand for what is now British Columbia. Polk fed this expansionist fever by laying claim in his inaugural address to all of the Oregon Country. Privately, however, he was willing to accept the 49th parallel as a dividing line. What made the situation so tense was that Polk was dedicated to an aggressive diplomacy of bluff and bluster.

In July 1845, Polk authorized Secretary of State James Buchanan to reply to the latest British request for terms by offering a boundary along the 49th parallel. The offer did not meet the British demand for all of Vancouver Island and free navigation of the Columbia River, and the British ambassador rejected the proposal out of hand. This rebuff infuriated Polk, who later called on Congress to terminate the agreement for joint occupation of the Pacific Northwest. Congress complied in April 1846.

Since abrogation of the joint agreement implied that the United States would attempt to extend its jurisdiction north to 54°40', the British government decided to take the diplomatic initiative in an effort to avert war, while at the same time dispatching warships to the Western Hemisphere in case conciliation failed. Their new proposal accepted the 49th parallel as the border, gave Britain all of Vancouver Island, and provided for British navigation rights on the Columbia River. The Senate recommended the treaty be accepted with the single change that British rights to navigate the Columbia be made temporary. It was ratified in that form on June 15.

Polk was prompted to settle the Oregon question because he now had a war with Mexico on his hands. His reckless and aggressive diplomacy had brought the nation within an eyelash of being involved in two wars at the same time. American policymakers got what they wanted from the Oregon treaty, namely the splendid natural deep-water harbor of Puget Sound and the strait that led into it south of Vancouver Island. By agreeing to compromise on the Oregon issue, however, Polk alienated expansionist advocates in the Old Northwest who had supported his call for "all of Oregon."

For many Northerners, the promise of new acquisitions in the Pacific Northwest was the only thing that made annexation of Texas palatable. They hoped new free states could be created to counterbalance the admission of slaveholding Texas to the Union. As this prospect receded, the charge of antislavery advocates that Texas annexation was a southern plot became more believable; to Northerners, Polk began to look more and more like a president concerned mainly with furthering the interests of his native region.

War with Mexico

While the United States was avoiding a war with Great Britain, it was getting into one with Mexico. Although they had recognized Texas independence in 1845, the Mexicans rejected the Lone Star Republic's dubious claim to the unsettled territory between the Nueces River and the Rio Grande. When the United States annexed Texas and assumed its claim to the disputed area, Mexico broke off diplomatic relations and prepared for armed conflict.

Polk responded by placing troops in Louisiana on the alert and by dispatching John Slidell as an emissary to Mexico City in the hope he could resolve the boundary dispute and also persuade the Mexicans to sell New Mexico and California to the United States. But the Mexican government refused to receive Slidell. Then in January 1846, Polk ordered General Zachary Taylor, commander of American forces in the Southwest, to advance well beyond the Nueces and proceed toward the Rio Grande, thus invading territory claimed by both sides.

By April, Taylor had taken up a position near Matamoros on the Rio Grande. On April 24, sixteen hundred Mexican soldiers crossed the river and the following day attacked a small American detachment, killing eleven and capturing the rest. After learning of the incident, Taylor sent word to the president: "Hostilities may now be considered as commenced."

The news was neither unexpected nor unwelcome. Polk in fact was already preparing his war message to Congress when he learned of the fighting on the Rio Grande. A short and decisive war, he had concluded, would force the cession of California and New Mexico to the United States.

This 1846 cartoon titled "This Is the House That Polk Built" shows President Polk sitting forlornly in a house of cards, which represents the delicately balanced issues facing him.

The war lasted much longer than expected because the Mexicans refused to make peace despite a succession of military defeats. In the first major campaign of the conflict, Taylor took Matamoros and overcame fierce resistance to capture Monterrey, a major city of northern Mexico.

Taylor's controversial decision to allow the Mexican garrison to go free and his unwillingness or inability to advance farther into Mexico angered Polk and led him to adopt a new strategy for winning the war and a new commander to implement it. General Winfield Scott was ordered to prepare an amphibious attack on Veracruz with the aim of placing an American army within striking distance of Mexico City itself. Taylor was left to hold his position in northern Mexico, where at Buena Vista in February 1847 he defeated a sizable Mexican army sent northward to dislodge him. Taylor was hailed as a national hero and a possible candidate for president.

Meanwhile, an expedition led by Stephen Kearny captured Santa Fe, proclaimed the annexation of New Mexico by the United States, and set off for California. There they found that American settlers, in cooperation with John C. Frémont's exploring expedition, had revolted against Mexican authorities and declared their independence as the Bear Flag Republic. With the addition of Kearny's troops, a relatively small number of Americans were able to take possession of California against scattered and disorganized Mexican opposition, a process that was completed by the beginning of 1847.

The decisive Veracruz campaign was slow to develop, but in March 1847, the main American army under General Scott finally laid siege to the crucial port city. Veracruz fell after eighteen days, and then Scott began his advance on Mexico City. In the most important single battle of the war, Scott met forces under General Santa Anna at Cerro Gordo on April 17 and 18. A daring flanking maneuver that required soldiers to scramble up mountainsides enabled Scott to win the decisive victory that opened the road to Mexico City. By August, American troops were drawn up in front of the Mexican capital. After a temporary armistice, a brief respite that the Mexicans used to regroup and improve their defenses, Scott ordered the massive assault that captured the city on September 14.

SETTLEMENT OF THE MEXICAN-AMERICAN WAR

Accompanying Scott's army was a diplomat, Nicholas P. Trist, who was authorized to negotiate a peace treaty whenever the Mexicans decided they had had enough. But even after the United States had achieved an overwhelming military victory, Trist found it difficult to exact an acceptable treaty from the Mexican government. In November, Polk ordered Trist to return to Washington.

Trist ignored Polk's instructions and continued to negotiate. On February 2, 1848, he signed a treaty that gained all the concessions he had been commissioned to obtain. The Treaty of Guadalupe Hidalgo ceded New Mexico and California to the United States for $15 million, established the Rio Grande as the border between Texas and Mexico, and promised that the U.S. government would assume the substantial claims of American citizens against Mexico. The treaty also provided that the Mexican residents of the new territories would become U.S. citizens. The Senate ratified the treaty on March 10.

As a result of the Mexican-American War, the United States gained 500,000 square miles of territory, enlarging the size of the nation by about 20 percent and adding to its domain the present states of California, Utah, New Mexico, Nevada, and Arizona and parts of Colorado and Wyoming. Soon those interested in a southern route for a transcontinental railroad pressed for even more territory along the southern border of the cession. That pressure led in 1853 to the Gadsden Purchase, through which the United States acquired the southernmost parts of present-day Arizona and New Mexico.

The war with Mexico divided the American public and provoked political dissension. A majority of the Whig party opposed the war in principle, arguing that the United States had no valid claims to the area south of the Nueces. Whig congressmen voted for military appropriations while the conflict was going on, but they constantly criticized the president for starting it. More ominous was the charge of some Northerners from both parties that the real purpose of the war was to spread the institution of slavery and increase the political power of the southern states. While battles were being fought in Mexico, Congress was debating the Wilmot Proviso, a proposal to prohibit slavery in any territories that might be acquired from Mexico. A bitter sectional quarrel over the status of slavery in new areas was a major legacy of the Mexican-American War.

The domestic controversies aroused by the war and the propaganda of Manifest Destiny put a damper on additional efforts to extend the nation's boundaries. Concerns about slavery and race impeded acquisition of new territory in Latin America and the Caribbean. Resolution of the Oregon dispute clearly indicated that the United States was not willing to go to war with a powerful adversary to obtain large chunks of British North America, and the old ambition of incorporating Canada faded. After 1848, Americans concentrated on populating and developing the vast territory already acquired.

INTERNAL EXPANSIONISM

Young American expansionists saw a clear link between acquisition of new territory and other forms of material growth and development. In 1844, Samuel F. B. Morse perfected and demonstrated his electric telegraph, a device that made it possible to communicate rapidly over the expanse of a continental nation. Simultaneously, the railroad was becoming increasingly important as a means of moving people and goods over the same great distances. Improvements in manufacturing and agricultural methods led to an upsurge in the volume and range of internal trade, and the beginnings of mass immigration were providing human resources for the exploitation of new areas and economic opportunities.

The discovery of gold in newly acquired California in 1848 attracted a flood of emigrants from the East and several foreign nations. The gold they unearthed spurred the national economy, and the rapid growth of population centers on the Pacific Coast inspired projects for transcontinental telegraph lines and railroad tracks.

The spirit of Manifest Destiny and the thirst for acquiring new territory waned after the Mexican-American War. The expansionist impulse was channeled instead into internal development. Although the nation ceased to grow in size, the technological advances and population increase of the 1840s continued during the 1850s. The result was an acceleration of economic growth, a substantial increase in industrialization and urbanization, and the emergence of a new American working class.

THE TRIUMPH OF THE RAILROAD

More than anything else, the rise of the railroad transformed the American economy during the 1840s and 1850s. The technology came from England, and in 1830 and 1831, two American railroads began commercial operation. After these pioneer lines had shown that steam locomotion was practical and profitable, several other railroads were built and began to carry passengers and freight during the 1830s. But this early success was somewhat limited, because canals proved to be strong competitors, especially for the freight business. Passengers might prefer the speed of trains, but the lower unit cost of transporting freight on the canalboats prevented most shippers from changing their habits. Furthermore, states such as New York and Pennsylvania had invested heavily in canals and resisted chartering a competitive form of transportation.

During the 1840s, rails extended beyond the northeastern and Middle Atlantic states, and mileage increased more than threefold, reaching a total of more than 9000 miles by 1850. Expansion was even greater in the following decade, and by 1860, all the states east of the Mississippi had rail service. Throughout the 1840s and 1850s, railroads cut deeply into the freight business of the canals and drove many of them out of business. The cost of hauling goods by rail decreased dramatically because of improved track construction and the introduction of powerful locomotives that could haul more cars.

The development of railroads had an enormous effect on the economy as a whole. Although the burgeoning demand for iron rails was initially met mainly by importation from England, it eventually spurred development of the domestic iron industry. Since railroads required an enormous outlay of capital, their promoters pioneered new methods for financing business enterprise. At a time when most manufacturing and mercantile concerns were still owned by families or partnerships, the railroad companies sold stock to the general public and helped to set the pattern for the separation of ownership and control that characterizes the modern corporation.

Private capital did not fully meet the desires of the early railroad barons. State and local governments, convinced that railroads were the key to their future prosperity, loaned the railroads money, bought their stock, and guaranteed their bonds. Despite the dominant philosophy of laissez-faire, the federal government became involved by surveying the routes of projected lines and providing land grants. In all, forty companies received such aid before 1860, setting a precedent for the massive land grants of the post–Civil War era.

THE INDUSTRIAL REVOLUTION TAKES OFF

While railroads were initiating a revolution in transportation, American industry was entering a new phase of rapid and sustained growth. The factory mode of production, which had originated before 1840 in the cotton mills of New England, was extended to a variety of other products. The weaving and processing of wool, instead of being carried on in different locations, was concentrated in single production units beginning in the 1830s, and by 1860 some of the largest textile mills in the country were producing wool cloth. In the coal and iron regions of eastern Pennsylvania, iron was being forged and rolled in factories by 1850. Among the other industries that adopted the factory system during this period were those producing firearms, clocks, and sewing machines.

The essential features of the emerging mode of production were the gathering of a supervised workforce in a single place, the payment of cash wages to workers, the use of interchangeable parts, and manufacture by "continuous process." Within a factory setting, standardized parts, manufactured separately

A revolution in farming followed the introduction of new farm implements such as Cyrus McCormick's reaper, which could do ten times the work of a single person. The lithograph, by an anonymous artist, is titled The Testing of the First Reaping Machine near Steele's Tavern, Virginia, 1831.

and in bulk, could be efficiently and rapidly assembled into a final product by an ordered sequence of continuously repeated operations. Mass production, which involved the division of labor into a series of relatively simple and repetitive tasks, contrasted sharply with the traditional craft mode of production, in which a single worker produced the entire product out of raw materials.

New technology often played an important role in the transition to mass production. Just as power looms and spinning machinery had made textile mills possible, the development of new and more reliable machines or industrial techniques revolutionized other industries. Elias Howe's invention of the sewing machine in 1846 laid the basis for the ready-to-wear clothing industry and also contributed to the mechanization of shoemaking. During the 1840s, iron manufacturers adopted the British practice of using coal rather than charcoal for smelting and thus produced a metal better suited to industrial needs. Charles Goodyear's discovery in 1839 of the process for the vulcanization of rubber made a new range of manufactured items available to the American consumer, most notably the overshoe.

Perhaps the greatest triumph of American technology during the mid-nineteenth century was the development of the world's most sophisticated and reliable machine tools. Such advances as the invention of the extraordinarily accurate measuring device known as the vernier caliper in 1851 and the first production of turret lathes in 1854 were signs of a special American aptitude for the kind of precision toolmaking that was essential to efficient industrialization.

Progress in industrial technology and organization did not mean the United States had become an industrial society by 1860. Factory workers remained a small fraction of the workforce, and agriculture retained first place both as a

THE AGE OF PRACTICAL INVENTION

YEAR*	INVENTOR	CONTRIBUTION	IMPORTANCE/DESCRIPTION
1787	John Fitch	Steamboat	First successful American steamboat
1793	Eli Whitney	Cotton gin	Simplified process of separating fiber from seeds; helped make cotton a profitable staple of southern agriculture
1798	Eli Whitney	Jig for guiding tools	Facilitated manufacture of interchangeable parts
1802	Oliver Evans	Steam engine	First American steam engine; led to manufacture of high-pressure engines used throughout eastern United States
1813	Richard B. Chenaworth	Cast-iron plow	First iron plow to be made in three separate pieces, thus making possible replacement of parts
1830	Peter Cooper	Railroad locomotive	First steam locomotive built in America
1831	Cyrus McCormick	Reaper	Mechanized harvesting; early model could cut six acres of grain a day
1836	Samuel Colt	Revolver	First successful repeating pistol
1837	John Deere	Steel plow	Steel surface kept soil from sticking; farming thus made easier on rich prairies of Midwest
1839	Charles Goodyear	Vulcanization of rubber	Made rubber much more useful by preventing it from sticking and melting in hot weather
1842	Crawford W. Long	First administered ether in surgery	Reduced pain and risk of shock during operations
1844	Samuel F. B. Morse	Telegraph	Made long-distance communication almost instantaneous
1846	Elias Howe	Sewing machine	First practical machine for automatic sewing
1846	Norbert Rillieux	Vacuum evaporator	Improved method of removing water from sugar cane; revolutionized sugar industry and was later applied to many other products
1847	Richard M. Hoe	Rotary printing press	Printed an entire sheet in one motion; vastly speeded up printing process
1851	William Kelly	"Air-boiling process"	Improved method of converting iron into steel (usually known as Bessemer process because English inventor Bessemer had more advantageous patent and financial arrangements)
1853	Elisha G. Otis	Passenger elevator	Improved movement in buildings; when later electrified, stimulated development of skyscrapers
1859	Edwin L. Drake	First American oil well	Initiated oil industry in the United States
1859	George M. Pullman	Pullman car	First sleeping car suitable for long-distance travel

*Dates refer to patent or first successful use.

Source: From *Freedom and Crisis: An American History,* 3rd ed., by Allen Weinstein and Frank Otto Gatell. Copyright © 1974, 1978, 1981 by Random House, Inc. Reprinted by permission of Random House, Inc.

In 1837, John Deere invented a plow with a smooth steel blade. Unlike the cast iron blades used previously, the new steel surface kept the rich prairie soil from sticking. Deere's plow quickly became popular with pioneer farmers in the Midwest as an essential tool for cultivating the land.

source of livelihood for individuals and as a contributor to the gross national product. But farming itself, at least in the North, was undergoing a technological revolution of its own. John Deere's steel plow, invented in 1837, enabled midwestern farmers to cultivate the tough prairie soils that had resisted cast-iron implements. The mechanical reaper, patented by Cyrus McCormick in 1834, offered an enormous saving in the labor required for harvesting grain. Other new farm implements that came into widespread use before 1860 included seed drills, cultivators, and threshing machines.

A dynamic interaction between advances in transportation, industry, and agriculture gave great strength and resiliency to the economy of the northern states during the 1850s. Railroads offered western farmers better access to eastern markets. After Chicago and New York were linked by rail in 1853, the flow of most midwestern farm commodities shifted from the north-south direction based on riverborne traffic, which had still predominated in the 1830s and 1840s, to an east-west pattern.

The mechanization of agriculture did more than lead to more efficient and profitable commercial farming; it also provided an additional impetus to industrialization, and its laborsaving features released workers for other economic activities. The growth of industry and the modernization of agriculture can thus be seen as mutually reinforcing aspects of a single process of economic growth.

MASS IMMIGRATION BEGINS

The original incentive to mechanize northern industry and agriculture came in part from a shortage of cheap labor. Compared with that of industrializing nations of Europe, the economy of the United States in the early nineteenth century was labor-scarce. Since it was difficult to attract able-bodied men to work for low wages in factories or on farms, women and children were used extensively in the early textile mills, and commercial farmers had to rely heavily on the labor of their family members. Labor-saving machinery eased but did not solve the labor

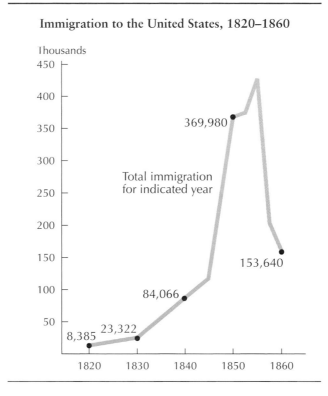

Immigration to the United States, 1820–1860

Thousands

Total immigration for indicated year

369,980

153,640

84,066

8,385 23,322

shortage problem. Factories required increasing numbers of operatives, and railroad builders needed construction gangs. The growth of industrial work opportunities helped attract a multitude of European immigrants during the two decades before the Civil War.

Between 1820 and 1840, an estimated 700,000 immigrants arrived in the United States, mainly from the British Isles and German-speaking areas of continental Europe. During the 1840s, this substantial flow suddenly became a flood. No fewer than 4.2 million people crossed the Atlantic between 1840 and 1860. The largest single source of the new mass immigration was Ireland, but Germany was not far behind. Smaller contingents came from Switzerland, Norway, Sweden, and the Netherlands.

The massive transatlantic movement had many causes; some people were "pushed" out of their homes while others were "pulled" toward America. The great push factor that caused 1.5 million Irish to forsake the Emerald Isle between 1845 and 1854 was the great potato blight, which brought famine to a population that subsisted on this single crop. Escape to America was made possible by the low fares then prevailing on sailing ships bound from England to North America. Ships involved in the timber trade carried their bulky cargoes from Boston or Halifax to Liverpool; as an alternative to returning to America partly in ballast, they packed Irish immigrants into their holds. The squalor and misery in these steerage accommodations were almost beyond belief.

Hundreds of Irish immigrants crowded into the disease-ridden slums and shanties of places such as Boston's Burgess Alley. The illustration of the deplorable living quarters of the city's immigrants is from the Report of the Committee on Internal Health on the Asiatic Cholera, issued in 1849.

The location of the ports involved in the lumber trade—Boston, Halifax, Saint John's, and Saint Andrews—meant that the Irish usually arrived in Canada or the northeastern states. Immobilized by poverty and a lack of the skills required for pioneering in the West, most of them remained in the Northeast. By the 1850s, they constituted a substantial portion of the total population of Boston, New York, Philadelphia, and many smaller cities of the New England and Middle Atlantic states. Forced to subsist on low-paid menial labor and crowded into festering urban slums, they were looked down on by most native-born Americans. Their devotion to Catholicism aroused Protestant resentment and mob violence.

The million or so Germans who also came in the late 1840s and early 1850s were somewhat more fortunate. Most of them were also peasants, but they had fled hard times rather than outright catastrophe. Those whose mortgages were foreclosed or who could no longer make regular payments to their landlords frequently opted for emigration to America. Unlike the Irish, they often escaped with a small amount of capital with which to make a fresh start in the New World. Many German immigrants were artisans and sought to ply their trades in cities such as New York, St. Louis, Cincinnati, and Milwaukee—all of which became centers of German-American population. But a large portion of those with peasant backgrounds went back to the land. The possession of diversified agricultural skills and small amounts of capital enabled many Germans to become successful midwestern farmers. In general, they encountered less prejudice and discrimination than the Irish.

What attracted most of the Irish, German, and other European immigrants to America was the promise of economic opportunity. Although a minority chose the United States because they admired its democratic political system, most immigrants were more interested in the chance to make a decent living than in voting or running for office. Peak periods of immigration—1845 to 1854 is a prime example—coincided very closely with times of domestic prosperity and high demand for labor. During depressed periods immigration dropped off significantly.

The arrival of large numbers of immigrants exacerbated the already serious problems of America's rapidly growing cities. The old "walking city" in which rich and poor lived in close proximity near the center of town was changing to a more segregated environment. The advent of railroads and horse-drawn streetcars enabled the affluent to move to the first American suburbs, while areas nearer commercial and industrial centers became the congested abode of newcomers from Europe. Emerging slums, such as the notorious Five Points district in New York City, were characterized by overcrowding, poverty, disease, and crime. Recognizing that these conditions created potential dangers for the entire urban population, middle-class reformers worked for the professionalization of police forces, introduction of sanitary water and sewage disposal systems, and the upgrading of housing standards. They made some progress in these endeavors in the period before the Civil War, but the lot of the urban poor, mainly immigrants, was not dramatically improved. For most of them, life remained unsafe, unhealthy, and unpleasant.

THE NEW WORKING CLASS

A majority of immigrants ended up as wage workers in factories, mines, and construction camps or as casual day laborers doing the many unskilled tasks required for urban and commercial growth. By providing a vast pool of cheap labor, they fueled and accelerated the Industrial Revolution.

In established industries and older mill towns of the Northeast, immigrants added to, or in some cases displaced, the native-born workers who had predominated in the 1830s and 1840s. This trend reveals much about the changing character of the American working class. In the 1830s, most male workers were artisans, and factory work was still largely the province of women and children. In the 1840s, the proportion of men engaged in factory work increased, although the workforce in the textile industry remained predominantly female. During that decade, work conditions in many mills deteriorated. Relations between management and labor became increasingly impersonal, and workers were pushed to increase their output. Workdays of twelve to fourteen hours were common.

The result was a new upsurge of labor militancy involving female as well as male factory workers. Mill girls in Lowell, for example, formed a union of their own—the Female Labor Reform Association—and agitated for shorter working hours. On a broader front, workers' organizations petitioned state legislatures to pass laws limiting the workday to ten hours. Some such laws were actually passed, but they turned out to be ineffective because employers could still require a prospective worker to sign a special contract agreeing to longer hours.

The employment of immigrants in increasing numbers between the mid-1840s and the late 1850s made it more difficult to organize industrial workers. Impoverished fugitives from the Irish potato famine tended to have lower economic expectations and more conservative social attitudes than did native-born workers. Consequently, the Irish immigrants were initially willing to work for less and were not so prone to protest bad working conditions.

But the new working class of former rural folk did not make the transition to industrial wage labor easily or without protesting in subtle and indirect ways. Tardiness, absenteeism, drunkenness, loafing on the job, and other forms of resistance to factory discipline reflected deep hostility to the unaccustomed and seemingly unnatural routines of industrial production. The adjustment to new styles and rhythms of work was painful and took time.

THE COSTS OF EXPANSION

By 1860, industrial expansion and immigration had created a working class of men and women who seemed destined for a life of low-paid wage labor. This reality stood in contrast to America's self-image as a land of opportunity and upward mobility. This ideal still had some validity in rapidly developing regions of the western states, but it was mostly myth when applied to the increasingly foreign-born industrial workers of the Northeast.

Both internal and external expansion had come at a heavy cost. Tensions associated with class and ethnic rivalries were only one part of the price of rapid economic development. The acquisition of new territories became politically divisive and would soon lead to a catastrophic sectional controversy. In the late 1840s and early 1850s Democratic Senator Stephen A. Douglas of Illinois (called the Little Giant because of his small stature and large public presence) sought political power for himself and his party by combining an expansionist foreign policy with the encouragement of economic development within the territories already acquired. Recognizing that the slavery question was the main obstacle to his program, he sought to neutralize it through compromise and evasion. His failure to win the presidency or even the Democratic nomination before 1860 showed that the dream of a patriotic consensus supporting headlong expansion and economic development could not withstand the tensions and divisions that expansionist policies created or brought to light.

CHRONOLOGY

1822	Santa Fe opened to American traders
1823	Earliest American settlers arrive in Texas
1830	Mexico attempts to halt American migration to Texas
1831	American railroads begin commercial operation
1834	Cyrus McCormick patents mechanical reaper
1835	Revolution breaks out in Texas
1836	Texas becomes independent republic
1837	John Deere invents steel plow
1841	President John Tyler inaugurated
1842	Webster-Ashburton Treaty fixes border between Maine and New Brunswick
1843	Mass migration to Oregon begins
	Mexico closes Santa Fe trade to Americans
1844	Samuel F. B. Morse demonstrates electric telegraph
	James K. Polk elected president on platform of expansionism
1845	Mass immigration from Europe begins
	United States annexes Texas
	John L. O'Sullivan coins slogan "Manifest Destiny"
1846	War with Mexico breaks out
	United States and Great Britain resolve diplomatic crisis over Oregon
1847	American conquest of California completed
	Mormons settle Utah
	American forces under Zachary Taylor defeat Mexicans at Buena Vista
	Winfield Scott's army captures Veracruz and defeats Mexicans at Cerro Gordo
	Mexico City falls to American invaders
1848	Treaty of Guadalupe Hidalgo consigns California and New Mexico to United States
	Gold discovered in California
1849	"Forty-niners" rush to California to dig for gold
1858	War between Utah Mormons and U.S. forces averted

14

→ —◆— ←

THE SECTIONAL CRISIS

On May 22, 1856, Representative Preston Brooks of South Carolina stormed onto the floor of the Senate looking for Charles Sumner, the antislavery senator from Massachusetts who had recently given a fiery oration condemning the South for plotting to extend slavery to the Kansas Territory. When he found Sumner seated at his desk, Brooks proceeded to batter him over the head with a cane. Amazed and stunned, Sumner made a desperate effort to rise and ripped his bolted desk from the floor. He then collapsed under a continued torrent of blows.

Sumner was so badly injured by the assault that he did not return to the Senate for three years. But his home state reelected him in 1857 and kept his seat vacant as testimony against southern brutality and "barbarism." Brooks, denounced in the North as a bully, was lionized by his fellow Southerners. When he resigned from the House after a vote of censure had narrowly failed because of solid southern opposition, his constituents reelected him overwhelmingly.

These contrasting reactions show how bitter sectional antagonism had become by 1856. Sumner spoke for the radical wing of the new Republican party, which was making a bid for national power by mobilizing the North against the alleged aggressions of "the slave power." Southerners viewed the very existence of this party as an insult to their section of the country and a threat to its vital interests. Sumner came closer to being an abolitionist than any other member of Congress, and nothing created greater fear and anxiety among Southerners than their belief that antislavery forces were plotting against their way of life. To many Northerners, "bully Brooks" stood for all the arrogant and violent slaveholders who were allegedly conspiring to extend their barbaric labor system. By 1856, therefore, the sectional cleavage that would lead to the Civil War had already undermined the foundations of national unity.

The crisis of the mid-1850s came only a few years after the elaborate compromise of 1850 had seemingly resolved the dispute over the future of slavery in the territories acquired as a result of the Mexican-American War. The

Kansas-Nebraska Act of 1854 renewed agitation over the extension of slavery and revived the sectional conflict that led to the emergence of the Republican party. From that point on, a dramatic series of events increased sectional confrontation and destroyed the prospects for a new compromise. The caning of Charles Sumner was one of these events, and violence on the Senate floor foreshadowed violence on the battlefield.

THE COMPROMISE OF 1850

The conflict over slavery in the territories began in the late 1840s. During the early phase of the sectional controversy, the leaders of two strong national parties, each with substantial followings in both the North and the South, had a vested interest in resolving the crisis. Furthermore, the less tangible features of sectionalism—emotion and ideology—were not as divisive as they would later become. Hence a fragile compromise was achieved through a kind of give-and-take that would not be possible in the changed environment of the mid-1850s.

THE PROBLEM OF SLAVERY IN THE MEXICAN CESSION

As the price of union between states committed to slavery and those in the process of abolishing it, the Founders had attempted to limit the role of the slavery issue in national politics. The Constitution gave the federal government the right to abolish the international slave trade but no definite authority to regulate or destroy the institution where it existed under state law. It was easy to condemn slavery in principle but very difficult to develop a practical program to eliminate it without defying the Constitution.

Radical abolitionists resolved this problem by rejecting the law of the land in favor of a "higher law" prohibiting human bondage. But radical abolitionists constituted only a small minority dedicated to freeing the North, at whatever cost, from the sin of condoning slavery. The majority of Northerners in the 1840s, while they disliked slavery, also detested abolitionism. They were inclined to view slavery as a backward and unwholesome institution and slaveholders as power-hungry aristocrats seeking more than their share of national political influence. But they regarded the Constitution as a binding contract between slave and free states and were likely to be prejudiced against blacks and reluctant to accept large numbers of them as free citizens. Consequently, they saw no legal or desirable way to bring about emancipation within the southern states.

But the Constitution had not predetermined the status of slavery in *future* states. Since Congress had the power to admit new states to the Union under any conditions it wished to impose, a majority could require the abolition of slavery as the price of admission. An effort to use this power had led to the Missouri crisis of 1819–1820 (see Chapter 9). The resulting compromise was designed to decide future cases by drawing a line between slave and free states and extending it westward. When specific territories were settled, organized, and prepared for statehood, slavery would be permitted south of the line of 36°30′ and prohibited north of it.

The tradition of providing both the free North and the slave South with opportunities for expansion and the creation of new states broke down when new territories were wrested from Mexico in the 1840s. The acquisition of Texas, New Mexico, and California—all south of the Missouri Compromise line—threatened to upset the parity between slave and free states. Since it was generally assumed in the North that Congress had the power to prohibit slavery in new territories, a movement developed in Congress to do just that.

THE WILMOT PROVISO LAUNCHES THE FREE-SOIL MOVEMENT

The Free-Soil crusade began in August 1846, only three months after the start of the Mexican-American War, when Congressman David Wilmot, a Pennsylvania Democrat, proposed an amendment to the military appropriations bill that would ban slavery in any territory that might be acquired from Mexico.

Wilmot spoke for the large number of northern Democrats who felt neglected and betrayed by the party's choice of Polk in 1844 and by the "prosouthern" policies of Polk's administration. Combining an appeal to racial prejudice with opposition to slavery as an institution, Wilmot proposed prohibiting not only slavery but also settlement by free African Americans in the territory obtained in the Mexican cession. He argued that such bans would protect the common folk of the North from job competition with slaves and free blacks. By linking racism with resistance to the spread of slavery, Wilmot appealed to a broad spectrum of northern opinion.

Northern Whigs backed the Wilmot Proviso because they too were concerned about the outcome of an unregulated competition between slave and free labor in the territories. Many northern Whigs had opposed the annexation of Texas and the Mexican-American War. If expansion was inevitable, however, they endorsed the view that acquisition of Mexican territory should not be used to increase the power of the slave states.

The first House vote on the Wilmot Proviso resulted in a sharp sectional cleavage. Every northern congressman with the exception of two Democrats voted for the amendment, and every Southerner except two Whigs went on record against it. The Proviso passed the House, but a combination of southern influence and Democratic loyalty to the administration blocked it in the Senate. When the appropriations bill went back to the House without the Proviso, the administration's arm-twisting succeeded in changing enough northern Democratic votes to pass the bill and thus send the Proviso down to defeat.

SQUATTER SOVEREIGNTY AND THE ELECTION OF 1848

After a futile attempt to extend the Missouri Compromise line to the Pacific—a proposal unacceptable to Northerners because most of the Mexican cession lay south of the line—Senator Lewis Cass of Michigan proposed a new approach, designed to appeal especially to Democrats. Cass, who described his formula as "squatter sovereignty," would leave the determination of the status of slavery in a territory to the actual settlers. From the beginning, this proposal contained an ambiguity that allowed it to be interpreted differently in the North and the

THE ELECTION OF 1848

CANDIDATE	PARTY	POPULAR VOTE	ELECTORAL VOTE
Taylor	Whig	1,360,967	163
Cass	Democratic	1,222,342	127
Van Buren	Free-Soil	291,263	—

South. For northern Democrats, squatter sovereignty—or popular sovereignty as it was later called—meant the settlers could vote slavery up or down at the first meeting of a territorial legislature. For the southern wing of the party, it meant a decision would be made only at the time a convention drew up a constitution and applied for statehood. It was in the interest of national Democratic leaders to leave this ambiguity unresolved for as long as possible.

Congress failed to resolve the future of slavery in the Mexican cession in time for the election of 1848, and the issue entered the arena of presidential politics. The Democrats nominated Cass on a platform of squatter sovereignty. The Whigs evaded the question by running war hero General Zachary Taylor without a platform. Taylor refused to commit himself on the status of slavery in the territories, but northern Whigs favoring restriction took heart from the general's promise not to veto any territorial legislation passed by Congress. Southern Whigs supported Taylor mainly because he was a southern slaveholder.

A third-party movement attracted northerners who had strongly supported the Wilmot Proviso. In August, a tumultuous convention in Buffalo nominated former president Martin Van Buren to carry the banner of the Free-Soil party. Support for the Free-Soilers came from antislavery Whigs dismayed by their party's nomination of a slaveholder and its evasiveness on the territorial issue, disgruntled Democrats who had backed the Proviso and resented southern influence in their party, and some of the former adherents of the abolitionist Liberty party. Van Buren himself was motivated less by antislavery zeal than by bitterness at being denied the Democratic nomination in 1844. The founding of the Free-Soil party was the first significant effort to create a broadly based sectional party addressing itself to voters' concerns about the extension of slavery.

After a noisy and confusing campaign, Taylor came out on top, winning a majority of the electoral votes in both the North and the South and a total of 1,360,967 popular votes to 1,222,342 for Cass and 291,263 for Van Buren. The Free-Soilers failed to carry a single state but did quite well in the North, coming in second behind Taylor in New York, Massachusetts, and Vermont.

TAYLOR TAKES CHARGE

Once in office, Taylor devised a bold plan to decide the fate of slavery in the Mexican cession. He tried to engineer the immediate admission of California and New Mexico to the Union as states, thus bypassing the territorial stage entirely and avoiding a congressional debate on the status of slavery in the federal domain. Under the administration's urging, California, which was filling up rapidly with settlers drawn by the lust for gold, convened a constitutional convention and applied for admission to the Union as a free state.

Instead of resolving the crisis, President Taylor's initiative only worsened it. Fearing that not only California but also New Mexico—where Mexican law had prohibited slavery—would be admitted as free states, Southerners of both parties accused the president of trying to impose the Wilmot Proviso in a new form. The prospect that only free states would emerge from the entire Mexican cession inspired serious talk of secession.

Senator John C. Calhoun of South Carolina saw in the crisis a chance to achieve his long-standing goal of creating a southern voting bloc that would cut across regular party lines. As state legislatures and conventions throughout the South denounced "northern aggression" against the rights of the slave states, Calhoun rejoiced that the South had never been so "united . . . bold, and decided." For an increasing number of southern political leaders, the survival of the Union would depend on the North's response to the demands of the southern rights movement.

FORGING A COMPROMISE

When it became clear that the president would not abandon or modify his plan in order to appease the South, Congress launched independent efforts to arrange a compromise. Hoping that he could again play the role of "great pacificator"

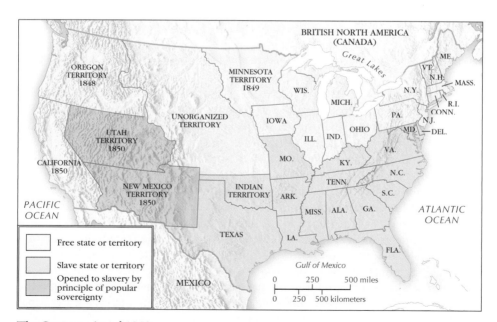

The Compromise of 1850
The compromise was actually a series of resolutions granting some concessions to the North—especially admission of California as a free state—and some to the South, such as a stricter Fugitive Slave Law.

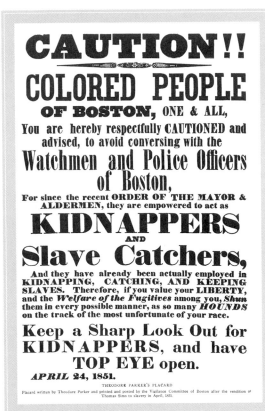

CAUTION!!

COLORED PEOPLE

OF BOSTON, ONE & ALL,

You are hereby respectfully CAUTIONED and
advised, to avoid conversing with the

Watchmen and Police Officers
of Boston,

For since the recent ORDER OF THE MAYOR &
ALDERMEN, they are empowered to act as

KIDNAPPERS

AND

Slave Catchers,

And they have already been actually employed in
KIDNAPPING, CATCHING, AND KEEPING
SLAVES. Therefore, if you value your LIBERTY,
and the *Welfare of the Fugitives* among you, *Shun*
them in every possible manner, as so many *HOUNDS*
on the track of the most unfortunate of your race.

Keep a Sharp Look Out for
KIDNAPPERS, and have
TOP EYE open.

APRIL 24, 1851.

THEODORE PARKER'S PLACARD

Placard written by Theodore Parker and printed and posted by the Vigilance Committee of Boston after the rendition of
Thomas Sims to slavery in April, 1851.

This abolitionist broadside was printed in response to a ruling that fugitive slave Thomas Sims must be returned to his master in Georgia.

as he had in the Missouri Compromise of 1820, Senator Henry Clay of Kentucky offered a series of resolutions meant to restore sectional harmony. On the critical territorial question, he proposed admitting California as a free state and organizing the rest of the Mexican cession with no explicit prohibition of slavery—in other words, without the Wilmot Proviso. He sought to resolve a major boundary dispute between New Mexico and Texas by granting the disputed region to New Mexico while compensating Texas through federal assumption of its state debt. As a concession to the North on another issue—the existence of slavery in the District of Columbia—he recommended prohibiting the buying and selling of slaves at auction and permitting the abolition of slavery itself with the consent of the District's white inhabitants. He also called for a more effective Fugitive Slave Law.

Clay's compromise plan, proposed in February 1850, took several months to get through Congress. One obstacle was President Taylor's firm resistance to the proposal; another was the difficulty of getting congressmen to vote for it in the form of a single package or "omnibus bill." Few politicians from either section were willing to go on record as supporting the key concessions to the *other* section. The logjam was broken in July by two crucial developments: President Taylor died and was succeeded by Millard Fillmore, who favored the compromise; and a decision was made to abandon the omnibus strategy in favor of a series of measures that could be voted on separately. After the breakup of the omnibus bill, some of Clay's proposals were modified to make them more acceptable to the South and the Democrats. Senator Stephen A. Douglas, a Democrat from Illinois, was particularly influential in maneuvering the separate provisions of the plan through Congress.

As the price of Democratic support, the popular sovereignty principle was included in the bills organizing New Mexico and Utah. Territorial legislatures in the Mexican cession were explicitly granted power over "all rightful subjects of legislation," which might include slavery. Half of the compensation to Texas for giving up its claims to New Mexico was paid directly to holders of Texas bonds.

Abolition of slave auctions and depots in the District of Columbia and a new Fugitive Slave Law were also enacted. The latter was a particularly outrageous piece of legislation. Suspected fugitives were now denied a jury trial, the right to testify in their own behalf, and other basic constitutional rights. As a result, there were no effective safeguards against false identification by accusers or against the kidnapping of blacks who were legally free.

The compromise passed because its key measures were supported by northern Democrats, southern Whigs, and representatives of both parties from the border states. No single bill was backed by a majority of the congressmen from both sections, and doubts persisted over the value of workability of a "compromise" that was really more like an armistice or a cease-fire.

Yet the Compromise of 1850 did serve for a short time as a basis for sectional peace. Southern moderate coalitions won out over radicals, but southern nationalism remained strong. Southerners demanded strict northern adherence to the compromise, especially to the Fugitive Slave Law, as the price for suppressing threats of secession. In the North, the compromise received greater support. The Fugitive Slave Law was unpopular in areas where abolitionism was particularly strong, and there were a few sensational rescues or attempted rescues of escaped slaves. But for the most part, the northern states adhered to the law during the next few years. When the Democrats and the Whigs approved or condoned the compromise in their 1852 platforms, it seemed that sharp differences on the slavery issue had once again been banished from national politics.

POLITICAL UPHEAVAL, 1852–1856

The second party system—Democrats versus Whigs—survived the crisis over slavery in the Mexican cession, but in the long run the Compromise of 1850 may have weakened it. Although both national parties had been careful during the 1840s not to take stands on the slavery issue that would alienate their supporters in either section of the country, they had in fact offered voters alternative ways of dealing with the question. Democrats had endorsed headlong territorial expansion with the promise of a fair division of the spoils between slave and free states. Whigs had generally opposed annexations or acquisitions, because they were likely to bring the slavery question to the fore and threaten sectional harmony. Each strategy could be presented to southern voters as a good way to protect slavery and to Northerners as a good way to contain it.

The consensus of 1852 meant the parties had to find other issues on which to base their distinctive appeals. Their failure to do so encouraged voter apathy and disenchantment with the major parties. When the Democrats sought to revive the Manifest Destiny issue in 1854, they reopened the explosive issue of slavery in the territories. By this time, the Whigs were too weak and divided to respond with a policy of their own, and a purely sectional Free-Soil party, the

THE ELECTION OF 1852

CANDIDATE	PARTY	POPULAR VOTE	ELECTORAL VOTE
Pierce	Democratic	1,601,117	254
Scott	Whig	1,385,453	42
Hale	Free-Soil	155,825	—

Republicans, came into existence and quickly gained prominence. The collapse of the second party system released sectional agitation from the earlier constraints imposed by the competition of strong national parties.

THE PARTY SYSTEM IN CRISIS

The presidential campaign of 1852 was singularly devoid of major issues. Some Whigs tried to revive interest in nationalistic economic policies but with business thriving under the Democratic program of limited government involvement, there was little support for Whig proposals for a protective tariff, a national bank, and internal improvements.

Another tempting issue was immigration. Many Whigs were upset by the massive influx from Europe, partly because most of the new arrivals were Catholics, and the Whig following was largely evangelical Protestant. In addition, the immigrants voted overwhelmingly Democratic. The Whig leadership was divided on whether to compete with the Democrats for the immigrant vote or to seek restrictions on immigrant voting rights.

The Whigs nominated war hero General Winfield Scott, who supported the faction that resisted nativism and sought to broaden the appeal of the party. But Scott and his supporters were unable to sway Catholic immigrants from their Democratic allegiance, and some nativist Whigs apparently sat out the election to protest their party's disregard of their cultural prejudices.

But the main cause for Scott's crushing defeat was the support he lost in the South when he allied himself with northern antislavery Whigs, led by Senator William Seward of New York. Democratic candidate Franklin Pierce of New Hampshire, a colorless nonentity compared to his rival, easily swept the Deep South and edged out Scott in most of the free states. The outcome revealed that the Whig party was in deep trouble because it lacked a program that would distinguish it from the Democrats and would appeal to voters in both sections of the country.

THE KANSAS-NEBRASKA ACT RAISES A STORM

In January 1854, Senator Stephen A. Douglas proposed a bill to organize the territory west of Missouri and Iowa. Since this region fell within the area where slavery had been banned by the Missouri Compromise, Douglas hoped to head off Southern opposition and keep the Democratic party united by disregarding the compromise line and setting up the territorial government in Kansas and Nebraska on the basis of popular sovereignty.

Douglas wanted to organize the Kansas-Nebraska area quickly because he was a strong supporter of the expansion of settlement and commerce. He hoped a railroad would soon be built to the Pacific with Chicago (or another midwestern city) as its eastern terminus. A long controversy over the status of slavery in the new territory would slow down the process of organization and settlement and might hinder the building of the railroad. Douglas also hoped his Kansas-Nebraska bill would revive the spirit of Manifest Destiny that had given the party cohesion and electoral success in the mid-1840s. As the main advocate for a new expansionism, he expected to win the Democratic nomination and the presidency.

The price of southern support, Douglas soon discovered, was the addition of an amendment explicitly repealing the Missouri Compromise. He reluctantly agreed, and in this more provocative form, the bill made its way through Congress, passing the Senate by a large margin and the House by a narrow one. Douglas's bill split his party rather than uniting it. A manifesto of "independent Democrats" denounced the bill as "a gross violation of a sacred pledge." For many Northerners, the Kansas-Nebraska Act was an abomination because it permitted the possibility of slavery in an area where it had previously been prohibited. Except for an aggressive minority, Southerners had not pushed for such legislation or even shown much interest in it, but now they felt obligated to support it. Their support provided deadly ammunition to those who were seeking to convince the northern public that there was a conspiracy to extend slavery.

Douglas's bill had a catastrophic effect on sectional harmony. It repudiated a compromise that many in the North regarded as binding. In defiance of the whole compromise tradition, it made a concession to the South on the issue of slavery extension without providing an equivalent concession to the North. It also shattered the fragile sectional accommodation of 1850 and made future compromises less likely. From now on, northern sectionalists would be fighting to regain what they had lost, while Southerners would battle to maintain rights already conceded.

The act also destroyed what was left of the second party system. The already weakened Whig party disintegrated when its congressional representation split cleanly along sectional lines on the Kansas-Nebraska issue. The Democratic party survived, but its ability to act as a unifying national force was seriously impaired. Northern desertions and southern gains (resulting from the recruitment of proslavery Whigs) combined to destroy the sectional balance within the party and place it under firm southern control.

The furor over Kansas-Nebraska also doomed the efforts of the Pierce administration to revive an expansionist foreign policy. Pierce and Secretary of State William Marcy were committed to acquiring Cuba from Spain. But Northerners interpreted the administration's plan, made public in a memorandum known as the Ostend Manifesto, as an attempt to create a "Caribbean slave empire." The resulting storm of protest forced Pierce and his cohorts to abandon their scheme.

AN APPEAL TO NATIVISM: THE KNOW-NOTHING EPISODE

The collapse of the Whigs created the opening for a new political party. The anti-Nebraska coalitions of 1854 suggested that such a party might be organized on the basis of northern opposition to the extension of slavery to the territories. Before such a prospect could be realized, however, an alternative emerged in the form of a major political movement based on hostility to immigrants. For a time, it appeared that the Whigs would be replaced by a nativist party rather than an antislavery one.

Massive immigration of Irish and Germans, most of whom were Catholic, led to increasing tension between ethnic groups during the 1840s and early 1850s. Native-born and even immigrant Protestants viewed the newcomers with suspicion and distrust. They expressed their fears in bloody anti-Catholic riots, in church and convent burnings, and in a barrage of propaganda and lurid literature. Nativist agitators charged that immigrants were agents of a foreign despotism, based in Rome, that was bent on overthrowing the American republic. The Irish were objects of particular disdain. They were often characterized as too uncivilized and degraded by poverty to become good citizens.

Political nativism first emerged during the 1840s in the form of local "American Republican" parties protesting immigrant influence in cities such as New York and Philadelphia. In 1849, a secret fraternal organization, the Order of the Star-Spangled Banner, was founded in New York as a vehicle for anti-immigrant attitudes. Members asked about the organization were instructed to reply, "I know nothing." The order grew rapidly in size, by 1854 reaching a membership of between 800,000 and 1,500,000. The political objective of the Know-Nothings was to extend the period of naturalization in order to undercut immigrant voting strength and to keep aliens in their place.

From 1854 to 1855, the nativist movement surfaced as a major political force, the American party. The party attracted Whigs looking for a new home, some ex-Democrats, and native-born workers who feared competition from low-paid immigrants. Many others supported the American party simply as an alternative to the Democrats. In the North, Know-Nothing candidates generally opposed the Kansas-Nebraska Act and drew some support from voters more anxious about the expansion of slavery than about the evils of immigration.

Know-Nothings often charged that immigrant voters were stealing American elections. In this cartoon, German and Irish immigrants, represented by German beer and Irish whiskey, steal a ballot box.

The success of the new party was so dramatic that it

was compared to a hurricane. In 1854 and 1855, it won control of several state governments from Massachusetts to Maryland to Texas, eventually emerging as the principal opposition to the Democrats everywhere except in the Midwest. By late 1855, the Know-Nothings showed every sign of displacing the Whigs as the nation's second party.

Yet, almost as rapidly as it had risen, the Know-Nothing movement collapsed. Its demise in 1856 is one of the great mysteries of American political history. Although it was a national party, it could not overcome the sectional differences that split its northern and southern delegates on the question of slavery in the territories.

Less clear is why the Know-Nothings failed to become the major opposition party to the Democrats in the North. The most persuasive explanation is that their Free-Soil Republican rivals, who were seeking to build a party committed to the containment of slavery, had an issue with wider appeal. In 1855 and 1856, the rate of immigration declined noticeably, and the conflict in Kansas heightened the concern about slavery. Consequently, voters who opposed both the expansion of slavery and unrestricted immigration were inclined to give priority to the former threat.

KANSAS AND THE RISE OF THE REPUBLICANS

The new Republican party was an outgrowth of the anti-Nebraska coalition of 1854. The Republican name was first used in the Midwest where Know-Nothingism failed to win a mass following. A new political label was required because Free-Soil Democrats—especially strong in the Midwest—refused to march under the Whig banner or even support any candidate for high office who called himself a Whig.

When the Know-Nothing party split over the Kansas-Nebraska issue in 1856, most of the northern nativists went over to the Republicans. Although the Republicans argued persuasively that the "slave-power conspiracy" was a greater threat to American liberty and equality than an alleged "popish plot," nativists did not have to abandon their ethnic and religious prejudices to become Republicans; the party showed a clear commitment to the values of native-born evangelical Protestants. On the local level, Republicans generally supported causes that reflected an anti-immigrant or anti-Catholic bias—such as prohibition of the sale of alcoholic beverages, observance of the Sabbath, defense of Protestant Bible reading in schools, and opposition to state aid for parochial education.

Unlike the Know-Nothings, the Republican party was led by seasoned professional politicians, men who had earlier been prominent Whigs or Democrats. Adept at organizing the grass roots, building coalitions, and employing all the techniques of popular campaigning, they built up an effective party apparatus in an amazingly short time. By early 1856, the new party was well established throughout the North and was preparing to make a serious bid for the presidency.

Underlying the rapid growth of the Republican party was the strong and growing appeal of its position on slavery in the territories. Republicans viewed the unsettled West as a land of opportunities, a place to which the ambitious and hardworking could migrate in the hope of improving their social and economic position. But if slavery was permitted to expand, the rights of "free labor" would be denied. Slaveholders would monopolize the best land, use their slaves to compete unfairly with free white workers, and block efforts at commercial and industrial development. Some Republicans also pandered to racial prejudice: They presented their policy as a way to keep African Americans out of the territories, thus preserving the new lands for exclusive white occupancy.

Although passage of the Kansas-Nebraska Act raised the territorial issue and gave birth to the Republican party, it was the turmoil associated with attempts to implement popular sovereignty in Kansas that kept the issue alive and enabled the Republicans to increase their following throughout the North. When Kansas was organized in the fall of 1854, a bitter contest began for control of the territorial government between militant Free-Soilers from New England and the Midwest and slaveholding settlers from Missouri. In the first territorial elections, thousands of Missouri residents crossed the border to vote illegally. The result was a decisive victory for the slave-state forces. The legislature then proceeded to pass laws that not only legalized slavery but made it a crime to speak or act against it.

Free-Soilers were already a majority of the actual residents of the territory when the fraudulently elected legislature denied them the right to agitate against slavery. To defend themselves and their convictions, they took up arms and established a rival territorial government under a constitution that outlawed slavery.

A small-scale civil war then broke out between the rival regimes, culminating in May 1856 when proslavery adherents raided the free-state capital at Lawrence. Portrayed in Republican propaganda as "the sack of Lawrence," this incursion resulted in substantial property damage but no loss of life. In reprisal, antislavery zealot John Brown and a few followers murdered five proslavery settlers in cold blood. During the next few months—until a truce was arranged by an effective territorial governor in the fall of 1856—a hit-and-run guerrilla war raged between free-state and slave-state factions.

The national Republican press exaggerated the extent of the violence in Kansas but correctly pointed out that the federal government was favoring rule by a proslavery minority over a Free-Soil majority. Since the "sack of Lawrence" occurred at about the same time that Charles Sumner was assaulted on the Senate floor, the Republicans launched their 1856 campaign under the twin slogans "Bleeding Kansas" and "Bleeding Sumner." The image of an evil and aggressive "slave power," using violence to deny constitutional rights to its opponents, was a potent device for arousing northern sympathies and winning votes.

SECTIONAL DIVISION IN THE ELECTION OF 1856

The Republican nominating convention revealed the strictly sectional nature of the new party. Only a handful of the delegates from the slave states attended, and all of these were from the upper South. The platform called for liberation of Kansas from the slave power and for congressional prohibition of slavery in all territories. The nominee was John C. Frémont, explorer of the West and participant in the conquest of California during the Mexican-American War.

THE ELECTION OF 1856

CANDIDATE	PARTY	POPULAR VOTE	ELECTORAL VOTE
Buchanan	Democratic	1,832,955	174
Frémont	Republican	1,339,932	114
Fillmore	American (Know-Nothing)	871,731	8

The Democrats nominated James Buchanan of Pennsylvania, who had a long career in public service. Their platform endorsed popular sovereignty in the territories. The American party, a Know-Nothing remnant that survived mainly as the rallying point for anti-Democratic conservatives in the border states and parts of the South, chose ex-President Millard Fillmore as its standard-bearer and received the backing of those northern Whigs who hoped to revive the tradition of sectional compromise.

The election was really two separate races—one in the North, where the main contest was between Frémont and Buchanan, and the other in the South, which pitted Fillmore against Buchanan. With strong southern support and narrow victories in four crucial northern states—Pennsylvania, New Jersey, Indiana, and Illinois—Buchanan won the election. But the Republicans did remarkably well for a party that was scarcely more than a year old. Frémont won eleven of the sixteen free states, sweeping the upper North with substantial majorities and winning a larger proportion of the northern popular vote than either of his opponents. Since the free states had a substantial majority in the electoral college, a future Republican candidate could win the presidency simply by overcoming a slim Democratic edge in the lower North.

In the South, the results of the election brought a momentary sense of relief tinged with deep anxiety about the future. The very existence of a sectional party committed to restricting the expansion of slavery constituted an insult to the Southerners' way of life. That such a party was genuinely popular in the North was profoundly alarming and raised grave doubts about the security of slavery within the Union. The continued success of a unified Democratic party under southern control was widely viewed as the last hope for the maintenance of sectional balance and "southern rights."

THE HOUSE DIVIDED, 1857–1860

The sectional quarrel deepened and became virtually "irreconcilable" in the years between Buchanan's election in 1856 and Lincoln's victory in 1860. A series of incidents provoked one side or the other, heightened the tension, and ultimately brought the crisis to a head. Behind the panicky reaction to public events lay a growing sense that the North and South were so different in culture and so opposed in basic interests that they could no longer coexist in the same nation.

CULTURAL SECTIONALISM

Signs of cultural and intellectual cleavage had appeared well before the triumph of sectional politics. In the mid-1840s, differing attitudes toward slaveholding split the Methodist and Baptist churches into northern and southern denominations. Informal northern and southern factions of Presbyterians went their separate ways on the slavery issue. Instead of unifying Americans around a common Protestant faith, the churches became nurseries of sectional discord. Increasingly, northern preachers and congregations denounced slaveholding as a sin, while most southern church leaders rallied to a biblical defense of the peculiar institution and became influential apologists for the southern way of life. In both the North and the South, religious leaders helped turn political questions into moral issues and reduced the prospects for a compromise.

American literature also became sectionalized during the 1840s and 1850s. Southern men of letters, including such notable figures as novelist William Gilmore Simms and Edgar Allan Poe, wrote proslavery polemics. In the North, prominent men of letters, including Ralph Waldo Emerson, Henry David Thoreau, and Herman Melville, expressed strong antislavery sentiments in prose and poetry.

Literary abolitionism reached a climax in 1852 when Harriet Beecher Stowe published *Uncle Tom's Cabin,* an enormously successful novel (it sold more than 300,000 copies in a single year) that fixed in the northern mind the image of the slaveholder as a brutal Simon Legree. Much of its emotional impact came from the book's portrayal of slavery as a threat to the family and the Cult of Domesticity. When the saintly Uncle Tom was sold away from his adoring wife and children, Northerners shuddered with horror and some Southerners felt a painful twinge of conscience.

Southern defensiveness gradually hardened into cultural and economic nationalism. Northern textbooks were banished from southern schools in favor of those with a prosouthern slant; young men of the planter class were induced to stay in the South for higher education rather than going North (as had been the custom); and a movement developed to encourage southern industry and commerce as a way of reducing dependence on the North. Almost without exception, prominent southern educators and intellectuals of the late 1850s rallied behind southern sectionalism, and many even endorsed the idea of a southern nation.

THE DRED SCOTT CASE

When James Buchanan was inaugurated on March 4, 1857, the dispute over the legal status of slavery in the territories was an open door through which sectional fears and hatreds could enter the political arena. Buchanan hoped to close that door by encouraging the Supreme Court to resolve the constitutional issue once and for all.

The Court was then about to render its decision in the case of *Dred Scott* v. *Sandford.* The plaintiff in the case was a Missouri slave who sued for his freedom

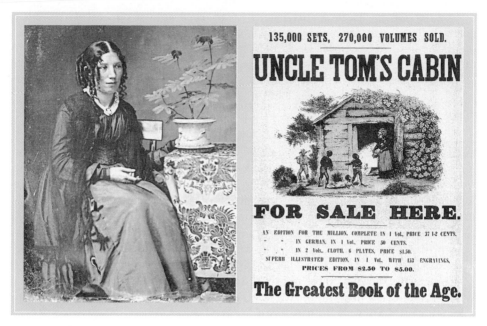

Harriet Beecher Stowe began writing the antislavery novel Uncle Tom's Cabin *in 1850, in part to protect passage of the Fugitive Slave Law. Within a year of the novel's publication in 1852, more than 300,000 copies had been sold. The poster pictured here advertises a German-language edition, published for German-speaking immigrants.*

on the grounds that he had lived for many years in the Wisconsin Territory, an area where slavery had been outlawed by the Missouri Compromise. President-elect Buchanan, in the days just before the inauguration, encouraged the Court to render a broad decision that would settle the slavery issue.

On March 6, Chief Justice Roger B. Taney announced that the Court had ruled against Scott, basing its decision on several arguments. The first was that Scott could not sue because he was not a citizen. Then Taney argued further that no African American—slave or free—could be a citizen of the United States. Finally, Taney announced that Scott would not have won his case even if he had been a legal plaintiff. His residence in the Wisconsin Territory established no right to freedom because Congress had no power to prohibit slavery there. The Missouri Compromise was thus declared unconstitutional and so, implicitly, was the main plank in the Republican platform.

In the North, especially among Republicans, the Court's verdict was viewed as the latest diabolical act of the "slave-power conspiracy." Strong circumstantial evidence supported the charge that the decision was a political maneuver. Five of the six judges who voted in the majority were proslavery Southerners, and their resolution of the territorial issue was close to the extreme southern rights position long advocated by John C. Calhoun.

Republicans denounced the decision as "a wicked and false judgment" and "the greatest crime in the annals of the republic," but they stopped short of openly defying the Court's authority. Instead, they argued on narrow technical grounds that the decision as written was not binding on Congress and that a ban on slavery in the territories could still be enacted. The decision actually helped the Republicans build support; it lent credence to their claim that an aggressive slave power was dominating all branches of the federal government and attempting to use the Constitution to achieve its own ends.

THE LECOMPTON CONTROVERSY

While the Dred Scott case was being decided, leaders of the proslavery faction in Kansas concluded that the time was ripe to draft a constitution and seek admission to the Union as a slave state. Since settlers with free-state views were now an overwhelming majority in the territory, the success of the plan required a rigged, gerrymandered election for convention delegates. When it became clear the election was fixed, the free-staters boycotted it. The resulting constitution, drawn up at Lecompton, was certain to be voted down if submitted to the voters in a fair election and sure to be rejected by Congress if no referendum of any kind was held.

To resolve the dilemma, supporters of the constitution decided to permit a vote on the slavery provision alone, giving the electorate the narrow choice of allowing or forbidding the future importation of slaves. Since there was no way to vote for total abolition, the free-state majority again boycotted, thus allowing ratification of a constitution that protected existing slave property and placed no restriction on importations. Meanwhile, the free-staters, who had finally gained control of the territorial legislature, authorized a second referendum on the constitution as a whole. This time, the proslavery party boycotted the election, and the Lecompton constitution was overwhelmingly rejected.

The Lecompton constitution was such an obvious perversion of popular sovereignty that Stephen A. Douglas spoke out against it. But the Buchanan administration tried to push it through Congress in early 1858, despite overwhelming evidence that the people of Kansas did not want to enter the Union as a slave state. The bill to admit Kansas as a slave state under the Lecompton constitution passed the Senate but was defeated in the House. A face-saving compromise was then devised. It allowed resubmission of the constitution to the Kansas voters on the pretext that a change in the provisions for a federal land grant was required. Finally, in August 1858, the people of Kansas killed the Lecompton constitution when they voted it down by a margin of 6 to 1.

The Lecompton controversy made the sectional quarrel truly "irreconcilable." Republicans viewed the administration's efforts to admit Kansas as a slave state as evidence of southern dominance of the Democratic party and the lengths to which proslavery conspirators would go to achieve their ends. The affair split the Democratic party between the followers of Douglas and the backers of the Buchanan administration.

For Douglas himself, however, the affair was a disaster; it destroyed his hopes of uniting the Democratic party and defusing the slavery issue through the application of popular sovereignty. In practice, popular sovereignty was an invitation to civil war. Furthermore, the Dred Scott decision protected

Southerners' rights to own human property in federal territories. Although his stand against Lecompton won him some popularity in the North, Douglas was denounced as a traitor in the South, and his hopes of being elected president were seriously diminished.

DEBATING THE MORALITY OF SLAVERY

Douglas's immediate problem was winning reelection to the Senate from Illinois in 1858. Here he faced surprisingly tough opposition from the Republican candidate, former Whig Congressman Abraham Lincoln. Lincoln set out to convince the voters that Douglas could not be relied on to oppose the extension of slavery, even though he had opposed the admission of Kansas under a proslavery constitution.

In the speech that opened his campaign, Lincoln tried to distance himself from his opponent by taking a more radical position. "'A house divided against itself cannot stand,'" he argued, paraphrasing a line from the Gospel of Mark. "I believe this government cannot endure, permanently half *slave* and half *free.*" He then described the chain of events between the Kansas-Nebraska Act and the Dred Scott decision as evidence of a plot to extend and nationalize slavery and tried to link Douglas to this proslavery conspiracy by pointing to his rival's unwillingness to take a stand on the morality of slavery, to his professed indifference about whether slavery was voted up or down in the territories. For Lincoln, the only security against the triumph of slavery and the slave power was moral opposition to human bondage.

In the series of debates that focused national attention on the Illinois senatorial contest, Lincoln hammered away at the theme that Douglas was a covert defender of slavery because he was not a principled opponent of it. Douglas responded by accusing Lincoln of endangering the Union by his talk of putting slavery on the path

Stephen Douglas, the "Little Giant" from Illinois, won election to Congress when he was just thirty years old. Four years later, he was elected to the Senate.

Abraham Lincoln, shown here in his first full-length portrait. Although Lincoln lost the contest for the Senate seat in 1858, the Lincoln-Douglas debates established his reputation as a rising star of the Republican party.

to extinction. Denying that he was an abolitionist, Lincoln made a distinction between tolerating slavery in the South, where it was protected by the Constitution, and allowing it to expand to places where it could legally be prohibited. Restriction of slavery, he argued, had been the policy of the Founders, and it was Douglas and the Democrats who had departed from the great tradition of containing an evil that could not be immediately eliminated.

In the debate at Freeport, Illinois, Lincoln questioned Douglas on how he could reconcile popular sovereignty with the Dred Scott decision. The Little Giant, as Douglas was called by his admirers, responded that slavery could not exist without supportive legislation to sustain it and that territorial legislatures could simply refrain from passing a slave code if they wanted to keep it out. Coupled with his anti-Lecompton stand, Douglas's "Freeport Doctrine" undoubtedly hardened southern opposition to his presidential ambitions.

Douglas's most effective debating point was charging that Lincoln's moral opposition to slavery implied a belief in racial equality. Lincoln, facing an intensely racist electorate, vigorously denied this charge and affirmed his commitment to white supremacy. He would grant blacks the right to the fruits of their own labor while denying them the "privileges" of citizenship. This was an inherently contradictory position, and Douglas made the most of it.

Although Republican candidates for the state legislature won a majority of the popular votes, the Democrats carried more counties and thus were able to send Douglas back to the Senate. Lincoln lost an office, but he won respect in

Republican circles throughout the country. By stressing the moral dimension of the slavery question and undercutting any possibility of fusion between Republicans and Douglas Democrats, he had sharpened his party's ideological focus and had stiffened its backbone against any temptation to compromise its Free-Soil position.

THE SOUTH'S CRISIS OF FEAR

After Kansas became a free territory instead of a slave state in August 1858, the issue of slavery in the territories became a symbolic issue rather than a practical one. The remaining unorganized areas, which were in the Rockies and northern Great Plains, were unlikely to attract slaveholding settlers. Nevertheless, Southerners continued to demand the "right" to take their slaves into the territories, and Republicans persisted in denying it to them. Although the Republicans repeatedly promised not to interfere with slavery where it already existed, Southerners refused to believe them and interpreted their unyielding stand against the extension of slavery as a threat to southern rights and security.

A chain of events in late 1859 and early 1860 turned southern anxiety about northern attitudes and policies into a "crisis of fear." The first of these incidents was John Brown's raid on Harpers Ferry, Virginia, in October 1859. Brown, who had the appearance and manner of an Old Testament prophet, thought of himself as God's chosen instrument "to purge this land with blood" and eradicate the sin of slaveholding. On October 16, he led a small band of men, including five free blacks, across the Potomac River from his base in Maryland and seized the federal arsenal and armory in Harpers Ferry.

Brown's aim was to launch a guerrilla war from havens in the Appalachians that would eventually extend to the plantation regions of the lower South. But the neighboring slaves did not rise up to join him, and Brown's raiders were driven out of the armory and arsenal by the local militia and forced to take refuge in a fire-engine house. There they held out until a force of U.S. Marines commanded by Colonel Robert E. Lee stormed their bastion. In the course of the fighting, ten of Brown's men were killed or mortally wounded, along with seven of the townspeople and soldiers who opposed them.

The wounded Brown and his remaining followers were put on trial for treason against the state of Virginia. The subsequent investigation produced evidence that several prominent northern abolitionists had approved of Brown's plan and had raised money for his preparations. This seemed to confirm southern fears that abolitionists were actively engaged in fomenting slave insurrection.

After Brown was sentenced to be hanged, Southerners were further stunned by the outpouring of sympathy and admiration that his impending fate aroused in the North. His actual execution on December 2 completed Brown's elevation to the status of a martyred saint of the antislavery cause. The day of his death was marked in parts of the North by the tolling of bells, the firing of cannons, and the holding of memorial services.

In this cartoon from the 1860 election, candidates Lincoln and Douglas struggle for control of the country, while Breckinridge tears away the South. John Bell of the Constitutional Union party futilely attempts to repair the damage to the torn nation.

Although Republican politicians were quick to denounce John Brown for his violent methods, Southerners interpreted the wave of northern sympathy as an expression of the majority opinion and the Republicans' "real" attitude. Within the South, the raid and its aftermath touched off a frenzy of fear, repression, and mobilization. Witch-hunts searched for the agents of a vast imagined conspiracy to stir up slave rebellion; vigilance committees were organized in many localities to resist subversion and ensure control of slaves; and orators pointed increasingly to secession as the only way to protect southern interests.

Brown was scarcely in his grave when another set of events put southern nerves on edge once more. Next to abolitionist-abetted rebellions, the slaveholding South's greatest fear was that the nonslaveholding majority would turn against the master class and the solidarity of southern whites behind the peculiar institution would crumble. When Congress met to elect a speaker of the House on December 5, Southerners bitterly denounced the Republican candidate—John Sherman of Ohio—because he had endorsed as a campaign document a condensed version of Hinton R. Helper's *Impending Crisis of the South*. Helper's book, which called on lower-class whites to resist planter dominance and abolish slavery in their own interest, was regarded by slaveholders as even more seditious than *Uncle Tom's Cabin*. They feared the spread of "Helperism" among poor whites almost as much as they feared the effect of "John Brownism" on the slaves.

The ensuing contest over the speaker's office lasted almost two months. Southern congressmen threatened secession if Sherman was elected, and feelings became so heated that some representatives began to carry weapons on the floor of the House. When it eventually became clear that Sherman could not be elected, his name was withdrawn in favor of a moderate Republican who had refrained from endorsing Helper's book. The impasse over the speakership was thus resolved, but the contest helped persuade Southerners that the Republicans were committed to stirring up class conflict among southern whites. The identification of Republicans with Helper's ideas may have been decisive in convincing many conservative planters in 1860 that a Republican president would be intolerable.

THE ELECTION OF 1860

The Republicans, sniffing victory and generally insensitive to the depth of southern feeling against them, met in Chicago on May 16 to nominate a presidential candidate. The initial front-runner, Senator William H. Seward of New York, proved unacceptable because of his reputation for radicalism and his record of strong opposition to the nativist movement. Most delegates wanted a less controversial nominee who could win two or three of the northern states that had gone Democratic in 1856. Abraham Lincoln met their specifications: He was from Illinois, a state the Republicans needed to win; he had a more moderate image than Seward; and he had kept his personal distaste for Know-Nothingism to himself. In addition, his rise from frontier poverty to legal and political prominence embodied the Republican ideal of equal opportunity for all.

The Republican platform, like the nominee, was meant to broaden the party's appeal in the North. Although a commitment to halt the expansion of slavery remained, economic matters received more attention than they had in 1856. The platform called for a high protective tariff, endorsed free homesteads, and supported federal aid for internal improvements, especially a transcontinental railroad. The platform was cleverly designed to attract ex-Whigs to the

THE ELECTION OF 1860

CANDIDATE	PARTY	POPULAR VOTE	ELECTORAL VOTE
Lincoln	Republican	1,865,593	180
Breckinridge	Democratic, Southern	848,356	72
Douglas	Democratic, Northern	1,382,713	12
Bell	Constitutional Union	592,906	39

Republican camp and accommodate enough renegade Democrats to give the party a solid majority in the northern states.

The Democrats failed to present a united front against this formidable challenge. When the party first met in Charleston in late April, Douglas commanded a majority of the delegates but was unable to win the two-thirds required for nomination because of unyielding southern opposition. He did succeed in getting the convention to endorse popular sovereignty as its slavery platform, but the price was a walkout by Deep South delegates who favored a federal slave code for the territories.

Unable to agree on a nominee, the convention adjourned to reconvene in Baltimore in June. Then a fight developed over whether to seat newly selected pro-Douglas delegations from some Deep South states in place of the bolters from the first convention. When the Douglas forces won most of the contested seats, another and more massive southern walkout took place. The result was a fracture of the Democratic party. The delegates who remained nominated Douglas and reaffirmed the party's commitment to popular sovereignty, while the bolters convened elsewhere to nominate John Breckinridge of Kentucky on a platform of federal protection for slavery in the territories.

By the time the campaign was under way, four parties were running presidential candidates. In addition to the Republicans, the Douglas Democrats, and the "Southern Rights" Democrats, a remnant of conservative Whigs and Know-Nothings nominated John Bell of Tennessee under the banner of the Constitutional Union party. Taking no explicit stand on the issue of slavery in the territories, the Constitutional Unionists tried to represent the spirit of sectional compromise. In effect, the race became a separate two-party contest in each section: In the North, the real choice was between Lincoln and Douglas; in the South, the only candidates with a fighting chance were Breckinridge and Bell.

When the results came in, the Republicans had achieved a stunning victory. Lincoln won a decisive majority—180 to 123 over his combined opponents. In the North, his 54 percent of the popular vote annihilated Douglas. In the South, where Lincoln was not even on the ballot, Breckinridge triumphed everywhere except in Virginia, Kentucky, and Tennessee, which went for Bell and the Constitutional Unionists. The Republican strategy of seeking power by trying to win decisively in the majority section was brilliantly successful. Although fewer than 40 percent of those who went to the polls throughout the nation actually voted for Lincoln, his support in the North was so solid that he would have won in the electoral college even if his opponents had been unified behind a single candidate.

Most Southerners saw the result of the election as a catastrophe. A candidate and a party with no support in their own section had won the presidency on a platform viewed as insulting to southern honor and hostile to vital southern interests. For the first time since the birth of the republic, Southern interests were in no way represented in the White House. Rather than accept permanent minority status in American politics and face the resulting dangers to black slavery and white "liberty," the political leaders of the lower South launched a movement for immediate secession from the Union.

EXPLAINING THE CRISIS

Generations of historians have searched for the underlying causes of the crisis leading to disruption of the Union but have failed to agree on exactly what they were. Some have stressed the clash of economic interests between agrarian and industrializing regions. But this interpretation does not reflect the way people at the time expressed their concerns. The main issues in the sectional debates of the 1850s were whether slavery was right or wrong and whether it should be extended or contained. Disagreements over protective tariffs and other economic measures benefiting one section or the other were clearly secondary.

Another group of historians have blamed the crisis on "irresponsible" politicians and agitators on both sides of the Mason-Dixon line. Public opinion, they argue, was whipped into a frenzy over issues that competent statesmen could have resolved. But this viewpoint has been sharply criticized for failing to acknowledge the depths of feeling that could be aroused by the slavery question and for underestimating the obstacles to a peaceful solution.

The dominant modern view is that the crisis was rooted in profound ideological differences over the morality and utility of slavery as an institution. Most interpreters now agree that the roots of the conflict lay in the fact that the South was a slave society and determined to stay that way, while the North was equally committed to a free-labor system. It is hard to imagine that secessionism would have developed if the South had followed the North's example and abolished slavery in the postrevolutionary period.

Nevertheless, the existence or nonexistence of slavery will not explain why the crisis came when it did and in the way that it did. Why did the conflict become "irreconcilable" in the 1850s and not earlier or later? Why did it take the form of a political struggle over the future of slavery in the territories? Adequate answers to both questions require an understanding of political developments that were not directly caused by tensions over slavery.

By the 1850s, the established Whig and Democratic parties were in trouble partly because they no longer offered the voters clear-cut alternatives on economic issues. This situation created an opening for new parties and issues. After the Know-Nothings failed to make attitudes toward immigrants the basis for a political realignment, the Republicans used the issue of slavery in the territories to build the first successful sectional party in American history. They called for "free soil" rather than freedom for blacks because abolitionism conflicted with the northern majority's commitment to white supremacy and its respect for the original constitutional compromise that established a hands-off policy toward slavery in the southern states. For Southerners, the Republican party now became the main issue, and they fought against it from within the Democratic party.

If politicians seeking new ways to mobilize an apathetic electorate are seen as the main instigators of sectional crisis, the reasons why certain appeals were more effective than others must still be explained. Why did the slavery extension issue arouse such strong feelings during the 1850s? The same issue had arisen earlier and had proved adjustable. If the expansion of slavery had been as vital and emotional a question in 1820 as it was in the 1850s, the declining Federalist party presumably would have revived in the form of a northern sectional party adamantly opposed to the admission of slave states to the Union.

Ultimately, therefore, the crisis of the 1850s must be understood as having a deep social and cultural dimension as well as a purely political one. Basic beliefs and values had diverged significantly in the North and the South between the 1820s and the 1850s. Both sections continued to profess allegiance to the traditional "republican" ideals of individual liberty and independence, and both were strongly influenced by evangelical religion. But differences in the economic and social development of each region transformed a common culture into two conflicting cultures. In the North, a rising middle class adapted to the new market economy with the help of an evangelical Christianity that sanctioned self-discipline and social reform. The South, on the other hand, embraced slavery as a foundation for the liberty and independence of whites. Its evangelicalism encouraged personal piety but not social reform. The notion that white liberty and equality depended on resistance to social and economic change and on continuing to have enslaved blacks to do menial labor became more deeply entrenched.

When politicians appealed to sectionalism during the 1850s, therefore, they could evoke conflicting views of what constituted the good society. To most Northerners, the South—with its allegedly idle masters, degraded unfree workers, and shiftless poor whites—seemed to be in flagrant violation of the Protestant work ethic and the ideal of open competition. Southerners tended to view the North as a land of hypocritical money-grubbers who denied the obvious fact that the virtue, independence, and liberty of free citizens was possible only when dependent laboring classes—especially racially inferior ones—were kept under the kind of rigid control that only slavery could provide. Once these contrary views of the world had become the main themes of political discourse, sectional compromise was no longer possible.

CHRONOLOGY

1846   David Wilmot introduces Proviso banning slavery in the Mexican cession

1848   Free-Soil party is founded

Zachary Taylor (Whig) elected president, defeating Lewis Cass (Democrat) and Martin Van Buren (Free-Soil)

1849   California seeks admission to the Union as a free state

1850   Congress debates sectional issues and enacts Compromise of 1850

1852   Harriet Beecher Stowe publishes *Uncle Tom's Cabin*

Franklin Pierce (Democrat) elected president by a large majority over Winfield Scott (Whig)

1854   Congress passes Kansas-Nebraska Act, repealing Missouri Compromise

Republican party founded in several northern states

Anti-Nebraska coalitions score victories in congressional elections in the North

1854–1855   Know-Nothing party achieves stunning successes in state politics

1854–1856   Free-state and slave-state forces struggle for control of Kansas Territory

1856   Preston Brooks assaults Charles Sumner on Senate floor

James Buchanan wins presidency despite strong challenge in the North from John C. Frémont

1857   Supreme Court decides Dred Scott case and legalizes slavery in all territories

1858   Congress refuses to admit Kansas to Union under the proslavery Lecompton constitution

Lincoln and Douglas debate slavery issue in Illinois

1859   John Brown raids Harpers Ferry, is captured and executed

1859–1860   Fierce struggle takes place over election of a Republican as speaker of the House (December–February)

1860   Republicans nominate Abraham Lincoln for presidency (May)

Democratic party splits into northern and southern factions with separate candidates and platforms (June)

Lincoln wins the presidency over Douglas, Breckinridge, and Bell

15

SECESSION AND THE CIVIL WAR

The man elected to the White House in 1860 was striking in appearance—
he was 6 feet 4 inches in height and seemed even taller because of his disproportionately long legs and his habit of wearing a high silk "stovepipe"
hat. But Abraham Lincoln's previous career provided no guarantee he would
tower over most of the other presidents in more than physical height. When
Lincoln sketched the main events of his life for a campaign biographer in June
1860, he was modest almost to the point of self-deprecation. Especially regret-
ting his "want of education," he assured the biographer that "he does what he
can to supply the want."

Born to poor and illiterate parents on the Kentucky frontier in 1809, Lincoln
received a few months of formal schooling in Indiana after the family moved
there in 1816. But mostly he educated himself, reading and rereading a few trea-
sured books by firelight. In 1831, when the family migrated to Illinois, he left
home to make a living for himself in the struggling settlement of New Salem.
After failing as a merchant, he found a path to success in law and politics. While
studying law on his own in New Salem, he won election to the state legislature
and in 1837, he moved to Springfield, the state capital. Lincoln combined exceptional political and legal skills with a down-to-earth, humorous way of addressing jurors and voters. Consequently, he became a leader of the Whig party in
Illinois and one of the most sought after of the lawyers who rode the central
Illinois judicial circuit.

The high point of his political career as a Whig was one term in Congress
(1847–1849), but his strong stand against the Mexican-American War alienated
much of his constituency, and he did not seek re-election. He campaigned vigorously for Zachary Taylor in the 1848 presidential contest, but the new president
failed to appoint Lincoln to a patronage job he coveted. Having been repudiated

This Mathew Brady photograph of Abraham Lincoln was taken when Lincoln arrived in Washington for his inauguration. In his inaugural address, Lincoln appealed for preservation of the Union.

by the electorate and ignored by the national leadership of a party he had served loyally and well, Lincoln concentrated on building his law practice.

The Kansas-Nebraska Act of 1854, with its advocacy of popular sovereignty, provided Lincoln with an opportunity to return to politics. For the first time, his driving ambition for political success and his personal convictions about what was best for the country were easy to reconcile. Lincoln had long believed slavery was an unjust institution that should be tolerated only to the extent the Constitution and the tradition of sectional compromise required. Attacking Democratic Senator Stephen A. Douglas's popular sovereignty plan because it broke with precedents for federal containment or control of the growth of slavery, Lincoln threw in his lot with the Republicans and assumed leadership of the new party in Illinois. He attracted national attention in his bid for Douglas's Senate seat in 1858 and turned out to have the right qualifications when the Republicans chose a presidential nominee in 1860. The fact that he had split rails as a young man was used in the campaign to show that he was a man of the people.

After Lincoln's election provoked southern secession and plunged the nation into the greatest crisis in its history, there was understandable skepticism about him in many quarters: Was the former rail-splitter from Illinois up to the responsibilities he faced? Lincoln had less experience relevant to a wartime presidency than any previous chief executive; he had never been a governor, senator, cabinet officer, vice president, or high-ranking military officer. But some of his training as a prairie politician would prove extremely useful in the years ahead.

Another reason for Lincoln's effectiveness as a war leader was that he identified wholeheartedly with the northern cause and could inspire others to make sacrifices for it. In his view, the issue in the conflict was nothing less than the survival of the kind of political system that gave men like himself a chance for high office.

The Civil War put on trial the very principle of democracy at a time when most European nations had rejected political liberalism and accepted the conservative view that popular government would inevitably collapse into anarchy. It also showed the shortcomings of a purely white man's democracy and brought the first hesitant steps toward black citizenship. As Lincoln put it in the Gettysburg Address, the only cause great enough to justify the enormous sacrifice of life on the battlefields was the struggle to preserve and extend the democratic ideal, or to ensure that "government of the people, by the people, for the people, shall not perish from the earth."

THE STORM GATHERS

Lincoln's election provoked the secession of seven states of the Deep South but did not lead immediately to armed conflict. Before the sectional quarrel would turn from a cold war into a hot one, two things had to happen: A final effort to defuse the conflict by compromise and conciliation had to fail, and the North needed to develop a firm resolve to maintain the Union by military action.

THE DEEP SOUTH SECEDES

South Carolina, which had long been in the forefront of southern rights and proslavery agitation, was the first state to secede, doing so on December 20, 1860, at a convention meeting in Charleston. The constitutional theory behind secession was that the Union was a "compact" among sovereign states, each of which could withdraw from the Union by the vote of a convention similar to the one that had ratified the Constitution in the first place. The South Carolinians justified seceding at that time by charging that "a sectional party" had elected a president "whose opinions and purposes are hostile to slavery."

In other states of the Cotton Kingdom, there was similar outrage at Lincoln's election but less certainty about how to respond to it. Those who advocated immediate secession by each state individually were opposed by the "cooperationists," who believed the slave states should act as a unit. If the cooperationists

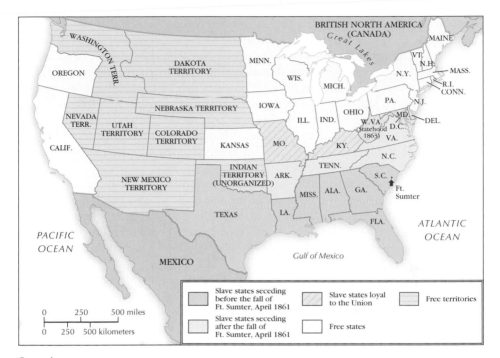

Secession

The fall of Fort Sumter was a watershed for the secessionist movement. With no room left for compromise, slave states of the upper South chose to join the Confederacy.

had triumphed, secession would have been delayed until a southern convention had agreed on it. Some of these moderates hoped a delay would provide time to extort major concessions from the North and thus remove the need for dissolving the Union. But South Carolina's unilateral action set a precedent that weakened the cooperationists' cause.

When conventions in six other Deep South states met in January 1861, delegates favoring immediate secession were everywhere in the majority. By February 1, seven states had removed themselves from the Union: South Carolina, Alabama, Mississippi, Florida, Georgia, Louisiana, and Texas. In the upper South, however, calls for immediate secession were unsuccessful; majority opinion in Virginia, North Carolina, Tennessee, and Arkansas did not subscribe to the view that Lincoln's election was a sufficient reason for breaking up the Union. In these states, with their stronger ties to the northern economy, moderate leaders were more willing than those in the lower South to seek a sectional compromise.

Delegates from the Deep South met in Montgomery, Alabama, on February 4 to establish the Confederate States of America. The convention acted as a provisional government while at the same time drafting a permanent constitution. Relatively moderate leaders dominated the proceedings and defeated or modified some of the pet schemes of a radical faction composed of extreme southern nationalists. Voted down were proposals to reopen the Atlantic slave trade, to abolish the three-fifths clause (in favor of counting all slaves in determining congressional representation), and to prohibit the admission of free states to the new Confederacy.

The resulting constitution was surprisingly similar to that of the United States. Most of the differences merely spelled out traditional southern interpretations of the federal charter: The central government was denied the authority to impose protective tariffs, subsidize internal improvements, or interfere with slavery in the states, and was required to pass laws protecting slavery in the territories. As provisional president and vice president, the convention chose Jefferson Davis of Mississippi and Alexander Stephens of Georgia, men who had resisted secessionist agitation.

The moderation shown in Montgomery resulted in part from a desire to win support for the cause of secessionism in the reluctant states of the upper South. But it also revealed that proslavery reactionaries had never succeeded in getting a majority behind them. Most Southerners had been opposed to dissolving the Union so long as there had been good reasons to believe slavery was safe from northern interference.

The panic following Lincoln's election destroyed that sense of security. But the actions of the Montgomery convention made it clear that the goal of the new converts to secessionism was not to establish a slaveholder's reactionary utopia. They only wished to re-create the Union as it had been before the rise of the new Republican party, and they opted for secession only when it seemed clear that separation was the only way to achieve their aim. Some optimists even predicted that all of the North except New England would eventually join the Confederacy.

Secession and the formation of the Confederacy amounted to a very conservative and defensive kind of "revolution." The only justification for southern independence on which a majority could agree was the need for greater security for the peculiar institution. Vice President Stephens spoke for all the founders of the Confederacy when he described the cornerstone of the new government as "the great truth that the negro is not equal to the white man—that slavery—subordination to the superior race—is his natural condition."

THE FAILURE OF COMPROMISE

While the Deep South was opting for independence, moderates in the North and border slave states were trying to devise a compromise that would stem the secessionist tide. In December 1860, Senator John Crittenden of Kentucky presented a plan that advocated extending the Missouri Compromise line to the Pacific to guarantee the protection of slavery in the southwestern territories. He also recommended a constitutional amendment that would forever prohibit the federal government from abolishing or regulating slavery in the states.

Initially, congressional Republicans showed some willingness to give ground and take the proposals seriously. However, Republican support quickly vanished when President-elect Lincoln sent word from Springfield that he was adamantly opposed to the extension of the compromise line. In the words of one of his fellow Republicans, he stood "firm as an oak."

The resounding no to the central provision of the Crittenden proposal stiffened the backbone of congressional Republicans, and they voted against compromise in the special committees to avert war that were set up in both the House and the Senate. Also voting against it, and thereby ensuring its defeat, were the remaining senators and congressmen of the seceding states, who had vowed in advance to support no compromise unless the majority of Republicans also endorsed it. Their purpose in taking this stand was to obtain guarantees that the northern sectional party would end its attacks on "southern rights." The Republicans did in the end agree to support Crittenden's "unamendable" amendment guaranteeing that slavery in the southern states would be immune from future federal action. This action was not really a concession to the South, because Republicans had always acknowledged that the federal government had no constitutional authority to meddle with slavery in the states.

Lincoln and those who took his advice had what they considered to be very good reasons for not making territorial concessions. They mistakenly believed that the secession movement reflected only a minority opinion in the South and that a strong stand would win the support of southern Unionists and moderates. It is doubtful, however, that Lincoln and his supporters would have given ground even if they had realized the secession movement was genuinely popular in the Deep South. In their view, extending the Missouri Compromise line of 36°30′ to the Pacific would not halt agitation for extending slavery to new areas. The only way to resolve the crisis over the future of slavery and to reunite "the house divided" was to remove any chance that slaveholders could enlarge their domain.

Lincoln was also convinced that backing down in the face of secessionist threats would fatally undermine the democratic principle of majority rule. In his inaugural address of March 4, 1861, he recalled that during the winter, many "patriotic men" had urged him to accept a compromise that would "shift the ground" on which he had been elected. But to do so would have signified that a victorious presidential candidate "cannot be inaugurated till he betrays those who elected him by breaking his pledges, and surrendering to those who tried and failed to defeat him at the polls." Making such a concession would mean that "this government and all popular government is already at an end."

AND THE WAR CAME

By the time of Lincoln's inauguration, seven states had seceded, formed an independent confederacy, and seized most federal forts and other installations in the Deep South without firing a shot. Lincoln's predecessor, James Buchanan, had denied the right of secession but had also refused to use "coercion" to maintain federal authority. Many Northerners agreed with his stand. The northern business community was reluctant to break commercial links with the cotton-producing South, and some antislavery Republicans and abolitionists opposed coercive action because they thought the nation might be better off if "the erring sisters" of the Deep South were allowed "to depart in peace."

The collapse of compromise efforts narrowed the choices to peaceful separation or war between the sections. By early March, the tide of public opinion was beginning to shift in favor of strong action to preserve the Union. Even the business community came to support coercive measures, reasoning that a temporary disruption of commerce was better than the permanent loss of the South as a market and source of raw materials.

In his inaugural address, Lincoln called for a cautious and limited use of force. He would defend federal forts and installations not yet in Confederate hands but would not attempt to recapture the ones already taken. He thus tried to shift the burden for beginning hostilities to the Confederacy, which would have to attack before it would be attacked.

As Lincoln spoke, only four military installations within the seceded states were still held by U.S. forces. The most important and vulnerable of these was Fort Sumter inside Charleston Harbor. The Confederacy demanded the surrender of a garrison that was within easy reach of shore batteries and running low on supplies. Shortly after taking office, Lincoln was informed that Sumter could not hold out much longer and that he would have to decide whether to reinforce it or let it fall.

Although the majority of Lincoln's cabinet initially opposed efforts to reinforce or provision Sumter, on April 4, Lincoln ordered that an expedition be prepared to bring food and other provisions to the beleaguered troops in Charleston Harbor. Two days later, he sent word to the governor of South Carolina that the relief expedition was being sent.

The expedition sailed on April 8 and 9, but before it arrived, Confederate authorities decided the sending of provisions was a hostile act and proceeded to attack the fort. Early on the morning of April 12, shore batteries opened fire; the bombardment continued for forty hours. Finally, on April 13, the Union forces under Major Robert Anderson surrendered, and the Confederate flag was raised over Fort Sumter. The South had won a victory but had also assumed responsibility for firing the first shot.

On April 15, Lincoln proclaimed that an insurrection against federal authority existed in the Deep South and called on the militia of the loyal states to provide 75,000 troops for short-term service to put it down. Two days later, Virginia voted to join the Confederacy. Within the next five weeks, Arkansas, Tennessee, and North Carolina followed suit. These slave states of the upper South had been unwilling to secede just because Lincoln was elected, but when he called on them to provide troops to "coerce" other southern states, they had to choose sides. Believing that secession was a constitutional right, they were quick to cut their ties with a government that opted for the use of force to maintain the Union.

In the North, the firing on Sumter evoked strong feelings of patriotism and dedication to the Union. Stephen A. Douglas, Lincoln's former political rival, pledged his full support for the crusade against secession and literally worked himself to death rallying midwestern Democrats behind the government. By firing on the flag, the Confederacy united the North. Everyone assumed the war would be short and not very bloody. It remained to be seen whether Unionist fervor could be sustained through a long and costly struggle.

The entire Confederacy, which now moved its capital from Montgomery to Richmond, Virginia, contained only eleven of the fifteen states in which slavery was lawful. In the border slave states of Maryland, Delaware, Kentucky, and

Missouri, a combination of local Unionism and federal intervention thwarted secession. Kentucky initially proclaimed itself neutral but eventually sided with the Union, mainly because Lincoln provoked the South into violating neutrality first by sending regular troops into the state. Maryland, which surrounded the nation's capital and provided it with access to the free states, was kept in the Union by more ruthless methods, which included the use of martial law to suppress Confederate sympathizers. In Missouri, the presence of regular troops, aided significantly by a staunchly pro-Union German immigrant population, stymied the secession movement. But pro-Union forces failed to maintain order and brutal guerrilla fighting made wartime Missouri an unsafe and bloody place.

Hence the Civil War was not, strictly speaking, a struggle between slave and free states. More than anything else, conflicting views on the right of secession determined the ultimate division of states and the choices of individuals in areas where sentiment was divided. Although concern about the future of slavery had driven the Deep South to secede in the first place, the actual lineup of states and supporters meant the two sides would initially define the war less as a struggle over slavery than as a contest to determine whether the Union was indivisible.

ADJUSTING TO TOTAL WAR

The Civil War was a "total war" involving every aspect of society because the North could achieve its aim of restoring the Union only by defeating the South so thoroughly that its separatist government would be overthrown. It was a long war because the Confederacy put up "a hell of a fight" before it would agree to be put to death. A total war is a test of societies, economies, and political systems, as well as a battle of wits between generals and military strategists.

PROSPECTS, PLANS, AND EXPECTATIONS

If the war was to be decided by sheer physical strength, then the North had an enormous edge in population, industrial capacity, and railroad mileage. But the South, too, had some advantages. To achieve its aim of independence, the Confederacy needed only to defend its own territory successfully. The North, on the other hand, had to invade and conquer the South. Consequently, the Confederacy faced a less serious supply problem, had a greater capacity to choose the time and place of combat, and could take advantage of familiar terrain and a friendly civilian population.

The nature of the war meant southern leaders could define their cause as defense of their homeland against Yankee invaders. The northern cause was not nearly as clear-cut as that of the South. It seemed doubtful in 1861 that Northerners would fervently support a war fought for the seemingly abstract principle that the Union was sacred and perpetual.

At the beginning of the war, leaders of both sides tried to find the best way to capitalize on their advantages and compensate for their limitations. The choice before President Davis, who assumed personal direction of the Confederate military effort, was whether to stay on the defensive or seek a sudden and dramatic

Resources of the Union and the Confederacy, 1861

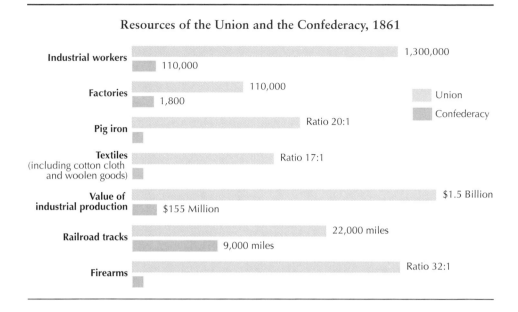

- Industrial workers — 1,300,000 / 110,000
- Factories — 110,000 / 1,800
- Pig iron — Ratio 20:1
- Textiles (including cotton cloth and woolen goods) — Ratio 17:1
- Value of industrial production — $1.5 Billion / $155 Million
- Railroad tracks — 22,000 miles / 9,000 miles
- Firearms — Ratio 32:1

Union

Confederacy

victory by invading the North. He chose to wage a mainly defensive war in the hope that the northern populace would soon tire of the blood and sacrifice and leave the Confederacy to go its own way. But this plan did not preclude invading the North when good opportunities presented themselves. Although their primary strategic orientation was defensive, it was an "offensive defense" that southern commanders put into effect.

Northern military planners had greater difficulty in working out a basic strategy, and it took a good deal of trial and error (mostly error) before there was a clear sense of what had to be done. Some optimists believed the war could be won quickly and easily by sending an army to capture the Confederate capital of Richmond, scarcely a hundred miles from Washington. The early battles in Virginia ended this optimistic "On to Richmond" strategy. The aged General Winfield Scott, who commanded the Union army during the early months of the war, recommended an "anaconda policy" calling for the North to squeeze the South into submission by blockading the southern coasts, seizing control of the Mississippi, and cutting off supplies of food and other essential commodities. This plan pointed to the West as the main locus of military operations.

Eventually Lincoln decided on a two-front war, keeping the pressure on Virginia and at the same time authorizing an advance down the Mississippi Valley with the aim of isolating Texas, Arkansas, and Louisiana. Lincoln also attached great importance to the coastal blockade and expected naval operations to seize the ports through which goods entered and left the Confederacy. His basic plan of applying pressure and probing for weaknesses at several points simultaneously took maximum advantage of the North's superiority in manpower and matériel. But it required better military leadership than the

North possessed at the beginning of the war and took a painfully long time to put into effect.

MOBILIZING THE HOME FRONTS

The North and South faced similar problems in trying to create the vast support systems needed by armies in the field. At the beginning of the conflict, both sides had more volunteers than could be armed and outfitted. But as hopes for a short and easy war faded, the pool of volunteers began to dry up. Many of the early recruits showed a reluctance to reenlist. To resolve this problem, the Confederacy passed a conscription law in April 1862, and the Union edged toward a draft in July when Congress gave Lincoln the power to assign manpower quotas to each state and resort to conscription if they were not met.

To produce the materials of war, both governments relied mainly on private industry. In the North, especially, the system of contracting with private firms and individuals resulted in much corruption, inefficiency, and shoddy and defective supplies. But the North's economy was strong at the core, and by 1863 its factories and farms were producing more than enough to provision the troops without significantly lowering the living standards of the civilian population.

The southern economy was much less adaptable to the needs of a total war. The South of 1861 depended on the outside world for most of its manufactured goods. As the Union blockade became more effective, the Confederacy had to rely increasingly on a government-sponsored crash program to produce war materials. In addition to encouraging and promoting private initiative, the government built its own munitions plants. Astonishingly, the Confederate Ordnance Bureau succeeded in producing or procuring sufficient armaments to keep southern armies well supplied throughout the conflict.

Southern agriculture, however, failed to meet the challenge. Planters were reluctant to shift from staples that could no longer be readily exported to foodstuffs that were urgently needed. But more significant was the inadequacy of the South's internal transportation system. Its limited rail network was designed to link plantation regions to port cities rather than to connect food-producing areas with centers of population.

When northern forces penetrated parts of the South, they created new gaps in the system. Although well armed, Confederate soldiers were increasingly undernourished, and by 1863 civilians in urban areas were rioting to protest shortages of food. To supply the troops, the Confederate commissary resorted to the impressment of available agricultural produce at below the market price, a policy resisted so vigorously by farmers and local politicians that it eventually had to be abandoned.

Both sides faced the challenge of financing an enormously costly struggle. Although both the North and South imposed special war taxes, neither side was willing to resort to the heavy taxation that was needed to maintain fiscal integrity. Besides floating loans and selling bonds, both treasuries deliberately inflated the currency by printing large quantities of paper money that could not be redeemed in gold and silver. Runaway inflation was the inevitable result. The problem was much less severe in the North because of the overall strength of its economy. War taxes on income were more readily collectable than in the South, and bond issues were more successful.

POLITICAL LEADERSHIP: NORTHERN SUCCESS AND SOUTHERN FAILURE

Total war also forced political adjustments, and both the Union and the Confederacy had to face the question of how much democracy and individual freedom could be permitted when military success required an unprecedented exercise of government authority. Since both constitutions made the president commander in chief of the army and navy, Lincoln and Davis took actions that would have been regarded as arbitrary or even tyrannical in peacetime.

Lincoln was especially bold in assuming new executive powers. He expanded the regular army and advanced public money to private individuals without authorization by Congress. On April 27, 1861, he declared martial law and suspended the writ of habeas corpus in the area between Philadelphia and Washington, an action deemed necessary because of mob attacks on Union troops passing through Baltimore. Suspension of the writ enabled the government to arrest Confederate sympathizers and hold them without trial, and in September 1862 Lincoln extended this authority to all parts of the United States where "disloyal" elements were active. He argued that preservation of the Union justified such actions. In fact, most of the thousands of civilians arrested by military authorities were suspected deserters and draft dodgers, refugees, smugglers, or people who were simply found wandering in areas under military control.

For the most part, the Lincoln administration showed restraint and tolerated a broad spectrum of political dissent. Although the government closed down a few newspapers for brief periods when they allegedly published false information or military secrets, generally anti-administration journals were allowed to criticize the president and his party at will. A few politicians were arrested for pro-Confederate activity, but a large number of "Peace Democrats"—who called for restoration of the Union by negotiation rather than force—ran successfully for office and thus had ample opportunity to present their views to the public. In fact, the persistence of vigorous two-party competition in the North during the Civil War strengthened Lincoln's hand. Since his war policies were also the platform of his party, he could usually rely on unified partisan backing for the most controversial of his decisions.

Lincoln was singularly adept at the art of party leadership; he was able to accommodate various factions and define party issues and principles in a way that would encourage unity and dedication to the cause. Since the Republican party served during the war as the main vehicle for mobilizing and maintaining devotion to the Union effort, these political skills assumed crucial importance. Lincoln held the party together by persuasion, patronage, and flexible policymaking; this cohesiveness was essential to Lincoln's success in unifying the nation by force.

Jefferson Davis, most historians agree, was a less effective war leader than Lincoln. He defined his powers as commander in chief narrowly and literally, which meant he assumed personal direction of the armed forces but left policymaking for the mobilization and control of the civilian population primarily to the Confederate Congress. Unfortunately, he overestimated his capacities as a strategist and lacked the tact to handle field commanders who were as proud and testy as he was.

Davis's greatest failing, however, was his lack of initiative and leadership in dealing with the problems of the home front. He devoted little attention to a deteriorating economic situation that caused great hardship and sapped Confederate morale. In addition, although the South had a much more serious problem of internal division and disloyalty than the North, he chose to be extremely cautious in his use of martial law.

As the war dragged on, Davis's political and popular support eroded. He was opposed and obstructed by state governors who resisted conscription and other Confederate policies that violated the tradition of states' rights. Southern newspapers and the Confederate Congress attacked Davis's conduct of the war. His authority was further undermined because he did not have an organized party behind him, for the Confederacy never developed a two-party system. As a result, it was difficult to mobilize the support required for hard decisions and controversial policies.

EARLY CAMPAIGNS AND BATTLES

The war's first major battle was a disaster for the North. Against his better judgment, General Winfield Scott responded to the "On to Richmond" clamor and ordered poorly trained Union troops under General Irvin McDowell to advance against the Confederate forces gathered at Manassas Junction, Virginia. They attacked the enemy position near Bull Run Creek on July 21, 1861. Confederate General Thomas J. Jackson earned the nickname "Stonewall" for holding the line against the northern assault until Confederate reinforcements arrived and routed the invading force. As they retreated toward Washington, the raw Union troops gave in to panic and broke ranks in their stampede to safety.

The humiliating defeat at Bull Run led to a shake-up of the northern high command. George McClellan replaced McDowell as commander of troops in the Washington area and then became general in chief when Scott was eased into retirement. A cautious disciplinarian, McClellan spent the fall and winter drilling his troops and whipping them into shape. President Lincoln, who could not understand why McClellan was taking so long to go into the field, became increasingly impatient and finally tried to order the army into action.

Before McClellan made his move, Union forces in the West won some important victories. In February 1862, a joint military-naval operation, commanded by General Ulysses S. Grant, captured Fort Henry on the Tennessee River and Fort Donelson on the Cumberland. The Confederate army was forced to withdraw from Kentucky and middle Tennessee. Southern forces in the West then massed at Corinth, Mississippi, just across the border from Tennessee. When a slow-moving Union army arrived just north of the Mississippi state line, the South launched a surprise attack on April 6. In the battle of Shiloh, one of the bloodiest of the war, only the timely arrival of reinforcements prevented the annihilation of

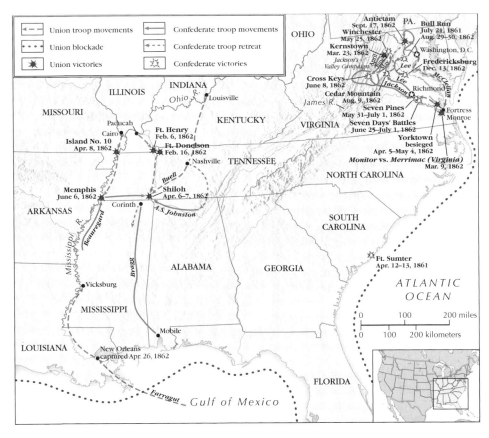

Civil War, 1861–1862

Defeats on the battlefield forced a change in the Union's initial military campaign of capturing Richmond, the Confederate capital. The Union's targets in the West were the key cities of Vicksburg and New Orleans.

Union troops backed up against the Tennessee River. After a second day of fierce fighting, the Confederates retreated to Corinth, leaving the enemy forces battered and exhausted.

Although the Union's military effort to seize control of the Mississippi Valley was temporarily halted at Shiloh, the Union navy soon contributed dramatically to the pursuit of that objective. On April 26, a fleet under Flag Officer David Farragut, coming up from the Gulf, captured the port of New Orleans. The occupation of New Orleans, besides securing the mouth of the Mississippi, climaxed a series of naval and amphibious operations around the edges of the Confederacy that provided strategically located bases to enforce a blockade of the southern coast. The last serious challenge to the North's naval supremacy ended on March 9, 1862, when the Confederate ironclad vessel *Virginia* (originally the USS *Merrimac*) was repulsed by the *Monitor,* an armored and turreted Union gunship.

Successes around the edges of the Confederacy did not relieve northern frustration at the inactivity or failure of Union forces on the eastern front. Only after

After Antietam, Lincoln visited McClellan's headquarters to urge the general to take action. McClellan is on the left facing the president.

Lincoln ordered him to take the offensive did McClellan start toward Richmond. Spurning the treacherous overland route, he moved his forces by water to the peninsula southeast of the Confederate capital. McClellan began moving up the peninsula in early April 1862. For a month he was bogged down before Yorktown, which he chose to besiege rather than assault directly. After Yorktown fell on May 4, he pushed ahead to a point twenty miles from Richmond, where he awaited the additional troops that he expected Lincoln to send.

The reinforcements were not forthcoming. While McClellan was inching his way up the peninsula, a relatively small southern force under Stonewall Jackson had pinned down a much larger Union army in the Shenandoah Valley. When it appeared by late May that Jackson might attack Washington, Lincoln decided to withhold troops from McClellan so they would be available to defend the Union capital.

At the end of May, the Confederates under Joseph E. Johnston took the offensive when they discovered McClellan's army was divided into two segments by the Chickahominy River. In the battle of Seven Pines, McClellan was barely able to hold his ground on the side of the river under attack until a corps from the other side crossed over just in time to save the day. During the battle, General Johnston was severely wounded; succeeding him in command of the Confederate Army of Northern Virginia was native Virginian and West Point graduate Robert E. Lee.

Toward the end of June, Lee began an all-out effort to expel McClellan from the outskirts of Richmond. In a series of battles that lasted for seven days, the two armies clawed at each other indecisively. Nevertheless, McClellan decided to retreat down the peninsula to a more secure base. This backward step convinced Lincoln that the peninsula campaign was an exercise in futility.

On July 11, Lincoln appointed General Henry W. Halleck as general in chief and through Halleck ordered McClellan to withdraw his troops from the peninsula and send reinforcements to an army under General John Pope that was preparing to move on Richmond by the overland route. At the end of August, in the second battle fought near Bull Run, Lee established his reputation for brilliant generalship; he sent Stonewall Jackson to Pope's rear, provoked the rash Union general to attack Jackson with full force, and then threw the main Confederate army against the Union's flank. Badly beaten, Pope retreated to the defenses of Washington, where he was stripped of command. A desperate Lincoln reappointed McClellan to head the Army of the Potomac.

Lee led his exuberant troops on an invasion of Maryland, hoping to isolate Washington from the rest of the North. McClellan caught up with him near Sharpsburg, and the bloodiest one-day battle of the war ensued. When the smoke cleared at Antietam on September 17, almost five thousand men had been killed on the two sides and more than eighteen thousand were wounded. The result was a draw, but Lee was forced to fall back south of the Potomac. McClellan was slow in pursuit, and Lincoln blamed him for letting the enemy escape.

Convinced that McClellan was fatally infected with "the slows," Lincoln put Ambrose E. Burnside in command of the Army of the Potomac. Burnside was aggressive enough, but he was also rather dense. His limitations were disastrously revealed at the battle of Fredericksburg, Virginia, on December 13, 1862, when he launched a direct assault to try to capture an entrenched and elevated position. The debacle at Fredericksburg, where Union forces suffered more than

This photograph of dead Confederate soldiers lined up for burial was taken by Alexander Gardner at Antietam, Maryland, after the deadliest one-day battle of the war. Several photographers working with Mathew Brady accompanied Union troops in battle. Their visual records of the campaigns and casualties stand as a testament to the hardships and horrors of war.

twice as many casualties as their opponents, ended a year of bitter failure for the North on the eastern front.

THE DIPLOMATIC STRUGGLE

The critical period of Civil War diplomacy was 1861–1862, when the South tried to induce major foreign powers to recognize its independence and break the Union blockade. The hope that England and France could be persuaded to intervene on the Confederate side stemmed from the fact that these nations depended on the South for three-quarters of their cotton supply.

The Confederate commissioners sent to England and France in May 1861 succeeded in gaining recognition of southern "belligerency," which meant the new government could claim some international rights of a nation at war, such as purchasing and outfitting privateers in neutral ports. As a result, Confederate raiders built and armed in British shipyards devastated northern shipping to such an extent that insurance costs eventually forced most of the American merchant marine off the high seas for the duration of the war.

In the fall of 1861, the Confederate government dispatched James M. Mason and John Slidell to be its permanent envoys to England and France, respectively, and instructed them to push for full recognition of the Confederacy. They took passage on the British steamer *Trent,* which was stopped and boarded in international waters by a U.S. warship. Mason and Slidell were taken into custody by the Union captain, causing a diplomatic crisis that nearly led to war between England and the United States. After a few weeks of ferocious posturing by both sides, Lincoln and Secretary of State Seward made the prudent decision to allow Mason and Slidell to proceed to their destinations.

These envoys may as well have stayed at home; they failed in their mission to obtain full recognition of the Confederacy from either England or France. The anticipated cotton shortage was slow to develop, for the bumper crop of 1860 had created a large surplus in British and French warehouses.

British opinion, both official and public, was seriously divided on how to respond to the American conflict. In 1861 and 1862, Lord Palmerston, the prime minister, and Lord Russell, the foreign secretary, played a cautious waiting game. Their government was sympathetic to the South but wary of the danger of war with the United States.

In September 1862, the British cabinet debated mediation and recognition as serious possibilities. Lord Russell pressed for a pro-Confederate policy because he was convinced the South was now strong enough to secure its independence. But Lord Palmerston overruled the foreign secretary and decided to maintain a hands-off policy. Only if the South won decisively on the battlefield would Britain risk the dangers of recognition and intervention.

The cotton famine finally hit in late 1862, causing massive unemployment in the British textile industry. But, contrary to southern hopes, public opinion did not compel the government to abandon its neutrality and use force to break the Union blockade. Influential interest groups that actually benefited from the famine provided the crucial support for continuing a policy of nonintervention. Among these groups were owners of large cotton mills, who had made bonanza profits on their existing stocks and were happy to see weaker competitors go under while they awaited new sources of supply. By early 1863, cotton from Egypt and India put the industry back on the track toward full production. Other beneficiaries of nonintervention were manufacturers of wool and linen textiles, munitions makers who supplied both sides, and shipping interests that profited from the decline of American competition on the world's sea-lanes. Since the British economy as a whole gained more than it lost from neutrality, it is not surprising that there was little effective pressure for a change in policy.

By early 1863, when it was clear that "King Cotton diplomacy" had failed, the Confederacy broke off formal relations with Great Britain. For the European powers, the advantages of getting involved were not worth the risk of a war with the United States. Independence for the South would have to be won on the battlefield.

Fight to the Finish

The last two and a half years of the struggle saw the implementation of more radical war measures. The most dramatic and important of these was the North's effort to follow through on Lincoln's decision to free the slaves and bring the black population into the war on the Union side. The tide of battle turned in the summer of 1863, but the South continued to resist valiantly for two more years, until it was finally overcome by the sheer weight of the North's advantages in manpower and resources.

The Coming of Emancipation

At the beginning of the war, when the North still hoped for a quick and easy victory, only dedicated abolitionists favored turning the struggle for the Union into a crusade against slavery. But as it became clear how hard it was going to be to subdue the "rebels," public and congressional sentiment developed for striking a blow at the South's economic and social system by freeing its slaves. In July 1862, Congress authorized the government to confiscate the slaves of masters who supported the Confederacy. By this time, slaves were deserting their plantations in areas where the Union forces were close enough to offer a haven. In this way, they put pressure on the government to determine their status and, in effect, offered themselves as a source of manpower to the Union on the condition that they be made free.

Although Lincoln favored freedom for blacks as an ultimate goal, he was reluctant to commit his administration to a policy of immediate emancipation. In the fall of 1861 and again in the spring of 1862, he had disallowed the orders of field commanders who sought to free slaves in areas occupied by their forces, thus angering abolitionists and the strongly antislavery Republicans known as Radicals. Lincoln's caution stemmed from a fear of alienating Unionist elements in the border slave states and from his own preference for a gradual, compensated form of emancipation.

In this allegorical painting, President Lincoln extends a copy of his proclamation to the goddess of liberty who is driving her chariot, Emancipation.

Lincoln was also aware that one of the main obstacles to any program leading to emancipation was the strong racial prejudice of most whites in both the North and the South. Pessimistic about prospects of equality for blacks in the United States, Lincoln coupled moderate proposals with a plea for government subsidies to support the voluntary "colonization" of freed blacks outside of the United States, and he actively sought places that would accept them.

But the slaveholding states that remained loyal to the Union refused to endorse Lincoln's gradual plan, and the failure of Union arms in the spring and summer of 1862 increased the public clamor for striking directly at the South's peculiar institution. The Lincoln administration also realized that emancipation would win sympathy for the Union cause in England and France and thus might counter the growing threat that these nations would come to the aid of the Confederacy. Lincoln drafted an emancipation proclamation in July, but he was persuaded not to issue it until the North had won a victory and could not be accused of acting out of desperation.

Finally, on September 22, 1862, Lincoln issued his preliminary Emancipation Proclamation. McClellan's success in stopping Lee at Antietam provided the occasion, but the president was also responding to growing political pressures. Most Republican politicians were now firmly committed to an emancipation policy, and many were on the verge of repudiating the administration for its inaction. Had Lincoln failed to act, his party would have been badly split, and he would have been in the minority faction. The proclamation gave the Confederate states one hundred days to give up the struggle without losing their slaves. In December, Lincoln proposed to Congress that it approve a series of constitutional amendments providing for gradual, compensated emancipation in slaveholding areas not actually in rebellion.

Since there was no response from the South and little enthusiasm in Congress for Lincoln's gradual plan, on January 1, 1863, the president declared that all slaves in those areas under Confederate control "shall be . . . thenceforward, and forever free." He justified the final proclamation as an act of "military necessity" sanctioned by the war powers of the president, and he authorized the enlistment of freed slaves in the Union army. The language and tone of the document—one historian has described it as having "all the moral grandeur of a bill of lading"— made it clear that blacks were being freed for reasons of state and not out of humanitarian conviction.

Despite its uninspiring origin and limited application—it did not extend to slave states loyal to the Union or to occupied areas and thus did not immediately free a single slave—the proclamation did commit the Union to the abolition of slavery as a war aim. It also accelerated the breakdown of slavery as a labor system, a process that was already well under way by early 1863. As word spread among the slaves that emancipation was now official policy, larger numbers of them were inspired to run off and seek the protection of approaching northern armies. Approximately one-quarter of the slave population gained freedom during the war under the terms of the Emancipation Proclamation and thus deprived the South of an important part of its agricultural workforce.

AFRICAN AMERICANS AND THE WAR

Almost 200,000 African Americans, most of them newly freed slaves, eventually served in the Union armed forces and made a vital contribution to the North's victory. Although they were enrolled in segregated units under white officers, were initially paid less than their white counterparts, and were used disproportionately for garrison duty or heavy labor behind the lines, "blacks in blue" fought heroically in several major battles during the last two years of the war.

Those freed during the war who did not serve in the military were often conscripted to serve as contract wage laborers on cotton plantations owned or leased by "loyal" white planters within the occupied areas of the Deep South. Abolitionists protested that the coercion used by military authorities to get blacks back into the cotton fields amounted to slavery in a new form, but those in power argued that the necessities of war and the northern economy required such "temporary" arrangements. To some extent, regimentation of freed slaves within the South was a way of assuring racially prejudiced Northerners that emancipation would not result in a massive migration of black refugees to their region of the country.

The heroic performance of African American troops (most notably at Fort Wagner in South Carolina and in Louisiana) and the easing of northern fears of being swamped by black migrants led to a deepening commitment to emancipation as a permanent and comprehensive policy. Realizing that his proclamation had a shaky constitutional foundation and might apply only to slaves actually freed while the war was going on, Lincoln sought to organize and recognize loyal state governments in southern areas under Union control on condition that they abolish slavery in their constitutions.

Finally, Lincoln pressed for an amendment to the federal constitution outlawing involuntary servitude. After supporting its inclusion as a central plank in the Republican platform of 1864, Lincoln used all his influence to win congressional approval for the new Thirteenth Amendment. On January 31, 1865, the House approved the amendment by a narrow margin. The cause of freedom for blacks and the cause of the Union had at last become one and the same. Lincoln, despite his earlier hesitations and misgivings, had earned the right to go down in history as the Great Emancipator.

THE TIDE TURNS

By early 1863, the Confederate economy was in shambles and its diplomacy had collapsed. The social order of the South was also showing signs of severe strain. Masters were losing control of their slaves, and nonslaveholding whites were becoming disillusioned with the hardships of a war that some of them described as "a rich man's war and a poor man's fight." Yet the North was slow to capitalize on the South's internal weaknesses because it had its own serious morale problems. The long series of defeats on the eastern front had engendered war weariness, and the new policies that "military necessity" forced the government to adopt encountered fierce opposition.

Although popular with Republicans, most Democrats viewed emancipation as a betrayal of northern war aims. Racism was a main ingredient in their opposition to freeing blacks. Riding a backlash against the preliminary proclamation, Democrats made significant gains in the congressional elections of 1862, especially in the Midwest, where they also captured the state legislatures of Illinois and Indiana.

The Enrollment Act of March 1863, which provided for outright conscription of white males but permitted men of wealth to hire substitutes or pay a fee to avoid military service, provoked a violent response from those unable to buy their way out of service and unwilling to fight for blacks. A series of antidraft riots broke out, culminating in one of the bloodiest domestic disorders in American history—the New York Riot of July 1863. The New York mob, composed mainly of Irish-American laborers, burned the draft offices, the homes of leading Republicans, and an orphanage for black children. They also lynched more than a dozen defenseless blacks who fell into their hands. At least 120 people died before federal troops restored order. Besides racial prejudice, the draft riots also reflected working-class anger at the wartime privileges and prosperity of the middle and upper classes; they showed how divided the North really was on the administration's conduct of the war.

To fight dissension and "disloyalty," the government used its martial law authority to arrest a few alleged ringleaders. Private patriotic organizations also issued a barrage of propaganda aimed at what they believed was a vast secret conspiracy to undermine the northern war effort. Historians disagree about the actual extent of covert and illegal antiwar activity, but militant advocates of "peace at any price"—popularly known as Copperheads—were certainly active in some areas, especially among the immigrant working classes of large cities and in southern Ohio, Indiana, and Illinois.

The only effective way to overcome the disillusionment that fed the peace movement was to start winning battles and thus convince the northern public that victory was assured. Before this could happen, the North suffered one more humiliating defeat on the eastern front. In early May 1863, Union forces under General Joseph Hooker were routed at Chancellorsville, Virginia, by a much smaller Confederate army commanded by Robert E. Lee. Lee sent his forces and Stonewall Jackson to make a devastating surprise attack on the Union right. The Confederacy prevailed, but it did suffer one major loss: Jackson himself died as a result of wounds he received in the battle.

In the West, however, a major Union triumph was taking shape. For more than a year, General Ulysses S. Grant had been trying to put his forces in position to capture Vicksburg, Mississippi, the almost inaccessible Confederate bastion that kept the North from controlling the Mississippi River. Finally, in late March 1863, he crossed to the west bank north of the city and moved his forces to a point south of it, where he joined up with naval forces that had run the Confederate batteries mounted on Vicksburg's high bluffs. In one of the boldest campaigns of the war, Grant crossed the river, deliberately cutting himself off from his sources of supply, and marched into the interior of Mississippi. Living off the land and out of communication with an anxious and perplexed Lincoln, his troops won a series of victories over two separate Confederate armies and advanced on Vicksburg from the east. After unsuccessfully assaulting the city's defenses, Grant settled down for a siege on May 22.

The Confederate government rejected proposals to mount a major offensive into Tennessee and Kentucky to draw Grant away from Vicksburg. Instead, President Davis approved Robert E. Lee's plan for an all-out invasion of the Northeast, an option that might lead to a dramatic victory that would more than compensate for the probable loss of Vicksburg. Lee's army crossed the Potomac in June and kept going until it reached Gettysburg, Pennsylvania. There Lee confronted a Union army that had taken up strong defensive positions on Cemetery Ridge and Culp's Hill.

A series of Confederate attacks on July 2 failed to dislodge General George Meade's troops from the high ground they occupied. The following day, Lee faced the choice of retreating to protect his lines of communication or launching a final, desperate assault. With more boldness than wisdom, he chose to make a direct attack on the strongest part of the Union line. The resulting charge on Cemetery Ridge was disastrous; advancing Confederate soldiers dropped like flies under the barrage of Union artillery and rifle fire. Only a few made it to the top of the ridge, and they were killed or captured.

Retreat was now inevitable, and Lee withdrew his battered troops to the Potomac, only to find that the river was at flood stage and could not be crossed for several days. But Meade failed to follow up his victory with a vigorous pursuit, and Lee was allowed to escape a predicament that could have resulted in his annihilation. Vicksburg fell to Grant on July 4, the same day Lee began his with-

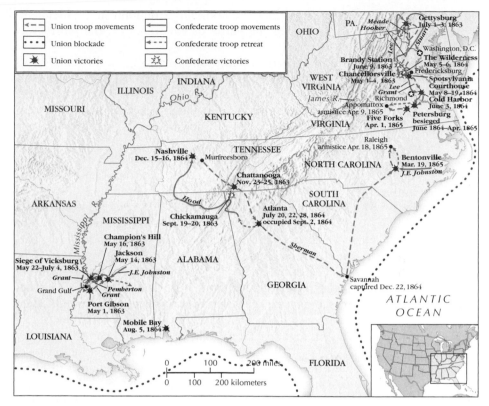

Civil War, 1863–1865

In the western theater of war, Grant's victories at Port Gibson, Jackson, and Champion's Hill cleared the way for his siege of Vicksburg. In the east, after the hard-won Union victory at Gettysburg, the South never again invaded the North. In 1864 and 1865, Union armies gradually closed in on Lee's Confederate forces in Virginia. Leaving Atlanta in flames, Sherman marched to the Georgia coast, took Savannah, then moved his troops north through the Carolinas. Grant's army, although suffering enormous losses, moved on toward Richmond, marching into the Confederate capital on April 3, 1865, and forcing surrender.

drawal, and Northerners rejoiced at the simultaneous Independence Day victories that turned the tide of the war. The Union had secured control of the Mississippi and had at last won a major battle in the East. But Lincoln's joy turned to frustration when he learned his generals had missed the chance to capture Lee's army and bring a quick end to the war.

LAST STAGES OF THE CONFLICT

Later in 1863, the North finally gained control of the middle South, an area where indecisive fighting had been going on since the beginning of the conflict. The main Union target was Chattanooga, "the gateway to the Southeast." In September, Union troops maneuvered the Confederates out of the city but were in turn eventually surrounded and besieged there by southern forces. Grant arrived from Vicksburg to take command, breaking the encirclement with daring assaults on the Confederate positions on Lookout Mountain and Missionary Ridge. As a result of its success in the battle of Chattanooga, the North was poised for an invasion of Georgia.

Grant's victories in the West earned him promotion to general in chief of all the Union armies. After assuming that position in March 1864, he ordered a multipronged offensive to finish off the Confederacy. The main movements were a march on Richmond under his personal command and a thrust by the western armies, now led by General William Tecumseh Sherman, to Atlanta and the heart of Georgia.

In May and early June, Grant and Lee fought a series of bloody battles in northern Virginia that tended to follow a set pattern. Lee would take up an entrenched position in the path of the invading force, and Grant would attack it, sustaining heavy losses but also inflicting casualties the shrinking Confederate army could ill afford. When his direct assault had failed, Grant would move to his left, hoping in vain to maneuver Lee into a less defensible position. In the battles of the Wilderness, Spotsylvania, and Cold Harbor, the Union lost about sixty thousand men—more than twice the number of Confederate casualties—without defeating Lee or opening the road to Richmond. After Cold Harbor, Grant decided to change his tactics and moved his army to the south of Richmond. There he drew up before Petersburg, a rail center that linked Richmond to the rest of the Confederacy; after failing to take it by assault, he settled down for a siege.

The siege of Petersburg was a long, drawn-out affair, and the resulting stalemate in the East caused northern morale to plummet during the summer of 1864. Lincoln was facing reelection, and his failure to end the war dimmed his prospects. Although nominated with ease in June—with Andrew Johnson, a proadministration Democrat from Tennessee, as his running mate—Lincoln con-

Bold and decisive, Confederate General Robert E. Lee (left) often faced an enemy army that greatly outnumbered his own troops. Union General Ulysses S. Grant (right) demonstrated a relentless determination that eventually triumphed.

THE ELECTION OF 1864

CANDIDATE	PARTY	POPULAR VOTE	ELECTORAL VOTE*
Lincoln	Republican	2,213,655	212
McClellan	Democratic	1,805,237	21

*Out of a total of 233 electoral votes. The eleven secessionist states—Alabama, Arkansas, Florida, Georgia, Louisiana, Mississippi, North Carolina, South Carolina, Tennessee, Texas, and Virginia—did not vote.

fronted growing opposition within his own party, especially from Radicals who disagreed with his apparently lenient approach to the future restoration of seceded states to the Union.

The Democrats seemed to be in a good position to capitalize on Republican divisions and make a strong bid for the White House. Their platform appealed to war weariness by calling for a cease-fire followed by negotiations to reestablish the Union. The party's nominee, General George McClellan, announced he would not be bound by the peace plank and would pursue the war. But he promised to end the conflict sooner than Lincoln could because he would not insist on emancipation as a condition for reconstruction. By late summer, Lincoln confessed privately that he would probably be defeated.

Northern military successes changed the political outlook. Sherman's invasion of Georgia went well. On September 2, Atlanta fell, and northern forces occupied the hub of the Deep South. The news unified the Republican party behind Lincoln. The election in November was almost an anticlimax: Lincoln won 212 of a possible 233 electoral votes and 55 percent of the popular vote. The Republican cause of "liberty and Union" was secure.

The concluding military operations revealed the futility of further southern resistance. Sherman marched unopposed through Georgia to the sea, destroying almost everything of possible military or economic value in a corridor 300 miles long and 60 miles wide. The Confederate army that had opposed him at Atlanta moved northward into Tennessee, where it was defeated and almost destroyed by Union forces at Nashville in mid-December. Sherman captured Savannah on December 22. He then turned north and marched through the Carolinas, intending to join up with Grant at Petersburg near Richmond.

While Sherman was bringing the war to the Carolinas, Grant finally ended the stalemate at Petersburg. When Lee's starving and exhausted army tried to break through the Union lines, Grant renewed his attack and forced the Confederates to abandon Petersburg and Richmond on April 2, 1865. He then pursued them westward for a hundred miles, placing his forces in position to cut off their line of retreat to the south. Recognizing the hopelessness of further resistance, Lee surrendered his army at Appomattox Courthouse on April 9.

But the joy of the victorious North turned to sorrow and anger when John Wilkes Booth, a pro-Confederate actor, assassinated Abraham Lincoln as the president watched a play at Ford's Theater in Washington on April 14. Although Booth had a few accomplices, popular theories that the assassination was the result of a vast conspiracy involving Confederate leaders or (according to another version) Radical Republicans have never been substantiated.

The man who had spoken of the need to sacrifice for the Union cause at Gettysburg had himself given "the last full measure of devotion" to the cause of "government of the people, by the people, for the people." Four days after Lincoln's death, the only remaining Confederate force of any significance (the troops under Joseph E. Johnston, who had been opposing Sherman in North Carolina) laid down its arms. The Union was saved.

EFFECTS OF THE WAR

The nation that emerged from four years of total war was not the same America that had split apart in 1861. More than 618,000 young men were in their graves, victims of enemy fire or the diseases that spread rapidly in military encampments in this era before modern medicine and sanitation. The widows and sweethearts they left behind temporarily increased the proportion of unmarried women in the population, and some members of this generation of involuntary "spinsters" sought new opportunities for making a living or serving the community that went beyond the purely domestic roles previously prescribed for women.

During the war, northern women pushed the boundaries of their traditional roles by participating on the home front as fund-raisers and in the rear lines as army nurses and members of the Sanitary Commission. The Sanitary Commission promoted health in the northern army's camps through attention to cleanliness, nutrition, and medical care. Women in the North simultaneously utilized their traditional position as nurturers to participate in the war effort while they advanced new ideas about their role in society. The large number who had served as nurses or volunteer workers during the war were especially responsive to calls for broadening "the woman's sphere." Some of the northern women who were prominent in wartime service organizations became leaders of postwar philanthropic and reform movements. The war did not destroy the barriers to gender equality that had long existed in American society, but the efforts of women during the Civil War broadened beliefs about what women could accomplish outside of the home.

The effect on white women in the Confederacy was different from the effect of the war on women in the victorious North. Southern women had always been intimately involved in the administration of the farms and plantations of the South, but the coming of the war forced them to shoulder even greater burdens at home. This was true for wealthy plantation mistresses, who had to take over the administration and maintenance of huge plantations without the benefit of extensive training or the assistance of male relatives. The wives of small

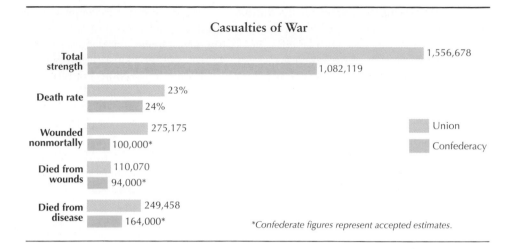

Casualties of War

Total strength
: Union 1,556,678
: Confederacy 1,082,119

Death rate
: Union 23%
: Confederacy 24%

Wounded nonmortally
: Union 275,175
: Confederacy 100,000*

Died from wounds
: Union 110,070
: Confederacy 94,000*

Died from disease
: Union 249,458
: Confederacy 164,000*

Union
Confederacy

*Confederate figures represent accepted estimates.

farmers found it hard to survive at all, especially at harvest time when they often had to do all the work themselves. The loss of fathers and brothers, the constant advance of Union troops, and the difficulty of controlling a slave labor force destroyed many southern women's allegiance to the Confederate cause. As in the North, the Civil War changed the situation of women in society. The devastation of the southern economy forced many women to play a more conspicuous public and economic role. These women responded by forming associations to assist returning soldiers, entering the workforce as educators, and establishing numerous benevolent and reform societies, or temperance organizations. Although these changes created a more visible presence of southern women in public, the South remained more conservative in its views about women's "proper place" than did the North.

At enormous human and economic cost, the nation had emancipated four million African Americans from slavery, but it had not yet resolved that they would be equal citizens. At the time of Lincoln's assassination, most northern states still denied blacks equality under the law and the right to vote. Whether the North would extend more rights to southern freedmen than it had granted to "free Negroes" was an open question.

The impact of the war on white working people was also unclear. Those in the industrializing parts of the North had suffered and lost ground economically because prices had risen much faster than wages during the conflict. But Republican rhetoric stressing "equal opportunity" and the "dignity of labor" raised hopes that the crusade against slavery could be broadened into a movement to improve the lot of working people in general. Foreign-born workers had additional reason to be optimistic; the fact that so many immigrants had fought and died for the Union cause had—for the moment—weakened nativist sentiment and encouraged ethnic tolerance.

What the war definitely decided was that the federal government was supreme over the states and had a broad grant of constitutional authority to act on matters affecting "the general welfare." The southern principle of state sovereignty and strict construction died at Appomattox, and the United States was on its way to becoming a true nation-state with an effective central government. States still had primary responsibility for most functions of government and the Constitution placed limits on what the national government could do; questions would continue to arise about where federal authority ended and states' rights began. Still, the war ended all question about where ultimate authority rested.

A broadened definition of federal powers had its greatest impact in the realm of economic policy. During the war, the Republican-dominated Congresses passed a rash of legislation designed to give stimulus and direction to the nation's economic development. Taking advantage of the absence of southern opposition, Republicans rejected the pre–Civil War tradition of virtual laissez-faire and enacted a Whiggish program of active support for business and agriculture. In 1862, Congress passed a high protective tariff, approved a homestead act intended to encourage settlement of the West by providing free land to settlers, granted huge tracts of public land to railroad companies to support the building of a transcontinental railroad, and gave the states land for the establishment of agricultural colleges. The following year, Congress set up a national banking system that required member banks to keep adequate reserves and invest one-third of their capital in government securities. The notes the national banks issued became the country's first standardized and reliable paper currency.

These wartime achievements added up to a decisive shift in the relationship between the federal government and private enterprise. The Republicans took a limited government that did little more than seek to protect the marketplace from the threat of monopoly and changed it into an activist state that promoted and subsidized the efforts of the economically ambitious and industrious.

The most pervasive effect of the war on northern society was to encourage an "organizational revolution." Aided by government policies, venturesome businessmen took advantage of the new national market created by military procurement to build larger firms that could operate across state lines. Philanthropists also developed more effective national associations. Efforts to care for the wounded influenced the development of the modern hospital and the rise of nursing as a female profession. Both the men who served in the army and those men and women who supported them on the home front or behind the lines became accustomed to working in large, bureaucratic organizations of a kind that had scarcely existed before the war.

The North won the war mainly because it had shown a greater capacity than the South to organize, innovate, and modernize. Its victory meant the nation as a whole would now be ready to embrace the concept of progress that the North had affirmed in its war effort—not only its advances in science and technology, but also its success in bringing together and managing large numbers of men and women for economic and social goals. The Civil War was thus a catalyst for the great transformation of American society from an individualistic society of small producers into the more highly organized and "incorporated" America of the late nineteenth century.

CHRONOLOGY

1860   South Carolina secedes from the Union (December)

1861   Rest of Deep South secedes: Confederacy is founded (January–February)

             Fort Sumter is fired upon and surrenders to Confederate forces (April)

             Upper South secedes (April–May)

             South wins first battle of Bull Run (July)

1862   Grant captures forts Henry and Donelson (February)

             Farragut captures New Orleans for the Union (April)

             McClellan leads unsuccessful campaign on the peninsula southeast of Richmond (March–July)

             South wins second battle of Bull Run (August)

             McClellan stops Lee at battle of Antietam (September)

             Lincoln issues preliminary Emancipation Proclamation (September)

             Lee defeats Union army at Fredericksburg (December)

1863   Lincoln issues final Emancipation Proclamation (January)

             Lee is victorious at Chancellorsville (May)

             North gains major victories at Gettysburg and Vicksburg (July)

             Grant defeats Confederate forces at Chattanooga (November)

1864   Grant and Lee battle in northern Virginia (May–June)

             Atlanta falls to Sherman (September)

             Lincoln is reelected president, defeating McClellan (November)

             Sherman marches through Georgia (November–December)

1865   Congress passes Thirteenth Amendment abolishing slavery (January)

             Grant captures Petersburg and Richmond; Lee surrenders at Appomattox (April)

             Lincoln assassinated by John Wilkes Booth (April)

             Remaining Confederate forces surrender (April–May)

16

THE AGONY OF
RECONSTRUCTION

During the Reconstruction period immediately following the Civil War,
African Americans struggled to become equal citizens of a democratic republic. A number of remarkable leaders won public office. Robert Smalls
of South Carolina was perhaps the most famous and widely respected southern
black leader of the Civil War and Reconstruction era.

Born a slave in 1839 to a white father, Smalls was allowed as a young man to
live and work independently, hiring his own time from a master who may have
been his half brother. Smalls worked as a sailor and trained himself to be a pilot
in Charleston Harbor. When the Union navy blockaded Charleston in 1862,
Smalls, who was then working on a Confederate steamship called the *Planter,*
saw a chance to win his freedom. At three o'clock in the morning on May 13,
1862, when the white officers of the *Planter* were ashore, he took command of
the vessel and its slave crew, sailed it out of the heavily fortified harbor, and surrendered it to the Union navy. The *Planter* was turned into a Union army transport, and Smalls was made its captain after being commissioned as an officer.
During the remainder of the war, he served as captain and pilot of Union vessels
off the coast of South Carolina.

Like a number of other African Americans who had fought valiantly for the
Union, Smalls went on to a distinguished political career during Reconstruction,
serving in the South Carolina constitutional convention, in the state legislature,
and for several terms in the U.S. Congress. He was also a shrewd businessman
and became the owner of extensive properties in and around Beaufort, South
Carolina. The electoral organization Smalls established was so effective that he
was able to control local government and get himself elected to Congress even after the election of 1876 had placed the state under the control of white conservatives bent on depriving blacks of political power. Organized mob violence defeated him in 1878, but he bounced back to win by decision of Congress a

With the help of several black crewmen, Robert Smalls—
then twenty-three years old—commandeered the Planter, a
Confederate steamship used to transport guns and ammunition, and surrendered it to the Union vessel, U.S.S.
Onward. Smalls provided distinguished service to the
Union during the Civil War and after the war went on to
become a successful politician and businessman.

contested congressional election in 1880. He did not leave
the House of Representatives
for good until 1886, when he
lost another contested election
that had to be decided by
Congress.

In their efforts to defeat
him, Smalls's white opponents
frequently charged that he had
a hand in the corruption that
was allegedly rampant in
South Carolina during
Reconstruction. But careful
historical investigation shows
that he was, by the standards
of the time, an honest and responsible public servant. In the
South Carolina convention of
1868 and later in the state legislature, he was a conspicuous
champion of free and compulsory public education. In
Congress, he fought for the enactment and enforcement of federal civil rights
laws. Like other middle-class black political leaders in Reconstruction-era South
Carolina, he can perhaps be faulted in hindsight for not doing more to help poor
blacks gain access to land of their own. But in 1875, he sponsored congressional
legislation that opened for purchase at low prices the land in his own district that
had been confiscated by the federal government during the war. As a result,
blacks were able to buy most of it, and they soon owned three-fourths of the
land in Beaufort and its vicinity.

Smalls spent the later years of his life as U.S. collector of customs for the port
of Beaufort, a beneficiary of the patronage that the Republican party continued
to provide for a few loyal southern blacks. But the loss of real political clout for
Smalls and men like him was one of the tragic consequences of the fall of
Reconstruction.

For a brief period of years, black politicians exercised more power in the South
than they would for another century. A series of political developments on the national and regional stage made Reconstruction "an unfinished revolution,"
promising but not delivering true equality for newly freed African Americans.
National party politics, shifting priorities among Northern Republicans, and white
Southerners' commitment to white supremacy, which was backed by legal restrictions as well as massive extra-legal violence against blacks, all combined to stifle
the promise of Reconstruction. Yet the Reconstruction era also saw major transfor-
mations in American society in the wake of the Civil War—new ways of organizing
labor and family life, new institutions within and outside of the government, and

new ideologies regarding the role of institutions and government in social and economic life. Many of the changes begun during Reconstruction laid the groundwork for later revolutions in American life.

THE PRESIDENT VERSUS CONGRESS

The problem of how to reconstruct the Union in the wake of the South's military defeat was one of the most difficult and perplexing challenges American policy-makers ever faced. The Constitution provided no firm guidelines, for the framers had not anticipated a division of the country into warring sections. Emancipation compounded the problem with a new issue: How far should the federal government go to secure freedom and civil rights for four million former slaves?

The debate that evolved led to a major political crisis. Advocates of a minimal Reconstruction policy favored quick restoration of the Union with no protection for the freed slaves beyond the prohibition of slavery. Proponents of a more radical policy wanted readmission of the southern states to be dependent on guarantees that "loyal" men would displace the Confederate elite in positions of power and that blacks would acquire basic rights of American citizenship. The White House favored the minimal approach, whereas Congress came to endorse the more radical and thoroughgoing form of Reconstruction. The resulting struggle between Congress and the chief executive was the most serious clash between two branches of government in the nation's history.

WARTIME RECONSTRUCTION

Tension between the president and Congress over how to reconstruct the Union began during the war. Occupied mainly with achieving victory, Lincoln never set forth a final and comprehensive plan for bringing rebellious states back into the fold. But he did take initiatives that indicated he favored a lenient and conciliatory policy toward Southerners who would give up the struggle and repudiate slavery. In December 1863, he offered a full pardon to all Southerners (with the exception of certain classes of Confederate leaders) who would take an oath of allegiance to the Union and acknowledge the legality of emancipation. Once 10 percent or more of the voting population of any occupied state had taken the oath, they were authorized to set up a loyal government. By 1864, Louisiana and Arkansas, states that were wholly or partially occupied by Union troops, had established Unionist governments. Lincoln's policy was meant to shorten the war. First, he hoped to weaken the southern cause by making it easy for disillusioned or lukewarm Confederates to switch sides. Second, he hoped to further his emancipation policy by insisting that the new governments abolish slavery.

Congress was unhappy with the president's Reconstruction experiments and in 1864 refused to seat the Unionists elected to the House and Senate from Louisiana and Arkansas. A minority of congressional Republicans—the strongly antislavery Radicals—favored protection for black rights (especially black male suffrage) as a precondition for the readmission of southern states. But a larger group of congressional moderates opposed Lincoln's plan, not on the basis of black rights but because they did not trust the repentant Confederates who would play a major role in the new governments.

Congress also believed the president was exceeding his authority by using executive powers to restore the Union. Lincoln operated on the theory that secession, being illegal, did not place the Confederate states outside the Union in a constitutional sense. Since individuals and not states had defied federal authority, the president could use his pardoning power to certify a loyal electorate, which could then function as the legitimate state government. The dominant view in Congress, on the other hand, was that the southern states had forfeited their place in the Union and that it was up to Congress to decide when and how they would be readmitted.

After refusing to recognize Lincoln's 10 percent governments, Congress passed a Reconstruction bill of its own in July 1864. Known as the Wade-Davis Bill, this legislation required that 50 percent of the voters take an oath of future loyalty before the restoration process could begin. Once this had occurred, those who could swear they had never willingly supported the Confederacy could vote in an election for delegates to a constitutional convention. Lincoln exercised a pocket veto by refusing to sign the bill before Congress adjourned. He justified his action by announcing that he did not want to be committed to any single Reconstruction plan. The sponsors of the bill responded with an angry manifesto, and Lincoln's relations with Congress reached their low.

Congress and the president remained stalemated on the Reconstruction issue for the rest of the war. During his last months in office, however, Lincoln showed some willingness to compromise. However, he died without clarifying his intentions, leaving historians to speculate whether his quarrel with Congress would have worsened or been resolved. Given Lincoln's past record of political flexibility, the best bet is that he would have come to terms with the majority of his party.

ANDREW JOHNSON AT THE HELM

Andrew Johnson, the man suddenly made president by an assassin's bullet, attempted to put the Union back together on his own authority in 1865. But his policies eventually set him at odds with Congress and the Republican party and provoked the most serious crisis in the history of relations between the executive and legislative branches of the federal government.

Johnson's background shaped his approach to Reconstruction. Born in dire poverty in North Carolina, he migrated as a young man to eastern Tennessee, where he made his living as a tailor. Lacking formal schooling, he did not learn to read and write until adult life. Entering politics as a Jacksonian Democrat, he became known as an effective stump speaker. His railing against the planter aristocracy made him the spokesman for Tennessee's nonslaveholding whites and the most successful politician in the state. He advanced from state legislator to congressman to governor and in 1857 was elected to the U.S. Senate.

When Tennessee seceded in 1861, Johnson was the only senator from a Confederate state who remained loyal to the Union and continued to serve in

Washington. But his Unionism and defense of the common people did not include antislavery sentiments. While campaigning in Tennessee, he had objected only to the fact that slaveholding was the privilege of a wealthy minority. He revealed his attitude when he wished that "every head of family in the United States had one slave to take the drudgery and menial service off his family."

While acting as military governor of Tennessee during the war, Johnson implemented Lincoln's emancipation policy as a means of destroying the power of the hated planter class rather than as a recognition of black humanity. He was chosen as Lincoln's running mate in 1864 because it was thought that a pro-administration Democrat, who was also a southern Unionist, would strengthen the ticket. No one expected that this fervent white supremacist would become president.

Some Radical Republicans initially welcomed Johnson's ascent to the nation's highest office. Like the Radicals, he was fiercely loyal to the Union and thought that ex-Confederates should be severely treated. Only gradually did the deep disagreement between the president and the Republican Congressional majority become evident.

The Reconstruction policy that Johnson initiated on May 29, 1865, disturbed some Radicals, but most Republicans were willing to give it a chance. Johnson appointed provisional state governors chosen mostly from among prominent southern politicians who had opposed the secession movement and had rendered no conspicuous service to the Confederacy. The governors were responsible for calling constitutional conventions and ensuring that only "loyal" whites were permitted to vote for delegates. Confederate leaders and former officeholders who had participated in the rebellion were excluded. To regain their political and property rights, those in the exempted categories had to apply for individual presidential pardons. Johnson made one significant addition to the list of the excluded: all those possessing taxable property exceeding $20,000 in value. In this fashion, he sought to prevent the wealthy planters from participating in the Reconstruction of southern state governments.

Johnson urged the convention delegates to do three things: declare the ordinances of secession illegal, repudiate the Confederate debt, and ratify the Thirteenth Amendment abolishing slavery. After governments had been reestablished under constitutions meeting these conditions, the president assumed that the Reconstruction process would be complete and that the ex-Confederate states could regain their full rights under the Constitution.

The conventions did their work in a way satisfactory to the president but troubling to many congressional Republicans. Rather than quickly accepting Johnson's recommendations, delegates in several states approved them begrudgingly or with qualifications. Furthermore, all the resulting constitutions limited suffrage to whites, disappointing the large number of Northerners who hoped that at least some African Americans would be given the vote.

Republican uneasiness turned to disillusionment and anger when the state legislatures elected under the new constitutions proceeded to pass Black Codes subjecting former slaves to a variety of special regulations and restrictions on their freedom. Vagrancy and apprenticeship laws forced African Americans to work and denied them a free choice of employers. In some states, blacks could

"Slavery Is Dead?" asks this 1866 cartoon by Thomas Nast. To the cartoonist, the Emancipation Proclamation of 1863 and the North's victory in the Civil War meant little difference to the treatment of the freed slaves in the South. Freed slaves convicted of crimes often endured the same punishments as had slaves—sale, as depicted in the left panel of the cartoon, or beatings, as shown on the right.

not testify in court on the same basis as whites and were subject to a separate penal code. To Radicals, the Black Codes looked suspiciously like slavery under a new guise. More upsetting to northern public opinion in general, a number of prominent ex-Confederate leaders were elected to Congress in the fall of 1865.

Johnson himself was partly responsible for this turn of events. Despite his lifelong feud with the planter class, he was generous in granting pardons to members of the old elite who came to him, hat in hand, and asked for them. The growing rift between the president and Congress came into the open in December, when the House and Senate refused to seat the recently elected southern delegation. Instead of recognizing the state governments Johnson had called into being, Congress established a joint committee to review Reconstruction policy and set further conditions for readmission of the seceded states.

CONGRESS TAKES THE INITIATIVE

The struggle over how to reconstruct the Union ended with Congress doing the job of setting policy all over again. The clash between Johnson and Congress was a matter of principle and could not be reconciled. President Johnson, an heir of the Democratic states' rights tradition, wanted to restore the prewar federal system as quickly as possible and without change except that states would not have the right to legalize slavery or to secede.

Most Republicans wanted firm guarantees that the old southern ruling class would not regain regional power and national influence by devising new ways to subjugate blacks. They favored a Reconstruction policy that would give the federal government authority to limit the political role of ex-Confederates and provide some protection for black citizenship.

Except for a few extreme Radicals, Republican leaders did not believe that blacks were inherently equal to whites. They did agree, however, that in a modern democratic state, all citizens must have the same basic rights and opportunities, regardless of natural abilities. Principle coincided easily with political expediency; southern blacks were likely to be loyal to the Republican party that had emancipated them and thus increase that party's political power in the South.

The disagreement between the president and Congress became irreconcilable in early 1866, when Johnson vetoed two bills that had passed with overwhelming Republican support. The first extended the life of the Freedmen's Bureau—a temporary agency set up to aid the former slaves by providing relief, education, legal help, and assistance in obtaining land or employment. The second was a civil rights bill meant to nullify the Black Codes and guarantee to freedmen "full and equal benefit of all laws and proceedings for the security of person and property as is enjoyed by white citizens."

Johnson's vetoes shocked moderate Republicans who had expected the president to accept the relatively modest measures. Johnson succeeded in blocking the Freedmen's Bureau bill, although a modified version later passed. But Congress overrode his veto of the Civil Rights Act, signifying that the president was now hopelessly at odds with most of the congressmen from what was supposed to be his own party. Never before had Congress overridden a presidential veto.

Johnson soon revealed that he intended to abandon the Republicans and place himself at the head of a new conservative party uniting the small minority of Republicans who supported him with a reviving Democratic party that was rallying behind his Reconstruction policy. He helped found the National Union movement to promote his plan to readmit the southern states to the Union without further qualifications. A National Union convention meeting in Philadelphia in August 1866 called for the election to Congress of men who endorsed the presidential plan for Reconstruction.

Meanwhile, the Republican majority on Capitol Hill, fearing that Johnson would not enforce civil rights legislation or that the courts would declare such federal laws unconstitutional, passed the Fourteenth Amendment. This, perhaps the most important of all our constitutional amendments, gave the federal government responsibility for guaranteeing equal rights under the law to all Americans. Section 1 defined national citizenship for the first time as extending to "all persons born or naturalized in the United States." The states were prohibited from abridging the rights of American citizens and could not "deprive any person of life, liberty, or property, without due process of law; nor deny to any person . . . equal protection of the laws." The amendment was sent to the states with the understanding that Southerners would have no chance of being readmitted to Congress unless their states ratified it.

RECONSTRUCTION AMENDMENTS, 1865–1870

AMENDMENT	MAIN PROVISIONS	CONGRESSIONAL PASSAGE (2/3 MAJORITY IN EACH HOUSE REQUIRED)	RATIFICATION PROCESS (3/4 OF ALL STATES REQUIRED, INCLUDING EX-CONFEDERATE STATES)
13	Slavery prohibited in United States	January 1865	December 1865 (27 states, including 8 southern states)
14	1. National citizenship 2. State representation in Congress reduced proportionally to number of voters disfranchised 3. Former Confederates denied right to hold office 4. Confederate debt repudiated	June 1866	Rejected by 12 southern and border states, February 1867; Radicals make readmission of southern states hinge on ratification; ratified July 1868
15	Denial of franchise because of race, color, or past servitude explicitly prohibited	February 1869	Ratification required for readmission of Virginia, Texas, Mississippi, Georgia; ratified March 1870

The congressional elections of 1866 served as a referendum on the Fourteenth Amendment. Johnson opposed the amendment on the grounds that it created a "centralized" government and denied states the right to manage their own affairs. All the southern states except Tennessee rejected the amendment. But the publicity resulting from bloody race riots in New Orleans and Memphis weakened the president's case for state autonomy. Atrocities against blacks made it clear that the existing southern state governments were failing abysmally to protect the "life, liberty, or property" of the ex-slaves.

Johnson further weakened his cause by taking the stump on behalf of candidates who supported his policies. He toured the nation, slandering his opponents in crude language. Johnson's behavior enraged northern voters, who repudiated the administration in the 1866 elections. The Republican majority in Congress increased to a solid two-thirds in both houses, and the Radical wing of the party gained strength at the expense of moderates and conservatives.

CONGRESSIONAL RECONSTRUCTION PLAN ENACTED

Congress was now in a position to implement its own plan of Reconstruction. In 1867 and 1868, it passed a series of acts that nullified the president's initiatives and reorganized the South on a new basis. Generally referred to as Radical Reconstruction, the measures actually represented a compromise between genuine Radicals and more moderate elements within the party.

Consistent Radicals such as Senator Charles Sumner of Massachusetts and Congressmen Thaddeus Stevens of Pennsylvania and George Julian of Indiana

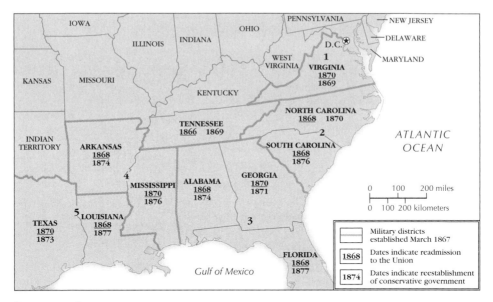

Reconstruction
During the Reconstruction era, the southern state governments passed through three phases: control by white ex-Confederates; domination by Republican legislators, both white and black; and, finally, the regaining of control by conservative white Democrats.

wanted to reshape southern society before readmitting ex-Confederates to the Union. Their plan required an extended period of military rule, confiscation and redistribution of large landholdings among the freedmen, and federal aid for schools to educate blacks and whites for citizenship. But the majority of Republican congressmen found such a program unacceptable because it broke too sharply with American traditions of federalism and regard for property rights.

The First Reconstruction Act, passed over Johnson's veto on March 2, 1867, reorganized the region into five military districts. But military rule would last for only a short time. Acts in 1867 and 1868 opened the way for the quick readmission of any state that framed and ratified a new constitution providing for black suffrage. Since blacks but not ex-Confederates were allowed to vote for delegates to the constitutional conventions or in the elections to ratify the conventions' work, Republicans thought they had found a way to ensure that "loyal" men would dominate the new governments.

Radical Reconstruction was based on the dubious assumption that once blacks had the vote, they would have the power to protect themselves against white supremacists' efforts to deny them their rights. The Reconstruction Acts thus signaled a retreat from the true Radical position that a sustained use of federal authority was needed to complete the transition from slavery to freedom and prevent the resurgence of the South's old ruling class. Most Republicans were unwilling to embrace centralized government and an extended period of military rule over civilians.

Even so, congressional Reconstruction did have a radical aspect. It strongly supported the cause of black male suffrage. Enabling people who were so poor and downtrodden to have access to the ballot box was a bold and innovative application of the principle of government by the consent of the governed. The problem was finding a way to enforce equal suffrage under conditions then existing in the postwar South.

THE IMPEACHMENT CRISIS

The first obstacle to enforcement of congressional Reconstruction was resistance from the White House. Johnson disapproved of the new policy and sought to thwart the will of Congress. He dismissed officeholders who sympathized with Radical Reconstruction, and he countermanded the orders of generals in charge of southern military districts who were zealous in their enforcement of the new legislation. Congress responded by passing laws designed to limit presidential authority over Reconstruction matters. One of the measures was the Tenure of Office Act, requiring Senate approval for the removal of cabinet officers and other officials whose appointment had needed the consent of the Senate. Another measure sought to limit Johnson's authority to issue orders to military commanders.

Johnson objected vigorously to the restrictions on the grounds that they violated the constitutional doctrine of the separation of powers. When it became clear that the president would do all in his power to resist the establishment of Radical regimes in the southern states, some congressmen began to call for his impeachment. When Johnson tried to discharge Secretary of War Edwin Stanton, the only Radical in the cabinet, the pro-impeachment forces gained in strength.

In January 1868, Johnson ordered General Grant to replace Stanton as head of the War Department. But Grant had his eye on the Republican presidential nomination and refused to defy Congress. Johnson then appointed General Lorenzo Thomas, who agreed to serve. Faced with this apparent violation of the Tenure of Office Act, the House voted overwhelmingly on February 24 to impeach the president, and he was placed on trial before the Senate.

Because seven Republican senators broke with the party leadership and voted for acquittal, the effort to convict Johnson and remove him from office fell one vote short of the necessary two-thirds. This outcome resulted in part from a skillful defense. Attorneys for the president argued for a narrow interpretation of the constitutional provision that a president could be impeached only for "high crimes and misdemeanors," asserting that this referred only to indictable offenses. Responding to the charge that Johnson had deliberately violated the Tenure of Office Act, the defense contended that the law did not apply to the removal of Stanton because he had been appointed by Lincoln, not Johnson.

The prosecution countered with a different interpretation of the Tenure of Office Act, but the core of their case was that Johnson had abused the powers of his office in an effort to sabotage the congressional Reconstruction policy. Obstructing the will of the legislative branch, they claimed, was sufficient grounds for conviction. The Republicans who voted for acquittal could not endorse such a broad view of the impeachment power. They feared that removal of a president for essentially political reasons would threaten the constitutional balance of powers and open the way to legislative supremacy over the executive.

The impeachment episode helped create an impression in the public mind that the Radicals were ready to turn the Constitution to their own use to gain their objectives. But the evidence of congressional ruthlessness and illegality is not as strong as most historians used to think. Modern legal scholars have found merit in the Radicals' claim that their actions did not violate the Constitution.

Failure to remove Johnson from office was an embarrassment to congressional Republicans, but the episode did ensure that Reconstruction in the South would proceed as the majority in Congress intended. During the trial, Johnson helped influence the verdict by pledging to enforce the Reconstruction Acts, and he held to this promise during his remaining months in office. Unable to depose the president, the Radicals had at least succeeded in neutralizing his opposition to their program.

RECONSTRUCTING SOUTHERN SOCIETY

The Civil War left the South devastated, demoralized, and destitute. Slavery was dead, but what this meant for future relationships between whites and blacks was still in doubt. Most southern whites wanted to keep blacks adrift between slavery and freedom—without political or civil rights. Blacks sought independence and viewed the acquisition of land, education, and the vote as the best means of achieving this goal. The thousands of Northerners who went south after the war hoped to extend Yankee "civilization" to what they viewed as an unenlightened and barbarous region. For most of them, this reformation required aiding the freed slaves.

The struggle of these groups to achieve their conflicting goals bred chaos, violence, and instability. This was scarcely an ideal setting for an experiment in interracial democracy, but one was attempted nonetheless. With massive and sustained support from the federal government, progressive reform could be achieved. When such support faltered, the forces of reaction and white supremacy were unleashed.

REORGANIZING LAND AND LABOR

The Civil War scarred the southern landscape and wrecked its economy. One devastated area—central South Carolina—looked to an 1865 observer "like a broad black streak of ruin and desolation." Several major cities—including Atlanta, Columbia, and Richmond—were gutted by fire. Most factories were dismantled or destroyed, and long stretches of railroad were torn up.

Nor was there adequate investment capital available for rebuilding. The substantial wealth represented by Confederate currency and bonds had melted away, and emancipation of the slaves had divested the propertied classes of their most valuable and productive assets. According to some estimates, the South's per capita wealth in 1865 was only about half what it had been in 1860.

Recovery could not even begin until a new labor system replaced slavery. It was widely assumed in both the North and the South that southern prosperity would continue to depend on cotton and that the plantation was the most efficient unit for producing the crop. Hindering efforts to rebuild the plantation economy were lack of capital, the deep-rooted belief of southern whites that blacks would work only under compulsion, and the freedpeople's resistance to labor conditions that recalled slavery.

Blacks strongly preferred to determine their own economic relationships, and for a time they had reason to hope the federal government would support their ambitions. Although they were grateful for the federal aid in ending slavery, freed slaves often had ideas about freedom that contradicted the plans of their northern allies. Many ex-slaves wanted to hold on to the family-based communal work methods that they utilized during slavery rather than adopt the individual piecework system northern capitalists promoted. They resisted becoming wage laborers who produced exclusively for a market. Finally, freed slaves often wanted to stay on the land their families had spent generations farming rather than move elsewhere to assume plots of land as individual farmers.

While not guaranteeing all of the freed slaves' hopes for economic self-determination, the northern military attempted to establish a new economic base for the freed men and women. General Sherman issued an order in January 1865 that set aside the islands and coastal areas of Georgia and South Carolina for exclusive black occupancy on 40-acre plots. The Freedmen's Bureau was given control of hundreds of thousands of acres of abandoned or confiscated land and was authorized to make 40-acre grants to black settlers for three-year periods. By June 1865, forty thousand black farmers were at work on 300,000 acres of what they thought would be their own land.

But for most of them the dream of "forty acres and a mule" was not to be realized. Neither President Johnson nor Congress supported any effective program of land confiscation and redistribution. Consequently, most blacks in physical possession of small farms failed to acquire title, and the mass of freedmen were left with little or no prospect of becoming landowners. Recalling the plight of southern blacks in 1865, an ex-slave later wrote that "they were set free without a dollar, without a foot of land, and without the wherewithal to get the next meal even."

Despite their poverty and landlessness, ex-slaves were reluctant to settle down and commit themselves to wage labor for their former masters. Many took to the road, hoping to find something better. Some were still expecting grants of land, but others were simply trying to increase their bargaining power. As the end of 1865 approached, many freedmen had still not signed up for the coming season; anxious planters feared that blacks were plotting to seize land by force. Within a few weeks, however, most holdouts signed for the best terms they could get.

The most common form of agricultural employment in 1866 was a contract labor system. Under this system, workers committed themselves for a year in return for fixed wages, a substantial portion of which was withheld until after the

The Civil War brought emancipation to slaves, but the sharecropping system kept many of them economically bound to their employers. At the end of a year the sharecropper tenants might owe most—or all—of what they had made to their landlord. Here a sharecropping family poses in front of their cabin. Ex-slaves often built their living quarters near woods in order to have a ready supply of fuel for heating and cooking. The cabin's chimney lists away from the house so that it can be easily pushed away from the living quarters should it catch fire.

harvest. The Freedmen's Bureau assumed responsibility for reviewing the contracts and enforcing them. But bureau officials had differing notions of what it meant to protect African Americans from exploitation. Some stood up strongly for the rights of the freedmen; others served as allies of the planters.

Growing up alongside the contract system and eventually displacing it was an alternative capital-labor relationship—sharecropping. Under this system, blacks worked a piece of land independently for a fixed share of the crop, usually one-half. Credit-starved landlords liked this arrangement because it did not require much expenditure in advance of the harvest and the tenant shared the risks of crop failure or a fall in cotton prices.

Blacks initially viewed sharecropping as a step up from wage labor in the direction of landownership. But during the 1870s, this form of tenancy evolved into a new kind of servitude. Croppers had to live on credit until their cotton was sold, and planters or merchants seized the chance to "provision" them at high prices and exorbitant rates of interest. Creditors were entitled to deduct what was owed to them out of the tenant's share of the crop, and this left most sharecroppers with no net profit at the end of the year—more often than not with a debt that had to be worked off in subsequent years.

BLACK CODES: A NEW NAME FOR SLAVERY?

While landless African Americans in the countryside were being reduced to economic dependence, those in towns and cities found themselves living in an increasingly segregated society. The Black Codes of 1865 attempted to require separation of the races in public places and facilities; when most of the codes were overturned by federal authorities as violations of the Civil Rights Act of 1866, the same end was often achieved through private initiative and community pressure. Blacks found it almost impossible to gain admittance to most hotels, restaurants, and other privately owned establishments catering to whites. Although separate black, or "Jim Crow," cars were not yet the rule on railroads, African Americans were often denied first-class accommodations. After 1868, black-supported Republican governments passed civil rights acts requiring equal access to public facilities, but little effort was made to enforce the legislation.

The Black Codes had other onerous provisions meant to control African Americans and return them to quasi-slavery. Most codes required blacks to make long-term contracts with white employers or be arrested for vagrancy. Others limited the rights of African Americans to own property or engage in occupations other than those of servant or laborer. Even after the codes were set aside, vagrancy laws remained in force across the South.

Furthermore, private violence and discrimination against blacks continued on a massive scale unchecked by state authorities. Hundreds, perhaps thousands, of blacks were murdered by whites in 1865–1866, and few of the perpetrators were brought to justice. The imposition of military rule in 1867 was designed in part to protect former slaves from such violence and intimidation, but the task was beyond the capacity of the few thousand troops stationed in the South. When new constitutions were approved and states readmitted to the Union under the congressional plan in 1868, the problem became more severe. White opponents of Radical Reconstruction adopted systematic terrorism and organized mob violence to keep blacks away from the polls.

The freed slaves tried to defend themselves by organizing their own militia groups. However, they were not powerful enough to overcome the growing power of the anti-Republican forces. As the military presence was progressively reduced, the new Republican regimes had to fight a losing battle against armed white supremacists.

REPUBLICAN RULE IN THE SOUTH

Hastily organized in 1867, the southern Republican party dominated the constitution making of 1868 and the regimes that came out of it. The party was an attempted coalition of three social groups: newly enfranchised blacks, poor white farmers, and businessmen seeking government aid for private enterprise. Many Republicans in this third group were recent arrivals from the North—the so-called carpetbaggers—but some were "scalawags," former Whig planters or merchants who were born in the South or had immigrated to the region before the war and now saw a chance to realize their dreams for commercial and industrial development.

White owners of small farms expected the party to favor their interests at the expense of the wealthy landowners and to come to their aid with special legislation when they faced the loss of their homesteads to creditors. Blacks formed the vast majority of the Republican rank and file in most states and were concerned mainly with education, civil rights, and landownership.

Under the best of conditions, these coalitions would have been difficult to maintain. Each group had its own distinct goals and did not fully support the aims of the other segments. White yeomen, for example, had a deeply rooted resistance to black equality. And for how long could one expect essentially conservative businessmen to support costly measures for the elevation or relief of the lower classes of either race? Some Democratic politicians exploited these divisions by appealing to disaffected white Republicans.

But during the relatively brief period when they were in power in the South, the Republicans chalked up some notable achievements. They established (on paper at least) the South's first adequate systems of public education, democratized state and local government, and appropriated funds for an enormous expansion of public services and responsibilities.

Important as these social and political reforms were, they took second place to the Republicans' major effort—to foster economic development and restore southern prosperity by subsidizing the construction of railroads and other internal improvements. But the policy of aiding railroads turned out to be disastrous. Extravagance, corruption, and routes laid out in response to local political pressure rather than on sound economic grounds made for an increasing burden of public debt and taxation; the policy did not produce the promised payoff of efficient, cheap transportation. Subsidized railroads frequently went bankrupt, leaving the taxpayers holding the bag. When the Panic of 1873 brought many southern state governments to the verge of bankruptcy and railroad building came to an end, it was clear the Republicans' "gospel of prosperity" through state aid to private enterprise had failed miserably. Their political opponents, many of whom had originally favored such policies, now saw an opportunity to take advantage of the situation by charging that Republicans had ruined the southern economy.

In general, the Radical regimes failed to conduct public business honestly and efficiently. Embezzlement of public funds and bribery of state lawmakers or officials were common occurrences. State debts and tax burdens rose enormously, mainly because governments had undertaken heavy new responsibilities, but partly because of waste and graft.

Yet southern corruption was not exceptional, nor was it a special result of the extension of suffrage to uneducated African Americans, as critics of Radical Reconstruction have claimed. It was part of a national pattern during an era when private interests considered buying government favors to be a part of the cost of doing business.

Blacks bore only a limited responsibility for the dishonesty of the Radical governments. Although sixteen African Americans served in Congress—two in the Senate—between 1869 and 1880, only in South Carolina did blacks constitute a majority of even one house of the state legislature. Furthermore, no black governors were elected during Reconstruction (although Pinkney B. S. Pinchback served for a time as acting governor of Louisiana). The biggest grafters were opportunistic whites. Some black legislators went with the tide and accepted "loans" from those railroad lobbyists who would pay most for their votes, but the same men could usually be depended on to vote the will of their constituents on civil rights or educational issues. Contrary to myth, the small number of African Americans elected to state or national office during Reconstruction demonstrated on the average more integrity and competence than their white counterparts.

If blacks served or supported corrupt and wasteful regimes, it was because they had no practical alternative. Although the Democrats, or Conservatives as they called themselves in some states, made sporadic efforts to attract African American voters, it was clear that if they won control, they would attempt to strip blacks of their civil and political rights. But opponents of Radical Reconstruction were able to capitalize on racial prejudice and persuade many Americans that "good government" was synonymous with white supremacy.

CLAIMING PUBLIC AND PRIVATE RIGHTS

As important as party politics to the changing political culture of the Reconstruction South were the ways that freed slaves claimed rights for themselves. They did so not only in negotiations with employers and in public meetings and convention halls, but also through the institutions they created, and perhaps most important, the households they formed.

As one black corporal in the Union Army told an audience of ex-slaves, "The Marriage covenant is at the foundation of all our rights. In slavery we could not have *legalized* marriage: *now* we have it . . . and we shall be established as a people." Through marriage, African Americans claimed citizenship. Freedmen hoped that marriage would allow them to take on not only political rights, but also the right to control the labor of wives and children.

While they were in effect in 1865–1866, many states' Black Codes included apprenticeship provisions, providing for freed children to be apprenticed by courts to some white person (with preference given to former masters) if their parents were paupers, unemployed, of "bad character," or even simply if it were found to be "better for the habits and comfort of a child." Ex-slaves struggled to win their children back from what often amounted to re-enslavement for arbitrary reasons. Freedpeople challenged the apprenticeship system in county courts, and through the Freedmen's Bureau.

While many former slaves lined up eagerly to formalize their marriages, many also retained their own definitions of marriage. Perhaps as many as 50 percent of ex-slaves chose not to marry legally. African American leaders worried about this refusal to follow white norms. Yet many poor blacks continued to recognize as husband and wife people who cared for and supported one another without benefit of legal sanction. The new legal system punished couples who deviated from the legal norm through laws against bastardy, adultery, and fornication. Furthermore, the Freedmen's Bureau made the marriage of freedpeople a priority so that husbands, rather than the federal government, would be legally responsible for families' support.

Some ex-slaves used the courts to assert rights against white people as well as other blacks, suing over domestic violence, child support, assault, and debt.

A Freedmen's school, one of the more successful endeavors supported by the Freedmen's Bureau. The Bureau, working with teachers from northern abolitionist and missionary societies, founded thousands of schools for freed slaves and poor whites.

Freedwomen sued their husbands for desertion and alimony, in order to enlist the Freedman's Bureau to help them claim property from men. Other ex-slaves mobilized kin networks and other community resources to make claims on property and family.

Immediately after the war, freedpeople flocked to create institutions that had been denied to them under slavery: churches, fraternal and benevolent associations, political organizations, and schools. Many joined all-black denominations such as the African Methodist Episcopal church, which provided freedom from white dominance and a more congenial style of worship. Black women formed all-black chapters of organizations like the Woman's Christian Temperance Union, and their own women's clubs to oppose lynching and work for "uplift" in the black community.

A top priority for most ex-slaves was the opportunity to educate their children; the first schools for freedpeople were all-black institutions established by the Freedmen's Bureau and various northern missionary societies. At the time, having been denied all education during the antebellum period, most blacks viewed separate schooling as an opportunity rather than as a form of discrimination. However, these schools were precursors to the segregated public school systems first instituted by Republican governments.

In a variety of ways, African American men and women during Reconstruction claimed freedom in the "private" realm as well as the public sphere, by claiming rights to their own families and building their own institutions. They did so in the face of the vigorous efforts of their former masters as well as the new government agencies to control their private lives and shape their new identities as husbands, wives, and citizens.

RETREAT FROM RECONSTRUCTION

The era of Reconstruction began coming to an end almost before it started. Although it was only a scant three years from the end of the Civil War, the impeachment crisis of 1868 represented the high point of popular interest in Reconstruction issues. That year, Ulysses S. Grant was elected president. Many historians blame Grant for the corruption of his administration and for the inconsistency and failure of his southern policy. He had neither the vision nor the sense of duty to tackle the difficult challenges the nation faced. From 1868 on, political issues besides southern Reconstruction moved to the forefront of national politics, and the plight of African Americans in the South receded in white consciousness.

RISE OF THE MONEY QUESTION

In the years immediately following the Civil War, another issue already competing for public attention was the "money question": whether to allow "greenbacks"—paper money issued during the war—to continue to circulate or to return to "sound" or "hard" money, meaning gold or silver. Supporters of paper money, known as greenbackers, were strongest in the credit-hungry West and among expansion-minded manufacturers. Defenders of hard money were mostly the commercial and financial interests in the East; they received crucial support from intellectuals who regarded government-sponsored inflation as immoral or contrary to the natural laws of classical economics.

In 1868, the money question surged briefly to the forefront of national politics. Faced with a business recession blamed on the Johnson administration's policy of contracting the currency, Congress voted to stop the retirement of greenbacks. The Democratic party, responding to Midwestern pressure, included in its platform for the 1868 national election a plan calling for the redemption of much of the Civil War debt in greenbacks rather than gold. Yet they nominated for president a sound-money supporter, so that the greenback question never became an issue in the 1868 presidential campaign. Grant, already a popular general, won the election handily with the help of the Republican-dominated Southern states.

In 1869 and 1870, a Republican-controlled Congress passed laws that assured payment in gold to most bondholders but eased the burden of the huge Civil War

THE ELECTION OF 1868

CANDIDATE	PARTY	POPULAR VOTE	ELECTORAL VOTE
Grant	Republican	3,012,833	214
Seymour	Democratic	2,703,249	80
Not voted*			23

*Unreconstructed states did not participate in the election.

debt by exchanging bonds soon coming due for those that would not be payable for ten, fifteen, or thirty years. In this way, the public credit was protected.

Still unresolved, however, was the problem of what to do about the $356 million in greenbacks that remained in circulation. Hard-money proponents wanted to retire them quickly; inflationists thought more should be issued to stimulate the economy. The Grant administration decided to allow the greenbacks to float until economic expansion would bring them to a par with gold, thus permitting a painless return to specie payments. But the Panic of 1873, which brought much of the economy to its knees, led to a revival of agitation to inflate the currency. Debt-ridden farmers, who would be the backbone of the greenback movement for years to come, now joined the soft-money clamor for the first time.

Responding to the money and credit crunch, Congress moved in 1874 to authorize a modest issue of new greenbacks. But Grant, influenced by the opinions of hard-money financiers, vetoed the bill. In 1875, Congress enacted the Specie Resumption Act, which provided for a limited reduction of greenbacks leading to full resumption of specie payments by January 1, 1879. Its action was widely interpreted as deflation in the midst of depression. Farmers and workers, who were already suffering acutely from deflation, reacted with dismay and anger.

The Democratic Party could not capitalize adequately on these sentiments because of the influence of its own hard-money faction, and in 1876 an independent Greenback party entered the national political arena. The party's nominee for president received an insignificant number of votes, but in 1878 the Greenback Labor party polled more than a million votes and elected fourteen congressmen. The Greenbackers were able to keep the money issue alive into the following decade.

FINAL EFFORTS OF RECONSTRUCTION

The Republican effort to make equal rights for blacks the law of the land culminated in the Fifteenth Amendment. Passed by Congress in 1869 and ratified by the states in 1870, the amendment prohibited any state from denying a citizen the right to vote because of race, color, or previous condition of servitude. A more radical version, requiring universal manhood suffrage, was rejected partly because it departed too sharply from traditional views of federal-state relations. States therefore could still limit the suffrage by imposing literacy tests, property qualifications, or poll taxes allegedly applying to all racial groups; such devices would eventually be used to strip southern blacks of the right to vote. But the makers of the amendment did not foresee this result.

Many feminists were bitterly disappointed that the amendment did not extend the vote to women as well as freedmen. A militant wing of the women's rights movement, led by Elizabeth Cady Stanton and Susan B. Anthony, was so angered that the Constitution was being amended in a way that, in effect, made gender a qualification for voting that they campaigned against ratification of the Fifteenth Amendment. Another group of feminists led by Lucy Stone supported the amendment on the grounds that this was "the Negro's hour" and that women could afford to wait a few years for the vote. This disagreement divided the woman suffrage movement for a generation to come.

The Grant administration was charged with enforcing the amendment and protecting black men's voting rights in the reconstructed states. Since survival of the Republican regimes depended on African American support, political partisanship dictated federal action, even though the North's emotional and ideological commitment to black citizenship was waning.

Between 1868 and 1872, the main threat to southern Republican regimes came from the Ku Klux Klan and other secret societies bent on restoring white supremacy by intimidating blacks who sought to exercise their political rights. First organized in

This 1868 photograph shows typical regalia of members of the Ku Klux Klan, a secret white supremacist organization. Before elections, hooded Klansmen terrorized African Americans to discourage them from voting.

Tennessee in 1866, the Klan spread rapidly to other states, adopting increasingly lawless and brutal tactics. A grassroots vigilante movement and not a centralized conspiracy, the Klan thrived on local initiative and gained support from whites of all social classes. Its secrecy, decentralization, popular support, and utter ruthlessness made it very difficult to suppress. As soon as blacks had been granted the right to vote, hooded "night riders" began to visit the cabins of those who were known to be active Republicans; some victims were only threatened, but others were whipped or even murdered.

In the presidential election of 1868, Grant lost in Louisiana and Georgia mainly because the Klan—or the Knights of the White Camellia, as the Louisiana variant was called—launched a reign of terror to prevent prospective black voters from exercising their rights. Political violence claimed more than a thousand lives in Louisiana, and more than two hundred Republicans, including a congressman, were assassinated in Arkansas. Thereafter, Klan terrorism was directed mainly at Republican state governments. Virtual insurrections broke out in Arkansas, Tennessee, North Carolina, and parts of South Carolina. Republican governors called out the state militia to fight the Klan, but only the Arkansas militia succeeded in bringing it to heel. In Tennessee, North Carolina, and Georgia, Klan activities helped undermine Republican control, thus allowing the Democrats to come to power in all of these states by 1870.

In 1870–1871, Congress passed a series of laws to enforce the Fifteenth Amendment by providing federal protection for black suffrage and authorizing use of the army against the Klan. The Ku Klux Klan or Force acts made interference with voting rights a federal crime and established provisions for government supervision of elections. The legislation also empowered the president to call out troops and suspend the writ of habeas corpus to quell insurrection. Thousands of suspected Klansmen were arrested by the military or U.S. marshals, and the writ was suspended in nine counties of South Carolina that had been virtually taken over by the secret order. Although most of the accused Klansmen were never brought to trial, were acquitted, or received suspended sentences, the enforcement effort was vigorous enough to put a damper on hooded terrorism and ensure relatively fair and peaceful elections in 1872.

A heavy black turnout in these elections enabled the Republicans to hold on to power in most states of the Deep South, despite efforts of the Democratic-Conservative opposition to cut into the Republican vote by taking moderate positions on racial and economic issues. This setback prompted the Democratic-Conservatives to make a significant change in their strategy and ideology. No longer did they try to take votes away from the Republicans by proclaiming support for black suffrage and government aid to business. Instead, they began to appeal openly to white supremacy and to the traditional Democratic and agrarian hostility to government promotion of economic development. Consequently, they were able to bring back to the polls a portion of the white electorate, mostly small farmers.

This new and more effective electoral strategy dovetailed with a resurgence of violence meant to reduce Republican, especially black Republican, voting. The new reign of terror differed from the previous Klan episode; its agents no longer wore masks but acted quite openly. They were effective because the northern public was increasingly disenchanted with federal intervention on behalf of what were widely viewed as corrupt and tottering Republican regimes. Grant used force in the South for the last time in 1874 when an overt paramilitary organization in Louisiana, known as the White League, tried to overthrow a Republican government accused of stealing an election. When an unofficial militia in Mississippi instigated a series of bloody race riots prior to the state elections of 1875, Grant refused the governor's request for federal troops. Intimidation kept black from the polls, and Mississippi fell to the Democratic-Conservatives.

By 1876, Republicans held on to only three southern states: South Carolina, Louisiana, and Florida. Partly because of Grant's hesitant and inconsistent use of presidential power, but mainly because the northern electorate would no longer tolerate military action to sustain Republican governments and black voting rights, Radical Reconstruction was falling into total eclipse.

SPOILSMEN VERSUS REFORMERS

One reason Grant found it increasingly difficult to take strong action to protect southern Republicans was the accusation by reformers that a corrupt national administration was propping up bad governments in the South for personal and partisan advantage.

The Republican party in the Grant era was losing the idealism and high purpose associated with the crusade against slavery. By the beginning of the 1870s, the men who had been the conscience of the party were either dead, out of office, or at odds with the administration. New leaders of a different stamp, whom historians have dubbed "spoilsmen" or "politicos," were taking their place. When he made common cause with hard-boiled manipulators such as senators Roscoe Conkling of New York and James G. Blaine of Maine, Grant lost credibility with reform-minded Republicans.

THE ELECTION OF 1872

CANDIDATE	PARTY	POPULAR VOTE	ELECTORAL VOTE*
Grant	Republican	3,597,132	286
Greeley	Democratic and Liberal Republican	2,834,125	Greeley died before the electoral college voted.

*Out of a total of 366 electoral votes. Greeley's votes were divided among the four minor candidates.

During Grant's first administration, an aura of scandal surrounded the White House but did not directly implicate the president. In 1869, the financial buccaneer Jay Gould enlisted the aid of a brother-in-law of Grant to further his fantastic scheme to corner the gold market. Gould failed in the attempt, but he did manage to save himself and come away with a huge profit.

Grant's first-term vice president, Schuyler Colfax of Indiana, was directly involved in the notorious Crédit Mobilier scandal. Crédit Mobilier was a construction company that actually served as a fraudulent device for siphoning off profits that should have gone to the stockholders of the Union Pacific Railroad, which was the beneficiary of massive federal land grants. In order to forestall government inquiry into this arrangement, Crédit Mobilier stock was distributed to influential congressmen, including Colfax (who was speaker of the House before he was elected vice president). The whole business came to light just before the campaign of 1872.

Republicans who could not tolerate such corruption or had other grievances against the administration broke with Grant in 1872 and formed a third party committed to "honest government" and "reconciliation" between the North and the South. These Liberal Republicans endorsed reform of the civil service to curb the corruption-breeding patronage system and advocated a laissez-faire economic policy of low tariffs, an end to government subsidies for railroads, and hard money. Despite their rhetoric of idealism and reform, the Liberal Republicans were extremely conservative in their notions of what government should do to assure justice for blacks and other underprivileged Americans.

The Liberal Republicans' national convention nominated Horace Greeley, editor of the respected New York *Tribune*. This was a curious and divisive choice, since Greeley was at odds with the founders of the movement on the tariff question and was indifferent to civil service reform. The Democrats also nominated Greeley, mainly because he promised to end Radical Reconstruction by restoring "self-government" to the South. Greeley, however, did not attract support and was soundly defeated by Grant.

Grant's second administration seemed to bear out the reformers' worst suspicions about corruption in high places. In 1875, the public learned that federal revenue officials had conspired with distillers to defraud the government of millions of dollars in liquor taxes. Grant's private secretary, Orville E. Babcock, was indicted as a member of the "Whiskey Ring" and was saved from conviction only by the president's personal intercession. The next year, Grant's secretary of war, William W. Belknap, was impeached by the House after an investigation revealed he had taken bribes for the sale of Indian trading posts. He avoided conviction in the Senate only by resigning from office before his trial.

There is no evidence that Ulysses S. Grant profited personally from any of the misdeeds of his subordinates. Yet he is not entirely without blame for the corruption in his administration. He failed to take firm action against the malefactors, and, even after their guilt had been clearly established, he sometimes tried to shield them from justice. Grant was the only president between Jackson and Wilson to serve two full and consecutive terms. But unlike other chief executives so favored by the electorate, Grant is commonly regarded as a failure. Although the problems he faced would have challenged any president, the shame of Grant's administration was that he made loyalty to old friends a higher priority than civil rights or sound economic principles.

REUNION AND THE NEW SOUTH

The end of Radical Reconstruction in 1877 opened the way to a reconciliation of North and South. But the costs of reunion were high for less privileged groups in the South. The civil and political rights of African Americans, left unprotected, were progressively and relentlessly stripped away by white supremacist regimes. Lower-class whites saw their interests sacrificed to those of capitalists and landlords. Despite the rhetoric hailing a prosperous "New South," the region remained poor and open to exploitation by northern business interests.

THE COMPROMISE OF 1877

The election of 1876 pitted Rutherford B. Hayes of Ohio, a Republican governor untainted by the scandals of the Grant era, against Governor Samuel J. Tilden of New York, a Democratic reformer. Honest government was apparently the electorate's highest priority. When the returns came in, Tilden had clearly won the popular vote and seemed likely to win a narrow victory in the electoral college. But the result was placed in doubt when the returns from the three southern states still controlled by the Republicans—South Carolina, Florida, and Louisiana—were contested. If Hayes were to be awarded these three states, plus one contested electoral vote in Oregon, Republican strategists realized, he would triumph in the electoral college by a single vote.

The outcome of the election remained undecided for months. To resolve the impasse, Congress appointed a special electoral commission of fifteen members to determine who would receive the votes of the disputed states. The commission split along party lines and voted 8 to 7 to award Hayes all of the disputed votes. But this decision still had to be ratified by Congress, and in the House there was strong Democratic opposition.

THE ELECTION OF 1876

CANDIDATE	PARTY	POPULAR VOTE	UNCONTESTED ELECTORAL VOTE	ELECTORAL TOTAL
Hayes	Republican	4,036,298	165	185
Tilden	Democratic	4,300,590	184	184
Cooper	Greenback	81,737	—	—

To ensure Hayes's election, Republican leaders negotiated secretly with conservative southern Democrats, some of whom seemed willing to abandon the filibuster if the last troops were withdrawn and "home rule" restored to the South. Eventually an informal bargain was struck, which historians have dubbed the Compromise of 1877. What precisely was agreed to and by whom remains a matter of dispute, but one thing at least was understood by both sides: Hayes would be president and southern blacks would be abandoned to their fate.

With southern Democratic acquiescence, the filibuster was broken, and Hayes took the oath of office. He immediately ordered the army not to resist a Democratic takeover of state governments in South Carolina and Louisiana. Thus fell the last of the Radical governments, and the entire South was firmly under the control of white Democrats. The trauma of the war and Reconstruction had destroyed the chances for a renewal of two-party competition among white Southerners.

"Redeeming" a New South

The men who came to power after the fall of Radical Reconstruction are usually referred to as the Redeemers. Some were members of the Old South's ruling planter class who had warmly supported secession and now sought to reestablish the old order with as few changes as possible. Others, of middle-class origin or outlook, favored commercial and industrial interests over agrarian groups and called for a New South committed to diversified economic development. A third group were professional politicians who shifted positions with the prevailing winds.

The Redeemers subscribed to no single coherent ideology but are perhaps best characterized as power brokers mediating among the dominant interest groups of the South in ways that served their own political advantage. In many ways, the "rings" that they established on the state and county level were analogous to the political machines developing at the same time in northern cities.

Redeemers did, however, agree on and endorse two basic principles: laissez-faire and white supremacy. Laissez-faire—the notion that government should be limited and should not intervene openly and directly in the economy—could unite planters, frustrated at seeing direct state support going to businessmen, and capitalist promoters who had come to realize that low taxes and freedom from government regulation were even more advantageous than state subsidies. It soon became clear that the Redeemers responded only to privileged and entrenched interest groups, especially landlords, merchants, and industrialists, and offered little or nothing to tenants, small farmers, and working people. As industrialization began to gather steam in the 1880s, Democratic regimes became increasingly accommodating to manufacturing interests and hospitable to agents of northern capital who were gaining control of the South's transportation system and its extractive industries.

White supremacy was the principal rallying cry that brought the Redeemers to power in the first place. Once in office, they found they could stay there by charging that opponents of ruling Democratic cliques were trying to divide "the white man's party" and open the way for a return to "black domination." Appeals to racism could also deflect attention from the economic grievances of groups without political clout.

The new governments were more economical than those of Reconstruction, mainly because they cut back drastically on appropriations for schools and other needed public services. But they were scarcely more honest—embezzlement of funds and bribery of officials continued to occur to an alarming extent.

The Redeemer regimes of the late 1870s and 1880s badly neglected the interests of small white farmers. Whites, as well as blacks, were suffering from the notorious crop lien system, which gave local merchants who advanced credit at high rates of interest during the growing season the right to take possession of the harvested crop on terms that buried farmers deeper and deeper in debt. As a result, increasing numbers of whites lost title to their homesteads and were reduced to tenancy. When a depression of world cotton prices added to the burden of a ruinous credit system, agrarian protesters began to challenge the ruling elite, first through the Southern Farmers' Alliance of the late 1880s and then by supporting its political descendant—the Populist party of the 1890s.

THE RISE OF JIM CROW

African Americans bore the greatest hardships imposed by the new order. From 1876 through the first decade of the twentieth century, Southern states imposed a series of restrictions on black civil rights known as "Jim Crow" laws. While segregation and disfranchisement began as informal arrangements, they culminated in a legal regime of separation and exclusion that took firm hold in the 1890s.

The rise of Jim Crow in the political arena was especially bitter for Southern blacks who realized that only political power could ensure other rights. The Redeemers had promised, in exchange for the end of federal intervention in 1877, to respect the rights of blacks as set forth in the Fourteenth and Fifteenth Amendments. But when blacks tried to vote Republican in the "redeemed" states, they encountered renewed violence and intimidation. Blacks who withstood the threat of losing their jobs or being evicted from tenant farms if they voted for Republicans were visited at night and literally whipped into line. The message was clear: Vote Democratic, or vote not at all.

Furthermore, white Democrats now controlled the electoral machinery and were able to manipulate the black vote by stuffing ballot boxes, discarding unwanted votes, or reporting fraudulent totals. Some states also imposed complicated new voting requirements to discourage black participation. Full-scale disfranchisement did not occur until literacy tests and other legalized obstacles to voting were imposed in the period from 1890 to 1910, but by that time, less formal and comprehensive methods had already made a mockery of the Fifteenth Amendment.

Nevertheless, blacks continued to vote freely in some localities until the 1890s; a few districts even elected black Republicans to Congress during the immediate post-Reconstruction period. The last of these, Representative George H. White of North Carolina, served until 1901. His farewell address eloquently conveyed the agony of southern blacks in the era of Jim Crow:

Perhaps no event better expresses the cruel and barbaric nature of the racism and white supremacy that swept the South after Reconstruction than lynching. Although lynchings were not confined to the South, most occurred there and African American men were the most frequent victims. Here two men lean out of a barn window above a black man who is about to be hanged. Others below prepare to set on fire the pile of hay at the victim's feet. Lynchings were often public events, drawing huge crowds to watch the victim's agonizing death.

These parting words are in behalf of an outraged, heart-broken, bruised, and bleeding but God-fearing people, faithful, industrious, loyal people—rising people, full of potential force. . . . The only apology that I have to make for the earnestness with which I have spoken is that I am pleading for the life, the liberty, the future happiness, and manhood suffrage of one-eighth of the entire population of the United States.

The dark night of racism that fell on the South after Reconstruction seemed to unleash all the baser impulses of human nature. Between 1889 and 1899, an average of 187 blacks were lynched every year for alleged offenses against white supremacy. Those convicted of petty crimes against property were often little better off; many were condemned to be leased out to private contractors whose brutality rivaled that of the most sadistic slaveholders. The convict-lease system enabled entrepreneurs, such as mine owners and extractors of forest products, to rent prisoners from the state and treat them as they saw fit. Unlike slaveowners, they suffered

SUPREME COURT DECISIONS AFFECTING BLACK CIVIL RIGHTS, 1875–1900

CASE	EFFECTS OF COURT'S DECISIONS
Hall v. DeCuir (1878)	Struck down Louisiana law prohibiting racial discrimination by "common carriers" (railroads, steamboats, buses). Declared the law a "burden" on interstate commerce, over which states had no authority.
United States v. Harris (1882)	Declared federal laws to punish crimes such as murder and assault unconstitutional. Declared such crimes to be the sole concern of local government. Ignored the frequent racial motivation behind such crimes in the South.
Civil Rights Cases (1883)	Struck down Civil Rights Act of 1875. Declared that Congress may not legislate on civil rights unless a state passes a discriminatory law. Declared the Fourteenth Amendment silent on racial discrimination by private citizens.
Plessy v. Ferguson (1896)	Upheld Louisiana statute requiring "separate but equal" accommodations on railroads. Declared that segregation is *not* necessarily discrimination.
Williams v. Mississippi (1898)	Upheld state law requiring a literacy test to qualify for voting. Refused to find any implication of racial discrimination in the law, although it permitted illiterate whites to vote if they "understood" the Constitution. Using such laws, southern states rapidly disfranchised blacks.

no loss when a forced laborer died from overwork. Finally, the dignity of blacks was cruelly affronted by the wave of segregation laws passed around the turn of the century, which served to remind them constantly that they were deemed unfit to associate with whites on any basis that implied equality. To some extent, the segregation laws were a white reaction to the refusal of many blacks to submit to voluntary segregation of railroads, streetcars, and other public facilities.

The North and the federal government did little or nothing to stem the tide of racial oppression in the South. A series of Supreme Court decisions between 1878 and 1898 gutted the Reconstruction amendments and the legislation passed to enforce them, leaving blacks virtually defenseless against political and social discrimination.

HENRY MCNEAL TURNER AND THE "UNFINISHED REVOLUTION"

The career of Henry McNeal Turner sums up the bitter side of the black experience in the South during and after Reconstruction. Born free in South Carolina in 1834, Turner became a minister of the African Methodist Episcopal (AME) Church just before the outbreak of the Civil War. During the war, he recruited African Americans for the Union army and later served as chaplain for black troops. After the fighting was over, he went to Georgia to work for the

Freedmen's Bureau but encountered racial discrimination from white Bureau officers and left government service for church work and Reconstruction politics. Elected to the 1867 Georgia constitutional convention and to the state legislature in 1868, he was one of a number of black clergymen who assumed leadership roles among the freedmen. But whites won control of the Georgia legislature and expelled all the black members. As the inhabitant of a state in which blacks never gained the degree of power that they achieved in some other parts of the South, Turner was one of the first black leaders to see the failure of Reconstruction as the betrayal of African American hopes for citizenship.

Becoming a bishop of the AME Church in 1880, Turner emerged as the late nineteenth century's leading proponent of black emigration to Africa. Because he believed that white Americans were so deeply prejudiced against blacks that they would never grant them equal rights, Turner became an early advocate of black nationalism and a total separation of the races. Emigration became a popular movement among southern blacks, who were especially hard hit by terror and oppression just after the end of Reconstruction, but a majority of blacks in the nation as a whole and even in Turner's own church refused to give up on the hope of eventual equality on American soil. But Bishop Turner's anger and despair were the understandable responses of a proud man to the way that he and his fellow African Americans had been treated in the post–Civil War period.

By the late 1880s, the wounds of the Civil War were healing, and white Americans were celebrating the spirit of sectional reconciliation and their common Americanism. But whites could come back together only because Northerners had tacitly agreed to give Southerners a free hand in their efforts to reduce blacks to a new form of servitude. The "outraged, heart-broken, bruised, and bleeding" African Americans of the South paid the heaviest price for sectional reunion.

CHRONOLOGY

1863	Lincoln sets forth 10 percent Reconstruction plan
1864	Wade-Davis Bill passes Congress but is pocket vetoed by Lincoln
1865	Johnson moves to reconstruct the South on his own initiative
	Congress refuses to seat representatives and senators elected from states reestablished under presidential plan (December)
1866	Johnson vetoes Freedmen's Bureau Bill (February)
	Johnson vetoes Civil Rights Act; it passes over his veto (April)
	Congress passes Fourteenth Amendment (June)
	Republicans increase their congressional majority in the fall elections
1867	First Reconstruction Act is passed over Johnson's veto (March)
1868	Johnson is impeached; he avoids conviction by one vote (February–May)
	Southern blacks vote and serve in constitutional conventions
	Grant wins presidential election, defeating Horatio Seymour
1869	Congress passes Fifteenth Amendment, granting African Americans the right to vote
1870–1871	Congress passes Ku Klux Klan Acts to protect black voting rights in the South
1872	Grant reelected president, defeating Horace Greeley, candidate of Liberal Republicans and Democrats
1873	Financial panic plunges nation into depression
1875	Congress passes Specie Resumption Act
	"Whiskey Ring" scandal exposed
1876–1877	Disputed presidential election resolved in favor of Republican Hayes over Democrat Tilden
1877	Compromise of 1877 ends military intervention in the South and causes fall of the last Radical governments

17

THE WEST
Exploiting an Empire

In 1863, federal Indian agents took a delegation of Cheyenne, Arapaho, Comanche, Kiowa, and Plains Apache to visit the eastern United States, hoping to impress them with the power of the white man. The visitors were, in fact, impressed. In New York City, they stared at the tall buildings and crowded streets, so different from the wide-open plains with which they were accustomed. They visited the museum of the great showman Phineas T. Barnum, who in turn put them on display; they even saw a hippopotamus.

In Washington, they met with President Abraham Lincoln. Lean Bear, a Cheyenne chief, assured Lincoln that Indians wanted peace but worried about the numbers of white people who were pouring into their country. Lincoln swore friendship, said the Indians would be better off if they began to farm, and promised he would do his best to keep the peace. But, he said, smiling at Lean Bear, "You know it is not always possible for any father to have his children do precisely as he wishes them to do."

Lean Bear, who had children of his own, had understood what Lincoln had had to say in Washington, at least in a way. Just a year later, back on his own lands, he watched as federal troops, Lincoln's "children," approached his camp. Wearing a peace medal that Lincoln had given him, Lean Bear rode slowly toward the troops to once again offer his friendship. When he was twenty yards away, they opened fire, then rode closer, and fired again and again into the fallen body.

In the last three decades of the nineteenth century, a flood of settlers ventured into the vast lands across the Mississippi River. Prospectors searched for "pay dirt," railroads crisscrossed the continent, eastern and foreign capitalists invested in cattle and land bonanzas, and farmers took up the promise of free western lands. In 1867, Horace Greeley, editor of the New York *Tribune*, told New York City's unemployed: "If you strike off into the broad, free West, and make yourself a farm from Uncle Sam's generous domain, you will crowd nobody, starve nobody, and neither you nor your children need evermore beg for something to do."

With the end of the Civil War, white Americans again claimed a special destiny to expand across the continent. In the process, they crushed the culture of the Native Americans and ignored the contributions of people of other races, such as the Chinese miners and laborers and the Mexican herdsmen. As millions moved west, the states of Colorado, Washington, Montana, the Dakotas, Idaho, Wyoming, and Utah were carved out of the lands across the Mississippi. At the turn of the century, only Arizona, New Mexico, and Oklahoma remained as territories.

The West became a great colonial empire, harnessed to eastern capital and tied increasingly to national and international markets. Its raw materials, sent east by wagon, train, and ship, helped fuel eastern factories. Western economies relied heavily on the federal government, which subsidized their railroads, distributed their land, and spent millions of dollars for the upkeep of soldiers and Indians.

By the 1890s, the West of the lands beyond the Mississippi had undergone substantial change. In place of buffalo and unfenced vistas, there were cities and towns, health resorts, homesteads, sheep ranches, and, in the arid regions, the beginnings of the irrigated agriculture that would reshape the West in the twentieth century. Ghost towns, abandoned farms, and the scars in the earth left by miners and farmers spoke to the less favorable side of settlement. As the new century dawned, the West had become a place of conquest and exploitation, as well as a mythic land of cowboys and quick fortunes.

Beyond the Frontier

The line of white settlement had reached the edge of the Missouri timber country by 1840. Beyond lay an enormous land of rolling prairies, parched deserts, and rugged, majestic mountains.

Early explorers like Zebulon Pike thought the country beyond the Mississippi was uninhabitable, fit only, Pike said, for "wandering and uncivilized aborigines." Mapmakers agreed; between 1825 and 1860, American maps showed this land as "The Great American Desert." As a result, settlement paused on the edge of the Plains, and most early settlers headed directly for California and Oregon.

Few rivers cut through the Plains. Rainfall usually did not reach 15 inches a year, not enough to support extensive agriculture. There was little lumber for homes and fences, and the tools of eastern settlement—the cast-iron plow, the boat, and the ax—were virtually useless on the tough and treeless Plains soil. "East of the Mississippi," historian Walter Prescott Webb noted, "civilization stood on three legs—land, water, and timber; west of the Mississippi not one but two of these legs were withdrawn—water and timber—and civilization was left on one leg—land."

Hot winds seared the Plains in summer, and northers, blizzards, and hailstorms froze them in winter. Wildlife roamed in profusion. The American bison, better known as the buffalo, grazed in enormous herds from Mexico to Canada. In 1865, perhaps fifteen million buffalo lived on the Plains, so many they seemed like "leaves in a forest" to an early observer. A single herd sighted in 1871 had four million head.

CRUSHING THE NATIVE AMERICANS

When Greeley urged New Yorkers to move West and "crowd nobody," he—like almost all white Americans—ignored the fact that large numbers of people already lived there. At the close of the Civil War, Native Americans inhabited nearly half the United States. By 1880, they had been driven onto smaller and smaller reservations and were no longer an independent people. A decade later, even their culture had crumbled under the impact of white domination.

In 1865, nearly a quarter million Native Americans lived in the western half of the country. Tribes such as the Winnebago, Menominee, Cherokee, and Chippewa were resettled there, forced out of their eastern lands by advancing white settlement. Other tribes were native to the region. In the Southwest there were the Pueblo groups, including the Hopi, Zuni, and Rio Grande Pueblo. Peaceful farmers and herders, they had built up complex traditions around a settled way of life.

The Pueblo groups were cultivators of corn. They lived on the subdesert plateau of present-day western New Mexico and eastern Arizona. Harassed by powerful neighboring tribes, they built communal houses of adobe brick on high mesas or in cracks in the cliffs. More nomadic were the Camp Dwellers, the Jicarilla Apache and Navajo who roamed eastern New Mexico and western Texas. Blending elements of the Plains and Plateau environments, they lived in te-pees or mud huts, grew some crops to supplement their hunting, and moved readily from place to place. The Navajo herded sheep and produced beautiful ornamental silver, baskets, and blankets. Fierce fighters, Apache horsemen were feared by whites and fellow Indians across the southwestern Plains.

Farther west were the tribes that inhabited present-day California. Divided into many small bands, they eked out a difficult existence living on roots, grubs, berries, acorns, and small game. In the Pacific Northwest, where fish and forest animals made life easier, the Klamath, Chinook, Yurok, and Shasta tribes developed a rich civilization. They built plank houses and canoes, worked extensively in wood, and evolved a complex social and political organization. Settled and determined, they resisted the invasion of the whites.

By the 1870s, most of these tribes had been destroyed or beaten into submission. The powerful Ute, crushed in 1855, ceded most of their Utah lands to the United States and settled on a small reservation near Great Salt Lake. The Navajo and Apache fought back fiercely, but between 1865 and 1873 they too were confined to reservations. The Native Americans of California succumbed to the contagious diseases carried by whites during the Gold Rush of 1849. Miners burned their villages, and by 1880, fewer than twenty thousand Indians lived in California.

LIFE OF THE PLAINS INDIANS

In the mid-nineteenth century, nearly two-thirds of the Native Americans lived on the Great Plains. The Plains tribes included the Sioux of present-day Minnesota and the Dakotas; the Blackfoot of Idaho and Montana; the Cheyenne, Crow, and Arapaho of the central Plains; the Pawnee of western Nebraska; and the Kiowa, Apache, and Comanche of present-day Texas and New Mexico.

Nomadic and warlike, the Plains Indians depended on the buffalo and horse. The modern horse, first brought by Spanish explorers in the 1500s, spread north from Mexico onto the Plains, and by the 1700s the Plains Indians' way of life had changed. The Plains tribes gave up farming almost entirely and hunted the buffalo, ranging widely over the rolling plains. The men became superb warriors and horsemen, among the best light cavalry in the world.

Migratory in culture, the Plains Indians formed tribes of several thousand people but lived in smaller bands of three to five hundred. Each band was governed by a chief and a council of elder men, and Indians of the same tribe transferred freely from band to band. Bands acted independently, making it difficult for the U.S. government to deal with the fragmented tribes.

The bands followed and lived off the buffalo. Buffalo provided food, clothing, and shelter; the Indians, unlike later white hunters, used every part of the animal. The meat was dried or "jerked" in the hot Plains air. The skins made tepees, blankets, and robes. Buffalo bones became knives; tendons were made into bowstrings; horns and hooves were boiled into glue. Buffalo "chips"—dried manure—were burned as fuel. All in all, the buffalo was "a galloping department store."

The Plains tribes divided labor tasks according to gender. Men hunted, traded, supervised ceremonial activities, and cleared ground for planting. They usually held the positions of authority, such as chief or medicine man. Women were responsible for child rearing and artistic activity. They also performed the camp work, grew vegetables, prepared buffalo meat and hides, and gathered berries and roots. In most tribes, women played an important role in political, economic, and religious activities. Among the Navajo and Zuni, kinship descended from the mother's side, and Navajo women were in charge of most of the family's property. In tribes such as the Sioux, there was little difference in status. Men were respected for hunting and war, women for their artistic skills with quill and paint.

"AS LONG AS WATERS RUN": SEARCHING FOR AN INDIAN POLICY

Before the Civil War, Americans used the land west of the Mississippi as "one big reservation." The government named the area "Indian Country," moved eastern tribes there with firm treaty guarantees, and in 1834 passed the Indian Intercourse Act, which prohibited any white person from entering Indian country without a license.

The situation changed in the 1850s. Wagon trains wound their way to California and Oregon, miners pushed into western goldfields, and there was talk of a transcontinental railroad. To clear the way for settlement, the federal government in 1851 abandoned "One Big Reservation" in favor of a new policy of concentration. For the first time, it assigned definite boundaries to each tribe. The Sioux, for example, were given the Dakota country north of the Platte River, the Crow a large area near the Powder River, and the Cheyenne and Arapaho the

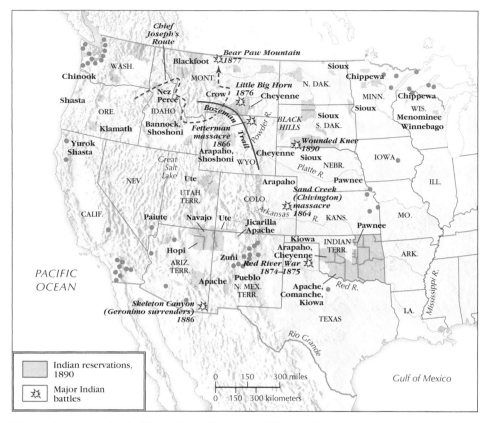

Native Americans in the West: Major Battles and Reservations

"They made us many promises, more than I remember, but they never kept but one; they promised to take our land, and they took it." So said Red Cloud of the Oglala Sioux, summarizing Native American–white relations in the 1870s.

Colorado foothills between the North Platte and Arkansas rivers for "as long as waters run and the grass shall grow."

The concentration policy lasted only a few years. Accustomed to hunting widely for buffalo, many Native Americans refused to stay within their assigned areas. White settlers poured into Indian lands, then called on the government to protect them. Indians were pushed out of Kansas and Nebraska in the 1850s, even as white reformers fought to hold those territories open for free blacks. In 1859, gold miners moved into the Pikes Peak country, touching off warfare with the Cheyenne and Arapaho.

In 1864, tired of the fighting, the two tribes asked for peace. Certain that the war was over, Chief Black Kettle led his seven hundred followers to camp on Sand Creek in southeastern Colorado. Early on the morning of November 29, 1864, a group of Colorado militia led by Colonel John M. Chivington attacked the sleeping group. "Kill and scalp all, big and little," Chivington told his men. "Nits make lice." Black Kettle tried to stop the ambush, raising first an American flag and then a white flag. Neither worked. The Native American men, women, and children were clubbed, stabbed, and scalped.

The Chivington massacre set off angry protests in Colorado and the East. Congress appointed an investigating committee, and the government concluded a treaty with the Cheyenne and Arapaho, condemning "the gross and wanton outrages." Still, the two tribes were forced to surrender their Sand Creek reservation in exchange for lands elsewhere. The Kiowa and Comanche were also ousted from areas they had been granted "forever" only a few years before. As the Sioux chief Spotted Tail said, "Why does not the Great Father put his red children on wheels so that he can move them as he will?"

Before long, the powerful Sioux were on the warpath in the great Sioux War of 1865–1867. Once again, an invasion of gold miners touched off the war, which flared even more intensely when the federal government announced plans to connect the various mining towns by building the Bozeman Trail through the heart of the Sioux hunting grounds in Montana. Red Cloud, the Sioux chief, determined to stop the trail. In December 1866, pursued by an army column under Captain William J. Fetterman, he lured the incautious Fetterman deep into the wilderness, ambushed him, and wiped out all eighty-two soldiers in his command.

The Fetterman massacre, coming so soon after the Chivington massacre, sparked a public debate over the nation's Indian policy. Like the policy itself, the debate reflected differing white views of the Native Americans. In the East, some reform, humanitarian, and church groups wanted a humane peace policy, directed toward educating and "civilizing" the tribes. Many white people, in the East and West, questioned this approach, convinced that Native Americans were savages unfit for civilization. Westerners, of course, had some reason to fear Indian attacks, and the fears often fed on wild rumors of scalped settlers and besieged forts. As a result, Westerners in general favored firm control over the Native Americans, including swift punishment of any who rebelled.

In 1867, the peace advocates won the debate. Halting construction on the Bozeman Trail, Congress created a Peace Commission of four civilians and three generals to end the Sioux War and eliminate permanently the causes of Indian wars. Setting out for the West, the Peace Commissioners agreed that only one policy offered a permanent solution: a policy of "small reservations" to isolate the Native Americans on distant lands, teach them to farm, and gradually "civilize" them.

FINAL BATTLES ON THE PLAINS

Few Native Americans settled peacefully into life on the new reservations. The reservation system not only changed their age-old customs; it chained them in a situation of poverty and isolation. Soon, young warriors and minor chiefs denounced the treaties and drifted back to the open countryside. In late 1868, warfare broke out again, and it took more than a decade of violence to beat the Indians into submission. The Kiowa and Comanche rampaged through the Texas Panhandle, looting and killing, until the U.S. Army crushed them in the Red River War of 1874–1875 and ended warfare in the Southwest.

On the northern Plains, fighting resulted from the Black Hills Gold Rush of 1875. As prospectors tramped across Native American hunting grounds, the Sioux gathered to stop them. They were led by Rain-in-the-Face, the great war chief Crazy Horse, and the famous medicine man Sitting Bull. The army sent several columns of troops after the Indians, but one, under flamboyant Lieutenant Colonel George Armstrong Custer, pushed recklessly ahead, eager to claim the victory. On the morning of June 25, 1876, thinking he had a small band of Native Americans surrounded in their village on the banks of the Little Bighorn River in Montana, Custer divided his column and took 265 men toward it. Instead of finding a small band, he discovered he had stumbled on the main Sioux camp with 2500 warriors. It was the largest Native American army ever assembled in the United States.

By midafternoon it was over; Custer and his men were dead. Custer was largely responsible for the loss, but "Custer's Last Stand," set in blazing headlines across the country, set off a nationwide demand for revenge. Within a few months, the Sioux were surrounded and beaten, three thousand of them surrendering in October 1876. Sitting Bull and a few followers who had fled to Canada gave up in 1881.

The Sioux War ended the major Indian warfare in the West, but occasional outbreaks occurred for several years thereafter. In 1890, the Teton Sioux of South Dakota, bitter and starving, became restless. Many of them turned to the Ghost Dances, a set of dances and rites that grew from a vision of a Paiute messiah named Wovoka. Performance of the dances, Wovoka said, would bring back

This pictogram by Oglala Sioux Amos Bad Heart Bull is a Native American version of the battle of the Little Bighorn, also known as Custer's Last Stand.

Native American lands and would cause the whites to disappear. All Native Americans would reunite, the earth would be covered with dust, and a new earth would come upon the old. The vanished buffalo would return in great herds.

The army intervened to stop the dancing, touching off violence that killed Sitting Bull and a number of other warriors. Frightened Native Americans fled southwest to join other Ghost Dancers under the aging chief Big Foot. Moving quickly, troops of the Seventh Cavalry, Custer's old regiment, caught up with Big Foot's band and took them to the army camp on Wounded Knee Creek in South Dakota. A Native American, it is thought, fired the first shot, returned by the army's new machine guns. Firing a shell a second, they shredded tepees and people. About two hundred men, women, and children were massacred in the snow.

THE END OF TRIBAL LIFE

The final step in Indian policy came in the 1870s and 1880s. Some reformers had long argued against segregating the Native Americans on reservations, urging instead that the nation assimilate them individually into white culture. These "assimilationists" wanted to use education, land policy, and federal law to eradicate tribal society.

Congress began to adopt the policy in 1871 when it ended the practice of treaty making with Native American tribes. Since tribes were no longer separate nations, they lost many of their political and judicial functions, and the power of the chiefs was weakened.

While Congress worked to break down the tribes, educators trained young Native Americans to adjust to white culture. In 1879, fifty Pawnee, Kiowa, and Cheyenne youths were brought east to the new Carlisle Indian School in Carlisle, Pennsylvania. Other Native American schools soon opened, including the Haskell Institute in Kansas and numerous day schools on the western reservations. The schools taught students to fix machines and farm; they forced young Indians to trim their long hair and made them speak English, banned the wearing of tribal paint or clothes, and forbade tribal ceremonies and dances. "Kill the Indian and save the man," said Richard H. Pratt, the army officer who founded the Carlisle School.

Land ownership was the final and most important link in the new policy. Native Americans who owned land, it was thought, would become responsible, self-reliant citizens. Deciding to give each Native American a farm, Congress in 1887 passed the Dawes Severalty Act, the most important legal development in Indian-white relations in more than three centuries.

Aiming to end tribal life, the Dawes Act divided tribal lands into small plots for distribution among members of the tribe. Each family head received 160 acres, single adults 80 acres, and children 40 acres. Through the Dawes Act, 47 million acres of land were distributed to Native Americans and their families. There were another 90 million acres in the reservations, and these lands, often the most fertile, were sold to white settlers. Many Native Americans knew little about farming. Their tools were rudimentary, and in the culture of the Plains

Tom Torlino, a Navajo Indian, photographed before and after his "assimilation." Torlino attended the Carlisle Indian School in Pennsylvania.

Indians, men had not ordinarily participated in farming. In 1934, the government returned to the idea of tribal land ownership, but by then 138 million acres of Indian land had shrunk to 48 million acres, half of which was barren.

The final blow to tribal life came not in the Dawes Act but in the virtual extermination of the buffalo, the Plains Indians' chief resource and the basis for their unique way of life. The killing began in the 1860s as the transcontinental railroads pushed west, and it stepped up as settlers found they could harm the Indians by harming the buffalo. "Kill every buffalo you can," an army officer said. "Every buffalo dead is an Indian gone." Then, in 1871, a Pennsylvania tannery discovered that buffalo hides made valuable leather. Professional hunters such as William F. "Buffalo Bill" Cody swarmed across the Plains, killing millions of the beasts.

Between 1872 and 1874, professional hunters slaughtered three million buffalo a year. In a frontier form of a factory system, riflemen, skinners, and transport wagons pushed through the vast herds, which shrank steadily behind them. A good hunter killed a hundred buffalo a day. Skinners took off the hides, removed the tongue, hump, and tallow, and left the rest. By 1883, the buffalo were almost gone. When the government set out to produce the famous "buffalo nickel," the designer had to go to the Bronx Zoo in New York City to find a buffalo.

By 1900, there were only 250,000 Native Americans in the country. (There were 600,000 within the limits of the present-day United States in 1800, and more than 5 million in 1492, when Columbus first set foot in the New World.) Most of the Indians lived on reservations. Many lived in poverty. Alcoholism and unemployment were growing problems, and Native Americans, no longer able to live off the buffalo, became wards of the state. They lost their cultural distinctiveness. Once possessors of the entire continent, they had been crowded into smaller and smaller areas, overwhelmed by the demand to become settled, literate, and English-speaking.

Even as the Native Americans lost their identity, they entered the romantic folklore of the West. Dime novels, snapped up by readers young and old, told tales of Indian fighting on the Plains. "Buffalo Bill" Cody turned it all into a profitable business. Beginning in 1883, his Wild West Show ran for more than three decades, playing to millions of viewers in the United States, Canada, and Europe. It featured Plains Indians chasing buffalo, performing a war dance, and attacking a settler's cabin. In 1885, Sitting Bull himself, victor over Custer at the battle of Little Bighorn, performed in the show.

SETTLEMENT OF THE WEST

Between 1870 and 1900, white—and some African, Hispanic, and Asian—Americans settled the enormous total of 430 million acres west of the Mississippi; they took over more land than had been occupied by Americans in all the years before 1870. People moved West for many reasons. Some sought adventure; others wanted to escape the drab routine of factory or city life. Many moved to California for their health. The Mormons settled Utah to escape religious persecution. Others followed the mining camps, the advancing railroads, and the farming and cattle frontier.

Whatever the specific reason, most people moved West to better their lot. On the whole, their timing was good, for as the nation's population grew, so did demand for the livestock and the agricultural, mineral, and lumber products of the expanding West. Contrary to older historical views, the West did not act as a major "safety valve," an outlet for social and economic tensions. The poor and unemployed did not have the means to move there and establish farms. "Moreover," as Douglass C. North, an economic historian, said, "most people moved West in good times . . . in periods of rising prices, of expanding demand, when the prospects for making money from this new land looked brightest; and this aspect characterized the whole pattern of settlement."

MEN AND WOMEN ON THE OVERLAND TRAIL

The first movement west aimed not for the nearby Plains but for California and Oregon on the continent's far shore. It started in the 1849 Gold Rush to California, and in the next three decades perhaps as many as half a million individuals made the long journey over the Overland Trail leading west. Some walked; others rode horses alone or in small groups. About half joined great caravans, numbering 150 wagons or more, that inched across the two thousand miles between the Missouri River and the Pacific Coast.

Individuals and wagon trains set out from various points along the Missouri River. Leaving in the spring and traveling through the summer, they hoped to reach their destination before the first snowfall. During April, travelers gradually assembled in spring camp just across the Missouri River, waiting for the new grass to ripen into forage. They packed and repacked the wagons and elected the trains' leaders, who would set the line of march, look for water and campsites, and impose discipline.

Setting out in early May, travelers divided the enormous route into manageable portions. The first leg of the journey followed the Platte River west to Fort Kearney in central Nebraska Territory, a distance of about three hundred miles. The land was even, with good supplies of wood, grass, and water. From a distance, the white-topped wagons seemed driven by a common force, but, in fact, internal discipline broke down almost immediately. Arguments erupted over the pace of the march, the choice of campsites, the number of guards to post, whether to rest or push on. Elected leaders quit; new ones were chosen. Every train was filled with individualists, and as the son of one train captain said, "If you think it's any snap to run a wagon train of 66 wagons with every man in the train having a different idea of what is the best thing to do, all I can say is that some day you ought to try it."

Men, women, and children had different tasks on the trail. Men concerned themselves almost entirely with hunting buffalo and antelope, guard duty, and transportation. They rose at 4 A.M. to hitch the wagons, and after breakfast began the day's march. At noon, they stopped and set the teams to graze. After the midday meal, the march continued until sunset. Then, while the men relaxed, the women fixed dinner and the next day's lunch, and the children kindled the fires, brought water to camp, and searched for wood or other fuel. Walking fifteen miles a day, in searing heat and mountain cold, travelers were exhausted by late afternoon.

For women, the trail was lonely, and they worked to exhaustion. Before long, some adjusted their clothing to the harsh conditions, adopting the new bloomer pants, shortening their skirts, or wearing regular "wash dresses"—so called because they had shorter hemlines that did not drag on the wet ground on washday. Both men and women carried firearms in case of Indian attacks, but most emigrants saw few Indians en route.

What they often did see was trash, miles of it, for the wagon trains were an early example of the impact of migration and settlement on the western environment. On the Oregon and other trails, travelers sidestepped mounds of garbage, tin cans, furniture, cooking stoves, kegs, tools, and clothing, all discarded by people who had passed through before.

The first stage of the journey was deceptively easy, and travelers usually reached Fort Kearney by late May. The second leg led another 300 miles up the Platte River to Fort Laramie on the eastern edge of Wyoming Territory. The heat of June had dried the grass, and there was no wood. Anxious to beat the early snowfalls, travelers rested a day or two at the fort, then hurried on to South Pass,

The migration westward on the overland trail was long and difficult. In this photograph from the 1870s, a caravan of covered wagons attempts to cross a river. Emigrants often chose oxen to pull the wagons because oxen were strong, less expensive than horses, and they could survive on a diet of prairie grasses.

280 miles to the west, the best route through the forbidding Rockies. The land was barren. It was now mid-July, but the mountain nights were so cold that ice formed in the water buckets.

Beyond South Pass, some emigrants turned south to the Mormon settlements on the Great Salt Lake, but most headed 340 miles north to Fort Hall on the Snake River in Idaho. It took another three months to cover the remaining 800 miles. California-bound travelers followed the Humboldt River through the summer heat of Nevada. Well into September, they began the final arduous push: first, a 55-mile stretch of desert; then 70 difficult miles up the eastern slopes of the Sierra Nevada, and finally the last 100 miles down the western slopes to the welcome sight of California's Central Valley in October.

Under the best of conditions the trip took six months, sixteen hours a day, dawn to dusk, of hard, grueling labor. Walking halfway across the continent was no easy task, and it provided a never-to-be-forgotten experience for those who did it. The wagon trains, carrying the dreams of thousands of individuals, reproduced society in small focus: individualistic, hopeful, mobile, divided by age and gender roles, apprehensive, yet willing to strike out for the distant and new.

LAND FOR THE TAKING

As railroads pushed west in the 1870s and 1880s, locomotive trains replaced wagon trains, but the shift was gradual, and until the end of the century, emigrants often combined both modes of travel.

Traffic flowed in all directions, belying the image of a simple "westward" movement. Many people did go west, of course, but others, such as migrants from Mexico, became westerners by moving north, and Asian Americans moved eastward from the Pacific Coast. Whatever their route, they all ended up in the meeting ground of cultures that formed the modern West.

Why did they come? "The motive that induced us to part with the pleasant associations and the dear friends of our childhood days," explained Phoebe Judson, an early emigrant, "was to obtain from the government of the United States a grant of land that 'Uncle Sam' had promised to give to the head of each family who settled in this new country." A popular camp song reflected the same motive:

Come along, come along—don't be alarmed,
Uncle Sam is rich enough to give us all a farm.

Uncle Sam owned about 1 billion acres of land in the 1860s, much of it mountain and desert land unsuited for agriculture. By 1900, the various land laws had distributed half of it. Between 1862 and 1890, the government gave away 48 million acres under the Homestead Act of 1862, sold about 100 million acres to private citizens and corporations, granted 128 million acres to railroad companies to tempt them to build across the unsettled West, and sold huge tracts to the states.

The Homestead Act of 1862, a law of great significance, gave 160 acres of land to anyone who would pay a $10 registration fee and pledge to live on it and cultivate it for five years. The offer set off a mass migration of land-hungry Europeans, dazzled by a country that gave its land away. Americans also seized on the act's provisions, and between 1862 and 1900, nearly 600,000 families claimed free homesteads under it.

Yet the Homestead Act did not work as Congress had hoped. Few farmers and laborers had the cash to move to the frontier, buy farm equipment, and wait out the year or two before the farm became self-supporting. Tailored to the timber and water conditions of the East, the act did not work as well in the semiarid West. In the fertile valleys of the Mississippi, 160 acres provided a generous farm. A farmer on the Great Plains needed either a larger farm for dry farming or a smaller one for irrigation.

Speculators made ingenious use of the land laws. Sending agents in advance of settlement, they moved along choice river bottoms or irrigable areas, accumulating large holdings to be held for high prices. In the arid West, where control of water meant control of the surrounding land, shrewd ranchers plotted their holdings accordingly. In Colorado, one cattleman, John F. Iliff, owned only 105 small parcels of land, but by placing them around the few water holes, he effectively dominated an empire stretching over 6,000 square miles.

Water, in fact, became a dominant western issue, since aside from the Pacific Northwest, northern California, parts of the Rocky Mountain West, and the eastern half of the Great Plains, much of the trans-Mississippi West was arid, receiving less than 20 inches of rainfall annually. People speculated in water as if it were gold and planned great irrigation systems in Utah, eastern Colorado, and California's Central Valley to "make the desert bloom."

Irrigators received a major boost in 1902 when the National Reclamation Act (the Newlands Act) set aside most of the proceeds from the sale of public lands in sixteen western states to finance irrigation projects in the arid states. Over the next decades, dams, canals, and irrigation systems channeled water into dry areas, creating a "hydraulic" society that was rich in crops and cities (such as Los Angeles and Phoenix), but ever thirstier and in danger of outrunning the precious water on which it all depended.

As beneficiaries of the government's policy of land grants for railway construction, the railroad companies were the West's largest landowners. Eager to have immigrants settle on the land they owned near the railroad right-of-way, and eager to boost their freight and passenger business, the companies sent agents to the East and Europe. Railroad lines set up land departments and bureaus of immigration. The land departments priced the land, arranged credit terms, and even gave free farming courses to immigrants. The bureaus of immigration employed agents in Europe, met immigrants at eastern seaports, and ran special cars for land seekers heading west.

Half a billion acres of western land were given or sold to speculators and corporations. At the same time, only 600,000 homestead patents were issued, covering 80 million acres. Thus, only one acre in every nine initially went to individual pioneers, the intended beneficiaries of the nation's largesse. Two-thirds of all homestead claimants before 1890 failed in their efforts to farm their new land.

THE SPANISH-SPEAKING SOUTHWEST

In the nineteenth century, almost all Spanish-speaking people in the United States lived in California, Arizona, New Mexico, Texas, and Colorado. Their numbers were small—California had only 8086 Mexican residents in 1900—but the influence of their culture and institutions was large. In some respects, the southwestern frontier was more Spanish American than Anglo-American.

Pushing northward from Mexico, the Spanish gradually established the present-day economic structure of the Southwest. They brought with them techniques of mining, stock raising, and irrigated farming. After winning independence in the 1820s, the Mexicans brought new laws and ranching methods as well as chaps and the burro. Both Spanish and Mexicans created the legal framework for distributing land and water, a precious resource in the Southwest.

In Southern California, the Californios, descendants of the original colonizers, began after the 1860s to lose their once vast landholdings to drought and mortgages. But as they died out, Mexican Americans continued the Spanish-Mexican influence. In 1880, one-fourth of the residents of Los Angeles County were Spanish speaking.

In New Mexico, Spanish-speaking citizens remained the majority ethnic group until the 1940s, and the Spanish-Mexican culture dominated the territory. Contests over land grants became New Mexico's largest industry; lawyers who dealt in them amassed huge holdings.

Throughout the Southwest, the Spanish-Mexican heritage gave a distinctive shape to society. Men headed the families and dominated economic life. Women had substantial economic rights (though few political ones), and they enjoyed a status their English American counterparts did not have. Wives kept full control of property acquired before their marriage; they also held half title to all property in a marriage, which later caused many southwestern states to pass community property laws.

In addition, the Spanish Mexican heritage fostered a modified economic caste system, a strong Roman Catholic influence, and the primary use of the Spanish language. Continuous immigration from Mexico kept language and cultural ties strong. Spanish was the region's first or second language. Confronted by Sheriff Pat Garrett in a darkened room, New Mexico's famous outlaw Billy the Kid died asking, "*Quién es? Quién es?*" ("Who is it? Who is it?").

The Bonanza West

Between 1850 and 1900, wave after wave of newcomers swept across the trans-Mississippi West. There were riches for the taking, hidden in gold-washed streams, spread lushly over grass-covered prairies, or available in the gullible minds of greedy newcomers. The nineteenth-century West took shape in the search for mining, cattle, and land bonanzas that drew eager settlers from the East and around the world.

As with all bonanzas, the consequences in the West were uneven growth, boom-and-bust economic cycles, and wasted resources. Society seemed constantly in the making. People moved here and there, following river bottoms, gold strikes, railroad tracks, and other opportunities. "Instant cities" arose. San Francisco, Salt Lake City, and Denver were the most spectacular examples, but every cow town and mining camp witnessed similar phenomena of growth. Boston needed more than two centuries to attract one-third of a million people; San Francisco did the same in a little more than twenty years.

Many Westerners had left home to get rich quickly, and they adopted institutions that reflected that goal. As a contemporary poem said:

> *Love to see the stir an' bustle*
> *In the busy town,*
> *Everybody on the hustle*
> *Saltin' profits down.*
> *Everybody got a wad a'*
> *Ready cash laid by;*
> *Ain't no flies on Colorado—*
> *Not a cussed fly.*

In their lives, the West was an idea as well as a region, and the idea molded them as much as they molded it.

THE MINING BONANZA

Mining was the first important magnet to attract people to the West. Many hoped to "strike it rich" in gold and silver, but at least half the newcomers had no intention of working in the mines. Instead, they provided food, clothing, and services to the thousands of miners.

The California Gold Rush of 1849 began the mining boom and set the pattern for subsequent strikes in other regions. Individual prospectors made the first strikes, discovering pockets of gold along streams flowing westward from the Sierra Nevada. To get the gold, they used a simple process called placer mining, which required little skill, technology, or capital. A placer miner needed only a shovel, a washing pan, and a good claim. As the placers gave out, a great deal of gold remained, but it was locked in quartz or buried deep in the earth. Mining became an expensive business, far beyond the reach of the average miner.

Large corporations moved in to dig the deep shafts and finance costly equipment. Quartz mining required heavy rock crushers, mercury vats to dissolve the gold, and large retorts to recapture it. Eastern and European financiers assumed control, labor became unionized, and mining towns took on some of the characteristics of the industrial city.

In 1859, fresh strikes were made near Pikes Peak in Colorado and in the Carson River Valley of Nevada. News of both discoveries set off wild migrations—100,000 miners were in Pikes Peak country by June 1859. The gold there quickly played out, but the Nevada find uncovered a thick bluish black ore that was almost pure silver and gold. A quick-witted drifter named Henry T. P. Comstock talked his way into partnership in the claim, and word of the Comstock Lode—with ore worth $3876 a ton—flashed over the mountains.

Thousands of miners climbed the Sierra Nevada that summer. The biggest strike was yet to come. In 1873, John W. Mackay and three partners formed a company to dig deep into the mountain, and at 1167 feet they hit the Big Bonanza, a seam of gold and silver more than 54 feet wide. It was the richest discovery in the history of mining. Between 1859 and 1879, the Comstock Lode produced gold and silver worth $306 million.

The final fling came in the Black Hills rush of 1874 to 1876. The army had tried to keep miners out of the area, the heart of the Sioux hunting grounds, and even sent a scientific party under Colonel George Armstrong Custer to disprove the rumors of gold and stop the miners' invasion. Instead, Custer found gold all over the hills, and the rush was on.

Towns such as Deadwood, in the Dakota Territory; Virginia City, Nevada; Leadville, Colorado; and Tombstone, Arizona, demonstrated a new development process in the frontier experience. The farming frontier had developed naturally in a rural setting. On the mining frontier, the germ of a city—the camp—appeared almost simultaneously with the first "strike." Periodicals, the latest fashions, theaters, schools, literary clubs, and lending libraries came quickly to the camps, providing civilized refinements not available on other frontiers. Urbanization also created the need for municipal government, sanitation, and law enforcement.

Mining camps were governed by a simple democracy. Soon after a strike, the miners in the area met to organize a mining "district" and adopted rules governing behavior in it. Rules regulated the size and boundaries of claims, established procedures for settling disputes, and set penalties for crimes. Petty criminals were banished from the district; serious offenders were hanged. In the case of a major dispute, the whole camp gathered, chose legal counsel for both sides, and heard the evidence. If all else failed, miners formed secret vigilance committees to hang a few offenders as a lesson to the rest. Early visitors to the mining country were struck by the way miners, solitary and competitive, joined together, founded a camp, and created a society.

In most camps, between one-quarter and one-half of the population was foreign born. The lure of gold drew large numbers of Chinese, Chileans, Peruvians, Mexicans, French, Germans, and English. Experienced miners, the Latin Americans brought valuable mining techniques. At least six thousand Mexicans joined the California rush of 1849, and by 1852, there were twenty-five thousand Chinese in California. Painstaking, the Chinese profitably worked claims others had abandoned. In the 1860s, almost one-third of the miners in the West were Chinese.

Hostility often surfaced against foreign miners, particularly the French, Latin Americans, and Chinese. In 1850, California passed a Foreign Miners' Tax that charged foreign miners a $20 monthly licensing fee. As intended, it drove out Mexicans and other foreigners. Riots against Chinese laborers occurred in the 1870s and 1880s in Los Angeles, San Francisco, Seattle, Reno, and Denver. Responding to pressure, Congress passed the Chinese Exclusion Act of 1882,

Leadville, Colorado, in the 1870s. Founded as a gold camp in 1860, by the 1880s Leadville, with thirty thousand residents, was the second largest city in the state, trailing only Denver.

which suspended immigration of Chinese laborers for ten years. The number of Chinese in the United States fell drastically.

By the 1890s, the early mining bonanza was over. All told, the western mines contributed billions of dollars to the economy. They had helped finance the Civil War and provided needed capital for industrialization. The vast boost in silver production from the Comstock Lode changed the relative value of gold and silver, the base of American currency. Bitter disputes over the currency affected politics and led to the famous "battle of the standards" in the presidential election of 1896 (see Chapter 20).

The mining frontier populated portions of the West and sped its process of political organization. Nevada, Idaho, and Montana were granted early statehood because of mining. Merchants, editors, lawyers, and ministers moved with the advancing frontier, establishing permanent settlements. Women in the mining camps helped to foster family life and raised the moral tone by campaigning against drinking, gambling, and prostitution. But not all the effects of the mining boom were positive. The industry also left behind painful scars in the form of invaded Indian reservations, pitted hills, and lonely ghost towns.

GOLD FROM THE ROOTS UP: THE CATTLE BONANZA

"There's gold from the grass roots down," said California Joe, a guide in the gold districts of Dakota in the 1870s, "but there's more gold from the grass roots up." Ranchers began to recognize the potential of the vast grasslands of the West. The Plains were covered with buffalo or grama grass, a wiry variety with short, hard stems. Cattle thrived on it.

For twenty years after 1865, cattle ranching dominated the "open range," a vast fenceless area extending from the Texas Panhandle north into Canada. The techniques of the business came from Mexico. Long before American cowboys moved herds north, their Mexican counterparts, the *vaqueros*, developed the essential techniques of branding, roundups, and roping. The cattle themselves, the famous Texas longhorns, also came from Mexico. Spreading over the grasslands of southern Texas, the longhorns multiplied rapidly. Although their meat was coarse and stringy, they fed a nation hungry for beef at the end of the Civil War.

The problem was getting the beef to eastern markets, and Joseph G. McCoy, a livestock shipper from Illinois, solved it. Looking for a way to market Texas beef, McCoy conceived the idea of taking the cattle to railheads in Kansas. He talked first with the president of the Missouri Pacific, who ordered him out of his office, and then with the head of the Kansas Pacific, who laughed at the idea. The persistent McCoy finally signed a contract in 1867 with the Hannibal and St. Joseph Railroad. Searching for an appropriate rail junction, he settled on the sleepy Kansas town of Abilene, "a very small, dead place," he remembered, with about a dozen log huts and one nearly bankrupt saloon.

In September 1867, McCoy shipped the first train of twenty cars of longhorn cattle. By the end of the year, a thousand carloads had followed, all headed for Chicago markets. In 1870, 300,000 head of Texas cattle reached Abilene, followed the next year—the peak year—by 700,000 head. The Alamo Saloon, crowded with tired cowboys at the end of the drive, now employed seventy-five bartenders, working three 8-hour shifts.

The profits were enormous. Drivers bought cheap Texas steers for $4 a head and sold them for $30 or $40 a head at the northern railhead. The most famous trail was the Chisholm, running from southern Texas through Oklahoma Territory to Ellsworth and Abilene, Kansas, on the Kansas Pacific Railroad.

Cowboys pushed steers northward in herds of two to three thousand. Novels and films have portrayed the cowboys as white, but at least a quarter of them were black, and possibly another quarter were Mexicans. A typical crew on the trail north might have eight men, half of them black or Mexican.

Like miners, cattlemen lived beyond the formal reach of the law and so established their own. Ranchers adopted rules for cattle ownership, branding,

Cattle Trails
Cattle raised in Texas were driven along the cattle trails to the northern railheads, and trains carried them to market.

roundups, and drives, and they formed associations to enforce them. The Wyoming Stock Growers' Association, the largest and most formidable, had four hundred members owning two million cattle; its reach extended well beyond Wyoming into Colorado, Nebraska, Montana, and the Dakotas.

By 1880, more than six million cattle had been driven to northern markets. But the era of the great cattle drive was ending. Farmers were planting wheat on the old buffalo ranges; barbed wire, a recent invention, cut across the trails and divided up the big ranches. Mechanical improvements in slaughtering, refrigerated transportation, and cold storage modernized the industry. Ranchers bred the Texas longhorns with heavier Hereford and Angus bulls, and as the new breeds proved profitable, more and more ranches opened on the northern ranges.

By the mid-1880s, some 4.5 million cattle grazed the High Plains, reminding people of the once great herds of buffalo. Stories of vast profits circulated, attracting outside capital. Large investments transformed ranching into big business, often controlled by absentee owners and subject to new problems.

The winter of 1886–1887 was one of the worst in western history. Temperatures dropped to 45 degrees below zero, and cattle that once would have saved themselves by drifting ahead of the storms came up against the new barbed wire fences. Cattle died by the tens of thousands. The cattle business recovered, but it took different directions. Outside capital, so plentiful in the boom years, dried up. Ranchers began fencing their lands, reducing their herds, and growing hay for winter food.

The last roundup on the northern ranges took place in 1905. Ranches grew smaller, and some ranchers, at first in the scrub country of the Southwest, then on the Plains themselves, switched to raising sheep. By 1900, there were nearly thirty-eight million sheep west of the Missouri River, far more than there were cattle.

Ranchers and sheepherders fought bitterly to control the grazing lands, but they had one problem in common: the troubles ahead. Homesteaders, armed with barbed wire and new strains of wheat, were pushing onto the Plains, and the day of the open range was over.

SODBUSTERS ON THE PLAINS: THE FARMING BONANZA

Like miners and cattle ranchers, millions of farmers moved into the West in the decades after 1870 to seek crop bonanzas and new ways of life. Some realized their dreams; many fought just to survive.

Between 1870 and 1900, farmers cultivated more land than ever before in American history. They peopled the Plains from Dakota to Texas, pushed the Indians out of their last sanctuary in Oklahoma, and poured into the basins and foothills of the Rockies. By 1900, the western half of the nation contained almost 30 percent of the population, compared to less than 1 percent just a half century earlier.

Unlike mining, farm settlement often followed predictable patterns, taking population from states east of the settlement line and moving gradually westward. Crossing the Mississippi, farmers settled first in western Iowa, Minnesota, Nebraska, Kansas, Texas, and South Dakota. The movement slumped during the depression of the 1870s, but then a new wave of optimism carried thousands more west. Several years of above average rainfall convinced farmers that the Dakotas, western Nebraska and Kansas, and eastern Colorado were the "rain belt of the Plains." Between 1870 and 1900, the population on the Plains tripled.

In some areas, the newcomers were blacks who had fled the South, fed up with beatings and murders, crop liens, and the Black Codes that institutionalized their subordinate status. In 1879, about six thousand African Americans known as the Exodusters left their homes in Louisiana, Mississippi, and Texas to establish new and freer lives in Kansas, the home of John Brown and the Free-Soil campaigns of the 1850s. Once there, they farmed or worked as laborers; women worked in the fields alongside the men or cleaned houses and took in washing to make ends meet. All told, the Exodusters homesteaded 20,000 acres of land, and though they met prejudice, it was not as extreme as they had known at home.

Other African Americans moved to Oklahoma, thinking they might establish the first African American state. Whether headed for Oklahoma or Kansas, they picked up and moved in sizable groups that were based on family units; they took with them the customs they had known, and in their new homes they were able, for the first time, to have some measure of self-government.

For blacks and whites alike, farming on the Plains presented new problems. There was little surface water, and wells ranged between 50 and 500 feet deep. Well drillers charged up to $2 a foot. Taking advantage of the steady Plains winds, windmills brought the water to the surface, but they too were expensive, and until 1900, many farmers could not afford them. Lumber for homes and fences was also scarce.

Unable to afford wood, farmers often started out in dreary sod houses. Cut into 3-foot sections, the thick prairie sod was laid like brick, with space left for two windows and a door. Since glass was scarce, cloth hung over the windows; a blanket was hung from the ceiling to make two rooms. Sod houses were small, provided little light and air, and were impossible to keep clean. When it rained, water seeped through the roof. Yet a sod house cost only $2.78 to build.

Disappointed with the failures of Reconstruction and fearful of the violence that surrounded them, many southern blacks migrated to Kansas in the 1870s and 1880s. Comparing their trek to the biblical story of the Israelites' exodus from Egypt, they became known as "Exodusters."

The Plains environment sorely tested the men and women who moved there. Neighbors were distant; the land stretched on as far as the eye could see. Always the wind blew.

In the winters, savage storms swept the open grasslands. Summertime temperatures stayed near 110 degrees for weeks at a time. Fearsome rainstorms, building in the summer's heat, beat down the young corn and wheat. The summers also brought grasshoppers, arriving without warning, flying in clouds so huge they shut out the sun. The grasshoppers ate everything in sight: crops, clothing, mosquito netting, tree bark, even plow handles. In the summer of 1874, they devastated the whole Plains from Texas to the Dakotas, eating everything "but the mortgage," as one farmer said.

NEW FARMING METHODS

Farmers adopted new techniques to meet conditions on the Plains. For one thing, they needed cheap and effective fencing material, and in 1874, Joseph F. Glidden, a farmer from De Kalb, Illinois, provided it with the invention of barbed wire. By 1883, his factory was turning out 600 miles of barbed wire every day, and farmers were buying it faster than it could be produced.

Dry farming, a new technique, helped compensate for the lack of rainfall. By plowing furrows 12 to 14 inches deep and creating a dust mulch to fill the furrow, farmers loosened the soil and slowed evaporation. Wheat farmers imported European varieties of plants that could withstand the harsh Plains winters.

Farm technology changed long before the Civil War, but later developments improved it. In 1877, James Oliver of Indiana patented a chilled-iron plow with a smooth-surfaced moldboard that did not clog in the thick prairie soils. The spring-tooth harrow (1869) sped soil preparation; the grain drill (1874) opened furrows and scientifically fed seed into the ground. The lister (1880) dug a deep furrow, planted corn at the bottom, and covered the seed— all in one operation.

The first baling press was built in 1866, and the hay loader was patented in 1876. The first successful harvester, the cord binder (1878), cut and tied bundles of grain, enabling two men and a team of horses to harvest 20 acres of wheat a day. Invented earlier, threshers grew larger; employing as many as nine men and ten horses, one machine could thresh 300 bushels of grain a day.

DISCONTENT ON THE FARM

Touring the South in the 1860s, Oliver H. Kelley, a clerk in the Department of Agriculture, was struck by the drabness of rural life. In 1867, he founded the National Grange of the Patrons of Husbandry, known simply as the Grange. The Grange provided social, cultural, and educational activities for its members. Its constitution banned involvement in politics, but Grangers often ignored the rules and supported railroad regulation and other measures.

The Grange grew rapidly during the depression of the 1870s, and by 1875, it had more than 800,000 members in 20,000 local Granges. Most were in the Midwest and South. The Granges set up cooperative stores, grain elevators, warehouses, insurance companies, and farm machinery factories. Many failed, but in the meantime the organization made its mark. Picking up where the Grange left off, farm-oriented groups such as the Farmers' Alliance, with branches in both the South and West, began to attract followers.

Like the cattle boom, the farming boom ended sharply after 1887. A severe drought that year cut harvests, and other droughts followed in 1889 and 1894. Thousands of new farmers were wiped out on the western Plains. Between 1888 and 1892, more than half the population of western Kansas left. Farmers grew angry and restless. They complained about declining crop prices, rising railroad rates, and heavy mortgages.

Although many farmers were unhappy, the peopling of the West in those years transformed American agriculture. The states beyond the Mississippi became the garden land of the nation. California sent fruit, wine, and wheat to eastern markets. Under the Mormons, Utah flourished with irrigation. Texas beef stocked the country's tables, and vast wheat fields, stretching to the horizon, covered Minnesota, the Dakotas, Montana, and eastern Colorado. All produced more than Americans could consume. By 1890, American farmers were exporting large amounts of wheat and other crops.

Farmers became more commercial and scientific. They needed to know more and work harder. Mail-order houses and rural free delivery diminished their isolation and tied them ever closer to the national future. "This is a new age to the farmer," said a statistician in the Department of Agriculture in 1889. "He is now, more than ever before, a citizen of the world."

THE FINAL FLING

As the West filled in with people, pressure mounted on the president and Congress to open the last Indian territory, Oklahoma, to settlers. In March 1889, Congress acted and forced the Creek and Seminole tribes, which had been moved into Oklahoma in the 1820s, to surrender their rights to the land. With arrangements complete, President Benjamin Harrison announced the opening of the Oklahoma District as of noon, April 22, 1889.

Preparations were feverish all along the frontier. On the morning of April 22, nearly a hundred thousand people lined the Oklahoma borders.

At noon, the starting flag dropped. Bugles and cannon signaled the opening of the "last" territory. Horsemen lunged forward; overloaded wagons collided and overturned.

By sunset that day, settlers claimed twelve thousand homesteads, and the 1.92 million acres of the Oklahoma District were officially settled. Homesteaders threw up shelters for the night. By evening, Oklahoma City, that morning merely a spot on the prairie with cottonwoods and grass, had ten thousand people.

The "Boomers" (those who waited for the signal) and "Sooners" (those who jumped the gun) reflected the speed of western settlement. "Creation!" a character in Edna Ferber's novel *Cimarron* declared. "Hell! That took six days. This was done in one. It was History made in an hour—and I helped make it."

THE MEANING OF THE WEST

Between the Civil War and 1900, the West witnessed one of the greatest migrations in history. With the Native Americans driven into smaller and smaller areas, farms, ranches, mines, and cities took over the vast lands from the Mississippi to the Pacific. The 1890 census noted that for the first time in the country's history, "there can hardly be said to be a frontier line." Picking up the theme, Frederick Jackson Turner, a young history instructor at the University of Wisconsin, examined its importance in an influential 1893 paper, "The Significance of the Frontier in American History."

"The existence of an area of free land," Turner wrote, "its continuous recession, and the advance of American settlement westward, explain American development." It shaped customs and character; gave rise to independence, self-confidence, and individualism; and fostered invention and adaptation. Historians have substantially modified Turner's thesis by pointing to frontier conservatism and imitativeness, the influence of varying racial groups, and the persistence of European ideas and institutions. Most recently, they have shown that family and community loomed as large as individualism on the frontier; men, women, and children played very much the same roles as they had back home.

Rejecting Turner almost completely, a group of "new Western historians" has advanced a different and complex view of the West, and one with few heroes and heroines. Emphasizing the region's racial and ethnic diversity, these historians stress the role of women as well as men, trace struggles between economic interests instead of fights between gunslingers, and question the impact of development on the environment. White English-speaking Americans, they suggest, could be said to have conquered the West rather than settled it.

The West, in this view, was not settled by a wave of white migrants moving west across the continent (Turner's "frontier") but by a set of waves—Anglo, Mexican American, African American, Asian American, and others—moving in many directions and interacting with each other and with Native American cultures to produce the modern West. Nor did western history end in 1890 as Turner would have it. Instead, migration, development, and economic exploitation continued into the twentieth century, illustrated in the fact that the number of people who moved to the West after 1900 far exceeded those who had moved there before.

In both the nineteenth and twentieth centuries, there can be no doubt that the image of the frontier and the West influenced American development. Western lands attracted European, Latin American, and Asian immigrants, adding to the society's talent and diversity. The mines, forests, and farms of the West fueled the economy, sent raw materials to eastern factories, and fed the growing cities. Though defeated in warfare, the Native Americans and Mexicans influenced art, architecture, law, and western folklore. The West was the first American empire, and it had a profound impact on the American mind and imagination.

Chronology

1849	Gold Rush to California
1859	More gold and silver discoveries in Colorado and Nevada
1862	Congress passes Homestead Act encouraging western settlement
1864	Nevada admitted to the Union
	Colonel John Chivington leads massacre of Indians at Sand Creek, Colorado
1865–1867	Sioux War against white miners and U.S. Army
1866	"Long drive" of cattle touches off cattle bonanzas
1867	Horace Greeley urges Easterners to "Go West, young man"
	National Grange of the Patrons of Husbandry (the Grange) founded to enrich farmers' lives
1867–1868	Policy of "small reservations" for Indians adopted
1873	Congress passes Timber Culture Act
	Big bonanza discovered on the Comstock Lode in Nevada
1874	Joseph F. Glidden invents barbed wire
	Discovery of gold in Dakota Territory sets off Black Hills Gold Rush
1876	Colorado admitted to the Union
	Custer and his men defeated and killed by the Sioux at battle of the Little Bighorn (June)
1883	Museum expedition discovers fewer than two hundred buffalo in the West
1886–1887	Severe drought and winter damage cattle and farming bonanzas
1887	Congress passes Dawes Severalty Act, making Indians individual landowners
	Hatch Act provides funds for establishment of agricultural experiment stations
1889	Washington, Montana, and the Dakotas admitted to the Union
	Oklahoma Territory opened to settlement
1890	Idaho and Wyoming admitted to the Union
	Teton Sioux massacred at battle of Wounded Knee, South Dakota (December)
1893	Young historian Frederick Jackson Turner analyzes closing of the frontier
1902	Congress passes National Reclamation Act (the Newlands Act)

18

❧ ———————— ❧

THE INDUSTRIAL SOCIETY

In 1876, Americans celebrated their first century of independence. Survivors of a recent civil war, they observed the centenary proudly and rather self-consciously, in song and speech, and above all in a grand Centennial Exposition held in Philadelphia, Pennsylvania.

Spread over several hundred acres, the exposition occupied 180 buildings and attracted nine million visitors, about one-fifth of the country's population at the time. Significantly, it focused more on the present than the past. Fairgoers strolled through exhibits of life in colonial times, then hurried off to see the main attractions: machines, inventions, and products of the new industrial era. They saw linoleum, a new, easy-to-clean floor covering. For the first time, they tasted root beer, supplied by a young druggist named Charles Hires, and the exotic banana, wrapped in foil and selling for a dime. They saw their first bicycle, an awkward high-wheeled contraption with solid tires.

A Japanese pavilion generated widespread interest in the culture of Japan. There was also a women's building, the first ever in a major exposition. Inside were displayed paintings and sculpture by women artists, along with rows of textile machinery staffed by female operators.

In the entire exposition, machinery was the focus, and Machinery Hall was the most popular building. Here were the products of an ever improving civilization. Long lines of the curious waited to see the telephone, Alexander Graham Bell's new device. ("My God, it talks!" the emperor of Brazil exclaimed.) Thomas A. Edison displayed several recent inventions, while nearby, whirring machines turned out bricks, chewing tobacco, and other products. Fairgoers saw the first public display of the typewriter, Elisha Otis's new elevator, and the Westinghouse railroad air brake.

But above all, they crowded around the mighty Corliss engine, the focal point of the exposition. A giant steam engine, it dwarfed everything else in Machinery Hall, its twin vertical cylinders towering almost four stories in the air. Alone, it supplied power for the eight thousand other machines, large and small, on the exposition grounds. Poorly designed, the Corliss was soon obsolete, but for the moment it captured the nation's imagination. It symbolized swift movement toward an industrial and urban society. John Greenleaf Whittier, the aging rural poet, likened it to the snake in the Garden of Eden and refused to see it.

As Whittier feared, the United States was fast becoming an industrial society. Developments earlier in the century laid the basis, but the most spectacular advances in industrialization came during the three decades after the Civil War. At the start of the war, the country lagged well behind industrializing nations such as Great Britain, France, and Germany. By 1900, it had vaulted far into the lead, with a manufacturing output that exceeded the *combined* output of its three European rivals. Over the same years, cities grew, technology advanced, and farm production rose. Developments in manufacturing, mining, agriculture, transportation, and communications changed society.

In this change, railroads, steel, oil, and other industries, all shaped by the hands of labor, played a leading role. Many Americans eagerly welcomed the new directions. William Dean Howells, a leading novelist, visited the Centennial Exposition and stood in awe before the Corliss. Comparing it to the paintings and sculpture on display, Howells preferred the machine: "It is in these things of iron and steel," he said, "that the national genius most freely speaks."

INDUSTRIAL DEVELOPMENT

American industry owed its remarkable growth to several considerations. It fed on an abundance of natural resources: coal, iron, timber, petroleum, waterpower. An iron manufacturer likened the nation to "a gigantic bowl filled with treasure." Labor was also abundant, drawn from American farm families and the hosts of European immigrants who flocked to American mines, cities, and factories. Nearly eight million immigrants arrived in the 1870s and 1880s; another fifteen million came between 1890 and 1914—large figures for a nation whose total population in 1900 was about seventy-six million people.

The burgeoning population led to expanded markets, which new devices such as the telegraph and telephone helped to exploit. The swiftly growing urban populations devoured goods, and the railroads, spreading pell-mell across the land, linked the cities together and opened a national market. Within its boundaries, the United States had the largest free trade market in the world, while tariff barriers partially protected its producers from outside competition.

Expansive market and labor conditions buoyed the confidence of investors, European and American, who provided large amounts of capital. Technological progress, so remarkable in these years, doomed some older industries (tallow, for example) but increased productivity in others, such as the kerosene industry, and created entirely new industries as well. Through inventions such as the harvester and the combine, it also helped foster a firm agricultural base, on which industrialization depended.

Eager to promote economic growth, government at all levels—federal, state, and local—gave manufacturers money, land, and other resources. Other benefits, too, flowed from the American system of government: stability, commitment to the concept of private property, and, initially at least, a reluctance to regulate industrial activity. Unlike their European counterparts, American manufacturers faced few legal or social barriers, and their main domestic rivals, the southern planters, had lost political power in the Civil War.

In this atmosphere, entrepreneurs flourished. Taking steps crucial for industrialization, they organized, managed, and assumed the financial risks of the new enterprises. Admirers called them captains of industry; foes labeled them robber barons. To some degree, they were both—creative *and* acquisitive. If sometimes they seemed larger than life, it was because they dealt in concepts, distances, and quantities often unknown to earlier generations.

Industrial growth, it must be remembered, was neither a simple nor steady nor inevitable process. It involved human decisions and brought with it large social benefits and costs. Growth varied from industry to industry and from year to year. It was concentrated in the Northeast, where in 1890, more than 85 percent of America's manufactured goods originated. The more sparsely settled West provided raw materials, while the South, although making major gains in iron, textiles, and tobacco, had to rebuild after wartime devastation.

Still, industrial development proceeded at an extraordinary pace. Between 1865 and 1914, the real gross national product—the total monetary value of all goods and services produced in a year, with prices held stable—grew at a rate of more than 4 percent a year, increasing about eightfold overall. As Robert Higgs, an economic historian, noted, "Never before had such rapid growth continued for so long."

AN EMPIRE ON RAILS

Genuine revolutions happen rarely, but a major one occurred in the nineteenth century: a revolution in transportation and communications. When the nineteenth century began, people traveled and communicated much as they had for centuries before; when it ended, the railroad, the telegraph, the telephone, and the oceangoing steamship had wrought enormous changes.

The steamship sliced in half the time of the Atlantic crossing and, not dependent on wind and tide, introduced new regularity in the movement of goods and passengers. The telegraph, flashing messages almost instantaneously along miles of wire (400,000 miles of it in the early 1880s), transformed communications, as did the telephone a little later. But the railroad worked the largest changes of all. Along with Bessemer steel, it was the most significant technical innovation of the century.

"EMBLEM OF MOTION AND POWER"

The railroad dramatically affected economic and social life. Economic growth would have occurred without it, of course; canals, inland steamboats, and the country's superb system of interior waterways already provided the outlines of an effective transportation network. But the railroad added significantly to the network and contributed advantages all its own.

Those advantages included more direct routes, greater speed, greater safety and comfort than other modes of land travel, more dependable schedules, a larger volume of traffic, and year-round service. The railroad went where canals and rivers did not go—directly to the loading platforms of great factories or across the arid West. As construction crews pushed tracks onward, vast areas of the continent opened for settlement.

Consequently, American railroads differed from European ones. In Europe, railroads were usually built between cities and towns that already existed; they carried mostly the same goods that earlier forms of transportation had. In the United States, they did that and more: They often created the very towns they then served, and they ended up carrying cattle from Texas, fruit from Florida, and other goods that had never been carried before.

Linking widely separated cities and villages, the railroad ended the relative isolation and self-sufficiency of the country's "island communities." It tied people together, brought in outside products, fostered greater interdependence, and encouraged economic specialization. Under its stimulus, Chicago supplied meat to the nation, Minneapolis supplied grain, and St. Louis supplied beer. For these and other communities, the railroad made possible a national market and in so doing pointed the way toward mass production and mass consumption, two of the hallmarks of twentieth-century society.

It also pointed the way toward later business development. The railroad, as Alfred D. Chandler, a historian of business, has written, was "the nation's first big business"; it worked out "the modern ways of finance, management, labor relations, competition, and government regulation."

A railroad corporation, far-flung and complex, was a new kind of business. It stretched over thousands of miles, employed thousands of people, dealt with countless customers, and required a scale of organization and decision making unknown in earlier business. Railroad managers never met most customers or even many employees; thus arose new problems in marketing and labor relations. Year by year, railroad companies consumed large quantities of iron, steel, coal, lumber, and glass, stimulating growth and employment in numerous industries.

No wonder, then, that the railroad captured so completely the country's imagination. For nearly a hundred years—the railroad era lasted through the 1940s—children gathered at depots, paused in the fields to wave as the fast express flashed by, listened at night to far-off whistles, and wondered what lay down the tracks. They lived in a world grown smaller.

BUILDING THE EMPIRE

When Lee surrendered at Appomattox in 1865, the country already had 35,000 miles of track, and much of the railroad system east of the Mississippi River was in place. Farther west, the rail network stood poised on the edge of settlement. Although southern railroads were in shambles from the war, the United States had nearly as much railroad track as the rest of the world.

After the Civil War, rail construction increased by leaps and bounds. From 35,000 miles in 1865, the network expanded to 93,000 miles in 1880; 166,000 in 1890; and 193,000 in 1900—more than in all Europe, including Russia. Mileage peaked at 254,037 miles in 1916, just before the industry began its long decline into the mid-twentieth century.

To build such an empire took vast amounts of capital. American and European investors provided some of the money; government supplied the rest. In all, local governments gave railroad companies about $300 million, and state governments added $228 million more. The federal government loaned nearly $65 million to a half dozen western railroads and donated millions of acres of the public domain.

The grants of cash and land promoted waste and corruption. The companies built fast and wastefully, eager to collect the subsidies that went with each mile of track. The grants also enabled railroads to build into territories that were pledged to the Indians, thus contributing to the wanton destruction of Indian life.

Yet, on balance, the grants probably worked more benefits than evils. As Congress had hoped, the grants were the lure for railroad building across the rugged, unsettled West, where it would be years before the railroads' revenues would repay their construction. Farmers, ranchers, and merchants poured into the newly opened areas, settling the country and boosting the value of government and private land nearby. The grants seemed necessary in a nation which, unlike Europe, expected private enterprise to build the railroads. In return for government aid, Congress required the railroads to carry government freight, troops, and mail at substantially reduced rates—resulting in savings to the government of almost $1 billion between 1850 and 1945. In no other cases of federal subsidies to carriers—canals, highways, and airlines—did Congress exact specific benefits in return.

LINKING THE NATION VIA TRUNK LINES

The early railroads may seem to have linked different regions, but in fact they did not. Built with little regard for through traffic, they were designed more to protect local interests than to tap outside markets. Many extended less than fifty miles. To avoid cooperating with other lines, they adopted conflicting schedules, built separate depots, and above all, used different gauges. Gauges, the distance between the rails, ranged from 4 feet $8\frac{1}{2}$ inches, which became the standard gauge, to 6 feet. Without special equipment, trains of one gauge could not run on tracks of another.

The Civil War showed the value of fast long-distance transportation, and after 1865, railroad managers worked to provide it. In a burst of consolidation, the large companies swallowed the small; integrated rail networks became a reality. Railroads also adopted standard schedules, signals, and equipment and finally, in 1886, the standard gauge. In 1866, in a dramatic innovation to speed traffic, railroad companies introduced fast freight lines that pooled cars for service between cities.

Over the rail system, passengers and freight moved in relative speed, comfort, and safety. Automatic couplers (1867), air brakes (1869), refrigerator cars (1867), dining cars, heated cars, electric switches, and stronger locomotives

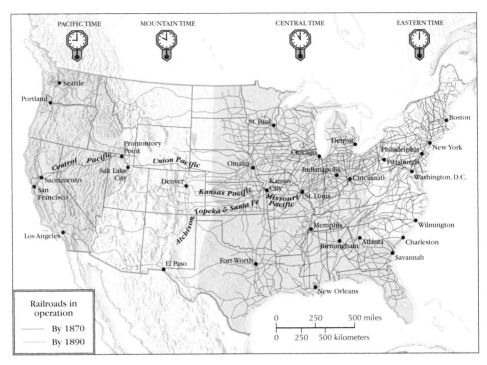

Railroads, 1870 and 1890
In the last quarter of the nineteenth century, railroads expanded into Texas, the far Southwest, and the Northwest, carrying settlers, businesses, and government to the far-flung areas.

transformed railroad service. George Pullman's lavish sleeping cars became popular. Handsome depots, such as New York's Grand Central Station and Washington's Union Station, were erected at major terminals.

In November 1883, the railroads even changed time. Ending the crazy quilt jumble of local times that caused scheduling difficulties, the American Railway Association divided the country into four time zones and adopted the modern system of standard time. Congress took thirty-five years longer; it adopted standard time in 1918, in the midst of World War I.

RAILS ACROSS THE CONTINENT

The dream of a transcontinental railroad, linking the Atlantic and Pacific oceans, stretched back many years but had always been lost to sectional quarrels over the route. In 1862 and 1864, with the South out of the picture, Congress moved to build the first transcontinental railroad. It chartered the Union Pacific Railroad Company to build westward from Nebraska and the Central Pacific Railroad Company to build eastward from the Pacific Coast.

Construction began simultaneously at Omaha and Sacramento in 1863, lagged during the war, and moved vigorously ahead after 1865. It became a race, each company vying for land, loans, and potential markets. General Grenville M. Dodge, a tough Union army veteran, served as construction chief for the Union

Pacific, while Charles Crocker, a former Sacramento dry goods merchant, led the Central Pacific crews. Dodge organized an army of ten thousand workers, many of them ex-soldiers and Irish immigrants. Pushing rapidly westward, he encountered frequent attacks from Native Americans defending their lands, but he had the advantage of building over flat prairie.

Crocker faced more trying conditions in the high Sierra Nevada along California's eastern border. After several experiments, he decided that Chinese laborers worked best, and he hired six thousand of them, most brought directly from China. "I built the Central Pacific," Crocker enjoyed boasting, but the Chinese crews in fact did the awesome work. Under the most difficult conditions, they dug, blasted, and pushed their way slowly east.

On May 10, 1869, the two lines met at Promontory, Utah, near the northern tip of the Great Salt Lake. Dodge's crews had built 1086 miles of track, Crocker's 689. The Union Pacific and Central Pacific presidents hammered in a golden spike, and the dreamed-of connection was made. The telegraph flashed the news east and west, setting off wild celebrations. A photograph was taken, but it included none of the Chinese who had worked so hard to build the road; they were all asked to step aside.

The transcontinental railroad symbolized American unity and progress. Along with the Suez Canal, completed the same year, it helped knit the world together. By the 1890s, business leaders talked comfortably of railroad systems

After the last spike was hammered in at Promontory, Utah, the pilots of the two locomotives exchanged champagne toasts. The chief engineers of the two lines are seen shaking hands. Conspicuously absent from the photograph are the Chinese laborers who helped build the railroad.

stretching deep into South America and across the Bering Strait to Asia, Europe, and Africa. In an age of progress, anything seemed possible.

PROBLEMS OF GROWTH

Overbuilding during the 1870s and 1880s caused serious problems for the railroads. Competition was severe, and managers fought desperately for traffic. They offered special rates and favors: free passes for large shippers; low rates on bulk freight, carload lots, and long hauls; and, above all, rebates—secret, privately negotiated reductions below published rates. Fierce rate wars broke out frequently, convincing managers that ruthless competition helped no one.

Managers such as Albert Fink, the brilliant vice president of the Louisville & Nashville, tried first to arrange pooling agreements, a way to control competition by sharing traffic, but none survived the intense pressures of competition. Failing to cooperate, railroad owners next tried to consolidate. Through purchase, lease, and merger, they gobbled up competitors and built "self-sustaining systems" that dominated entire regions. But many of the systems, expensive and unwieldy, collapsed in the Panic of 1893. By mid-1894, a quarter of the railroads were bankrupt. The victims of the panic included such legendary names as the Erie, Santa Fe, Northern Pacific, and Union Pacific.

Needing money, railroads turned naturally to bankers, who finally imposed order on the industry. J. Pierpont Morgan, head of the New York investment house of J. P. Morgan and Company, took the lead. Massively built, with eyes so piercing they seemed like the headlights of an onrushing train, Morgan was the most powerful figure in American finance. He liked efficiency, combination, and order. He disliked "wasteful" competition.

After 1893, Morgan and a few other bankers refinanced ailing railroads, and in the process they took control of the industry. Their methods were direct: fixed costs and debt were ruthlessly cut, new stock was issued to provide capital, rates were stabilized, rebates and competition were eliminated, and control was vested in a "voting trust" of handpicked trustees. Between 1894 and 1898, Morgan reorganized—critics said "Morganized"—the Southern Railway, the Erie, the Northern Pacific, and the Baltimore & Ohio. In addition, he took over a half dozen other important railroads. By 1900, he was a dominant figure in American railroading.

As the new century began, the railroads had pioneered the patterns followed by most other industries. Seven giant systems controlled nearly two-thirds of the mileage, and they in turn answered to a few investment banking firms such as the house of Morgan. For good and ill, a national transportation network, centralized and relatively efficient, was now in place.

AN INDUSTRIAL EMPIRE

The new industrial empire was based on a number of dramatic innovations, including steel, oil, and inventions of all kinds that transformed ordinary life. In this process, steel was as important as the railroads. Harder and more durable than other kinds of iron, steel wrought changes in manufacturing, agriculture, transportation, and architecture. It permitted construction of longer bridges, taller buildings, stronger railroad track, deadlier weapons, better plows, heavier machinery, and faster ships. Made in great furnaces by strong men, it symbolized the tough, often brutal nature of industrial society. From the 1870s onward, steel output became the worldwide accepted measure of industrial progress, and nations around the globe vied for leadership.

The Bessemer process, developed in the late 1850s by Henry Bessemer in England and independently by William Kelly in the United States, made increased steel production possible. Both Bessemer and Kelly discovered that a blast of air forced through molten iron burned off carbon and other impurities, resulting in steel of a more uniform and durable quality. The discovery transformed the industry. While earlier methods produced amounts a person could lift, a Bessemer converter handled 5 tons of molten metal at a time. The mass production of steel was now possible.

CARNEGIE AND STEEL

Bessemer plants demanded extensive capital investment, abundant raw materials, and sophisticated production techniques. Using chemical and other processes, the plants required research departments, which became critical components of later American industries. Costly to build, they limited entry into the industry to the handful who could afford them.

Great steel districts arose in Pennsylvania, Ohio, and Alabama—in each case around large coal deposits that fueled the huge furnaces. Pittsburgh became the center of the industry, its giant mills employing thousands of workers. Output shot up. In 1874, the United States produced less than half the amount of pig iron produced in Great Britain. By 1890, it took the lead, and in 1900, it produced four times as much as Britain.

Like the railroads, steel companies grew larger and larger. In 1880, only nine companies could produce more than 100,000 tons a year. By the early 1890s, several companies exceeded 250,000 tons, and two—including the great Carnegie Steel Company—produced more than 1 million tons a year. As operations expanded, managers needed more complex skills. Product development, marketing, and consumer preferences became important.

Andrew Carnegie emerged as the undisputed master of the industry. Born in Scotland, he came to the United States in 1848 at the age of 12. Settling near Pittsburgh, he went to work as a bobbin boy in a cotton mill, earning $1.20 a week. He soon took a job in a telegraph office, where in 1852 his hard work and skill caught the eye of Thomas A. Scott of the Pennsylvania Railroad. Starting as Scott's personal telegrapher, Carnegie spent a total of twelve years on the Pennsylvania, a training ground for company managers. By 1859, he had become a divisional superintendent. He was 24 years old.

Soon rich from shrewd investments, Carnegie plunged into the steel industry in 1872. On the Monongahela River south of Pittsburgh, he built the giant J. Edgar Thomson Steel Works, named after the president of the Pennsylvania

International Steel Production, 1880–1914

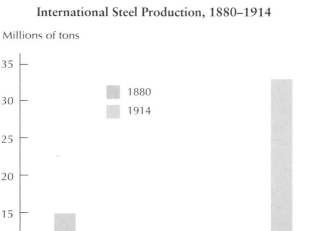

Millions of tons

35
30
25
20
15
10
5

1880
1914

Germany   France   Great Britain   Russia   United States

Railroad, his biggest customer. With his warmth and salesmanship, he attracted able partners and subordinates such as Henry Clay Frick and Charles M. Schwab, whom he drove hard and paid well. Although he had written magazine articles defending the rights of workers, Carnegie kept the wages of the laborers in his mills low and disliked unions. With the help of Frick, he crushed a violent strike at his Homestead works in 1892 (see p. 484).

In 1878, he won the steel contract for the Brooklyn Bridge. During the next decade, as city building boomed, he converted the huge Homestead works near Pittsburgh to the manufacture of structural beams and angles, which went into the New York City elevated railway, the first skyscrapers, and the Washington Monument. Carnegie profits mounted: from $2 million in 1888 to $40 million in 1900. That year, Carnegie Steel alone produced more steel than Great Britain. Employing twenty thousand people, it was the largest industrial company in the world.

In 1901, Carnegie sold it. Believing that wealth brought social obligations, he wanted to devote his full time to philanthropy. He found a buyer in J. Pierpont Morgan, who in the late 1890s had put together several steel companies, including Federal Steel, Carnegie's chief rival. Carnegie Steel had blocked Morgan's well-known desire for control, and in mid-1900, when a war loomed between the two interests, Morgan decided to buy Carnegie out. In early January 1901, Morgan told Charles M. Schwab: "Go and find his price." Schwab cornered Carnegie on the golf course; Carnegie listened, and the next day he handed

Schwab a note, scribbled in blunt pencil, asking almost a half billion dollars. Morgan glanced at it and said, "I accept this price."

Drawing other companies into the combination, Morgan on March 3, 1901, announced the creation of the United States Steel Corporation. The new firm was capitalized at $1.4 billion, the first billion-dollar company. Soon there were other giants, including Bethlehem Steel, Republic Steel, and National Steel. As the nineteenth century ended, steel products—rare just thirty years before—had altered the landscape. Huge firms, investment bankers, and professional managers dominated the industry.

ROCKEFELLER AND OIL

Petroleum worked comparable changes in the economic and social landscape, although mostly after 1900. Distilled into oil, it lubricated the machinery of the industrial age. There seemed little use for gasoline (the internal combustion engine had only just been developed), but kerosene, another major distillate, brought inexpensive illumination into almost every home. Whale oil, cottonseed oil, and even tallow candles were expensive to burn; consequently, many people went to bed at nightfall. Kerosene lamps opened the evenings to activity, altering the patterns of life.

Like other changes in these years, the oil boom happened with surprising speed. In the mid-1850s, petroleum was a bothersome, smelly fluid that occasionally rose to the surface of springs and streams. In 1859, Edwin L. Drake drilled the first oil well near Titusville in northwest Pennsylvania, and the "black gold" fever struck. Chemists soon discovered ways to transform petroleum into lubricating oil, grease, paint, wax, varnish, naphtha, and paraffin. Within a few years, there was a world market in oil.

At first, growth of the oil industry was chaotic. Early drillers and refiners produced for local markets, and since drilling wells and even erecting refineries cost little, competition flourished. Output fluctuated dramatically; prices rose and fell, with devastating effect.

A young merchant from Cleveland named John D. Rockefeller imposed order on the industry. "I had an ambition to build," he later recalled, and beginning in 1863 at the age of 24, he built the Standard Oil Company, soon to become one of the titans of corporate business. Like Morgan, Rockefeller considered competition wasteful, small-scale enterprise inefficient, and consolidation the path of the future.

Methodically, Rockefeller absorbed or destroyed competitors in Cleveland and elsewhere. Like Carnegie, he demanded efficiency, relentless cost cutting, and the latest technology.

Paying careful attention to detail, Rockefeller counted the stoppers in barrels, shortened barrel hoops to save metal, and, in one famous incident, reduced the number of drops of solder on kerosene cans from forty to thirty-nine. In large-scale production, Rockefeller realized, even small reductions meant huge savings. Research uncovered other ways of lowering costs and improving products, and Herman Frasch, a brilliant Standard chemist, solved problem after problem in the refining of oil.

John D. Rockefeller, satirized in a 1901 Puck *cartoon, is enthroned on oil, the base of his empire; his crown is girded by other holdings.*

In the end, Rockefeller triumphed over his competitors by marketing products of high quality at the lowest unit cost. But he employed other, less savory methods as well. He threatened rivals and bribed politicians. He employed spies to harass the customers of competing refiners. Above all, he extorted railroad rebates that lowered his transportation costs and undercut competitors. By 1879, he controlled 90 percent of the country's entire oil-refining capacity.

Vertically integrated, Standard Oil owned wells, timberlands, barrel and chemical plants, refineries, warehouses, pipelines, and fleets of tankers and oil cars. Its marketing organization served as the model for the industry. Standard exported oil to Asia, Africa, and South America; its 5-gallon kerosene tin, like Coca-Cola bottles and cans of a later era, was a familiar sight in the most distant parts of the world.

To manage it all, the company developed a new plan of business organization, the trust, which had profound significance for American business. In 1881, Samuel C. T. Dodd, Standard's attorney, set up the Standard Oil Trust, with a board of nine trustees empowered "to hold, control, and manage" all Standard's properties. Stockholders exchanged their stock for trust certificates, on which dividends were paid. On January 2, 1882, the first of the modern trusts was born. As Dodd intended, it immediately centralized control of Standard's far-flung empire.

Competition almost disappeared; profits soared. A trust movement swept the country as industries with similar problems—whiskey, lead, and sugar, among others—followed Standard's example. The word *trust* became synonymous with monopoly, amid vehement protests from the public. *Antitrust* became a watchword for a generation of reformers from the 1880s through the era of Woodrow Wilson. But Rockefeller's purpose had been *management* of a monopoly, not monopoly itself, which he had already achieved.

Other companies followed suit, including American Sugar Refining, the Northern Securities Company, and the National Biscuit Company. Merger followed merger. By 1900, 1 percent of the nation's companies controlled more than one-third of its industrial production.

In 1897, Rockefeller retired with a fortune of nearly $900 million, but for Standard Oil and petroleum in general, the most expansive period was yet to come. The great oil pools of Texas and Oklahoma had not yet been discovered. Plastics and other oil-based synthetics were several decades in the future. There were only four usable automobiles in the country, and the day of the gasoline engine, automobile, and airplane lay just ahead.

THE BUSINESS OF INVENTION

"America has become known the world around as the home of invention," boasted the commissioner of patents in 1892. It had not always been so; until the last third of the nineteenth century, the country had imported most of its technology. Then an extraordinary group of inventors and tinkerers—"specialists in invention," Thomas A. Edison called them—began to study the world around them. Some of their inventions gave rise to new industries; a few actually changed the quality of life.

The number of patents issued to inventors reflected the trend. During the 1850s, fewer than 2000 patents were issued each year. By the 1880s and 1890s, the figure reached more than 20,000 a year. Between 1790 and 1860, the U.S. Patent Office issued just 36,000 patents; in the decade of the 1890s alone, it issued more than 200,000.

Some of the inventions, such as the transatlantic cable, transformed communications. The typewriter (1867), stock ticker (1867), cash register (1879), calculating machine (1887), and adding machine (1888) helped business transactions. High-speed spindles, automatic looms, and electric sewing machines transformed the clothing industry, which for the first time in history turned out ready-made clothes for the masses. In 1890, the Census Bureau first used machines to sort and tabulate data on punched cards, a portent of a new era of information storage and processing.

In 1879, George Eastman patented a process for coating gelatin on photographic dry plates, which led to celluloid film and motion pictures. By 1888, he was marketing the Kodak camera, which weighed 35 ounces, took 100 exposures, and cost $25. Even though early Kodaks had to be returned to the factory, camera and all, for film developing, they revolutionized photography. Now almost anyone could snap a picture.

Other innovations changed the diet. There were new processes for flour, canned meat, vegetables, condensed milk, and even beer (from an offshoot of Louis Pasteur's discoveries about bacteria). Packaged cereals appeared on breakfast tables. Refrigerated railroad cars, ice-cooled, brought fresh fruit from Florida and California to all parts of the country.

No innovation, however, rivaled the importance of the telephone and the use of electricity for light and power. The telephone was the work of Alexander Graham Bell, a shrewd and genial Scot who settled in Boston in 1871. Interested in the problems of the deaf, Bell experimented with ways to transmit speech electrically, and after several years he had developed electrified metal disks that, much like the human ear, converted sound waves to electrical impulses and back again. On March 10, 1876, he transmitted the first sentence over a telephone: "Mr. Watson, come here; I want you." Later that year, he exhibited the new device to excited crowds at the Centennial Exposition in Philadelphia.

In 1878—the year a telephone was installed in the White House—the first telephone exchange opened in New Haven, Connecticut. Fighting off competitors who challenged the patent, the young Bell Telephone Company dominated the growing industry. By 1895, there were about 310,000 phones; a decade later, there were 10 million—about one for every ten people. American Telephone and Telegraph Company, formed by the Bell interests in 1885, became another of the vast holding companies, consolidating more than a hundred local systems.

If the telephone dissolved communication barriers as old as the human race, Thomas Alva Edison, the "Wizard of Menlo Park," invented processes and products of comparable significance. Born in 1847, Edison had little formal education, although he was an avid reader. Like Carnegie, he went into the new field of telegraphy. Tinkering in his spare time, he made several important improvements, including a telegraph capable of sending four messages over a single wire. Gathering teams of specialists to work on specific problems, Edison built the first modern research laboratory at Menlo Park, New Jersey. It may have been his most important invention.

The laboratory, Edison promised, would turn out "a minor invention every ten days and a big thing every six months or so." In 1877, it turned out a big thing, the phonograph, and in 1879, an even bigger one, the incandescent lamp.

Thomas Edison poses with his favorite invention, the tinfoil phonograph, in Mathew Brady's studio in Washington, D.C., in 1878.

Sir Joseph William Swan, an English inventor, had already experimented with the carbon filament, but Edison's task involved more than finding a durable filament. He set out to do nothing less than change light. A trial-and-error inventor, Edison tested sixteen hundred materials before producing, late in 1879, the carbon filament he wanted. Then he had to devise a complex system of conductors, meters, and generators by which electricity could be divided and distributed to homes and businesses.

With the financial backing of J. P. Morgan, he organized the Edison Illuminating Company and built the Pearl Street power station in New York City, the testing ground of the new apparatus. On September 4, 1882, as Morgan and others watched, Edison threw a switch and lit the house of Morgan, the stock exchange, the *New York Times,* and a number of other buildings. Amazed, a *Times* reporter marveled that writing stories in the office at night "seemed almost like writing in daylight." Power stations soon opened in Boston, Philadelphia, and Chicago. In a nation alive with light, the habits of centuries changed. A flick of the switch lit homes and factories at any hour of the day or night.

In a rare blunder, Edison based his system on low-voltage direct current, which could be transmitted only about two miles. George Westinghouse, the inventor of the railroad air brake, demonstrated the advantages of high-voltage alternating current for transmission over great distances. In 1886, he formed the Westinghouse Electric Company and with the inventor Nikola Tesla, a Hungarian immigrant, developed an alternating-current motor that could convert electricity into mechanical power. Electricity could light a lamp or illuminate a skyscraper, pull a streetcar or drive an entire railroad, run a sewing machine or power a mammoth assembly line. Transmitted easily over long distances, it freed factories and cities from location near water or coal. Electricity, in short, brought a revolution.

THE SELLERS

The increased output of the industrial age alone was not enough to ensure huge profits. The products still had to be sold, and that gave rise to a new "science" of marketing. Some business leaders—such as Swift in meatpacking, James B. Duke in tobacco, and Rockefeller in oil—built extensive marketing organizations of their own. Others relied on retailers, merchandising techniques, and advertising, developing a host of methods to convince consumers to buy.

Bringing producer and consumer together, nationwide advertising was the final link in the national market. From roadside signs to newspaper ads, it pervaded American life.

R. H. Macy in New York, John Wanamaker in Philadelphia, and Marshall Field in Chicago turned the department store into a national institution. There people could browse (a relatively new concept) and buy. Innovations in pricing, display, and advertising helped customers develop wants they did not know they had. In 1870, Wanamaker took out the first full-page newspaper ad, and Macy, an aggressive advertiser, touted "goods suitable for the millionaire at prices in reach of the millions."

A cutaway view of the "bee-hive" headquarters of mail-order giant Montgomery Ward & Co. of Chicago. By the time Ward moved into this building in 1899, rival retailer Sears, Roebuck & Co. was challenging Ward's mail-order business.

The "chain store"—an American term—spread across the country. The A & P grocery stores, begun in 1859, numbered sixty-seven by 1876, all marked by a familiar red-and-gold facade. By 1915, there were a thousand of them. In 1880, F. W. Woolworth, bored with the family farm, opened the first "Five and Ten Cent Store" in Utica, New York. He had fifty-nine stores in 1900, the year he adopted the bright red storefront and heaping counters to lure customers in and persuade them to buy.

In similar fashion, Sears, Roebuck and Montgomery Ward sold to rural customers through mail-order catalogs— a means of selling that depended on effective transportation and a high level of customer literacy. As a traveler for a dry goods firm, Aaron Montgomery Ward had seen an unfulfilled need of people in the rural West. He started the mail-order trend in 1872, with a one-sheet price list offered from a Chicago loft. By 1884, he offered almost ten thousand items in a catalog of 240 pages.

Richard W. Sears also saw the possibilities in the mail-order business. Starting with watches and jewelry, he gradually expanded his list. In the early 1880s, he moved to Chicago and with Alvah C. Roebuck founded Sears, Roebuck and Company. Sears sold anything and everything, prospering in a business that relied on mutual faith between unseen customers and distant distributors. Sears catalogs, soon more than five hundred pages long, exploited four-color illustration and other new techniques. By the early 1900s, Sears distributed six million catalogs annually.

Advertising, brand names, chain stores, and mail-order houses brought Americans of all varieties into a national market. Even as the country grew, a certain homogeneity of goods bound it together, touching cities and farms, East and West, rich and poor. There was a common language of consumption.

Americans had become a community of consumers, surrounded by goods unavailable just a few decades before, and able to purchase them. They had learned to make, want, and buy. "Because you see the main thing today is— shopping," Arthur Miller, a twentieth-century playwright, said in *The Price:*

Years ago a person, he was unhappy, didn't know what to do with himself—he'd go to church, start a revolution—something. Today you're unhappy? Can't figure it out? What is the salvation? Go shopping.

THE WAGE EARNERS

Although entrepreneurs were important, it was the labor of millions of men and women that built the new industrial society. In their individual stories, nearly all unrecorded, lay much of the achievement, drama, and pain of these years.

In a number of respects, their lot improved during the last quarter of the nineteenth century. Real wages rose, working conditions improved, and the workers' influence in national affairs increased. Between 1880 and 1914, wages of the average worker rose about $7 a year. Like others, workers also benefited from expanding health and educational services.

WORKING MEN, WORKING WOMEN, WORKING CHILDREN

Still, life for workers was not easy. Before 1900, most wage earners worked at least ten hours a day, six days a week. If skilled, they earned about 20 cents an hour; if unskilled, just half that. On average, workers earned between $400 and $500 a year. It took about $600 for a family of four to live decently.

There were few holidays or vacations, and there was little respite from the grueling routine. Skilled workers could turn the system to their own ends—New York City cigar makers, for example, paid someone to read to them while they worked—but the unskilled seldom had such luxury. They were too easily replaced. "A bit of advice to you," said a guidebook for immigrant Jews in the 1890s: "Do not take a moment's rest. Run, do, work, and keep your own good in mind."

Work was not only grueling; it was very dangerous. Safety standards were low, and accidents were common, more common in fact than in any other industrial nation in the world at that time. On the railroads, 1 in every 26 workers was injured and 1 in every 399 was killed each year. Thousands suffered from chronic illness, unknowing victims of dust, chemicals, and other pollutants.

The breadwinner might be a woman or a child; both worked in increasing numbers. In 1870, about 15 percent of women over the age of 16 were employed for wages; in 1900, 20 percent (5.3 million women) were. In 1900, 1 out of every 10 girls and 1 out of every 5 boys between the ages of 10 and 15 held jobs.

There were so many children in the labor force that when people spoke of child labor, they often meant boys and girls under the age of 14. Boys were paid little enough, but girls made even less. Girls, it was argued, were headed for marriage; those who worked were just doing so in order to help out their families. "We try to employ girls who are members of families," a box manufacturer said, "for we don't pay the girls a living wage in this trade."

Most working women were young and single. Many began working at 16 or 17, worked a half dozen years or so, married, and quit. In 1900, only 5 percent of all married women were employed outside the home, although African American women were an important exception. Among them, 25 percent of

It was not unusual for children in some cities to grow up along with their peers in the factory instead of on the playground, like these girls working in the garment industry.

married women worked in 1900, usually on southern farms or as low-paid laundresses or domestic servants. As clerical work expanded, women learned new skills such as typing and stenography. Moving into formerly male occupations, they became secretaries, bookkeepers, typists, telephone operators, and clerks in the new department stores.

A few women—very few—became ministers, lawyers, and doctors. Arabella Mansfield, admitted to the Iowa bar in 1869, was the first woman lawyer in the country. But change was slow, and in the 1880s, some law schools still were refusing to admit women because they "had not the mentality to study law." Among women entering the professions, the overwhelming majority became nurses, schoolteachers, and librarians. In such professions, a process of "feminization" occurred: Women became a majority of the workers, a small number of men took the management roles, and most men left for other jobs, lowering the profession's status.

In general, adults earned more than children, the skilled more than the unskilled, native born more than foreign born, Protestants more than Catholics or Jews, and whites more than blacks and Asians. On average, women made a little more than half as much as men, according to contemporary estimates. In some cases, employers defended the differences—the foreign born, for example, might not speak English—but most simply reflected bias against race, creed, or gender. In the industrial society, white, native-born Protestant men—the bulk of the male population—reaped the greatest rewards.

Blacks labored on the fringes, usually in menial occupations. The last hired and first fired, they earned less than other workers at almost every level of skill. On the Pacific Coast, the Chinese—and later the Japanese—lived in enclaves and suffered periodic attacks of discrimination. In 1882, Congress passed the Chinese Exclusion Act, prohibiting the immigration of Chinese workers for ten years.

Culture of Work

Among almost all groups, industrialization shattered age-old patterns, including work habits and the culture of work, as Herbert G. Gutman, a social historian, noted. It made people adapt "older work routines to new necessities and strained those wedded to premodern patterns of labor." Adaptation was difficult and often demeaning. Virtually everyone went through it, and newcomers repeated the experiences of those who came before.

Men and women fresh from farms were not accustomed to the factory's disciplines. Now they worked indoors rather than out, paced themselves to the clock rather than the movements of the sun, and followed the needs of the market rather than the natural rhythms of the seasons. They had supervisors and hierarchies and strict rules.

As industries grew larger, work became more impersonal. Machines displaced skilled artisans, and the unskilled tended the machines for employers they never saw. Workers picked up and left their jobs with startling frequency, and factories drew on a churning, highly mobile labor supply. Historian Stephan

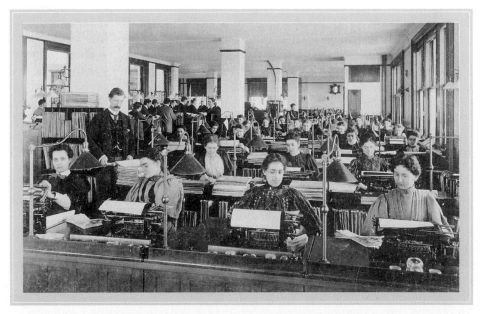

A typing pool in the audit division of the Metropolitan Life Insurance Company, 1897. As demand for clerical workers grew, women took over many of the secretarial duties formerly performed by men. Despite their prominence in the workplace, however, the women were usually overseen by male supervisors.

Thernstrom, who carefully studied the census records, found that only about half the people recorded in any census still lived in the same community ten years later. "The country had an enormous reservoir of restless and footloose men, who could be lured to new destinations when opportunity beckoned."

Thernstrom and others have also found substantial economic and social mobility. The rags-to-riches stories of Horatio Alger, of course, had always said so, and careers of men such as Andrew Carnegie—the impoverished immigrant boy who made good—seemed to confirm it. The actual record was considerably more limited. Most business leaders in the period came from well-to-do or middle-class families of old American stock. Of 360 iron and steel barons in Pittsburgh, Carnegie's own city, only 5 fit the Carnegie characteristics, and one of those was Carnegie himself. Still, if few workers became steel magnates, many workers made major progress during their lifetimes. Thernstrom discovered that a quarter of the manual laborers rose to middle-class positions, and working-class children were even more likely to move up the ladder.

The chance for advancement played a vital role in American industrial development. It gave workers hope, wedded them to the system, and tempered their response to the appeal of labor unions and working-class agitation. Very few workers rose from rags to riches, but a great many rose to better jobs and higher status.

LABOR UNIONS

Weak throughout the nineteenth century, labor unions never included more than 2 percent of the total labor force or more than 10 percent of industrial workers. To many workers, unions seemed "foreign," radical, and out of step with the American tradition of individual advancement. Craft, ethnic, and other differences fragmented the labor force, and its extraordinary mobility made organization difficult. Employers opposed unions. "I have always had one rule," said an executive of U.S. Steel. "If a worker sticks up his head, hit it."

As the national economy emerged, however, national labor unions gradually took shape. In 1869, Uriah S. Stephens and a group of Philadelphia garment workers founded one of the first successful organizations, the Noble and Holy Order of the Knights of Labor. A secret fraternal order, it grew slowly through the 1870s, until Terence V. Powderly, the new Grand Master Workman elected in 1879, ended the secrecy and embarked on an aggressive recruitment program. Wanting to unite all labor, the Knights welcomed everyone who "toiled," regardless of skill, creed, gender, or color. Unlike most unions, it organized women workers, and at its peak, it had 60,000 black members.

Harking back to the Jacksonians, the Knights set the "producers" against monopoly and special privilege. As members they excluded only "nonproducers"—bankers, lawyers, liquor dealers, and gamblers. Since employers were "producers," they could join; and since workers and employers had common interests, the Knights maintained that workers should not strike. The order's platform included the eight-hour day and the abolition of child labor, but more often it focused on uplifting, utopian reform. Powderly, the eloquent and idealistic leader, spun dreams of a new era of harmony and cooperation.

Membership grew steadily—from 42,000 in 1882 to 110,000 in 1885. In March 1885, ignoring Powderly's dislike of strikes, local Knights in St. Louis, Kansas City, and other cities won a victory against Jay Gould's Missouri Pacific Railroad, and membership soared. It soon reached almost 730,000, but neither Powderly nor the union's loose structure could handle the growth. In 1886, the wily Gould struck back, crushing the Knights on the Texas and Pacific Railroad. The defeat punctured the union's growth and revealed the ineffectiveness of its national leaders. Tens of thousands of unskilled laborers, who had recently rushed to join, deserted the ranks. The Haymarket Riot turned public sympathy against unions like the Knights. By 1890, the order had shrunk to 100,000 members, and a few years later, it was virtually defunct.

Even as the Knights waxed and waned, another organization emerged that was to endure. Founded in 1886, the American Federation of Labor (AFL) was a loose alliance of national craft unions. It organized only skilled workers along craft lines, avoided politics, and worked for specific practical objectives. "I have my own philosophy and my own dreams," said Samuel Gompers, the founder and longtime president, "but first and foremost I want to increase the working-man's welfare year by year."

Born in a London tenement in 1850, Gompers was a child of the union movement. Settling in New York, he worked as a cigar maker, took an active hand in union activities, and experimented for a time with socialism and working-class politics. As leader of the AFL, he adopted a pragmatic approach to labor's needs. Gompers accepted capitalism and did not argue for fundamental changes in it. For labor he wanted simply a recognized place within the system and a greater share of the rewards.

Unlike Powderly, Gompers and the AFL assumed that most workers would remain workers throughout their lives. The task, then, lay in improving lives in "practical" ways: higher wages, shorter hours, and better working conditions. The AFL offered some attractive assurances to employers. As a trade union, the AFL would use the strike and boycott, but only to achieve limited gains; if treated fairly, the organization would provide a stable labor force. The AFL would not oppose monopolies and trusts, as Gompers said, "so long as we obtain fair wages."

By the 1890s, the AFL was the most important labor group in the country, and Gompers, the guiding spirit, was its president, except for one year, until his death in 1924. Membership expanded from 140,000 in 1886, past 250,000 in 1892, to more than 1 million by 1901. The AFL then included almost one-third of the country's skilled workers. By 1914, it had more than 2 million members. The great majority of workers—skilled and unskilled—remained unorganized, but Gompers and the AFL had become a significant force in national life.

The AFL either ignored or opposed women workers. Only two of its national affiliates accepted women as members; others prohibited them outright, and Gompers himself often complained that women workers undercut the pay scales for men. Working conditions improved after 1900, but even then, unions were largely a man's world. In 1910, when there were 6.3 million women at work, only 125,000 of them were in unions.

The AFL did not expressly forbid black workers from joining, but member unions used high initiation fees, technical examinations, and other means to discourage black membership. The AFL's informal exclusion practices were, all in all, a sorry record, but Gompers defended his policy toward blacks, women, and the unskilled by pointing to the dangers that unions faced. Only by restricting membership, he argued, could the union succeed.

LABOR UNREST

Workers used various means to adjust to the factory age. To the dismay of managers and "efficiency" experts, the employees often dictated the pace and quality of their work and set the tone of the workplace. Friends and relatives of newly arrived immigrants found jobs for them, taught them how to deal with factory conditions, and humanized the workplace.

Workers also formed their own institutions to deal with their jobs. Overcoming differences of race or ethnic origin, they often banded together to help each other. They joined social or fraternal organizations, and their unions did more than argue for higher wages. Unions offered companionship, news of job openings, and much needed insurance plans for sickness, accident, or death. Workers went to the union hall to play cards or pool, sing union songs, and hear older workers tell of past labor struggles. Unions provided food for sick members, and there were dances, picnics, and parades.

Many employers believed in an "iron law of wages" in which supply and demand, not the welfare of their workers, dictated wages. Wanting a docile labor force, employers fired union members, hired scabs to replace strikers, and used a new weapon, the court injunction, to quell strikes.

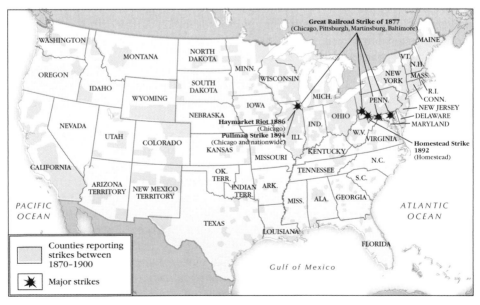

Labor Strikes, 1870–1890
More than 14,000 strikes occurred in the 1880s and early 1890s, involving millions of workers.

In the rioting that followed the bomb explosion in Haymarket Square in Chicago, seven police offi-cers and four workers died and more than seventy officers were wounded, many of them by fellow police. August Spies, one of the anarchists convicted of murder and sent to the gallows, said at his trial, "Let the world know that in A.D. 1886, in the state of Illinois, eight men were sentenced to death because they believed in a better future; because they had not lost their faith in the ultimate victory of liberty and justice!" (Actually, seven of the agitators were sentenced to death, the eighth to imprisonment.)

The injunction, which forbade workers to interfere with their employers' business, was used to break the great Pullman strike of 1894, and the Supreme Court upheld use of the injunction in *In re Debs* (1895).

As employers' attitudes hardened, strikes and violence broke out. The United States had the greatest number of violent confrontations between capital and la-bor in the industrial world. Between 1880 and 1900, there were more than 23,000 strikes involving 6.6 million workers. The great railroad strike of 1877 paralyzed railroads from West Virginia to California, resulted in the deaths of more than a hundred workers, and required federal troops to suppress it. Another outburst of labor unrest occurred during the mid-1880s; in 1886, the peak year, 610,000 workers were off the job because of strikes and lockouts.

The worst incident took place at Haymarket Square in Chicago, where work-ers had been campaigning for an eight-hour workday. In early May 1886, police, intervening in a strike at the McCormick Harvester works, shot and killed two workers. The next evening, May 4, labor leaders called a protest meeting at Haymarket Square near downtown Chicago. The meeting was peaceful, even a bit dull. About three thousand people were there; police ordered them to disperse, and someone threw a dynamite bomb that instantly killed one policeman and fatally wounded six others. Police fired into the crowd and killed four people.

The authorities never discovered who threw the bomb, but many Americans—not just business leaders—demanded action against labor "radicalism." Cities strengthened their police forces and armories. Uncertain who threw the bomb, Chicago police rounded up eight anarchists, who were convicted of murder. Although there was no evidence of their guilt, four were hanged, one committed suicide, and three remained in jail until pardoned by the governor in 1893. Linking labor and anarchism in the public mind, the Haymarket Riot weakened the national labor movement.

Violence again broke out in the unsettled conditions of the 1890s. In 1892, Carnegie and Henry Clay Frick, Carnegie's partner and manager, cut wages nearly 20 percent at the Homestead steel plant. The Amalgamated Iron and Steel Workers, an AFL affiliate, struck, and Frick responded by locking the workers out of the plant. The workers surrounded it, and Frick, furious, hired a small private army of Pinkerton detectives to drive them off. But alert workers spotted the detectives, pinned them down with gunfire, and forced them to surrender. Three detectives and ten workers died in the battle.

A few days later, the Pennsylvania governor ordered the state militia to impose peace at Homestead. On July 23, an anarchist named Alexander Berkman, who was not one of the strikers, walked into Frick's office and shot him twice, then stabbed him several times. Incredibly, Frick survived, watched the police take Berkman away, called in a doctor to bandage his wounds, and stayed in the office until closing time. In late July, the Homestead works reopened under military guard, and in November the strikers gave up.

Events like the Homestead Strike troubled many Americans who wondered whether industrialization, for all its benefits, might carry a heavy price in social upheaval, class tensions, and even outright warfare. Most workers did not share in the immense profits of the industrial age, and as the nineteenth century came to a close, there were some who rebelled against the inequity.

INDUSTRIALIZATION'S BENEFITS AND COSTS

In the half century after the Civil War, the United States became an industrial nation—the leading one, in fact, in the world. On one hand, industrialization meant "progress," growth, world power, and in some sense, fulfillment of the American promise of abundance. National wealth grew from $16 billion in 1860 to $88 billion in 1900; wealth per capita more than doubled. For the bulk of the population, the standard of living—a particularly American concept—rose.

But industrialization also meant rapid change, social instability, exploitation of labor, and growing disparity in income between rich and poor. Industry flourished, but control rested in fewer and fewer hands. Maturing quickly, the young system became a new corporate capitalism: giant businesses, interlocking in ownership, managed by a new professional class, and selling an expanding variety of goods in an increasingly controlled market. As goods spread through the society, so did a sharpened, aggressive materialism. Workers felt the strains of the shift to a new social order.

In 1902, a well-to-do New Yorker named Bessie Van Vorst decided to see what it was like to work for a living in a factory. Disguising herself in coarse woolen clothes, she went to Pittsburgh and got a job in a canning factory. She worked ten hours a day, six days a week, including four hours on Saturday afternoons when she and the other women, on their hands and knees, scrubbed the tables, stands, and entire factory floor. For that she earned $4.20 a week, $3 of which went for food alone.

Van Vorst was lucky—when she tired of the life, she could go back to her home in New York. The working men and women around her were not so fortunate. They stayed on the factory floor and, by dint of their labor, created the new industrial society.

CHRONOLOGY

1859	First oil well drilled near Titusville, Pennsylvania
1866	William Sylvis establishes National Labor Union
1869	Transcontinental railroad completed at Promontory, Utah
	Knights of Labor organize
1876	Alexander Graham Bell invents the telephone
	Centennial Exposition held in Philadelphia
1877	Railroads cut workers' wages, leading to bloody and violent strike
1879	Thomas A. Edison invents the incandescent lamp
1882	Rockefeller's Standard Oil Company becomes nation's first trust
	Edison opens first electric generating station in New York
1883	Railroads introduce standard time zones
1886	Samuel Gompers founds American Federation of Labor (AFL)
	Labor protest erupts in violence in Haymarket Riot in Chicago
	Railroads adopt standard gauge
1892	Workers strike at Homestead steel plant in Pennsylvania
1893	Economic depression begins
1901	J. P. Morgan announces formation of U.S. Steel Corporation, nation's first billion-dollar company

19

TOWARD AN URBAN SOCIETY, 1877–1900

One day around 1900, Harriet Vittum, a settlement house worker in Chicago, went to the aid of a young Polish girl who lived in a nearby slum. The girl, aged 15, had discovered she was pregnant and had taken poison. An ambulance was on the way, and Vittum, told of the poisoning, rushed over to do what she could.

Quickly, she raced up the three flights of stairs to the floor where the girl and her family lived. Pushing open the door, she found the father, several male boarders, and two or three small boys asleep on the kitchen floor. In the next room, the mother was on the floor among several women boarders and one or two small children. Glancing out the window, Vittum saw the wall of another building so close she could reach out and touch it.

There was a third room; in it lay the 15-year-old girl, along with two more small children who were asleep. Looking at the scene, Vittum thought about the girl's life in the crowded tenement. Should she try to save her? Vittum asked herself. Should she even try to bring the girl back "to the misery and hopelessness of the life she was living in that awful place?"

The young girl died, and in later years, Vittum often told her story. It was easy to see why. The girl's life in the slum, the children on the floor, the need to take in boarders to make ends meet, the way the mother and father collapsed at the end of a workday that began long before sunup—all reflected the experiences of millions of people living in the nation's cities.

Vittum and people like her were attempting to respond to the overwhelming challenges of the nation's burgeoning cities. People poured into cities in the last part of the nineteenth century, lured by glitter and excitement, by friends and relatives who were already there, and, above all, by the greater opportunities for jobs and higher wages. Between 1860 and 1910, the rural population of the United States almost doubled; the number of people living in cities increased sevenfold.

Little of the increase came from natural growth, since urban families had high rates of infant mortality, a declining fertility rate, and a high death rate from injury and disease. Many of the newcomers came from rural America, and many more came from Europe, Latin America, and Asia. In one of the most significant migrations in American history, thousands of African Americans began in the 1880s to move from the rural South to northern cities. By 1900, there were large black communities in New York, Baltimore, Chicago, Washington, D.C., and other cities. Yet to come was the even greater black migration during World War I.

Two major forces reshaped American society between 1870 and 1920. One was industrialization; the other was urbanization, the headlong rush of people from their rural roots into the modern urban environment. In these years, cities grew upward and outward, attracting millions of newcomers and influencing politics, education, entertainment, and family life. By 1920, they had become the center of American economic, social, and cultural life.

THE LURE OF THE CITY

Between 1870 and 1900, the city—like the factory—became a symbol of a new America. Drawn from farms, small towns, and foreign lands, newcomers swelled the population of older cities and created new ones almost overnight. At the beginning of the Civil War, only one-sixth of the American people lived in cities of eight thousand people or more. By 1900, one-third did; by 1920, one-half.

The movement to urban life brought explosive growth. Thousands of years of history had produced only a handful of cities with more than a half million in population. In 1900, the United States had six such cities, including three—New York, Chicago, and Philadelphia—with populations greater than one million.

SKYSCRAPERS AND SUBURBS

Like so many things in these years, the city was transformed by a revolution in technology. Beginning in the 1880s, the age of steel and glass produced the skyscraper; the streetcar produced the suburbs and new residential patterns.

On the eve of the change, American cities were a crowded jumble of small buildings. Church steeples stood out on the skyline, clearly visible above the roofs of factories and office buildings. Buildings were usually made of masonry, and since the massive walls had to support their own weight, they could be no taller than a dozen or so stories. Steel frames and girders ended that limitation and allowed buildings to soar higher and higher. "Curtain walls," which concealed the steel framework, were no longer load bearing; they were pierced by many windows that let in fresh air and light. Completed in 1885, the Home Insurance Building in Chicago was the country's first metal-frame structure.

To a group of talented Chicago architects, the new trends served as a springboard for innovative forms. The leaders of the movement were John Root and Louis H. Sullivan, both of whom were attracted by the chance to rebuild Chicago after the great fire of 1871. Noting that the fire had fed on fancy exterior ornamentation, Root developed a plain, stripped-down style, bold in mass and form—the keynotes of modern architecture. He had another important insight, too. In an age of business, Root thought, the office tower, more than a church or a government building, symbolized the society, and he designed office buildings that carried out, as he said, "the ideas of modern business life: simplicity, stability, breadth, dignity."

Sullivan had studied at the Massachusetts Institute of Technology (MIT) and in Paris before settling in Chicago. In 1886, at the age of 30, he had a "flash of imagination," the skyscraper, which soon changed the urban skyline.

In the Wainwright Building in St. Louis (1890), the Schiller Building (1892) and the Carson, Pirie, and Scott department store (1899) in Chicago, and the Prudential Building in Buffalo (1895), Sullivan developed the new forms. Architects must discard "books, rules, precedents," he announced; responding to the new, they should design for a building's function. "Form follows function," Sullivan believed, and he passed the idea on to a talented disciple, Frank Lloyd Wright. The modern city should stretch to the sky. A skyscraper "must be every inch a proud and soaring thing, rising in sheer exaltation . . . from bottom to top."

Electric elevators, first used in 1871, carried passengers upward in the new skyscrapers. During the same years, streetcars, another innovation, carried the people outward to expanded boundaries that transformed urban life. Cities were no longer largely "walking cities," confined to a radius of two or three miles, the distance an individual might walk. Streetcar systems extended the radius and changed the urban map. Cable lines, electric surface lines, and elevated rapid transit brought shoppers and workers into central business districts and sped them home again. Offering a modest five-cent fare with a free transfer, the mass transit systems fostered commuting and widely separated business and residential districts sprang up. The middle class moved farther and farther out to the leafy greenness of the suburbs.

As the middle class moved out of the cities, the immigrants and working class poured in. They took over the older brownstones, row houses, and workers' cottages, turning them, under the sheer weight of numbers, into the slums of the central city. In the cities of the past, classes and occupations had been thrown together; without streetcars and subways, there was no other choice. The streetcar city, sprawling and specialized, became a more fragmented and stratified society with middle-class residential rings surrounding a business and working-class core.

TENEMENTS AND THE PROBLEMS OF OVERCROWDING

In the shadow of the skyscrapers, grimy rows of tenements filled the central city and crowded people into cramped apartments. In the late 1870s, architect James E. Ware won a competition for tenement design with the "dumbbell tenement." Rising seven or eight stories in height, the dumbbell tenement packed about 30 four-room apartments on a lot only 25 by 100 feet. Between four and sixteen families lived on a floor; two toilets in the hall of each floor served their needs. Narrowed at the middle, the tenement resembled a giant dumbbell in shape. The indented middle created an air shaft between adjoining buildings that provided a little light and ventilation. In case of fire, it also carried flames from one story to the next, making the buildings notorious firetraps. In 1890, nearly half the dwellings in New York City were tenements.

That year, more than 1.4 million people lived on Manhattan Island, one of whose wards had a population density of 334,000 people per square mile. Many people lived in alleys and basements so dark they could not be photographed until flashlight photography was invented in 1887. Exploring the city, William Dean Howells, the prominent author, inhaled "the stenches of the neglected street . . . [and] the yet fouler and dreadfuller poverty smell which breathes from the open doorways."

Howells smelled more than poverty. In the 1870s and 1880s, cities stank. One problem was horse manure, hundreds of tons of it a day in every city. Another was the privy, "a single one of which," said a leading authority on public health, "may render life in a whole neighborhood almost unendurable in the summer." In 1880, the Chicago *Times* said that a "solid stink" pervaded the city. "No other word expresses it so well as stink. A stench means something finite. Stink reaches the infinite and becomes sublime in the magnitude of odiousness."

Cities dumped their wastes into the nearest body of water, then drew drinking water from the same site. Many built modern purified waterworks but could not keep pace with spiraling growth. In 1900, fewer than one in ten city dwellers drank filtered water. Factories, the pride of the era, polluted the urban air. At night, Pittsburgh looked and sounded like "Hell with the lid off," according to contemporary observers. Smoke poured from seventy-three glass factories, forty-one iron and steel mills, and twenty-nine oil refineries. The choking air helped prevent lung diseases and malaria—or so the city's advertising claimed.

Crime was another growing problem. The nation's homicide rate nearly tripled in the 1880s, much of the increase coming in the cities. After remaining constant for many decades, the suicide rate rose steadily between 1870 and 1900, according to a study of Philadelphia. Alcoholism also rose, especially among men, though recent studies have shown that for working-class men, the urban saloon was as much a gathering spot as it was a place to drink. Nonetheless, a 1905 survey of Chicago counted as many saloons as grocery stores, meat markets, and dry goods stores combined.

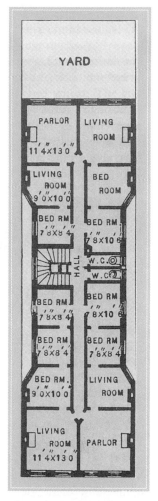

This 1879 dumbbell floor plan was meant to provide four apartments to a floor. However, a whole family might live in each room. Crowded, unsanitary conditions contributed to the spread of tuberculosis, the chief cause of death in the United States until 1909.

The tenement district of New York City's Lower East Side. As millions emigrated to the United States during the last quarter of the nineteenth century, they crammed into already overpopulated ethnic neighborhoods, seeking others who spoke their language, practiced their religion, and followed their customs.

STRANGERS IN A NEW LAND

While some of the new city dwellers came from farms and small towns, many more came from abroad. Most came from Europe, where unemployment, food shortages, and increasing threats of war sent millions fleeing across the Atlantic to make a fresh start. Often they knew someone already in the United States, a friend or relative who had written them about prospects for jobs and freer lives in a new land.

All told, the immigration figures were staggering. Between 1877 and 1890, more than 6.3 million people entered the United States. In one year alone, 1882, almost 789,000 people came. By 1890, about 15 percent of the population, 9 million people, were foreign born.

Most newcomers were job seekers. Nearly two-thirds were males, and the majority were between the ages of 15 and 40. Most were unskilled laborers. Most settled on the eastern seaboard. In 1901, the Industrial Relocation Office was established to relieve overcrowding in the eastern cities; opening Galveston, Texas, as a port of entry, it attracted many Russian Jews to Texas and the Southwest. But most immigrants preferred the shorter, more familiar journey to

Immigration to the United States, 1870–1900

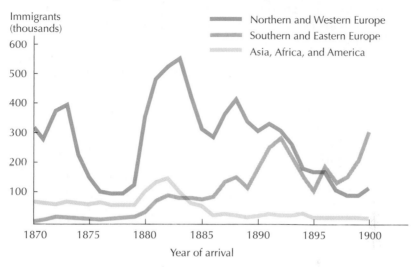

Note: For purposes of classification, "Northern and Western Europe" includes Great Britain, Ireland, Scandinavia, the Netherlands, Belgium, Luxembourg, Switzerland, France, and Germany. "Southern and Eastern Europe" includes Poland, Austria-Hungary, Russia and the Baltic States, Romania, Bulgaria, European Turkey, Italy, Spain, Portugal, and Greece. "Asia, Africa, and America" includes Asian Turkey, China, Japan, India, Canada, the Caribbean, Latin America, and all of Africa.

Source: U.S. Bureau of the Census, *Historical Statistics of the United States, Colonial Times to 1970*, Bicentennial Edition, Washington, D.C., 1975.

New York. Entering through Ellis Island in New York harbor, as four in every ten immigrants did, most tended to crowd into northern and eastern cities, settling in areas where others of their nationality or religion lived.

Cities had increasingly large foreign-born populations. In 1900, four-fifths of Chicago's population was foreign born or of foreign-born parentage, two-thirds of Boston's, and one-half of Philadelphia's. New York City, where most immigrants arrived and many stayed, had more Italians than lived in Naples, more Germans than lived in Hamburg, and twice as many Irish as lived in Dublin. Four out of five New York City residents in 1890 were of foreign birth or foreign parentage.

Beginning in the 1880s, the sources of immigration shifted dramatically away from northern and western Europe, the chief source of immigration for over two centuries. More and more immigrants came from southern and eastern Europe: Italy, Greece, Austria-Hungary, Poland, and Russia. Between 1880 and 1910, approximately 8.4 million people came from these lands. The "new" immigrants tended to be Catholics or Jews rather than Protestants. Like their predecessors, most were unskilled rather than skilled, and they often spoke "strange" languages. Most were poor and uneducated; sticking together in close-knit communities, they clung to their native customs, languages, and religions.

More than any previous group, the so-called new immigrants troubled the mainstream society. Could they be assimilated? Did they share "American" values? Such questions preoccupied groups like the American Protective Association, a midwestern anti-Catholic organization that expanded in the 1890s and worked to limit or end immigration.

Anti-Catholicism and anti-Semitism flared up again, as they had in the 1850s. The Immigration Restriction League, founded in 1894, demanded a literacy test for immigrants from southern and eastern Europe. Congress passed such a law in 1896, but President Cleveland vetoed it.

IMMIGRANTS AND THE CITY

Industrial capitalism—the world of factories and foremen and grimy machines—tested the immigrants and placed an enormous strain on their families. Many immigrants came from peasant societies where life proceeded according to outdoor routine and age-old tradition. In their new city homes, they found both new freedoms and new confinements, a different language, and a novel set of customs and expectations. Historians have only recently begun to discover the remarkable ways in which they learned to adjust.

Like native-born families, most immigrant families were nuclear in structure—they consisted of two parents and their children. Though variations occurred from group to group, men and women occupied roles similar to those in native families: men were wage earners, women were housekeepers and mothers. Margaret

In a Puck *cartoon titled "Looking Backward," the shadows of their immigrant origins loom over the rich and powerful who wanted to deny the "new" immigrants from central and southern Europe admission to America. The caption on the cartoon reads, "They would close to the newcomer the bridge that carried them and their fathers over."*

Byington, who studied steelworkers' homes in Homestead in the early 1900s, learned that the father played a relatively small role in child rearing or managing the family's finances. "His part of the problem is to earn and hers to spend."

Although patterns varied among ethnic groups, and between economic classes within ethnic groups, immigrants tended to marry within the group more than did the native born. Immigrants also tended to marry at a later age than natives, and they tended to have more children, a fact that worried nativists opposed to immigration.

Immigrants shaped the city as much as it shaped them. Most of them tried to retain their traditional culture for themselves and their children while at the same time adapting to life in their new country. To do this, they spoke their native language, practiced their religious faith, read their own newspapers, and established special parochial or other schools. They observed traditional holidays and formed a myriad of social organizations to maintain ties among members of the group.

Immigrant associations offered fellowship in a strange land. They helped newcomers find jobs and homes; they provided important services such as unemployment insurance and health insurance. Some groups were no larger than a neighborhood; others spread nationwide. In 1914, the Deutsch-Amerikanischer Nationalbund, the largest of the associations, had more than two million members in dozens of cities and towns.

Every major city had dozens of foreign language newspapers, with circulations large and small. The first newspaper published in the Lithuanian language appeared in the United States, not in Lithuania. Eagerly read, the papers not only carried news of events in the homeland but also reported on local ethnic leaders, told readers how to vote and become citizens, and gave practical tips on adjusting to life in the United States.

Church, school, and fraternal societies shaped the way in which immigrants adjusted to life in America. Eastern European Jews established synagogues and religious schools wherever they settled; they taught the Hebrew language and raised their children in a heritage they did not want to leave behind. Among such groups as the Irish and the Poles, the Roman Catholic Church provided spiritual and educational guidance. In the parish schools, Polish priests and nuns taught Polish American children about Polish as well as American culture in the Polish language. By preserving language, religion, and heritage, they also shaped the country itself.

THE HOUSE THAT TWEED BUILT

Closely connected with explosive urban growth was the emergence of the powerful city political machine. As cities grew, lines of responsibility in city governments became hopelessly confused, increasing the opportunity for corruption and greed. Burgeoning populations required streets, buildings, and public services; immigrants needed even more services. In this situation, political party machines played an important role.

The machines traded services for votes. Loosely knit, they were headed by a strong, influential leader—the "boss"—who tied together a network of ward and precinct captains, each of whom looked after his local constituents. William M. Tweed, head of the famed Tweed Ring in New York, provided the model for them all. Nearly six feet tall, weighing almost three hundred pounds, Tweed rose through the ranks of Tammany Hall, the famous Democratic party organization that dominated city politics during much of the nineteenth century. A man of culture and warmth, he moved easily between the rough back alleys of New York and the parlors and clubs of the city's elite. Behind the scenes, he headed a ring that plundered New York for tens of millions of dollars.

The New York County Courthouse—"the house that Tweed built"—was his masterpiece. Nestled in City Hall Park in downtown Manhattan, the three-story structure was designed to cost $250,000, but the bills ran a bit higher. Furniture, carpets, and window shades alone came to more than $5.5 million. Andrew Garvey, the "prince of plasterers," charged $500,000 for plasterwork, and then $1 million to repair the same work. His total bill came to $2,870,464.06. (The *New York Times* suggested that the six cents be donated to charity.) In the end, the building cost more than $13 million—and in 1872, when Tweed fell, it was still not finished.

The role of the political bosses can be overemphasized. Power structures in the turn-of-the-century city were complex, involving a host of people and institutions. Banks, real estate investors, insurance companies, architects, and engineers, among others, played roles in governing the city. Viewed in retrospect, many city governments were remarkably successful. With populations that in some cases doubled every decade, city governments provided water and sewer lines, built parks and playgrounds, and paved streets. When it was over, Boston had the world's largest public library and New York City had the Brooklyn Bridge and Central Park, two of the finest achievements in city planning and architecture of any era. By the 1890s, New York also had 660 miles of water lines, 464 miles of sewers, and 1800 miles of paved streets, far more than comparable cities in Europe.

Bosses, moreover, differed from city to city. "Honest" John Kelly earned his nickname serving as a watchdog over the New York City treasury. Tweed was one of the early backers of the Brooklyn Bridge. Some bosses were plainly corrupt; others believed in *honest graft,* a term Tammany's George Washington Plunkitt coined to describe "legitimate" profits made from advance knowledge of city projects.

Why did voters keep the bosses in power? The answers are complex, but two reasons were skillful political organization and the fact that immigrants and others made up the bosses' constituency. Most immigrants had little experience with democratic government and proved easy prey for well-oiled machines. For the most part, however, the bosses stayed in power because they paid attention to the needs of the least privileged city voters. They offered valued services in an era when neither government nor business lent a hand.

Most bosses became wealthy; they were not Robin Hoods who took from the rich to give to the poor. They took for themselves as well. Reformers occasionally ousted them; Tweed fell from power in 1872. But the reformers rarely stayed in power long. Drawn mainly from the middle and upper classes, they had little understanding of the needs of the poor. Before long, they returned to private concerns, and the bosses, who had known that they would all along, cheerily took power again.

"What tells in holdin' your grip on your district," the engaging Plunkitt once said, "is to go right down among the poor families and help them in the different ways they need help. . . . It's philanthropy, but it's politics, too—mighty good politics. . . . The poor are the most grateful people in the world."

SOCIAL AND CULTURAL CHANGE, 1877–1900

The rise of cities and industry between 1877 and the 1890s affected all aspects of American life. Mores changed; family ties loosened. Factories turned out consumer goods, and the newly invented cash register rang up record sales. Public and private educational systems burgeoned, illiteracy declined, life expectancy increased. While many people worked harder and harder just to survive, others found they had a greater amount of leisure time. The roles of women and children changed in a number of ways, and the family took on functions it had not had before. Thanks to advancing technology, news flashed quickly across the oceans, and for the first time in history, people read of the day's events in distant lands when they opened their daily newspapers.

FAMILY LIFE AND HEALTH

Though the rush to the cities was about to begin, most people of 1877 still lived on farms or in small towns. Their lives revolved around the farm, the church, and the general store. In 1880, nearly 75 percent of the population lived in communities of fewer than 2500 people. In 1900, in the midst of city growth, 60 percent still did. The average family in 1880 had three children, dramatically fewer than at the beginning of the century, and life expectancy was about 43 years. By 1900, it had risen to 47 years, a result of improved health care. For blacks and other minorities, who often lived in unsanitary rural areas, life expectancy was substantially lower: 33 years in 1900.

Meals tended to be heavy, and so did people. Food prices were low. Families ate fresh homegrown produce in the summer and "put up" their fruits and vegetables for the long winters. Toward the end of the century, eating habits changed. New packaged breakfast cereals became popular; fresh fruit and vegetables came in on fast trains from Florida and California, and commercially canned food became safer and cheaper. The newfangled icebox, cooled by blocks of ice, kept food fresher and added new treats such as ice cream.

Medical science was in the midst of a major revolution. Louis Pasteur's recent discovery that germs cause infection and disease created the new science of microbiology and led the way to the development of vaccines and other preventive measures. But tuberculosis, typhoid, diphtheria, and pneumonia—all now curable—were still the leading causes of death. Infant mortality declined between

1877 and 1900, but the decline was gradual; a great drop did not come until after 1920.

There were few hospitals and no hospital insurance. Most patients stayed at home, although medical practice, especially surgery, expanded rapidly. Once brutal and dangerous, surgery in these years became relatively safe and painless. Anesthetics—ether and chloroform—eliminated pain, and antiseptic practices helped prevent postoperative infections. Antiseptic practices at childbirth also cut down on puerperal fever, an infection that for centuries had killed many women and newborn infants. The new science of psychology began to explore the mind, hitherto uncharted. William James, a leading American psychologist and philosopher, laid the foundations of modern behavioral psychology, which stressed the importance of the environment on human development.

Manners and Mores

The code of Victorian morality, its name derived from the British queen who reigned throughout the period, set the tone for the era. The code prescribed strict standards of dress, manners, and sexual behavior. It was both obeyed and disobeyed, and it reflected the tensions of a generation that was undergoing a change in moral standards.

In 1877, children were to be seen and not heard. They spoke when spoken to, listened rather than chattered—or at least that was the rule. Older boys and girls were often chaperoned, although they could always find moments alone. They played post office and spin the bottle; they puffed cigarettes behind the barn. Counterbalancing such youthful exuberance was strong pride in virtue and self-control. "Thank heaven I am absolutely pure," Theodore Roosevelt, the future president, wrote in 1880 after proposing to Alice Lee. "I can tell Alice everything I have ever done."

Gentlemen of the middle class dressed in heavy black suits, derby hats, and white shirts with paper collars. Women wore tight corsets, long dark dresses, and black shoes reaching well above the ankles. As with so many things, styles changed dramatically toward the end of the century, spurred in part by new sporting fads such as golf, tennis, and bicycling, which required looser clothing.

Religious and patriotic values were strong. A center of community life, the church often set the tenor for family and social relationships. In the 1880s, eight out of ten church members were Protestants; most of the rest were Roman Catholics.

With slavery abolished, reformers turned their attention to new moral and political issues. One group, known as the Mugwumps, worked to end corruption in politics. Drawn mostly from the educated and upper class, they included Thomas Nast, the famous political cartoonist, and E. L. Godkin, editor of the influential *Nation*. Other zealous reformers campaigned for prohibition of the sale of intoxicating liquors, hoping to end the social evils that stemmed from drunkenness. In 1874, women who advocated total abstinence from alcoholic beverages formed the Woman's Christian Temperance Union (WCTU). Their leader,

MARCH 1900 TEN CENTS

THE LADIES' HOME JOURNAL

THE CURTIS PUBLISHING COMPANY, PHILADELPHIA

Victorian fashion ideals for women emphasized elaborate, confining dress styles with a tiny waistline and full skirts that reached to the floor. Throughout the 1890s, as women began to participate in some of the new sports or go to work in factories, stores, or business offices, styles gradually became less restrictive. This 1900 cover of Ladies' Home Journal *shows women wearing tailored jackets and simple pleated skirts hemmed above the ankle playing golf with men.*

Frances E. Willard, served as president of the group from 1879 until her death in 1898. By then, the WCTU had 10,000 branches and 500,000 members.

LEISURE AND ENTERTAINMENT

In the 1870s, people tended to rise early. On getting up, they washed from the pitcher and bowl in the bedroom, first breaking the layer of ice if it was winter. After dressing and eating, they went off to work and school. Without large refrigerators, housewives marketed almost daily. In the evening, families gathered in the "second parlor" or living room, where the children did their lessons, played games, sang around the piano, and listened to that day's verse from the Bible.

The newest outdoor game was croquet, so popular that candles were mounted on the wickets to allow play at night. Croquet was the first outdoor game designed for play by both sexes, and it frequently served as a setting for courtship. Early manuals advised girls how to assume attractive poses while hitting the ball.

Sentimental ballads such as "Silver Threads Among the Gold" (1873) remained the most popular musical form, but the insistent syncopated rhythms of ragtime were being heard, reflecting the influence of the new urban culture. By the time the strains of Scott Joplin's "Maple Leaf Rag" (1899) popularized ragtime, critics complained that "a wave of vulgar, filthy and suggestive music has inundated the land." Classical music flourished. The New England Conservatory

(1867), the Cincinnati College of Music (1878), and the Metropolitan Opera (1883) were new sources of civic pride; New York, Boston, and Chicago launched first-rate symphony orchestras between 1878 and 1891.

Fairs, horse races, balloon ascensions, bicycle tournaments, and football and baseball contests attracted avid fans. The years between 1870 and 1900 saw the rise of organized spectator sports, a trend reflecting both the rise of the city and the new uses of leisure. Baseball's first professional team, the Cincinnati Red Stockings, appeared in 1869, and baseball soon became the preeminent national sport. Modern rules were adopted. Umpires were designated to call balls and strikes; catchers wore masks and chest protectors and moved closer to the plate instead of staying back to catch the ball on the bounce. Fielders had to catch the ball on the fly rather than on one bounce in their caps. By 1890, professional baseball teams were drawing crowds of sixty thousand daily. In 1901, the American League was organized, and two years later the Boston Red Sox beat the Pittsburgh Pirates in the first modern World Series.

In 1869, Princeton and Rutgers played the first intercollegiate football game. Soon, other schools picked up the sport, and by the early 1890s, crowds of fifty thousand or more attended the most popular contests. Basketball, invented in 1891, gained a large following.

As gas and electric lights brightened the night, and streetcars crisscrossed city streets, leisure habits changed. Delighted with the new technology, people took advantage of an increasing variety of things to do. They stayed home less often. New York City's first electric sign—"Manhattan Beach Swept by Ocean Breezes"—appeared in 1881, and people went out at night, filling the streets on their way to the theater, vaudeville shows, and dance halls or just out for an evening stroll.

CHANGES IN FAMILY LIFE

Under the impact of industrialization and urbanization, family relationships were changing. On the farm, parents and children worked more or less together, and the family was a producing unit. In factories and offices, family members rarely worked together. In working-class families, mothers, fathers, and children separated at dawn and returned, ready for sleep, at dark.

Working-class families of the late nineteenth century, like the family of the young Polish girl that Harriet Vittum saw, often lived in complex household units—taking in relatives and boarders to pay the rent. As many as one-third of all households contained people who were not members of the immediate family. Although driven apart by the daily routine, family ties among the working class tended to remain strong, cemented by the need to join forces in order to survive in the industrial economy.

The middle-class wife and children, however, became increasingly isolated from the world of work. Turning inward, the middle-class family became more self-contained. Older children spent more time in adolescence, and periods of formal schooling were lengthier. Families took in fewer apprentices and boarders. By the end of the century, most middle-class offspring continued to live with their parents into their late teens and their twenties, a larger proportion than today.

Fewer middle-class wives participated directly in their husbands' work. As a result, they and their children occupied what contemporaries called a "separate sphere of domesticity," set apart from the masculine sphere of income-producing work. The family home became a "walled garden," a place to retreat from the crass materialism of the outside world. Middle-class fathers began to move their families out of the city to the suburbs, commuting to work on the new streetcars and leaving wives and children at home and school.

The middle-class family had once functioned in part to transmit a craft or skill, arrange marriages, and offer care for dependent kin. Now, as these functions declined, the family took on new emotional and ideological responsibilities. In a society that worried about the weakening hold of other institutions, the family became more and more important as a means of social control. It also placed new burdens on wives.

Magazines such as the *Ladies' Home Journal*, which started in 1889, glorified motherhood and the home, but its articles and ads featured women as homebound, child-oriented consumers. While society's leaders spoke fondly of the value of homemaking, the status of housewives declined under the factory system, which emphasized money rewards and devalued household labor.

Underlying all these changes was one of the modern world's most important trends, a major decline in fertility rates that lasted from 1800 to 1939. Though blacks, immigrants, and rural dwellers continued to have more children than white native-born city dwellers, the trend affected all classes and races; among white women, the birthrate fell from 7 in 1800 to just over 4 in 1880 to about 3 in 1900. People everywhere tended to marry later and have fewer children.

Since contraceptive devices were not yet widely used, the decline reflected abstinence and a conscious decision to postpone or limit families. Some women decided to devote greater attention to a smaller number of children, others to pursue their own careers. There was a marked increase in the number of young unmarried women working for wages or attending school, an increase in the number of women delaying marriage or not marrying at all, and a gradual decline in rates of illegitimacy and premarital pregnancy.

In large part, the decline in fertility stemmed from people's responses to the social and economic forces around them, the rise of cities and industry. In a host of individual decisions, they decided to have fewer children, and the result reshaped some of the fundamental attitudes and institutions of American society.

CHANGING VIEWS:
A GROWING ASSERTIVENESS AMONG WOMEN

In and out of the family, there was growing recognition of self-sufficient working women, employed in factory, telephone exchange, or business office, who were entering the workforce in increasing numbers. In 1880, 2.6 million women were gainfully employed; in 1890, 4 million. In 1882, the Census Bureau took the first census of working women; most were single and worked out of necessity rather than choice.

Many regarded this "new woman" as a corruption of the ideal vision of the American woman, in which man worshiped "a diviner self than his own,"

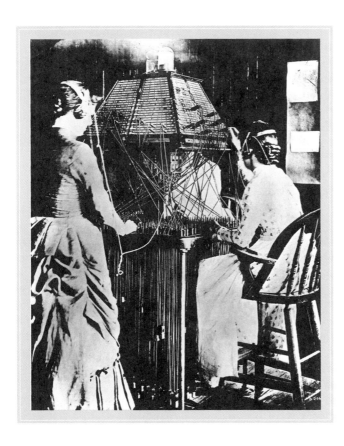

Female operators, called "hello girls," were hired to work telephone switch-boards after it was discovered that male operators tended to argue too much with subscribers.

innocent, helpless, and good. Women were to be better than the world around them. They were brought up, said Ida Tarbell, a leading political reformer, "as if wrongdoing were impossible to them."

Views changed, albeit slowly. One important change occurred in the legal codes pertaining to women, particularly in the common law doctrine of *femme couverte*. Under that doctrine, wives were chattel of their husbands; they could not legally control their own earnings, property, or children unless they had drawn up a specific contract before marriage. By 1890, many states had substantially revised the doctrine to allow wives control of their earnings and inherited property. In cases of divorce, the new laws also recognized women's rights to custody or joint custody of their children. Although divorce was still far from being socially acceptable, divorce rates more than doubled during the last third of the century. By 1905, one in twelve marriages was ending in divorce.

In the 1870s and 1880s, a growing number of women were asserting their own humanness. They fought for the vote, lobbied for equal pay, and sought self-fulfillment. The new interest in psychology and medicine strengthened their causes. Charlotte Perkins Gilman, author of *Women and Economics* (1898), joined other women in questioning the ideal of womanly "innocence," which, she argued, actually meant ignorance. In medical and popular literature, menstruation, sexual intercourse, and childbirth were becoming viewed as natural functions instead of taboo topics.

Women espoused causes with new fervor. Susan B. Anthony, a veteran of many reform campaigns, tried to vote in the 1872 presidential election and was fined $100, which she refused to pay. In 1890, she helped form the National American Woman Suffrage Association to work for the enfranchisement of women. On New York's Lower East Side, the Ladies Anti–Beef Trust Association, which formed to protest increases in the price of meat, established a boycott of butcher shops. When their demands were ignored, the women invaded the shops, poured kerosene on the meat, and set fire to it. "We don't riot," Rebecca Ablowitz told the judge. "But if all we did was to weep at home, nobody would notice it; so we have to do something to help ourselves."

EDUCATING THE MASSES

Continuing a trend that stretched back a hundred years, childhood was becoming an even more distinct time of life. There was still only a vague concept of adolescence—the special nature of the teenage years—but the role of children was changing. Less and less were children perceived as "little adults," valued for the additional financial gain they might bring into the family. Now children were to grow and learn and be nurtured rather than rushed into adulthood.

As a result, schooling became more important, and American children came closer than ever before to universal education. By 1900, thirty-one states and territories (out of fifty-one) had enacted laws making school attendance compulsory, though most required attendance only until the age of 14. In 1870, there were only 160 public high schools; in 1900, there were 6000. In the same years, illiteracy declined from 20 percent to just over 10 percent of the population. Still, even as late as 1900, the average adult had only five years of schooling.

Educators saw the school as the primary means to train people for life and work in an industrializing society. Hence teachers focused on basic skills—reading and mathematics—and on values—obedience and attentiveness to the clock. Most schools had a highly structured curriculum, built around discipline and routine. School began early; boys attended all day, but girls often stayed home after lunch, since it was thought they needed less in the way of learning. On the teacher's command, students stood and recited from *Webster's Spellers* and *McGuffey's Eclectic Readers*, the period's two most popular textbooks, which taught ethics, values, and religion as well as reading. In the *Readers*, boys grew up to be heroes, girls to be mothers, and hard work always meant success:

> Shall birds, and bees, and ants, be wise,
>   While I my moments waste?
> O let me with the morning rise,
>   And to my duty haste.

The South lagged far behind in education. The average family size there was about twice as large as in the North, and a greater proportion of the population

Schools, regarded primarily as training grounds for a life of work, stressed conformity and deportment— feet on the floor, hands folded and resting atop the desk. The teacher was drillmaster and disciplinarian as well as instructor.

lived in isolated rural areas. State and local authorities mandated fewer weeks in the average school year, and many southern states refused to adopt compulsory education laws.

Even more important was the effect of southern "Jim Crow" laws, passed in the 1890s and after to keep African Americans from voting, serving on juries, and participating in other aspects of southern life. Southerners used these laws to maintain separate school systems to segregate the races. Supported by the U.S. Supreme Court decision of 1896 in *Plessy* v. *Ferguson*, segregated schooling added a devastating financial burden to education in the South.

North Carolina and Alabama mandated segregated schools in 1876, South Carolina and Louisiana in 1877, Mississippi in 1878, and Virginia in 1882. A series of Supreme Court decisions in the 1880s and 1890s upheld the concept of segregation. In the *Civil Rights Cases* (1883), the Court ruled that the Fourteenth Amendment barred state governments from discriminating on account of race but did not prevent private individuals or organizations from doing so. *Plessy* v. *Ferguson* (1896) established the doctrine of "separate but equal" and upheld a Louisiana law requiring different railroad cars for whites and blacks. The Court applied the doctrine directly to schools in *Cumming* v. *County Board of Education* (1899), which approved the creation of separate schools for whites, even if there were no comparable schools for blacks.

Southern school laws often implied that the schools would be "separate but equal," and they were often separate but rarely equal. Black schools were usually dilapidated, and black teachers were paid considerably less than white teachers.

In 1890, only 35 percent of black children attended school in the South; 55 percent of white children did. That year nearly two-thirds of the country's black population was illiterate.

Educational techniques changed after the 1870s. Educators paid more attention to early elementary education, a trend that placed young children in school and helped the growing number of mothers who worked outside the home. The kindergarten movement, started in St. Louis in 1873, spread across the country. In kindergartens, 4- to 6-year-old children learned by playing, not by keeping their knees and toes in order. For older children, social reformers advocated "practical" courses in manual training and homemaking.

HIGHER EDUCATION

Nearly 150 new colleges and universities opened in the twenty years between 1880 and 1900. The Morrill Land Grant Act of 1862 gave large grants of land to the states for the establishment of colleges to teach "agriculture and the mechanic arts." The act fostered 69 "land-grant" institutions, including the great state universities of Wisconsin, California, Minnesota, and Illinois.

Private philanthropy, born of the large fortunes of the industrial age, also spurred growth in higher education. Leland Stanford gave $24 million to endow Stanford University on his California ranch, and John D. Rockefeller, founder of the Standard Oil Company, gave $34 million to found the University of Chicago. Other industrialists established Cornell (1865), Vanderbilt (1873), and Tulane (1884).

As colleges expanded, their function changed and their curriculum broadened. No longer did they exist primarily to train young men for the ministry. They moved away from the classical curriculum of rhetoric, mathematics, Latin, and Greek toward "reality and practicality," as President David Starr Jordan of Stanford University said. The Massachusetts Institute of Technology (MIT), founded in 1861, focused on science and engineering.

Charles W. Eliot, who became president of Harvard in 1869 at the age of 35, moved to end, as an admirer said, the "old fogyism" that marked the institution. Revising the curriculum, Eliot set up the elective system, in which students chose their own courses rather than following a rigidly prescribed curriculum. Lectures and discussions replaced rote recitation, and courses in the natural and social sciences, fine arts, and modern languages multiplied. In the 1890s, Eliot's Harvard moved to the forefront of educational innovation.

Women still had to fight for educational opportunities. Before the Civil War, only three private colleges admitted women to study with men. After the war, educational opportunities increased for women. A number of women's colleges opened, including Vassar (1865), Wellesley (1875), Smith (1875), Bryn Mawr (1885), Barnard (1889), and Radcliffe (1893). The land-grant colleges of the Midwest, open to women from the outset, spurred a nationwide trend toward coeducation, although some physicians, such as Harvard Medical School's Dr. Edward H. Clarke in his popular *Sex in Education* (1873), continued to argue that the strain of learning made women sterile. By 1900, women made up about 40 percent of college students, and four out of five colleges admitted them.

Fewer opportunities existed for African Americans and other minorities. Jane Stanford encouraged the Chinese who had worked on her husband's Central Pacific Railroad to apply to Stanford University, but her policy was unusual. Most colleges did not accept minority students, and only a few applied. W. E. B. Du Bois, the brilliant African American sociologist and civil rights leader, attended Harvard in the late 1880s but found the society of Harvard Yard closed against him. Disdained and disdainful, he "asked no fellowship of my fellow students." Chosen as one of the commencement speakers, Du Bois picked as his topic "Jefferson Davis," treating it, said an onlooker, with "an almost contemptuous fairness."

Black students turned to black colleges such as the Hampton Normal and Industrial Institute in Virginia and the Tuskegee Institute in Alabama. These colleges were often supported by whites who favored manual training for blacks. Booker T. Washington, an ex-slave, put into practice his educational ideas at Tuskegee, which opened in 1881. Washington began Tuskegee with limited funds, four run-down buildings, and only thirty students; by 1900, it was a model industrial and agricultural school. Spread over forty-six buildings, it offered instruction in thirty trades to fourteen hundred students.

Washington stressed patience, manual training, and hard work. "The wisest among my race understand," he said in a widely acclaimed speech at the Atlanta Exposition in 1895, "that the agitation of questions of social equality is the extremest folly." Blacks should focus on economic gains; they should go to school,

Booker T. Washington, who served as the first president of Tuskegee Institute, advocated work efficiency and practical skills as keys to advancement for African Americans. Students like these at Tuskegee studied academic subjects and received training in trades and professions.

learn skills, and work their way up the ladder. "No race," he said at Atlanta, "can prosper till it learns that there is as much dignity in tilling a field as in writing a poem. It is at the bottom of life we must begin, and not at the top." Southern whites should help out because they would then have "the most patient, faithful, law-abiding, and unresentful people that the world has seen."

Outlined most forcefully in Washington's speech in Atlanta, the philosophy became known as the Atlanta Compromise, and many whites and some blacks welcomed it. Acknowledging white domination, it called for slow progress through self-improvement, not through lawsuits or agitation. Rather than fighting for equal rights, blacks should acquire property and show they were worthy of their rights. But Washington did believe in black equality. Often secretive in his methods, he worked behind the scenes to organize black voters and lobby against harmful laws. In his own way, he bespoke a racial pride that contributed to the rise of black nationalism in the twentieth century.

Du Bois wanted a more aggressive strategy. Born in Massachusetts in 1868, the son of poor parents, he studied at Fisk University in Tennessee and the University of Berlin before he went to Harvard. Unable to find a teaching job in a white college, he took a low-paying research position at the University of Pennsylvania. He had no office but did not need one. Du Bois used the new discipline of sociology, which emphasized factual observation in the field, to study the condition of blacks.

Notebook in hand, he set out to examine crime in Philadelphia's black seventh ward. He interviewed five thousand people, mapped and classified neighborhoods, and produced *The Philadelphia Negro* (1898). The first study of the effect of urban life on blacks, it cited a wealth of statistics, all suggesting that crime in the ward stemmed not from inborn degeneracy but from the environment in which blacks lived. Change the environment, and people would change, too; education was a good way to go about it.

In *The Souls of Black Folk* (1903), Du Bois openly attacked Booker T. Washington and the philosophy of the Atlanta Compromise. He urged African Americans to aspire to professional careers, to fight for the restoration of their civil rights, and, wherever possible, to get a college education. Calling for integrated schools with equal opportunity for all, Du Bois urged blacks to educate their "talented tenth," a highly trained intellectual elite, to lead them.

Du Bois was not alone in promoting careers in the professions. Throughout higher education there was increased emphasis on professional training, particularly in medicine, dentistry, and law. Enrollments swelled, even as standards of admission tightened. The number of medical schools in the country rose from 75 in 1870 to 160 in 1900, and the number of medical students—including more and more women—almost tripled. Schools of nursing grew from only 15 in 1880 to 432 in 1900. Doctors, lawyers, and others became part of a growing middle class that shaped the concerns of the Progressive Era of the early twentieth century.

Although less than 5 percent of the college-age population attended college during the 1877–1890 period, the new trends had great impact. A generation of men and women encountered new ideas that changed their views of themselves and society. Many students emerged from American colleges with a heightened sense of the social problems facing the nation and the belief that they could help cure society's ills.

THE STIRRINGS OF REFORM

When Henry George, one of the era's leading reformers, asked a friend what could be done about the problem of political corruption in American cities, his friend replied: "Nothing! You and I can do nothing at all. . . . We can only wait for evolution. Perhaps in four or five thousand years evolution may have carried men beyond this state of things."

This stress on the slow pace of change reflected the doctrine of social Darwinism, based on the writings of English social philosopher Herbert Spencer. In several influential books, Spencer took the evolutionary theories of Charles Darwin and applied Darwinian principles of natural selection to society, combining biology and sociology in a theory of "social selection" that tried to explain human progress. Like animals, society evolved, slowly, by adapting to the environment. The "survival of the fittest"—a term that Spencer, not Darwin, invented—preserved the strong and weeded out the weak.

Social Darwinism had a number of influential followers in the United States, including William Graham Sumner, a professor of political and social science at Yale University. One of the country's best known academic figures, Sumner was forceful and eloquent. In writings such as *What Social Classes Owe to Each Other* (1883) and "The Absurd Effort to Make the World Over" (1894), he argued that government action on behalf of the poor or weak interfered with evolution and sapped the species. Reform tampered with the laws of nature.

The influence of social Darwinism on American thinking has been exaggerated, but in the powerful hands of Sumner and others it did influence some journalists, ministers, and policymakers. Between 1877 and the 1890s, however, it came under increasing attack. In fields like religion, economics, politics, literature, and law, thoughtful people raised questions about established conditions and suggested the need for reform.

PROGRESS AND POVERTY

Read and reread, passed from hand to hand, Henry George's nationwide best-seller *Progress and Poverty* (1879) led the way to a more critical appraisal of American society in the 1880s and beyond. The book jolted traditional thought. "It was responsible," one historian has said, "for starting along new lines of thinking an amazing number of the men and women" who became leaders of reform.

Disturbed by the depression of the 1870s and labor upheavals such as the great railroad strikes of 1877, George saw modern society—rich, complex, with material goods hitherto unknown—as sadly flawed.

"The present century," he wrote, "has been marked by a prodigious increase in wealth-producing power. . . . It was natural to expect, and it was expected, that . . . real poverty [would become] a thing of the past." Instead, he argued:

it becomes no easier for the masses of our people to make a living. On the con-
trary, it is becoming harder. The wealthy class is becoming more wealthy; but
the poorer class is becoming more dependent. The gulf between the employed
and the employer is growing wider; social contrasts are becoming sharper; as
liveried carriages appear, so do barefooted children.

George proposed a simple solution. Land, he thought, formed the basis of
wealth, and a few people could grow wealthy just because the price of their land
rose. Since the rise in price did not result from any effort on their part, it represented an "unearned increment," which, George argued, should be taxed for the
good of society. A "single tax" on the increment, replacing all other taxes, would
help equalize wealth and raise revenue to aid the poor. "Single-tax" clubs sprang
up around the country, but George's solution, simplistic and unappealing, had
much less impact than his analysis of the problem itself. He raised questions a
generation of readers set out to answer.

NEW CURRENTS IN SOCIAL THOUGHT

George's emphasis on deprivation in the environment excited a young country
lawyer in Ashtabula, Ohio—Clarence Darrow. Unlike the social Darwinists,
Darrow was sure that criminals were made and not born. They grew out of "the
unjust condition of human life." In the mid-1880s, he left for Chicago and a
forty-year career working to convince people that poverty lay at the root of
crime. "There is no such thing as crime as the word is generally understood," he
told a group of startled prisoners in the Cook County jail. "If every man, woman
and child in the world had a chance to make a decent, fair, honest living there
would be no jails and no lawyers and no courts."

As Darrow rejected the implications of social Darwinism, in similar fashion
Richard T. Ely and a group of young economists poked holes in traditional economic thought. Fresh from graduate study in Germany, Ely in 1884 attacked
classical economics for its dogmatism, simple faith in laissez-faire, and reliance
on self-interest as a guide for human conduct. The "younger" economics, he
said, must no longer be "a tool in the hands of the greedy and the avaricious for
keeping down and oppressing the laboring classes. It does not acknowledge
laissez-faire as an excuse for doing nothing while people starve."

Edward Bellamy dreamed of a cooperative society in which poverty, greed,
and crime no longer existed. A lawyer from western Massachusetts, Bellamy
published *Looking Backward, 2000–1887,* in 1887 and became a national reform figure virtually overnight. The novel's protagonist, Julian West, falls asleep
in 1887 and awakes in the year 2000. Wide-eyed, he finds himself in a socialist
utopia: The government owns the means of production, and citizens share the
material rewards. Cooperation, rather than competition, is the watchword.

The world of *Looking Backward* had limits; it was regimented, paternalistic, and filled with the gadgets and material concerns of Bellamy's own day.
But it had a dramatic effect on many readers. The book sold at the rate of ten
thousand copies a week, and its followers formed Nationalist Clubs to work
for its objectives.

Some Protestant sects stressed individual salvation and a better life in the next world, not in this one. Poverty was evidence of sinfulness; the poor had only themselves to blame. "God has intended the great to be great and the little to be little," said Henry Ward Beecher, the country's best known pastor. Wealth and destitution, suburbs and slums—all formed part of God's plan.

Challenging those traditional doctrines, a number of churches in the 1880s began establishing missions in the city slums. William Dwight Porter Bliss, an Episcopal clergyman, founded the Church of the Carpenter in a working-class district of Boston. Lewis M. Pease worked in the grim Five Points area of New York; Alexander Irvine, a Jewish missionary, lived in a flophouse in the Bowery. Irvine walked his skid row neighborhood every afternoon to lend a hand to those in need. Living among the poor and homeless, the urban missionaries grew impatient with religious doctrines that endorsed the status quo.

Many of the new trends were reflected in an emerging religious philosophy known as the Social Gospel. As the name suggests, the Social Gospel focused on society as well as individuals, on improving living conditions as well as saving souls. Sermons in Social Gospel churches called on church members to fulfill their social obligations, and adults met before and after the regular service to discuss social and economic problems. Children were excused from sermons, organized into age groups, and encouraged to make the church a center for social as well as religious activity. Soon churches included dining halls, gymnasiums, and even theaters.

The most active Social Gospel leader was Washington Gladden, a Congregational minister and prolific writer. Linking Christianity to the social and economic environment, Gladden spent a lifetime working for "social salvation." He saw Christianity as a fellowship of love and the church as a social agency. In *Applied Christianity* (1886) and other writings, he denounced competition, urged an "industrial partnership" between employers and employees, and called for efforts to help the poor.

THE SETTLEMENT HOUSES

A growing number of social reformers living in the urban slums shared Gladden's concern. Like Tweed and Plunkitt, they appreciated the dependency of the poor; unlike them, they wanted to eradicate the conditions that underlay it. To do so, they formed settlement houses in the slums and went to live in them to experience the problems they were trying to solve.

Youthful, idealistic, and mostly middle class, these social workers took as their model Toynbee Hall, founded in 1884 in the slums of East London to provide community services. The idea spread swiftly. By 1900, there were more than a hundred settlements in the country; five years later, there were more than two hundred, and by 1910, more than four hundred.

The settlements included Jane Addams's famous Hull House in Chicago (1889), Robert A. Woods's South End House in Boston (1892), and Lillian Wald's Henry Street Settlement in New York (1893). The reformers wanted to bridge the socioeconomic gap between rich and poor and to bring education, culture, and hope to the slums. They sought to create in the heart of the city the values and sense of community of small-town America.

Many of the settlement workers were women, some of them college graduates, who found that society had little use for their talents and energy. Jane Addams, a graduate of Rockford College in Illinois, opened Hull House on South Halsted Street in the heart of the Chicago slums. Twenty-nine years old, endowed with a forceful and winning personality, she intended "to share the lives of the poor" and humanize the industrial city. "American ideals," she said, "crumbled under the overpowering poverty of the overcrowded city."

Occupying an old, rundown house, Hull House stressed education, offering classes in elementary English and Shakespeare, lectures on ethics and the history of art, and courses in cooking,

Jane Addams founded Chicago's Hull House in 1889. The settlement house provided recreational and day-care facilities; offered extension classes in academic, vocational, and artistic subjects; and, above all, sought to bring hope to poverty-stricken slum dwellers.

sewing, and manual skills. A pragmatist, Addams believed in investigating a problem and then doing something to solve it. Noting the lack of medical care in the area, she established an infant welfare clinic and free medical dispensary. Because the tenements lacked bathtubs, she installed showers in the basement of the house and built a bathhouse for the neighbors. Because there was no local library, she opened a reading room. Gradually, Hull House expanded to occupy a dozen buildings sprawling over more than a city block.

Like settlement workers in other cities, Addams and her colleagues studied the immigrants in nearby tenements. Laboriously, they identified the background of every family in a one-third-square-mile area around Hull House. Finding people of eighteen different nationalities, they taught them American history and the English language, yet Addams also encouraged them—through folk festivals and art—to preserve their own heritage.

Florence Kelley, an energetic graduate of Cornell University, taught night school one winter in Chicago. Watching children break under the burden of poverty, she devoted her life to the problem of child labor. Convinced of the need for political activism, she worked with Addams and others to push through the Illinois Factory Act of 1893, which mandated an eight-hour day for women in factories and for children under the age of 14.

The settlement house movement had its limits. Hull House, one of the best, attracted two thousand visitors a week, still just a fraction of the seventy thousand people who lived within six blocks. Immigrants sometimes resented the middle-class "strangers" who told them how to live. Dressed always in a brown suit and dark stockings, Harriet Vittum, the head resident of Chicago's Northwestern University Settlement (who told the story of the suicide victim at the beginning of this chapter), was known in the neighborhood as "the police lady in brown." She once stopped a dance because it was too wild, and then watched in disgust as the boys responded by "making vulgar sounds with their lips." Though her attempts to help were sincere, in private Vittum called the people she was trying to help "ignorant foreigners, who live in an atmosphere of low morals . . . surrounded by anarchy and crime."

Although Addams tried to offer a few programs for blacks, most white reformers did not, and after 1900, a number of black reformers opened their own settlements. Like the whites, they offered employment information, medical care, and recreational facilities, along with concerts, lectures, and other educational events. White and black, the settlement workers made important contributions to urban life.

A CRISIS IN SOCIAL WELFARE

The depression of 1893 jarred the young settlement workers, many of whom had just begun their work. Addams and the Hull House workers helped form the Chicago Bureau of Charities to coordinate emergency relief. Kelley, recently appointed the chief factory inspector of Illinois, worked even harder to end child labor, and in 1899, she moved to New York City to head the National Consumers League, which marshaled the buying power of women to encourage employers to provide better working conditions.

In cities and towns across the country, traditional methods of helping the needy foundered in the crisis. Churches, charity organization societies, and community chests did what they could, but their resources were limited, and they functioned on traditional lines. Many of them still tried to change rather than aid individual families, and people were often reluctant to call on them for help.

Gradually, a new class of professional social workers arose to fill the need. Unlike the church and charity volunteers, these social workers wanted not only to feed the poor but to study their condition and alleviate it. Revealingly, they called themselves "case workers" and daily collected data on the income, housing, jobs, health, and habits of the poor. Prowling tenement districts, they gathered information about the number of rooms, number of occupants, ventilation, and sanitation of the buildings, putting together a fund of useful data.

Studies of the poor popped up everywhere. W. E. B. Du Bois did his pioneering study of urban blacks; Lillian Pettengill took a job as a domestic servant to see "the ups and downs of this particular dog-life from the dog's end of the chain." Others became street beggars, miners, lumberjacks, and factory laborers.

William T. Stead, a prominent British editor, visited the Chicago World's Fair in 1893 and stayed to examine the city. He roamed the flophouses and tenements and dropped in at Hull House to drink hot chocolate and talk over conditions with Jane Addams. Later he wrote an influential book, *If Christ Came to Chicago* (1894), and in a series of mass meetings during 1893, he called for a civic revival. In response, Chicagoans formed the Civic Federation, a group of forty leaders who aimed to make Chicago "the best governed, the healthiest city in this country." Setting up task forces for philanthropy, moral improvement, and legislation, the new group helped spawn the National Civic Federation (1900), a nationwide organization devoted to reform of urban life.

THE PLURALISTIC SOCIETY

"The United States was born in the country and moved to the city," historian Richard Hofstadter said. Much of that movement occurred during the nineteenth century when the United States was the most rapidly urbanizing nation in the Western world. American cities bustled with energy; they absorbed millions of migrants who came from Europe and other distant and not-so-distant parts of the world. That migration, and the urban growth that accompanied it, reshaped American politics and culture.

By 1920, the census showed that, for the first time, most Americans lived in cities. By then, too, almost half the population was descended from people who had arrived after the American Revolution. As European, African, and Asian cultures met in the American city, a culturally pluralistic society emerged. Dozens of nationalities produced a culture whose members considered themselves Polish Americans, African Americans, and Irish Americans. The melting pot sometimes softened distinctions between the various groups, but it only partially blended them into a unified society.

"Ah, Vera," said a character in Israel Zangwill's popular play *The Melting Pot* (1908), "what is the glory of Rome and Jerusalem where all nations and races come to worship and look back, compared with the glory of America, where all races and nations come to labour and look forward!" Critics scorned the play as "romantic claptrap," and indeed it was. But the metaphor of the melting pot clearly depicted a new national image. In the decades after the 1870s a jumble of ethnic and racial groups struggled for a place in society.

That society, it is clear, experienced a crisis between 1870 and 1900. Together, the growth of cities and the rise of industrial capitalism brought jarring change, the exploitation of labor, ethnic and racial tensions, poverty—and, for a few, wealth beyond the imagination. At Homestead, Pullman, and a host of other places, there was open warfare between capital and labor. As reformers struggled to mediate the situation, they turned more and more to state and federal government to look after human welfare, a tendency the Supreme Court stoutly resisted. In the midst of the crisis, the depression of the 1890s struck, adding to the turmoil and straining American institutions. Tracing the changes wrought by waves of urbanization and industrialization, Henry George described the country as "the House of Have and the House of Want," almost in paraphrase of Lincoln's earlier metaphor of the "house divided." The question was, could this house, unlike that one, stand?

CHRONOLOGY

1862 Morrill Land Grant gives land to states for establishment of colleges

1869 Rutgers and Princeton play in nation's first intercollegiate football game

Cincinnati Red Stockings, baseball's first professional team, organized

1873 Comstock Law bans obscene articles from U.S. mail

Nation's first kindergarten opens in St. Louis, Missouri

1874 Women's Christian Temperance Union formed to crusade against evils of liquor

1876 Johns Hopkins University opens first separate graduate school

1879 Henry George analyzes problems of urbanizing America in *Progress and Poverty*

Salvation Army arrives in United States

1880 Polish National Alliance formed to help Polish immigrants adjust to life in America

1881 Booker T. Washington opens Tuskegee Institute in Alabama

Dr. John H. Kellogg advises parents to teach their children about sex in *Plain Facts for Old and Young*

1883 Metropolitan Opera opens in New York

1885 Home Insurance Building, country's first metal-frame structure, erected in Chicago

American Economic Association formed to advocate government intervention in economic affairs

1887 Edward Bellamy promotes idea of socialist utopia in *Looking Backward, 2000–1887*

1889 Jane Addams opens Hull House in Chicago

1890 National Woman Suffrage Association and the American Woman Suffrage Association, both formed in 1869, merge to consolidate the woman suffrage movement

1894 Immigration Restriction League formed to limit immigration from southern and eastern Europe

1896 Supreme Court decision in *Plessy* v. *Ferguson* establishes constitutionality of "separate but equal" facilities

John Dewey's Laboratory School for testing and practice of new educational theory opens at University of Chicago

20

POLITICAL REALIGNMENTS
IN THE 1890S

I n June 1894, Susan Orcutt, a young farm woman from western Kansas, sat down to write the governor of her state a letter. She was desperate. The nation was in the midst of a devastating economic depression, and, like thousands of other people, she had no money and nothing to eat. "I take my Pen In hand to let you know that we are Starving to death," she wrote. Hail had ruined the Orcutts' crops, and none of the household could find work. "My Husband went away to find work and came home last night and told me that we would have to Starve. [H]e has bin in ten countys and did not Get no work. . . . I havent had nothing to Eat today and It is three oclock[.]"

As bad as conditions were on the farms, they were no better in the cities. "There are thousands of homeless and starving men in the streets," reported a journalist in Chicago in the winter of 1893. "I have seen more misery in this last week than I ever saw in my life before." Charity societies and churches tried to help, but they could not handle the huge numbers of people who were in need. The records of the Massachusetts state medical examiner told a grim story:

F.S., 29   *Suicide by arsenic*

Boston   *January 1, 1896*

Much depressed for several weeks. Loss of employment. At 7:50 A.M. Jan. 1, she called her father and told him she had taken poison and wished to die.

R.N., 23   *Suicide by bullet wound of brain*

Boston   *June 22, 1896*

Out of work. Mentally depressed. About 3 P.M. June 21 shot himself in right temple. . . . Left a letter explaining that he killed himself to save others the trouble of caring for him.

Lasting until 1897, the depression was the decisive event of the decade. At its height, three million people were unemployed—fully 20 percent of the work-force. The human costs were enormous, even among the well-to-do. "They were for me years of simple Hell," shattering "my whole scheme of life," said Charles Francis Adams, Jr., the descendant of two American presidents.

Like the Great Depression of the 1930s that gave rise to the New Deal, the depression of the 1890s had profound and lasting effects. Bringing to a head many of the tensions that had been building in the society, it increased rural hos-tility toward the cities, brought about a bitter fight over the currency, and changed people's thinking about government, unemployment, and reform. There were outbreaks of warfare between capital and labor; farmers demanded a fairer share of economic and social benefits; the new immigrants came under fresh at-tack. The depression of the 1890s changed the course of American history, as did another event of that decade: the war with Spain in 1898.

Under the cruel impact of the depression, ideas changed in many areas, in-cluding in politics. A realignment of the American political system, which had been developing since the end of Reconstruction, finally reached its fruition in the 1890s, establishing new patterns that gave rise to the Progressive Era and lasted well into the twentieth century.

POLITICS OF STALEMATE

Politics was a major fascination of the late nineteenth century, its mass entertain-ment and favorite sport. Political campaigns were events that involved the whole community, even though in most states men were the only ones who could vote. During the weeks leading up to an election, there were rallies, parades, picnics, and torchlight processions. Americans turned out in enormous numbers to vote. In the six presidential elections from 1876 to 1896, an average of almost 79 per-cent of the electorate voted, a higher percentage than voted before or after.

White males made up the bulk of the electorate; until after the turn of the century, women could vote in national elections only in Wyoming, Utah, Idaho, and Colorado. The National Woman Suffrage Association early sued for the vote, but in 1875, the Supreme Court (*Minor* v. *Happersett*) upheld the power of the states to deny this right to women. On several occasions, Congress refused to pass a constitutional amendment for woman suffrage, and between 1870 and 1910, nearly a dozen states defeated referenda to grant women the vote.

Black men were another group kept from the polls. In 1877, Georgia adopted the poll tax to make voters pay an annual tax for the right to vote. The technique, aimed at impoverished blacks, was quickly copied across the South.

In 1890, Mississippi required voters to be able to read and interpret the fed-eral Constitution to the satisfaction of registration officials, all of them white. Such literacy tests, which the Supreme Court upheld in the case of *Williams* v. *Mississippi* (1898), excluded poor white voters as well as blacks. In 1898, Louisiana avoided the problem by adopting the famous "grandfather clause," which used a literacy test to disqualify black voters but permitted men who had

A delegation of women's rights advocates addressed the judiciary committee of the House of Representatives to present their arguments in favor of woman suffrage. Reading the argument is Victoria Claflin Woodhull, one of the more radical activists in the women's movement.

failed the test to vote anyway if their fathers and grandfathers had voted before 1867—a time, of course, when no blacks could vote. The number of black voters decreased dramatically. In 1896, there were 130,334 registered black voters in Louisiana; in 1904, there were 1,342.

THE PARTY DEADLOCK

The 1870s and 1880s were still dominated by the Civil War generation, the unusual group of people who rose to power in the turbulent 1850s. Five of the six presidents elected between 1865 and 1900 had served in the war, as had many civic, business, and religious leaders. In 1890, well over one million veterans of the Union army were still alive, and Confederate veterans numbered in the hundreds of thousands.

Party loyalties—rooted in Civil War traditions, ethnic and religious differences, and perhaps class distinctions—were remarkably strong. Voters clung to their old parties, shifts were infrequent, and there were relatively few "independent" voters. Although linked to the defeated Confederacy, the Democrats revived quickly after the war. In 1874, they gained control of the House of Representatives, which they maintained for all but four of the succeeding twenty years. The Democrats rested on a less sectional base than the Republicans. Identification with civil rights and military rule cut Republican strength in the South, but the Democratic party's principles of states' rights, decentralization,

A toy scale pitting the presidential candidates of 1888 (Harrison and Cleveland) against each other invites participation in determining the election outcome. More than a plaything, the scale symbolized the high level of voter participation during the late nineteenth century when elections hung in balance until the last vote was counted.

and limited government won supporters everywhere.

While Democrats wanted to keep government local and small, the Republicans pursued policies for the nation as a whole, in which government was an instrument to promote moral progress and material wealth. The Republicans passed the Homestead Act (1862), granted subsidies to the transcontinental railroads, and pushed other measures to encourage economic growth. They enacted legislation and constitutional amendments to protect civil rights. They advocated a high protective tariff as a tool of economic policy, to keep out foreign products while "infant industries" grew.

In national elections, sixteen states, mostly in New England and the North, consistently voted Republican; fourteen states, mostly in the South, consistently voted Democratic. Elections, therefore, depended on a handful of "doubtful" states, which could swing elections either way. These states—New York, New Jersey, Connecticut, Ohio, Indiana, and Illinois—received special attention at election time.

The two parties were evenly matched, and elections were closely fought. In three of the five presidential elections from 1876 to 1892, the victor won by less than 1 percent of the vote; in 1876 and 1888, the losing candidates actually had more popular votes than the winners but lost in the electoral college. Only twice during these years did one party control both the presidency and the two houses of Congress—the Republicans in 1888 and the Democrats in 1892.

Historians once believed that political leaders accomplished little between 1877 and 1900, but those who saw few achievements were looking in the wrong location. With the impeachment of Andrew Johnson, the authority of the presidency dwindled in relation to congressional strength. For the first time in many years, attention shifted away from Washington itself. North and South, people who were weary of the centralization brought on by war and Reconstruction looked first to state and local governments to deal with the problems of an urban-industrial society.

EXPERIMENTS IN THE STATES

Across the country, state bureaus and commissions were established to regulate the new industrial society. Many of the early commissions were formed to oversee the railroads, at the time the nation's largest businesses. People who shipped goods over the railroads, especially farmers and merchants, wanted to end the policies of rate discrimination and other harmful practices. In 1869, Massachusetts established the first commission to regulate the railroads; by 1900, twenty-eight states had taken such action.

Most of the early commissions were advisory in nature. They collected statistics and published reports on rates and practices—serving, one commissioner said, "as a sort of lens" to focus public attention. Impatient with the results, legislatures in the Midwest and on the Pacific Coast established commissions with greater power to fix rates, outlaw rebates, and investigate rate discrimination. These commissions, experimental in nature, served as models for later policy at the federal level.

Illinois had one of the most thoroughgoing provisions. Responding to local merchants who were upset with existing railroad rate policies, the Illinois state constitution of 1870 declared railroads to be public highways and authorized the legislature to pass laws establishing maximum rates and preventing rate discrimination. In the important case of *Munn* v. *Illinois* (1877), the Supreme Court upheld the Illinois legislation, declaring that private property "affected with the public interest . . . must submit to being controlled by the public for the common good."

But the Court soon weakened that judgment. In the *Wabash* case of 1886 (*Wabash, St. Louis, & Pacific Railway Co.* v. *Illinois*), it narrowed the *Munn* ruling and held that states could not regulate commerce extending beyond their borders. Only Congress could. The *Wabash* decision turned people's attention back to the federal government. It spurred Congress to pass the Interstate Commerce Act (1887), which created the Interstate Commerce Commission (ICC) to investigate and oversee railroad activities. The act outlawed rebates and pooling agreements, and the ICC became the prototype of the federal commissions that today regulate many parts of the economy.

REESTABLISHING PRESIDENTIAL POWER

Johnson's impeachment, the scandals of the Grant administrations, and the controversy surrounding the 1876 election weakened the presidency. During the last two decades of the nineteenth century, presidents fought to reassert their authority, and by 1900, under William McKinley, they had succeeded to a remarkable degree. The late 1890s, in fact, marked the birth of the modern powerful presidency.

Rutherford B. Hayes entered the White House with his title clouded by the disputed election of 1876. Opponents called him "His Fraudulency" and "Rutherfraud B. Hayes," but soon he began to reassert the authority of the presidency. Hayes worked for reform in the civil service, placed well-known reformers in high offices, and, ordering the last troops out of South Carolina and Louisiana, ended military Reconstruction.

James A. Garfield, a Union army hero and longtime member of Congress, succeeded Hayes. Winning by a handful of votes in 1880, he took office energetically, determined to lower the tariff to cut taxes and assert American economic and strategic interests in Latin America. Ambitious and eloquent, Garfield had looked forward to the presidency, yet within a few weeks he said to friends, "My God! What is there in this place that a man should ever want to get into it?"

THE ELECTION OF 1880

CANDIDATE	PARTY	POPULAR VOTE	ELECTORAL VOTE
Garfield	Republican	4,454,416	214
Hancock	Democratic	4,444,952	155
Weaver	Greenback	308,578	0

Office seekers, hordes of them, evoked Garfield's anguish. Each one wanted a government job, and each one thought nothing of cornering the president on every occasion. Garfield planned to leave Washington on July 2, 1881, for a vacation in New England. Walking toward his train, he was shot in the back by Charles J. Guiteau, a deranged lawyer and disappointed office seeker. Suffering through the summer, Garfield died on September 19, 1881, and Vice President Chester A. Arthur became president.

Arthur was a better president than many had expected. He approved the construction of the modern American navy. Arthur worked to lower the tariff, and in 1883, with his backing, Congress passed the Pendleton Act to reform the civil service. In part a reaction to Garfield's assassination, the act created a bipartisan Civil Service Commission to administer competitive examinations and appoint officeholders on the basis of merit. Initially, the act affected only about 14,000 of some 100,000 government offices, but it laid the basis for the later expansion of the civil service.

In the election of 1884, Grover Cleveland, the Democratic governor of New York, narrowly defeated Republican nominee, James G. Blaine. The first Democratic president since 1861, Cleveland was slow and ponderous, known for his honesty, stubbornness, and hard work. His term in the White House from 1885 to 1889 reflected the Democratic party's desire to curtail federal activities.

THE ELECTION OF 1884

CANDIDATE	PARTY	POPULAR VOTE	ELECTORAL VOTE
Cleveland	Democratic	4,874,986	219
Blaine	Republican	4,851,981	182
Butler	Greenback	175,370	0
St. John	Prohibition	150,369	0

THE ELECTION OF 1888

CANDIDATE	PARTY	POPULAR VOTE	ELECTORAL VOTE
Harrison	Republican	5,439,853	233
Cleveland	Democratic	5,540,309	168
	Minor Parties	396,441	0

Cleveland vetoed more than two-thirds of the bills presented to him, more than all his predecessors combined.

Late in 1887, Cleveland devoted his annual message to an attack on the tariff, "the vicious, inequitable, and illogical source of unnecessary taxation," and committed himself and the Democratic party to lowering the tariff.

The Republicans accused him of undermining American industries, and in 1888, they nominated for the presidency Benjamin Harrison, a defender of the tariff. Cleveland garnered ninety thousand more popular votes than Harrison but won the electoral votes of only two northern states and the South. Harrison won the rest of the North, most of the "doubtful" states, and the election.

REPUBLICANS IN POWER: THE BILLION-DOLLAR CONGRESS

Despite Harrison's narrow margin, the election of 1888 was the most sweeping victory for either party in almost twenty years; it gave the Republicans the presidency and both houses of Congress. The Republicans, it seemed, had broken the party stalemate and become the majority party in the country.

TARIFFS, TRUSTS, AND SILVER

As if a dam had burst, law after law poured out of the Republican Congress during 1890. The Republicans passed the McKinley Tariff Act, which raised tariff duties about 4 percent, higher than ever before; it also included a novel reciprocity provision that allowed the president to lower duties if other countries did the same. A Dependent Pensions Act granted pensions to Union army veterans and their widows and children. The pensions were modest—$6 to $12 a month—but the number of pensioners doubled by 1893, when nearly 1 million individuals received about $160 million in pensions.

With little debate, the Republicans and Democrats joined in passing the Sherman Antitrust Act, the first federal attempt to regulate big business. As the initial attempt to deal with the problem of trusts and industrial growth, the act shaped all later antitrust policy. It declared illegal "every contract, combination in the form of trust or otherwise, or conspiracy, in restraint of trade or commerce." Penalties for violation were stiff, including fines and imprisonment and the dissolution of guilty trusts. Experimental in nature, the act's terms were often vague and left precise interpretation to later experience and the courts.

One of the most important laws Congress passed, the Sherman Antitrust Act made the United States virtually the only industrial nation to regulate business combinations. It tried to harness big business without harming it. Many members of Congress did not expect the new law to have much effect on businesses, and for a decade, in fact, it did not. The Justice Department rarely filed suit under it, and in the *United States* v. *E. C. Knight Co.* decision (1895), the first judicial interpretation of the law, the Supreme Court severely crippled it. Though the E. C. Knight Co. controlled 98 percent of all sugar refining in the country, the Court drew a sharp distinction between commerce and manufacturing, holding that the company, as a manufacturer, was not subject to the law. But judicial interpretations changed after the turn of the century, and the Sherman Antitrust Act gained fresh power.

Another measure, the Sherman Silver Purchase Act, tried to end the troublesome problem presented by silver. As one of the two most commonly used precious metals, silver had once played a large role in currencies around the world,

In this 1886 cartoon illustrating the silver standard versus gold standard controversy, Uncle Sam bicycles to national bankruptcy on an enormous silverite dollar.

but by the mid-1800s, it had slipped into disuse. With the discovery of the great bonanza mines in Nevada, American silver production quadrupled between 1870 and 1890, glutting the world market, lowering the price of silver, and persuading many European nations to demonetize silver in favor of the scarcer metal, gold. The United States kept a limited form of silver coinage with congressional passage of the Bland-Allison Act in 1878.

Support for silver coinage was especially strong in the South and West, where people thought it might inflate the currency, raise wages and crop prices, and challenge the power of the gold-oriented Northeast. Eager to avert the free coinage of silver, which would require the coinage of all silver presented at the U.S. mints, President Harrison and other Republican leaders pressed for a compromise that took shape in the Sherman Silver Purchase Act of 1890.

The act directed the Treasury to purchase 4.5 million ounces of silver a month and to issue legal tender in the form of Treasury notes in payment for it. The act was a compromise. Opponents of silver were pleased that it did not include free coinage. Silverites, on the other hand, were delighted that the monthly purchases would buy up most of the country's silver production. The Treasury notes, moreover, could be cashed for either gold or silver at the bank, a gesture toward a true bimetallic system based on silver and gold.

As a final measure, Republicans in the House courageously passed a federal elections bill to protect the voting rights of blacks in the South. Although restrained in language and intent, it set off a storm of denunciation among the Democrats, who called it a "force bill" that would station army troops in the South. Because of the outcry, the bill failed in the Senate; it was the last major effort until the 1950s to enforce the Fifteenth Amendment to the Constitution.

THE 1890 ELECTIONS

The Republican Congress of 1890 was one of the most important Congresses in American history. It passed a record number of significant laws that helped shape later policy and asserted the authority of the federal government to a degree the country would not then accept. Sensing the public reaction, the Democrats labeled it the "Billion-Dollar Congress" for spending that much in appropriations and grants.

"This is a billion-dollar country," Speaker Reed replied, but the voters disagreed. The 1890 elections crushed the Republicans, who lost an extraordinary seventy-eight seats in the House. Political veterans went down to defeat, and new leaders vaulted into sudden prominence. Nebraska elected a Democratic governor for the first time in its history. The state of Iowa, once so staunchly Republican that a local leader had predicted that "Iowa will go Democratic when Hell goes Methodist," went Democratic in 1890.

THE RISE OF THE POPULIST MOVEMENT

The elections of 1890 drew attention to a fast-growing movement among farmers that soon came to be known far and wide as populism. During the summer of 1890, wagonloads of farm families in the South and West converged on campgrounds and picnic areas to socialize and discuss common problems. They came by the thousands, weary of drought, mortgages, and low crop prices. At the campgrounds, they picnicked, talked, and listened to recruiters from an organization called the National Farmers' Alliance and Industrial Union, which promised unified action to solve agricultural problems.

THE FARM PROBLEM

Farm discontent was a worldwide phenomenon between 1870 and 1900. With the new means of transportation and communication, farmers everywhere were caught up in a complex international market they neither controlled nor entirely understood.

American farmers complained bitterly about declining prices for their products, rising railroad rates for shipping them, and burdensome mortgages. Some of their grievances were valid. Farm profits were certainly low. The prices of farm commodities fell between 1865 and 1890, but they did not fall as low as did other commodity prices. Despite the fact that farmers received less for their crops, their purchasing power actually increased.

Neither was the farmers' second grievance—rising railroad rates—entirely justified. Railroad rates actually fell during these years, benefiting shippers of all products. Farm mortgages, the farmers' third grievance, were common because many farmers mortgaged their property to expand their holdings or buy new farm machinery. While certainly burdensome, most mortgages did not bring hardship. They were often short, with a term of four years or less, after which farmers could renegotiate at new rates, and the new machinery the farmers bought enabled them to triple their output and increase their income.

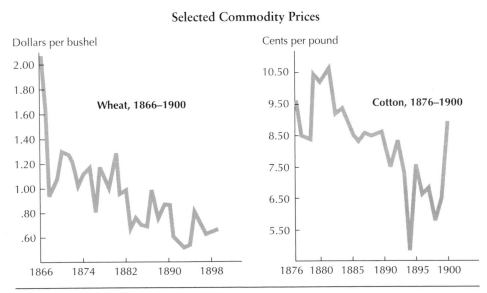

Selected Commodity Prices

Source: U.S. Bureau of the Census, *Historical Statistics of the United States, Colonial Times to 1970*, Bicentennial Edition, Washington, D.C., 1975.

Some farmers had valid grievances, though many understandably tended to exaggerate them. More important, many farmers were sure their condition had declined, and this perception—as bitterly real as any actual fact—sparked a growing anger. Equally upsetting, everyone in the 1870s and 1880s seemed excited about factories, not farms. Farmers had become "hayseeds," a word that first appeared in 1889, and they watched their offspring leave for city lights and new careers.

THE FAST-GROWING FARMERS' ALLIANCE

Originally a social organization for farmers, the Grange lost many of its members as it turned more and more toward politics in the late 1870s. In its place, a multitude of farm societies sprang into existence. By the end of the 1880s, they had formed into two major organizations: the National Farmers' Alliance, located on the Plains west of the Mississippi and known as the Northwestern Alliance, and the Farmers' Alliance and Industrial Union, based in the South and known as the Southern Alliance.

The Southern Alliance began in Texas in 1875 but did not assume major proportions until Dr. Charles W. Macune, an energetic and farsighted person, took over the leadership in 1886. Rapidly expanding, the Alliance absorbed other agricultural societies. Its agents spread across the South, where farmers were fed up with crop liens, depleted lands, and sharecropping. In 1890, the Southern Alliance claimed more than a million members. It welcomed to membership the farmers' "natural friends"—country doctors, schoolteachers, preachers, and mechanics. It excluded lawyers, bankers, cotton merchants, and warehouse operators.

Loosely affiliated with the Southern Alliance, a separate Colored Farmers' National Alliance and Cooperative Union enlisted black farmers in the South. Claiming more than 1 million members, it probably had closer to 250,000, but even that figure was sizable in an era when "uppity" blacks faced not merely defeat, but death. In 1891, black cotton pickers struck for higher wages near Memphis, Tennessee. Led by Ben Patterson, a 30-year-old picker, they walked off several plantations, but a posse hunted them down and, following violence on both sides, lynched fifteen strikers, including Patterson. The abortive strike ended the Colored Farmers' Alliance.

On the Plains, the Northwestern Alliance, a smaller organization, was formed in 1880. Its objectives were similar to those of the Southern Alliance, but it disagreed with the Southerners' emphasis on secrecy, centralized control, and separate organizations for blacks. In 1889, the Southern Alliance changed its name to the National Farmers' Alliance and Industrial Union and persuaded the three strongest state alliances on the Plains—those in North Dakota, South Dakota, and Kansas—to join. Thereafter, the renamed organization dominated the Alliance movement.

The Alliance mainly sponsored social and economic programs, but it turned early to politics. In the West, its leaders rejected both the Republicans and Democrats and organized their own party; in June 1890, Kansas Alliance members formed the first major People's party. The Southern Alliance resisted the

Populist Mary E. Lease advised farmers to "raise less corn and more hell." She also said, "If one man has not enough to eat three times a day and another man has $25 million, that last man has something that belongs to the first."

idea of a new party for fear it might divide the white vote, thus undercutting white supremacy. The Southerners instead followed leaders such as Benjamin F. Tillman of South Carolina, who wanted to capture control of the dominant Democratic party.

Thomas E. Watson and Leonidas L. Polk, two politically minded Southerners, reflected the high quality of Alliance leadership. Georgia-born, Watson was a talented orator and organizer; he urged Georgia farmers, black and white, to unite against their oppressors. The president of the National Farmers' Alliance, Polk believed in scientific farming and cooperative action. Also from Kansas, Mary E. Lease—Mary Ellen to her friends, "Mary Yellin" to her opponents—helped head a movement remarkably open to female leadership. A captivating speaker, she made 160 speeches during the summer of 1890, calling on farmers to rise against Wall Street and the industrial East.

Meeting in Ocala, Florida, in 1890, the Alliance adopted the Ocala Demands, the platform the organization pushed as long as it existed. First and foremost, the demands called for the creation of a "sub-treasury system," which would allow farmers to store their crops in government warehouses. In return, they could claim Treasury notes for up to 80 percent of the local market value of the crop, a loan to be repaid when the crops were sold. Farmers could thus hold their crops for the best price. The Ocala Demands also urged the free coinage of silver, an end to protective tariffs and national banks, a federal income tax, the direct election of senators by voters instead of state legislatures, and tighter regulation of railroad companies.

The Alliance strategy worked well in the elections of 1890. In Kansas, the Alliance-related People's party, organized just a few months before, elected four congressmen and a U.S. senator. Across the South, the Alliance won victories based on the "Alliance yardstick," a demand that Democratic party candidates pledge support for Alliance measures. Alliance leaders claimed thirty-eight Alliance supporters elected to Congress, with at least a dozen more pledged to Alliance principles.

THE PEOPLE'S PARTY

After the 1890 elections, Northern Alliance leaders urged the formation of a national third party to promote reform, although the Southerners remained reluctant, still hopeful of capturing control of the Democratic party. Plans for a new party were discussed at Alliance conventions in 1891 and the following year. In July 1892, a convention in Omaha, Nebraska, formed the new People's (or Populist) party. Southern Alliance leaders joined in, convinced now that there was no reason to cooperate with the Democrats who exploited Alliance popularity but failed to adopt its reforms.

In the South, some Populists had worked to unite black and white farmers. "They are in the ditch just like we are," a white Texas Populist said. Blacks and whites served on Populist election committees; they spoke from the same platforms, and they ran on the same tickets.

Many of the delegates at the Omaha convention had planned to nominate Leonidas L. Polk for president, but he died suddenly in June, and the convention turned instead to James B. Weaver of Iowa, a former congressman, Union army general, and third-party candidate for president in 1880 (on the Greenback-Labor party ticket). As its platform, the People's party adopted many of the Ocala Demands.

Weaver waged an active campaign but with mixed results. He won 1,027,329 votes, the first third-party presidential candidate ever to attract more than a million. He carried Kansas, Idaho, Nevada, and Colorado, along with portions of North Dakota and Oregon, for a total of twenty-two electoral votes, a measure of agrarian unrest. The Populists elected governors in Kansas and North Dakota, ten congressmen, five senators, and about fifteen hundred members of state legislatures.

Despite the Populists' victories, the election brought disappointment. Southern Democrats used intimidation, fraud, and manipulation to hold down Populist votes. Weaver was held to less than a quarter of the vote in every southern state except Alabama. In most of the country, he lost heavily in urban areas, with the exception of some mining towns in the Far West. He also failed to win

THE ELECTION OF 1892

CANDIDATE	PARTY	POPULAR VOTE	ELECTORAL VOTE
Cleveland	Democratic	5,556,918	277
Harrison	Republican	5,176,108	145
Weaver	People's (Populist)	1,027,329	22
	Minor Parties	264,133	0

over most farmers. In no midwestern state except Kansas and North Dakota did he win as much as 5 percent of the vote.

In the election of 1892, many voters switched parties, but they tended to realign with the Democrats rather than the Populists, whose platform on silver and other issues had relatively little appeal among city dwellers or factory workers. Although the Populists did run candidates in the next three presidential elections, they had reached their peak in 1892. That year, Farmers' Alliance membership dropped for the second year in a row, and the organization, which was once the breeding ground of the People's party, was broken.

While it lived, the Alliance was one of the most powerful protest movements in American history. Catalyzing the feelings of hundreds of thousands of farmers, it attempted to solve specific economic problems while at the same time advancing a larger vision of harmony and community, in which people who cared about each other were rewarded for what they produced.

THE CRISIS OF THE DEPRESSION

It was economic crisis, however, not harmony and community, that dominated the last decade of the century. Responding to the heady forces of industrialization, the American economy had expanded too rapidly in the 1870s and 1880s. Railroads had overbuilt, gambling on future growth. Companies had grown beyond their markets; farms and businesses had borrowed heavily for expansion.

THE PANIC OF 1893

The mood changed early in 1893. In mid-February, panic suddenly hit the New York stock market. In one day, investors dumped one million shares of a leading company, the Philadelphia and Reading Railroad, and it went bankrupt. Business investment dropped sharply in the railroad and construction industries, touching off the worst economic downturn to that point in the country's history.

Frightened, people hurriedly sold stocks and other assets to buy gold. The overwhelming demand depleted the gold reserve of the U.S. Treasury. Eroding almost daily, in March 1893, the Treasury's reserve slumped toward the $100 million mark, an amount that stood for the government's commitment to maintain the gold standard. On April 22, for the first time since the 1870s, the reserve fell below $100 million.

The news shattered business confidence—the stock market broke. On Wednesday, May 3, railroad and industrial stocks plummeted, and the next day, several major firms went bankrupt. When the market opened on Friday, crowds filled its galleries, anticipating a panic. Within minutes, leading stocks plunged to record lows, and there was pandemonium on the floor and in the streets outside.

Afterward, banks cut back on loans. Unable to get capital, businesses failed at an average rate of two dozen a day during the month of May. On July 26, the Erie Railroad, one of the leading names in railroading history, failed. August 1893 was the worst month. Across the country, factories and mines shut down.

Customers line up in front of the Farmers and Mechanics Bank in Minneapolis, Minnesota, in May 1893 to try to withdraw their savings. Many banks had loaned out most of their deposits and kept only a small portion of cash in reserve. When they could not meet depositors' demands for cash withdrawals, banks closed their doors.

On August 15, the Northern Pacific Railroad went bankrupt; the Union Pacific and the Santa Fe soon followed. Some economists estimated unemployment at 2 million people, or nearly 15 percent of the labor force.

The year 1894 was even worse. The gross national product dropped again, and by midyear the number of unemployed stood at 3 million. One out of every five workers was unemployed. In the summer, a heat wave and drought struck the farm belt west of the Mississippi River, creating conditions unmatched until the devastating Dust Bowl of the 1930s. Corn withered in the fields. In the South, the price of cotton fell below five cents a pound, far under the break-even point.

People became restless and angry. As one newspaper said in 1896: "On every corner stands a man whose fortune in these dull times has made him an ugly critic of everything and everybody." There was even talk of revolution and bloodshed. Some of the unemployed wandered across the country—singly, in small groups, and in small armies. During 1894, there were some fourteen hundred strikes involving more than a half million workers.

THE PULLMAN STRIKE

Discontent mounted. The great Pullman strike—one of the largest strikes in the country's history—began when the employees of the Pullman Palace Car Company, living in a company town just outside Chicago (a town in which everything was owned and meted out by the company), struck to protest wage cuts, continuing high rents, and layoffs. On June 26, 1894, the American Railway Union (ARU) under Eugene V. Debs joined the strike by refusing to handle trains that carried Pullman sleeping cars.

Within hours, the strike paralyzed the western half of the nation. Grain and livestock could not reach markets. Factories shut down for lack of coal. The strike extended into twenty-seven states and territories, tying up the economy and renewing talk of class warfare. In Washington, President Grover Cleveland, who had been reelected to the presidency in 1892, decided to break the strike on the grounds that it obstructed delivery of the mail.

On July 2, he secured a court injunction against the ARU, and he ordered troops to Chicago. When they arrived on the morning of Independence Day, the city was peaceful. Before long, however, violence broke out, and mobs, composed mostly of nonstrikers, overturned freight cars, looted, and burned. Restoring order, the army occupied railroad yards in Illinois, California, and other places. By late July, the strike was over; Debs was jailed for violating the injunction.

The Pullman strike had far-reaching consequences for the development of the labor movement. Working people resented Cleveland's actions in the strike, particularly as it became apparent that he sided with the railroads. Upholding Debs's sentence in *In re Debs* (1895), the Supreme Court endorsed the use of the injunction in labor disputes, thus giving business and government an effective antilabor weapon that hindered union growth in the 1890s.

THE MINERS OF THE MIDWEST

The plight of coal miners in the Midwest illustrated the personal and social impact of the depression. Even in the best of times, mining was a dirty and dangerous business. One miner in twelve died underground; one in three suffered injury. Mines routinely closed for as long as six months a year, and wages fell with the depression.

Midwestern mining was often a family occupation, passed down from father to son. It demanded delicate judgments about when to blast, where to follow a seam, and how to avoid rockfalls. Until 1890, English and Irish immigrants dominated the business. They migrated from mine to mine, and they nearly always lived in flimsy shacks owned by the company.

After 1890, immigration from southern and eastern Europe, hitherto a trickle, became a flood. Italians, Lithuanians, Poles, Slovaks, Magyars, Russians, Bohemians, and Croatians came to the mines to find work. In some mining towns, Italian and Polish miners soon made up almost half the population.

As the depression deepened, tensions grew between miners and their employers and between "old" miners and the "new." Many "new" miners spoke no English, and often they were "birds of passage," transients who had come to the United States to make money to take back home. Lacking the skills handed down by the "old" miners, they were often blamed for accidents, and they worked longer hours for less pay. At many a tavern after work, "old" miners grumbled about the different-looking newcomers and considered ways to get rid of them.

In April 1894, a wave of wage reductions sparked an explosion of labor unrest in the mines. The United Mine Workers, a struggling union formed just four years earlier, called for a strike of bituminous coal miners, and on April 21, virtually all midwestern and Pennsylvania miners—some 170,000 in all—quit working. The flow of crucial coal slackened; cities faced blackouts; factories closed.

The violence that soon broke out followed a significant pattern. Over the years, the English and Irish miners had built up a set of unspoken understandings with their employers. The "new" miners had not, and they were more prone to violent action to win a strike. The depression hit them especially hard, frustrating their plans to earn money and return home. In many areas, anger and frustration turned the 1894 strikes into outright war.

For nearly two weeks in June 1894, fighting rocked the Illinois, Ohio, and Indiana coalfields. Mobs ignited mine shafts, dynamited coal trains, and defied state militias. Shocked by the violence, public opinion shifted against the strikers. The strike ended in a matter of weeks, but its effects lingered. English and Irish miners moved out into other jobs or up into supervisory positions. Jokes and songs poked cruel fun at the "new" immigrants, and the Pennsylvania and Illinois legislatures adopted laws to keep them out of the mines. Thousands of "old" miners voted Populist in 1894—the Populist platform called for restrictions on immigration—in one of the Populists' few successes that year.

Occurring at the same time, the Pullman strike pulled attention away from the crisis in the coalfields, yet the miners' strike involved three times as many workers and provided a revealing glimpse of the tensions within American society. The miners of the Midwest were the first large group of skilled workers seriously affected by the flood of immigrants from southern and eastern Europe. Buffeted by depression, they reflected the social and economic discord that permeated every industry.

A BELEAGUERED PRESIDENT

Building on the Democratic party's sweeping triumph in the midterm elections of 1890, Grover Cleveland decisively defeated the Populist candidate, James B. Weaver, and the incumbent president, Benjamin Harrison, in 1892. The Democrats increased their strength in the cities and among working-class voters. For the first time since the 1850s, they controlled the White House and both branches of Congress.

The Democrats, it now seemed, had broken the party stalemate, but unfortunately for Cleveland, the Panic of 1893 struck almost as he took office. He was sure that he knew its cause. The Sherman Silver Purchase Act of 1890, he believed, had damaged business confidence, drained the Treasury's gold reserve, and caused the panic. The solution to the depression was equally simple: repeal the act.

In June 1893, Cleveland summoned Congress into special session. The silverites were on the defensive, although they pleaded for a compromise. Rejecting the pleas, Cleveland pushed the repeal bill through Congress, and on November 1, 1893, he signed it into law. Always sure of himself, he had staked everything on a single measure—a winning strategy if he succeeded, a devastating one if he did not.

Repeal of the Sherman Silver Purchase Act was probably a necessary action. It responded to the realities of international finance, reduced the flight of gold out of the country, and, over the long run, boosted business confidence. Unfortunately, it contracted the currency at a time when inflation might have helped. It did not bring economic revival. The stock market remained listless, businesses continued to close, unemployment spread, and farm prices dropped.

The repeal battle of 1893, discrediting the conservative Cleveland Democrats who had dominated the party since the 1860s, reshaped the politics of the country. It confined the Democratic party largely to the South, helped the Republicans become the majority party in 1894, and strengthened the position of the silver Democrats in their bid for the presidency in 1896. It also focused national attention on the silver issue and thus intensified the silver sentiment Cleveland had intended to dampen. In the end, repeal did not even solve the Treasury's gold problem. By January 1894, the reserve had fallen to $65 million. A year later, it fell to $44.5 million.

BREAKING THE PARTY DEADLOCK

The Democrats were buried in the elections of 1894. Suffering the greatest defeat in congressional history, they lost 113 House seats, while the Republicans gained 117. In twenty-four states, not a single Democrat was elected to Congress. The Democrats even lost some of the "solid South," and in the Midwest, a crucial battleground of the 1890s, the party was virtually destroyed.

Wooing labor and the unemployed, the Populists made striking inroads in parts of the South and West, yet their progress was far from enough. In a year in which thousands of voters switched parties, the People's party elected only four senators and four congressmen. Southern Democrats again used fraud and violence to keep the Populists' totals down. In the Midwest, the Populists won double the number of votes they had received in 1892, yet still attracted less than 7 percent of the vote. Across the country, the discontented tended to vote for the Republicans, not the Populists, a discouraging sign for the Populist party.

The elections of 1894 marked the end of the party deadlock that had existed since the 1870s. The Democrats lost, the Populists gained somewhat, and the Republicans became the majority party in the country. In the midst of the depression, the Republican doctrines of activism and national authority, which voters had repudiated in the elections of 1890, became more attractive. This was a development of great significance, because as Americans became more accepting of the use of government power to regulate the economy and safeguard individual welfare, the way lay open to the reforms of the Progressive Era, the New Deal, and beyond.

CHANGING ATTITUDES

The depression, brutal and far-reaching, did more than shift political alignments. Across the country, it undermined traditional views and caused people to rethink older ideas about government, the economy, and society. As men and women concluded that established ideas had failed to deal with the depression, they looked for new ones.

In prosperous times, Americans had thought of unemployment as the result of personal failure, affecting primarily the lazy and immoral. In the midst of depression, such views were harder to maintain, since everyone knew people who were both worthy and unemployed. Next door, a respected neighbor might be laid off; down the block, an entire factory might be shut down.

People debated issues they had long taken for granted. New and reinvigorated local institutions—discussion clubs, women's clubs, reform societies, university extension centers, church groups, farmers' societies—gave people a place to discuss alternatives to the existing order. Pressures for reform increased, and demand grew for government intervention to help the poor and unemployed.

"EVERYBODY WORKS BUT FATHER"

Women and children had been entering the labor force for years, and the depression accelerated the trend. As husbands and fathers lost their jobs, more and more women and children went to work. Even as late as 1901, well after the depression had ended, a study of working-class families showed that more than half the principal breadwinners were out of work. So many women and children worked that in 1905 there was a popular song titled "Everybody Works But Father."

During the 1890s, the number of working women rose from 4 million to 5.3 million. Trying to make ends meet, they took in boarders and found jobs as laundresses, cleaners, or domestics. Where possible, they worked in offices and factories. Far more black urban women than white worked to supplement their husbands' meager earnings. In New York City in 1900, nearly 60 percent of all black women worked, compared to 27 percent of the foreign-born and 24 percent of native-born white women. Men still dominated business offices, but during the 1890s, more and more employers noted the relative cheapness of female labor. Women telegraph and telephone operators nearly tripled in number during the decade. Women worked as clerks in the new five-and-tens and department stores, and as nurses; in 1900, a half million were teachers. They increasingly entered office work as stenographers and typists.

The depression also caused an increasing number of children to work. During the 1890s, the number of children employed in southern textile mills jumped more than 160 percent, and boys and girls under 16 years of age made up nearly one-third of the labor force of the mills. Youngsters of 8 and 9 years worked twelve hours a day for pitiful wages. In most cases, however, children worked not in factories but in farming and city street trades such as peddling and shoe shining.

Concerned about child labor, middle-class women in 1896 formed the League for the Protection of the Family, which called for compulsory education to get children out of factories and into classrooms. The Mothers Congress of 1896 gave rise to the National Congress of Parents and Teachers, the spawning ground of thousands of local Parent-Teacher Associations. The National Council of Women and the General Federation of Women's Clubs took up similar issues. By the end of the 1890s, the Federation had 150,000 members who

Tiny children peddling newspapers and women domestics serving the rich—their meager earnings were desperately needed.

worked for various civic reforms in the fields of child welfare, education, and sanitation.

CHANGING THEMES IN LITERATURE

The depression also gave point to a growing movement in literature toward realism and naturalism. In the years after the Civil War, literature often reflected the mood of romanticism—sentimental and unrealistic.

The novels of Horatio Alger, which provided simple lessons about how to get ahead in business and life, continued to attract large numbers of readers. They told of poor youngsters who made their way to the top through hard work, thrift, honesty, and luck. Louisa May Alcott's *Little Women* (1868–1869) related the daily lives of four girls in a New England family; Anna Sewell's *Black Beauty* (1877) charmed readers with the story of an abused horse that found a happy home.

After the 1870s, however, a number of talented authors began to reject romanticism and escapism, turning instead to realism. Determined to portray life as it was, they studied local dialects, wrote regional stories, and emphasized the "true" relationships between people. In doing so, they reflected broader trends in the society, such as industrialism; evolutionary theory, which emphasized the effect of the environment on humans; and the new philosophy of pragmatism, which stressed the relativity of values.

Mark Twain became the country's most outstanding realist author. Growing up along the Mississippi River in Hannibal County, Missouri, the young Samuel

Langhorne Clemens observed life around him with a humorous and skeptical eye. Adopting a pen name from the river term "mark twain" (two fathoms), he wrote a number of important works that drew on his own experiences. *Life on the Mississippi* (1883) described his career as a steamboat pilot. *The Adventures of Tom Sawyer* (1876) and *The Adventures of Huckleberry Finn* (1884) gained international prominence. In these books, Twain used dialect and common speech instead of literary language, touching off a major change in American prose style.

Other writers, the naturalists, became impatient even with realism. Pushing Darwinian theory to its limits, they wrote of a world in which a cruel and merciless environment determined human fate. Often focusing on economic hardship, naturalist writers studied the poor, the lower classes, and the criminal mind; they brought to their writing the social worker's passion for direct and honest experience.

Stephen Crane spent a night in a seven-cent lodging house on the Bowery and in "An Experiment in Misery" captured the smells and sounds of the poor. Crane depicted the carnage of war in *The Red Badge of Courage* (1895) and the impact of poverty in *Maggie: A Girl of the Streets* (1893). His poetry suggested the unimportance of the individual in an uncaring world.

Frank Norris assailed the power of big business in two dramatic novels, *The Octopus* (1901) and *The Pit* (1903), both the story of individual futility in the face of the heartless corporations. Jack London, another naturalist author, traced the power of nature over civilized society in novels such as *The Sea Wolf* (1904) and *The Call of the Wild* (1903), his classic tale of a sled dog that preferred the difficult life of the wilderness to the world of human beings.

Theodore Dreiser, the foremost naturalist writer, grimly portrayed a dark world in which human beings were tossed about by forces beyond their understanding or control. In his great novel *Sister Carrie* (1901), he followed a young farm girl who took a job in a Chicago shoe factory. He described the exhausting nature of factory work: "Her hands began to ache at the wrists and then in the fingers, and towards the last she seemed one mass of dull, complaining muscle, fixed in an eternal position, and performing a single mechanical movement."

Like other naturalists, Dreiser focused on environment and character. He thought writers should tell the truth about human affairs, not fabricate romance, and *Sister Carrie,* he said, was "not intended as a piece of literary craftsmanship, but was a picture of conditions."

THE PRESIDENTIAL ELECTION OF 1896

The election of 1896 was known as the "battle of the standards" because it focused primarily on the gold and silver standards of money. As an election, it was exciting and decisive. New voting patterns replaced old, a new majority party confirmed its control of the country, and national policy shifted to suit new realities.

THE MYSTIQUE OF SILVER

Sentiment for free silver coinage grew swiftly after 1894, dominating the South and West, appearing even in the farming regions of New York and New England. Prosilver literature flooded the country.

People wanted quick solutions to the economic crisis. During 1896, unemployment shot up and farm income and prices fell to the lowest point in the decade. "I can remember back as far as 1858," an Iowa hardware dealer said in February 1896, "and I have never seen such hard times as these are." The silverites offered a solution, simple but compelling: the free and independent coinage of silver at the ratio of 16 ounces of silver to every ounce of gold. Free coinage meant that the U.S. mints would coin all the silver offered to them. Independent coinage meant that the country would coin silver regardless of the policies of other nations, nearly all of which were on the gold standard.

It is difficult now to understand the kind of faith the silverites placed in silver as a cure for the depression. But faith it was, and of a sort that some observers compared to religious fervor. Underlying it all was a belief in a quantity theory of money: The silverites believed the amount of money in circulation determined the level of activity in the economy. If money was short, that meant there was a limit on economic activity and ultimately a depression. If the government coined silver as well as gold, that meant more money in circulation, more business for everyone, and thus prosperity. Farm prices would rise; laborers would go back to work.

By 1896, silver was also a symbol. It had moral and patriotic dimensions—by going to a silver standard, the United States could assert its independence in the world—and it stood for a wide range of popular grievances. For many, it reflected rural values rather than urban ones, suggested a shift of power away from the Northeast, and spoke for the downtrodden instead of the well-to-do. Silver represented the common people.

Silver was more than just a political or economic issue. It was a social movement, one of the largest in American history, but its life span turned out to be brief. As a mass phenomenon, it flourished between 1894 and 1896, then succumbed to electoral defeat, the return of prosperity, and the onset of fresh concerns. But in its time, the silver movement bespoke a national mood and won millions of followers.

THE REPUBLICANS AND GOLD

Scenting victory over the discredited Democrats, numerous Republicans fought for the party's presidential nomination, including a Republican favorite, William McKinley of Ohio.

Able, calm, and affable, McKinley had served in the Union army during the Civil War. In 1876, he won a seat in Congress, where he became the chief sponsor of the tariff act named for him. In the months before the 1896 national convention, Marcus A. Hanna, his campaign manager and trusted friend, built a powerful national organization that featured McKinley as "the advance agent of prosperity," an alluring slogan in a country beset with depression. When the convention met in June, McKinley had the nomination in hand, and he secured a platform that favored the gold standard against the free coinage of silver.

THE DEMOCRATS AND SILVER

Silver, meanwhile, had captured large segments of the Democratic party in the South and West. Despite President Cleveland's opposition, more than twenty Democratic state platforms came out for free silver in 1894. Power in the party shifted to the South, where it remained for decades. The party's base narrowed; its outlook increasingly reflected southern views on silver, race, and other issues. In effect, the Democrats became a sectional—no longer a national—party.

The anti-Cleveland Democrats had their issue, but they lacked a leader. Out in Nebraska, William Jennings Bryan saw the opportunity to take on that role. He was barely 36 years old and had relatively little political experience. But he had spent months wooing support, and he was a captivating public speaker— tall, slender, and handsome, with a resounding voice that, in an era without microphones, projected easily into every corner of an auditorium.

From the outset of the 1896 Democratic convention, the silver Democrats were in charge, and they put together a platform that stunned the Cleveland wing of the party. It demanded the free coinage of silver and attacked Cleveland's actions in the Pullman strike. On July 9, as delegates debated the platform, Bryan's moment came. Striding to the stage, he stood for an instant, a hand raised for silence, waiting for the applause to die down. He would not contend with the previous speakers, he began, for "this is not a contest between persons. The humblest citizen in all the land, when clad in the armor of a righteous cause, is stronger than all the hosts of error. I come to speak to you in defense of a cause as holy as the cause of liberty—the cause of humanity."

The delegates were captivated. Like a trained choir, they rose, cheered each point, and sat back to listen for more. Easterners, Bryan said, liked to praise businessmen but forgot that plain people—laborers, miners, and farmers—were businessmen, too. Shouts rang through the hall, and delegates pounded on chairs. Savoring each cheer, Bryan defended silver. Then came the famous closing: "Having behind us the producing masses of this nation and the world . . . we will answer their demand for a gold standard by saying to them: 'You shall not press down upon the brow of labor this crown of thorns, you shall not crucify mankind upon a cross of gold.'"

Bryan moved his fingers down his temples, suggesting blood trickling from his wounds. He ended with his arms outstretched as on a cross. Letting the silence hang, he dropped his arms, stepped back, then started to his seat. Suddenly, there was pandemonium. Delegates shouted and cheered. When the tumult subsided, they adopted the anti-Cleveland platform, and the next day, Bryan won the presidential nomination.

The religious symbolism in Bryan's "Cross of Gold" speech is satirized in this cartoon, but his stirring rhetoric captivated his audience and won him the Democratic presidential nomination for the election of 1896.

CAMPAIGN AND ELECTION

The Democratic convention presented the Populists with a dilemma. The People's party had staked everything on the assumption that neither major party would endorse silver. Now it faced a painful choice: nominate an independent ticket and risk splitting the silverite forces, or nominate Bryan and give up its separate identity as a party.

The choice was unpleasant, and it shattered the People's party. Meeting late in July, the party's national convention nominated Bryan, but rather than accept the Democratic candidate for vice president, it named Tom Watson instead. The Populists' endorsement probably hurt Bryan as much as it helped. It won him relatively few votes, since many Populists would have voted for him anyway. It also identified him as a Populist, which he was not, allowing the Republicans to accuse him of heading a ragtag army of malcontents. The squabble over Watson seemed to prove that the Democratic-Populist alliance could never stay together long enough to govern.

In August 1896, Bryan set off on a campaign that became an American legend. He took his campaign directly to the voters, the first presidential candidate in history to do so in a systematic way. By his own count, Bryan traveled 18,009 miles, visited 27 states, and spoke 600 times to a total of some 3 million people.

THE ELECTION OF 1896

CANDIDATE	PARTY	POPULAR VOTE	ELECTORAL VOTE
McKinley	Republican	7,104,779	271
Bryan	Democratic	6,502,925	176
	Minor Parties	265,155	0

He built skillfully on a new "merchandising" style of campaign in which he worked to educate and persuade voters.

Bryan summoned voters to an older America: a land where farms were as important as factories, where the virtues of rural and religious life outweighed the doubtful lure of the city, where common people still ruled and opportunity existed for all. He drew on the Jeffersonian tradition of rural virtue, distrust of central authority, and abiding faith in the powers of human reason.

Urged to take the stump against Bryan, McKinley replied, "I might just as well put up a trapeze on my front lawn and compete with some professional athlete as go out speaking against Bryan." The Republican candidate let voters come to him. Railroads brought them by the thousands into McKinley's hometown of Canton, Ohio, and he spoke to them from his front porch. Through use of the press, he reached fully as many people as Bryan's more strenuous effort. Appealing to labor, immigrants, well-to-do farmers, businessmen, and the middle class, McKinley defended economic nationalism and the advancing urban-industrial society.

On election day, voter turnout was extraordinarily high, a measure of the intense interest. By nightfall, the outcome was clear: McKinley won 50 percent of the vote to Bryan's 46 percent. He won the Northeast and Midwest and carried four border states. In the cities, McKinley crushed Bryan.

The election struck down the Populists, whose totals sagged nearly everywhere. Many Populist proposals were later adopted under different leadership. The graduated income tax, crop loans to farmers, the secret ballot, and direct election of U.S. senators all were early Populist ideas. But the People's party never could win over a majority of the voters, and failing that, it vanished after 1896.

THE MCKINLEY ADMINISTRATION

The election of 1896 cemented the voter realignment of 1894 and initiated a generation of Republican rule. For more than three decades after 1896, with only a brief Democratic resurgence under Woodrow Wilson, the Republicans remained the country's majority party.

McKinley took office in 1897 under favorable circumstances. To everyone's relief, the economy had begun to revive. The stock market rose, factories once again churned out goods, and farmers prospered. Farm prices climbed sharply during 1897 on bumper crops of wheat, cotton, and corn. Discoveries of gold in Australia and Alaska—together with the development of a new cyanide process for extracting gold from ore—enlarged the world's gold supply, decreased its price, and inflated the currency as the silverites had hoped. For the first time since 1890, the 1897 Treasury statements showed a comfortable gold reserve.

McKinley and the Republicans basked in the glow. They became the party of progress and prosperity, an image that helped them win victories until another depression hit in the 1930s. McKinley's popularity soared. An activist president, he set the policies of the administration. Conscious of the limits of power, he maintained close ties with Congress and worked hard to educate the public on national choices and priorities. McKinley struck new relations with the press and traveled far more than previous presidents. In some ways, he began the modern presidency.

Shortly after taking office, he summoned Congress into special session to revise the tariff. In July 1897, the Dingley Tariff passed the House and Senate. It raised average tariff duties to a record level, and as the final burst of nineteenth-century protectionism, it caused trouble for the Republican party. By the end of the 1890s, consumers, critics, and the Republicans themselves were wondering if the tariff had outlived its usefulness in the maturing American economy.

From the 1860s to the 1890s, the Republicans had built their party on a pledge to *promote* economic growth through the use of state and national power. By 1900, with the industrial system firmly in place, the focus had shifted. The need to *regulate*, to control the effects of industrialism, became a central public concern of the new century. McKinley prodded the Republicans to meet that shift, but he died before his plans matured.

McKinley toyed with the idea of lowering the tariff, but one obstacle always stood in the way: The government needed revenue, and tariff duties were one of the few taxes the public would support. The Spanish-American War of 1898 persuaded people to accept greater federal power and, with it, new forms of taxation. In 1899, McKinley spoke of lowering tariff barriers in a world that technology had made smaller. "God and man have linked the nations together," he said in his last speech at Buffalo, New York, in 1901. "Isolation is no longer possible or desirable."

In 1898 and 1899, the McKinley administration focused on the war with Spain, the peace treaty that followed, and the dawning realization that the war had thrust the United States into a position of world power. In March 1900, Congress passed the Gold Standard Act, which declared gold the standard of currency and ended the silver controversy that had dominated the 1890s.

The presidential campaign of 1900 was a replay of the McKinley-Bryan fight of 1896. McKinley's running mate was Theodore Roosevelt, hero of the Spanish-American War and former governor of New York, who was nominated for vice president to capitalize on his popularity and, his enemies hoped, to sidetrack his political career into oblivion. Bryan stressed the issues of imperialism and the trusts; McKinley stressed his record at home and abroad. The result in 1900 was a landslide.

On September 6, 1901, a few months after his second inauguration, McKinley stood in a receiving line at the Pan-American Exposition in Buffalo. Leon

The Election of 1900

CANDIDATE	PARTY	POPULAR VOTE	ELECTORAL VOTE
McKinley	Republican	7,207,923	292
Bryan	Democratic	6,358,133	155
Woolley	Prohibition	209,004	0
Debs	Socialist	94,768	0

Czolgosz, a 28-year-old unemployed laborer and anarchist, moved through the line and, reaching the president, shot him. Surgeons probed the wound but could find nothing. A recent discovery called the X ray was on display at the exposition, but it was not used. On September 14, McKinley died, and Vice President Theodore Roosevelt became president. A new century had begun.

A Decade's Dramatic Changes

As the funeral train carried McKinley's body back to Ohio, Mark Hanna, McKinley's old friend and ally, sat slumped in his parlor car. "I told William McKinley it was a mistake to nominate that wild man at Philadelphia," he mourned. "I asked him if he realized what would happen if he should die. Now look, that damned cowboy is president of the United States!"

Hanna's world had changed, and so had the nation's—not so much because "that damned cowboy" was suddenly president, but because events of the 1890s had had powerful effects. In the course of that decade, political patterns shifted, the presidency acquired fresh power, and massive unrest prompted social change. The war with Spain brought a new empire and worldwide responsibilities. Economic hardship posed questions of the most difficult sort about industrialization, urbanization, and the quality of American life. Worried, people embraced new ideas and causes. Reform movements begun in the 1890s flowered in the Progressive Era after 1900.

Technology continued to alter the way Americans lived. In 1896, Henry Ford produced a two-cylinder, four-horsepower car, the first of the famous line that bore his name. In 1899, the first automobile salesroom opened in New York, and some innovative thinkers were already imagining a network of service stations to keep the new cars running. At Kitty Hawk, North Carolina, Wilbur and Orville Wright, two bicycle manufacturers, neared the birth of powered flight.

The realignments that reached their peak in the 1890s seem distant, yet they are not. Important decisions in those years shaped nearly everything that came after them. In character and influence, the 1890s were as much a part of the twentieth century as of the nineteenth and continue to have repercussions into the twenty-first century.

CHRONOLOGY

1876	Mark Twain publishes *The Adventures of Tom Sawyer*
1877	Disputed election of 1876 results in awarding of presidency to Republican Rutherford B. Hayes
1880	Republican James A. Garfield elected president
1881	Garfield assassinated; Vice President Chester A. Arthur becomes president
1884	Democrat Grover Cleveland elected president, defeating Republican James G. Blaine
1887	Cleveland calls for lowering of tariff duties
1888	Republican Benjamin Harrison wins presidential election
1889	National Farmers' Alliance and Industrial Union formed to address problems of farmers
1890	Republican-dominated "Billion-Dollar" Congress enacts McKinley Tariff Act, Sherman Antitrust Act, and Sherman Silver Purchase Act
	Farmers' Alliance adopts the Ocala Demands
1892	Democrat Cleveland defeats Republican Harrison for presidency
	People's party formed
1893	Financial panic touches off depression lasting until 1897
	Sherman Silver Purchase Act repealed
	World Columbian Exposition opens in Chicago
1894	Pullman employees strike
1896	Republican McKinley defeats William Jennings Bryan, Democratic and Populist candidate, in "battle of the standards"
1897	Gold discovered in Alaska
	Dingley Tariff Act raises tariff duties
1900	McKinley reelected, again defeating Bryan
	Gold Standard Act establishes gold as standard of currency
1901	McKinley assassinated; Vice President Theodore Roosevelt assumes presidency
	Naturalist writer Theodore Dreiser publishes *Sister Carrie*

21

TOWARD EMPIRE

Many Americans regretted the start of the war with Spain that began in April 1898, but many others welcomed it. Many highly respected people believed that nations must fight every now and then to prove their power and test the national spirit.

Theodore Roosevelt, 39 years old in 1898, was one of them. Nations needed to fight in order to survive, he thought. For months, Roosevelt argued strenuously for war with Spain for three reasons: first, on grounds of freeing Cuba and expelling Spain from the hemisphere; second, because of "the benefit done to our people by giving them something to think of which isn't material gain"; and third, because the army and navy needed the practice.

In April 1898, Roosevelt was serving in the important post of assistant secretary of the navy. When war broke out, he quickly resigned to join the army, rejecting the advice of the secretary of the navy, who warned he would only "ride a horse and brush mosquitoes from his neck in the Florida sands." The secretary was wrong—dead wrong—and later had the grace to admit it. "Roosevelt was right," he said. "His going into the Army led straight to the Presidency."

Joining a friend, Roosevelt chose to enlist his own regiment, and after a few telephone calls to friends, and telegrams to the governors of Arizona, New Mexico, and Oklahoma asking for "good shots and good riders," he had more than enough men. The First United States Volunteer Cavalry, an intriguing mixture of Ivy League athletes and western frontiersmen, was born.

Known as the Rough Riders, it included men from the Harvard, Yale, and Princeton clubs of New York City; the Somerset Club of Boston; and New York's exclusive Knickerbocker Club. Former college athletes—football players, tennis players, and track stars—enlisted. Woodbury Kane, a wealthy yachtsman, signed up and promptly volunteered for kitchen duty.

Other volunteers came from the West—natural soldiers, Roosevelt called them, "tall and sinewy, with resolute, weather-beaten faces, and eyes that looked a man straight in the face without flinching." Among the cowboys, hunters, and

Colonel Theodore Roosevelt poses in his custom-designed uniform. With surgeon Leonard Wood, Roosevelt organized the First U.S. Volunteer Cavalry—the Rough Riders—for service in the Spanish-American War.

prospectors, there were Bucky O'Neill, a legendary Arizona sheriff and Indian fighter; a half dozen other sheriffs and Texas Rangers; a large number of Indians; a famous broncobuster; and an ex-marshal of Dodge City, Kansas.

The troops howled with joy when orders came to join the invasion army for Cuba. They set sail on June 14, 1898, and Lieutenant Colonel Roosevelt, who had performed a war dance for the troops the night before, caught their mood: "We knew not whither we were bound, nor what we were to do; but we believed that the nearing future held for us many chances of death and hardship, of honor and renown. If we failed, we would share the fate of all who fail; but we were sure that we would win, that we should score the first great triumph in a mighty world-movement."

That "world movement," Roosevelt was sure, would establish the United States as a world power, whose commerce and influence would extend around the globe, particularly in Latin America and Asia. As he hoped, the nation in the 1890s underwent dramatic expansion, building on the foreign policy approaches of administrations from Lincoln to William McKinley. Policymakers fostered business interests abroad, strengthened the navy, and extended American influence into Latin America and the Pacific. Differences over Cuba resulted in a war with Spain that brought new colonies and colonial subjects, establishing for the first time an American overseas empire.

AMERICA LOOKS OUTWARD

The overseas expansion of the 1890s differed in several important respects from earlier expansionist moves of the United States. From its beginning, the American republic had been expanding. After the first landings in Jamestown and Plymouth, settlers pushed westward: into the trans-Appalachian region, the Louisiana Territory, Florida, Texas, California, Arizona, and New Mexico. Most of these lands were contiguous with existing territories of the United States, and most were intended for settlement, usually agricultural.

The expansion of the 1890s was different. It sought to gain island possessions, the bulk of them already thickly populated. The new territories were intended less for settlement than for use as naval bases, trading outposts, or commercial centers on major trade routes. More often than not, they were viewed as colonies, not as states-in-the-making.

Historian Samuel F. Bemis described the overseas expansion of the 1890s as "the great aberration," a time when the country adopted expansionist policies that did not fit with prior experience. Other historians, pointing to expansionist tendencies in thought and foreign policy that surfaced during the last half of the nineteenth century, have found a developing pattern that led naturally to the overseas adventures of the 1890s. In the view of Walter LaFeber, "the United States did not set out on an expansionist path in the late 1890s in a sudden, spur-of-the-moment fashion. The overseas empire that Americans controlled in 1900 was not a break in their history, but a natural culmination."

CATCHING THE SPIRIT OF EMPIRE

Most people in most times in history tend to look at domestic concerns, and Americans in the years following the Civil War were no exception. Among other things, they focused on Reconstruction, the movement westward, and simply making a living. Throughout the nineteenth century, Americans enjoyed "free security" without fully appreciating it. Sheltered by two oceans and the British navy, they could enunciate bold policies such as the Monroe Doctrine, which instructed European nations to stay out of the affairs of the Western Hemisphere, while remaining virtually impregnable to foreign attack.

In the 1870s and after, however, Americans began to take an increasing interest in events abroad. There was a growing sense of internationalism, which stemmed in part from the telegraphs, telephones, and undersea cables that kept people better informed about political and economic developments in distant lands. Many Americans continued to be interested in expansion of the country's borders; relatively few were interested in imperialism. Expansion meant the kind of growth that had brought California and Oregon into the American system. Imperialism meant the imposition of control over other peoples through annexation, military conquest, or economic domination.

Several developments in these years combined to shift attention outward across the seas. The end of the frontier, announced officially in the census report of 1890, sparked fears about diminishing opportunities at home. Further growth, it seemed to some, must take place abroad. Factories and farms multiplied, producing more goods than the domestic market could consume. Both farmers and industrialists looked for new overseas markets, and the growing volume of exports—including more and more manufactured goods—changed the nature of American trade relations with the world.

Political leaders such as James G. Blaine began to argue for the vital importance of foreign markets to continued economic growth. Blaine, secretary of state under Garfield and again under Harrison, aggressively sought wider markets in Latin America, Asia, and Africa, using tariff reciprocity agreements and other measures. To some extent, he and others were also caught up in a worldwide scramble for empire. In the last third of the century, Great Britain, France, and Germany divided up Africa and looked covetously at Asia. The idea of imperialistic expansion was in the air, and the great powers measured their greatness by the colonies they acquired.

Intellectual currents that supported expansion drew on Charles Darwin's theories of evolution. Adherents pointed, for example, to *The Origin of Species,* which mentioned in its subtitle *The Preservation of Favoured Races in the Struggle for Life.* Applied to human and social development, biological concepts seemed to call for the triumph of the fit and the elimination of the unfit. "In this world," said Theodore Roosevelt, who thought of himself as one of the fit, "the nation that has trained itself to a career of unwarlike and isolated ease is bound, in the end, to go down before other nations which have not lost the manly and adventurous qualities."

The career of Josiah Strong, a Congregational minister and fervent expansionist, suggested the strength of the developing ideas. A champion of overseas missionary work, Strong traveled extensively through the West for the Home Missionary Society, and in 1885, drawing on his experiences, he published a book titled *Our Country: Its Possible Future and Its Present Crisis.* An immediate best-seller, the book called on foreign missions to civilize the world under the Anglo-Saxon races. Strong became a national celebrity.

Our Country argued for expanding American trade and dominion. Trade was important, it said, because the desire for material things was one of the hallmarks of civilized people. So was the Christian religion, and by exporting both trade and religion, Americans could civilize and Christianize "inferior" races around the world. Anglo-Saxons already owned one-third of the earth, Strong said, and in a famous passage he concluded that they would take more. In "the final competition of races," they would win and "move down upon Mexico, down upon Central and South America, out upon the islands of the sea, over upon Africa and beyond."

Taken together, these developments in social, political, and economic thought prepared Americans for a larger role in the world. The change was gradual, and there was never a day when people awoke with a sudden realization of their interests overseas. But change there was, and by the 1890s, Americans were ready to reach out into the world in a more determined and deliberate fashion than ever before. For almost the first time, they felt the need for a foreign "policy."

FOREIGN POLICY APPROACHES, 1867–1900

Rarely consistent, American foreign policy in the last half of the nineteenth century took different approaches to different areas of the world. In relation to Europe, seat of the dominant world powers, policymakers promoted trade and tried to avoid diplomatic entanglements. In North and South America, they based policy on the Monroe Doctrine, a recurrent dream of annexing Canada or Mexico, a hope for extensive trade, and Pan-American unity against the nations of the Old World. In the Pacific, they coveted Hawaii and other outposts on the sea-lanes to China.

Secretary of State William Henry Seward, who served from 1861 to 1869, aggressively pushed an expansive foreign policy. Seward developed a vision of an American empire stretching south into Latin America and west to the shores of Asia. His vision included Canada and Mexico; islands in the Caribbean as strategic bases to protect a canal across the isthmus; and Hawaii and other islands as stepping-stones to Asia, which Seward and many others considered a virtually bottomless outlet for farm and manufactured goods.

In 1867, he annexed the Midway Islands, a small atoll group twelve hundred miles northwest of Hawaii, and concluded a treaty with Russia for the purchase of Alaska (which was promptly labeled "Seward's Folly") partly to sandwich western Canada between American territory and lead to its annexation. As the American empire spread, Seward thought, Mexico City would become its capital.

Secretary of State Hamilton Fish, an urbane New Yorker, followed Seward in 1869, serving under President Ulysses S. Grant. An avid expansionist, Grant wanted to extend American influence in the Caribbean and Pacific, though the more conservative Fish often restrained him. They moved first to repair relations with Great Britain. The first business was settlement of the *Alabama* claims—demands that Britain pay the United States for damages to Union ships caused by Confederate vessels which, like the *Alabama*, had been built and outfitted in British shipyards. Negotiating patiently, Fish signed the Treaty of Washington in 1871, providing for arbitration of the *Alabama* issue and other nettlesome controversies. The treaty, one of the landmarks in the peaceful settlement of international disputes, marked a significant step in cementing Anglo-American relations.

James G. Blaine served briefly as secretary of state under President James Garfield and laid extensive plans to establish closer commercial relations with Latin America. Blaine's successor, Frederick T. Frelinghuysen, changed Blaine's approach but not his strategy. Like Blaine, Frelinghuysen wanted to find Caribbean markets for American goods; he negotiated separate reciprocity treaties with Mexico, Cuba and Puerto Rico, the British West Indies, Santo Domingo, and Colombia. Using these treaties, Frelinghuysen hoped not only to obtain markets for American goods but to bind these countries to American interests.

When Blaine returned to the State Department in 1889 under President Benjamin Harrison, he moved again to expand markets in Latin America. Drawing on earlier ideas, he envisaged a hemispheric system of peaceful intercourse, arbitration of disputes, and expanded trade. He also wanted to annex Hawaii.

Harrison and Blaine toyed with naval acquisitions in the Caribbean and elsewhere, but in general they focused on Pan-Americanism and tariff reciprocity. Blaine presided over the first Inter-American Conference in Washington on October 2, 1889, where delegates from nineteen American nations were present. They negotiated several agreements to promote trade and created the International Bureau of the American Republics, later renamed the Pan-American Union, for the exchange of general information, including political, scientific, and cultural knowledge. The conference, a major step in hemispheric relations, led to later meetings promoting trade and other agreements.

Grover Cleveland, Harrison's successor, also pursued an aggressive policy toward Latin America. In 1895, he brought the United States precariously close to war with Great Britain over a boundary dispute between Venezuela and British Guiana. Cleveland sympathized with Venezuela, and he and Secretary of State Richard Olney urged Britain to arbitrate the dispute. When Britain failed to act, Olney drafted a stiff diplomatic note affirming the Monroe Doctrine and denying European nations the right to meddle in Western Hemisphere affairs.

Four months passed before Lord Salisbury, the British foreign secretary, replied. Rejecting Olney's arguments, he sent two letters, the first bluntly repudiating the Monroe Doctrine as international law. The second letter, carefully reasoned and sometimes sarcastic, rejected Olney's arguments for the Venezuelan boundary. Enraged, Cleveland defended the Monroe Doctrine, and he asked Congress for authority to appoint a commission to decide the boundary and enforce its decision.

Preoccupied with larger diplomatic problems in Africa and Europe, Britain changed its position. In November 1896, the two countries signed a treaty of arbitration, under which Great Britain and Venezuela divided the disputed territory. Though Cleveland's approach was clumsy, the Venezuelan incident demonstrated a growing determination to exert American power in the Western Hemisphere. Cleveland and Olney had persuaded Great Britain to recognize the United States' dominance, and they had increased American influence in Latin America. The Monroe Doctrine assumed new importance. In averting war, an era of Anglo-American friendship was begun.

THE LURE OF HAWAII AND SAMOA

The islands of Hawaii offered a tempting way station to Asian markets. In the early 1800s, they were already called the "Crossroads of the Pacific," and trading ships of many nations stopped there. In 1820, the first American missionaries arrived to convert the islanders to Christianity. Like missionaries elsewhere, they advertised Hawaii's economic and other benefits and attracted new settlers.

After the Civil War, the United States tightened its connections with the islands. The reciprocity treaty of 1875 allowed Hawaiian sugar to enter the United States free of duty and bound the Hawaiian monarchy to make no territorial or economic concessions to other powers. The treaty increased Hawaiian economic dependence on the United States; its political clauses effectively made Hawaii an American protectorate. In 1887, a new treaty reaffirmed these arrangements and granted the United States exclusive use of Pearl Harbor, a magnificent harbor that had early caught the eye of naval strategists.

Following the 1875 treaty, white Hawaiians became more and more influential in the islands' political life. The McKinley Tariff Act of 1890 ended the special status given Hawaiian sugar and at the same time awarded American producers a bounty of two cents a pound. Hawaiian sugar production dropped dramatically, unemployment rose, and property values fell. The following year, the weak King Kalakaua died, bringing to power a strong-willed nationalist, Queen Liliuokalani. Resentful of white minority rule, she decreed a new constitution that gave greater power to native Hawaiians.

Unhappy, the American residents revolted in early 1893 and called on the United States for help. John L. Stevens, the American minister in Honolulu, sent 150 marines ashore from the cruiser *Boston*, and within three days, the bloodless revolution was over. Queen Liliuokalani surrendered "to the superior force of the United States," and the victorious rebels set up a provisional government. On February 14, 1893, Harrison's secretary of state, John W. Foster, and delegates of the new government signed a treaty annexing Hawaii to the United States.

The first step toward American annexation of Hawaii came in 1893 when Queen Liliuokalani was removed from the throne. Hawaii was annexed to the United States as a possession in 1898 and became a U.S. territory in 1900.

But only two weeks remained in Harrison's term, and the Senate refused to ratify the agreement. Five days after taking office, Cleveland withdrew the treaty; he then sent a representative to investigate the cause of the rebellion. The investigation revealed that the Americans' role in it had been improper, and Cleveland decided to restore the queen to her throne. He made the demand, but the provisional government in Hawaii politely refused and instead established the Republic of Hawaii, which the embarrassed Cleveland, unable to do otherwise, recognized.

The debate over Hawaiian annexation, continuing through the 1890s, foreshadowed the later debate over the treaty to end the Spanish-American War. People in favor of annexation pointed to Hawaii's strategic location, argued that Japan or other powers might seize the islands if the United States did not, and suggested that Americans had a responsibility to civilize and Christianize the native Hawaiians. Opponents warned that annexation might lead to a colonial army and colonial problems, the inclusion of a "mongrel" population in the United States, and rule over an area not destined for statehood.

Annexation came swiftly in July 1898 in the midst of excitement over victories in the Spanish-American War. The year before, President William McKinley had sent a treaty of annexation to the Senate, but opposition quickly arose, and the treaty stalled. In 1898, annexationists redoubled arguments about Hawaii's commercial and military importance. McKinley and congressional leaders switched strategies to seek a joint resolution, rather than a treaty, for annexation. A joint resolution required only a majority of both houses, while a treaty needed a two-thirds vote in the Senate. Bolstered by the new strategy, the annexation measure moved quickly through Congress, and McKinley signed it on July 7, 1898.

Hawaii represented a step toward China; the Samoan Islands, 3000 miles to the south, sat astride the sea lanes of the South Pacific. In 1878, the United States acquired the use of Pago Pago, a harbor on the island of Tutuila. Great Britain and Germany also secured treaty rights in Samoa, and thereafter the three nations jockeyed for position.

The situation grew tense in 1889, when warships from all three countries gathered in a Samoan harbor. But a sudden typhoon damaged the fleets, and tensions eased. A month later, delegates from the three countries met in Berlin to negotiate the problem. For a time, the indigenous population was granted some degree of authority, but in 1899, the United States and Germany divided Samoa and compensated Britain with lands elsewhere in the Pacific.

THE NEW NAVY

Large navies were vital in the scramble for colonies, and in the 1870s the United States had almost no naval power. One of the most powerful fleets in the world during the Civil War, the American navy had fallen into rapid decline. By 1880, there were fewer than two thousand vessels, only forty-eight of which could fire a gun. Ships rotted, and many officers left the service.

Conditions changed during the 1880s. A group of rising young officers, steeped in a new naval philosophy, argued for an expanded navy equipped with fast, aggressive fleets capable of fighting battles across the seas. Big-navy proponents pointed to the growing fleets of Great Britain, France, and Germany, arguing that the United States needed greater fleet strength to protect its economic and other interests in the Caribbean and Pacific.

In 1883, Congress authorized construction of four steel ships, marking the beginning of the new navy. Between 1885 and 1889, Congress budgeted funds for thirty additional ships. The initial building program focused on lightly armored fast cruisers for raiding enemy merchant ships and protecting American shores, but after 1890, the program shifted to the construction of a seagoing offensive battleship navy capable of challenging the strongest fleets of Europe.

Alfred Thayer Mahan and Benjamin F. Tracy were two of the main forces behind the new navy. Austere and scholarly, Mahan was the era's most influential naval strategist. His reasoning was simple and, to that generation, persuasive. Industrialism, he argued, produced vast surpluses of agricultural and manufactured goods, for which markets must be found. Markets involved distant ports; reaching them required a large merchant marine and a powerful navy to protect it. Navies, in turn, needed coaling stations and repair yards. Coaling stations meant colonies, and colonies became strategic bases, the foundation of a nation's wealth and power. The bases might serve as markets themselves, but they were more important as stepping-stones to other objectives, such as the markets of Latin America and Asia.

Mahan called attention to the worldwide race for power, a race, he warned, the United States could not afford to lose. To compete in the race, Mahan argued, the United States must expand. It needed strategic bases, a powerful ocean-going navy, a canal across the isthmus to link the East Coast with the Pacific, and Hawaii as a way station on the route to Asia.

Mahan influenced a generation of policymakers in the United States and Europe; one of them, Benjamin F. Tracy, became Harrison's secretary of the navy in 1889. Tracy organized the Bureau of Construction and Repair to design and build new ships, established the Naval Reserve in 1891, and ordered construction of the first American submarine in 1893. Above all, he joined with big-navy advocates in Congress to push for a far-ranging battleship fleet capable of attacking distant enemies. He wanted two fleets of battleships, eight ships in the Pacific and twelve in the Atlantic. He got four first-class battleships.

In 1889, when Tracy entered office, the United States ranked twelfth among world navies; in 1893, when he left, it ranked seventh and was climbing rapidly. By the end of the decade, the navy had seventeen steel battleships, six armored cruisers, and many smaller craft. It ranked third in the world.

WAR WITH SPAIN

The war with Spain in 1898 built a mood of national confidence; altered older, more insular patterns of thought; and reshaped the way Americans saw themselves and the world. Its outcome pleased some people but troubled others, who raised questions about war itself, colonies, and subject peoples. The war left a lingering strain of isolationism and antiwar feeling that affected later policy. It also left an

American empire, small by European standards, but quite new to the American experience by virtue of its overseas location. When the war ended, American possessions stretched into the Caribbean and deep into the Pacific. American influence went further still, and the United States was recognized as a "world power."

The Spanish-American War established the United States as a dominant force for the twentieth century. It brought America colonies and millions of colonial subjects; it brought the responsibilities of governing an empire and protecting it. For better or worse, it involved the country in other nations' arguments and affairs. The war strengthened the office of the presidency, swept the nation together in a tide of emotion, and confirmed the long-standing belief in the superiority of the New World over the Old. When it was over, Americans looked outward as never before, touched, they were sure, with a special destiny.

A WAR FOR PRINCIPLE

By the 1890s, Cuba and the nearby island of Puerto Rico comprised nearly all that remained of Spain's once vast empire in the New World. Several times, Cuban insurgents had rebelled against Spanish rule, including a decade-long rebellion from 1868 to 1878 that failed to settle the conflict. The depression of 1893 damaged the Cuban economy. Discontent with Spanish rule heightened, and in late February 1895, revolt again broke out.

Recognizing the importance of the nearby United States, Cuban insurgents established a junta in New York City to raise money, buy weapons, and wage a propaganda war to sway American public opinion. Conditions in Cuba were grim. Spain in January 1896 sent a new commander, General Valeriano Weyler y Nicolau. Relentless and brutal, Weyler gave the rebels ten days to lay down their arms. He then put into effect a "reconcentration" policy designed to move the native population into camps and destroy the rebellion's popular base. Herded into fortified areas, Cubans died by the thousands, victims of unsanitary conditions, overcrowding, and disease.

There was a wave of sympathy for the insurgents, stimulated by the newspapers, but so-called yellow or sensationalist journalism did not cause the war. The conflict stemmed from larger disputes in policies and perceptions between Spain and the United States. Grover Cleveland, under whose administration the rebellion began, preferred Spanish rule to the kind of turmoil that might invite foreign intervention. Opposed to the annexation of Cuba, he issued a proclamation of neutrality and tried to restrain public opinion.

Taking office in March 1897, President McKinley also urged neutrality but leaned slightly toward the insurgents. He immediately sent a trusted aide on a fact-finding mission to Cuba; the aide reported in mid-1897 that Weyler's policy had wrapped Cuba "in the stillness of death and the silence of desolation." The report in hand, McKinley offered to mediate the struggle, but, concerned over the suffering, he protested against Spain's "uncivilized and inhuman" conduct. The United States, he made clear, did not contest Spain's right to fight the rebellion but insisted it be done within humane limits.

Late in 1897, a change in government in Madrid brought a temporary lull in the crisis. The new government recalled Weyler and agreed to offer the Cubans

This print titled"Bohío de Reconcentrados" ("A Reconcentrado Shack") depicts Cubans suffering brutal conditions in one of General Weyler's "reconcentration" camps. Such images appearing in American newspapers and magazines strengthened U.S. sympathy for the Cubans.

some form of autonomy. It also declared an amnesty for political prisoners and released Americans from Cuban jails. The new initiatives pleased McKinley, though he again warned Spain that it must find a humane end to the rebellion. Then, in January 1898, Spanish army officers led riots in Havana against the new autonomy policy, shaking the president's confidence in Madrid's control over conditions in Cuba.

McKinley ordered the battleship *Maine* to Havana to demonstrate strength and protect American citizens if necessary. On February 9, 1898, the *New York Journal,* a leader of the yellow press, published a letter stolen from Enrique Dupuy de Lôme, the Spanish ambassador in Washington. In the letter, which was private correspondence to a friend, de Lôme called McKinley "weak," "a would-be politician," and "a bidder for the admiration of the crowd." Many Americans were angered by the insult; McKinley himself was more worried about other sections of the letter that revealed Spanish insincerity in the negotiations. De Lôme immediately resigned and went home, but the damage was done.

A few days later, on February 15, an explosion tore through the hull of the *Maine,* riding at anchor in Havana harbor. The ship, a trim symbol of the new steel navy, sank quickly; 266 lives were lost. McKinley cautioned patience and promised an immediate investigation. Crowds gathered quietly on Capitol Hill and outside the White House, mourning the lost men. Soon there was a new slogan: "Remember the *Maine* and to Hell with Spain!"

Recent studies of the *Maine* incident blame the sinking on an accidental internal explosion, caused perhaps by spontaneous combustion in poorly ventilated coal bunkers. In 1898, Americans blamed it on Spain. Roosevelt, William Jennings Bryan, and others urged war, but McKinley delayed, hopeful that Spain might yet agree to an armistice and perhaps Cuban independence.

In early March 1898, wanting to be ready for war if it came, McKinley asked Congress for $50 million in emergency defense appropriations, a request Congress promptly approved. The unanimous vote stunned Spain; allowing the president a latitude that was highly unusual for the era, it appropriated the money "for the National defense and for each and every purpose connected therewith to be expended at the discretion of the President." In late March, the report of the investigating board blamed the sinking of the *Maine* on an external (and thus presumably Spanish) explosion. Pressures for war increased.

On March 27, McKinley cabled Spain his final terms. He asked Spain to declare an armistice, end the reconcentration policy, and—implicitly—move toward Cuban independence. When the Spanish answer came, it conceded some things, but not, in McKinley's judgment, the important ones. Spain offered a suspension of hostilities (but not an armistice) and left the Spanish commander in Cuba to set the length and terms of the suspension. It also revoked the reconcen-

Headlines like these in William Randolph Hearst's New York Journal *left little doubt among his readers that Spain had sunk the* Maine.

tration policy. But the Spanish response made no mention of a true armistice, McKinley's offer to mediate, or Cuba's independence.

Reluctantly McKinley prepared his war message, and Congress heard it on April 11, 1898. On April 19, Congress passed a joint resolution declaring Cuba independent and authorizing the president to use the army and navy to expel the Spanish from it. An amendment by Colorado senator Henry M. Teller pledged that the United States had no intention of annexing the island.

On April 21, Spain severed diplomatic relations. The following day, McKinley proclaimed a blockade of Cuba and called for 125,000 volunteers. On Monday, April 25, Congress passed a declaration of war. Late that afternoon, McKinley signed it.

Some historians have suggested that in leading the country toward war, McKinley was weak and indecisive, a victim of war hysteria in the Congress and the country; others have called him a wily manipulator for war and imperial gains. In truth, he was neither. Throughout the Spanish crisis, McKinley pursued a moderate middle course that sought to end the suffering in Cuba, promote Cuba's independence, and allow Spain time to adjust to the loss of the remnant of empire. He also wanted peace, as did Spain, but in the end, the conflicting national interests of the two countries brought them to war.

"A Splendid Little War"

Ten weeks after the declaration of war, the fighting was over. For Americans, they were ten glorious, dizzying weeks, with victories to fill every headline and slogans to suit every taste. No war can be a happy occasion for those who fight it, but the Spanish-American War came closer than most. Declared in April, it ended in August. Relatively few Americans died, and the quick victory seemed to verify burgeoning American power. John Hay, soon to be McKinley's secretary of state, called it "a splendid little war."

At the outset, the United States was militarily unprepared. The regular army consisted of only 28,000 officers and men, most of them more experienced in quelling Indian uprisings than fighting large-scale battles. The Indian wars did produce effective small-scale forces, well trained and tightly disciplined, but the army was unquestionably too small for war against Spain.

When McKinley called for 125,000 volunteers, as many as 1 million young Americans responded. Keeping the regular army units intact, War Department officials enlisted the volunteers in National Guard units that were then integrated into the national army. Men clamored to join. The secretary of war feared "there is going to be more trouble to satisfy those who are not going than to find those who are willing to go."

In an army inundated with men, problems of equipment and supply quickly appeared. The regulars had the new .30-caliber Krag-Jorgensen rifles, but National Guard units carried Civil War Springfield rifles that used old black-powder cartridges. The cartridges gave off a puff of smoke when fired, neatly marking the troops' position. Spanish troops were better equipped; they had modern Mausers with smokeless powder, which they used to devastating effect. Food was also a problem, as was sickness.

Americans then believed that "a foreign war should be fought by the home-town military unit acting as an extension of their community." Soldiers identified with their hometowns, dressed in the local fashion, and thought of themselves as members of a town unit in a national army. Not surprisingly, then, National Guard units mirrored the social patterns of their communities. Since everyone knew each other, there was an easygoing familiarity, tempered by the deference that went with hometown wealth, occupation, education, and length of resi-dence. Enlisted men resented officers who grabbed too much authority, and they expected officers and men to call each other by their first names.

Each community thought of the hometown unit as its own unit, an extension of itself. In later wars, the government censored news and dominated press rela-tions; there was little censorship in the war with Spain, and the freshest news ar-rived in the latest letter home. Small-town newspapers printed news of the men; towns sent food, clothing, and occasionally even local doctors to the front.

"SMOKED YANKEES"

When the invasion force sailed for Cuba, nearly one-fourth of it was African American. In 1898, the regular army included four regiments of African American soldiers, the Twenty-fourth and Twenty-fifth Infantry and the Ninth and Tenth Cavalry. Black regiments had served with distinction in campaigns against the Indians in the West. Most African American troops in fact were posted in the West; no eastern community would accept them. A troop of the Ninth Cavalry was stationed in Virginia in 1891, but whites protested and the troop was ordered back to the West.

When the war broke out, the War Department called for five black volunteer regiments. The army needed men, and military authorities were sure that black men had a natural immunity to the climate and diseases of the tropics. But most state governors refused to accept black volunteers. African American leaders protested the discrimination. The McKinley administration intervened, and in the end, the volunteer army included more than ten thousand black troops.

Orders quickly went out to the four black regular army regiments in the West to move to camps in the South to prepare for the invasion of Cuba. Crowds and cheers followed the troop trains across the Plains, but as they crossed into Kentucky and Tennessee, the cheering stopped. Welcoming crowds were kept away from the trains, and the troops were hustled onward. Station restaurants refused to serve them; all waiting rooms were segregated. "It mattered not if we were soldiers of the United States, and going to fight for the honor of our coun-try," Sergeant Frank W. Pullen of the Twenty-fourth Infantry wrote; "we were 'niggers' as they called us and treated us with contempt."

Many soldiers were not prepared to put up with the treatment. Those stationed near Chickamauga Park, Tennessee, shot "at some whites who insulted them" and forcibly desegregated the railroad cars on the line into Chattanooga. Troops train-ing near Macon, Georgia, refused to ride in the segregated "trailers" attached to the trolleys, and fights broke out.

More than four thousand black troops training near Tampa and Lakeland, Florida, found segregated saloons, cafes, and drugstores. "Here the Negro is not

Charge of the 24th and 25th Colored Infantry and Rescue of the Rough Riders at San Juan Hill, July 2, 1898, *colored lithograph by Kurz and Allison, 1899. The 24th and 25th Colored Infantry regiments served with exceptional gallantry in the Spanish-American War.*

allowed to purchase over the same counter in some stores as the white man purchases over," Chaplain George W. Prioleau charged. "Why sir, the Negro of this country is a freeman and yet a slave. Talk about fighting and freeing poor Cuba and of Spain's brutality; of Cuba's murdered thousands, and starving recon-centradoes. Is America any better than Spain?"

When the invasion force sailed a few days later, segregation continued on some of the troop-ships. Blacks were assigned to the lowest decks, or whites and blacks were placed on different sides of the ship. But the confusion of war often ended the problem, if only

Charles Young, an 1889 graduate of West Point, was the only African American officer in the army during the Spanish-American War except for a few chaplains.

temporarily. Blacks took command as white officers died, and Spanish troops soon came to fear the "smoked Yankees," as they called them. Black soldiers played a major role in the Cuban campaign and probably staved off defeat for the Rough Riders at San Juan Hill. In Cuba, they won twenty-six Certificates of Merit and five Congressional Medals of Honor.

THE COURSE OF THE WAR

Mahan's Naval War College had begun studying strategy for a war with Spain in 1895. By 1898, it had a detailed plan for operations in the Caribbean and Pacific. Naval strategy was simple: destroy the Spanish fleet, damage Spain's merchant marine, and harry the colonies or the coast of Spain. Planners were excited; two steam-powered armored fleets had yet to meet in battle anywhere in the world. The army's task was more difficult. It must defend the United States, invade Cuba and probably Puerto Rico, and undertake possible action in far-flung places such as the Philippines or Spain.

Even before war was declared, the secretary of war arranged joint planning between the army and navy. Military intelligence was plentiful, and planners knew the numbers and locations of the Spanish troops. Earlier they had rejected a proposal to send an officer in disguise to map Cuban harbors; such things, they said, were simply not done in peacetime. Still, the War Department's new Military Information Division, a sign of the increasing professionalization of the army, had detailed diagrams of Spanish fortifications in Havana and other points. On the afternoon of April 20, 1898, McKinley summoned the strategists to the White House; to the dismay of those who wanted a more aggressive policy, they decided on the limited strategy of blockading Cuba, sending arms to the insurgents, and annoying the Spanish with small thrusts by the army.

Victories soon changed the strategy. In case of war, long-standing naval plans had called for a holding action against the Spanish base in the Philippines. On May 1, 1898, with the war barely a week old, Commodore George Dewey, commander of the Asiatic Squadron located at Hong Kong, crushed the Spanish fleet in Manila Bay. Suddenly, Manila and the Philippines lay within American grasp. At home, Dewey portraits, songs, and poems blossomed everywhere, and his calm order to the flagship's captain—"You may fire when ready, Gridley"—hung on every tongue. Dewey had two modern cruisers, a gunboat, and a Civil War paddle steamer. He sank eight Spanish warships. Dewey had no troops to attack the Spanish army in Manila, but the War Department, stunned by the speed and size of the victory, quickly raised an expeditionary force. On August 13, 1898, the troops accepted the surrender of Manila, and with it, the Philippines.

McKinley and his aides were worried about Admiral Pascual Cervera's main Spanish fleet, thought to be headed across the Atlantic for an attack on Florida. On May 13, the navy found Cervera's ships near Martinique in the Caribbean but then lost them again. A few days later, Cervera slipped secretly into the harbor of Santiago de Cuba, a city on the island's southern coast. But a spy in the Havana telegraph office alerted the Americans, and on May 28, a superior American force under Admiral William T. Sampson bottled Cervera up.

In early June, a small force of Marines seized Guantánamo Bay, the great harbor on the south of the island. They established depots for the navy to refuel and pinned down Spanish troops in the area. On June 14, an invasion force of about seventeen thousand men set sail from Tampa. Seven days later, they landed at Daiquiri on Cuba's southeastern coast. All was confusion, but the Spanish offered no resistance. Helped by Cuban insurgents, the Americans immediately pushed west toward Santiago, which they hoped to surround and capture. At first, the advance through the lush tropical countryside was peaceful.

The first battle broke out at Las Guasimas, a crossroads on the Santiago road. After a sharp fight, the Spanish fell back. On July 1, the Rough Riders, troops from the four black regiments, and the other regulars reached the strong fortifications at El Caney and San Juan Hill. Black soldiers of the Twenty-fifth Infantry charged the El Caney blockhouses, surprising the Spanish defenders with Comanche yells. For the better part of a day, the defenders fought stubbornly and held back the army's elite corps. In the confusion of battle, Roosevelt rallied an assortment of infantry and cavalry to take Kettle Hill, adjacent to San Juan Hill.

They charged directly into the Spanish guns, Roosevelt at their head, mounted on a horse, a blue polka-dot handkerchief floating from the brim of his sombrero. "I waved my hat and we went up the hill with a rush," he recalled in his autobiography. Actually, it was not quite so easy. Losses were heavy; eighty-nine Rough Riders were killed or wounded in the attack. Dense foliage concealed the enemy; smokeless powder gave no clue to their position. At nightfall, the surviving Spanish defenders withdrew, and the Americans prepared for the counterattack.

American troops now occupied the ridges overlooking Santiago. They were weakened by sickness, a fact unknown to the Spanish, who decided the city was lost. The Spanish command in Havana ordered Cervera to run for the open sea, although he knew the attempt to escape was hopeless. On the morning of July 3, Cervera's squadron steamed down the bay and out through the harbor's narrow channel, but the waiting American fleet closed in, and in a few hours every Spanish vessel was destroyed. Two weeks later, Santiago surrendered.

Soon thereafter, army troops, meeting little resistance, occupied Puerto Rico. Cervera had commanded Spain's only battle fleet, and when it sank, Spain was helpless against attacks on the colonies or even its own shores. The war was over. Lasting 113 days, it took relatively few lives, most of them the result of accident, yellow fever, malaria, and typhoid in Cuba. Of the 5500 Americans who died in the war, only 379 were killed in battle. The navy lost one man in the battle at Santiago Bay, and only one to heatstroke in the stunning victory in Manila Bay.

ACQUISITION OF EMPIRE

Late in the afternoon of August 12, 1898, representatives of Spain and the United States met in McKinley's White House office to sign the preliminary instrument of peace. Secretary of State William R. Day beckoned a presidential aide over to a large globe, remarking, "Let's see what we get by this."

What the United States got was an expansion of its territory and an even larger expansion of its responsibilities. According to the preliminary agreement, Spain granted independence to Cuba, ceded Puerto Rico and the Pacific island of Guam to the United States, and allowed Americans to occupy Manila until the two countries reached final agreement on the Philippines. To McKinley, the Philippines were the problem. Puerto Rico was close to the mainland, and it appealed even to many of the opponents of expansion. Guam was small and unknown; it escaped attention. The Philippines, on the other hand, were huge, sprawling, and thousands of miles from America.

McKinley weighed a number of alternatives for the Philippines, but he liked none of them. He believed he could not give the islands back to Spain; public opinion would not allow it. He might turn them over to another nation, but then they would fall, as he later said, "a golden apple of discord, among the rival powers." Germany, Japan, Great Britain, and Russia had all expressed interest in acquiring them. Germany even sent a large fleet to Manila and laid plans to take the Philippines if the United States let them go.

Rejecting those alternatives, McKinley considered independence for the islands but was soon talked out of it. People who had been there, reflecting the era's racism, told him the Filipinos were not ready for independence. He thought of establishing an American protectorate but discarded the idea, convinced it would bring American responsibilities without full American control. Sifting the alternatives, McKinley decided there was only one practical policy: annex the Philippines, with an eye to future independence after a period of tutelage.

At first hesitant, American opinion was swinging to the same conclusion. Religious and missionary organizations appealed to McKinley to hold on to the Philippines in order to "Christianize" them. Some merchants and industrialists saw them as the key to the China market and the wealth of Asia. Many Americans simply regarded them as the legitimate fruits of war. In October 1898, representatives of the United States and Spain met in Paris to discuss a peace treaty. Spain agreed to recognize Cuba's independence, assume the Cuban debt, and cede Puerto Rico and Guam to the United States.

Acting on instructions from McKinley, the American representatives demanded the cession of the Philippines. In return, the United States offered a payment of $20 million. Spain resisted but had little choice, and on December 10, 1898, the American and Spanish representatives signed the Treaty of Paris.

THE TREATY OF PARIS DEBATE

Submitted to the Senate for ratification, the treaty set off a storm of debate throughout the country. Industrialist Andrew Carnegie, reformer Jane Addams, labor leader Samuel Gompers, Mark Twain, and a host of others argued forcefully against annexing the Philippines. Annexation of the Philippines, the anti-imperialists protested over and over again, violated the very principles of independence and self-determination on which the United States was founded.

Some labor leaders feared the importation of cheap labor from new Pacific colonies. Gompers warned about the "half-breeds and semi-barbaric people" who might undercut wages and the union movement. Other anti-imperialists argued against assimilation of different races. Such racial views were also common among those favoring expansion, and the anti-imperialists usually focused on different arguments. If the United States established a tyranny abroad, they were sure, there would soon be tyranny at home. "This nation," declared William Jennings Bryan, "cannot endure half republic and half colony—half free and half vassal."

Charles Francis Adams, Jr., warned that the possession of colonies meant big armies, government, and debts ("an income tax looms up in the largest possible proportions," he said). Bryan scoffed at the argument that colonies were good for trade, pointing out, "It is not necessary to own people to trade with them." Many others thought there was no way to reconcile the country's republican ideals with the practice of keeping people under heel abroad. To Booker T. Washington, the country had more important things to think about at home, including its treatment of Indians and blacks.

In November 1898, opponents of expansion formed the Anti-Imperialist League to fight against the peace treaty. Membership centered in New England; the cause was less popular in the West and South. It enlisted more Democrats than Republicans, though never a majority of either. The anti-imperialists were weakened by the fact that they lacked a coherent program. Some favored keeping naval bases in the conquered areas. Some wanted Hawaii and Puerto Rico but not the Philippines. Others wanted nothing at all to do with any colonies.

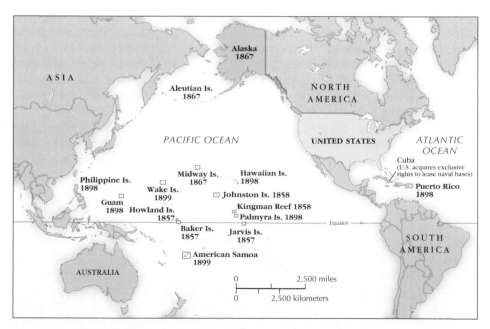

American Empire, 1900
With the Treaty of Paris, the United States gained an expanded colonial empire stretching from the Caribbean to the far Pacific. It embraced Puerto Rico, Alaska, Hawaii, part of Samoa, Guam, the Philippines, and a chain of Pacific islands. The dates on the map refer to the date of U.S. acquisition.

The treaty debate in the Senate lasted a month. Pressing hard for ratification, McKinley earlier toured the South to rally support and consulted closely with senators. Though opposed to taking the Philippines, Bryan supported ratification in order to end the war; his support influenced some Democratic votes. Still, on the final weekend before the vote, the treaty was two votes short. That Saturday night, news reached Washington that fighting had broken out between American troops and Filipino insurgents who demanded immediate independence. The news increased pressure to ratify the treaty, which the Senate did on February 6, 1899, with two votes to spare. An amendment promising independence as soon as the Filipinos established a stable government lost by one vote. The United States had a colonial empire.

GUERRILLA WARFARE IN THE PHILIPPINES

Historians rarely write of the Philippine-American War, but it was an important event in American history. The war with Spain was over a few months after it began, but war with the Filipinos lasted more than three years. Four times as many American soldiers fought in the Philippines as in Cuba. For the first time, Americans fought men of a different color in an Asian guerrilla war. The Philippine-American War of 1898–1902 took a heavy toll: 4300 American lives and untold thousands of Filipino lives (estimates range from 50,000 to 200,000).

Emilio Aguinaldo, the Filipino leader, was 29 years old in 1898. An early organizer of the anti-Spanish resistance, he had gone into exile in Hong Kong, from where he welcomed the outbreak of the Spanish-American War. Certain the United States would grant independence, he worked for an American victory. Filipino insurgents helped guide Dewey into Manila Bay, and Dewey himself sent a ship to Hong Kong to bring back Aguinaldo to lead a native uprising against the Spanish. On June 12, 1898, the insurgents proclaimed their independence.

Cooperating with the Americans, they drove the Spanish out of many areas of the islands. In the liberated regions, Aguinaldo established local governments with appointed provincial governors. He waited impatiently for American recognition, but McKinley and others had concluded that the Filipinos were not ready. Soon, warfare broke out between the Filipinos and Americans over the question of Filipino independence.

By late 1899, the American army had defeated and dispersed the organized Filipino army, but claims of victory proved premature. Aguinaldo and his advisers shifted to guerrilla tactics, striking suddenly and then melting into the jungle or friendly native villages. There were terrible atrocities on both sides. The Americans found themselves using brutal, Weyler-like tactics. After any attack on an American patrol, the Americans burned all the houses in the nearest district. They tortured people and executed prisoners. They established protected "zones" and herded Filipinos into them. Seizing or destroying all food outside the zones, they starved many guerrillas into submission.

Bryan tried to turn the election of 1900 into a debate over imperialism, but the attempt failed. For one thing, he himself refused to give up the silver issue,

Emilio Aguinaldo (seated, in vest) and his advisers in the Philippines, 1896. Aguinaldo's forces helped the Americans drive Spain out of the Philippines, expecting that the United States would recognize Filipino independence. When the United States failed to do so, Aguinaldo led his forces in warfare against the Americans.

which cost him some support among anti-imperialists in the Northeast who were for gold. McKinley, moreover, was able to take advantage of the surging economy, and he could defend expansion as an accomplished fact. Riding a wave of patriotism and prosperity, McKinley won the election handily—by an even larger margin than he had in 1896.

In 1900, McKinley sent a special Philippine Commission to the islands under William Howard Taft, a prominent Ohio judge. Directed to establish a civil government, the commission organized municipal administrations and, in stages, created a government for the Philippines. In March 1901, five American soldiers tricked their way into Aguinaldo's camp deep in the mountains and took him prisoner. Back in Manila, he signed a proclamation urging his people to end the fighting. Some guerrillas held out for another year, but to no avail. On July 4, 1901, authority was transferred from the army to Taft, who was named civilian governor of the islands, and his civilian commission. McKinley reaffirmed his purpose to grant the Filipinos self-government as soon as they were deemed ready for it.

Given broad powers, the Taft Commission introduced many changes. New schools provided education and vocational training for Filipinos of all social classes. The Americans built roads and bridges, reformed the judiciary, restructured the tax system, and introduced sanitation and vaccination programs. They established local governments built on Filipino traditions and hierarchies. Taft encouraged Filipino participation in government. During the following decades, other measures broadened Filipino rights. Independence finally came on July 4, 1946, nearly fifty years after Aguinaldo proclaimed it.

GOVERNING THE EMPIRE

Ruling the colonies raised new and perplexing questions. How could—and how should—the distant dependencies be governed? Did their inhabitants have the rights of American citizens? Some people contended that acquisition did not automatically incorporate the new possessions into the United States and endow them with constitutional privileges. Others argued that "the Constitution followed the flag," meaning that acquisition made the possessions part of the nation and thus entitled them to all constitutional guarantees. A third group suggested that only "fundamental" constitutional guarantees—citizenship, the right to vote, and the right to trial by jury—not "formal" privileges—the right to use American currency, the right to be taxed, and the right to run for the presidency—were applicable to the new empire.

In a series of cases between 1901 and 1904 (*De Lima* v. *Bidwell, Dooley* v. *U.S.,* and *Downes* v. *Bidwell*), the Supreme Court asserted the principle that the Constitution did not automatically and immediately apply to the people of an annexed territory and did not confer upon them all the privileges of U.S. citizenship. Instead, Congress could specifically extend such constitutional provisions as it saw fit. "Ye-es," the secretary of war said of the Court's ambiguous rulings, "as near as I can make out the Constitution follows the flag—but doesn't quite catch up with it."

Four dependencies—Hawaii, Alaska, Guam, and Puerto Rico—were organized quickly. In 1900, Congress granted territorial status to Hawaii, gave American citizenship to all citizens of the Hawaiian republic, authorized an elective legislature, and provided for a governor appointed from Washington. A similar measure made Alaska a territory in 1912. Guam and American Samoa were simply placed under the control of naval officers.

Unlike the Filipinos, Puerto Ricans readily accepted the war's outcome, and McKinley early withdrew troops from the island. The Foraker Act of 1900 established civil government in Puerto Rico. It organized the island as a territory, made its residents citizens of Puerto Rico (U.S. citizenship was extended to them in 1917), and empowered the president to appoint a governor general and a council to serve as the upper house of the legislature. A lower house of delegates was to be elected.

Cuba proved a trickier matter. McKinley asserted the authority of the United States over conquered territory and promised to govern the island until the Cubans had established a firm and stable government of their own. "I want you to go down there to get the people ready for a republican form of government," he instructed General Leonard Wood, commander of the army in Cuba until 1902. "I leave the details of procedure to you. Give them a good school system, try to straighten out their ports, and put them on their feet as best you can. We want to do all we can for them and to get out of the island as soon as we safely can."

Wood moved quickly to implement the instructions. Early in 1900, he completed a census of the Cuban population, conducted municipal elections, and arranged the election of delegates to a constitutional convention. The convention adopted a constitution modeled on the U.S. Constitution and, at Wood's prodding, included provisions for future relations with the United States. Known as the Platt Amendment to the new Cuban Constitution, the provisions stipulated that Cuba should make no treaties with other powers that might impair its independence, acquire no debts it could not pay, and lease naval bases such as Guantánamo Bay to the United States. Most important, the amendment empowered the United States to intervene in Cuba to maintain orderly government.

Between 1898 and 1902, the American military government worked hard for the economic and political revival of the island, though it often demonstrated a paternalistic attitude toward the Cubans themselves. It repaired the damage of the civil war, built roads and schools, and established order in rural areas. A public health campaign headed by Dr. Walter Reed, an army surgeon, wiped out yellow fever. When the last troops left in May 1902, the Cubans at last had a form of independence, but they were still under the clear domination of their neighbor to the north.

THE OPEN DOOR

Poised in the Philippines, the United States had become an Asian power on the doorstep of China. Weakened by years of warfare, China in 1898 and 1899 was unable to resist foreign influence. Japan, England, France, Germany, and Russia eyed it covetously, dividing parts of the country into "spheres of influence." They forced China to grant "concessions" that allowed them exclusive rights to develop particular areas and threatened American hopes for extensive trade with the country.

McKinley first outlined a new China policy in September 1898 when he said that Americans sought more trade, "but we seek no advantages in the Orient which are not common to all. Asking only the open door for ourselves, we are ready to accord the open door to others." In September 1899, Secretary of State John Hay addressed identical diplomatic notes to England, Germany, and Russia, and later to France, Japan, and Italy, asking them to join the United States in establishing the "Open Door policy." The policy urged three agreements: Nations possessing a sphere of influence would respect the rights and privileges of other nations in that sphere; the Chinese government would continue to collect tariff duties in all spheres; and nations would not discriminate against other nations in levying port dues and railroad rates within their respective spheres of influence.

Under the Open Door policy, the United States would retain many commercial advantages it might lose if China was partitioned into spheres of influence. McKinley and Hay also attempted to preserve for the Chinese some semblance of national authority. Great Britain most nearly accepted the principle of the Open Door. Russia declined to approve it, and the other powers, sending evasive

In this 1899 cartoon, "Putting His Foot Down" from Puck, *the nations of Europe are getting ready to cut up China to expand their spheres of influence, but Uncle Sam stands firm on American commitments to preserve China's sovereignty.*

replies, stated they would agree only if all the other nations did. Hay turned the situation to American advantage by boldly announcing in March 1900 that all the powers had accepted the Open Door policy.

The policy's first test came just three months later with the outbreak of the Boxer Rebellion in Peking (now Beijing). In June 1900, a secret, intensely nationalistic Chinese society called the Boxers tried to oust all foreigners from their country. Overrunning Peking, they drove foreigners into their legations and penned them up for nearly two months. In the end, the United States joined Britain, Germany, and other powers in sending troops to lift the siege.

Fearing that the rebellion gave some nations, especially Germany and Russia, an excuse to expand their spheres of influence, Hay took quick action to emphasize American policy. In July, he sent off another round of Open Door notes affirming U.S. commitment to equal commercial opportunity and respect for China's independence. While the first Open Door notes had implied recognition of China's continued independence, the second notes explicitly stated the need to preserve it. Together, the two notes comprised the Open Door policy, which became a central element in American policy in the Far East.

To some degree, the policy tried to help China, but it also led to further American meddling in the affairs of another country. Moreover, by committing itself to a policy that Americans were not prepared to defend militarily, the McKinley administration left the opportunity for later controversy with Japan and other expansion-minded powers in the Pacific.

OUTCOME OF THE WAR WITH SPAIN

The war with Spain over, Roosevelt and the Rough Riders sailed for home in mid-August 1898. They sauntered through the streets of New York, the heroes of the city. A few weeks later, Roosevelt bade them farewell. Close to tears, he told them, "I am proud of this regiment beyond measure." Soon, Roosevelt was governor of New York and on his way to the White House.

Other soldiers were also glad to be home, although they were sometimes resentful of the reception they found. "The war is over now," said Winslow Hobson, a black trooper from the Ninth Ohio, "and Roosevelt . . . and others (white of course) have all there is to be gotten out of it." Bravery in Cuba and the Philippines won some recognition for black soldiers, but the war itself set back the cause of civil rights. It spurred talk about "inferior" races, at home and abroad, and united whites in the North and South. "The Negro might as well know it now as later," a black editor said, "the closer the North and South get together by this war, the harder he will have to fight to maintain a footing." A fresh outburst of segregation and lynching occurred during the decade after the war.

McKinley and the Republican party soared to new heights of popularity. Firmly established, the Republican majority dominated politics until 1932. Scandals arose about the food and the conduct of the War Department, but there was none of the sharp sense of deception and betrayal that was to mark the years after World War I. In a little more than a century, the United States had grown from thirteen states stretched along a thin Atlantic coastline into a world power that reached from the Caribbean to the Pacific. As Seward and others had hoped, the nation now dominated its own hemisphere, dealt with European powers on more equal terms, and was a major power in Asia.

CHRONOLOGY

1867 United States purchases Alaska from Russia

Midway Islands are annexed

1871 Treaty of Washington between United States and Great Britain sets precedent for peaceful settlement of international disputes

1875 Reciprocity treaty with Hawaii binds Hawaii economically and politically to United States

1878 United States acquires naval base in Samoa

1883 Congress approves funds for construction of first modern steel ships; beginning of modern navy

1887 New treaty with Hawaii gives United States exclusive use of Pearl Harbor

1889 First Inter-American Conference meets in Washington, D.C.

1893 American settlers in Hawaii overthrow Queen Liliuokalani; provisional government established

1895 Cuban insurgents rebel against Spanish rule

1898 Battleship *Maine* explodes in Havana harbor (February)

Congress declares war against Spain (April)

Commodore Dewey defeats Spanish fleet at Manila Bay (May)

United States annexes Hawaii (July)

Americans defeat Spanish at El Caney, San Juan Hill (actually Kettle Hill), and Santiago (July)

Spain sues for peace (August)

Treaty of Paris ends Spanish-American War (December)

1899 Congress ratifies Treaty of Paris

United States sends Open Door notes to Britain, Germany, Russia, France, Japan, and Italy

Philippine-American War erupts

1900 Foraker Act establishes civil government in Puerto Rico

1901 Platt Amendment authorizes American intervention in Cuba

1902 Philippine-American War ends with American victory

22

THE PROGRESSIVE ERA

In 1902, Samuel S. McClure, the shrewd owner of *McClure's Magazine*, sensed something astir in the country that his reporters were not covering. Like *Life, Munsey's,* the *Ladies' Home Journal,* and *Cosmopolitan, McClure's* was reaching more and more people—more than a quarter million readers a month. Americans were snapping up the new popular magazines filled with eye-catching illustrations and up-to-date fiction.

McClure was always chasing new ideas and readers, and in 1902, certain that something was happening in the public mood, he told one of his editors, 36-year-old Lincoln Steffens, a former Wall Street reporter, to find out what it was. "Get out of here, travel, go—somewhere," he said to Steffens. "Buy a railroad ticket, get on a train, and there, where it lands you, there you will learn to edit a magazine."

Steffens traveled west. In St. Louis, he came across a young district attorney named Joseph W. Folk who had found a trail of corruption linking politics and some of the city's respected business leaders. Eager for help, Folk did not mind naming names to the visiting editor from New York. "It is good business men that are corrupting our bad politicians," he stressed again and again. Steffens's story, "Tweed Days in St. Louis," appeared in the October 1902 issue of *McClure's.*

The November *McClure's* carried the first installment of Ida Tarbell's scathing "History of the Standard Oil Company," and in January 1903, Steffens was back with "The Shame of Minneapolis," another tale of corrupt partnership between business and politics. McClure had what he wanted, and in the January issue he printed an editorial, "Concerning Three Articles in This Number of *McClure's,* and a Coincidence That May Set Us Thinking." Steffens on Minneapolis, Tarbell on Standard Oil, and an article on abuses in labor unions—all, McClure said, on different topics but actually on the same theme: corruption in American life. "Capitalists, workingmen, politicians, citizens—all breaking the law, or letting it be broken."

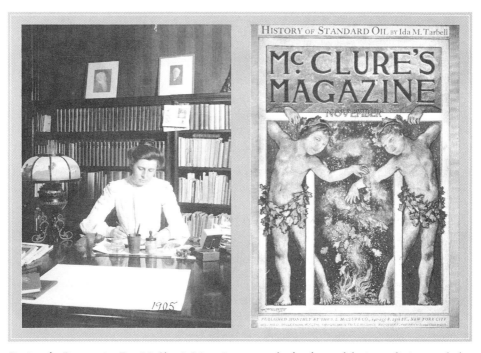

During the Progressive Era, McClure's Magazine *was at the forefront of the journalistic crusade for reform, which took the form of muckraking articles by such writers as Ida Tarbell (left). The November 1902 edition shown here featured the first installment of Tarbell's two-year series on Standard Oil that exposed the corrupt practices and deals that had helped create the company.*

Readers were enthralled, and articles and books by other muckrakers— Theodore Roosevelt coined the term *muckraking* in 1906 to describe the practice of exposing the corruption of public and prominent figures—spread swiftly. *Collier's* had articles on questionable stock market practices, patent medicines, and the beef trust. Novelist Upton Sinclair tackled the meatpackers in *The Jungle* (1906).

Muckraking flourished from 1903 to 1909, and while it did, good writers and bad investigated almost every corner of American life: government, labor unions, big business, Wall Street, health care, the food industry, child labor, women's rights, prostitution, ghetto living, and life insurance.

The muckrakers were a journalistic voice of a larger movement in American society. Called *progressivism,* it lasted from the mid-1890s through World War I. Like muckraking itself, progressivism reflected worry about the state of society, the effects of industrialization and urbanization, social disorder, political corruption, and a host of other issues. With concerns so large, progressivism often had a sense of crisis and urgency, although it was rooted in a spirit of hopefulness and confidence in human progress. For varying reasons, thousands of people became concerned about their society, and, separately and together, they set out to cure some of the ills they saw around them. The efforts of the so-called progressives changed the nation and gave the era its name.

THE CHANGING FACE OF INDUSTRIALISM

As the new century turned, conditions in America were better than just a few years before. Farms and factories were once again prosperous; in 1901, for the first time in years, the economy reached full capacity. Farm prices rose almost 50 percent between 1900 and 1910. Unemployment dropped. Not everyone was progressing. Many of the problems that had angered people in the 1890s continued into the new century, and millions of Americans still suffered from poverty and disease. Racism sat even more heavily on African Americans in both South and North, and there was increasing hostility against immigrants from southern and eastern Europe and from Mexico and Asia. Yet economic conditions were better for many people, and as a result, prosperity became one of the keys to understanding the era and the nature of progressive reform.

The start of the new century was another key as well, for it influenced people to take a fresh look at themselves and their times. Excited about beginning the twentieth century, people believed technology and enterprise would shape a better life. Savoring the word *new,* they talked of the new poetry, new cinema, new history, new democracy, new woman, new art, new immigration, new morality, and new city. Presidents Theodore Roosevelt and Woodrow Wilson called their political programs the New Nationalism and the New Freedom.

The word *mass* also cropped up frequently. Victors in the recent war with Spain, Americans took pride in teeming cities, burgeoning corporations, and other marks of the mass society. They enjoyed the fruits of mass production, read mass circulation newspapers and magazines, and took mass transit from the growing spiral of suburbs into the central cities.

Behind mass production lay significant changes in the nation's industrial system. Businesses grew at a rapid rate. They were large in the three decades after the Civil War, but in the years between 1895 and 1915, industries became mammoth, employing thousands of workers and equipped with assembly lines to turn out huge quantities of the company's product. Inevitably, changes in management attitudes, business organization, and worker roles influenced the entire society. Inevitably, too, the growth of giant businesses gave rise to a widespread fear of "trusts" and a desire among many progressive reformers to break them up or regulate them.

THE INNOVATIVE MODEL T

In the movement toward large-scale business and mass production, the automobile industry was one of those that led the way. In 1895, there were only four cars on the nation's roads; in 1917, there were nearly five million, and the automobile had already helped work a small revolution in industrial methods and social mores.

In 1903, Henry Ford and a small group of associates formed the Ford Motor Company, the firm that transformed the business. Ford was 40 years old. He had tried farming and hated it. During the 1890s, he worked as an engineer, but spent his spare time designing internal combustion engines and automobiles. At first, like many others in the industry, he concentrated on building luxury and racing cars.

In 1903, Ford sold the first Ford car. The price was high, and in 1905, Ford raised prices still higher. Sales plummeted. In 1907, he lowered the price; sales and revenues rose. Ford learned an important lesson of the modern economy: A smaller unit profit on a large number of sales meant enormous revenues. Early in 1908, he introduced the Model T, a four-cylinder, 20-horsepower "Tin Lizzie," costing $850, and available only in black. Eleven thousand were sold the first year.

"I am going to democratize the automobile," Ford proclaimed. "When I'm through everybody will be able to afford one, and about everyone will have one." The key was mass production, and after many experiments, Ford copied the techniques of meatpackers who moved animal carcasses along overhead trolleys from station to station. Adapting the process to automobile assembly, Ford in 1913 set up moving assembly lines in his plant in Highland Park, Michigan, that dramatically reduced the time and cost of producing cars. Emphasizing continuous movement, he strove for a nonstop flow from raw material to finished product. In 1914, he sold 248,000 Model T cars.

That year, Ford workers assembled a car in 93 minutes, one-tenth the time it had taken just eight months before. On a single day in 1925, Ford set a record by turning out 9109 Model Ts, a new car for every 10 seconds of the work day.

THE BURGEONING TRUSTS

As businesses like Ford's grew, capital and organization became increasingly important, and the result was the formation of a growing number of trusts. Between 1898 and 1903, a series of mergers and consolidations swept the econ-

Business Consolidations (Mergers), 1895–1905

omy. Many smaller firms disappeared, swallowed up in giant corporations. By 1904, large-scale combinations of one form or another controlled nearly two-fifths of the capital in manufacturing in the country.

The result was not monopoly but oligopoly—control of a commodity or service by a small number of large, powerful companies. Six great financial groups dominated the railroad industry; a handful of holding companies controlled utilities and steel. Rockefeller's Standard Oil owned about 85 percent of the oil business. After 1898, financiers and industrialists formed the Amalgamated Copper Company, Consolidated Tobacco, U.S. Rubber, and a host of others. By 1909, just 1 percent of the industrial firms were producing nearly half of all manufactured goods.

Although the trend has been overstated, finance capitalists such as J. P. Morgan tended to replace the industrial capitalists of an earlier era. Able to finance the mergers and reorganizations, investment bankers played a greater and greater role in the economy. A multibillion-dollar financial house, J. P. Morgan and Company operated a network of control that ran from New York City to every industrial and financial center in the nation. Like other investment firms, it held directorships in many corporations, creating "interlocking directorates" that allowed it to control many businesses.

Massive business growth set off a decade-long debate over what government should do about the trusts. Some critics who believed that the giant companies were responsible for stifling individual opportunity and raising prices wanted to break them up into small competitive units. Others argued that large-scale business was a mark of the times, and that it produced more goods and better lives.

The debate over the trusts was one of the issues that shaped the Progressive Era, but it was never a simple contest between high-minded reformers and greedy business titans. Some progressives favored big business; others wanted it broken up. Business leaders themselves were divided in their viewpoints, and some welcomed reform-led assaults on giant competitors. As a rule, both progressives and business leaders drew on similar visions of the country: complex, expansive, hopeful, managerially minded, and oriented toward results and efficiency. They both believed in private property and the importance of economic progress. In fact, in working for reform, the progressives often drew on the managerial methods of a business world they sought to regulate.

MANAGING THE MACHINES

Mass production changed the direction of American industry. Size, system, organization, and marketing became increasingly important. Management focused on speed and product, not on workers. Assembly-line technology changed tasks and, to some extent, values. The goal was no longer to make a unique product that would be better than the one before. "The way to make automobiles," Ford said as early as 1903, "is to make one automobile like another automobile, to make them all alike, to make them come through the factory just alike."

In a development that rivaled assembly lines in importance, businesses established industrial research laboratories where scientists and engineers developed new products. General Electric founded the first one in 1900, housed in a barn. It soon attracted experts who designed improvements in light bulbs, invented the cathode-ray tube, worked on early radio, and even tinkered with atomic theory. Du Pont opened its labs in 1911, Eastman Kodak in 1912, and Standard Oil in 1919. As the source of new ideas and technology, the labs altered life in the twentieth century.

Through all this, business became large-scale, mechanized, and managed. While many shops still employed fewer than a dozen workers, the proportion of such shops shrank. By 1920, close to one-half of all industrial workers toiled in factories employing more than 250 people. More than one-third worked in factories that were part of multiplant companies.

Industries that processed materials—iron and steel, paper, cement, and chemicals—were increasingly automated and operated continuously. Workers in those industries could not fall behind. Foremen still managed the laborers on the factory floor, but more and more, the rules came down from a central office where trained professional managers supervised production flow. Systematic record keeping, cost accounting, and inventory and production controls became widespread. In the automobile industry, output per worker-hour multiplied an extraordinary four times between 1909 and 1919.

Workers caught up in the changing industrial system experienced the benefits of efficiency and productivity; in some industries, they earned more. But they suffered important losses as well. Performing repetitive tasks, they seemed part of the machinery, moving to the pace and needs of their mechanical pacesetters. Bored, they might easily lose pride of workmanship, though many workers, it is clear, did not. Efficiency engineers experimented with tools and methods, a process many workers found unsettling. Yet the goal was to establish routine—to work out, as someone said of a garment worker, "one single precise motion each second, 3,600 in one hour, and all exactly the same." Praising that worker, the manager said, "She is a sure machine."

Fire nets were of no avail to the workers at the Triangle Shirtwaist Company who jumped from the upper stories to escape the flames. Speaking to a mass meeting after the fire, labor organizer Rose Schneiderman (right) inveighed against a system that treated human beings as expendable commodities.

Jobs became not only monotonous but dangerous. As machines and assembly lines sped up, boredom or miscalculation could bring disaster. In March 1911, a fire at the Triangle Shirtwaist Company in New York focused nationwide attention on unsafe working conditions. When the fire started, five hundred men and women, mostly Italians and Jews from eastern Europe, were just finishing their workday. Firefighters arrived within minutes, but they were already too late. Terrified seamstresses raced to the exits to try to escape the flames, but most exit doors were closed, locked by the company to prevent theft and shut out union organizers. Many died in the stampede down the narrow stairways or the single fire escape. Still others, trapped on the building's top stories far above the reach of the fire department's ladders, jumped to their deaths on the street below. One hundred forty-six people died.

A few days later, eighty thousand people marched silently in the rain in a funeral procession up Fifth Avenue. A quarter million people watched. At a mass meeting held to protest factory working conditions, Rose Schneiderman, a dynamic 29-year-old organizer for the Women's Trade Union League, told New York City's civic and religious leaders that they had not done enough, they had not cared. "Every week I must learn of the untimely death of one of my sister workers. Every year thousands of us are maimed. The life of men and women is so cheap and property is so sacred."

The outcry impelled New York's governor to appoint a State Factory Investigating Commission that recommended laws to shorten the workweek and improve safety in factories and stores.

SOCIETY'S MASSES

Spreading consumer goods through society, mass production not only improved people's lives but sometimes cost lives, too. Tending the machines took hard, painful labor, often under dangerous conditions. As businesses expanded, they required more and more people, and the labor force increased tremendously to keep up with the demand for workers in the factories, mines, and forests. Women, African Americans, Asian Americans, and Mexican Americans played larger and larger roles. Immigration soared. Between 1901 and 1910, nearly 8.8 million immigrants entered the United States; between 1911 and 1920, another 5.7 million came.

For many of these people, life was harsh, spent in crowded slums and long hours on the job. Fortunately, the massive unemployment of the 1890s was over, and in many skilled trades, such as cigar making, there was plenty of work to go around. Although the economic recovery helped nearly everyone, the less skilled continued to be the less fortunate. Migrant workers, lumberjacks, ore shovelers, and others struggled to find jobs that paid decently.

Under such circumstances, many people fought to make a living, and many, too, fought to improve their lot. Their efforts, along with the efforts of the reform-minded people who came to their aid, became another important hallmark of the Progressive Era.

Better Times on the Farm

While people continued to flee the farms—by 1920, fewer than one-third of all Americans lived on farms, and fewer than one-half lived in rural areas—farmers themselves prospered, the beneficiaries of greater production and expanding urban markets. Rural free delivery, begun in 1896, helped diminish the farmers' sense of isolation and changed farm life. The delivery of mail to the farm door opened that door to a wider world; it exposed farmers to urban thinking, national advertising, and political events.

Parcel post (1913) permitted the sending of packages through the U.S. mail. Mail-order houses flourished; rural merchants suffered. Within a year, 300 million packages were being mailed annually. While telephones and electricity did not reach most rural areas for decades, better roads, mail-order catalogs, and other innovations knit farmers into the larger society. Early in the new century, Mary E. Lease—who in her Populist days had urged Kansas farmers to raise less corn and more Hell—moved to Brooklyn.

Farmers still had problems. Land prices rose with crop prices, and farm tenancy increased, especially in the South. Tenancy grew from one-quarter of all farms in 1880 to more than one-third in 1910. Many southern tenant farmers were African Americans, and they suffered from farm-bred diseases. In one of the reforms of the Progressive Era, in 1909, the Rockefeller Sanitary Commission, acting on recent scientific discoveries, began a sanitation campaign that eventually wiped out the hookworm disease.

In the arid West, irrigation transformed the land as the federal government and private landholders joined to import water from mountain watersheds. The dry lands bloomed, and so did a rural class structure that sharply separated owners from workers. Under the Newlands Act of 1902, the secretary of the interior formed the U.S. Reclamation Service, which gathered a staff of thousands of engineers and technicians, "the largest bureaucracy ever assembled in irrigation history."

Dams and canals channeled water into places such as California's Imperial Valley, and as the water streamed in, cotton, cantaloupes, oranges, tomatoes, lettuce, and a host of other crops streamed out to national markets. By 1920, Idaho, Montana, Utah, Wyoming, Colorado, and Oregon had extensive irrigation systems, all drawing on scarce water supplies; California, the foremost importer of water, had 4.2 million acres under irrigation, many of them picked by migrant workers from Mexico, China, and Japan.

Women and Children at Work

Women worked in larger and larger numbers. In 1900, more than five million worked—one-fifth of all adult women—and among those aged 14 to 24, the employment rate was almost one-third. Of those employed, single women outnumbered married women by seven to one, yet more than one-third of married women worked. Most women held service jobs. Only a small number held higher-paying jobs as professionals or managers.

LAD FELL TO DEATH IN BIG COAL CHUTE

Dennis McKee Dead and Arthur All-becker Had Leg Burned In the Lee Mines.

Falling into a chute at the Chauncey colliery of the George S. Lee Coal Company at Avondale, this afternoon, Dennis McKee, aged 18, of West Nanticoke, was smothered to death and Arthur Allbecker, aged 13, had both of his legs burned and injured. Dr. Bird, of Plymouth, was summoned and dressed the burns of the injured boy.

He was removed to his home at Avondale.

Both boys were employed as breaker boys, and going too close to the chutes fell in. Fellow workmen rushed to their assistance and soon had them out of the chutes. When taken out, McKee was found to be dead. His remains were removed to his home at West Nanticoke. Allbecker will recover.

Breaker boys, who picked out pieces of slate from the coal as it rushed past, often became bent-backed after years of working fourteen hours a day in the coal mines. Accidents—and deaths—were common in the mines.

More women than men graduated from high school, and with professions like medicine and science largely closed to them, they often turned to the new "business schools" that offered training in stenography, typing, and bookkeeping. In 1920, more than one-quarter of all employed women held clerical jobs. Many others taught school.

Black women had always worked, and in far larger numbers than their white counterparts. The reason was usually economic; an African American man or woman alone could rarely earn enough to support a family. Unlike many white women, black women tended to remain in the labor force after marriage or the start of a family. They also had less opportunity for job advancement, and in 1920, between one-third and one-half of all African American women who were working were restricted to personal and domestic service jobs.

Critics charged that women's employment endangered the home, threatened their reproductive functions, and even, as one man said, stripped them of "that modest demeanor that lends a charm to their kind." Adding to these fears, the birthrate continued to drop between 1900 and 1920, and the divorce rate soared, in part because working-class men took advantage of the newer moral freedom and deserted their families in growing numbers. By 1916, there was one divorce for every nine marriages as compared to one for twenty-one in 1880.

Many children also worked. In 1900, about three million children—nearly 20 percent of those between the ages of 5 and 15—held full-time or almost full-time jobs. Twenty-five thousand boys under 16 worked in mining; twenty thousand children under 12, mainly girls, worked in southern cotton mills. Gradually, as public indignation grew, the use of child labor shrank.

Determined to do something about the situation, the Women's Trade Union League lobbied the federal Bureau of Labor to investigate the conditions under which women and children worked. Begun in 1907, the investigation took four years and produced nineteen volumes of data, some of it shocking, all of it factual. In 1911, spurred by the data, the Children's Bureau was formed within the U.S. Bureau of Labor, with Grace Abbott, a social worker, at its head. It immediately began its own investigations, showing among other things the need for greater protection of maternal and infant health. In 1921, Congress passed the Sheppard-Towner Maternity and Infancy Protection Act, which helped fund maternity and pediatric clinics. Providing a precedent for the Social Security Act of 1935, it demonstrated the increasing effectiveness of women reformers in the Progressive Era.

Numerous middle-class women became involved in the fight for reform, while many others, reflecting the ongoing changes in the family, took increasing pride in homemaking and motherhood. Mother's Day, the national holiday, was formally established in 1913. Women who preferred smaller numbers of children turned increasingly to birth control, which became a more acceptable practice. Margaret Sanger, a nurse and outspoken social reformer, led a campaign to give physicians broad discretion in prescribing contraceptives.

THE NIAGARA MOVEMENT AND THE NAACP

At the turn of the century eight of every ten African Americans still lived in rural areas, mainly in the South. Most were poor sharecroppers. Jim Crow laws segregated many schools, railroad cars, hotels, and hospitals. Poll taxes and other devices disfranchised blacks and many poor whites. Violence was common; from 1900 to 1914, white mobs murdered more than a thousand black people.

Few blacks belonged to labor unions, and blacks almost always earned less than whites in the same job. Black songs such as "I've Got a White Man Workin' for Me" (1901) voiced more hope than reality. The illiteracy rate among African Americans dropped from 45 percent in 1900 to 30 percent in 1910, but nowhere were they given equal school facilities, teachers' salaries, or educational materials. In 1910, scarcely eight thousand African American youths were attending high schools in all the states of the Southeast.

African American leaders grew increasingly impatient with this kind of treatment, and in 1905 a group of them, led by sociologist W. E. B. Du Bois, met near Niagara Falls, New York (they met on the Canadian side of the Falls, since no hotel on the American side would take them). There they pledged action in the matters of voting, equal access to economic opportunity, integration, and equality before the law. Rejecting Booker T. Washington's gradualist approach, the Niagara Movement claimed for African Americans "every single right that belongs to a freeborn American, political, civil and social; and until we get these rights we will never cease to protest."

The Niagara Movement focused on equal rights and the education of African American youth. Keeping alive a program of militant action, it spawned later civil rights movements. Du Bois was its inspiration. In *The Souls of Black Folk* (1903) and other works, he called eloquently for justice and equality.

Still, race riots broke out in Atlanta, Georgia, in 1906 and in Springfield, Illinois, in 1908, the latter the home of Abraham Lincoln. Unlike the riots of the

The wish to have "our children . . . enjoy fairer conditions than have fallen to our lot" was the impetus behind the NAACP, which sponsored this parade in New York City.

1960s, white mobs invaded black neighborhoods, burning, looting, and killing. They lynched two blacks—one 84 years old—in Springfield.

Outrage was voiced by William E. Walling, a wealthy southerner and settlement house worker; Mary Ovington, a white anthropology student; and Oswald Garrison Villard, grandson of the famous abolitionist William Lloyd Garrison. Along with other reformers, white and black (among them Jane Addams and John Dewey), they issued a call for the conference that organized the National Association for the Advancement of Colored People, which swiftly became the most important civil rights organization in the country. Created in 1909, within four years the NAACP grew to fifty branches and more than six thousand members. Walling headed it, and Du Bois, the only African American among the top officers, directed publicity and edited *The Crisis,* the voice of the organization.

Joined by the National Urban League, which was created in 1911, the NAACP pressured employers, labor unions, and the government on behalf of African Americans. It had some victories. In 1918, in the midst of World War I, the NAACP and the National Urban League persuaded the federal government to form a special Bureau of Negro Economics within the Labor Department to look after the interests of African American wage earners.

Despite these gains, African Americans continued to experience disfranchisement, poor job opportunities, and segregation. As Booker T. Washington said in

1913, "I have never seen the colored people so discouraged and so bitter as they are at the present time."

"I HEAR THE WHISTLE": IMMIGRANTS IN THE LABOR FORCE

While women and African Americans worked in growing numbers, much of the huge increase in the labor force in these years came from outside the country, particularly from Europe and Mexico. Between 1901 and 1920, the extraordinarily high total of 14.5 million immigrants entered the country, more than in any previous twenty-year period. Continuing the trend begun in the 1880s, many came from southern and eastern Europe. Still called the "new" immigrants, they met hostility from "older" immigrants of northern European stock who questioned their values, religion (often Catholic or Jewish), traditions, and appearance.

Older residents lumped the newcomers together, ignoring geographic, religious, and other differences. Preserving important regional distinctions, Italians tended to settle as Calabreses, Venetians, Abruzzis, and Sicilians. Old-stock Americans viewed them all simply as Italians. Henry Ford and other employers tried to erase the differences through English classes and deliberate "Americanization" programs. The Ford Motor Company ran a school where immigrant employees were first taught to say, "I am a good American." At the graduation ceremony, the pupils acted out a gigantic pantomime in which, clad in their old-country dress, they filed into a large "melting pot." When they

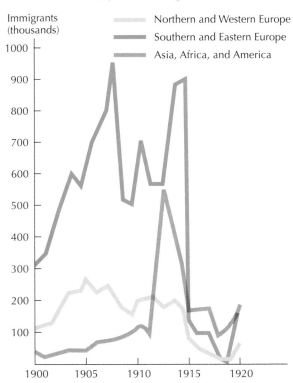

Immigration to the United States, 1900–1920 (by area of origin)

Immigrants (thousands)

— Northern and Western Europe
— Southern and Eastern Europe
— Asia, Africa, and America

Note: For purposes of classification, "Northern and Western Europe" includes Great Britain, Ireland, Scandinavia, the Netherlands, Belgium, Luxembourg, Switzerland, France, and Germany. "Southern and Eastern Europe" includes Poland, Austria-Hungary, Russia and the Baltic States, Romania, Bulgaria, European Turkey, Italy, Spain, Portugal, and Greece. "Asia, Africa, and America" includes Asian Turkey, China, Japan, India, Canada, the Caribbean, Latin America, and all of Africa.

Source: U.S. Bureau of the Census, *Historical Statistics of the United States, Colonial Times to 1970*, Bicentennial Edition, Washington, D.C., 1975.

emerged, they were wearing identical American-made clothes, and each was waving a little American flag.

In similar fashion, the International Harvester Corporation taught Polish laborers to speak English, but it had other lessons in view as well. According to Lesson One, drilled into the Polish "pupils":

> *I hear the whistle. I must hurry.*
> *I hear the five minute whistle.*
> *It is time to go into the shop.*
> *I take my check from the gate board and hang it on the department board.*
> *I change my clothes and get ready to work.*
> *The starting whistle blows.*
> *I eat my lunch.*
> *It is forbidden to eat until then.*
> *The whistle blows at five minutes of starting time.*
> *I get ready to go to work.*
> *I work until the whistle blows to quit.*
> *I leave my place nice and clean.*
> *I put all my clothes in the locker.*
> *I must go home.*

Labor groups soon learned to counter these techniques. The Women's Trade Union League (WTUL) urged workers to ignore business-sponsored English lessons because they did not "tell the girl worker the things she really wants to know. They do not suggest that $5 a week is not a living wage. They tell her to be respectful to her employer." Designing its own educational program, the WTUL in 1912 published "New World Lessons for Old World Peoples," which provided quite a different kind of English lesson:

> *A Union girl takes me into the Union.*
> *The Union girls are glad to see me.*
> *They call me sister.*
> *I will work hard for our Union.*
> *I will come to all the Union meetings.*

In another significant development at the beginning of the twentieth century, Mexicans for the first time immigrated in large numbers, especially after a revolution in Mexico in 1910 forced many to flee across the northern border into Texas, New Mexico, Arizona, and California. Their exact numbers were unknown. American officials did not count border crossings until 1907, and even then, many migrants avoided the official immigration stations. Almost all came from the Mexican lower class, eager to escape peonage and violence in their native land. Labor agents called *coyotes*—usually in the employ of large corporations or working for ranchers—recruited Mexican workers.

Between 1900 and 1910, the Mexican population of Texas and New Mexico nearly doubled; in Arizona, it more than doubled; in California, it quadrupled. In all four states, it doubled again between 1910 and 1920. After the turn of the century, almost 10 percent of the total population of Mexico moved to the American Southwest.

In time, these Mexican Americans and their children transformed the Southwest. They built most of the early highways in Texas, New Mexico, and Arizona; dug the irrigation ditches that watered crops throughout the area; laid railroad track; and picked the cotton and vegetables that clothed and fed millions of Americans. Many lived in shacks and shanties along the railroad tracks, isolated in a separate Spanish-speaking world. Like other immigrant groups, they also formed enclaves in the cities; these *barrios* became cultural islands of family life, foods, church, and festivals.

Fewer people immigrated from China in these years, deterred in part by anti-Chinese laws and hostility. Like many other immigrants, most Chinese who came did not intend to remain. Wanting to make money and return home, they mined, farmed, and worked as common laborers. In their willingness to work hard for low wages, their desire to preserve clan and family associations from China, and their maintenance of strong ties with their home villages, Chinese Americans resembled other immigrant groups, but they differed in two important respects. As late as 1920, men outnumbered women by ten to one in the Chinese American population, and with a male median age of 42, their communities were generally dominated by the elderly.

The Chinese American population differed in another respect as well. Unlike other immigrant groups, whose numbers tended to grow, the number of Chinese

Asian immigrants in a waiting room at Angel Island, near San Francisco. Quota systems and exclusionary laws severely limited Asian immigration, while other laws placed restrictions on the immigrants, curtailing their right to own or even rent agricultural land. Some Asian immigrants, after months of detention at Angel Island, were refused permission to enter the United States and were forced to return to their homelands. Courtesy of the California Historical Society, FN-18240.

Americans shrank in these years—from about 125,000 in the early 1880s to just over 60,000 in 1920. After 1910, the U.S. government set up a special immigration facility at Angel Island in San Francisco Bay, but unlike European immigrants who landed at Ellis Island in New York and were quickly sent on, Chinese immigrants were kept for weeks and months, examined and reexamined, before being allowed to cross the narrow band of water to San Francisco. Angel Island remained open until 1940.

Many Japanese also arrived at Angel Island, and though at first fewer in numbers than the Chinese, they developed communities along the Pacific coast, where they settled mainly on farms. The number of Japanese Americans grew. In 1907, the heaviest year of immigration from Japan, nearly 31,000 Japanese entered the United States; by 1920, there were 111,000 Japanese in the country, nearly three-quarters of them in California.

As the newcomers arrived from Asia, Europe, and Mexico, nativist sentiment, which had criticized earlier waves of immigrants, intensified. Old-stock Americans sneered at their dress and language. Racial theories emphasized the superiority of northern Europeans, and the new "science" of eugenics suggested the need to control the population growth of "inferior" peoples. Hostility toward Catholics and Jews was common but touched other groups as well.

In 1902, Congress enacted a law prohibiting immigration from China. Statutes requiring literacy tests designed to curtail immigration from southern and eastern Europe were vetoed by William Howard Taft in 1913 and by Woodrow Wilson in 1915 and 1917. In 1917, such a measure passed despite Wilson's veto. Other measures tried to limit immigration from Mexico and Japan.

CONFLICT IN THE WORKPLACE

Assembly lines, speedups, long hours, and low pay produced a dramatic increase in American industrial output (and profits) after 1900; they also gave rise to numerous strikes and other kinds of labor unrest. Sometimes strikes took place through the action of unions; sometimes workers just decided they had had enough and walked off the job. Whatever the cause, strikes were frequent. In one industry, in one city—the meatpacking industry in Chicago—there were 251 strikes in 1903 alone.

Strikes and absenteeism increased after 1910; labor productivity dropped 10 percent between 1915 and 1918, the first such decline in memory. In many industries, labor turnover became a serious problem; workers changed jobs in droves. Union membership grew. In 1900, only about a million workers—less than 4 percent of the workforce—belonged to unions. By 1920, five million workers belonged, increasing the unionized portion of the workforce to about 13 percent.

As tensions grew between capital and labor, some people in the middle class became fearful that, unless something was done to improve the workers' situation, there might be violence or even revolution. This fear motivated some of the labor-oriented reforms of the Progressive Era. While some reform supporters genuinely wanted to improve labor's lot, others embraced reform because they were afraid of something else.

ORGANIZING LABOR

Samuel Gompers's American Federation of Labor increased from 250,000 members in 1897 to 1.7 million in 1904. By far the largest union organization, it remained devoted to the interests of skilled craftspeople. While it aimed partly at better wages and working conditions, it also sought to limit entry into the crafts and protect worker prerogatives. Within limits, the AFL found acceptance among giant business corporations eager for conservative policies and labor stability.

Of the 8 million female workers in 1910, only 125,000 belonged to unions. Gompers continued to resist organizing them, saying they were too emotional and, as union organizers, "had a way of making serious mistakes." Margaret Dreier Robins, an organizer of proven skill, scoffed at that. "These men died twenty years ago and are just walking around dead!" she protested.

Robins helped found the Women's Trade Union League in 1903. The WTUL led the effort to organize women into trade unions, to lobby for legislation protecting female workers, and to educate the public on the problems and needs of working women. It took in all working women who would join, regardless of skill (although not, at first, African American women), and it won crucial financial support from well-to-do women such as Anne Morgan, daughter of the feared financier J. P. Morgan. Robins's close friend Jane Addams belonged, as did Dr. Alice Hamilton, a pioneer in American research on the causes of industrial disease.

The WTUL never had many members—a few thousand at most—but its influence extended far beyond its membership. In 1909, it supported the "Uprising of the 20,000," a strike of shirtwaist workers in New York City. When female employees of the Triangle Shirtwaist Company tried to form a union, the company fired them, and they walked out; 20,000 men and women in 500 other shops followed. Strike meetings were conducted in three languages—English, Yiddish, and Italian—and before being forced to go back to work, the strikers won a shorter workweek and a few other gains. Sadly, the Triangle women lost out on another important demand—for unlocked shop doors and safe fire escapes. Their loss proved lethal in the famous Triangle Shirtwaist Company fire of 1911.

Labor Union Membership, 1897–1920

Source: U.S. Bureau of the Census, *Statistical Abstract of the United States: 1982–83* (103rd ed.), Washington, D.C., 1982.

The WTUL also backed a strike in 1910 against Hart, Schaffner and Marx, Chicago's largest manufacturer of men's clothing. One day, Annie Shapiro, the 18-year-old daughter of Russian immigrants, was told her wages were being cut from $7 a week to $6.20. That was a large cut, and along with sixteen other young women, Shapiro refused to accept it and walked out. "We had to be recognized as people," she said later. Soon other women walked out, and the revolt spread.

In a matter of days, some forty thousand garment workers were on strike, about half of them women. Manufacturers hurried to negotiate, and the result was the important Hart, Schaffner agreement, which created an arbitration committee composed of management and labor to handle grievances and settle disputes. The first successful experiment in collective bargaining, the Hart, Schaffner agreement became the model for the kind of agreements that govern industrial relations today.

Another union, the Industrial Workers of the World (IWW), attracted by far the greatest attention (and the most fears) in these years. Unlike the WTUL, it welcomed everyone regardless of gender or race. Unlike the AFL, it tried to organize the unskilled and foreign-born laborers who worked in the mass production industries. Founded in Chicago in 1905, it aimed to unite the American working class into a mammoth union to promote labor's interests. Its motto—"An injury to one is an injury to all"—stressed labor solidarity, as had the earlier Knights of Labor. But unlike the Knights, the IWW, or Wobblies as they were often known, urged social revolution.

"It is our purpose to overthrow the capitalist system by forcible means if necessary," William D. "Big Bill" Haywood, one of its founders, said; he went on in his speeches to say he knew of nothing a worker could do that "will bring as much anguish to the boss as a little sabotage in the right place."

The IWW led a number of major strikes. Strikes in Lawrence, Massachusetts (1912), and Paterson, New Jersey (1912), attracted national attention: in Lawrence, when the strikers sent their children, ill-clad and hungry, out of the city to stay with sympathetic families; in Paterson, when they rented New York's Madison Square Garden for a massive labor pageant. IWW leaders welcomed the revolutionary tumult sweeping Russia and other countries. In the United States, they thought, a series of local strikes would bring about capitalist repression, then a general strike, and eventually a workers' commonwealth.

The IWW fell short of these objectives, but during its lifetime—from 1905 to the mid-1920s—it made major gains among immigrant workers in the Northeast, migrant farm laborers on the Plains, and loggers and miners in the South and Far West. In factories like Ford's, it recruited workers resentful of the speedups on the assembly lines. Although IWW membership probably amounted to no more than 100,000 at any one time, workers came and left so often that its total membership may have reached as high as 1 million.

Working with Workers

Concerned about labor unrest, some business leaders used violence and police action to keep workers in line, but others turned to the new fields of applied psychology and personnel management. A school of industrial psychology emerged, led by Frederick Winslow Taylor, an innovative mechanical engineer, who wrote an influential book, *The Principles of Scientific Management* (1911). Like Taylor, industrial psychologists studied workers' routines, and, further, they showed that output was also affected by job satisfaction. While most businesses pushed ahead with efficiency campaigns, a few did establish industrial relations departments, hire public relations firms to improve their corporate image, and link productivity to job safety and worker happiness. To please employees, companies printed newsletters and organized softball teams; they awarded prizes and celebrated retirements. Ford created a "sociology department" staffed by 150 experts who showed workers how to budget their incomes and care for their health. They even taught them how to shop for meat.

On January 5, 1914, Ford took another significant step. He announced the five-dollar day, "the greatest revolution," he said, "in the matter of rewards for workers ever known to the industrial world." With a stroke, he doubled the wage rate for common labor, reduced the working day from nine hours to eight, and established a personnel department to place workers in appropriate jobs. The next day, ten thousand applicants stood outside the gates.

As a result, Ford had the pick of the labor force. Turnover declined; absenteeism, previously as much as one-tenth of all Ford workers every day, fell to 0.3 percent. Output increased; the IWW at Ford collapsed. The plan increased wages, but it also gave the company greater control over a more stable labor force. Workers had to meet a behavior code in order to qualify for the five-dollar day. At first scornful of the "utopian" plan, business leaders across the country soon copied it, and on January 2, 1919, Ford announced the six-dollar day.

AMOSKEAG

In size, system, and worker relations, the record of the Amoskeag Company textile mills was revealing. Located beside the Merrimack River in Manchester, New Hampshire, the mills—an enormous complex of factories, warehouses, canals, and machinery—had been built in the 1830s. By the turn of the century, they were producing nearly 50 miles of cloth an hour, more cloth each day than any other mills in the entire world.

The face of the mills, an almost solid wall of red brick, stretched nearly a mile. Archways and bridges pierced the facade. Amoskeag resembled a walled medieval city within which workers found "a total institution, a closed and almost self-contained world." At first the mills employed young women for labor, but by 1900, more and more immigrant males staffed the machines. French Canadians, Irish, Poles, and Greeks—seventeen thousand in all—worked there, and their experiences revealed a great deal about factory work and life at the turn of the century.

The company hired and fired at will, and it demanded relentless output from the spindles and spinning frames. Yet it also viewed employees as its "children" and looked for total loyalty in return, an expectation often realized. Workers identified with Amoskeag and, decades later, still called themselves Amoskeag men and women. "We were all like a family," one said.

Most Amoskeag workers preferred the industrial world of the mills to the farms they had left behind. They did not feel displaced; they knew the pains of industrial life; and they adapted in ways that fit their own needs and traditions. Families played a large role. They neither disintegrated nor lost their relationships. French Canadians and others often came in family units. One or two family members left the farm for the mills, maintained close ties with those back home, and then sent for others, creating a form of "chain migration."

Once in Manchester, families often toiled in the same workrooms. Looking after each other, they asked for transfers and promotions for relatives; they taught their children technical skills and how to get along with bosses and fellow workers. Although low paid, Amoskeag employees took pride in their work, and for many of them, a well-turned-out product provided dignity and self-esteem.

As part of its paternal interest in employee welfare, in 1910 the company inaugurated a welfare and efficiency program, which aimed to increase productivity, accustom immigrants to industrial work, instill company loyalty, and curb labor unrest. Playgrounds and visiting nurses, home-buying plans, a cooking school, and dental service were part of the plan. The Amoskeag Textile Club held employee dinners and picnics, organized shooting clubs and a baseball team, sponsored Christmas parties for the children, and put out the *Amoskeag Bulletin,* a monthly magazine of employee news.

From 1885 to 1919, no strike touched the mills. Thereafter, however, labor unrest increased. Overproduction and foreign competition took their toll, and Amoskeag closed in 1935.

A New Urban Culture

For many Americans, the quality of life improved significantly between 1900 and 1920. Jobs were relatively plentiful, and, in a development of great importance, more and more people were entering the professions as doctors, lawyers, teachers, and engineers. With comfortable incomes, a growing middle class could take advantage of new lifestyles, inventions, and forms of entertainment. Mass production could not have worked without mass consumption, and Americans in these years increasingly became a nation of consumers.

PRODUCTION AND CONSUMPTION

In 1900, business firms spent about $95 million on advertising; twenty years later, they spent more than $500 million. Ads and billboards touted cigarettes, cars, perfumes, and cosmetics. Advertising agencies boomed. Using new sampling techniques, they developed modern concepts of market testing and research. Sampling customer preferences affected business indirectly as well, making it more responsive to public opinion on social and political issues.

Mass production swept the clothing industry and dressed more Americans better than any people ever before. Using lessons learned in making uniforms during the Civil War, manufacturers for the first time developed standard clothing and shoe sizes that fit most bodies. Clothing prices dropped; the availability of inexpensive "off-the-rack" clothes lessened distinctions between rich and poor. By 1900, nine of every ten men and boys wore the new "ready-to-wear" clothes.

Rural Americans gained access to the same array of consumer goods that urban dwellers had when mail-order companies, such as Sears, Roebuck and Company, offered goods through the mail. Parcel post delivery, begun in 1913, made shopping by mail easier than visiting the local general store.

In 1900, people employed in manufacturing earned on average $418 a year. Two decades later, they earned $1342 a year, though inflation took much of the increase. While the middle class expanded, the rich also grew richer. In 1920, the new income tax showed the first accurate tabulation of income, and it confirmed what many had suspected all along: Five percent of the population received almost one-fourth of all income.

LIVING AND DYING IN AN URBAN NATION

In 1920, the median age of the population was only 25. (It is now 36.5.) Immigration accounted for part of the population's youthfulness, since most immigrants were young. Thanks to medical advances and better living conditions, the death rate dropped in the early years of the century; the average life span increased. Between 1900 and 1920, life expectancy rose from 49 to 56 years for white women and from 47 to 54 years for white men. It rose from 33 to 45 years for blacks and other racial minorities.

Despite the increase in life expectancy, infant mortality remained high; nearly 10 percent of white babies and 20 percent of minority babies died in the first year of life. In comparison to today, fewer babies on average survived to adolescence, and fewer people survived beyond middle age. In 1900, the death rate among people between 45 and 65 was more than twice the modern rate. As a result, there were relatively fewer older people—in 1900, only 4 percent of the population was older than 65 compared to nearly 13 percent today. Fewer children than today knew their grandparents. Still, improvements in health care helped people live longer, and as a result, the incidence of cancer and heart disease increased.

Cities grew, and by any earlier standards, they grew on a colossal scale. Downtowns became a central hive of skyscrapers, department stores, warehouses, and hotels. Strips of factories radiated from the center. As street railways spread, cities took on a systematic pattern of socioeconomic segregation, usually in rings. The innermost ring filled with immigrants, circled by a belt of working-class housing. The remaining rings marked areas of rising affluence outward toward wealthy suburbs, which themselves formed around shopping strips and grid patterns of streets that restricted social interaction.

The giants were New York, Chicago, and Philadelphia, industrial cities that turned out every kind of product from textiles to structural steel. Smaller cities such as Rochester, New York, or Cleveland, Ohio, specialized in manufacturing a specific line of goods or processing regional products for the national market. Railroads instead of highways tied things together; in 1916, the rail network, the largest in the world, reached its peak—254,000 miles of track that carried more than three-fourths of all intercity freight tonnage.

Step by step, cities adopted their twentieth-century forms. Between 1909 and 1915, Los Angeles, a city of 300,000 people, passed a series of ordinances that gave rise to modern urban zoning. For the first time, the ordinances divided a city into three districts of specified use: a residential area, an industrial area, and an area open to residence and a limited list of industries. Other cities followed. Combining several features, the New York zoning law of 1916 became the model for the nation; within a decade, 591 cities copied it.

Zoning ordered city development, keeping skyscrapers out of factory districts, factories out of the suburbs. It also had powerful social repercussions. In the South, zoning became a tool to extend racial segregation; in northern cities, it acted against ethnic minorities. Jews in New York, Italians in Boston, Poles in Detroit, African Americans in Chicago—zoning laws held them all at arm's length. Like other migrants, African Americans often preferred to settle together, but zoning also helped put them there. By 1920, ten districts in Chicago were more than three-quarters black. In Los Angeles, Cleveland, Detroit, and Washington, D.C., most blacks lived in only two or three wards.

POPULAR PASTIMES

Thanks to changing work rules and mechanization, many Americans enjoyed more leisure time. The average workweek for manufacturing laborers fell from 60 hours in 1890 to 51 in 1920. By the early 1900s, white-collar workers might spend only 8 to 10 hours a day at work and a half day on weekends. Greater leisure time gave more people more opportunity for play and people flocked to places of entertainment. Baseball entrenched itself as the national pastime.

Football also drew fans, although critics attacked the sport's violence and the use of "tramp athletes," nonstudents whom colleges paid to play. In 1905, the worst year, 18 players were killed and 150 seriously injured.

Alarmed, President Theodore Roosevelt—who had once said, "I am the father of three boys [and] if I thought any one of them would weigh a possible broken bone against the glory of being chosen to play on Harvard's football team I would disinherit him"—called a White House conference to clean up college sports. The conference founded the Intercollegiate Athletic Association, which in 1910 became the National Collegiate Athletic Association (NCAA).

Movie theaters opened everywhere. By 1910, there were 10,000 of them, drawing a weekly audience of 10 million people. Admission was usually 5 cents, and movies stressing laughter and pathos appealed to a mass market. In 1915, D. W. Griffith, a talented and creative director—as well as a racist—produced the first movie spectacular: *Birth of a Nation*. Griffith adopted new film techniques, including close-ups, fade-outs, and artistic camera angles.

Phonographs brought ready-made entertainment into the home. By 1901, phonograph and record companies included the Victor Talking Machine Company, the Edison Speaking Machine Company, and Columbia Records. Ornate mahogany Victrolas became standard fixtures in middle-class parlors. In 1919, 2.25 million phonographs were produced; two years later, more than 100 million records were sold.

As record sales grew, families sang less and listened more. Music became a business. In 1909, Congress enacted a copyright law that provided a two-cent royalty on each piece of music on phonograph records or piano rolls. The royalty, small as it was, offered welcome income to composers and publishers, and in 1914, composer Victor Herbert and others formed the American Society of Composers, Authors, and Publishers (ASCAP) to protect musical rights and royalties.

The faster rhythms of syncopated ragtime became the rage, especially after 1911, when Irving Berlin, a Russian immigrant, wrote "Alexander's Ragtime Band." Ragtime set off a nationwide dance craze. Secretaries danced on their lunch hour, the first nightclubs opened, and restaurants and hotels introduced dance floors. Waltzes and polkas gave way to a host of new dances, many with animal names: the fox-trot, bunny hop, turkey trot, snake, and kangaroo dip. Partners were not permitted to dance too close; bouncers tapped them on the shoulder if they got closer than 9 inches.

Vaudeville, increasingly popular after 1900, reached maturity around 1915. Drawing on the immigrant experience, it voiced the variety of city life and included skits, songs, comics, acrobats, and magicians. Dances and jokes showed an earthiness new to mass audiences. By 1914, stage runways extended into the crowd; women performers had bared their legs and were beginning to show glimpses of the midriff. Fanny Brice; Ann Pennington, the "shimmy" queen; and Eva Tanguay, who sang "It's All Been Done Before But Not the Way I Do It," starred in Florenz Ziegfeld's Follies, the peak of vaudeville.

In songs such as "St. Louis Blues" (1914), W. C. Handy took the black southern folk music of the blues to northern cities. Gertrude "Ma" Rainey, the daughter of minstrels, sang in black vaudeville for nearly thirty-five years. Performing in Chattanooga, Tennessee, about 1910, she came across a 12-year-old orphan, Bessie Smith, who became the "Empress of the Blues." Smith's voice was huge and sweeping. Recording for the Race division of Columbia Records, she made more than eighty records that together sold nearly ten million copies.

Another musical innovation came north from New Orleans. Charles (Buddy) Bolden, a cornetist; Ferdinand "Jelly Roll" Morton, a pianist; and a youngster named Louis Armstrong played an improvisational music that had no formal name. Reaching Chicago, it became "jas," then "jass," and finally "jazz." Jazz jumped, and jazz musicians relied on feeling and mood.

Popular fiction reflected changing interests. Kate Douglas Wiggins's *Rebecca of Sunnybrook Farm* (1903) and Lucy M. Montgomery's *Anne of Green Gables* (1908) showed the continuing popularity of rural themes. Westerns also sold well, but readers turned more and more to detective thrillers with hard-bitten city detectives and science fiction featuring the latest dream in technology. The Tom Swift series, begun in 1910, looked ahead to spaceships, ray guns, and gravity nullifiers.

Edward L. Stratemeyer, the mind behind Tom Swift, brought the techniques of mass production to book writing. In 1906, he formed the Stratemeyer Literary Syndicate, which employed a stable of writers to turn out hundreds of Tom Swift, Rover Boys, and Bobbsey Twins stories for young readers. Burt Standish, another prolific author, took the pen name Gilbert Patten and created the character of Frank Merriwell, wholesome college athlete. As Patten said, "I took the three qualities I most wanted him to represent—frank and merry in nature, well in body and mind—and made the name Frank Merriwell." The Merriwell books sold twenty-five million copies.

EXPERIMENTATION IN THE ARTS

"There is a state of unrest all over the world in art as in all other things," the director of New York's Metropolitan Museum said in 1908. "It is the same in literature, as in music, in painting, and in sculpture."

Isadora Duncan and Ruth St. Denis transformed the dance. Departing from traditional ballet steps, both women stressed improvisation, emotion, and the human form. "Listen to the music with your soul," Duncan told her students. "Unless your dancing springs from an inner emotion and expresses an idea, it will be meaningless." Draped in flowing robes, she revealed more of her legs than some thought tasteful, and she proclaimed that the "noblest art is the nude." Duncan died tragically in 1927, her neck broken when her long red scarf caught in the wheel of a racing car.

The lofts and apartments of New York's Greenwich Village attracted artists, writers, and poets interested in experimentation and change. To these artists, the city was the focus of national life and the sign of a new culture. Robert Henri and the realist painters—known to their critics as the Ashcan School—relished the city's excitement. They wanted, a friend said, "to paint truth and to paint it with strength and fearlessness and individuality."

To the realists, a painting carried into the future the look of life as it happened. Their paintings depicted street scenes, colorful crowds, and slum children swimming in the river. In paintings such as the *Cliff Dwellers*, George W. Bellows captured the color and excitement of the tenements; John Sloan, one of Henri's most talented students, painted the vitality of ordinary people and familiar scenes.

In 1913, a show at the New York Armory presented sixteen hundred modernist paintings, prints, and sculptures. The work of Picasso, Cézanne, Matisse, Brancusi, Van Gogh, and Gauguin dazed and dazzled American observers. Critics attacked the show as worthless and depraved; a Chicago official wanted it banned from the city because the "idea that people can gaze at this sort of thing without [it] hurting them is all bosh."

The postimpressionists changed the direction of twentieth-century art and influenced adventuresome American painters. John Marin, Max Weber, Georgia O'Keeffe, Arthur Dove, and other modernists experimented in ways foreign to Henri's realists. Defiantly avant-garde, they shook off convention and experimented with new forms. Using bold colors and abstract patterns, they worked to capture the energy of urban life.

There was an extraordinary outburst of poetry. In 1912, Harriet Monroe started the magazine *Poetry* in Chicago, the hotbed of the new poetry; Ezra Pound and Vachel Lindsay, both daring experimenters with ideas and verse, published in the first issue. T. S. Eliot published the classic "Love Song of J. Alfred Prufrock" in *Poetry* in 1915. Attacked bitterly by conservative critics, the poem established Eliot's leadership among a group of poets, many of them living and writing in London, who rejected traditional meter and rhyme as artificial constraints. Eliot, Pound, and Amy Lowell, among others, believed the poet's task was to capture fleeting images in verse.

Others experimenting with new techniques in poetry included Robert Frost (*North of Boston*, 1914), Edgar Lee Masters (*Spoon River Anthology*, 1915), and Carl Sandburg (*Chicago Poems*, 1916). Sandburg's poem "Chicago" celebrated the vitality of the city:

> *Come and show me another city with lifted head*
>   *singing so proud to be*
>   *alive and coarse and strong and cunning*
> . . . .
> *Fierce as a dog with tongue lapping for action,*
>   *cunning as a savage*
>   *pitted against the wilderness,*
>   *Bareheaded,*
>   *Shoveling,*
>   *Wrecking,*
>   *Planning,*
>   *Building, breaking, rebuilding,*
> . . . .
> *Bragging and laughing that under his wrist is the*
>   *pulse, and under his*

> *ribs the heart of the people,*
> *Laughing!*
> *Laughing the stormy, husky, brawling laughter of*
> *Youth, half-naked,*
> *sweating, proud to be Hog Butcher, Tool*
> *Maker, Stacker of Wheat,*
> *Player with Railroads and Freight Handler to*
> *the Nation.*

A FERMENT OF DISCOVERY AND REFORM

Manners and morals change slowly, and many Americans overlooked the importance of the first two decades of the twentieth century. Yet sweeping change was under way; anyone who doubted it could visit a gallery, see a film, listen to music, or read one of the new literary magazines. Garrets and galleries were filled with a breathtaking sense of change. "There was life in all these new things," Marsden Hartley, a modernist painter, recalled. "There was excitement, there was healthy revolt, investigation, discovery, and an utterly new world out of it all."

The ferment of progressivism in city, state, and nation reshaped the country. In a burst of reform, people built playgrounds, restructured taxes, regulated business, won the vote for women, shortened working hours, altered political systems, opened kindergartens, and improved factory safety. They tried to fulfill the national promise of dignity and liberty.

Marsden Hartley, it turned out, had voiced a mood that went well beyond painters and poets. Across society, people in many walks of life were experiencing a similar sense of excitement and discovery. Racism, repression, and labor conflict were present, to be sure, but there was also talk of hope, progress, and change. In politics, science, journalism, education, and a host of other fields, people believed for a time that they could make a difference, and in trying to do so, they became part of the progressive generation.

CHRONOLOGY

1898	Mergers and consolidations begin to sweep the business world, leading to fear of trusts
1903	Ford Motor Company formed
	W. E. B. Du Bois calls for justice and equality for African Americans in *The Souls of Black Folk*
	Women's Trade Union League (WTUL) formed to organize women workers
1905	Industrial Workers of the World (IWW) established
	African American leaders inaugurate the Niagara Movement, advocating integration and equal opportunity for African Americans
1909	Shirtwaist workers in New York City strike in the Uprising of the 20,000
	Campaign by Rockefeller Sanitary Commission wipes out hookworm disease
1910	NAACP founded
	Strike at Hart, Schaffner and Marx leads to pioneering collective bargaining agreement
	National Collegiate Athletic Association (NCAA) formed
1911	Fire at the Triangle Shirtwaist Company kills 146 people
	Irving Berlin popularizes rhythm of ragtime with "Alexander's Ragtime Band"
	Frederick Winslow Taylor publishes *The Principles of Scientific Management*
1912	Harriet Monroe begins publishing magazine *Poetry*
	IWW leads strikes in Massachusetts and New Jersey
1913	Ford introduces the moving assembly line in Highland Park, Michigan, plant
	Mother's Day becomes national holiday
1915	D. W. Griffith produces the first movie spectacular, *Birth of a Nation*
	T. S. Eliot publishes "The Love Song of J. Alfred Prufrock"
1916	Margaret Sanger forms New York Birth Control League
	Federal Aid Roads Act creates national road network
	New York zoning law sets the pattern for zoning laws across the nation
1917	Congress passes law requiring literacy test for all immigrants
1921	Congress passes the Sheppard-Towner Act to help protect maternal and infant health

23

FROM ROOSEVELT TO WILSON IN THE AGE OF PROGRESSIVISM

O n a sunny spring morning in 1909, Theodore Roosevelt, wearing the greatcoat of a colonel of the Rough Riders, left New York for a safari in Africa. An ex-president at the age of 50, he had turned over the White House to his chosen successor, William Howard Taft, and was now off for "the joy of wandering through lonely lands, the joy of hunting the mighty and terrible lords" of Africa, "where death broods in the dark and silent depths."

Some of Roosevelt's enemies hoped he would not return. "I trust some lion will do its duty," Wall Street magnate J. P. Morgan said. Always prepared, Roosevelt took nine extra pairs of eyeglasses, and, just in case, several expert hunters accompanied him. When the nearsighted Roosevelt took aim, three others aimed at the same moment. "Mr. Roosevelt had a fairly good idea of the general direction," the safari leader said, "but we couldn't take chances with the life of a former president."

It was all good fun, but less happily, he followed events back home where, in the judgment of many friends, Taft was not working out as president. At almost every stop there were letters waiting for him from disappointed Republicans.

For his part, Taft was puzzled by it all. Honest and warmhearted, he had intended to continue Roosevelt's policies, even writing Roosevelt that he would "see to it that your judgment in selecting me as your successor and bringing about that succession shall be vindicated." But events turned out differently. The conservative and progressive wings of the Republican party split, and Taft often sided with the conservatives. Among progressive Republicans, Taft's troubles stirred talk of a Roosevelt "back from Elba" movement, akin to Napoleon's return from exile.

Thousands gathered to greet Roosevelt on his return from Europe. He sailed into New York harbor on June 18, 1910, to the sound of naval guns and loud cheers. In characteristic fashion, he had helped make the arrangements: "If there

Teddy Roosevelt, with his hunting party in Africa, poses with one of the more than three hundred animals he and his group took down. As president, Roosevelt had supported measures protecting wildlife in the United States, including designating Pelican Island, Florida, as the nation's first wildlife refuge.

is to be a great crowd, do arrange it so that the whole crowd has a chance to see me and that there is as little disappointment as possible."

Roosevelt carried with him a touching letter from Taft, received just before he left Europe. "I have had a hard time—I do not know that I have had harder luck than other Presidents, but I do know that thus far I have succeeded far less than have others. I have been conscientiously trying to carry out your policies but my method of doing so has not worked smoothly." Relations between the two friends cooled.

A year later, there was a desperate fight between Taft and Roosevelt for the Republican presidential nomination. Taft won the nomination, but, angry and ambitious, Roosevelt bolted and helped form a new party, the Progressive (or "Bull Moose") party, to unseat Taft and capture the White House. With Taft, Roosevelt, Woodrow Wilson (the Democratic party's candidate), and Socialist party candidate Eugene V. Debs all in the race, the election of 1912 became one of the most exciting in American history.

It was also one of the most important. People were worried about the social and economic effects of urban-industrial growth. The election of 1912 provided a forum for those worries, and, to a degree unusual in American politics, it pitted deeply opposed candidates against one another and outlined differing views of the nation's future. In the spirited battle between Roosevelt and Wilson, it also brought to the forefront some of the currents of progressive reform.

Those currents built on a number of important developments, including the rise of a new professional class, reform movements designed to cure problems in the cities and states, and the activist, achievement-oriented administrations of Roosevelt and Wilson. Together they produced the age of progressivism.

THE SPIRIT OF PROGRESSIVISM

In one way or another, progressivism touched all aspects of society. Politically, it fostered a reform movement that sought cures for the problems of city, state, and nation. Intellectually, it drew on the expertise of the new social sciences and reflected a shift from older absolutes such as religion to newer schools of thought that emphasized relativism and the role of the environment in human development. Culturally, it inspired fresh modes of expression in dance, film, painting, literature, and architecture. Touching individuals in different ways, progressivism became a set of attitudes as well as a definable movement.

Although broad and diverse, progressivism as a whole had a half dozen characteristics that gave it definition. First, the progressives acted out of concern about the effects of industrialization and the conditions of industrial life. While their viewpoints varied, they did not, as a rule, set out to harm big business, but instead sought to humanize and regulate it.

In pursuing these objectives, the progressives displayed a second characteristic: a fundamental optimism about human nature, the possibilities of progress, and the capacity of people to recognize problems and take action to solve them. Progressives believed they could "investigate, educate, and legislate"—learn about a problem, inform people about it, and, with the help of an informed public, find and enforce a solution.

Third, more than many earlier reformers, the progressives were willing to intervene in people's lives, confident that it was their right to do so. They knew best, some of them thought, and as a result, there was an element of coercion in a number of their ideas. Fourth, while progressives preferred if possible to use voluntary means to achieve reform, they tended to turn more and more to the authority of the state and government at all levels in order to put into effect the reforms they wanted.

As a fifth characteristic, many progressives drew on a combination of evangelical Protestantism (which gave them the desire—and, they thought, the duty—to purge the world of sins such as prostitution and drunkenness) and the natural and social sciences (whose theories made them confident that they could understand and control the environment in which people lived). Progressives tended to view the environment as a key to reform, thinking—in the way some economists, sociologists, and other social scientists were suggesting—that if they could change the environment, they could change the individual.

Finally, progressivism was distinctive because it touched virtually the whole nation. Not everyone, of course, was a progressive, and there were many who opposed or ignored the ideas of the movement. There were also those who were untouched by progressive reforms and those whom the movement overlooked. But in one way or another, a remarkable number of people were caught up in it, giving progressivism a national reach and a mass base.

That was one of the features, in fact, that set it off from populism, which had grown mostly in the rural South and West. Progressivism drew support from across society. "The thing that constantly amazed me," said William Allen White, a leading progressive journalist, "was how many people were with us." Progressivism appealed to the expanding middle class, prosperous farmers, and skilled laborers; it also attracted significant support in the business community.

The progressives believed in progress and disliked waste. No single issue or concern united them all. Some progressives wanted to clean up city governments, others to clean up city streets. Some wanted to purify politics or control corporate abuses, others to eradicate poverty or prostitution. Some demanded social justice in the form of women's rights, child labor laws, temperance, and factory safety. They were Democrats, Republicans, Socialists, and independents.

Progressives believed in a better world and in the ability of people to achieve it. Progress depended on knowledge. The progressives stressed individual morality and collective action, the scientific method, and the value of expert opinion. Like contemporary business leaders, they valued system, planning, management, and predictability. They wanted not only reform but efficiency.

Historians once viewed progressivism as the triumph of one group in society over another. In this view, farmers took on the hated and powerful railroads; upstart reformers challenged the city bosses; business interests fought for favorable legislation; youthful professionals carved out their place in society. Now, historians stress the way progressivism brought people together rather than drove them apart. Disparate groups united in an effort to improve the well-being of many groups in society.

THE RISE OF THE PROFESSIONS

Progressivism fed on an organizational impulse that encouraged people to join forces, share information, and solve problems. Between 1890 and 1920, a host of national societies and associations took shape—nearly four hundred of them in just three decades. Groups such as the National Child Labor Committee, which lobbied for legislation to regulate the employment and working conditions of children, were formed to attack specific issues. Other groups reflected one of the most significant developments in American society at the turn of the century— the rise of the professions.

Growing rapidly in these years, the professions—law, medicine, religion, business, teaching, and social work—were the source of much of the leadership of the progressive movement. The professions attracted young, educated men and women, who in turn were part of a larger trend: a dramatic increase in the number of individuals working in administrative and professional jobs. In businesses, these people were managers, architects, technicians, and accountants. In city governments, they were experts in everything from education to sanitation. They organized and ran the urban-industrial society.

Together these professionals formed part of a new middle class whose members did not derive their status from birth or inherited wealth, as had many members of the older middle class. Instead, they moved ahead through education and personal accomplishment. They had worked to become doctors, lawyers, ministers, and teachers. Proud of their skills, they were ambitious and self-confident, and they thought of themselves as experts who could use their knowledge for the benefit of society.

As a way of asserting their status, they formed professional societies to look after their interests and govern entry into their professions. Just a few years before, for example, a doctor had become a doctor simply by stocking up on patent medicines and hanging out a sign. Now doctors began to insist they were part of a medical profession, and they wanted to set educational requirements and minimum standards for practice. In 1901, they reorganized the American Medical Association (AMA) and made it into a modern national professional society.

Other groups and professions showed the same pattern. Lawyers formed bar associations, created examining boards, and lobbied for regulations restricting entry into the profession. Teachers organized the National Education Association (1905) and pressed for teacher certification and compulsory education laws. Social workers formed the National Federation of Settlements (1911); business leaders created the National Association of Manufacturers (1895) and the U.S. Chamber of Commerce (1912); and farmers joined the National Farm Bureau Federation to spread information about farming and to try to improve their lot.

Working both as individuals and groups, members of the professions had a major impact on the era, as the career of one of them, Dr. Alice Hamilton, illustrated. Hamilton early decided to devote her life to helping the less fortunate. Choosing medicine, she went to the University of Michigan Medical School, one of a shrinking number of medical schools that admitted women, and then settled in Chicago, where she met Jane Addams and took a room in Hull House. Soon thereafter, she traced a local typhoid epidemic to flies carrying germs from open privies.

Combining field study with meticulous laboratory techniques, she pioneered research into the causes of lead poisoning and other industrial disease. In 1908, the governor of Illinois appointed her to a commission on occupational diseases; two years later, she headed a statewide survey of industrial poisons. Thanks to her work, in 1911, Illinois passed the first state law providing compensation for industrial disease caused by poisonous fumes and dust. By the end of the 1930s, all the major industrial states had such laws.

One of the new professionals, Hamilton had used her education and skill to broaden knowledge of her subject, change industrial practices, and improve the lives of countless workers. "For me," she said later in a comment characteristic of the progressives, "the satisfaction is that things are better now, and I had some part in it."

THE SOCIAL-JUSTICE MOVEMENT

As Alice Hamilton's career exemplified, progressivism began in the cities during the 1890s. It first took form around settlement workers and others interested in freeing individuals from the crushing impact of cities and factories.

Ministers, intellectuals, social workers, and lawyers joined in a social-justice movement that focused national attention on the need for tenement house laws, more stringent child labor legislation, and better working conditions for women. They brought pressure on municipal agencies for more and better parks, playgrounds, day nurseries, schools, and community services. Blending private and public action, settlement leaders turned increasingly to government aid.

Social-justice reformers were more interested in social cures than individual charity. Unlike earlier reformers, they saw problems as endless and interrelated; individuals became part of a city's larger patterns. With that insight, social-service casework shifted from a focus on an individual's well-being to a scientific analysis of neighborhoods, occupations, and classes.

Social-justice reformers, banding together to work for change, formed the National Conference of Charities and Corrections, which in 1915 became the National Conference of Social Work. Controlled by social workers, the conference reflected the growing professionalization of reform. Through it, social workers discovered each other's efforts, shared methodology, and tried to establish themselves as a separate field within the social sciences. They founded professional schools at Chicago, Harvard, and other major universities. Instead of piecemeal reforms, they aimed at a comprehensive program of minimum wages, maximum hours, workers' compensation, and widows' pensions.

THE PURITY CRUSADE

Working in city neighborhoods, social-justice reformers were often struck by the degree to which alcohol affected the lives of the people they were trying to help. Workers drank away their wages; some men spent more time at the saloon than at home. Drunkenness caused violence, and it angered employers who did not want intoxicated workers on the job. In countless ways, alcohol wasted human resources, the reformers believed, and they launched a crusade to remove the evils of drink from American life.

At the head of the crusade was the Woman's Christian Temperance Union (WCTU), which had continued to grow since it was founded in the 1870s. By 1911, the WCTU had nearly a quarter of a million members; it was the largest organization of women in American history to that time. In 1893, it was joined by the Anti-Saloon League, and together the groups pressed to abolish alcohol and the places where it was consumed. In the midst of the moral fervor of World War I, they succeeded, and the Eighteenth Amendment to the Constitution, prohibiting the manufacture, sale, and transportation of intoxicating liquors, took effect in January 1920.

The amendment encountered troubles later in the 1920s as the social atmosphere changed, but at the time it passed, progressives thought prohibition was a major step toward eliminating social instability and moral wrong. In a similar fashion, some progressive reformers also worked to get rid of prostitution, convinced that poverty and ignorance drove women to the trade. By 1915, nearly every state had banned brothels, and in 1910, Congress passed the Mann Act, which prohibited the interstate transportation of women for immoral purposes.

Woman suffrage was a key element in the social-justice movement. Without the right to vote, women working actively for reform had little real power to influence elected officials to support their endeavors.

WOMAN SUFFRAGE, WOMEN'S RIGHTS

Women played a large role in the social-justice movement. Feminists were particularly active, especially in the political sphere, between 1890 and 1914. Some working-class women pushed for higher wages and better working conditions. College-educated women—five thousand a year graduated after 1900—took up careers in the professions, from which some of them supported reform. From 1890 to 1910, the work of a number of national women's organizations, including the National Council of Jewish Women, the National Congress of Mothers, and the Women's Trade Union League, furthered the aims of the progressive movement.

Excluded from most of these organizations, African American women formed their own groups. The National Association of Colored Women was founded in 1895, fifteen years before the better known male-oriented National Association for the Advancement of Colored People (NAACP). Aimed at social welfare, the women's organization was the first African American social-service agency in the country.

From 200,000 members in 1900, the General Federation of Women's Clubs grew to more than 1 million by 1912. The clubs met, as they had before, for coffee and literary conversation, but they also began to look closely at conditions around them.

Woman Suffrage Before 1920
State-by-state gains in woman suffrage were limited to the Far West and were agonizingly slow in the early years of the twentieth century.

Forming an Industrial Section and a Committee on Legislation for Women and Children, the federation supported reforms to safeguard child and women workers, improve schools, ensure pure food, and beautify the community. Reluctant at first, the federation finally lent support in 1914 to woman suffrage, a cause that dated back to the first women's rights convention in Seneca Falls, New York, in 1848. Divided over tactics since the Civil War, the suffrage movement suffered from disunity, male opposition, indecision over whether to seek action at the state or at the national level, resistance from the Catholic Church, and opposition from liquor interests, who linked the cause to prohibition.

Because politics was an avenue for reform, growing numbers of women activists became involved in the suffrage movement. After years of disagreement, the two major suffrage organizations, the National Woman Suffrage Association and the American Woman Suffrage Association, merged in 1890 to form the National American Woman Suffrage Association. The merger opened a new phase of the suffrage movement, characterized by unity and a tightly controlled national organization.

In 1900, Carrie Chapman Catt, a superb organizer, became president of the National American Woman Suffrage Association, which by 1920 had nearly two million members. Catt and Anna Howard Shaw, who became the association's head in 1904, believed in organization and peaceful lobbying to win the vote. Alice Paul and Lucy Burns, founders of the Congressional Union, were more militant; they interrupted public meetings, focused on Congress rather than the states, and in 1917 picketed the White House.

Significantly, Catt, Paul, and others made a major change in the argument for woman suffrage. When the campaign began in the nineteenth century, suffragists had claimed the vote as a natural right, owed to women as much as men. Now, they stressed a pragmatic argument: Since women were more sensitive to moral issues than men, they would use their votes to help create a better society. They would support temperance, clean government, laws to protect workers, and other reforms. In 1918, the House passed a constitutional amendment stating simply that the right to vote shall not be denied "on account of sex." The Senate and enough states followed, and, after three generations of suffragist efforts, the Nineteenth Amendment took effect in 1920.

A FERMENT OF IDEAS: CHALLENGING THE STATUS QUO

A dramatic shift in ideas became one of the most important forces behind progressive reform. Most of the ideas focused on the role of the environment in shaping human behavior. Progressive reformers accepted society's growing complexity, called for factual treatment of piecemeal problems, allowed room for new theories, and, above all, rejected age-encrusted divine or natural "laws" in favor of thoughts and actions that worked.

A new doctrine called pragmatism emerged in this ferment of ideas. It came from William James, a brilliant Harvard psychologist who became the key figure in American thought from the 1890s to World War I. A warm, tolerant person, James was impatient with theories that regarded truth as abstract. Truth, he believed, should work for the individual, and it worked best not in abstraction, but in action.

People, James thought, not only were shaped by their environment; they shaped it. In *Pragmatism* (1907), he praised "tough-minded" individuals who could live effectively in a world with no easy answers. The tough-minded accepted change; they knew how to pick manageable problems, gather facts, discard ideas that did not work, and act on those that did. Ideas that worked became truth.

The most influential educator of the Progressive Era, John Dewey, applied pragmatism to educational reform. A friend and disciple of William James, he argued that thought evolves in relation to the environment and that education is directly related to experience. In 1896, Dewey founded a separate School of Pedagogy at the University of Chicago, with a laboratory in which educational theory based on the newer philosophical and psychological studies could be tested and practiced.

Dewey introduced an educational revolution that stressed children's needs and capabilities. He opposed memorization, rote learning, and dogmatic, authoritarian teaching methods; he emphasized personal growth, free inquiry, and creativity.

Rejecting the older view of the law as universal and unchanging, lawyers and legal theorists instead viewed it as a reflection of the environment—an instrument for social change. Law reflected the environment that shaped it. A movement grew among judges for "sociological jurisprudence" that related the law to social reform instead of only to legal precedent, a shift most evident in the famous "Brandeis brief" in a case that came before the Supreme Court in 1908.

Socialism, a reformist political philosophy, grew dramatically before World War I. Eugene V. Debs, president of the American Railway Union, in 1896 formed the Social Democratic party. Gentle and reflective, not at all the popular image of the wild-eyed radical, Debs was thrust into prominence by the Pullman strike. In 1901, he formed the important Socialist party of America. Neither Debs nor the party ever developed a cohesive platform, nor was Debs an effective organizer. But he was eloquent, passionate, and visionary. An excellent speaker, he captivated audiences, attacking the injustices of capitalism and urging a workers' republic.

The Socialist party of America enlisted some intellectuals, factory workers, disillusioned Populists, tenant farmers, miners, and lumberjacks. By 1911, there were Socialist mayors in thirty-two cities. Although its doctrines were aimed at an urban proletariat, the Socialist party drew support in rural Texas, Missouri, Arkansas, Idaho, and Washington. In Oklahoma, it attracted as much as one-third of the vote. Most Socialists who won promised progressive reform rather than threatening to overthrow capitalists.

Although torn by factions, the Socialist party doubled in membership between 1904 and 1908, then tripled in the four years after that. Running for president, Debs garnered 100,000 votes in 1900; 400,000 in 1904; and 900,000 in 1912, the party's peak year.

REFORM IN THE CITIES AND STATES

Progressive reformers realized government could be a crucial agent in accomplishing their goals. They wanted to curb the influence of "special interests" and, through such measures of political reform as the direct primary and the direct election of senators, make government follow the public will. Once it did, they welcomed government action at whatever level was appropriate.

As a result of this thinking, the use of federal power increased, as did the power and prestige of the presidency. Progressives not only lobbied for government-sponsored reform but also worked actively in their home neighborhoods, cities, and states; much of the significant change occurred in local settings, outside the national limelight. Most important, the progressives believed in the ability of experts to solve problems. At every level—local, state, and federal—thousands of commissions and agencies took form. Staffed by trained experts, they oversaw a multitude of matters ranging from railroad rates to public health.

INTEREST GROUPS AND THE DECLINE OF POPULAR POLITICS

Placing government in the hands of experts was one way to get it out of the hands of politicians and political parties. The direct primary, which allowed voters rather than parties to choose candidates for office, was another way. These initiatives and others like them were part of a fundamental change in the way Americans viewed their political system.

As one sign of the change, fewer and fewer people were going to the polls. Voter turnout dropped dramatically after 1900, when the intense partisanship of the decades after the Civil War gave way to media-oriented political campaigns based largely on the personalities of the candidates. From 1876 to 1900, the average turnout in presidential elections was 77 percent. From 1900 to 1916, it was 65 percent, and in the 1920s, it dropped to 52 percent, close to the average today. Turnout was lowest among young people, immigrants, the poor, and, ironically, the newly enfranchised women.

There were numerous causes for the falloff, but among the most important was the fact that people had found another way to achieve some of the objectives they had once assigned to political parties. They had found the "interest group," a means of action that assumed importance in this era and became a major feature of politics ever after. Professional societies, trade associations, labor organizations, farm lobbies, and scores of other interest groups worked outside the party system to pressure government for things their members wanted. Social workers, women's clubs, reform groups, and others learned to apply pressure in similar ways, and the result was much significant legislation of the Progressive Era.

REFORM IN THE CITIES

During the early years of the twentieth century, urban reform movements, many of them born in the depression of the 1890s, spread across the nation. In 1894, the National Municipal League was organized, and it became the forum for debate over civic reform, changes in the tax laws, and municipal ownership of public utilities. Within a few years, nearly every city had a variety of clubs and organizations directed at improving the quality of city life.

In city after city, reformers reordered municipal government. Tightening controls on corporate activities, they broadened the scope of utility regulation and restricted city franchises. They updated tax assessments, often skewed in favor of corporations, and tried to clean up the electoral machinery. Devoted to efficiency, they developed a trained civil service to oversee planning and operations. The generation of the 1880s also had believed in civil service, but the goal then was mostly negative: to get spoilsmen out and "good" people in. Now the goal was efficiency and, above all, results.

In constructing their model governments, urban reformers often turned to recent advances in business management and organization. They stressed continuity and expertise, a system in which professional experts staffed a government overseen by elected officials. At the top, the elected leader surveyed the breadth of city, state, or national affairs and defined directions. Below, a corps of experts—trained in the various disciplines of the new society—funneled the definition into specific scientifically based policies.

Reformers created a growing number of regulatory commissions and municipal departments. They hired engineers to oversee utility and water systems, physicians and nurses to improve municipal health, and city planners to oversee park and highway development.

In the race for reform, a number of city mayors won national reputations—among them Seth Low in New York City and Hazen S. Pingree in Detroit—working to modernize taxes, clean up politics, lower utility rates, and control the awarding of valuable city franchises.

In Cleveland, Ohio, Tom L. Johnson demonstrated an innovative approach to city government. A millionaire who had made his fortune manipulating city franchises, Johnson one day read Henry George's *Progress and Poverty* and turned to reform. Elected mayor of Cleveland, he served from 1901 to 1909.

Tom L. Johnson (in derby hat) and companions in a car known as the "Red Devil," the first automobile used in a political campaign. Johnson, who made his fortune in the streetcar business, served as mayor of Cleveland from 1901 to 1909. His administration, noted for its efficiency and many municipal reforms, also waged a long and bitter fight with streetcar business interests opposed to Johnson's efforts to lower streetcar fares to make them affordable for working-class people. Muckraking journalist Lincoln Steffens praised Johnson's Cleveland as "the best-governed city in America."

Believing in an informed citizenry, he held outdoor meetings in huge tents. He used colorful charts to give Cleveland residents a course in utilities and taxation. He cut down on corruption, cut off special privilege, updated taxes, and gave Cleveland a reputation as the country's best-governed city.

ACTION IN THE STATES

Reformers soon discovered, however, that many problems lay beyond a city's boundaries, and they turned for action to the state governments. From the 1890s to 1920, reformers worked to stiffen state laws regulating the labor of women and children, to create and strengthen commissions to regulate railroads and utilities, to impose corporate and inheritance taxes, to improve mental and penal institutions, and to allocate more funds for state universities, which were viewed as the training ground for the experts and educated citizenry needed for the new society.

To regulate business, virtually every state created regulatory commissions empowered to examine corporate books and hold public hearings. Building on earlier experience, state commissions after 1900 were given new power to initiate actions, rather than await complaints, and in some cases to set maximum prices and rates. Dictating company practices, they pioneered regulatory methods later adopted in federal legislation of 1906 and 1910.

Historians have long praised the regulation movement, but the commissions did not always act wisely or even in the public interest. Elective commissions often produced commissioners who had little knowledge of corporate affairs. In addition, to win election, some promised specific rates or reforms, obligations that might bias the commission's investigative functions. Appointive commissions sometimes fared better, but they too had to oversee extraordinarily complex businesses such as the railroads.

To the progressives, commissions offered a way to end the corrupt alliance between business and politics. There was another way, too, and that was to "democratize" government by reducing the power of politicians and increasing the influence of the electorate. To do that, progressives backed three measures to make officeholders responsive to popular will: the initiative, which allowed voters to propose new laws; the referendum, which allowed them to accept or reject a law at the ballot box; and the recall, which gave them a way to remove an elected official from office.

Oregon adopted the initiative and referendum in 1902; by 1912, twelve states had them. That year Congress added the Seventeenth Amendment to the Constitution to provide for the direct election of U.S. senators. By 1916, all but three states had direct primaries, which allowed the people, rather than nominating conventions, to choose candidates for office.

Robert M. La Follette became the most famous reform governor. In 1901, he became governor of Wisconsin, and in the following six years, he put together the "Wisconsin Idea," one of the most important reform programs in the history of state government. He established an industrial commission, the first in the country, to regulate factory safety and sanitation. He improved education, workers' compensation, public utility controls, and resource conservation. He lowered railroad rates and raised railroad taxes. Under La Follette's prodding, Wisconsin became the first state to adopt a direct primary for all political nominations. It also became the first to adopt a state income tax. Theodore Roosevelt called La Follette's Wisconsin "the laboratory of democracy," and the Wisconsin Idea soon spread to many other states.

After 1905, the progressives looked more and more to Washington. For one thing, Teddy Roosevelt was there, with his zest for publicity and his alluring grin. But progressives also had a growing sense that many concerns—corporations and conservation, factory safety and child labor—crossed state lines. Federal action seemed desirable; specific reforms fit into a larger plan perhaps best seen from the nation's center. Within a few years, the focus of progressivism shifted to Washington.

THE REPUBLICAN ROOSEVELT

When President William McKinley died of gunshot wounds in September 1901, Vice President Theodore Roosevelt succeeded him in the White House. The new president initially vowed to carry on McKinley's policies. He continued some, developed others of his own, and in the end brought to them all the particular exuberance of his own personality.

At age 42, Roosevelt was then the youngest president in American history. In contrast to the dignified McKinley, he was open, aggressive, and high-spirited. At his desk by 8:30 every morning, he worked through the day, usually with visitors for breakfast, lunch, and dinner. Politicians, labor leaders, industrialists, poets, artists, and writers paraded through the White House.

If McKinley cut down on presidential isolation, Roosevelt virtually ended it. The presidency, he thought, was the "bully pulpit," a forum of ideas and leadership for the nation. The president was "a steward of the people bound actively and affirmatively to do all he could for the people." Self-confident, Roosevelt enlisted talented associates, including Elihu Root, secretary of war and later secretary of state; William Howard Taft, secretary of war; Gifford Pinchot, the nation's chief forester and leading conservationist; and Oliver Wendell Holmes, Jr., whom he named to the Supreme Court.

In 1901, Roosevelt invited Booker T. Washington, the prominent African American educator, to dinner at the White House. Many Southerners protested— "a crime equal to treason," a newspaper said—and they protested again when Roosevelt appointed several African Americans to important federal offices in South Carolina and Mississippi. At first, Roosevelt considered building a biracial "black-and-tan" southern Republican party, thinking it would foster racial progress and his own renomination in 1904.

But Roosevelt soon retreated. In some areas of the South, he supported "lily-white" Republican organizations, and his policies often reflected his own belief in African American inferiority. He said nothing when a race riot broke out in Atlanta in 1906, although twelve persons died. He joined others in blaming African American soldiers stationed near Brownsville, Texas, after a night of violence there in August 1906. Acting quickly and on little evidence, he discharged "without honor" three companies of African American troops. Six of the soldiers who were discharged held the Congressional Medal of Honor.

BUSTING THE TRUSTS

"There is a widespread conviction in the minds of the American people that the great corporations known as trusts are in certain of their features and tendencies hurtful to the general welfare," Roosevelt reported to Congress in 1901. Like most people, however, the president wavered on the trusts. Large-scale production and industrial growth, he believed, were natural and beneficial; they needed only to be controlled. Still he distrusted the trusts' impact on local enterprise and individual opportunity. Distinguishing between "good" and "bad" trusts, he pledged to protect the former while controlling the latter.

In 1903, Roosevelt asked Congress to create a Department of Commerce and Labor, with a Bureau of Corporations empowered to investigate corporations engaged in interstate commerce. Congress balked; Roosevelt called in reporters and, in an off-the-record interview, charged that John D. Rockefeller had organized the opposition to the measure. The press spread the word, and in the outcry that followed, the proposal passed easily in a matter of weeks. Roosevelt

A cartoon illustrating Theodore Roosevelt's promise to break up only those "bad trusts" that were hurtful to the general welfare. Despite his reputation as a trust buster, Roosevelt dissolved relatively few trusts.

was delighted. With the new Bureau of Corporations publicizing its findings, he thought, the glare of publicity would eliminate most corporate abuses.

Roosevelt also undertook direct legal action. On February 18, 1902, he instructed the Justice Department to bring suit against the Northern Securities Company for violation of the Sherman Antitrust Act. It was a shrewd move. A mammoth holding company, Northern Securities controlled the massive rail networks of the Northern Pacific, Great Northern, and Chicago, Burlington & Quincy railroads.

In 1904, the Supreme Court, in a 5 to 4 decision, upheld the suit against Northern Securities and ordered the company dissolved. Roosevelt was jubilant, and he followed up the victory with several other antitrust suits. In 1902, he had moved against the beef trust, an action applauded by western farmers and urban consumers alike. After a lull, he initiated suits in 1906 and 1907 against the American Tobacco Company, the Du Pont Corporation, the New Haven Railroad, and Standard Oil.

But Roosevelt's policies were not always clear, nor his actions always consistent. He asked for (and received) business support in his bid for reelection in 1904. Large donations came in from industrial leaders, and J. P. Morgan himself later testified that he gave $150,000 to Roosevelt's campaign. In 1907, acting in part to avert a threatened financial panic, the president permitted Morgan's U.S. Steel to absorb the Tennessee Coal and Iron Company, an important competitor.

Roosevelt, in truth, was not a trust buster, although he was frequently called that. William Howard Taft, his successor in the White House, initiated forty-three antitrust indictments in four years—nearly twice as many as the twenty-five Roosevelt initiated in the seven years of his presidency. Instead, Roosevelt used antitrust threats to keep businesses within bounds. Regulation, he believed, was a better way to control large-scale enterprise.

"SQUARE DEAL" IN THE COALFIELDS

A few months after announcing the Northern Securities suit, Roosevelt intervened in a major labor dispute involving the anthracite coal miners of northeastern Pennsylvania. Led by John Mitchell, a moderate labor leader, the United Mine Workers demanded wage increases, an eight-hour workday, and company recognition of the union. The coal companies refused, and in May 1902, 140,000 miners walked off the job. The mines closed.

As the months passed and the strike continued, coal prices rose. With winter coming on, schools, hospitals, and factories ran short of coal. Public opinion turned against the companies. Morgan and other industrial leaders privately urged them to settle, but George F. Baer, head of one of the largest companies, refused.

Roosevelt was furious. Complaining of the companies' arrogance, he invited both sides in the dispute to an October 1902 conference at the White House. There, Mitchell took a moderate tone and offered to submit the issues to arbitration, but the companies again refused to budge. Roosevelt ordered the army to prepare to seize the mines and then leaked word of his intent to Wall Street leaders.

Alarmed, Morgan and others again urged settlement of the dispute, and at last the companies retreated. They agreed to accept the recommendations of an independent commission the president would appoint. In late October, the strikers returned to work, and in March 1903, the commission awarded them a 10 percent wage increase and a cut in working hours. It recommended, however, against union recognition. The coal companies, in turn, were encouraged to raise prices to offset the wage increase.

More and more, Roosevelt saw the federal government as an honest and impartial "broker" between powerful elements in society. Rather than leaning toward labor, he pursued a middle way to curb corporate and labor abuses, abolish privilege, and enlarge individual opportunity. Conservative by temperament, he sometimes backed reforms in part to head off more radical measures.

During the 1904 campaign, Roosevelt called his actions in the coal miners' strike a "square deal" for both labor and capital, a term that stuck to his administration. Roosevelt was not the first president to take a stand for labor, but he was the first to bring opposing sides in a labor dispute to the White House to settle it.

ROOSEVELT PROGRESSIVISM AT ITS HEIGHT

In the election of 1904, the popular Roosevelt soundly drubbed his Democratic opponent, Alton B. Parker of New York, and the Socialist party candidate, Eugene V. Debs of Indiana. Roosevelt attracted a large campaign chest and won

THE ELECTION OF 1904

CANDIDATE	PARTY	POPULAR VOTE	ELECTORAL VOTE
T. Roosevelt	Republican	7,623,486	336
Parker	Democrat	5,077,911	140
Debs	Socialist	402,400	0
Swallow	Prohibition	258,596	0

votes everywhere. After a landslide victory, he pledged that "under no circumstances will I be a candidate for or accept another nomination," a statement he later regretted.

REGULATING THE RAILROADS

Following his election, Roosevelt in late 1904 laid out a reform program that included railroad regulation, employers' liability for federal employees, greater federal control over corporations, and laws regulating child labor, factory inspection, and slum clearance in the District of Columbia. He turned first to railroad regulation. In 1903, he had worked with Congress to pass the Elkins Act to prohibit railroad rebates and increase the powers of the Interstate Commerce Commission (ICC). The Elkins Act, a moderate law, was framed with the consent of railroad leaders. In 1904 and 1905, the president wanted much more, and he urged Congress to empower the ICC to set reasonable and nondiscriminatory rates and prevent inequitable practices.

Widespread demand for railroad regulation strengthened Roosevelt's hand. In the Midwest and Far West, the issue was a popular one, and reform governors La Follette in Wisconsin and Albert B. Cummins in Iowa urged federal action. Roosevelt maneuvered cannily. As the legislative battle opened, he released figures showing that Standard Oil had reaped $750,000 a year from railroad rebates. He also skillfully traded congressional support for a strong railroad measure in return for his promise to postpone a reduction of the tariff, a stratagem that came back to plague President Taft.

Triumph came with passage of the Hepburn Act of 1906. A significant achievement, the act strengthened the rate-making power of the Interstate Commerce Commission. It increased membership on the ICC from five to seven, empowered it to fix reasonable maximum railroad rates, and broadened its jurisdiction to include oil pipeline, express, and sleeping car companies. ICC orders were binding, pending any court appeals, thus placing the burden of proof of injustice on the companies. Delighted, Roosevelt viewed the Hepburn Act as a major step in his plan for continuous expert federal control over industry.

CLEANING UP FOOD AND DRUGS

Soon Roosevelt was dealing with two other important bills, these aimed at regulating the food and drug industries. Muckraking articles had touched frequently on filthy conditions in meatpacking houses, but Upton Sinclair's *The Jungle* (1906) set off a storm of indignation. Ironically, Sinclair had set out to write a novel about the packinghouse workers, the "wage slaves of the Beef Trust," hoping to do for wage slavery what Harriet Beecher Stowe had done for chattel slavery. But readers largely ignored his story of the workers and seized instead on the graphic descriptions of the things that went into their meat.

Sinclair was disappointed at the reaction. "I aimed at the public's heart," he later said, "and by accident I hit it in the stomach." He had, indeed. After reading *The Jungle,* Roosevelt ordered an investigation. The result, he said, was "hideous," and he threatened to publish the entire "sickening report" if Congress did not act. Meat sales plummeted in the United States and Europe.

A poster for the movie version of Upton Sinclair's The Jungle *promises a "wonderful story of the beef packing industry." The conditions that Sinclair described in the book brought to public attention the scandals of the meatpacking industry knowingly selling diseased meat and the filthy, disease-ridden, dangerous conditions in which the workers toiled for their subsistence wages.*

Demand for reform grew. Alarmed, the meatpackers themselves supported a reform law, which they hoped would be just strong enough to still the clamor. The Meat Inspection Act of 1906, stronger than the packers wanted, set rules for sanitary meatpacking and government inspection of meat products.

A second measure, the Pure Food and Drug Act, passed more easily. Samuel Hopkins Adams, a muckraker, exposed the dangers of patent medicines in several sensational articles in *Collier's*. Patent medicines, Adams pointed out, contained mostly alcohol, drugs, and "undiluted fraud." Dr. Harvey W. Wiley, the chief chemist in the Department of Agriculture, led a "poison squad" of young assistants who experimented with the medicines. With evidence in hand, Wiley pushed for regulation; Roosevelt and the recently reorganized American Medical Association joined the fight, and the act passed on June 30, 1906. Requiring manufacturers to list certain ingredients on the label, it represented a pioneering effort to ban the manufacture and sale of adulterated, misbranded, or unsanitary food or drugs.

CONSERVING THE LAND

An expert on birds, Roosevelt loved nature and the wilderness, and some of his most enduring accomplishments came in the field of conservation. Working closely with Gifford Pinchot, chief of the Forest Service, he established the first

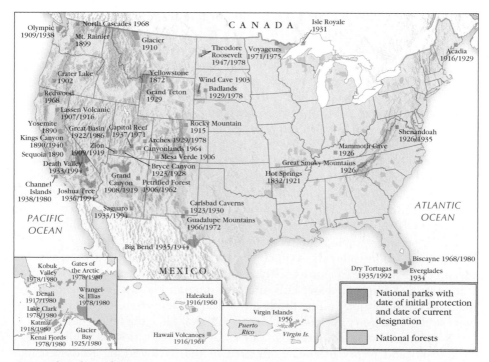

National Parks and Forests
During the presidency of Theodore Roosevelt, who considered conservation his most important domestic achievement, millions of acres of land were set aside for national parks and forests.

comprehensive national conservation policy. To Roosevelt, conservation meant the wise use of natural resources, not locking them away, so those who thought the wilderness should be preserved rather than developed generally opposed his policies.

Using experts in the federal government, Roosevelt undertook a major reclamation program, created the federal Reclamation Service, and strengthened the forest preserve program in the Department of Agriculture. Broadening the concept of conservation, he placed power sites, coal lands, and oil reserves as well as national forest in the public domain. When Roosevelt took office in 1901, there were 45 million acres in government preserves. In 1908, there were almost 195 million.

Immensely popular, Roosevelt prepared in 1908 to turn over the White House to William Howard Taft, his close friend and colleague. As expected, Taft soundly defeated the Democratic standard-bearer William Jennings Bryan, who was making his third try for the presidency. The Republicans retained control of Congress. Taft prepared to move into the White House, ready and willing to carry on the Roosevelt legacy.

THE ORDEAL OF WILLIAM HOWARD TAFT

The Republican national convention that nominated Taft had not satisfied either Roosevelt or Taft. True, Taft won the presidential nomination as planned, but conservative Republicans beat back the attempts of progressive Republicans to influence the convention. They named a conservative, James S. Sherman, for vice president and built a platform that reflected conservative views on labor, the courts, and other issues. Taft wanted a pledge to lower the tariff but got only a promise of revision, which might lower—or raise—it. La Follette, Cummins, Jonathan P. Dolliver of Iowa, Albert J. Beveridge of Indiana, and other progressive Republicans were openly disappointed.

Taking office in 1909, Taft felt "just a bit like a fish out of water." The son of a distinguished Ohio family and a graduate of Yale Law School, he became an Ohio judge, solicitor general of the United States, and a judge of the federal circuit court. In 1900, McKinley asked him to head the Philippine Commission, charged with the difficult and challenging task of forming a civil government in the Philippines. Later Taft was named the first governor general of the Philippines. In 1904, Roosevelt appointed him secretary of war. In all these positions, Taft made his mark as a skillful administrator. He worked quietly behind the scenes, avoided controversy, and shared none of Roosevelt's zest for politics. A good-natured man, Taft had personal charm and infectious humor. He fled from fights rather than seeking them out, and he disliked political maneuvering, preferring instead quiet solitude. "I don't like politics," he said. "I don't like the limelight."

Weighing close to 300 pounds, Taft enjoyed conversation, golf and bridge, good food, and plenty of rest. Compared to the hardworking Roosevelt and Wilson, he was lazy. He was also honest, kindly, and amiable, and in his own way he knew how to get things done.

THE ELECTION OF 1908

CANDIDATE	PARTY	POPULAR VOTE	ELECTORAL VOTE
Taft	Republican	7,678,908	321
Bryan	Democrat	6,409,104	162
Debs	Socialist	402,820	0
Chafin	Prohibition	252,821	0

Taft's years as president were not happy. As it turned out, he presided over a Republican party torn with tensions that Roosevelt had either brushed aside or concealed. The tariff, business regulation, and other issues split conservatives and progressives, and Taft often wavered or sided with the conservatives. Taft revered the past and distrusted change; although an ardent supporter of Roosevelt, he never had Roosevelt's faith in the ability of government to impose reform and alter individual behavior. He named five corporation attorneys to his cabinet, leaned more to business than to labor, and spoke of a desire to "clean out the unions."

At that time and later, Taft's reputation suffered by comparison to the flair of Roosevelt and the moral majesty of Woodrow Wilson. He deserved better. Taft was an honest and sincere president, who—sometimes firm, sometimes befuddled— faced a series of important and troublesome problems during his term of office.

PARTY INSURGENCY

Taft started his term with an attempt to curb the powerful Republican speaker of the House, Joseph "Uncle Joe" Cannon of Illinois. Using the powers of his position, Cannon had been setting House procedures, appointing committees, and virtually dictating legislation. Straightforward and crusty, he often opposed reform. In March 1909, thirty Republican congressmen joined Taft's effort to curb Cannon's power, and the president sensed success. But Cannon retaliated and, threatening to block all tariff bills, forced a compromise. Taft stopped the anti-Cannon campaign in return for Cannon's pledge to help with tariff cuts.

Republicans were divided over the tariff, and there was a growing party insurgency against high rates. The House quickly passed a bill providing for lower rates, but in the Senate, protectionists raised them. Senate leader Nelson W. Aldrich of Rhode Island introduced a revised bill that added more than eight hundred amendments to the rates approved in the House.

Angry, La Follette and other Republicans attacked the bill as the child of special interests. In speeches on the Senate floor they called themselves "progressives," invoked Roosevelt's name, and urged Taft to defeat the high-tariff proposal.

Caught between protectionists and progressives, Taft wavered, then tried to compromise. In the end, he backed Aldrich. The Payne-Aldrich Act, passed in November 1909, called for higher rates than the original House bill, though it lowered them from the Dingley Tariff of 1897. An unpopular law, Payne-Aldrich helped discredit Taft and revealed the tensions in the Republican party.

Republican progressives and conservatives drifted apart. Thin-skinned, Taft resented the persistent pinpricks of the progressives who criticized him for virtually everything he did. He tried to find middle ground but leaned more and more toward the conservatives. By early 1910, progressive Republicans in Congress no longer looked to Taft for leadership. As before, they challenged Cannon's power, and Taft wavered. In an outcome embarrassing to the president, the progressives won, managing to curtail Cannon's authority to dictate committee assignments and schedule debate. In progressive circles there was growing talk of a Roosevelt return to the White House.

THE BALLINGER-PINCHOT AFFAIR

The conservation issue dealt another blow to relations between Roosevelt and President Taft. In 1909, Richard A. Ballinger, Taft's secretary of the interior, offered for sale a million acres of public land that Pinchot, who had stayed on as Taft's chief forester, had withdrawn from sale. Pinchot, fearing that Ballinger would hurt conservation programs, protested and, seizing on a report that Ballinger had helped sell valuable Alaskan coal lands to a syndicate that included J. P. Morgan, asked Taft to intervene. After investigating, Taft supported Ballinger on every count, although he asked Pinchot to remain in office.

Pinchot refused to drop the matter. Behind the scenes, he provided material for two anti-Ballinger magazine articles. Taft had had enough. He fired the insubordinate Pinchot, an action which, though appropriate, again lost support for Taft. Newspapers followed the controversy for months, and muckrakers assailed the administration's "surrender" to Morgan and other "despoilers of the national heritage."

The Ballinger-Pinchot controversy obscured Taft's important contributions to conservation. He won from Congress the power to remove lands from sale, and he used it to conserve more land than Roosevelt did. Still, the controversy tarred Taft, and it upset his old friend Roosevelt.

TAFT ALIENATES THE PROGRESSIVES

Interested in railroad regulation, Taft backed a bill in 1910 to empower the ICC to fix maximum railroad rates. Progressive Republicans favored that plan but attacked Taft's suggestion of a special Commerce Court to hear appeals from ICC decisions because most judges were traditionally conservative in outlook and usually rejected attempts to regulate railroad rates. They also thought the railroads had been consulted too closely in drawing up the bill. Democratic and Republican progressives tried to amend the bill to strengthen it; Taft made support of it a test of party loyalty.

The Mann-Elkins Act of 1910 gave something to everyone. It gave the ICC power to set rates, stiffened long- and short-haul regulations, and placed telephone and telegraph companies under ICC jurisdiction. These provisions delighted progressives. The act also created a Commerce Court, pleasing conservatives. In a trade-off, conservative Republican Senate leaders pledged their support for a statehood bill for Arizona and New Mexico, which were both predicted to be Democratic. In return, enough Democratic senators promised to vote for the Commerce Court provision to pass the bill. While pleased with the act, Taft and the Republican party lost further ground. In votes on key provisions of the Mann-Elkins Act, Taft raised the issue of party regularity, and progressive Republicans defied him.

The 1910 election results were a major setback for Taft and the Republicans—especially conservative Republicans. A key issue in the election, the high cost of living, gave an edge to the progressive wings in both major parties, lending support to their attack on the tariff and the trusts. In party primaries, progressive Republicans overwhelmed most Taft candidates, and in the general election, they tended to fare better than the conservatives, which increased progressive influence in the Republican party.

For Republicans of all persuasions, however, it was a difficult election. The Democrats swept the urban-industrial states from New York to Illinois. New York, New Jersey, Indiana, and even Taft's Ohio elected Democratic governors. For the first time since 1894, Republicans lost control of both the House and the Senate. Disappointed, Taft called it "not only a landslide, but a tidal wave and holocaust all rolled into one general cataclysm."

Despite the defeat, Taft pushed through several important measures before his term ended. With the help of the new Democratic House, he backed laws to regulate safety in mines and on railroads, create a Children's Bureau in the federal government, establish employers' liability for all work done on government contracts, and mandate an eight-hour workday for government workers.

In 1909, Congress initiated a constitutional amendment authorizing an income tax, which, along with woman suffrage, was one of the most significant legislative measures of the twentieth century. The Sixteenth Amendment took effect early in 1913. A few months later, an important progressive goal was realized when the direct election of senators was ratified as the Seventeenth Amendment to the Constitution.

An ardent supporter of competition, Taft relentlessly pressed a campaign against trusts. The Sherman Antitrust Act, he said in 1911, "is a good law that ought to be enforced, and I propose to enforce it." That year, the Supreme Court in cases against Standard Oil and American Tobacco established the "rule of reason," which allowed the Court to determine whether a business presented "reasonable" restraint on trade. Taft thought the decisions gave the Court too much discretion, and he pushed ahead with the antitrust effort.

In October 1911, he sued U.S. Steel for its acquisition of the Tennessee Coal and Iron Company in 1907. Roosevelt had approved the acquisition, and the suit seemed designed to impugn his action. Enraged, he attacked Taft, and Taft, for

According to this 1913 cartoon, the new income tax legislation distributed the tax burden more evenly, so that contributions from the wealthy eased some of the burden on the working class.

once, fought back. He accused Roosevelt of undermining the conservative tradition in the country and began working to undercut the influence of the progressive Republicans. Increasingly now, Roosevelt listened to anti-Taft Republicans who urged him to run for president in 1912. In February 1912, he announced, "My hat is in the ring."

DIFFERING PHILOSOPHIES IN THE ELECTION OF 1912

Delighted Democrats looked on as Taft and Roosevelt fought for the Republican nomination. As the incumbent president, Taft controlled the party machinery, and when the Republican convention met in June 1912, he took the nomination. In early July, the Democrats met in Baltimore and, confident of victory for the first time in two decades, struggled through forty-six ballots before finally nominating Woodrow Wilson, the reform-minded governor of New Jersey.

A month later, some of the anti-Taft and progressive Republicans—now calling themselves the Progressive party—whooped it up in Chicago. Roosevelt was there to give a stirring "Confession of Faith." Naming Roosevelt for president at its convention, the Progressive party—soon known as the Bull Moose party—set the stage for the first important three-cornered presidential contest since 1860.

Taft was out of the running before the campaign even began. "I think I might as well give up so far as being a candidate is concerned," he said in July. "There are so many people in the country who don't like me." Taft stayed at home and made no speeches before the election. Roosevelt campaigned strenuously, even completing one speech after being shot in the chest by an anti-third-term fanatic. "I have a message to deliver," he said, "and will deliver it as long as there is life in my body."

Roosevelt's message involved a program he called the New Nationalism. An important phase in the shaping of twentieth-century American political thought, it demanded a national approach to the country's affairs and a strong president to deal with them. The New Nationalism called for efficiency in government and society. It exalted the executive and the expert; urged social-justice reforms to protect workers, women, and children; and accepted "good" trusts. The New Nationalism encouraged large concentrations of labor and capital, serving the nation's interests under a forceful federal executive.

For the first time in the history of a major political party, the Progressive campaign enlisted women in its organization. Jane Addams, the well-known settlement worker, seconded Roosevelt's nomination at Chicago, and she and other women played a leading role in his campaign. Some labor leaders, who saw potential for union growth, and some business leaders, who saw relief from destructive competition and labor strife, supported the new party.

Wilson, in contrast, set forth a program called the New Freedom that emphasized business competition and small government. A states' rights Democrat, he wanted to rein in federal authority, using it only to sweep away special privilege, release individual energies, and restore competition. Drawing on the thinking of Louis D. Brandeis, the brilliant shaper of reform-minded law, he echoed the Progressive party's social-justice objectives, while continuing to attack Roosevelt's planned state. For Wilson, the vital issue was not a planned economy but a free one. "The history of liberty is the history of the limitation of governmental power," he said in October 1912. "If America is not to have free enterprise, then she can have freedom of no sort whatever."

In the New Nationalism and New Freedom, the election of 1912 offered competing philosophies of government. Both Roosevelt and Wilson saw the central problem of the American nation as economic growth and its effect on individuals and society. Both focused on the government's relation to business, both believed in bureaucratic reform, and both wanted to use government to protect the ordinary citizen. But Roosevelt welcomed federal power, national planning, and business growth; Wilson distrusted them all.

THE ELECTION OF 1912

CANDIDATE	PARTY	POPULAR VOTE	ELECTORAL VOTE
Wilson	Democrat	6,293,454	435
Roosevelt	Progressive (Bull Moose)	4,119,538	88
Taft	Republican	3,484,980	8
	Minor Parties	1,135,697	0

On election day, Wilson won 6.3 million votes to 4.1 million for Roosevelt (who had recovered quickly from his wound) and 900,000 for Eugene V. Debs, the Socialist party candidate. Taft, the incumbent president, finished third with 3.5 million votes; he carried only Vermont and Utah for 8 electoral votes. The Democrats also won outright control of both houses.

WOODROW WILSON'S NEW FREEDOM

If under Roosevelt social reform took on the excitement of a circus, "under Wilson it acquired the dedication of a sunrise service." Born in Virginia in 1856 and raised in the South, Wilson was the son of a Presbyterian minister. As a young man, he wanted a career in public service, and he trained himself carefully in history and oratory. A moralist, he reached judgments easily. Once reached, almost nothing shook them. Opponents called him stubborn and smug.

After graduating from Princeton University and the University of Virginia Law School, Wilson found that practicing law bored him. Shifting to history,

Woodrow Wilson and outgoing President William Taft share a carriage ride en route to Wilson's inauguration following his victory in the election of 1912. The Republican party split over the election with the Progressives supporting Theodore Roosevelt and his Bull Moose ticket and the party machine supporting Taft. Even though the Republican split encouraged the Democrats to hope for victory, it still took forty-six ballots before they could agree on Wilson as their candidate.

from 1890 to 1902 he served as professor of jurisprudence and political economy at Princeton. In 1902, he became president of the university. Eight years later, he was governor of New Jersey, where he led a campaign to reform election procedures, abolish corrupt practices, and strengthen railroad regulation.

Wilson's rise was rapid, and he knew relatively little about national issues and personalities. But he learned fast, and in some ways the lack of experience served him well. He had few political debts to repay, and he brought fresh perspectives to older issues. Ideas intrigued Wilson; details bored him. Although he was outgoing at times, he could also be cold and aloof, and aides soon learned that he preferred loyalty and flattery to candid criticism.

Prone to self-righteousness, Wilson often turned differences of opinion into bitter personal quarrels. Like Roosevelt, he believed in strong presidential leadership. A scholar of the party system, he cooperated closely with Democrats in Congress, and his legislative record placed him among the most effective presidents in terms of passing bills that he supported. Forbidding in individual conversation, Wilson could move crowds with graceful oratory. Unlike Taft, and to a greater degree than Roosevelt, he could inspire.

His inaugural address was eloquent. "The Nation," he said, "has been deeply stirred, stirred by a solemn passion, stirred by the knowledge of wrong, of ideals lost, of government too often debauched and made an instrument of evil. The feelings with which we face this new age of right and opportunity sweep across our heartstrings like some air out of God's own presence."

THE NEW FREEDOM IN ACTION

On the day of his inauguration, Wilson called Congress into special session to lower the tariff. When the session opened on April 8, 1913, Wilson himself was there, the first president since John Adams in 1801 to appear personally before Congress. In forceful language, he urged Congress to reduce tariff rates.

As the bill moved through Congress, Wilson showed exceptional skill. He worked closely with congressional leaders, and when lobbyists threatened the bill in the Senate, he appealed for popular support. The result was a triumph for Wilson and the Democratic party. The Underwood Tariff Act, passed in 1913, lowered rates about 15 percent and removed duties from sugar, wool, and several other consumer goods.

To make up for lost revenue, the act also levied a modest graduated income tax, authorized under the just ratified Sixteenth Amendment. Marking a significant shift in the American tax structure, it imposed a 1 percent tax on individuals and corporations earning more than $4,000 annually and an additional 1 percent tax on incomes more than $20,000. Above all, the act reflected a new unity within the Democratic party, which had worked together to pass a difficult tariff law.

Encouraged by his success, Wilson decided to keep Congress in session through the hot Washington summer. Now he focused on banking reform, and the result in December 1913 was the Federal Reserve Act, the most important domestic law of his administration.

Meant to provide the United States with a sound yet flexible currency, the act established the country's first efficient banking system since Andrew Jackson killed the second Bank of the United States in 1832. It created twelve regional banks, each to serve the banks of its district. The regional banks answered to a Federal Reserve Board, appointed by the president, which governed the nationwide system.

A compromise law, the act blended public and private control of the banking system. Private bankers owned the federal reserve banks but answered to the presidentially appointed Federal Reserve Board. The reserve banks were authorized to issue currency, and through the discount rate—the interest rate at which they loaned money to member banks—they could raise or lower the amount of money in circulation. Monetary affairs no longer depended solely on the price of gold. Within a year, nearly half the nation's banking resources were in the Federal Reserve System.

The Clayton Antitrust Act (1914) completed Wilson's initial legislative program. Like previous antitrust measures, it reflected confusion over how to discipline a growing economy without putting a brake on output. In part it was a response to the revelations of the Pujo Committee of the House, publicized by Brandeis in a disquieting series of articles, "Other People's Money." In its investigation of Wall Street, the committee discovered a pyramid of money and power capped by the Morgan-Rockefeller empire that, through "interlocking directorates," controlled companies worth $22 billion, more than one-tenth of the national wealth.

The Clayton Act outlawed such directorates and prohibited unfair trade practices. It forbade pricing policies that created monopoly, and it made corporate officers personally responsible for antitrust violations. Delighting Samuel Gompers and the labor movement, the act declared that unions were not conspiracies in restraint of trade, outlawed the use of injunctions in labor disputes unless necessary to protect property, and approved lawful strikes and picketing. To Gompers's dismay, the courts continued to rule against union activity.

A related law established a powerful Federal Trade Commission to oversee business methods. Composed of five members, the commission could demand special and annual reports, investigate complaints, and order corporate compliance, subject to court review. At first, Wilson opposed the commission concept, which was an approach more suitable to Roosevelt's New Nationalism, but he changed his mind and, along with Brandeis, called it the cornerstone of his antitrust plan. To reassure business leaders, he appointed a number of conservatives to the new commission and to the Federal Reserve Board.

In November 1914, Wilson proudly announced the completion of his New Freedom program. Tariff, banking, and antitrust laws promised a brighter future, he said, and it was now "a time of healing because a time of just dealing." Many progressives were aghast. That Wilson could think society's ills were so easily cured, the *New Republic* said, "casts suspicion either upon his own sincerity or upon his grasp of the realities of modern social and industrial life."

WILSON MOVES TOWARD THE NEW NATIONALISM

Distracted by the start of war in Europe, Wilson gave less attention to domestic issues for more than a year. When he returned to concern with reform, he adopted more and more of Roosevelt's New Nationalism and blended it with the New Freedom to set it off from his earlier policies.

One of Wilson's problems was the Congress. To his dismay, the Republicans gained substantially in the 1914 elections. Reducing the Democratic majority in the House, they swept key industrial and farm states. At the same time, a recession struck the economy, which had been hurt by the outbreak of the European war in August 1914. Some business leaders blamed the tariff and other New Freedom laws. On the defensive, Wilson soothed business sentiment and invited bankers and industrialists to the White House. He allowed companies fearful of antitrust actions to seek advice from the Justice Department.

Preoccupied with such problems, Wilson blocked significant action in Congress through most of 1915. He refused to support a bill providing minimum wages for women workers, sidetracked a child labor bill on the ground that it was unconstitutional, and opposed a bill to establish long-term credits for farmers. He also refused to endorse woman suffrage, arguing that the right to vote was a state matter, not a federal one.

Wilson's record on race disappointed African Americans and many progressives. He had appealed to African American voters during the 1912 election, and a number of African American leaders campaigned for him. Soon after the inauguration, Oswald Garrison Villard, a leader of the NAACP, proposed a National Race Commission to study the problem of race relations. Initially sympathetic, Wilson rejected the idea because he feared he might lose southern Democratic votes in Congress. A Virginian himself, he appointed many Southerners to high office, and for the first time since the Civil War, southern views on race dominated the nation's capital.

At one of Wilson's first cabinet meetings, the postmaster general proposed the segregation of all African Americans in the federal service. No one dissented, including Wilson. Several government bureaus promptly began to segregate workers in offices, shops, rest rooms, and restaurants. Employees who objected were fired. African American leaders protested, and they were joined by progressive leaders and clergymen. Surprised at the protest, Wilson backed quietly away from the policy, although he continued to insist that segregation benefited African Americans.

As the year 1916 began, Wilson made a dramatic switch in focus and again pushed for substantial reforms. The result was a virtual river of reform laws, which was significant because it began the second, more national-minded phase of the New Freedom. With scarcely a glance over his shoulder, Wilson embraced important portions of Roosevelt's New Nationalism campaign.

In part, he was motivated by the approaching presidential election. A minority president, Wilson owed his victory in 1912 to the split in the Republican party, now almost healed. Roosevelt was moving back into Republican ranks, and there were issues connected with the war in Europe that he might use against Wilson. Moreover, many progressives were voicing disappointment with Wilson's limited reforms and his failure to support more advanced reform legislation on matters such as farm credits, child labor, and woman suffrage.

Moving quickly to patch up the problem, Wilson named Brandeis to the Supreme Court in January 1916. Popular among progressives, Brandeis was also the first person of Jewish faith to serve on the Court. When conservatives in the Senate tried to defeat the nomination, Wilson stood firm and won, earning further praise from progressives, Jews, and others.

Wilson was already popular within the labor movement. Going beyond Roosevelt's policies, which had sought a balance between business and labor, he defended union recognition and collective bargaining. In 1913, he appointed William B. Wilson, a respected leader of the United Mine Workers, as the first head of the Labor Department, and he strengthened the department's Division of Conciliation. In 1914, in Ludlow, Colorado, state militia and mine guards fired machine guns into a tent colony of coal strikers, killing twenty-one men, women, and children. Outraged, Wilson stepped in and used federal troops to end the violence while negotiations to end the strike went on.

Miners in Ludlow, Colorado, went on strike in September 1913 for better working conditions and union recognition. Expecting eviction from company housing, they built a tent colony near the company town. The company, John D. Rockefeller's Colorado Fuel and Iron Company, hired guards to break the strike. On April 20, 1914, state troops and guards sprayed the tents with gunfire, then soaked the tents with kerosene and set the colony afire. Twenty-one of the colonists died, including eleven children.

In August 1916, a threatened railroad strike again revealed Wilson's sympathies with labor. Like Roosevelt, he invited the two sides to the White House, where he urged the railroad companies to grant an eight-hour day and labor leaders to abandon the demand for overtime pay. Labor leaders accepted the proposal; railroad leaders did not. "I pray God to forgive you, I never can," Wilson said as he left the room. Soon he signed the Adamson Act (1916) that imposed the eight-hour day on interstate railways and established a federal commission to study the railroad problem. Ending the threat of a strike, the act marked a milestone in the expansion of the federal government's authority to regulate industry.

With Wilson leading the way, the flow of reform legislation continued until the election. The Federal Workmen's Compensation Act established workers' compensation for government employees. The Keating-Owen Act, the first federal child labor law, prohibited the shipment in interstate commerce of products manufactured by children under the age of 14. It too expanded the authority of the federal government, although it was soon struck down by the Supreme Court.

In September, Wilson signed the Tariff Commission Act creating an expert commission to recommend tariff rates. The same month, the Revenue Act of 1916 boosted income taxes and furthered tax reform. Four thousand members of the National American Woman Suffrage Association cheered when Wilson finally came out in support of woman suffrage. Two weeks later he endorsed the eight-hour day for all the nation's workers.

The 1916 presidential election was close, but Wilson won it on the issues of peace and progressivism. By the end of 1916, he and the Democratic party had enacted most of the important parts of Roosevelt's Progressive party platform of 1912. To do it, Wilson abandoned portions of the New Freedom and accepted much of the New Nationalism, including greater federal power and commissions governing trade and tariffs. In mixing the two programs, he blended some of the competing doctrines of the Progressive Era, established the primacy of the federal government, and foreshadowed the pragmatic outlook of Franklin D. Roosevelt's New Deal of the 1930s.

THE FRUITS OF PROGRESSIVISM

The election of 1916 showed how deeply progressivism had reached into American society. "We have in four years," Wilson said that fall, "come very near to carrying out the platform of the Progressive party as well as our own; for we are also progressives." In retrospect, however, 1916 also marked the beginning of progressivism's decline. At most, the years of progressive reform lasted from the 1890s to 1921, and in large measure they were compressed into a single decade between 1906 and American entry into World War I in 1917. Many problems the progressives addressed but did not solve; and some important ones, such as race, they did not even tackle. Yet their regulatory commissions, direct primaries, city improvements, and child labor laws marked an era of important and measured reform.

The institution of the presidency expanded. From the White House radiated executive departments that guided a host of activities. Independent commissions, operating within flexible laws, supplemented executive authority.

These developments owed a great deal to both Roosevelt and Wilson. To manage a complex society, Roosevelt developed a simple formula: expert advice; growth-minded policies; a balancing of business, labor, and other interests; the use of publicity to gather support; and stern but often permissive oversight of the economy. Roosevelt strengthened the executive office, and he called on the newer group of professional, educated, public-minded citizens to help him. "I believe in a strong executive," he said; "I believe in power."

At first, Wilson had different ideas, wanting to dismantle much of Roosevelt's governing apparatus. But driven by outside forces and changes in his own thinking, Wilson soon moved in directions similar to those Roosevelt had championed. Starting out to disperse power, he eventually consolidated it.

Through such movements, government at all levels accepted responsibility for the welfare of various elements in the social order. A reform-minded and bureaucratic society took shape, in which men and women, labor and capital, political parties and social classes competed for shares in the expansive framework of twentieth-century life. But there were limits to reform. As both Roosevelt and Wilson found, the new government agencies, understaffed and underfinanced, depended on the responsiveness of those they sought to regulate.

Soon there was a far darker cloud on the horizon. The spirit of progressivism rested on a belief in human potential, peace, and progress. After Napoleon's defeat in 1815, a century of peace began in western Europe, and as the decades passed, war seemed a dying institution. It was not to be. In 1914, the most devastating of wars broke out in Europe, and within three years, Americans were fighting on the battlefields of France.

CHRONOLOGY

1894	National Municipal League formed to work for reform in cities
1900	Galveston, Texas, is first city to try commission form of government
1901	Theodore Roosevelt becomes president
	Robert M. La Follette elected reform governor of Wisconsin
	Doctors reorganize the American Medical Association
	Socialist party of America organized
1902	Roosevelt sues Northern Securities Company for violation of Antitrust Act
	Coal miners in northeastern Pennsylvania strike
	Maryland is first state to pass workers' compensation law
	Oregon adopts the initiative and referendum
1904	Roosevelt elected president
1906	Hepburn Act strengthens Interstate Commerce Commission (ICC)
	Upton Sinclair attacks meatpacking industry in *The Jungle*
	Congress passes Meat Inspection Act and Pure Food and Drug Act
1908	Taft elected president
	Supreme Court upholds Oregon law limiting working hours for women in *Muller* v. *Oregon*
1909	Payne-Aldrich Tariff Act divides Republican party
1910	Mann-Elkins Act passed to regulate railroads
	Taft fires Gifford Pinchot, head of U.S. Forest Service
	Democrats sweep midterm elections
1912	Progressive party formed; nominates Roosevelt for president
	Woodrow Wilson elected president
1913	Underwood Tariff Act lowers rates
	Federal Reserve Act reforms U.S. banking system
	Sixteenth Amendment authorizes Congress to collect taxes on incomes
1914	Clayton Act strengthens antitrust legislation
1916	Wilson wins reelection
1918	Supreme Court strikes down federal law limiting child labor in *Hammer* v. *Dagenhart*
1920	Nineteenth Amendment gives women the right to vote

24

THE NATION AT WAR

On the morning of May 1, 1915, the German government took out an advertisement in the *New York World* warning Americans and other voyagers against setting sail for England: "Travellers intending to embark on the Atlantic voyage are reminded that a state of war exists between Germany and her allies and Great Britain and her allies"; anyone sailing "in the war zone on ships of Great Britain or her allies do so at their own risk." At 12:30 that afternoon, the British steamship *Lusitania* set sail from New York to Liverpool. Secretly, it carried a load of ammunition as well as passengers.

The steamer was two hours late in leaving, but it held several speed records and could easily make up the time. Six days later, back on schedule, it reached the coast of Ireland. German U-boats were known to patrol the dangerous waters. When the war began in 1914, Great Britain imposed a naval blockade of Germany. In return, Germany in February 1915 declared the area around the British Isles a war zone; all enemy vessels, armed or unarmed, were at risk. Germany had only a handful of U-boats, but the submarines were a new and frightening weapon. On behalf of the United States, President Woodrow Wilson protested the German action, and on February 10, he warned Germany of its "strict accountability" for any American losses resulting from U-boat attacks.

Off Ireland, the passengers lounged on the deck of the *Lusitania*. As if it were peacetime, the ship sailed straight ahead, with no zigzag maneuvers to throw off pursuit. But the submarine U-20 was there, and its commander, seeing a large ship, fired a single torpedo. Seconds after it hit, a boiler exploded and blew a hole in the *Lusitania*'s side. The ship listed immediately, hindering the launching of lifeboats, and in eighteen minutes it sank. Nearly 1200 people died, including 128 Americans. As the ship's bow lifted and went under, the U-20 commander for the first time read the name: *Lusitania*.

The sinking, the worst since the *Titanic* went down with 1500 people in 1912, horrified Americans. Theodore Roosevelt called it "an act of piracy" and demanded war. Most Americans, however, wanted to stay out of war; like

900 Die as Lusitania Goes to Bottom; 400 Americans on Board Torpedoed Ship; Washington Stirred as When Maine Sank

With the sinking of the Lusitania, *the American people learned firsthand of the horrors of total war. President Wilson's decision to protest the incident through diplomacy kept the United States out of the war—but only temporarily.*

Wilson, they hoped negotiations could solve the problem. "There is such a thing," Wilson said a few days after the sinking, "as a man being too proud to fight. There is such a thing as a nation being so right that it does not need to convince others by force."

In a series of diplomatic notes, Wilson demanded a change in German policy. The first *Lusitania* note (May 13, 1915) called on Germany to abandon unrestricted submarine warfare, disavow the sinking, and compensate for lost American lives. Germany sent an evasive reply, and Wilson drafted a second *Lusitania* note (June 9) insisting on specific pledges. Fearful the demand would lead to war, Secretary of State William Jennings Bryan resigned rather than sign the note. Wilson sent it anyway and followed with a third note (July 21)—almost an ultimatum—warning Germany that the United States would view similar sinkings as "deliberately unfriendly."

Unbeknownst to Wilson, Germany had already ordered U-boat commanders not to sink passenger liners without warning. In August 1915, a U-boat mistakenly torpedoed the British liner *Arabic,* killing two Americans. Wilson protested, and Germany, eager to keep the United States out of the war, backed down. The *Arabic* pledge (September 1) promised that U-boats would stop and warn liners, unless they tried to resist or escape. Germany also apologized for American deaths on the *Arabic,* and for the rest of 1915, U-boats hunted freighters, not passenger liners.

Although Wilson's diplomacy had achieved his immediate goal, the *Lusitania* and *Arabic* crises contained the elements that led to war. Trade and travel tied the world together, and Americans no longer hid behind safe ocean barriers. New weapons, such as the submarine, strained old rules of international law. But while Americans sifted the conflicting claims of Great Britain and Germany, they hoped for peace. A generation of progressives, inspired with confidence in human progress, did not easily accept war.

Wilson also hated war, but he found himself caught up in a worldwide crisis that demanded the best in American will and diplomacy. In the end, diplomacy failed, and in April 1917, the United States entered a war that changed the nation's history. Building on several major trends in American foreign policy since the 1890s, the years around World War I firmly established the United States as a world power, confirmed the country's dominance in Latin America, and ended with a war with Germany and her allies that had far-reaching results, including establishing the United States as one of the world's foremost economic powers.

A NEW WORLD POWER

As they had in the late nineteenth century, Americans after 1900 continued to pay relatively little attention to foreign affairs. Newspapers and magazines ran stories every day about events abroad, but people paid closer attention to what was going on at home. For Americans at the time, foreign policy was something to be left to the president in office, an attitude that suited the interests of Roosevelt, Taft, and Wilson.

American foreign policy from 1901 to 1920 was aggressive and nationalistic. During these years, the United States intervened in Europe, the Far East, and Latin America. It dominated the Caribbean.

In 1898, the United States left the peace table possessing the Philippines, Puerto Rico, and Guam. Holding distant possessions required a colonial policy; it also required a change in foreign policy, reflecting an outward approach. From the Caribbean to the Pacific, policymakers paid attention to issues and countries they had earlier ignored. Like other nations in these years, the United States built a large navy, protected its colonial empire, and became increasingly involved in international affairs.

The nation also became more and more involved in economic ventures abroad. Turning out goods from textiles to steel, mass production industries sold products overseas, and financiers invested in Asia, Africa, Latin America, and Europe. During the years between the Spanish-American War and World War I, investments abroad rose from $445 million to $2.5 billion. While investments and trade never wholly dictated American foreign policy, they fostered greater involvement in foreign lands.

"I Took the Canal Zone"

Convinced the United States should take a more active international role, Theodore Roosevelt spent his presidency preparing the nation for world power. Working with Secretary of War Elihu Root, he modernized the army, using lessons learned from the war with Spain. Determined to end dependence on the British fleet, Roosevelt doubled the strength of the navy during his term in office.

Stretching his authority to the limits, Roosevelt took steps to consolidate the country's new position in the Caribbean and Central America. European powers, which had long resisted American initiatives there, now accepted

American supremacy. Preoccupied with problems in Europe and Africa, Great Britain agreed to U.S. plans for an Isthmian canal in Central America and withdrew much of its military force from the area.

Roosevelt wanted a canal to link the Atlantic and Pacific oceans across the isthmus connecting North and South America. Secretary of State John Hay negotiated with Britain the Hay-Pauncefote Treaty of 1901 that permitted the United States to construct and control an isthmian canal, providing it would be free and open to ships of all nations.

Delighted, Roosevelt began selecting the route. One route, fifty miles long, wandered through the rough, swampy terrain of the Panama region of Colombia. To the northwest, another route ran through mountainous Nicaragua. Although two hundred miles in length, it followed natural waterways, a factor that would make construction easier.

An Isthmian Canal Commission investigated both routes in 1899 and recommended the shorter route through Panama. Roosevelt backed the idea, and he authorized Hay to negotiate an agreement with the Colombian chargé d'affaires, Thomas Herrán. The Hay-Herrán Convention (1903) gave the United States a 99-year lease, with option for renewal, on a canal zone 6 miles in width. In exchange, the United States agreed to pay Colombia a onetime fee of $10 million and an annual rental of $250,000.

To Roosevelt's dismay, the Colombian Senate rejected the treaty, in part because it infringed on Colombian sovereignty. The Colombians also wanted more money. Roosevelt considered seizing Panama, then hinted he would welcome a Panamanian revolt from Colombia. In November 1903, the Panamanians took the hint, and Roosevelt moved quickly to support them. Sending the cruiser *Nashville* to prevent Colombian troops from putting down the revolt, he promptly recognized the new Republic of Panama.

Two weeks later, the Hay-Bunau-Varilla Treaty with Panama granted the United States control of a canal zone 10 miles wide across the Isthmus of Panama. In return, the United States guaranteed the independence of Panama and agreed to pay the same fees offered Colombia. On August 15, 1914, the first ocean steamer sailed through the completed canal, which had cost $375 million to build.

Roosevelt's actions angered many Latin Americans. Trying to soothe feelings, Wilson agreed in 1914 to pay Colombia $25 million in cash, give it preferential treatment in using the canal, and express "sincere regret" over American actions. Roosevelt was furious, and his friends in the Senate blocked the agreement. Colombian-American relations remained strained until 1921, when the two countries signed a treaty that included Wilson's first two provisions but omitted the apology.

For his part, Roosevelt took great pride in the canal, calling it "by far the most important action in foreign affairs." Defending his methods, he said in 1911, "If I had followed traditional conservative methods, I would have submitted a dignified state paper of 200 pages to Congress and the debate on it would have been going on yet; but I took the Canal Zone and let Congress debate; and while the debate goes on the Canal does also."

THE ROOSEVELT COROLLARY

With interests in Puerto Rico, Cuba, and the canal, the United States developed a Caribbean policy to ensure its dominance in the region. It established protectorates over some countries and subsidized others to keep them dependent.

From 1903 to 1920, the United States intervened often in Latin America to protect the canal, promote regional stability, and exclude foreign influence. One problem worrying American policymakers was the scale of Latin American debts to European powers. Many countries in the Western Hemisphere owed money to European governments and banks, and often these nations were poor, prone to revolution, and unable to pay. The situation invited European intervention. In 1902, Venezuela defaulted on debts; England, Germany, and Italy sent Venezuela an ultimatum and blockaded its ports. American pressure forced a settlement of the issue, but the general problem remained.

Roosevelt was concerned about it, and in 1904, when the Dominican Republic defaulted on its debts, he was ready with a major announcement. Known as the Roosevelt Corollary of the Monroe Doctrine, the policy warned Latin American nations to keep their affairs in order or face American intervention.

Applying the new policy immediately, Roosevelt in 1905 took charge of the Dominican Republic's revenue system. American officials collected customs and saw to the payment of debt. Within two years, Roosevelt also established protectorates in Cuba and Panama. Continued by Taft, Wilson, and other presidents,

A cartoon from Judge *titled "The World's Constable." The Roosevelt Corollary claimed the right of the United States to exercise "an international police power," enforced by what many referred to as a "big stick" diplomacy.*

the Roosevelt Corollary guided American policy in Latin America until the 1930s, when Franklin D. Roosevelt's Good Neighbor policy replaced it.

VENTURES IN THE FAR EAST

The Open Door policy toward China and possession of the Philippine Islands shaped American actions in the Far East. Roosevelt wanted to balance Russian and Japanese power, and he was not unhappy at first when war broke out between them in 1904. As Japan won victory after victory, however, Roosevelt grew worried. In August 1905, he convened a peace conference at Portsmouth, New Hampshire. The conference ended the war, but Japan emerged as the dominant force in the Far East. Adjusting policy, Roosevelt sent Secretary of War Taft to Tokyo to negotiate the Taft-Katsura Agreement (1905), which recognized Japan's dominance over Korea in return for its promise not to invade the Philippines. Giving Japan a free hand in Korea violated the Open Door policy, but Roosevelt argued that he had little choice.

In case Japan viewed his policy as a sign of weakness, Roosevelt sent sixteen battleships of the new American fleet around the world, including a stop in Tokyo in October 1908. European naval experts felt certain Japan would attack the fleet, but the Japanese welcomed it. For the moment, Japanese-American relations improved, and in 1908 the two nations, in an exchange of diplomatic notes, reached the comprehensive Root-Takahira Agreement in which they promised to maintain the status quo in the Pacific, uphold the Open Door, and support Chinese independence.

TAFT AND DOLLAR DIPLOMACY

In foreign as well as domestic affairs, President Taft tried to continue Roosevelt's policies. For secretary of state he chose Philander C. Knox, Roosevelt's attorney general, and together they pursued a policy of "dollar diplomacy" to promote American financial and business interests abroad. The policy had profit-seeking motives, but it also aimed to substitute economic ties for military alliances with the idea of increasing American influence and bringing lasting peace.

Intent, like Roosevelt, on supremacy in the Caribbean, Taft worked to replace European loans with American ones, thereby reducing the danger of outside meddling. In 1909, he asked American bankers to assume the Honduran debt in order to fend off English bondholders, and in 1911 he helped Nicaragua secure a large loan in return for American control of Nicaragua's National Bank. When Nicaraguans revolted against the agreement, Taft sent marines to put them down.

In the Far East, Knox worked closely with Willard Straight, an agent of American bankers, who argued that dollar diplomacy was the financial arm of the Open Door. Straight had close ties to Edward H. Harriman, the railroad magnate, who wanted to build railroads in Manchuria in northern China. Roosevelt had tacitly promised Japan he would keep American investors out of the area, and Knox's plan reversed the policy. Trying to organize an international syndicate to loan China money to purchase the Manchurian railroads,

Knox approached England, Japan, and Russia. In January 1910, all three turned him down.

The outcome was a blow to American policy and prestige in Asia. Russia and Japan found reasons to cooperate with each other and staked out spheres of influence in violation of the Open Door. Japan resented Taft's initiatives in Manchuria, and China's distrust of the United States deepened. Instead of cultivating friendship, as Roosevelt had envisioned, Taft had started an intense rivalry with Japan for commercial advantage in China.

FOREIGN POLICY UNDER WILSON

When he took office in 1913, Woodrow Wilson knew little about foreign policy. During the 1912 campaign he mentioned foreign policy only when it affected domestic concerns. "It would be the irony of fate if my administration had to deal chiefly with foreign affairs," he said to a friend before becoming president. And so it was. During his two terms, Wilson faced crisis after crisis in foreign affairs, including the outbreak of World War I.

The idealistic Wilson believed in a principled, ethical world in which militarism, colonialism, and war were brought under control. He stressed moral purposes over material interests and said during one crisis, "The force of America is the force of moral principle." Rejecting the policy of dollar diplomacy, Wilson initially chose a course of moral diplomacy, designed to bring right to the world, preserve peace, and extend to other peoples the blessings of democracy.

CONDUCTING MORAL DIPLOMACY

William Jennings Bryan, whom Wilson appointed as secretary of state, was also an amateur in foreign relations. He was a fervent pacifist, and like Wilson, he believed in the American duty to "help" less favored nations.

In 1913 and 1914, he embarked on an idealistic campaign to negotiate treaties of arbitration throughout the world. Known as "cooling-off" treaties, they provided for submitting all international disputes to permanent commissions of investigation. Neither party could declare war or increase armaments until the investigation ended, usually within one year. The idea drew on the era's confidence in commissions and the sense that human reason, given time for emotions to fade, could settle problems without war. Bryan negotiated cooling-off treaties with thirty nations, including Great Britain, France, and Italy. Germany refused to sign one. Based on a generous idea, the treaties were naive, and they did not work.

Wilson and Bryan promised a dramatic new approach in Latin America, concerned not with the "pursuit of material interest" but with "human rights" and "national integrity." Signaling the change, in 1913 they negotiated the treaty with Colombia apologizing for Roosevelt's Panamanian policy. Yet in the end, Wilson, distracted by other problems and impatient with the results of his idealistic approach, continued the Roosevelt-Taft policies. He defended the Monroe

Doctrine, gave unspoken support to the Roosevelt Corollary, and intervened in Latin America more than had either Roosevelt or Taft.

In 1914, Wilson negotiated a treaty with Nicaragua to grant the United States exclusive rights to build a canal and lease sites for naval bases. This treaty made Nicaragua an American satellite. In 1915, he sent marines into Haiti to quell a revolution; they stayed until 1934. In 1916, he occupied the Dominican Republic, establishing a protectorate that lasted until 1924. By 1917, American troops "protected" Nicaragua, Haiti, the Dominican Republic, and Cuba—four nations that were U.S. dependencies in all but name.

TROUBLES ACROSS THE BORDER

Wilson's moral diplomacy encountered one of its greatest challenges across the border in Mexico. Porfirio Díaz, president of Mexico for thirty-seven years, was overthrown in 1911, and a liberal reformer, Francisco I. Madero, succeeded him. But Madero could not keep order in the troubled country, and opponents of his reforms undermined him. With support from wealthy landowners, the army, and the Catholic Church, General Victoriano Huerta ousted Madero in 1913, threw him in jail, and arranged his murder. Most European nations immediately recognized Huerta, but Wilson, calling him a "butcher," refused to do so. Instead, he announced a new policy toward revolutionary regimes in Latin America. To win American recognition, they must not only exercise power but reflect "a just government based upon law, not upon arbitrary or irregular force."

On that basis, Wilson withheld recognition from Huerta and maneuvered to oust him. Early in 1914, he stationed naval units off Mexico's ports to cut off arms shipments to the Huerta regime. The action produced trouble. On April 9, 1914, several American sailors, who had gone ashore in Tampico to purchase supplies, were arrested. They were promptly released, but the American admiral demanded an apology and a 21-gun salute to the American flag. Huerta agreed— if the Americans also saluted the Mexican flag.

Wilson asked Congress for authority to use military force if needed; then, just as Congress acted, he learned that a German ship was landing arms at Veracruz on Mexico's eastern coast. With Wilson's approval, American warships shelled the harbor, and marines went ashore. Against heavy resistance, they took the city. Outraged, Mexicans of all factions denounced the invasion, and for a time the two countries hovered on the edge of war.

Retreating hastily, Wilson explained that he desired only to help Mexico. Argentina, Brazil, and Chile came to his aid with an offer to mediate the dispute, and tensions eased. In July 1914, weakened by an armed rebellion, Huerta resigned. Wilson recognized the new government, headed by Venustiano Carranza, an associate of Madero. Early in 1916, Francisco ("Pancho") Villa, one of Carranza's generals, revolted. Hoping to goad the United States into an action that would help him seize power, he raided border towns, injuring American civilians.

Stationing militia along the border, Wilson ordered General John J. Pershing on a punitive expedition to seize Villa in Mexico. Pershing led six thousand troops deep into Mexican territory. At first, Carranza agreed to the drive, but as the Americans pushed farther and farther into his country, he changed his mind. As the wily Villa eluded Pershing, Carranza protested bitterly, and Wilson, worried about events in Europe, ordered Pershing home.

Wilson's policy had laudable goals; he wanted to help the Mexicans achieve political and agrarian reform. But his motives and methods were condescending. Wilson tried to impose gradual progressive reform on a society sharply divided along class and other lines. With little forethought, he interfered in the affairs of another country, and in doing so he revealed the themes—moralism, combined with pragmatic self-interest and a desire for peace—that also shaped his policies in Europe.

TOWARD WAR

In May 1914, Colonel Edward M. House, Wilson's close friend and adviser, sailed to Europe on a fact-finding mission. Tensions there were rising. "The situation is extraordinary," he reported to Wilson. ". . . There is too much hatred, too many jealousies."

In Germany, the ambitious Kaiser Wilhelm II coveted a world empire to match those of Britain and France. Germany had military treaties with Turkey and Austria-Hungary, a sprawling central European country of many nationalities. Linked in another alliance, England, France, and Russia agreed to aid each other in case of attack.

On June 28, 1914, a Bosnian assassin linked to Serbia murdered Archduke Franz Ferdinand, heir to the Austro-Hungarian throne. Within weeks, Germany, Turkey, and Austria-Hungary (the Central Powers) were at war with England, France, and Russia (the Allied Powers). Americans were shocked at the events. Wilson immediately proclaimed neutrality and asked Americans to remain "impartial in thought as well as in action."

The war, he said, was one "with which we have nothing to do, whose causes cannot touch us." In private, Wilson was stunned. A man who loved peace, he had long admired the British parliamentary system, and he respected the leaders of the British Liberal party, who supported social programs akin to his own. "Everything I love most in the world," he said, "is at stake."

THE NEUTRALITY POLICY

In general, Americans accepted neutrality. They saw no need to enter the conflict, especially after the Allies in September 1914 halted the first German drive toward Paris. America resisted involvement in other countries' problems, with the notable exception of Latin America, and had a tradition of freedom from foreign entanglements.

Many of the nation's large number of progressives saw additional reasons to resist. War, they thought, violated the very spirit of progressive reform. Why demand safer factories in which people could work and then kill them by the millions in war? To many progressives, moreover, England represented international finance, an institution they detested. Germany, on the other hand, had pioneered some of their favorite social reforms. Above all, progressives were sure that war would end reform. It consumed money and attention; it inflamed emotions.

As a result, Jane Addams, Florence Kelley, Frederic C. Howe, Lillian Wald, and other progressives fought to keep the United States out of war. In late 1915, they formed the American Union Against Militarism, to throw, they said, "a monkey wrench into the machinery" of war. In 1915, Addams and Wald helped organize the League to Limit Armament, and shortly thereafter, Addams and Carrie Chapman Catt formed the Woman's Peace Party to organize women against the war.

The war's outbreak also tugged at the emotions of millions of immigrant Americans. At the deepest level, a majority in the country, bound by common language and institutions, sympathized with the Allies and blamed Germany for the war. Like Wilson, many Americans admired English literature, customs, and law; they remembered Lafayette and the times when France had helped the United States in its early years. Germany, on the other hand, seemed arrogant and militaristic. When the war began, it invaded Belgium to strike at France and violated a treaty that the German chancellor called "just a scrap of paper."

Both sides sought to sway American opinion, and fierce propaganda campaigns flourished. German propaganda tended to stress strength and will; Allied propaganda called on historical ties and took advantage of German atrocities, both real and alleged. In the end, the propaganda probably made little difference. Ties of heritage and the course of the war, not propaganda, decided the American position. At the outset, no matter which side they cheered for, Americans of all persuasions preferred simply to remain at peace.

FREEDOM OF THE SEAS

The demands of trade tested American neutrality and confronted Wilson with difficult choices. Under international law, neutral countries were permitted to trade in nonmilitary goods with all belligerent countries. But Great Britain controlled the seas, and it intended to cut off shipments of war materials to the Central Powers.

As soon as war broke out, Britain blockaded German ports and limited the goods Americans could sell to Germany. American ships had to carry cargoes to neutral ports from which, after examination, they could be carried to Germany. As time passed, Britain stepped up the economic sanctions by forbidding the shipment to Germany of all foodstuffs and most raw materials, seizing and censoring mail, and "blacklisting" American firms that dealt directly with the Central Powers.

Again and again, Wilson protested against such infringements on neutral rights. Sometimes Britain complied, sometimes not, and Wilson often grew angry. But needing American support and supplies, Britain pursued a careful strategy to disrupt German-American trade without disrupting Anglo-American relations. When necessary, it promised to reimburse American businesses after the war's end.

Other than the German U-boats, there were no constraints on trade with the Allies, and a flood of Allied war orders fueled the American economy. To finance the purchases, the Allies turned to American bankers for loans. By 1917, loans to Allied governments exceeded $2 billion; loans to Germany came to only $27 million.

In a development that influenced Wilson's policy, the war produced the greatest economic boom in the nation's history. Loans and trade drew the United States ever closer to the Allied cause. And even though Wilson often protested English maritime policy, the protests involved American goods and money, whereas Germany's submarine policy threatened American lives.

THE U-BOAT THREAT

A relatively new weapon, the *Unterseeboot,* or submarine, strained the guidelines of international law. Traditional law required a submarine to surface, warn the target to stop, send a boarding party to check papers and cargo, then allow time for passengers and crew to board lifeboats before sinking the vessel. Flimsy and slow, submarines could ill afford to surface while the prey radioed for help. If they did surface, they might be rammed or blown up by deck guns.

When Germany announced the submarine campaign in February 1915, Wilson protested sharply, calling the sinking of merchant ships without checking cargo "a wanton act." The Germans promised not to sink American ships—an agreement that lasted until 1917—and thereafter the issue became the right of Americans to sail on the ships of belligerent nations. In March, an American citizen aboard the British liner *Falaba* perished when the ship was torpedoed off the Irish coast. Bryan urged Wilson to forbid Americans to travel in the war zones, but the president, determined to stand by the principles of international law, refused.

Wilson reacted more harshly in May and August of 1915 when U-boats sank the *Lusitania* and the *Arabic.* He demanded that the Germans protect passenger vessels and pay for American losses. At odds with Wilson's understanding of neutrality, Bryan resigned as secretary of state and was replaced by Robert Lansing, a lawyer and counselor in the State Department. Lansing brought a very different spirit to the job. He favored the Allies and believed that democracy was threatened in a world dominated by Germany. He urged strong stands against German violations of American neutrality.

In February 1916, Germany declared unrestricted submarine warfare against all armed ships. Lansing protested and told Germany it would be held strictly accountable for American losses. A month later, a U-boat torpedoed the unarmed French channel steamer *Sussex* without warning, injuring several Americans. Arguing that the sinking violated the *Arabic* pledge, Lansing urged Wilson to break relations with Germany. Wilson rejected the advice, but on April 18 he sent an ultimatum to Germany, stating that unless the Germans immediately called off attacks on cargo and passenger ships, the United States would sever relations.

The kaiser, convinced he did not yet have enough submarines to risk war, yielded. In the *Sussex* pledge of May 4, 1916, he agreed to Wilson's demands and promised to shoot on sight only ships of the enemy's navy.

A new and terrifying weapon of the war was the German U-boat, which attacked silently and without warning.

The *Sussex* pledge marked the beginning of a short period of friendly relations between Germany and the United States. The agreement applied not only to passenger liners but to all merchant ships, belligerent or not. There was one problem: Wilson had taken such a strong position that if Germany renewed submarine warfare on merchant shipping, war was likely. Most Americans, however, viewed the agreement as a diplomatic stroke for peace by Wilson, and the issues of peace and preparedness dominated the presidential election of 1916.

"HE KEPT US OUT OF WAR"

The "preparedness" issue pitted antiwar groups against those who wanted to prepare for war. Bellicose as always, Teddy Roosevelt led the preparedness campaign. He called Wilson "yellow" for not pressing Germany harder and scoffed at the popular song "I Didn't Raise My Boy to Be a Soldier," which he compared to singing "I Didn't Raise My Girl to Be a Mother." Defending the military's state of readiness, Wilson refused to be stampeded just because "some amongst us are nervous and excited."

Wilson's position was attacked from both sides as preparedness advocates charged cowardice, while pacifists denounced any attempt at military readiness. The difficulty of his situation, plus the growing U-boat crisis, soon changed Wilson's mind. In mid-1915, he asked the War Department to increase military planning, and he quietly notified congressional leaders of a switch in policy.

THE ELECTION OF 1916

CANDIDATE	PARTY	POPULAR VOTE	ELECTORAL VOTE
Wilson	Democrat	9,129,606	277
Hughes	Republican	8,538,221	254
	Minor Parties	819,022	0

Later that year, Wilson approved large increases in the army and navy, a move that upset many peace-minded progressives.

For their standard-bearer in the presidential election of 1916, the Republicans nominated Charles Evans Hughes, a moderate justice of the Supreme Court. Hughes seemed to have all the qualifications for victory. A former reform governor of New York, he could lure back the Roosevelt progressives while at the same time appealing to the Republican conservatives. To woo the Roosevelt wing, Hughes called for a tougher line against Germany, thus allowing the Democrats to label him the "war" candidate.

The Democrats renominated Wilson in a convention marked by spontaneous demonstrations for peace. The campaign slogan "He kept us out of war" was repeated again and again, and just before the election, the Democrats took full-page ads in leading newspapers:

> *You Are Working*—Not Fighting!
> *Alive and Happy*—Not Cannon Fodder!
> *Wilson and Peace with Honor?*
>
>   *or*
>
> *Hughes with Roosevelt and War?*

On election night, Hughes had swept most of the East, and Wilson retired at 10 P.M. thinking he had lost. During the night, the results came in from California, New Mexico, and North Dakota; all supported Wilson—California by a mere 3773 votes. Wilson won with 9.1 million votes against 8.5 million for Hughes. Holding the Democratic South, he carried key states in the Midwest and West and took large portions of the labor and progressive vote. Women—who were then allowed to vote in presidential elections in twelve states—also voted heavily for Wilson.

THE FINAL MONTHS OF PEACE

Just before election day, Great Britain further limited neutral trade, and there were reports from Germany of a renewal of unrestricted submarine warfare. Fresh from his victory, Wilson redoubled his efforts for peace. Aware that time was running out, he hoped to start negotiations to end the bloodshed and create a peaceful postwar world.

In December 1916, he sent messages to both sides asking them to state their war aims. Should they do so, he pledged the "whole force" of the United States to end the war. The Allies refused, although they promised privately to negotiate if the German terms were reasonable. The Germans replied evasively and in January 1917 revealed their real objectives. Close to forcing Russia out of the war, Germany sensed victory and wanted territory in eastern Europe, Africa, Belgium, and France.

On January 22, in an eloquent speech before the Senate, Wilson called for a "peace without victory." Outlining his own ambitious aims, he urged respect for all nations, freedom of the seas, arms limitations, and a League of Nations to keep the peace. The speech made a great impression on many Europeans, but it was too late. The Germans had decided a few weeks before to unleash the submarines and gamble on a quick end to the war. Even as Wilson spoke, U-boats were in the Atlantic west of Ireland, preparing to attack.

On January 31, the German ambassador in Washington informed Lansing that beginning February 1, U-boats would sink on sight all ships—passenger or merchant, neutral or belligerent, armed or unarmed—in the waters around England and France. Staking everything on a last effort, the Germans calculated that if they could sink 600,000 tons of shipping a month, they could defeat England in six months. As he had pledged in 1916, Wilson broke off relations with Germany, although he still hoped for peace.

On February 25, the British government privately gave Wilson a telegram intercepted from Arthur Zimmermann, the German foreign minister, to the German

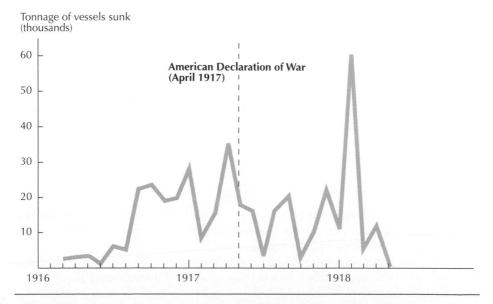

U.S. Losses to the German Submarine Campaign, 1916–1918

ambassador in Mexico. A day later, Wilson asked Congress for authority to arm merchant ships to deter U-boat attacks. When La Follette and a handful of others threatened to filibuster, Wilson divulged the contents of the Zimmermann telegram. It proposed a German alliance with Mexico in case of war with the United States, offering financial support and recovery of Mexico's "lost territory" in New Mexico, Texas, and Arizona.

Spurred by a wave of public indignation toward the Germans, the House passed Wilson's measure, but La Follette and others still blocked action in the Senate. On March 9, 1917, Wilson ordered merchant ships armed on his own authority. Three days later, he announced the arming, and on March 13, the navy instructed all vessels to fire on submarines. Between March 12 and March 21, U-boats sank five American ships, and Wilson decided to wait no longer.

He called Congress into special session and at 8:30 in the evening on April 2, 1917, asked for a declaration of war. "It is a fearful thing to lead this great peaceful people into war, into the most terrible and disastrous of all wars, civilization itself seeming to be in the balance. But the right is more precious than peace, and we shall fight for the things which we have always carried nearest our hearts,—for democracy, . . . for the rights and liberties of small nations, for a universal dominion of right by such a concert of free peoples as shall bring peace and safety to all nations and make the world itself at last free."

Congressmen broke into applause and crowded the aisles to congratulate Wilson. "My message today was a message of death for our young men," he said afterward. "How strange it seems to applaud that."

Pacifists in Congress continued to hold out, and for four days they managed to postpone action. Finally, on April 6, the declaration of war passed, with fifty members of the House and six senators voting against it. Even then, the country was divided over entry into the war.

OVER THERE

With a burst of patriotism, the United States entered a war its new allies were in danger of losing. That same month, the Germans sank 881,000 tons of Allied shipping, the highest amount for any one month during the war. There were mutinies in the French army; a costly British drive in Flanders stalled. In November, the Bolsheviks seized power in Russia, and, led by V. I. Lenin, they soon signed a separate peace treaty with Germany, freeing German troops to fight in the West. German and Austrian forces routed the Italian army on the southern flank, and the Allies braced for a spring 1918 offensive.

MOBILIZATION

The United States was not prepared for war. Some Americans hoped the declaration of war itself might daunt the Germans; there were those who thought that naval escorts of Allied shipping would be enough.

Bypassing older generals, Wilson named John J. ("Black Jack") Pershing, leader of the Mexican campaign, to head the American Expeditionary Force (AEF).

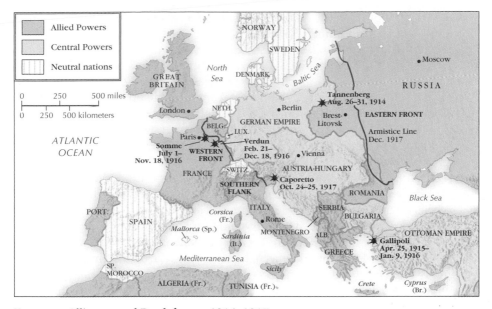

European Alliances and Battlefronts, 1914–1917
Allied forces suffered early defeats on the eastern front (Tannenberg) and in the Dardanelles (Gallipoli). In 1917, the Allies were routed on the southern flank (Caporetto); the western front then became the critical theater of the war.

Pershing inherited an army unready for war. In April 1917, it had 200,000 officers and men, equipped with 300,000 old rifles, 1500 machine guns, 55 out-of-date airplanes, and 2 field radio sets. Its most recent battle experience had been chasing Pancho Villa around northern Mexico. It had not caught him.

Although some in Congress preferred a voluntary army of the kind that had fought in the Spanish-American War, Wilson turned to conscription, which he believed was both efficient and democratic. In May 1917, Congress passed the Selective Service Act, providing for the registration of all men between the ages of 21 and 30 (later changed to 18 and 45). Early in June, 9.5 million men registered for the draft. By the end of the war, the act had registered 24.2 million men, about 2.8 million of whom were inducted into the army.

The draft included black men as well as white, and four African American regiments were among the first sent into action. Despite their contributions, however, no black soldiers were allowed to march in the victory celebrations that eventually took place in Paris. Nor were they included in a French mural of the different races in the war, even though black servicemen from English and French colonies were represented.

WAR IN THE TRENCHES

World War I may have been the most terrible war of all time, more terrible even than World War II and its vast devastation. After the early offensives, the European armies dug themselves into trenches only hundreds of yards apart in places. Artillery, poison gas, hand grenades, and a new weapon—rapid-fire machine guns—kept them pinned down.

The first American soldiers reached France in June 1917. By March of the following year, 300,000 Americans were there, and by war's end, 2 million men had crossed the Atlantic. No troop ships were sunk, a credit to the British and American navies. In the summer of 1917, Admiral William S. Sims, a brilliant American strategist, pushed through a convoy plan that used Allied destroyers to escort merchant vessels across the ocean. At first resisted by English captains who liked to sail alone, the plan soon cut shipping losses in half.

As expected, on March 21, 1918, the Germans launched a massive assault in western Europe. Troops from the Russian front added to the force, and by May they had driven Allied forces back to the Marne River, just 50 miles from Paris. There, the Americans saw their first action. The American forces blocked the Germans at the town of Château-Thierry and four weeks later forced them out of Belleau Wood, a crucial stronghold. On July 15, the Germans threw everything into a last drive for Paris, but they were halted at the Marne, and in three days of battle they were finished.

With the German drive stalled, the Allies counterattacked along the entire front. On September 12, 1918, a half million Americans and a smaller contingent of French drove the Germans from the St. Mihiel salient, 12 miles south of Verdun. Two weeks later, 896,000 American soldiers attacked between the Meuse River and the Argonne Forest. Focusing their efforts on a main railroad supply line for the German army in the West, American troops broke through in early November, cut the line, and drove the Germans back along the whole front.

In The Victorious Retreat Back to the Rhine *(1918), American illustrator and painter Frank Schoonover captures the intensity of aerial bombardment supporting the gathering momentum of Allied ground forces to drive back the Germans in the final stages of the war.*

The German high command knew that the war was lost. On October 6, 1918, Germany appealed to Wilson for an armistice, and by the end of the month, Turkey, Bulgaria, and Austria-Hungary were out of the war. At 4 A.M. on November 11, Germany signed the armistice. The AEF lost 48,909 dead and 230,000 wounded; losses to disease brought the total of dead to more than 112,000.

The American contribution, although small in comparison to the enormous costs to European nations, was vital. Fresh, enthusiastic American troops raised Allied morale; they helped turn the tide at a crucial point in the war.

OVER HERE

Victory at the front depended on economic and emotional mobilization at home. Consolidating federal authority, Wilson moved quickly in 1917 and 1918 to organize war production and distribution. An idealist who knew how to sway public opinion, he also recognized the need to enlist American emotions. To him, the war for people's minds, the "conquest of their convictions," was as vital as events on the battlefield.

THE CONQUEST OF CONVICTIONS

A week after war was declared, Wilson formed the Committee on Public Information (CPI) and asked George Creel, an outspoken progressive journalist, to head it. Creel hired progressives such as Ida Tarbell and Ray Stannard Baker and recruited thousands of people in the arts, advertising, and film industries to publicize the war.

Anti-German sentiment spread rapidly. Many schools stopped offering instruction in the German language—California's state education board called it a language "of autocracy, brutality, and hatred." Sauerkraut became "liberty cabbage"; saloonkeepers removed pretzels from the bar. Orchestral works by Bach, Beethoven, and Brahms vanished from some symphonic programs, and the New York Philharmonic agreed not to perform the music of living German composers.

Rather than curbing the repression, Wilson encouraged it. "Woe be to the man or group of men that seeks to stand in our way," he told peace advocates soon after the war began. At his request, Congress passed the Espionage Act of 1917, which imposed sentences of up to twenty years in prison for persons found guilty of aiding the enemy, obstructing recruitment of soldiers, or encouraging disloyalty. It allowed the postmaster general to remove from the mails materials that incited treason or insurrection. The Trading-with-the-Enemy Act of 1917 authorized the government to censor the foreign language press.

In 1918, Congress passed the Sedition Act, imposing harsh penalties on anyone using "disloyal, profane, scurrilous, or abusive language" about the government, flag, or armed forces uniforms. In all, more than fifteen hundred persons were arrested under the new laws.

The sedition laws clearly went beyond any clear or present danger. There were, to be sure, German spies in the country, Germans who wanted to encourage strikes in American arms factories. Moreover, the U.S. government and other national leaders were painfully aware of how divided Americans had been about entering the war. They set out to promote unity—by force, if necessary—in order to convince Germany that the nation was united behind the war.

But none of these matters warranted a nationwide program of repression. Conservatives took advantage of wartime feelings to try to stamp out American socialists, who in fact were vulnerable because, unlike their European counterparts, they continued to oppose the war even after their country had entered it. Using the sedition laws, conservatives harried the Socialist party and another favorite target, the Industrial Workers of the World.

In 1918, Eugene V. Debs, the Socialist party leader, delivered a speech denouncing capitalism and the war. He was convicted for violation of the Espionage Act and spent the war in a penitentiary in Atlanta. Nominated as the Socialist party candidate in the presidential election of 1920, Debs—prisoner 9653—won nearly a million votes, but the Socialist movement never fully recovered from the repression of the war.

In fostering hostility toward anything that smacked of dissent, the war also gave rise to the great "Red Scare" that began in 1919. Pleased at first with the Russian revolution, Americans in general turned quickly against it, especially after Lenin and the Bolsheviks seized control late in 1917. The Americans feared Lenin's anticapitalist program, and they denounced his decision in early 1918 to make peace with Germany because it freed German troops to fight in France.

Once again, Wilson himself played a prominent role in the development of anti-Bolshevik sentiment. In the summer of 1918, he sent fifteen thousand American troops into the Soviet Union, where they joined other Allied soldiers. Wilson and others hoped to bring down the fledgling Bolshevik government, fearful it would spread revolution around the world. American troops remained in Russia until April 1920, and on the whole, American willingness to interfere soured Russian-American relations for decades to come.

A BUREAUCRATIC WAR

Quick, effective action was needed to win the war. To meet the need, Wilson and Congress set up an array of new federal agencies, nearly five thousand in all. Staffed largely by businessmen, the agencies drew on funds and powers of a hitherto unknown scope.

At first, Wilson tried to organize the wartime economy along decentralized lines, almost in the fashion of his early New Freedom thinking. But that proved unworkable, and he moved instead to a series of highly centralized planning boards, each with broad authority over a specific area of the economy. There were boards to control virtually every aspect of transportation, agriculture, and manufacturing. Though only a few of them were as effective as Wilson had hoped, they did coordinate the war effort to some degree.

The War Industries Board (WIB), one of the most powerful of the new agencies, oversaw the production of all American factories. Headed by millionaire Bernard M. Baruch, a Wall Street broker and speculator, it determined priorities, allocated raw materials, and fixed prices. It told manufacturers what they could and could not make. Working closely with business, Baruch for a time acted as the dictator of the American economy.

Herbert Hoover, the hero of a campaign to feed starving Belgians, headed a new Food Administration, and he set out with customary energy to supply food to the armies overseas. Appealing to the "spirit of self-sacrifice," Hoover convinced people to save food by observing "meatless" and "wheatless" days. He fixed prices to boost production, bought and distributed wheat, and encouraged people to plant "victory gardens" behind homes, churches, and schools. One householder— Wilson—set an example by grazing sheep on the White House lawn.

At another new agency, the Fuel Administration, Harry A. Garfield, the president of Williams College, introduced daylight saving time, rationed coal and oil, and imposed gasless days when motorists could not drive. A fourth agency, the Railroad Administration, dictated rail traffic over nearly 400,000 miles of track— standardizing rates, limiting passenger travel, and speeding arms shipments. The War Shipping Board coordinated shipping, the Emergency Fleet Corporation supervised shipbuilding, and the War Trade Board oversaw foreign trade.

As never before, the government intervened in American life. When strikes threatened the telephone and telegraph companies, the government simply seized and ran them. Businessmen, paid a nominal dollar a year, flocked to Washington to run the new agencies, and the partnership between government and business grew closer. As government expanded, business expanded as well, responding to wartime contracts. Industries such as steel, aluminum, and cigarettes boomed, and corporate profits increased threefold between 1914 and 1919.

LABOR IN THE WAR

The war also brought organized labor into the partnership with government, although the results were more limited than in the business-government alliance. Samuel Gompers, president of the AFL, served on Wilson's Council of National Defense, an advisory group formed to unify business, labor, and government. Gompers hoped to trade labor peace for labor advances, and he formed a War Committee on Labor to enlist workers' support for the war. With the blessing of the Wilson administration, union membership grew rapidly during the war.

Hoping to encourage production and avoid strikes, Wilson adopted many of the objectives of the social-justice reformers. He supported an eight-hour day in war-related industries and improved wages and working conditions. In May 1918, he named Felix Frankfurter, a brilliant young law professor, to head a new War Labor Board (WLB). The agency standardized wages and hours, and at Wilson's direction, it protected the right of labor to organize and bargain collectively. Although it did not forbid strikes, it used various tactics to discourage them.

The WLB also ordered that women be paid equal wages for equal work in war industries. In 1914, the flow of European immigrants suddenly stopped because of the war, and in 1917, the draft began to take large numbers of American men. The result was a labor shortage, filled by women, African Americans, and Mexican Americans. One million women worked in war industries. Some of them took jobs previously held by men, but for the most part, they moved from

Housewives did not leave home for the factory en masse in 1917 as they later did during World War II, but many women already employed outside the home found new, well-paying opportunities in jobs previously held by men.

one set of "women's jobs" into another. From the beginning of the war to the end, the number of women in the workforce held steady at about eight million, and unlike the experience in World War II, large numbers of housewives did not leave the home for machine shops and arms plants.

Still, there were some new opportunities and in some cases higher pay. In food, airplane, and electrical plants, women made up one-fifth or more of the workforce. As their wages increased, so did their expectations; some became more militant, and conflict grew between them and male coworkers. To set standards for female employment, a Women's Bureau was established in the Department of Labor, but the government's influence varied. In the federally run railroad industry, women often made wages equal to those of men; in the federally run telephone industry, they did not.

Looking for more people to fill wartime jobs, corporations found another major source among southern blacks. Beginning in 1916, northern labor agents traveled across the South, promising jobs, high wages, and free transportation. Soon the word spread, and the movement northward became a flood. Between 1916 and 1918, more than 450,000 African Americans left the Old South for the booming industrial cities of St. Louis, Chicago, Detroit, and Cleveland. In the decade before 1920, Detroit's black population grew by more than 600 percent, Cleveland's by more than 300 percent, and Chicago's by 150 percent.

Most of the newcomers were young, unmarried, and skilled or semiskilled. The men found jobs in factories, railroad yards, steel mills, packinghouses, and coal mines; black women worked in textile factories, department stores, and restaurants. In their new homes, African Americans found greater racial freedom but also different living conditions. If the South was often hostile, the North could be impersonal and lonely. Accustomed to the pace of the farm—ruled by the seasons and the sun—those blacks who were able to enter the industrial sector now worked for hourly wages in mass production industries, where time clocks and line supervisors dictated the daily routine.

Racial tensions increased, resulting in part from growing competition for housing and jobs. In mid-1917, a race war in East St. Louis, Illinois, killed nine whites and about forty blacks. In July 1919, the month President Wilson returned from the peace conference in Paris, a race riot in Washington, D.C., killed six people. Riots in Chicago that month killed thirty-eight—fifteen whites and twenty-three blacks—and there were later outbreaks in New York City and Omaha. Lynch mobs killed forty-eight blacks in 1917, sixty-three in 1918, and seventy-eight in 1919. Ten of the victims in 1919 were war veterans, several still in uniform.

Blacks were more and more inclined to fight back. Two hundred thousand blacks served in France—forty-two thousand as combat troops. Returning home, they expected better treatment. "I'm glad I went," a black veteran said. "I done my part and I'm going to fight right here till Uncle Sam does his." Roscoe Jameson, Claude McKay, and other black poets wrote biting poetry, some of it—such as Fenton Johnson's "The New Day"—drawn from the war experience:

> *For we have been with thee in No Man's Land,*
> *Through lake of fire and down to Hell itself;*
> *And now we ask of thee our liberty,*
> *Our freedom in the land of Stars and Stripes.*

"Lift Ev'ry Voice and Sing," composed in 1900, became known as the "Negro National Anthem." Parents bought black dolls for their children, and W. E. B. Du Bois spoke of a "New Negro," proud and more militant: "We return. We return from fighting. We return fighting."

Eager for cheap labor, farmers and ranchers in the Southwest persuaded the federal government to relax immigration restrictions, and between 1917 and 1920, more than 100,000 Mexicans migrated into Texas, Arizona, New Mexico, and California. The Mexican American population grew from 385,000 in 1910 to 740,000 in 1920. Tens of thousands of Mexican Americans moved to Chicago, St. Louis, Omaha, and other northern cities to take wartime jobs. Often scorned and insecure, they created urban barrios similar to the Chinatowns and Little Italys around them.

Like most wars, World War I affected patterns at home as much as abroad. Business profits grew, factories expanded, and industries turned out huge amounts of war goods. Government authority swelled, and people came to expect different things of their government. Labor made some gains, as did women

The 369th infantry regiment returning from the war on the Stockholm *in February 1919. They were awarded the Croix de Guerre for bravery in the Meuse-Argonne.*

and blacks. Society assimilated some of the shifts, but social and economic tensions grew, and when the war ended, they spilled over in the strikes and violence of the Red Scare that followed.

The United States emerged from the war the strongest economic power in the world. In 1914, it was a debtor nation, and American citizens owed foreign investors about $3 billion. Five years later, the United States had become a creditor nation. Foreign governments owed more than $10 billion, and foreign citizens owed American investors nearly $3 billion. The war marked a shift in economic power rarely equaled in history.

THE TREATY OF VERSAILLES

Long before the fighting ended, Wilson began to formulate plans for the peace. Like many others, he was disconcerted when the new Bolshevik government in Russia began revealing the terms of secret agreements among Britain, France, and czarist Russia to divide up Germany's colonies. To try to place the war on a higher plane, he appeared before Congress on January 8, 1918, and outlined terms for a far-reaching, nonpunitive settlement. Wilson's Fourteen Points were generous and farsighted, but they failed to satisfy wartime emotions that sought vindication.

England and France distrusted Wilsonian idealism as the basis for peace. They wanted Germany disarmed and crippled; they wanted its colonies; and they

WOODROW WILSON'S FOURTEEN POINTS, 1918: SUCCESS AND FAILURE IN IMPLEMENTATION

1. Open covenants of peace openly arrived at	Not fulfilled
2. Absolute freedom of navigation on the seas in peace and war	Not fulfilled
3. Removal of all economic barriers to the equality of trade among nations	Not fulfilled
4. Reduction of armaments to the level needed only for domestic safety	Not fulfilled
5. Impartial adjustments of colonial claims	Not fulfilled
6. Evacuation of all Russian territory; Russia to be welcomed into the society of free nations	Not fulfilled
7. Evacuation and restoration of Belgium	**Fulfilled**
8. Evacuation and restoration of all French lands; return of Alsace-Lorraine to France	**Fulfilled**
9. Readjustment of Italy's frontiers along lines of Italian nationality	Compromised
10. Self-determination for the former subjects of the Austro-Hungarian Empire	Compromised
11. Evacuation of Romania, Serbia, and Montenegro; free access to the sea for Serbia	Compromised
12. Self-determination for the former subjects of the Ottoman Empire; secure sovereignty for Turkish portion	Compromised
13. Establishment of an independent Poland, with free and secure access to the sea	**Fulfilled**
14. Establishment of a League of Nations affording mutual guarantees of independence and territorial integrity	Not fulfilled

Sources: Data from G. M. Gathorne-Hardy, *The Fourteen Points and the Treaty of Versailles* (Oxford Pamphlets on World Affairs, no. 6, 1939), pp. 8–34; Thomas G. Paterson et al., *American Foreign Policy: A History Since 1900,* 2nd ed., vol. 2, pp. 282–93.

were skeptical of the principle of self-determination. As the end of the war neared, the Allies, who had in fact made secret commitments with one another, balked at making the Fourteen Points the basis of peace. When Wilson threatened to negotiate a separate treaty with Germany, however, they accepted.

Wilson had won an important victory, but difficulties lay ahead. As Georges Clemenceau, the 78-year-old French premier, said, "God gave us the Ten Commandments, and we broke them. Wilson gives us the Fourteen Points. We shall see."

A PEACE AT PARIS

Wilson soon announced he would attend the peace conference. This was a dramatic break from tradition, and his personal involvement drew attacks from Republicans. They renewed criticism when he named the rest of the delegation: Secretary of State Lansing; Colonel House; General Tasker H. Bliss, a military expert; and Henry White, a career diplomat. Wilson named no member of the Senate, and the only Republican in the group was White.

In selecting the delegation, Wilson passed over Henry Cabot Lodge, the powerful Republican senator from Massachusetts who opposed the Fourteen

Points and would soon head the Senate Foreign Relations Committee. He also decided not to appoint Elihu Root or ex-President Taft, both of them enthusiastic internationalists. Never good at accepting criticism or delegating authority, Wilson wanted a delegation he could control—an advantage at the peace table but not in any battle over the treaty at home.

Upon his arrival, Wilson received a tumultuous welcome in England, France, and Italy. Never before had such crowds acclaimed a democratic political figure. In Paris, two million people lined the Champs-Elysées, threw flowers at him, and shouted, "Wilson le Juste [the just]" as his carriage drove by. Overwhelmed, Wilson was sure that the people of Europe shared his goals and would force their leaders to accept his peace. He was wrong. Like their leaders, many people on the Allied side hated Germany and wanted victory unmistakably reflected in the peace.

Opening in January 1919, the Peace Conference at Paris continued until May. Although twenty-seven nations were represented, the "Big Four" dominated it: Wilson; Clemenceau of France, tired and stubborn, determined to end the German threat forever; David Lloyd George, the crafty British prime minister who had pledged to squeeze Germany "until the pips squeak"; and the Italian prime minister, Vittorio Orlando. A clever negotiator, Wilson traded various "small" concessions for his major goals—national self-determination, a reduction in tensions, and a League of Nations to enforce the peace.

Wilson had to surrender some important principles. Departing from the Fourteen Points by violating the principle of self-determination, the treaty created two new independent nations—Poland and Czechoslovakia—with large German-speaking populations. It divided up the German colonies in Asia and Africa. Instead of a peace without victory, it made Germany accept responsibility for the war and demanded enormous reparations—which eventually totaled $33 billion. It made no mention of disarmament, free trade, or freedom of the seas. Instead of an open covenant openly arrived at, the treaty was drafted behind closed doors.

But Wilson deflected some of the most extreme Allied demands, and he won his coveted Point 14, a League of Nations, designed "to achieve international peace and security." The League included a general assembly; a smaller council composed of the United States, Great Britain, France, Italy, Japan, and four nations to be elected by the assembly; and a court of international justice. League members pledged to submit to arbitration every dispute threatening peace and to enjoin military and economic sanctions against nations resorting to war. Article X, for Wilson the heart of the League, obliged members to look out for one another's independence and territorial integrity.

The draft treaty in hand, Wilson returned home in February 1919 to discuss it with Congress and the people. Most Americans, the polls showed, favored the League. But over dinner with the Senate and House Foreign Relations Committees, Wilson learned of the strength of congressional opposition to it. On March 3, Senator Lodge produced a "round robin" signed by thirty-seven senators declaring they would not vote for the treaty without amendment. Should the numbers hold, Lodge had enough votes to defeat it.

Returning to Paris, Wilson attacked his critics, while he worked privately for changes to improve the chances of Senate approval. In return for major conces-

New and reconstituted nations

FINLAND

NORWAY

SWEDEN

North Sea

ESTONIA

LATVIA

DENMARK

Danzig (Free City)

LITHUANIA

GER.

GREAT BRITAIN

SOVIET UNION

NETH.

GERMANY

POLAND

BELG.

LUX.

CZECHOSLOVAKIA

FRANCE

SWITZ.

AUSTRIA

HUNGARY

ROMANIA

YUGOSLAVIA

SPAIN

Corsica (Fr.)

ITALY

BULGARIA

Mallorca (Sp.)

Sardinia (It.)

ALBANIA

Mediterranean Sea

GREECE

ALGERIA (Fr.)

TUNISIA (Fr.)

Sicily

Crete

Europe After the Treaty of Versailles, 1919

The treaty changed the map of Europe, creating a number of new and reconstituted nations. (Note the boundary changes from the war map on p. 641.)

sions, the Allies amended the League draft treaty, agreeing that domestic affairs remained outside League jurisdiction (exempting the Monroe Doctrine) and allowing nations to withdraw after two years' notice. On June 28, 1919, they signed the treaty in the Hall of Mirrors at Versailles, and Wilson started home for his most difficult fight.

REJECTION IN THE SENATE

There were ninety-six senators in 1919, forty-nine of them Republicans. Fourteen Republicans, led by William E. Borah of Idaho, were the "irreconcilables" who opposed the League on any grounds. Frank B. Kellogg of Minnesota led a group of twelve "mild reservationists" who accepted the treaty but wanted to insert several reservations that would not greatly weaken it. Finally, there were the Lodge-led "strong reservationists," twenty-three of them in all, who wanted major changes that the Allies would have to approve.

With only four Democratic senators opposed to the treaty, the Democrats and Republicans willing to compromise had enough votes to ratify it, once a few reservations were inserted. Democratic leaders urged Wilson to appeal to the Republican "mild reservationists," but he refused: "Anyone who opposes me in that I'll crush!"

Fed up with Lodge's tactics, Wilson set out in early September to take the case directly to the people. Crossing the Midwest, his speeches aroused little emotion, but on the Pacific Coast he won ovations, which heartened him. On his

Humanity is the accuser, the U.S. Senate is the assassin, and the Treaty of Versailles is the victim in this commentary on the Senate's rejection of the treaty. Isolationists, who wanted to keep the United States out of European affairs, opposed the treaty because it included the Covenant for the League of Nations.

way back to Washington, he stopped in Pueblo, Colorado, where he delivered one of the most eloquent speeches of his career. People wept as he talked of Americans who died in battle and the hope that they would never fight again in foreign lands. That night Wilson felt ill. He returned to Washington, and on October 2, Mrs. Wilson found him lying unconscious on the floor of the White House, the victim of a stroke that paralyzed his left side.

After the stroke, Wilson could not work more than an hour or two at a time. No one was allowed to see him except family members, his secretary, and his physician. For more than seven months, he did not meet with the cabinet. Focusing his remaining energy on the fight over the treaty, Wilson lost touch with other issues, and critics charged that his wife, Edith Bolling Wilson, ran the government.

On November 6, 1919, while Wilson convalesced, Lodge finally reported the treaty out of committee, along with "Fourteen Reservations," one for each of Wilson's points. The most important reservation stipulated that implementation of Article X, Wilson's key article, required the action of Congress before any American intervention abroad.

On November 19, the treaty—with the Lodge reservations—failed, 39 to 55. Following Wilson's instructions, the Democrats voted against it. A motion to approve without the reservations lost 38 to 53, with only one Republican voting in favor. The defeat brought pleas for compromise, but neither Wilson nor Lodge would back down. When the treaty with reservations again came up for vote on March 19, 1920, Wilson ordered the Democrats to hold firm against it. Although twenty-one of them defied him, enough obeyed his orders to defeat it, 49 to 35, seven votes short of the necessary two-thirds majority.

THE ELECTION OF 1920

CANDIDATE	PARTY	POPULAR VOTE	ELECTORAL VOTE
Harding	Republican	16,152,200	404
Cox	Democrat	9,147,353	127
Debs	Socialist	917,799	0

To Wilson, walking now with the help of a cane, one chance remained: the presidential election of 1920. For a time, he thought of running for a third term himself, but his party shunted him aside. The Democrats nominated Governor James M. Cox of Ohio, along with the young and popular Franklin D. Roosevelt, assistant secretary of the navy, for vice president. Wilson called for "a great and solemn referendum" on the treaty. The Democratic platform endorsed the treaty but agreed to accept reservations that clarified the American role in the League.

On the Republican side, Senator Warren G. Harding of Ohio, who had nominated Taft in 1912, won the presidential nomination. Harding waffled on the treaty, but that issue made little difference. Voters wanted a change. Harding won in a landslide, taking 61 percent of the vote and beating Cox by seven million votes. Without a peace treaty, the United States remained technically at war, and it was not until July 1921, almost three years after the last shot was fired, that Congress passed a joint resolution ending the war.

POSTWAR DISILLUSIONMENT

After 1919, there was disillusionment. World War I was feared before it started, popular while it lasted, and hated when it ended. To a whole generation that followed, it appeared futile, killing without cause, sacrificing without benefit. Books, plays, and movies—Hemingway's *A Farewell to Arms* (1929), John Dos Passos's *Three Soldiers* (1921), Laurence Stallings and Maxwell Anderson's *What Price Glory?* (1924), among others—showed it as waste, horror, and death.

The war and its aftermath damaged the humanitarian, progressive spirit of the early years of the century. It killed "something precious and perhaps irretrievable in the hearts of thinking men and women." Progressivism survived well into the 1920s and the New Deal, but it no longer had the old conviction and broad popular support. Bruising fights over the war and the League drained people's energy and enthusiasm.

Confined to bed, Woodrow Wilson died in Washington in 1924, three years after Harding, the new president, promised "not heroics but healing; not nostrums but normalcy; not revolution but restoration." Nonetheless, the "war to end all wars" and the spirit of Woodrow Wilson left an indelible imprint on the country.

CHRONOLOGY

1901 Hay-Pauncefote Treaty with Great Britain empowers United States to build Isthmian canal

1904 Theodore Roosevelt introduces corollary to Monroe Doctrine

1904–1905 Russo-Japanese War

1905 Taft-Katsura Agreement recognizes Japanese power in Korea

1908 Root-Takahira Agreement vows to maintain status quo in the Pacific

Roosevelt sends the fleet around the world

1911 Revolution begins in Mexico

1913–1914 Bryan negotiates "cooling-off" treaties to end war

1914 World War I begins

U.S. Marines take Veracruz

Panama Canal completed

1915 Japan issues Twenty-one Demands to China (January)

Germany declares water around British Isles a war zone (February)

Lusitania torpedoed (May)

Bryan resigns; Robert Lansing becomes secretary of state (June)

Arabic pledge restricts submarine warfare (September)

1916 Germany issues *Sussex* pledge (March)

General John J. Pershing leads unsuccessful punitive expedition into Mexico to seize Pancho Villa (April)

Wilson wins reelection

1917 Wilson calls for "peace without victory" (January)

Germany resumes unrestricted U-boat warfare (February)

United States enters World War I (April)

Congress passes Selective Service Act (May)

First American troops reach France (June)

War Industries Board established (July)

1918 Wilson outlines Fourteen Points for peace (January)

Germany asks for peace (October)

Armistice ends the war (November)

1919 Peace negotiations begin in Paris (January)

Treaty of Versailles defeated in Senate

1920 Warren G. Harding elected president

25

TRANSITION TO
MODERN AMERICA

The moving assembly line that Henry Ford perfected in 1913 for manufacture of the Model T marked only the first step toward full mass production and the beginning of America's worldwide industrial supremacy. A year later, Ford began buying large plots of land along the Rouge River southeast of Detroit, Michigan. He already had a vision of a vast industrial tract where machines, moving through a sequence of carefully arranged manufacturing operations, would transform raw materials into finished cars, trucks, and tractors. The key would be control over the flow of goods at each step along the way—from lake steamers and railroad cars bringing in the coal and iron ore, to overhead conveyor belts and huge turning tables carrying the moving parts past the stationary workers on the assembly line. "Everything must move," Ford commanded, and by the mid-1920s at River Rouge, as the plant became known, it did.

Ford began fulfilling his industrial dream in 1919 when he built a blast furnace and foundry to make engine blocks for both the Model T and his tractors. By 1924, more than forty thousand workers were turning out nearly all the metal parts used in making Ford vehicles. One tractor factory was so efficient that it took just over twenty-eight hours to convert raw ore into a new farm implement.

Visitors from all over the world came to marvel at River Rouge. Some were disturbed by the jumble of machines (by 1926, there were forty-three thousand in operation) and the apparent congestion on the plant floor, but industrial experts recognized that the arrangement led to incredible productivity because "the work moves and the men stand still."

In May 1927, after producing more than fifteen million Model Ts, Ford closed the assembly line at Highland Park. For the next six months, his engineers worked on designing a more compact and efficient assembly line at River Rouge for the Model A, which went into production in November. By then,

River Rouge had more than justified Ford's vision. "Ford had brought together everything at a single site and on a scale no one else had ever attempted," concluded historian Geoffrey Perrett. "The Rouge plant became to a generation of engineers far more than a factory. It was a monument."

Mass production, born in Highland Park in 1913 and perfected at River Rouge in the 1920s, became the hallmark of American industry. Soon Ford's emphasis on the flow of parts moving past stationary workers became the standard in nearly every American factory. The moving assembly line—with its emphasis on uniformity, speed, precision, and coordination—took away the last vestiges of craftsmanship and turned workers into near robots. It led to amazing efficiency that produced both high profits for manufacturers and low prices for buyers. By the mid-1920s, the cost of the Model T had dropped from $950 to $290.

Most important, mass production contributed to a consumer goods revolution. American factories turned out a flood of automobiles, electrical appliances, and other items that made life easier and more pleasant for most Americans. The result was the creation of a distinctively modern America, one marked by the material abundance that has characterized American society ever since.

But the abundance came at a price. The 1920s have been portrayed as a decade of escape and frivolity, and for many Americans they were just that. But those years also were an era of transition: a time when the old America of individualistic rural values gave way to a new America of conformist urban values. The transition was often wrenching, and many Americans clung desperately to the old ways. Modernity finally won, but not without a struggle.

THE SECOND INDUSTRIAL REVOLUTION

The first Industrial Revolution in the late nineteenth century had catapulted the United States into the forefront among the world's richest and most highly developed nations. With the advent of the new consumer goods industries, the American people by the 1920s enjoyed the highest standard of living of any nation on earth. After a brief postwar depression, 1922 saw the beginning of a great boom that peaked in 1927 and lasted until 1929. In this brief period, American industrial output nearly doubled, and the gross national product rose by 40 percent. Most of this explosive growth took place in industries producing consumer goods—automobiles, appliances, furniture, and clothing. Equally important, the national per capita income increased by 30 percent to $681 in 1929. American workers became the highest paid in history. Combined with the expansion of installment credit programs that allowed customers to buy now and pay later, this income growth allowed a purchasing spree like nothing the nation had ever experienced.

The key to the new affluence lay in technology. Electric motors replaced steam engines as the basic source of energy in factories; by 1929, 70 percent of all industrial power came from electricity. Efficiency experts broke down the industrial process into minute parts, using time and motion studies, and then showed managers and workers how to maximize the output of their labor. Production per

On the assembly line at Ford's River Rouge plant, workers performed repetitive tasks on the car chassis that rushed by at a rate of 6 feet per minute.

worker-hour increased an amazing 75 percent over the decade; in 1929, a workforce no larger than that of 1919 was producing almost twice as many goods.

THE AUTOMOBILE INDUSTRY

The nature of the consumer goods revolution can best be seen in the automobile industry, which became the nation's largest in the 1920s. Rapid growth was its hallmark. In 1920, there were ten million cars in the nation; by the end of the decade, twenty-six million were on the road. Production jumped from fewer than two million units a year to more than five million by 1929.

The automobile boom, at its peak from 1922 to 1927, depended on the apparently insatiable appetite of the American people for cars. But as the decade continued, the market became saturated as more and more of those who could afford the new luxury had become car owners. Marketing became as crucial as production. Automobile makers began to rely heavily on advertising and annual model changes, seeking to make customers dissatisfied with their old vehicles and eager to order new ones. Despite these efforts, sales slumped in 1927 when Ford stopped making the Model T, picked up again the next year with the new Model A, but began to slide again in 1929. The new industry revealed a basic weakness in the consumer goods economy; once people had bought an item with a long life, they would be out of the market for a few years.

In the affluent 1920s, few noticed the emerging economic instability. Instead, contemporary observers focused on the stimulating effect the automobile had on the rest of the economy. The mass production of cars required huge quantities of steel; entire new rolling mills had to be built to supply sheet steel for car bodies. Rubber factories boomed with the demand for tires, and paint and glass suppliers had more business than ever before. The auto changed the pattern of city life, leading to a suburban explosion. Real estate developers, no longer dependent on streetcars and railway lines, could now build houses in ever wider concentric circles around the central cities.

Patterns of Economic Growth

Automobiles were the most conspicuous of the consumer products that flourished in the 1920s, but certainly not the only ones. The electrical industry grew almost as quickly. Central power stations, where massive steam generators converted coal into electricity, brought current into the homes of city and town dwellers. Two-thirds of all American families enjoyed electricity by the end of the decade, and they spent vast sums on washing machines, vacuum cleaners, refrigerators, and ranges. The new appliances eased the burdens of housework and ushered in an age of leisure.

Radio broadcasting and motion picture production also boomed in the 1920s. The early success of KDKA in Pittsburgh stimulated the growth of more than eight hundred independent radio stations, and by 1929, NBC had formed the first successful radio network. The film industry thrived in Hollywood, reaching its maturity in the mid-1920s when in every large city there were huge theaters seating as many as four thousand people. With the advent of the "talkies" by 1929, average weekly movie attendance climbed to nearly 100 million.

The corporation continued to be the dominant business structure in the 1920s. Corporations now had hundreds of thousands of stockholders. The enormous profits the corporations generated provided ample funds to finance growth and expansion, freeing companies from their earlier dependence on investment bankers like J. P. Morgan. Operating independently, free of outside restraint, the corporate managers were accountable only to other managers.

Another wave of mergers accompanied the growth of corporations during the 1920s. By the end of the decade, the two hundred largest nonfinancial corporations owned almost half of the country's corporate wealth.

The most distinctive feature of the new consumer-oriented economy was the emphasis on marketing. Advertising earnings rose from $1.3 billion in 1915 to $3.4 billion in 1926. Skillful practitioners such as Edward Bernays and Bruce Barton sought to control public taste and consumer spending by identifying the good life with the possession of the latest product of American industry, whether it be a car, a refrigerator, or a brand of cigarettes.

Uniformity and standardization, the characteristics of mass production, now prevailed. The farmer in Kansas bought the same kind of car, the same groceries, and the same pills as the factory worker in Pennsylvania. Sectional differences in dress, food, and furniture began to disappear. Even the regional accents that distinguished Americans in different parts of the country were threatened with extinction by the advent of radio and films, which promoted a standard national dialect devoid of any local flavor.

Economic Weaknesses

The New Era, as business leaders labeled the decade, was not as prosperous as it first appeared. The revolution in consumer goods disguised the decline of many traditional industries in the 1920s. Railroads suffered from poor management and from the competition of the growing trucking industry. The coal industry was also troubled, with petroleum and natural gas beginning to replace coal as a fuel. The use of cotton textiles declined with the development of rayon and other synthetic fibers. The New England mills moved south in search of cheap labor, leaving behind thousands of unemployed workers and virtual ghost towns in the nation's oldest industrial center.

Hardest hit of all was agriculture. American farmers had expanded production to meet the demands of World War I, when they fed their own nation and most of Europe as well. After the war, farm prices and exports fell sharply. Throughout the 1920s, the farmers' share of the national income dropped, until by 1929, the per capita farm income was only $273, compared to the national average of $681.

Urban workers were better off than farmers in the 1920s, but they did not share fully in the decade's affluence. The industrial labor force remained remarkably steady during this period of economic growth; technical innovations meant the same number of workers could produce far more than before. Most new jobs appeared in the lower-paying service industry. During the decade, factory wage rates rose only a modest 11 percent; by 1929, nearly half of all American families had an income of less than $1500. At the same time, however, conditions of life improved. Prices remained stable, even dropping somewhat in the early 1920s, so workers enjoyed a gain in real wages.

Organized labor proved unable to advance the interests of workers in the 1920s. Conservative leadership in the AFL neglected the task of organizing the vast number of unskilled laborers in the mass production industries. Aggressive management weakened the appeal of unions by portraying them as radical organizations after a series of strikes in 1919. The net result was a decline in union membership from a postwar high of five million to less than three million by 1929.

Black workers remained on the bottom, both economically and socially. Nearly half a million African Americans had migrated northward from the rural South during World War I. Some found jobs in northern industries, but many more worked in menial service areas, collecting garbage, washing dishes, and sweeping floors. Yet even these jobs offered them a better life than they found on the depressed southern farms, where millions of African Americans still lived in poverty, and so the migration continued. The black ghettos in northern cities grew rapidly in the 1920s; Chicago's African American population doubled during the decade, while New York's rose from 152,467 to 327,706, with most African Americans living in Harlem.

Middle- and upper-class Americans were the groups who thrived in the 1920s. The rewards of this second Industrial Revolution went to the managers—the engineers, bankers, and executives—who directed the new industrial economy. Corporate profits nearly doubled in ten years, and income from dividends rose 65 percent, nearly six times the rate of increase in workers' wages. Bank accounts, reflecting the accumulated savings of the upper-middle and wealthy classes, rose from $41.1 billion to $57.9 billion. These were the people who bought the fine new houses in the suburbs and who could afford more than one car.

The economic trends of the decade had both positive and negative implications for the future. On the one hand, there was the solid growth of new consumer-based industries. Automobiles and appliances were not passing fancies; their production and use became a part of the modern American way of life. The future pattern of American culture—cars and suburbs, shopping centers and skyscrapers—was determined by the end of the 1920s.

But at the same time, there were ominous signs of danger. The unequal distribution of wealth, the growth of consumer debt, the saturation of the market for cars and appliances, and the rampant speculation all contributed to economic instability. The boom of the 1920s would end in a great crash; yet the achievements of the decade would survive even that dire experience to shape the future of American life.

CITY LIFE IN THE JAZZ AGE

The city replaced the countryside as the focal point of American life in the 1920s. The 1920 census revealed that for the first time, slightly more than half of the population lived in cities (defined broadly to include all places of more than 2500 people). During the decade, the metropolitan areas grew rapidly as both whites and blacks from rural areas came seeking jobs in the new consumer industries. Between 1920 and 1930, cities with populations of 250,000 or more had added some 8 million people to their ranks. New York City grew by nearly 25 percent, while Detroit more than doubled its population during the decade.

The skyscraper soon became the most visible feature of the city. Faced with inflated land prices, builders turned upward—developing a distinctively American architectural style in the process. New York led the way with the ornate Woolworth Building in 1913. The sleek 102-story Empire State Building, completed in 1931, was for years the tallest building in the world. Other cities erected their own jagged skylines. By 1929, there were 377 buildings more than 20 stories tall across the nation. Most significantly, the skyscraper came to symbolize the new mass culture.

In the metropolis, life was different. The old community ties of home, church, and school were absent, but there were important gains to replace them—new ideas, new creativity, new perspectives. Some city dwellers became lost and lonely without the old institutions; others thrived in the urban environment.

WOMEN AND THE FAMILY

The urban culture of the 1920s witnessed important changes in the American family. This vital institution began to break down under the impact of economic and social change. A new freedom for women and children seemed to be emerging in its wake.

Although World War I accelerated the process by which women left the home for work, the postwar decade witnessed a return to the slower pace of the prewar years. During the 1920s there was no permanent gain in the number of working women. Two million more women were employed in 1930 than in 1920, but this represented an increase of only 1 percent. Most women workers, moreover, had low-paying jobs, ranging from stenographers to maids. For the

September 11, 1920

Price—15 Cents
Subscription Price $7.00 a year

Le~li~'s

Illustrate ~~~ *paper*

VOTING
BOOTH NO 1

*Women finally realized the
hard-won right to vote.
The cover of* Leslie's
Illustrated Newspaper *for
September 11, 1920, cele-
brates the fact.*

most part, the professions were reserved for men, with women relegated to such fields as teaching and nursing.

Women had won the right to vote in 1920, but the Nineteenth Amendment proved to have less impact than its proponents had hoped. Adoption of the amendment robbed women of a unifying cause, and the exercise of the franchise itself did little to change prevailing sex roles. Men remained the principal bread-winners in the family; women cooked, cleaned, and reared the children.

The feminist movement, however, still showed signs of vitality in the 1920s. Social feminists pushing for humanitarian reform won enactment of the Sheppard-Towner Act of 1921, which provided for federal aid to establish state programs for maternal and infant health care. Although the failure to enact the child labor amendment in 1925 marked the beginning of a decline in humanitarian reform, for the rest of the decade, women's groups continued to work for good-government measures, for the inclusion of women on juries, and for consumer legislation.

In 1923, the National Woman's Party succeeded in having an Equal Rights Amendment (ERA) introduced in Congress. Most other women's organizations, notably the League of Women Voters, opposed the amendment because it threatened gender-specific legislation such as the Sheppard-Towner Act that women had fought so hard to enact. The drive for the ERA in the 1920s failed.

Growing assertiveness had a profound impact on feminism in the 1920s. Instead of crusading for social progress, young women concentrated on individual self-expression by rebelling against Victorian restraints. In the larger cities, some quickly adopted what critic H. L. Mencken called the flapper image, portrayed most strikingly by artist John Held, Jr. Cutting their hair short, raising their skirts above the knee, and binding their breasts, "flappers" set out to compete on equal terms with men on the golf course and in the speakeasy. The flappers assaulted the traditional double standard in sex, demanding that equality with men should include sexual fulfillment before and during marriage. New and more liberal laws led to a sharp rise in the divorce rate; by 1928, there were 166 divorces for every 1000 marriages, compared to only 81 in 1900.

The sense of woman's emancipation was heightened by a continuing drop in the birthrate and by the abundance of consumer goods. With fewer children to care for and with washing machines and vacuum cleaners to ease their household labor, it seemed that women of the 1920s would have more leisure time. Yet appearances were deceptive. Advertisers eagerly sought out women as buyers of laborsaving consumer products, but wives exercised purchasing power only as delegated by their husbands. In addition, many women were not in the position to put the new devices to use—one-fourth of the homes in Cleveland lacked running water in the 1920s, and three-quarters of the nation's families did not have washing machines.

The family, however, did change. It became smaller as easier access to effective birth control methods enabled couples to limit the number of their offspring. More and more married women took jobs outside the home, bringing in an income and gaining a measure of independence (although their rate of pay was always lower than that for men). Young people, who had once joined the labor force when they entered their teens, now discovered adolescence as a stage of life. A high school education was no longer uncommon, and college attendance increased.

THE ROARING TWENTIES

Excitement ran high in the cities as both crime waves and highly publicized sports events flourished. Prohibition ushered in such distinctive features of the decade as speakeasies, bootleggers, and bathtub gin. Crime rose sharply as middle- and upper-class Americans willingly broke the law to gain access to alcoholic beverages. City streets became the scene of violent shoot-outs between rival bootleggers; by 1929, Chicago had witnessed more than five hundred gangland murders.

Sports became a national mania in the 1920s as people found more leisure time. Golf boomed, with some two million men and women playing on nearly five thousand courses across the country. Spectator sports attracted even more attention. Boxing drew huge crowds to see fighters such as Jack Dempsey and Gene Tunney. Baseball attendance soared. More than twenty million fans attended games in 1927, the year Babe Ruth became a national idol by hitting sixty home runs.

In what Frederick Lewis Allen called "the ballyhoo years," the popular yearning for excitement led people to seek vicarious thrills in all kinds of ways—applauding Charles Lindbergh's solo flight across the Atlantic, cheering Gertrude

Ederle's swim across the English Channel, and flocking to such bizarre events as six-day bicycle races, dance marathons, and flagpole sittings.

Sex became another popular topic in the 1920s as Victorian standards began to crumble. Sophisticated city dwellers seemed to be intent on exploring a new freedom in sexual expression. Plays and novels focused on adultery, and the new urban tabloids—led by the *New York Daily News*—delighted in telling their readers about love nests and kept women. The popular songs of the decade, such as "Hot Lips" and "Burning Kisses," were less romantic and more explicit than those of years before. Hollywood exploited the obsession with sex by producing movies with such provocative titles as *Up in Mabel's Room, A Shocking Night,* and *Women and Lovers.* Young people embraced the new permissiveness joyfully, with the automobile giving couples an easy way to escape parental supervision.

There is considerable debate, however, over the extent of the sexual revolution in the 1920s. Actual changes in sexual behavior are beyond the historian's reach, hidden in the privacy of the bedroom, but the old Victorian prudishness was a clear casualty of the 1920s. At least in urban areas, sex was no longer a taboo subject; men and women now could and did discuss it openly.

FLOWERING OF THE ARTS

The greatest cultural advance of the 1920s was visible in the outpouring of literature. The city gave rise to a new class of intellectuals—writers who commented on the new industrial society. Many were bewildered by the rapidly changing social patterns of the 1920s and appalled by the materialism of American culture. Some fled to Europe to live as expatriates, congregating in Paris cafés to bemoan the loss of American innocence and purity. Others stayed at home, observing and condemning the excesses of a business civilization. All shared a sense of disillusionment and wrote pessimistically of the flawed promise of American life. Yet, ironically, their body of writing revealed a profound creativity that suggested America was coming of age intellectually.

The exiles included the poets T. S. Eliot and Ezra Pound and the novelist Ernest Hemingway. Pound discarded rhyme and meter in a search for clear, cold images that conveyed reality. Like many of the writers of the 1920s, he reacted against World War I, expressing a deep regret for the tragic waste of a whole generation in defense of a "botched civilization."

Eliot, who was born in Missouri but became a British citizen, displayed even more profound despair. In *The Waste Land,* which appeared in 1922, he evoked images of fragmentation and sterility that had a powerful impact on the other disillusioned writers of the decade. He reached the depths in *The Hollow Men* (1925), a biting description of the emptiness of modern man.

Ernest Hemingway sought redemption from the modern plight in the romantic individualism of his heroes. Preoccupied with violence, he wrote of men alienated from society who found a sense of identity in their own courage and quest for personal honor. His own experiences, ranging from driving an ambulance in the war to stalking lions in Africa, made him a legendary figure; his greatest impact on other writers, however, came from his sparse, direct, and clean prose style.

The writers who stayed home were equally disdainful of contemporary American life. F. Scott Fitzgerald chronicled American youth in *This Side of Paradise* (1920) and *The Great Gatsby* (1925), writing in bittersweet prose about "the beautiful and the damned." Amid the glitter of life among the wealthy on Long Island's North Shore came the haunting realization of emptiness and lack of human concern.

Most savage of all was H. L. Mencken, the Baltimore newspaperman and literary critic who founded *American Mercury* magazine in 1923. Declaring war on "Homo boobiens," Mencken mocked everything he found distasteful in America, from the Rotary Club to the Ku Klux Klan. It was not difficult to discover Mencken's dislikes (including Jews, as his published diary makes clear); the hard part was finding out what he affirmed, other than wit and a clever turn of phrase.

The cultural explosion of the 1920s was surprisingly broad. It included novelists such as Sherwood Anderson and John Dos Passos, who described the way the new machine age undermined such traditional American values as craftsmanship and a sense of community, and playwrights such as Eugene O'Neill, Maxwell Anderson, and Elmer Rice, who added greatly to the stature of American theater. Women writers were particularly effective in dealing with regional themes. Edith Wharton continued to write penetratingly about eastern aristocrats in books such as *The House of Mirth* (1905) and *The Age of Innocence* (1921); Willa Cather and Ellen Glasgow focused on the plight of women in the Midwest and the South, respectively, in their short stories and novels. These writers portrayed their heroines in the traditional roles of wives and mothers; playwright Zona Gale, on the other hand (who won the Pulitzer Prize for drama in 1920 for *Miss Lulu Bett*), used her title character to depict the dilemmas facing an unmarried woman in American society.

Art and especially music made significant advances as well. Edward Hopper and Charles Burchfield captured the ugliness of city life and the loneliness of its inhabitants in their realistic paintings. Aaron Copland and George Gershwin added a new vitality to American music. But African Americans migrating northward brought the most significant contribution: the spread of jazz—first to St. Louis, Kansas City, and Chicago, and finally to New York. The form of jazz known as the blues, so expressive of the suffering of African Americans, became an authentic national folk music, and performers such as Louis Armstrong enjoyed popularity around the world.

The cultural growth of the 1920s was the work of blacks as well as whites. W. E. B. Du Bois, the editor of the newspaper *The Crisis*, became the intellectual voice of the black community developing in New York City's Harlem. In 1917, James Weldon Johnson, who had been a professor of literature at Fisk University, published *Fifty Years and Other Poems*, in which the title poem commented on the half century of suffering that had followed the Emancipation Proclamation. As other African American writers gathered around them, Du Bois and Johnson became the leaders of the Harlem Renaissance. The NAACP moved its headquarters to Harlem, and in 1923, the Urban League began publishing *Opportunity*, a magazine devoted to scholarly studies of racial issues.

Art and music also flourished during Harlem's golden age. Plays and concerts at the 135th Street YMCA; floor shows at Happy Rhone's nightclub (at-

W. E. B. Du Bois (left), editor of The Crisis, *was one of the intellectual and political leaders of the Harlem Renaissance, which fostered the rise of literary figures such as Zora Neale Hurston (center) and Langston Hughes (right). Hurston wrote four novels and two books of black folklore that "helped to remind the Renaissance . . . of the richness in racial heritage." In his poetry, fiction, and nonfiction, Hughes described to the world the black experience in the United States.*

tended by many white celebrities); rent parties where jazz musicians played to raise money to help writers, artists, and neighbors pay their bills—all were part of the ferment that made Harlem "the Negro Capital of the World" in the 1920s.

Although its most famous writers were identified with New York's Harlem, the new African American cultural awareness spread to other cities in the form of poetry circles and theater groups. The number of African Americans graduating from college rose from 391 in 1920 to 1903 by 1929. Although blacks were still an oppressed minority in the America of the 1920s, they had taken major strides toward achieving cultural and intellectual fulfillment.

In retrospect, there is a striking paradox about the literary flowering of the 1920s. Nearly all the writers, black as well as white, cried out against conformity and materialism. Few took any interest in politics or in social reform. They retreated instead into individualism, seeking an escape into their art from the prevailing business civilization. Whether they went abroad or stayed home, the writers of the 1920s turned inward to avoid being swept up in the consumer goods revolution. Yet despite their withdrawal, and perhaps because of it, they produced an astonishingly rich and varied body of work. American writing had a greater intensity and depth than in the past; American writers, despite their alienation, had placed their country in the forefront of world literature.

THE RURAL COUNTERATTACK

The shift of population from the countryside to the city led to heightened social tensions in the 1920s. Intent on preserving traditional social values, rural Americans saw in the city all that was evil in contemporary life. Saloons, whorehouses, little Italys and little Polands, communist cells, free love, and atheism—all were identified with the city. Accordingly, the countryside struck back at the newly dominant urban areas, aiming to restore the primacy of the Anglo-Saxon and predominantly Protestant culture they revered. This counterattack won considerable support in the cities from those so recently uprooted from their rural backgrounds.

Other factors contributed to the intensity of the counterattack. The war had unleashed a nationalistic spirit that craved unity and conformity. In a nation where one-third of the people were foreign born, the attack on immigrants and the call for 100 percent Americanism took on a frightening zeal. When the war was over, groups such as the American Legion tried to root out "un-American" behavior and insisted on cultural as well as political conformity. The prewar progressive reform spirit added to the social tension. Stripped of much of its former idealism, progressivism focused on such social problems as drinking and illiteracy to justify repressive measures such as prohibition and immigration restriction. The result was tragic. Amid the emergence of a new urban culture, the movements aimed at preserving the values of an earlier America succeeded only in complicating life in an already difficult period of cultural transition.

THE RED SCARE

The first and most intense outbreak of national alarm came in 1919. The heightened nationalism of World War I, aimed at achieving unity at the expense of ethnic diversity, found a new target in bolshevism. The Russian Revolution and the triumph of Marxism frightened many Americans. A growing turn to communism among American radicals (especially the foreign born) accelerated these fears. Although the numbers involved were tiny—at most there were sixty thousand communists in the United States in 1919—they were highly visible. Located in the cities, their influence appeared to be magnified with the outbreak of widespread labor unrest.

A general strike in Seattle, a police strike in Boston, and a violent strike in the iron and steel industry thoroughly alarmed the American people in the spring and summer of 1919. A series of bombings led to panic. First the mayor of strike-bound Seattle received a small brown package containing a homemade bomb; then an alert New York postal employee detected sixteen bombs addressed to a variety of famous citizens (including John D. Rockefeller); and finally, on June 2, a bomb shattered the front of Attorney General A. Mitchell Palmer's home. Although the man who delivered it was blown to pieces, authorities quickly identified him as an Italian anarchist from Philadelphia.

In the ensuing public outcry, Attorney General Palmer led the attack on the alien threat. A Quaker and progressive, Palmer abandoned his earlier liberalism to launch a massive roundup of foreign-born radicals. In a series of raids that began on November 7, federal agents seized suspected anarchists and communists and held them for deportation with no regard for due process of law. In December, 249 aliens were sent to Russia aboard the *Buford*, dubbed the "Soviet Ark" by the press. Nearly all were innocent of the charges against them.

For a time, it seemed that the Red Scare reflected the prevailing views of the American people. Instead of condemning their government's action, citizens voiced their approval and even urged more drastic steps. One patriot said his solution to the alien problem was simple: "S.O.S.—ship or shoot." General Leonard Wood, the former army chief of staff, favored placing Bolsheviks on "ships of stone with sails of lead," while evangelist Billy Sunday preferred to take "these ornery, wild-eyed Socialists" and "stand them up before a firing squad and save space on our ships."

The very extremism of the Red Scare led to its rapid demise. In early 1920, courageous government officials from the Department of Labor insisted on due process and full hearings before anyone else was deported. Prominent public leaders began to speak out against the acts of terror. Finally, Palmer himself, with evident presidential ambition, went too far. In April 1920, he warned of a vast revolution to occur on May 1; the entire New York City police force, some eleven thousand strong, was placed on duty to prepare for imminent disaster. When no bombings or violence took place on May Day, the public began to react against Palmer's hysteria. Despite a violent explosion on Wall Street in September that killed thirty-three people, the Red Scare died out by the end of 1920. Palmer passed into obscurity, the tiny Communist party became torn with factionalism, and the American people tried hard to forget their loss of balance.

Yet the Red Scare exerted a continuing influence on American society in the 1920s. The foreign born lived in the uneasy realization that they were viewed with hostility and suspicion. Two Italian aliens in Massachusetts, Nicola Sacco and Bartolomeo Vanzetti, were arrested in May 1920 for a payroll robbery and murder. They faced a prosecutor and jury who condemned them more for their ideas than for any evidence of criminal conduct and a judge who referred to them as "those anarchist bastards." Despite a worldwide effort that became the chief liberal cause of the 1920s, the courts rejected all appeals. Sacco, a shoemaker, and Vanzetti, a fish peddler, died in the electric chair on August 23, 1927. Their fate symbolized the bigotry and intolerance that lasted through the 1920s and made that decade one of the least attractive in American history.

PROHIBITION

In December 1917, Congress adopted the Eighteenth Amendment, prohibiting the manufacture and sale of alcoholic beverages. A little over a year later, Nebraska was the necessary thirty-sixth state to ratify, and prohibition became the law of the land.

Beginning January 16, 1920, the Volstead Act, which implemented prohibition, banned most commercial production and distribution of beverages containing more than one-half of 1 percent of alcohol by volume. (Exceptions were made for medicinal and religious uses of wine and spirits. Production for one's own private use was also allowed.) Prohibition was the result of both a rural effort of the Anti-Saloon League, backed by Methodist and Baptist clergymen, and the urban progressive concern over the social disease of drunkenness, especially among industrial workers. The moral issue had already led to the enactment of prohibition laws in twenty-six states by 1920; the real tragedy would occur in the effort to extend this "noble experiment" to the growing cities, where it was deeply resented by ethnic groups such as the Germans and the Irish and was almost totally disregarded by the well-to-do and the sophisticated.

Prohibition did in fact lead to a decline in drinking. Americans consumed much less alcohol in the 1920s than in the prewar years. Rural areas became totally dry, and in the cities, the consumption of alcoholic beverages dropped sharply among the lower classes, who could not afford the high prices for bootleg liquor. Among the middle class and the wealthy, however, drinking became fashionable; Americans consumed some 150 million quarts of liquor a year in the 1920s. Bootleggers took in nearly $2 billion annually, about 2 percent of the gross national product.

Urban resistance to prohibition finally led to its repeal in 1933. But in the intervening years, it damaged American society by breeding a profound disrespect for the law. The flamboyant excesses of bootleggers were only the more obvious evils spawned by prohibition. In city after city, police openly tolerated the traffic in liquor, and judges and prosecutors agreed to let bootleggers pay merely token fines, creating almost a system of licenses. Prohibition satisfied the countryside's desire for vindication, yet rural and urban America alike suffered from this overzealous attempt to legislate morals.

The Ku Klux Klan

The most ominous expression of protest against the new urban culture was the rebirth of the Ku Klux Klan. On Thanksgiving night in 1915, on Stone Mountain in Georgia, Colonel William J. Simmons and thirty-four followers founded the modern Klan. Only "native born, white, gentile Americans" were permitted to join. Membership grew slowly during World War I, but after 1920, fueled by postwar fears and shrewd promotional techniques, the Klan mushroomed. In villages, towns, and small cities across the nation, Anglo-Saxon Protestant men flocked into the newly formed chapters, seeking to relieve their anxiety over a changing society by embracing the Klan's unusual rituals and by demonstrating their hatred against blacks, aliens, Jews, and Catholics.

The Klan of the 1920s, unlike the night riders of the post–Civil War era, was not just antiblack; the threat to American culture, as Klansmen perceived it, came from aliens—Italians and Russians, Jews and Catholics. They attributed much of the tension and conflict in society to the prewar flood of immigrants, foreigners who spoke different languages, worshiped in strange churches, and lived in distant, threatening cities. The Klansmen struck back by coming together and enforcing their own values. They punished blacks who did not know their place, women who practiced the new morality, and aliens who refused to conform. Beating, flogging, burning with acid—even murder—were condoned. They also tried more peaceful methods of coercion, formulating codes of behavior and seeking communitywide support.

The Klan entered politics, at first hesitantly, then with growing confidence. The KKK gained control of the legislatures in Texas, Oklahoma, Oregon, and Indiana; in 1924, it blocked a resolution of censure at the Democratic national convention. With an estimated five million members by the mid-1920s, the Klan seemed to be fully established.

Yet the Klan fell even more quickly than it rose. Its more violent activities—which included kidnapping, lynching, setting fire to synagogues and Catholic churches, and, in one case, murdering a priest—began to offend the nation's con-

A 1925 Ku Klux Klan demonstration in Cincinnati, Ohio, attended by nearly thirty thousand robed members and marked by the induction of eight thousand young boys in the Junior Order. Only native-born, white Americans "who believe in the tenets of the Christian religion" were admitted into the Klan. The original Klan, formed during the Reconstruction era to terrorize former slaves, disbanded in 1869. The Klan that formed in 1915 declined after the mid-1920s but did not officially disband until 1944. Two years later, a third Klan emerged, focusing on the civil rights movement and communism.

science. Misuse of funds and sexual scandals among Klan leaders, notably in Indiana, repelled many of the rank and file; effective counterattacks by traditional politicians ousted the KKK from control in Texas and Oklahoma. Membership declined sharply after 1925; by the end of the decade, the Klan had virtually disappeared. But its spirit lived on, testimony to the recurring demons of nativism and hatred that have surfaced periodically throughout the American experience.

IMMIGRATION RESTRICTION

The nativism that permeated the Klan found its most successful outlet in the immigration legislation of the 1920s. The sharp increase in immigration in the late nineteenth century had led to a broad-based movement, spearheaded by organized labor and by New England aristocrats such as Henry Cabot Lodge, to restrict the flow of people from Europe. In 1917, over Wilson's veto, Congress enacted a literacy test that reduced the number of immigrants allowed into the country. The war caused a much more drastic decline—from an average of 1 million a year between 1900 and 1914 to only 110,000 in 1918.

After the armistice, however, rumors began to spread of an impending flood of people seeking to escape war-ravaged Europe. Congress in 1921 passed an emergency immigration act. The new quota system restricted immigration from Europe to 3 percent of the number of nationals from each country living in the United States in 1910. In 1924, Congress adopted the National Origins Quota

Act, which limited immigration from Europe to 150,000 a year; allocated most of the available slots to immigrants from Great Britain, Ireland, Germany, and Scandinavia; and banned all Asian immigrants. The measure passed Congress with overwhelming rural support.

The new restrictive legislation marked the most enduring achievement of the rural counterattack. Unlike the Red Scare, prohibition, and the Klan, the quota system would survive until the 1960s, enforcing a racist bias that excluded Asians and limited the immigration of Italians, Greeks, and Poles to a few thousand a year while permitting a steady stream of Irish, English, and Scandinavian immigrants. Yet even here the victory was not complete. A growing tide of Mexican laborers, exempt from the quota act, flowed northward across the Rio Grande to fill the continuing need for unskilled workers on the farms and in the service trades. The Mexican immigrants, as many as 100,000 a year, marked the strengthening of an element in the national ethnic mosaic that would grow in size and influence until it became a major force in modern American society.

THE FUNDAMENTALIST CHALLENGE

The most significant—and, as it turned out, longest-lasting—challenge to the new urban culture was rooted in the traditional religious beliefs of millions of Americans who felt alienated from city life, from science, and from much of what modernization entailed. Sometimes this challenge was direct, as when Christian fundamentalists campaigned against the teaching of evolution in the public schools. Their success in Tennessee touched off a court battle, the Scopes trial, that drew the attention of the entire country to the small town of Dayton in the summer of 1925. There, William Jennings Bryan engaged in a crusade against the theory of evolution, appearing as a chief witness against John Scopes, a high school biology teacher who had deliberately violated a new Tennessee law that forbade the teaching of Darwin's theory.

In the trial, Bryan testified under oath that he believed Jonah had been swallowed by a big fish and declared, "It is better to trust in the Rock of Ages than in the age of rocks." Chicago defense attorney Clarence Darrow succeeded in making Bryan look ridiculous. The court found Scopes guilty but let him off with a token fine; Bryan, exhausted by his efforts, died a few days later. H. L. Mencken, who covered the trial in person, rejoiced in the belief that fundamentalism was dead.

Other aspects of the fundamentalist challenge were more subtle but no less important in countering the modernizing trend. As middle- and upper-class Americans drifted into a genteel Christianity that stressed good works and respectability, the Baptist and Methodist churches continued to hold on to the old faith. In addition, aggressive fundamentalist sects such as the Churches of Christ, the Pentecostals, and Jehovah's Witnesses grew rapidly. While church membership increased from 41.9 million in 1916 to 54.5 million in 1926, the number of churches actually declined during the decade. More and more rural dwellers drove their cars into town instead of going to the local crossroads chapel.

POLITICS OF THE 1920s

The tensions between the city and the countryside also shaped the course of politics in the 1920s. On the surface, it was a Republican decade. The GOP ("Grand Old Party") controlled the White House from 1921 to 1933 and had majorities in both houses of Congress from 1919 to 1931. The Republicans used their return to power after World War I to halt further reform legislation and to establish a friendly relationship between government and business. Important shifts were taking place, however, in the American electorate. The Democrats, although divided into competing urban and rural wings, were laying the groundwork for the future by winning over millions of new voters, especially among the ethnic groups in the cities. The rising tide of urban voters indicated a fundamental shift away from the Republicans toward a new Democratic majority.

HARDING, COOLIDGE, AND HOOVER

The Republicans regained the White House in 1920 with the election of Warren G. Harding of Ohio. A dark-horse contender, Harding won the GOP nomination when the convention deadlocked and he became the compromise choice. Handsome and dignified, Harding reflected both the virtues and blemishes of small-town America. Conventional in outlook, Harding was a genial man who lacked the capacity to govern and who, as president, broadly delegated power.

He made some good cabinet choices, notably Charles Evans Hughes as secretary of state and Herbert C. Hoover as secretary of commerce, but two corrupt officials—Attorney General Harry Daugherty and Secretary of the Interior Albert Fall—sabotaged his administration. Daugherty became involved in a series of questionable deals that led ultimately to his forced resignation; Fall was the chief figure in the Teapot Dome scandal. Two oil promoters gave Fall nearly $400,000 in loans and bribes; in return, he helped them secure leases on naval oil reserves in Elk Hills, California, and Teapot Dome, Wyoming. The scandal came to light after Harding's death from a heart attack in 1923. Fall eventually served a year in jail, and the reputation of the Harding administration never recovered.

Vice President Calvin Coolidge assumed the presidency upon Harding's death, and his honesty and integrity quickly reassured the nation. Coolidge, born in Vermont of old Yankee stock, had first gained national attention in 1919 as governor of Massachusetts when he had dealt firmly with a Boston police strike by declaring, "There is no right to strike against the public safety by anybody, anywhere, any time." A reserved, reticent man, Coolidge became famous for his epigrams, which contemporaries mistook for wisdom. "The business of America is business," he proclaimed. "The man who builds a factory builds a temple; the man who works there worships there." Consistent with this philosophy, he believed his duty was simply to preside benignly, not govern the nation. Satisfied with the prosperity of the mid-1920s, the people responded favorably. Coolidge was elected to a full term by a wide margin in 1924.

When Coolidge announced in 1927 that he did not "choose to run," Herbert Hoover became the Republican choice to succeed him. By far the ablest GOP leader of the decade, Hoover epitomized the American myth of the self-made man. Orphaned as a boy, he had worked his way through Stanford University and had gained both wealth and fame as a mining engineer. During World War I, he had displayed admirable administrative skills in directing Wilson's food program at home and relief activities abroad. Sober, intelligent, and immensely hardworking, Hoover embodied the nation's faith in individualism and free enterprise.

As secretary of commerce under Harding and Coolidge, he had sought co-operation between government and business. Instead of viewing business and government as antagonists, he saw them as partners, working together to achieve efficiency and affluence for all Americans. His optimistic view of the future led him to declare in his speech accepting the Republican presidential nomination in 1928 that "we in America today are nearer to the final triumph over poverty than ever before in the history of any land."

REPUBLICAN POLICIES

During the 1920 campaign, Warren Harding urged a return to "normalcy," a coined word that became the theme for the Republican administrations of the 1920s. Aware that the public was tired of zealous reform-minded presidents such as Teddy Roosevelt and Woodrow Wilson, Harding and his successors sought a return to traditional Republican policies. In some areas they were successful, but in others the Republican leaders were forced to adjust to the new realities of a mass production society. The result was a mixture of traditional and innovative measures that was neither wholly reactionary nor entirely progressive.

The most obvious attempt to go back to the Republicanism of William McKinley came in tariff and tax policy. Fearful of a flood of postwar European imports, Congress passed an emergency tariff act in 1921 and followed it a year later with the protectionist Fordney-McCumber Tariff Act.

Secretary of the Treasury Andrew Mellon, a wealthy Pittsburgh banker and industrialist, worked hard to achieve a similar return to normalcy in taxation. Using the new budget system adopted by Congress in 1921, he reduced government spending from its World War I peak of $18 billion to just over $3 billion by 1925, thereby creating a slight surplus. Congress responded in 1926 by cutting the highest income tax bracket to a modest 20 percent.

The revenue acts of the 1920s greatly reduced the burden of taxation; by the end of the decade, the government was collecting one-third less than it had in 1921, and the number of people paying income taxes dropped from more than 6.5 million to 4 million. Yet the greatest relief went to the wealthy. The public was shocked to learn in the 1930s that J. P. Morgan and his nineteen partners had paid no income tax at all during the depths of the Great Depression.

The growing crisis in American farming during the decade forced the Republican administrations to seek new solutions. The end of the European war led to a sharp decline in farm prices and a return to the problem of overproduction. Southern and western lawmakers formed a farm bloc in Congress to press for special legislation for American agriculture. The farm bloc supported the

higher tariffs, which included protection for constituents' crops, and helped secure passage of legislation to create federal supervision over stockyards, packinghouses, and grain trading.

Despite Republican rhetoric, the government's role in the economy increased
rather than lessened in the 1920s. Herbert Hoover led the way in the Commerce
Department, establishing new bureaus to help make American industry more efficient in housing, transportation, and mining. Under his leadership, the government encouraged corporations to develop welfare programs that undercut trade
unions, and he tried to minimize labor disturbances by devising new federal machinery to mediate disputes. Instead of going back to the laissez-faire tradition of
the nineteenth century, the Republican administrations of the 1920s were pioneering a close relationship between government and private business.

THE DIVIDED DEMOCRATS

While the Republicans ruled in the 1920s, the Democrats seemed bent on self-
destruction. The Wilson coalition fell apart in 1920 as pent-up dissatisfaction
stemming from the war enabled Harding to win by a landslide. The pace of the
second Industrial Revolution and the growing urbanization split the party in
two. One faction was centered in the rural South and West. Traditional
Democrats who had supported Wilson stood for prohibition, fundamentalism,
the Klan, and other facets of the rural counterattack against the city. In contrast,
a new breed of Democrat was emerging in the metropolitan areas of the North
and Midwest. Immigrants and their descendants began to become active in the
Democratic party. Catholic or Jewish in religion and strongly opposed to prohibition, they had little in common with their rural counterparts.

The split within the party surfaced dramatically at the national convention
in New York in 1924. Held in Madison Square Garden, the convention soon
degenerated into what one observer described as a "snarling, cursing, tenuous,
suicidal, homicidal roughhouse." An urban resolution to condemn the Ku Klux
Klan led to a spirited response from the rural faction and its defeat by a single
vote. Then for nine days, in the midst of a stifling heat wave, the delegates divided between Alfred E. Smith, the governor of New York, and William G.
McAdoo of California, Wilson's secretary of the treasury. When it became clear
that neither the city nor the rural candidate could win a majority, both men
withdrew; on the 103rd ballot, the weary Democrats finally chose John W.
Davis, a former West Virginia congressman and New York corporation lawyer,
as their compromise nominee.

In the ensuing election, the conservative Davis had difficulty setting his views
apart from those of Republican president Calvin Coolidge. For the discontented,
Senator Robert La Follette of Wisconsin offered an alternative by running on an
independent Progressive party ticket. Coolidge won easily, receiving 15 million
votes to 8 million for Davis and nearly 5 million for La Follette. Davis had made
the poorest showing of any Democratic candidate in the twentieth century.

Yet the Democrats were in far better shape than this setback indicated.
Beginning in 1922, the party had made heavy inroads into the GOP majority in

THE ELECTION OF 1924

CANDIDATE	PARTY	POPULAR VOTE	ELECTORAL VOTE
Coolidge	Republican	15,725,016	382
Davis	Democrat	8,386,503	136
La Follette	Progressive	4,822,856	13

Congress. The Democrats took seventy-eight seats away from Republicans in that election, many of them in the cities of the East and Midwest. In New York alone, they gained thirteen new congressmen, all but one in districts with heavy immigrant populations. In 1926, the Democrats came within one vote of controlling the Senate and had picked up nine more seats in the House in metropolitan areas. The large cities were swinging clearly into the Democratic column; all the party needed was a charismatic leader who could fuse the older rural elements with the new urban voters.

THE ELECTION OF 1928

The selection of Governor Al Smith of New York as the Democratic candidate in 1928 indicated the growing power of the city. Born on the Lower East Side of Manhattan of mixed Irish-German ancestry, Smith was the prototype of the urban Democrat. He was Catholic; he was associated with a big-city machine; he was a "wet" who wanted to end prohibition. Rejected by rural Democrats in 1924, he still had to prove he could unite the South and West behind his leadership. His lack of education, poor grammar, and distinctive New York accent all hurt him, as did his eastern provincialism. When reporters asked him about his appeal in the states west of the Mississippi, he replied, "What states are west of the Mississippi?"

The choice facing the American voter in 1928 seemed unusually clear-cut. Herbert Hoover was a Protestant, a dry, and an old-stock American, who stood for efficiency and individualism; Smith was a Catholic, a wet, and a descendant of immigrants, who was closely associated with big-city politics. Just as Smith appealed to new voters in the cities, so Hoover won the support of many old-line Democrats who feared the city, Tammany Hall, and the pope.

The 1928 election was a dubious victory for the Republicans. Hoover won easily, defeating Smith by more than six million votes and carrying such traditionally Democratic states as Oklahoma, Texas, and Florida. But Smith succeeded for the first time in winning a majority of votes for the Democrats in the nation's twelve largest cities. A new Democratic electorate was emerging, consisting of Catholics and Jews, Irish and Italians, Poles and Greeks. Now the task was to unite the traditional Democrats of the South and West with the urban voters of the Northeast and Midwest.

THE ELECTION OF 1928

CANDIDATE	PARTY	POPULAR VOTE	ELECTORAL VOTE
Hoover	Republican	21,391,381	444
Smith	Democrat	15,016,443	87
	Minor Parties	330,725	—

THE OLD AND THE NEW

The election-night celebrations at Hoover campaign headquarters were muted by prohibition and by the president elect's natural reserve. Had Hoover known what lay just ahead for the country, and for his presidency, no doubt the party would have been even more somber.

During the 1920s, America struggled to enter the modern era. The economics of mass production and the politics of urbanization drove the country forward, but the persistent appeal of individualism and rural-based values held it back. Americans achieved greater prosperity than ever before, but the prosperity was unevenly distributed. Further, as the outbursts of nativism, ethnic and racial bigotry, and intolerance revealed, prosperity hardly guaranteed generosity or unity. Nor, for that matter, did it guarantee continued prosperity, even for those who benefited initially. As much as America changed during the 1920s, in one crucial respect the country remained as before. The American economy, for all its remarkable productive capacity, was astonishingly fragile. This was the message Hoover was soon to learn.

CHRONOLOGY

1919 U.S. agents arrest 1700 in Red Scare raids

Congress passes Volstead Act over Wilson's veto (October)

1920 Budget Bureau set up to oversee federal spending

Nineteenth Amendment passed, granting women the right to vote

Transcontinental airmail service inaugurated (September)

WWJ-Detroit broadcasts first commercial radio program (November)

1921 Congress enacts quotas for European immigrants

1923 Newspapers expose Ku Klux Klan graft, torture, and murder

Henry Luce begins publishing *Time* magazine (March)

1924 Senate probes Teapot Dome scandal

Veterans' World War I bonus bill passed

1925 John Scopes convicted of teaching theory of evolution in violation of Tennessee law (July)

1926 First Martha Graham modern dance recital (April)

1927 Charles Lindbergh completes first nonstop transatlantic flight from New York to Paris (May)

Coolidge vetoes farm price-control bill

Sacco and Vanzetti executed (August)

The movie *The Jazz Singer* features singing-talking soundtrack

26

━◆━━━◆━

FRANKLIN D. ROOSEVELT
AND THE NEW DEAL

Oscar Heline never forgot the terrible waste of the Great Depression. "Grain was being burned," he told interviewer Studs Terkel. "It was cheaper than coal." Heline lived in Iowa, in the heart of the farm belt. "A county just east of here, they burned corn in their courthouse all winter. . . . You couldn't hardly buy groceries for corn." Farmers, desperate for higher prices, resorted to destruction. As Heline recalled, "People were determined to withhold produce from the market—livestock, cream, butter, eggs, what not. If they would dump the produce, they would force the market to a higher level. The farmers would man the highways, and cream cans were emptied in ditches and eggs dumped out. They burned the trestle bridge, so the trains wouldn't be able to haul grain."

Film critic Pauline Kael recounted a different memory of the 1930s. Kael was a college student in California during the Great Depression, and was struck by the number of students who were missing fathers. "They had wandered off in disgrace because they couldn't support their families. Other fathers had killed themselves, so the family could have the insurance. Families had totally broken down." Kael and many of her classmates struggled to stay in school. "There were kids who didn't have a place to sleep, huddling under bridges on the campus. I had a scholarship, but there were times when I didn't have any food. The meals were often three candy bars."

No American who lived through the Great Depression ever forgot the experience. As the stories of Heline and Kael show, the individual memories were of hard times, but also of determination, adaptation, and survival.

The depression decade had an equally profound effect on American institutions. To cope with the problems of poverty and dislocation, Americans looked to government as never before, and in doing so transformed American politics and public life. The agent of the transformation—the man America turned to in its moment of trial—was Franklin D. Roosevelt. His answer to the country's demands for action was an ambitious program of relief and reform called the New Deal.

THE GREAT DEPRESSION

The depression of the 1930s came as a shock to Americans who had grown used to the prosperity of the 1920s. The consumer revolution of that earlier decade had fostered a general confidence that the American way of life would continue to improve. But following the collapse of the stock market in late 1929, factories closed, machines fell silent, and millions of Americans walked the streets looking for jobs that didn't exist.

THE GREAT CRASH

The consumer goods revolution contained the seeds of its own demise. The productive capacity of the automobile and appliance industries grew faster than the effective demand. Each year after 1924, the rate of increase in the sale of cars and refrigerators and ranges slowed, a natural consequence as more and more people already owned these durable goods. Production began to falter, and in 1927, the nation underwent a mild recession. The sale of durable goods declined, and construction of houses and buildings fell slightly. If corporate leaders had heeded these warning signs, they might have responded by raising wages or lowering prices, both effective ways to stimulate purchasing power and sustain the consumer goods revolution. Or if government officials had recognized the danger signals and forced a halt in installment buying and slowed bank loans, the nation might have experienced a sharp but brief depression.

Neither government nor business leaders were so farsighted. The Federal Reserve Board lowered the discount rate, charging banks less for loans in an attempt to stimulate the economy. Much of this additional credit, however, went not into solid investment in factories and machinery but instead into the stock market, touching off a new wave of speculation that obscured the growing economic slowdown and ensured a far greater crash to come.

Individuals with excess cash began to invest heavily in the stock market, betting the already impressive rise in security prices would bring them even greater windfall profits. The market had advanced in spurts during the decade; the value of all stocks listed on the New York Stock Exchange rose from $27 billion in 1925 to $67 billion in early 1929. People bet their savings on speculative stocks. Corporations used their large cash reserves to supply money to brokers who in turn loaned it to investors on margin; in 1929, for example, the Standard Oil Company of New Jersey loaned out $69 million a day in this fashion.

Investors could now play the market on credit, buying stock listed at $100 a share with $10 down and $90 on margin, the broker's loan for the balance. If the stock advanced to $150, the investor could sell and reap a gain of 500 percent on the $10 investment. And in the bull market climate of the 1920s, everyone was sure the market would go up.

Unemployment, 1929–1942

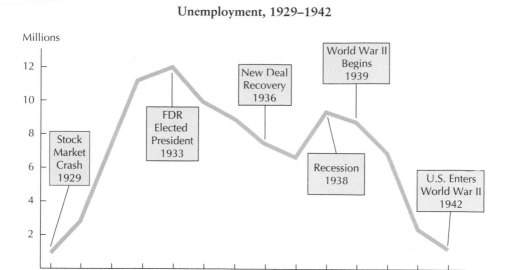

By 1929, it seemed the whole nation was engaged in speculation. In city after city, brokers opened branch offices, each complete with a stock ticker and a huge board covered with the latest Wall Street quotations. In reality, though, more people were spectators than speculators; fewer than three million Americans owned stocks in 1929, and only about a half million were active buyers and sellers. But the bull market became a national obsession, assuring everyone that the economy was healthy and preventing any serious analysis of its underlying flaws.

And then things changed, almost overnight. On October 24—later known as Black Thursday—the rise in stock prices faltered, and when it did investors nervously began to sell. Such leading stocks as RCA and Westinghouse plunged, losing nearly half their value in a single day. Speculators panicked as their creditors demanded new collateral, and the panic caused prices to plummet still further. Within weeks the gains of the previous two years had vanished.

The great crash of the stock market soon spilled over into the larger economy. Banks and other financial institutions suffered heavy losses in the market and were forced to curtail lending for consumer purchases. As consumers came up short, factories cut back production, laying off some workers and reducing hours for others. The layoffs and cutbacks lowered purchasing power even further, so fewer people bought cars and appliances. More factory layoffs resulted, and some plants closed entirely, leading to the availability of even less money for the purchase of consumer goods.

This downward economic spiral continued for four years. By 1932, unemployment had swelled to 25 percent of the workforce, while the gross national product fell to 67 percent of the 1929 level. The bright promise of mass production had ended in a nightmare.

The basic explanation for the Great Depression lies in the fact that U.S. factories produced more goods than the American people could consume. The problem was not that the market for such products was fully saturated. In 1929, there were still millions of Americans who did not own cars or radios or refrigerators, but many of them could not afford the new products. There were other contributing causes—unstable economic conditions in Europe, the agricultural decline since 1919, corporate mismanagement, and excessive speculation—but it all came down to the fact that people did not have enough money to buy the consumer products coming off the assembly lines. Installment sales helped bridge the gap, but by 1929 the burden of debt was just too great.

The new economic system had failed to distribute wealth more broadly. Too much money had gone into profits, dividends, and industrial expansion, and not enough had gone into the hands of the workers, who were also consumers. If the billions that went into stock market speculation had been used instead to increase wages—which would then have increased consumer purchasing power—production and consumption could have been brought into balance. Yet it is too much to expect that the prophets of the new era could have foreseen this flaw and corrected it. They were pioneering a new industrial system, and only out of the bitter experience of the Great Depression would they discover the full dynamics of the consumer goods economy.

EFFECT OF THE DEPRESSION

It is difficult to measure the human cost of the Great Depression. The material hardships were bad enough. Men and women lived in lean-tos made of scrap wood and metal, and families went without meat and fresh vegetables for months, existing on a diet of soup and beans. The psychological burden was even greater: Americans suffered through year after year of grinding poverty with no letup in sight. The unemployed stood in line for hours waiting for relief checks; veterans sold apples or pencils on street corners, their manhood—once prized so highly by the nation—now in question.

Few escaped the suffering. African Americans who had left the poverty of the rural South for factory jobs in the North were among the first to be laid off. Mexican immigrants, who had flowed in to replace European immigrants, met with competition from angry citizens now willing to do stoop labor in the fields and work as track layers on the railroads. Immigration officials used technicalities to halt the flow across the Rio Grande and even to reverse it; nearly a half million Mexicans were deported in the 1930s, including families with children born in the United States.

The poor—black, brown, and white—survived because they knew better than most Americans how to exist in poverty. They stayed in bed in cold weather, both to keep warm and to avoid unnecessary burning up of calories; they patched their shoes with pieces of rubber from discarded tires, heated only the kitchens of their homes, and ate scraps of food that others would reject.

The middle class, which had always lived with high expectations, was hit hard. Professionals and white-collar workers refused to ask for charity even while their families went without food; one New York dentist and his wife turned on the gas

The Great Depression devastated millions who lost their jobs and often then the means to provide food and shelter for themselves and their families. Overwhelmed local and private charities could not keep up with the demands for assistance, and many looked to the federal government for direct relief from their suffering. Breadlines stretched as far as the eye could see as impoverished workers lined up in the hope of obtaining some meager rations for their hungry families.

and left a note saying, "We want to get out of the way before we are forced to accept relief money." People who fell behind in their mortgage payments lost their homes and then faced eviction when they could not pay the rent.

Even the well-to-do were affected, giving up many of their former luxuries and weighed down with guilt as they watched former friends and business associates join the ranks of the impoverished. "My father lost everything" became an all-too-familiar refrain among young people who dropped out of college.

Many Americans sought escape in movement. Men, boys, and some women rode the rails in search of jobs, hopping freights to move south in the winter or west in the summer. One town in the Southwest hired special police to keep vagrants from leaving the boxcars. Those who became tramps had to keep on the move, but they did find a sense of community in the hobo jungles that sprang up along the major railroad routes. Here the unfortunate could find a place to eat and sleep, and people with whom to share their misery.

FIGHTING THE DEPRESSION

The Great Depression presented an enormous challenge for American political leadership. The inability of the Republicans to overcome the economic catastrophe provided the Democrats with the chance to regain power. Although they failed to achieve full recovery before the outbreak of World War II, the Democrats did succeed in alleviating some of the suffering and establishing political dominance.

HOOVER AND VOLUNTARISM

Herbert Hoover was the Great Depression's most prominent victim. When the economic downturn began in late 1929, he tried to rally the nation with bold forecasts of better days ahead. His repeated assertion that prosperity was just around the corner bred cynicism and mistrust. Expressing complete faith in the American economic system, Hoover blamed the depression on foreign causes, especially unstable European banks. The president rejected proposals for bold government action and relied instead on voluntary cooperation within business to halt the slide.

Hoover also believed in voluntary efforts to relieve the human suffering brought about by the depression. He called on private charities and local governments to help feed and clothe those in need. But when these sources were exhausted, he rejected all requests for direct federal relief, asserting that such handouts would undermine the character of proud American citizens.

As the depression deepened, Hoover reluctantly began to move beyond voluntarism to undertake more sweeping government measures. A new Federal Farm Board loaned money to aid cooperatives and bought up surplus crops in the open market in a vain effort to raise farm prices. At Hoover's request, Congress cut taxes in an attempt to restore public confidence and adopted a few federal public works projects, such as Boulder (Hoover) Dam, to provide jobs for idle men.

To help imperiled banks and insurance companies, Hoover proposed the Reconstruction Finance Corporation (RFC), which Congress established in early 1932. The RFC loaned government money to financial institutions to save them from bankruptcy. Hoover's critics, however, pointed out that while he favored aid to business, he still opposed measures such as direct relief and massive public works that would help the millions of unemployed.

By 1932, Hoover's efforts to overcome the depression had clearly failed. The Democrats had gained control of the House of Representatives in the 1930 elections and were pressing the president to take bolder action, but Hoover stubbornly resisted. His public image suffered its sharpest blow in the summer of 1932 when he ordered General Douglas MacArthur to clear out the

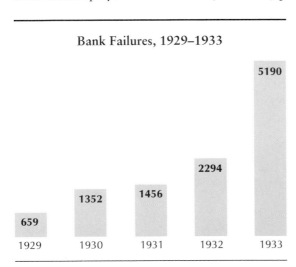

Bank Failures, 1929–1933

1929	1930	1931	1932	1933
659	1352	1456	2294	5190

Source: Data compiled from C. D. Bremer, *American Bank Failures* (New York: Columbia University Press, 1935), p. 42.

"bonus army." This ragged group of some twenty-two thousand World War I veterans had come to Washington in the summer of 1932 to lobby Congress to pay immediately a bonus for military service that was due them in 1945.

Meanwhile, the nation's banking structure approached collapse. Bank failures rose steadily in 1931 and 1932 as customers responded to rumors of bankruptcy by rushing in to withdraw their deposits. The banking crisis completed the nation's disenchantment with Hoover; people were ready for a new leader in the White House.

THE EMERGENCE OF ROOSEVELT

The man who came forward to meet this national need was Franklin D. Roosevelt. Born into the old Dutch colonial aristocracy of New York, FDR was a distant cousin of the Republican Teddy. He grew up with all the advantages of wealth—private tutors, his own sailboat and pony, frequent trips to Europe, and education at Groton and Harvard. After graduation from Harvard, he briefly attended law school but left to plunge into politics. He served in the New York legislature and then went to Washington as assistant secretary of the navy under Wilson, a post he filled capably during World War I. Defeated as the Democratic vice presidential candidate in 1920, Roosevelt had just begun a banking career when he suffered an attack of polio in the summer of 1921. Refusing to give in, he fought back bravely, and although he never again walked unaided, he reentered politics in the mid-1920s and was elected governor of New York in 1928.

Roosevelt took advantage of the opportunity offered by the Great Depression. With the Republicans discredited, he cultivated the two wings of the divided Democrats, appealing to both the traditionalists from the South and West and the new urban elements in the North. After winning the party's nomination in 1932, he broke with tradition by flying to Chicago and accepting in person, telling the cheering delegates, "I pledge you—I pledge myself to a new deal for the American people."

In the fall, he defeated Herbert Hoover in a near landslide for the Democrats. Roosevelt tallied 472 electoral votes as he swept the South and West and carried nearly all the large industrial states as well. Farmers and workers, Protestants and Catholics, immigrants and native born rallied behind the new

THE ELECTION OF 1932

CANDIDATE	PARTY	POPULAR VOTE	ELECTORAL VOTE
Roosevelt	Democratic	22,821,857	472
Hoover	Republican	15,761,841	59
	Minor Parties	1,153,306	—

leader who promised to restore prosperity. Roosevelt not only met the challenge of the depression but also solidified the shift to the Democratic party and created an enduring coalition that would dominate American politics for a half century.

THE HUNDRED DAYS

When Franklin Roosevelt took the oath of office on March 4, 1933, the nation's economy was on the brink of collapse. Unemployment stood at nearly thirteen million, one-fourth of the labor force; banks were closed in thirty-eight states. Speaking from the steps of the Capitol, FDR declared boldly, "First of all, let me assert my firm belief that the only thing we have to fear is fear itself—nameless, unreasoning, unjustified terror." Then he announced he would call Congress into special session and request "broad executive power to wage a war against the emergency, as great as the power that would be given to me if we were in fact invaded by a foreign foe."

Within the next ten days, Roosevelt won his first great New Deal victory by saving the nation's banks. On March 5, he issued a decree closing the banks and called Congress back into session. His aides drafted new banking legislation and presented it to Congress on March 9; a few hours later, both houses passed it, and FDR signed the new legislation that evening. The measure provided for government supervision and aid to the banks. Strong ones would be reopened with federal support, weak ones closed, and those in difficulty bolstered by government loans.

On March 12, FDR addressed the nation by radio in the first of his fireside chats. In conversational tones, he told the public what he had done. Some banks would begin to reopen the next day, with the government standing behind them. Other banks, once they became solvent, would open later, and the American people could safely put their money back into these institutions. The next day, March 13, the nation's largest and strongest banks opened their doors; at the end of the day, customers had deposited more cash than they withdrew. The crisis was over; gradually, other banks opened, and the runs and failures ceased.

"Capitalism was saved in eight days," boasted one of Roosevelt's advisers. Most surprising was the conservative nature of FDR's action. Instead of nationalizing the banks, he had simply thrown the government's resources behind them and preserved private ownership. Though some other New Deal measures would be more radical, Roosevelt set a tone in the banking crisis. He was out to reform and restore the American economic system, not change it drastically.

For the next three months, until it adjourned in June, Congress responded to a series of presidential initiatives. During these "Hundred Days," Roosevelt sent fifteen major requests to Congress and received back fifteen pieces of legislation. A few created permanent agencies that have become a part of American life: the Tennessee Valley Authority (TVA) proved to be the most successful and enduring of all Roosevelt's New Deal measures. This innovative effort at regional planning resulted in the building of a series of dams in seven states along the Tennessee River to control floods, ease navigation, and produce electricity.

With his fireside chats, FDR became the first president to use radio to reach and reassure the American people.

Other New Deal agencies were temporary in nature, designed to meet the specific economic problems of the Great Depression. None were completely successful; the depression would continue for another six years, immune even to Roosevelt's magic. But psychologically, the nation turned the corner in the spring of 1933. Under FDR, the government seemed to be responding to the economic crisis, enabling people for the first time since 1929 to look to the future with hope.

ROOSEVELT AND RECOVERY

Two major New Deal programs launched during the Hundred Days were aimed at industrial and agricultural recovery. The first was the National Recovery Administration (NRA), FDR's attempt to achieve economic advance through planning and cooperation among government, business, and labor. In the midst of the depression, businessowners were intent on stabilizing production and raising prices for their goods. Labor leaders were equally determined to spread work through maximum hours and to put a floor under workers' income with minimum wages.

The NRA hoped to achieve both goals by permitting companies in each major industry to cooperate in writing codes of fair competition that would set realistic limits on production, allocate percentages to individual producers, and set firm guidelines for prices. Section 7a of the enabling act mandated protection for labor in all the codes by establishing maximum hours, minimum wages, and the guarantee of collective bargaining by unions. No company could be compelled to join, but the New Deal sought complete participation by appealing to patriotism. Each firm that took part could display a blue eagle and stamp the symbol on its products. By the summer of 1933, more than five hundred industries had adopted codes that covered 2.5 million workers.

The NRA quickly bogged down in a huge bureaucratic morass. The codes proved to be too detailed to enforce easily. Written by the largest companies, the rules favored big business at the expense of smaller competitors. Labor quickly became disenchanted with Section 7a. The minimum wages were often near starvation level, while business avoided the requirement for collective bargaining by creating company unions that did not represent the real needs of workers. After a brief upsurge in the spring of 1933, industrial production began to sag as disillusionment with the NRA grew. When the Supreme Court finally invalidated the NRA in 1935 on constitutional grounds, few mourned its demise. The idea of trying to overcome the depression by relying on voluntary cooperation between competing businesses and labor leaders had collapsed in the face of individual self-interest and greed.

The New Deal's attempt at farm recovery fared a little better. Henry A. Wallace, FDR's secretary of agriculture, came up with an answer to the farmers' old dilemma of overproduction. The government would act as a clearinghouse for producers of major crops, arranging for them to set production limits for wheat, cotton, corn, and other leading crops. The Agricultural Adjustment Administration (AAA) created by Congress in May 1933 would allocate acreage among individual farmers, encouraging them to take land out of production by paying them subsidies (raised by a tax on food processors). Unfortunately, Wallace preferred not to wait until the 1934 planting season to implement this program, and so farmers were paid in 1933 to plow under crops they had already planted and to kill livestock they were raising. Faced with the problem of hunger in the midst of plenty, the New Deal seemed to respond by destroying the plenty.

The AAA program worked better in 1934 and 1935 as land removed from production led to smaller harvests and rising farm prices. Farm income rose for the first time since World War I, increasing from $2 billion in 1933 to $5 billion by 1935. Severe weather, especially Dust Bowl conditions on the Great Plains, contributed to the crop-limitation program, but most of the gain in farm income came from the subsidy payments themselves rather than from higher market prices.

On the whole, large farmers benefited most from the program. Possessing the capital to buy machinery and fertilizer, they were able to farm more efficiently than before on fewer acres of land. Small farmers, tenants, and sharecroppers did not fare as well, receiving very little of the government payments and often being driven off the land as owners took the acreage previously cultivated by tenants and sharecroppers out of production.

The Supreme Court eventually found the AAA unconstitutional in 1936, but Congress reenacted it in modified form that year and again in 1938. The system of allotments, now financed directly by the government, became a standard feature of the farm economy. The result of the New Deal for American farming was

Drought and soil erosion brought on by overfarming turned the agricultural land of the Great Plains into a giant dust bowl during the 1930s. Especially hard hit were western Kansas and Oklahoma, eastern Colorado, and the Texas Panhandle. Giant dust storms, such as the one approaching this Oklahoma ranch, forced many farmers from their land.

to hasten its transformation into a business in which only the efficient and well capitalized would thrive.

ROOSEVELT AND RELIEF

The New Deal was far more successful in meeting the most immediate problem of the 1930s—relief for the millions of unemployed and destitute citizens. Roosevelt never shared Hoover's distaste for direct federal support; on May 12, 1933, in response to FDR's March request, Congress authorized the Reconstruction Finance Corporation (RFC) to distribute $500 million to the states to help individuals and families in need.

Roosevelt brought in Harry Hopkins to direct the relief program. A former social worker who seemed to live on black coffee and cigarettes, Hopkins set up a desk in the hallway of the RFC building and proceeded to spend more than $5 million in less than two hours. The relief payments were modest in size, but they enabled millions to avoid starvation and stay out of humiliating breadlines.

Another, more imaginative early effort was the Civilian Conservation Corps (CCC), which was Roosevelt's own idea. The CCC enrolled young males from city families on relief and sent them to work on the nation's public lands, cutting

Federal work relief programs helped millions maintain their self-respect. Workers in the CCC received $30 a month for planting trees and digging drainage ditches.

trails, planting trees, building bridges, and paving roads. Ultimately, more than two million young people served in the CCC, contributing both to their families' incomes and to the nation's welfare.

Hopkins realized the need to do more than just keep people alive, and he soon became an advocate of work relief. Hopkins argued that the government should put the jobless to work, not just to encourage self-respect, but also to enable them to earn enough to purchase consumer goods and thus stimulate the entire economy. In the fall of 1933, Roosevelt created the Civil Works Administration (CWA) and charged Hopkins with getting people off the unemployment lines and relief rolls and back to work. Hopkins had more than four million men and women at work by January 1934, building roads, schools, playgrounds, and athletic fields. Many of the workers were unskilled, and some of the projects were shoddy, but the CWA at least enabled people to work and earn enough money to survive the winter. Roosevelt, appalled at the huge expenditures involved, shut down the CWA in 1934.

The final commitment to the idea of work relief came in 1935 when Roosevelt established the Works Progress Administration (WPA) to spend nearly $5 billion authorized by Congress for emergency relief. The WPA, under Hopkins, put the unemployed on the federal payroll so they could earn enough to meet their basic needs and help stimulate the stagnant economy. Conservatives complained that the WPA amounted to nothing more than hiring the jobless to do make-work tasks with no real value. But Hopkins cared less about what was accomplished than about helping those who had been unemployed for years to get off the dole and gain self-respect by working again.

In addition to funding the usual construction and conservation projects, the WPA tried to preserve the skills of American artists, actors, and writers. The Federal Theatre Project produced plays, circuses, and puppet shows that enabled entertainers to practice their crafts and to perform before people who often had never seen a professional production before. Similar projects for writers and artists led to a series of valuable state guidebooks and to murals that adorned public buildings across the land.

The WPA helped ease the burden for the unemployed, but it failed to overcome the depression. Rather than spending too much, as his critics charged, Roosevelt's greatest failure was not spending enough. The WPA never employed at any one time more than three million of the ten million jobless. The wages, although larger than relief payments, were still pitifully low, averaging only $52 a month. Thus the WPA failed to prime the American economy by increasing consumer purchasing power. Factories remained closed and machinery idle because the American people still did not have the money, either from relief or the WPA, to buy cars, radios, appliances, and the other consumer goods that had been the basis for the prosperity of the 1920s. By responding to basic human needs, Roosevelt had made the Great Depression bearable. The New Deal's failure, however, to go beyond relief to achieve prosperity led to a growing frustration and the appearance of more radical alternatives that challenged the conservative nature of the New Deal and forced FDR to shift to the left.

ROOSEVELT AND REFORM

In 1935, the focus of the New Deal shifted from relief and recovery to reform. During his first two years in office, FDR had concentrated on fighting the depression by shoring up the sagging American economy. Roosevelt was developing a "broker-state" concept of government, responding to pressures from organized elements such as corporations, labor unions, and farm groups while ignoring the needs and wants of the dispossessed who had no clear political voice. The early New Deal tried to assist bankers and industrialists, large farmers, and members of the labor unions, but it did little to help unskilled workers and sharecroppers.

The continuing depression and high unemployment began to build pressure for more sweeping changes. Roosevelt faced the choice of either providing more radical programs, ones designed to end historical inequities in American life, or deferring to others who put forth solutions to the nation's ills. Bolstered by an impressive Democratic victory in the 1934 congressional elections, Roosevelt responded by embracing a reform program that marked the climax of the New Deal.

CHALLENGES TO FDR

The signs of discontent were visible everywhere by 1935. In the upper Midwest, progressives and agrarian radicals were calling for government action to raise farm and labor income. Upton Sinclair, the muckraking novelist, nearly won the governorship of California in 1934 running on the slogan "End poverty in California," while in the East a violent strike in the textile industry shut down plants in twenty states. The most serious challenge to Roosevelt's leadership, however, came from three demagogues who captured national attention in the mid-1930s.

The first was Father Charles Coughlin, a Roman Catholic priest from Detroit, who had originally supported FDR. Speaking to a rapt nationwide radio audience in his rich, melodious voice, Coughlin appealed to the discontented with a strange mixture of crank monetary schemes and anti-Semitism. He broke with the New Deal in late 1934, denouncing it as the "Pagan Deal," and founded his own National Union for Social Justice.

A more benign but equally threatening figure appeared in California. Francis Townsend, a 67-year-old physician, came forward in 1934 with a scheme to assist the elderly, who were suffering greatly during the depression. The Townsend Plan proposed giving everyone over the age of 60 a monthly pension of $200 with the proviso that it must be spent within thirty days. Although designed less as an old-age pension plan than as a way to stimulate the economy, the proposal understandably had its greatest appeal among the elderly. Despite the criticism from economists that the plan would transfer more than half the national income to less than 10 percent of the population, more than ten million people signed petitions endorsing the Townsend Plan, and few politicians dared oppose it.

The third new voice of protest was that of Huey Long, the flamboyant senator from Louisiana. Like Coughlin, an original supporter of the New Deal, Long turned against FDR and by 1935 had become a major political threat to the president. In 1934, he announced a nationwide "Share the Wealth" movement. He spoke grandly of taking from the rich to make "every man a king," guaranteeing each American a home worth $5000 and an annual income of $2500. To finance the plan, Long advocated seizing all fortunes of more than $5 million and levying a tax of 100 percent on incomes greater than $1 million. By 1935, Long claimed to have founded twenty-seven thousand Share the Wealth clubs. Threatening to run as a third-party candidate in 1936, Long generated fear among Democratic leaders that he might attract three to four million votes, possibly enough to swing the election to the Republicans. Although an assassin killed Huey Long in Louisiana in late 1935, his popularity showed the need for the New Deal to do more to help those still in distress.

SOCIAL SECURITY

When the new Congress met in January 1935, Roosevelt was ready to support a series of reform measures designed to take the edge off national dissent. The recent elections had increased Democratic congressional strength significantly, with the

Republicans losing thirteen seats in the House and retaining less than one-third of the Senate. Many of the Democrats were to the left of Roosevelt, favoring increased spending and more sweeping federal programs. "Boys—this is our hour," exulted Harry Hopkins. "We've got to get everything we want . . . now or never."

The most significant reform enacted in 1935 was the Social Security Act. The Townsend movement had reminded Americans that the United States, alone among modern industrial nations, had never developed a welfare system to aid the aged, the disabled, and the unemployed. A cabinet committee began studying the problem in 1934, and President Roosevelt sent its recommendations to Congress the following January.

The proposed legislation had three major parts. First, it provided for old-age pensions financed equally by a tax on employers and workers, without government contributions. In addition, it gave states federal matching funds to provide modest pensions for the destitute elderly. Second, it set up a system of unemployment compensation on a federal-state basis, with employers paying a payroll tax and with each state setting benefit levels and administering the program locally. Finally, it provided for direct federal grants to the states, on a matching basis, for welfare payments to the blind, handicapped, needy elderly, and dependent children.

Although there was criticism from conservatives who mourned the passing of traditional American reliance on self-help and individualism, the chief objections came from those who argued that the administration's measure did not go far enough. Democratic leaders, however, defeated efforts to incorporate Townsend's proposal for $200 monthly pensions and increases in unemployment benefits. Congress then passed the Social Security Act by overwhelming margins.

Critics began to point out its shortcomings, as they have ever since. The old-age pensions were paltry. Designed to begin in 1942, they ranged from $10 to $85 a month. Not everyone was covered; those who most needed protection in their old age, such as farmers and domestic servants, were not included. The regressive feature of the act was even worse. All participants, regardless of income or economic status, paid in at the same rate, with no supplement from the general revenue.

Other portions of the act were equally open to question. The cumbersome unemployment system offered no aid to those currently out of work, only to people who would lose their jobs in the future. The outright grants to the handicapped and dependent children were minute in terms of the need; in New York City, for example, a blind person received only $5 a week in 1937.

The conservative nature of the legislation reflected Roosevelt's own fiscal orthodoxy, but even more it was a product of his political realism. Despite the severity of the depression, he realized that establishing a system of federal welfare went against deeply rooted American convictions. He insisted on a tax on participants to give those involved in the pension plan a vested interest in Social Security. He wanted them to feel they had earned their pensions and that in the future no one would dare take them away. "With those taxes in there," he explained privately, "no damned politician can ever scrap my social security program." Above all,

FDR had succeeded in establishing the principle of government responsibility for the aged, the handicapped, and the unemployed. Whatever the defects of the legislation, Social Security stood as a landmark of the New Deal, creating a system to provide for the welfare of individuals in a complex industrial society.

LABOR LEGISLATION

The other major reform achievement in 1935 was passage of the National Labor Relations Act. Senator Robert Wagner of New York introduced legislation in 1934 to outlaw company unions and other unfair labor practices in order to ensure collective bargaining for unions. FDR, who had little knowledge of labor-management relations and apparently little interest in them, opposed the bill. In 1935, however, Wagner began to gather broad support for his measure, which passed the Senate in May with only twelve opposing votes, and the president, seeing passage as likely, gave it his approval. The bill moved quickly through the House, and Roosevelt signed it into law in July.

The Wagner Act, as it became known, created a National Labor Relations Board to preside over labor-management relations and enable unions to engage in collective bargaining with federal support. The act outlawed a variety of union-busting tactics and in its key provision decreed that whenever the majority of a company's workers voted for a union to represent them, management would be compelled to negotiate with the union on all matters of wages, hours, and working conditions. With this unprecedented government sanction, labor unions could now recruit the large number of unorganized workers throughout the country. The Wagner Act, the most far-reaching of all New Deal measures, led to the revitalization of the American labor movement and a permanent change in labor-management relations.

Three years later, Congress passed a second law that had a lasting impact on American workers—the Fair Labor Standards Act. A long-sought goal of the New Deal, this measure aimed to establish both minimum wages and maximum hours of work per week. Since labor unions usually were able to negotiate adequate levels of pay and work for their members, the act was aimed at unorganized workers and met with only grudging support from unions.

The Fair Labor Standards Act provided for a minimum wage of 40 cents an hour by 1940 and a standard workweek of forty hours, with time and a half for overtime. Despite its loopholes, the legislation did lead to pay raises for the twelve million workers earning less than 40 cents an hour. More important, like Social Security it set up a system—however inadequate—that Congress could build on in the future to reach more generous and humane levels.

All in all, Roosevelt's record in reform was similar to that in relief and recovery—modest success but no sweeping victory. A cautious and pragmatic leader, FDR moved far enough to the left to overcome the challenges of Coughlin, Townsend, and Long without venturing too far from the mainstream. His reforms improved the quality of life in America significantly, but he made no effort to correct all the nation's social and economic wrongs.

IMPACT OF THE NEW DEAL

The New Deal had a broad influence on the quality of life in the United States in the 1930s. Government programs reached into areas hitherto untouched. Many of them brought about long-overdue improvements, but others failed to make any significant dent in historic inequities. The most important advances came with the dramatic growth of labor unions; the conditions for working women and minorities in nonunionized industries showed no comparable advance.

RISE OF ORGANIZED LABOR

Trade unions were weak at the onset of the Great Depression, with a membership of fewer than three million workers. Most were in the American Federation of Labor (AFL), composed of craft unions that served the needs of skilled workers. The nation's basic industries, such as steel and automobiles, were unorganized; the great mass of unskilled workers thus fared poorly in terms of wages and working conditions.

John L. Lewis, head of the United Mine Workers, took the lead in forming the Committee on Industrial Organization (CIO) in 1935. The son of a Welsh coal miner, Lewis was a dynamic and ruthless man. He had led the mine workers since 1919 and was determined to spread the benefits of unions throughout industry. Lewis first battled with the leadership of the AFL, and then—after being expelled—he renamed his group the Congress of Industrial Organizations and announced in 1936 that he would use the Wagner Act to extend collective bargaining to the nation's auto and steel industries.

Within five years, Lewis had scored a remarkable series of victories. Some came easily. The big steel companies, led by U.S. Steel, surrendered without a fight in 1937; management realized that federal support put the unions in a strong position. There was greater resistance in the automobile industry. When General Motors, the first target, resisted, the newly created United Automobile Workers (UAW) developed an effective strike technique. In late December 1936, GM workers in Flint, Michigan, simply sat down in the factory, refusing to leave until the company recognized their union, and threatening to destroy the valuable tools and machines if they were removed forcibly. General Motors conceded defeat and signed a contract with the UAW. Chrysler quickly followed suit, and after a hard fight, so did Ford.

By the end of the 1930s, the CIO had some five million members, slightly more than the AFL. The successes were remarkable—in addition to the automaking and steel unions, organizers for the CIO and the AFL had been successful in the textile, rubber, electrical, and metal industries. For the first time, unskilled as well as skilled were unionized. Because women and blacks made up a substantial proportion of the unskilled workforce, they too benefited from the creation of the CIO.

Yet despite these impressive gains, only 28 percent of all Americans (excluding farmworkers) belonged to unions by 1940. Employer resistance and traditional hostility to unions blocked further progress, as did the aloof attitude of

President Roosevelt. The Wagner Act had helped open the way, but labor leaders deserved most of the credit for union achievements.

THE NEW DEAL RECORD ON HELP TO MINORITIES

The Roosevelt administration's attempts to aid the downtrodden were least effective with African Americans and other racial minorities. The Great Depression had hit blacks with special force. Sharecroppers and tenant farmers had seen the price of cotton drop from 18 to 6 cents a pound, far below the level to sustain a family on the land. In the cities, the saying "Last hired, First fired" proved all too true; by 1933, more than 50 percent of urban blacks were unemployed. Hard times sharpened racial prejudice. "No jobs for niggers until every white man has a job" became a rallying cry for many whites in Atlanta.

The New Deal helped African Americans survive the depression, but it never tried to confront squarely the racial injustice built into the federal relief programs. Although the programs served blacks as well as whites, in the South the weekly payments blacks received were much smaller. Nor did later reform measures help very much. Neither the minimum wage nor Social Security covered those working as farmers or domestic servants, categories that comprised 65 percent of all African American workers. Thus an NAACP official commented that Social Security "looks like a sieve with the holes just large enough for the majority of Negroes to fall through."

Despite this bleak record, African Americans rallied behind Roosevelt's leadership, abandoning their historic ties to the Republican party. In 1936, more than 75 percent of those African Americans who voted supported FDR. In part, this switch came in response to Roosevelt's appointment of a number of prominent blacks to high-ranking government positions. Eleanor Roosevelt spoke out eloquently throughout the decade against racial discrimination, most notably in 1939 when the Daughters of the American Revolution refused to let African American contralto Marian Anderson sing in Constitution Hall. The First Lady and Interior Secretary Harold Ickes arranged for the singer to perform at the Lincoln Memorial, where 75,000 people gathered to hear her on Easter Sunday.

Perhaps the most influential factor in the African Americans' political switch was the color-blind policy of Harry Hopkins. He had more than one million blacks working for the WPA by 1939, many of them in teaching and artistic positions as well as in construction jobs. Overall, the New Deal provided assistance to 40 percent of the nation's blacks during the depression. Uneven as his record was, Roosevelt had still done more to aid this oppressed minority than any previous president since Lincoln.

The New Deal did far less for Mexican Americans. Engaged primarily in agricultural labor, these people found their wages in California fields dropping from 35 to 14 cents an hour by 1933. The pool of unemployed migrant labor expanded rapidly with Dust Bowl conditions in the Great Plains and the subsequent flight of "Okies" and "Arkies" to the cotton fields of Arizona and the truck farms of California. The Roosevelt administration cut off any further influx from Mexico by barring entry of any immigrant "likely to become a public

With the statue of Abraham Lincoln as a backdrop, African American contralto Marian Anderson sang on the steps of the Lincoln Memorial in a concert given April 9, 1939.

charge"; local authorities rounded up migrants and shipped them back to Mexico to reduce the welfare rolls.

Native Americans, after decades of neglect, fared slightly better under the New Deal. Roosevelt appointed John Collier, a social worker who championed Indian rights, to serve as commissioner of Indian affairs. In 1934, Congress passed the Indian Reorganization Act, a reform measure designed to stress tribal unity and autonomy instead of attempting (as previous policy had done) to transform Indians into self-sufficient farmers by granting them small plots of land. Despite modest gains, however, the nation's one-third million Indians remained the most impoverished citizens in America.

WOMEN AT WORK

The decade witnessed no significant gain in the status of American women. In the midst of the depression, there was little concern expressed for protecting or extending their rights. The popular idea that women worked for "pin money" while men were the breadwinners for their families led employers to discriminate in favor of men when cutting the workforce. Working women "are holding jobs that rightfully belong to the God-intended providers of the household," declared a Chicago civic group. More than three-fourths of the nation's school boards refused to hire married women, and more than half of them fired women teachers who married. Federal regulations prohibited more than one member of a family

Roosevelt appointed John Collier as commissioner of Indian affairs to bring the New Deal to Native Americans. Under the Indian Reorganization Act of 1934, more than 7 million acres of land were restored to Native American control. Still, many Indians continued to distrust the government and its New Deal programs. Collier is shown here with a group of Flathead Indian chiefs standing behind Secretary of the Interior Harold L. Ickes on October 28, 1935, as Ickes signs the first constitution providing for Indian self-rule. Previously, the Bureau of Indian Affairs had directed the government of the Indians.

from working in the civil service, and almost always it was the wife who had to defer to her husband.

Many of the working women in the 1930s were either single or the sole supporters of an entire family. Yet their wages remained lower than those for men, and their unemployment rate ran higher than 20 percent throughout the decade. The New Deal offered little encouragement. NRA codes sanctioned lower wages for women, permitting laundries, for example, to pay them as little as 14 cents an hour. The minimum wage did help those women employed in industry, but too many worked as maids and waitresses—jobs not covered by the law—for the new law to have much overall effect on women's income.

The one area of advance in the 1930s came in government. Eleanor Roosevelt set an example that encouraged millions of American women. Instead of presiding sedately over the White House, she traveled continually around the country, always eager to uncover wrongs and bring them to the president's attention. Frances Perkins, the secretary of labor, became the first woman cabinet member, and FDR appointed women as ambassadors and federal judges for the first time.

Women also were elected to office in larger numbers in the 1930s. Hattie W. Caraway of Arkansas succeeded her husband in the Senate, winning a full term in 1934. That same year, voters elected six women to the House of

Eleanor Roosevelt visited many sites in her efforts to bring the New Deal to the forgotten and the dispossessed. She is shown here visiting an African American nursery school run by the WPA in Des Moines, Iowa.

Representatives. Public service, however, was one of the few professions open to women. The nation's leading medical and law schools discouraged women from applying, and the percentage of female faculty members in colleges and universities continued to decline in the 1930s. In sum, a decade that was grim for most Americans was especially hard on American women.

END OF THE NEW DEAL

The New Deal reached its high point in 1936, when Roosevelt was overwhelmingly reelected and the Democratic party strengthened its hold on Congress. This political triumph was deceptive. In the next two years, Roosevelt met with a series of defeats in Congress. Yet despite the setbacks, he remained a popular political leader who had restored American self-confidence as he strove to meet the challenges of the Great Depression.

THE ELECTION OF 1936

Franklin Roosevelt enjoyed his finest political hour in 1936. A man who loved the give-and-take of politics, FDR faced challenges from both the left and the right as he sought reelection. Father Coughlin helped organize a Union party,

THE ELECTION OF 1936

CANDIDATE	PARTY	POPULAR VOTE	ELECTORAL VOTE
Roosevelt	Democratic	27,751,597	523
Landon	Republican	16,679,583	8

with North Dakota Progressive Congressman William Lemke heading the ticket. At the other extreme, a group of wealthy industrialists formed the Liberty League to fight what they saw as the New Deal's assault on property rights. The Liberty League endorsed the Republican presidential candidate, Governor Alfred M. Landon of Kansas. A moderate, colorless figure, Landon disappointed his backers by refusing to campaign for repeal of the popular New Deal reforms.

Roosevelt ignored Lemke and the Union party, focusing attention instead on the assault from the right. In his speeches, FDR condemned the "economic royalists" who were "unanimous in their hatred for me." "I welcome their hatred," he declared, and promised that in his second term, these forces would meet "their master."

This frank appeal to class sympathies proved enormously successful. Roosevelt won easily, receiving five million more votes than he had in 1932 and outscoring Landon in the electoral college by 523 to 8. The Democrats did almost as well in Congress, piling up margins of 331 to 89 in the House and 76 to 16 in the Senate (with 4 not aligned with either major party).

Equally important, the election marked the stunning success of a new political coalition that would dominate American politics for the next three decades. FDR, building on the inroads into the Republican majority that Al Smith had begun in 1928, carried urban areas by impressive margins, winning 3.6 million more votes than his opponents in the nation's twelve largest cities. He held on to the traditional Democratic votes in the South and West and added to them by appealing strongly to the diverse religious and ethnic groups in the northern cities—Catholics and Jews, Italians and Poles, Irish and Slavs. The strong support of labor, together with three-quarters of the black vote, indicated that the nation's new alignment followed economic as well as cultural lines. The poor and the oppressed, who in the depression years included many middle-class Americans, became attached to the Democratic party, leaving the GOP in a minority position, limited to the well-to-do and to rural and small-town Americans of native stock.

THE SUPREME COURT FIGHT

FDR proved to be far more adept at winning electoral victories than in achieving his goals in Congress. In 1937, he attempted to use his recent success to overcome the one obstacle remaining in his path—the Supreme Court. During his first term, the Court had ruled several New Deal programs unconstitutional, most notably the NRA and the AAA. Only three of the nine justices were sympathetic to the need for emergency measures in the midst of the depression. Two others were unpredictable, sometimes approving New Deal measures and sometimes opposing them. Four justices were bent on using the Constitution to block Roosevelt's proposals.

When Congress convened in 1937, the president offered a startling proposal to overcome the Court's threat to the New Deal. Instead of seeking a constitutional amendment either to limit the Court's power or to clarify the constitutional issues, FDR chose an oblique attack. Declaring the Court was falling behind schedule because of the age of its members, he asked Congress to appoint a new justice for each member of the Court over the age of 70, up to a maximum of six.

Although this "court-packing" scheme, as critics quickly dubbed it, was perfectly legal, it outraged not only conservatives but also liberals, who realized it could set a dangerous precedent for the future. Republicans wisely kept silent, letting prominent Democrats lead the fight against Roosevelt's plan. Despite all-out pressure from the White House, resistance in the Senate blocked early action on the proposal.

The Court defended itself well. Chief Justice Charles Evans Hughes testified tellingly to the Senate Judiciary Committee, pointing out that in fact the Court was up to date and not behind schedule as Roosevelt charged. The Court then surprised observers with a series of rulings approving such controversial New Deal measures as the Wagner Act and Social Security. Believing he had proved his point, the president allowed his court-packing plan to die in the Senate.

During the next few years, Roosevelt was able to appoint such distinguished jurists as Hugo Black, William O. Douglas, and Felix Frankfurter to the Supreme Court. Yet the price was high. The court fight had badly weakened the president's relations with Congress, opening deep rifts with members of his own party. Many senators and representatives who had voted reluctantly for Roosevelt's measures during the depths of the depression now felt free to oppose any further New Deal reforms.

THE NEW DEAL IN DECLINE

The legislative record during Roosevelt's second term was meager. Aside from the minimum wage and maximum-hour law passed in 1938, Congress did not extend the New Deal into any new areas. Disturbed by the growing congressional resistance, Roosevelt set out in the spring of 1938 to defeat a number of conservative Democratic congressmen and senators, primarily in the South. His targets gleefully charged the president with interference in local politics; only one of the men he sought to defeat lost in the primaries. The failure of this attempted purge further undermined Roosevelt's strained relations with Congress.

The worst blow came in the economic sector. The slow but steady improvement in the economy suddenly gave way to a sharp recession in the late summer of 1937. In the following ten months, industrial production fell by one-third, and nearly four million workers lost their jobs. Critics of the New Deal quickly labeled the downturn "the Roosevelt recession," and business executives claimed that it reflected a lack of confidence in FDR's leadership.

The criticism was overblown but not without basis. In an effort to reduce expanding budget deficits, Roosevelt had cut back sharply on WPA and other government programs after the election. For several months, Roosevelt refused to heed calls from economists to renew heavy government spending. Finally, in April 1938, Roosevelt asked Congress for a $3.75 billion relief appropriation, and the economy began to revive. But FDR's premature attempt to balance the budget had meant two more years of hard times and had marred his reputation as the energetic foe of the Great Depression.

The political result of the attempted purge and the recession was a strong Republican upsurge in the elections of 1938. The GOP won an impressive 81 seats in the House and 8 more in the Senate, as well as 13 governorships. The Democrats still held a sizable majority in Congress, but their margin in the House was particularly deceptive. There were 262 Democratic representatives to 169 Republicans, but 93 southern Democrats held the balance of power. More and more often after 1938, anti–New Deal Southerners voted with Republican conservatives to block social and economic reform measures. Thus not only was the New Deal over by the end of 1938, but a new bipartisan conservative coalition that would prevail for a quarter century had formed in Congress.

EVALUATION OF THE NEW DEAL

The New Deal lasted a brief five years, and most of its measures came in two legislative bursts in the spring of 1933 and the summer of 1935. Yet its impact on American life was enduring. Nearly every aspect of economic, social, and political development in the decades that followed bore the imprint of Roosevelt's leadership.

The least impressive achievement of the New Deal came in the economic realm. Whatever credit Roosevelt is given for relieving human suffering in the depths of the Great Depression must be balanced against his failure to achieve recovery in the 1930s. The moderate nature of his programs, especially the unwieldy NRA, led to slow and halting industrial recovery. Although much of the improvement that was made came as a result of government spending, FDR never embraced the concept of planned deficits, striving instead for a balanced budget. As a result, the nation had barely reached the 1929 level of production a decade later, and there were still nearly ten million men and women unemployed.

Equally important, Roosevelt refused to make any sweeping changes in the American economic system. Aside from the TVA, there were no broad experiments in regional planning and no attempt to alter free enterprise beyond imposing some limited forms of government regulation. The New Deal did nothing to alter the basic distribution of wealth and power in the nation. The outcome was the preservation of the traditional capitalist system with a thin overlay of federal control.

More significant change occurred in American society. With the adoption of Social Security, the government acknowledged for the first time its responsibility to provide for the welfare of those unable to care for themselves in an industrial society. The Wagner Act helped stimulate the growth of labor unions to balance corporate power, and the minimum wage law provided a much needed floor for many workers. Yet the New Deal tended to help only the more vocal and organized groups, such as union members and commercial farmers. People without effective voices or political clout received little help from the New Deal. For all the appealing rhetoric about the "forgotten man," Roosevelt did little more than Hoover in responding to the long-term needs of the dispossessed.

The most lasting impact of the Roosevelt leadership came in politics. Taking advantage of the emerging power of ethnic voters and capitalizing on the frustration growing out of the depression, FDR proved to be a genius at forging a new coalition. Overcoming the friction between rural and urban Democrats that had prolonged Republican supremacy in the 1920s, he attracted new groups to the Democratic party, principally African Americans and organized labor. His political success led to a major realignment that lasted long after he left the scene.

His political achievement also reveals the true nature of Roosevelt's success. He was a brilliant politician who recognized the essence of leadership in a democracy—appealing directly to the people and giving them a sense of purpose. He succeeded in infusing them with the same indomitable courage and jaunty optimism that had marked his own battle with polio. Thus, despite his limitations as a reformer, Roosevelt proved to be the leader the American people needed in the 1930s—a president who provided the psychological lift that helped them endure and survive the Great Depression.

CHRONOLOGY

1932   Franklin D. Roosevelt elected president

1933   Emergency Banking Relief Act passed in one day (March)

Twenty-first Amendment repeals prohibition (December)

1934   Securities and Exchange Commission authorized (June)

1935   Works Progress Administration (WPA) hires unemployed (April)

Wagner Act grants workers collective bargaining (July)

Congress passes Social Security Act (August)

1936   FDR wins second term as president

1937   United Automobile Workers sit-down strike forces General Motors contract (February)

FDR loses court-packing battle (July)

"Roosevelt recession" begins (August)

1938   Congress sets minimum wage at 40 cents an hour (June)

27

AMERICA AND THE WORLD, 1921–1945

On August 27, 1928, U.S. Secretary of State Frank B. Kellogg, French Foreign Minister Aristide Briand, and representatives of twelve other nations met in Paris to sign a treaty outlawing war. Several hundred spectators crowded into the ornate clock room of the Quai d'Orsay to watch the historic ceremony. Six huge klieg lights illuminated the scene so photographers could record the moment for a world eager for peace. Briand opened the ceremony with a speech in which he declared, "Peace is proclaimed," and then Kellogg signed the document with a foot-long gold pen given to him by the citizens of Le Havre as a token of Franco-American friendship. In the United States, a senator called the Kellogg-Briand Pact "the most telling action ever taken in human history to abolish war."

In reality, the Pact of Paris was the result of a determined American effort to avoid involvement in the European alliance system. In June 1927, Briand had sent a message to the American people inviting the United States to join with France in signing a treaty to outlaw war between the two nations. The invitation struck a sympathetic response, especially among pacifists who had advocated the outlawing of war throughout the 1920s, but the State Department feared correctly that Briand's true intention was to establish a close tie between France and the United States. The French had already created a network of alliances with the smaller countries of eastern Europe; an antiwar treaty with the United States would at least ensure American sympathy, if not involvement, in case of another European war. Kellogg delayed several months and then outmaneuvered Briand by proposing the pledge against war not be confined just to France and the United States, but instead be extended to all nations.

Eventually the signers of the Kellogg-Briand Pact included nearly every nation in the world, but the effect was negligible. All promised to renounce war as an instrument of national policy, except in matters of self-defense. Enforcement of the treaty relied solely on the moral force of world opinion. The Pact of Paris was, as one senator shrewdly commented, only "an international kiss."

Unfortunately, the Kellogg-Briand Pact was symbolic of American foreign policy in the years immediately following World War I. Instead of asserting the role of world leadership its resources and power commanded, the United States retreated from involvement with other nations. America went its own way, extending trade and economic dominance but refusing to take the lead in maintaining world order. This retreat from responsibility seemed unimportant in the 1920s when exhaustion from World War I ensured relative peace and tranquility. But in the 1930s, when threats to world order arose in Europe and Asia, the American people retreated even deeper, searching for an isolationist policy that would spare them the agony of another great war.

There was no place to hide in the modern world. The Nazi onslaught in Europe and the Japanese expansion in Asia finally convinced America to reverse its isolationist stance and become involved in World War II in late 1941, at a time when the chances for an Allied victory seemed most remote. With incredible swiftness, the nation mobilized its military and industrial strength. American armies were soon fighting on three continents, the U.S. Navy controlled the world's oceans, and the nation's factories were sending a vast stream of war supplies to more than twenty Allied countries.

When Allied victory came in 1945, the United States was by far the most powerful nation in the world. But instead of the enduring peace that might have permitted a return to a less active foreign policy, the onset of the Cold War with the Soviet Union brought on a new era of tension and rivalry. This time the United States could not retreat from responsibility. World War II was a coming of age for American foreign policy.

RETREAT, REVERSAL, AND RIVALRY

"The day of the armistice America stood on the hilltops of glory, proud in her strength, invincible in her ideals, acclaimed and loved by a world free of an ancient fear at last," wrote journalist George Creel in 1920. "Today we writhe in a pit of our own digging; despising ourselves and despised by the betrayed peoples of earth." The bitter disillusionment Creel described ran through every aspect of American foreign policy in the 1920s. In contrast to diplomatic actions under Wilsonian idealism, American diplomats in the 1920s made loans, negotiated treaties and agreements, and pledged the nation's good faith, but they were careful not to make any binding commitments on behalf of world order. The result was neither isolation nor involvement but rather a cautious middle course that managed to alienate friends and encourage foes.

RETREAT IN EUROPE

The United States emerged from World War I as the richest nation on earth, displacing England from its prewar position of economic primacy. The Allied governments owed the United States a staggering $10 billion in war debts, money they had borrowed during and immediately after the conflict. Each year of the 1920s saw the nation increase its economic lead as the balance of trade tipped heavily in America's favor. By 1929, American exports totaled more than $7 billion a year, three times the prewar level, and American overseas investment had risen to $17.2 billion.

The European nations could no longer compete on equal terms. The high American tariff, first imposed in 1922 and then raised again in 1930, frustrated attempts by England, France, and a defeated Germany to earn the dollars necessary to meet their American financial obligations. The Allied partners in World War I asked Washington to cancel the $10 billion in war debts, but American leaders from Wilson to Hoover indignantly refused the request, claiming the ungrateful Allies were trying to repudiate their sacred obligations.

Only a continuing flow of private American capital to Germany allowed the payment of reparations to the Allies and the partial repayment of the Allies' war debts in the 1920s. The financial crash of 1929 halted the flow of American dollars across the Atlantic and led to subsequent default on the debt payments, with accompanying bitterness on both sides of the ocean.

Political relations fared little better. The United States never joined the League of Nations, nor did it take part in the attempts by England and France to negotiate European security treaties. The Republican administrations of the 1920s refused to compromise American freedom of action by embracing collective security, the principle on which the League was founded. And FDR made no effort to renew Wilson's futile quest. Thus the United States remained aloof from the European balance of power and refused to stand behind the increasingly shaky Versailles settlement.

The U.S. government ignored the Soviet Union throughout the 1920s. American businessmen, however, actively traded with the Soviets and pressed for diplomatic recognition of the Bolshevik regime. In 1933, Franklin Roosevelt finally signed an agreement opening up diplomatic relations between the two countries.

COOPERATION IN LATIN AMERICA

U.S. policy was both more active and more enlightened in the Western Hemisphere than in Europe. When FDR took office in 1933, relations with Latin America were far better than they had been under Wilson, but American trade in the hemisphere had fallen drastically as the Great Depression worsened. Roosevelt moved quickly to solidify the improved relations and gain economic benefits. With his usual flair for the dramatic, he proclaimed a Good Neighbor Policy and then proceeded to win goodwill by renouncing the imperialism of the past.

In 1933, Secretary of State Cordell Hull signed a conditional pledge of nonintervention at a Pan-American conference in Montevideo, Uruguay. A year later, the United States renounced the right to intervene in Cuban affairs it had asserted under the Platt Amendment and loosened its grip on Panama. By 1936, American troops were no longer occupying any Latin American nation.

The United States had not changed its basic goal of political and economic dominance in the hemisphere; rather, the new policy of benevolence reflected Roosevelt's belief that cooperation and friendship were more effective tactics than threats and armed intervention. American commerce with Latin America increased fourfold in the 1930s, and investment rose substantially from its Great Depression low. Most important, FDR succeeded in forging a new policy of regional collective security. As the ominous events leading to World War II unfolded in Europe and Asia, the nations of the Western Hemisphere looked to the United States for protection against external danger.

RIVALRY IN ASIA

In the years following World War I, the United States and Japan were on a collision course in the Pacific. The Japanese, lacking the raw materials to sustain their developing industrial economy, were determined to expand onto the Asian mainland. They had taken Korea by 1905 and during World War I had extended their control over the mines, harbors, and railroads of Manchuria, the industrial region of northeast China. The American Open Door policy remained the primary obstacle to complete Japanese dominion over China. The United States thus faced the clear-cut choice of either abandoning China or forcefully opposing Japan's expansion. American efforts to avoid making this painful decision postponed the eventual showdown but not the growing rivalry.

The first attempt at a solution came in 1921 when the United States convened the Washington Conference, which included delegates from the United States, Japan, Great Britain, and six other nations. The major objective was a political settlement of the tense Asian situation, but the most pressing issue was a dangerous naval race between Japan and the United States. Both nations were engaged in extensive shipbuilding programs begun during the war; Great Britain was forced to compete in order to preserve its traditional control of the sea.

After three months of negotiation, the delegates signed a Five Power Treaty limiting capital ships (battleships and aircraft carriers) in a ratio of 5:5:3 for the United States, Britain, and Japan, respectively, and 1.67:1.67 for France and Italy. England reluctantly accepted equality with the United States, while Japan agreed to the lower ratio only in return for an American pledge not to fortify Pacific bases such as the Philippines and Guam. The Washington Conference produced two other major agreements: the Nine Power Treaty and the Four Power Treaty. The first simply pledged all the countries involved to uphold the Open Door policy, while the other compact replaced the old Anglo-Japanese alliance with a new Pacific security pact signed by the United States, Great Britain, Japan, and France. Neither document contained any enforcement provision beyond a promise to consult in case of a violation. In essence, the Washington treaties formed a parchment peace, a pious set of pledges that attempted to freeze the status quo in the Pacific.

This compromise lasted less than a decade. In September 1931, Japanese forces violated the Nine Power Treaty and the Kellogg-Briand Pact by overrunning Manchuria in a brutal act of aggression. The United States, paralyzed by the Great Depression, responded feebly. Secretary of State Henry L. Stimson issued notes in January 1932 vowing the United States would not recognize the legality of the Japanese seizure of Manchuria. Despite concurrence by the League on nonrecognition, the Japanese ignored the American moral sanction and incorporated the former Chinese province, now renamed Manchukuo, into their expanding empire.

Aside from the Good Neighbor approach in the Western Hemisphere, American foreign policy faithfully reflected the prevailing disillusionment with world power that gripped the country after World War I. The United States avoided taking any constructive steps toward preserving world order, preferring instead the empty symbolism of the Washington treaties and the Kellogg-Briand Pact.

ISOLATIONISM

The retreat from an active world policy in the 1920s turned into a headlong flight back to isolationism in the 1930s. Two factors were responsible. First, the Great Depression made foreign policy seem remote and unimportant to most Americans. Second, the danger of war abroad, when it did finally penetrate the American consciousness, served only to strengthen the desire to escape involvement.

Three powerful and discontented nations were on the march in the 1930s: Germany, Italy, and Japan. In Germany, Adolf Hitler came to power in 1933 as the head of a National Socialist, or Nazi, movement. A shrewd and charismatic leader, Hitler capitalized on both domestic discontent and bitterness over World War I. Blaming the Jews for all of Germany's ills and asserting the supremacy of the "Aryan" race of blond, blue-eyed Germans, he quickly imposed a totalitarian dictatorship in which the Nazi party ruled and the Führer was supreme. Hitler took Germany out of the League of Nations, reoccupied the Rhineland, and formally denounced the Treaty of Versailles. His boasts of uniting all Germans into a Greater Third Reich that would last a thousand years filled his European opponents with terror, blocking any effective challenge to his regime.

In Italy, another dictator, Benito Mussolini, had come to power in 1922. Emboldened by Hitler's success, he embarked on an aggressive foreign policy in 1935. His invasion of the independent African nation of Ethiopia led its emperor, Haile Selassie, to call on the League of Nations for support. With England and France far more concerned about Hitler, the League's halfhearted measures utterly failed to halt Mussolini's conquest.

Japan formed the third element in the threat to world peace. Militarists began to dominate the government in Tokyo by the mid-1930s, using tactics of fear and even assassination against their liberal opponents. By 1936, Japan had left the League of Nations and had repudiated the Washington treaties. A year later, its armies began an invasion of China that marked the beginning of the Pacific phase of World War II.

The resurgence of militarism in Germany, Italy, and Japan undermined the Versailles settlement and threatened to destroy the existing balance of power. In 1937, the three totalitarian nations signed an anti-Comintern pact completing a Berlin-Rome-Tokyo axis. Their alliance ostensibly was aimed at the Soviet Union, but in fact it threatened the entire world. Only a determined American response could unite the other nations against the Axis threat. Unfortunately, the United States deliberately abstained from assuming the role of leadership until it was nearly too late.

THE LURE OF PACIFISM AND NEUTRALITY

The growing danger of war abroad led to a rising American desire for peace and noninvolvement. Memories of World War I contributed heavily. Erich Maria Remarque's novel *All Quiet on the Western Front,* as well as the movie based on it, reminded people of the brutality of war. Historians began to treat the Great War as a mistake, criticizing Wilson for failing to preserve American neutrality and claiming the clever British had duped the United States into entering the war. American youth made clear their determination not to repeat the errors of their elders. Pacifism swept across college campuses. A Brown University poll indicated 72 percent of the students opposed military service in wartime. At Princeton, undergraduates formed the Veterans of Future Wars, a parody on veterans' groups, to demand a bonus of $1000 apiece before they marched off to a foreign war.

The pacifist movement found a scapegoat in the munitions industry. The publication of several books exposing the unsavory business tactics of large arms dealers such as Krupp in Germany and Vickers in Britain led to a demand to curb these "merchants of death." Senator Gerald Nye of North Dakota headed a special Senate committee that spent two years investigating American munitions dealers. The committee revealed the enormous profits firms such as Du Pont reaped from World War I, but Nye went further, charging that bankers and munitions makers were responsible for American intervention in 1917. No proof was forthcoming, but the public—prepared to believe the worst of businessmen during the depression—accepted the "merchants of death" thesis.

The Nye Committee's revelations culminated in neutrality legislation. In 1935, Senator Nye and another Senate colleague introduced measures to ban arms sales and loans to belligerents and to prevent Americans from traveling on belligerent ships. By outlawing the activities that led to World War I, they hoped, the United States could avoid involvement in the new conflict. This "never again" philosophy proved irresistible. In August 1935, Congress passed the first of three neutrality acts. The 1935 law banned the sale of arms to nations at war and warned American citizens not to sail on belligerent ships. In 1936, a second act added a ban on loans, and in 1937, a third neutrality act made these prohibitions permanent and required, on a two-year trial basis, that all trade other than munitions be conducted on a cash-and-carry basis.

President Roosevelt played a passive role in the adoption of the neutrality legislation. Privately, he expressed some reservations, but publicly he bowed to the prevailing isolationism. Yet FDR did take a few steps to try to limit the nation's retreat into isolationism. His failure to invoke the neutrality act after the Japanese invasion of China in 1937 enabled the hard-pressed Chinese to continue buying arms from the United States. FDR's strongest public statement came in Chicago in October 1937, when he denounced "the epidemic of world lawlessness" and called for an international effort to "quarantine" the disease.

WAR IN EUROPE

The neutrality legislation played directly into the hands of Adolf Hitler. Bent on the conquest of Europe, he could now proceed without worrying about American interference. In March 1938, he seized Austria in a bloodless coup. Six

Hitler sent his armies into Poland with tremendous force and firepower, devastating the country. When Jews, such as these residents of the Warsaw Ghetto, fell into the hands of the Nazi occupiers, they were deported to slave labor camps that soon became the sites of mass extermination.

months later, he was demanding the Sudetenland, a province of Czechoslovakia with a large German population. When the British and French leaders approved Hitler's move at their Munich conference, FDR gave his tacit consent.

Six months after the meeting at Munich, Hitler violated his promises by seizing nearly all of Czechoslovakia. In the United States, Roosevelt permitted the State Department to press for neutrality revision. The administration proposal to repeal the arms embargo and place *all* trade with belligerents, including munitions, on a cash-and-carry basis soon met stubborn resistance from isolationists. They argued that cash-and-carry would favor England and France, which controlled the sea. The House rejected the measure by a narrow margin, and the Senate's Foreign Relations Committee voted 12 to 11 to postpone any action on neutrality revision.

On September 1, 1939, Hitler began World War II by invading Poland. England and France responded two days later by declaring war, although there was no way they could prevent the German conquest of Poland. Russia had played a key role, refusing Western overtures for a common front against Germany and finally signing a nonaggression treaty with Hitler in late August. The Nazi-Soviet Pact enabled Germany to avoid a two-front war; the Russians were rewarded with a generous slice of eastern Poland.

President Roosevelt reacted to the outbreak of war by proclaiming American neutrality, but the successful aggression by Nazi Germany brought into question the isolationist assumption that American well-being did not depend on the

European balance of power. Strategic as well as ideological considerations began to undermine the earlier belief that the United States could safely pursue a policy of neutrality and noninvolvement. Americans came to realize that their own democracy and security were at stake in the European war.

THE ROAD TO WAR

For two years, the United States tried to remain at peace while war raged in Europe and Asia. In contrast to the climate of the country while Wilson attempted to be impartial during most of World War I, however, the American people displayed an overwhelming sympathy for the Allies and total distaste for Germany and Japan. Roosevelt made no secret of his preference for an Allied victory, but a fear of isolationist criticism compelled him to move slowly, and often deviously, in adopting a policy of aid for England and France.

FROM NEUTRALITY TO UNDECLARED WAR

Two weeks after the outbreak of war in Europe, Roosevelt called Congress into special session to revise the neutrality legislation. He wanted to repeal the arms embargo in order to supply weapons to England and France, but he refused to state this aim openly. Instead he asked Congress to replace the arms embargo with cash-and-carry regulations. Belligerents would be able to purchase war supplies in the United States, but they would have to pay cash and transport the goods in their own ships. Public opinion strongly supported the president, and Congress passed the revised neutrality policy by heavy margins in early November 1939.

A series of dramatic German victories had a profound impact on American opinion. Quiet during the winter of 1939–1940, the Germans struck with lightning speed and devastating effect in the spring. In April, they seized Denmark and Norway, and on May 10, 1940, they unleashed the *blitzkrieg* (lightning war) on the western front. Within three weeks, the British were driven off the Continent. In another three weeks, France fell to Hitler's victorious armies.

Americans were stunned. Hitler had taken only six weeks to achieve what Germany had failed to do in four years of fighting in World War I. Suddenly they realized they did have a stake in the outcome; if England fell, Hitler might well gain control of the British navy. The Atlantic would no longer be a barrier; instead, it would be a highway for German penetration of the New World.

Roosevelt responded by invoking a policy of all-out aid to the Allies, short of war. Denouncing Germany and Italy as representing "the gods of force and hate" he pledged American support for England and its allies. It was too late to help France, but in early September, FDR announced the transfer of fifty old destroyers to England in exchange for rights to build air and naval bases on eight British possessions in the Western Hemisphere.

Isolationists cried out against this departure from neutrality. A bold headline in the *St. Louis Post-Dispatch* read, "Dictator Roosevelt Commits Act of War." A group of Roosevelt's opponents in the Midwest formed the America First Committee to protest the drift toward war. Voicing belief in a "Fortress America," they denied that Hitler threatened American security and claimed that the nation had the strength to defend itself regardless of what happened in Europe.

To support the administration's policies, opponents of the isolationists organized the Committee to Defend America by Aiding the Allies. Eastern Anglophiles, moderate New Dealers, and liberal Republicans made up the bulk of the membership, with Kansas newspaper editor William Allen White serving as chairman. The White Committee, as it became known, advocated unlimited assistance to England short of war. Above all, the interventionists challenged the isolationist premise that events in Europe did not affect American security. "The future of western civilization is being decided upon the battlefield of Europe," White declared.

In the ensuing debate, the American people gradually came to agree with the interventionists. The battle of Britain helped. "Every time Hitler bombed London, we got a couple of votes," noted one interventionist. Frightened by the events in Europe, Congress approved large sums for preparedness, increasing the defense budget from $2 billion to $10 billion during 1940. Roosevelt courageously asked for a peacetime draft, the first in American history, to build up the army; in September, Congress agreed.

The sense of crisis affected domestic politics. Roosevelt ran for an unprecedented third term in 1940 because of the European war; the Republicans nominated Wendell Willkie, a former Democratic businessman who shared FDR's commitment to aid for England. Both candidates made appeals to peace sentiment during the campaign, but Roosevelt's decisive victory made it clear that the nation supported his increasing departure from neutrality.

After the election, FDR took his boldest step. Responding to British Prime Minister Winston Churchill's warning that England was running out of money, the president asked Congress to approve a new program to lend and lease goods and weapons to countries fighting against aggressors.

Isolationists angrily denounced Lend-Lease as both unnecessary and untruthful. "Lending war equipment is a good deal like lending chewing gum," commented Senator Taft. "You don't want it back." In March 1941, however, Congress voted by substantial margins to authorize the president to "sell, transfer title to, exchange, lease, lend, or otherwise dispose of" war supplies to "any country the President deems vital to the defense of the United States." The ac-

The Election of 1940

CANDIDATE	PARTY	POPULAR VOTE	ELECTORAL VOTE
Roosevelt	Democratic	27,244,160	449
Willkie	Republican	22,305,198	82

companying $7 billion appropriation ended the "cash" part of cash-and-carry and ensured Britain full access to American war supplies.

The "carry" problem still remained. German submarines were sinking more than 500,000 tons of shipping a month. England desperately needed the help of the American navy in escorting convoys across the U-boat–infested waters of the North Atlantic. Roosevelt, fearful of isolationist reaction, responded with naval patrols in the western half of the ocean. Hitler placed his submarine commanders under strict restraints to avoid drawing America into the European war.

Nevertheless, incidents were bound to occur. On October 17, 1941, a German submarine damaged the U.S. destroyer *Kearney;* ten days later, another U-boat sank the *Reuben James,* killing more than one hundred American sailors. FDR issued orders for the destroyers to shoot U-boats on sight. He also asked Congress to repeal the "carry" section of the neutrality laws and permit American ships to deliver supplies to England. In mid-November, Congress approved these moves by slim margins. Now American merchant ships as well as destroyers would become targets for German attacks. By December, it seemed only a matter of weeks—or months at most—until repeated sinkings would lead to a formal declaration of war against Germany.

In leading the nation to the brink of war in Europe, Roosevelt opened himself to criticism from both sides in the domestic debate. Interventionists believed he had been too cautious in dealing with the danger to the nation from Nazi Germany. Isolationists were equally critical of the president, claiming he had misled the American people by professing peace while plotting for war. Roosevelt was certainly less than candid, relying on executive discretion to engage in highly provocative acts in the North Atlantic. He agreed with the interventionists that in the long run a German victory in Europe would threaten American security. But he also was aware that a poll taken in September 1941 showed nearly 80 percent of the American people wanted to stay out of World War II. Realizing that leading a divided nation into war would be disastrous, FDR played for time, inching the country toward war while waiting for the Axis nations to make the ultimate move. Japan finally obliged at Pearl Harbor.

SHOWDOWN IN THE PACIFIC

Japan had taken advantage of the war in Europe to expand farther in Asia. Although successful after 1937 in conquering the populous coastal areas of China, the Japanese had been unable to defeat Chiang Kai-shek, whose forces retreated into the vast interior of the country. The German defeat of France and the Netherlands in 1940, however, left their colonial possessions in the East Indies and Indochina vulnerable and defenseless. Japan now set out to incorporate these territories—rich in oil, tin, and rubber—into a Greater East Asia Co-Prosperity Sphere.

The Roosevelt administration countered with economic pressure. Japan depended heavily on the United States for petroleum and scrap metal. In July 1940, President Roosevelt signed an order setting up a licensing and quota system for the export of these crucial materials to Japan and banned the sale of aviation gasoline altogether.

Tokyo appeared to be unimpressed. In early September, Japanese troops occupied strategic bases in the northern part of French Indochina. Later in the month, Japan signed the Tripartite Pact with Germany and Italy, a defensive treaty that confronted the United States with a possible two-ocean war. The new Axis alignment confirmed American suspicions that Japan was part of a worldwide totalitarian threat. Roosevelt and his advisers, however, saw Germany as the primary danger; thus they pursued a policy of all-out aid to England while hoping that economic measures alone would deter Japan.

The embargo on aviation gasoline, extended to include scrap iron and steel in late September 1940, was a burden Japan could bear, but a possible ban on all oil shipments was a different matter. Japan lacked petroleum reserves of its own and was entirely dependent on imports from the United States and the Dutch East Indies. In an attempt to ease the economic pressure through negotiation, Japan sent a new envoy to Washington in the spring of 1941.

In July 1941, Japan invaded southern Indochina, beginning the chain of events that led to war. Washington knew of this aggression before it occurred. Naval intelligence experts had broken the Japanese diplomatic code and were intercepting and reading all messages between Tokyo and the Japanese embassy in Washington. President Roosevelt responded on July 25, 1941, with an order freezing all Japanese assets in the United States. Trade with Japan, including the vital oil shipments, came to a complete halt. When the Dutch government in exile took similar action, Japan faced a dilemma: In order to have oil shipments resumed, Tokyo would have to end its aggression; the alternative would be to seize the needed petroleum supplies in the Dutch East Indies, an action that would mean war.

After one final diplomatic effort failed, General Hideki Tojo, an army militant, became the new premier of Japan. To mask its war preparations, Tokyo sent yet another envoy to Washington with new peace proposals. Army and navy leaders urged President Roosevelt to seek at least a temporary settlement with Japan to give them time to prepare American defenses in the Pacific. Secretary of State Cordell Hull, however, refused to allow any concession; on November 26, he sent a stiff ten-point reply to Tokyo that included a demand for Japanese withdrawal from China.

The Japanese response came two weeks later. On the evening of December 6, 1941, the first thirteen parts of the reply to Hull's note arrived in Washington, with the fourteenth part to follow the next morning. Naval intelligence actually decoded the message faster than the Japanese embassy clerks. A messenger delivered the text to President Roosevelt late that night; after glancing at it, he commented, "This means war." The next day, December 7, the fourteenth part arrived, revealing that Japan totally rejected the American position.

Officials in Washington immediately sent warning messages to American bases in the Pacific, but they failed to arrive in time. At 7:55 in the morning, just before 1 P.M. in Washington, squadrons of Japanese carrier-based planes caught the American fleet at Pearl Harbor totally by surprise. In little more than an hour, they crippled the American Pacific fleet and its major base, sinking eight battleships and killing more than twenty-four hundred American sailors.

American ships were destroyed in the surprise attack on Pearl Harbor, December 7, 1941. Caught completely off guard, U.S. forces still managed to shoot down twenty-nine enemy planes.

Speaking before Congress the next day, President Roosevelt termed December 7 "a date which will live in infamy" and asked for a declaration of war on Japan. With only one dissenting vote, both branches passed the measure. On December 11, Germany and Italy declared war against the United States; the nation was now fully involved in World War II.

The whole country united behind Roosevelt's leadership to seek revenge for Pearl Harbor and to defeat the Axis threat to American security. After the war, however, critics charged that FDR had entered the conflict by a back door, claiming the president had deliberately exposed the Pacific fleet to attack. Subsequent investigations uncovered negligence in both Hawaii and Washington but no evidence to support the conspiracy charge. Both military experts and FDR had badly underestimated the daring and skill of the Japanese, but there was no plot. Perhaps the most frightening aspect of the whole episode is that it took the shock of the Japanese sneak attack to make the American people aware of the extent of the Axis threat to their well-being and lead them to end the long American retreat from responsibility.

TURNING THE TIDE AGAINST THE AXIS

In the first few months after the United States entered the war, the outlook for victory was bleak. In Europe, Hitler's armies controlled virtually the entire continent, from Norway in the north to Greece in the south. Despite the nonaggression pact, German armies had penetrated deep into Russia after an initial invasion in June 1941. Although they had failed to capture either Moscow or Leningrad, the Nazi forces had conquered the Ukraine and by the spring of 1942 were threatening to sweep across the Volga River and seize vital oil fields in the Caucasus. In North Africa, General Erwin Rommel's Afrika Korps had pushed the British back into Egypt and threatened the Suez Canal (see the map on p. 726).

The situation was no better in Asia. The Pearl Harbor attack had enabled the Japanese to move unopposed across Southeast Asia. Within three months, they had conquered Malaya and the Dutch East Indies, with its valuable oil fields, and were pressing the British back both in Burma and New Guinea. American forces under General Douglas MacArthur had tried vainly to block the Japanese conquest of the Philippines. MacArthur finally escaped by torpedo boat to Australia; the American garrison at Corregidor surrendered after a long siege, the survivors then enduring the cruel death march across the Bataan peninsula. With the American navy still recovering from the devastation at Pearl Harbor, Japan controlled the western half of the Pacific (see the map on p. 717).

Over the next two years, the United States and its allies would finally halt the German and Japanese offensives in Europe and Asia. But then they faced the difficult process of driving back the enemy, freeing the vast conquered areas, and finally defeating the Axis powers on their home territory. It would be a difficult and costly struggle that would require great sacrifice and heavy losses; World War II would test American will and resourcefulness to the utmost.

WARTIME PARTNERSHIPS

The greatest single advantage that the United States and its partners possessed was their willingness to form a genuine coalition to bring about the defeat of the Axis powers. Although there were many strains within the wartime alliance, it did permit a high degree of coordination. In striking contrast was the behavior of Germany and Japan, each fighting a separate war without any attempt at cooperation.

The United States and Britain achieved a complete wartime partnership. The close cooperation between President Roosevelt and Prime Minister Churchill ensured a common strategy. The leaders decided at the outset that a German victory posed the greater danger and thus gave priority to the European theater in the conduct of the war. In a series of meetings in December 1941, Roosevelt and Churchill signed a Declaration of the United Nations, eventually subscribed to by twenty-six countries, that pledged them to fight together until the Axis powers were defeated.

Relations with the other members of the United Nations coalition in World War II were not quite so harmonious. The decision to defeat Germany first displeased the Chinese, who had been at war with Japan since 1937. France posed a more delicate problem. FDR virtually ignored the Free French government in exile under General Charles de Gaulle; Roosevelt preferred to deal with the Vichy regime.

The greatest strain of all within the wartime coalition was with the Soviet Union. Although Roosevelt had ended the long period of nonrecognition in 1933, close ties had failed to develop. The great Russian purge trials and the temporary Nazi-Soviet alliance from 1939 to 1941, along with deep-seated cultural and ideological differences, made wartime cooperation difficult.

Ever the pragmatist, Roosevelt tried hard to break down the old hostility and establish a more cordial relationship with Russia during the war. Even before Pearl Harbor, he extended Lend-Lease aid to Russia, and after American entry into the war, this economic assistance grew rapidly, limited only by the difficulty of delivering the supplies. Eager to keep Russia in the war, the president promised a visiting Russian diplomat in May 1942 that the United States would create a second front in Europe by the end of that year—a pledge he could not fulfill. In January 1943, Roosevelt and Churchill met in Casablanca, Morocco, where they declared a policy of unconditional surrender, vowing that the Allies would fight until the Axis nations were completely defeated.

Despite these promises, the Soviet Union bore the brunt of battle against Hitler in the early years of the war, fighting alone against more than two hundred German divisions. The United States and England, grateful for the respite to build up their forces, could do little more than offer promises of future help and send Lend-Lease supplies. The result was a rift that never fully healed—one that did not prevent the defeat of Germany but did ensure future tensions and uncertainties between the Soviet Union and the Western nations.

HALTING THE GERMAN BLITZ

From the outset, the United States favored an invasion across the English Channel. Army planners, led by Chief of Staff George C. Marshall and his protégé, Dwight D. Eisenhower, were convinced such a frontal assault would be the quickest way to win the war. Roosevelt concurred, in part because it fulfilled his second-front commitment to the Soviets.

The initial plan, drawn up by Eisenhower, called for a full-scale invasion of Europe in the spring of 1943. Marshall surprised everyone by placing Eisenhower, until then a relatively junior general, in charge of implementing the plan.

But the British, remembering the heavy casualties of trench warfare in World War I, preferred a perimeter approach, with air and naval attacks around the edge of the Continent until Germany was softened up for the final invasion. British strategists assented to the basic plan but strongly urged a preliminary invasion of North Africa in the fall of 1942. Roosevelt agreed and American and British troops landed on the Atlantic and Mediterranean coasts of Morocco and Algeria in November 1942.

The British launched an attack against Rommel at El Alamein in Egypt and soon forced the Afrika Korps to retreat across Libya to Tunisia. Eisenhower, despite initial setbacks, advanced from Algeria, and by May 1943, Germany had been driven from Africa, leaving behind nearly 300,000 troops.

During these same months, the Soviet Union's Red Army had broken the back of German military power in the battle of Stalingrad. Turned back at the critical bend in the Volga, Hitler had poured in division after division in what was ultimately a losing cause; never again would Germany be able to take the offensive in Europe.

At Churchill's insistence, FDR agreed to follow up the North African victory with the invasion first of Sicily and then Italy in the summer of 1943. Italy dropped out of the war when Mussolini fled to Germany, but the Italian campaign proved to be a strategic dead end.

More important, these Mediterranean operations delayed the second front, postponing it eventually to the spring of 1944. Meanwhile, the Soviets began to push the Germans out of Russia and looked forward to the liberation of Poland, Hungary, and Romania, where they could establish "friendly" communist regimes. Having borne the brunt of the fighting against Nazi Germany, Russia was ready to claim its reward—the postwar domination of eastern Europe.

CHECKING JAPAN IN THE PACIFIC

Both the decision to defeat Germany first and the vast expanses of the Pacific dictated the nature of the war against Japan. The United States conducted amphibious island-hopping campaigns rather than attempting to reconquer the Dutch East Indies, Southeast Asia, and China. There would be two separate American operations. One, led by Douglas MacArthur based in Australia, would move from New Guinea back to the Philippines, while the other, commanded by Admiral Chester Nimitz from Hawaii, was directed at key Japanese islands in the Central Pacific.

Success in the Pacific depended above all else on control of the sea. The devastation at Pearl Harbor gave Japan the initial edge, but fortunately, the United States had not lost any of its four aircraft carriers. The turning point came in June 1942 at Midway. A powerful Japanese task force threatened to seize this remote American outpost more than a thousand miles west of Pearl Harbor; Japan's real objective was the destruction of what remained of the American Pacific fleet. Superior American airpower enabled Nimitz's forces to engage the enemy at long range. The battle of Midway ended with the loss of four Japanese aircraft carriers compared to just one American carrier. It was the first defeat the modern Japanese navy had ever suffered, and it left the United States in control of the Central Pacific.

Encouraged by the victory, American forces launched their first Pacific offensive in the Solomon Islands, east of New Guinea, in August 1942. Both sides suffered heavy losses, but six months later the last Japanese were driven from the key island of Guadalcanal. At the same time, MacArthur began the long, slow, and bloody job of driving the Japanese back along the north coast of New Guinea.

By early 1943, the defensive phase of the war with Japan was over. The enemy surge had been halted in both the central and the southwestern Pacific, and

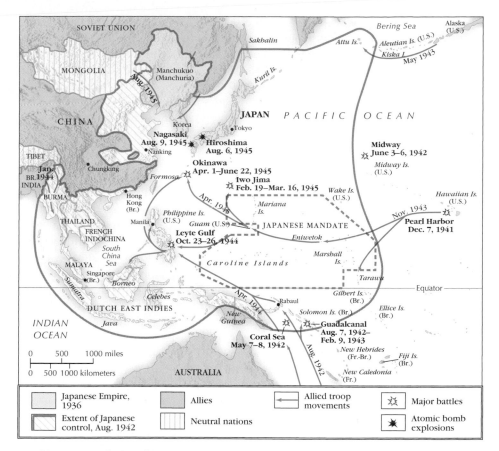

World War II in the Pacific
The tide of battle turned in the Pacific the same year as in Europe. The balance of sea power shifted back to the United States from Japan after the naval victories of 1942.

the United States was preparing to penetrate the Gilbert, Marshall, and Caroline Islands and recapture the Philippines. Just as Russia had broken German power in Europe, so the United States, fighting alone except for Australia and New Zealand, had halted the Japanese. And, like the USSR with its plans for eastern Europe, America expected to reap the rewards of victory by dominating the Pacific in the future.

THE HOME FRONT

World War II had a greater impact than the Great Depression on American life. While American soldiers and sailors fought abroad, the nation underwent sweeping social and economic changes at home. American industry worked to capacity to meet the need for war materials. Increased production in both industry and agriculture benefited workers and farmers alike. The expansion of war-related industries encouraged many people to move to where new jobs had sprung up. Women moved out of the home into the paid workforce; rural dwellers relocated to urban areas, and northerners and easterners sought new opportunities and new homes in the South and West. Another beneficiary of the return to prosperity brought on by the war was FDR, who had seen the nation through the dark days of the depression. The nation's economic recovery helped him win reelection to the presidency for a fourth term in 1944.

THE ARSENAL OF DEMOCRACY

American industry made the nation's single most important contribution to victory. Even though more than fifteen million Americans served in the armed forces, it was the nearly sixty million who worked on farms and factories who achieved the miracle of production that ensured the defeat of Germany and Japan. The manufacturing plants that had run at half capacity through the 1930s now hummed with activity. In Detroit, automobile assembly lines were converted to produce tanks and airplanes. Henry J. Kaiser, a California industrialist, constructed huge West Coast shipyards to meet the demand for cargo vessels and landing craft. His plant in Richmond, California, reduced the time to build a merchant ship from 105 to 14 days. In part, America won the battle of the Atlantic by building ships faster than German U-boats could sink them.

This vast industrial expansion, however, created many problems. In 1942, President Roosevelt appointed Donald Nelson, a Sears, Roebuck executive, to head a War Production Board (WPB). A jovial, easygoing man, Nelson soon was outmaneuvered by the army and the navy, which preferred to negotiate directly with large corporations. Shortages of critical materials such as steel, aluminum, and copper led to an allocation system based on military priorities. Rubber, cut off by the Japanese conquest of Southeast Asia, was particularly scarce; the administration finally began gasoline rationing in 1943 to curb pleasure driving and prolong tire life.

Roosevelt revealed the same tendency toward compromise in directing the economic mobilization as he did in shaping the New Deal. When the Office of Price Administration—which tried to curb inflation by controlling prices and rationing scarce goods such as sugar, canned food, and shoes—clashed with the WPB, FDR appointed James Byrnes to head an Office of Economic Stabilization. Byrnes, a former South Carolina senator and Supreme Court justice, used political judgment to settle disputes between agencies and keep all groups happy.

A result of the wartime economic explosion was a growing affluence. Despite the federal incentives to business, heavy excess-profit taxes and a 94 percent tax rate for the very rich kept the wealthy from benefiting unduly. The huge increase in federal spending, from $9 billion in 1940 to $98 billion in 1944, spread through American society. A government agreement with labor unions in 1943 held wage rates to a 15 percent increase, but the long hours of overtime resulted in doubling and sometimes tripling the weekly paychecks of factory workers. Farmers shared in the new prosperity as their incomes

American war production was twice that of all the Axis countries. Here, Boeing aircraft workers celebrate the completion of their five-thousandth bomber.

quadrupled between 1940 and 1945. Most important, this rising income ensured postwar prosperity. Workers and farmers saved their money, channeling much of it into government war bonds, waiting for the day when they could buy the cars and home appliances they had done without during the long years of depression and war.

A NATION ON THE MOVE

The war led to a vast migration of the American population. Young men left their homes for training camps and then for service overseas. Defense workers and their families, some nine million people in all, moved to work in the new booming shipyards, munitions factories, and aircraft plants. Rural areas lost population while coastal regions, especially along the Pacific and the Gulf of Mexico, drew millions of people. The location of army camps in the South and West created boom conditions in the future Sunbelt, as did the concentration of aircraft factories and shipyards in this region. California had the greatest gains, adding nearly two million to its population in less than five years.

This movement of people caused severe social problems. Housing was in short supply. Migrating workers crowded into house trailers and boardinghouses, bringing unexpected windfalls to landlords. Family life suffered under these

As men left for military service in World War II and U.S. industry expanded to keep up with the defense needs, millions of women joined the paid labor force. By 1944, the peak year for female wartime employment, women made up 36 percent of the American workforce. Women took jobs that before had been done by men, such as riveting, welding, and operating heavy equipment. The women shown here are operating a bolt cutting machine at a factory in Erie, Pennsylvania.

crowded living conditions; an increase in the number of marriages was offset by a rising divorce rate. In addition, schools and other social agencies were hard pressed to service the remarkable baby boom that began during the war.

The demand for workers led to a dramatic rise in women's employment, from fourteen million working women in 1940 to nineteen million by 1945. Most of the new women workers were married and many were middle-aged, thus broadening the composition of the female workforce, which in the past had been composed primarily of young single women. Women entered industries once viewed as exclusively male; by the end of the war, they worked alongside men tending blast furnaces in steel mills and welding hulls in shipyards. Women enjoyed the hefty weekly paychecks, which rose by 50 percent from 1941 to 1943, and they took pride in their contributions to the war effort. "To hell with the life I have had," commented a former fashion designer. "This war is too damn serious, and it is too damn important to win it."

African Americans shared in the wartime migration, but racial prejudice limited their social and economic gains. Nearly one million served in the armed forces, but relatively few saw combat. The army placed black soldiers in segregated units, usually led by white officers, and used them for service and construction tasks. The navy was even worse, relegating them to menial jobs until late in the war. African Americans were denied the chance to become petty officers, Secretary of the Navy Frank Knox explained, because experience had shown that "men of the colored race . . . cannot maintain discipline among men of the white race."

African American civilians fared a little better. In 1941, black labor leader A. Philip Randolph threatened a massive march on Washington to force President Roosevelt to end racial discrimination in defense industries and government employment and to integrate the armed forces. FDR compromised, persuading Randolph to call off the march and drop his integration demand in return for an executive order creating a Fair Employment Practices Committee (FEPC) to ban racial discrimination in war industries. As a result, black employment by the federal government rose from 60,000 in 1941 to 200,000 by the end of the war. The FEPC proved less successful in the private sector. The nationwide shortage of labor was more influential than the FEPC in accounting for the rise in black employment during wartime. African Americans moved from the rural South to northern and western cities, finding jobs in the automobile, aircraft, and shipbuilding industries.

The movement of an estimated 700,000 people helped transform black-white relations from a regional issue into a national concern that could no longer be ignored. The limited housing and recreational facilities for both black and white war workers created tensions that led to race riots in Detroit and New York City. These outbursts of racial violence fueled the resentments that would grow into the postwar civil rights movement. For most African Americans, despite economic gains, World War II was a reminder of the inequality of American life. "Just carve on my tombstone," remarked one black soldier in the Pacific, "'Here lies a black man killed fighting a yellow man for the protection of a white man.'"

One-third of a million Mexican Americans served in the armed forces and shared some of the same experiences as African Americans. Although they were not as completely segregated, many served in the 88th Division, made up largely of Mexican American officers and troops, which earned the nickname "Blue Devils" in the Italian campaign. At home, Spanish-speaking people left the rural areas of the Southwest for jobs in the cities, especially in aircraft plants and petroleum refineries. Despite low wages and union resistance, they improved their economic position substantially. But they still faced discrimination based both on skin color and language. The racial prejudice heightened feelings of ethnic identity and led returning Mexican American veterans to form organizations such as the American G.I. Forum to press for equal rights in the future.

A tragic counterpoint to the voluntary movement of American workers in search of jobs was the forced relocation of 120,000 Japanese Americans from the West Coast. Responding to racial fears in California after Pearl Harbor, President Roosevelt approved an army order in February 1942 to move all Japanese Americans on the West Coast to concentration camps in the interior. More than two-thirds of those detained were *Nisei*, native-born Americans whose only crime was their Japanese ancestry. Forced to sell their farms and businesses at distress prices, the Japanese Americans lost not only their liberty but also most of their worldly goods. Herded into ten hastily built detention centers in seven western and southern states, they lived as prisoners in tar-papered barracks behind barbed wire, guarded by armed troops.

Appeals to the Supreme Court proved fruitless; in 1944, six justices upheld relocation on grounds of national security in wartime. Beginning in 1943, individual Nisei could win release by pledging their loyalty and finding a job away from the West Coast. Some thirty-five thousand left the camps during the next two years, including more than thirteen thousand who joined the armed forces. The all-Nisei 442nd Combat Team served gallantly in the European theater,

A mother and son, interned at a temporary relocation camp, pose with a picture of her older son wearing his U.S. Army uniform. Japanese Americans living on the West Coast were first ordered to large assembly centers such as the racetrack at Santa Anita, California. There whole families were assigned to individual horse stalls while they awaited relocation to one of the internment camps located in isolated areas of California, Arizona, Idaho, Utah, Colorado, Wyoming, and Arkansas. Conditions in the camps were equally dismal. Whole families lived in a single room furnished with little more than a few cots, some blankets, and a single light bulb.

losing more than five hundred men in battle and winning more than a thousand citations for bravery.

For other Nisei, the experience was bitter. More than five thousand renounced their American citizenship and chose to live in Japan at the war's end. Japanese Americans never experienced the torture and mass death of the German concentration camps, but their treatment was a disgrace to a nation fighting for freedom and democracy. Finally, in 1988, Congress voted an indemnity of $1.2 billion for the estimated sixty thousand surviving Japanese Americans detained during World War II. Susumi Emori, who had been moved with his wife and four children from his farm in Stockton, California, to a camp in Arkansas, felt vindicated. "It was terrible," he said, with tears in his eyes, "but it was a time of war. Anything can happen. I didn't blame the United States for that."

WIN-THE-WAR POLITICS

Franklin Roosevelt used World War II to strengthen his leadership and maintain Democratic political dominance. As war brought about prosperity and removed the economic discontent that had sustained the New Deal, FDR announced that "Dr. New Deal" had given way to "Dr. Win-the-War." Congress,

THE ELECTION OF 1944

CANDIDATE	PARTY	POPULAR VOTE	ELECTORAL VOTE
Roosevelt	Democrat	25,602,504	432
Dewey	Republican	22,006,285	99

already controlled by a conservative coalition of southern Democrats and northern Republicans, had almost slipped into GOP hands in 1942. With a very low voter turnout, the Republicans won forty-four new seats in the House and nine in the Senate and elected governors in New York and California as well.

In 1944, Roosevelt responded to the Democratic slippage by dropping Henry Wallace, his liberal and visionary vice president, for Harry Truman, a moderate and down-to-earth Missouri senator who was acceptable to all factions of the Democratic party. Equally important, FDR received increased political support from organized labor.

The Republicans nominated Thomas E. Dewey, who had been elected governor of New York after gaining fame as a prosecutor of organized crime. Dewey, moderate in his views, played down opposition to the New Deal and instead tried to make Roosevelt's age and health the primary issues, along with the charge that the Democrats were soft on communism. His foreign policy statements were far more internationalist than previous Republican policy. Indeed, Dewey pioneered a bipartisan approach to foreign policy. He accepted wartime planning for the future United Nations and kept the issue of an international organization out of the campaign.

Reacting to the issues of his age and health, especially after a long bout with influenza in the spring, FDR took a five-hour drive in an open car through the rain-soaked streets of New York City just before the election. His vitality impressed the voters, and in November 1944 he swept back into office for a fourth term, although the margin of 3.6 million votes was his smallest yet. The campaign, however, had taken its toll. The president, suffering from high blood pressure and congestive heart failure, had only a few months left to lead the nation.

VICTORY

World War II ended with surprising swiftness. By 1943, the Axis tide had been turned in Europe and Asia, and it did not take long for Russia, the United States, and England to mount the offensives that drove Germany and Japan back across the vast areas they had conquered and set the stage for their final defeat.

The long-awaited second front finally came on June 6, 1944. For two years, the United States and England concentrated on building up an invasion force of nearly three million troops and a vast armada of ships and landing craft to carry them across the English Channel. In hopes of catching Hitler by surprise, Eisenhower chose the Normandy peninsula, where the absence of good harbors had led to lighter German fortifications.

D-Day was originally set for June 5, but bad weather forced a delay. Relying on a forecasted break in the storm, Eisenhower gambled on going ahead on June 6. During the night, three divisions parachuted down behind the German defenses; at dawn, the British and American troops fought their way ashore at five points along a sixty-mile stretch of beach, encountering stiff German resistance at several points. By the end of the day, however, Eisenhower had won his beachhead; a week later, more than one-third of a million men were slowly pushing back the German forces through the hedgerows of Normandy. The breakthrough came on July 25 when General Omar Bradley decimated the enemy with a massive artillery and aerial bombardment at Saint-Lô, opening a gap for General George Patton's Third Army. American tanks raced across the French countryside, trapping thousands of Germans and liberating Paris by August 25. Allied troops reached the Rhine River by September, but a shortage of supplies, especially gasoline, forced a three-month halt.

Hitler took advantage of this breathing spell to deliver a daring counterattack. In mid-December, the remaining German armored divisions burst through a weak point in the Allied lines in the Ardennes Forest, planning a breakout to the coast that would have cut off nearly one-third of Eisenhower's forces. But an airborne division dug in at the key crossroads of Bastogne, in Belgium, and held off a much larger German force. Allied reinforcements and clearing weather then combined to end the attack. By committing nearly all his reserves to the Battle of the Bulge, Hitler had delayed Eisenhower's advance into Germany, but he also had fatally weakened German resistance in the west.

The end came quickly. A massive Russian offensive began in mid-January and swept across the Oder River toward Berlin. General Bradley's troops, finding a bridge left virtually intact by the retreating Germans, crossed the Rhine on March 7. The Allied forces advanced on a broad front, capturing the industrial Ruhr basin and meeting the Russians at the Elbe by the last week in April. With the Red Army already in the suburbs of Berlin, Adolf Hitler committed suicide on April 30. A week later, on May 7, 1945, Eisenhower accepted the unconditional surrender of all German forces. Just eleven months and a day after the landings in Normandy, the Allied forces had brought the war in Europe to a successful conclusion.

After they entered Germany, American troops found horrifying evidence of the Holocaust—Hitler's eradication of six million European Jews. American soldiers were shocked at the conditions within the German concentration camps—lethal gas chambers, huge ovens for cremation, bodies stacked like cords of wood, and most vivid of all, the emaciated, skeleton-like survivors with their

Victims at the Bergen-Belsen concentration camp were buried in a mass grave. The camp was liberated by the Allies on April 14, 1945, less than a month before Germany's surrender.

blank stares. One battle-hardened veteran commented on the scene at Nordhausen, where his unit had found 3000 dead and only 700 survivors:

> *The odors, well there is no way to describe the odors. . . . Many of the boys I am talking about now—these were tough soldiers, there were combat men who had been all the way through the invasion—were ill and vomiting, throwing up, just at the sight of this.*

These awful discoveries removed any doubt in the minds of the American people about the evil nature of the Nazi regime they had just helped to destroy.

WAR AIMS AND WARTIME DIPLOMACY

The American contribution to Hitler's defeat was relatively minor compared to the damage inflicted by the Soviet Union. At the height of the German invasion of Russia, more than 300 Soviet divisions had been locked in battle with 250 German ones, a striking contrast to the 58 divisions the United States and Britain used in the Normandy invasion. As his armies overran Poland and the Balkan countries, Joseph Stalin was determined to retain control over this region, which had been the historic pathway for Western invasion into Russia. Delay in opening the second front and an innate distrust of the West convinced the Soviets that

World War II in Europe and North Africa
The tide of battle shifted in this theater during the winter of 1942–1943. The massive German assault on the eastern front was turned back by the Russians at Stalingrad, and the Allied forces recaptured North Africa.

they should maximize their territorial gains by imposing communist regimes on eastern Europe.

American postwar goals were quite different. Now believing the failure to join the League of Nations in 1919 had led to the coming of World War II, the American people and their leaders vowed to put their faith in a new attempt at collective security. At Moscow in 1943, Secretary of State Cordell Hull had won Russian agreement to participate in a future world organization at the war's end. The first wartime Big Three conference brought together Roosevelt, Churchill, and Stalin at Teheran, Iran, in late 1943. Stalin reaffirmed this commitment and also indicated to President Roosevelt that Russia would enter the war against Japan once Germany was defeated.

By the time the Big Three met again at Yalta, in February 1945, the military situation favored the Russians. Stalin drove a series of hard bargains. He refused to give up his plans for communist domination of Poland and the Balkans, although he did agree to Roosevelt's request for a Declaration of Liberated Europe, which called for free elections without providing for any method of enforcement or supervision. More important for the United States, Stalin promised to enter the Pacific war three months after Germany surrendered. In return, Roosevelt offered extensive concessions in Asia, including Russian control over Manchuria. While neither a sellout nor a betrayal, as some critics have charged, Yalta was a significant diplomatic victory for the Soviets—one that reflected Russia's major contribution to a victory in Europe.

For the president, the long journey to Yalta proved to be too much. His health continued to fail after his return to Washington. In early April, FDR left the capital for Warm Springs, Georgia, where he had always been able to relax. He was sitting for his portrait at midday on April 12, 1945, when he suddenly complained of a "terrific headache," then slumped forward and died.

The nation mourned a man who had gallantly met the challenge of depression and global war. Unfortunately, FDR had taken no steps to prepare his successor for the difficult problems that lay ahead. The defeat of Nazi Germany dissolved the one strong bond between the United States and the Soviet Union. With very different histories, cultures, and ideologies, the two nations were bound to drift apart. It was now up to the inexperienced Harry Truman to manage the growing rivalry that was destined to develop into the future Cold War.

TRIUMPH AND TRAGEDY IN THE PACIFIC

The total defeat of Germany in May 1945 turned all eyes toward Japan. Although the combined chiefs of staff had originally estimated it would take eighteen months after Germany's surrender to conquer Japan, American forces moved with surprising speed. Admiral Nimitz swept through the Gilbert, Caroline, and Marshall Islands in 1944, while General MacArthur cleared New Guinea of the last Japanese defender and began planning his long-heralded return to the Philippines. American troops landed on the island of Leyte on October 20, 1944, and Manila fell in early February 1945. The Japanese navy launched a daring three-pronged attack on the American invasion fleet in Leyte Gulf. The U.S. Navy rallied to blunt all three Japanese thrusts, sinking four carriers and ending any further Japanese naval threat.

The defeat of Japan was now only a matter of time. The United States had three possible ways to proceed. The military favored a full-scale invasion, beginning on the southernmost island of Kyushu in November 1945 and culminating with an assault on Honshu (the main island of Japan) and a climactic battle for Tokyo in 1946; casualties were expected to run into the hundreds of thousands. Diplomats suggested a negotiated peace, urging the United States to modify the unconditional surrender formula to permit Japan to retain the institution of the emperor.

The third possibility involved the highly secret Manhattan Project. Since 1939, the United States had spent $2 billion to develop an atomic bomb based on the fission of radioactive uranium and plutonium. Scientists, many of them refugees from Europe, worked to perfect this deadly new weapon at the University of Chicago; Oak Ridge, Tennessee; Hanford, Washington; and a remote laboratory in Los Alamos, New Mexico. In the New Mexico desert on July 16, 1945, they successfully tested the first atomic bomb.

Truman had been unaware of the existence of the Manhattan Project before he became president on April 12. Now he simply followed the recommendation of a committee headed by Secretary of War Henry L. Stimson to drop the bomb on a Japanese city. Neither Truman nor Stimson had any qualms about the decision to drop the bomb without warning. They viewed it as a legitimate wartime measure, one designed to save the lives of hundreds of thousands of Americans— and Japanese—that would be lost in a full-scale invasion.

Weather conditions on the morning of August 6 dictated the choice of Hiroshima as the bomb's target. The explosion incinerated 4 square miles of the city, instantly killing more than sixty thousand. Two days later, Russia entered

The atomic bomb dropped on Nagasaki, a provincial capital and naval base in southern Japan, on August 9, 1945, virtually obliterated the city and killed about 40,000 people. Only buildings made with reinforced concrete remained standing after the blast.

the war against Japan, and the next day, August 9, the United States dropped a second bomb on Nagasaki. The emperor personally broke a deadlock in the Japanese cabinet and persuaded his ministers to surrender unconditionally on August 14, 1945. Three weeks later, Japan signed a formal capitulation agreement on the decks of the battleship *Missouri* in Tokyo Bay to bring World War II to its official close.

Many years later, scholars charged that Truman had more in mind than defeating Japan when he decided to use the atomic bomb. Citing air force and naval officers who claimed Japan could be defeated by a blockade or by conventional air attacks, these revisionists suggested the real reason for dropping the bomb was to impress the Soviet Union with the fact that the United States had exclusive possession of the ultimate weapon. The available evidence indicates that while Truman and his associates were aware of the possible effect on the Soviet Union, their primary motive was to end World War II as quickly and effortlessly as possible. The saving of American lives, along with a desire for revenge for Pearl Harbor, were uppermost in the decision to bomb Hiroshima and Nagasaki. Yet in using the atomic bomb to defeat Japan, the United States virtually guaranteed a postwar arms race with the Soviet Union.

THE TRANSFORMING POWER OF WAR

The second great war of the twentieth century has had a lasting impact on American life. For the first time, the nation's military potential had been reached. In 1945, the United States was unquestionably the strongest country on the earth. In the future, the United States would be involved in all parts of the world, from western Europe to remote jungles in Asia, from the nearby Caribbean to the distant Persian Gulf. And despite its enormous strength in 1945, the nation's new world role would encompass failure and frustration as well as power and dominion.

The legacy of war was equally strong at home. Four years of fighting brought about industrial recovery and unparalleled prosperity. The old pattern of unregulated free enterprise was as much a victim of the war as of the New Deal; big government and huge deficits had now become the norm as economic control passed from New York and Wall Street to Washington and Pennsylvania Avenue. The war led to far-reaching changes in American society that would become apparent only decades later. Such distinctive patterns of recent American life as the baby boom and the growth of the Sunbelt can be traced back to wartime origins. World War II was a watershed in twentieth-century America, ushering in a new age of global concerns and domestic upheaval.

CHRONOLOGY

1922	Washington Naval Conference limits tonnage
1926	World Court rejects qualified U.S. entry
1928	Kellogg-Briand Pact outlaws war (August)
	Clark Memorandum repudiates Roosevelt Corollary (December)
1931	Japan occupies China's Manchurian province
1933	FDR extends diplomatic recognition to USSR
1936	Hitler's troops reoccupy Rhineland
1937	FDR signs permanent Neutrality Act (May)
	FDR urges quarantine of aggressor nations (October)
	Japanese planes sink USS *Panay* in China (December)
1938	Ludlow war referendum buried in Congress (January)
	Munich Conference appeases Hitler (September)
1939	Germany invades Poland; World War II begins
1941	Germany invades USSR
	Japan attacks Pearl Harbor; United States enters World War II
1942	U.S. defeats Japanese at battle of Midway (June)
	Allies land in North Africa (November)
1943	Soviets smash Nazis at Stalingrad
1944	Allies land on Normandy beachheads
1945	Big Three meet at Yalta (February)
	FDR dies; Harry Truman becomes president (April)
	Germany surrenders unconditionally (May)
	United States drops atomic bombs on Hiroshima and Nagasaki; Japan surrenders (August)

28

❧ ———— ❧

THE ONSET OF THE
COLD WAR

" I am getting ready to go see Stalin and Churchill," President Truman wrote to his mother in July 1945, "and it is a chore." On board the cruiser *Augusta,* the new president continued to complain about the upcoming Potsdam conference in his diary. "How I hate this trip!" he confided. "But I have to make it win, lose, or draw and we must win. I am giving nothing away except to save starving people and even then I hope we can only help them to help themselves."

Halfway around the world, Joseph Stalin left Moscow a day late because of a slight heart attack. The Russian leader hated to fly, so he traveled by rail. Moreover, he ordered the heavily guarded train to detour around Poland for fear of an ambush, further delaying his arrival. When he made his entrance into Potsdam, a suburb of Berlin miraculously spared the total destruction that his forces had created in the German capital, he was ready to claim the spoils of war.

These two men, one the veteran revolutionary who had been in power for two decades, the other an untested leader in office for barely three months, symbolized the enormous differences that now separated the wartime allies. Stalin was above all a realist. Brutal in securing total control at home, he was more flexible in his foreign policy, bent on exploiting Russia's victory in World War II rather than aiming at world domination. Cunning and caution were the hallmarks of his diplomatic style. Small in stature, ungainly in build, he radiated a catlike quality as he waited behind his unassuming facade, ready to dazzle an opponent with his "brilliant, terrifying tactical mastery." Truman, in contrast, personified traditional Wilsonian idealism. Lacking Roosevelt's guile, the new president placed his faith in international cooperation. Like many Americans, he believed implicitly in his country's innate goodness. Self-assured to the point of cockiness, he came to Potsdam clothed in the armor of self-righteousness.

Truman and Stalin met for the first time on July 17, 1945. "I told Stalin that I am no diplomat," the president recorded in his diary, "but usually said yes and no to questions after hearing all the argument." The Russian dictator's reaction to Truman remains a mystery, but Truman believed the first encounter went well. "I can deal with Stalin," he wrote. "He is honest—but smart as hell."

Together with Winston Churchill and his replacement, Clement Attlee, whose Labour party had just triumphed in British elections, Truman and Stalin clashed for the next ten days over such difficult issues as reparations, the Polish border, and the fate of eastern Europe. Truman presented the ideas and proposals formulated by his advisers; he saw his task as essentially procedural, and when he presided, he moved the agenda along in brisk fashion. In an indirect way, he informed Stalin of the existence of the atomic bomb, tested successfully in the New Mexico desert just before the conference began. Truman offered no details, and the impassive Stalin asked for none, commenting only that he hoped the United States would make "good use of it against the Japanese."

Reparations proved to be the crucial issue at Potsdam. The Russians wanted to rebuild their war-ravaged economy with German industry; the United States feared it would be saddled with the entire cost of caring for the defeated Germans. A compromise was finally reached. Each side would take reparations primarily from its own occupation zone, a solution that foreshadowed the future division of Germany. "Because they could not agree on how to govern Europe," wrote historian Daniel Yergin, "Truman and Stalin began to divide it." The other issues were referred to the newly created Council of Foreign Ministers, which would meet in the fall in London.

The conference thus ended on an apparent note of harmony; beneath the surface, however, the bitter antagonism of the Cold War was festering. America and Russia, each distrustful of the other, were preparing for a long and bitter confrontation. A dozen years later, Truman reminisced to an old associate about Potsdam. "What a show that was!" Describing himself as "an innocent idealist" surrounded by wolves, he claimed that all the agreements reached there were "broken as soon as the unconscionable Russian Dictator returned to Moscow!" He added ruefully, "And I liked the little son of a bitch."

Potsdam marked the end of the wartime alliance. America and Russia, each distrustful of the other, began to engage in a long and bitter confrontation. For the next decade, the two superpowers would vie for control of postwar Europe, and later clash over the spread of communism to Asia. By the time Truman's and Stalin's successors met for the next summit conference, at Geneva in 1955, the Cold War was at its height.

THE COLD WAR BEGINS

The conflict between the United States and the Soviet Union began gradually. For two years, the nations tried to adjust their differences over the division of Europe, postwar economic aid, and the atomic bomb through discussion and negotiation. The Council of Foreign Ministers provided the forum. Beginning in London during the fall of 1945 and meeting with their Russian counterparts in Paris, New York, and Moscow, American diplomats searched for a way to live in peace with a suspicious Soviet Union.

THE DIVISION OF EUROPE

The fundamental disagreement was over who would control postwar Europe. In the east, the Red Army had swept over Poland and the Balkans, laying the basis for Soviet domination there. American and British forces had liberated western Europe from Scandinavia to Italy. The Russians, mindful of past invasions from the west across the plains of Poland, were intent on imposing communist governments loyal to Moscow in the Soviet sphere. The United States, on the other hand, upheld the principle of national self-determination, insisting the people in each country should freely choose their postwar rulers. The Soviets saw the demand for free elections as subversive, since they knew that popularly chosen regimes would be unfriendly to Russia. Suspecting American duplicity, Stalin brought down an "iron curtain" (Churchill's phrase) from the Baltic to the Adriatic as he created a series of satellite governments.

Germany was the key. The temporary zones of occupation gradually hardened into permanent lines of division. Ignoring the Potsdam Conference agreement that the country be treated as an economic unit, the United States and Great Britain were by 1946 refusing to permit the Russians to take reparations from the industrial western zones. The initial harsh occupation policy gave way to more humane treatment of the German people and a slow but steady economic recovery. The United States and England merged their zones and championed the idea of the unification of all Germany. Russia, fearing a resurgence of German military power, responded by intensifying the communization of its zone, which included the jointly occupied city of Berlin.

The Soviet Union consolidated its grip on eastern Europe in 1946 and 1947. One by one, communist regimes replaced coalition governments in Poland, Hungary, Romania, and Bulgaria. Moving cautiously to avoid provoking the West, Stalin used communism as a means to dominate half of Europe, both to protect the security of the Soviet state and to advance its international power. The climax came in March 1948 when a coup in Czechoslovakia overthrew a democratic government and gave the Soviets a strategic foothold in central Europe.

The division of Europe was an inevitable aftereffect of World War II. Both sides were intent on imposing their values in the areas liberated by their troops. A frank recognition of competing spheres of influence might have avoided further escalation of tension. But the Western nations, remembering Hitler's aggression in the 1930s, began to see Stalin as an equally dangerous threat to their well-being. Instead of accepting him as a cautious leader bent on protecting Russian security, they perceived him as an aggressive dictator leading a communist drive for world domination.

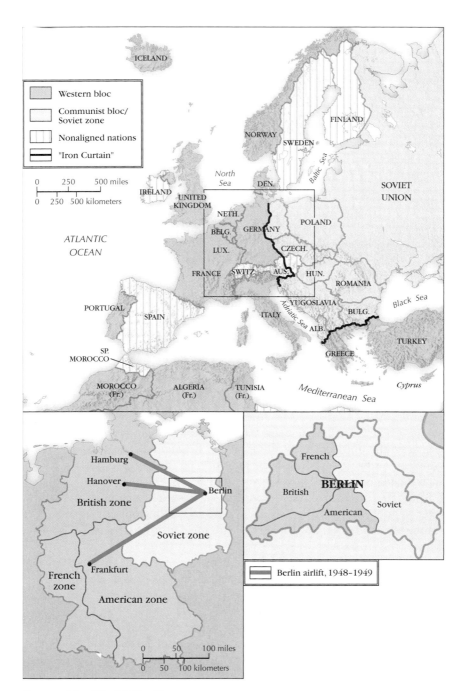

Europe After World War II

The heavy line splitting Germany shows in graphic form the division of Europe between the Western and Soviet spheres of influence. "From Stettin in the Baltic to Trieste in the Adriatic," said Churchill in a speech at Fulton, Missouri, in 1946, "an iron curtain has descended across the Continent."

WITHHOLDING ECONOMIC AID

World War II had inflicted enormous damage on Russia. The brutal fighting had taken between fifteen and twenty million Russian lives, destroyed more than thirty thousand factories, and torn up forty thousand miles of railroad track. The industrialization that Stalin had achieved at such great sacrifice in the 1930s had been badly set back; even agricultural production had fallen by half during the war. Outside aid and assistance were vital for the reconstruction of the Soviet Union.

American leaders knew of Russia's plight and hoped to use it to good advantage. President Truman was convinced that economically "we held all the cards and the Russians had to come to us." In 1945, the United States terminated Lend-Lease aid to Russia and rejected a Soviet request for a $6 billion loan.

Deprived of American assistance, the Russians were forced to rebuild their economy through reparations. The Soviets systematically removed factories and plants from areas they controlled, including their zone of Germany, eastern Europe, and Manchuria. Slowly, the Russian economy recovered from the war, but the bitterness over the American refusal to extend aid convinced Stalin of Western hostility and thus deepened the growing antagonism between the Soviet Union and the United States.

THE ATOMIC DILEMMA

Overshadowing all else was the atomic bomb. Used by the United States with deadly success at Hiroshima and Nagasaki, the new weapon raised problems that would have been difficult for even friendly nations to resolve. Given the uneasy state of Soviet-American relations, the effect was disastrous.

The wartime policy followed by Roosevelt and Churchill ensured a postwar nuclear arms race. Instead of informing their major ally of the developing atomic bomb, they kept it a closely guarded secret. Stalin learned of the Manhattan Project through espionage and responded by starting a Soviet atomic program in 1943. By the time Truman informed Stalin of the weapon's existence at Potsdam, the Russians, aided by a steady stream of information from spies in the United States, were well on the way to making their own bomb.

After the war, President Truman appointed financier Bernard Baruch to present a proposal for atomic disarmament to the United Nations. The Baruch Plan called for American retention of the bomb while an international agency secured control of all fissionable material and nuclear processing plants. The emphasis on inspection and the denial of United Nations veto power ensured the opposition of the Soviets, who countered with a simple plan to outlaw the bomb and to destroy all existing nuclear weapons.

No agreement was possible. Neither the United States nor the Soviet Union could abandon its position without surrendering a vital national interest. Wanting to preserve its monopoly, America stressed inspection and control; hoping to neutralize the U.S. advantage, Russia advocated immediate disarmament. The nuclear dilemma, inherent in the Soviet-American rivalry, blocked any negotiated settlement. Instead, the two superpowers agreed to disagree. Trusting neither each other nor any form of international cooperation, each concentrated on taking maximum advantage of its wartime gains. Thus the Russians exploited the territory they had conquered in Europe while the United States retained its economic and strategic advantages over the Soviet Union. The result was the Cold War.

CONTAINMENT

A major departure in American foreign policy occurred in January 1947, when General George C. Marshall, the wartime army chief of staff, became secretary of state. He had the capacity to think in broad, strategic terms. An extraordinarily good judge of ability, he relied on gifted subordinates to handle the day-to-day implementation of his policies. In the months after taking office, he came to rely on two men in particular: Dean Acheson and George Kennan.

Acheson, an experienced Washington lawyer and bureaucrat, was appointed undersecretary of state and given free rein by Marshall to conduct American diplomacy. A man of keen intelligence, he had a carefully cultivated reputation for arrogance and a low tolerance for mediocrity. Recalling the lesson of Munich, he opposed appeasement and advocated a policy of negotiating only from strength.

George Kennan, Marshall's other mainstay, headed the newly created Policy Planning Staff. A career foreign service officer, Kennan had become a Soviet expert, mastering Russian history and culture as well as speaking the language fluently. He served in Moscow after U.S. recognition in 1933 and again during World War II, developing there a profound distrust for the Soviet regime. In a crucial telegram in 1946, he advocated a policy of containment, arguing that only strong and sustained resistance could halt the outward flow of Russian power.

In the spring of 1947, a sense of crisis impelled Marshall, Acheson, and Kennan to set out on a new course in American diplomacy. Dubbed "containment," after an article by Kennan in *Foreign Affairs*, the new policy both consolidated the evolving postwar anticommunism and established guidelines that would shape America's role in the world for more than two decades. What Kennan proposed was "a long-term, patient but firm, and vigilant containment of Russian expansive tendencies." Such a policy of halting Soviet aggression would not lead to any immediate victory, Kennan warned. In the long run, however, he believed that the United States could force the Soviet Union to adopt more reasonable policies and live in peace with the West.

THE TRUMAN DOCTRINE

The initial step toward containment came in response to an urgent British request. Since March 1946, England had been supporting the Greek government in a bitter civil war against communist guerrillas. On February 21, 1947, the British informed the United States that they could no longer afford to aid Greece or Turkey, the latter under heavy pressure from the Soviets for access to the Mediterranean. Believing the Russians responsible for the strife in Greece (in fact, they were not), Marshall, Acheson, and Kennan quickly decided the United States would have to assume Britain's role in the eastern Mediterranean.

Worried about congressional support, especially since the Republicans had gained control of Congress in 1946, Marshall called a meeting with the legislative leadership in late February. He outlined the problem; then Acheson took over to warn that "a highly possible Soviet breakthrough might open three continents to Soviet penetration."

The bipartisan group of congressional leaders was deeply impressed. Finally, Republican Senator Arthur M. Vandenberg spoke up, saying he would support the president, but adding that to ensure public backing, Truman would have to "scare hell" out of the American people.

The president followed the senator's advice. On March 12, 1947, he asked Congress for $400 million for military and economic assistance to Greece and Turkey. In stating what would become known as the Truman Doctrine, he made clear that more was involved than just these two countries—the stakes in fact were far higher. "It must be the policy of the United States," Truman told the Congress, "to support free peoples who are resisting attempted subjugation by armed minorities or by outside pressure." After a brief debate, both the House and the Senate approved the program by margins of better than three to one.

The Truman Doctrine marked an informal declaration of cold war against the Soviet Union. Truman used the crisis in Greece to secure congressional approval and build a national consensus for the policy of containment. In less than two years, the civil war in Greece ended, but the American commitment to oppose communist expansion, whether by internal subversion or external aggression, placed the United States on a collision course with the Soviet Union around the globe.

THE MARSHALL PLAN

Despite American interest in controlling Soviet expansion into Greece, western Europe was far more vital to U.S. interests than was the eastern Mediterranean. Yet by 1947, many Americans believed that western Europe was open to Soviet penetration. The problem was economic in nature. Despite $9 billion in piecemeal American loans, England, France, Italy, and the other European countries had great difficulty in recovering from World War II. Food was scarce, with millions existing on less than fifteen hundred calories a day; industrial machinery was broken down and obsolete; and workers were demoralized by years of depression and war. Resentment and discontent led to growing communist voting strength, especially in Italy and France. If the United States could not reverse the process, it seemed as though all Europe might drift into the communist orbit.

In the weeks following proclamation of the Truman Doctrine, American officials dealt with this problem. Secretary of State Marshall, returning from a frustrating Council of Foreign Ministers meeting in Moscow, warned that "the patient is sinking while the doctors deliberate." The experts drew up a plan for the massive infusion of American capital to finance the economic recovery of Europe. Speaking at a Harvard commencement on June 5, 1947, Marshall presented the broad outline. He offered extensive economic aid to all the nations of Europe if they could reach agreement on ways to achieve "the revival of a working economy in the world. . . ."

The fate of the Marshall Plan depended on the reaction of the Soviet Union and the U.S. Congress. Marshall had taken, in the words of one American diplomat, "a hell of a gamble" by including Russia in his offer of aid. At a meeting of the European nations in Paris in July 1947, the Soviet foreign minister ended the suspense by abruptly withdrawing. Neither the Soviet Union nor its satellites would take part. The other European countries then made a formal request for $17 billion in assistance over the next four years.

Congress responded cautiously to the proposal. The administration lobbied vigorously, pointing out that the Marshall Plan would help the United States by stimulating trade with Europe as well as checking Soviet expansion. It was the latter argument that proved decisive. When the Czech coup touched off a war scare in March 1948, Congress quickly approved the Marshall Plan by heavy majorities. Over the next four years, the huge American investment paid rich dividends, generating a broad industrial revival in western Europe that became self-sustaining by the 1950s. The threat of communist domination faded, and a prosperous Europe proved to be a bonanza for American farmers, miners, and manufacturers.

THE WESTERN MILITARY ALLIANCE

The third and final phase of containment came in 1949 with the establishment of the North Atlantic Treaty Organization (NATO). NATO grew out of European fears of Russian military aggression. Recalling Hitler's tactics in the 1930s, the people of western Europe wanted assurance that the United States would protect them from attack as they began to achieve economic recovery.

In January 1949, President Truman called for a broad defense pact including the United States; ten European nations, from Norway in the north to Italy in the south, joined the United States and Canada in signing the North Atlantic Treaty in Washington on April 4, 1949. This historic departure from the traditional policy of isolation caused extensive debate, but the Senate ratified it in July by a vote of 82 to 13.

There were two main features of NATO. First, the United States committed itself to the defense of Europe in the key clause, which stated that "an armed attack against one or more shall be considered an attack against them all." In effect, the

The Soviet view of the Cold War, as depicted in this Soviet cartoon, shows the United States stretching out long arms to take hold of Korea, Iran, Turkey, Taiwan, and Vietnam.

United States was extending its atomic shield over Europe. The second feature was designed to reassure worried Europeans that the United States would honor this commitment. In late 1950, President Truman authorized the stationing of four American divisions in Europe to serve as the nucleus of the NATO army. It was believed that the threat of American troop involvement in any Russian assault would deter the Soviet Union from making such an attack.

The Western military alliance escalated the developing Cold War. Whatever its advantage in building a sense of security among worried Europeans, it represented an overreaction to the Soviet danger. Americans and Europeans alike were attempting to apply the lesson of Munich to the Cold War. But Stalin was not Hitler, and the Soviets were not the Nazis. There was no evidence of any Russian plan to invade western Europe. NATO only intensified Russian fears of the West and thus increased the level of international tension.

THE BERLIN BLOCKADE

The main Russian response to containment came in 1948 at the West's most vulnerable point. American, British, French, and Soviet troops each occupied a sector of Berlin, but the city was located more than a hundred miles within the Russian zone of Germany (see the map of postwar Europe on p. 734). Stalin decided to test his opponents' resolve by cutting off all rail and highway traffic to Berlin on June 20, 1948.

The timing was very awkward for Harry Truman. He faced a difficult reelection effort against a strong Republican candidate, Governor Thomas E. Dewey of New York. Immersed in election-year politics, Truman was caught unprepared by the Berlin blockade. The United States could withdraw its forces and lose not just a city, but the confidence of all Europe; it could try to send in reinforcements and fight for Berlin; or it could sit tight and attempt to find a diplomatic solution. Truman made the basic decision in characteristic fashion, telling the military that there would be no thought of pulling out. "We were going to stay, period," an aide reported Truman as saying.

In the next few weeks, the president and his advisers adopted a two-phase policy. The first part was a massive airlift of food, fuel, and supplies for the ten thousand troops and the two million civilians in Berlin. A fleet of fifty-two C-54s and eighty C-47s began making two daily round-trip flights to Berlin, carrying 2500 tons every twenty-four hours. Then, to guard against Soviet interruption of the airlift, Truman transferred sixty American B-29s, planes capable of delivering atomic bombs, to bases in England. The president was bluffing; the B-29s were not equipped with atomic bombs, but at the time, the threat was effective.

For a few weeks, the world teetered on the edge of war. Stalin did not attempt to disrupt the flights to Berlin, but he rejected all American diplomatic initiatives. Governor Dewey patriotically supported the president's policy, thus removing foreign policy from the presidential campaign.

Slowly, the tension eased. The Russians did not shoot down any planes, and the daily airlift climbed to nearly 7000 tons. Truman, a decided underdog, won a surprising second term in November over a complacent Dewey, in part because the Berlin crisis had rallied the nation behind his leadership. In early 1949, the

The Berlin airlift of 1948–1949 broke the Soviet blockade. Called Operation Vittles, it provided food and fuel for West Berliners. Here children wait for the candy that American pilots dropped in tiny handkerchief parachutes.

Soviets gave in, ending the blockade in return for another meeting of the Council of Foreign Ministers on Germany—a conclave that proved as unproductive as all the earlier ones.

The Berlin crisis marked the end of the initial phase of the Cold War. The airlift had given the United States a striking political victory, showing the world the triumph of American ingenuity over Russian stubbornness. Yet it could not disguise the fact that the Cold War had cut Europe in two. Behind the Iron Curtain, the Russians had consolidated control over the areas won by their troops in the war, while the United States had used the Marshall Plan to revitalize western Europe. But a divided continent was a far cry from the wartime hopes for a peaceful world. And the rivalry that began in Europe would soon spread into a worldwide contest between the superpowers.

The Cold War Expands

The rivalry between the United States and the Soviet Union grew in the late 1940s and early 1950s. Both sides began to rebuild their military forces with new methods and new weapons. Equally significant, the diplomatic competition spread from Europe to Asia as each of the superpowers sought to enhance its influence in the Far East. By the time Truman left office in early 1953, the Cold War had taken on global proportions.

The Military Dimension

After World War II, American leaders were intent on reforming the nation's military system in light of their wartime experience. Two goals were uppermost. First, nearly everyone agreed in the aftermath of Pearl Harbor that the U.S. armed services should be unified into an integrated military system. The developing Cold War reinforced this decision. Equally important, planners realized, was the need for new institutions to coordinate military and diplomatic strategy so the nation could cope effectively with threats to its security.

In 1947, Congress passed the National Security Act. It established a Department of Defense, headed by a civilian secretary of cabinet rank presiding over three separate services—the army, the navy, and the new air force. In addition, the act created the Central Intelligence Agency (CIA) to coordinate the intelligence-gathering activities of various government agencies. Finally, the act provided for a National Security Council (NSC)—composed of the service secretaries, the secretary of defense, and the secretary of state—to advise the president on all matters regarding the nation's security.

Despite the appearance of equality among the services, the air force quickly emerged as the dominant power in the atomic age, based on its capability both to deter an enemy from attacking and to wage war if deterrence failed. President Truman, intent on cutting back defense expenditures, favored the air force in his 1949 military budget, allotting this branch more than one-half the total sum.

When the Soviet Union exploded its first atomic bomb in the fall of 1949, President Truman appointed a high-level committee to explore mounting an all-out effort to build a hydrogen bomb to maintain American nuclear supremacy.

Some scientists had technical objections to the H-bomb, which was still far from being perfected, while others opposed the new weapon on moral grounds, claiming that its enormous destructive power (intended to be one thousand times greater than the atomic bomb) made it unthinkable. Dean Acheson—who succeeded Marshall as secretary of state in early 1949—believed it was imperative that the United States develop the hydrogen bomb before the Soviet Union. When Acheson presented the committee's favorable report to the president in January 1950, Truman took only seven minutes to decide to go ahead with the awesome new weapon.

At the same time, Acheson ordered the Policy Planning Staff to draw up a new statement of national defense policy. NSC-68, as the document eventually became known, called for a massive expansion of American military power so the United States could halt and overcome the Soviet threat and proposed an increase in defense spending from $13 to $45 billion annually. Approved in principle by the National Security Council in April 1950, NSC-68 stood as a symbol of the Truman administration's determination to win the Cold War regardless of cost.

THE COLD WAR IN ASIA

The Soviet-American conflict developed more slowly in Asia. At Yalta, the two superpowers had agreed to a Far Eastern balance of power, with the Russians dominating Northeast Asia and the Americans in control of the Pacific, including both Japan and its former island empire.

The United States moved quickly to consolidate its sphere of influence. General Douglas MacArthur, in charge of Japanese occupation, denied the Soviet Union any role in the reconstruction of Japan. Instead, he supervised the transition of the Japanese government into a constitutional democracy, shaped along Western lines, in which communists were barred from all government posts. The Japanese willingly renounced war in their new constitution, relying instead on American forces to protect their security.

As defined at Yalta, China lay between the Soviet and American spheres. When World War II ended, the country was torn between Chiang Kai-shek's Nationalists in the South and Mao Tse-tung's Communists in the North. Chiang had many advantages, including American political and economic backing and official Soviet recognition. But corruption was widespread among the Nationalist leaders, and a raging inflation that soon reached 100 percent a year devastated the Chinese middle classes and thus eroded Chiang's base of power. Mao used tight discipline and patriotic appeals to strengthen his hold on the peasantry and extend his influence. When the Soviets abruptly vacated Manchuria in 1946, Mao inherited control of this rich northern province. Ignoring American advice, Chiang rushed north to occupy Manchurian cities, overextending his supply lines and exposing his forces to Communist counterattack.

American policy sought to prevent a Chinese civil war. Before he became secretary of state, George Marshall undertook the difficult task of forming a coalition government between Chiang and Mao. There was no basis for compromise. Chiang insisted he "was going to liquidate Communists," while Mao was trying to play the United States against Russia in his bid for power. By 1947, as China plunged into full-scale civil war, the Truman administration had given up any meaningful effort to influence the outcome. Political mediation had failed, military intervention was out of the question so soon after World War II, and a policy of continued American economic aid served only to appease domestic supporters of Chiang Kai-shek; 80 percent of the military supplies ended up in Communist hands.

The Chinese conflict climaxed at the end of the decade. Mao's forces drove the Nationalists out of Manchuria in late 1948 and advanced across the Yangtze by mid-1949. Acheson released a lengthy report justifying American policy in China. Republican senators, however, disagreed, blaming American diplomats for sabotaging the Nationalists and terming Acheson's report "a 1,054-page white-wash of a wishful, do-nothing policy." While the domestic debate raged, Chiang's forces fled the mainland for sanctuary on Formosa (Taiwan) in December 1949. Two months later, Mao and Stalin signed a Sino-Soviet treaty of mutual assistance that clearly placed China in the Russian orbit.

The American response to the Communist triumph in China was twofold. First, the State Department refused to recognize the legitimacy of the new regime in Peking, maintaining instead formal diplomatic relations with the Nationalists on Formosa. Then, to compensate for the loss of China, the United States focused on Japan as its main ally in Asia. The State Department encouraged the buildup of Japanese industry, and the Pentagon expanded American bases on the Japanese home islands and Okinawa. A Japanese-American security pact led to the end of American occupation by 1952. The Cold War had now split east Asia in two.

THE KOREAN WAR

The showdown between the United States and the Soviet Union in Asia came in Korea. Traditionally the cockpit of international rivalry in northeast Asia, Korea had been divided at the 38th parallel in 1945. The Russians occupied the industrial North, installing a communist government under the leadership of Kim Il-Sung. In the agrarian South, Syngman Rhee, a conservative nationalist, emerged as the American-sponsored ruler. Neither regime heeded a UN call for elections to unify the country. The two superpowers pulled out most of their occupation forces by 1949. The Russians, however, helped train a well-equipped army in the North, while the United States—fearful Rhee would seek unification through armed conquest—gave much more limited military assistance to South Korea.

On June 25, 1950, the North Korean army suddenly crossed the 38th parallel in great strength. We now know that Stalin had approved this act of aggression in advance. In April 1950, when Kim Il-Sung came to Moscow to gain approval for the assault on South Korea, Stalin gave it willingly, apparently in the belief that the United States was ready to abandon Syngman Rhee. Despite expressing some reservations, Mao Tse-tung also approved the planned North Korean aggression.

Both Stalin and Mao had badly miscalculated the American response. President Truman saw the invasion as a clear-cut case of Soviet aggression reminiscent of the 1930s. "Communism was acting in Korea just as Hitler, Mussolini, and the Japanese had acted ten, fifteen, and twenty years earlier," he commented in his memoirs. Following Acheson's advice, the president convened the UN Security Council and, taking advantage of a temporary Soviet boycott, secured a resolution condemning North Korea as an aggressor and calling on the member nations to engage in a collective security action. Within a few days, American troops from Japan were in combat in South Korea. The conflict, which would last for more than three years, was technically a police action fought under UN auspices; in reality, the United States was at war with a Soviet satellite in Asia.

In the beginning, the fighting went badly as the North Koreans continued to drive down the peninsula. But by August, American forces had halted the communist advance near Pusan. In September, General MacArthur changed the whole complexion of the war by carrying out a brilliant amphibious assault at Inchon, on the waist of Korea, cutting off and destroying most of the North Korean army in the South. Encouraged by this victory, Truman began to shift from his original goal of restoring the 38th parallel to a new one: the unification of Korea by military force.

The administration ignored warnings from Peking against an American invasion of North Korea. "I should think it would be sheer madness for the Chinese to intervene," commented Acheson. MacArthur was even more confident. "We are no longer fearful of their intervention," he told Truman at a Wake Island conference in mid-October.

Rarely has an American president received worse advice than Truman did from Acheson and MacArthur. The UN forces crossed the 38th parallel in October, advanced confidently to the Yalu in November, and then were completely routed by a massive Chinese counterattack that drove them out of all North Korea by December. MacArthur finally stabilized the fighting near the 38th parallel, but when Truman decided to give up his attempt to unify Korea, the general protested to Congress, calling for a renewed offensive and proclaiming, "There is no substitute for victory."

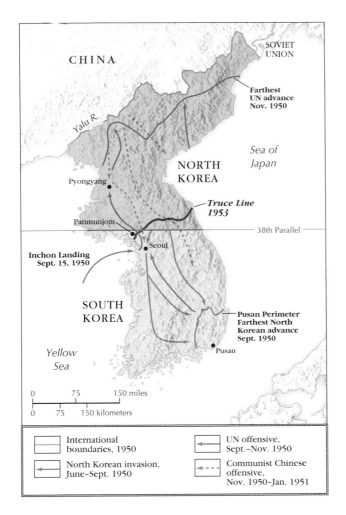

The Korean War, 1950–1953

After a year of rapid movement up and down the Korean peninsula, the fighting stalled just north of the 38th parallel. The resulting truce line has divided North and South Korea since the July 1953 armistice.

Truman courageously relieved the popular hero of the Pacific of his command on April 11, 1951. At first, MacArthur seemed likely to force the president to back down. Huge crowds came forward to welcome him home and hear him call for victory over the communists in Asia. At a special congressional hearing, the administration struck back effectively by warning that MacArthur's strategy would expose all Europe to Soviet attack.

Congress and the American people came to accept MacArthur's recall. The Korean War settled into a stalemate near the 38th parallel as truce talks with the communists bogged down for the rest of Truman's term in office. The president could take heart from the fact that he had achieved his primary goal, defense of South Korea and the principle of collective security. Yet by taking the gamble to unify Korea by force, he had confused the American people and humiliated the United States in the eyes of the world.

In the last analysis, the most significant result of the Korean conflict was the massive American rearmament it brought about. The army expanded to 3.5 million troops, the defense budget increased to $50 billion a year by 1952, and the United States acquired distant military bases from Saudi Arabia to Morocco. America was now committed to waging a global contest against the Soviet Union with arms as well as words.

THE COLD WAR AT HOME

The Cold War cast a long shadow over American life in the late 1940s and early 1950s. Truman tried to carry on the New Deal reform tradition he had inherited from FDR, but the American people were more concerned about events abroad. The Republican party used both growing dissatisfaction with postwar economic adjustment and fears of communist penetration of the United States to revive its sagging fortunes and regain control of the White House in 1952 for the first time in twenty years.

TRUMAN'S TROUBLES

Matching his foreign policy successes with equal achievements at home was not easy for Harry S. Truman. As a loyal supporter of Franklin D. Roosevelt's New Deal programs during his Senate career, Truman had earned a reputation for being a hardworking, reliable, and intensely partisan legislator. But he was relatively unknown to the general public, and his background as a Missouri county official associated with Kansas City machine politics did little to inspire confidence in his ability to lead the nation. Surprisingly well-read—especially in history and biography—Truman possessed sound judgment, the ability to reach decisions quickly, and a fierce and uncompromising sense of right and wrong.

Two weaknesses marred his performance in the White House. One was a fondness for old friends, which resulted in the appointment of many Missouri and Senate cronies to high office. The president's other serious limitation was his lack of political vision. Failing to pursue a coherent legislative program of his own, he tried to perpetuate FDR's New Deal and, as a result, engaged in a running battle with Congress.

The postwar mood was not conducive to an extension of New Deal reforms. Americans were weary of shortages and sacrifices; they wanted the chance to buy the consumer goods denied them under wartime conditions. Prices and wages rose quickly as Congress voted to end wartime controls. With prices going up 25 percent in two years, workers demanded higher wages to offset the loss of overtime pay. A wave of labor unrest swept over the country in the spring of 1946.

In the face of rising discontent, Truman's efforts to extend the New Deal met with little success. The only measure Congress passed was the Employment Act of 1946. This legislation created the Council of Economic Advisers to assist the president and asserted the principle that the government was responsible for the state of the economy, but it failed to address Truman's original goal of mandatory federal planning to achieve full employment.

The Republicans took advantage of increasing public dissatisfaction with postwar economic woes to attack the Democrats. "To err is Truman," the GOP

THE ELECTION OF 1948

CANDIDATE	PARTY	POPULAR VOTE	ELECTORAL VOTE
Truman	Democratic	24,105,695	303
Dewey	Republican	21,969,170	189
Thurmond	States' Rights	1,169,021	39
	Minor Parties	1,296,898	—

proclaimed and then adopted a very effective two-word slogan for the 1946 congressional elections: "Had enough?" The American people, weary of inflation and labor unrest, responded by electing Republican majorities in both the House and Senate for the first time since 1930.

TRUMAN VINDICATED

The president's relations with Congress became even stormier after the 1946 election. Congress overrode his veto of the Taft-Hartley Act in 1947. Designed to correct the imbalance in labor-management relations created by the Wagner Act, the Taft-Hartley Act outlawed specific labor union activities—including the closed shop and secondary boycotts. Despite Truman's claim that it was a "slave-labor" bill, unions were able to survive its provisions.

President Truman's political fortunes reached their lowest ebb in early 1948. Former vice president Henry A. Wallace, claiming to represent the New Deal, announced his third-party (Progressive) candidacy in the presidential contest that year. The Democrats reluctantly nominated Truman. His prospects for victory in the fall, however, looked very dim—especially after disgruntled Southerners bolted the Democratic party in protest over a progressive civil rights platform. The Dixiecrats, as they became known, nominated Strom Thurmond, the governor of South Carolina, on a States' Rights party ticket.

The defection of the Dixiecrats in the South and Wallace's liberal followers in the North led political experts to predict an almost certain Republican victory. Governor Thomas E. Dewey of New York, the GOP candidate, was so certain of winning that he waged a cautious and bland campaign designed to give him a free hand once he was in the White House. With nothing to lose, Truman barnstormed around the country denouncing the "do-nothing" Republican Eightieth Congress. To the amazement of the pollsters, Truman won a narrow but decisive victory in November. The old Roosevelt coalition—farmers, organized labor, urban ethnic groups, and blacks—had held together, enabling Truman to remain in the White House and the Democrats to regain control of Congress.

There was one more reason for Truman's win in 1948. During this election, held at the height of the Berlin crisis, the GOP failed to challenge Truman's conduct of the Cold War. The Republicans, committed to support the biparti-

A jubilant Harry Truman, on the morning after his 1948 election win, displays the headline blazoned on the front page of the Chicago Daily Tribune—*a newspaper that believed the pollsters.*

san policy of containment, had allowed the Democrats to preempt the foreign policy issue. Until they found a way to challenge Truman's Cold War policies, GOP leaders had little chance to regain the White House.

THE LOYALTY ISSUE

Despite Truman's surprising victory in 1948, there was one area on which the Democrats were vulnerable. The fear of communism abroad that had led to the bipartisan containment policy could be used against them at home by politicians who were willing to exploit the public's deep-seated anxiety.

The Cold War heightened the traditional belief that subversion from abroad endangered the republic. Bold rhetoric from members of the Truman administration, portraying the men in the Kremlin as inspired revolutionaries bent on world conquest, frightened the American people. They viewed the Soviet Union as a successor to Nazi Germany—a totalitarian police state that threatened the basic liberties of a free people.

A series of revelations of communist espionage activities reinforced these fears. Canadian officials uncovered a Soviet spy ring in 1946, and the House Un-American Activities Committee held hearings indicating that communist agents had flourished in the Agriculture and Treasury departments in the 1930s.

Although Truman tried to dismiss the loyalty issue as a "red herring," he felt compelled to take protective measures, thus lending substance to the charges of subversion. In March 1947, he had initiated a loyalty program, ordering security checks of government employees in order to root out communists. Thousands of government workers lost their jobs, charged with guilt by association with radicals or with membership in left-wing organizations. Often those who were charged had no chance to face their accusers.

The most famous disclosure came in August 1948, when Whittaker Chambers, a repentant communist, accused Alger Hiss of having been a Soviet spy in the 1930s. When Hiss, who had been a prominent State Department official, denied the charges, Chambers led investigators to a hollowed-out pumpkin on his Maryland farm. Inside the pumpkin were microfilms of confidential government documents. Chambers claimed that Hiss had passed the State Department materials to him in the late 1930s. Although the statute of limitations prevented a charge of treason against Hiss, he was convicted of perjury in January 1950 and sentenced to a five-year prison term.

Events abroad intensified the sense of danger. The communist triumph in China in the fall of 1949 came as a shock; soon there were charges that "fellow travelers" in the State Department were responsible for "the loss of China." In September 1949, when the Truman administration announced that the Russians had detonated their first atomic bomb, the end of America's nuclear monopoly was blamed on Soviet espionage.

In 1950, the government charged American communists Ethel and Julius Rosenberg with conspiracy to transmit atomic secrets to the Soviet Union. A year later, a jury found the Rosenbergs guilty of treason, and Judge Irving Kaufman sentenced them to die for what he termed their "loathsome offense." Despite their insistent claims of innocence and worldwide appeals on their behalf, the Rosenbergs were electrocuted on June 19, 1953. Thus by the early 1950s, nearly all the ingredients were at hand for a new outburst of hysteria—fear of Russia, evidence of espionage, and a belief in a vast unseen conspiracy. The only element missing was a leader to release the new outburst of intolerance.

McCARTHYISM IN ACTION

On February 12, 1950, Senator Joseph R. McCarthy of Wisconsin delivered a routine Lincoln's Birthday speech in Wheeling, West Virginia. This little known Republican suddenly attracted national attention when he declared, "I have here in my hand a list of 205—a list of names that were made known to the secretary of state as being members of the communist party and who nevertheless are still working and shaping policy in the State Department." The charge that there were communists in the State Department was never substantiated. But McCarthy's Wheeling speech triggered a four-and-a-half-year crusade to hunt down alleged communists in government. The stridency and sensationalism of the senator's accusations soon won the name "McCarthyism."

McCarthy's basic technique was the multiple untruth. He leveled a bevy of charges of treasonable activities in government. While officials were refuting his initial accusations, he brought forth a steady stream of new ones, so the corrections never caught up with the latest blast. He failed to unearth a single confirmed communist in government, but he kept the Truman administration in turmoil.

The secret of McCarthy's power was the fear he engendered among his Senate colleagues. In 1950, Maryland Senator Millard Tydings, who headed a committee critical of McCarthy's activities, failed to win reelection when McCarthy opposed him; after that, other senators ran scared. McCarthy delighted in making sweeping, startling charges of communist sympathies against prominent public figures; a favorite target was patrician Secretary of State Dean Acheson. Nor were fellow Republicans immune. One GOP senator was described as "a living miracle in that he is without question the only man who has lived so long with neither brains nor guts."

Senator Joseph McCarthy maintained a steady stream of unsubstantiated charges, always ready to make new accusations of communist infiltration before the preceding ones could be proven untrue. McCarthy's ruthless, vicious attacks cost hundreds of people their jobs and careers.

The attacks on the wealthy, famous, and privileged won McCarthy a devoted national following, although at the height of his influence in early 1954, he gained the approval of only 50 percent of the respondents in a Gallup poll. He offered a simple solution to the complicated Cold War: defeat the enemy at home rather than continue to engage in costly foreign aid programs and entangling alliances abroad. Above all, McCarthy appealed to conservative Republicans in the Midwest who shared his right-wing views and felt cheated by Truman's upset victory in 1948.

THE REPUBLICANS IN POWER

In 1952, the GOP capitalized on a growing sense of national frustration to capture the presidency. The stalemate in Korea and the fear of communism created a desire for political change; revelations of scandals by several individuals close to Truman intensified the feeling that someone needed to clean up "the mess in Washington." In Dwight D. Eisenhower, the Republican party found the perfect candidate to explore what one senator called K_1C_2—Korea, communism, and corruption.

Immensely popular because of his amiable manner, winning smile, and heroic stature, Eisenhower alone appeared to have the ability to unite a divided nation. In the 1952 campaign, Ike displayed hidden gifts as a politician in running against Adlai Stevenson, the eloquent Illinois governor whose appeal was

THE ELECTION OF 1952

CANDIDATE	PARTY	POPULAR VOTE	ELECTORAL VOTE
Eisenhower	Republican	33,778,963	442
Stevenson	Democratic	27,314,992	89

limited to diehard Democrats and liberal intellectuals. Eisenhower delivered the most telling blow of all on the Korean War. Speaking in Detroit in late October, just after the fighting had intensified again in Korea, Ike promised if elected he would go personally to the battlefield in an attempt "to bring the Korean War to an early and honorable end."

"That does it—Ike is in," several reporters exclaimed after they heard this pledge. The hero of World War II had clinched his election by committing himself to end an unpopular war. Ten days later, he won the presidency handily, carrying thirty-nine states, including four in the formerly solid Democratic South. The Republican party, however, did not fare as well in Congress; it gained just a slight edge in the House and controlled the Senate by only one seat.

Once elected, Eisenhower moved quickly to fulfill his campaign pledge. He spent three days in early December touring the battlefront in Korea, quickly ruling out the new offensive the military favored. Instead he turned to diplomacy, relying on subtle hints to China on the possible use of nuclear weapons to break the stalemated peace talks. These tactics, together with the death of Joseph Stalin in early March, finally led to the signing of an armistice on July 27, 1953, which ended the fighting but left Korea divided—as it had been before the war—near the 38th parallel.

The new president was less effective in dealing with the problem raised by Senator McCarthy's continuing witch-hunt. Instead of toning down his anticommunist crusade after the Republican victory in 1952, McCarthy used his new position as chairman of the Senate Committee on Government Operations as a base for ferreting out communists on the federal payroll. Eisenhower's advisers urged the president to use his own great prestige to stop McCarthy. But Ike refused such a confrontation, saying, "I will not get into a pissing contest with a skunk." Eisenhower preferred to play for time, hoping the American people would eventually come to their senses.

The Wisconsin senator finally overreached himself. In early 1954, he uncovered an army dentist suspected of disloyalty and proceeded to attack the upper echelons of the U.S. Army, telling one much decorated general that he was "not fit to wear the uniform." The controversy culminated in the televised Army-McCarthy hearings. Viewers were repelled by his frequent outbursts that began with the insistent cry, "Point of order, Mr. Chairman, point of order," and by his attempt to slur the reputation of a young lawyer associated with army counsel Joseph Welch.

Courageous Republicans, led by Senators Ralph Flanders of Vermont and Margaret Chase Smith of Maine, joined with Democrats to bring about the Senate's censure of McCarthy in December 1954, by a vote of 67 to 22. Once rebuked, McCarthy fell quickly from prominence. He died three years later virtually unnoticed and unmourned.

Yet his influence was profound. Not only did he paralyze national life with what a Senate subcommittee described as "the most nefarious campaign of half-truth and untruth in the history of the Republic," but he also helped impose a political and cultural conformity that froze dissent for the rest of the 1950s. Long after McCarthy's passing, the nation tolerated loyalty oaths for teachers, the banning of left-wing books in public libraries, and the blacklisting of entertainers in radio, television, and films.

While Dwight Eisenhower could claim that his policy of giving McCarthy enough rope to hang himself had worked, it is possible that a bolder and more forthright presidential attack on the senator might have spared the nation some of the excesses of the anticommunist crusade.

EISENHOWER WAGES THE COLD WAR

Dwight D. Eisenhower came into the presidency in 1952 unusually well prepared to lead the nation at the height of the Cold War. His long years of military service had exposed him to a wide variety of international issues, both in Asia and in Europe, and to an even broader array of world leaders, such as Winston Churchill and Charles de Gaulle. He was not only an experienced military strategist but a gifted politician and diplomat as well. He was blessed with a sharp, pragmatic mind and organizational genius that enabled him to plan and carry out large enterprises. Above all, he had a serene confidence in his own ability. At the end of his first day in the White House, he confided in his diary: "Plenty of worries and difficult problems. But such has been my portion for a long time—the result is that this just seems like a continuation of all I've been doing since July 1941."

Eisenhower chose John Foster Dulles as his secretary of state. The myth soon developed that Ike had given Dulles free rein to conduct American diplomacy. Appearances were deceptive. Eisenhower preferred to work behind the scenes. He let Dulles make the public speeches and appearances before congressional committees, where the secretary's hard-line views placated GOP extremists. But Dulles carefully consulted with the president before every appearance, meeting frequently with Eisenhower at the White House and telephoning him several times a day. Ike respected his secretary of state's broad knowledge of foreign policy and skill in conducting American diplomacy, but he made all the major decisions himself.

From the outset, Eisenhower was determined to bring the Cold War under control. In part, he was motivated by a deeply held concern about the budget. Defense spending had increased from $13 billion to $50 billion under Truman; Ike was convinced the nation was in danger of going bankrupt unless military spending was reduced. As president, he inaugurated a "new look" for American defense, cutting back on the army and navy and relying even more heavily than Truman had on the air force and its nuclear striking power. As a result, the defense budget dropped below $40 billion annually. In 1954, Dulles announced reliance on massive retaliation—in fact a continuance of Truman's policy of deterrence. Rather than becoming involved in limited wars such as Korea, the United States would consider the possibility of using nuclear weapons to halt any communist aggression that threatened vital U.S. interests anywhere in the world.

While he permitted Dulles to make his veiled nuclear threats, Eisenhower's fondest dream was to end the arms race. Sobered by the development of the hydrogen bomb, successfully tested by the United States in November 1952 and by the Soviet Union in August 1953, the president began a new effort at disarmament with the Russians. Yet before this initiative could take effect, Ike had to weather a series of crises around the world that tested his skill and patience to the utmost.

ENTANGLEMENT IN INDOCHINA

The first crisis facing the new president came in Indochina. Since 1950, the United States had been giving France military and economic aid in a war in Indochina against communist guerrillas led by Ho Chi Minh. The Chinese increased their support to Ho's forces, known as the Vietminh, after the Korean War ended; by the spring of 1954, the French were on the brink of defeat. The Vietminh had surrounded nearly ten thousand French troops at Dien Bien Phu deep in the interior of northern Indochina; in desperation, France turned to the United States for help. Admiral Arthur Radford, chairman of the Joint Chiefs of Staff, proposed an American air strike to lift the siege.

Eisenhower decided against Radford's bold proposal, but he killed it in his typically indirect fashion. Fearful that an air attack would lead inevitably to the use of ground troops, Ike insisted that both Congress and American allies in Europe approve the strike in advance. Congressional leaders, recalling the recent Korean stalemate, were reluctant to agree; the British were appalled and ruled out any joint action. The president used these objections to reject intervention in Indochina in 1954.

Dien Bien Phu fell to the Vietminh in May 1954. At an international conference held in Geneva a few weeks later, Indochina was divided at the 17th parallel. Ho gained control of North Vietnam, while the French continued to rule in the South. The United States gradually took over from the French in South Vietnam, sponsoring a new government in Saigon headed by Ngo Dinh Diem, a Vietnamese nationalist from a northern Catholic family. While Eisenhower can be given credit for refusing to engage American forces on behalf of French colonialism in Indochina, his determination to resist communist expansion had committed the United States to a long and eventually futile struggle to prevent Ho Chi Minh from achieving his long-sought goal of a unified, independent Vietnam.

CONTAINING CHINA

The communist government in Peking posed a serious challenge for the Eisenhower administration. Senate Republicans, led by William Knowland of California, blamed the Democrats for the "loss" of China. They viewed Mao as

A French soldier stands guard over a truckload of Vietnamese nationalists captured in the fighting in Indochina. French efforts to quash the rebellion in Vietnam ended on May 7, 1954, when the Vietminh took the French stronghold at Dien Bien Phu.

a puppet of the Soviet Union and insisted the United States recognize the Nationalists on Formosa as the only legitimate government of China. While State Department experts realized there were underlying tensions between China and Russia, Mao's intervention in the Korean War had convinced most Americans that the Chinese communists were an integral part of a larger communist effort at world domination.

Eisenhower and Dulles chose to accentuate the potential conflict between Russia and China. By taking a strong line against China, the United States could make the Chinese realize that Russia was unable to protect their interests; at the same time, such a hawkish policy would please congressional conservatives such as Knowland. Ultimately, Eisenhower and Dulles hoped that a policy of firmness would not only contain communist Chinese expansion in Asia but also drive a wedge between Moscow and Peking.

A crisis in the Formosa Straits provided the first test of the new policy. In the fall of 1954, communist China threatened to seize coastal islands, notably Quemoy and Matsu, occupied by the Nationalists. Fearful that seizure of these offshore islands would be the first step toward an invasion of Formosa, Eisenhower permitted Dulles to sign a security treaty with Chiang Kai-shek committing the United States to defend Formosa. When the communists began shelling the offshore islands, Eisenhower persuaded Congress to pass a resolution authorizing him to use force to defend Formosa and "closely related localities."

Despite repeated requests, however, the president refused to say whether he would use force to repel a Chinese attack on Quemoy or Matsu. Instead he and Dulles hinted at the use of nuclear weapons. The Chinese leaders, unsure whether Eisenhower was bluffing, decided not to test American resolve. The shelling ended in 1955, and when the communists resumed it again in 1958, another firm but equally ambiguous American response forced them to desist. The apparent refusal of the Soviet Union to come to China's aid in these crises with the United States contributed to a growing rift between the two communist nations by the end of the 1950s.

TURMOIL IN THE MIDDLE EAST

The gravest crisis for Eisenhower came in the Middle East when Egyptian leader Gamal Nasser seized the Suez Canal in July 1956. England and France were ready to use force immediately; their citizens owned the canal company, and their economies were dependent on the canal for the flow of oil from the Persian Gulf. President Eisenhower, however, was staunchly opposed to intervention. For three months, Dulles did everything possible to restrain the European allies, but finally they decided to take a desperate gamble—they invaded Egypt and seized the canal, relying on the United States to prevent any Russian interference.

Eisenhower was furious when England and France launched their attack in early November. Campaigning for reelection against Adlai Stevenson on the slogan of keeping the peace, Ike had to abandon domestic politics to deal with the threat of war. Unhesitatingly, he instructed Dulles to sponsor a UN resolution calling for British and French withdrawal from Egypt. Yet when the Russians supported the American proposal and went further, threatening rocket attacks on British and French cities and even offering to send "volunteers" to fight in Egypt, Eisenhower made it clear he would not tolerate Soviet interference. He put the Strategic Air Command on alert and said of the Russians, "If those fellows start something, we may have to hit 'em—and, if necessary, with everything in the bucket."

Just after noon on election day, November 6, 1956, British Prime Minister Anthony Eden called the president to inform him that England and France were ending their invasion. Eisenhower breathed a sigh of relief. American voters rallied behind Ike, electing him to a second term by a near landslide. As a result of the Suez crisis, the United States replaced England and France as the main Western influence in the Middle East. With Russia strongly backing Egypt and Syria, the Cold War had found yet another battleground.

COVERT ACTIONS

Amid these dangerous crises, the Eisenhower administration worked behind the scenes in the 1950s to expand the nation's global influence. In 1953, the CIA was instrumental in overthrowing a popularly elected government in Iran and placing the shah in full control of that country. American oil companies were rewarded with lucrative concessions, and Eisenhower believed he had gained a valuable ally on the Russian border. But these short-run gains created a deep-seated animosity among Iranians that would haunt the United States in the future.

Closer to home, in Latin America, Eisenhower once again relied on covert action. In 1954, the CIA masterminded the overthrow of a leftist regime in Guatemala. The immediate advantage was in denying the Soviets a possible foothold in the Western Hemisphere, but Latin Americans resented the thinly disguised interference of the United States in their internal affairs. More important, when Fidel Castro came to power in Cuba in 1959, the Eisenhower administration—after a brief effort at conciliation—adopted a hard line that helped drive Cuba into the Soviet orbit and led to new attempts at covert action.

Eisenhower's record as a cold warrior was thus mixed. His successful ending of the Korean War and his peacekeeping efforts in Indochina and Formosa and in the Suez crisis are all to his credit. Yet his reliance on coups and subversion directed by the CIA in Iran and Guatemala reveal Ike's corrupting belief that the ends justified the means.

Nevertheless, Eisenhower did display an admirable ability to stay calm and unruffled in moments of great tension, reassuring the nation and the world. And above all, he could boast, as he did in 1962, of his ability to keep the peace. "In those eight years," he reminded the nation, "we lost no inch of ground to tyranny. One war was ended and incipient wars were blocked."

WAGING PEACE

Eisenhower hoped to ease Cold War tensions by ending the nuclear arms race. The advent of the hydrogen bomb intensified his concern over nuclear warfare; by 1955, both the United States and the Soviet Union had added this dread new weapon to their arsenals. With new long-range ballistic missiles being perfected, it was only a matter of time before Russia and the United States would be capable of destroying each other completely. Peace, as Winston Churchill noted, now depended on a balance of terror.

Throughout the 1950s, Eisenhower sought a way out of the nuclear dilemma. In April 1953, shortly after Stalin's death, he gave a speech in which he called on the Russians to join him in a new effort at disarmament. When the Soviets ignored this appeal, Eisenhower tried again. At a summit conference in Geneva, Switzerland, in 1955, Ike proposed to Nikita Khrushchev, just emerging as Stalin's successor after a two-year struggle for power, a way to break the disarmament deadlock. "Open skies," as reporters dubbed the plan, would overcome the traditional Russian objection to on-site inspection by having both superpowers open their territory to mutual aerial surveillance. Unfortunately, Khrushchev dismissed open skies as "a very transparent espionage device," and the conference ended without any significant breakthrough in the Cold War.

Amid rising worldwide concern over global fallout from nuclear testing, Eisenhower and Khrushchev suspended further weapons tests in the atmosphere in October 1958 while diplomats met at Geneva to negotiate a test ban treaty. A dispute over how to detect underground tests prevented them from reaching agreement, but neither the United States nor the Soviet Union resumed atmospheric tests for the remainder of Ike's term in office.

The suspension of testing halted the pollution of the world's atmosphere, but it did not lead to the improvement in Soviet-American relations that Eisenhower sought. Instead, the Soviet feat in launching *Sputnik,* the first artificial satellite to orbit the earth, intensified the Cold War. Fearful that the Russians were several years ahead of the United States in the development of intercontinental ballistic missiles (ICBMs), Democrats criticized Eisenhower for not spending enough on defense and warned that a dangerous missile gap would open up by the early 1960s—a time when the Russians might have such a commanding lead in ICBMs that they could launch a first strike and destroy America. Despite the president's belief that the American missile program was in good shape, he allowed increased defense spending to speed up the building of American ICBMs and the new Polaris submarine–launched intermediate range missile (IRBM).

The most serious threat came in November 1958, when the Russian leader declared that within six months he would sign a separate peace treaty with East Germany, calling for an end to American, British, and French occupation rights in Berlin.

Eisenhower met the second Berlin crisis as firmly as Truman had the first. He not only refused to abandon the city but also tried to avoid a military show-down. Prudent diplomacy forced Khrushchev to extend his deadline indefi-nitely. After a trip to the United States, culminating in a personal meeting with Eisenhower at Camp David, the Russian leader agreed to attend a summit con-ference in Paris in May 1960.

This much heralded meeting never took place. On May 1, two weeks before the leaders were to convene in Paris, the Soviets shot down an American U-2 plane piloted by Francis Gary Powers. The United States had been overflying Russia since 1956 in the high-altitude spy planes, gaining vital information about

"Handshake" is the title of this cartoon depicting a British view of relations between Soviet Premier Khrushchev and U.S. President Eisenhower dur-ing the Cold War. But the "handshake" between the two superpowers is more a contest of strength than a gesture of cooperation.

Russians view the wreckage of the U-2 reconnaissance plane piloted by Francis Powers that was shot down over Soviet territory on May 1, 1960. Although Eisenhower originally disavowed any knowledge of Powers's mission, Khrushchev produced photographs of Soviet military and industrial sites, which he said had been taken by the U-2 pilot. Powers was held in a Soviet prison for two years before he was released in exchange for a Russian spy.

the Soviet missile program. After initially denying any knowledge, Eisenhower took full responsibility for Powers's overflight, and Khrushchev responded with a scathing personal denunciation and a refusal to meet with the American president.

THE CONTINUING COLD WAR

The breakup of the Paris summit marked the end of Eisenhower's attempt to moderate the Cold War. The disillusioned leader told an aide that "the stupid U-2 mess" had destroyed all his efforts for peace. Khrushchev marked time for the next nine months, waiting for the American people to choose a new president. Eisenhower did make a final effort at peace, however. Three days before leaving office, he delivered a farewell address in which he gave a somber warning about the danger of massive military spending. "In the councils of government," he declared, "we must guard against the acquisition of unwarranted influence, whether sought or unsought, by the military-industrial complex."

Rarely has an American president been more prophetic. In the next few years, the level of defense spending would skyrocket as the Cold War escalated. The military-industrial complex reached its peak in the 1960s when the United States realized the full implications of Truman's doctrine of containment.

Eisenhower had succeeded in keeping the peace for eight years, but he had failed to halt the momentum of the Cold War he had inherited from Harry Truman. Ike's efforts to ease tension with the Soviet Union were dashed by his own distrust of communism and by Khrushchev's belligerent rhetoric and behavior. Still, he had begun to relax tensions, a process that would survive the troubled 1960s and, after several false starts, would finally begin to erode the Cold War by the end of the 1980s.

CHRONOLOGY

1945	Truman meets Stalin at Potsdam Conference (July)
	World War II ends with Japanese surrender (August)
1946	Winston Churchill gives "Iron Curtain" speech
1947	Truman Doctrine announced to Congress (March)
	George Marshall outlines Marshall Plan (June)
	Truman orders loyalty program for government employees (March)
1948	Soviets begin blockade of Berlin (June)
	Truman scores upset victory in presidential election
1949	NATO treaty signed in Washington (April)
	Soviet Union tests its first atomic bomb (August)
1950	Truman authorizes building of hydrogen bomb (January)
	Senator Joseph McCarthy claims communists in government (February)
	North Korea invades South Korea (June)
1951	Truman recalls MacArthur from Korea
1952	Dwight D. Eisenhower elected president
1953	Julius and Ethel Rosenberg executed for atomic-secrets spying (June)
	Korean War truce signed at Panmunjom (July)
1954	Fall of Dien Bien Phu to Vietminh ends French control of Indochina
1956	England and France touch off Suez crisis
1957	Russia launches *Sputnik* satellite
1959	Fidel Castro takes power in Cuba
1960	American U-2 spy plane shot down over Russia

29

AFFLUENCE AND ANXIETY

On May 7, 1947, William Levitt announced plans to build two thousand rental houses in a former potato field on Long Island, thirty miles from Midtown Manhattan. Using mass production techniques he had learned while erecting navy housing during the war, Levitt quickly built four thousand homes and rented them to young veterans eager to leave crowded city apartments or their parents' homes to begin raising families. A change in government financing regulations led him to begin offering his houses for sale in 1948 for a small amount down and a low monthly payment. Young couples quickly bought the first four thousand; by the time Levittown—as he called the new community—was completed in 1951, it contained more than seventeen thousand homes. So many babies were born in Levittown that it soon became known as "Fertility Valley" and "the Rabbit Hutch."

Levitt eventually built two more Levittowns, one in Pennsylvania and one in New Jersey; each contained the same curving streets, neighborhood parks and playgrounds, and community swimming pools characteristic of the first development. The secret of Levittown's appeal was the basic house, a 720-square-foot Cape Cod design built on a concrete slab. It had a kitchen, two bedrooms and bath, a living room complete with a fireplace and 16-foot picture window, and an expansion attic with room for two more bedrooms. Levitt built only one interior, but there were four different facades to break the monotony. The original house sold for $6990 in 1948; even the improved model, a ranch-style house, sold for less than $10,000 in 1951.

Levitt's houses were ideal for young people just starting out in life. They were cheap, comfortable, and efficient, and each home came with a refrigerator, cooking range, and washing machine. Despite the conformity of the houses, the three Levittowns were surprisingly diverse communities; residents had a wide variety of religious, ethnic, and occupational backgrounds. African Americans, however, were rigidly excluded.

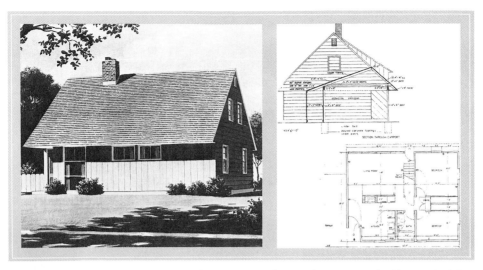

A photograph, floor plan, and elevation for a Levittown house. The Levittown builders applied the principles of mass production used in auto manufacturing to house construction. One important difference was the fact that the product stood stationary while workers came to the site to perform their specialized tasks. Construction was broken down into twenty-seven separate tasks, and a house could be assembled in fifteen minutes.

Levittown symbolized the most significant social trend of the postwar era in the United States—the flight to the suburbs. The residential areas surrounding cities such as New York and Chicago nearly doubled in the 1950s. While central cities remained relatively stagnant during the decade, suburbs grew by 46 percent; by 1960, some sixty million people, one-third of the nation, lived in suburban rings around the cities. This massive shift in population from the central city was accompanied by a baby boom that started during World War II. Young married couples began to have three, four, or even five children (compared with only one or two children in American families during the 1930s). These larger families led to a 19 percent growth in the nation's population between 1950 and 1960, the highest growth rate since 1910.

The economy boomed as residential construction soared. By 1960, one-fourth of all existing homes were less than ten years old, and factories were turning out large quantities of appliances and television sets for the new households. A multitude of new consumer products—ranging from frozen foods to cars equipped with automatic transmissions and tubeless tires—appeared in stores and showrooms.

A new affluence replaced the poverty and hunger of the Great Depression for most Americans, but many had haunting memories of the 1930s. The obsession with material goods took on an almost desperate quality, as if a profusion of houses, cars, and home appliances could guarantee that the nightmare of depression would never return. Critics were quick to disparage the quality of life in suburban society, charging the newly affluent with forsaking traditional American individualism to live in identical houses, drive look-alike cars, and accumulate the same material possessions.

Events abroad added to the feeling of anxiety in the postwar years. Nuclear war became a frighteningly real possibility. The rivalry with the Soviet Union had led to the second Red Scare, with charges of treason and disloyalty being leveled at loyal Americans. Many Americans joined Senator Joseph McCarthy in searching for the communist enemy at home rather than abroad. Loyalty oaths and book burning revealed how insecure Americans had become in the era of the Cold War. The 1950s also witnessed a growing demand by African Americans for equal opportunity in an age of abundance. The civil rights movement, along with strident criticism of the consumer culture, revealed that beneath the bland surface of suburban affluence, forces for change were at work.

THE POSTWAR BOOM

For fifteen years following World War II, the nation witnessed a period of unparalleled economic growth. A pent-up demand for consumer goods fueled a steady industrial expansion. Heavy government spending during the Cold War added an extra stimulus to the economy, offsetting brief recessions in 1949 and 1953 and moderating a steeper one in 1957–1958. By the end of the 1950s, the American people had achieved an affluence that finally erased the lingering fears of the Great Depression.

POSTWAR PROSPERITY

The economy began its upward surge as the result of two long-term factors. First, American consumers—after being held in check by depression and then by wartime scarcities—finally had a chance to indulge their suppressed appetites for material goods. At the war's end, personal savings in the United States stood at more than $37 billion, providing a powerful stimulus to consumption. Initially, American factories could not turn out enough automobiles and appliances to satisfy the horde of buyers. By 1950, however, production lines had finally caught up with the demand.

The Cold War provided the additional stimulus the economy needed when postwar expansion slowed. The Marshall Plan and other foreign aid programs financed a heavy export trade. In 1952, the nation spent $44 billion, two-thirds of the federal budget, on national defense. Although Eisenhower managed to bring about some modest reductions, defense spending continued at a level of $40 billion throughout the decade.

The nation achieved an affluence in the 1950s that made the persisting fear of another Great Depression seem irrational. The baby boom and the spectacular growth of suburbia served as great stimulants to the consumer goods industries. Manufacturers turned out an ever increasing number of refrigerators, washing machines, and dishwashers to equip the kitchens of Levittown and its many imitators across the country. The automobile industry thrived with suburban expansion as two-car families became more and more common.

Commercial enterprises snapped up office machines and the first generation of computers; industry installed electronic sensors and processors as it underwent extensive automation; and the military displayed an insatiable appetite for electronic devices for its planes and ships. As a result, American industry averaged more than $10 billion a year in capital investment, and the number of persons employed rose above the long-sought goal of sixty million nationwide.

Yet the economic abundance of the 1950s was not without its problems. While some sections of the nation (notably the emerging Sunbelt areas of the South and West) benefited enormously from the growth of the aircraft and electronics industries, older manufacturing regions, such as New England, did not fare as well. The steel industry increased its capacity during the decade, but it began to fall behind the rate of national growth. Agriculture continued to experience bumper crops and low prices, so rural regions failed to share in the general affluence.

None of these flaws, however, could disguise the fact that the nation was prospering to an extent no one dreamed possible in the 1930s. The GNP grew to $440 billion by 1960, more than double the 1940 level. By the mid-1950s, the average American family had twice as much real income to spend as its counterpart had possessed in the boom years of the 1920s. From 1945 to 1960, per capita disposable income rose by $500—to $1845—for every man, woman, and child in the country. The American people, in one generation, had moved from poverty and depression to the highest standard of living the world had ever known.

LIFE IN THE SUBURBS

Sociologists had difficulty describing the nature of suburban society in the 1950s. Some saw it as classless, while others noted the absence of both the very rich and the very poor and consequently labeled it "middle class." Rather than forming a homogeneous social group, though, the suburbs contained a surprising variety of people, whether classified as "upper lower," "lower middle," and "upper middle" or simply as blue collar, white collar, and professional. Doctors and lawyers often lived in the same developments as salesclerks and master plumbers. The traditional distinctions of ancestry, education, and size of residence no longer differentiated people as easily as they had in the past.

Life in all the suburban communities depended on the automobile. Highways and expressways allowed fathers to commute to jobs in the cities, often an hour or more away. Children might ride buses to and from school, but mothers had to drive them to piano lessons and Little League ballgames. Two cars became a necessity for almost every suburban family, thus helping spur the boom in automobile production.

In the new drive-in culture, people shopped at the stores that grew up first in "miracle miles" along the highways and later at the shopping centers that spread across the countryside by the mid-1950s. There were only eight shopping centers in the entire country in 1946; hundreds appeared over the next fifteen years.

Despite the increased mobility provided by the car, the home became the focus for activities and aspirations. The postwar shortage of housing that often forced young couples to live with their parents or in-laws created an intense demand for new homes in the suburbs. When questioned, prospective buyers expressed a desire for "more space," for "comfort and roominess," and for "privacy and freedom of action" in their new residences.

But there were some less attractive consequences of the new suburban lifestyle. The extended family, in which several generations had lived in close proximity, was a casualty of the boom in small detached homes. As historian Kenneth Jackson has noted, suburban life "ordained that most children would grow up in intimate contact only with their parents and siblings." For many families, grandparents, aunts and uncles, cousins, and more distant relatives would become remote figures, seen only on special occasions.

The nuclear family, typical of the suburb, did little to encourage the development of feminism. The end of the war saw many women who had entered the workforce return to the home, where the role of wife and mother continued to be viewed as the ideal for women in the 1950s. Trends toward getting married earlier and having larger families reinforced the pattern of women devoting all their efforts to housework and child raising rather than acquiring professional skills and pursuing careers outside the home.

Nonetheless, the number of working wives doubled between 1940 and 1960. By the end of the 1950s, 40 percent of American women, and nearly one-third of all married women, had jobs outside the home. The heavy expenses involved in rearing and educating children led wives and mothers to seek ways to augment the family income, inadvertently preparing the way for a new demand for equality in the 1960s.

THE GOOD LIFE?

Consumerism became the dominant social theme of the 1950s. Yet even with an abundance of creature comforts and added hours of leisure time, the quality of life left many Americans anxious and dissatisfied.

AREAS OF GREATEST GROWTH

Organized religion flourished in the climate of the 1950s. Ministers, priests, and rabbis all commented on the rise in church and synagogue attendance in the new communities. Will Herberg claimed that religious affiliation had become the primary identifying feature of modern American life, dividing the nation into three separate segments—Protestant, Catholic, and Jewish.

Some observers condemned the bland, secular nature of suburban churches, which seemed to be an integral part of the consumer society. "On weekdays one shops for food," wrote one critic, "on Saturdays one shops for recreation, and on Sundays one shops for the Holy Ghost." But the popularity of religious writer Norman Vincent Peale, with his positive gospel that urged people to "start thinking faith, enthusiasm and joy," suggested that the new churches filled a genuine if shallow human need.

Schools provided an immediate problem for the growing new suburban communities. The increase in the number of school-age children, from twenty to thirty million in the first eight grades, overwhelmed the resources of many local

Entertainment for all age levels was the focus of television in the 1950s. Then, as now, shows were targeted for specific age groups, such as these children watching intently the antics of the puppets and live actors on the "Howdy Doody Show." The television became the focal center of rooms where families gathered to spend their leisure time.

districts, leading to demands for federal aid. Congress granted limited help for areas affected by defense plants and military bases, but Eisenhower's reluctance to unbalance the budget blocked further federal assistance prior to 1957, when the government reacted to *Sputnik*.

The largest advances were made in the exciting new medium of television. From a shaky start just after the war, TV boomed in the 1950s, pushing radio aside and undermining many of the nation's magazines. By 1957, three networks controlled the airwaves, reaching forty million sets over nearly five hundred stations.

At first, the insatiable demand for programs encouraged a burst of creativity. Playwrights such as Reginald Rose, Rod Serling, and Paddy Chayefsky wrote a series of notable dramas for *Playhouse 90, Studio One,* and the *Goodyear Television Playhouse.* Broadcast live from cramped studios, these productions thrived on tight dramatic structures, movable scenery, and frequent close-ups of the actors.

Advertisers, however, quickly became disillusioned with the live anthology programs, wanting shows that stressed excitement, glamour, and instant success. Aware that audiences were fascinated by contestants with unusual expertise (a shoemaker answering tough questions on operas, a grandmother stumping experts on baseball), producers began giving away huge cash prizes on *The $64,000 Question* and *Twenty-one*. In 1959, the nation was shocked when Charles Van

Doren, a Columbia University professor, confessed he had been given the answers in advance to win $129,000 on *Twenty-one.* The three networks quickly dropped all the big-prize quiz programs, replacing them with comedy, action, and adventure shows. Despite its early promise of artistic innovation, television had become a technologically sophisticated but safe conveyor of the consumer culture.

CRITICS OF THE CONSUMER SOCIETY

One striking feature of the 1950s was the abundance of self-criticism. A number of widely read books explored the flaws in the new suburbia. John Keats's *The Crack in the Picture Window* described the endless rows of tract houses "vomited up" by developers as "identical boxes spreading like gangrene." Their occupants lost any sense of individuality in their obsession with material goods.

The most sweeping indictment came in William H. Whyte's *The Organization Man* (1956), based on a study of the Chicago suburb of Park Forest. Whyte perceived a change from the old Protestant ethic, with its emphasis on hard work and personal responsibility, to a new social ethic centered on "the team" with the ultimate goal of "belongingness." The result was a stifling conformity and the loss of personal identity.

The most influential social critic of the 1950s was Harvard sociologist David Riesman. His book *The Lonely Crowd* appeared in 1950 and set the tone for intellectual commentary about suburbia for the rest of the decade. Riesman described the shift from the "inner-directed" Americans of the past who had relied on such traditional values as self-denial and frugality to the "other-directed" Americans of the consumer society who constantly adapted their behavior to conform to social pressures. The resulting decline in individualism produced a bland and tolerant society of consumers lacking creativity and a sense of adventure.

C. Wright Mills was a far more caustic commentator on American society in the 1950s. Anticipating government statistics that revealed white-collar workers (salesclerks, office workers, bank tellers) now outnumbered blue-collar workers (miners, factory workers, millhands), Mills described the new middle class in ominous terms in his books *White Collar* (1951) and *Power Elite* (1956). The industrial assembly line had given way to an even more dehumanizing workplace, the modern office.

This disenchantment with the consumer culture reached its most eloquent expression with the "beats," literary groups that rebelled against the materialistic society of the 1950s. Jack Kerouac's novel *On the Road,* published in 1957, set the tone for the new movement. The name came from the quest for beatitude, a state of inner grace sought in Zen Buddhism. Flouting the respectability of suburbia, the "beatniks"—as middle America termed them—were easily identified by their long hair and bizarre clothing; they also had a penchant for sexual promiscuity and drug experimentation.

Despite the disapproval they evoked from mainstream Americans, the beat generation had some compassion for their detractors. "We love everything," Kerouac proclaimed, "Billy Graham, the Big Ten, Rock and Roll, Zen, apple pie,

Eisenhower—we dig it all." Yet as highly visible nonconformists in an era of stifling conformity, the beats demonstrated a style of social protest that would flower into the counterculture of the 1960s.

THE REACTION TO *SPUTNIK*

The profound insecurity that underlay American life throughout the 1950s burst into view in October 1957, when the Soviets sent the satellite *Sputnik* into orbit. People around the world applauded the scientific feat, but in the United States the reaction was one of dismay at being bested by a communist rival. Americans became afraid that their nation had somehow lost its previously unquestioned primacy in the eyes of the world.

The national sense of humiliation only deepened in December, when TV cameras showed the rocket bearing the first American satellite exploding only a few feet after liftoff. Finally, on January 31, 1958, the United States launched *Explorer,* its first orbiting satellite. Although the *Explorer* was tiny compared to *Sputnik,* it carried a much more advanced set of scientific instruments to probe the mysteries of space.

In the late 1950s, the president and Congress moved to restore national confidence. Eisenhower appointed James R. Killian, president of the Massachusetts Institute of Technology (MIT), as his special assistant for science and technology and to oversee a crash program in missile development. The House and Senate followed by creating the National Aeronautics and Space Administration (NASA) in 1958. Congress appropriated vast sums to allow the agency to com-

The Soviets' successful launching of Sputnik *shook American confidence and triggered new interest and activity in the "space race." Both houses of Congress established space committees, and President Eisenhower created the National Aeronautics and Space Administration (NASA).*

pete with the Russians in the space race. Soon a new group of heroes, the astronauts, began the training that led to suborbital flights and eventually to John Glenn's five-hour flight around the globe in 1962.

Congress also sought to match the Soviet educational advances by passing the National Defense Education Act (NDEA). This legislation authorized federal financing of scientific and foreign language programs in the nation's schools and colleges. Soon American students were hard at work mastering the "new physics" and the "new math."

The belief persisted, however, that the faults lay deeper, that in the midst of affluence and abundance Americans had lost their competitive edge. Economists pointed to the higher rate of Soviet economic growth, and social critics bemoaned a supermarket culture that stressed consumption over production, comfort over hard work.

FAREWELL TO REFORM

It is not surprising that the spirit of reform underlying the New Deal failed to flourish in the postwar years. Growing affluence took away the sense of grievance and the cry for change that was so strong in the 1930s. Eager to enjoy the new prosperity after years of want and sacrifice, the American people turned away from federal regulation and welfare programs.

TRUMAN AND THE FAIR DEAL

Harry Truman was in a buoyant mood when he gave his State of the Union address on January 5, 1949. Heartened by his upset victory in 1948 and by the substantial Democratic majorities in Congress, he looked forward to advancing a liberal legislative agenda. In addition to stressing traditional New Deal goals such as broadening Social Security and increasing the minimum wage, he advocated new areas of reform. "Every segment of our population and every individual," the president declared, "has a right to expect from our Government a fair deal."

Three measures made up Truman's Fair Deal. The first was a plan for medical insurance for all Americans, designed to provide a comprehensive solution to the nation's health problem. Equally controversial was his civil rights proposal, which called for a compulsory Fair Employment Practices Commission (FEPC) to open up employment opportunities for African Americans. Third, the president called for federal aid to education in order to help the states and local school districts meet the demands created by the postwar baby boom.

Truman's ambitious Fair Deal met with total defeat. Doctors branded the administration's health insurance plan as socialized medicine and lobbied effectively against it. Southern senators threatened a filibuster against the FEPC proposal, quickly ending any chance for action on civil rights. And, despite the need for more funding for schools, those favoring local control were able to defeat measures for federal aid. Congress thus failed to act on all three of the Fair Deal reforms.

Truman's only successes came in expanding Social Security to cover 10 million more Americans and in raising the minimum wage to 75 cents an hour.

Despite nominal Democratic control of the House and Senate, a conservative coalition blocked all efforts at further reform. Southern Democrats and northern Republicans combined to defeat any effort to extend government regulation, especially into sensitive areas such as health care and civil rights. At the same time, Truman can be faulted for trying to do too much, too soon. His attempt to pass such a sweeping program in the face of the bipartisan conservative coalition proved hopeless. Yet Truman must be given credit for defending and consolidating the New Deal legacy of the 1930s. By going on the offensive, he blocked any effort by conservatives to undo reforms such as Social Security. Moreover, Truman succeeded in expanding his party's reform agenda. By calling for action on civil rights, health care, and federal aid to education, he was laying the groundwork for legislative action on these vital issues in the future.

EISENHOWER'S MODERN REPUBLICANISM

Moderation was the keynote of the Eisenhower presidency. His major goal from the outset was to restore calm and tranquility to a badly divided nation. Unlike FDR and Truman, he had no commitment to social change or economic reform, yet he had no plans to dismantle the social programs of the New Deal. He sought instead to work toward balancing the budget, to keep military spending in check, to encourage as much private initiative as possible, and to reduce federal activities to the bare minimum. Defining his position as "Modern Republicanism," he claimed that he was "conservative when it comes to money and liberal when it comes to human beings."

On domestic issues, Eisenhower preferred to delegate authority and to play a passive role. He concentrated his own efforts on the Cold War abroad. The men he chose to run the nation reflected his preference for successful corporation executives. Thus George Humphrey, an Ohio industrialist, carried out a policy of fiscal stringency as secretary of the treasury, while Charles E. Wilson, the former head of General Motors, sought to keep the Pentagon budget under control as secretary of defense. Neither man was wholly successful, and both were guilty of tactless public statements. Humphrey warned that unless Congress showed budgetary restraint, "we're gonna have a depression which will curl your hair," and Wilson gained notoriety by proclaiming that "what was good for our country was good for General Motors, and vice versa."

Eisenhower was equally reluctant to play an active role in dealing with Congress. A fervent believer in the separation of powers, Ike did not want to engage in intensive lobbying. Republican losses in the midterm election of 1954 weakened Eisenhower's position with Congress. The Democrats regained control of both houses and kept it throughout the 1950s. The president had to rely on two Texas Democrats, Senate Majority Leader Lyndon B. Johnson and Speaker of the House Sam Rayburn, for legislative action; at best, it was an awkward and uneasy relationship.

The result was a very modest legislative record. Eisenhower did continue the basic social measures of the New Deal. In 1954, he signed bills extending Social

Security benefits to more than seven million Americans, raising the minimum wage to $1 an hour, and adding four million workers to those eligible for unemployment benefits. But Ike steadfastly opposed Democratic plans for compulsory health insurance—which he condemned as the "socialization of medicine"—and comprehensive federal aid to education, preferring to leave everything except school construction in the hands of local and state authorities. This lack of presidential support and the continuing grip of the conservative coalition in Congress blocked any further reform in the 1950s.

The one significant legislative achievement of the Eisenhower years came with the passage of the Highway Act of 1956. After a twelve-year delay, Congress appropriated funds for a 41,000-mile interstate highway system consisting of multilane divided expressways that would connect the nation's major cities. Justified on grounds of national defense, the 1956 act pleased a variety of highway users: the trucking industry, automobile clubs, organized labor (eager for construction jobs), farmers (needing to speed their crops to market), and state highway officials (anxious for the 90 percent funding contributed by the federal government). Built over the next twenty years, the interstate highway system stimulated the economy and shortened travel time dramatically, while at the same time intensifying the nation's dependence on the automobile and distorting metropolitan growth patterns into long strips paralleling the new expressways.

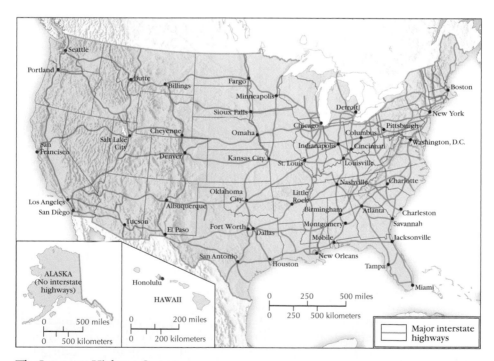

The Interstate Highway System
The 1956 plan to create an interstate highway system drastically changed America's landscape and culture. Today, the system covers about forty-five thousand miles, only a few thousand more miles than called for in the original plan.

THE ELECTION OF 1956

CANDIDATE	PARTY	POPULAR VOTE	ELECTORAL VOTE
Eisenhower	Republican	35,575,420	457
Stevenson	Democratic	26,033,066	73

Overall, the Eisenhower years marked an era of political moderation. The American people, enjoying the abundance of the 1950s, seemed quite content with legislative inaction. The president was sensitive to the nation's economic health; when recessions developed in 1953 and again in 1957 after his landslide reelection victory, he quickly abandoned his goal of a balanced budget in favor of a policy advocating government spending to restore prosperity. Eisenhower was able to balance the budget in only three of his eight years in office, and the $12 billion deficit in 1959 was larger than any ever before recorded in peacetime. In this manner, Eisenhower was able to maintain the New Deal legacy of federal responsibility for social welfare and the state of the economy while at the same time successfully resisting demands for more extensive government involvement in American life.

THE STRUGGLE OVER CIVIL RIGHTS

Despite President Eisenhower's reluctance to champion the cause of reform, powerful pressures for change forced long-overdue action in one area of American life—the denial of basic rights to the nation's black minority. In the midst of the Cold War, the contradiction between the denunciation of the Soviet Union for its human rights violations and the second-class status of African Americans began to arouse the national conscience. Fighting for freedom against communist tyranny abroad, Americans had to face the reality of the continued denial of freedom to a submerged minority at home.

African Americans had benefited economically from World War II, but they were still a seriously disadvantaged group. Those who had left the South for better opportunities in northern and western cities were concentrated in blighted and segregated neighborhoods, working at low-paying jobs, suffering economic and social discrimination, and failing to share fully in the postwar prosperity.

In the South, conditions were much worse. State laws forced blacks to live almost totally segregated from white society. Not only did African Americans attend separate (and almost always inferior) schools, but they also were rigidly segregated in all public facilities. "Segregation was enforced at all places of public entertainment, including libraries, auditoriums, and circuses," Chief Justice Earl Warren noted. "There was segregation in the hospitals, prisons, mental institutions, and nursing homes. Even ambulance service was segregated."

CIVIL RIGHTS AS A POLITICAL ISSUE

Truman was the first president to attempt to alter the historic pattern of racial discrimination in the United States. In 1946, he appointed a presidential commission on civil rights. A year later, in a sweeping report titled "To Secure These Rights," the commission recommended the reinstatement of the wartime Fair Employment Practices Committee (FEPC), the establishment of a permanent civil rights commission, and the denial of federal aid to any state that condoned segregation in schools and public facilities. But southern resistance blocked any action by Congress.

African American voters in the North overwhelmingly backed Truman over Dewey in the 1948 election. The African American vote in key cities—Los Angeles, Cleveland, and Chicago—ensured the Democratic victory in California, Ohio, and Illinois. Truman responded by including civil rights legislation in his Fair Deal program in 1949. Once again, however, determined southern opposition blocked congressional action.

Even though President Truman was unable to secure any significant legislation, he did succeed in adding civil rights to the liberal agenda. From this time forward, it would be an integral part of the Democratic reform program. Also, Truman used his executive power to assist African Americans, most notably in 1948 when he issued an order calling for the desegregation of the armed forces. The navy and the air force quickly complied, but the army resisted until the personnel needs of the Korean War finally overcame the military's objections. By the end of the 1950s, the armed forces had become far more integrated than American society at large.

DESEGREGATING THE SCHOOLS

The nation's schools soon became the primary target of civil rights advocates. The NAACP concentrated first on universities, successfully waging an intensive legal battle to win admission for qualified African Americans to graduate and professional schools. Led by Thurgood Marshall, NAACP lawyers then took on the broader issue of segregation in the country's public schools. Challenging the 1896 Supreme Court decision (*Plessy* v. *Ferguson*) that upheld the constitutionality of separate but equal public facilities, Marshall argued that even substantially equal but separate schools did profound psychological damage to African American children and thus violated the Fourteenth Amendment.

The Supreme Court was unanimous in its 1954 decision in the case of *Brown* v. *Board of Education of Topeka*. Chief Justice Earl Warren, recently appointed by President Eisenhower, wrote the landmark opinion flatly declaring that "separate educational facilities are inherently unequal." Warren, however, realized it would be difficult to change historic patterns of segregation quickly. Accordingly, in 1955 the Court ruled that desegregation of the schools should proceed "with all deliberate speed" and left the details to the lower federal courts.

"All deliberate speed" proved to be agonizingly slow. Officials in the border states quickly complied with the Court's ruling, but states deeper in the South responded with a policy of massive resistance. Local white citizens' councils organized to fight for retention of racial separation; school boards found a variety of ways to evade the Court's ruling. These stalling tactics led to long disputes in the federal courts; by the end of the decade, fewer than 1 percent of the black children in the Deep South attended school with whites.

A conspicuous lack of presidential support further weakened the desegregation effort. Dwight Eisenhower believed that people's attitudes could not be altered by "cold lawmaking"—only "by appealing to reason, by prayer, and by constantly working at it through our own efforts" could change be enacted. Quietly and unobtrusively, he worked to achieve desegregation in federal facilities, particularly in veterans' hospitals, navy yards, and the District of Columbia school system. Yet he refrained from endorsing the *Brown* decision.

Southern leaders mistook Ike's silence for tacit support of segregation. In 1957, Governor Orval Faubus of Arkansas called out the national guard to prevent the integration of Little Rock's Central High School on grounds of a threat to public order. After 270 armed troops turned back 9 young African American students, a federal judge ordered the guardsmen removed; but when the black students entered the school, a mob of 500 jeering whites surrounded the building. Eisenhower, who had told Faubus that "the Federal Constitution will be upheld by me by every legal means at my command," sent in 1000 paratroopers to ensure the rights of the Little Rock Nine to attend Central High. The students finished the school year under armed guard. Then Little Rock authorities closed Central High School for the next two years; when it reopened, there were only three African Americans in attendance.

Linda Brown (left). Her parents were the plaintiffs in the Brown *v.* Board of Education of Topeka *landmark Supreme Court case. Thurgood Marshall (right), a leading African American civil rights lawyer, was chief counsel for the Browns.*

Angry whites taunt one of the African American students trying to pass through the lines of Arkansas National Guardsmen to enroll in Little Rock's Central High School in 1957.

Despite the snail's pace of school desegregation, the *Brown* decision led to other advances. In 1957, the Eisenhower administration proposed the first general civil rights legislation since Reconstruction. Despite congressional compromises, the final act did create a permanent Commission for Civil Rights, one of Truman's original goals. It also provided for federal efforts aimed at "securing and protecting the right to vote."

Like the desegregation effort, the attempt to ensure African American voting rights in the South was still largely symbolic. Southern registrars used a variety of devices, ranging from intimidation to unfair tests, to deny African Americans suffrage. Yet the actions of Congress and the Supreme Court marked a vital turning point in national policy toward racial justice.

THE BEGINNINGS OF BLACK ACTIVISM

The most dynamic force for change came from African Americans themselves. The shift from legal struggles in the courts to protest in the streets began with an incident in Montgomery, Alabama. On December 1, 1955, Rosa Parks—a black seamstress who had been active in the local NAACP chapter—violated a city ordinance by refusing to give up her seat to a white person on a local bus. Her action, often viewed as spontaneous, grew out of a long tradition of black protest against the rigid segregation of the races in the South.

Rosa Parks's arrest sparked a massive protest movement in Montgomery. Black women played a particularly important role in the protest, printing and handing out 50,000 leaflets to rally the African American community behind

Parks. The movement also led to the emergence of Martin Luther King, Jr., as an eloquent new spokesman for African Americans.

King agreed to lead the subsequent bus boycott. The son of a famous Atlanta preacher, he had recently taken his first church in Montgomery after years of studying theology while earning a Ph.D. at Boston University. Now he would be able to combine his wide learning with his charismatic appeal in behalf of a practical goal—fair treatment for the African Americans who made up the bulk of the riders on the city's buses.

The Montgomery bus boycott started out with a modest goal. Instead of challenging the legality of segregated seating, King simply asked that seats be taken on a first-come, first-served basis, with African Americans being seated from the back and the whites from the front of each bus. An effective system of car pools enabled the protesters to avoid using the city buses and soon they were insisting on a complete end to segregated seating.

The boycott ended in victory a year later when the Supreme Court ruled the Alabama segregated seating law unconstitutional. The protest movement had won far more than this limited dent in the wall of segregation, however. King had emerged as the charismatic leader of a new civil rights movement—a man who won acclaim not only at home but around the world. He led a triumphant Prayer Pilgrimage to Washington in 1957 on the third anniversary of the *Brown* decision, stirring the crowd of thirty thousand with his ringing demand for the right to vote. His cry "Give us the ballot" boomed in salvos that civil rights historian Taylor Branch likened to "cannon bursts in a diplomatic salute." His remarkable voice became familiar to the entire nation.

Even more important, he had a strategy and message that fitted perfectly with the plight of his followers. King came out of the bus boycott with the concept of passive resistance. "If cursed," he had told protesters in Montgomery, "do not curse back. If struck, do not strike back, but evidence love and goodwill at all times." The essence of his strategy was to use the apparent weakness of southern blacks—their lack of power—and turn it into a conquering weapon.

His ultimate goal was to unite the broken community through bonds of Christian love. He hoped to use nonviolence to appeal to middle-class white America, "to the conscience of the great decent majority who through blindness, fear, pride or irrationality have allowed their consciences to sleep." The result, King prophesied, would be to enable future historians to say of the effort, "There lived a great people—a black people—who injected new meaning and dignity into the veins of civilization."

The Continuing Civil Rights Movement

A year after the successful bus boycott, King founded the Southern Christian Leadership Conference (SCLC) to direct the crusade against segregation. Then in February 1960, another spontaneous event sparked a further advance for passive

In February 1960, black students from North Carolina A &T College staged a sit-in at a "whites only" Woolworth's lunch counter in Greensboro, North Carolina. Their act of nonviolent protest spurred similar demonstrations in public spaces across the South in an effort to draw national attention to racial injustice, to demand desegregation of public facilities, and to prompt the federal government to take a more active role to end segregation.

resistance. Four African American students from North Carolina Agricultural and Technical College sat down at a dime-store lunch counter in Greensboro, North Carolina, and refused to move after being denied service. Other students, both whites and blacks, joined in similar "sit-ins" across the South. By the end of the year, some fifty thousand young people had succeeded in desegregating public facilities in more than a hundred southern cities, leading to the formation of the Student Nonviolent Coordinating Committee (SNCC) in April 1960. From this time on, the SCLC and SNCC, with their tactic of direct, although peaceful, confrontation, would replace the NAACP and its reliance on court action in the forefront of the civil rights movement. The change would eventually lead to dramatic success for the movement, but it also ushered in a period of heightened tension and social turmoil in the 1960s.

The 1950s ended with the national mood less troubled than when the decade began amid the turmoil of the second Red Scare and the Korean War, yet hardly as tranquil or confident as Eisenhower had hoped it would be. The American people felt reassured about the state of the economy, no longer fearing a return to the grim years of the Great Depression. At the same time, however, they were aware that abundance alone did not guarantee the quality of everyday life and realized that there was still a huge gap between American ideals and the reality of race relations, in the North as well as the South.

CHRONOLOGY

1946	Republicans win control of both houses of Congress in November elections
1947	William Levitt announces first Levittown
1948	Truman orders end to segregation in armed forces
1949	Minimum wage raised from 40 to 75 cents an hour
1950	Gwendolyn Brooks becomes first African American woman to be awarded Pulitzer Prize
1951	Remington Rand unveils UNIVAC, the first electronic digital computer to be marketed commercially
1952	Edward R. Murrow inaugurates television news show *See It Now*
1953	McDonald's chooses golden arches design for its hamburger shops
1954	Supreme Court orders schools desegregated in *Brown* v. *Board of Education of Topeka*
1955	Dr. Jonas Salk reports success of antipolio vaccine (April)
	African Americans begin boycott of Montgomery, Alabama, bus company (December)
1956	Eisenhower signs legislation creating the interstate highway system
1957	Congress passes first Civil Rights Act since Reconstruction
1958	Charles Van Doren confesses to cheating on television quiz show *Twenty-one*
1960	African American college students stage sit-in in Greensboro, North Carolina

30

THE TURBULENT SIXTIES

On Monday evening, September 26, 1960, John F. Kennedy and Richard M. Nixon faced each other in the nation's first televised debate between two presidential candidates. Kennedy, the relatively unknown Democratic challenger, had proposed the debates; Nixon, confident of his mastery of television, had accepted even though, as Eisenhower's vice president and the early front-runner in the election, he had more to lose and less to gain.

Richard Nixon arrived an hour early at the CBS studio in Chicago, looking tired and ill at ease. He was still recovering from a knee injury that had slowed his campaign and left him pale and weak as he pursued a hectic catch-up schedule. Makeup experts offered to hide Nixon's heavy beard and soften his prominent jowls, but the GOP candidate declined, preferring to let an aide apply a light coat of Max Factor's "Lazy Shave," a pancake cosmetic. John Kennedy, tanned from open-air campaigning in California and rested by a day spent nearly free of distracting activity, wore very light makeup.

At 8:30 P.M. central time, moderator Howard K. Smith welcomed a viewing audience estimated at seventy-seven million. Kennedy led off, echoing Abraham Lincoln by saying that the nation faced the question of "whether the world will exist half-slave and half-free." Although the ground rules limited the first debate to domestic issues, Kennedy argued that foreign and domestic policy were inseparable. He accused the Republicans of letting the country drift at home and abroad. "I think it's time America started moving again," he concluded. Nixon, caught off guard, seemed to agree with Kennedy's assessment of the nation's problems, but he contended that he had better solutions. "Our disagreement," the vice president pointed out, "is not about the goals for America but only about the means to reach those goals."

For the rest of the hour, the two candidates answered questions from a panel of journalists. Radiating confidence and self-assurance, Kennedy used a flow of statistics and details to create the image of a man deeply knowledgeable about all aspects of government. Nixon fought back with a defense of the Eisenhower record, but he seemed nervous and unsure of himself.

Polls taken during the following few weeks revealed a sharp swing to Kennedy. Many Democrats and independents who had thought him too young or too inexperienced were impressed by his performance. Nixon suffered more from his unattractive image than from what he said. In the three additional debates held during the campaign, Nixon improved his performance notably. But the damage had been done. A postelection poll revealed that of four million voters who were influenced by the debates, three million voted for Kennedy.

The televised debates were only one of many factors influencing the outcome of the 1960 election. In essence, Kennedy won because he took full advantage of all his opportunities. Lightly regarded by Democratic leaders, he won the nomination by appealing to the rank and file in the primaries, but then he astutely chose Lyndon Johnson of Texas as his running mate to blunt Nixon's southern strategy.

During the fall campaign, Kennedy exploited the national mood of frustration that had followed *Sputnik*. At home, he promised to stimulate the lagging economy and carry forward long-overdue reforms in education, health care, and civil rights under the banner of the "New Frontier." Abroad, he pledged a renewed commitment to the Cold War, vowing he would lead the nation to victory over the Soviet Union. He met the issue of his Catholicism head on, telling a group of Protestant ministers in Houston that as president he would always place country above religion.

The Democratic victory in 1960 was paper-thin. Kennedy's edge in the popular vote was only two-tenths of 1 percent, and his wide margin in the electoral college (303 to 219) was tainted by voting irregularities in several states—notably Illinois and Texas—which went Democratic by very slender majorities. Yet even though he had no mandate, Kennedy's triumph did mark a sharp political shift. In contrast to the aging Eisenhower, Kennedy symbolized youth, energy, and ambition. His mastery of the new medium of television reflected his sensitivity to the changes taking place in American life in the 1960s. Over the next eight years, he and Lyndon Johnson achieved many of their goals. Yet the nation also became engulfed in angry protests, violent demonstrations, and sweeping social change in one of the stormiest decades in American history.

THE ELECTION OF 1960

CANDIDATE	PARTY	POPULAR VOTE	ELECTORAL VOTE
Kennedy	Democratic	34,227,096	303
Byrd	States' Rights	—	15
Nixon	Republican	34,108,546	219
	Minor Parties	502,363	—

KENNEDY INTENSIFIES THE COLD WAR

John F. Kennedy was determined to succeed where he believed Eisenhower had failed. Critical of his predecessor for holding down defense spending and apparently allowing the Soviet Union to open up a dangerous lead in ICBMs, Kennedy sought to warn the nation of its peril and lead it to victory in the Cold War.

In his inaugural address, the young president sounded the alarm. Ignoring the domestic issues aired during the campaign, he dealt exclusively with the world. "Let every nation know, whether it wishes us well or ill, that we shall pay any price, bear any burden, meet any hardship, support any friend, oppose any foe," Kennedy declared, "to assure the survival and success of liberty. We will do all this and more."

From the day he took office, John F. Kennedy gave foreign policy top priority. In part, the decision reflected the perilous world situation, the immediate dangers ranging from the unresolved Berlin crisis to the emergence of Fidel Castro as a Soviet ally in Cuba. But it also corresponded to Kennedy's personal priorities. As a congressman and senator, he had been an intense cold warrior. Bored by committee work and legislative details, he had focused on foreign policy in the Senate.

His appointments reflected his determination to win the Cold War. His choice of Dean Rusk, an experienced but unassertive diplomat, to head the State Department indicated that Kennedy planned to be his own secretary of state. He surrounded himself with young pragmatic advisers who prided themselves on toughness: McGeorge Bundy, dean of Harvard College, became national security adviser; Walt W. Rostow, an MIT economist, was Bundy's deputy; and Robert McNamara, the youthful president of the Ford Motor Company, took over as secretary of defense. These New Frontiersmen, later dubbed "the best and the brightest" by journalist David Halberstam, all shared a hard-line view of the Soviet Union and the belief that American security depended on superior force and the willingness to use it.

FLEXIBLE RESPONSE

The first goal of the Kennedy administration was to build up the nation's armed forces. During the 1960 campaign, Kennedy had warned that the Soviets were opening a missile gap. In fact, due largely to Eisenhower's foresight, the United States had a significant lead in nuclear striking power by early 1961. Nevertheless, the new administration, intent on putting the Soviets on the defensive, authorized the construction of an awesome nuclear arsenal that included 1000 Minuteman solid-fuel ICBMs and 32 Polaris submarines carrying 656 missiles. The United States thus opened a missile gap in reverse, creating the possibility of a successful American first strike.

At the same time, the Kennedy administration augmented conventional military strength, leading to a $6 billion jump in the defense budget in 1961 alone. The president took a personal interest in counterinsurgency. He expanded the Special Forces unit at Fort Bragg, North Carolina, and insisted, over army objections, that it adopt a distinctive green beret as a symbol of its elite status.

The purpose of this buildup was to create an alternative to Eisenhower's policy of massive retaliation. Instead of responding to communist moves with nuclear threats, the United States could now call on a wide spectrum of force—ranging from ICBMs to Green Berets. Thus, as Secretary of Defense Robert McNamara explained, the new strategy of flexible response meant the United States could "choose among several operational plans." The danger was that such a powerful arsenal might tempt the new administration to test its strength against the Soviet Union.

CRISIS OVER BERLIN

The first confrontation came in Germany. Since 1958, Soviet Premier Khrushchev had been threatening to sign a peace treaty that would put access to the isolated western zones of Berlin under the control of East Germany. The steady flight of skilled workers to the West through the Berlin escape route weakened the East German regime dangerously, and the Soviets believed they had to resolve this issue quickly.

At a summit meeting in Vienna in June 1961, Kennedy and Khrushchev focused on Berlin as the key issue. The Russian leader called the current situation "intolerable" and announced the Soviet Union would proceed with an East German peace treaty. Kennedy was equally adamant, defending the American presence in Berlin. "I want peace," Khrushchev declared, "but, if you want war, that is your problem." When the Soviet leader said he would sign a German peace treaty by December, Kennedy replied, "It will be a cold winter."

The climax came sooner than either man expected. On July 25, Kennedy delivered an impassioned televised address to the American people in which he called the defense of Berlin "essential" to "the entire Free World" and announced a series of arms increases, including $3 billion more in defense spending.

Aware of superior American nuclear striking power, Khrushchev settled for a stalemate. On August 13, the Soviets began the construction of the Berlin Wall to stop the flow of brains and talent to the West. For a brief time, Russian and American tanks maneuvered within sight of each other at Checkpoint Charlie (where the American and Soviet zones met), but by fall, the tension gradually eased. Berlin—like Germany and, indeed, all of Europe—remained divided between the East and the West. Neither side could claim a victory, but Kennedy believed that at least he had proved to the world America's willingness to honor its commitments.

CONTAINMENT IN SOUTHEAST ASIA

Two weeks before Kennedy's inauguration, Khrushchev gave a speech in Moscow in which he declared Soviet support for "wars of national liberation." The Russian leader's words were actually aimed more at China than the United States; the two powerful communist nations were now rivals for influence in the Third World. But the new American president, ignoring the growing Sino-Soviet split, concluded the United States and Russia were locked in a struggle for the hearts and minds of the uncommitted in Asia, Africa, and Latin America.

East German soldiers repair a breach in the Berlin Wall made when an East German mechanic rammed an armored car into the wall while making his escape into West Berlin. On the other side of the wall, West Berliners observe the repair work.

Calling for a new policy of nation building, Kennedy advocated financial and technical assistance designed to help Third World nations achieve economic modernization and stable pro-Western governments. Measures ranging from the formation of the idealistic Peace Corps to the ambitious Alliance for Progress—a massive economic aid program for Latin America—were part of this effort.

Southeast Asia offered the gravest test. Ngo Dinh Diem sought to establish a separate government in South Vietnam with large-scale American economic and military assistance. By the time Kennedy entered the White House, however, the communist government in North Vietnam, led by Ho Chi Minh, was directing the efforts of Vietcong rebels in the South. As the guerrilla war intensified in the fall of 1961, the president sent two trusted advisers, Walt Rostow and General Maxwell Taylor, to South Vietnam. They returned favoring the dispatch of eight thousand American combat troops.

The president decided against sending in combat troops in 1961, but he authorized substantial increases in economic aid to Diem and in the size of the military mission in Saigon. The number of American advisers in Vietnam grew from fewer than one thousand in 1961 to more than sixteen thousand by late 1963. Yet, by 1963, the situation had again become critical. Diem had failed to win the support of his own people; Buddhist monks set themselves aflame in public protests against him; and even Diem's own generals plotted his overthrow.

Flames engulf a Buddhist monk, the Reverend Quang Duc, who set himself afire at an intersection in Saigon, Vietnam, to protest persecution of Buddhists by Vietnam president Ngo Dinh Diem and his government. Other monks placed themselves in front of the wheels of nearby fire trucks to prevent them from reaching Duc.

President Kennedy was in a quandary. He realized that the fate of South Vietnam would be determined not by America but by the Vietnamese. "In the final analysis," he said in September 1963, "it is their war. They are the ones who have to win it or lose it." But at the same time, Kennedy was not prepared to accept the possible loss of all Southeast Asia. Although aides later claimed he planned to pull out after the 1964 election, Kennedy raised the stakes by tacitly approving a coup that led to Diem's overthrow and death on November 1, 1963. The resulting power vacuum in Saigon made further American involvement in Vietnam almost certain.

CONTAINING CASTRO: THE BAY OF PIGS FIASCO

Kennedy's determination to check global communist expansion reached a peak of intensity in Cuba with Fidel Castro. In the 1960 campaign he had accused the Republicans of permitting a "communist satellite" to arise on "our very doorstep." Kennedy had even issued a statement backing "anti-Castro forces in exile," calling them "fighters for freedom" who held out hope for "overthrowing Castro."

In reality, the Eisenhower administration had been training a group of Cuban exiles in Guatemala since March 1960 as part of a CIA plan to topple the Castro regime. Many of the new president's advisers had doubts about the proposed invasion. Kennedy, however, committed by his own campaign rhetoric and assured of success by the military, decided to proceed.

On April 17, 1961, fourteen hundred Cuban exiles moved ashore at the Bay of Pigs on the southern coast of Cuba. Even though the United States had masterminded the entire operation, Kennedy insisted on covert action, even canceling at the last minute a planned American air strike on the beachhead. With air superiority, Castro's well-trained forces had no difficulty in quashing the invasion. They killed nearly five hundred exiles and forced the rest to surrender within forty-eight hours.

Aghast at the swiftness of the defeat, President Kennedy took personal responsibility for the failure. In his address to the American people, however, he showed no remorse for arranging the violation of a neighboring country's sovereignty, only regret at the outcome. For the remainder of his presidency, Kennedy continued to harass the Castro regime, imposing an economic blockade on Cuba, supporting a continuing series of raids by exile groups operating out of Florida, and failing to stop the CIA from experimenting with bizarre plots to assassinate Fidel Castro.

CONTAINING CASTRO: THE CUBAN MISSILE CRISIS

The climax of Kennedy's crusade came in October 1962 with the Cuban missile crisis. Throughout the summer and early fall, the Soviets engaged in a massive arms buildup in Cuba, ostensibly to protect Castro from an American invasion. Kennedy delivered a stern warning against the introduction of any offensive weapons, believing their presence would directly threaten American security. Khrushchev publicly denied any such intent, but secretly he took a daring gamble, building sites for twenty-four medium-range (1000-mile) and eighteen intermediate-range (2000-mile) missiles in Cuba. Later he claimed his purpose was purely defensive, but most likely he was responding to the pressures from his own military to close the enormous strategic gap in nuclear striking power that Kennedy had opened.

Unfortunately, the Kennedy administration had stopped direct U-2 overflights of Cuba in August. Fearful that recently installed Soviet surface-to-air missiles could bring down the American spy plane, the White House, over the objections of CIA Director John McCone, limited U-2 flights to the air space bordering the island. McCone finally prevailed on the president to resume direct overflights, and on October 14 the first such mission brought back indisputable photographic evidence of the missile sites, which were now nearing completion.

As soon as President Kennedy was informed of this development, he decided to keep it secret while he consulted with a hand-picked group of advisers. In the ExComm, as this group became known, the initial preference for an immediate air strike gradually gave way to discussion of either a full-scale invasion of Cuba or a naval blockade of the island. The president and his advisers ruled out diplomacy, rejecting a proposal to offer the withdrawal of obsolete American Jupiter missiles from Turkey in return for a similar Russian pullout in Cuba. Kennedy finally agreed to a two-step procedure. He would proclaim a quarantine of Cuba to prevent the arrival of new missiles and threaten a nuclear confrontation to force the removal of those already there. If the Russians did not cooperate, then the United States would invade Cuba and dismantle the missiles by force.

On the evening of October 22, the president informed the nation of the existence of the Soviet missiles and his plans to remove them. He accused Khrushchev of making a "provocative threat to world peace," and soberly promised "a full retaliatory response upon the Soviet Union" if any of the missiles in Cuba were launched.

For the next six days, the world hovered on the brink of nuclear catastrophe. At mid-week, sixteen Soviet ships approached the blockade line 500 miles from

Aerial photographs taken by a U-2 reconnaissance plane flying over Cuba revealed the presence of Russian missile sites under construction on the island. Recently released information about the type and number of Soviet nuclear warheads in Cuba confirms the imminence of the threat of nuclear war had not the Soviets capitulated to U.S. demands for removal of the missiles.

Cuba, but then suddenly turned back to avoid a confrontation with the American navy. Later in the week, Khrushchev sent a letter to Kennedy indicating a willingness to withdraw the missiles from Cuba in return for an American promise never to invade the island.

On Saturday, October 27, however, a second Soviet message raised the stakes, demanding an American withdrawal of the Jupiter missiles from Turkey. While allowing the military to prepare for an invasion of Cuba, the president followed his brother's advice and sent a cable to Khrushchev ignoring the proposed missile swap and instead accepting the Russian leader's original offer. To make clear that this was the last chance to avoid a nuclear showdown, Robert Kennedy met privately that evening with Soviet ambassador Anatoly Dobrynin. Warning that the Soviet Union must agree to remove the missiles by the next day, Kennedy remarked that if Khrushchev did not back down, "there would be not only dead Americans but dead Russians as well."

In reality, John F. Kennedy was not quite so ready to risk nuclear war. He instructed his brother to assure Dobrynin that the Jupiter missiles would soon be removed from Turkey. The president preferred that the missile swap be done privately, but twenty-five years later, Secretary of State Dean Rusk revealed that JFK had instructed him to arrange a deal through the United Nations involving "the removal of both the Jupiters and the missiles in Cuba." In recently released transcripts of his meetings with his advisers, the president reaffirmed his intention of making a missile trade with Khrushchev publicly as a last resort to avoid nuclear war.

President Kennedy never had to make this final concession. At nine the next morning, Khrushchev agreed to remove the missiles in return only for Kennedy's promise not to invade Cuba. The crisis was over.

The world, however, had come perilously close to a nuclear conflict. We now know the Soviets had nuclear warheads in Cuba, not only for twenty of the medium-range missiles, but also for short-range tactical launchers designed to be used against an American invading force. If Kennedy had approved the military's recommendations for an invasion of Cuba, the consequences might have been disastrous.

The peaceful resolution of the Cuban missile crisis became a personal and political triumph for John F. Kennedy. His party successfully overcame the Republican challenge in the November elections, and his own popularity reached new heights.

The Cuban missile crisis had more substantial results as well. Shaken by their close call, Kennedy and Khrushchev agreed to install a "hot line" to speed direct communication between Washington and Moscow in an emergency. Long-stalled negotiations over the reduction of nuclear testing suddenly resumed, leading to the limited test ban treaty of 1963, which outlawed tests in the atmosphere while still permitting them underground. Above all, Kennedy displayed a new maturity as a result of the crisis. In a speech at American University in June 1963, he said to the Russians, "Our most basic common link is the fact that we all inhabit this planet. We all breathe the same air. We all cherish our children's future. And we are all mortal."

Despite these hopeful words, the missile crisis also had an unfortunate consequence. Those who believed that the Russians understood only the language of force were confirmed in their penchant for a hard line. The Russian leaders drew similar conclusions. After 1962, the Soviets embarked on a crash program to build up their navy and to overtake the American lead in nuclear missiles. Within five years, they had the nucleus of a modern fleet and had surpassed the United States in ICBMs. Kennedy's fleeting moment of triumph thus ensured the escalation of the arms race. His legacy was a bittersweet one of short-term success and long-term anxiety.

THE NEW FRONTIER AT HOME

Kennedy hoped to change the course of history at home as well as abroad. His election marked the arrival of a new generation of leadership. For the first time, people born in the twentieth century who had entered political life after World War II were in charge of national affairs. Kennedy's inaugural call to get the nation moving again was particularly attractive to young people, who had shunned political involvement during the Eisenhower years.

The new administration reflected Kennedy's aura of youth and energy. Major cabinet appointments went to activists—notably Connecticut governor Abraham Ribicoff as secretary of health, education, and welfare; labor lawyer Arthur J. Goldberg as secretary of labor; and Arizona congressman Stuart Udall as secretary of the interior. The most controversial choice was Robert F. Kennedy, the president's brother, as attorney general. Critics scoffed at his lack of legal experience; in fact, the president prized his brother's loyalty and shrewd political advice.

Kennedy's greatest asset was his own personality. A cool, attractive, and intelligent man, he possessed a sense of style that endeared him to the American public. He invited artists and musicians as well as corporate executives to White House functions, and he sprinkled his speeches with references to Emerson and Shakespeare. He seemed to be a new Lancelot, bent on calling forth the best in national life; admirers likened his inner circle to King Arthur's court at Camelot.

THE CONGRESSIONAL OBSTACLE

Neither Kennedy's wit nor his charm proved strong enough to break the logjam in Congress. Since the late 1940s, a series of reform bills ranging from health care to federal aid to education had been stalled on Capitol Hill. Despite JFK's victory, the election of 1960 clouded the outlook for his New Frontier program. The Democrats had lost twenty seats in the House and two in the Senate; even though they retained majorities in both branches, a conservative coalition of northern Republicans and southern Democrats opposed all efforts at reform.

Faced with this obstacle, Kennedy gave up the fight for health care in 1961 and settled instead for a modest increase in the minimum wage. He had no more success in 1962 and 1963 when the conservative coalition stood firmly against education and health care reform measures. Kennedy's greater interest in foreign policy and his distaste for congressional infighting also contributed to the failure to enact his New Frontier program.

ECONOMIC ADVANCE

Kennedy gave a higher priority to the sluggish American economy. During the last years of Eisenhower's administration, the rate of economic growth had slowed to just over 2 percent annually, while unemployment rose to new heights with each recession. JFK was determined to stimulate the economy to achieve a much higher rate of long-term growth.

Kennedy received conflicting advice from the experts. Those who claimed the problem was essentially a technological one urged manpower training and area-redevelopment programs to modernize American industry. Others called for federal spending to rebuild the nation's public facilities. Kennedy sided with the first group, largely because Congress was opposed to massive spending on public works.

The actual stimulation of the economy, however, came not from social programs but from greatly increased appropriations for defense and space. A $6 billion increase in the arms budget in 1961 gave the economy a great lift, and Kennedy's decision to send an astronaut to the moon eventually cost $25 billion. By 1962, more than half the federal budget was devoted to space and defense.

The administration's desire to keep the inflation rate low led to a serious confrontation with the business community. Kennedy relied on informal wage and price guidelines to hold down the cost of living. But in April 1962, just after the president had persuaded the steelworkers' union to accept a new contract with no wage increases and only a few additional benefits, U.S. Steel head Roger Blough informed Kennedy that his company was raising steel prices by $6 a ton. Outraged, the president publicly called the increase "a wholly unjustifiable and irresponsible defiance of the public interest" and accused Blough of displaying "contempt for the interests of 185 million Americans."

Roger Blough soon gave way. The president's tongue-lashing, along with a cutoff in Pentagon steel orders and the threat of an antitrust suit, forced him to reconsider. When several smaller steel companies refused to raise their prices in hopes of expanding their share of the market, U.S. Steel rolled back its prices. The business community deeply resented the president's action.

Troubled by his strained relations with business and by the continued lag in economic growth, the president decided to adopt a more unorthodox approach in 1963. Walter Heller, chairman of the Council of Economic Advisers, had been arguing since 1961 for a major cut in taxes in the belief it would stimulate consumer spending and give the economy the jolt it needed. In January 1963, the president proposed a tax reduction of $13.5 billion. When finally enacted by Congress in 1964, the massive tax cut led to sustained economic advance for the rest of the decade.

Kennedy's economic policy was far more successful than his legislative efforts. Although the rate of economic growth doubled to 4.5 percent by the end of 1963 and unemployment was reduced substantially, the cost of living rose only 1.3 percent a year. Personal income went up 13 percent in the early 1960s, but the greatest gains came in corporate profits—up 67 percent in the period. Despite the overall economic growth, the public sector continued to be neglected. "I am not sure what the advantage is," complained economist John Kenneth Galbraith, "in having a few more dollars to spend if the air is too dirty to breathe, the water too polluted to drink, the commuters are losing out in the struggle to get in and out of the cities, the streets are filthy, and the schools so bad that the young, perhaps wisely, stay away."

MOVING SLOWLY ON CIVIL RIGHTS

Kennedy faced a genuine dilemma over the issue of civil rights. Despite his own lack of a strong record while in the Senate, he had portrayed himself during the 1960 campaign as a crusader for African American rights. He had promised to launch an attack on segregation in the Deep South, but his fear of alienating the large bloc of southern Democrats forced him to downplay civil rights legislation.

The president's solution was to defer congressional action in favor of executive leadership in this area. He directed his brother, Attorney General Robert Kennedy, to continue and expand the Eisenhower administration's efforts to achieve voting rights for southern blacks. In two years, the Kennedy administration increased the number of voting rights suits fivefold. Yet the attorney general could not force the FBI to provide protection for the civil rights volunteers who risked their lives by encouraging African Americans to register.

Kennedy did succeed in appointing a number of African Americans to high government positions; Thurgood Marshall, who pleaded the *Brown* v. *Board of Education* school desegregation case before the Supreme Court, was named to the U.S. Circuit Court. On the other hand, among his judicial appointments, Kennedy included one Mississippi jurist who referred to African Americans in court as "niggers" and once compared them to "a bunch of chimpanzees."

The civil rights movement refused to accept Kennedy's indirect approach. In May 1961, the Congress of Racial Equality (CORE) sponsored a "freedom ride" in which a biracial group attempted to test a 1960 Supreme Court decision outlawing segregation in all bus and train stations used in interstate commerce. When they arrived in Birmingham, Alabama, the freedom riders were attacked by a mob of angry whites. The attorney general quickly dispatched several hundred federal marshals to protect the freedom riders, but the president, deeply involved in the Berlin crisis, was more upset at the distraction the protesters created.

In September, after the attorney general finally convinced the Interstate Commerce Commission to issue an order banning segregation in interstate terminals and buses, the freedom rides ended. The Kennedy administration then sought to prevent further confrontations by involving civil rights activists in its voting drive.

A pattern of belated reaction to southern racism marked the basic approach of the Kennedys. When James Meredith courageously sought admission to the all-white University of Mississippi in 1962, the president and the attorney general worked closely with Mississippi governor Ross Barnett to avoid violence. Despite Barnett's later promise of cooperation, the night before Meredith enrolled at the University of Mississippi, a mob attacked the federal marshals and national guard troops sent to protect him. The violence left 2 dead and 375 injured, including 166 marshals and 12 guardsmen, but Meredith attended the university and eventually graduated.

"I HAVE A DREAM"

Martin Luther King, Jr., finally forced Kennedy to abandon his cautious tactics and come out openly in behalf of racial justice. In the spring of 1963, King began a massive protest in Birmingham, one of the South's most segregated cities. Public marches and demonstrations aimed at integrating public facilities and opening up jobs for African Americans quickly led to police harassment and many arrests, including that of King himself.

This repression played directly into King's hands. On May 3, as six thousand children marched in place of the jailed protesters, authorities broke up a demonstration with clubs, snarling police dogs, and high-pressure water hoses strong enough to take the bark off a tree. With a horrified nation watching scene after scene of this brutality on television, the Kennedy administration quickly intervened to arrange a settlement with the Birmingham civic leaders that ended the violence and granted the protesters most of their demands.

The attempts of African Americans to end discrimination and secure their civil rights met with violent resistance in Birmingham, Alabama, where police used snarling dogs, fire hoses, clubs, and electric cattle prods to turn back the unarmed demonstrators.

More important, Kennedy finally ended his long hesitation. Declaring, "We are confronted primarily with a moral issue," the president sponsored civil rights legislation providing equal access to all public accommodations as well as an extension of voting rights for African Americans.

Despite pleas from the government for an end to demonstrations and protests, civil rights leaders kept pressure on the administration. They scheduled a massive march on Washington for August 1963. On August 28, more than 200,000 marchers gathered for a daylong rally in front of the Lincoln Memorial where they listened to hymns, speeches, and prayers for racial justice. The climax of the event was Martin Luther King, Jr.'s eloquent description of his dream for America. It concluded:

> When we let freedom ring, when we let it ring from every village and every hamlet, from every state and every city, we will be able to speed up that day when all God's children, black men and white men, Jews and Gentiles, Protestants and Catholics, will be able to join hands and sing, in the words of that old Negro spiritual, "Free at last! Free at last! Thank God almighty, we are free at last!"

By the time of Kennedy's death in November 1963, his civil rights legislation was well on its way to passage in Congress. Unlike Eisenhower, he had provided presidential leadership for the civil rights movement. His emphasis on executive action gradually paid off, especially in extending voting rights. By early 1964, 40 percent of southern blacks had the franchise, compared to only 28 percent in 1960. Moreover, Kennedy's sense of caution and restraint, painful and frustrating as it was to African American activists, had proved well founded. Avoiding an early, and possibly fatal, defeat in Congress, he had waited until a national consensus emerged and then had carefully channeled it behind effective legislation.

Reverend Martin Luther King, Jr., addresses the crowd at the March on Washington in August 1963. The largest single demonstration of the early 1960s, the march reflected the spirit and determination of many devoted to the cause of equality for African Americans. In his speech, King recounted the difficulties of blacks' struggle for freedom, then stirred the crowd with the description of his dream for America: "I have a dream that one day this nation will rise up and live out the true meaning of its creed— we hold these truths to be self-evident, that all men are created equal."

THE SUPREME COURT AND REFORM

The most active impulse for social change in the early 1960s came from a surprising source: the usually staid and conservative Supreme Court. Under the leadership of Earl Warren, a pragmatic jurist more noted for his political astuteness than his legal scholarship, the Court ventured into new areas.

The Warren Court issued a series of landmark decisions designed to extend to state and local jurisdictions the traditional rights afforded the accused in federal courts. Thus in *Gideon v. Wainwright* (1963), *Escobedo v. Illinois* (1964), and *Miranda v. Arizona* (1966), the majority decreed that defendants had to be provided lawyers, had to be informed of their constitutional rights, and could not be interrogated or induced to confess to a crime without defense counsel being present. In effect, the Court extended to the poor and the ignorant those constitutional guarantees that had always been available to the rich and to the legally informed—notably hardened criminals.

The most far-reaching Warren Court decisions came in the area of legislative reapportionment. In 1962, the Court ruled in *Baker v. Carr* that Tennessee had to redistribute its legislative seats to give citizens in Memphis equal representation. Subsequent decisions reinforced the ban on rural overrepresentation as the Court proclaimed that places in all legislative bodies, including the House of

Representatives, had to be allocated on the basis of "people, not land or trees or pastures." The principle of "one man, one vote" greatly increased the political power of cities at the expense of rural areas.

The activism of the Supreme Court stirred up a storm of criticism. The rulings that extended protection to criminals and those accused of subversive activity led some Americans to charge that the Court was encouraging crime and weakening national security. Legal scholars worried more about the weakening of the Court's prestige as it became more directly involved in the political process. On balance, however, the Warren Court helped achieve greater social justice by protecting the rights of the underprivileged and by permitting dissent and free expression to flourish.

"LET US CONTINUE"

The New Frontier came to a sudden and violent end on November 22, 1963, when Lee Harvey Oswald assassinated John F. Kennedy as the president rode in a motorcade in downtown Dallas. The shock of losing the young president, who had become a symbol of hope and promise for a whole generation,

President Kennedy smiles at the crowd as his motorcade moves through downtown Dallas, Texas, on November 22, 1963. Minutes later, the president was assassinated.

stunned the entire world. The American people were bewildered by the rapid sequence of events: the brutal killing of their beloved president; the televised slaying of Oswald by Jack Ruby in the basement of the Dallas police station; the composure and dignity of Kennedy's widow, Jacqueline, at the ensuing state funeral; and the hurried Warren Commission report, which identified Oswald as the lone assassin. Afterward, critics would charge that Oswald had been part of a vast conspiracy, but at the time, the prevailing national reaction was a numbing sense of loss.

Vice President Lyndon B. Johnson moved quickly to fill the vacuum left by Kennedy's death. Sworn in on board Air Force One as he returned to Washington, Johnson soon met with a stream of world leaders to reassure them of American political stability. Five days after the tragedy in Dallas, Johnson spoke eloquently to a special joint session of Congress. Recalling JFK's inaugural summons, "Let us begin," the new president declared, "Today in the moment of new resolve, I would say to all my fellow Americans, 'Let us continue.'"

JOHNSON IN ACTION

Lyndon Johnson suffered from the inevitable comparison with his young and stylish predecessor. LBJ was acutely aware of his own lack of polish; he sought to surround himself with Kennedy advisers and insiders, hoping their sophistication would rub off on him. Johnson's assets were very real—he possessed an intimate knowledge of Congress, an incredible energy and determination to succeed, and a fierce ego.

LBJ's height and intensity gave him a powerful presence; he dominated any room he entered, and he delighted in using his physical power of persuasion. One Texas politician explained why he had given in to Johnson: "Lyndon got me by the lapels and put his face on top of mine and he talked and talked and talked. I figured it was either getting drowned or joining."

Yet LBJ found it impossible to project his intelligence and vitality to large audiences. Unlike Kennedy, he wilted before the camera, turning his televised speeches into stilted and awkward performances. Trying to belie his reputation as a riverboat gambler, he came across like a foxy grandpa, clever, calculating, and not to be trusted.

Whatever his shortcomings in style, however, Johnson possessed far greater ability than Kennedy in dealing with Congress. He entered the White House with more than thirty years of experience in Washington as a legislative aide, congressman, and senator. His encyclopedic knowledge of the legislative process and his shrewd manipulation of individual senators had enabled him to become the most influential Senate majority leader in history.

Above all, Johnson sought consensus. Indifferent to ideology, he had moved easily from New Deal liberalism to oil-and-gas conservatism as his career advanced. He had performed a balancing act on civil rights, working with the Eisenhower administration on behalf of the 1957 Voting Rights Act, yet carefully weakening it to avoid alienating southern Democrats. When Kennedy dashed Johnson's own intense presidential ambitions in 1960, LBJ had gracefully agreed

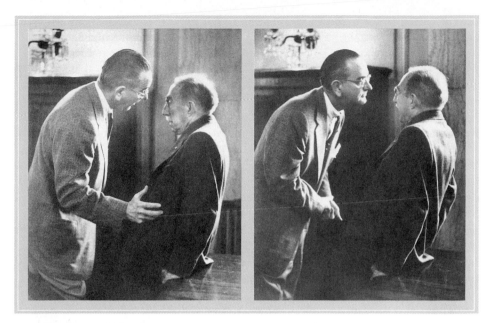

President Johnson applies the "Johnson treatment" to Senator Theodore Francis Green of Rhode Island. A shrewd politician and master of the legislative process, Johnson always knew which votes he could count on, those he couldn't, and where and how to apply pressure to swing votes his way.

to be his running mate and had endured the humiliation of the vice presidency loyally and silently. Suddenly thrust into power, Johnson used his gifts wisely. Citing his favorite scriptural passage from Isaiah, "Come now, and let us reason together, saith the Lord," he concentrated on securing passage of Kennedy's tax and civil rights bills in 1964.

The tax cut came first. Aware of the power wielded by Senate Finance Committee Chairman Harry Byrd, a Virginia conservative, Johnson astutely lowered Kennedy's projected $101.5 billion budget for 1965 to $97.9 billion. In February, Congress reduced personal income taxes by more than $10 billion, touching off a sustained economic boom.

Johnson was even more influential in passing the Kennedy civil rights measure. He refused all efforts at compromise, counting on growing public pressure to force northern Republicans to abandon their traditional alliance with southern Democrats. Everett M. Dirksen of Illinois, the GOP leader in the Senate, met repeatedly with Johnson at the White House. When LBJ refused to yield, Dirksen finally led a Republican vote to end a 57-day filibuster.

The 1964 Civil Rights Act, signed on July 2, made illegal the segregation of African Americans in public facilities, established an Equal Employment Opportunity Commission to lessen racial discrimination in employment, and protected the voting rights of African Americans. An amendment sponsored by segregationists in an effort to weaken the bill added gender to the prohibition of discrimination in Title VII of the act; in the future, women's groups would use the clause to secure government support for greater equality in employment and education.

THE ELECTION OF 1964

Passage of two key Kennedy measures within six months did not satisfy Johnson, who wanted now to win the presidency in his own right. Eager to surpass Kennedy's narrow victory in 1960, he hoped to win by a great landslide.

Searching for a cause of his own, LBJ found one in the issue of poverty. Beginning in the late 1950s, economists had warned that the prevailing affluence disguised a persistent and deep-seated problem of poverty. Johnson quickly took over poverty proposals that Kennedy had been developing. In his January 1964 State of the Union address LBJ announced, "This administration, today, here and now, declares unconditional war on poverty in America." During the next eight months, Johnson fashioned a comprehensive poverty program under the direction of R. Sargent Shriver, Kennedy's brother-in-law. The president added $500 million to existing programs to come up with a $1 billion effort that Congress passed in August 1964.

The new Office of Economic Opportunity (OEO) set up a wide variety of programs, ranging from Head Start for preschoolers to the Job Corps for high school dropouts in need of vocational training. The level of funding was never high enough to meet the OEO's ambitious goals. Nonetheless, the war on poverty, along with the economic growth provided by the tax cut, helped reduce the ranks of the poor by nearly ten million between 1964 and 1967.

The new program established Johnson's reputation as a reformer in an election year, but he still faced two challenges to his authority. The first was Robert F. Kennedy, the late president's brother, who continued as attorney general but who wanted to become vice president and Johnson's eventual successor in the White House. Desperate to prove his ability to succeed without Kennedy help, LBJ commented, "I don't need that little runt to win" and chose Hubert Humphrey as his running mate.

The second challenge was the Republican candidate, Senator Barry Goldwater, an outspoken conservative from Arizona. An attractive and articulate man, Goldwater advocated a rejection of the welfare state and a return to unregulated free enterprise. To Johnson's delight, Goldwater chose to place ideology ahead of political expediency. The senator spoke out boldly against the Tennessee Valley Authority, denounced Social Security, and advocated a hawkish foreign policy.

Johnson stuck carefully to the middle of the road, embracing the liberal reform program—which he now called the Great Society—while stressing his concern for balanced budgets and fiscal orthodoxy. On election day, LBJ received 61.1 percent of the popular vote and an overwhelming majority in the electoral college. Equally important, the Democrats achieved huge gains in Congress, controlling the House by a margin of 295 to 140 and the Senate by 68 to 32. Kennedy's legacy and Goldwater's candor had enabled Johnson to break the conservative grip on Congress for the first time in a quarter century.

THE ELECTION OF 1964

CANDIDATE	PARTY	POPULAR VOTE	ELECTORAL VOTE
Johnson	Democratic	43,126,506	486
Goldwater	Republican	27,176,799	52

THE TRIUMPH OF REFORM

LBJ moved quickly to secure his legislative goals. Despite solid majorities in both Houses, Johnson knew he would have to enact the Great Society as swiftly as possible. "You've got to give it all you can, that first year," he told an aide. "Doesn't matter what kind of majority you come in with. You've got just one year when they treat you right, and before they start worrying about themselves."

Johnson gave two traditional Democratic reforms—health care and education—top priority. Aware of strong opposition to a comprehensive medical program, LBJ settled for Medicare, which mandated health insurance under the Social Security program for Americans over age 65, and a supplementary Medicaid program for the indigent. To symbolize the end of a long struggle, Johnson flew to Independence, Missouri, so Truman could witness the ceremonial signing of the Medicare law, which had its origins in Truman's 1949 health insurance proposal.

LBJ overcame the religious hurdle on education by supporting a child-benefit approach, allocating federal money to advance the education of students in parochial as well as public schools. The Elementary and Secondary Education Act of 1965 provided more than $1 billion in federal aid, the largest share going to school districts with the highest percentage of impoverished pupils.

Civil rights proved to be the most difficult test of Johnson's leadership. Martin Luther King, concerned that three million southern blacks were still denied the right to vote, in early 1965 chose Selma, Alabama, as the site for a test case. The white authorities in Selma, led by Sheriff James Clark, used cattle prods and bullwhips to break up the demonstrations. Johnson intervened in March, after TV cameras showed Sheriff Clark's deputies brutally halting a march from Selma to Montgomery. The president ordered the Alabama National Guard to federal duty to protect the demonstrators, had the Justice Department draw up a new voting rights bill, and personally addressed the Congress on civil rights.

Five months later, Congress passed the Voting Rights Act of 1965. Once again Johnson had worked with Senate Republican leader Dirksen to break a southern filibuster and assure passage of a measure. The act banned literacy tests in states and counties in which less than half the population had voted in 1964 and provided for federal registrars in these areas to assure African Americans the franchise.

AFRICAN AMERICAN VOTER REGISTRATION BEFORE AND AFTER THE 1965 VOTING RIGHTS ACT

STATE	1960	1966	INCREASE	PERCENTAGE OF INCREASE OVER 1960
Alabama	66,000	250,000	184,000	278.8
Arkansas	73,000	115,000	42,000	57.5
Florida	183,000	303,000	120,000	65.6
Georgia	180,000	300,000	120,000	66.7
Louisiana	159,000	243,000	84,000	52.8
Mississippi	22,000	175,000	153,000	695.4
North Carolina	210,000	282,000	72,000	34.3
South Carolina	58,000	191,000	133,000	229.3
Tennessee	185,000	225,000	40,000	21.6
Texas	227,000	400,000	173,000	76.2
Virginia	100,000	205,000	105,000	105.0

Compiled from U.S. Bureau of the Census, *Statistical Abstract of the United States.*

The results were dramatic. In less than a year, 166,000 African Americans were added to the voting rolls in Alabama; African American registration went up 400 percent in Mississippi. For the first time since Reconstruction, African Americans had become active participants in southern politics.

Before the 89th Congress ended its first session in the fall of 1965, it had passed eighty-nine bills. These included measures to create two new cabinet departments (Transportation, and Housing and Urban Affairs); acts to provide for highway safety and to ensure clean air and water; and large appropriations for higher education, public housing, and the continuing war on poverty. In nine months, Johnson had enacted the entire Democratic reform agenda.

The man responsible for this great leap forward, however, had failed to win the public adulation he so deeply desired. His legislative skills had made the most of the opportunities offered by the 1964 Democratic landslide, but the people did not respond to Johnson's leadership with the warmth and praise they had showered on Kennedy. Reporters continued to portray him as a crude wheeler-dealer; as a maniac who drove around Texas back roads at 90 miles an hour, one hand on the wheel and the other holding a can of beer.

The dilemmas of the Cold War began to divert his attention from domestic concerns and eventually, in the case of Vietnam, would overwhelm him. Yet his legislative achievements were still remarkable. In one brief outburst of reform, he had accomplished more than any president since FDR.

Difficulties abroad would dim the luster of the Johnson presidency, but they could not diminish the lasting impact of the Great Society on American life. Federal aid to education, the enactment of Medicare and Medicaid, and, above all, the civil rights acts of 1964 and 1965 changed the nation irrevocably. The aged and the poor now were guaranteed access to medical care; communities saw an infusion of federal funds to improve local education; and African Americans could now begin to attend integrated schools, enjoy public facilities, and gain political power by exercising the right to vote. But even at this moment of triumph for liberal reform, new currents of dissent and rebellion were brewing.

JOHNSON ESCALATES THE VIETNAM WAR

Lyndon Johnson stressed continuity in foreign policy just as he had in enacting Kennedy's domestic reforms. He not only inherited the policy of containment from his fallen predecessor, but he shared the same Cold War assumptions and convictions. And, feeling less confident about dealing with international issues, he tended to rely heavily on Kennedy's advisers—notably Secretary of State Rusk, Secretary of Defense McNamara, and McGeorge Bundy, the national security adviser.

Johnson had broad exposure to national security affairs. He had served on the Naval Affairs Committee in the House before and during World War II, and as Senate majority leader he had been briefed and consulted regularly on the crises of the 1950s. A confirmed cold warrior, he had also seen in the 1940s the devastating political impact on the Democratic party of the communist triumph in China. "I am not going to lose Vietnam," he told the American ambassador to Saigon just after taking office in 1963. "I am not going to be the president who saw Southeast Asia go the way China went."

Aware of the problem Castro had caused John Kennedy, LBJ moved firmly to contain communism in the Western Hemisphere. In 1965, to block the possible emergence of a Castro-type government, LBJ sent twenty thousand American troops to the Dominican Republic. Johnson's flimsy justifications served only to alienate liberal critics in the United States, particularly Senate Foreign Relations Committee Chairman J. William Fulbright, a former Johnson favorite. The intervention ended in 1966 with the election of a conservative government. Senator Fulbright, however, continued his criticism of Johnson's foreign policy by publishing *The Arrogance of Power,* a biting analysis of the fallacies of containment. Fulbright's defection symbolized a growing gap between the president and liberal intellectuals; the more LBJ struggled to uphold the Cold War policies he had inherited from Kennedy, the more he found himself under attack from Congress, the media, and the universities.

THE VIETNAM DILEMMA

It was Vietnam rather than Latin America that became Lyndon Johnson's obsession and led ultimately to his political downfall. Inheriting an American commitment that dated back to Eisenhower to support an independent South Vietnam, the new president believed he had little choice but to continue Kennedy's policy in Vietnam. The crisis created by Diem's overthrow only three weeks before Kennedy's assassination led to a vacuum of power in Saigon.

Resisting pressure from the Joint Chiefs of Staff for direct American military involvement, LBJ continued Kennedy's policy of economic and technical assistance. He sent in seven thousand more military advisers and an additional $50 million in aid. While he insisted it was still up to the Vietnamese themselves to win the war, he expanded American support for covert operations, including amphibious raids on the North.

These undercover activities led directly to the Gulf of Tonkin affair. On August 2, 1964, North Vietnamese torpedo boats attacked the *Maddox,* an American destroyer engaged in electronic intelligence gathering in the Gulf of Tonkin. The *Maddox* escaped unscathed, but to show American resolve, the navy sent in another destroyer, the *C. Turner Joy.* On the evening of August 4, the two destroyers, responding to sonar and radar contacts, opened fire on North Vietnamese gunboats in the area. Johnson ordered retaliatory air strikes on North Vietnamese naval bases. Later investigation indicated that the North Vietnamese gunboats had not launched a second attack on the American ships.

The next day, the president asked Congress to pass a resolution authorizing him to take "all necessary measures to repel any armed attack against the forces of the United States and to prevent further aggression." Later, critics charged that LBJ wanted a blank check from Congress to carry out the future escalation of the Vietnam War, but such a motive is unlikely. In part, he wanted the Gulf of Tonkin Resolution to demonstrate to North Vietnam the American determination to defend South Vietnam at any cost. He also wanted to preempt the Vietnam issue from his Republican opponent, Barry Goldwater, who had been advocating a tougher policy. By taking a firm stand on the Gulf of Tonkin incident, Johnson could both impress the North Vietnamese and outmaneuver a political rival at home.

Congress responded with alacrity. The House acted unanimously, and only two senators voted against the Gulf of Tonkin Resolution. In the long run this easy victory proved costly. Having used force once against North Vietnam, LBJ was more likely to do so in the future. And although he apparently had no intention of widening the conflict in August 1964, the congressional resolution was phrased broadly enough to enable him to use whatever level of force he wanted—including unlimited military intervention. Above all, when he did wage war in Vietnam, he left himself open to the charge of deliberately misleading Congress. Presidential credibility proved ultimately to be Johnson's Achilles' heel; his political downfall began with the Gulf of Tonkin Resolution.

ESCALATION

Full-scale American involvement in Vietnam began in 1965 in a series of steps designed primarily to prevent a North Vietnamese victory. With the political situation in Saigon growing more hopeless every day, the president's advisers urged the bombing of the North. As McGeorge Bundy reported after a visit to Pleiku (site of a Vietcong attack on an American base that took nine lives), "Without new U.S. action defeat appears inevitable—probably not in a matter of weeks or perhaps even months, but within the next year or so." In February 1965,

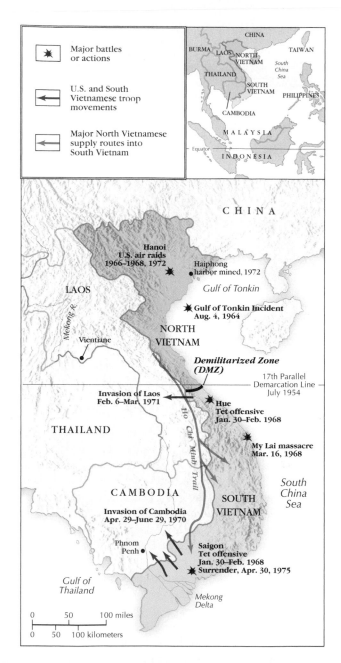

Southeast Asia and the Vietnam War
American combat forces in South Vietnam rose from sixteen thousand in 1963 to a half million in 1968, but a successful conclusion to the conflict was no closer.

Johnson cited the Pleiku attack in ordering a long-planned aerial bombardment of selected North Vietnamese targets.

The air strikes, aimed at impeding the communist supply line and damaging Hanoi's economy, proved ineffective. In April, Johnson authorized the use of American combat troops in South Vietnam, restricting them to defensive operations intended to protect American air bases. In mid-July, Secretary of Defense

U.S. troops wade through marshland during an operation on South Vietnam's Mekong Delta. Although the United States conducted thousands of air strikes over North Vietnam and committed a half million troops to the South, it failed to win the advantage. North Vietnamese regulars and Vietcong guerillas were better able to use the jungle terrain to advantage than their American adversaries.

McNamara recommended sending a hundred thousand combat troops to Vietnam, more than doubling the American forces there. He believed this escalation would lead to a "favorable outcome," but he also told the president that an additional hundred thousand soldiers might be needed in 1966. At the same time, other advisers, most notably Undersecretary of State George Ball, spoke out against military escalation in favor of a political settlement. Warning that the United States was likely to suffer "national humiliation," Ball told the president that he had "serious doubt that an army of westerners can successfully fight Orientals in an Asian jungle."

Lyndon Johnson was genuinely torn, asking his advisers at one point, "Are we starting something that in two to three years we simply can't finish?" But he finally decided he had no choice but to persevere in Vietnam. In late July, the president permitted a gradual increase in the bombing of North Vietnam and allowed American ground commanders to conduct offensive operations in the South. Most ominously, he approved the immediate dispatch of fifty thousand troops to Vietnam and the future commitment of fifty thousand more.

These July decisions formed "an open-ended commitment to employ American military forces as the situation demanded," wrote historian George Herring, and they were "the closest thing to a formal decision for war in Vietnam." Convinced that withdrawal would destroy American credibility before the world and that an invasion of the North would lead to World War III, Johnson settled for a limited war. He committed a half million American troops to battle in Southeast Asia, all the while pretending it was a minor engagement and refusing to ask the American people for the support and sacrifice required for victory.

Lyndon Johnson was not solely responsible for the Vietnam War. He inherited both a policy that assumed Vietnam was a vital national interest and a deteriorating situation in Saigon that demanded a more active American role. But LBJ bears full responsibility for the way he tried to resolve his dilemma. The failure to confront the people with the stark choices the nation faced in Vietnam, the insistence on secrecy and deceit, the refusal to acknowledge that he had committed the United States to a dangerous military involvement—these were Johnson's sins in Vietnam. His lack of self-confidence in foreign policy and fear of domestic reaction led directly to his undoing.

STALEMATE

For the next three years, Americans waged an intensive war in Vietnam and succeeded only in preventing a communist victory. American bombing of the North proved ineffective. The rural, undeveloped nature of the North Vietnamese economy meant there were few industrial targets. Nor were the efforts to destroy supply lines any more successful. American planes pounded the Ho Chi Minh trail that ran down through Laos and Cambodia, but the North Vietnamese used the jungle canopy effectively to hide their shipments. In fact, the American air attacks, with their inadvertent civilian casualties, gave North Vietnam a powerful propaganda weapon, which it used to sway world opinion against the United States.

The war in the South went no better. Despite the steady increase in American ground forces, from 184,000 in late 1965 to more than 500,000 by early 1968, the Vietcong still controlled much of the countryside. The search-and-destroy tactics employed by the American commander, General William Westmoreland, proved ill suited to the situation. In a vain effort to destroy the enemy, Westmoreland used superior American firepower wantonly, devastating the countryside, causing many civilian casualties, and driving the peasantry into the arms of the guerrillas.

The main premise of Westmoreland's strategy was to wage a war of attrition that would finally reach a "crossover point" when communist losses each month would be greater than the number of new troops they could recruit. He hoped to lure the Vietcong and the North Vietnamese regulars into pitched battles in which American firepower would inflict heavy casualties. But soon it was the communists who were deciding where and when the fighting would take place, provoking American attacks in remote areas of South Vietnam that favored the defenders. By the end of 1967, the nearly half million American troops Johnson had sent to Vietnam had failed to defeat the enemy. At best, LBJ had only achieved a bloody stalemate that gradually turned the American people against a war they had once eagerly embraced.

YEARS OF TURMOIL

The Vietnam War became the focal point for a growing movement of youthful protest that made the 1960s the most turbulent decade of the twentieth century. Disenchantment with conventional middle-class values, a rapid increase in college enrollments as a result of the post–World War II baby boom, a reaction against the crass materialism of the affluent society—with its endless suburbs and shopping malls—all led American youth to embrace an alternative lifestyle based on the belief that people are "sensitive, searching, poetic, and capable of love." They were ready to create a counterculture.

The agitation of the 1960s was at its height between 1965 and 1968, the years that marked the escalation of the Vietnam War. Disturbances on college campuses reflected growing discontent in other parts of society, from the urban ghettos to the lettuce fields of the Southwest. All who felt disadvantaged—students, African Americans, Hispanics, Native Americans, women, hippies—took to the streets to give vent to their feelings.

THE STUDENT REVOLT

The first sign of student rebellion came in the fall of 1964 at the prestigious University of California at Berkeley. A small group of radical students resisted university efforts to deny them a place to solicit volunteers and funds for off-campus causes. Forming the Free Speech movement, they struck back by occupying administration buildings and blocking the arrest of a nonstudent protester. For the next two months, the campus was in turmoil until the protesters won the rights of free speech and association that they championed.

The Free Speech movement at Berkeley offered many insights into the causes of campus unrest. It was fueled in part by student suspicion of an older, Depression-born generation that viewed affluence as the answer to all problems. Students viewed higher education as the faithful servant of a corporate culture: The university trained hordes of technicians, harbored research laboratories that perfected dreadful weapons, and used IBM punch cards to regiment students.

Student protest found its full expression in the explosive growth of the Students for a Democratic Society (SDS). Founded in Port Huron, Michigan, in 1962, this radical organization wanted to rid American society of poverty, racism, and violence. Although the SDS embraced many traditional liberal reforms, its founders advocated a new approach called participatory democracy. Personal control of one's life and destiny, not the creation of new bureaucracies, was the hallmark of the New Left.

In the next few years, the SDS grew phenomenally. Spurred on by the Vietnam War and massive campus unrest, the SDS could count more than a hundred thousand followers and was responsible for disruptions at nearly a thousand colleges in 1968. Yet its very emphasis on the individual and its fear of bureaucracy left it leaderless and subject to division and disunity. By 1970, a split between factions, some of which were given to violence, led to its complete demise.

The meteoric career of the SDS symbolized the turbulence of the 1960s. For a brief time, it seemed as though the nation's youth had gone berserk, indulging in a wave of experimentation with drugs, sex, and rock music. Not all American youth joined in the cultural insurgency; the rebellion was generally limited to children of the upper middle class. But like the flappers of the 1920s, the protesters set the tone for an entire era and left a lasting impression on American society.

PROTESTING THE VIETNAM WAR

The most dramatic aspect of the youthful rebellion came in opposing the Vietnam War. The first student "teach-ins" began at the University of Michigan in March 1965; soon they spread to campuses across the nation. More than twenty thousand protesters, under SDS auspices, gathered in Washington in April to listen to entertainers Joan Baez and Judy Collins sing antiwar songs. "End the War in Vietnam Now, Stop the Killing" read the signs.

As the fighting in Southeast Asia intensified in 1966 and 1967, the protests grew larger and the slogans more extreme. "Hey, Hey, LBJ, how many kids did you kill today?" chanted students as they proclaimed, "Hell, no, we won't go!" At the Pentagon in October 1967, more than a hundred thousand demonstrators confronted a cordon of military policemen guarding the heart of the nation's war machine.

Antiwar protesters came face-to-face with military police in the October 1967 March on the Pentagon. Leaders of the march announced that the demonstration marked the end of peaceful protest against the war and the beginning of a new stage of "active resistance." Borrowing techniques from the civil rights movement, some of the demonstrators staged a sit-down in the Pentagon parking lot.

The climax came in the spring of 1968. Driven by both opposition to the war and concern for social justice, the SDS and African American radicals at Columbia University joined forces in April. They seized five buildings, effectively paralyzing one of the country's leading colleges. After eight days of tension, the New York City police regained control. The brutal repression quickened the pace of protest elsewhere; students held sit-ins and marches at more than one hundred colleges.

The students failed to stop the war, but they did succeed in gaining a voice in their education. University administrations allowed undergraduates to sit on faculty curriculum-planning committees and gave up their once rigid control of dormitory and social life. But the students' greatest impact lay outside politics and the campus. They spawned a cultural uprising that transformed the manners and morals of America.

THE CULTURAL REVOLUTION

In contrast to the elitist political revolt of the SDS, the cultural rebellion by youth in the 1960s was pervasive. Led by college students, young people challenged the prevailing adult values in clothing, hairstyles, sexual conduct, work habits, and music. Blue jeans and love beads took the place of business suits and wristwatches; long hair and unkempt beards for men, bare feet and bralessness for women became the new uniform of protest.

Music became the touchstone of the new departure. Folksingers such as Joan Baez and Bob Dylan, popular for their songs of social protest in the mid-1960s, gave way first to rock groups such as the Beatles, whose lyrics were often suggestive of drug use, and then to "acid rock" as symbolized by the Grateful Dead. The climactic event of the decade came at the Woodstock concert at Bethel in upstate New York when 400,000 young people indulged in a three-day festival of rock music, drug experimentation, and public sexual activity.

Former Harvard psychology professor Timothy Leary encouraged youth to join him in trying out the drug scene. Millions accepted his invitation to "tune in, turn on, drop out" literally, as they experimented with marijuana and with LSD, a new and dangerous chemical hallucinogen. The ultimate expression of insurgency was the Yippie movement, led by Jerry Rubin and Abbie Hoffman. Shrewd buffoons who mocked the consumer culture, they delighted in capitalizing on the mood of social protest to win attention.

"BLACK POWER"

The civil rights movement, which had spawned the mood of protest in the 1960s, fell on hard times later in the decade. The legislative triumphs of 1964 and 1965 were relatively easy victories over southern bigotry; now the movement faced the far more complex problem of achieving economic equality in the cities of the North, where more than half of the nation's African Americans lived in poverty. The civil rights movement had raised the expectations of urban African Americans for improvement; frustration mounted as they failed to experience any significant economic gain.

The first sign of trouble came in the summer of 1964, when African American teenagers in Harlem and Rochester, New York, rioted. The next summer, a massive outburst of rage and destruction swept over the Watts area of Los Angeles as the inhabitants burned buildings and looted stores. Riots in the summer of 1966 were less destructive, but in 1967 the worst ones yet took place in Newark and in Detroit, where forty-three people were killed and thousands were injured. The mobs attacked the shops and stores, expressing a burning grievance against a consumer society from which they were excluded by their poverty.

The civil rights coalition fell apart, a victim of both its legislative success and economic failure. Black militants took over the leadership of the Student Nonviolent Coordinating Committee (SNCC); they disdained white help and even reversed Martin Luther King's insistence on nonviolence. SNCC's new leader, Stokely Carmichael, told blacks they should seize power in those parts of the South where they outnumbered whites. Soon his calls for "black power" became a rallying cry for more militant blacks.

King suffered the most from this extremism. His denunciation of the Vietnam War cost him the support of the Johnson administration and alienated him from the more conservative civil rights groups such as the NAACP and the Urban League. He finally seized on poverty as the proper enemy for attack, but before he could lead his Poor People's March on Washington in 1968, he was assassinated in Memphis in early April.

Both blacks and whites realized the nation had lost its most eloquent voice for racial harmony. His tragic death elevated King to the status of a martyr, but it also led to one last outbreak of urban violence. African Americans exploded in angry riots in 125 cities across the nation; the worst rioting took place in Washington, D.C., where buildings were set on fire within a few blocks of the White House.

Yet there was a positive side to the emotions engendered by black nationalism. Leaders urged African Americans to take pride in their ethnic heritage, to embrace their blackness as a positive value. African Americans began to wear Afro hairstyles and dress in dashikis, stressing their African roots. Students began to demand new black studies programs in the colleges; the word *Negro*—identified with white supremacy of the past—virtually disappeared from usage overnight, replaced by the favored *Afro-American* or *black*. Singer James Brown best expressed the sense of racial identity: "Say It Loud—I'm Black and I'm Proud."

ETHNIC NATIONALISM

Other groups quickly emulated the African American phenomenon. Native Americans decried the callous use of their identity as football mascots; in response, universities such as Stanford changed their symbols. Puerto Ricans demanded their history be included in school and college texts. Polish, Italian, and Czech groups insisted on respect for their nationalities. Congress acknowledged these demands with passage of the Ethnic Heritage Studies Act of 1972.

Mexican Americans were in the forefront of the ethnic groups that became active in the 1970s. The primary impulse came from the efforts of César Chávez to organize the poorly paid grape pickers and lettuce workers in California into

In March 1966, César Chávez, shown here talking with workers, led striking grape pickers on a 250-mile march from Delano, California, to the state capital at Sacramento to dramatize the plight of the migrant farmworkers. With the slogan "God is beside you on the picket line," the march took on the character of a religious pilgrimage.

the National Farm Workers Association (NFWA). Chávez appealed to ethnic nationalism in mobilizing Mexican American field hands to strike against grape growers in the San Joaquin Valley in 1965. The five-year struggle resulted in a union victory in 1970, but at an enormous cost—95 percent of the farmworkers involved had lost their homes and their cars. Nevertheless, Chávez succeeded in raising the hourly wage of farmworkers in California to $3.53 by 1977 (it had been $1.20 in 1965).

Chávez's efforts helped spark an outburst of ethnic consciousness among Mexican Americans that swept through the urban barrios of the Southwest. Mexican American leaders campaigned for bilingual programs and improved educational opportunities. Young activists began to call themselves Chicanos, which had previously been a derogatory term, and to take pride in their cultural heritage.

WOMEN'S LIBERATION

Active as they were in the civil rights and antiwar movements, women soon learned that the male leaders of these causes were little different from corporate executives—they expected women to fix the food and type the communiqués while the men made the decisions. Understandably, women soon realized that they could only achieve respect and equality by mounting their own protest.

In some ways, the position of women in American society was worse in the 1960s than it had been in the 1920s. After forty years, a lower percentage of women were enrolled in the nation's colleges and professional schools. Women were still relegated to stereotyped occupations such as nursing and teaching. And gender roles, as portrayed on television commercials, continued to call for the husband to be the breadwinner and the wife to be the homemaker.

Betty Friedan was one of the first to seize on the sense of grievance and discrimination that developed among white middle-class women in the 1960s. The beginning of the effort to raise women's consciousness was her 1963 book, *The Feminine Mystique.* Calling the American home "a comfortable concentration camp," she attacked the prevailing view that women were completely contented with their housekeeping and child-rearing tasks.

The 1964 Civil Rights Act helped women attack economic inequality head-on by making it illegal to discriminate in employment on the basis of gender. Women filed suit for equal wages, and demanded that companies provide day care for their infants and preschool children. As the women's liberation movement grew, its advocates began to attack laws banning abortion and waged a campaign to toughen the enforcement of rape laws.

The women's movement met with many of the same obstacles as other protest groups in the 1960s. The moderate leadership of the National Organization for Women (NOW), founded by Betty Friedan in 1966, soon was challenged by those with more extreme views. Many women were repelled by the harsh rhetoric of the extremists and expressed satisfaction with their lives. But despite these disagreements, most women supported the effort to achieve equal status with men, and in 1972, Congress responded by voting to send the Equal Rights Amendment to the state legislatures for ratification.

THE RETURN OF RICHARD NIXON

The turmoil of the 1960s reached a crescendo in 1968 as the American people responded to the two dominant events of the decade—the war in Vietnam and the cultural insurgency at home. In an election marked by a series of bizarre events, including riots and an assassination, Richard Nixon staged a remarkable comeback to win the post denied him in 1960.

VIETNAM UNDERMINES LYNDON JOHNSON

A controversial Vietcong offensive in early 1968 proved to be the decisive event in breaking the stalemate in Vietnam and driving Lyndon Johnson from office. Using deceptive tactics, the North Vietnamese began a prolonged siege of an American marine base at Khe Sanh, deep in the northern interior. Fearing another Dien Bien Phu, Westmoreland rushed in reinforcements, sending more than 40 percent of all American infantry and armor battalions into the two northern-most provinces of South Vietnam.

The Vietcong then used the traditional lull in the fighting at Tet, the lunar New Year, to launch a surprise attack in the heavily populated cities. Beginning on January 30, 1968, the VC struck at thirty-six of the forty-four provincial capitals. The most daring raid came at the American embassy compound in Saigon. Although the guerrillas were unable to penetrate the embassy proper, for six hours television cameras caught the dramatic battle that ensued in the courtyard before military police finally overcame the attackers.

Tet proved to be the turning point of the Vietnam War. Although the communists failed to win control of the cities and suffered heavy losses, they still held on to most of the rural areas and had scored an impressive political victory. CBS-TV newscaster Walter Cronkite took a quick trip to Saigon to find out what had happened. Horrified at what he saw, he exclaimed to his guides, "What the hell is going on? I thought we were winning the war." He returned home to tell the American people, "It seems now more certain than ever that the bloody experience of Vietnam is to end in a stalemate."

President Johnson reluctantly came to the same conclusion after the Joint Chiefs of Staff requested an additional 205,000 troops to achieve victory in Vietnam following the Tet offensive. He began to listen to his new secretary of defense, Clark Clifford, who had replaced Robert McNamara in January 1968. In mid-March, the president decided to limit the bombing of North Vietnam in an effort to open up peace negotiations with Hanoi. In a speech to the nation on Sunday evening, March 31, 1968, Johnson outlined his plans for a new effort at ending the war peacefully and then concluded by saying, as proof of his sincerity, "I shall not seek, and I will not accept, the nomination of my party for another term as your president."

In the fourteen years since the siege of Dien Bien Phu, American policy had gone full cycle in Vietnam. Even though Eisenhower had decided against using force to rescue the French, his commitment to the Diem regime in Saigon had led eventually to American military involvement on a massive scale. Three years of inconclusive fighting and a steadily mounting loss of American lives had disillusioned the American people and finally cost Lyndon Johnson the presidency.

THE DEMOCRATS DIVIDE

Lyndon Johnson's withdrawal from the presidential race after the Tet offensive set the tone for the 1968 election. LBJ's decision had come in response to political as well as military realities. By 1966, the antiwar movement had spread from the college campuses to Capitol Hill. Chairman J. William Fulbright gave the protests a new respectability when his Senate Foreign Relations Committee held probing hearings on the war, broadcast on television to the entire country.

The essentially leaderless protest against the war took on a new quality on January 3, 1968, when Senator Eugene McCarthy, a Democrat from Minnesota, announced he was challenging LBJ for the party's presidential nomination. College students flocked to his campaign, shaving their beards and cutting their hair to be "clean for Gene." In the New Hampshire primary in early March, the nation's earliest political test, McCarthy shocked the political experts by coming within a few thousand votes of defeating President Johnson.

McCarthy's strong showing in New Hampshire led Robert Kennedy, who had been weighing the risks in challenging Johnson, to enter the presidential race. Elected senator from New York in 1964, Bobby Kennedy had become an effective voice for the disadvantaged, as well as an increasingly severe critic of the Vietnam War.

Lyndon Johnson's dramatic withdrawal caused an uproar in the Democratic party. With Johnson's tacit backing and strong support from party regulars and organized labor, Vice President Hubert H. Humphrey immediately declared his candidacy. Humphrey, aware that he was totally unacceptable to the antiwar movement, decided to avoid the primaries and work for the nomination within the framework of the party.

Kennedy and McCarthy, the two antiwar candidates, were thus left to compete in the spring primaries, requiring agonizing choices among those who desired change. Kennedy won everywhere except in Oregon, but his narrow victory in California ended in tragedy when a Palestinian immigrant, Sirhan Sirhan, assassinated him in a Los Angeles hotel.

With his strongest opponent struck down, Hubert Humphrey had little difficulty at the Chicago convention. The vice president relied on party leaders to defeat an antiwar resolution and win the nomination on the first ballot by a margin of more than two to one.

Humphrey's triumph was marred by violence outside the heavily guarded convention hall. Radical groups had urged their members to come to Chicago to agitate; epithets and cries of "pigs" brought on a savage response from the police. "The cops had one thing on their mind," commented journalist Jimmy Breslin. "Club and then gas, club and then gas, club and then gas."

What an official investigation later termed a "police riot" marred Humphrey's nomination and made a sad mockery out of his call for "the politics of joy." The Democratic party itself had become the next victim of the Vietnam War.

THE REPUBLICAN RESURGENCE

The primary beneficiary of the Democratic debacle was Richard Nixon. Written off as politically dead after his unsuccessful race for governor of California in 1962, Nixon had slowly rebuilt his place within the party by working loyally for Barry Goldwater in 1964 and for GOP congressional candidates two years later. At the GOP convention in Miami Beach, Nixon won an easy first-ballot nomination and chose Maryland governor Spiro Agnew as his running mate.

In the fall campaign, Nixon opened up a wide lead by avoiding controversy and reaping the benefit of discontent with the Vietnam War. He played the peace issue shrewdly, appearing to advocate an end to the conflict without ever taking a definite stand. Above all, he chose the role of reconciler for a nation torn by emotion, a leader who promised to bring a divided country together again.

Humphrey, in contrast, found himself hounded by antiwar demonstrators who heckled him constantly. He walked a tightwire, desperate for the continued support of President Johnson but handicapped by LBJ's stubborn refusal to end all bombing of North Vietnam. Only when he broke with Johnson in late September by announcing that if elected he would "stop the bombing of North Vietnam as an acceptable risk for peace" did his campaign begin to gain momentum.

Unfortunately for Humphrey, a third-party candidate cut deeply into the normal Democratic majority. George Wallace had first gained national attention

The Election of 1968

CANDIDATE	PARTY	POPULAR VOTE	ELECTORAL VOTE
Nixon	Republican	31,770,237	301
Humphrey	Democratic	31,270,533	191
Wallace	American Independent	9,906,141	46
	Minor Parties	239,908	—

as the racist governor of Alabama whose motto was "Segregation now . . . segregation tomorrow . . . segregation forever." By attacking both black leaders and their liberal white allies, Wallace appealed to the sense of powerlessness among the urban working classes. "Liberals, intellectuals, and longhairs have run the country for too long," Wallace told his followers. "When I get to Washington," he promised, "I'll throw all these phonies and their briefcases into the Potomac."

Running on the ticket of the American Independent Party, Wallace was a close third in the September polls. But as the election neared, his following declined. Humphrey continued to gain, especially after Johnson agreed in late October to end all bombing of North Vietnam.

Nixon won the election with the smallest share of the popular vote of any winning candidate since 1916. But he swept a broad band of states from Virginia and the Carolinas through the Midwest to the Pacific for a clear-cut victory in the electoral college. Humphrey held on to the urban Northeast; Wallace took just five states in the Deep South.

The End of an Era

The election marked a repudiation of the politics of protest and the cultural insurgency of the mid-1960s. The combined popular vote for Nixon and Wallace, 56.5 percent of the electorate, signified there was a silent majority that was fed up with violence and confrontation. A growing concern over psychedelic drugs, rock music, long hair, and sexual permissiveness had offset the usual Democratic advantage on economic issues and led to the election of a Republican president.

At the election of Richard Nixon, an era came to an end with the passing of two concepts that had guided American life since the 1930s. First, the liberal reform impulse, which reached its zenith with the Great Society legislation in 1965, had clearly run its course. Nixon's triumph signaled a strong reaction against the growth of federal power. At the same time, the Vietnam fiasco spelled the end of an activist foreign policy that had begun with American entry into World War II.

Containment, so successful in protecting western Europe against the Soviet threat, had proved a disastrous failure when applied on a global scale. The last three decades of the twentieth century would witness a struggle to replace outmoded liberal internationalism with new policies at home and abroad.

CHRONOLOGY

1961	JFK establishes Peace Corps (March)
	U.S.-backed Bay of Pigs invasion crushed by Cubans (April)
1962	Astronaut John H. Glenn, Jr., becomes first American to orbit the earth (February)
	President Kennedy forces U.S. Steel to roll back price hike (April)
	Cuban missile crisis takes world to brink of nuclear war (October)
1963	United States, Great Britain, and USSR sign Limited Nuclear Test Ban treaty (August)
	JFK assassinated; Lyndon B. Johnson sworn in as president (November)
1964	President Johnson declares war on poverty (January)
	Congress overwhelmingly passes Gulf of Tonkin Resolution (August)
	Johnson wins presidency in landslide (November)
1965	LBJ commits fifty thousand American troops to combat in Vietnam (July)
	Congress enacts Medicare and Medicaid (July)
1966	National Organization for Women (NOW) formed
1967	Israel wins Six Day War in Middle East (June)
	Riots in Detroit kill forty-three, injure two thousand, leave five thousand homeless (July)
1968	Vietcong launch the Tet offensive (January)
	Johnson announces he will not seek reelection (March)
	Martin Luther King, Jr., assassinated in Memphis (April)
	Robert Kennedy assassinated in Los Angeles (June)

31

TO A NEW CONSERVATISM, 1969–1988

In October 1964, the Republican National Committee sponsored a televised address by Hollywood actor Ronald Reagan on behalf of Barry Goldwater's presidential candidacy. Reagan's speech had originally been aired on a Los Angeles station; the resulting outpouring of praise and campaign contributions led to its national rebroadcast.

In contrast to Goldwater's strident rhetoric, Reagan used relaxed, confident, and persuasive terms to put forth the case for a return to individual freedom. Instead of the usual choice between increased government activity and less government involvement, often couched in terms of the left and the right, Reagan presented the options of either going up or down—"up to the maximum of human freedom consistent with law and order, or down to the ant heap of totalitarianism." Then, borrowing a phrase from FDR, he told his audience: "You and I have a rendezvous with destiny. We can preserve for our children this the last best hope of man on earth, or we can sentence them to take the first step into a thousand years of darkness."

Although the speech did not rescue Goldwater's unpopular candidacy, it marked the beginning of Ronald Reagan's remarkable political career. A popular actor whose movie career had begun to fade in the 1950s, Reagan had become an effective television performer as host of *The General Electric Theater*. His political views, once liberal, moved steadily to the right as he became a spokesperson for a major American corporation. In 1965, a group of wealthy friends persuaded him, largely on the basis of the success of "the speech," to run for the California governorship.

Reagan proved to be an attractive candidate. His approachable manner and his mastery of television enabled him to present his strongly conservative message without appearing to be a rigid ideologue of the right. He won handily by appealing effectively to rising middle-class suburban resentment over high taxes, expanding welfare programs, and bureaucratic regulation.

In two terms as governor, Reagan displayed natural ability as a political leader. Instead of insisting on implementing all of his conservative beliefs, he proved surprisingly flexible.

By the time Reagan left the governor's office in 1974, many signs pointed to a growing conservative mood across the nation. In a popular rebellion against escalating property taxes in 1978, California's voters passed Proposition 13, which slashed property taxes in half and resulted in a gradual reduction in social services. Conservatives were especially outraged over the 1962 Supreme Court ruling in *Engel* v. *Vitale* outlawing school prayer. One Alabama congressman denounced the Supreme Court justices, proclaiming, "They put the Negroes in the schools and now they're driving God out."

Concern over school prayer, along with rising abortion and divorce rates, impelled religious groups to engage in political activity to defend what they viewed as traditional family values. Jerry Falwell, a successful Virginia radio and television evangelist, founded the Moral Majority, a fundamentalist group dedicated to preserving the "American way of life."

The population shift of the 1970s, especially the rapid growth of the Sunbelt region in the South and West, added momentum to the conservative upsurge. Those moving to the Sunbelt tended to be white, middle- and upper-class suburbanites—mainly skilled workers, young professionals, and business executives who were attracted both by economic opportunity and by a political climate stressing low taxes, less government regulation, and more reliance on the marketplace. The political impact of population shifts from East to West and North to South during the 1970s was reflected in the congressional gains (seventeen seats) by Sunbelt and Far West states after the 1980 census.

Conservatives also succeeded, for the first time since World War II, in making their cause intellectually respectable. Scholars and academics on the right flourished in new "think tanks." They denounced liberals for being too soft on the communist threat abroad and too willing to compromise high standards at home in the face of demands for equality from African Americans, women, and the disadvantaged.

By the end of the 1970s, a decade marked by military defeat in Vietnam, political scandal that destroyed the administration of Richard Nixon, economic ills that vexed the country under Gerald Ford and Jimmy Carter, and unprecedented social strains on families and traditional institutions, millions of Americans had come to believe that Cold War liberalism had run its course. Ronald Reagan, as the acknowledged leader of the conservative resurgence, was ideally placed to capitalize on this discontent. His personal charm softened the hard edges of his right-wing call to arms, and his conviction that America could regain its traditional self-confidence by reaffirming basic ideals had a broad appeal to a nation facing new challenges at home and abroad. In 1976, Reagan had barely lost to President Ford at the Republican convention; four years later, he overcame an early upset by George Bush in Iowa to win the GOP presidential nomination handily.

In his acceptance speech at the Republican convention in Detroit, Reagan set forth the themes that endeared him to conservatives: less government, a balanced budget, family values, and peace through greater military spending. Reagan offered reassurance and hope for the future. In Ronald Reagan, the Republicans had found the perfect figure to lead Americans into a new conservative era.

THE TEMPTING OF RICHARD NIXON

Following the divisive campaign of 1968, Richard Nixon's presidency proved to be one of the most controversial in American history. Nixon's domestic policies had limited success, and though his diplomacy broke new ground in relations with China and the Soviet Union and ended American fighting in Vietnam, he was forced to resign the presidency under the dark cloud of the Watergate scandal.

PRAGMATIC LIBERALISM

Nixon began his first term on a hopeful note, promising the nation peace and respite from the chaos of the 1960s. Rejecting the divisions that had driven Americans apart, he pledged in his inaugural address to bring the country together. "We cannot learn from one another," he said, "until we stop shouting at one another—until we speak quietly enough so that our words can be heard as well as our voices."

Nixon's moderate language appeared to herald a return to the politics of accommodation that had characterized the Eisenhower era. Faced with a Democratic Congress, Nixon, like Ike, reconciled himself to the broad outlines of the welfare state. Instead of trying to overthrow the Great Society, he focused on making the federal bureaucracy function more efficiently. In some areas he actually expanded federal programs and responsibilities.

On civil rights, for example, Nixon was the first president to adopt affirmative action as an explicit policy. His labor secretary, George Shultz, applied the "Philadelphia plan," which had evolved to ensure the hiring of minority contractors in Pennsylvania's largest city, to other cities and eventually to all federal contracts worth more than $50,000. Nixon also expanded affirmative action to include women, vastly increasing the scope of the policy. The goal, a Nixon executive order explained, was for the federal government to achieve "the prompt and full utilization of minorities and women at all levels in all segments of its work force."

Nixon broke new ground in other areas associated with liberalism. He approved the creation of the Occupational Safety and Health Administration (OSHA), which assumed responsibility for reducing workplace injuries. He oversaw the establishment of the Environmental Protection Agency (EPA), the federal watchdog on environmental affairs. He signed the Clean Air Act, which provided the basis for tackling smog and other air pollutants. He supported automatic cost-of-living increases to Social Security, ensuring that the elderly not lose ground to the inflation that increasingly vexed the American economy.

Many liberals suspected Nixon's motives, and not without reason. Nixon's liberalism was pragmatic, even opportunistic, rather than principled. In private conversations he could be demeaning of African Americans, Jews, and other minorities. But, planning big changes in American foreign policy, he chose not to pick fights with congressional Democrats or buck the liberal tide that was still flowing from the 1960s.

He did try to shape that tide. Nixon was successful in shifting responsibility for social problems from Washington to state and local authorities. He developed the concept of revenue sharing by which federal funds would be dispersed to state, county, and city agencies to meet local needs. In 1972, Congress finally approved a measure to share $30.1 billion with local governments over a five-year period.

Nixon's civil rights policy was similarly calculating. Action by Congress and the outgoing Johnson administration had ensured that massive desegregation of southern schools would begin just as Nixon took office. Nixon and his attorney general, John Mitchell, decided to shift responsibility for this process to the courts. In the summer of 1969, the Justice Department asked a federal judge to delay the integration of thirty-three school districts in Mississippi. The Supreme Court quickly ruled against the Justice Department. Thus, in the minds of southern white voters it was the hated Supreme Court, not Richard Nixon, who had forced them to integrate their schools. The upshot of Nixon's domestic policies

High school students in Woodville, Mississippi, board a school bus after their first day of class in a now all-black school. The school, which was formerly predominantly white, was one of thirty Mississippi schools under court order to speed desegregation.

was to extend the welfare state in some areas, reshape it in others, and leave liberals and conservatives alike wondering just where Nixon stood.

DÉTENTE

Foreign policy was Nixon's pride and joy. He had thought long about the state of the world, and he was determined to improve it. To assist him in this endeavor, he appointed Henry Kissinger to be national security adviser. A refugee from Nazi Germany, Kissinger had become a professor of government at Harvard, the author of several influential books, and an acknowledged authority on international affairs. Nixon and Kissinger approached foreign policy from a practical, realistic perspective. Instead of viewing the Cold War as an ideological struggle for survival with communism, they saw it as a traditional great-power rivalry, one to be managed and controlled rather than to be won.

Nixon and Kissinger had a grand design. Realizing that recent events, especially the Vietnam War and the rapid Soviet arms buildup of the 1960s, had eroded America's position of primacy in the world, they planned a strategic retreat. Russia had great military strength, but its economy was weak and it had a dangerous rival in China. Nixon planned to use American trade—notably grain and high technology—to induce Soviet cooperation, while at the same time improving U.S. relations with China.

Nixon and Kissinger shrewdly played the China card as their first step toward achieving détente—a relaxation of tension—with the Soviet Union. In February 1972, accompanied by a planeload of reporters and television camera crews, Nixon visited China, meeting with the communist leaders and ending more than two decades of Sino-American hostility. Nixon agreed to establish an American liaison mission in Beijing as a first step toward diplomatic recognition.

The Soviets, who viewed China as a dangerous adversary, responded by agreeing to an arms control pact with the United States. The Strategic Arms Limitation Talks (SALT) had been under way since 1969. During a visit to Moscow in May 1972, Nixon signed two vital documents with Soviet leader Leonid Brezhnev. The first limited the two superpowers to two hundred antiballistic missiles (ABMs) apiece; the second froze the number of offensive ballistic missiles for a five-year period. The SALT I agreements recognized the existing Soviet lead in missiles, but the American deployment of multiple independently targeted reentry vehicles (MIRVs) ensured a continuing strategic advantage for the United States.

ENDING THE VIETNAM WAR

Vietnam remained the one foreign policy challenge that Nixon could not overcome. He had a three-part plan to end the conflict—gradual withdrawal of American troops, accompanied by training of South Vietnamese forces to take over the combat role; renewed bombing; and a hard line in negotiations with Hanoi. The number of American soldiers in Vietnam fell from 540,000 in early 1969 to less than 30,000 by 1972; domestic opposition to the war declined sharply with the accompanying drop in casualties and reductions in the draft call.

The renewed bombing of North Vietnam and invasion of Cambodia ordered by Nixon in hopes of ending the conflict precipitated student protests at many campuses. At Kent State University in Ohio, demonstrators and bystanders were shot by national guardsmen.

Renewed bombing proved the most controversial part of the plan. In April 1970, Nixon ordered both air and ground strikes into Cambodia, causing a massive outburst of antiwar protests at home. Students demonstrated against the invasion of Cambodia on campuses across the nation. Tragedy struck at Kent State University in Ohio in early May. After rioters had firebombed an ROTC building, the governor sent in national guard troops who were taunted and harassed by irate students. The guardsmen then opened fire, killing four students and wounding eleven more. The victims were innocent bystanders; two were young women caught in the fusillade on their way between classes. A week later, two African American student demonstrators were killed at Jackson State College in Mississippi; soon riots and protests raged on more than four hundred campuses across the country.

Nixon's third tactic, negotiation with Hanoi, finally proved successful. In the summer and fall of 1972, the two sides neared agreement, but South Vietnamese objections blocked a settlement before the 1972 election. When the North Vietnamese tried to make last-minute changes, Nixon ordered a series of heavy B-52 raids on Hanoi that finally led to the signing of a truce on January 27, 1973. In return for the release of all American prisoners of war, the United States agreed to remove its troops from South Vietnam within sixty days. The political clauses allowed the North Vietnamese to keep their troops in the South, thus virtually guaranteeing future control of all Vietnam by the communists.

For two years after the accords the communists waited, weighing, among other things, the willingness of Americans to continue to support South Vietnam. As Nixon became enmeshed in the Watergate scandal (see below), his grip on foreign policy weakened, and by the time he was forced from office in August 1974 most Americans simply wanted to forget Vietnam. The following spring the communists mounted a major offensive and in just weeks completed their takeover of Vietnam. Ten years after the American escalation of the war, and

after the loss of sixty thousand American lives, the American effort to preserve
South Vietnam from communism had proved a tragic failure.

THE WATERGATE SCANDAL

Nixon's Vietnam problems and especially his formulation of détente made him
sensitive to the unauthorized release of information about American foreign
policy. The White House established an informal office of covert surveillance—
the "plumbers," its operatives were called—which began by investigating the
national security breaches but, during the presidential campaign of 1972,
branched out into spying on Nixon's Democratic opponents and engaging in political dirty tricks.

Five of the "plumbers" were arrested in June 1972 during a break-in at the
headquarters of the Democratic National Committee at the Watergate office
complex in Washington. The Nixon White House took pains to conceal its connection to what its spokesman dismissed as a "third-rate burglary attempt."
Nixon personally ordered the cover-up. "I want you to stonewall it, let them
plead the Fifth Amendment, cover-up, or anything else," Nixon told John
Mitchell, his former attorney general and then campaign director.

The cover-up succeeded long enough to ensure Nixon's landslide reelection
victory over Democrat George S. McGovern of South Dakota, but in the months
after the election the cover-up began to unravel. James McCord, one of the
Watergate burglars, was the first to break the silence. Sentenced to a long jail term
by Judge John Sirica, McCord asked for leniency, informing Sirica he had received
money from the White House and had been promised a presidential pardon in return for his silence. By April 1973, Nixon was compelled to fire aide John Dean,
who had directed the cover-up but who now refused to become a scapegoat. Two
other aides, H. R. Haldeman and John Ehrlichman, were forced to resign.

The Senate then appointed a special committee to investigate the unfolding
Watergate scandal. In a week of dramatic testimony, Dean revealed the president's personal involvement in the cover-up. Still, it was basically a matter of
whose word was to be believed—the president's or a discredited aide's—and
Nixon hoped to weather the storm.

The committee's discovery of the existence of tape recordings of conversations in the Oval Office, made regularly since 1970, proved the beginning of the
end for Nixon. At first, the president tried to invoke executive privilege to with-

THE ELECTION OF 1972

CANDIDATE	PARTY	POPULAR VOTE	ELECTORAL VOTE
Nixon	Republican	46,740,323	520
McGovern	Democratic	28,901,598	17

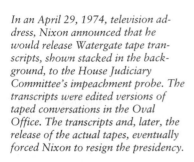

In an April 29, 1974, television address, Nixon announced that he would release Watergate tape transcripts, shown stacked in the background, to the House Judiciary Committee's impeachment probe. The transcripts were edited versions of taped conversations in the Oval Office. The transcripts and, later, the release of the actual tapes, eventually forced Nixon to resign the presidency.

hold the tapes. Then Nixon tried to release only a few of the less damaging ones, but the Supreme Court ruled unanimously in June 1974 that the tapes had to be turned over to Judge Sirica.

By that time, the House Judiciary Committee, acting on evidence compiled by the staff of the Senate committee, had voted three articles of impeachment, charging Nixon with obstruction of justice, abuse of power, and contempt of Congress. Faced with the release of tapes that directly implicated him in the cover-up, the president chose to resign on August 9, 1974.

Nixon's resignation proved to be the culmination of the Watergate scandal. The entire episode revealed both the weaknesses and strengths of the American political system. Most regrettable was the abuse of presidential authority. Realizing he had reached the White House almost by accident, Nixon did everything possible to retain his hold on his office. He used the plumbers to maintain executive secrecy, and he directed the Internal Revenue Service and the Justice Department to punish his enemies and reward his friends.

But Watergate also demonstrated the vitality of a democratic society. The press showed how investigative reporting could unlock even the most closely guarded executive secrets. Judge Sirica proved that an independent judiciary was still the best bulwark for individual freedom. And Congress rose to the occasion, both by carrying out a successful investigation of executive misconduct and by following a scrupulous and nonpartisan impeachment process that left Nixon with no chance to escape his fate.

THE ECONOMY OF STAGFLATION

In the midst of Watergate, the outbreak of war in the Middle East threatened a vital national interest: the unimpeded and inexpensive flow of oil to the United States. The resulting energy crisis helped spark a raging price inflation that had a profound impact on the national economy and on American society at large.

WAR AND OIL

On October 6, 1973, Egypt and Syria launched a surprise attack on Israel. The fighting followed decades of tension between Israel and its Arab neighbors, which had grown only worse upon the stunning Israeli victory in the Six Day War of 1967. In that conflict, the Israelis routed the Arabs, seizing the Golan Heights from Syria, the Sinai Peninsula from Egypt, and Jerusalem and the West Bank from Jordan. The Arabs ached for revenge, and in 1973 the Egyptians and Syrians attacked. Catching Israel off guard, they won early battles but eventually lost the initiative and were forced to give up the ground they had recovered. The Israelis would have delivered another devastating defeat to the Arabs if not for the diplomatic intervention of Nixon and Kissinger, who, despite America's previous strong support for Israel, believed a decisive Israeli victory would destabilize the Middle East even more.

The American diplomatic triumph, however, was offset by an unforeseen consequence of the October War (also called the Yom Kippur War, as it started on the Jewish holy day). On October 17, the Arab members of the Organization of Petroleum Exporting Countries (OPEC) announced a 5 percent cut in oil production, and vowed additional cuts of 5 percent each month until Israel surrendered the lands it had taken in 1967. Three days later, following Nixon's announcement of an emergency aid package for Israel, Saudi Arabia cut off oil shipments to the United States.

The Arab oil embargo had a disastrous impact on the American economy. With Arab producers cutting production by 25 percent from the September 1973 level, world supplies fell by 10 percent. For the United States, which imported one-third of its daily consumption, this meant a loss of nearly 2 million barrels a day. Long lines formed at gas stations as motorists who feared running out of fuel kept filling their tanks.

A dramatic increase in oil prices proved to be a far more significant result of the embargo. After the Arab embargo began, OPEC, led by the shah of Iran, raised crude oil prices fourfold. In the United States, gasoline prices at the pumps nearly doubled in a few weeks' time, while the cost of home heating fuel rose even more.

Nixon responded with a series of temporary measures, including pleas to Americans to turn down their thermostats in homes and offices and avoid driving simply for pleasure. When the Arab oil embargo ended in March, after Kissinger negotiated an Israeli pullback in the Sinai, the American public relaxed. Gasoline once again became plentiful, thermostats were raised, and people resumed their love affair with the automobile.

The energy crisis, however, did not end with the lifting of the embargo. The Arab action marked the beginning of a new era in American history. The United States, with only 6 percent of the world's population, had been responsible for nearly 40 percent of the world's energy consumption. In 1970, domestic oil production began to decline; the embargo served only to highlight the fact that the

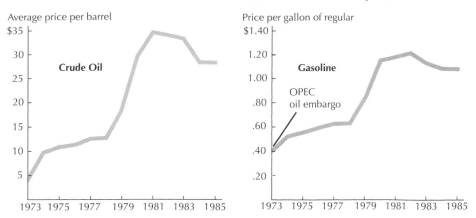

The Oil Shocks: Price Increases of Crude Oil and Gasoline, 1973–1985

nation was now dependent on other countries, notably those in the Persian Gulf, for its economic well-being. A nation that based its way of life on abundance and expansion suddenly was faced with the reality of limited resources and economic stagnation.

THE GREAT INFLATION

The price spike from the October War was merely the first of the oil shocks of the 1970s. Cheap energy had been a primary contributor to the relentless growth of the American economy after World War II. The GNP had more than doubled between 1950 and 1973; the American people had come to base their standard of living on oil prices that yielded gas at about 35 cents a gallon. Large cars, sprawling suburbs, detached houses heated by fuel oil and natural gas and cooled by central air-conditioning produced a dependence on inexpensive energy Americans took for granted.

The quadrupling of oil prices in 1973–1974 suddenly put all this at risk. Because oil or its equivalent in energy is required for the production and transportation of manufactured goods, the rising oil prices caused the prices of nearly everything else to increase as well. Most services require energy; their costs went up as well.

Other factors added to the trend of rising prices. The Vietnam War created federal budget deficits that grew from $63 billion for the entire decade of the 1960s to a total of $420 billion in the 1970s. A worldwide shortage of food, resulting from both rapid population increases and poor harvests around the globe in the mid-1970s, triggered a 20 percent rise in American food prices in 1973 alone. But above all else, the primary source of the great inflation of the 1970s was the sixfold increase in petroleum prices.

The impact on consumers was staggering. The price of an automobile jumped 72 percent between 1973 and 1978. During the decade, the price of a hamburger doubled, milk went from 28 to 59 cents a quart, and a loaf of bread rose from 24 to 89 cents. Corresponding wage increases failed to keep pace with inflation; in 1980, the real income of the average American family fell by 5.5 percent.

Often inflation signals economic exuberance, and rising prices indicate a rapid rate of growth. Not so with the inflation of the 1970s, which reflected economic weakness. The great inflation contributed to the worst recession in the United States since World War II. American GNP dropped by 6 percent in 1974, and unemployment rose to more than 9 percent, the highest level since the Great Depression of the 1930s.

President Gerald R. Ford, who followed Richard Nixon into the White House (see p. 830), responded belatedly to the economic crisis by proposing a tax cut to stimulate consumer spending. Congress passed a $23 billion reduction in taxes in early 1975, which led to a gradual recovery by 1976. The resulting budget deficits, however, helped keep inflation above 5 percent and prevented a return to full economic health.

Jimmy Carter of Georgia, who succeeded Ford (see p. 831), had little more success in reviving the economy. Continued federal deficits and relatively high interest rates kept the economy sluggish throughout 1977 and 1978. Then in 1979, the outbreak of the Iranian Revolution and the overthrow of the shah touched off another oil shock. The members of the OPEC cartel took advantage of the situation to double prices over the next eighteen months. A barrel of crude oil now cost more than $30. Gasoline prices climbed to more than $1 a gallon at American service stations, leading to an even greater wave of inflation than in 1973.

Finally, in late 1979, the Federal Reserve Board, led by Carter appointee Paul Volcker, began a sustained effort to halt inflation by mandating increased bank reserves to curtail the supply of money in circulation. The new tight-money policy served only to heighten inflation in the short run by driving interest rates up to record levels. By the spring of 1980, the prime interest rate reached 20 percent.

THE SHIFTING AMERICAN ECONOMY

Inflation and the oil shocks helped bring about significant changes in American business and industry in the 1970s. The most obvious result was the slowing of the rate of economic growth. More important, American industry began to lose its position of primacy in world markets. In 1959, U.S. firms had been the leaders in eleven of thirteen major industrial sectors, ranging from manufacturing to banking. By 1976, American companies led in only seven areas, and in all but one category—aerospace—U.S. corporations had declined in relation to Japanese and western European competitors.

The foreign competition did the greatest damage to the automobile industry. The oil shocks led to a consumer demand for small, efficient cars. German and Japanese automakers seized the opportunity to expand their once low volume of sales in the United States. By 1977, imported cars had captured nearly a fifth of the American market, with Japan leading the way. In response, Detroit spent $70 billion retooling to produce a new fleet of smaller, lighter front-wheel-drive cars; but American manufacturers barely survived the foreign invasion. Only government-backed loans helped the Chrysler Corporation stave off bankruptcy.

The decline in manufacturing led to significant shifts in the labor movement. The industrial unions such as the United Automobile Workers (UAW) lost members steadily in the 1960s and 1970s. At the same time, public employee unions enjoyed rapid growth and acceptance. The Great Society legislation, the baby boom with the resulting need for many more teachers, and the growth of social agencies on the state and local level opened up new jobs for social workers, teachers, and government employees. The rise of public employee unions also

Increasing imports of foreign cars, many of them smaller and more fuel-efficient than American-made autos, alarmed U.S. automobile manufacturers, who scrambled to produce lighter and more economical cars. Here, dockworkers unload imports at Baltimore's Dundalk Marine Terminal, the nation's largest entry port for foreign automobiles.

opened the way for greater participation by African Americans and women than in the older trade and industrial unions.

Just as public employee unions prospered from the shifts in the American economy in the 1970s, so did many American corporations. The multinationals that had emerged in the boom years of the 1960s continued to thrive. The growth of high-technology industries proved to be the most profitable new trend of the 1970s. Computer companies and electronics firms grew at a rapid rate, especially after the development of the silicon chip, a small, wafer-thin microprocessor capable of performing complex calculations almost instantly.

The result was a geographic shift of American industry from the East and Midwest to the Sunbelt. Electronics manufacturers flourished in California, Texas, and North Carolina, where they grew up around major universities. The absence of entrenched labor unions, the availability of skilled labor, and the warm and attractive climate of the southern and western states lured many new concerns to the Sunbelt. At the same time, the decline of the steel and auto industries was leading to massive unemployment and economic stagnation in the northern industrial heartland.

A NEW ENVIRONMENTALISM

The oil shocks had another effect: They injected new life into the environmental movement. The high price of gasoline made pocketbook conservationists of millions of Americans who hadn't thought twice about their country's heavy dependence on foreign oil; it also spurred Congress to press automakers to improve the fuel efficiency of the cars they built. The 1975 Energy Policy and Conservation Act set corporate standards for gas mileage; manufacturers who failed to achieve the mandated averages faced stiff fines and other sanctions. Between the high prices and the federal requirements, American drivers began squeezing more miles out of each tank of gas.

Environmentalists and consumers meanwhile began searching for alternative sources of energy. Solar power appealed to some as being clean and endlessly renewable. But it was also expensive (solar panels and related technologies remained underdeveloped) and intermittent (clouds cut off the power). Hydropower—electricity generated by falling water—was better proven and more reliable, but most of the suitable dam sites had already been built upon. Wind power worked in some areas (where the wind blew frequently and without obstruction), but those were precisely the areas where few people lived. Coal power was reliable, proven, and cheap, but it was also dirty (the gases emitted by coal plants fouled the air) and dangerous (to the men and women who mined the coal).

Nuclear power had its advocates. It had been in use in America since the 1950s, and its characteristics were well known. Its fuel—uranium—was essentially inexhaustible, and nuclear reactors, in normal operations, produced no noxious gases. Nor did they produce any "greenhouse gases"—carbon dioxide and other heating-trapping gases—that contribute to global warming, a rise in average temperatures that was just beginning to worry some earth scientists (and would worry them much more in coming decades).

But nuclear power made many environmentalists nervous. The waste products of the reactors were radioactive, and would remain so for thousands of years. Guaranteeing that the wastes not contaminate water supplies—for fifty generations into the future—was a daunting challenge. And occasionally nuclear reactors malfunctioned in terrifying ways. In March 1979, a reactor at Three Mile Island, near Harrisburg, Pennsylvania, nearly melted down when cooling systems failed. Tens of thousands of people living in the vicinity fled, and though the reactor didn't explode, as authorities had feared it might, the close call inspired grave second thoughts about nuclear power. A more severe accident in 1986 at Chernobyl, in the Soviet Ukraine, which released large amounts of radiation into the atmosphere and caused many deaths, reinforced the fears.

PRIVATE LIVES, PUBLIC ISSUES

Sweeping changes in the private lives of the American people began in the 1970s and continued for the rest of the century. The traditional American family, with the husband as wage earner and the wife as homemaker, gave way to much more diverse living arrangements. The number of working women, including wives and mothers, increased sharply; the wage gap between the sexes narrowed, but women still lagged noticeably behind men in earnings. Then, in the years following 1970 came the emergence of an active gay rights movement as more and more gay, lesbian, and bisexual Americans began to disclose their sexual identities and demand an end to discrimination.

THE CHANGING AMERICAN FAMILY

Family life underwent a number of significant shifts after 1970. The most notable was a decline in the number of families with two parents and one or more children under 18. By the end of the 1980s, in only one two-parent family out of five was the mother solely engaged in child rearing. A few fathers stayed at home with the children, but in the great majority of these families, both parents worked outside the home.

The traditional nuclear family of the 1950s no longer prevailed in America by the end of the twentieth century. The number of married couple households with children dropped from 30 percent in the 1970s to 23 percent by 2000. The number of unmarried couples doubled in the 1990s, while adults living alone surpassed the number of married couples with children for the first time in American history.

The divorce rate, which doubled between the mid-1960s and the late 1970s, leveled off for the rest of the century. Nevertheless, half of all first marriages still ended in divorce. After a sharp fall in the 1970s, the birthrate climbed again as the baby boom generation began to mature. There was a marked increase in the number of births to women over age 30, as well as a very high proportion of children born to single mothers.

For better or worse, the American family structure changed significantly in the last three decades of the twentieth century, with a large number of people either never marrying or postponing marriage until late in the childbearing period. The traditional family unit, with the working father and the mother rearing the children at home, rapidly declined. Women without partners headed more than one-third of all impoverished families, and children made up 40 percent of the nation's poor.

GAINS AND SETBACKS FOR WOMEN

American women experienced significant changes in their way of life and their place in society in the last quarter of the twentieth century. The prevailing theme concerned the increasing percentage of working women. There was a rapid movement of women into the labor force in the 1970s; six million more married women held jobs by the end of the decade as two incomes became increasingly necessary to keep up with inflation. The trend continued through the 1980s. Fully 61 percent of the nearly nineteen million new jobs created during the decade were filled by women; many of these new jobs, however, were entry-level or low-paying service positions.

Women scored some impressive breakthroughs. They began to enter corporation boardrooms, became presidents of major universities, and were admitted to the nation's military academies. Women entered blue-collar, professional, and small-business fields traditionally dominated by men. Ronald Reagan's appointment of Sandra Day O'Connor to the Supreme Court in 1981 marked a historic first; Bill Clinton doubled the number of women on the Court with his selection of Ruth Bader Ginsburg.

Yet at the same time, women encountered a great deal of resistance. Most women continued to work in female-dominated fields—as nurses, secretaries, teachers, and waitresses. Those who entered such "male" areas as management and administration soon encountered the so-called glass ceiling, which kept them from advancing beyond mid-level executive status. The economic boom of the 1990s, however, led to a steady increase in the number of women executives; in 1998, there was an increase of 514,000.

Even with these gains, however, by 2002 women's wages still averaged only 77.5 percent of men's earnings. Older women, who often had no other source of support, fared poorly; those over the age of 50 earned only 64 percent as much as men their age. Feminists had once hoped to close the gender gap by the year 2000, but experts predicted women would not reach pay equity with men until 2018.

Beyond equal pay and greater economic opportunity, the women's movement had two goals. The first was ratification of the Equal Rights Amendment (ERA). Approved by Congress in 1972, the ERA stated simply, "Equality of rights under the law shall not be denied or abridged by the United States or any state on account of sex." Within a year, twenty-two states had approved the amendment, but the efforts gradually faltered just three states short of ratification. The opposition came in part from working-class women who feared, as one union leader explained, that those employed as "maids, laundry workers, hospital cleaners, or dishwashers" would lose the protection of state laws that regulated wages and hours of work for women. Right-wing activist Phyllis Schlafly

Voting on the Equal Rights Amendment
By the end of 1974, thirty-four states had ratified the ERA; Indiana finally approved the amendment in 1977, but the remaining fifteen states held out, leaving ratification three states short of the required three-fourths majority.

led an organized effort to defeat the ERA, claiming the amendment would lead to unisex toilets, homosexual marriages, and the drafting of women. The National Organization of Women (NOW) fought back, persuading Congress to extend the time for ratification by three years and waging intense campaigns for approval in Florida and Illinois. But the deadline for ratification finally passed on June 30, 1982, with the ERA forces still three states short.

The women's movement focused even more of its energies on protecting the major victory it had won in 1973 in the case of *Roe* v. *Wade,* which affirmed women's right to abortions. "Right-to-life" groups, consisting mainly of ortho- dox Catholics, fundamentalist Protestants, and conservatives, fought back. In 1978, with strong support from President Carter, Congress passed the Hyde amendment, which denied the use of federal funds to pay for abortions for poor women. Nevertheless, prochoice groups organized privately funded family plan- ning agencies and abortion clinics to give more women a chance to exercise their constitutional right to abortion.

As Presidents Reagan and Bush appointed more conservative judges to the Court, however, prochoice groups began to fear the future overturn of *Roe* v. *Wade.* The Court avoided a direct challenge, contenting itself with lesser actions that upheld the rights of states to regulate abortion clinics, impose a 24-hour waiting period, and require the approval of one parent or a judge before a minor could have an abortion. Even the exercise of the right to abortion proved diffi- cult and sometimes dangerous in view of the often violent protests of prolife groups outside abortion clinics. For many women, abortion was a hard-won right they still had to struggle to protect.

THE GAY LIBERATION MOVEMENT

On the night of June 27, 1969, a squad of New York policemen raided the Stonewall Inn, a Greenwich Village bar frequented by "drag queens" and les- bians. As the patrons were being herded into vans, a crowd of gay onlookers be- gan to jeer and taunt the police. A riot quickly broke out. The next night, more than four hundred police officers battled two thousand gay demonstrators through the streets of Greenwich Village. The two-day Stonewall Riots marked the beginning of the modern gay liberation movement. Refusing to play the role of victims any longer, gays and lesbians decided to affirm their sexual orientation and demand an end to discrimination against them.

Within a few days, two new organizations were formed in New York: the Gay Liberation Front and the Gay Activist Alliance, with branches and offshoots quickly appearing in cities across the country. The basic theme of gay liberation was to urge all gays and lesbians to "come out of the closet" and affirm with pride their sexual identity.

In the course of the 1970s, hundreds of thousands of gays and lesbians re- sponded to this call. They formed more than a thousand local clubs and organi- zations and won a series of notable victories. In 1974, the American Psychiatric Association stopped classifying homosexuality as a mental disorder, and by the end of the decade, half the states had repealed their sodomy statutes. Gays fought hard in cities and states for laws forbidding discrimination against homosexuals in housing and employment, and in 1980, they finally succeeded in getting a gay rights plank in the Democratic National Platform.

In the 1980s, the onset of the AIDS (acquired immune deficiency syndrome) epidemic (see p. 829) forced the gay liberation movement onto the defensive. Amid accusations that AIDS was a "gay disease"—it was first noticed in the United States among gay men—male homosexuals faced new public condemnation at a time when they were trying desperately to care for the growing number of victims of the disease within their ranks. The gay organizations formed in the 1970s to win new rights now were channeling their energies into caring for the ill, promoting safe sex practices, and fighting for more public funding to help conquer AIDS.

The movement also continued to stimulate gay consciousness in the 1980s. In 1987, an estimated 600,000 gays and lesbians took part in a march on Washington on behalf of gay rights. Every year afterward, gay groups held a National Coming Out Day in October to encourage homosexuals to proclaim proudly their sexual identity. In a more controversial move, some gay leaders encouraged "outing"—releasing the names of prominent homosexuals, primarily politicians and movie stars, in an effort to make the nation aware of how many Americans were gay or lesbian. Gay leaders claimed there were more than twenty million gays and lesbians in the nation, an estimate viewed as too high by sociologists. Whatever the actual number, it was clear by the 1990s that gays and lesbians formed a significant minority that had succeeded in forcing the nation, however grudgingly, to respect its rights.

There was one battle, however, in which victory eluded the gay liberation movement. In the 1992 election, gays and lesbians strongly backed Democratic candidate Bill Clinton, who promised, if elected, to end the ban on homosexuals in the military. In his first days in office, however, President Clinton stirred up great resistance in the Pentagon and Congress when he tried to issue an executive order forbidding such discrimination. The Joint Chiefs of Staff and many Democrats, led by Georgia Senator Sam Nunn, warned that acceptance of gays and lesbians would destroy morale and seriously weaken the armed forces. Clinton finally settled for the Pentagon's compromise "Don't ask, don't tell" policy that would permit homosexuals to continue serving in the military as they had in the past as long as they did not reveal their sexual preference and refrained from homosexual conduct. However disappointed gays and lesbians were in Clinton's retreat, their leaders understood that the real problem was the resistance of mainstream America to full acceptance of homosexuality.

Public attitudes toward gays and lesbians seemed to be changing in the 1990s, but the growing tolerance had definite limits. In a 1996 poll, 85 percent of those questioned believed that gays should be treated equally in the workplace, up from 76 percent in 1992. Violence against gays, however, continued, most notably in the 1998 fatal beating of Matthew Shepard, a 21-year-old gay college student, in Wyoming. The brutal attack spurred calls for hate-crime legislation and the judge in the case, banning a so-called gay-panic defense, sentenced Shepard's assailant to two consecutive terms of life imprisonment.

The issue of same-sex marriage came to a head at the end of the century. In 1996, President Clinton signed the Defense of Marriage Act, which decreed that states did not have to recognize same-sex marriages performed elsewhere. But in 2000, following a state supreme court ruling, the Vermont legislature legalized "civil unions" between individuals of the same sex, enabling gays and lesbians to receive all the legal benefits available to married couples. Whether sanctioned by law or not, the number of gay and lesbian households steadily increased; the 2000 census revealed that there were nearly 600,000 homes in America headed by same-sex couples.

THE AIDS EPIDEMIC

The outbreak of AIDS (acquired immune deficiency syndrome) in the early 1980s took most Americans by surprise. Even health experts had difficulty grasping the nature and extent of the new public health threat. The Centers for Disease Control noted the phenomenon in a June 1981 bulletin, but it was several years before researchers finally identified it as a hitherto unknown human immuno-deficiency virus (HIV). HIV apparently originated in Central Africa and spread to the United States, where it found its first victims primarily among gay men.

Initially, AIDS was perceived as a threat only to gay men. With a growing sense of urgency as the death toll mounted, gay men began to practice safer sex, using condoms and confining themselves to trusted partners. It soon became clear, however, that AIDS could not be so easily contained. It began to appear among intravenous (IV) drug users who shared the same needles and eventually among hemophiliacs and others receiving frequent blood transfusions. The threat of a contaminated national blood supply terrified middle-class America. Scientists tried to reassure the public by explaining that the virus could be spread only by the exchange of bodily fluids, primarily blood and semen, and not by casual contact. The integrity of hospital blood supplies caused the most realistic concern; in 1985, a new test gave reassurance that transfusions could be performed safely.

The Reagan administration proved slow and halting in its approach to the AIDS epidemic. The lack of sympathy for gays and a need to reduce the deficit worked against any large increase in health spending; what little money was devoted to AIDS went almost entirely for research rather than for educational measures to slow its spread. But growing public concern finally led to action. After a special commission report in 1988 criticized the administration's AIDS efforts and recommended a new effort that included antidiscrimination legislation and explicit prevention education, Congress voted to spend $1.3 billion to fight AIDS.

Despite the new efforts, the epidemic continued to grow. The U.S. Centers for Disease Control in Atlanta reported more than 200,000 cases at the end of 1991; the total had increased to more than 500,000 by mid-1996. By then, 345,000 AIDS victims had died, making it the leading cause of death for Americans aged 25 to 44.

The most encouraging development was a drop in the death rate from AIDS that began in the mid-1990s. Health officials attributed the decline to heavier spending on treatment and prevention and, above all, to powerful new drug combinations. By 2001, however, the drop in new cases and deaths from AIDS began to level off. "The latest data," commented one expert in August 2001, "suggest that the era of dramatic declines is now over." There was a particularly alarming increase in the number of new cases among young gay men, who apparently believed that the new treatment had made the disease manageable. And even more disturbing was the growing realization that AIDS was threatening to decimate the population of Third World countries, especially in sub-Saharan Africa.

POLITICS AND DIPLOMACY AFTER WATERGATE

The economic and social disruptions of the era contributed to problems of governance left over from Watergate. Even as many Americans worried about shrinking paychecks and disintegrating families, Congress increasingly challenged the prerogatives of the presidency. This made life in the White House difficult for Richard Nixon's immediate successors—and it made solving America's pressing problems nearly impossible.

THE FORD ADMINISTRATION

Gerald R. Ford had the distinction of being the first president who had not been elected to national office. Richard Nixon had appointed him to the vice presidency to succeed Spiro Agnew, who had been forced to resign in order to avoid prosecution for accepting bribes while he was governor of Maryland. Ford, an amiable and unpretentious Michigan congressman who had risen to the post of House minority leader, seemed ready to restore public confidence in the presidency when he replaced Nixon in August 1974.

Ford's honeymoon lasted only a month. On September 8, 1974, he shocked the nation by announcing he had granted Richard Nixon a full and unconditional pardon for all federal crimes he may have committed. Some critics charged darkly that Nixon and Ford had made a secret bargain; others pointed out how unfair it was for Nixon's aides to serve their prison terms while the chief criminal went free. Ford apparently acted in an effort to end the bitterness over Watergate, but his attempt backfired, eroding public confidence in his leadership and linking him indelibly with the scandal.

Ford soon found himself fighting an equally difficult battle on behalf of the beleaguered CIA. The Watergate scandal and the Vietnam fiasco had eroded public confidence in the government and lent credibility to a startling series of disclosures about past covert actions. The president allowed the CIA to confirm some of the charges, and then he made things worse by blurting out to the press the juiciest item of all: The CIA had been involved in plots to assassinate foreign leaders. Senate and House select committees appointed to investigate the CIA now focused on the assassination issue, eventually charging that the agency had been involved in no less than eight separate attempts to kill Fidel Castro.

In late 1975, President Ford finally moved to limit the damage to the CIA. He appointed George H. W. Bush, then a respected former Republican congressman, as the agency's new director and gave him the authority both to reform the CIA and to strengthen its role in shaping national security policy. Most notably, Ford issued an executive order outlawing assassination as an instrument of American foreign policy. To prevent future abuses, Congress created permanent House and Senate intelligence committees to exercise general oversight for covert CIA operations.

Ford proved less successful in his dealings with Congress on other issues. Although he prided himself on his good relations with members of both houses, he opposed Democratic measures such as federal aid to education and control over strip mining. In a little more than a year, he vetoed thirty-nine separate bills. In fact, Ford, who as a congressman had opposed virtually every Great Society measure, proved far more conservative than Nixon in the White House.

CARTER AND AMERICAN MALAISE

Ford's lackluster record and the legacy of Watergate made the Democratic nomination a prize worth fighting for in 1976. A large field of candidates entered the contest, but a virtual unknown, former Georgia governor James Earl Carter, quickly became the front-runner. Aware of the voters' disgust with politicians of both parties, Jimmy Carter ran as an outsider, portraying himself as a Southerner who had no experience in Washington and one who could thus give the nation fresh and untainted leadership. On television, the basic Carter commercial showed him at his Georgia peanut farm, dressed in blue jeans, looking directly into the camera and saying, "I'll never tell a lie."

Voters took Carter at his word, and elected him over Ford in a close contest. Unfortunately, Carter's outsider status, while attractive in a campaign, made governing as president difficult. He had no discernible political philosophy, no clear sense of direction. He called himself a populist, but that label meant little more than an appeal to the common man, a somewhat ironic appeal, given Carter's personal wealth.

Lacking both a clear set of priorities and a coherent political philosophy, the Carter administration had little chance to succeed. The president strove hard for a balanced budget but was forced to accept mounting deficits. Federal agencies fought to save the environment and help consumers but served only to anger industry.

THE ELECTION OF 1976

CANDIDATE	PARTY	POPULAR VOTE	ELECTORAL VOTE
Carter	Democratic	40,828,587	297
Ford	Republican	39,147,613	241

In the crucial area of social services, Joseph Califano, secretary of Health, Education, and Welfare (HEW), failed repeatedly in efforts to carry out long-overdue reforms. His attempts to overhaul the nation's welfare program, which had become a $30 billion annual operation serving some thirty million Americans, won little support from the White House. Carter's unwillingness to take the political risks involved in revamping the overburdened Social Security system by reducing benefits and raising the retirement age blocked Califano's efforts.

Informed by his pollsters in 1979 that he was losing the nation's confidence, Carter sought desperately to redeem himself. After a series of meetings at Camp David with a wide variety of advisers, he gave a speech in which he seemed to blame his failure on the American people, accusing them of creating "a crisis of confidence . . . that strikes at the very heart and soul and spirit of our national will." Then, a week after what his critics termed the "national malaise" speech, he requested the resignation of Califano and the secretary of the treasury. But neither the attempt to pin responsibility on the American people nor the firing of cabinet members could hide the fact that Carter, despite his good intentions and hard work, had failed to provide the bold leadership the nation needed.

TROUBLES ABROAD

In the aftermath of the Vietnam War, most Americans wanted to have little to do with the world. Military intervention had failed in Southeast Asia, and with the American economy in trouble, the country's economic leverage appeared minimal. Moreover, the point of détente was to diminish the need for American intervention abroad by directing the superpower contest with the Soviet Union into political channels.

Yet various groups in the Third World didn't get the message of détente. Central America, for example, witnessed numerous uprisings against entrenched authoritarian regimes. In mid-1979, dictator Anastasio Somoza capitulated to the Sandinista forces in Nicaragua. Despite American attempts to moderate the Sandinista revolution, the new regime moved steadily to the left, developing close ties with Castro's Cuba. In neighboring El Salvador, a growing leftist insurgency against a repressive regime put the United States in an awkward position. Unable to find a workable alternative between the extremes of reactionary dictatorship and radical revolution in Central America, Carter tried to use American economic aid to encourage the military junta in El Salvador to carry out democratic reforms. But after the guerrillas launched a major offensive in January 1981, he authorized large-scale military assistance to the government for its war against the insurgents, setting a precedent for the future.

Carter initially had better luck in the Middle East. In 1978 he invited Egyptian president Anwar Sadat and Israeli prime minister Menachem Begin to negotiate a peace treaty under his guidance at Camp David. For thirteen days, Carter met with Sadat and Begin, finally emerging with the Camp David accords. A framework for negotiations rather than an actual peace settlement, the Camp David accords nonetheless paved the way for a 1979 treaty between these princi-

A *highlight of Carter's presidency was his role in helping negotiate the Camp David accords between Israeli Prime Minister Menachem Begin (right) and Egyptian President Anwar Sadat (left). The agreements set the stage for a peace treaty between Israel and Egypt.*

pal antagonists in the Arab-Israeli conflict. The treaty provided for the gradual return of the Sinai to Egypt but left the fate of the Palestinians, the Arab inhabitants of the West Bank and the Gaza Strip, unsettled.

Any sense of progress in the Middle East was quickly offset in 1979 with the outbreak of the Iranian Revolution. Under Nixon and Kissinger, the United States had come to depend heavily on the shah for defense of the vital Persian Gulf. Carter continued the close relationship with the shah, despite growing signs of domestic discontent with his leadership. By 1978, Iran was in chaos as the exiled Ayatollah Ruholla Khomeini led a fundamentalist Muslim revolt against the shah, who was forced to flee the country.

In October 1979, Carter permitted the shah to enter the United States for medical treatment. Irate mobs in Iran denounced the United States, and on November 4, militants seized the U.S. embassy in Tehran and took fifty-three Americans prisoner. The prolonged Iranian hostage crisis revealed the extent to which American power had declined in the 1970s. Carter relied first on diplomacy and economic reprisals in a vain attempt to free the hostages. In April 1980, the president authorized a desperate rescue mission that ended in failure when several helicopters broke down in the Iranian desert and an accident cost the lives of eight crewmen. The hostage crisis dragged on through the summer

Blindfolded American hostages stand among their Iranian captors after Iranian militants captured the American embassy in Tehran on November 4, 1979. The Iranians' capture of fifty-three Americans as hostages and their violent attacks on the embassy shocked U.S. citizens. The hostage crisis dragged on for the rest of Carter's administration; the hostages were not released until January 1981.

and fall of 1980, a symbol of American weakness that proved to be a powerful political handicap to Carter in the upcoming presidential election.

THE COLLAPSE OF DÉTENTE

The policy of détente was already in trouble when Carter took office in 1977. Congressional refusal to relax trade restrictions on the Soviet Union had doomed Kissinger's attempts to win political concessions from the Soviets through economic incentives. The Kremlin's repression of the growing dissident movement and its harsh policy restricting the emigration of Soviet Jews had caused many Americans to doubt the wisdom of seeking accommodation with the Soviet Union.

President Carter's emphasis on human rights appeared to the Russians to be a direct repudiation of détente. In his inaugural address, Carter reaffirmed his concern over the mistreatment of human beings anywhere in the world, declaring that "our commitment to human rights must be absolute." The Soviets found these words to be threatening, particularly after Carter received Soviet exiles in the White House.

Zbigniew Brzezinski, Carter's national security adviser, worked from the outset to reverse the policy of détente, favoring confrontation with the Kremlin. Brzezinski was successful in persuading the president to use China to outmaneuver the Soviets. On January 1, 1979, the United States and China exchanged ambassadors, thereby completing the reconciliation that Nixon had begun in 1971. The new relationship between Beijing and Washington presented the Soviet Union with the problem of a link between its two most powerful enemies.

The Cold War, in abeyance for nearly a decade, resumed with full fury in December 1979 when the Soviet Union invaded Afghanistan. Although this move was designed to ensure a regime friendly to the Soviet Union, it appeared to many the beginning of a Soviet thrust toward the Indian Ocean and the Persian Gulf. Carter responded to this aggression by declaring a Carter Doctrine threatening armed opposition to any further Soviet advance toward the Gulf. The president banned the sale of high technology to Russia, embargoed the export of grain, resumed draft registration, and even boycotted the 1980 Moscow Olympics.

The Soviet action and the American reaction doomed détente. Carter had signed a SALT II treaty with Russia in 1979, lowering the ceiling on nuclear delivery systems to 2250, but he now withdrew it from the Senate, aware that he could not get the necessary two-thirds vote of approval. The hopeful phrases of détente gave way to belligerent rhetoric as groups such as the Committee on the Present Danger called for an all-out effort against the Soviet Union. Jimmy Carter, who had come into office hoping to advance human rights and control the nuclear arms race, now found himself a victim of a renewed Cold War.

THE REAGAN REVOLUTION

After the turmoil of the 1960s, the economic and political troubles of the 1970s made Americans' turn to conservatism almost inevitable. The Watergate scandal won the Democrats a brief reprieve, but when the Republicans discovered an attractive candidate in Ronald Reagan, a decisive Republican victory was essentially assured.

THE ELECTION OF 1980

In 1980, Jimmy Carter, who had used the Watergate trauma to win the presidency, found himself in serious trouble. Inflation, touched off by the second oil shock of the 1970s, reached double-digit figures. The Federal Reserve Board's effort to tighten the money supply had led to a recession, with unemployment climbing to nearly 8 percent by July 1980. What Ronald Reagan dubbed the "misery index," the combined rate of inflation and unemployment, hit 28 percent early in 1980 and stayed above 20 percent throughout the year.

Foreign policy proved almost as damaging to Carter. The Soviet invasion of Afghanistan had exploded hopes for continued détente and made Carter appear naive. The continuing hostage crisis in Iran underlined the administration's helplessness.

Ronald Reagan and his running mate, George H. W. Bush, hammered away at the state of the economy and the world. Reagan scored heavily among traditionally Democratic blue-collar groups by blaming Carter for inflation, which robbed workers of any gain in real wages. Reagan also accused Carter of allowing the Soviets to outstrip the United States militarily and promised a massive buildup of American forces if he was elected. Carter's position was further hurt by the independent candidacy of liberal Republican John Anderson of Illinois, who appealed to voters disenchanted with Carter but not yet ready to embrace Reagan.

The president fought back by claiming that Reagan was too reckless to conduct American foreign policy in the nuclear age. Charging that the election

Republican presidential candidate Ronald Reagan greets supporters in Cincinnati during his 1980 campaign. Reagan won the election, carrying all but six states.

would decide "whether we have peace or war," Carter tried to portray his Republican challenger as a warmonger. Reagan deflected the charge and summarized the case against the administration by putting a simple question to voters: "Are you better off now than you were four years ago?"

Voters answered with a resounding "no." Reagan carried forty-four states and gained 51 percent of the popular vote. Carter won only six states and 41 percent of the popular vote, while John Anderson received the remaining 8 percent but failed to carry a single state. Reagan clearly benefited from the growing political power of the Sunbelt; he carried every state west of the Mississippi except Minnesota, the home state of Carter's running mate, Walter Mondale. In the South, Reagan lost only Georgia, Carter's home state. Even more impressive were Reagan's inroads into the old New Deal coalition. He received 50.5 percent of the blue-collar vote and 46 percent of the Jewish vote, the best showing by a Republican since 1928. Only one group remained loyal to Carter: African American voters gave him 85 percent of their ballots.

THE ELECTION OF 1980

CANDIDATE	PARTY	POPULAR VOTE	ELECTORAL VOTE
Reagan	Republican	43,901,812	489
Carter	Democratic	35,483,820	49
Anderson	Independent	5,719,437	—
	Minor Parties	921,188	—

Republican gains in Congress were even more surprising. For the first time since 1954, the GOP gained control of the Senate, 53 to 46, and the party picked up 33 seats in the House to narrow the Democratic margin from 114 to 50.

Though the full implications of the 1980 election remained to be seen, the outcome suggested that the Democratic coalition that had dominated American politics since the days of Franklin Roosevelt was falling apart. In the eight presidential elections from 1952 to 1980, Republican candidates received 52.3 percent of the popular vote, compared with 47.7 percent for the Democrats. Reagan's victory in 1980 thus marked the culmination of a Republican presidential realignment that ended a half-century of Democratic dominance.

Cutting Taxes and Spending

When Ronald Reagan took office in January 1981, the ravages of inflation had devastated the economy. Interest rates hovered near 20 percent, while the value of the dollar, compared to 1960, had dropped to just 36 cents. The new president blamed what he termed "the worst economic mess since the Great Depression" on high federal spending and excessive taxation. "Government is not the solution to our problems," Reagan announced in his inaugural address. "Government is the problem."

The president embraced the concept of supply-side economics as the remedy for the nation's economic ills. Supply-side economists believed that the private sector, if encouraged by tax cuts, would shift its resources from tax shelters to productive investment, leading to an economic boom that would provide enough new income to offset the lost revenue. Although many economists worried that the 30 percent cut in income taxes that Reagan favored would lead to large deficits, the president was confident that his program would both stimulate the economy and reduce the role of government.

The president made federal spending his first target. Quickly deciding not to attack such popular middle-class entitlement programs as Social Security and Medicare, and sparing critical social services for the "truly deserving needy," the so-called safety net, the Republicans concentrated on slashing $41 billion from the budget by cutting heavily into other social services such as food stamps and by reducing public service jobs, student loans, and support for urban mass transit. Reagan used his charm and powers of persuasion to woo conservative Democrats from the West and South. Appearing before a joint session of Congress only weeks after the attempt on his life, Reagan won a commanding 253 to 176 margin of victory for his budget in the House, and an even more lopsided vote of 78 to 20 in the Senate in May. A jubilant Reagan told a Los Angeles audience that he had achieved "the greatest reduction in government spending that has ever been attempted."

The president proved equally successful in trimming taxes. He initially advocated annual cuts of 10 percent in personal income taxes for three consecutive years. When the Democrats countered with a two-year plan that would reduce taxes by only 15 percent, Reagan compromised with a proposal to cut taxes by

5 percent the first year but insisted on the full 10 percent reduction for the second and third years. In July, both houses passed the tax cut by impressive margins.

In securing reductions in spending and lowering taxes, Reagan demonstrated beyond doubt his ability to wield presidential power effectively. As *Time* magazine commented, no president since FDR had "done so much of such magnitude so quickly to change the economic direction of the country."

UNLEASHING THE PRIVATE SECTOR

Reagan met with only mixed success in his other efforts to restrict government activity and reduce federal regulation of the economy. Cutting back on the scope of federal agencies and limiting their impact on American business was a central tenet of the president's political philosophy. To achieve his goal of deregulation he appointed men and women who shared his belief in relying on the marketplace rather than the bureaucracy to direct the nation's economy. To the outrage of environmentalists, Secretary of the Interior James Watt opened up federal land

The Professional Air Traffic Controllers' Organization (PATCO) was one of the few unions to support Reagan in the 1980 campaign. But when PATCO struck in August 1981, Reagan unhesitatingly fired the striking air traffic controllers and refused to rehire them when the strike collapsed.

to coal and timber production, halted the growth of national parkland, and made more than a billion acres available for offshore oil drilling. Though Watt was eventually forced to resign, the Reagan administration continued its policy of reducing government intervention in business long after Watt's departure.

Transportation Secretary Drew Lewis proved to be the most effective cabinet member in the administration's first two years. He helped relieve the troubled American automobile industry of many of the regulations adopted in the 1970s to reduce air pollution and increase passenger safety. At the same time, he played a key role in the behind-the-scenes negotiations that led Japan to agree in the spring of 1981 to restrict its automobile exports to the United States for the next three years. This unilateral Japanese action enabled the Reagan administration to help Detroit's carmakers without openly violating its free market position by endorsing protectionist measures.

Lewis gained notoriety in opposing a strike by the air traffic controllers' union (PATCO) in the summer of 1981. The president fired the striking workers, decertified the union, and ordered Lewis to hire and train thousands of new air traffic controllers at a cost of $1.3 billion. For the Reagan administration, the price was worth paying to prove that no group of government employees had the right to defy the public interest.

The Reagan administration was less successful in trying to cut back on the entitlement programs that it viewed as the primary cause of the growing budget deficits. Social Security was the greatest offender. A 500 percent increase in Social Security benefits in the 1970s threatened to bankrupt the system's trust fund by the end of the century. Reagan, overconfident from his budget victory, met a sharp rebuff when he tried to make substantial cuts in future benefits. The president then appointed a bipartisan commission to recommend ways to protect the system's endangered trust fund. In March 1983, Congress approved a series of changes that guaranteed the solvency of Social Security by gradually raising the retirement age, delaying cost-of-living increases for six months, and taxing pensions paid to the well-to-do elderly.

The administration's record in dealing with women's concerns and civil rights proved clumsy and divisive. Although feminist groups were disappointed by the administration's strong rhetorical attacks on legalized abortion, the appointment of Sandra Day O'Connor to the Supreme Court pleased them. His appointments to the lower federal courts were a better indication of his administration's relatively low regard for

Chief Justice Warren Burger swears in Sandra Day O'Connor, the first woman to serve on the U.S. Supreme Court, in September 1981.

women. Of the first seventy-two Reagan nominees to the federal judiciary, only three were women; just one of the sixty-nine men was African American.

The administration's civil rights record proved especially revealing. Aware of how few African Americans had supported the GOP in 1980, Reagan made no effort to reward this group with government jobs or favors. Instead, the Justice Department actively opposed busing to achieve school integration and affirmative action measures that resulted in minority hiring quotas.

REAGAN AND THE WORLD

Reagan was determined to reverse the course of American policy abroad no less than at home. He believed that under Carter, American prestige and standing in the world had dropped to an all-time low. Intent on restoring traditional American pride and influence, Reagan devoted himself to strengthening America's defenses and recapturing world supremacy from the Soviet Union.

CHALLENGING THE "EVIL EMPIRE"

The president scored his first foreign policy victory on the day he took office, thanks to diplomatic efforts begun under Carter. On January 20, 1981, Iran released the fifty-three Americans held hostage and thus enabled Reagan to begin his presidency on a positive note.

He built upon this accomplishment by embarking on a major military expansion. Here again he continued efforts begun by Carter, who after the Soviet invasion of Afghanistan had persuaded Congress to fund a 5 percent increase in defense spending. The Reagan expansion went far beyond Carter's. Secretary of Defense Caspar Weinberger proposed a plan that would more than double defense spending. The emphasis was on new weapons, ranging from the B-1 bomber and the controversial MX nuclear missile to the expansion of the navy from 456 to 600 ships. Despite some opposition in Congress, Reagan and Weinberger got most of what they wanted, and by 1985 the defense budget grew to more than $300 billion.

The justification for all the new weapons was Reagan's belief that the Soviet Union was a deadly enemy that threatened the well-being and security of the United States. Reagan saw the Russians as bent on world revolution, ready "to commit any crime, to lie, to cheat" to advance their cause.

Given this view of Russia as "the focus of evil in the modern world," it is not surprising that the new president continued the hard line that Carter had adopted after the invasion of Afghanistan. Abandoning détente, Reagan proceeded to implement a 1979 decision to place 572 Pershing II and cruise missiles in western Europe within range of Moscow and other Russian population centers to match Soviet deployment of medium-range missiles aimed at NATO countries. Despite strong protests from the Soviet Union, as well as growing uneasiness in Europe and an increasingly vocal nuclear freeze movement at home, the United States began putting the weapons in bases in Great Britain and Germany in November

1983. The Soviets, claiming the move gave them only ten minutes of warning time in case of an American attack, responded by breaking off disarmament negotiations in Geneva.

The nuclear arms race had now reached a more dangerous level than ever before. The United States stepped up research and development of the Strategic Defense Initiative (SDI), an antimissile system based on the use of lasers and particle beams to destroy incoming missiles in outer space. SDI was quickly dubbed "star wars" by the media. Critics doubted that SDI could be perfected, but they warned that even if it were, the result would be to escalate the arms race by forcing the Russians to build more offensive missiles in order to overcome the American defense system. The Reagan administration, however, defended SDI as a legitimate attempt to free the United States from the deadly trap of deterrence, with its reliance on the threat of nuclear retaliation to keep the peace.

CONFRONTATION IN CENTRAL AMERICA

Reagan perceived the Soviet challenge as extending across the globe. In Central America, an area marked by great extremes of wealth, with a small landowning elite and masses of peasants mired in poverty, the United States had traditionally looked for moderate middle-class regimes to support. But these were hard to find, and Washington often ended up backing repressive right-wing dictatorships rather than the leftist groups that raised the radical issues of land reform and redistribution of wealth. Yet it was often oppression by U.S.-supported regimes that drove those seeking political change to embrace revolutionary tactics.

This is what happened in Nicaragua, where the leftist Sandinista coalition finally succeeded in overthrowing the authoritarian Somoza regime in 1979. In an effort to strengthen the many middle-class elements in the original Sandinista government and to avoid forcing Nicaragua into the Cuban and Soviet orbit, Carter extended American economic aid.

The Reagan administration quickly reversed this policy. Secretary of State Alexander Haig cut off aid to Nicaragua in the spring of 1981, accusing the Sandinistas of driving out the moderates, welcoming Cuban advisers and Soviet military assistance, and serving as a supply base for leftist guerrillas in nearby El Salvador. The criticism became a self-fulfilling prophecy as Nicaragua became even more dependent on Cuba and the Soviet Union.

The United States and Nicaragua were soon on a collision course. In April 1983, Reagan asked Congress for the money and authority to oust the Sandinistas. When Congress, fearful of repeating the Vietnam fiasco, refused, Reagan opted for covert action. The CIA began supplying the Contras, exiles fighting against the Sandinistas from bases in Honduras and Costa Rica. The U.S.-backed rebels tried to disrupt the Nicaraguan economy, raiding villages, blowing up oil tanks, and even mining harbors. Then, in 1984, Congress passed the Boland Amendment prohibiting any U.S. agency from spending money in Central America. The withdrawal of U.S. financial backing left the Contras in a precarious position.

MORE TROUBLE IN THE MIDDLE EAST

Reagan tried to continue Carter's basic policy in the turbulent Middle East. In April 1982, the Israelis honored a Camp David pledge by making their final withdrawal from the Sinai. Reagan hoped to achieve the other Camp David objective of providing a homeland for the Palestinian Arabs on the West Bank, but Israel instead continued to extend Jewish settlements into the disputed area. The threat of the Palestine Liberation Organization (PLO), based in southern Lebanon and frequently raiding across the border into Israel, seemed to be the major obstacle to further progress.

On June 6, 1982, with tacit American encouragement, Israel invaded southern Lebanon in order to secure its northern border and destroy the PLO. The Reagan administration made no effort to halt the offensive but did join with France and Italy in sending a multinational force to permit the PLO to evacuate to Tunisia. Unfortunately, the United States soon became enmeshed in the Lebanese civil war, which had been raging since 1975. American marines, sent to Lebanon as part of the multinational force to restore order, were caught up in the renewed hostilities between Muslim and Christian militias. The Muslims perceived the marines as aiding the Christian-dominated government of Lebanon instead of acting as neutral peacekeepers, and they began firing on the vulnerable American troops.

In the face of growing congressional demands for the withdrawal of the marines, Reagan declared they were there to protect Lebanon from the designs of Soviet-backed Syria. But finally, after terrorists drove a truck loaded with explosives into the American barracks, killing 239 marines, the president saw no choice but to pull out. The last American unit left Beirut in late February 1984. Despite his good intentions, Reagan had experienced a humiliation similar to Carter's in Iran—one that left Lebanon in shambles and the Arab-Israeli situation worse than ever.

TRADING ARMS FOR HOSTAGES

Reagan's Middle Eastern troubles didn't prevent his easy re-election in 1984. Voters gave him credit for curbing inflation, reviving the economy, and challenging communism; compared to these major achievements, the miscue in Lebanon appeared minor. Democratic candidate Walter Mondale, formerly

THE ELECTION OF 1984

CANDIDATE	PARTY	POPULAR VOTE	ELECTORAL VOTE
Reagan	Republican	54,455,075	525
Mondale	Democratic	37,577,185	13

Jimmy Carter's vice president, provided a jolt to the campaign by choosing Representative Geraldine Ferraro of New York as his running mate. But even the presence of the first woman on the national ticket of a major American party couldn't dent Reagan's enormous popularity. He swept to victory with 59 percent of the popular vote and carried every state but Mondale's home, Minnesota.

Yet the troubles abroad persisted. Not long after Reagan's second inauguration, his administration's policies in the Middle East and Central America converged in the Iran-Contra affair. In mid-1985, Robert McFarlane, who had become national security adviser a year earlier, began a new initiative designed to restore American influence in the troubled Middle East. Concerned over the fate of six Americans held hostage in Lebanon by groups thought to be loyal to Iran's Ayatollah Khomeini, McFarlane proposed trading American antitank missiles to Iran in return for the hostages' release. The Iranians, desperate for weapons in the war they had been waging against Iraq since 1980, seemed willing to comply.

McFarlane soon found himself in over his head. He relied heavily on a young marine lieutenant colonel assigned to the National Security Council (NSC), Oliver North, and North in turn sought the assistance of CIA director William Casey, who interpreted the Iran initiative as an opportunity to use the NSC to mount the kind of covert operation denied the CIA under the post-1975 congressional oversight policy. By early 1986, when John Poindexter, a naval officer with little political experience, replaced a burned-out McFarlane as national security adviser, Casey was able to persuade the president to go ahead with shipments of weapons to Iran.

The arms deal with Iran was bad policy, but what came next was criminal. Ever since the Boland Amendment in late 1984 had cut off congressional funding, the Reagan administration had been searching for ways to supply the Contras in Nicaragua. Oliver North was put in charge of soliciting donations from wealthy right-wing Americans. In early 1986, North realized he could use the enormous profits from the sale of weapons to Iran to finance the Contras. North's ploy was clearly not only illegal but unconstitutional, since it meant usurping the congressional power of the purse.

Ultimately the secret got out. Administration officials tried to shield Reagan from blame, and even after a congressional investigation it was unclear whether the president had approved the Contra diversion. Reagan's reputation survived the scandal, albeit tarnished. Several of his subordinates, including North and Poindexter, were prosecuted. William Casey might have joined them in the dock but died suddenly of a brain tumor.

REAGAN THE PEACEMAKER

Americans' tolerance of Reagan's mistakes in the Iran-Contra affair resulted in part from the progress he was making on the larger issue of U.S.-Soviet relations. Elected as an anticommunist hard-liner, Reagan softened during his second term to become an advocate of cooperation with Moscow.

Reagan and Gorbachev in Red Square. During the summits between the two leaders, the American public grew to admire the Soviet premier for his policies of perestroika *(restructuring) and* glasnost (openness).

A momentous change in leadership in the Soviet Union had much to do with the change in Reagan's approach. The illness and death of Leonid Brezhnev in 1982, followed in rapid succession by the deaths of his aged successors, Yuri Andropov and Konstantin Chernenko, led finally to the selection of Mikhail Gorbachev, a younger and more dynamic Soviet leader. Gorbachev was intent on improving relations with the United States as part of his new policy of *perestroika* (restructuring the Soviet economy) and *glasnost* (political openness). Soviet economic performance had been deteriorating steadily and the war in Afghanistan had become a major liability. Gorbachev needed a breathing spell in the arms race and a reduction in Cold War tensions in order to carry out his sweeping changes at home.

A series of summit meetings between Reagan and Gorbachev broke the chill in superpower relations and led in December 1987 to an Intermediate Nuclear

Forces Treaty, by which Reagan and Gorbachev agreed to remove and destroy all intermediate-range missiles in Europe. The most important arms-control agreement since SALT I of 1972, the INF treaty raised hopes that an end to the Cold War was finally in sight.

During the president's last year in office, the Soviets cooperated with the United States in pressuring Iran and Iraq to end their long war. Most significant of all, Gorbachev moved to end the war in Afghanistan. The first Soviet units pulled out in April 1988, with the final evacuation due to be completed early the next year. By the time Reagan left office in January 1989, he had scored a series of foreign policy triumphs that offset the Iran-Contra fiasco and thus helped redeem his presidency.

CHALLENGING THE NEW DEAL

Though trouble dogged the final years of his presidency, the overall effect of Reagan's two terms was to reshape the landscape of American politics. The Democratic coalition forged by Franklin Roosevelt during the New Deal finally broke down as the Republicans captured the South and made deep inroads into organized labor.

More significantly, Reagan challenged the liberal premises of the New Deal by asserting that the private sector, rather than the federal government, ought to be the source of remedies to most of America's ills. Reagan prudently left intact the centerpieces of the welfare state—Social Security and Medicare—but he trimmed other programs and made any comparable expansion of federal authority nearly impossible. By the time he left office, small-government conservatism seemed the undeniable wave of the American future.

CHRONOLOGY

1969 Stonewall Riots in New York's Greenwich Village spark gay rights movement

American astronauts land on the moon

1970 U.S. forces invade Cambodia

Ohio National Guardsmen kill four students at Kent State University

1971 States ratify Twenty-sixth Amendment to the Constitution, giving 18-year-olds the right to vote

President Nixon freezes wages and prices for ninety days

1972 President Nixon visits China

U.S. and USSR sign SALT I accords in Moscow

White House "plumbers" unit breaks into Democratic headquarters in Watergate complex

Richard Nixon wins re-election in landslide victory over George McGovern

1973 United States and North Vietnam sign truce

Arab oil embargo creates energy crisis in the United States

1974 Supreme Court orders Nixon to surrender White House tapes

Richard M. Nixon resigns presidency

1975 Last evacuation helicopter leaves roof of U.S. embassy in Saigon, South Vietnam

1976 Nation celebrates bicentennial with fireworks, patriotic music, and parade of sailing ships

Jimmy Carter defeats Gerald Ford in presidential election

1977 President Carter signs Panama Canal treaties restoring sovereignty to Panama

Sales of imported cars, mainly from Japan, surpass two million a year for first time

1978 President Carter signs law raising mandatory retirement age from 65 to 70

Over nine hundred followers of Rev. Jim Jones die in a mass suicide in Guyana

1979 Iranian militants take fifty-three Americans hostage in U.S. embassy in Tehran

Soviet invasion of Afghanistan leads to U.S. withdrawal from 1980 Moscow Olympics

Congress approves loan of $1.5 billion to rescue the ailing Chrysler Corporation

1980 Ronald Reagan wins presidency in landslide

1981 American hostages in Iran released after 444 days in captivity

Sandra Day O'Connor becomes first woman U.S. Supreme Court justice

1982 Equal Rights Amendment fails state ratification

Unemployment reaches postwar record high of 10.4 percent

1983 Soviets shoot down Korean airliner

U.S. invades Grenada

1984 Russia boycotts summer Olympics in Los Angeles

Ronald Reagan re-elected president

1985 Mikhail Gorbachev becomes leader of the Soviet Union

1986 Space shuttle *Challenger* explodes, killing seven astronauts

Iran-Contra affair made public

1987 Reagan and Gorbachev sign INF treaty at Washington summit

1988 George Bush defeats Michael Dukakis decisively in presidential election

32

To the Twenty-first Century, 1989–2006

On the evening of August 1, 1990, George H. W. Bush sat in a T-shirt in the medical office in the basement of the White House. He had strained a shoulder muscle hitting golf balls, and now he rested on the exam table while a therapist applied deep heat. He planned a quiet evening and hoped the soreness would be gone by morning.

Two unexpected visitors altered his plans. Brent Scowcroft, Bush's national security adviser, and Richard Haass, the Middle East expert of the National Security Council, appeared at the door of the exam room. "Mr. President, it looks very bad, " Scowcroft said. "Iraq may be about to invade Kuwait."

For months, the Bush administration had been monitoring a territorial and financial dispute between Iraq and Kuwait. Iraqi dictator Saddam Hussein was rattling the saber against the much smaller Kuwait, but Saddam had rattled sabers before without actually using them. The previous week Saddam had spoken with the American ambassador in Iraq, April Glaspie, who came away from the meeting with the belief that his bellicose talk was chiefly for political effect. The United States had indicated its displeasure with Saddam's threats, and Glaspie judged that he had gotten the message. "He does not want to further antagonize us," she wrote to Washington.

For this reason, Saddam's decision to invade Kuwait at the beginning of August caught the Bush administration by surprise. American intelligence agencies detected Iraq's mobilization; this was what brought Scowcroft and Haass to the White House on the evening of August 1. Haass suggested that the president call Saddam and warn him not to go through with the attack. But even as Bush considered this suggestion, Scowcroft received a message from the State Department that the American embassy in Kuwait had reported shooting in downtown Kuwait City. "So much for calling Saddam," Bush said. Within hours the Iraqi forces crushed all resistance in Kuwait.

Bush, Scowcroft, and other American officials recognized that the Iraqi takeover of Kuwait constituted the first crisis of the post–Cold War era. As Lawrence Eagleburger, the deputy secretary of state, asserted in an emergency meeting of the National Security Council, "This is the first test of the postwar system. As the bipolar world is relaxed, it permits this, giving people more flexibility because they are not worried about the involvement of the superpowers." During the Cold War, a de facto division of labor had developed, with the United States and the Soviet Union each generally keeping its clients and allies in line, typically by threatening to withhold weapons or other assistance. Had the Soviet Union still been a superpower, Saddam, a longtime recipient of Soviet aid, likely would have heeded Moscow's warnings to settle his dispute with Kuwait peacefully. But in 1990 the Soviet system was disintegrating, and the Kremlin's clients were on their own. "Saddam Hussein now has greater flexibility because the Soviets are tangled up in domestic issues," Eagleburger explained. The world was watching. "If he succeeds, others may try the same thing."

It was this belief that shaped the Bush administration's response to the crisis. The president and his advisers understood that they were entering uncharted territory after the Cold War. As the sole remaining superpower, the United States had the opportunity to employ its military and economic resources more freely than at any time in history. But with that freedom came unprecedented responsibility. During the Cold War the United States could cite the threat of Soviet retaliation as reason to avoid intervening in the affairs of other countries; with that threat gone, American leaders would have to weigh each prospective intervention on its own merits. If one country attacked another, should the United States defend the victim? If the government of a country oppressed its own people, should the United States move to stop the oppression? These questions—and the answers American presidents gave to them—would define American foreign policy in the era after the Cold War.

Bush sensed this, and he responded accordingly. He convened his principal deputies for a series of White House meetings. The particular stakes with Iraq and in the surrounding Persian Gulf were discussed at length. "The rest of the world badly needs oil," Defense Secretary Dick Cheney observed, restating the obvious. Saddam's seizure of Kuwait gave him control of a large part of the world's oil supply, but the real prize was Saudi Arabia. "Saudi Arabia and others will cut and run if we are weak," Cheney predicted.

Bush consulted America's oldest allies. Britain's Margaret Thatcher urged the president to oppose Saddam most vigorously. "If Iraq wins, no small state is safe," the prime minister declared. She offered to help. "We must win this. . . . We cannot give in to dictators."

Bush asked his generals what his military options were. "Iraq is not ten feet tall, but it is formidable," Norman Schwarzkopf, the U.S. commander for the Middle East, replied. American air power could punish Saddam and perhaps soften him up, but ground forces—in large numbers—would be required to guarantee victory.

By August 5 Bush had made up his mind. As he exited the helicopter that brought him back to the White House from another high-level meeting, at

Camp David, reporters crowded the South Lawn. What was he planning to do? they asked.

"I'm not going to discuss what we're doing in terms of moving forces, anything of that nature," Bush answered. "But I view it very seriously, not just that but any threat to any other countries." Bush was no orator, and these remarks were unscripted. But one sentence summarized the policy that soon began to unfold: "This will not stand, this aggression against Kuwait."

THE FIRST PRESIDENT BUSH

Elected on the strength of his association with Ronald Reagan, George H. W. Bush appeared poised to confirm the ascendancy of the conservative values Reagan forced to the center stage of American life. But events, especially abroad, distracted Bush, whose principal contribution proved to be in the area of foreign affairs. Bush brought the Cold War to a peaceful and triumphant conclusion, and he launched America toward the twenty-first century, an era in which the United States would face new opportunities and new challenges.

REPUBLICANS AT HOME

Democrats approached the 1988 presidential election with high hopes, having regained control of the Senate in 1986 and not having to face the popular Reagan. But Vice President George H. W. Bush proved a stronger candidate than almost anyone had expected, and in a contest that confirmed the Republicans' hold on the Sunbelt, he defeated Massachusetts governor Michael Dukakis.

Many people expected the policies of the Bush administration to reflect the reputation of the new president—bland and cautious, lacking in vision but safely predictable. At home, he lived up (or down) to his reputation, sponsoring few initiatives in education, health care, or environmental protection while continuing the Reagan theme of limiting federal interference in the everyday lives of American citizens. He vetoed family leave legislation, declined to endorse meaningful health care reform, and watered down civil rights proposals in Congress.

The one exception was the Americans with Disabilities Act (ADA), passed by Congress in 1991, which prohibited discrimination against the disabled in hiring, transportation, and public accommodations. Beginning in July 1992, the ADA

THE ELECTION OF 1988

CANDIDATE	PARTY	POPULAR VOTE	ELECTORAL VOTE
Bush	Republican	48,886,097	426
Dukakis	Democratic	41,809,074	111

called for all public buildings, restaurants, and stores to be made accessible to those with physical handicaps and required that businesses with twenty-five or more workers hire new employees without regard to disability.

ENDING THE COLD WAR

Bush might have accomplished more in domestic affairs had not the international developments begun during the Reagan years accelerated dramatically. Bush had been in office only months when the communist system of the Cold War began falling apart. In country after country, communism gave way to democracy as the old order collapsed more quickly than anyone had expected.

The collapse began in eastern Europe in mid-1989. In June, Lech Walesa and his Solidarity movement came to power in free elections in Poland. Soon the winds of change were sweeping over the former Iron Curtain countries. A new regime in Hungary opened its borders to the West in September, allowing thousands of East German tourists in Hungary to flee to freedom. One by one, the repressive governments of East Germany, Czechoslovakia, Bulgaria, and Romania fell. The most heartening scene of all took place in East Germany in early November when the new communist leaders suddenly announced the opening of the Berlin Wall. Workers quickly demolished a 12-foot-high section of this despised physical symbol of the Cold War, joyously singing a German version of "For He's a Jolly Good Fellow."

Most people realized it was Mikhail Gorbachev who was responsible for the liberation of eastern Europe. In late 1988, the Soviet leader signaled the spread of his reforms to the Soviet satellites by announcing that the Brezhnev doctrine, which called for Soviet control of eastern Europe, was now replaced with "the Sinatra doctrine," which meant that the people of this region could now do things "their way." It was Gorbachev's refusal to use armed force to keep repressive regimes in power that permitted the long-delayed liberation of the captive peoples of central and eastern Europe.

Yet by the end of 1991, both Gorbachev and the Soviet Union had become victims of the demise of communism. On August 19, 1991, right-wing plotters placed Gorbachev under arrest. Boris Yeltsin, the newly elected president of the Russian Republic, broke up the coup by mounting a tank in Moscow and demanding Gorbachev's release. The Red Army rallied to Yeltsin's side. The coup failed and Gorbachev was released, only to resign in December 1991 after the fifteen republics dissolved the Soviet Union. Russia, by far the largest and most powerful of the former Soviet republics, took the lead in joining with ten others to form a loose alignment called the Commonwealth of Independent States (CIS). Yeltsin then disbanded the Communist party and continued the reforms begun by Gorbachev to establish democracy and a free market system in Russia.

The Bush administration, although criticized for its cautious approach, welcomed the demise of communism. Bush facilitated the reunification of Germany and offered economic assistance to Russia and the other members of the new CIS. On the critical issue of nuclear weapons, Bush and Gorbachev in 1991 signed START I, agreeing to reduce nuclear warheads to less than ten thousand

1. **Poland.** Solidarity Party sweeps elections, June 1989.

2. **Czechoslovakia.** Communist leadership ousted, Nov. 1989; country divided into Czech Republic and Slovakia, Jan. 1, 1993.

3. **Germany.** Berlin Wall breached, Nov. 1989; East and West Germany reunited, Oct. 1990.

4. **Yugoslavia.** Country disintegrates, 1991–92; civil war begins in Bosnia and Herzegovina, 1992.

5. **Romania.** Communist dictator Ceausescu overthrown and executed, Dec. 1989; Salvation Front led by dissident former Communists wins elections, May 1990.

6. **Lithuania** declares independence, Mar. 1990.

7. **Latvia and Estonia** begin process of separation from Soviet Union, Apr. 1990.

8. **Hungary.** Free election sweeps non-Communists into power, Apr. 1990.

9. **Bulgaria.** Government pledges free elections and new constitution in 1990; free elections sweep non-Communists into power.

10. **Albania.** Free elections sweep non-Communists into power.

11. **Soviet Union.** Dissolved, Dec. 1991; Russia and 10 former Soviet republics form Commonwealth of Independent States.

The End of the Cold War
Free elections in Poland in June 1989 triggered the domino effect in the fall of communism in Eastern Europe and the former Soviet Union. Changes in policy came quickly, but the restructuring of social and economic institutions continues to take time.

apiece. In late 1992, Bush and Yeltsin agreed on the terms of START II, which would eliminate land missiles with multiple warheads and reduce the number of nuclear weapons on each side to just over three thousand, a level not seen since the mid-1960s.

THE GULF WAR

Amid the disintegration of the Soviet system, Iraq in August 1990 invaded Kuwait. Although Bush quickly concluded that Saddam Hussein's aggression must be reversed, actually removing Iraq from Kuwait took time and great effort. The president started by persuading Saudi Arabia to accept a huge American troop buildup, dubbed Desert Shield. This American presence would prevent Saddam from advancing beyond Kuwait into Saudi Arabia; it would also allow the United States to launch a ground attack against Iraqi forces if and when the president determined such an attack was necessary.

While the American buildup took place, Bush arranged an international coalition to condemn the Iraqi invasion and endorse economic sanctions against Iraq. Not every member of the coalition subscribed to the "new world order" that Bush said the liberation of Kuwait would help establish, but all concurred in the general principle of deterring international aggression. Essential to the success of Bush's diplomatic offensive was the support of the Soviet Union, which during the Cold War had regularly blocked American initiatives in the United Nations. Soviet leaders may have been sincere in wanting to see Saddam punished, but they also hoped to receive American aid in restructuring their economy.

Congress required somewhat more convincing. Many Democrats supported economic sanctions against Iraq but opposed the use of force. Yet as the troop buildup in the Persian Gulf proceeded—as Operation Desert Shield evolved into what would be called Operation Desert Storm—and as the sanctions failed to dislodge Iraq from Kuwait, some of the skeptics gradually came around. After securing UN support for military action, Bush persuaded Congress (with just five votes to spare in the Senate) to approve the use of force to liberate Kuwait.

On January 17, 1991, the president unleashed a devastating aerial assault on Iraq. After knocking out the Iraqi air defense network in a few hours, F-117A stealth fighters and Tomahawk cruise missiles hit key targets in Baghdad. The air attack, virtually unchallenged by the Iraqis, wiped out command and control centers and enabled the bombers of the United States and its coalition partners (chiefly Britain) to demoralize the beleaguered enemy troops. After five weeks of this, Bush gave the order for the ground assault. Led by General Schwarzkopf, American and allied armored units swept across the desert in a great flanking operation while a combined force of U.S. marines and Saudi troops drove directly into Kuwait City. In just one hundred hours, the American-led offensive liberated Kuwait and sent Saddam Hussein's vaunted Republican Guard fleeing back into Iraq.

In a controversial decision, President Bush, acting on the advice of General Colin Powell, chairman of the Joint Chiefs, halted the advance and agreed to an armistice with Iraq. Critics claimed that with just a few more days of fighting, perhaps even just a few more hours, American forces could have encircled the

Antiaircraft fire lights up the sky over Baghdad, Iraq, during the 1991 Persian Gulf War. A month of strikes on Iraqi targets was followed by a ground offensive that lasted only one hundred hours before Iraqi troops began to surrender and President Bush ordered a cease-fire. Critics of Bush's decision argued that stopping the advance allowed an unvanquished Saddam Hussein to remain in power in Iraq.

Republican Guard and ended Saddam's cruel regime. But the president, fearful of disrupting the allied coalition and of having American troops mired down in a guerrilla war, stopped when he had achieved his announced goal of liberating Kuwait. Moreover, he hoped that a chastened Saddam would help balance the threat of Iran in the volatile Persian Gulf region.

THE CHANGING FACES OF AMERICA

From the *Mayflower* to the covered wagon, movement has always characterized the American people. The final years of the twentieth century and the early years of the twenty-first witnessed two significant shifts in the American population: continued movement internally to the Sunbelt region of the South and West, and a remarkable influx of immigrants from developing nations. These changes led to increased urbanization, greater ethnic diversity, and growing social unrest.

A PEOPLE ON THE MOVE

By the 1990s, a majority of Americans lived in the Sunbelt of the South and West. Best defined as a broad band running across the country below the 37th parallel from the Carolinas to Southern California, the Sunbelt had begun to flourish with the buildup of military bases and defense plants during World War II. Rapid population growth continued with the stimulus of heavy Cold War defense spending and accelerated in the 1970s when both new high-technology firms and more established industries were attracted by lower labor costs and the favorable climate of the Sunbelt states. Florida, Texas, and California led the way, each gaining more than two million new residents in the 1970s.

The flow continued at a slightly lower rate over the next two decades. The Northeast and the Middle West continued losing people to the South and West, and in 1994 Texas surpassed New York as the nation's second most populous state. The 2000 census revealed that while all regions had gained population in the 1990s, the South and West had expanded by nearly 20 percent, compared to around 6 percent for the Northeast and Middle West.

The increasing urbanization of America had positive and negative aspects. People living in the large metropolitan areas were both more affluent and better educated than their rural counterparts. Family income among people living in the bigger cities and their suburbs ran $9000 a year more, and three-fourths of the urban population had graduated from high school, compared to two-thirds of other Americans. A metropolitan American was twice as likely to be a college graduate as a rural resident. Yet these advantages were offset by higher urban crime rates, longer commuting time in heavy traffic, and higher living costs. Nevertheless, the big cities and their suburbs continued to thrive, accounting for 80 percent of all Americans by 2000.

Another striking population trend was the nationwide rise in the number of the elderly. At the beginning of the twentieth century, only 4.1 percent of the population was aged 65 or older; by 2000, those over 65 made up more than 12 percent of the population, with the nearly four million over 85 the fastest growing group of all. Census Bureau projections suggest that by the year 2030, one out of every five Americans will be over age 65.

THE REVIVAL OF IMMIGRATION

The flow of immigrants into the United States reached record proportions in the 1990s as a result of the new policies adopted in 1965. The number of arrivals continued to grow during the first decade of the new century, with nearly 8 million immigrants reaching America between the beginning of 2000 and early 2005. By 2005, a record high of 35 million foreign-born persons lived in the United States, constituting 12 percent of the total population.

The new wave of immigrants came mainly from Latin America and Asia. By 2005, over half the foreign-born population of the United States came from Latin America, about one-quarter from Asia, and about one out of seven from Europe. The new immigrants tended to settle in urban areas in six states: California, Texas, New York, Florida, Illinois, and New Jersey. In California, the influx of immigrants from Asia and Mexico created growing pressure on public services, especially during the recessions of the early 1990s and the early 2000s.

The arrival of so many immigrants was bound to lead to controversy over whether immigrants were a benefit or a liability to American society. A study by the National Academy of Sciences in 1997 reported that while government

Newly sworn in citizens of the United States wave U.S. flags during a naturalization ceremony in Miami on April 28, 2006. Days later, more than one million immigrants participated in a nationwide boycott called "A Day Without Immigrants" to protest the proposed tightening of U.S. immigration laws.

services used by immigrants—schools, welfare, health clinics—cost more initially than was collected from them in taxes, in the long run, immigrants and their families more than paid their way. In regard to employment, immigrants tended to help consumers and employers by working for relatively low wages in restaurants, the textile industry, and farming, but they hurt low-skilled U.S. workers, notably high school dropouts and many African Americans, by keeping wages low. Economist George J. Borjas, a refugee from Cuba, claimed that immigrants from developing countries lacked the education and job skills needed to achieve the level of prosperity attained by newcomers in the past; instead of entering the mainstream of American life, they were likely to remain a permanent underclass.

EMERGING HISPANICS

People of Hispanic origin became the nation's largest ethnic group in 2002, surpassing African Americans for the first time. The rapidly growing Hispanic population climbed to over 41 million by 2005, accounting for 14 percent of the nation's population. "It doesn't surprise me," commented the leader of the League of Latin American Citizens. "Anybody that travels around . . . can see Latinos everywhere, working everywhere, trying to reach the American dream."

The Census Bureau identified four major Hispanic groups: Mexican Americans, Puerto Ricans, Cuban Americans, and other Hispanics, including many from Central America. Even though most of the Hispanic population was concentrated in cities such as New York, Los Angeles, San Antonio, and Miami, the 2000 census showed a surprising geographical spread. Hispanics made up 20 percent of the population in individual counties in states such as Georgia, Iowa, and Minnesota.

The Hispanic groups had several features in common. All were relatively youthful, with a median age of 22 and a high fertility rate. They tended to be relatively poor, with one-fourth falling below the poverty line, and to be employed in low-paying positions as manual laborers, domestic servants, and migrant workers. Although the position of Hispanics had improved considerably in the boom years of the 1980s and 1990s, they still lagged behind mainstream America. The poverty rate among Hispanics was twice the national average, and family median income in 2005 was $34,000, or roughly two-thirds the level for whites.

Lack of education was a key factor in preventing economic progress for Hispanics. Fewer Hispanics graduated from high school than other minorities and their school dropout rate was the nation's highest at more than 50 percent. Hispanic leaders warned that these figures boded ill not just for their own group, but for society as a whole. "You either educate us," claimed a San Antonio activist, "or you pay for building more jails or for more welfare."

The entry of several million illegal immigrants from Mexico, once derisively called "wetbacks" and now known as undocumented aliens, created a substantial social problem for the nation and especially for the Southwest. Critics charged that the flagrant violation of the nation's border with Mexico had led to a subculture beyond the boundaries of law and ordinary custom. They argued that the aliens took jobs from U.S. citizens, kept wages artificially low, and received extensive welfare and medical benefits that strained budgets in states such as Texas and California.

Defenders of the undocumented aliens contended that the nation gained from the abundant supply of workers who were willing to work in fields and factories at backbreaking jobs shunned by most Americans. Moreover, defenders stated, illegal entrants usually paid sales and withholding taxes but rarely used government services for fear of being deported. Whichever view was correct, an exploited class of illegal aliens was living on the edge of poverty.

Concern over economic competition from Mexican "illegals" had led Congress to pass legislation in 1986 that penalized employers who hired undocumented workers. Congress permitted those aliens who could show that they were living in the United States before 1982 to become legal residents; nearly three million accepted this offer of amnesty to become legal residents. The reform effort, however, failed to stem the continued flow of undocumented workers northward from Mexico in the 1990s and early 2000s—more than 500,000 in some years. While experts debated the exact number, the Congressional Research Service estimated that more than 9 million foreigners, mainly from Mexico and Central America, were living illegally in the United States in 2002.

Despite stepped-up border enforcement efforts after the September 11, 2001, terrorist attacks, illegal immigrants continued to move northward from Mexico and Central America. The trip could be dangerous, even lethal. Mexican experts estimated that more than 2000 migrants lost their lives attempting to enter the

United States illegally between 1997 and 2003. Yet the movement continued. As one rural Mexican official commented, "There are great problems in the countryside. And that famous American dream keeps calling."

ADVANCE AND RETREAT FOR AFRICAN AMERICANS

African Americans formed the second largest of the nation's ethnic minorities. In 2004, there were just over 39 million blacks in the United States, 13.4 percent of the population. Although the heaviest concentration of African Americans was in northern cities, notably New York and Chicago, there was a significant movement back to the South. This shift, which began in the 1970s and accelerated during the 1990s, meant that by 2000 nearly 54 percent of those identifying themselves as black for the census lived in the sixteen states of the Sunbelt. Family ties and a search for ancestral roots explained much of this movement, but it also reflected the same economic incentives that drew so many Americans to the Sunbelt in the last three decades of the twentieth century.

African Americans made substantial gains in certain areas of life. In 2004, some 81 percent of blacks aged 25 and older had earned a high school diploma, an increase of 8 percent during the previous decade. Eighteen percent of African Americans possessed a college degree, 5 percent more than a decade earlier. The number of black-owned businesses topped 1.2 million, up more than 45 percent since 1997.

Yet in other respects African Americans did less well. The black poverty rate was nearly 25 percent, and the median income for black families was less than two-thirds of that for whites. Blacks remained clustered in entry-level jobs, where they faced increasing competition from immigrants. The African American incarceration rate was much higher than the national average; in 2002, more than 10 percent of black males aged 25–29 were in prison, and more than one out of four black men could expect to spend time in a state or federal prison during their lives. Blacks were also more likely to be victims of crime, especially violent crime. Homicide was the leading cause of death among black males between the ages of 15 and 34.

Two events, one from 1991 and the other from 2005, summarized much of the frustration African Americans felt. In March 1991, a bystander videotaped four Los Angeles policemen brutally beating Rodney King, an African American who had been stopped for a traffic violation. The pictures of the rain of blows on King shocked the nation. Nearly a year later, when an all-white jury acquitted the four officers of charges of police brutality, rioting erupted in South Central Los Angeles that for a time threatened the entire city when the police failed to respond promptly. In the aftermath of the riot, which took fifty-three lives (compared to thirty-four deaths in the 1965 riot in the nearby Watts area) and did more than $1 billion in damage, government and state agencies promised new efforts to help the inner-city dwellers. But the efforts produced little effect, and life for many urban blacks remained difficult and dangerous.

A tragedy of a different sort occurred fourteen years later. In August 2005, Hurricane Katrina ravaged the Gulf Coast and broke levees in New Orleans. The

In August 2005, the catastrophic Hurricane Katrina devastated much of the Louisiana and Mississippi Gulf Coast. In the wake of the storm, the levee system of New Orleans failed and flooded nearly 80 percent of the city. Particularly hard hit were low-lying areas such as the Lower Ninth Ward, where police rescue boats are shown here rescuing residents. All levels of government were criticized for halting, inadequate responses to the disaster.

high winds and water killed more than a thousand persons, destroyed hundreds of thousands of homes, and forced the evacuation of millions of men, women, and children. Television cameras captured the plight of the several thousand who took refuge in the New Orleans Superdome, only to be stranded when state and federal relief efforts failed. Most conspicuous in the footage was the fact that the vast majority of those suffering the worst in New Orleans were black. Their neighborhoods were the lowest-lying in the city, and hence the worst flooded. Many lacked the cars necessary to flee the city in advance of the hurricane; others lacked the means to pay for hotels or apartments had they been able to get out. Though the relief efforts were largely color-blind (despite early allegations to the contrary), the entire experience demonstrated that poverty in America most certainly was not.

AMERICANS FROM ASIA AND THE MIDDLE EAST

Asian Americans were the fasting-growing minority group at the beginning of the twenty-first century. According to the 2000 census, there were more than 12 million Americans of Asian or Pacific Island descent. Although they represented only 4 percent of the total population, they were increasing at seven times the national rate, and future projections indicated that by 2050 one in ten Americans would be of Asian ancestry. The Chinese formed the largest single group of Asian

Americans, followed by Filipinos, Japanese, Indians, Koreans, and Vietnamese. Immigration was the primary reason for the rapid growth of all these groups except the Japanese; during the 1980s, Asia had provided nearly half of all immigrants to the United States. Though the influx subsequently slowed, the children of the immigrants added to the Asian numbers.

Compared to other minorities, Asian Americans were well educated and affluent. Three out of four Asian youths graduated from high school, compared to less than one out of two for blacks and Hispanics. Asian Americans also had the highest percentage of college graduates and recipients of doctoral degrees of any minority group; in fact, they were better represented in colleges and universities than the white majority. Many Asians entered professional fields, and in part as a result, the median income for Asian American families in 2004 was nearly 20 percent higher than the national average.

Not all Asian Americans fared so well, however. Refugees from Southeast Asia experienced both economic hardship and persecution. The median family income for Vietnamese Americans fell substantially below the national average. Nearly half the Laotian refugees living in Minnesota were unemployed because they had great difficulty learning to read and write English. Vietnamese fishermen who settled on the Gulf Coast of Texas and Louisiana experienced repeated attacks on their livelihood and their homes. In the Los Angeles riots in 1992, Korean stores and shops became a main target for looting and firebombing.

But the overall experience of Asian Americans was a positive one. They came to America seeking economic opportunity, or as many put it, "to climb the mountain of gold." "People are looking for a better life," a Chinese spokeswoman explained. "It's as simple as that, and we will continue to come here, especially if the situations over there [in Asia] stay tight, or get worse."

The number of Americans from the Middle East grew almost as fast as the number of those from Asia in the 1990s. The 2000 census counted 1.5 million Americans of Middle Eastern ancestry, up from 200,000 thirty years earlier. Most came from Arab countries, as well as Israel and Iran. Concentrated in California, New York, and Michigan, Middle Eastern Americans were well-educated, with nearly half having college degrees. Many Arab Americans felt nervous after the terrorist attacks of September 11, 2001, committed by Arab extremists; some experienced actual violence at the hands of persons who wanted to blame anyone of Arab descent for the shocking mass murders. Yet most Arab Americans carried on as before, pursuing their interpretation of the American dream.

THE NEW DEMOCRATS

The Democrats, victims of the runaway inflation of the 1970s, became the beneficiaries of the lingering recession of the early 1990s. Moving away from its traditional liberal reliance on big government, the party regained strength by choosing moderate candidates and tailoring its programs to appeal to the hard-pressed middle class. These tactics enabled the Democrats to regain the White

House in 1992 and retain it in 1996, despite a Republican sweep of Congress in 1994. The key figure in this political shift was Bill Clinton, who overcame some early setbacks to reap the rewards of a sustained economic boom.

THE ELECTION OF 1992

The persistence of the recession that had begun two years earlier became a major political issue in 1992. Although mild by postwar standards, the economic downturn that began in July 1990 proved unusually stubborn, especially in states such as California that relied heavily on the defense industry, which was hurt by the end of the Cold War. The recovery, which started just after the end of the Persian Gulf War in the spring of 1991, proved slow and uneven. Unemployment remained high for eighteen months and the gross domestic product rose only an anemic 2.9 percent in the same period.

The political impact was devastating for the Bush administration. Three million Americans joined the ranks of the unemployed, and many were white-collar employees rather than factory workers typically hit by hard times. Although the economy began to advance more briskly in 1992, unemployment persisted as businesses still hesitated to hire new workers. As a result, the average American worker was ready to look beyond the Republican party for relief.

As Bush's popularity plummeted, two men sought to capitalize on the dismal state of the U.S. economy. First, Arkansas governor Bill Clinton defeated a field of five other challengers for the Democratic nomination by becoming the champion of economic renewal. Forgoing traditional liberal appeals to interest groups, Clinton stressed the need for investment in the nation's future—rebuilding roads and bridges, training workers for high-tech jobs, and solving the growing national health care crisis.

Despite his victories in the Democratic primaries, however, Clinton faced a new rival in H. Ross Perot. An eccentric Texas billionaire, Perot singled out the deficit as the nation's gravest problem and agreed to run as an independent candidate in response to a grassroots movement (which he financed) to place his name on the November ballot.

When Clinton and his running mate, Senator Albert Gore, Jr., of Tennessee, succeeded in unifying the Democratic party and gaining agreement on a moder-

THE ELECTION OF 1992

CANDIDATE	PARTY	POPULAR VOTE	ELECTORAL VOTE
Clinton	Democratic	44,908,254	370
Bush	Republican	39,102,343	168
Perot	Independent	19,741,065	—

ate platform promising economic change, Perot stunned his supporters by suddenly dropping out of the race in July. Clinton immediately became the front-runner, rising from 30 percent to more than 50 percent in the polls, leaving Bush far behind.

A relentless Democratic attack on the administration's lackluster economic performance overcame all the president's efforts to remind the nation of Reagan prosperity and Bush triumphs abroad. Even GOP assaults on Clinton's character, notably his evasion of the draft during the Vietnam War, failed to halt the Democratic momentum. The message that Clinton's political advisers tacked up at the Democratic candidate's headquarters in Little Rock—"The economy, stupid"—provided the key to victory in November. Clinton wound up with 43 percent of the popular vote but with a commanding lead in the electoral college, 370 to 168 for Bush. Perot, who had reentered the race, won 19 percent of the popular vote but failed to carry a single state.

CLINTON AND CONGRESS

In the White House, Bill Clinton proved to be the most adept politician since Franklin Roosevelt. Born in Hope, Arkansas, in 1946, Clinton weathered a difficult childhood with an alcoholic stepfather by developing skills at dealing with people and using personal charm to achieve his goals. Intelligent and ambitious, he completed his undergraduate work at Georgetown University, studied law at Yale, and spent two years as a Rhodes scholar at Oxford University in England. Entering politics after teaching law briefly at the University of Arkansas, he won election first as Arkansas attorney general and then as governor. Defeated after his first term in 1980, Clinton won the nickname "Comeback Kid" by regaining the governor's office in 1982. He was elected three more times, earning a reputation as one of the nation's most successful young political leaders.

In keeping with the theme of his campaign, Clinton concentrated at first on the economy. The federal budget he proposed to Congress in February 1993 called for tax increases and spending cuts to achieve a balanced budget. Congress was skeptical of such unpopular measures, but Clinton cajoled, shamed, and threatened sufficient members to win approval of $241 billion in new taxes and $255 billion in spending cuts, for a total deficit reduction of $496 billion over four years. This major achievement earned Clinton the confidence of financial markets and helped fuel the economic boom of the 1990s.

Clinton scored another victory when Congress approved the North American Free Trade Agreement (NAFTA) in the fall of 1993. NAFTA, initiated and nearly completed by Bush, was a free trade plan that united the United States, Mexico, and Canada into a common market without tariff barriers. Clinton endorsed the treaty as a way of securing American prosperity and spreading American values. Critics complained that free trade would cost American workers their jobs as American companies moved production overseas; Ross Perot, the defeated 1992 third-party candidate, predicted a "giant sucking sound" as American jobs went south to Mexico. But Clinton carried the day, winning a bruising fight in the House and an easier contest in the Senate.

Although Clinton's NAFTA coalition included many congressional Republicans, on other issues the GOP staunchly opposed the president. Republicans decried his budget as entailing "the biggest tax increase in the history of the world," and they scuttled an ambitious attempt to revamp the nation's health care system. Leading the opposition was a young congressman from Georgia, Newton Leroy "Newt" Gingrich, who asked all GOP candidates in the 1994 congressional races to sign a ten-point "Contract with America." The contract consisted of familiar conservative goals, including a balanced budget amendment to the Constitution, term limits for members of Congress, a line-item veto for the president, and a middle-class tax cut. For the first time in recent political history, a party sought to win Congress on ideological issues rather than relying on individual personalities.

A series of embarrassing disclosures involving Bill Clinton's character made this tactic particularly effective in 1994. During the 1992 campaign, the *New York Times* had raised questions about a bankrupt Arkansas land development called Whitewater in which the Clintons had lost a modest investment. Additional scandals cropped up over activities that had taken place after Clinton was elected president. Travelgate was the name given to the firing, apparently at the urging of First Lady Hillary Clinton, of several White House employees who arranged travel for the press covering the president. Then in early 1994, Paula Jones, a former Arkansas state employee, filed a sexual harassment suit against Clinton, charging that in 1991 then-Governor Clinton had made sexual advances to her.

The outcome of the November 1994 vote stunned political observers. The Republicans gained 9 seats in the Senate and an astonishing 53 in the House to take control of both houses. Newt Gingrich, who had worked so hard to ensure the change in leadership in the Congress, became speaker of the House. The GOP also captured 32 governorships, including those of New York, California, and Texas, where George W. Bush, the son of the man Clinton beat in 1992, won handily.

The Republicans claimed a mandate to resume the Reagan Revolution: to cut taxes, diminish the scope of government, and empower the private sector. Clinton and the Democrats managed to keep the Republicans in check on matters of substance, but the Republicans in turn contrived to hobble Clinton. The administration and the Republicans collaborated on welfare reform and a modest increase in the minimum wage, but otherwise deadlock descended on Washington.

Clinton turned the deadlock to his benefit in 1996 after the Republicans, having failed to force him to accept cuts in Medicare, college loans, and other social services, refused to pass a budget bill, and thereby shut down the federal government. Clinton proved defter at finger-pointing than Gingrich and the Republicans did, and he succeeded in persuading voters that they were to blame. He carried this theme into his 1996 re-election campaign. The Republican nominee, Robert Dole of Kansas, lacked Clinton's charisma and failed to shake the impression that the Republicans were flint-hearts who wanted to cut the pet programs of the American people. Clinton won decisively, holding the presidency for the Democrats even while the Republicans continued to control Congress.

THE ELECTION OF 1996

CANDIDATE	PARTY	POPULAR VOTE	ELECTORAL VOTE
Clinton	Democratic	45,590,703	379
Dole	Republican	37,816,307	159
Perot	Independent	7,866,284	—

SCANDAL IN THE WHITE HOUSE

Despite Clinton's re-election, rumors of wrongdoing still clung to his presidency. The special prosecutor appointed to probe the Whitewater transactions, Kenneth Starr, turned over stone after stone in search of evidence of malfeasance, till he came across rumors that Clinton had conducted a clandestine affair with a White House intern, Monica Lewinsky.

Clinton initially denied the affair. "I did not have sexual relations with that woman, Miss Lewinsky," he said in January 1998. But Starr subpoenaed Lewinsky, who eventually gave a detailed account of her sexual encounters with the president and provided crucial physical evidence implicating Clinton.

Realizing that he could no longer deny the affair, the president sought to limit the damage. On August 17, 1998, he appeared before Starr's grand jury and admitted to having "inappropriate intimate contact" with Lewinsky. That evening Clinton spoke briefly to the nation. Claiming that he had given the grand jury "legally accurate" answers, the president for the first time admitted to a relationship with Lewinsky that was "not appropriate" and "wrong." He said he regretted misleading the people and especially his wife, but he refused to apologize for his behavior or his false denials.

Clinton's fate hung in the balance. For the first time, some Democrats began to speak out. But just when Clinton seemed most vulnerable, the special prosecutor inadvertently rescued him. In early September, Starr sent a 452-page report to Congress outlining eleven possible impeachment charges against Clinton. The key one was perjury, and Starr provided painstakingly graphic detail on all of the sexual encounters between Clinton and Lewinsky to prove that the president had lied when he denied engaging in sexual relations with the intern.

Many Americans responded by condemning Starr rather than the president. Shocked by the sordid details, they blamed the prosecutor for exposing families to distasteful sexual practices on the evening news. When Hillary Clinton stood staunchly by her husband, a majority of the public seemed to conclude that however bad the president's conduct, it was a private matter, one to be settled between a husband and a wife, not in the public arena.

Republican leaders ignored the public sentiment and pressed ahead with impeachment proceedings. In December, the House (where the 1998 midterm

Members of the House Judiciary Committee listen to President Clinton's testimony during the hearings on his impeachment in December 1998. The Committee sent four articles of impeachment to the full House, and the House adopted two—one count of perjury and one of obstruction of justice. The Senate could not muster the two-thirds majority required for conviction, and so Clinton was acquitted of both articles.

elections had narrowed the GOP advantage to six) voted on four articles of impeachment, rejecting two, but approving two others—perjury and obstruction of justice—by small margins in nearly straight party-line votes.

The final showdown in the Senate was anticlimactic. With a two-thirds vote required to find the president guilty and remove him from office, there was no chance of conviction in the highly charged partisan mood that prevailed. On February 12, 1999, the GOP was unable to muster even a majority on the perjury charge, with 45 in favor and 55 opposed. After a second, closer vote, 50 to 50, on obstruction of justice, the presiding officer, Chief Justice William Rehnquist, declared, "Acquitted of the charges."

CLINTON AND THE WORLD

Neither Clinton's scandals nor his struggle with Congress allowed Americans to forget about the rest of the world, much though many would have liked to do so. The Cold War had ended, and with it America's forty-year struggle with communism. But the post–Cold War world was plenty threatening, and while the United States was the only superpower still standing, America's power could not preserve Americans from having to make difficult decisions about how to use that power.

OLD RIVALS IN NEW LIGHT

Inheriting the chaos left by the breakup of the Soviet Union, Clinton concentrated on two issues in dealing with Russia and its neighbors. First, as Bush had done, he strongly supported Russian President Boris Yeltsin. In 1993, Clinton persuaded Congress to provide a $2.5 billion aid package to help Yeltsin carry out his free market reforms of the devastated Russian economy. The Clinton administration backed Yeltsin and his successor, Vladimir V. Putin, despite Russia's continuing brutal war with Chechnya. Although the expansion of NATO to include Poland, Hungary, and the Czech Republic, and plans for a missile defense system, created some tension, the Clinton administration succeeded in maintaining good relations with Russia.

Clinton was even more successful on the second big issue left over from the Cold War against the Soviets: preventing the proliferation of nuclear weapons among the former republics of the Soviet Union. With patient diplomacy, Secretary of State Warren Christopher won agreements from Belarus and Kazakhstan to scrap their deadly ICBMs. Ukraine proved more difficult, but Clinton persuaded the president of Ukraine in 1994 to surrender his country's entire nuclear stockpile. Clinton's effort on behalf of nuclear nonproliferation in the former Soviet Union was perhaps his most important, if least heralded, achievement.

The president's policy toward China was more questionable. Clinton ignored China's dismal human rights record and continued Bush's policy of annually extending most favored nation status to Beijing. The growing importance of trade with China, whose economic output in 1993 exceeded Britain's, led Clinton to overlook the memory of the Tiananmen Square massacre and the continued persecution of dissidents in China. As trade with China began to rival that with Japan, the president announced a policy of "constructive engagement." It was better, he contended, to keep talking, and trading, with China than to harden Chinese resentment against the West by harping on moral issues. In 2000, Clinton won a notable victory for free trade when the House voted to give China permanent most favored nation status.

The Chinese, however, proved to be less than fully cooperative. China ignored U.S. protests of its export of missiles to Iran and nuclear technology to Pakistan, and it continued to stifle dissent at home. China conducted provocative missile tests near Taiwan, which Beijing still claimed for China. When the Clinton administration sent aircraft carriers to patrol the waters off Taiwan, a Chinese official talked casually about raining nuclear bombs upon Los Angeles. Constructive engagement clearly had its limits.

TO INTERVENE OR NOT

The most difficult foreign policy decisions for the Clinton administration came over the use of American troops abroad. The absence of the Cold War threat, with its implicit need to counter communist rivals, made it much more difficult for the president and his advisers to decide when the national interest required sending American servicemen and servicewomen into harm's way. Between 1993 and 1999, Clinton opted for foreign intervention in four areas—Somalia, Haiti, Bosnia, and Kosovo—with decidedly mixed results.

Clinton inherited the Somalian venture from Bush, who in December 1992 had sent 25,000 American troops to that starving country on a humanitarian mission. Under Clinton, however, the original aim of using troops to protect the flow of food supplies and relief workers gradually shifted to supporting a UN effort at nation building. Tragedy struck in October 1993 when eighteen American soldiers died in a botched attempt to capture a local warlord in Mogadishu. After television cameras recorded the naked corpse of a U.S. helicopter pilot being dragged through the streets of Somalia's capital, an angry Congress demanded a quick end to the intervention. American forces left Somalia by the end of March 1994 in what was unquestionably the low point of Clinton's foreign policy.

The lack of clear criteria governing intervention that had brought on the disaster in Somalia almost led to another fiasco in Haiti. Seeking to halt the flow into Florida of thousands of Haitians fleeing both poverty and tyranny, Clinton worked to compel the military rulers of Haiti to abdicate in favor of the man they had overthrown in 1991, Jean-Bertrand Aristide. After nearly a year of trade sanctions and increasing diplomatic pressure, the president prepared to use force to remove the military regime. At the last minute, a three-member peace mission led by former President Jimmy Carter worked out a compromise that allowed U.S. troops to land unopposed in late September 1994. Aristide returned to Haiti, but he could do little either to restore democracy or achieve economic progress in view of his country's bankrupt treasury, ruined economy, and deep political divisions. By the time Aristide turned over the presidency to his elected successor in 1996, Haiti remained mired in hopeless poverty. The reality of Haiti's plight had frustrated Clinton's effort to use American power righteously.

Two other U.S. interventions, in Bosnia and Kosovo on the Balkan Peninsula, were more difficult but more successful. The breakup of Yugoslavia in 1991 led the Muslim president of Bosnia to ask the European community to recognize the independence of Bosnia-Herzegovina. But Bosnia's ethnic and religious makeup— 44 percent Muslim, 31 percent Serb, and 17 percent Croat—contributed to a civil

The lack of any clear principle or philosophy guiding President Clinton's foreign policy hampered the effort to define the proper role for and responsibilities of the United States, the only remaining superpower, in the post–Cold War era.

war in which the Bosnian Serbs used the weapons of the former Yugoslavian army to seize more than 70 percent of Bosnian territory. The Muslim and Croatian forces were unable to prevent the Serb bombardment of the capital, Sarajevo, or the Serb policy of "ethnic cleansing"—driving Muslims and Croats from their ancestral homes.

Clinton initially backed a plan to divide Bosnia into ten ethnic provinces. When the Serbs rejected the proposal in the spring of 1993, the president fell back on using American air power to patrol no-fly zones over Bosnia designed to protect UN peacekeeping efforts. Meanwhile, Serb artillery continued to pour a withering fire on the civilian population of Sarajevo, and journalists reported a series of brutal atrocities in which Serb troops slaughtered thousands of Muslim men and raped thousands of Muslim women.

These reports forced Clinton's hand. In the summer of 1995, American planes under NATO auspices began a series of air strikes on the Serb forces, shelling Sarajevo from the surrounding mountains. The air campaign, which lasted two weeks, along with a major counteroffensive by better equipped Croatian and Muslim forces, led to a cease-fire in October 1995. The three warring factions sent delegations to Dayton, Ohio, to discuss a settlement. After three weeks of talks, U.S. mediator Richard Holbrooke secured agreement to create a weak central government for all Bosnia at Sarajevo and to divide the rest of the country into two parts: a Muslim-Croatian federation with 51 percent of the territory and a Serbian enclave with 49 percent. The Dayton plan called for free elections, the return of refugees to their former homes, and a NATO force to oversee the peace process.

The U.S. intervention in Kosovo was similarly rooted in the breakup of Yugoslavia. Serbian leader Slobodan Milosevic had ended Kosovo's autonomy within Yugoslavia and imposed Serbian rule, even though 90 percent of the province's population was ethnic Albanian. When these Kosovars launched a guerrilla war against the Serbian police, Milosevic responded with a campaign of repression that outraged world opinion. Diplomatic efforts failed to achieve a cease-fire, prompting Clinton and the heads of government of other NATO countries in March 1999 to order an aerial assault on Serbia, in an effort to end the persecution of the Kosovars.

At first it appeared that Clinton had miscalculated. The initial air attacks, directed at empty barracks and remote military bases, failed to persuade Milosevic to seek peace. Instead, he stepped up the ethnic cleansing in Kosovo, forcing hundreds of thousands of Kosovars to leave their homes and flee to neighboring Albania and Macedonia.

Clinton and the NATO governments shifted the focus of the air assault to Serbia's infrastructure, targeting bridges, oil refineries, and, most important of all, power stations. By the end of May 1999, Serbia had lost 60 percent of its electrical capacity, and domestic pressure on Milosevic began to mount. With Russian diplomats acting as go-betweens, Milosevic finally agreed to halt his attempts to purge Kosovo of its Albanian inhabitants. An agreement signed on June 10, 1999, called for the withdrawal of all Serb forces and placed Kosovo under UN supervision, with NATO troops acting as peacekeepers.

REPUBLICANS TRIUMPHANT

Clinton's eight years in the White House gave Democrats hope that the conservative gains of the 1980s had been only temporary. They pointed to the booming economy of the 1990s and the absence of any serious threat to American security as reasons for voters to leave the presidency in Democratic hands. The election of 2000 proved a bitter disappointment—all the more bitter by reason of the way in which it made Republican George W. Bush president.

THE DISPUTED ELECTION OF 2000

If history had been the guide, the prosperity of the 1990s should have guaranteed victory to Clinton's protégé, Vice President Al Gore. The state of the economy generally determines the outcome of presidential elections, and entering 2000 the American economy had never appeared stronger. The stock market soared, spreading wealth among tens of millions of Americans; the federal deficit of the Reagan years had given way to large and growing surpluses.

But Clinton's personal problems muddled the issue. Clinton had survived his impeachment trial, yet the experience tainted his record and left many voters unwilling to reward the Democrats by promoting his vice president.

Certain other domestic problems unnerved voters, as well. The 1995 bombing of a federal building in Oklahoma City by two domestic terrorists killed 168 people and suggested that irrational violence threatened the daily lives of ordinary Americans. This feeling was reinforced by a 1999 shooting rampage at Columbine High School near Denver, which left twelve students and a teacher dead, besides the two shooters, who killed themselves. The apparent conflict between material abundance and eroding personal values resulted in the closest election in more than a century.

The two candidates, Vice President Gore of Tennessee and Governor Bush of Texas, had little in common beyond being the sons of successful political fathers. Gore had spent eighteen years in Washington as a congressman, senator, and vice president. Somewhat stiff and aloof in manner, he had mastered the intricacies of all the major policy issues and had the experience and knowledge to lead the nation. Bush, by contrast, had pursued a business career before winning the governorship of Texas in 1994. Personable and outgoing, Bush had the temperament for leadership but lacked not only experience but a full grasp of national issues. Journalists were quick to seize on the weaknesses of both men, accusing Gore of frequent and misleading exaggeration and Bush of mangling words and speaking only in generalities.

The candidacy of consumer advocate Ralph Nader, who ran on the Green party ticket, complicated the political reckoning. Nader never seemed likely to win more than a small percentage of the votes, but in a close election a few points could make all the difference. Nader's mere presence pushed Gore to the left, leaving room for Bush among independent-minded swing voters.

The race appeared close until election day, and even closer on election night. Gore seemed the likely winner when the major television networks predicted a Democratic victory in Florida. They reconsidered as Bush swept the South, in-

THE ELECTION OF 2000

CANDIDATE	PARTY	POPULAR VOTE	ELECTORAL VOTE
Bush	Republican	50,456,167	271
Gore	Democratic	50,996,064	266*
Nader	Green	2,864,810	—

*One District of Columbia Gore elector abstained.

cluding the Clinton-Gore home states of Arkansas and Tennessee. After midnight, the networks again called Florida, but this time for Bush, and the vice president telephoned the governor to concede, only to recant an hour later when it became clear that the Bush margin in Florida was paper thin.

There things stuck, and for the next month all eyes were on Florida. Gore had 200,000 more popular votes nationwide than Bush, and 267 electoral votes to Bush's 246. Yet with Florida's 25 electoral votes, Bush could win the presidency. Both sides sent teams of lawyers to Florida. Bush's team, working with Florida's Republican secretary of state, sought to certify the results that showed the GOP candidate with a lead of 930 votes out of nearly 6 million cast. Citing many voting problems disclosed by the media, Gore asked for a recount in three heavily Democratic counties in south Florida. All three used antiquated punch card machines that resulted in some ballots not being clearly marked for any presidential candidate when the chads, the bits of paper removed when a card is punched, were not completely detached from the cards. For weeks, the results in Florida, and hence of the entire election, appeared to depend on how one divined the intent of a voter based on hanging, dimpled, or bulging chads.

The decision finally came in the courts. Democrats appealed the initial attempt to certify Bush as the victor to the Florida Supreme Court. The Florida court twice ordered recounts, the second time for all counties in the state, but Bush's lawyers appealed to the United States Supreme Court. On December 12, five weeks after the election, the Court overruled the state court's call for a recount, in a 5 to 4 decision that reflected a long-standing ideological divide among the nine justices. The next day, Gore gracefully conceded, and Bush finally became president-elect.

GEORGE W. BUSH AT HOME

Bush's first order of business was a large tax cut, which required intense lobbying from the White House. The president had to win over enough conservative southern Democrats to compensate for losing Republican moderates who insisted on reducing the federal debt before cutting taxes. Bush managed the feat, and in June 2005 Congress passed legislation that slashed taxes by a staggering

$1.35 trillion over a ten-year period. Many of the cuts would take effect only in future years, but Congress offered an immediate stimulus to the economy by authorizing rebate payments to taxpayers: $600 for couples and $300 for individuals earning more than $6000 a year. While critics saw this measure as a betrayal of the long effort to balance the budget, Bush contended that future budget surpluses would more than offset the loss of tax revenue.

A slowdown in the American economy, which soon turned the projected budget surplus into annual deficits, failed to halt the Bush administration's tax cut momentum. In 2003, arguing that a further reduction in taxes would stimulate the stalled economy, Bush prevailed upon Congress to adopt another $350 billion in cuts. Like the 2001 cuts, the new reductions were temporary in order to preserve the possibility of a balanced budget by 2010. Opponents charged that if a future Congress made these tax cuts permanent, as seemed likely, the total cost would rise to nearly $1 trillion. While Clinton had favored a policy of eliminating the deficit, Bush made tax reduction the centerpiece of his economic policy.

Although it took a bit longer, the president also succeeded in persuading Congress to enact a program of education reform. Borrowing the label, "No Child Left Behind," from liberal Democrats, the administration pushed hard for a new policy requiring states to give annual performance tests to all elementary school students. Democrats countered with demands for increased federal funding of public education to assist states and local school boards in raising their standards. Bush shrewdly cultivated the support of Senator Edward Kennedy, a leading liberal Democrat, to forge a bipartisan consensus. The final measure increased federal aid to education by $4 billion, to a total of $22 billion annually, and mandated state tests in reading and math for all students in grades three through eight, and at least once during grades ten to twelve.

By this time the economic slowdown had become a full-blown recession, the first in ten years. A glut of unsold goods forced manufacturers to curtail production and lay off workers. Unemployment rose, eventually to 6 percent, despite the efforts of the Federal Reserve to stem the decline by cutting interest rates. The tax rebates authorized by Congress had boosted the economy slightly during the summer of 2001, but then the September 11 terrorist attacks on New York and the Pentagon led to a further decline. In 2002, the economy once again began to recover, only to relapse late in the year amid concern over the threat of war with Iraq.

One of the most troubling aspects of the economic downturn was the implosion of several major corporations and the subsequent revelation of shocking financial practices. WorldCom, Inc., a major telecommunications company, became the largest corporation in American history to declare bankruptcy, while a New York grand jury charged executives of Tyco International, a large electronics company, with stealing more than $600 million from shareholders through stock fraud, false expense reports, and unauthorized bonuses.

These scandals, however, paled before the misdeeds of Enron, a Houston energy company that failed in late 2001 as the result of astonishingly corrupt business practices, including fraudulent accounting and private partnerships designed to inflate profits and hide losses. When investors began to sell their overvalued Enron stock, shares that were once worth nearly $100 fell to less than $1. Enron declared bankruptcy and the remaining shareholders lost over $50 billion, while rank-and-file employees lost not only their jobs but much of their retirement savings, invested largely in now worthless Enron stock.

THE WAR ON TERROR

On the morning of September 11, 2001, nineteen Islamic militant terrorists hijacked four U.S. airliners and turned them to attack targets in New York City and Washington, D.C. The hijackers took over two planes flying out of Boston's Logan Airport en route to California, and flew them into the World Trade Center (WTC) in New York. One plane slammed into the north tower just before 9 A.M. and the second hit the south tower only 20 minutes later. Within two hours, both towers had collapsed, taking the lives of nearly 3000 victims trapped in the buildings or crushed by the debris and more than 300 firefighters and other rescue workers who attempted to save them.

In Washington, an American Airlines flight that left Dulles Airport bound for Los Angeles met a similar fate. Taken over by five terrorists, the Boeing 757 plowed into the Pentagon, destroying one wing of the building and killing 189 military personnel and civilian workers. The terrorists had seized a fourth plane, United Airlines flight 93, scheduled to fly from Newark, New Jersey, to San Francisco. Over Pennsylvania, as the hijackers attempted to turn the plane toward the nation's capital, the passengers fought to regain control of the plane. They failed to do so, but prevented the plane from hitting another target in Washington—perhaps the White House or the Capitol building. Flight 93 crashed in southern Pennsylvania, killing all forty-four passengers and crew as well as the hijackers.

"None of us will forget this day," President Bush told the American people in a televised speech that evening. Bush vowed to find and punish those responsible for the attacks, as well as any who assisted them. "We will make no distinction between those who planned these acts and those who harbor them."

Bush didn't have to look long to discover the mastermind behind the September 11 attacks. Osama bin Laden, a wealthy Saudi, released videotapes claiming responsibility on behalf of his terrorist organization, al Qaeda ("the Base" in Arabic). Bin Laden had originally been part of the international Muslim resistance to the Soviet invasion of Afghanistan that had received support and weapons from the CIA in the 1980s. He turned against the United States at the time of the 1991 Persian Gulf War, outraged by the presence of large numbers of American troops in his native Saudi Arabia. Evidence linked bin Laden and al Qaeda to the bombing of two American embassies in East Africa in 1998 and an attack on the American destroyer USS *Cole* in Yemen in 2000.

The United States had been trying to neutralize al Qaeda for a decade without success. Ordered out of Saudi Arabia in 1991, bid Laden had sought refuge in the Sudan and later in Afghanistan after the Taliban, another extremist Muslim group, took over that country. In Afghanistan, bin Laden set up camps to train hundreds of would-be terrorists, mainly from Arab countries but including recruits from the Philippines, Indonesia, and Central Asia. After the 1998 embassy bombings, President Clinton ordered cruise missile attacks on several of

As rescue efforts continued in the rubble of the World Trade Center, President Bush toured the site on September 14, 2001. In CNN's televised coverage of the visit, Bush is shown here addressing rescue workers through a bullhorn. Firefighter Bob Beckwith stands beside him.

these camps in the hope of killing bin Laden. The al Qaeda leader survived, though, leaving one of the targets only a few hours before the strike.

Bush's determination to go after those harboring terrorists made Afghanistan the prime target for the American counterattack. The president ordered the Pentagon and the CIA, which already had agents on the scene, to launch an invasion of Afghanistan to destroy the Taliban, wipe out al Qaeda, and capture or kill Osama bin Laden.

In early October 2001, the CIA and Army Special Forces began the operation, relying on the Northern Alliance, an Afghan political coalition resisting the Taliban. Using a variety of methods, ranging from bribes of local warlords to air strikes, American forces quickly routed the Taliban and by December had installed a U.S.-friendly regime in Kabul. Most of Afghanistan, however, remained in chaos, and despite extensive efforts and several near misses, bin Laden avoided capture.

While waging the war on terror abroad, the Bush administration also focused on the problem of securing the United States from any further terrorist assaults. At the president's urging, Congress approved a new Department of Homeland Security, combining the Customs Bureau, the Coast Guard, the Immigration and Naturalization Service (INS), and other government bureaus.

A primary focus of homeland security was on ensuring the safety of airline travel in the wake of the September 11 hijackings. In November 2001, Bush signed legislation replacing private companies with government employees at all airport screening stations. The airlines were required to replace cockpit doors with secure barriers and to permit armed air marshals to ride among the passengers. The understandable public fear of flying after September 11 nevertheless had a devastating effect on the airline industry, forcing the cancellation of many flights and the laying off of thousands of pilots and other workers. Despite a $15 billion government bailout approved in late September 2001, the airlines continued to experience heavy losses. Several, including United Airlines, filed for bankruptcy. Although air travel began to revive slowly in 2002, the industry, along with other forms of tourism, continued to be a drag on an already sluggish economy.

The war on terror raised an even more fundamental question than economic stagnation. Attorney General John Ashcroft, using new powers granted by Congress under the Patriot Act, conducted a broad crackdown on possible terrorists, detaining many Muslim Americans on flimsy evidence and insisting that concern for national security outweighed traditional civil liberties. Opponents quickly challenged Ashcroft, arguing that the terrorists would win their greatest victory if the United States violated its own historic principles of individual freedom in the name of fighting terrorism. It was a debate that troubled many Americans who had difficulty reconciling the need for security with respect for civil liberties.

A New American Empire?

The terrorist attacks on the United States were the catalyst for a major change in direction for American foreign policy. Not only did the Bush administration wage an intensive effort to avenge the September 11 attacks and prevent further assaults, it initiated a new global policy of American preeminence. For the first time since the end of the Cold War, the United States had a clear, if controversial, blueprint for international affairs.

The new administration rejected traditional forms of international cooperation. President Bush withdrew U.S. participation in the Kyoto Protocol to control global warming and announced plans to terminate the 1972 Antiballistic Missile (ABM) treaty with Russia. And he was outspoken in refusing to expose American servicemen and women to the jurisdiction of the International Criminal Court for possible crimes committed in worldwide peacekeeping efforts.

The new direction of American foreign policy became clear on January 29, 2002, when Bush delivered his second State of the Union address to Congress and the nation. He repeated his vow to punish all nations sponsoring terrorism, and he specified three countries in particular. Iraq, Iran, and North Korea, he declared in a memorable phrase, constituted an "axis of evil." Nine months later, in September 2002, the Bush administration released a fully developed statement of its new world policy, "National Security Strategy (NSS) of the United States." The goal of American policy, Bush's NSS declared, was to "extend the peace by encouraging free and open societies on every continent."

There were two main components of the new strategy, which critics quickly called unilateralism. The first was to accept fully the role the nation had been playing since the end of the Cold War: global policeman. The United States would not shrink from defending freedom anywhere in the world—with allies if possible, by itself if necessary. To implement this policy, NSS asserted that the Bush administration would maintain "military strength beyond challenge." "Our forces," the NSS declared, "will be strong enough to dissuade potential adversaries from pursuing a military buildup in hopes of surpassing, or equaling, the power of the United States."

In playing the role of world cop, Bush and his advisers asserted the right to the preventive use of force. Reacting to September 11, the NSS continued, "We cannot let our enemies strike first." Although promising to seek the support of the international community before using force, the NSS stated, "we will not hesitate to act alone, if necessary, to exercise our right of self-defense." In other words, the Bush administration, aware that the United States was far stronger militarily and economically than any other nation, accepted its new role as final arbiter of all international disputes.

Iraq quickly became the test case for this new shift in American foreign policy. After his "axis of evil" speech in January, President Bush focused on what he and his Pentagon advisers called weapons of mass destruction (WMD) that they claimed Saddam Hussein had been secretly amassing in large quantities. The United States demanded that Iraq permit UN inspectors (forced out of the country in 1998) to search for such weapons. Meanwhile the Bush administration perfected plans for a unilateral American military solution to the Iraq question.

Slowly, but inevitably, the United States moved toward war with Iraq in late 2002 and early 2003. Congress approved a resolution in October authorizing the president to use force against Saddam Hussein's regime. A month later, the UN Security Council voted unanimously to send its team of inspectors back into Iraq, warning Saddam of "severe consequences" if he failed to comply. Despite the failure of the international inspectors to find any evidence of chemical, biological, or nuclear weapons in Iraq, the Bush administration kept pressing for a Security Council resolution authorizing the use of force to compel Saddam to disarm. When France and Russia vowed to veto any such measure, Bush and his advisers decided to ignore the world body and proceed on their own. Preemption would have its first real test.

The ensuing war with Iraq surprised both the backers and the critics of unilateralism. In March 2003 three columns of American troops, a total of 65,000, began to execute a two-pronged invasion of Iraq from bases in Kuwait. Britain, the only major power to join the United States in the fighting, helped by besieging the city of Basra and taking control of southern Iraq. Within two weeks, the U.S. army had captured the Baghdad international airport, and on April 8, just three weeks after the fighting had begun, marines marched virtually unopposed into the heart of the city. The American people watched the televised scene of joyous Iraqis toppling a statue of Saddam in Fardos Square. An Iraqi major summed up the magnitude of his country's defeat: "Losing a war is one thing, but losing Baghdad is another," he explained. "It was like losing the dearest thing in life."

The rapid success of the anti-Saddam offensive seemed to confirm the wisdom of Bush's decision for war. But the subsequent failure to find any weapons of mass destruction led critics to question the validity of the war. In response, the president's defenders stressed the importance of deposing Saddam by pointing to his brutal prisons and to the killing fields south of Baghdad where thousands of Shi'ite rebels had been slaughtered in 1991.

The problems of restoring order and rebuilding the shattered Iraqi economy quickly overshadowed the debate over the war's legitimacy. Daily attacks on

In a memorable image from the war in Iraq, Iraqi civilians and U.S. soldiers pull down a statue of Saddam Hussein in Baghdad on April 9, 2003. Eight months later, U.S. soldiers captured the former Iraqi president near Tikrit.

American troops in the Sunni triangle north of Baghdad began in the summer of 2003 and increased in intensity during the fall, killing an average of three American soldiers each week. By October, more troops had died from these attacks than had been killed during the combat phase in March and April. Widespread looting, sabotage of oil pipelines, and difficulties in repairing and operating outdated power plants and oil facilities made economic recovery very slow and halting. U.S. efforts to involve occupation forces from other UN members yielded only a few troops.

The December 2003 arrest of Saddam, who had eluded capture till then despite determined efforts to find him, revived American optimism. Yet the overall situation remained troubling. Despite slow but steady progress in restoring public services such as electric power and the gradual recovery of the Iraq oil industry, the armed insurrection continued. Mortar attacks on Baghdad hotels, roadside bombs aimed at American armored convoys, and hand-held missile attacks on American helicopters made Iraq a very dangerous place. Equally disturbing, conflicts of interest between Shi'ite and Sunni Muslims, as well as the Kurdish demand for autonomy, threatened the American goal of creating a stable Iraqi government.

BUSH RE-ELECTED

Not surprisingly, the war in Iraq became the central issue in the 2004 presidential race. Bush cast himself as the resolute commander in the war on terror; he and his supporters contended that it would be reckless to change commanders in mid-conflict. Democrats initially favored former Vermont governor Howard Dean, who had opposed the invasion of Iraq and still strongly criticized Bush's conduct of the war. But the nomination ultimately went to Senator John Kerry of Massachusetts, a decorated Vietnam War veteran who voted for the war but later criticized Bush for misleading the country regarding the causes of the conflict, and who contended that the war in Iraq, rather than contributing to the war on terror, actually distracted from it.

The campaign was the most vitriolic in years. Democrats accused Bush of having stolen the election of 2000 (with the help of the Supreme Court) and of lying about Saddam's weapons. Republicans called Kerry's belated opposition to the war in Vietnam an insult to those Americans who had died there, and they cited certain of his votes in the Senate as evidence of a fatal inconsistency. Both sides (following the example of Howard Dean in the primaries) employed the Internet to rally the faithful, raise money, and spread rumors.

The strong emotions produced a record turnout: 12 million more than in 2000. Bush won the popular vote by 2.5 percent, becoming the first victor since his father in 1988 to gain an absolute popular majority. The electoral race was comparably close, with 286 for Bush and 252 for Kerry. Taken together with the congressional elections, which increased the Republican majorities in both the Senate and the House of Representatives, the 2004 race confirmed the "red state/blue state" split in America, with the Republicans dominating the South, the Plains, and the Rockies, while the Democrats carried the Northeast, the Great Lakes, and the West Coast.

Despite his modest margin of victory, Bush claimed a mandate. He proposed to privatize part of the Social Security system and promised to stay the course in Iraq. His Social Security plan went nowhere, but the situation in Iraq briefly seemed to improve. Elections there in January 2005 took place more calmly than many observers expected and appeared to place Iraq well on the road to self-government.

Yet an escalation of the insurgency during 2005 and early 2006 pushed American deaths in Iraq beyond 2000, and the violence grew more clearly sectarian. As the country verged on civil war, the American public grew more disillusioned than ever. An opinion poll in February 2006 revealed that 72 percent of Americans thought U.S. troops should be withdrawn from Iraq within a year; 24 percent called for an immediate pullout.

THE ELECTION OF 2004

CANDIDATE	PARTY	POPULAR VOTE	ELECTORAL VOTE
Bush	Republican	60,693,281	286
Kerry	Democratic	57,355,978	252

CHALLENGES OF THE NEW CENTURY

The war in Iraq was merely one example of the challenges facing Americans in the new century. Americans remained as divided as ever over cultural issues. A revival of the American economy after its recession masked a growing inequality between rich and poor and increasing insecurity even among those comparatively well off. The nation's health care and retirement systems sagged under the increasing demands placed upon them. Environmental worries rose along with rising global temperatures.

THE CULTURE WARS CONTINUE

The war in Iraq and the broader concerns about terrorism sometimes overshadowed but did not erase the divisions among Americans on social and cultural issues. The race question remained alive and contentious, as affirmative action policies came under increasing scrutiny. The *Bakke* decision of 1978 had allowed the use of race as one factor in determining admission to colleges and universities, so long as rigid racial quotas weren't employed. This dissatisfied many conservatives, who during the 1980s and 1990s attacked affirmative action politically and in the courts. In 1992, Cheryl Hopwood, an unsuccessful white applicant to the University of Texas Law School, challenged her rejection, contending that the school had admitted less-qualified African American applicants. In 1996, the Fifth Circuit Court of Appeals decided in her favor, and the *Hopwood* decision raised the hopes of anti–affirmative action groups that the Supreme Court would overturn *Bakke*. But in a 2003 case involving the University of Michigan, the Supreme Court ruled that "student body diversity is a compelling state interest that can justify the use of race in university admissions." In other words, affirmative action in higher education could continue. But the 5–4 vote indicated that the court remained split, and it suggested that affirmative action would continue to spark controversy.

Even more controversial was abortion. The issue had roiled American politics for years, but it did so particularly after the death of Chief Justice William Rehnquist in September 2005 and the concurrent retirement of Associate Justice Sandra Day O'Connor allowed George W. Bush to nominate their replacements. Rehnquist had been a reliable conservative, but O'Connor was a swing vote, and liberals feared that a more conservative successor would tip the balance against abortion rights, among other contentious issues. Yet John Roberts, Bush's nominee for chief justice, and Samuel Alito, the nominee for associate justice, dodged Democrats' questions in hearings, and though the Democrats briefly threatened to filibuster Alito, both nominations succeeded. Almost immediately, South Dakota passed a law essentially banning abortion, and the law, which directly challenged the abortion rights guaranteed by the 1973 *Roe* decision, appeared bound for the newly reconfigured court.

Gay rights provoked fresh controversy as gay advocates pushed for equal marital rights. After the Massachusetts supreme court in 2004 struck down a state law barring same-sex marriages, gay advocates celebrated, but conservatives in dozens of states pressed for laws and constitutional amendments reaffirming traditional

Marriage ceremony of Hillary, left, and Julie Goodridge in Boston on May 17, 2004, the first day of state-sanctioned same-sex marriage in the United States. The couple were the lead plaintiffs in the landmark lawsuit in which the Massachusetts supreme court struck down a state law barring same-sex marriages. In the first year, more than 6,000 gay and lesbian couples wed in the state.

views on the subject and defining marriage as the union of one man and one woman. Nearly all the efforts were successful, suggesting that, on this front at least, the advances gay men and women had achieved since the 1960s had hit a wall.

Science and religion continued to battle in America's classrooms. Opponents of evolution revised their challenge to Darwin, replacing creationism with "intelligent design" and demanding that this version of their beliefs be aired in biology classes. School board elections hinged on the issue; Ohio embraced intelligent design only to reject it following an adverse 2005 court decision in a case from the Dover school district. For the moment the evolutionists held their own, but given that public opinion polls consistently showed a majority of Americans rejecting evolution in favor of divine creation, the fight was sure to continue.

PROSPERITY—FOR WHOM?

After the recession of George W. Bush's first term, the economy gradually recovered. The economy as a whole grew steadily, and the jobless rate fell to less than 5 percent, not far from the level of the booming 1990s. Corporate profits soared, registering double-digit increases for three years running.

But the good news disguised some unsettling trends. The median family income declined slightly, and although corporate executives commanded seven-

and eight-digit pay packages, ordinary workers watched their compensation diminish. Wages were flat, while medical and retirement benefits fell. The poverty rate increased; in 2004, some 37 million Americans, or 12.7 percent of the population, lived below the poverty line. Nearly 46 million Americans lacked health insurance, which, besides jeopardizing their health, often meant that personal bankruptcy was a broken arm or ruptured appendix away.

Uncertainty came in other forms as well. The globalization of the economy placed continued pressure on American jobs. The automobile industry, long a mainstay of the American economy, suffered grievously. General Motors lost billions and was forced to slash tens of thousands of jobs. In early 2006, Ford announced the closing of fourteen plants in the United States and Canada. Even workers in industries formerly thought exempt from the export of jobs found themselves facing direct foreign competition. Telephone call centers moved from the American Midwest to Ireland; computer and other high-tech companies relocated research facilities to India and China. What Silicon Valley in California had been to the birth of the personal computer industry in the 1970s, Bangalore in India promised—or threatened—to be to the industry's maturation in the 2010s.

Rising oil prices—triggered by the turmoil in the Middle East but also by rising demand from China—threatened the status quo in other ways. The rise this

Employees at a busy call center in Bangalore, India, provide service support to international customers. India is the leading market to which developed nations such as the United States outsource high-technology jobs.

time took place more gradually than during the 1970s—the price required a year, rather than weeks, to double, to more than $60 a barrel in early 2006—and though nothing quite like the oil shocks of that earlier decade occurred, the higher price of oil did contribute to higher prices for a wide array of other goods, and it rekindled fears of inflation. At the gas pump, prices leaped to more than $3 a gallon. As was often the case, persons at the lower end of the income scale were hit harder than those higher up, as transportation took a larger share of their income. In the long term, the higher prices would prompt the purchase of more efficient cars; in the meantime, drivers simply had to grin and bear $40 fill-ups as best they could.

DOUBTING THE FUTURE

During most of American history, every generation had been better off materially than the generation before. Events of the early twenty-first century called this implicit guarantee into question. To an unprecedented extent, the American economy was at the mercy of developments beyond American shores. The pressure on American jobs would continue and probably intensify; no less alarming, as a result of America's large and growing trade deficit, foreign investors held huge quantities of America's public debt. Should these investors lose confidence in America's economic future, or for whatever other reason decide to divest themselves of their dollar holdings, interest rates in the United States would probably balloon, touching off a major recession. Already some of the foreign investors were diversifying from Treasury bonds into ownership of American capital assets, making the American economy—and even American physical safety—further subject to foreign influence. When, in early 2006, a firm from the United Arab Emirates applied to purchase the concession to operate six American port facilities, a public outcry arose that American security was in danger.

Internal problems appeared hardly more tractable. As the baby boom generation neared retirement, the load on the Social Security system increased. Everyone realized something would have to be done to keep the pension program afloat, but after the rejection of George W. Bush's privatization scheme, no one could figure out how to make the necessary changes politically palatable. Middle-aged Americans faced the prospect of delayed retirement, smaller pensions, or both. Not surprisingly, they resisted. Younger Americans resisted the tax increases that could have spared the elders such sacrifice.

The trend in health care costs was even more alarming. For years, medical costs had grown rapidly and, as the population aged, they appeared certain to claim an ever larger share of the nation's income. Combined with the growth in the number of Americans without medical insurance, the health care system seemed to require a major overhaul. But, again, the status quo stubbornly resisted changing, and the situation only grew worse.

Immigration became more controversial than at any time since the 1920s. The number of persons entering the country illegally soared, but efforts to rectify the situation—as by tighter enforcement at the border, by sanctions on employers hiring undocumented aliens, by temporary visas for guest workers—stalled on the opposition of immigrant advocates, of businesses, and of assorted other groups.

Environmental problems demanded attention, which they got, and solutions, which they didn't. A consensus emerged among the scientific community that global warming had to be addressed, but the proposed solutions—higher mileage standards for automobiles, a "carbon tax" on emissions of greenhouse gases, greater reliance on nuclear energy, among others—were costly, intrusive, unproven, or environmentally problematic in their own ways. As on other issues, there was broad agreement that current trends were unsustainable, but little agreement on what should replace them.

THE PARADOX OF POWER

Events of the early twenty-first century highlighted a paradox of contemporary American life. Never in their history had Americans been more powerful relative to the rest of the world, yet rarely in their history had they felt more at risk. Their superpower status couldn't preserve them from the terrorist attacks of September 11, nor could it guarantee victory over the insurgents in Iraq. Had the United States been less powerful, it might not have become the target of al Qaeda's hijackers; had it been less powerful, it probably wouldn't have been tempted to invade Iraq. Power excited envy, and invited hubris. America might be the only remaining superpower, but it wasn't omnipotent, and it wasn't invulnerable.

Nor were Americans invulnerable to the challenges that crowded domestic life as the new century took shape. The American economy was still far and away the most powerful and dynamic in the world, but it was increasingly subject to unsettling foreign influences, and it failed distressingly often to deliver on the promise of equality to the most vulnerable in society. Conservatives and liberals fought over the values that ought to guide the country; different racial and ethnic groups proposed competing models of American pluralism.

The fundamental challenge for Americans of the twenty-first century would be to balance their power against their vulnerabilities. This wasn't new; it has been the challenge for Americans of every generation. At times, they have met the challenge brilliantly; at other times, they've done less well. How they would fare this time was for the present generation to determine—guided, ideally, by the lessons of the past.

CHRONOLOGY

1989 *Exxon Valdez* oil spill pollutes over 500 square miles of Alaskan waters
San Francisco rocked by massive earthquake
Berlin Wall crumbles

1990 Saddam Hussein invades Kuwait
Bush breaks "no new taxes" campaign pledge, supports $500 billion budget deal

1991 Operation Desert Storm frees Kuwait and crushes Iraq
Soviet Union dissolved, replaced by Commonwealth of Independent States

1992 Riots devastate South Central Los Angeles after verdict in Rodney King case
Bill Clinton elected president

1993 General Motors announces loss of $23.4 billion, the largest one-year loss in U.S. corporate history

1994 Former football star O. J. Simpson charged with killing ex-wife Nicole Brown Simpson and her friend Ronald Goldman
Republicans gain control of both houses of Congress

1995 U.S. troops arrive in Bosnia as part of international peacekeeping force

1996 FBI arrests Theodore Kaczynzki, suspected Unabomber, in Montana
Clinton signs major welfare reform measure

1997 Federal jury gives Timothy McVeigh death sentence for Oklahoma City bombing

1998 Terrorists bomb American embassies in Kenya and Tanzania

1999 Senate acquits Clinton of impeachment charges
Dow Jones Industrial Average goes over 10,000 for first time

2000 Y2K furor proves unfounded
George W. Bush wins contested presidential election

2001 American economy goes into recession, ending the longest period of expansion in U.S. history
Terrorist attacks on World Trade Center and the Pentagon
Anthrax spores found in mail
United States military action against the Taliban regime in Afghanistan

2002 Department of Homeland Security created

2003 U.S. troops invade Iraq and overthrow Saddam Hussein's regime
Saddam Hussein captured

2004 Insurgency in Iraq escalates
Global warming gains international attention
George W. Bush re-elected

2005 Bush's plan for Social Security reform fails
Hurricane Katrina devastates Gulf Coast and forces evacuation of New Orleans

2006 Proposed constitutional amendment to ban same-sex marriage fails to achieve required two-thirds majority in the Senate

APPENDIX

The Declaration of Independence

The Constitution of the United States of America

Amendments to the Constitution

Recommended Reading

Suggested Web Sites

Physical and Political Map of the United States

Political Map of the World

The Declaration of Independence

In Congress, July 4, 1776

The Unanimous Declaration
of the Thirteen United States of America,

When, in the course of human events, it becomes necessary for one people to dissolve the political bonds which have connected them with another, and to assume, among the powers of the earth, the separate and equal station to which the laws of nature and of nature's God entitle them, a decent respect to the opinions of mankind requires that they should declare the causes which impel them to the separation.

We hold these truths to be self-evident: That all men are created equal; that they are endowed by their Creator with certain unalienable rights; that among these are life, liberty, and the pursuit of happiness; that, to secure these rights, governments are instituted among men, deriving their just powers from the consent of the governed; that whenever any form of government becomes destructive of these ends, it is the right of the people to alter or to abolish it, and to institute new government, laying its foundation on such principles, and organizing its powers in such form, as to them shall seem most likely to effect their safety and happiness. Prudence, indeed, will dictate that governments long established should not be changed for light and transient causes; and accordingly all experience hath shown that mankind are more disposed to suffer, while evils are sufferable, than to right themselves by abolishing the forms to which they are accustomed. But when a long train of abuses and usurpations, pursuing invariably the same object, evinces a design to reduce them under absolute despotism, it is their right, it is their duty, to throw off such government, and to provide new guards for their future security. Such has been the patient sufferance of these colonies; and such is now the necessity which constrains them to alter their former systems of government. The history of the present King of Great Britain is a history of repeated injuries and usurpations, all having in direct object the establishment of an absolute tyranny over these states. To prove this, let facts be submitted to a candid world.

He has refused his assent to laws, the most wholesome and necessary for the public good.

He has forbidden his governors to pass laws of immediate and pressing importance, unless suspended in their operation till his assent should be obtained; and, when so suspended, he has utterly neglected to attend to them.

He has refused to pass other laws for the accommodation of large districts of people, unless those people would relinquish the right of representation in the legislature, a right inestimable to them, and formidable to tyrants only.

He has called together legislative bodies at places unusual, uncomfortable, and distant from the depository of their public records, for the sole purpose of fatiguing them into compliance with his measures.

He has dissolved representative houses repeatedly, for opposing, with manly firmness, his invasions on the rights of the people.

He has refused for a long time, after such dissolutions, to cause others to be elected; whereby the legislative powers, incapable of annihilation, have returned to the people at large for their exercise; the state remaining, in the mean time, exposed to all the dangers of invasions from without and convulsions within.

He has endeavored to prevent the population of these states; for that purpose obstructing the laws for naturalization of foreigners; refusing to pass others to encourage their migration hither, and raising the conditions of new appropriations of lands.

He has obstructed the administration of justice, by refusing his assent to laws for establishing judiciary powers.

He has made judges dependent on his will alone, for the tenure of their offices, and the amount and payment of their salaries.

He has erected a multitude of new offices, and sent hither swarms of officers to harass our people and eat out their substance.

He has kept among us, in times of peace, standing armies, without the consent of our legislatures.

He has affected to render the military independent of, and superior to, the civil power.

He has combined with others to subject us to a jurisdiction foreign to our constitution, and unacknowledged by our laws, giving his assent to their acts of pretended legislation:

For quartering large bodies of armed troops among us;

For protecting them, by a mock trial, from punishment for any murder which they should commit on the inhabitants of these states;

For cutting off our trade with all parts of the world;

For imposing taxes on us without our consent;

For depriving us, in many cases, of the benefits of trial by jury;

For transporting us beyond seas, to be tried for pretended offenses;

For abolishing the free system of English laws in a neighboring province, establishing therein an arbitrary government, and enlarging its boundaries, so as to render it at once an example and fit instrument for introducing the same absolute rule into these colonies;

For taking away our charters, abolishing our most valuable laws, and altering fundamentally the forms of our governments;

For suspending our own legislatures, and declaring themselves invested with power to legislate for us in all cases whatsoever.

He has abdicated government here, by declaring us out of his protection and waging war against us.

He has plundered our seas, ravaged our coasts, burned our towns, and destroyed the lives of our people.

He is at this time transporting large armies of foreign mercenaries to complete the works of death, desolation, and tyranny already begun with circumstances of cruelty and perfidy scarcely paralleled in the most barbarous ages, and totally unworthy the head of a civilized nation.

He has constrained our fellow-citizens, taken captive on the high seas, to bear arms against their country, to become the executioners of their friends and brethren, or to fall themselves by their hands.

He has excited domestic insurrection among us, and has endeavored to bring on the inhabitants of our frontiers the merciless Indian savages, whose known rule of warfare is an undistinguished destruction of all ages, sexes, and conditions.

In every stage of these oppressions we have petitioned for redress in the most humble terms; our repeated petitions have been answered only by repeated injury. A prince, whose character is thus marked by every act which may define a tyrant, is unfit to be the ruler of a free people.

Nor have we been wanting in our attentions to our British brethren. We have warned them, from time to time, of attempts by their legislature to extend an unwarrantable jurisdiction over us. We have reminded them of the circumstances of our emigration and settlement here. We have appealed to their native justice and magnanimity; and we have conjured them, by the ties of our common kindred, to disavow these usurpations, which would inevitably interrupt our connections and correspondence. They, too, have been deaf to the voice of justice and of consanguinity. We must, therefore, acquiesce in the necessity which denounces our separation, and hold them, as we hold the rest of mankind, enemies in war, in peace friends.

We, therefore, the representatives of the United States of America, in General Congress assembled, appealing to the Supreme Judge of the world for the rectitude of our intentions, do, in the name and by the authority of the good people of these colonies, solemnly publish and declare, that these United Colonies are, and of right ought to be, FREE AND INDEPENDENT STATES; that they are absolved from all allegiance to the British crown, and that all political connection between them and the state of Great Britain is, and ought to be, totally dissolved; and that, as free and independent states, they have full power to levy war, conclude peace, contract alliances, establish commerce, and do all other acts and things which independent states may of right do. And for the support of this declaration, with a firm reliance on the protection of Divine Providence, we mutually pledge to each other our lives, our fortunes, and our sacred honor.

JOHN HANCOCK

BUTTON GWINNETT	THOS. NELSON, JR.	RICHD. STOCKTON
LYMAN HALL	FRANCIS LIGHTFOOT LEE	JNO. WITHERSPOON
GEO. WALTON	CARTER BRAXTON	FRAS. HOPKINSON
WM. HOOPER	ROBT. MORRIS	JOHN HART
JOSEPH HEWES	BENJAMIN RUSH	ABRA. CLARK
JOHN PENN	BENJA. FRANKLIN	JOSIAH BARTLETT
EDWARD RUTLEDGE	JOHN MORTON	WM. WHIPPLE
THOS. HEYWARD, JUNR.	GEO. CLYMER	SAML. ADAMS
THOMAS LYNCH, JUNR.	JAS. SMITH	JOHN ADAMS
ARTHUR MIDDLETON	GEO. TAYLOR	ROBT. TREAT PAINE
SAMUEL CHASE	JAMES WILSON	ELBRIDGE GERRY
WM. PACA	GEO. ROSS	STEP. HOPKINS
THOS. STONE	CAESAR RODNEY	WILLIAM ELLERY
CHARLES CARROLL OF	GEO. READ	ROGER SHERMAN
CARROLLTON	THO. M'KEAN	SAM'EL HUNTINGTON
GEORGE WYTHE	WM. FLOYD	WM. WILLIAMS
RICHARD HENRY LEE	PHIL. LIVINGSTON	OLIVER WOLCOTT
TH. JEFFERSON	FRANS. LEWIS	MATTHEW THORNTON
BENJ. HARRISON	LEWIS MORRIS	

The Constitution of the United States of America

PREAMBLE

We the People of the United States, in Order to form a more perfect Union, establish Justice, insure domestic Tranquility, provide for the common defence, promote the general Welfare, and secure the Blessings of Liberty to ourselves and our Posterity, do ordain and establish this Constitution for the United States of America.

ARTICLE I

Section 1

All legislative Powers herein granted shall be vested in a Congress of the United States, which shall consist of a Senate and House of Representatives.

Section 2

The House of Representatives shall be composed of Members chosen every second Year by the People of the several States, and the Electors in each State shall have the Qualifications requisite for Electors of the most numerous Branch of the State Legislature.

No Person shall be a Representative who shall not have attained to the Age of twenty five Years, and been seven Years a Citizen of the United States, and who shall not, when elected, be an inhabitant of that State in which he shall be chosen.

Representatives and direct Taxes shall be apportioned among the several States which may be included within this Union, according to their respective Numbers, *which shall be determined by adding to the whole Number of free Persons, including those bound to Service for a Term of Years, and excluding Indians not taxed, three fifths of all other Persons.* The actual Enumeration shall be made within three Years after the first Meeting of the Congress of the United States, and within every subsequent Term of ten Years, in such Manner as they shall by Law direct. The Number of Representatives shall not exceed one for every thirty Thousand, but each State shall have at Least one Representative; *and until such enumeration shall be made, the State of New Hampshire shall be entitled to chuse three, Massachusetts eight, Rhode-Island and Providence Plantations one, Connecticut five, New York six, New Jersey four, Pennsylvania eight, Delaware one, Maryland six, Virginia ten, North Carolina five, South Carolina five, and Georgia three.*

When vacancies happen in the Representation from any State, the Executive Authority thereof shall issue Writs of Election to fill such Vacancies.

The House of Representatives shall chuse their Speaker and other Officers; and shall have the sole Power of Impeachment.

Section 3

The Senate of the United States shall be composed of two Senators from each State, *chosen by the Legislature thereof,* for six Years; and each Senator shall have one Vote.

Immediately after they shall be assembled in Consequence of the first Election, they shall be divided as equally as may be into three Classes. The Seats of the Senators of the first Class shall be vacated at the Expiration of the second Year, of the second Class at the Expiration of the fourth Year, and of the third Class at the Expiration of the sixth Year so that one third may be chosen every second Year; and if Vacancies happen by Resignation, or otherwise, during the Recess of the Legislature

---

*Passages no longer in effect are printed in italic type.

of any state, the Executive thereof may make temporary Appointments until the next Meeting of the Legislature, which shall then fill such Vacancies.

No Person shall be a Senator who shall not have attained to the Age of thirty Years, and been nine Years a Citizen of the United States, and who shall not, when elected, be an Inhabitant of that State for which he shall be chosen.

The Vice President of the United States shall be President of the Senate, but shall have no Vote, unless they be equally divided.

The Senate shall chuse their other Officers, and also a President *pro tempore*, in the Absence of the Vice President, or when he shall exercise the Office of President of the United States.

The Senate shall have the sole Power to try all Impeachments. When sitting for that Purpose, they shall be on Oath or Affirmation. When the President of the United States is tried the Chief Justice shall preside: And no Person shall be convicted without the Concurrence of two thirds of the Members present.

Judgment in Cases of Impeachment shall not extend further than to removal from Office, and disqualification to hold and enjoy any Office of honor, Trust or Profit under the United States: but the Party convicted shall nevertheless be liable and subject to Indictment, Trial, Judgment and Punishment, according to Law.

Section 4

The Times, Places and Manner of holding Elections for Senators and Representatives, shall be prescribed in each State by the Legislature thereof; but the Congress may at any time by Law make or alter such Regulations, except as to the Places of chusing Senators.

The Congress shall assemble at least once in every Year, *and such Meeting shall be on the first Monday in December, unless they shall by Law appoint a different Day.*

Section 5

Each House shall be the Judge of the Elections, Returns and Qualifications of its own Members, and a Majority of each shall constitute a Quorum to do Business; but a smaller Number may adjourn from day to day, and may be authorized to compel the Attendance of absent Members, in such Manner, and under such Penalties as each House may provide.

Each House may determine the Rules of its Proceedings, punish its Members for disorderly Behaviour, and, with the Concurrence of two thirds, expel a Member.

Each House shall keep a Journal of its Proceedings, and from time to time publish the same, excepting such Parts as may in their Judgment require Secrecy; and the Yeas and Nays of the Members of either House on any question shall, at the Desire of one fifth of those Present, be entered on the Journal.

Neither House, during the Session of Congress, shall, without the Consent of the other, adjourn for more than three days, nor to any other Place than that in which the two Houses shall be sitting.

Section 6

The Senators and Representatives shall receive a Compensation for their Services, to be ascertained by Law, and paid out of the Treasury of the United States. They shall in all Cases, except Treason, Felony and Breach of the Peace, be privileged from Arrest during their Attendance at the Session of their respective Houses, and in going to and returning from the same; and for any Speech or Debate in either House, they shall not be questioned in any other Place.

No Senator or Representative shall, during the Time for which he was elected, be appointed to any civil Office under the Authority of the United States, which shall have been created, or the Emoluments whereof shall have been encreased during such time, and no Person holding any Office under the United States, shall be a Member of either House during his Continuance in Office.

Section 7

All Bills for raising Revenue shall originate in the House of Representatives; but the Senate may propose or concur with Amendments as on other Bills.

Every Bill which shall have passed the House of Representatives and the Senate, shall, before it become a Law, be presented to the President of the United States; If he approve he shall sign it, but if not he shall return it, with his Objections to the House in which it shall have originated, who shall enter the Objections at large on their Journal, and proceed to reconsider it. If after such Reconsideration two thirds of that House shall agree to pass the Bill, it shall be sent, together with the Objections, to the other House, by which it shall likewise be reconsidered, and if approved by two thirds of that House, it shall become a Law. But in all such Cases the Votes of both Houses shall be determined by yeas and Nays, and the Names of the Persons voting for and against the Bill shall be entered on the Journal of each House respectively. If any Bill shall not be returned by the President within ten Days (Sundays excepted) after it shall have been presented to him, the Same shall be a Law, in like Manner as if he had signed it, unless the Congress by their Adjournment prevent its Return, in which Case it shall not be a Law.

Every Order, Resolution, or Vote to which the Concurrence of the Senate and House of Representatives may be necessary (except on a question of Adjournment) shall be presented to the President of the United States; and before the Same shall take Effect, shall be approved by him, or being disapproved by him, shall be repassed by two thirds of the Senate and House of Representatives, according to the Rules and Limitations prescribed in the Case of a Bill.

Section 8

The Congress shall have Power To lay and collect Taxes, Duties, Imposts and Excises, to pay the Debts and provide for the common Defence and general Welfare of the United States; but all Duties, Imposts and Excises shall be uniform throughout the United States;

To borrow Money on the credit of the United States;

To regulate Commerce with foreign Nations, and among the several States, and with the Indian Tribes;

To establish an uniform Rule of Naturalization, and uniform Laws on the subject of Bankruptcies throughout the United States;

To coin Money, regulate the Value thereof, and of foreign Coin, and fix the Standard of Weights and Measures;

To provide for the Punishment of counterfeiting the Securities and current Coin of the United States;

To establish Post Offices and post Roads;

To promote the Progress of Science and useful Arts, by securing for limited Times to Authors and Inventors the exclusive Right to their respective Writings and Discoveries;

To constitute Tribunals inferior to the supreme Court;

To define and punish Piracies and Felonies committed on the high Seas, and Offences against the Law of Nations;

To declare War, grant Letters of Marque and Reprisal, and make Rules concerning Captures on Land and Water;

To raise and support Armies, but no Appropriation of Money to that Use shall be for a longer Term than two Years;

To provide and maintain a Navy;

To make Rules for the Government and Regulation of the land and naval Forces;

To provide for calling forth the Militia to execute the Laws of the Union, suppress Insurrections and repel Invasions;

To provide for organizing, arming, and disciplining, the Militia, and for governing such Part of them as may be employed in the Service of the United States, reserving to the States respectively, the Appointment of the Officers, and the Authority of training the Militia according to the discipline prescribed by Congress;

To exercise exclusive Legislation in all Cases whatsoever, over such District (not exceeding ten Miles square) as may, by Cession of particular States, and the Acceptance of Congress, become the Seat of the Government of the United States, and to exercise like Authority over all Places purchased by the Consent of the Legislature of the State in which the Same shall be, for the Erection of Forts, Magazines, Arsenals, dock-Yards, and other needful Buildings;—And

To make all Laws which shall be necessary and proper for carrying into Execution the foregoing Powers, and all other Powers vested by this Constitution in the Government of the United States, or in any Department of Officer thereof.

Section 9

The Migration or Importation of such Persons as any of the States now existing shall think proper to admit, shall not be prohibited by the Congress prior to the Year one thousand eight hundred and eight, but a Tax or duty may be imposed on such Importation, not exceeding ten dollars for each Person.

The Privilege of the Writ of Habeas Corpus shall not be suspended, unless when in Cases of Rebellion or Invasion the public Safety may require it.

No Bill of Attainder or ex post facto Law shall be passed.

No Capitation, or other direct, Tax shall be laid, unless in Proportion to the Census or Enumeration herein before directed to be taken.

No Tax or Duty shall be laid on Articles exported from any State.

No Preference shall be given by any Regulation of Commerce or Revenue to the Ports of one State over those of another: nor shall Vessels bound to, or from, one State, be obliged to enter, clear, or pay Duties in another.

No Money shall be drawn from the Treasury, but in Consequence of Appropriations made by Law; and a regular Statement and Account of the Receipts and Expenditures of all public Money shall be published from time to time.

No Title of Nobility shall be granted by the United States: And no Person holding any Office of Profit or Trust under them, shall, without the Consent of the Congress, accept of any present, Emolument, Office, or Title, of any kind whatever, from any King, Prince, or foreign State.

Section 10

No State shall enter into any Treaty, Alliance, or Confederation; grant Letters of Marque and Reprisal; coin Money; emit Bills of Credit; make any Thing but gold and silver Coin a Tender in Payment of Debts; pass any Bill of Attainder, ex post facto Law, or Law impairing the obligation of Contracts, or grant any Title of Nobility.

No State shall, without the Consent of the Congress, lay any Imposts or Duties on Imports or Exports, except what may be absolutely necessary for executing its inspection Laws: and the net Produce of all Duties and Imposts, laid by any State on Imports or Exports, shall be for the Use of the Treasury of the United States; and all such Laws shall be subject to the Revision and Controul of the Congress.

No State shall, without the Consent of Congress, lay any Duty of Tonnage, keep Troops, or Ships of War in time of Peace, enter into any Agreement or Compact with another State, or with a foreign Power, or engage in War, unless actually invaded, or in such imminent Danger as will not admit of delay.

ARTICLE II

Section 1

The executive Power shall be vested in a President of the United States of America. He shall hold his Office during the Term of four Years, and, together with the Vice President, chosen for the same Term, be elected, as follows:

Each State shall appoint, in such Manner as the Legislature thereof may direct, a Number of Electors, equal to the whole Number of Senators and Representatives to which the State may be entitled in the Congress: but no Senator or Representative, or Person holding an Office of Trust or Profit under the United States, shall be appointed an Elector.

The Electors shall meet in their respective States, and vote by Ballot for two Persons, of whom one at least shall not be an Inhabitant of the same State with themselves. And they shall make a List of all the Persons voted for, and of the Number of Votes for each; which List they shall sign and certify, and transmit sealed to the Seat of the Government of the United States, directed to the President of the Senate. The President of the Senate shall, in the Presence of the Senate and House of Representatives, open all the Certificates, and the Votes shall then be counted. The Person having the greatest Number of Votes shall be the President, if such Number be a Majority of the whole number of Electors appointed; and if there be more than one who have such Majority, and have an equal Number of Votes, then the House of Representatives shall immediately chuse by Ballot one of them for President; and if no Person have a Majority, then from the five highest on the List the said House shall in like Manner chuse the President. But in chusing the President, the Votes shall be taken by States, the Representation from each State having one Vote; A quorum for this Purpose shall consist of a Member or Members from two thirds of the States, and a Majority of all the States shall be nec-essary to a Choice. In every Case, after the Choice of the President, the Person having the greatest Number of Votes of the Electors shall be the Vice President. But if there should remain two or more who have equal Votes, the Senate shall chuse from them by Ballot the Vice President.

The Congress may determine the time of chusing the Electors, and the Day on which they shall give their Votes; which Day shall be the same throughout the United States.

No person except a natural born Citizen, *or a Citizen of the United States, at the time of the Adoption of this Constitution,* shall be eligible to the Office of President; neither shall any Person be eligible to that Office who shall not have attained to the Age of thirty five Years, and been fourteen Years a Resident within the United States.

In Case of the Removal of the President from Office, or of his Death, Resignation, or Inability to discharge the Powers and Duties of the said Office, the Same shall devolve on the Vice President, and the Congress may by Law provide for the Case of Removal, Death, Resignation or Inability, both of the President and Vice President, declaring what Officer shall then act as President, and such Officer shall act accordingly, until the Disability be removed, or a President shall be elected.

The President shall, at stated Times, receive for his Services, a Compensation, which shall neither be encreased nor diminished during the Period for which he shall have been elected, and he shall not receive within that period any other Emolument from the United States, or any of them.

Before he enter on the Execution of his Office, he shall take the following Oath or Affirmation:—"I do solemnly swear (or affirm) that I will faithfully execute the Office of President of the United States, and will to the best of my Ability, preserve, protect and defend the Constitution of the United States."

Section 2

The President shall be Commander in Chief of the Army and Navy of the United States, and of the Militia of the several States, when called into the actual Service of the United States; he may require the Opinion, in writing, of the principal Officer in each of the executive Departments, upon any Subject relating to the Duties of their respective Offices, and he shall have Power to grant Reprieves and Pardons for Offences against the United States, except in Cases of Impeachment.

He shall have Power, by and with the Advice and Consent of the Senate, to make Treaties, pro-vided two thirds of the Senators present concur; and he shall nominate, and by and with the Advice and Consent of the Senate, shall appoint Ambassadors, other public Ministers and Consuls, Judges of the supreme Court, and all other Officers of the United States, whose Appointments are not herein otherwise provided for, and which shall be established by Law: but the Congress may by Law vest the Appointment of such inferior Officers, as they think proper in the President alone, in the Courts of Law, or in the Heads of Departments.

The President shall have Power to fill up all Vacancies that may happen during the Recess of the Senate, by granting Commissions which shall expire at the End of their next Session.

Section 3

He shall from time to time give to the Congress Information of the State of the Union, and recom-mend to their Consideration such Measures as he shall judge necessary and expedient; he may, on ex-traordinary Occasions, convene both Houses, or either of them, and in Case of disagreement between them, with Respect to the Time of Adjournment, he may adjourn them to such Time as he shall think proper; he shall receive Ambassadors and other public Ministers; he shall take Care that the Laws be faithfully executed, and shall Commission all the officers of the United States.

Section 4

The President, Vice President and all civil Officers of the United States, shall be removed from Office on Impeachment for, and Conviction of, Treason, Bribery or other high Crimes and Misdemeanors.

ARTICLE III

Section 1

The judicial Power of the United States, shall be vested in one supreme Court, and in such inferior Courts as the Congress may from time to time ordain and establish. The Judges, both of the supreme and inferior Courts, shall hold their offices during good Behaviour, and shall, at stated Times, receive for their Services, a Compensation, which shall not be diminished during their Continuance in Office.

Section 2

The judicial Power shall extend to all Cases, in Law and Equity, arising under this Constitution, the Laws of the United States, and Treaties made, or which shall be made, under their Authority;— to all Cases affecting Ambassadors, other public Ministers and Consuls;—to all Cases of admiralty and maritime Jurisdiction;—to Controversies to which the United States shall be a Party;—to Controversies between two or more States;—between a State and Citizens of another State;— *between Citizens of different States;*—between Citizens of the same State claiming Lands under Grants of different States, and between a State, or the Citizens thereof, and foreign States, Citizens or Subjects.

In all Cases affecting Ambassadors, other public Ministers and Consuls, and those in which a State shall be Party, the supreme Court shall have original Jurisdiction. In all the other Cases before mentioned, the supreme Court shall have appellate Jurisdiction, both as to Law and Fact, with such Exceptions, and under such Regulations as the Congress shall make.

The Trial of all Crimes, except in Cases of Impeachment, shall be by Jury; and such Trial shall be held in the State where the said Crimes shall have been committed; but when not committed within any State, the Trial shall be at such Place or Places as the Congress may by Law have directed.

Section 3

Treason against the United States, shall consist only in levying War against them, or in adhering to their Enemies, giving them Aid and Comfort. No person shall be convicted of Treason unless on the Testimony of two Witnesses to the same overt Act, or on Confession in open Court.

The Congress shall have Power to declare the Punishment of Treason, but no Attainder of Treason shall work Corruption of Blood, or Forfeiture except during the Life of the Person attainted.

ARTICLE IV

Section 1

Full Faith and Credit shall be given in each State to the public Acts, Records, and judicial Proceedings of every other State. And the Congress may by general Laws prescribe the Manner in which such Acts, Records and Proceedings shall be proved, and the Effect thereof.

Section 2

The Citizens of each State shall be entitled to all Privileges and Immunities of Citizens in the several States.

A Person charged in any State with Treason, Felony, or other Crime, who shall flee from Justice, and be found in another State, shall on Demand of the executive Authority of the State from which he fled, be delivered up, to be removed to the State having Jurisdiction of the Crime.

No Person held to Service or Labour in one State, under the Laws thereof, escaping into another, shall, in Consequence of any Law or Regulation therein, be discharged from such Service or Labour, but shall be delivered up on Claim of the Party to whom such Service or Labour may be due.

Section 3

New States may be admitted by the Congress into this Union; but no new State shall be formed or erected within the Jurisdiction of any other State; nor any State be formed by the Junction of two or more States, or Parts of States, without the Consent of the Legislatures of the States concerned as well as of the Congress.

The Congress shall have Power to dispose of and make all needful Rules and Regulations respecting the Territory or other Property belonging to the United States; and nothing in this Constitution shall be so construed as to Prejudice any Claims of the United States, or of any particular States.

Section 4

The United States shall guarantee to every State in this Union a Republican Form of Government, and shall protect each of them against Invasion; and on Application of the Legislature, or of the Executive (when the Legislature cannot be convened) against domestic violence.

ARTICLE V

The Congress, whenever two thirds of both Houses shall deem it necessary, shall propose Amendments to this Constitution, or, on the Application of the Legislatures of two thirds of the several States, shall call a Convention for proposing Amendments, which, in either Case, shall be valid to all Intents and Purposes, as Part of this Constitution, when ratified by the Legislatures of three fourths of the several States, or by Conventions in three fourths thereof, as the one or the other Mode of Ratification may be proposed by the Congress; *Provided that no Amendment which may be made prior to the Year One thousand eight hundred and eight shall in any Manner affect the first and fourth Clauses in the Ninth Section of the first Article;* and that no State, without its Consent, shall be deprived of its equal Suffrage in the Senate.

ARTICLE VI

All Debts contracted and Engagements entered into, before the Adoption of this Constitution, shall be as valid against the United States under this Constitution, as under the Confederation.

This Constitution, and Laws of the United States which shall be made in Pursuance thereof; and all Treaties made, or which shall be made, under the Authority of the United States, shall be the supreme Law of the Land; and the Judges in every State shall be bound thereby, any Thing in the Constitution or Laws of any State to the Contrary notwithstanding.

The Senators and Representatives before mentioned, and the Members of the several State Legislatures, and all executive and Judicial Officers, both of the United States and of the several States, shall be bound by Oath or Affirmation, to support this Constitution; but no religious Test shall ever be required as a Qualification to any Office of public Trust under the United States.

ARTICLE VII

The Ratification of the Conventions of nine States, shall be sufficient for the Establishment of this Constitution between the States so ratifying the Same.

Done in Convention by the Unanimous Consent of the States present the Seventeenth Day of September in the Year of our Lord one thousand seven hundred and Eighty seven and of the Independence of the United States of America the Twelfth* IN WITNESS whereof We have hereunto subscribed our Names,

---

The Constitution was submitted on September 17, 1787, by the Constitutional Convention, was ratified by the Convention of several states at various dates up to May 29, 1790, and became effective on March 4, 1789.

GEORGE WASHINGTON
President and Deputy from Virginia

Delaware
GEORGE READ
GUNNING BEDFORD, JR.
JOHN DICKINSON
RICHARD BASSETT
JACOB BROOM

Maryland
JAMES MCHENRY
DANIEL OF ST. THOMAS JENIFER
DANIEL CARROLL

Virginia
JOHN BLAIR
JAMES MADISON, JR.

North Carolina
WILLIAM BLOUNT
RICHARD DOBBS SPRAIGHT
HUGH WILLIAMSON

South Carolina
JOHN RUTLEDGE
CHARLES COTESWORTH PINCKNEY
CHARLES PINCKNEY
PIERCE BUTLER

Georgia
WILLIAM FEW
ABRAHAM BALDWIN

New Hampshire
JOHN LANGDON
NICHOLAS GILMAN

Massachusetts
NATHANIEL GORHAM
RUFUS KING

Connecticut
WILLIAM SAMUEL JOHNSON
ROGER SHERMAN

New York
ALEXANDER HAMILTON

New Jersey
WILLIAM LIVINGSTON
DAVID BREARLEY
WILLIAM PATERSON
JONATHAN DAYTON

Pennsylvania
BENJAMIN FRANKLIN
THOMAS MIFFLIN
ROBERT MORRIS
GEORGE CLYMER
THOMAS FITZSIMONS
JARED INGERSOLL
JAMES WILSON
GOUVERNEUR MORRIS

Amendments to the Constitution

AMENDMENT I

Congress shall make no law respecting an establishment of religion, or prohibiting the free exercise thereof; or abridging the freedom of speech, or of the press; or the right of the people peaceably to assemble, and to petition the Government for a redress of grievances.

AMENDMENT II

A well regulated Militia being necessary to the security of a free State, the right of the people to keep and bear Arms, shall not be infringed.

AMENDMENT III

No Soldier shall, in time of peace be quartered in any house, without the consent of the Owner, nor in time of war, but in a manner to be prescribed by law.

AMENDMENT IV

The right of the people to be secure in their persons, houses, papers, and effects, against unreasonable searches and seizures, shall not be violated, and no Warrants shall issue, but upon probable cause, supported by Oath or affirmation, and particularly describing the place to be searched, and the persons or things to be seized.

AMENDMENT V

No person shall be held to answer for a capital, or otherwise infamous crime, unless on a presentment or indictment of a Grand Jury, except in cases arising in the land or naval forces, or in the Militia, when in actual service in time of War or public danger; nor shall any person be subject for the same offense to be twice put in jeopardy of life or limb; nor shall be compelled in any criminal case to be a witness against himself, nor be deprived of life, liberty, or property, without due process of law; nor shall private property be taken for public use, without just compensation.

AMENDMENT VI

In all criminal prosecutions, the accused shall enjoy the right to a speedy and public trial, by an impartial jury of the State and district wherein the crime shall have been committed, which district shall have been previously ascertained by law, and to be informed of the nature and cause of the accusation; to be confronted with the witnesses against him; to have compulsory process for obtaining witnesses in his favor, and to have the Assistance of Counsel for his defence.

AMENDMENT VII

In Suits at common law, where the value in controversy shall exceed twenty dollars, the right of trial by jury shall be preserved, and no fact tried by a jury, shall be otherwise re-examined in any Court of the United States, than according to the rules of the common law.

AMENDMENT VIII

Excessive bail shall not be required, nor excessive fines imposed, nor cruel and unusual punishments inflicted.

AMENDMENT IX

The enumeration in the Constitution, of certain rights, shall not be construed to deny or disparage others retained by the people.

AMENDMENT X*

The powers not delegated to the United States by the Constitution, nor prohibited by it to the States, are reserved to the States respectively, or to the people.

AMENDMENT XI
[ADOPTED 1798]

The Judicial power of the United States shall not be construed to extend to any suit in law or equity, commenced or prosecuted against one of the United States by Citizens of another State, or by Citizens or Subjects of any Foreign State.

AMENDMENT XII
[ADOPTED 1804]

The Electors shall meet in their respective states, and vote by ballot for President and Vice President, one of whom, at least, shall not be an inhabitant of the same state with themselves; they shall name in their ballots the person voted for as President, and in distinct ballots the person voted for as Vice President, and they shall make distinct lists of all persons voted for as President, and of all persons voted for as Vice President, and of the number of votes for each, which lists they shall sign and certify, and transmit sealed to the seat of the government of the United States, directed to the President of the Senate;—The President of the Senate shall, in the presence of the Senate and House of Representatives, open all the certificates and the votes shall then be counted;—The person having the greatest number of votes for President, shall be the President, if such number be a majority of the whole number of Electors appointed; and if no person have such majority, then from the persons having the highest numbers not exceeding three on the list of those voted for as President, the House of Representatives shall choose immediately, by ballot, the President. But in choosing the President, the votes shall be taken by states, the representation from each state having one vote; a quorum for this purpose shall consist of a member or members from two-thirds of the states, and a majority of all the states shall be necessary to a choice. And if the House of Representatives shall not choose a President whenever the right of choice shall devolve upon them, before *the fourth day of March* next following, then the Vice President shall act as President, as in the case of the death or other constitutional disability of the President.—The person having the greatest number of votes as Vice President, shall be the Vice President, if such number be a majority of the whole number of Electors appointed, and if no person have a majority, then from the two highest numbers on the list, the Senate shall choose the Vice President; a quorum for the purpose shall consist of two-thirds of the whole number of Senators, and a majority of the whole number shall be necessary to a choice. But no person constitutionally ineligible to the office of President shall be eligible to that of Vice President of the United States.

AMENDMENT XIII
[ADOPTED 1865]

Section 1

Neither slavery nor involuntary servitude, except as a punishment for crime whereof the party shall have been duly convicted, shall exist within the United States, or any place subject to their jurisdiction.

Section 2

Congress shall have power to enforce this article by appropriate legislation.

The first ten amendments (the Bill of Rights) were ratified, and their adoption was certified, on December 15, 1791.

AMENDMENT XIV
[ADOPTED 1868]

Section 1

All persons born or naturalized in the United States, and subject to the jurisdiction thereof, are citizens of the United States and of the State wherein they reside. No State shall make or enforce any law which shall abridge the privileges or immunities of citizens of the United States; nor shall any State deprive any person of life, liberty, or property, without due process of law; nor deny to any person within its jurisdiction the equal protection of the laws.

Section 2

Representatives shall be apportioned among the several States according to their respective numbers, counting the whole number of persons in each State, excluding Indians not taxed. But when the right to vote at any election for the choice of electors for President and Vice President of the United States, Representatives in Congress, the Executive and Judicial officers of a State, or the members of the Legislature thereof, is denied to any of the male inhabitants of such State, being twenty-one years of age, and citizens of the United States, or in any way abridged, except for participation in rebellion, or other crime, the basis of representation therein shall be reduced in the proportion which the number of such male citizens shall bear to the whole number of male citizens twenty-one years of age in such State.

Section 3

No person shall be a Senator or Representative in Congress, or elector of President and Vice President, or hold any office, civil or military, under the United States, or under any State, who, having previously taken an oath, as a member of Congress, or as an officer of the United States, or as a member of any State legislature, or as an executive or judicial officer of any State, to support the Constitution of the United States, shall have engaged in insurrection or rebellion against the same, or given aid or comfort to the enemies thereof. But Congress may by a vote of two-thirds of each House, remove such disability.

Section 4

The validity of the public debt of the United States, authorized by law, including debts incurred for payment of pensions and bounties for services in suppressing insurrection or rebellion, shall not be questioned. But neither the United States nor any State shall assume or pay any debt or obligation incurred in aid of insurrection or rebellion against the United States, or any claim for the loss or emancipation of any slave; but all such debts, obligations and claims shall be held illegal and void.

Section 5

The Congress shall have power to enforce, by appropriate legislation, the provisions of this article.

AMENDMENT XV
[ADOPTED 1870]

Section 1

The right of citizens of the United States to vote shall not be denied or abridged by the United States or by any State on account of race, color, or previous condition of servitude.

Section 2

The Congress shall have power to enforce this article by appropriate legislation.

AMENDMENT XVI
[ADOPTED 1913]

The Congress shall have power to lay and collect taxes on incomes, from whatever source derived, without apportionment among the several States, and without regard to any census or enummeration.

AMENDMENT XVII
[ADOPTED 1913]

The Senate of the United States shall be composed of two Senators from each State, elected by the people thereof, for six years; and each Senator shall have one vote. The electors in each State shall have the qualifications requisite for electors of the most numerous branch of the State legislatures.

When vacancies happen in the representation of any State in the Senate, the executive authority of such State shall issue writs of election to fill such vacancies: *Provided,* That the legislature of any State may empower the executive thereof to make temporary appointments until the people fill the vacancies by election as the legislature may direct.

This amendment shall not be so construed as to affect the election or term of any Senator chosen before it becomes valid as part of the Constitution.

AMENDMENT XVIII
[ADOPTED 1919, REPEALED 1933]

Section 1

After one year from the ratification of this article the manufacture, sale, or transportation of intoxicating liquors within, the importation thereof into, or the exportation thereof from the United States and all territory subject to the jurisdiction thereof for beverage purposes is hereby prohibited.

Section 2

The Congress and the several States shall have concurrent power to enforce this article by appropriate legislation.

Section 3

This article shall be inoperative unless it shall have been ratified as an amendment to the Constitution by the legislatures of the several States, as provided in the Constitution, within seven years from the date of the submission hereof to the States by the Congress.

AMENDMENT XIX
[ADOPTED 1920]

The right of citizens of the United States to vote shall not be denied or abridged by the United States or by any State on account of sex.

Congress shall have power to enforce this article by appropriate legislation.

AMENDMENT XX
[ADOPTED 1933]

Section 1

The terms of the President and Vice President shall end at noon on the 20th day of January, and the terms of Senators and Representatives at noon on the 3d day of January, of the years in which such terms would have ended if this article had not been ratified and the terms of their successors shall then begin.

Section 2

The Congress shall assemble at least once in every year, and such meeting shall begin at noon on the 3d day of January, unless they shall by law appoint a different day.

Section 3

If, at the time fixed for the beginning of the term of the President, the President elect shall have died, the Vice President elect shall become President. If a President shall not have been chosen before the time fixed for the beginning of his term, or if the President elect shall have failed to qualify, then the Vice President elect shall act as President until a President shall have qualified; and the Congress may by law provide for the case wherein neither a President elect nor a Vice President elect shall have qualified, declaring who shall then act as President, or the manner in which one who is to act shall be selected, and such person shall act accordingly until a President or Vice President shall have qualified.

Section 4

The Congress may by law provide for the case of the death of any of the persons from whom the House of Representatives may choose a President whenever the right of choice shall have devolved upon them, and for the case of the death of any of the persons from whom the Senate may choose a Vice President whenever the right of choice shall have devolved upon them.

Section 5

Sections 1 and 2 shall take effect on the 15th day of October following the ratification of this article.

Section 6

This article shall be inoperative unless it shall have been ratified as an amendment to the Constitution by the legislatures of three fourths of the several States within seven years from the date of its submission.

Amendment XXI
[Adopted 1933]

Section 1

The eighteenth article of amendment to the Constitution of the United States is hereby repealed.

Section 2

The transportation or importation into any State, Territory, or possession of the United States for delivery or use therein of intoxicating liquors in violation of the laws thereof, is hereby prohibited.

Section 3

This article shall be inoperative unless it shall have been ratified as an amendment to the Constitution by conventions in the several States, as provided in the Constitution, within seven years from the date of the submission hereof to the States by the Congress.

Amendment XXII
[Adopted 1951]

Section 1

No person shall be elected to the office of the President more than twice, and no person who has held the office of President, or acted as President, for more than two years of a term to which some other person was elected President shall be elected to the office of the President more than once. But this Article shall not apply to any person holding the office of President when this Article was proposed by the Congress, and shall not prevent any person who may be holding the office of President, or acting as President, during the term within which this Article becomes operative from holding the office of President or acting as President during the remainder of such term.

Section 2

This article shall be inoperative unless it shall have been ratified as an amendment to the Constitution by the legislatures of three-fourths of the several States within seven years from the date of its submission to the States by the Congress.

AMENDMENT XXIII
[ADOPTED 1961]

Section 1

The District constituting the seat of Government of the United States shall appoint in such manner as the Congress shall direct:

A number of electors of President and Vice President equal to the whole number of Senators and Representatives in Congress to which the District would be entitled if it were a State, but in no event more than the least populous State; they shall be in addition to those appointed by the States, but they shall be considered, for the purposes of the election of President and Vice President, to be electors appointed by a State; and they shall meet in the District and perform such duties as provided by the twelfth article of amendment.

Section 2

The Congress shall have power to enforce this article by appropriate legislation.

AMENDMENT XXIV
[ADOPTED 1964]

Section 1

The right of citizens of the United States to vote in any primary or other election for President or Vice President, for electors for President or Vice President, or for Senator or Representative in Congress, shall not be denied or abridged by the United States or any state by reason of failure to pay any poll tax or other tax.

Section 2

The Congress shall have the power to enforce this article by appropriate legislation.

AMENDMENT XXV
[ADOPTED 1967]

Section 1

In case of the removal of the President from office or his death or resignation, the Vice President shall become President.

Section 2

Whenever there is a vacancy in the office of the Vice President, the President shall nominate a Vice President who shall take the office upon confirmation by a majority vote of both houses of Congress.

Section 3

Whenever the President transmits to the President pro tempore of the Senate and the Speaker of the House of Representatives his written declaration that he is unable to discharge the powers and duties of his office, and until he transmits to them a written declaration to the contrary, such powers and duties shall be discharged by the Vice President as Acting President.

Section 4

Whenever the Vice President and a majority of either the principal officers of the executive departments or of such other body as Congress may by law provide, transmit to the President pro tempore of the Senate and the Speaker of the House of Representatives their written declaration that the President is unable to discharge the powers and duties of his office, the Vice President shall immediately assume the powers and duties of the office as Acting President.

Thereafter, when the President transmits to the President pro tempore of the Senate and the Speaker of the House of Representatives his written declaration that no inability exists, he shall resume the powers and duties of his office unless the Vice President and a majority of either the principal officers of the executive department or of such other body as Congress may by law provide, transmit within four days to the President pro tempore of the Senate and the Speaker of the House of Representatives their written declaration that the President is unable to discharge the powers and duties of his office. Thereupon Congress shall decide the issue, assembling within 48 hours for that purpose if not in session. If the Congress, within 21 days after receipt of the latter written declaration, or, if Congress is not in session, within 21 days after Congress is required to assemble, determines by two-thirds vote of both houses that the President is unable to discharge the powers and duties of his office, the Vice President shall continue to discharge the same as Acting President; otherwise, the President shall resume the powers and duties of his office.

AMENDMENT XXVI
[ADOPTED 1971]

Section 1

The right of citizens of the United States, who are 18 years of age or older, to vote shall not be denied or abridged by the United States or any state on account of age.

Section 2

The Congress shall have the power to enforce this article by appropriate legislation.

AMENDMENT XXVII
[ADOPTED 1992]

No law, varying the compensation for the services of the Senators and Representatives shall take effect, until an election of Representatives shall have intervened.

Recommended Reading

CHAPTER 1 | NEW WORLD ENCOUNTERS

The histories of three different peoples coming together for the first time in the New World have sparked innovative scholarship. Charles C. Mann describes Native American societies before Conquest in *1491: New Revelations of the Americas Before Columbus* (2005). These titles bring fresh insights to the Native Americans' response to radical environmental and social change: Inga Clendinnen, *Aztecs: An Interpretation* (1991); James H. Merrell, *The Indians' New World: Catawbas and Their Neighbors From European Contact Through the Era of Removal* (1989); and James F. Brooks, *Captives and Cousins: Slavery, Kinship and Community in the Southwest Borderlands* (2002). Other broad-ranging volumes examine how early European invaders imagined the New World: Stephen Greenblatt, *Marvelous Possessions: The Wonder of the New World* (1991), and Anthony Pagden, *European Encounters with the New World: From Renaissance to Romanticism* (1992). The impact of the environment is the topic of three pioneering investigations: A. W. Crosby, *The Columbian Voyages, The Columbian Exchange,* and *Their Historians* (1987); William Cronon, *Changes in the Land: Indians, Colonists, and the Ecology of New England* (1983); and Shepard Krech III, *The Ecological Indian: Myth and History* (1999). The best overview of the European response to the Conquest is John H. Elliott, *The Old World and New, 1492–1650* (1970). For the Irish experience consult Nicholas Canny, *Making Ireland British 1580–1650* (2001). Two outstanding interpretations of the English Reformation are Ethan H. Shagan, *Popular Politics and the English Reformation* (2003) and Eamon Duffy, *The Stripping of the Altars: Traditional Religion in England 1400–1580* (1992). A book that offers a boldly original interpretation of the Conquest is Kirkpatrick Sale, *The Conquest of Paradise: Christopher Columbus and the Columbian Legacy* (1990).

CHAPTER 2 | ENGLAND'S COLONIAL EXPERIMENTS: THE SEVENTEENTH CENTURY

A good introduction to England's participation in an Atlantic World is Nicholas Canny, ed., *The Oxford History of the British Empire, vol. 1, The Origins of Empire: English Overseas Enterprise from the Beginning to the Close of the Seventeenth Century* (1998). The best single work on Puritanism remains Perry Miller, *The New England Mind: From Colony to Province* (1956). David D. Hall explores popular religious practice in New England in *Worlds of Wonder, Days of Judgment: Popular Religious Belief in Early New England* (1989). On the challenge of creating new social and political institutions in early Massachusetts, see Kenneth A. Lockridge, *A New England Town: The First Hundred Years* (1970). Two brilliantly original studies of the founding of Virginia are Edmund S. Morgan, *American Slavery, American Freedom: The Ordeal of Colonial Virginia* (1975) and Kathleen M. Brown, *Good Wives, Nasty Wenches, and Anxious Patriarchs: Gender, Race, and Power in Colonial Virginia* (1996). T. H. Breen compares the development of seventeenth-century New England and the Chesapeake in *Puritans and Adventurers: Change and Persistence in Early America* (1980). The forces that drove migration to the New World during this period are the subject of David Cressy's *Coming Over: Migration and Communication Between England and New England in the Seventeenth Century* (1987). For the founding of Virginia, see James Horn, *A Land as God Made It: Jamestown and the Birth of America* (2005).

CHAPTER 3 | PUTTING DOWN ROOTS: FAMILIES IN AN ATLANTIC EMPIRE

The most innovative research of chapters covered in this chapter explores the history of New World slavery during the period before the American Revolution. Among the more impressive contributions are Ira Berlin, *Many Thousands Gone: The First Two Centuries of Slavery in North America* (2000); Philip Morgan, *Slave Counterpoint: Black Culture in the Eighteenth-Century Chesapeake and Lowcountry* (1998); and Robin Blackburn, *The Making of New World Slavery, 1492–1800* (1997). A pioneering work of high quality is Winthrop D. Jordan, *White Over Black: American Attitudes Toward the Negro, 1550–1812* (1968). Peter Wood provides an original interpretation of the evolution of race relations in *Black Majority: Negroes in Colonial South Carolina from 1670 Through the Stono Rebellion* (1974). The world of Anthony Johnson, a free black planter in early Virginia, is reconstructed in T. H. Breen and Stephen Innes, *"Myne Owne Ground": Race and Freedom on Virginia's Eastern Shore, 1640–1676,* rev. ed. (2004). The most recent account of the Salem witch trials can be found in Mary Beth Norton, *In the Devil's Snare: The Salem Witchcraft Crisis of 1692* (2002). Richard Godbeer offers a solid account of the Puritans' intimate lives in

Sexual Revolution in Early America (2002), but one should also consult Laurel T. Ulrich, *Good Wives: Image and Reality in the Lives of Women in Northern New England, 1650–1750* (1982). A provocative discussion of cultural tensions within the British Empire can be found in Linda Colley, *Captives: The Story of Britain's Pursuit of Empire and How its Soldiers and Civilians Were Held Captive by the Dream of Global Supremacy, 1600–1850* (2002).

CHAPTER 4 | COLONIES IN AN EMPIRE: EIGHTEENTH-CENTURY AMERICA

A good introduction to the imperial dimension of eighteenth-century experience is P. J. Marshall, ed., *The Oxford History of the British Empire, vol. 2, The Eighteenth Century* (1998). In *Britons: Forging the Nation, 1707–1837* (1992), Linda Colley provides an excellent discussion of the aggressive spirit of the British nationalism that the Americans came to celebrate. The arrival of new ethnic groups is examined in Eric Hinderaker and Peter C. Mancall, *At the Edge of Empire: The Backcountry in British North America* (2003); Patrick Griffin, *The People with No Name: Ulster's Presbyterians in a British Atlantic World, 1688–1763* (2001); Bernard Bailyn, *The Peopling of British North America: An Introduction* (1988); and Bernard Bailyn and Philip D. Morgan, eds., *Strangers Within the Realm: Cultural Margins of the First British Empire* (1991). Richard White has transformed how we think about Native American resistance during this period in *The Middle Ground: Indians, Empires, and Republics in the Great Lakes Region* (1991). Two other fine books explore the Indians' response to the expanding European empires: Timothy Shannon, *Indians and Colonists at the Crossroads of Empire: The Albany Congress of 1754* (2000) and Gregory Evans Dowd, *War Under Heaven: Pontiac, The Indian Nations and the British Empire* (2002). The complex story of Spanish colonization of the Southwest is told masterfully in David J. Weber, *The Spanish Frontier in North America* (1992). Fred Anderson offers the most complete treatment of war and empire in *Crucible of War: The Seven Years' War and the Fate of Empire in British North America, 1754–1766* (2000). A splendid examination of Benjamin Franklin as a colonial voice of the Enlightenment is Edmund S. Morgan, *Benjamin Franklin* (2002). The extraordinary impact of evangelical religion on colonial life is addressed in Mark A. Noll, *America's God: From Jonathan Edwards to Abraham Lincoln* (2002); Frank Lambert, *"Pedlar of Divinity": George Whitefield and the Transatlantic Revivals, 1734–1770* (1994); and Timothy D. Hall, *Contested Boundaries: Itinerancy and the Reshaping of the Colonial Religious World* (1994).

CHAPTER 5 | THE AMERICAN REVOLUTION: FROM ELITE PROTEST TO POPULAR REVOLT, 1763–1783

Several books have had a profound impact on how historians think about the ideas that energized the Revolution. Edmund S. Morgan and Helen M. Morgan explore how Americans interpreted the first great imperial controversy: *The Stamp Act Crisis: Prologue to Revolution* (1953). In his classic study, *The Ideological Origins of the American Revolution* (1967), Bernard Bailyn maps an ideology of power that informed colonial protest. Gordon Wood extends this argument in *The Radicalism of the American Revolution* (1992). In *Marketplace of Revolution: How Consumer Politics Shaped American Independence* (2004), T. H. Breen attempts to integrate more fully the experiences of ordinary men and women into the analysis of popular mobilization. Works that focus productively on popular mobilization in specific colonies include Rhys Isaac, *The Transformation of Virginia, 1740–1790* (1983); Robert A. Gross, *The Minutemen and Their World* (1976); Woody Holton, *Forced Founders: Indians, Debtors, Slaves and the Making of the American Revolution in Virginia* (1999); and T. H. Breen, *Tobacco Culture: The Mentality of the Great Tidewater Planters on the Eve of Revolution* (1985). The tragedy that visited the Native Americans is examined in Colin C. Calloway, *American Revolution in Indian Country: Crisis and Diversity in Native American Communities* (1995) and Gregory Evans Dowd, *War Under Heaven: Pontiac, The Indian Nations and the British Empire* (2002). A useful study of the aspirations and disappointments of American women during this period is Linda Kerber, *Women of the Republic: Intellect and Ideology in Revolutionary America* (1980). Sidney Kaplan, *The Black Presence in the Era of the American Revolution* (1973), documents the hopes of African Americans during a period of radical political change.

CHAPTER 6 | THE REPUBLICAN EXPERIMENT

The best way to comprehend the major issues debated at the Philadelphia Convention and then later at the separate state ratifying conventions is to examine the key documents of the period. James Madison, *Journal of the Federal Constitution* (reprinted in many modern editions), is our only detailed account of what actually occurred during the closed debates in Philadelphia. A good introduction to the contest between the Federalists and Antifederalists over ratification is Bernard Bailyn, ed., *The Debate on the Constitution: Federalist and Antifederalist Speeches, Articles, and Letters During the Struggle Over Ratification* (1993). Gordon S. Wood analyzes late-eighteenth-century republican political thought in *The Creation of the American Republic, 1776–1787* (1969). Several recent titles interpret the complex political experience of the 1780s: Jack N. Rakove, *Original Meanings: Politics and Ideas in the Making of the Constitution* (1996); Peter Onuf, *Statehood and Union: A History of the Northwest Ordinance* (1987); and Max M. Edling, *A Revolution in Favor of Government: Origins of the U.S. Constitution and the Making of the American State* (2003). Larry D. Kramer provides a valuable new perspective in *The People Themselves: Popular Constitutionalism and Judicial Review* (2004). On the expectations of African Americans and women during this period, see the final sections of Winthrop Jordan, *White Over Black: American Attitudes Toward the Negro, 1550–1812* (1968); T. H. Breen, "Making History: The Force of Public Opinion and the Last Years of Slavery in Revolutionary Massachusetts," in Ronald Hoffman, et al., eds., *Through a Glass Darkly: Reflections on Personal Identity in Early America* (1997), 67–95; and Ronald Hoffman and Peter J. Albert, eds., *Women in the Age of the American Revolution* (1990).

CHAPTER 7 | DEMOCRACY AND DISSENT: THE VIOLENCE OF PARTY POLITICS, 1788–1800

These recent accounts capture the sense of anger and disappointment that informed the deeply partisan political culture of the 1790s: Joanne B. Freeman, *Affairs of Honor: National Politics in the New Republic* (2001) and Joseph J. Ellis, *Founding Brothers: The Revolutionary Generation* (2000). Joyce Appleby provides useful insights into the ideological tensions that divided former allies in *Liberalism and Republicanism in the Historical Imagination* (1992). Jack N. Rakove offers a fine short introduction to James Madison's political thought in *James Madison and the Creation of the American Republic* (1990). An excellent discussion of the conflicting economic visions put forward by Hamilton and Jefferson can be found in Drew McCoy, *The Elusive Republic: The Political Economy in Jeffersonian America* (1980). Anyone curious about the controversial rise of political parties should consult Richard Hofstadter, *The Idea of a Party System: The Rise of Legitimate Opposition in the United States, 1780–1840* (1997) and Stanley Elkins and Eric McKitrick, *The Age of Federalism: The Early Republic* (1993). One can obtain many useful and readable biographies of the dominant leaders of the period. Two more analytic studies are Peter Onuf, ed., *Jeffersonian Legacies* (1993) and Paul K. Longmore, *The Invention of George Washington* (1999). How Americans constructed a convincing sense of national identity is examined in David Waldstreicher, *In the Midst of Perpetual Fetes: The Making of American Nationalism, 1776–1820* (1997). Conor Cruise O'Brien helps explain why foreign affairs, especially with the leaders of the French Revolution, disrupted domestic politics: *The Long Affair: Thomas Jefferson and the French Revolution, 1785–1800* (1996).

CHAPTER 8 | REPUBLICAN ASCENDANCY: THE JEFFERSONIAN VISION

The fullest account of Thomas Jefferson's administration can be found in Merrill D. Peterson, *Thomas Jefferson and the New Nation: A Biography* (1970). Three more recent books examine Jefferson's complex character as well as the impact of Republican policies on the larger society: Peter S. Onuf, *Jeffersonian America* (2001); Joseph J. Ellis, *American Sphinx: The Character of Thomas Jefferson* (1997); and James Horn, et al., eds., *The Revolution of 1800: Democracy, Race, and the New Republic* (2002). The tensions that made this political culture so explosive are treated in Roger Sharp, *American Politics in the Early Republic: The New Nation in Crisis* (1993) and Bernard A. Weisberger, *America Afire: Jefferson, Adams, and the Revolutionary Election of 1800* (2000). The controversies over how best to interpret the Constitution and the politics of the Supreme Court are explored in Jean Edward Smith, *John Marshall: Definer of a Nation* (1996). The Louisiana Purchase is the subject of Alexander DeConde, *The Affair of Louisiana* (1976). On the Lewis and Clark Expedition, see James P. Ronda, *Lewis and Clark Among the Indians* (1984) and Donald Jackson, *Thomas Jefferson and the Stony Mountains: Exploring the West from Monticello* (1981). Henry Wiencek tells how Washington confronted the problem of slavery in *An Imperfect God: George Washington, His Slaves, and the Creation of America* (2003). On foreign relations, see Peter S. Onuf, ed., *America and the World: Diplomacy, Politics, and War* (1991); J. C. A. Stagg, *Mr. Madison's War: Politics, Diplomacy, and Warfare in the Early American Republic* (1983); James E. Lewis, Jr., *The American Union and the Problem of Neighborhood: The United States and the Collapse of the Spanish Empire, 1783–1829* (1998); and Franklin Lambert, *The Barbary Wars: American Independence in the Atlantic World* (2005). Two splendid works demonstrate how Evangelical Protestantism shaped early nineteenth-century public culture: Nathan O. Hatch, *The Democratization of American Christianity* (1989) and Mark A. Noll, *America's God: From Jonathan Edwards to Abraham Lincoln* (2002).

CHAPTER 9 | NATION BUILDING AND NATIONALISM

The standard surveys of the period between the War of 1812 and the age of Jackson are two works by George Dangerfield: *The Era of Good Feelings* (1952) and *Awakening of American Nationalism, 1815–1828* (1965); but see also the early chapters of Charles Sellers, *The Market Revolution: Jacksonian America, 1815–1846* (1991). For a positive account of the venturesome, entrepreneurial spirit of the age, see Joyce Appleby, *Inheriting the Revolution: The First Generations of Americans* (2000). On westward expansion, see John Mack Faragher, *Women and Men on the Overland Trail* (1979); Stephen Aron, *How the West Was Lost: The Transformation of Kentucky from Daniel Boone to Henry Clay* (1996); and Richard White, *It's Your Misfortune and None of My Own* (1992). On Native American life in the antebellum Southeast, see William G. McLoughlin, *Cherokee Renascence in the New Republic* (1986), and Theda Perdue, *Slavery and the Evolution of Cherokee Society, 1540–1866* (1979).

Outstanding studies of economic transformation and the rise of a market economy are George R. Taylor, *The Transportation Revolution, 1815–1860* (1951); Paul W. Gates, *The Farmer's Age: Agriculture, 1815–1860* (1960); Stuart Bruchey, *Enterprise: The Dynamic Economy of a Free People* (1990); and Douglas C. North, *The Economic Growth of the United States, 1790–1860* (1961). Early manufacturing is described in David J. Jeremy, *Transatlantic Industrial Revolution* (1981) and Robert F. Dalzell, *The Boston Associates and the World They Made* (1987). On early mill workers, see Thomas Dublin, *Women at Work: The Transformation of Work and Community in Lowell, Massachusetts, 1826–1860* (1979).

On the Marshall Court and legal change in this era, see Morton Horwitz, *The Transformation of American Law, 1780–1865* (1977), and G. Edward White, *The Marshall Court and Cultural Change, 1815–1835* (1991). Samuel F. Bemis, *John Quincy Adams and the Foundations of American Policy* (1949) provides the classic account of the statesmanship that led to the Monroe Doctrine. But see also Ernest May, *The Making of the Monroe Doctrine* (1976), for a persuasive interpretation of how the doctrine originated.

CHAPTER 10 | THE TRIUMPH OF WHITE MEN'S DEMOCRACY

Arthur M. Schlesinger, Jr., *The Age of Jackson* (1945), sees Jacksonian democracy as a progressive protest against big business and stresses the participation of urban workers. Marvin Meyers, *The Jacksonian Persuasion: Politics and Belief* (1960), argues that Jacksonians appealed to nostalgia for an older America. Lee Benson, *The Concept of Jacksonian Democracy: New York as a Test Case* (1964), finds an ethnocultural basis for democratic allegiance. A sharply critical view of Jacksonian leadership can be found in Edward Pessen, *Jacksonian America: Society, Personality, and Politics*, rev. ed. (1979). An excellent survey of Jacksonian politics is Harry L. Watson, *Liberty and Power* (1990). Daniel Feller, *Jacksonian Promise: America, 1815–1840* (1995), focuses on the optimism that marked all sides of the political conflict and points to the similarities between the political parties. Development of the view that Jacksonianism was a negative reaction to the rise of market capitalism can be found in Charles Sellers, *The Market Revolution* (1991).

The classic study of the new party system is Richard P. McCormick, *The Second Party System: Party Formation in the Jacksonian Era* (1966). On who the anti-Jacksonians were, what they stood for, and what they accomplished, see Michael Holt's magisterial, *The Rise and Fall of the American Whig Party* (1999). James C. Curtis, *Andrew Jackson and the Search for Vindication* (1976), provides a good introduction to Jackson's career and personality. On Jackson's popular image, see John William Ward, *Andrew Jackson: Symbol for an Age* (1955). His Indian removal policy is the subject of Anthony F. C. Wallace, *The Long Bitter Trail: Andrew Jackson and the Indians* (1993). On the other towering political figures of the period, see Merrill D. Peterson, *The Great Triumvirate: Webster, Clay, and Calhoun* (1987). The culture of the period is well surveyed in Russel B. Nye, *Society and Culture in America, 1830–1860* (1960). Alexis de Tocqueville, *Democracy in America*, 2 vols. (1945), is a foreign visitor's wise and insightful analysis of American life in the 1830s.

On the role of race in the formation of political parties and social divisions during this period, see David Roediger, *The Wages of Whiteness: Race and the Making of the American Working Class* (1991); Jean H. Baker, *Affairs of Party: The Political Culture of Northern Democrats in the Mid-Nineteenth Century* (1983); and Alexander Saxton, *The Rise and Fall of the White Republic: Class, Politics, and Mass Culture in Nineteenth-Century America* (1990).

CHAPTER 11 | SLAVES AND MASTERS

Major works that take a broad view of slavery are Kenneth M. Stampp, *The Peculiar Institution: Slavery in the Antebellum South* (1956), which stresses its coercive features; John W. Blassingame, *The Slave Community: Plantation Life in the Antebellum South* (1972), which focuses on slave culture and psychology; and Eugene D. Genovese, *Roll, Jordan, Roll: The World the Slaves Made* (1974), which probes the paternalistic character of the institution and the way in which slaves made a world for themselves within its bounds. An insightful interpretation of antebellum southern society is James Oakes, *Slavery and Freedom: An Interpretation of the Old South* (1990). For an overview of the history of slavery, see Peter Kolchin, *American Slavery, 1619–1877* (1993).

On the economics of slavery, see Gavin Wright, *The Political Economy of the Cotton South: Households, Markets, and Wealth in the Nineteenth Century* (1978). On women in the Old South, see Laura F. Edwards, *Scarlett Doesn't Live Here Anymore: Southern Women in the Civil War Era* (2000) and Deborah Gray White, *Ar'n't I a Woman: Female Slaves in the Plantation South* (1985). On the slave trade, see two excellent studies: Michael Tadman, *Speculators and Slaves: Masters, Traders, and Slaves in the Old South* (1989) and Walter Johnson, *Soul by Soul: Life Inside the Antebellum Slave Market* (1999). For the history of the slave family, see Herbert Gutman, *The Black Family in Slavery and Freedom, 1750-1925* (1976); Brenda Stevenson, *Life in Black and White: Family and Community in the Slave South* (1996); and Marie Jenkins Schwartz, *Born in Bondage: Growing Up Enslaved in the Antebellum South* (2000). For southern law and slavery, see Thomas D. Morris, *Southern Slavery and the Law, 1619–1860* (1996) and Ariela J. Gross, *Double Character: Slavery and Mastery in the Antebellum Southern Courtroom* (2000).

Black resistance to slavery is described in Vincent Harding, *There Is a River: The Black Struggle for Freedom in America* (1981). Slave culture is examined in Albert J. Raboteau, *Slave Religion: The "Invisible Institution" in the Antebellum South* (1978); Lawrence W. Levine, *Black Culture and Consciousness: Afro-American Folk Thought from Slavery to Freedom* (1977); Sterling Stuckey, *Slave Culture: Nationalist Theory and the Foundations of Black America* (1987); and Sharla M. Fett, *Healing, Health, and Power on Southern Slave Plantations* (2002).

CHAPTER 12 | THE PURSUIT OF PERFECTION

Ronald G. Walters, *American Reformers, 1815–1860,* rev. ed. (1997), and Steven Mintz, *Moralists and Modernizers: America's Pre–Civil War Reformers* (1995), provide good overviews of pre-Civil War reform activities. A particularly useful collection of documents on reform movements and other aspects of antebellum culture is David Brion Davis, *Antebellum American Culture: An Interpretive Anthology* (1979). Lori D. Ginzberg, *Women and the Work of Benevolence: Morality, Politics and Class in the Nineteenth Century United States* (1990), and Bruce Dorsey, *Reforming Men and Women: Gender in the Antebellum City* (2002), relate reform politics to gender and class politics.

A general survey of the religious ferment of this period is Nathan O. Hatch, *The Democratization of American Christianity* (1989). Paul E. Johnson, *A Shopkeeper's Millennium: Society and Revivals in Rochester, New York, 1815–1837* (1978), incisively describes the impact of the revival on a single community. The connection between religion and reform is described in Robert H. Abzug, *Cosmos Crumbling: American Reform and the Religious Imagination* (1994).

Sara Evans, *Born for Liberty: A History of Women in America,* provides an excellent synthesis of women's history. On the rise of the domestic ideology, see Nancy F. Cott, *The Bonds of Womanhood: "Woman's Sphere" in New England, 1780–1835* (1977). The condition of working-class women is incisively treated in Christine Stansell, *City of Women: Sex and Class in New York, 1789–1860* (1986).

David J. Rothman, *The Discovery of the Asylum: Social Order and Disorder in the New Republic* (1971), provides a penetrating analysis of the movement for institutional reform. For good surveys of abolitionism, see James Brewer Stewart, *Holy Warriors: The Abolitionists and American Slavery* (1976) and Paul Goodman, *Of One Blood: Abolitionism and Racial Equality* (1998). Patrick Rael, *Black Identity and Black Protest in the Antebellum North* (2002), is an excellent treatment of black abolitionists. On transcendentalism, see Charles Capper and Conrad E. Wright, *Transient and Permanent: The Transcendentalist Movement and Its Contexts* (1999).

CHAPTER 13 | AN AGE OF EXPANSIONISM

An overview of expansion to the Pacific is Ray A. Billington, *The Far Western Frontier, 1830–1860* (1956). The impulse behind Manifest Destiny has been variously interpreted. Albert K. Weinberg's classic *Manifest Destiny: A Study of National Expansionism in American History* (1935) describes and stresses the ideological rationale as does Anders Stephenson, *Manifest Destiny: American Expansion and the Empire of Right* (1995). Frederick Merk, *Manifest Destiny and Mission in American History* (1963), analyzes public opinion and shows how divided it was on the question of territorial acquisitions. Norman A. Graebner, *Empire on the Pacific: A Study in American Continental Expansionism* (1956), highlights the desire for Pacific harbors as a motive for adding new territory. The most complete and authoritative account of the diplomatic side of expansionism in this period is David M. Pletcher, *The Diplomacy of Annexation: Texas, Oregon, and the Mexican War* (1973). Charles G. Sellers, *James K. Polk: Continentalist, 1843–1846* (1966), is the definitive work on Polk's election and the expansionist policies of his administration. A very good account of the Mexican-American War is John S. D. Eisenhower, *So Far from God: The U.S. War with Mexico* (1989). On gold rushes, see Malcolm J. Rohrbough, *Days of Gold: The California Gold Rush and the American Nation* (1997) and Elliott West, *The Contested Plains: Indians, Goldseekers, and the Rush to Colorado* (1998).

Economic developments of the 1840s and 1850s are well covered in George R. Taylor, *The Transportation Revolution, 1815–1960* (1952) and Albert Fishlow, *American Railroads and the Transformation of the Ante-Bellum Economy* (1965). For an overview of immigration in this period, see the early chapters of Roger Daniels, *Coming to America: Immigration and Ethnicity in American Life* (1990). A standard work on the antebellum working class is Sean Wilentz, *Chants Democratic: New York City and the Rise of the American Working Class, 1788–1850* (1984); for the newer approach to labor history that emphasizes working-class culture, see Herbert G. Gutman, *Work, Culture, and Society in Industrializing America* (1976). For the rich public life of antebellum cities, see Mary P. Ryan, *Civic Wars: Democracy and Public Life in the American City During the Nineteenth Century* (1997). A pathbreaking and insightful study of workers in the textile industry is Thomas Dublin, *Women at Work: The Transformation of Work and Community in Lowell, Massachusetts, 1826–1860* (1979).

Chapter 14 | The Sectional Crisis

The best general account of the politics of the sectional crisis is David M. Potter, *The Impending Crisis, 1848–1861* (1976). For a shorter overview, see Bruce C. Levine, *Half Slave and Half Free: The Roots of the Civil War* (1991). On the demise of the Whigs, see Michael F. Holt, *The Rise and Fall of the American Whig Party* (1999). The best treatment of the Know-Nothing movement is Tyler Anbinder, *Nativism and Slavery: The Northern Know-Nothings and the Politics of the 1850s* (1992). The most important studies of northern political sectionalism are Eric Foner, *Free Soil, Free Labor, Free Men: The Ideology of the Republican Party Before the Civil War* (1970), and William E. Gienapp, *The Origins of the Republican Party, 1852–1856* (1987), on the Republican party generally; and Don E. Fehrenbacher, *Prelude to Greatness: Lincoln in the 1850s* (1962), on Lincoln's rise to prominence. On the climactic events of 1857, see Don E. Fehrenbacher, *The Dred Scott Case: Its Significance in American Law and Politics* (1978) and Kenneth M. Stampp, *America in 1857: A Nation on the Brink* (1990). On the background of southern separatism, see William W. Freehling, *The Road to Disunion: Secessionists at Bay, 1776–1854* (1990) and William L. Barney, *The Road to Secession: A New Perspective on the Old South* (1972).

Chapter 15 | Secession and the Civil War

The best one-volume history of the Civil War is James M. McPherson, *Battle Cry of Freedom: The Civil War Era* (1988). Other valuable surveys of the war and its aftermath are J. G. Randall and David Herbert Donald, *The Civil War and Reconstruction*, 2nd ed. (1969), and James M. McPherson, *Ordeal by Fire: The Civil War and Reconstruction* (1981). An excellent shorter account is David Herbert Donald, *Liberty and Union* (1978). The Confederate experience is covered in Clement Eaton, *A History of the Southern Confederacy* (1954), and Emory M. Thomas, *The Confederate Nation, 1861–1865* (1979). Gary W. Gallagher, *The Confederate War* (1997) argues, contrary to a common view, that the South lost the war simply because it was overpowered and not because of low morale or lack of a will to win. On the North's war effort, see Phillip Paludan, *A People's Contest: The Union and the Civil War, 1861–1865* (1988). The best one-volume introduction to the military side of the conflict is still Bruce Catton, *This Hallowed Ground: The Story of the Union Side of the Civil War* (1956).

Lincoln's career and wartime leadership are well treated in David Herbert Donald, *Lincoln* (1995). Another competent biography is Stephen B. Oates, *With Malice Toward None: The Life of Abraham Lincoln* (1977). For a shorter life of Lincoln, see William Gienapp, *Abraham Lincoln and Civil War America* (2002). A penetrating analysis of events immediately preceding the fighting is Kenneth M. Stampp, *And the War Came: The North and the Sectional Crisis* (1950). John Hope Franklin, *The Emancipation Proclamation* (1963), is a good short account of the North's decision to free the slaves. An incisive account of the transition from slavery to freedom is Barbara Jeanne Fields, *Slavery and Freedom on the Middle Ground: Maryland in the Nineteenth Century* (1985). The circumstances and activities of southern women during the war are covered in Drew Faust, *Mothers of Invention: Women of the Slaveholding States in the American Civil War* (1996) and in Laura F. Edwards, *Scarlett Doesn't Live Here Anymore: Southern Women in the Civil War Era* (2002). The experiences of northern women are described in Elizabeth D. Leonard, *Yankee Women: Gender Battles in the Civil War* (1994). A brilliant study of the writings of those who experienced the war is Edmund Wilson, *Patriotic Gore: Studies in the Literature of the American Civil War* (1962). On the intellectual impact of the war, see George M. Fredrickson, *The Inner Civil War: Northern Intellectuals and the Crisis of the Union*, 2nd ed. (1993).

Chapter 16 | The Agony of Reconstruction

The best one-volume account of Reconstruction is Eric Foner, *Reconstruction: America's Unfinished Revolution* (1988). Two excellent short surveys are Kenneth M. Stampp, *The Era of Reconstruction, 1865–1877* (1965), and John Hope Franklin, *Reconstruction: After the Civil War* (1961). W. E. B. DuBois, *Black Reconstruction in America, 1860–1880* (1935), remains brilliant and provocative. On the politics of Reconstruction, see Stephen

David Kantrowitz, *Ben Tillman and the Reconstruction of White Supremacy* (2001); Laura F. Edwards, *Gendered Strife and Confusion: The Political Culture of Reconstruction* (1997); J. Morgan Kousser and James M. McPherson, eds., *Region, Race, and Reconstruction: Essays in Honor of C. Vann Woodward* (1982); and Eric Foner, *Nothing But Freedom: Emancipation and Its Legacy* (1983).

Leon F. Litwack, *Been in the Storm So Long: The Aftermath of Slavery* (1979), provides a moving portrayal of the black experience of emancipation. On changing society and family life during Reconstruction, see Noralee Frankel, *Freedom's Women: Black Women and Families in Reconstruction Era Mississippi* (1999), Dylan Penningroth, *Claiming Kin and Property: African American Life Before and After Emancipation* (2003), and Amy Dru Stanley, *From Bondage to Contract: Wage Labor, Marriage, and the Market in the Age of Slave Emancipation* (1998). On what freedom meant in economic terms, see Gerald David Jaynes, *Branches Without Roots: Genesis of the Black Working Class in the American South, 1862–1882* (1986). A work that focuses on ex-slaves' attempts to create their own economic order is Julie Saville, *The Work of Reconstruction: Free Slave to Wage Laborer in South Carolina, 1860–1870* (1994). The best overview of the postwar southern economy is Gavin Wright, *Old South, New South* (1986). On the end of Reconstruction, see David W. Blight, *Race and Reunion: The Civil War in American Memory* (2000). On the character of the post–Reconstruction South, see the classic work by C. Vann Woodward, *Origins of the New South, 1877–1913* (1951) and Edward Ayers, *The Promise of the New South* (1992).

Chapter 17 | The West: Exploiting an Empire

The best traditional account of the movement west is Ray Allen Billington, *Westward Expansion* (1967), which also has a first-rate bibliography. Walter Prescott Webb, *The Great Plains* (1931), offers a fascinating analysis of development on the Plains.

For examples of the work of "new Western historians," see Donald Worster, *Rivers of Empire* (1985), a powerful study of the "hydraulic" society, and his *Under Western Skies: Nature and History in the American West* (1992); William Cronon, *Nature's Metropolis: Chicago and the Great West* (1991), a provocative analysis of the relationship of Chicago and the West; Patricia Nelson Limerick, *The Legacy of Conquest* (1987); and Richard White, *"It's Your Misfortune and None of My Own": A History of the American West* (1991).

More recent authors have taken fresh and stimulating looks at older or ignored questions. Robert R. Dykstra, *The Cattle Towns* (1968), examines five Kansas cattle towns, with interesting results. Elliott West discusses the Plains in *The Contested Plains: Indians, Goldseekers, and the Rush to Colorado* (1998). Eugene P. Moehring, *Urbanism and Empire in the Far West, 1840–1890* (2004), and David M. Wrobel, *Promised Lands: Promotion, Memory, and the Creation of the American West* (2002), offer engaging interpretations of frontier history. Recent studies of the environment include Andrew C. Isenberg, *The Destruction of the Bison: An Environmental History, 1750–1920* (2000); Shepard Krech III, *The Ecological Indian: Myth and History* (1999); and Dan L. Flores, *The Natural West: Environmental History in the Great Plains and Rocky Mountains* (2001). Susan Lee Johnson, *Roaring Camp: The Social World of the California Gold Rush* (2000), is a fascinating examination of the gold camps. On the Native Americans, there are a number of valuable works, including Colin G. Calloway, *One Vast Winter Count: The Native American West before Lewis and Clark* (2003); Steven Conn, *History's Shadow: Native Americans and Historical Consciousness in the Nineteenth Century* (2004); R. Douglas Hurt's excellent *Indian Agriculture in America* (1987); Janet A. McDonnell, *The Dispossession of the American Indian, 1887–1934* (1991); Paul H. Carlson, *The Plains Indians* (1998); and John William Sayer, *Ghost Dancing the Law: The Wounded Knee Trials* (1997). Nell Irvin Painter, *Exodusters: Black Migration to Kansas After Reconstruction* (1976); William A. Dobak and Thomas D. Phillips, *The Black Regulars, 1866–1898* (2001); and James N. Leiker, *Racial Borders: Black Soldiers along the Rio Grande* (2002), tell the story of the Exodusters and black soldiers on the frontier. Julie Roy Jeffrey, *Frontier Women: The Trans-Mississippi West* (1979); Virginia Scharff, *Twenty Thousand Roads: Women, Movement, and the West* (2003); Quitard Taylor and Shirley Ann Wilson Moore, *African American Women Confront the West, 1600–2000* (2003); Joanna L. Stratton, *Pioneer Women: Voices from the Kansas Frontier* (1981); and Deena J. González, *Refusing the Favor: The Spanish-Mexican Women of Santa Fe, 1820–1880* (1999), are perceptive works on a neglected topic.

Chapter 18 | The Industrial Society

Samuel P. Hays, *The Response to Industrialism: 1885–1914* (1957), is an influential interpretation of the period. Douglass C. North, *Growth and Welfare in the American Past: A New Economic History* (1966), is stimulating. David Montgomery, *The Fall of the House of Labor* (1987), is an outstanding study of labor in the period. Richard Franklin Bensel, *The Political Economy of American Industrialization, 1877–1900* (2000), and Charles Perrow, *Organizing America: Wealth, Power, and the Origins of Corporate Capitalism* (2002), trace the underlying ideas of the new industrialization.

Alfred D. Chandler, *The Visible Hand: The Managerial Revolution in American Business* (1978); Olivier Zunz, *Making America Corporate, 1870–1920* (1990); and JoAnne Yates, *Control Through Communication: The Rise of*

System in American Management (1989), are perceptive. The railroad empire is treated in John R. Stilgoe, *Metropolitan Corridor: Railroads and the American Scene* (1983); Claire Strom, *Profiting from the Plains: The Great Northern Railway and Corporate Development of the American West* (2003); John Hoyt Williams, *A Great and Shining Road: The Epic Story of the Transcontinental Railroad* (1988); and John F. Stover, *American Railroads* (1961). On the steel industry, see Peter Temin, *Iron and Steel in Nineteenth-Century America* (1964).

Two superb books by Sam Bass Warner, Jr., *Streetcar Suburbs: The Process of Growth in Boston, 1870–1900* (1962), and *The Urban Wilderness: A History of the American City* (1973), examine technology and city development. The wage earner is examined in Herbert G. Gutman, *Work, Culture, and Society in Industrializing America* (1976), and Joshua L. Rosenbloom, *Looking for Work, Searching for Workers: American Labor Markets during Industrialization* (2002). Two books by Stephan Thernstrom, *Poverty and Progress: Social Mobility in the Nineteenth-Century City* (1964) and *The Other Bostonians: Poverty and Progress in the American Metropolis, 1880–1970* (1973), examine mobility. Walter A. Friedman, *Birth of a Salesman: The Transformation of Selling in America* (2004), looks at the growing importance of advertising. Philip S. Foner, *Women and the American Labor Movement*, 2 vols. (1979); Susan E. Kennedy, *If All We Did Was to Weep at Home* (1979); Barbara Mayer Wertheimer, *We Were There: The Story of Working Women in America* (1977); and Alice Kessler-Harris, *Out to Work: A History of Wage-Earning Women in the United States* (1982), are excellent on the subject of women in the workplace.

CHAPTER 19 | TOWARD AN URBAN SOCIETY, 1877–1900

On urban America, see Sam Bass Warner, Jr., *Streetcar Suburbs* (1962) and *The Urban Wilderness* (1972). William R. Taylor, *In Pursuit of Gotham: Culture and Commerce in New York* (1992); Eric H. Monkkonen, *America Becomes Urban* (1988); John Jakle, *City Lights: Illuminating the American Night* (2003); Jon. A. Peterson, *The Birth of City Planning in the United States, 1840–1917* (2003); John Henry Hepp IV, *The Middle-Class City: Transforming Space and Time in Philadelphia, 1876–1926* (2003); Sven Beckert, *The Monied Metropolis: New York City and the Consolidation of the American Bourgeoisie, 1850–1896* (2001); and David Schuyler, *The New Urban Landscape* (1986), are also valuable.

For family life, see Joseph Kett, *Rites of Passage: Adolescence in America* (1977); Elaine Tyler May, *Great Expectations: Marriage and Divorce in Post-Victorian America* (1980); Steven Mintz, *A Prison of Expectations: The Family in Victorian Culture* (1983); Helen Lefkowitz Horowitz, *Rereading Sex: Battles over Sexual Knowledge and Suppression in Nineteenth-Century America* (2002); Maureen A. Flanagan, *Seeing With Their Hearts: Chicago Women and the Vision of the Good City, 1871–1933* (2002); Stephen M. Frank, *Life With Father: Parenthood and Masculinity in the Nineteenth-Century American North* (1998); and Norma Basch, *In the Eyes of the Law: Women, Marriage, and Property in Nineteenth-Century New York* (1982). Karen Lystra, *Searching the Heart: Women, Men, and Romantic Love in Nineteenth-Century America* (1989), is valuable, as is Jean V. Matthews, *The Rise of the New Woman: The Women's Movement in America, 1875–1930* (2003).

Urban reform is examined in Judith Ann Trolander, *Professionalism and Social Change: From the Settlement House Movement to Neighborhood Centers, 1886 to the Present* (1987); Shannon Jackson, *Lines of Activity: Performance, Historiography, Hull-House Domesticity* (2001); Allen F. Davis, *Spearheads for Reform: The Social Settlements and the Progressive Movement, 1890–1914* (1967); and *American Heroine: The Life and Legend of Jane Addams* (1973). Also, see the more recent Victoria Bissell Brown, *The Education of Jane Addams* (2004).

CHAPTER 20 | POLITICAL REALIGNMENTS IN THE 1890s

The best study of the 1890s depression is Charles Hoffman, *The Depression of the Nineties: An Economic History* (1970). H. Wayne Morgan, *From Hayes to McKinley: National Party Politics, 1877–1896* (1969); Michael E. McGerr, *The Decline of Popular Politics: The American North, 1865–1928* (1986); Mark Lawrence Kornbluh, *Why America Stopped Voting: The Decline of Participatory Democracy and the Emergence of Modern American Politics* (2000); and Richard J. Jensen, *The Winning of the Midwest* (1971), are good on politics. David P. Thelen, *The New Citizenship: Origins of Progressivism in Wisconsin, 1885–1900* (1972); Carl Smith, *Urban Disorder and the Shape of Belief: The Great Chicago Fire, the Haymarket Bomb, and the Model Town of Pullman* (1995); Susan Eleanor Hirsch, *After the Strike: A Century of Labor Struggle at Pullman* (2003); and Douglas W. Steeples and David O. Whitten, *Democracy in Desperation: The Depression of 1893* (1998), stress the impact of the depression on ideas and attitudes. C. Vann Woodward examines the South in *Origins of the New South, 1877–1913* (1951). Also, see Michael Perman, *Struggle for Mastery: Disfranchisement in the South, 1888–1908* (2001) and Thomas Adams Upchurch, *Legislating Racism: The Billion Dollar Congress and the Birth of Jim Crow* (2004).

On Populism, see John D. Hicks, *The Populist Revolt* (1931); Lawrence Goodwyn, *Democratic Promise: The Populist Moment in America* (1976); James L. Hunt, *Marion Butler and American Populism* (2003); Steven Hahn, *The Roots of Southern Populism* (1983); and Elizabeth Sanders, *Roots of Reform: Farmers, Workers, and the American State, 1877–1917* (1999). Steven W. Usselman, *Regulating Railroad Innovation: Business, Technology, and Politics in America, 1840–1920* (2002), looks at regulatory reform.

CHAPTER 21 | TOWARD EMPIRE

The best general account of the development of American foreign policy during the last part of the nineteenth century is Walter LaFeber, *The New Empire: An Interpretation of American Expansion, 1860–1898* (1963). William Appleman Williams, *The Tragedy of American Diplomacy* (1959), examines the economic motives for expansion. See also Paul Wolman, *Most Favored Nation: The Republican Revisionists and U.S. Tariff Policy, 1897–1912* (1992); Thomas Schoonover, *Uncle Sam's War of 1898 and the Origins of Globalization* (2003); Eric T. L. Lowe, *Race Over Empire: Racism and U.S. Imperialism, 1865–1900* (2004); and Laura Wexler, *Tender Violence: Domestic Visions in an Age of U.S. Imperialism* (2000). Lewis L. Gould persuasively reassesses McKinley's diplomacy and wartime leadership in *The Presidency of William McKinley* (1980). Also helpful are Michael H. Hunt, *Ideology and Foreign Policy* (1987); Tom E. Terrill, *The Tariff, Politics, and American Foreign Policy, 1874–1901* (1973); and Matthew Frye Jacobson, *Barbarian Virtues: The United States Encounters Foreign Peoples at Home and Abroad, 1876–1917* (2000).

Graham A. Cosmas presents a detailed account of military organization and strategy in *An Army for Empire: The United States Army in the Spanish-American War* (1971); Willard B. Gatewood, Jr., offers a fascinating glimpse of the thoughts of some black soldiers in the war in *"Smoked Yankees" and the Struggle for Empire: Letters from Negro Soldiers, 1898–1902* (1971). Also, see Vincent H. Cirillo, *Bullets and Bacilli: The Spanish-American War and Military Medicine* (2004). Ivan Musicant, *Empire by Default: The Spanish-American War and the Dawn of the American Century* (1998); Kristin L. Hoganson, *Fighting for American Manhood: How Gender Politics Provoked the Spanish-American and Philippine-American Wars* (1998); and John L. Offner, *An Unwanted War: The Diplomacy of the United States and Spain over Cuba, 1895–1898* (1992), trace the background to the war with Spain. Brian McAllister Linn, *The Philippine War, 1899–1902* (2000), examines the often forgotten war against the Filipinos. Gerald F. Linderman relates the war to the home front in *The Mirror of War: American Society and the Spanish-American War* (1974).

CHAPTER 22 | THE PROGRESSIVE ERA

There are several important analyses of the Progressive Era, including Robert H. Wiebe, *The Search for Order, 1877–1920* (1967); Richard Hofstadter, *The Age of Reform* (1955); Michael McGerr, *A Fierce Discontent: The Rise and Fall of the Progressive Movement in America, 1870–1920* (2003); Samuel P. Hays, *The Response to Industrialism* (1957); and Gabriel Kolko, *The Triumph of Conservatism* (1963). C. Vann Woodward, *Origins of the New South 1877–1913* (1951), is a superb account of developments in the South, along with William A. Link, *The Paradox of Southern Progressivism, 1880–1930* (1992) and Steven Hahn, *A Nation Under Our Feet: Black Political Struggles in the Rural South from Slavery to the Great Migration* (2003).

George William Shea, *Spoiled Silk: The Red Mayor and the Great Paterson Textile Strike* (2001); Greg Hall, *Harvest Wobblies: The Industrial Workers of the World and Agricultural Laborers in the American West, 1905–1930* (2001); and Elliot J. Gorn, *Mother Jones: The Most Dangerous Woman in America* (2001), look at radical labor movements; David I. Macleod, *The Age of the Child: Children in America, 1890–1920* (1998), at children; Tom Holm, *The Great Confusion in Indian Affairs: Native Americans and Whites in the Progressive Era* (2005), and Alan Trachtenberg, *Shades of Hiawatha: Staging Indians, Making Americans, 1880–1930* (2004), at Native Americans; Nancy C. Unger, *Fighting Bob LaFollette: The Righteous Reformer* (2000); Joyce A. Hanson, *Mary McCloud Bethune and Black Women's Political Activism* (2003); and Patricia A. Schechter, *Ida B. Wells-Barnett and American Reform, 1880–1930* (2001), at specific reformers. Gary Scott Smith, *The Search for Social Salvation: Social Christianity and America, 1880–1925* (2000), and Thomas Winter, *Making Men, Making Class: The YMCA and Workingmen, 1877–1920* (2002), examine the role of religion. Steven L. Piott, *Giving Voters a Voice: The Origins of the Initiative and Referendum in America* (2003), and Rebecca J. Mead, *How the Vote Was Won: Woman Suffrage in the Western United States, 1868–1914* (2003), look at important political issues. James T. Kloppenberg, *Uncertain Victory: Social Democracy and Progressivism in European and American Thought, 1870–1920* (1986), examines progressivism at home and abroad. C. Vann Woodward, *The Strange Career of Jim Crow* (1955), traces the civil rights setbacks of the Progressive Era.

CHAPTER 23 | FROM ROOSEVELT TO WILSON IN THE AGE OF PROGRESSIVISM

George Mowry, *The Era of Theodore Roosevelt* (1958), and Arthur S. Link, *Woodrow Wilson and the Progressive Era* (1954), trace the social and economic conditions of the period. See also John M. Blum's perceptive and brief *The Republican Roosevelt* (1954); Sarah Watts, *Rough Rider in the White House: Theodore Roosevelt and the Politics of Desire* (2003); and Kathleen Dalton, *Theodore Roosevelt: A Strenuous Life* (2002). The definitive biography of Wilson is Arthur S. Link, *Wilson*, 5 vols. (1947–1965).

Samuel P. Hays offers an influential interpretation of progressivism in *Conservation and the Gospel of Efficiency* (1959) as does Nancy Cohen, *The Reconstruction of American Liberalism, 1865–1914* (2002), for the broader period. Albro Martin, *Enterprise Denied: Origins of the Decline of American Railroads, 1897–1917* (1971), argues persuasively that reformers damaged as well as regulated. Samuel Haber, *The Quest for Authority and Honor in the American Professions, 1750–1900* (1991), examines the changing nature of the professions.

CHAPTER 24 | THE NATION AT WAR

American foreign policy between 1901 and 1921 has been the subject of considerable study. Richard W. Leopold, *The Growth of American Foreign Policy* (1962), is balanced and informed. Robert E. Osgood, *Ideals and Self-Interest in America's Foreign Relations* (1953); Robert E. Hannigan, *The New World Power: American Foreign Policy, 1898–1917* (2002); and William Appleman Williams, *Roots of the Modern American Empire* (1969), explore the forces underlying American foreign policy.

For American policy toward Latin America, see Dana G. Munro's detailed account, *Intervention and Dollar Diplomacy in the Caribbean, 1900–1920* (1964); Mary A. Renda, *Taking Haiti: Military Occupation and the Culture of U.S. Imperialism, 1915–1940* (2001); and Emily S. Rosenberg, *Financial Missionaries to the World: The Politics and Culture of Dollar Diplomacy, 1900–1930* (1999). Arthur S. Link examines Wilson's foreign policy in his exceptional five-volume biography, *Wilson* (1947–1965), and in *Woodrow Wilson: Revolution, War, and Peace* (1979). Arthur Walworth, *America's Moment, 1918: American Diplomacy at the End of World War I* (1977), and John Milton Cooper, Jr., *Breaking the Heart of the World: Woodrow Wilson and the Fight for the League of Nations* (2001), examine Wilson's attempt to create a peaceful world order.

Studies of events at home during the war include David M. Kennedy, *Over Here* (1980); Alan Dawley, *Changing the World: American Progressives in War and Revolution* (2003); Christopher M. Sterba, *Good Americans: Italian and Jewish Immigrants during the First World War* (2003); Robert D. Cuff, *The War Industries Board* (1973); and Maurine W. Greenwald, *Women, War, and Work* (1980). Susan Zeiger, *In Uncle Sam's Service: Women Workers with the American Expeditionary Force, 1917–1919* (1999), and Kathleen Kennedy, *Disloyal Mothers and Scurrilous Citizens: Women and Subversion During World War I* (1999), look at the role of women; Jennifer D. Keene, *Doughboys, the Great War, and the Remaking of America* (2001), at the war's effects on the soldiers; and Mark Robert Schneider, *"We Return Fighting": The Civil Rights Movement in the Jazz Age* (2001), Mark Ellis, *Race, War, and Surveillance: African Americans and the United States Government during World War I* (2001), and Theodore Kornweibel, Jr., *"Investigate Everything": Federal Efforts to Compel Black Loyalty During World War I* (2002), at its impact on African Americans.

CHAPTER 25 | TRANSITION TO MODERN AMERICA

William Leuchtenburg provides the best overview of the 1920s in *The Perils of Prosperity, 1914–1932* (1958). Ellis Hawley, *The Great War and the Search for a Modern Order* (1979), and Donald McCoy, *Coming of Age* (1973), are also valuable as surveys of the period. Frederick Lewis Allen, *Only Yesterday: An Informal History of the 1920s* (1931), is a classic, and still delightfully readable. The changing political alignments of the 1920s are covered in David Burner, *The Politics of Provincialism* (1968). The essays in John Braeman, Robert H. Bremner, and David Brody, eds., *Change and Continuity in Twentieth-Century America: The 1920s* (1968), provide various perspectives on important facets of the period.

Economic developments of the 1920s are the subject of George Soule, *Prosperity Decade* (1947). Helen Lynd and Robert Lynd, *Middletown* (1929), examine the social and cultural trends of the decade. David J. Goldberg, *Discontented America* (1999), finds unhappiness beneath the apparent prosperity. Edward J. Larson, *Summer for the Gods* (1998), is the most recent and accessible account of the Scopes trial. The lives of public figures of the 1920s are traced in David Levering Lewis, *W. E. B. Du Bois*, vol. 2 (2000); Terry Teachout, *The Skeptic* (2002), on H. L. Mencken; Elisabeth Israels Perry, *Belle Moskowitz* (2000); and Robert A. Slayton, *Empire Statesman* (2001), and Christopher M. Finan, *Alfred E. Smith* (2002), both on the leading Democrat of the 1920s.

CHAPTER 26 | FRANKLIN D. ROOSEVELT AND THE NEW DEAL

The best overall account of political developments in the 1930s is William Leuchtenburg, *Franklin D. Roosevelt and the New Deal* (1963). For a more critical view, see James MacGregor Burns, *Roosevelt: The Lion and the Fox* (1956), which portrays FDR as an overly cautious political leader; and Robert A. McElvaine, *The Great Depression: America, 1929–1941* (1984), which laments the New Deal's failure to make more sweeping changes in American life. Gene

Smiley, *Rethinking the Great Depression* (2002), succinctly challenges conventional wisdom on the subject. Alonzo Hamby, *For the Survival of Democracy* (2004), compares the American New Deal to reform in other countries.

David M. Kennedy provides a comprehensive portrait of American life during both the Great Depression and World War II in *Freedom from Fear* (1999). More succinct is Gerald D. Nash, *The Crucial Era: The Great Depression and World War II, 1929–1945* (1992). For a sympathetic examination of the New Deal through 1936, see Arthur M. Schlesinger, Jr., *The Age of Roosevelt,* 3 vols. (1957–1960); Paul Conkin offers a brief but provocative critique of Roosevelt's policies in *The New Deal* (1967). George McJimsy, *The Presidency of Franklin Delano Roosevelt* (2000), is the most recent and best-balanced account.

John Kenneth Galbraith, *The Great Crash, 1929* (1961), has long been the standard treatment of that event, but Maury Klein, *Rainbow's End* (2001), may displace it. Alan Brinkley, *Voices of Protest* (1982), assesses the challenges to Roosevelt from the left and the right. Lizabeth Cohen, *Making a New Deal: Industrial Workers in Chicago, 1919–1939* (1990), examines the effects of the Great Depression and the New Deal on the working class.

CHAPTER 27 | AMERICA AND THE WORLD, 1921–1945

The best general account of American attitudes toward the world in the 1920s can be found in Warren I. Cohen, *Empire Without Tears* (1987). Robert Dallek provides a thorough account of FDR's diplomacy in *Franklin D. Roosevelt and American Foreign Policy, 1932–1945* (1979). For a more critical view, see Robert A. Divine, *Roosevelt and World War II* (1969). David M. Kennedy, *Freedom from Fear* (1999), sets Roosevelt's foreign and wartime policies against the background of domestic politics.

Two good books on the continuing controversy over Pearl Harbor are Roberta Wohlstetter, *Pearl Harbor: Warning and Decision* (1962), and Gordon W. Prange, *At Dawn We Slept* (1981). In his brief overview of wartime diplomacy, *American Diplomacy During the Second World War,* 2nd ed. (1985), Gaddis Smith stresses the tensions within the victorious coalition. So does Mark Stoler in *Allies and Adversaries* (2000). Kenneth S. Davis, *FDR: The War President* (2000), Thomas Fleming, *The New Dealers' War* (2001), and Michael Beschloss, *The Conquerors* (2002), portray American leadership during the war. Robert S. Norris, *Racing for the Bomb* (2002), and Gregg Herken, *Brotherhood of the Bomb* (2002), describe the Manhattan Project and what it led to.

The best accounts of the home front are Kennedy, *Freedom from Fear;* Richard Polenberg, *War and Society* (1972); John M. Blum, *V Was for Victory* (1976); and Doris Kearns Goodwin, *No Ordinary Time* (1995). Daniel Kryder, *Divided Arsenal* (2000); Ronald Takaki, *Double Victory* (2000); and Greg Robinson, *By Order of the President* (2001), trace the war's effects on racial and ethnic minorities in the United States.

CHAPTER 28 | THE ONSET OF THE COLD WAR

The best general guide to American diplomacy since World War II is Walter LaFeber, *America, Russia and the Cold War, 1945–2000,* 9th ed. (2002). On the much debated question of the origins of the Cold War, the most balanced account is Daniel Yergin, *Shattered Peace* (1977); for a dissenting view, see Thomas G. Paterson, *On Every Front* (1979). John Lewis Gaddis, *We Now Know* (1997), integrates new disclosures from Soviet and Chinese archives to provide the best rounded account of the Cold War through the early 1960s.

The classic account of containment is still the lucid recollection of its chief architect, George Kennan, *Memoirs, 1925–1950* (1967). John Lewis Gaddis uses Kennan's ideas as a point of departure for his account of the changing nature of American Cold War policy in *Strategies of Containment* (1982). Melvyn P. Leffler offers a full account of the development of containment in *A Preponderance of Power* (1992); Arnold A. Offner is more critical of Truman's policies in *Another Such Victory* (2002). Kai Bird and Martin J. Sherwin probe Robert Oppenheimer's opposition to development of the hydrogen bomb in their biography, *American Prometheus* (2005). For developments in the Far East, consult the perceptive book by Akira Iriye, *The Cold War in Asia* (1974). On the Korean conflict, see Burton Kaufman, *The Korean War,* 2nd ed. (1997), and Bruce Cumings, *The Origins of the Korean War,* 2 vols. (1981 and 1991).

The best book on the Truman period is Alonzo L. Hamby, *Man of the People* (1995), which provides a balanced portrait of a controversial leader. Richard M. Fried offers a perceptive overview of the postwar anticommunist crusade in *Nightmare in Red: The McCarthy Era in Perspective* (1990); the best biography of McCarthy is David Oshinsky, *A Conspiracy So Immense* (1983).

Stephen A. Ambrose evaluates Dwight D. Eisenhower positively in the second volume of his biography, *Eisenhower: The President* (1985). For an equally favorable analysis, see Robert A. Divine, *Eisenhower and the Cold War* (1981). Richard H. Immerman provides a balanced portrait of Eisenhower's secretary of state in *John Foster Dulles* (1999).

CHAPTER 29 | AFFLUENCE AND ANXIETY

Two excellent books survey the social, cultural, and political trends in the United States during the postwar period. In *One Nation Divisible* (1980), Richard Polenberg analyzes class, ethnic, and racial changes; James T. Patterson offers a perceptive overview of American life from the end of World War II through the mid-1970s in *Grand Expectations* (1996).

Richard Pells provides a sweeping survey of the American intellectual community's response to the Cold War in *The Liberal Mind in a Conservative Age* (1985). The broadest account of American life during the decade is David Halberstam, *The Fifties* (1993). Other important books on social and cultural trends include Elaine Tyler May, *Homeward Bound: American Families in the Cold War Era* (1988); Kenneth A. Jackson, *Crabgrass Frontier* (1986); Lisabeth Cohen, *A Consumer's Republic* (2003); and Serge Guilbaut, *How New York Stole the Idea of Modern Art* (1983).

Charles Alexander provides a balanced view of the Eisenhower years in *Holding the Line* (1975). Fred Greenstein, *The Hidden Hand Presidency* (1982), explores Eisenhower's fondness for indirect leadership. For the impact of *Sputnik* and the space program, see Walter A. MacDougall, *The Heavens and the Earth* (1985) and Robert A. Divine, *The Sputnik Challenge* (1993).

Taylor Branch gives a comprehensive account of the genesis of the civil rights movement in *Parting the Waters: America in the King Years, 1954–1963* (1988). Three fine biographies—David L. Lewis's *King* (1970), Stephen B. Oates's *Let the Trumpet Sound* (1982), and David Garrow's *Bearing the Cross* (1986)—present perceptive portraits of Martin Luther King, Jr., the movement's most influential leader. On civil rights, see also Adam Fairclough, *To Redeem the Soul of America* (1987); Joanne Grant, *Ella Baker* (1999); and James T. Patterson, *Brown* v. *Board of Education* (2001). The fullest account of the passage of the 1957 civil rights act is the third volume of Robert Caro's biography of Lyndon Johnson, *Master of the Senate* (2002).

CHAPTER 30 | THE TURBULENT SIXTIES

The best general account of the 1960s is Jim F. Heath, *Decade of Disillusionment* (1975), which stresses the continuity in policy between the Kennedy and Johnson administrations. Arthur M. Schlesinger, Jr., *A Thousand Days* (1965), is the classic history of the Kennedy administration; for a more balanced view, see Richard Reeves, *President Kennedy* (1993). The best study of Kennedy's foreign policy is Michael R. Beschloss, *The Crisis Years: Kennedy and Khrushchev, 1960–1963* (1991); for the Cuban missile crisis, consult Graham Allison and Philip Zelikow, *Essence of Decision*, 2nd ed. (1999) and Sheldon Stern, *The Week the World Stood Still* (2005).

Robert Dallek offers a balanced view of Johnson's presidential years in *Flawed Giant* (1998). For the impact of the 1965 immigration legislation, see Hugh Davis Graham, *Collision Course* (2002). For LBJ's foreign policy, see H. W. Brands, *The Wages of Globalism* (1995). The best introduction to the Vietnam War is the balanced survey by George Herring, *America's Longest War*, 4th ed. (2002). For differing views of Johnson's responsibility for the Vietnam conflict, see Fredrik Logevall, *Choosing War* (1999), highly critical; Lloyd Gardner, *Pay Any Price* (1995), more understanding; and Garth Porter, *Perils of Dominance* (2005).

The best overview of civil rights developments in the 1960s is Hugh Davis Graham, *The Civil Rights Era, 1960–1972* (1990). The most comprehensive account of the student protests is Terry Anderson, *The Movement and the Sixties* (1995), but see also Todd Gitlin, *The Sixties* (1987), more sympathetic to the youthful protesters; W. J. Rorabaugh, *Berkeley at War* (1989); and Rhodri Jeffrey-Jones, *Peace Now!* (1999).

Garry Wills provides the most revealing portrait of Richard Nixon's character and prepresidential career in *Nixon Agonistes* (1970). The best account of the 1968 election is Lewis L. Gould, *1968: The Election That Changed America* (1993).

CHAPTER 31 | TO A NEW CONSERVATISM, 1969–1988

The most comprehensive account of Nixon's political career and presidency is the three-volume biography by Stephen E. Ambrose, *Nixon* (1987–1992). Melvin Small offers a balanced assessment of Nixon's White House years in *The Presidency of Richard Nixon* (1999); for a more detailed view, see Richard Reeves, *President Nixon* (2001). Stanley Kutler provides a thorough account of the scandal that drove Nixon from office in *The Wars of Watergate* (1990).

H. W. Brands surveys American foreign policy from the mid-1970s through the mid-1990s in *Since Vietnam* (1995). For foreign policy under Nixon, see William P. Bundy, *A Tangled Web* (1998), and Jeffrey Kimball, *Nixon's Vietnam War* (1998). Raymond L. Garthoff, *Détente and Confrontation* (1985), covers relations with the Soviet Union in the 1970s. The best study of Henry Kissinger's diplomacy is Jussi Hanhimaki, *The Flawed Architect* (2004). James Bamford, *Body of Secrets* (2001), deals with the highly secretive National Security Agency.

In *The Prize* (1991), Daniel Yergin puts the energy crisis of the 1970s in historical perspective. Richard Barnet gives a thorough description of the impact of the energy crisis and foreign competition on the American economy in the 1970s in *The Lean Years* (1980). For economic policy under Carter, see W. Carl Biven, *Jimmy Carter's Economy* (2002). Two books survey popular culture in the 1970s: David Frum, *How We Got Here: The 70's* (2000) and Bruce J. Schulman, *The Seventies* (2001).

For the Ford and Carter administrations, see John R. Greene, *The Presidency of Gerald R. Ford* (1995), and Burton I. Kaufman, *The Presidency of Jimmy Carter* (1993). Gaddis Smith surveys Carter's foreign policy in *Morality, Reason, and Power* (1985). For the crisis with Iran, see Barry Rubin, *Paved with Good Intentions* (1980). On the rise of Ronald Reagan, see Lou Cannon, *Governor Reagan* (2003). The most insightful account of the Reagan presidency is Richard Reeves, *President Reagan* (2005).

CHAPTER 32 | TO THE TWENTY-FIRST CENTURY, 1989–2006

John Robert Greene provides a balanced view of the Bush administration in *The Presidency of George Bush* (2000). The best biography of the president is Herbert Parmet, *George Bush* (1997). For foreign policy, see George Bush and Brent Scowcroft, *A World Transformed* (1998). Bob Woodward traces the decisions leading to the Gulf War in *The Commanders* (1991) The best overview of the military operations is Michael R. Gordon and Bernard F. Trainor, *The Generals' War* (1995).

Bill Clinton's *My Life* (2004) is one of the most revealing of presidential memoirs. Sidney Blumenthal, *The Clinton Wars* (2003), settles accounts with some former colleagues from the Clinton administration even as he reveals how the administration operated. Joe Klein, *The Natural* (2002), is sympathetic to Clinton. Rich Lowry, *Legacy* (2003), is not. Richard A. Posner, *An Affair of State* (1999), and Michael Isikoff, *Uncovering Clinton* (2000), dissect the Monica Lewinsky scandal and the ensuing impeachment proceedings.

Haynes Johnson, *The Best of Times* (2001), provides a journalistic account of the 1990s. John Cassidy, *dot.com* (2002), treats the Internet boom. The best survey of foreign policy in the Clinton years is David Halberstam, *War in a Time of Peace* (2001). On Bosnia, see Richard Holbrooke, *To End a War* (2001). David Fromkin covers the other Balkan crisis in *Kosovo Crossing* (1999).

The most balanced account of the disputed 2000 election is Howard Gillman, *The Votes that Counted* (2001). Contrasting views of George W. Bush can be found in Frank Bruni, *Ambling into History* (2002); David Frum, *The Right Man* (2003); and Maureen Dowd, *Bushworld* (2004). On the terrorist attacks of September 11, 2001, see Richard Bernstein, et. al., *Out of the Blue* (2002). Bob Woodward, *Plan of Attack* (2004), provides the most detailed account of the decision for war against Iraq (the second time around). George Packer, *The Assassin's Gate* (2005), offers a ground-level view of Iraq after the overthrow of Saddam Hussein.

Terry H. Anderson, *The Pursuit of Fairness* (2004), provides a history of affirmative action. Kevin Phillips, *Wealth and Democracy* (2002), traces the rise of economic inequality in America. Thomas L. Friedman, *The World is Flat* (2005), assesses the impact of globalization. Reasonable voices on the culture wars are hard to hear; one is Alan Wolfe, *One Nation after All* (1999).

Suggested Web Sites

CHAPTER 1 | NEW WORLD ENCOUNTERS

Vikings in the New World
emuseum.mnsu.edu/prehistory/vikings/vikhome.html
This site explores the history of some of the earliest European visitors to America.

Ancient Mesoamerican Civilizations
www.angelfire.com/ca/humanorigins/index.html
Kevin L. Callahan of the University of Minnesota Department of Anthropology maintains this page that supplies information regarding Mesoamerican civilizations with well-organized essays and photos.

1492: An Ongoing Voyage
www.loc.gov/exhibits/1492
An exhibit of the Library of Congress, Washington, D.C. With brief essays and images about early civilizations and contact in the Americas.

Cahokia Mounds
www.cahokiamounds.com/
The Cahokia Mounds State Historical Site gives information about a fascinating pre-Columbian culture in North America.

Mexican Pre-Columbian History
www.mexonline.com/precolum.htm
This site "provides information on the Aztecs, Maya, Mexica, Olmecs, Toltec, Zapotecs and other pre-European cultures, as well as information on museums, archeology, language, and education."

CHAPTER 2 | ENGLAND'S COLONIAL EXPERIMENTS: THE SEVENTEENTH CENTURY

The Plymouth Colony Archive Project at the University of Virginia
etext.virginia.edu/users/deetz
This site contains comprehensive and fairly extensive information about late seventeenth-century Plymouth Colony.

Jamestown Rediscovery
www.apva.org
This site mounted by the Association for the Preservation of Virginia Antiquity has excellent material on archaeological excavations at Jamestown.

Lost Worlds: Georgia Before Oglethorpe
www.lostworlds.org/ga_before_oglethorpe.html
This resources guide informs about Native American Georgia in the seventeenth century.

William Penn, Visionary Proprietor
xroads.virginia.edu/~CAP/PENN/pnhome.html
William Penn had an interesting life, and this site is a good introduction to the man and some of his achievements.

CHAPTER 3 | PUTTING DOWN ROOTS:
FAMILIES IN AN ATLANTIC EMPIRE

DPLS Archive: Slave Movement During the 18th and 19th Centuries (Wisconsin)
dpls.dacc.wisc.edu/slavedata/index.html
This site explores the slave ships and the slave trade that carried thousands of Africans to the New World.

Excerpts from Slave Narratives
www.vgskole.net/prosjekt/slavrute/primary.htm
Accounts of slavery from the seventeenth through nineteenth centuries speak volumes about the many impacts of slavery.

Salem Witch Trials: Documentary Archive and Transcription Project
www.iath.virginia.edu/salem/home.html
Extensive archive of the 1692 trials and life in late seventeenth-century Massachusetts.

Colonial Documents
www.yale.edu/lawweb/avalon/18th.htm
The key documents of the Colonial Era are reproduced here, as are some important documents from earlier and later periods in American history.

Africans in America
www.pbs.org/wgbh/aia/home.html
This PBS site contains images and documents recounting slavery in America.

CHAPTER 4 | COLONIES IN AN EMPIRE:
EIGHTEENTH-CENTURY AMERICA

History Buff—American History Library
www.historybuff.com/library
Brief journalistic essays on newspaper coverage of sixteenth- to eighteenth-century American history.

Benjamin Franklin Documentary History Web Site
www.english.udel.edu/lemay/franklin/
University of Delaware professor J. A. Leo Lemay tells the story of Franklin's varied life in seven parts on this intriguing site.

Jonathan Edwards
www.jonathanedwards.com/
Speeches by this famous preacher of the Great Awakening are on this site.

Religion and the Founding of the American Republic
lcweb.loc.gov/exhibits/religion/religion.html
This Library of Congress site is an on-line exhibit about religion and the creation of the United States.

The French and Indian War
web.syr.edu/~laroux/
This site is about French soldiers who came to New France between 1755 and 1760 to fight in the French and Indian War.

Smithsonian Institution: You Be the Historian
www.americanhistory.si.edu/hohr/springer
Part of the Smithsonian's on-line museum, this exhibit enables students to examine artifacts from the home of New Castle, Delaware, residents Thomas and Elizabeth Springer and interpret the lives of a late eighteenth-century American family.

CHAPTER 5 | THE AMERICAN REVOLUTION: FROM ELITE PROTEST TO POPULAR REVOLT, 1763–1783

Canada History
www.civilization.ca/indexe.asp
Canada and the United States shared a colonial past but developed differently in the long run. This site is a part of the virtual museum of the Canadian Museum of Civilization Corporation.

Georgia's Rare Map Collection
scarlett.libs.uga.edu/darchive/hargrett/maps/colamer.html
scarlett.libs.uga.edu/darchive/hargrett/maps/revamer.html
These two sites contain maps for Colonial and Revolutionary America.

Maryland Loyalism and the American Revolution
users.erols.com/candidus/index.htm
This look at Maryland's loyalists promotes the author's book, but the site has good information about an underappreciated phenomenon, including loyalist songs and poems.

The American Revolution
revolution.h-net.msu.edu/
This site accompanies the PBS series *Revolution* with essays and resource links.

CHAPTER 6 | THE REPUBLICAN EXPERIMENT

Independence Hall National Historical Park
www.nps.gov/inde/visit.html
This site includes images and historical accounts of Independence Hall and other Philadelphia buildings closely associated with the nation's founding.

Biographies of the Founding Fathers
www.colonialhall.com/
This site provides interesting information about the men who signed the Declaration of Independence and includes a trivia section.

The Federalist Papers
www.law.emory.edu/FEDERAL/federalist/
This site is a collection of the most important Federalist Papers, a series of documents designed to convince people to support the new Constitution and the Federalist party.

The Constitution and the Amendments
www.law.emory.edu/FEDERAL/usconst.html
A searchable site to the Constitution, especially useful for its information about the Bill of Rights and other constitutional amendments.

Documents from the Continental Congress and the Constitutional Convention, 1774–1789
memory.loc.gov/ammem/bdsds/bdsdhome.html
The Continental Congress Broadside Collection and the Constitutional Convention Broadside Collection contain 274 documents relating to the work of Congress and the drafting and ratification of the Constitution.

CHAPTER 7 | DEMOCRACY AND DISSENT: THE VIOLENCE OF PARTY POLITICS

Temple of Liberty—Building the Capitol for a New Nation
www.lcweb.loc.gov/exhibits/us.capitol/s0.html
Compiled from holdings in the Library of Congress, this site contains detailed information on the design and early construction of the Capitol building in Washington, D.C.

George Washington Papers at the Library of Congress, 1741–1799
memory.loc.gov/ammem/gwhtml/gwhome.html
This site is "the complete George Washington Papers from the Manuscript Division at the Library of Congress and consists of approximately 65,000 documents. This is the largest collection of original Washington documents in the world."

Archiving Early America
earlyamerica.com/
Old newspapers are excellent windows into the issues of the past. This site includes the Keigwin and Matthews collection of historic newspapers.

John Adams
www.ipl.org/div/potus/jadams.html
This Internet Public Library page contains biographical information about the second president, his inaugural address, and links to more information.

CHAPTER 8 | REPUBLICAN ASCENDANCY: THE JEFFERSONIAN VISION

Thomas Jefferson
www.pbs.org/jefferson/
A companion site to the Public Broadcasting Service series on Jefferson, especially important because it contains a fine collection of other people's view of Jefferson.

White House Historical Association
www.whitehousehistory.org/
This site contains a timeline of the history of the White House and several interesting photos and links.

Thomas Jefferson Digital Archive at the University of Virginia
etext.virginia.edu/jefferson/
Mr. Jefferson's University—the University of Virginia—houses this site with numerous on-line resources about Jefferson and his times, including electronic versions of texts by Jefferson, a page of selected quotations, and a comprehensive annotated bibliography of works on Jefferson from 1826 to 1997.

PBS Online—Lewis and Clark
www.pbs.org/lewisandclark/
This is a companion site to Ken Burns's documentary on Lewis and Clark containing a timeline of the expedition, a collection of related links, a bibliography, and more than 800 minutes of unedited, full-length RealPlayer interviews with seven experts featured in the film.

The War of 1812
members.tripod.com/~war1812/index.html
In-depth and varied information about the War of 1812.

CHAPTER 9 | NATION BUILDING AND NATIONALISM

The Era of the Mountain Men
www.xmission.com/~drudy/amm.html
Private letters can speak volumes about the concerns and environment of the writers and recipients. Letters from early settlers west of the Mississippi River are offered on this site.

Pioneering the Upper Midwest
memory.loc.gov/ammem/umhtml/umhome.html
This collection of firsthand accounts and memoirs vividly depicts life on the Midwestern frontier.

Prairietown, Indiana
www.connerprairie.org/explore/prairietown.html
This fictional model of a town and its inhabitants on the early frontier says much about America's movement westward and the everyday lives of Americans.

The Seminole Tribe of Florida
www.seminoletribe.com/
Before he was president, Andrew Jackson began a war against the Seminole Indians. This site presents information on their history and culture.

Erie Canal On-line
www.syracuse.com/features/eriecanal
This site, built around the diary of a 14-year-old girl who traveled from Amsterdam to Syracuse, New York, in the early nineteenth century, explores the construction and importance of the Erie Canal.

Whole Cloth: Discovering Science and Technology Through American Textile History
www.si.edu/lemelson/centerpieces/whole_cloth/
The Jerome and Dorothy Lemelson Center for the Study of Invention and Innovation/Society for the History of Technology put together this site, which includes excellent activities and sources concerning early American manufacturing and industry.

CHAPTER 10 | THE TRIUMPH OF WHITE MEN'S DEMOCRACY

Indian Affairs: Laws and Treaties, compiled and edited by Charles J. Kappler (1904)
digital.library.okstate.edu/kappler
This digitized text at Oklahoma State University includes preremoval treaties with the Five Civilized Tribes and other tribes.

Medicine of Jacksonian America
www.connerprairie.org/historyonline/jmed.html
Survival was far from certain in the Jacksonian Era. This site discusses some of the reasons and some of the possible cures of the times.

The University of Pennsylvania in 1830
www.archives.upenn.edu/histy/features/1830/
This virtual tour shows what a fairly typical campus looked like and what student life was like at one of the larger universities in the Antebellum Era.

19th Century Scientific American On-line
www.history.rochester.edu/Scientific_American/
Magazines and journals are windows through which we can view society. This site provides on-line editions of one of the more interesting nineteenth-century journals.

National Museum of the American Indian
www.si.edu/nmai
The Smithsonian Institution maintains this site, providing information about the museum, which is dedicated to the history and culture of Native Americans.

The Alexis de Tocqueville Tour: Exploring Democracy in America
www.tocqueville.org/
Text, images, and teaching suggestions are a part of this companion site to C-SPAN's programming on de Tocqueville.

CHAPTER 11 | SLAVES AND MASTERS

"Been Here So Long": Selections from the WPA American Slave Narratives
newdeal.feri.org/asn/index.htm
Slave narratives are some of the more interesting primary sources about slavery.

Amistad Trials (1839–1840)
www.law.umkc.edu/faculty/projects/ftrials/amistad/AMISTD.HTM
Images, chronology, court and official documents comprise this site by Dr. Doug Linder at University of Missouri–Kansas City Law School.

Slave Narratives
docsouth.unc.edu/neh/neh.html
This site presents the telling narratives of several slaves housed at the Documents of the American South collection and the University of North Carolina.

Colonization: The African-American Mosaic
www.loc.gov/exhibits/african/afam002.html
This site contains images and text relating to the colonization movement to return African Americans to Africa.

Images of African Americans from the Nineteenth Century
digital.nypl.org/schomburg/images_aa19/
The New York Public Library–Schomburg Center for Research in Black Culture site contains numerous visuals.

Images of African American Slavery and Freedom
www.loc.gov/rr/print/list/082_slave.html
This site contains numerous photographs and other images of slaves and free blacks from the Library of Congress.

St. Louis Circuit Court Historical Records Project
stlcourtrecords.wustl.edu/resources.php
This site contains links to full-text reproductions of slaves' freedom suits in Missouri, including Dred Scott's case, and many other African American history links.

CHAPTER 12 | THE PURSUIT OF PERFECTION

America's First Look into the Camera: Daguerreotype Portraits and Views, 1839–1862
memory.loc.gov/ammem/daghtml/daghome.html
The Library of Congress's daguerreotype collection consists of more than 650 photographs dating from 1839 to 1862. Portraits, architectural views, and some street scenes make up most of the collection.

Women in America, 1820 to 1842
xroads.virginia.edu/~HYPER/DETOC/FEM/home.htm
This University of Virginia site takes a look at women in antebellum America.

Votes for Women: Selections from the National American Woman Suffrage Association Collection, 1848–1921
memory.loc.gov/ammem/naw/nawshome.html
This Library of Congress site contains 167 books, pamphlets, and other artifacts documenting the suffrage campaign.

Godey's Lady's Book On-line
www.history.rochester.edu/godeys/
Here is on-line text of this interesting nineteenth-century journal.

Influence of Prominent Abolitionists
www.loc.gov/exhibits/african/afam006.html
An exhibit site from the Library of Congress, with pictures and text, which discusses some key African American abolitionists and their efforts to end slavery.

CHAPTER 13 | AN AGE OF EXPANSIONISM

Pioneering the Upper Midwest: Books from Michigan, Minnesota, and Wisconsin, ca. 1820–1910
memory.loc.gov/ammem/umhtml/umhome.html
This Library of Congress site looks at first-person accounts, biographies, promotional literature, local histories, ethnographic and antiquarian texts, colonial archival documents, and other works from the seventeenth to the early twentieth century. It covers many topics and issues that affected Americans in the settlement and development of the Upper Midwest.

The Mexican-American War Memorial Homepage
sunsite.dcaa.unam.mx/revistas/1847/
Images and text explain the causes, courses, and outcomes of the Mexican-American War.

On the Trail in Kansas
www.kancoll.org/galtrl.htm
This Kansas Collection site holds several good primary sources with images concerning the Oregon trail and America's early movement westward.

Mountain Men and the Fur Trade
www.xmission.com/~drudy/amm.html
Private letters can speak volumes about the concerns and environment of the writers and recipients. Letters from early settlers west of the Mississippi River are offered on this site, along with other resources relating to explorers, trappers, and traders.

CHAPTER 14 | THE SECTIONAL CRISIS

Secession Era Editorials Project
history.furman.edu/~benson/docs/
Furman University is digitizing editorials about the secession crisis and already includes scores of them on this site.

John Brown Trial Links
www.law.umkc.edu/faculty/projects/ftrials/Brown.html
For information about the trial of John Brown, this site provides a list of excellent links.

Abraham Lincoln and Slavery
odur.let.rug.nl/~usa/H/1990/ch5_p6.htm
This site discusses Lincoln's views and actions concerning slavery, especially the Lincoln-Douglas debate.

Bleeding Kansas
www.kancoll.org/galbks.htm
Contemporary and later accounts of America's rehearsal for the Civil War comprise this Kansas Collection site.

The Compromise of 1850 and the Fugitive Slave Act
www.pbs.org/wgbh/aia/part4/4p2951.html
From the series on Africans in America, an analysis of the Compromise of 1850 and of the effects of the Fugitive Slave Act on black Americans.

Words and Deeds in American History
lcweb2.loc.gov/ammem/mcchtml/corhome.html
A Library of Congress site containing links to Frederick Douglass; the Compromise of 1850; speeches by John C. Calhoun, Daniel Webster, and Henry Clay; and other topics from the Civil War era.

CHAPTER 15 | SECESSION AND THE CIVIL WAR

The American Civil War Homepage
sunsite.utk.edu/civil-war/warweb.html
This site has a great collection of hypertext links to the most useful identified electronic files about the American Civil War.

The Valley of the Shadow: Living the Civil War in Pennsylvania and Virginia
jefferson.village.virginia.edu/vshadow/vshadow.html
This project tells the histories of two communities on either side of the Mason-Dixon line during the Civil War. It includes narrative and an electronic archive of sources.

Abraham Lincoln Association
www.alincolnassoc.com/
This site allows the search of digital versions of Lincoln's papers.

U.S. Civil War Center
www.cwc.lsu.edu/
This site offers private and public data regarding the Civil War.

The Papers of Jefferson Davis Home Page
jeffersondavis.rice.edu
This site tells about the collection of Jefferson Davis papers and includes a chronology of his life, a family genealogy, some key Davis documents on-line, and a collection of related links.

History of African Americans in the Civil War
www.itd.nps.gov/cwss/history/aa_history.htm
This National Park Service site explores the history of the United States Colored Troops.

Civil War Women
scriptorium.lib.duke.edu/collections/civil-war-women.html
This site includes original documents, links, and biographical information about several women and their lives during the Civil War.

Selected Civil War Photographs
memory.loc.gov/ammem/cwphtml/cwphome.html
Library of Congress site with more than one thousand photographs, many from Matthew Brady.

CHAPTER 16 | THE AGONY OF RECONSTRUCTION

Diary and Letters of Rutherford B. Hayes
www.ohiohistory.org/onlinedoc/hayes/index.cfm
The Rutherford B. Hayes Presidential Center in Fremont, Ohio, maintains this searchable database of Hayes's writings.

Images of African Americans from the Nineteenth Century
digital.nypl.org/schomburg/images_aa19/
The New York Public Library–Schomburg Center for Research in Black Culture site contains numerous visuals.

Freedmen and Southern Society Project (University of Maryland-College Park)
www.inform.umd.edu/ARHU/Depts/History/Freedman/home.html
This site contains a chronology and sample documents from several print collections or primary sources about emancipation and freedom in the 1860s.

Andrew Johnson
www.whitehouse.gov/WH/glimpse/presidents/html/aj17.html
White House history of Johnson.

Ulysses S. Grant
www.whitehouse.gov/WH/glimpse/presidents/html/ug18.html
White House history of Grant.

CHAPTER 17 | THE WEST: EXPLOITING AN EMPIRE

Native American Documents Project
www.csusm.edu/projects/nadp/nadp.htm
California State University at San Marcos has several digital documents relating to Native Americans on this site.

The Northern Great Plains, 1880–1920
memory.loc.gov/ammem/award97/ndfahtml/ngphome.html
This American Memory site from the Library of Congress contains 900 photographs of the northern Great Plains at the turn of the century from the Fred Hultstrand and F. A. Pazandak collections from the Institute for Regional Studies at North Dakota State University.

On the Trail in Kansas
www.kancoll.org/galtrl.htm
This Kansas Collection site holds several good primary sources with images concerning the Oregon trail and America's early movement westward.

"California as I Saw It": First-Person Narratives of California's Early Years, 1849–1900
memory.loc.gov/ammem/cbhtml/cbhome.html
This site is a part of the American Memory series and contains full texts and illustrations of works documenting California's history through eyewitness accounts.

Home on the Range/Cowboy Heritage
www.vlib.us/old_west/cowboy.html
This site tells the history of the cattle trails and towns such as Dodge City, with useful text, links, documents, and maps.

The Evolution of the Conservation Movement, 1850–1920
memory.loc.gov/ammem/amrvhtml/conshome.html
This American Memory site brings together scores of primary sources and photographs about the movement to conserve and protect America's natural heritage.

CHAPTER 18 | THE INDUSTRIAL SOCIETY

Alexander Graham Bell Family Papers at the Library of Congress
memory.loc.gov/ammem/bellhtml/bellhome.html
This site contains papers from 1862 to 1939, but includes a chronology, images, selected documents, and interpretive essays about Bell.

The Richest Man in the World: Andrew Carnegie
www.pbs.org/wgbh/amex/carnegie/
This American Experience/PBS site provides images and text about Carnegie's life and activities.

John D. Rockefeller and the Standard Oil Company
www.micheloud.com/FXM/SO/
This study with accompanying images by François Micheloud tells of the rise of Rockefeller and his mammoth company.

Labor-Management Conflict in American History
www.history.osu.edu/projects/laborconflict/
This Ohio State University site includes primary accounts of some of the major events in the history of labor-management conflict in the late nineteenth and early twentieth centuries.

Samuel Gompers Papers at the University of Maryland
www.history.umd.edu/Gompers/index.htm
This site includes information about the papers project but also has a photo gallery, selected documents, and a brief history of the first president of the American Federation of Labor.

The Strike at Homestead
history.osu.edu/projects/homesteadstrike1892/
This site provides a collection of historical documents on the strike and reactions to it.

CHAPTER 19 | TOWARD AN URBAN SOCIETY, 1877–1900

The American Experience: America 1900
www.pbs.org/wgbh/amex/1900/
Companion to the PBS documentary, this site includes audio clips of respected historians on the economics, politics, and culture of 1900, a primary source database, a timeline of the year, downloadable software to compile a family tree, and other materials.

Touring Turn-of-the-Century America: Photographs from the Detroit Publishing Company, 1880–1920
memory.loc.gov/ammem/detroit/dethome.html
This Library of Congress collection has thousands of photographs from turn-of-the-century America.

United States History: The Gilded Age (1890) to World War I
www.emayzine.com/lectures/Gilded~1.htm
This site consists of a good overview essay of the era.

Jane Addams Hull-House Museum
www.uic.edu/jaddams/hull/hull_house.html
This site offers information on Addams, her settlement house programs, and the neighborhoods they served.

African American Perspectives: Pamphlets from the Daniel A. P. Murray Collection, 1818–1907
memory.loc.gov/ammem/aap/aaphome.html
This collection includes writings of famous African Americans, including Frederick Douglass, Booker T. Washington, Ida B. Wells-Barnett, Benjamin W. Arnett, Alexander Crummel, and Emanuel Love.

CHAPTER 20 | POLITICAL REALIGNMENTS IN THE 1890s

World's Columbian Exposition: Idea, Experience, Aftermath
xroads.virginia.edu/~MA96/WCE/title.html
This site has a virtual tour of the fair, along with contemporary reactions and modern analysis.

Pullman Links on the Web—Historic Pullman Foundation
www.pullmanil.org/links.htm
This page offers several links to sites with Pullman related information, including a section of sites on the Pullman strike and labor history.

Election of 1896
jefferson.village.virginia.edu/seminar/unit8/home.htm
This University of Virginia site contains biographical information, images, cartoons, and related links about the pivotal 1896 election.

The Era of William McKinley
history.osu.edu/Projects/McKinley/default.cfm
This site contains numerous images from various stages of William McKinley's career along with a brief biographical essay. This Ohio State University site also has a section with an excellent collection of cartoons from the era.

CHAPTER 21 | TOWARD EMPIRE

The Spanish-American War in Motion Pictures
memory.loc.gov/ammem/sawhtml/sawhome.html
This Library of Congress Web presentation features sixty-eight films of the Spanish American War, the first war to be documented in motion pictures.

The World of 1898: The Spanish-American War
www.loc.gov/rr/hispanic/1898/
This Library of Congress site offers resources and documents about the Spanish-American War and the people who participated in or commented about it.

Sentenaryo/Centennial: The Philippine Revolution and Philippine-American War
www.boondocksnet.com/centennial/index.html
Jim Zwick organizes primary documents, images, and essays focusing on the Philippines and American involvement.

Anti-Imperialism in the United States, 1898–1935
www.boondocksnet.com/ail98-35.html
Jim Zwick edits this extensive site, collating a large number of primary documents about anti-imperialism in America.

The Age of Imperialism
www.smplanet.com/imperialism/toc.html
Focusing on the period around the turn of the century, this site puts much information about American imperialism in one place.

Theodore Roosevelt Association
www.theodoreroosevelt.org/
This site contains much biographical and research information about Roosevelt.

CHAPTER 22 | THE PROGRESSIVE ERA

NAACP Online
www.naacp.org/
The National Association for the Advancement of Colored People official Web site explains its mission and includes a primary document explaining the start of the NAACP.

The Triangle Shirtwaist Factory Fire, March 25, 1911
www.ilr.cornell.edu/trianglefire/
The Kheel Center for Labor-Management Documentation and Archives at Cornell University put together this excellent site composed of oral histories, cartoons, images, and essays.

Touring Turn-of-the-Century America: Photographs from the Detroit Publishing Company, 1880–1920
memory.loc.gov/ammem/detroit/dethome.html
This Library of Congress collection has thousands of photographs from turn-of-the-century America.

Inside an American Factory: The Westinghouse Works, 1904
lcweb2.loc.gov/ammem/papr/west/westhome.html
Part of the American Memory Project at the Library of Congress, this site provides a glimpse inside a turn-of-the-century factory.

African American Women Writers of the Nineteenth Century
digital.nypl.org/schomburg/writers_aa19/
The New York Public Library–Schomburg Center for Research in Black Culture maintains this site that contains a large number of digital texts by African American women of the nineteenth century.

Margaret Sanger Papers Project
www.nyu.edu/projects/sanger/
This site at New York University contains information about Margaret Sanger and digital versions of several of her works.

CHAPTER 23 | FROM ROOSEVELT TO WILSON IN THE AGE OF PROGRESSIVISM

Theodore Roosevelt Association
www.theodoreroosevelt.org/
This site contains much biographical and research information about Theodore Roosevelt.

History of the Suffrage Movement
www.rochester.edu/SBA
This site includes a chronology, important texts relating to woman suffrage, and biographical information about Susan B. Anthony and Elizabeth Cady Stanton.

Woodrow Wilson
www.ipl.org/div/potus/wwilson.html
This page contains basic factual data about Wilson's election and presidency, speeches, and on-line biographies.

Women and Social Movements in the United States, 1775–2000
womhist.binghamton.edu
This site offers essays and primary documents on women in social movements.

CHAPTER 24 | THE NATION AT WAR

Woodrow Wilson
www.ipl.org/div/potus/wwilson.html
This page contains basic factual data about Wilson's election and presidency, speeches, and on-line biographies.

World War I Document Archive
www.lib.byu.edu/~rdh/wwi/
This archive contains sources about World War I in general, not just America's involvement.

World War One: Trenches on the Web
www.worldwar1.com/index.htm
This site provides a mass of data concerning the prosecution of the world's first global war.

The Great Migration in Chicago
lcweb.loc.gov/exhibits/african/afam011.html
This site looks at the black experience in the Great Migration at one prominent destination.

The American Experience: Influenza
www.pbs.org/wgbh/amex/influenza
This PBS site reveals the impact of the great flu epidemic of 1918.

CHAPTER 25 | TRANSITION TO MODERN AMERICA

Harlem 1900–1940: An African American Community
www.si.umich.edu/CHICO/Harlem/
The New York Public Library–Schomburg Center for Research in Black Culture hosts this site that includes a database, a timeline, and an exhibit.

The Scopes Trial
www.law.umkc.edu/faculty/projects/ftrials/scopes/scopes.htm
This site provides a detailed discussion of the trial, biographies of the major figures, images, and excerpts from the trial transcript.

American Temperance and Prohibition
prohibition.osu.edu/
This site looks at the temperance movement over time and contains many informative links.

The Jazz Age: Flapper Culture and Style
www.geocities.com/flapper_culture
This site contains many links to information about the popular culture of the 1920s with special reference to the flapper.

The Calvin Coolidge Experience
www.geocities.com/CapitolHill/4921/
This site is an unusual look at one of America's less colorful presidents.

CHAPTER 26 | FRANKLIN D. ROOSEVELT AND THE NEW DEAL

Voices from the Dust Bowl: The Charles L. Todd and Robert Sonkin Migrant Worker Collection, 1940–1941
memory.loc.gov/ammem/afctshtml/tshome.html
Farm Security Administration (FSA) studies of migrant work camps in central California in 1940 and 1941 are the bulk of this site. The collection includes audio recordings, photographs, manuscript materials, and publications.

New Deal Network
newdeal.feri.org/
This database includes photographs, political cartoons, and texts—including speeches, letters, and other historic documents—from the New Deal period.

Franklin Delano Roosevelt
www.ipl.org/div/potus/fdroosevelt.html
This site provides information about FDR, the only president to serve more than two terms.

A New Deal for the Arts
www.archives.gov/exhibits/new_deal_for_the_arts/index.html
Artwork, documents, and photographs recount the federal government's efforts to fund artists in the 1930s in the National Archives site.

America from the Great Depression to World War II: Photographs from the FSA and OWI, ca. 1935–1945
memory.loc.gov/ammem/fsowhome.html
These images in the Farm Security Administration–Office of War Information Collection show Americans from all over the nation experiencing everything from despair to triumph in the 1930s and 1940s.

Chapter 27 | America and the World, 1921–1945

A People at War
www.archives.gov/exhibits/a_people_at_war/a_people_at_war.html
This National Archives exhibit takes a close look at the contributions millions of Americans made to the war effort.

Powers of Persuasion—Poster Art of World War II
www.archives.gov/exhibits/powers_of_persuasion/powers_of_persuasion_home.html
These powerful posters at the National Archives were part of the battle for the hearts and minds of the American people.

A-Bomb WWW Museum
www.csi.ad.jp/ABOMB/
This site offers information about the impact of the first atomic bomb as well as the background and context of weapons of total destruction.

The United States Holocaust Memorial Museum
www.ushmm.org/
This is the official Web site of the Holocaust Museum in Washington, D.C.

Tuskegee Airmen
www.wpafb.af.mil/museum/history/prewwii/ta.htm
The Air Force Museum at Wright-Patterson Air Force Base maintains this site about the African American pilots of World War II.

World War II Resources: Primary Source Materials on the Web
www.ibiblio.org/pha/index.html
This site has a large number of searchable primary texts from all aspects of World War II.

Chapter 28 | The Onset of the Cold War

Harry S Truman
www.ipl.org/div/potus/hstruman.html
This page contains basic factual data about his election and presidency, speeches, and on-line biographies.

Harry S Truman Library and Museum
www.trumanlibrary.org
This presidential library site has numerous photos and various important primary documents relating to Truman.

Cold War
cnn.com/SPECIALS/cold.war/
This is the companion site to the CNN Perspectives series on the Cold War. It contains information including interactive timelines and a quiz.

Korean War Project
www.koreanwar.org
This site has information about the Korean War and is a guide to resources on the struggle.

Senator Joe McCarthy—A Multimedia Celebration
webcorp.com/mccarthy/
This webcorp site includes audio and visual clips of McCarthy's speeches.

CHAPTER 29 | AFFLUENCE AND ANXIETY

Fifties Website Home Page
www.fiftiesweb.com/
This entertaining site tells about and samples music and television from the 1950s. It also includes a related links page.

1950s America
www.english.upenn.edu/~afilreis/50/home.html
This site by Professor Al Filreis of the University of Pennsylvania contains a large array of 1950s literature and images in an alphabetical index.

Levittown: Documents of an Ideal American Suburb
www.uic.edu/~pbhales/Levittown/
The postwar boom in housing made suburban living the cultural norm in America and shaped a generation. The story of the classic suburb, Levittown, is told on this site in pictures and text.

Dwight David Eisenhower
www.ipl.org/div/potus/ddeisenhower.html
This site contains basic factual data about Eisenhower's election and presidency, including speeches and other materials.

CHAPTER 30 | THE TURBULENT SIXTIES

The Avalon Project: The Cuban Missile Crisis
www.yale.edu/lawweb/avalon/diplomacy/forrel/cuba/cubamenu.htm
Part of the foreign relations series of the Avalon Project at Yale Law School, this site includes a collection of on-line documents pertaining to the Cuban Missile Crisis and its aftermath.

The Kennedy Assassination
mcadams.posc.mu.edu/home.htm
This well-organized site has images, essays, and photos on the assassination.

Lyndon B. Johnson Library and Museum
www.lbjlib.utexas.edu/
This presidential library contains images and on-line exhibits.

Investigating the Vietnam War
www.spartacus.schoolnet.co.uk/vietintro.htm
This site from Spartacus Educational Publishing, U.K., has an excellent list of annotated links to the best Vietnam-related sites.

Free Speech Movement: Student Protest–U.C. Berkeley, 1964–65
www.lib.berkeley.edu/BANC/FSM/
The Bancroft Library at U.C. Berkeley houses this exhibit with oral histories, a chronology, and documents.

Vietnam On-line
www.pbs.org/wgbh/pages/amex/vietnam/index.html
From PBS and the *American Experience,* this site contains a detailed, interactive timeline of the war, interpretive essays, and autobiographical reflections.

Martin Luther King, Jr. Papers Project
www.stanford.edu/group/King/
This site at Stanford University has links and selected digital documents by and concerning Martin Luther King, Jr.

National Civil Rights Museum
www.mecca.org/~crights/nc2.html
This site allows a virtual tour of the museum with its interpretive exhibits.

The Sixties Project
lists.village.virginia.edu/sixties/
This University of Virginia site has extensive exhibits, documents, and personal narratives from the 1960s.

Civil Rights Oral History Bibliography
www-dept.usm.edu/~mcrohb/
This University of Southern Mississippi site includes complete transcripts of the selected oral resources.

1969 Woodstock Festival and Concert
www.woodstock69.com/index.htm
This site provides pictures and lists of songs from the famous rock festival.

CHAPTER 31 | TO A NEW CONSERVATISM, 1969–1988

May 4 Collection Home Page
speccoll.library.kent.edu/4may70
This site commemorates the May 4, 1970, shootings at Kent State University with a detailed chronology and other information.

Documents from the Women's Liberation Movement
scriptorium.lib.duke.edu/wlm/
Primary documents on-line from the Special Collections Library at Duke University provide first-hand information about the women's liberation movement.

Revisiting Watergate
www.washingtonpost.com/wp-srv/national/longterm/watergate/front.htm
This site features a chronology, images, searchable articles, and a good deal of background information about the burglary and its consequences, as well as an update on the revelation of Deep Throat's identity in 2005.

CNN 1970s Interactive Timeline
cnn.com/SPECIALS/1999/century/episodes/08/
CNN has a series of interactive timelines. This one covers the years from 1970 to 1979.

Richard Milhous Nixon
www.ipl.org/div/potus/rmnixon.html
This site contains information about Nixon's election and presidency, speeches, and on-line biographies.

Gerald Rudolph Ford
www.ipl.org/div/potus/grford.html
This site contains information about Ford's election and presidency, speeches, and on-line biographies.

James Earl Carter, Jr.
www.ipl.org/div/potus/jecarter.html
This site contains information about Carter's election and presidency, speeches, and on-line biographies.

Ronald Wilson Reagan
www.ipl.org/div/potus/rwreagan.html
This site contains information about Reagan's election and presidency, speeches, and on-line biographies.

U.S. Environmental Protection Agency
www.epa.gov/history
This history of the EPA includes a timeline, topical information, publications, and a document collection.

The 80s Server
www.80s.com/
Contains information on life in the 1980s.

In Their Own Words
aidshistory.nih.gov
National Institutes of Health researchers recall the early years of HIV/AIDS.

CHAPTER 32 | TO THE TWENTY-FIRST CENTURY, 1989–2006

George Herbert Walker Bush
www.ipl.org/div/potus/ghwbush.html
This site contains information about Bush's election and presidency, speeches, and on-line biographies.

The Gulf War
www.pbs.org/pages/frontline/gulf/index.html
This *Frontline* and PBS site combines personal accounts with a chronology and general information about the war.

Bill Clinton
www.ipl.org/div/potus/wjclinton.html
This site contains information about Clinton's election and presidency, speeches, and on-line biographies.

Census 2000
www.census.gov/main/www/cen2000.html
U.S. Census Bureau gateway to its snapshot of the American people at the beginning of the new millennium.

George Walker Bush
www.ipl.org/div/potus/gwbush.html
Contains information about the second Bush presidency.

9-11 Commission Report
www.9-11commission.gov/
The findings of the commission that investigated the terrorist attacks.

War in Iraq
www.cnn.com/SPECIALS/2003/iraq/
A CNN special report on the war, including maps and video.

History of the Internet
www.isoc.org/internet/history/brief.shtml
The technology that wired the world.

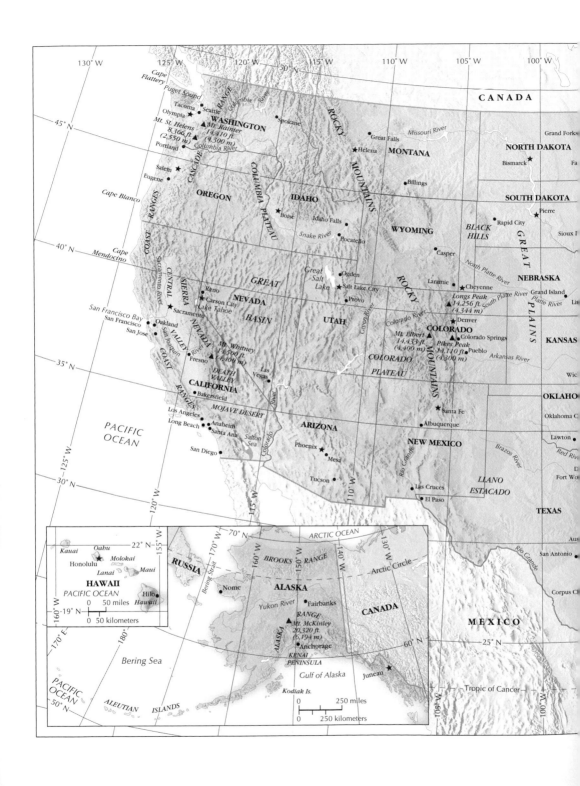

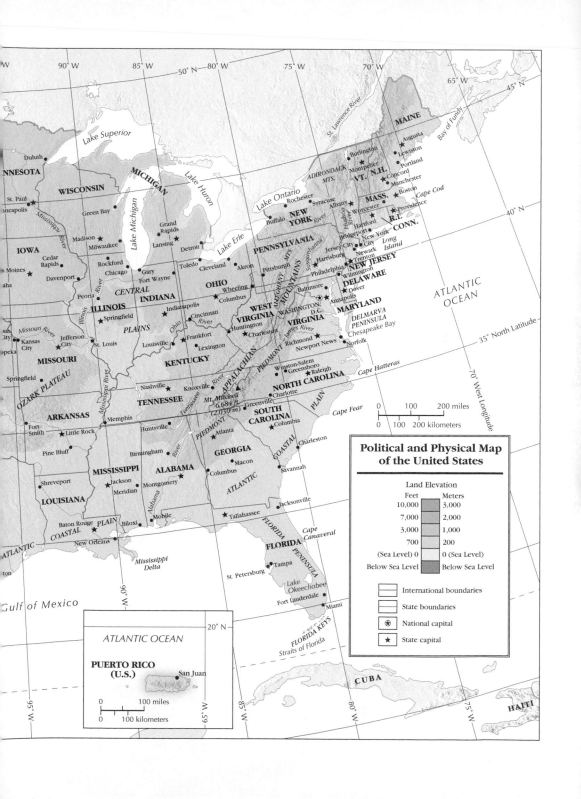

Political and Physical Map of the United States

Land Elevation

Feet	Meters
10,000	3,000
7,000	2,000
3,000	1,000
700	200
(Sea Level) 0	0 (Sea Level)
Below Sea Level	Below Sea Level

International boundaries

State boundaries

⊛ National capital

★ State capital

ATLANTIC OCEAN

PUERTO RICO (U.S.)

San Juan

0   100 miles

0   100 kilometers

CUBA

HAITI

Gulf of Mexico

ATLANTIC OCEAN

0   100   200 miles

0   100   200 kilometers

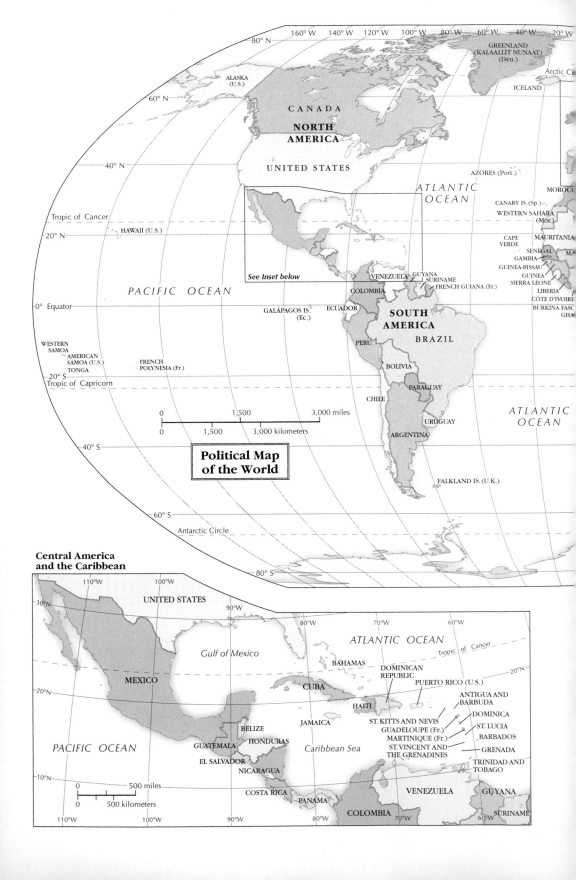

Political Map of the World

Central America and the Caribbean

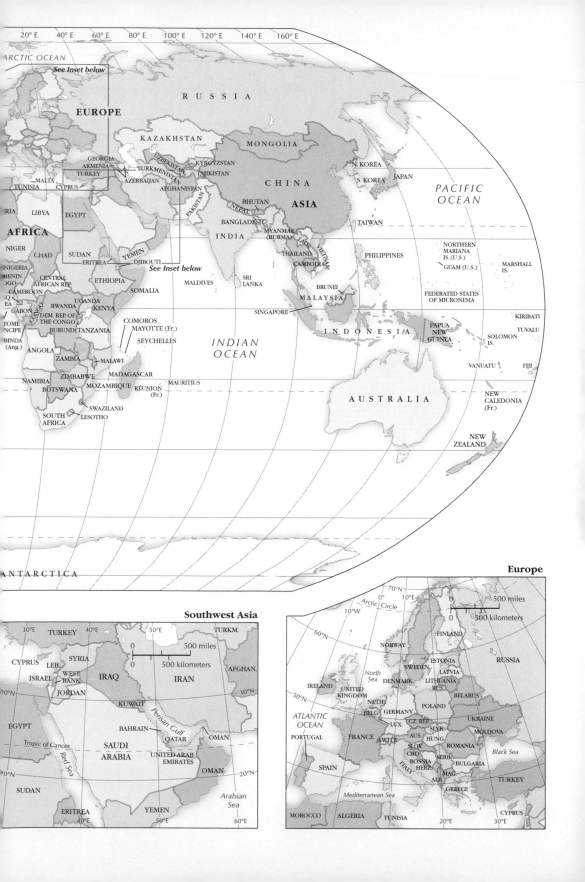

20° E 40° E 60° E 80° E 100° E 120° E 140° E 160° E

ARCTIC OCEAN

See Inset below

EUROPE

R U S S I A

KAZAKHSTAN

MONGOLIA

UZBEKISTAN KYRGYZSTAN

GEORGIA
ARMENIA   TURKMENISTAN TAJIKISTAN
TURKEY   AZERBAIJAN   AFGHANISTAN

C H I N A   **ASIA**

N. KOREA

S. KOREA   JAPAN

*PACIFIC
OCEAN*

TUNISIA   CYPRUS
MALTA

IRIA
LIBYA   EGYPT

PAKISTAN   BHUTAN
NEPAL   BANGLADESH

AFRICA

NIGER   CHAD   SUDAN   YEMEN
ERITREA   DJIBOUTI
See Inset below

I N D I A   MYANMAR   LAOS
(BURMA)   VIETNAM
THAILAND
CAMBODIA

TAIWAN

NORTHERN
MARIANA
IS. (U.S.)

GUAM (U.S.)

MARSHALL
IS.

BENIN   CENTRAL
NIGERIA   AFRICAN REP
OGO   ETHIOPIA
CAMEROON
EQ.
GABON
TOMÉ   RWANDA UGANDA
NCIPE   DEM. REP. OF KENYA
        THE CONGO
BINDA   BURUNDI TANZANIA
(Ang.)

SOMALIA

MALDIVES

SRI
LANKA

BRUNEI

M A L A Y S I A

SINGAPORE

PHILIPPINES

FEDERATED STATES
OF MICRONESIA

KIRIBATI

CONGO

COMOROS
MAYOTTE (Fr.)

SEYCHELLES

*INDIAN
OCEAN*

I N D O N E S I A

PAPUA
NEW
GUINEA

SOLOMON
IS.

TUVALU

ANGOLA

ZAMBIA   MALAWI

NAMIBIA   MADAGASCAR
        ZIMBABWE
BOTSWANA MOZAMBIQUE RÉUNION
                    (Fr.)

MAURITIUS

VANUATU   FIJI

A U S T R A L I A

NEW
CALEDONIA
(Fr.)

SWAZILAND
SOUTH   LESOTHO
AFRICA

NEW
ZEALAND

ANTARCTICA

Southwest Asia

30°E   TURKEY   40°E   50°E   TURKM.

CYPRUS   SYRIA
LEB.
ISRAEL WEST   IRAQ   IRAN
        BANK
        JORDAN   AFGHAN.

0   500 miles
0   500 kilometers

KUWAIT

BAHRAIN
QATAR   Persian Gulf   OMAN

EGYPT

SAUDI
ARABIA

UNITED ARAB
EMIRATES

OMAN

Tropic of Cancer

Red Sea

SUDAN

ERITREA   YEMEN
40°E

30°N

20°N

Arabian
Sea

50°E   60°E

Europe

70°N
Arctic Circle
0°   10°E
10°W

60°N

NORWAY   FINLAND

0   500 miles
0   500 kilometers

SWEDEN   ESTONIA
         LATVIA

RUSSIA

IRELAND
UNITED
KINGDOM

North
Sea   DENMARK

LITHUANIA
RUS.

50°N

ATLANTIC
OCEAN

NETH.
BELG. GERMANY
       LUX.
FRANCE CZ. REP.
        SWITZ. AUS.

POLAND

BELARUS

UKRAINE

MOLDOVA

PORTUGAL

HUNG.
SLOV.
CRO.
BOSNIA-
HERZ.

ROMANIA

SERB.   Black Sea
BULGARIA

SPAIN

ITALY

MAC.
ALB.

GREECE

TURKEY

CYPRUS

Mediterranean Sea

MOROCCO   ALGERIA   TUNISIA

20°E   30°E

CREDITS

CHAPTER 1   5 Cahokia Mounds State Historic Site, painting by William R. Iseminger 11 The Granger Collection, NY 12 Werner Foreman/Art Resource 14 Clement N'Taye/AP/Wide World Photos 15 © Parcs Canada 19 Joseph Furtenback, *Architectura Navalis*, Ulm, 1629 20 The Granger Collection, NY 21 Theodor de Bry, *America*, 1595, New York Public Library, Astor, Lenox and Tilden Foundations 27 © Copyright The Trustees of The British Museum

CHAPTER 2   36 National Portrait Gallery, Smithsonian Institution/Art Resource, NY 37 The Granger Collection, NY 39 Historic St. Mary's City, MD 44 Courtesy, American Antiquarian Society 46 © Paul Skillings 55 The Library Company of Philadelphia

CHAPTER 3   69 Network Aspen 75 Abby Aldrich Rockefeller Folk Art Center, Williamsburg, VA 80 © Shelburne Museum, Shelburne, Vermont 82 New York Public Library, Astor, Lenox and Tilden Foundations

CHAPTER 4   88 Rare Book Division, New York Public Library, Astor, Lenox and Tilden Foundations 91 "Pa. German Painted Wooden Box" by Elmer G. Anderson. Index of American Design, Image © 2004 Board of Trustees, National Gallery of Art, Washington, c. 1937, watercolor and graphite on paper, .463 × .369 (18 ¼ × 14 ½) 92 The New-York Historical Society 94 Richard Cummins/Corbis 96 Atwater Kent Museum of Philadelphia, Courtesy of Historical Society of Pennsylvania Collection/Bridgeman Art Library 101 By courtesy of the National Portrait Gallery, London 108 © Copyright The Trustees of The British Museum

CHAPTER 5   118 Courtesy of the John Carter Brown Library at Brown University, Providence, RI 128 The Library of Congress 130 Courtesy, American Antiquarian Society 133 Chicago Historical Society, ICHi-20449 134 By courtesy of the National Portrait Gallery, London 142 Anne S. K. Brown Military Collection, Brown University Library, Providence, RI

CHAPTER 6   149 The Library Company of Philadelphia 153 Friends Historical Library of Swarthmore College, Swarthmore, PA 166 National Portrait Gallery, Smithsonian Institution/Art Resource, NY

CHAPTER 7   178 Courtesy, American Antiquarian Society 179 National Portrait Gallery, Smithsonian Institution/Art Resource, NY 180   National Museum of American History, Smithsonian Institution 182 L Independence National Historical Park Collection 182 R Independence National Historical Park Collection 189 Bibliotheque Nationale/Art Resource, NY 191 Ohio Historical Society

CHAPTER 8   207 The Library of Congress 212 Chicago Historical Society, (P & S-1932.0018) 218 Courtesy JP Morgan Chase Archives, Photo by Vincent Colabella Photography 220 Abby Aldrich Rockefeller Folk Art Museum, Williamsburg, VA 222 The New-York Historical Society, (#7278) 225 Collection of Davenport West, Jr. 228 Getty Images

CHAPTER 9   234 L Courtesy, Colorado Historical Society, (F17954A) 234 R National Museum of the American Indian, Smithsonian Institution, (15/4658.) Photo by David Heald 234 B Alfred Miller, *Rendezvous*, 1837. The Walters Art Museum, Baltimore, MD 236 Courtesy of The Newberry Library, Chicago, IL

239 Wisconsin Historical Society, WHI-649 (28199) 241 New York Public Library, Astor, Lenox and Tilden Foundations 242 The Granger Collection, NY 246 Massachusetts Historical Society 252 Chester Harding, John Marshall, ca.1829. Washington & Lee University, Lexington, VA

CHAPTER 10   259 John Lewis Krimmel, *Village Tavern*, 1813–14. The Toledo Museum of Art, Purchased with funds from the Florence Scott Libbey Bequest in Memory of her Father, Maurice A. Scott 261 William Sidney Mount, *Rustic Dance After a Sleigh Ride*, 1830. Museum of Fine Arts, Boston, Bequest of Martha C. Karolik for the M. and M. Karolik Collection of American Paintings, 1815–1865, 48.458. Reproduced with Permission. © 2007 Museum of Fine Arts, Boston. All Rights Reserved. 266 Thomas Sully, *General Andrew Jackson*, 1845. In the collection of The Corcoran Gallery of Art, Washington D. C. Gift of William Wilson Corcoran 275 Chicago Historical Society, (ICHi-12739) 277 George Caleb Bingham (1811–79). Private Collection. The Bridgeman Art Library.

CHAPTER 11   283 The New-York Historical Society 285 The Library of Congress 286 John Antrobus, *Plantation Burial*, ca.1860. The Historic New Orleans Collection 288 State Historical Society of Wisconsin (Image 1926) 293 The Library of Congress 296 The New-York Historical Society, (#3087)

CHAPTER 12   307 Chicago Historical Society, (ICHi-22019) 310 Fruitlands Museums, Harvard, Massachusetts 312 The New-York Historical Society, (#1941.910) 317 Courtesy of The Newberry Library, Chicago 318 Bettmann/Corbis 320 Massachusetts Historical Society, MHS image #0031 322 National Portrait Gallery, Smithsonian Institution/Art Resource, NY 324 New York Public Library, Astor, Lenox and Tilden Foundations 327 L & R Courtesy, Concord Free Public Library

CHAPTER 13   335 "Handcart Pioneers" by CCA Christensen. © by Intellectual Reserve, Inc. Courtesy of Museum of Church History and Art. Used by Permission 341 Bettmann/Corbis 345 Chicago Historical Society, (ICHi-00013) 347 Agriculture Department, Smithsonian Institution

CHAPTER 14   362 New York Public Library, Astor, Lenox and Tilden Foundations 367 L Harriet Beecher Stowe Center, Stowe-Day Foundation 367 R The New-York Historical Society, Bella C. Landauer Collection of Business and Advertising Art, (#38219) 369 The Library of Congress 370 The Library of Congress 372 The Library of Congress

CHAPTER 15   391 The Library of Congress 392 The Library of Congress 395 Francis G. Mayer/Corbis 400 L & R The Library of Congress

CHAPTER 16   407 The Library of Congress 418 The New-York Historical Society, (#50475) 422 Valentine Museum/Richmond History Center 425 Rutherford B. Hayes Presidential Center, Fremont, Ohio 432 Corbis

CHAPTER 17   442 Amos Bad Heart Bull, *A Pictographic History of the Oglala Sioux*, text by Helen Blish, University of Nebraska Press 444 L Arizona Historical Society/Tucson, (#19831) 444 R Arizona Historical Society/Tucson, (#19830) 447 Corbis 452 Denver Public Library, Western History Department

CHAPTER 18   467 Union Pacific Railroad Museum Collection 474 Edison National Historical Site/U. S. Department of the Interior, National Park Service 476 Chicago Historical Society, (ICHi-01622) 478 The Library of Congress 479 Courtesy, Metropolitan Life Insurance Company 483 Bettmann/Corbis

CHAPTER 19   490 The Library of Congress 492 New York Public Library, Astor, Lenox and Tilden Foundations 497 The Advertising Archive 500 AT&T Archives 502 Brown Brothers 504 The Library of Congress 509 Time Life Pictures/Getty Images

CHAPTER 20   515 The Library of Congress 520 Bettmann/Corbis 524 Kansas State Historical Society 527 Minnesota Historical Society/Corbis 532 L Bettmann/Corbis 532 R Valentine Museum/Richmond History Center 536 Culver Pictures

INDEX

PENGUIN BOOKS

The partnership between Penguin USA and Longman Publishers offers your students a discount on many titles when bundled with any Longman survey. For a full list, please visit www.ablongman.com/penguin.

Available titles include the following:

Horatio Alger, Jr., *Ragged Dick and Struggling Upward*

Louis Auchincloss, *Woodrow Wilson*

Edward Bellamy, *Looking Backward*

Roy Blout, Jr., *Robert E. Lee*

Clayborne Carson (Editor), *Eyes on The Prize Civil Rights Reader*

Willa Cather, *O Pioneers!*

Ina Chang, *A Separate Battle*

Charles W. Chesnutt, *The Marrow of Tradition*

Alexis De Tocqueville, *Democracy in America*

Frederick Douglass, *Narrative of the Life of Frederick Douglass*

W. E. B. DuBois, *Souls of Black Folk*

William Fletcher, *Rebel Private: Front and Rear*

Benjamin Franklin, *Ben Franklin: The Autobiography and Other Writings*

Nelson George, *The Death of Rhythm and Blues*

Al Gore, *Earth in the Balance*

Joel Chandler Harris (Editor), *Nights with Uncle Remus*

Gordon Hunter (Editor), *Immigrant Voices*

Harriet Jacobs, *Incidents in the Life of a Slave Girl*

Thomas Jefferson, *Notes on the State of Virginia*

Jack Kerouac, *On the Road*

Ralph Ketcham, *The Anti-Federalist Papers and the Constitutional Convention Debates*

Martin Luther King, Jr., *Why We Can't Wait*

Julius Lester, *From Slave Ship to Freedom Road*

David Lewis, *The Portable Harlem Renaissance Reader*

Sinclair Lewis, *Babbitt*

Brian Macarthur, *The Penguin Book of Twentieth-Century Speeches*

James McBride, *The Color of Water*

Herman Melville, *Moby-Dick*

John Stuart Mill, *On Liberty*

Arthur Miller, *Death of A Salesman*

Toni Morrison, *The Bluest Eye*

George Orwell, *1984*

George Orwell, *Animal Farm*

Thomas Paine, *Common Sense*

Dorothy Parker, *The Portable Dorothy Parker*

Rosa Parks, *Rosa Parks: My Story*

Upton Sinclair, *The Jungle*

John Steinbeck, *The Grapes Of Wrath*

Sojourner Truth, *Narrative of Sojourner Truth*

Mark Twain, *The Adventures of Huckleberry Finn*

Various, *The Classic Slave Narratives*

Various, *The Federalist Papers*

Rebecca Walker, *Black, White, and Jewish: Autobiography of a Shifting Self*

Booker T. Washington, *Up From Slavery*

Phyllis Wheatley, *Complete Writings*

August Wilson, *Fences*

Hamet L. Wilson, *Our Nig*